Transport decisions in an age of uncertainty

Les décisions sur les transports dans une période d'incertitude

Transport decisions in an age of uncertainty

Proceedings of the third
World Conference on Transport Research
Rotterdam, 26 - 28 April, 1977

A Conference organized by
The Netherlands Institute of Transport

supported by
The Netherlands Government

and under the patronage of
OECD (Organisation for Economic Co-operation and Development)
ECMT (European Conference of Ministers of Transport)

edited by
Evert J. Visser
The Netherlands Institute of Transport

MARTINUS NIJHOFF, THE HAGUE - BOSTON

Martinus Nijhoff ISBN: 90 247 2061 3

PUBLISHER:
MARTINUS NIJHOFF, THE HAGUE

SOLE DISTRIBUTOR FOR THE U.S.A. AND CANADA:
KLUWER BOSTON, INC.
160 OLD DERBY STREET
HINGHAM, MASSACHUSETTS 02043

PRINTED IN THE NETHERLANDS

Steering Committee World Conference on Transport Research

Comité de Direction de la Conférence Mondiale sur la Recherche dans les Transports

Table of Contents

Avant-propos

Comme cela a déjà été énoncé durant la première Conférence Mondiale sur la Recherche dans les Transports à Bruges, Belgique en 1973, le transport est aujourd'hui une profession reconnue. C'est également vrai en 1977, année à laquelle fut organisée à Rotterdam, Pays-Bas, la troisième Conférence Mondiale. Le transport a véritablement émergé pour s'identifier à une profession multi-modale et multi-disciplinaire.

Le thème choisi pour cette troisième Conférence Mondiale sur la Recherche dans les Transports était: "Les Décisions sur les Transports dans une Période d'Incertitude.

Le Comité de Direction de la Conférence Mondiale a estimé utile de réunir ceux qui à travers le monde, sont engagés dans tous les aspects de la recherche relative aux problèmes de transport, et ceux qui s'occupent de formuler et de mettre en oeuvre les décisions en matière de politique des transports. La Conférence a reçu l'appui du Gouvernement Néerlandais et en outre le patronage de la Conférence Européenne des Ministres des Transports (C.E.M.T.) et de l'Organisation de Coopération et de Développement Economiques (O.C.D.E.).

Il s'est agi d'une Conférence Mondiale car elle a couvert à la fois les pays développés et les pays en voie de développement. Elle a été multi-modale, couvrant tous les modes de transport, de voyageurs comme de marchandises, multi-sectorielle présentant les vues de tous les secteurs, multi-disciplinaire incluant les perspectives des différentes disciplines.

Les thèmes de la Conférence ont été les suivants:

Thème 1. Appréciation
Une appréciation critique du rapport entre la recherche et les décisions de politique et de planification:
A quelles décisions essentielles seront confrontés les décideurs en matière de transport dans l'avenir immédiat? Quelles décisions essentielles se sont déjà présentées dans le passé?
Comment la recherche a-t-elle influencé ces décisions? Dans quelle mesure a-t-elle échoué?

Thème 2. Orientations actuelles des recherches
Un examen des résultats des recherches actuelles dans les domaines choisis:
Quelles sont les nouvelles approches actuellement développées?
Où sont les lacunes dans la recherche actuelle?
Quels sont les domaines prometteurs pour les recherches futures?

Thème 3. Les Directions de Recherche sur les Transports pour la décennie à venir (planification)
Appréciations des priorités futures:
Comment peut-on appliquer effectivement la recherche existante aux décisions en matière de politique et de planification?
A quelles nouvelles recherches faut-t-il accorder la plus grande priorité?

Maintenant que la Conférence s'est achevée, nous pouvons revenir sur cette Conférence qui fut un plein succès.

Foreword

As already indicated during the first World Conference on Transport Research in Bruges, Belgium in 1973, today transportation is a recognized profession. This is equally true in 1977, the year that the third World Conference was organized in Rotterdam, The Netherlands. Transportation has truly emerged as an identifiable multi-modal and multi-disciplinary profession.

The theme chosen for this third World Conference on Transport Research has been: "Transport Decisions in an Age of Uncertainty".

The Steering Committee of the World Conference thought it useful to bring together those engaged throughout the world in all aspects of research on transport problems, with others concerned with formulating and implementing transport policy decisions. The Conference has been supported by the Netherlands Government and further has been under the patronage of the European Conference of Ministers of Transport (E.C.M.T.) and the Organization for Economic coöperation and Development (O.E.C.D.).

The Conference has been world-wide in that it covered both development and developing areas. It has been multi-modal covering all modes for both passengers and freight, multi-sectoral presenting the views of all sectors as well as multi-diciplinary including the perspectives of various disciplines.

The topics of the Conference have been as follows:

Topic 1. Appraisal
A critical appraisal of the relation of research to policy planning decisions:
What key decisions will transport decision makers face in the near future?
What key decisions were faced in the past?
How has research influenced these decisions?
How has it failed?

Topic 2. Current Research Directions
An examination of current research results in selected areas:
What new approaches are being developed?
Where are the gaps in present research?
What are especially promising areas for future research?

Topic 3. Transport Research Directions for the next decade (planning)
Appraisal of future priorities:
How can existing research be applied more effectively to policy and planning decisions?
What new research is of highest priority?
Now that the Conference is over we can look back at a highly successful Conference.

We would like to thank the members of the Steering Committee who contributed to developing the technical programme and above all Evert J. Visser of the Netherlands Institute of Transport, whose organizational talents were absolutely invaluable and who will also act as editor of the proceedings.

We also express our appreciation to those who served as Chairmen of the various sessions and workshops (listed below).

Nous voudrions remercier les membres du Comité de Direction qui ont contribué à l'élaboration du programme technique et aussi tout particulièrement Evert J. Visser de l'Institut Néerlandais des Transports, dont les talents d'organisateur furent tout à fait inestimables et qui se chargera aussi de l'édition des Actes de la Conférence.

Nous exprimons aussi notre satisfaction à tous ceux qui ont eu la tâche de présider les différentes sessions et ateliers de recherche (liste ci-dessous).

Nous voudrions remercier spécialement les Gouvernements néerlandais, britannique et allemand de même que l'O.C.D.E. pour leur soutien financier, qui a permis à un si grand nombre de délégations de pays en voie de développement de pouvoir participer. Nous adressons aussi tous nos remerciements à la C.E.MT. et à l'O.C.D.E. pour leur patronage.

H.J. Noortman,
Président du Comité de Direction de la Conférence Mondiale sur la Recherche dans les Transports.

We especially like to thank the Dutch, English and German Governments as well as the O.E.C.D. for their financial support, which made it possible that so many delegates from developing countries could participate. We also are very thankful to the E.C.M.T. and O.E.C.D. for their patronage.

H.J. Noortman,
Chairman of the Steering Committee of the World Conference on Transport Research.

List of Chairmen

Liste des Présidents

P. Baron
M.E. Ben-Akiva
B. Bjørkman
J. Dousset
M. Frybourg
D. Genton
E.P. Holland
A. Kanafani
H. Klumpp

I.B.F. Kormoss
W. Leutzbach
M.L. Manheim
F.E.A. Nderitu
H.J. Noortman
E.M. van de Poll
A. Silverleaf
J. Vrebos
A. De Waele

Welcome speech

by

H. J. NOORTMAN
Chairman of the Steering Committee of the
World Conference on Transport Research

M ay I welcome you on behalf of the Steering Committee at this opening session of the World Conference on Transport Research.

It is a great pleasure to us that so many delegates were able to participate in this Conference, in which - as I have been told - about 50 countries are represented.

We are very honoured indeed that so many prominent representatives of those countries grace this conference with their presence.

The theme of this Conference is "Transport Decisions in an age of uncertainty".

I think it is beyond discussion that the decision makers in the transport world are confronted with a wide range of uncertainties as far as future developments are concerned.

Just to mention a few:

– Under what conditions, social and economic, will the "family of men" approach the end of this century?

– What will be the final objectives as far as the future economic development is concerned, both in the structure of the economy and in the distribution of these activities over the limits of growth which are set by the availability of scarce resources?

– It would be too difficult to add to this list of uncertainties at least 10 other major questions. But I think it suffices now to say that the decision makers can not stop the world and that they have to take the responsibility for their decisions, notwithstanding the broad margins within which future developments will probably be directed.

Since the extrapolation of past trends does not make much sense under these conditions, other forms of policy oriented research are needed.

The Steering Committee, whose members are closely associated with transport research, thought it useful therefor to bring together those engaged in the various aspects of research on transport problems, with others concerned with formulating and implementing transport policy decisions.

The Conference continues a tradition which was established by two earlier conferences in the sphere of policy oriented research at Bruges, Belgium in 1973 and in Paris in 1975. This tradition started out of the desire, felt by a number of research workers, to bring together those who are active in the same type of policy oriented research in various parts of the world.

Those who took the initiative wanted to open the possibility to exchange experiences and to optimise the effects of research work. In that period the greater part of the participants were from the more developed countries.

In the second half of the seventies, however, it is unthinkable to limit the exchange of ideas and experiences to these countries. The necessity to approach funde-

mental problems on a world wide scale is evident. This perhaps especially holds for fundamental transport problems, where transport has the function of bridging gaps. Gaps between human beings, whether they live within the same or in differing economic or social systems.

The Steering Committee therefor has tried to organize this Conference on a real world wide scale, covering both developed and developing areas.

As I mentioned before, the delegates now together at this Conference represent about 50 countries.

The Steering Committee has the feeling that the world wide set-up has been succesful, because more than half of this total number, belongs to the developing areas.

This certainly would not have been possible without the strong support that has been received from so many sides. Here should be mentioned the Netherlands Government, that via its Ministry of Transport and its Ministry of Foreign Affairs opened the possibility to reach the decision makers in many developing countries. Further should be mentioned the organization for Economic Co-operation and Development and the European Conference of Ministers of Transport, that gave their patronage to the Conference, and the World Bank that opened too its channels to reach the developing areas.

Beside these organizations the Steering Committee would like to express its gratitude for the support it received from many international organizations of companies and persons active in the field of transport, that encouraged their members to participate. As such can be mentioned:

– the Union International des Chemins de fer
– the International Road Union
– the International Cargo Handling Co-ordination Association
– the Transport Research Board
– the Transport Research Forum

and last but not least the many authors should be mentioned who gave their time and efforts to prepare the many papers which form the basis for the coming discussions.

Because the Steering Committee wanted to bring together those people engaged in transport research with the decision makers in transport policy, this objective had of course consequences for the set-up of the Conference. The Committee therefor chose an approach in three steps: in the first place it seemed desirable to come to a critical appraisal of the way in which research has been given support to policy and planning decissons up to now. Beside the keynote speakers of this morning, 4 sessions and a workshop will be dedicated to this appraisal.

As a second step the current research results will be

examined, in which all modes for both passengers and freight transport will be discussed.

In 8 sessions and 3 workshops this topic will be discussed. Given the character of the Conference the Steering Committee has asked for papers that give a survey of the state of the art. Highly specialised papers on research techniques seemed to be less appropriate for this Conference.

Then, as the third step of this Conference, the Steering Committee hopes that the panel discussions on Thursday afternoon, in which decision makers and research people will be brought together, will result in some answers to the question how existing research can be applied more effectively to policy and planning decisions, both in developed and developing countries.

May I end with expressing the sincere hope that this Conference will bring the delegates the results they were looking for, when coming to this World Conference on Transport Research.

Trends in thinking on traffic and transport policy in recent decades and the role of research on which policy is based

by

T. E. WESTERTERP

Minister of Transport and Public Works, The Netherlands

I t cannot be denied that in this age of uncertainty anyone who organises a meeting between the research world and that of day-to-day politics - the latter being a particularly precarious sphere - is demonstrating considerable courage. If they then attach the epithet 'World Conference' to it they might even be accused of being audacious.

Nevertheless, I am very enthusiastic about the initiative shown by the Netherlands Institute of Transport. One thing is certain, the choice of speakers and the number of participants from many countries are proof in any event that the conference is living up to its name of being a 'world' one.

I do not think I exaggerate when I say that given this great variety, expectations are high - at least mine are. I can perhaps describe the field in which I have such high expectations if I sketch the trends in the relationship between research and transport policy in my own country. This provides the basis for future plans.

THE NETHERLANDS
Policy guided by demand and policy guiding demand

After the second world war Holland had a national policy which was designed to create a thriving economy. This involved a traffic and transport policy which was mainly guided by demand, and so it remained until it became obvious that if restraint was not imposed traffic would increase out of all proportion. So in the early seventies the findings of a national transport and traffic study were published in which a forecast was made of the demand for passenger and goods transport in 1980, 1990 and 2000. The study also indicated the infrastructure which would be needed for the estimated traffic flows. The policy makers were shocked by the findings.

The development predicted was all the more frightening because it was becoming increasingly obvious that the growth entailed negative external consequences, in other words: nuisance to others.

The objective which up to then had been to 'meet the demand for transport from one place to another' became "to meet the demand only in so far as social well-being on balance is positively affected".

To provide a basis for policy, a detailed investigation was carried out into factors which determine the existing transport pattern of persons and goods. After all, if we understand this we have something on which to construct our policy. A study was also made of ways of altering the modal split to the favour of means of transport which are preferable on planning and environmental grounds.

Sector and Integrated policy

Gradually we have also become convinced in the Ne-therlands that the sector by sector approach was too narrow. As long as policy was guided by demand, we could manage with a policy which gave priority to transport and traffic aspects and in particular rapid and comfortable connections. We became aware, however, of the negative effects of encouraging traffic. At the same time we were becoming aware of these things, the public began to react to these side effects, sometimes more violently than at others. We then realised that we needed to curb the unbridled growth in the number of cars on the road especially in urban areas and at certain times of the day. Policy, if it is to be really effective, will have to attack the roots of the problem. The reasons for greater mobility will have to be dealt with. The main reason was the increase in the average trip length: in the Amsterdam conurbation this rose from 2.7 to 4 kilometres for all modes of transport between 1960 and 1975, an increase of 50%. The prime cause was the rise in car ownership and activities becoming spread further afield due to more space being used for living and working. To try to restrain this growth the first prerequisite is an integration of traffic and transport policy and land use planning policy. In the last five to six years, therefore, we have switched to an integrated approach to the problems.

Traffic and transport policy in the medium-term and long-term is formulated in close cooperation with the Ministry of Housing and Physical Planning. By the same token policy concerning land use in urban and rural areas has been geared to the traffic policy which we have chosen to follow. The aspects of both transport and land use planning are considered in the research designed to help in policy formulation. Up to now it has been assumed in transport policy models that the spatial arrangement is static. The effect of certain policy alternatives on land use planning cannot yet be incorporated into the models, although there is a need for this. It is precisely this aspect of transport research which should be given a high priority. In the meantime it has become clear that more attention has to be paid to concentrating places of work around points where public transport stops.

Long-term policy and medium-term policy

A development which is also very apparent is the shift from long-term to medium-term policy, a development in fact which is a corollary to those already mentioned.

The more a policy is geared to guiding demand the more it is likely to become medium-term. The effects of medium-term policy will have to be assessed regularly and adjusted accordingly. Formulating a concrete policy for the long-term is impossible, especially when conducting an integrated policy, given the number of factors

17

which exercise an influence, the many ways in which they interact and the large number of unpredictable reactions they will produce. Switching from target planning to process planning would seem to be the course for the future. If policy is also going to be able to respond to undesirable trends or sudden occurrences in transport and traffic behaviour and correct them, research will have to put forward suggestions for corrective measures. The least research will have to do therefore is keep up with society's feelings about transport and traffic behaviour but it should preferably be one step ahead.

National, regional, conurbation and urban policy

Another noticeable shift in policy-making is the increasing emphasis on a regional or conurbation approach. At the moment we make a clear distinction between the problems which occur in the transport sector in urban areas and those in rural areas. We sketch a general policy for the country as a whole which is then shaded in in more detail for the urban areas.

An integrated approach and a policy which guides events do not only require a shift from long-term to medium-term policy, they also profit from a general division into areas which have their own individual transport problems.

As I have already said, the towns in particular are experiencing pressing traffic problems which are urgently in need of a solution. In the last few years various studies have been carried out into these very problems of urban traffic. As examples we can quote strategic studies performed for some Dutch urban agglomerations. An investigation was also carried out into the possibility and desirability of introducing zoned fares for public transport.

Quantitive and qualitive research

Casting a glance over all these trends I would summarise the pattern in policy as follows: we have gradually switched from a policy which was guided by various trends to a more flexible policy, one providing a guide, a strategic policy. Pausing a moment to look at the studies already conducted we notice that for a long time research has mainly been quantitive, but that increasing emphasis is being placed on qualitative aspects. The quantitive character of research was linked with the recognition of the merits of computers. Computers were introduced on a major scale and seemed to be the key to solving many of the problems. For a long time the slogan, "If you can't count it, it doesn't count" applied. But gradually it was realised that the input absolutely determined the output of the computer and attention was switched to the factors that played a role in the input. This was not just restricted to the structure of the models and the way they operated; much time and energy was, and still is, spent on research into the variables which explain the pattern of the movement of persons and goods. Subjective assessments of waiting and journey times when using public transport are expressed in standards.

Research is becoming more qualitive because we have been forced to listen to the many protests from the community at the negative side affects of transport and traffic. It is important for policy not only to concentrate on what happened yesterday but also to try to indicate what is going to happen tomorrow. In other words people who are involved in transport research, and many are here today, will have to give more attention to the qualitive aspects of traffic and transport systems.

EUROPE

Having outlined the changing relationship between research and transport policy in the Netherlands, I should like to move on to other trends in a wider context which run parallel. Some examples will serve to illustrate this: First of all the recently completed report on the future development of passenger transport in Europe over long distances, COST 33. The political follow-up to this report will be discussed in the ECMT in Athens in June. Apart from the results of the report, the approach to the problems themselves is unique. For the first time the three branches of transport have been considered together on a European scale, taking account of the way they depend on one another and effect one another. The report also plumped for the strategic approach; that is to say that four strategies have been formulated, each of which puts forward a different idea of European transport policy for the future. The environment, land use planning and social policy aspects play a large part in these, so that one can justifiably talk of an integrated approach. Here, too, we encounter the recurrent motifs of "integrated" and "strategic". As I have already said the ECMT has taken it upon itself to get the political follow-up under way. I hope first and foremost that there will be a stimulating exchange of ideas in the Council of Ministers in Athens so that the impetus towards an European approach provided by the report, can make itself felt in as many sectors of transport policy as possible.

Another study, one which complements the OECD one, is the forecast of European goods transport, currently being carried out by the EEC countries and Spain. Here too an obvious choice has been made for an approach which is both integrated and strategic.

Besides these two major European studies there is the research work of the ECMT which has been going on for years. It is interesting to note that here too the same shift has been taking place. At the first symposium in 1964 it was still considered very important to investigate the implications of general economic theory for transport economy with special emphasis on the quantitative aspects, but in 1969 integration of policy with that of land use planning was already being given priority. In 1973 and especially at the 1975 symposium (after the energy crisis) we concentrated on the quality of life and scarcity of raw materials.

Is it a coincidence that for the coming Seventh symposium in London, at least one facet of this Conference, the contribution of economic research to transport policy, has been chosen as a central theme. Thus it too will be a consideration of what has been achieved and a reformulation of the desires for the future. I hope that this Conference will prepare the ground as fully as possible for this next stage of our joint efforts.

DEVELOPING COUNTRIES

Given the world-wide character of the conference, I must look beyond Europe. There we are confronted with countries which are wrestling with the same, or practically the same, problems as those in Europe so that the relationship between research and transport policy is following a similar trend. I am thinking of countries like the United States and Japan. And then there are the developing countries where problems connected with transport policy are cast in an entirely different mould. To cite an example: there are the urban traffic problems. Urban traffic in developing countries is in an alarming state. Although relatively few people have cars, congestion is an enormous problem. If present trends are not halted the congestion will only become worse. The main cause, the tremendous growth of the urban population, will most probably remain a factor to be reckoned with. Obviously an individual problem such as this requires a made-to-measure solution. The amount of space in towns and cities allocated for infrastructure is relatively small in many developing countries. In the first place, therefore, traffic engineering will have to try to find solutions to the problem. In some cases these solutions will relieve the situation but they alone will not suffice. Urban infrastructure is expensive and not built to cope with the ever-increasing demand. This is why it is a good idea to be thinking about a policy which guides demand besides resorting to measures which meet it. For instance measures such as giving priority to public transport, and congestion levies on private cars. Perhaps one of the best solutions is to separate the various types of transport. After all public transport, taxis and bicycles, and you must realise that as a Dutchman the bicycle as a mode of transport is one that is particularly dear to my heart, would be used more if they had their own lanes separated from other traffic. It is obvious that a strategic approach to the problem would be a help here. Research should develop a number of general strategies which include the appropriate instruments and measures to be offered to the policy makers and which take into account the different potential uses of urban space and the individual forms of transport needed. A challenge indeed.

I have given you a birds'eye view of trends in the relationship between research and transport policy. I have stressed developments in the Netherlands, but elswhere, although the problems are of totally different proportions, such as in the developing countries, the same trends can be observed. At the same time I have attempted to extrapolate some policy developments into the future and on the basis of this to formulate policy makers' expectations of research. Research will increasingly have to be in tune with an integrated and a strategic approach.

I hope that this conference with its great diversity of expertise can help to make it clear to us that even with a multitude of uncertainties, applied research can provide a more secure basis for our decisions in the traffic and transport sector.

Allocution

par
GÉRARD ELDIN
Organisation de Coopération
et de Développement Economiques

Je suis heureux d'apporter ici le salut de l'OCDE à cette importante conférence mondiale placée sous son patronage, et qui va rassembler ici tant d'éminentes personnalités. Je voudrais rendre hommage à l'Institut Néerlandais des Transports qui a assuré l'organisation de cette manifestation dans cette ville de Rotterdam, ce carrefour de routes terrestres et maritimes qui, cette fois, sera, j'en suis sûr, un carrefour d'idées nouvelles et fécondes.

Les trois thèmes de cette rencontre convergent vers un problème très actuel: Comment établir un lien satisfaisant et efficace entre la recherche et la prise de décisions?", et je me propose de vous faire part de quelques réflexions à ce sujet.

Pourquoi ce problème est-il urgent?

1 – D'abord, parce que nous vivons dans une époque d'incertitude. Celle-ci ne caractérise pas seulement l'avenir immédiat de nos économies, mais aussi et surtout l'horizon à long terme de nos sociétés industrielles.

On peut et on doit s'efforcer de réduire cette incertitude tout en sachant que la prévision n'est pas la prédiction car, selon le mot de Paul Valéry "l'avenir est doué d'imprévisibilité essentielle". Réduire (et non éliminer) l'incertitude, c'est la tâche très noble des organes de prévision et de planification dans les gouvernements et dans les entreprises.

2 – La seconde circonstance qui donne de l'actualité à votre conférence c'est le malaise qui me paraît affecter la recherche elle-même. Ce malaise comporte deux symptômes:

– un sentiment de frustration de la part des chercheurs qui, parce que leur travail est plus parcellaire qu'autrefois, n'ont pas toujours une claire perception de l'utilité sociale incontestable de leur travail;

– un sentiment d'injustice aussi lorsque l'opinion publique blâme les techniciens pour des erreurs d'orientation qui ne leur sont pas imputables.

Le monde des transports n'échappe pas à ces remous. Il suffit de noter que certains modes de transports sont aujourd'hui mis en accusation par la société - ou du moins par certains segments de la société-comme facteurs de bruit, de pollution, d'insécurité et de consommation excessive d'énergie.

Votre programme est impressionnant, à la fois par la qualité des participants et par le nombre et l'intérêt des communications prévues. C'est pourquoi je suis assuré que la conférence sera en mesure de projeter quelque lumière sur les relations qui ont existé jusqu'à présent entre la recherche et la prise de décision et, en partant de cette expérience, d'indiquer comment la recherche pourrait à l'avenir contribuer à une meilleure information des responsables de la décision.

Pour ma part, je voudrais, cependant, mettre en garde contre l'ambiguïté qui pourrait résulter de l'emploi inconcidéré de mots tels que "science", "technologie" et "recherche".

Il est bien évident, en effet, que l'on ne peut - dans le domaine qui nous intéresse, celui des transports - mettre sur le même plan la recherche technique portant sur de nouveaux produits ou de nouveaux procédés, et la recherche qui s'attache aux systèmes de transports et qui a un caractère socio-économique plus large.

En schématisant beaucoup, on pourrait dire que la recherche technique doit de plus en plus être l'auxiliaire de décisions déjà prises, tandis que la recherche socio-économique doit concourir à la prise de décisions elle-même.

I – Permettez-moi, tout d'abord, de faire quelques remarques sur la place de la *recherche technique* en ce domaine des transports:

a. Si j'ai dit qu'elle devait de plus en plus être une auxiliaire, loin de moi l'idée de diminuer, par cette formule, son importance! Il ne faut pas oublier, en effet, combien toute notre vie économique et sociale est affectée par les technologies nouvelles: c'est une platitude que de rappeler, par exemple, à quel point la centralisation économique et politique en France s'est appuyée sur les chemins de fer ou encore tous les traits que la société américaine doit à l'automobile.

Ces technologies nouvelles sont elles-mêmes déstabilisantes: elles le sont par définition, puisque l'innovation est précisément ce qui rompt avec le cours prévisible des choses. Ainsi, des catégories entières de connaissances, de techniques et de qualifications professionnelles peuvent être rapidement frappées d'obsolescence.

Mais la recherche et l'innovation appraissent aussi comme la principale source d'actions correctives. C'est donc dans un processus complexe et dialectique que se situent l'innovation technologique, avec ses avantages et ses dangers, et un autre cycle de recherches qui tend à compléter l'oeuvre initiale.

A partir de ces constatations, je voudrais tirer deux conclusions du point de vue des décideurs:

– La première, c'est qu'ils ne seront jamais entièrement maîtres du processus d'innovation, car celui-ci ne se commande pas;

– La seconde est qu'ils doivent eux-mêmes tenir compte des possibilités d'innovation technique qui, sans être certaines, ont un caractère de probabilité suffisant pour affecter l'avenir.

b. Ma deuxième remarque a trait aux conditions dans lesquelles doit s'exercer aujourd'hui la recherche technique.

Le temps n'est plus où celle-ci était exclusivement l'oeuvre d'individus isolés. L'essentiel de l'innovation technique résulte, au contraire, d'un travail d'équipe qui peut être lui-même orienté et planifié. A l'approche traditionnelle d'une recherche "tous azimuths" se substitue celle d'une approche plus "focalisée" ou "canalisée".

Le fait est que beaucoup d'inventions du passé ne se sont pas matérialisées, soit parce qu'elles n'ont pas franchi le mur de la rentabilité, soit parce qu'elles ne répondaient pas aux besoins réels de l'époque. Il suffit de feuilleter quelques vieux magazines du XIXe siècle pour s'en convaincre. Ainsi, par exemple, du système RAMMEL de chemin de fer pneumatique expérimenté en 1865 près de Londres et que l'on pensait déjà, à l'époque, pouvoir appliquer au Tunnel sous la Manche! (N'est-ce pas le même principe que l'on retrouve aujourd'hui dans le système UNIFLO?)

Il me semble qu'aujourd'hui la tendance est moins de se tourner exclusivement vers l'innovation technique et de lui rechercher un débouché a posteriori que d'identifier, à partir d'études de systèmes, des besoins qui sont autant de défis lancés aux techniciens.

Nous restons sans doute convaincus les uns et les autres que l'innovation technique s'épanouira plus facilement si la liberté nécessaire est laissée aux chercheurs. Mais cette liberté est relative, en ce sens qu'elle s'exerce de plus en plus à l'intérieur de corridors préalablement définis. Le secteur des transports n'échappe pas à la règle. Je pense en particulier aux domaines de recherches que constituent les ensembles "énergie et transport", "environnement et transports", "sécurité et transports".

c. Ma troisième remarque, qui découle en réalité des deux autres, est que la recherche technique doit procéder de manière *associative*, et non de manière isolée.

J'entends par là que dans chaque direction de recherche, des efforts combinés sont nécessaires, mettant en jeu diverses disciplines. A quoi servirait en effet de développer un mode de transport très rapide ou très efficace si, parallèlement, n'étaient pas résolus les problèmes de bruit ou de sécurité qu'il pourrait susciter? Pas plus que nous n'en sommes, en économie, au simple jeu du "laissez faire", nous n'en sommes, en technologie, au simple jeu du "laissez innover".

Ces quelques remarques montrent que la recherche technique est de nos jours étroitement liée à la recherche socio-économique, qui procède elle-même d'une prospective des besoins.

II – La recherche socio-économique, qui - ne nous faisons pas d'illusions - en est encore à ses débuts, peut être caractérisée comme une *aide à la décision*:

A – Dans cet effort de rationalisation, on peut distinguer deux degrés d'ambition, selon qu'il s'agit simplement de mieux informer le ou les responsables de la décision ou d'améliorer le processus de décision lui-même.

1. Mieux informer les choix sociaux, cela consiste essentiellement à poser les problèmes dans toutes leurs diverses dimensions.

– Il va de soi que les choix en matière de nouveaux systèmes de transports ont une dimension économique et financière qui est fondamentale.

– Mais, de plus en plus, intervient une dimension sociale (ou sociétale) qu'il convient de prendre en compte dans l'analyse prospective des coûts et avantages.

Au cours des dernières années, la somme d'informations produites pour les décideurs n'a cessé de s'accroître à mesure que les dimensions de l'analyse se développèrent dans l'espace et dans le temps.

Mais cela devait fatalement entraîner un autre problème lié à la surabondance de l'information: celui de l'intégration et de la pondération des données.

2. Le problème des aides à la décision est aujourd'hui l'un de ceux qui passionnent également scientifiques et politiques.

Dans ce domaine, les outils n'ont cessé de se perfectionner. En ce qui concerne l'analyse prévisionnelle, des modèles mathématiques de plus en plus raffinés ont été développés, en même temps que des méthodes tenant compte du caractère aléatoire de l'avenir. Parallèlement, l'étude traditionnelle de rentabilité a cédé le pas à l'analyse coûts-avantages faisant intervenir des paramètres sociaux. Les gouvernements eux-mêmes ont, dans une certaine mesure, mis en application ces méthodes nouvelles par exemples sous la forme du PPBS aux Etats-Unis ou de la RCB en France.

Toutes ces méthodes mettent l'accent sur l'amélioration des résultats et de l'efficacité des analyses, sur la transparence et le caractère de relatif des données considérées. Elles ont fait la preuve de leur utilité dans l'évaluation des technologies des transports et dans l'étude détaillée des moyens intellectuels ou matériels permettant le mieux d'assurer diverses fonctions, y compris l'examen des caractéristiques et des coûts comparés des systèmes concurrents, et des performances des systèmes en vigueur.

Est-ce à dire que le problème de la décision ait été résolu?

Certes pas, et je voudrais ici évoquer un certain nombre de difficultés sur lesquelles votre conférence pourrait utilement se pencher.

1 – La première difficulté est de nature purement pratique: les méthodes d'analyse de systèmes sont séduisantes. Elles représentent un progrès incontestable par rapport aux méthodes étroites et rigides du passé. Mais elles impliquent le maniement d'un grand nombre d'informations.

A la limite, cette surabondance d'information ne risque-t-elle pas d'être un facteur paralysant? Je n'ignore pas que nos techniques de traitement de l'information ont fait de grands progrès. Je remarque, cependant, que l'analyse de systèmes pose inévitablement la question difficile de la taille optimale du système.

2 – La deuxième difficulté a trait aux *jugements de valeur*. Toutes les méthodes que je viens d'évoquer s'appliquent convenablement dès lors que les divers éléments qui entrent en ligne de compte sont quantifiables et cumulables. Leur emploi suppose une définition claire des objectifs (aussi claire, par exemple, que celle qui consiste pour l'entreprise à maximiser son *cash-flow*), et une certaine stabilité des normes, des institutions et des valeurs. Elles n'apportent pas de réponse à la question fondamentale à laquelle achoppent les "décideurs", à savoir celle de la *fonction d'utilité* qui doit prévaloir.

Quel secours pouvons-nous attendre à cet égard des politologues? Ceux-ci ont mis au point divers modèles permettant de classer les décisions politiques suivant les domaines d'activité, les "groupes-cibles", les niveaux d'autorité, les instruments et techniques propres à obtenir l'adhésion de toutes les parties concernées, les procédures de répartition des coûts et des avantages entre les divers groupes d'intérêt de la collectivité.

Considérant le bilan de ces efforts, d'autres politologues soulignent qu'en dépit de la prolifération de ces études et de ces méthodes, il ne semble pas que de grands progrès aient été accomplis dans la compréhension des mécanismes d'élaboration des mesures gouvernementales.

Néanmoins, une leçon importante se dégage de toutes ces tentatives: c'est que les choix des "décideurs" ne peuvent être effectués que dans certaines limites, qui tiennent à l'étendue des attributions de l'organisme décideur, au nombre des problèmes jugés importants, au rôle des différents acteurs en jeu, à la nature des solutions politiquement acceptables, aux règles et procédures qu'il convient d'observer pour, qu'en somme, le processus démocratique demeure ouvert.

3 − Enfin, je voudrais mentionner ce qui est, à mon sens, un problème majeur: celui de la communication entre les analystes et les "décideurs". C'est le reflet d'une sorte d'incompréhension mutuelle: d'un côté, le décideur, l'homme politique, est souvent rebuté par l'appareil scientifique de l'analyste, le langage souvent cryptique qu'il utilise ou encore les nuances qui caractérisent son approche scientifique. D'où une certaine méfiance, parfois justifiée d'ailleurs de sa part. L'analyste, de son côté, peut être heurté par le manque apparent de rationalité des hommes qui ont à décider ou par l'introduction de considérations bassement politiciennes qui sacrifient souvent les exigences du long terme aux impératifs du court terme.

Une symbiose plus étroite est évidemment souhaitable entre analystes et décideurs. Cette symbiose suppose, de part et d'autre, un rapprochement des manières de penser et de travailler. A l'analyste, il sera demandé de mieux comprendre les objectifs, les moyens d'action et les problèmes du décideur, afin de lui fournir les informations scientifiques et techniques sur lesquelles il puisse fonder ses décisions. Réciproquement, le décideur devra entrer dans les raisons du technicien, contribuer à établir des objectifs et des critères valables pour la mesure des performances, et surtout être capable de faire pénétrer les résultats des analyses scientifiques dans la sphère de l'action politique. Cela ne peut se faire que par un échange continu d'informations, un commerce plus suivi entre décideurs et techniciens, et une réitération convergente des opérations correspondant à chaque stade de l'analyse.

Ces difficultés, Monsieur le Président, loin de nous conduire à un quelconque découragement, doivent, au contraire, nous inciter à améliorer nos moyens de connaissance et d'action.

Il est clair, en effet, que dans le domaine des transports comme dans beaucoup d'autres, une approche intégrée est une garantie de progrès. Cette approche doit s'étendre autant que possible à l'ensemble des interactions entre le système de transports et son contexte économique et social. C'est seulement dans ce cadre que peuvent être prises en compte les données et résultats venant de disciplines aussi différentes et aussi interdépendantes que les sciences de l'ingénieur, l'économie des transports, l'urbanisme et l'aménagement du territoire, sans oublier l'écologie.

Mais il faut aller plus loin: nous devons aborder les problèmes en jeu avec la modestie qui sied aux chercheurs et non avec la suffisance de ceux qui croient détenir la science infuse. Il ne faut jamais oublier, en effet, que la prise de décisions ne se ramène pas simplement à un exercice de résolution des problèmes, ou à la recherche des solutions les plus rationnelles sur le plan des coûts. Elle oblige à effectuer des choix pour lesquels les ressources sont, de toute façon, limitées et dont les divers groupes sociaux vont tirer un avantage inégal: comme les intérêts en cause sont loin d'être toujours convergents, la prise de décisions a nécessairement une "dimension politique". Bref, au delà du problème technique, nous devons accepter d'en affronter les implications fondamentalement humaines et sociales.

Technique d'un côté, décision de l'autre: c'est bien en rapprochant ces deux univers qu'on peut espérer surmonter les obstacles. Vous ne m'en voudrez pas, Monsieur le Président, de rappeler pour conclure la formule d'un philosophe qui, bien avant notre siècle technologique, a réfléchi sur la technique et les problèmes qu'elle pose aux hommes politiques - et déjà il s'agissait de transports: "A quoi sert la science de la navigation, si nous ne savons pas où aller?".

Cette question, posée par Platon, il me semble qu'elle est, très explicitement, au coeur de vos débats, dont je souhaite le plein succès.

Allocution

par
G. BILLET
Conférence Européenne des
Ministres des Transports

L'actualité vous a amenés à vous interroger sur l'apport de la recherche aux prises de décision politique. En effet, la situation que nous vivons impose à ce sujet une réflexion profonde, voire même une remise en cause.

La CEMT que j'ai l'honneur de représenter devant votre auditoire est particulièrement atachée à ce problème et ce à plusieurs titres qui convergent d'ailleurs tous vers l'élaboration d'un équilibre entre la théorie et la pratique.

Depuis bientôt vingt-cinq ans, la CEMT qui groupe en son sein dix neuf pays d'Europe et quatre Etats associés se propose de promouvoir le transport entre ses Etats membres. Pratiquement depuis le début de son existence elle consacre une de ses activités essentielles aux problèmes que pose la prévision des trafics, activité qui sert de support à l'intégration et à l'adaptation des réseaux internationaux de transport.

Chemin faisant, il est apparu aux pays membres que la consolidation et l'élargissement de cette activité scientifique était indispensable à la continuation et à l'orientation de leur activité politique.

C'est ainsi que fonctionne depuis dix ans au Secrétariat de la CEMT un Centre de Recherches et de Documentation suivant une ligne de conduite originale et pragmatique. Plutôt que de créer un nouvel et tantième institut international de recherches, nos instances ont jugé plus efficace de se baser sur les institutions qui existaient déjà et de faire fonctionner son propre centre comme un lieu de rencontre et d'information. Chaque fois qu'un problème politique paraît requérir un éclairage scientifique, la CEMT invite les experts en la matière à lui faire part de leur expérience sous forme de Tables Rondes sur des thèmes bien déterminés. Une plus vaste rencontre qui permet un échange général d'idées sur des questions d'actualité est offerte tous les deux ans sous forme de Symposiums.

En procédant de la sorte, la CEMT s'informe donc systématiquement et régulièrement sur les progrès qu'accomplissent les universités et les centres de recherche dans le domaine des sciences humaines du transport. En retour, elle fournit à ces institutions une documentation périodique sur les recherches en cours afin de faciliter les contacts et la coopération entre chercheurs.

Sans ignorer pour autant les aspects fondamentaux inhérents à tout progrès scientifique, la CEMT, de par son objectif même, est appelée tout naturellement à considérer la recherche en liaison avec ses préoccupations politiques. Elle a réalisé progressivement un précieux réseau de contacts et un point de rencontres qui, à leur tour, permet aux scientifiques de s'informer de ces préoccupations politiques. Il va sans dire que ce réseau de relations humaines fonctionnant dans les deux sens est fort apprécié de tous les partenaires politiques et

scientifiques.

De toute évidence, cette expérience me place à un poste d'observation privilégié pour introduire vos débats et aussi pour vous faire part de quelques réflexions bien muries sur les grandeurs et sur les servitudes de la recherche vus dans l'optique du décideur qui a l'habitude de s'entourer de conseils scientifiques.

Je parle essentiellement des sciences humaines du transport que nous enveloppons schématiquement sous le vocable "économie des transports" mais qui comprend aussi la sociologie, la psychologie, la géographie, bref tout cet ensemble de branches qui se proposent de connaître les besoins ainsi que les moyens pour les satisfaire.

Politiquement, la solution des problèmes que pose le transport inclut bon nombre d'aspects qui sont extérieurs au transport. Il en a toujours été ainsi mais cette diversification des objectifs s'est beaucoup accentuée au cours des dernières années. L'aménagement du territoire, l'environnement, la qualité de vie, la logistique industrielle constituent autant de préoccupations récentes et importantes qui viennent interférer avec la politique des transports, au point d'aller même jusqu'à remettre en question les propres justifications la politique des transports.

Certes, cette complexité d'objectifs interactés rend nécessaire une approche globale, mais elle ne supprime pas les approches sectorielles; il y a là une question de niveaux et en bousculant les secteurs qu'on apportera plus de clarté.

De surcroît, ces dernières années ont apporté à l'intérieur des transports un développement qui justifie plus que jamais une approche sectorielle; il s'agit du renchérissement plus que proportionnel de certaines prestations de transport qui réclament la fixation d'une ligne de conduite.

Sur le plan global, la mobilité toujours croissante implique toute une nouvelle problématique pour ce qui est de l'utilisation des ressources d'espace, d'énergie, du temps, etc. . Là également nous nous trouvons au seuil de nouvelles orientations politiques dont les premières manifestations se concrétisent déjà.

En conséquence, il est parfaitement logique de plaider pour une plus grande coopération de la recherche qui doit guider ces actions politiques, coopération qui devrait se réaliser à la fois entre les disciplines et entre les institutions et organisations.

En effet, la recherche qui est née naguère d'initiative d'individus, risque de perdre beaucoup de son efficacité si elle reste une affaire de goûts et d'aspirations individuelles. Trop souvent, on a l'impression de voir toujours recommencer à d'autres endroits les mêmes recherches sur les mêmes problèmes; il y a là un danger évident d'attirer un discrédit à une activité qui n'apporterait plus

23

le guidage indispensable qu'on est en droit d'attendre d'elle.

Il est donc souhaitable que la recherche s'organise davantage en fonction de son rôle social et que son activité soit conçue davantage comme un apport fonctionnel à une société qui en a besoin.

L'efficacité de la recherche ne dépend pas seulement de son organisation interdisciplinaire et coopérante, mais également, et même avant toutes choses de son objectivité vis-à-vis des intérêts et des tendances de l'actualité.

La liberté du chercheur, face aux intérêts impliqués, est une nécessité qui n'a pas besoin dêtre démontrée. Cependant, il y a plus: l'évolution précipitée et le rôle déterminant des moyens d'information contribuent à conférer une actualité aussi brutale que passagère à certaines questions. Il faut alors que les équipes de recherche fassent la preuve d'un recul, d'une critique et d'une culture suffisants pour situer correctement ces "modes scientifiques" dans un contexte de valeurs. Il n'est guère besoin de rappeler certains exemples récents pour démontrer à quel point certains intérêts et certaines modes peuvent entraîner une part importante de la recherche dans l'impasse de l'aventure intellectuelle. La crédibilité de la recherche ne sort pas grandie de pareilles péripéties et ce n'est que par une meilleure conscience de la fonction sociale qu'on pourra les éviter à l'avenir.

Même à l'intérieur de l'Europe, il existe de sensibles différences entre les niveaux de développement des pays. Une recherche désintéressée et de haute qualité peut avoir des effets stimulants pour les pays moins développés, notamment en les aidant dans le choix judicieux des moyens à engager et en les laissant profiter de nos expériences positives ou négatives. Dans la réalité, il faut constater que ce type de recherche fait encore trop souvent défaut dans le dévelopment de certains pays et qu'il y prédomine une prétendue recherche qui n'est qu'une forme embellie du marketing ou de la publicité pour tel ou tel article.

En définitive, la CEMT a pu s'assurer le concours sélectif des résultats de la recherche dans des domaines qui la préoccupent sur le plan politique; elle a pu évaluer les possibilités et les limites; elle a pu déceler des possibilités d'amélioration. Elle est bien placée pour estimer les chercheurs et particulièrement ceux parmi eux qui s'avèrent être des trouveurs.

Ce sont les appréciations de la CEMT, fruits d'une expérience déjà longue, sur l'organisation de la recherche en matière de transports, l'esprit dans lequel elle devrait être conduite et l'objectif qu'elle devrait poursuivre que j'ai essayé de vous livrer dans mon court propos.

Précisément, vous allez discuter au cours du présent congrès d'une question essentielle, celle du passage de l'approche théorique à la mise en oeuvre pratique des résultats de la recherche ou, plus exactement, de l'appui réciproque que l'exploration scientifique qui cherche à avoir un caractère objectif et les orientations politiques peuvent s'apporter dans le choix de la solution la plus efficace et la plus conforme à l'intérêt général.

On est loin, en fait, d'avoir trouvé le terrain de rencontre souhaité et souhaitable et la situation jusqu'alors crée plutôt des insatisfactions. Insatisfaction des chercheurs qui estiment qu'on a trop souvent tendance à négliger les résultats des travaux qu'ils ont conduits avec tout le sérieux désirable, insatisfaction des décideurs qui estiment ne pas trouver le plus souvent dans les travaux de recherche des éléments suffisants d'éclairage de leur choix, même en tenant compte des aspects aléatoires des études et des prévisions dans le domaine de l'économie des transports.

Je souhaite que les travaux du présent congrès puissent permettre de progresser dans la voie de la compréhension, des préoccupations, des contraintes d'approche des problèmes, des limites d'appréciation quant aux choix et aux décisions ainsi que du cadre et du contexte de réflexion des deux séries d'acteurs dont la mission est de rechercher la solution aux problèmes des transports la plus adéquate eu égard à tous les paramètres du passé parfois, du présent sans doute et si possible de l'avenir qu'il convient d'intégrer.

Cette liaison constante entre la spéculation prospective et les nécessités de l'action concrète est d'autant plus indispensable pour les investissements dans le secteur des transports que dans ce domaine il s'agit le plus souvent d'investissements "lourds" et pour lesquels toute erreur d'appréciation a des conséquences importantes, car ces investissements engagent généralement l'avenir pour un temps important.

Pour ma part, je considère que la recherche doit avoir dans le temps présent une place encore plus importante que par le passé précisément parce que, comme il est retenu dans le thème même de votre congrès, nous sommes en présence d'une période d'incertitude en ce qui concerne les choix à opérer et les orientations à prendre en matière de politique des transports. Il importe peut-être plus que jamais que la recherche apporte aux décideurs des éléments pouvant les aider à mieux percevoir les voies à suivre. Mais il importe aussi aux chercheurs de définir les voies et moyens de leur intervention qui permettront de répondre à la contribution qu'on attend de leur part.

A development banker's view

CHRISTOPHER R. WILLOUGHBY

Transportation Department, World Bank

I count it a great honor to be invited to participate in a world conference on the important subject of transportation research. Particularly so when the conference is sponsored by a country which has played such an innovative role as the Netherlands have in the main job of our era, the search for paths of reconciliation and constructive cooperation between rich North and poor South, between all Worlds, from first to fourth. And, too, particularly so when the conference takes place in Rotterdam, greatest hub of the global transport system which is the physical expression of growing interdependence among countries. I would like to pay special tribute to the foresight and several years' hard work of Dr. Noortman and the Netherlands Institute of Transport in taking the initiative to organize the conference.

One example of the good foresight of those who have arranged our meeting is to have emphasized the word 'Uncertainty' in the Conference title. We know now that the uncertainties in the world economy borne in upon us by the events of the early 1970s have not, as some hoped, been overcome by a rapid return to normalcy. We who work in transportation know too that we cannot take the easy way out that has become favored by some - to leave the forecasting to foolhardy seers and to act on a day-to-day basis. Most transportation investments and policies have much too long gestation periods and operating lives. And they have too wide and deep an impact on all other spheres and aspects of living to warrant taking long-range planning casually. Rather, we have to be humble about the failures of our foresight in the 1960s and to seek the lessons of experience.

For guilty people like ourselves a famous eighteenth-century countryman of mine had an interesting comment that is still often quoted: "When a man knows he is to be hanged in a fortnight, it concentrates his mind wonderfully". That assertion has always mystified me a little. I would have thought that fear and remorse might, on the contrary, dissipate his mind. But we are more fortunate that the rude shocks to our forecasts of a few years ago do not yet bring any ultimate penalties. In fact, I think, they force upon us a better opportunity than Samuel Johnson's poor convict had to concentrate calmly but intensively on identifying what was really significant in what we were and are doing.

Our business in the World Bank is to confront the future with concrete decisions about investments, in countries which have suffered some of the most painful shocks of the economic uncertainties of the last years. With the valuable cooperation of several of you here, we do a little research ourselves - some of which will be covered in papers to be discussed in the coming days. More broadly, we are a major user of research by others, and we are very aware of the significance of it in helping us avoid mistakes. In the transportation field we have loaned upwards of US $ 12,000 million more than for any other single purpose - distributed among some 80

different countries. About one-half has been for roads and highways, one third for railways, and the remainder for ports, shipping, aviation and pipelines. Currently we are committing each year about US $ 1,500 million in support of some 30-40 transport development projects with a total cost of around US $ 5,000 million. In addition, in the transport field, we lend several hundred million dollars each year for transportation components of some 20-30 projects primarily oriented to other purposes such as rural or urban regional development, exploitation of minerals, or tourism.

Before drawing on our experience of past investment projects to identify outstanding uncertainties, let me start with some certainties, some facts which may help broadly to locate the countries I am referring to on the world spectrum. In 1975 world population reached about 4,000 million. Nearly one-third, or 1,200 million of those people lived in very poor countries, mainly in Asia and Africa, with per capita annual incomes averaging $ 150. And nearly twenty percent, or over 700 million, lived in middle-income developing countries with per capita incomes above $ 250 and averaging $ 800. It is essentially this one-half of the world's population to whom we lend - on the basis of resources borrowed from, or contributed by, two sources: the twenty percent of the world's population in the 'North', with an average per capita income above $ 5,000 in 1975, and the three per cent of world population in major oil-exporting countries with per capita incomes averaging nearly $ 2,000.

Overall transportation investment capabilities are probably best expressed in relation to the number of people entering the labor force and requiring a job each year; for that stage in life roughly corresponds to the time when a person starts an independent family and requires corresponding housing and related infrastructure. In the 'North' we have been able to invest in our transportation systems each year of the middle 1970s an average of some $ 40-50 thousand for each new entrant to the labor force in that year. The corresponding figure for the middle-income developing countries is about one-fifteenth of this, or $ 3,000. And for the by far most numerous group, the very poor countries, it is under $ 500, or one-hundredth of that in the rich North. The proportions are so much wider apart than for per capita incomes because of the interaction of higher labor-force growth rates in the developing countries and lower share of overall resources in the very poor countries that can be spared for investment, including whatever small foreign assistance is presently given.

In Holland, and before this group, I do not have to apologize for focussing attention on countries which account for one-half of world population but only about 15% of annual worldwide investment in transportation (outside the Communist countries). It is morally impossible to turn away from the desperate needs of the hundreds of millions of poverty-stricken people in both very

25

poor and middle-income developing countries. And it is politically unrealistic to believe that a normalcy can be successfully recreated which did so little to give them a share in the world economy. The problems of these people should, and will, get an increasing proportion of world attention.

Looking back at our World Bank efforts to assist the transportation dimension of development, we can of course identify a myriad ways in which uncertainty impinged to throw off forecasts and to cause probable shortfalls from some precise optimum. But what are the important things that Johnson would have us concentrate on? What was the difference on 'the bottom line', as the Americans would say? Actually, according to the ex-post evaluations we now do of each individual project financed with World Bank assistance, much less than one might think. The very large majority of projects assisted has turned out to be as economically worthwhile as expected. A certain 'law of compensation' has worked - increases in traffic have offset the effects of increased construction costs, shortfalls in one type of traffic have been counterbalanced by greater than expected increases in another type - and economic agents have shown a remarkable capacity to adjust to changed situations.

But there are four areas where one cannot be so sanguine and which therefore suggest themselves, from our experience, as very high priorities for further research. Let me try briefly to depict them to you and to indicate the kind of research efforts that seem to be needed.

First, and undoubtedly the most serious problem in terms of number of projects significantly affected, is the issue of socio-economic impact of a transport facility in the area it opens up or makes more accessible. The debate has been long and inconclusive between those who have seen transport as a leading sector, capable of inducing other economic activity, and those who have seen transport investments as needing to respond only to given traffic demands. Both sides of the argument can be supported from World Bank experience. But the difficulty is that we still do not really know why transport has led effectively in some cases and not in others. The tendency in the Bank has been increasingly to insist upon comprehensive, or at least multisectoral, regional development programs being prepared for very undeveloped regions before embarking on transport investments. We do not assume spontaneous response. Research is needed in the form of more and deeper case studies than have so far generally been done to explain the causal relationships. It is also needed to help develop frameworks, properly parsimonious in data requirements, for optimal selection of roads in an undeveloped area and for identifying the critical minimum of complementary public action required in different circumstances. It is not so much a matter of improving traffic forecasting as of maximizing development impact.

Second is the problem of reducing unit costs of investment. We all know that high benefit-cost ratios can be misleading, unless complemented by an analysis to show that the solution propounded is the minimum-cost course of action for carrying the expected traffic. There are continuing doubts in our Bank as to whether the designs proposed by consultant engineers are to the best-adapted standards for the country and location in question; whether they take sufficient advantage of the scope for stage construction; and whether they make maximum feasible use of local resources. It must be very rare that a design standard used in a developed country would also be most appropriate for a country able to invest in transportation only one-hundredth the amount per new entrant in the labor force. I was most interested to observe at a recent national Roads Congress in India the great emphasis placed on research to increase the use of locally available road-building materials, to improve the efficiency of traditional local vehicles such a bullock-carts, and to strengthen traditional labor-intensive civil construction techniques. More generally, the most vital contribution that research can make to helping provide vehicular transportation for the hundreds of millions of people still without significant access to it in Africa, Asia an Latin America is, in my opinion, work to help reduce costs, for instance (a) filling the gap in knowledge of local materials and of how they can best be used for construction, (b) improving techniques for analyzing alternative design standards in light of local conditions, (c) overcoming the organizational problems which are a major obstacle to wider use of labor-intensive construction techniques, and (d) helping to upgrade traditional vehicles and possibly to develop a new inexpensive motorized vehicle adapted for farm use in poor countries.

Third is the problem of looking broadly enough at possible system-alternatives, and the nagging question that sometimes arises as to whether a wholly different system, network or combination of modes might not have been a more efficient solution to a transport need. One example of this problem of narrowness of view is the insufficient attention usually given to the potential for better traffic management and particularly for pricing mechanisms to allocate transport space more efficiently, so as to get a better use of existing infrastructure. The very interesting experiments in road space pricing now underway in Singapore and Malaysia are unique. Another example is the way that transport discussion and planning still tend to be excessively modal in nature, without sufficient attention to what can be done by cooperation between modes: highways have sometimes needlessly duplicated railways, railway networks have been preserved at excessive scale, and the potential for coastal shipping has suffered from neglect. And again, transport alternatives are too seldom considered in combination with alternative possible future patterns of regional distribution of population and economic activity. Broader approaches of these sorts are likely to become increasingly necessary with the growing pressure on transportation to release investment resources for use in other needy sectors and with the prospects for the emergence of metropolitan regions of unparalleled population size. Perhaps the priority needs for research in this area, from the point of view of the developing countries, are for development of framework methods - without the excessive sophistication that has sometimes been a failing here - for analyzing the broad system alternatives fifteen years ahead and helping strategic choices; studies of the problems of inter-modal transfer points; and expanded experimental work on congestion pricing.

The fourth area, last but by no means least, to which I would like to draw your attention is operational efficiency in the use of transport investment once installed. Disappointing operational efficiency - and here I include maintenance operations as well as train operations - has probably been the most serious single factor in causing many of the railway projects we have supported to show less satisfactory economic results than expected. But the problem has not been absent in Highway Departments, especially in regard to maintenance, where performance has rather frequently fallen short of expectation. There is increasing evidence that it also affects the trucking industry in developing countries, whether due to excessive regulation, fragmentation or lack of market organization and of terminals. Priority needs for research in this area seem to be on maintenance, particularly on convincing economic methods for analyzing and demonstrating the appropriate amounts to be done, and equally important ways of effectively organizing and motivating those

26

responsible for it; and on the problems confronting the trucking industry, so far little studied, in developing countries.

Despite the effort to concentrate on problems which emerge entirely from practice, the research priorities I have sketched are large. No figures are available on the amounts of resources being devoted to transportation research in the developing countries themselves. Work on their problems in developed countries is limited to a very few institutions, most notably the British Transport and Road Research Laboratory, which has taken initiatives in several of the fields I have mentioned. But it is safe to say that the total share of transportation research resources being devoted to the developing countries' problems is less even than their 15% share of total transportation investment - and even more disproportionately small if proper allowance is made for their relative lack of the systematized back-ground knowledge on transport and relevant local resources which has been accumulated over the years for the more developed countries. More is vitally needed.

It would, moreover, be very wrong to assume that the problems can be solved simply by transferring solutions, as and when discovered in the more developed countries, to the poorer nations. An even more unfortunate by-product of commercial pressures in the advanced world is sometimes to use developing countries as guinea-pigs for advanced technology prototypes untried even in the rich countries. Some advances in the better-off countries can of course be useful to developing ones too - for instance, fuel-economizing vehicles and urban bikeways. Advances in labor- and time-saving, capital-using directions, on the other hand, are seldom helpful, unless of extraordinary overall efficiency. In our experience few efforts to assist the developing countries have turned out less successful than those where the Foreign advisers hired decided merely to translate into the local language or institutional nomenclature a manual from North America of Europe; or where the consultant team just drew a blue-print of a project or a program without reference to local capacities to fully understand and update it and gather the requisite data on a regular basis. The manual and the blue-print may have been technically superior to what could have been achieved with giving more attention, respect and responsibility to local people and local resources, but they had little or no life beyond the consultants' departure. Real assistance to developing countries cannot be a by-product and requires special effort.

The need to involve local people may be particularly important in so far as most of the priorities turn out not to be in hardware or purely physical sciences but rather in the use and maintenance of facilities and planning, obviously very dependent on behavioural considerations. Indeed I am surprised how often the subjects that emerged in my priority list require interdisciplinary work by economists, engineers, sociologists and others. Take, for instance, even the seemingly technical problem of road maintenance, and design standards. One approach has been to build to seemingly appropriate initial standards and to urge Goverment to undertake adequate regular maintenance - often unsuccessfully in light of extreme shortages of resources and the pressures felt by Ministers to complete new roads. Another approach has been to assume from the start that maintenance will in practice get neglected and to build to unusually expensive but durable standards. A third approach, developed particularly in Mexico for rural roads, is to build initially to somewhat lower standards but with labor-intensive techniques organized by the local community. That way both understanding of the need for maintenance, and capacity to carry it out, are generated locally by the very

process of construction. Clearly this approach has advantages in terms of being potentially cheaper in capital cost and saving foreign exchange, as well as easing the maintenance problem. But it requires a type of organization in which few economists or engineers have any experience.

This example seems to me illustrative too of some of the need for, and considerable interest inherent in, cooperation from outside in the transportation research and development activities in developing countries. Some of the transportation research work underway in developing countries - such as that on congestion pricing or highway maintenance strategies - may have considerable direct relevance to more developed countries too. Even the problem of inducing appropriate complementary action for desirable socio-economic impact of transport investment is of broader relevance, as shown by current discussion in France of how to ensure that the Paris-Lyons high-speed train will have a decongesting rather than a further concentrating effect. In our small transportation research effort at the World Bank, we have the good fortune to be working with local institutions in Brazil, India, Kenya, Singapore and elsewhere. Just as I stressed before the limits to the role the foreigner can play in transportation research, so I would like to emphasize the real appreciation that is expressed for someone who brings, and conveys, a particular expertise that is needed but not locally available. I believe that those from other countries who have been involved in these research projects have found the experience intellectually most rewarding.

I recognize the very significant contribution that research can make to the developing world by discovering and propagating less costly solutions to the transport problems of the advanced nations thereby freeing a part of the very high proportion of world transport investment currently spent there, for use in countries of greater need. But I would go further and beg humbly to raise the question with you whether the research community might be able to organize its work in such a way as to give more support directly to resolving some of the pressing questions confronting the developing countries in their transportation planning and policy-making. I am aware that over the last ten years, there has been an increasing amount of cooperation among developed countries in certain types of transportation research, for instance in railway equipment development and some aspects of highway design. I wonder whether there may be scope for further international division of labor and elimination of duplication, for instance by leaving to different agreed lead-institutions full responsibility for particular technical areas. That could free resources for active collaboration on the problems arising in the much more dissimilar circumstances of the developing countries. Perhaps more institutes in the developed countries should have separate units orientated to overseas cooperation. In some cases adjustment of personnel, to include the more diversified range of disciplines I referred to earlier, might be appropriate. It may be desirable for more of the institutes in developed countries to have standing partnership arrangements with individual corresponding institutes in developing countries. The transport development projects which we help finance tend increasingly to have research dimensions and may sometimes provide a useful framework for such collaboration.

I have dwelt at some length on these questions of technical cooperation and transfer of technology before returning to the fundamental problem of Uncertainty, precisely because it seems to me that one of the most important measures that can be taken to confront an uncertain world is to build up and strengthen local capacities to respond to changing situations. The blue print plan has such limited value simply because there have almost always been at least one or two deviations from underlying forecasts even before the final printing is complete. My emphasis, earlier, on simple order-of-magnitude methods and analytical frameworks, with minimum date requirements and understandable to the maximum possible number of people, serves the same end. Excessively sophisticated hardware only adds to uncertainty. Local human capacities to respond effectively and in timely fashion to change are the heart of any answer to an Age of Uncertainty.

Sheer accumulation of knowledge and data, such as I have been suggesting on certain key issues, can also be a major contribution to reducing the uncertainties we face in trying to make sound investment decisions. And reductions in costs - whether by development of the better-adapted designs and construction techniques I was urging or by the more thorough analysis of system-wide alternatives - can have the very valuable attribute of reducing the cost equally of something that turns out to have been a mistake, hence devaluing the significance of uncertainty.

But there is also no question but that risk and uncertainty need to be taken into account more explicitly than they now typically are in actual investment decisions. I do not see the problem as being a very complicated one.

Rather it is a matter of getting away from unrealistically precise point estimates, and of weighing alternative sets of costs and benefits by their estimated probablilities of occurrence. Stage-construction would be favored, for example, where a road's traffic depends heavily on uncertain complementary investment. More limited berth provision would be preferred where a port could easily extend its working day. But practical implementation of such approaches in investment analysis has proven more difficult. And one of the many reasons why I look forward to the coming days' discussions is the hope to learn some more efficient mechanisms to cope with that problem.

Gentlemen, morally and politically the needs of the developing countries are the overriding issue of our epoch. The experience of the last few years teaches us: to "concentrate the mind wonderfully",; to avoid being beguiled by the beauties of theoretical perfection or the chimera of precise forecasts; and to focus our limited resources more than ever on finding practical, lower-cost answers to urgent strategic questions. I beg you to take the opportunity over the next days, among the many other things that will preoccupy you, to consider and discuss what collaboration you might bring to help deal with the key practical problems confronting the developing countries' transport development.

Keynote Address

by
R. P. BAFFOUR
Ghana Highway Authority, Ghana

I t is to me a very rare privilege indeed to be present at this conference and to participate in it. I cannot claim to represent developing countries generally, because as the last speaker said we are spread all over the world, covering practically three quarters of the globe and we have our very distinct social, economic and development problems and thus we cannot be grouped together in one sense and no one can say that he actually represents the interests of these developing countries in their various forms.

We in my little country, Ghana, in West Africa have distinct problems. These problems stretching over the past 30 years, present forms which are of great significance on the thinking and the planning and the discussions that we are having here. Indeed I think I am right in saying that the force of the significance of this conference is emphasized by the preliminent participation in it by the representatives of developing countries. And I would like to pay great tribute here to the paper presented before me by Mr. Willoughby. He more or less outlines the problems precisely that we face in developing countries. I like to make reference here that 25 years ago, I even think almost to the date, I came to Rotterdam for the first time, to discuss with the port authorities here the outlines of development that would enable us to decide where the major port of Ghana was to be. We had one in Takoradi, about 130 miles west of the capital and it became necessary for the government of Ghana, which was then colonial in some respects, to decide on where to place this big new port. We had in mind the planning of the water river dam and the electric power associated with it, which is near to Accra and so I came here to see the organization of the Rotterdam port and to hold discussions with prof. Thyssen of Delft University, who was then director of the hydraulics division of the University of Delft.

I made reference to Rotterdam to give you an idea as to the problems that beset us in the early beginning of our development. We did not only have to think of transportation, the building of roads, but we had to think ot our ports, the organization of our shipping, our air traffic systems and so on. All those problems came to the fall in the early days and some people had to sit together to draw up a blue print, which may have been hypothetical, which may have been based on false precepts, false factors or indefinite ideas, but some people had to sit down and draw up this blue print or a system to follow, however faulty.

We were unlucky because we had no research organization in Ghana at the time and practically no means of taking decisions whatsoever of a technical or even socio-economic nature on the transportation need in the country. So we had to make use of exterior advisors in the matter. I was, at the time, connected with the urban transportation of Accra. We were operating, at the time, with converted army vehicles, 30 of them on the urban bus transport system. It was with the advice of efficient British people that we embarked for the first time in constructing our own buses with proper bodies which we helped to design and had manufactured in the prototype in Birmingham. Then together we built 180 buses comparatively cheaper than when they would have been produced entirely in Great Britain. It was a very efficient new bus, because we based our designs on the best that the British could export at the time though better suited to our particular type of country and terrain.

We have the Leylands and we built all our buses on the Leyland design and we trained our men specifically to work on them and though the results were never satisfactory, they were encouraging. We were able to turn out 90% of bus servicability and the service was all right.

Then came a situation where the government had to decide on expanding the service. Then came the importance of influencing the policy of decision-makers. That is when we found our biggest draw-back.

When the time came to spend hardwon foreign currency on expanding our transportation system, other kinds of interests came in. There were foreign influences who urged the deviation from the standard types of vehicles we knew. The result was chaos and disaster. What would have been in 6 years a fleet of 400, was reduced to 70. They were all wrecks. Of course the analysis is quite simple, the population and thus the need of transportation was creasing, the passenger carrying capacity of the buses became less and less significant and the few buses there were, were overloaded to breaking capacity, like the old warrior horses with a broken back. So the result was a total wreck and since then we have not recovered. Various stages of experimentation with different types of buses have led to disaster. One type after the other has been tried. The result is that the population of one million in Accra, which should have an operating fleet of 350 buses, has now to do with 50. So you can imagine the number of passengers queuing sometimes half a mile long, waiting for 3 hours to get home after work. Some have to walk 2 miles to their work instead of waiting for transportation.

This gives you an idea of the situation which some developing countries face, not because of incapability to follow up, but because of the unavailability of research facilities and the inadequacy or ineffectiveness of the decision-making machinery. These are very important factors.

I can tell you what happened a hundred years ago. Our people walked from one part of the country to another on the roads, 25 miles a day, free from highwaymen and so on. There were unwritten laws that guided the traveller from one village to another, protecting him and his goods, unwritten laws which were very strong and abided by the people.

So transportation was free and easy. One would have thought that with the advance in science and technology, transportation would improve. But has it? No, it has not.

Even interurban transportation is at a very low ebb.

Roads have been built to all sorts of standards and I would like to praise Mr. Willoughby's emphasis on the standards achieved and the standards prepared by outside research organizations for developing countries. Some are terribly inadequate, unrealistic. They are merely a copy book of blue prints of research endeavours, research decisions which have been taken in other countries, imposed on developing countries, completely unrelated to the practical issues to be faced, entirely theoretical, and in many cases the results of their influence are so fundamental that it will take generations to correct them.

I had a similar case some 6 months ago, a decision had to be taken by the highway authority. Contracts had been awarded for the construction of 180 miles of very important trans-routes through the country. The specifications had been passed long before the authority had the opportunity to examine them more closely. We found to our dismay that the specifications were so unrealistic as to expect not more than 5 years of life of the roads. We had to urge the government to stop and suspend their order of contract until the specifications had been re-examined. Subsequently after the re-examination, new specifications were drawn up where we did ensure the best use of local material and give the roads a life of not less than 15 years. We had to do this, although as a matter of fact it annoyed the government, but it listened when the highway authority put forward this very strong case and urged the afore-mentioned revision of the specifications.

These are some of the problems we have to face, and indeed we have established very good working relationships with the British road service organization, which we have maintained and which are giving great benfits, and we hope that as was emphasized by Mr. Willoughby, that developed countries should endeavour to establish links with research organizations in the country and where they do not exist, encourage the establishment of such organizations, so that the links between developed and developing countries may be strengthened to the better mind of both the developed and developing countries. This should not be a relationship in which the developed countries treat the developing ones as a dumping ground or as research guinea-pigs but as a realistic positive approach to the program of a world of collaboration because, after all, we have to look in terms of the whole research and discussions here as a global responsibility, where we are all responsible for what happens on this globe and not necessarily for what concerns us alone or only concerns the developed countries but what concerns developing countries much more, because it is they who form the strength of the chain, the weaker element determining the strength of the global chain of transportation.

We have problems, and I must admit political ones as well, over which perhaps we have no control and I would like to raise this point. I look forward to the day on which transportation will be looked upon as a world responsibility, having influence, not power, over the decision-making organizations and bodies in the various countries, particularly in developing countries, so that the decisions may be taken in the right, the positive, direction.

Quite recently we had the big problem of port congestion in Lagos, the capital of Nigeria. You all may have heard that at one time there were as many as 500 ships lying outside of the port of Lagos with a three months' waiting time. The situation got very serious, with many of these ships waiting with cement rapidly deteriorating in the heat of the tropics, so that some solution had to be found. The Ghana government offered help and Nigeria accepted it very willingly. Meetings were held in Accra, in which I took part and regulations were drawn up to govern the use of Temor port as an extension of Lagos, whereby many of the container ships would be diverted to Accra to take the load off the Lagos congestion. To organize this was quite simple, the first ships started arriving and the intention was to organize fleets of heavy trucks to carry the containers across by road, only 500 kilometers from Accra to Lagos.

Now we did not realize at the time that there were all sorts of imponderable problems that we did not anticipate. The first containers took off and then various problems began to erupt. The political differences between the countries cropped up to the extent that the system had to be stopped.

We were worried, in the first instance, of this road, because it was constructed during the war in 1940/41 and we did not know whether it could take the strain. We did a survey which showed that it could take the strain for 4 years and we thought it was well worth the risk. We advised the government to go ahead with the scheme not realizing at the time that the political reservations were so significant that as a result the Lagos congestion had to remain as it was and be solved as the situation would allow.

These are some of the problems that developing countries have to face. In the first place we have very few research organizations and whenever there are, they are fundamental and rudimentary. We look forward to greater participation, greater encouragement from developed countries to help to set up organizations; first of all to create and establish the training of research people with interchange arrangements and also to make it possible to raise the standard and status of developing countries with research organizations, to influence them more deeply; to raise the status of research organizations before their various governments, so that they may listen more closely to their decisions. The reason is, that in the past, politicians have not been technical or scientific and if they were at all, they were quite suspicious, and very rightly too, of decisions that technicians and scientists would pass on to them. Until and unless they have greater confidence in them, this can be emphasized by the right decisions that the collaborating research organizations in the developed world can exercise on them.

This is the appeal I would like to make on the developed countries particularly. This is the line in which the developing countries can be helped to establish themselves more fully and play a part in the advancement of transportation in the world. I would like to emphasize again that transportation is a global exercise. We are willing and ready to assist in any help that you can give us towards an advance in the use of our materials, in developing our research efforts and of making sure that we have sufficient good and wise material, in order to make the right decisions in the future.

An agenda for urban transportation

by

C. KENNETH ORSKI

Urban Mass Transportation Administration

U.S. Department of Transportation

W inston Churchill once said "We shape our buildings; and then the buildings shape us". The same, I think, can be said of transportation. We shape our transportation facilities, but then we allow the transportation facilities to mold us, our lives and our cities. In managing the UMTA program we have been mindful of this pervasive influence of transportation. And we have tried to make our grant decisions and exercise our other authority accordingly.

Having said this, the question remains: what should be the federal role in urban transportation? What precisely should the federal mass transportation program seek to accomplish? These are not easy questions, but they need to be answered. For in these days of growing competition for limited federal resources, we need to understand what special reasons there might be to justify the Federal presence in this field, and what payoffs are to be realized from a continued federal involvement in urban mass transportation.

In my remarks this morning I propose to share with you some thoughts on this subject. I shall argue that the UMTA program has a threefold mission to accomplish. The first is to help preserve the transit option for the millions of people who currently depend on it; the second is to assist in the national efforts to revitalize the Nations's cities; and the third is to help guide urban growth over the long run into more orderly and efficient settlement patterns that will help the Nation to adapt to an era of limited energy resources.

Let me discuss each of these in turn.

MAINTAINING AND IMPROVING EXISTING TRANSIT SYSTEMS

To begin with, the UMTA program must assist in the job of maintaining and modernizing existing transit systems in cities large and small. We often tend to forget that even today, with transit ridership drastically reduced from its former pre-World War II levels, the transit systems of this country still carry some 16 million daily riders.

These riders are part of our transit dependent public. While most of them are not too poor to own a car or too old to drive, they are nonetheless "captives" of the public transit systems because they have no other effective or economical way of moving about. Clearly, a Federal program devoted to the support of public transportation cannot ignore the needs of these millions of transit users nor their legitimate desire for more convenient, reliable and comfortable service.

Not only are there substantial numbers of transit patrons whose travel conditions deserve to be improved, the maintenance of existing transit systems is also essential to the survival and efficient functioning of our metropolitan areas. This is especially true of the older industrial cities of the Northeast and Midwest. One can no more imagine cities like Boston, New York or Chicago getting along without their transit systems than one can conceive of them functioning without telephones or electricity. Transit for these cities represents more than long term insurance against an energy constrained future - it is an essential public service without which the cities would quickly collapse.

USING TRANSIT TO REVITALIZE CITIES

The mission of transit and the UMTA program, however, is not confined to improving mobility. Transit investment, we believe, must also be part of a broader national strategy to revitalize our cities.

The Federal mass transportation assistance program has an enormous impact on the major cities. In those cities which are building or operating rail transit systems, the annual dollar impact of UMTA assistance typically exceeds that of the HUD community development program and general revenue sharing combined. Particularly significant, of course, are the huge rail transit construction grants. These grants usually support the largest single public works projects ever undertaken in the city in question.

These projects can do more than just help to move people faster and more efficiently. They have a massive impact in terms of real estate development, land use, economic activity and job creation. When used creatively, they can help to stem the decline and promote the recovery of our older metropolitan areas.

The Federal transit assistance program, in other words, should have a much broader mission than has been traditionally assigned to it. The UMTA program should be enlisted in the national effort to preserve and strengthen our cities, and its success should be measured not just in terms of increased ridership but in terms of its salutary influence on the urban economy and the quality of the urban environment. Dedicating the Federal transit program to the cause of urban rejuvenation is also a way of broadening public support of mass transportation. And transit needs that broader urban constituency if it intends to claim a secure share of public resources.

Joint Development and Value Capture

One way for these major transit investments to pay off in broader terms is through joint development projects involving multipurpose activity centers built around and integrated with transit stations. The payoff to the city is obvious. There can be a redevelopment and renewal impact on a deteriorating station site area. Joint development can add significant tax rateables from new office and commercial construction. And it can be a magnet for center city housing which, of course, is high on most of the major cities' agenda.

For transit, too, there is a payoff from joint development activity. New development, new activity centers, higher density around transit stations - all of these generate ridership and rail transit needs high ridership in order to justify and sustain its growing capital and operating costs. We have tried to do whatever we can through our management of the discretionary grant program to reward and stimulate joint development activity. We even have some specific legislative authority - as yet unused - through the so-called Young Amendment to permit UMTA funds to flow into public and quasi-public development entities for joint development activities. The leverage possibilities of this mechanism are enormous.

Another way to exploit the economic development impact of major transit construction is through the technique of value capture. Value capture involves recovering a portion of the increased real estate values created as a result of the transit investment and dedicating them to help support a transit system. It seems eminently reasonable that some of the cost of the system should be met in part out of the appreciation in land value which the system itself has helped to create.

There is another reason why the concept of value capture is particularly appropriate in connection with transit development. Fares will never approach the levels necessary to carry operating coasts, let alone to amortize capital investment. But if transit users cannot alone be expected to bear the full burden of supporting the cost of public transportation, perhaps other beneficiaries of the transit system should assume some of the residual cost. As a matter of equity, it is not unreasonable to expect that all who benefit from a public project should help to pay part of its cost.

Value capture financing can support transit in a variety of ways. For example, revenues from air rights leasing, tax increment financing or special tax districts could help finance second stage construction of the system; they could be directed to offset operating deficits; or they could help support some of the capital costs associated with joint development activities or other improvements around transit stations, such as pedestrian malls, skywalks, etc.

One city which has made a creative use of the principle of value capture is Toronto. This city purchased land adjacent to transit stations before construction began and leased lands to real estate developers through 99-year leases. Toronto hopes to pay off the entire capital construction costs of the system in 30 years from this mutually advantageous use of the value capture mechanism.

Although we cannot yet say that value capture will be unfailingly successful in defraying the capital costs of transit development in American cities, it offers a major untapped source of transit revenue which, in these days of fiscal constraints, we can no longer afford to ignore.

Leveraging Private Investment

The major capital grants can be used not only to encourage real estate development at the "micro" level, i.e., around transit station sites, but also to leverage complementary private investment throughout the metropolitan area. The large UMTA grants, in other words, can act as stimuli for private capital commitments to revitalize economically depressed cities and create new jobs in areas of high unemployment.

With this in mind, several of UMTA's recent major grant actions - Detroit, Philadelphia, and Boston, for example - have been conditioned on obtaining commitments to fund private commercial and office development and job training programs. To the extent possible, physical integration or linking of the new development with the transit system should be encouraged in order to reinforce the viability of the transit investment.

Targeting Transit Investment on Central Cities

Using federal assistance to encourage private investment would be particularly effective if the combined resources could be targeted on areas of particular need, such as the older central cities and inner suburbs. In this way the economic and job creation impact of the transit program would be concentrated where it is most needed.

Targeting transit investment on central cities is also a way of restoring a measure of balance to the federal transportation assistance program. For years our federal transportation investments have facilitated long distance commuting, and thus unwittingly contributed to the outmigration of people and jobs to the suburbs. By focusing new transit investment on improved circulation in the core area we might help the central city to resist more effectively the suburban "pull".

This, in fact, has been the principal rationale behind UMTA's Downtown People Mover Program. Contrary to what one might expect, this program is not designed to test new hardware or to experiment with advanced technology. Rather, the aim of this demonstration program is to assess the economic impact of improved circulation systems on the central city.

The downtown people mover can perform two important transportation functions. In the words of Colin Buchanan, it can help commuters "wiggle in" and "wiggle out" of the congested downtown area with a minimum of delay and inconvenience. And it can facilitate the myriad of trips that make up the internal circulation within the central business district. In either of its two modes the DPM can give a great boost to a central city. It can promote a better economic functioning of the business district, open up declining downtown areas of re-development, and stimulate investor confidence in the future of the corporate city.

Transit Improvements to Enhance Urban Neighbourhoods

So far I have talked about the urban revitalization impact of large capital grants. But much can be accomplished also through more modest efforts. In city after city, downtown merchants, in-town residents, local developers and lending institutions, banded together in a variety of cooperative efforts, have demonstrated that downtown districts and residential neighbourhoods can be revitalized and preserved without a massive expenditure of funds.

Baltimore, Seattle, Minneapolis, Boston, Cincinnati, Philadelphia, Hartford, and New Orleans are just a few examples of cities where neighbourhood groups and local merchants' associations in cooperation with local officials, have embarked on successful programs of housing renovation and rehabilitation, turning incipiently declining areas into thriving inner city residential neighbourhoods.

All these efforts have certain things in common. They are neighbourhood-oriented; they draw heavily on local citizen initiative and private sector resources; they spring from an emerging ethic of urban conservation which stresses the best use of existing urban assets before undertaking massive new construction programs; and they are motivated by a new concern for neighbourhood preservation, which is grounded in the belief that stable and cohesive urban neighbourhoods are the key to the continued vitality of the nation's cities. Low cost transportation improvements should form an integral part of these neighbourhood preservation efforts. Next to housing rehabilitation, they are probably the most effective way of restoring a sense of livability to urban neighbourhoods.

These transportation improvements can take a variety of forms. They can curb of discourage the use of automobiles and trucks in heavily congested shopping streets and quiet residential ares; they can improve the pedestrian environment through creation of malls, transitways, skywalks connecting downtown office and commercial buildings, vest pocket parks, etc; and they can provide local transit services in residential neighbourhoods and downtown retail areas. Just changing the nature of the street with planting, gateways at entrances or different pavements can often transform a street into a "place" and enhance immeasurably the quality of the neighbourhood environment.

BUILDING FOR AN ENERGY-SCARCE FUTURE

The third objective of transport and of the UMTA program should be to prepare the way for a gradual transition from an era of abundant resources to an economy of scarcity.

Our urban transportation systems and the spread patterns of development that have come to characterize our metropolitan areas are a legacy of the old faith that we and endless amounts of land to build on and unlimited energy to burn.

We now realize that our fuel supplies are finite and that the continued outward expansion of our urban areas can be sustained only at a growing financial and environmental cost. Each new subdivision, each "leap frog" development adds to the strain on municipal services, takes away valuable agricultural land, and places an added burden on fiscal and energy resources. Sooner of later we must end our profligate use of resources and start on the road toward more compact, energy conserving forms of settlement and land use patterns that reduce the need for unnecessary movement.

Can transportation help us in this effort? The answer to this question depends on whether you believe that transit can serve to guide the forces of urban growth and stem the trend toward low density dispersion.

Transit as a Tool of Metropolitan Development

Those who have recently visited Toronto would be inclined to answer in the affirmative. Since 1964 the Yonge Street subway line and its extensions have served as a magnet for nearly 80 percent of all office and residential high rise development in the metropolian area. A large proportion of this construction has taken place within a five-minute walk of the subway stations.

An especially striking aspect of the Toronto experience is the way in which the incremental extension of the subway system anticipated growth in population and economic activity, and encouraged planned, clustered development of residential areas as well as of the booming central business district.

Can the Toronto experience be replicated in our own cities? The evidence so far in inconclusive. The Bay Area's BART has stimulated a good deal of office construction in the central business districs of San Francisco and Oakland, but as yet there is little sign of high density development elsewhere. Only a few new office buildings have been built near any outlying stations, and even these buldings had difficulty finding tenants. Most suburban stations still stand in virtual isolation from any development activity in their sub-region, seemingly ignored by all except commuters who park their cars in adjoining lots.

One explanation may be that most BART stations are located in established neighbourhoods with strong community pressure to maintain the established single family housing pattern. Another reason may be that the Bay Area is endowed with an excellent freeway network which renders most locations within the area already highly accessible. The BART system has improved that accessibility only marginally - not sufficiently it has been suggested, to influence location decisions of many households and firms.

Whether this situation will continue into the future is still a matter of conjecture. One likely scenario is that, with the price of gasoline rising, automobile use will become expensive enough to begin influencing location decisions. More and more people will want to live and work within easy distance of public transit. Land in the vicinity of transit stations will increase in value, thus creating an economic incentive for more intensive development. In time, concentrations of office, commercial and residential activity will spring up in compact clusters around many suburban stations.

Such is the classic scenario of the influence of rising fuel prices on metropolitan form. These effects, however, may take a long time to become manifest, because the shift in the comparitive economics of metropolitan location - especially in auto-dominated areas - is likely to be gradual. Thus, it may be too early for any firm conclusions about BART's impact on the Bay Area's development. Any definitive judgments about rail transit's ability to restructure a region may have to be deferred for another ten years or more.

Compatible Land Use and Development Policies

There is, however, a way of accelerating the process I have just described through a deliberate policy of growth management. Such policy would involve the use of various local incentives and controls to reinforce the developmental impact of a rail transit system. These could include incentive zoning, allowance of land write-downs, tax abatements, provision of local feeder bus services to transit stations, and automobile management policies. Their purpose would be to facilitate the process of high density development and to channel the forces of growth into preselected patterns of settlement.

This does not mean that the Federal government should impose a national land use policy favoring high density living patterns and actively discouraging scattered development. Instead, it is a matter of requiring consistency and coordination between the rail transit plan and the local land use and development policies - and according preference to those communities which, at their own volition, are prepared to support such policies and implementing arrangements.

This accounts, in part, for UMTA's willingness to go forward with a rapid transit grant to Miami, where the adopted land use plan is based upon activity centers linked by transit, and where the Dade County government has the institutional and jurisdictional breadth necessary to implement transit and land use plans jointly.

A showing of compatibility between the proposed rail investment and the region's land use and development objectives has also become a condition of the "letters of commitment" that have been addressed to Los Angeles, Detroit, Honolulu and other major grantees. UMTA is saying to those cities that, while land use plans and development objectives remain a matter of local decision, it does not make sense for the Federal government or for local communities to commit hundreds of millions of public dollars for new fixed facilities unless there is a local commitment to actions and policies that will make it possible for the transit investment to be part of some broader regional growth management and energy conservation strategy.

Improved Linkages Among Federal Programs

The process of restructuring metropolitan areas into

more energy efficient forms of settlement would also be facilitated if our transit policy became part of a broader policy of urban growth within which all our urban-related programs could operate.

This is not the case today. Indeed, many of the current federal programs and policies inadvertently promote dispersal rather than concentration. Our tax code, water and sewer grants, housing mortgage guarantees, highway programs, all have spurred development farther and farther away from the urban core, scattering housing projects thinly through areas in a more or less haphazard fashion.

In these circumstances the transit program can at best be compensatory in character. It can only compensate for the consequences of the spatial organization and living patterns which other federal programs - and our own preferences as to living patterns - have unwittingly encouraged.

If transit investment is to be allowed to realize its full form-giving potential it must be linked with a number of other Federal programs and initiatives to support a comprehensive and coordinated urban growth policy. The opportunities for such linkages are numerous.

For example, HUD mortgages and community development grants could be oriented toward multi-use acti-vity centers related to rail transit stations. Commerce Department (EDA) and Small Business Administration funds and Department of Labor's manpower training and CEDA grants could finance a wide variety of supportive public works and job creation programs in association with transit construction. HUD's "701" planning grants could be directed toward station impact zone planning to ensure that broader community development goals in those neighbourhoods are served. EPA's water and sewer grants could be coordinated with transit construction grants so that no large developments are allowed to occur in places where no adequate public transportation service is planned to be provided. Finally, HUD's rehabilitation loans and financial support from the National Foundation on the Arts could be joined with DOT's neighbourhood transportation and pedestrian improvement programs to preserve and revitalize city residential neighbourhoods and declining central business districts.

The aim, in other words, would be to link all federal programs that have major developmental impact for the common purpose of promoting the goals of orderly metropolitan growth and urban revitalization.

The UMTA program, I believe, is an essential component of any such comprehensive urban strategy.

Tendances de la recherche dans les transports urbains
Un point de vue

par

A. BIEBER

Institut de Recherche des Transports, France

C omment résumer, en quelques pages, les "composantes principales" d'une activité aussi foisonnante que la recherche sur les transports urbains? Il n'est bien entendu pas question d'en dresser un "bilan", en se référant à une structure de recherche d'efficacité (objectifs, moyens, résultats) qui ne s'applique pas à la recherche. Aussi doit-on se rebattre sur l'exposé d'une interprétation personnelle de quelques faits marquants de la recherche. J'ai choisi de le faire sous la forme d'un schéma très simplifié, caricatural en quelque sorte, des liaisons entre les états successifs du développement économique, les politiques en matière de transports urbains et les grands objectifs assignés plus ou moins implicitement de la recherche.

Je proposerais donc d'examiner l'activité de recherche en relation avec les deux états successifs de la croissance que nous avons récemment connus: croissance rapide jusqu'en 1970 environ, croissance ralentie depuis quelques années.

1. LA RECHERCHE DANS LA PHASE DE CROISSANCE ECONOMIQUE RAPIDE
(1950-1970)

Dans le prolongement des efforts de reconstruction de l'après-guerre, les priorités politiques en matière d'aménagement urbain ont été, dans les années 1950, l'équipement au meilleur coût des vastes zones d'urbanisation créées par l'expansion à la périphérie des grandes agglomérations. Cette primauté du nouveau sur l'existant, de la périphérie sur le centre, de l'infrastructure sur l'exploitation, s'est traduite par une orientation de la planification privilégiant, au niveau méthodologique, les approches:

– à objectifs dimensionnels: le problème a été souvent réduit à celui d'un dimensionnement des infrastructures,

– à objectifs statiques: "l'objet" planifié a été plus un état final avant d'être un processus de transformation,

– sans innovation: l'espace urbain futur a été vu comme résultant d'une croissance "homothétique" de l'espace actuel: l'innovation sociale et l'innovation technique ont été évacuées de la réflexion, notamment par le biais des "modèles de trafic".

Ces orientations correspondent, est-il nécessaire de le rappeler, à une vision très "mécaniste" de la prospective économique, marquée par un postulat de continuité de l'expansion, sans problèmes d'environnement, sans problèmes énergétiques, sans problèmes sociaux.

C'est sur l'idée d'une satisfaction homogène des besoins d'écoulement de flux de déplacement (liés à une prospective, finement découpée dans l'espace, de l'utilisation du sol) que repose la méthodologie "classique" de ingéniosité des transports urbains.

C'est enfin à ces bases qu'il faut, me semble-t-il, rattacher l'attachement que nous éprouvons tous pour les "modèles de demande".

On peut comprendre, avec le recul, les raisons du succès prodigieux de cette approche, dans les milieux techniques, et la bonne réceptivité des milieux politiques dans le contexte de l'expansion économique.

L'observation de la demande permet en effet d'établir une méthodologie officielle sur le seul "canal" politiquement neutre de révélation des besoins de déplacement. Elle assure sans difficulté la légitimité d'une intervention technique visant à transcender les arbitrages sociaux que représente toute politique de transport. Elle rend positive toute action destinée à augmenter quelque part la mobilité de quelqu'un, puisqu'elle fait de la satisfaction de toute demande de transport l'objet même de la démarche planificatrice. Le problème des effets de cette recherche de mobilité sur les conditions de vie n'est pas posé.

Dans ces conditions, la recherche "classique" paraît entièrement dominée par le problème de l'amélioration de la boucle prédictive: (Utilisation du sol, Déplacements effets sur les localisations) au moyen de modélisations fondées sur l'observation de corrélations statistiques agrégées.

Si l'approche statistique agrégée a permis d'améliorer quelque peu notre compréhension des phénomènes de production de déplacements, comme le montreront sans aucun doute les débats de ce colloque, il n'en est malheureusement pas de même pour tout ce qui concerne les localisations et la nature de la croissance urbaine. La concentration des pouvoirs économiques des sociétés modernes, le "jeu économique" qu'elle implique au niveau des décisions de localisation des grands complexes industriels, commerciaux, et même résidentiels, est fort peu compatible avec l'approche modélisatrice statistique: faut-il s'étonner dans ces conditions de la crédibilité quasi-nulle des modèles de développement urbain?

Ainsi, l'approche planificatrice classique, orientée sur la seule satisfaction de la "demande" de transport, s'est d'abord heurtée dans notre pays à une difficulté technique. Nous pouvons la résumer en disant que la prospective des déplacements n'a pu, à elle seule, constituer une méthode de planification valable en l'absence d'une prospective urbaine (et de ce fait sociale) crédible.

Mais elle s'est ensuite heurtée à une difficulté beaucoup plus profonde, à mes yeux, lorsque le ralentissement de la croissance a fait se poser la question fondamentale de la répartition des bienfaits d'une recherche d'amélioration de la mobilité.

2. LA RECHERCHE DANS LA PHASE DE RALENTISSEMENT DE LA CROISSANCE
2.1. La recherche socio-économique
Nous ne ferons qu'évoquer les problèmes de "nui-

sances", effets externes au système de transport que la motorisation de masse, l'urbanisation incontrôlée, des réalisations techniques insuffisamment étudiées ont créées un peu partout: non pas parce que je les juge secondaires, mais parce qu'ils ne constituent pas un champ de recherche spécifique au domaine des transports.

Par contre, l'interrogation qui se fait jour dans certains milieux de la recherche sociale, au sujet d'une forme plus insidieuse, mais plus profonde, des effets négatifs de l'accroissement de mobilité sur les modes de vie me paraît très important pour l'avenir de la recherche urbaine. Si je résume en quelques mots cette thèse, défendue d'un point de vue général par Karl Vopper puis développée par Illitch et Dupuy dans le secteur des transports, l'accroissement de mobilité des plus mobiles (et c'est bien dans ce sens que nous conduit une planification basée sur la satisfaction des "demandes" observées et extrapolées) s'accompagnerait nécessairement d'un appauvrissement des opportunités d'échanges (certains diraient d'insertion sociale) des plus pauvres et renforcerait donc l'inégalité entre groupes sociaux.

Comment concrétiser mieux qu'Illitch, ce phénomène lorsqu'il écrit "l'industrie du transport" dicte la configuration de l'espace social. Les autoroutes font reculer les champs, les ambulances éloignent les médecins du voisinage de leurs malades, le camion fait disparaître le marché local puis le village (et qu'en résultat) l'industrie façonne une nouvelle espèce d'hommes: les usagers ... exaspérés par l'inégalité croissante, la pénurie du temps et leur propre impuissance ... attendant leur salut de changements techniques, vivant de l'espoir de transports qui permettraient de se déplacer plus vite et du jour où, propulsés d'un réseau à un autre, programmés à rencontrer leurs semblables, ils seront définitivement pris en charge par le "monopole" de l'industrie des transports [1].

Cette vision peut paraître pessimiste et inutilement "radicalisée". Pouvons-nous pour autant nier que les "progrès" apportés à la mobilité se sont surtout traduits, du fait des facilités qu'ils accordaient du même coup à la concentration industrielle et commerciale et à la ségrégation urbaine, par un alourdissement des budgets-temps en des budgets-coûts du transport pour une part de plus en plus importante de la population?

La traduction de cette idéologie en principes pour l'action est, comme l'a bien noté Illitch, très ambigue. C'est d'abord la volonté égalitariste qui s'exprime au sein des associations d'usager [2] mais c'est aussi la revendication pour "plus de transport" (principalement sous forme de transports collectifs) qui s'affirme même dans les environnements où la présence de très puissants moyens de transport a fortement contribué à créer des ensembles urbains, générateurs d'inégalités structurelles, insupportables par leur dimension et la ségrégation spatiale qui les caractérisent.

Une question importante est donc posée à tout planificateur dans les sociétés développées: elle consiste à déceler dans l'ensemble des propositions d'améliorations de la mobilité celles qui seront les plus favorables au plan de l'équité sociale à long terme.

Sous cet éclairage, les outils de la planification classique paraissent peu adaptés et il ne faut pas s'étonner de leur faible impact dans les études conduites avec une forte participation des associations d'usagers.

Les tentatives pour relancer sur une autre voie le processus de planification peuvent être brièvement évoquées. Elles reposent sur l'idée d'une "valorisation" plus substantielle de la mobilité urbaine, au moyen d'une *relation directe entre états du système de transport et éléments de la qualité de vie urbaine*, sans "passage obligé" par l'expression du flux de déplacement.

1 - Les recherches d'indicateurs d'accessibilité, internes au secteur des transports, n'englobant pas la relation du transport et du mode de vie des groupes sociaux.

Ces recherches sont satisfaisantes aux yeux de ceux qui sont motivés par l'idée de refléter par un indicateur unique même très imparfait, les problèmes d'équité en matière de transports urbaines. Mais le concept d'accessibilité a déjà reçu de nombreuses critiques, liées au fait qu'il n'échappe pas au défaut fondamental de séparer le composant "transport" de l'ensemble des autres composants des modes de vie. C'est ainsi qu'il apparaît aux yeux des critiques les plus radicaux (Dupuy) comme un artifice destiné à glorifier les services de transport encore plus que ne pouvait le fair le calcul économique néoclassique.

2 - La recherche d'indicateurs *reliés aussi directement que possible aux séquences d'activités (et de déplacements) caractéristiques des modes de vie des différents groupes sociaux.* Sans entrer dans les détails, nous rappellerons que ces recherches [3] fournissent une base d'évaluation des politiques de transport en proposant de vérifier comment les modes de vie (schématisés par une séquence d'activités-types) peuvent se développer normalement en tel ou tel lieu d'une agglomération, en fonction des services de transport mis en place pour la desserte des divers quartiers de l'agglomération concernée.

La situation actuelle des recherches relatives au cadre d'évaluation des politiques de transports urbaines est ainsi particulièrement ouverte: si la grande majorité des chercheurs a abandonné l'espoir d'éclairer des décisions par les procédures de comptabilisation des gains de temps de la méthodologie classique, aucune des directions de recherche relatives aux indicateurs sociaux citées plus haut n'a atteint à notre connaissance un niveau de développement tel qu'il soit possible d'en espérer un support méthodologique puissant dans les prochaines années. Dans ces conditions, l'idée d'un effort soutenu de recherche fondamentale sur les relations entre mobilité et modes de vie doit être acceptée par les grands "programmateurs" de la recherche, au niveau national. En effet, du point de vue de la recherche sur les comportements, l'émergence des questions relatives à la valorisation de la mobilité change profondément la nature des besoins de connaissance sur les comportements de mobilité. Disons, pour schématiser, qu'elle remplace dans beaucoup de cas un besoin de projection sans compréhension, par un besoin de compréhension sans projection. C'est ainsi qu'il devient nécessaire d'aborder le problème de la mobilité plus par le biais de l'analyse des comportements individuels que par celui des agrégats de population, plus par l'analyse du vécu des déplacements, en liaison avec les modes de vie, que par la corrélation statistique.

On notera ainsi que de nombreuses recherches en cours renvoient les questions posées sur la mobilité à l'ensemble de ses déterminants sociaux "primaires", en étudiant pour citer des exemples marquants:
– les liens entre mobilité et insertion sociale
– les liens entre mobilité et motorisation
– les liens entre mobilité et organisation sociale

Parallèlement, une nouvelle forme d'appréciation statistique de la mobilité peut paraître particulièrement pertinente, parce que plus étroitement liée au mode de vie de l'individu: il s'agit du budget-temps transport qui a déjà suscité d'intéressantes recherches dans plusieurs pays d'Europe.

Contrairement à ce qui se passe aux Etats-Unis, une attention relativement modeste a été donnée jusqu'à présent en Europe aux "modèles désagrégés" qui seront l'objet de sessions spécialisées de ce colloque. Leur intérêt scientifique potentiel paraît cependent important car

36

leurs résultats éclairent les déterminantes de la mobilité individuelle.

L'apport des sciences sociales marque profondément, comme l'a récemment très bien noté D. Brand l'ensemble de la recherche appliquée sur ce que beaucoup de praticiens appellent encore la "prévision de la demande", alors même que les objectifs de l'investigation scientifique sur la mobilité ont déjà largement dépassé ce stade strictement utilitaire [4].

2.2. La recherche technique

Notons tout d'abord deux caractéristiques de notre secteur de recherche: d'une part, du côté des "consommateurs" du transport urbain, la diversité des situations économiques, la complexité des phénomènes sociaux qui génèrent les déplacements et fixent les localisations, d'autre part, du côté de la production du transport urbain, la puissance et la concentration des milieux de la production automobile principalement. Aucun secteur ne mérite, me semble-t-il, plus que celui des transports urbains, que lui soit appliqué le slogan mis à la mode, il y a quelques années, par un mouvement de consommateurs américains: "Unis nous produisons, divisés nous consommons".

Dans un contexte aussi inégal, la recherche technique doit essentiellement faire face à une inertie considérable des milieux industriels, au demeurant peu préoccupés jusqu'à présent par les problèmes spécifiquement urbains (à l'exception du bruit et de la pollution). Pour l'automobile, cette insensibilité industrielle est, semble-t-il, à rapprocher du fait que l'automobile est (tout au moins en cas de mono-motorisation) acquise en tout état de cause par des usagers avides de liberté de mouvement dans l'espace des loisirs, espace régional et interurbain et non urbain. Pour les transports collectifs, il suffit de jeter un regard sur les volumes de production (et les chiffres d'affaires) de la branche "autobus" de n'importe quel producteur de poids lourd ou de la branche "métro" de n'importe quel constructeur ferroviaire pour comprendre que le matériel de transports urbains ne peut être qu'un sousproduit de faible importance dans la stratégie industrielle des groupes concernés.

On a cherché dans le passé à vaincre cette insensibilité de diverses façons et en particulier par l'utilisation des capacités "aéro-spatiales". Trop exclusivement axées sur les techniques de pointe, reposant sur l'idée de l'automatisation de conduite et le site propre intégral, ces recherches ont semble-t-il échoué, au moins provisoirement, si l'on s'en tient à leurs objectifs propres, qui étaient de créer des systèmes de transport collectif de très haute qualité de service capables de rivaliser en attractivité avec la voiture individuelle. Si l'on en juge par leurs effets d'entrainement sur les techniques classiques, le résultat est sans doute moins négatif. L'intérêt porté, depuis quelques années, par l'industrie classique à une nouvelle génération d'autobus, de trolleybus voire de tramways, n'est sans doute pas étranger aux efforts développés par les industries de pointe pour développer des moyens de transport "nouveaux".

Malgré tout, la tendance générale est au désenchantement en matière de recherche technologique. Je préciserai, très rapidement, pourquoi cette attitude est à la fois très compréhensible, si l'on en juge par le passé, et très dangereuse pour l'avenir.

Elle est très compréhensible parce que nous ne pouvons pas empêcher de porter un jugement d'ensemble sur la recherche technologique en nous référant à un "moment" très particulier de cette recherche: celui des techniques de pointe étudiées dans les dernières années de la phase d'expansion économique incontrôlée. Adaptées aux conditions économiques de l'époque, ces techniques de pointe privilégient très fortement les recherches d'économie de main -d'oeuvre aux dépens des as-

pects infrastructurels et énergétiques: elles sont de ce fait dépréciées par le renversement des valeurs qui s'est produit depuis en faveur de moyens moins dispendieux en énergie et en infrastructure, quitte à reposer sur une main-d'oeuvre un peu plus abondante.

Mais le problème de la recherche technique ne doit pas être posé sous un jour conjoncturel. Si l'on s'en tient à la source d'énergie, déterminant principal de toutes les innovations techniques du passé, il est très probable qu'une organisation nouvelle des transports accompagnera une forme nouvelle de production d'énergie, quel que soit le niveau de cette production d'ailleurs.

Une prospective paraît particulièrement difficile en ce moment, du fait de l'incertitude qui règne dans le domaine énergétique. Mais la difficulté ne devrait pas masquer la nécessité de l'opération: il serait en effet dangereux de considérer que les considérations actuellement avancées de stabilité technologique, raisonnables à moyen terme, seront également valables à long terme.

De ce fait, nous avons souligné dans notre pays, la nécessité de revoir assez profondément l'organisation de la recherche technique. Contrairement à ce qui se passait, il y a encore cinq ans, il n'est plus possible de voir dans l'innovation technique la solution miracle des problèmes de transport urbain à court et à moyen terme.

Mais il est par contre nécessaire de préparer, par une recherche technique plus fondamentale, portant sur les systèmes de propulsion et de transmission qui les complètent, les solutions pour le long terme. Un nouveau type d'organisation de la recherche technique est sans doute nécessaire, plus diversifié dans ses objectifs, moins directement lié aux intérêts industriels immédiats.

3. CONCLUSION

Il est difficile de répondre à la question posée en exergue dans le document introductif du Colloque. Qu'avons-nous découvert d'essentiel dans le domaine des transports urbains? Peut-être d'abord, sous forme de boutade, qu'il n'y a précisément rien de vraiment essentiel dans un secteur aussi intimement lié à l'ensemble des déterminants sociaux, techniques et même culturels de la vie quotidienne. La phase du "tout est possible" économique étant désormais derrière nous, ce sont deux aspects de l'évolution récente des idées qui me paraissent dominer:

1. D'une part, l'abandon d'une optique de la planification des transports limitée au "service à la mobilité".

La contestation locale des grands projets et la renaissance de dynamiques locales - prise de conscience d'élus locaux, formation d'associations de défense et d'usagers conduit à la formulation d'hypothèses de recherche bien différentes de celles de classiques "études de trafic". Le point de vue a profondément changé: la recherche n'est plus exclusivement au service des professions du transport et de l'aménagement mais cherche à se placer au service des transportés eux-mêmes. Outre la nécessité de mieux connaître les aspects pratiques de la prise de décision et les modalités de participation du public dans ce secteur particulier, c'est la nécessité de se référer, dans l'évaluation des politiques de transport, à des besoins plus fondamentaux que le besoin de déplacement qui se fait sentir. Nous notons bien, aiguillonnés par des pensées libres et fortes de quelques chercheurs fondamentaux, qu'il devient difficile d'orienter une politique de déplacements en se basant uniquement sur l'idéologie du "service à la mobilité" puisque la mise en oeuvre des pratiques qui en découlent s'est traduite par un isolement social croissant de groupes importants de la population urbaine dans le passé.

Il faut donc envisager une approche susceptible d'englober les aspect du mode de vie (déplacements compris) des différents groupes sociaux peut permettre à nos acti-

37

vités scientifiques de susciter un intérêt au niveau politique local.

2. D'autre part, la fin de certaines illusions technologiques nous fait découvrir la nécessité d'aborder la recherche technique dans un esprit différent, moins détaché des réalités de la consommation sociale de transport, plus détaché des intérêts industriels immédiats de la production des moyens de transport.

Dans l'un et l'autre cas, la technicité d'une approche sectorielle transport doit faire place à la "globalité" d'une approche sociale, certes difficile à codifier mais seule susceptible, semble-t-il, de redonner un sens à une intervention "planificatrice" dans les transports urbains.

NOTES EN BAS DE PAGES

1. monopole "radical" ajoute Illitch par son "caractère dissimulé, son retranchement, son pouvoir de structurer la société".

2. cf. la "Charte des transports" de la Convention Nationale des Usagers des transports en France: *le droit au transport* doit être reconnu. Il doit être satisfait par une amélioration considérable des services offerts par les transports collectifs. Piétons et utilisateurs de deux roues doivent pouvoir se déplacer partout en sécurité et de manière agréable, etc.

3. Voir par exemple les travaux de l'école de Lünd (Hagerstrand, Lemdorp)

4. NOTA: L'orientation des recherches sur la mobilité reflète l'importance croissante dans notre domaine des concepts de base de la psychologie sociale et, tout particulièrement, du concept des champs sociologiques (théorie du "Gestalt" de K. Levin). Cette façon d'analyser le problème des déplacements a pour conséquence directe de réinsérer les pratiques de déplacement observés dans l'ensemble des activités des individus observés. Elle rend plus complexe, mais plus riche, l'appréhension des régularités de comportement utiles à la planification. Elle renvoie directement à l'optique de l'école de Lünd, discutée plus haut au titre de l'évaluation.

Urban mass transportation in India

by

K. C. AGARWAL

Association of State Road Transport Undertakings
(Ministry of Shipping and Transport, Government of India)

INTRODUCTION

The urban transporation problem though often taken to be relatively new and associated with an increasing demand for mobility is both global and historic. The City of Man is becoming more and more immobile and this is common to the various world urban centres. The present metropolitan immobility is the result of perpetual imbalance between the transportation demand and the available transport capacity. To an Engineer or an Architect, the City of Man no more represents houses and buildings as one thought decades ago. It is much more than that. Neither an Engineer nor an Architect can produce city structures unless proper infa-structure is provided for mobility of the citizens.

The function of any urban system is to provide for movement of men and materials. A passenger movement ranges from a pedestrian movement to the mass of commuters daily entering and leaving the various activity centres. It includes automobiles, omnibuses, rail roads. It comprises many travel routes for a variety of purposes, viz. work, education, shopping, pleasure, etc. The combination of these demands for transport and the transportation units to serve them compound the equation for the system. It embraces walk-ways, services, streets, major streets, highways, freeways, railways, etc. The total urban transportation system has a variety of functions to serve. The urban environment largely depends on this transportation system so as to be attractive to the society.

Every one of us has a different picture of the city. This is because every urban centre not only in India but in the world is facing a crisis because of growing imbalances between demands and available capacities for almost all the amenities. Man is failing miserably in cities because of too many students for schools, too much sludge for sewers, too many sick for the hospitals, too much crime for the police, too many fumes for the atmosphere to bear, too many chemicals for the water to carry, too many cars for the highways, too many commuters for the transport system, etc.

The city populations are exploding. Some people think that this can be avoided by planned dispersal and effective constraints on migration. It is, however, very doubtful indeed whether city populations can be effectively controlled and planned, particularly in a developing economy where cities become nerve-centres of industrial activities and this would be the picture obtainable in India for some decades to come. The only solution, therefore, available to India and every other country placed in similar economic conditions would lie in using technology to create human conditions within an inhuman frame. The populations in these cities would continue to grow in geometric progression and this growth can be faced by connecting cities into a continuous network. Within a city itself, there must be a powerful transport network to connect the various parts so that urban mobility is adequately ensured. Advancement of every phase of civic life is not possible without efficient arteries for transportation of the people.

It is in this context that I propose to present this paper to this August Conference detailing the present Indian scene in the urban mass transportation sector.

URBANISATION

The population in India as in other countries is steadily becoming urban intensive. Cities with a population of over 100,000 (one hundred thousand) each are growing in number, area and population decade after decade. Trends in rural and urban population as shown in the table below denote the increasing urbanisation of the country:

Table 1 – Indices of Population Growth

Population	1911	1921	1931	1941	1951	1961	1971
Urban Population	100	108	129	170	241	304	421
Rural Population	871	860	946	1058	1151	1388	1692

The cities in India are thus in the process of a rapid growth. The two thickly populated cities viz. Bombay and Calcutta have approached a level of development as regards amenities comparable to many developed European towns. Apart from the state of urbanisation, mass transportation problems in some of the major Indian cities are becoming as acute as in other parts of the world. The four jumbo cities as they are called, namely Bombay, Calcutta, Dehli and Madras, have reached a stage when expansion and modernisation of the public transport system need preference over other important municipal investments. With the rate at which urbanisation is growing in the country, the urban transportation system is becoming more complex than ever before. Mere addition to the road kilometerage, number of omnibuses and capacity of suburban railways will not offer any lasting solution as expanding population together with the rising incomes is paralysing existing transportation facilities in every urban centre. At the same time, the financial constraints put limitations on ambitious projects like an under-ground railway. It is in this context that we in India have to think of solutions to relieve traffic congestion in urban centres.

SURFACE TRAFFIC

Because of changing urban growth pattern, urban motor vehicle travel has risen sharply for the last three decades in India. The number of automobiles is increasing quite fast and as is usually the case, a large portion of these vehicles is concentrated in urban areas. The present number of motor vehicles on the road would be around two million as compared to 0.2 million in 1947. Bombay is the commercial capital of the country and a study of the growth of different types of motor vehicles in this city would give a fair idea of what is happening in major cities in the country. Table 2 below indicates the magnitude of growth of different types of motor vehicles in Greater Bombay.

Table 2

Types of Vehicles	1951	YEAR 1956	1961	1966	1971
1 Motor Cycle & Rickshaws	2188	2352	5341	8977	24799
2 Motor Cars	19701	25800	36899	46119	82586
3 Taxi Cabs	1495	3390	5150	7543	15924
4 Stage Carriages	409	672	1067	1310	1569
5 Heavy Vehicles	6870	7363	11653	17335	24013
6 Ambulances, School buses & Service Vehicles	107	114	413	589	970
7 Trailers &Tractors	—	—	770	1026	1290
8 Others	111	519	88	109	328

The above figures reveal that during the two decades from 1951 to 1971, the total vehicles in Greater Bombay increased about 5 times, motor cycles about 12 times, motor cars nearly 4.5 times, taxi cabs about 10 times and heavy vehicles nearly 3.5 times. The growth during the five years 1966-71 is particularly significant.

This tremendous increase in the number of motor vehicles in urban centres in India has seriously aggravated traffic conditions for daily movement of the citizens. In a city like Bombay, the present car ownership is about one car per 80 persons. The riding habit has reached a figure of approx. 365. Thus even if the occupation ratio for a car is taken to be 4, actually it is around 1.7. The transportation demand in respect of the other 76 trips has to be met through public transportation system. This demand becomes particularly important as the majority of the trips are required to be made to reach work-places in the morning and residences in the evening. A study recently carried out in Bombay indicates that about 80% of the total trips made are work-trips.

The system of suburban railways is one of the principal modes of transport only in Bombay. In the other cities, this mode has not developed yet to any appreciable degree to the extent that it can serve the line-haul component of the work-trip as is the case in Bombay. The percentage of trips made by bicycles and the bus system, therefore, would increase in these cities.

The picture that emerges is that for Indian conditions, people in urban centres move mainly for work, and therefore their mobility becomes of prime importance for economic development. Secondly, movement by omnibuses is, and would continue to be for some decades to come, the backbone of the overall transportation system. With constraints on finances, it would be difficult to develop even the surface railways, let alone costly systems like grade-separated metropolitan railways in cities where these facilities do not exist. Therefore, the study of urban mass transportation system in India centralises around the system of road transport by passenger buses.

The distribution of person trips by various mechanical modes on an average week day in Bombay is illustrated in the chart:

DISTRIBUTION OF PERSON TRIPS BY VARIOUS MECHANICAL MODES ON AN AVERAGE WEEK DAY GREATER BOMBAY AREA –1968

MODE	PERCENTAGE
SUBURBAN RAILWAYS	39·0
BEST BUSES	39·0
CARS	10·6
SCHOOL BUSES	1·5
TAXIS	9·3
BICYCLES MOTOR CYCLES & OTHERS	0·6
TOTAL No OF DAILY TRIPS = 4,721,611	100·0

PROBLEM OF MASS TRANSPORTATION

Having concluded that the majority of commuter trips are work trips, the mass transportation problem has to be mainly a peak hour problem. The major percentage of trips is for journey to work in the morning and these trips are naturally concentrated in a few hours on certain corridors. The trips are repeated on the same corridors in the evening but in the opposite direction. The hourly passenger carrying capacity, therefore, becomes the criterian to decide the configuration of the overall transportation system. For a given conveyance the passenger flow would have a limit which would depend on the maximum number of passages that can be made by transportation units and also on the carrying capacity of each unit. Considering the present urban street pattern in India, it has been observed that the auto system has an hourly passenger carrying capacity of around 3,500. In the case of buses, this figure reaches 12,000 to 15,000. In the case of railways, it is around 35,000 to 40,000. As far as the bus system is concerned, there would then be two major considerations. One is the carrying capacity of the vehicle which would be governed by considerations of type of chassis, community preferences in service quality, climatic conditions, etc. The other consideration would be the speed of movement. Apart from the considerations of engine design etc. it is mainly governed by factors such as street congestion, traffic management, traffic engineering, etc. which are external as far as the operator is concerned.

The expression Mass Transportation indicates a system in which great volumes of passengers are on the move. In urban centres, it would be necessary to adopt large capacity modes of transportation, particularly along the corridors of heavy traffic demand. The choice of mode of transportation, however, must be made within reasonable practical and economical limits. It would not be economically feasible to introduce a high speed metropolitan railway on stretches where a bus every few minutes would easily perform the task. Nor would it be technically feasible to operate on a narrow street a bus service for which passenger volume requires an hourly carrying capacity of 40,000 to 50,000 passengers. It would therefore, be necessary to integrate several modes of transportation, namely buses, tramways, metropolitan railways, etc. in such a way that the total traffic demand is met efficiently and economically.

In India, considering the financial constraints for introduction of powerful modes like railways, surface or otherwise, the main part of the total strategy becomes the optimisation of the bus system by adopting various low capital cost traffic management measures and the solution to the problem depends on such issues and on an approach which would not result in undue strain on finances and at the same time ensure the required priority to the town and transportation planning.

APPROACH TO THE PROBLEM
Considering the availability of resources, it has now been accepted by the planners in India that the success of any transportation system depends on how closely its planning is co-ordinated with the land use. Transport is only a service industry, not an end in itself and must be co-ordinated with development in communications and with the land use planning to make the city life more pleasant.

Considering the low car ownership in India, it is certain that undue priority cannot be given to the car traffic. On the other hand, top priority has to be given to the needs of public transportation systems and this is probably the most important aspect of the overall urban transportation planning. The policy should be to move more people and less vehicles. It has now been understood in India that the entire transportation planning in cities must emerge from this basic requirement.

Another important aspect is the fact that movement of people in urban areas is being considered as a welfare activity by the community, as such fares for this movement are low and cannot meet the operational cost which keeps growing. In such considerations, every system has necessarily to be productivity conscious as far as the operator is concerned and has to be suitably subsidised as far as Government is concerned. The approach will therefore, have to be towards maximising operational efficiency, thus minimising operational costs. This approach will only enable the level of subsidy to be as low as possible.

As said earlier, the mass transportation problem being mainly a peak hour problem, the hourly carrying capacity of the various modes of transport becomes important. Every mode has certain limitations in this respect. In case of the bus system as said earlier, the modal capacity cannot exceed approx. 15,000 passengers per hour. In growing urban centres like Bombay and Calcutta, unlimited addition of buses will not only fail to solve the problem, but will add to the already prevailing traffic chaos on roads. This fact has been well recognised, and the construction of an underground railway corridor is already at hand in Calcutta. In Bombay, two additional railway corridors have been planned. One of these corridors will be largely underground. The construction of these corridors however, is not in sight for want of funds.

It has, however, been recognised that judicious distribution of traffic among the several forms of transport is an important factor in the sound economic yield of the whole transport system. The various modes available have to complement each other and should not compete among themselves. Major cities like Bombay and Calcutta would have a mass transportation system built around the hard core of rapid rail transit, while in other cities a system will be built around a well organised bus transportation system.

KEY TO SUCCESS
It is thus clear that while in developed countries it is possible to build the overall transportation system around the most powerful mode like a metropolitan railway, in developing countries where the bus system would continue to play the main part for public transportation in urban areas, emphasis is necessary on low capital intensive measures to reduce transportation congestion and to improve mobility of the people. We have thus recognised in India that it is necesary to optimise the bus system by wide use of technological and management controls with a view to combating congestion in major travel corridors that lead to and from work places. The bus system is able to collect and discharge passengers in an adoptable, flexible way and yet can proceed to give rapid service for thousands of commuters in congested corridors leading to the central business district, if optimally operated. Bus transit in India has just begun to realize its potential and the future undoubtedly will see many more applications of this concept. Further improvements would be seen in the vehicles and travel ways. Vehicle improvements can be anticipated with respect to aesthetics, passenger comfort, performance and environmental effects, guidance and control features, etc.

It is certain that the key to making the urban population adequately mobile in developing countries like India, is by insisting on a more comprehensive approach to managing urban transportation. It is imperative to cope with increasing travel demands without major capital works as an immediate solution. Demand on available road space has inevitably become more fierce, and under these circumstances it must be recognised that unless special arrangements are made for buses, bus operations tend to suffer disproportionately with a consequent downward economical spiral. With this background in India, the low cost measures for optimising the urban bus transportation facilities become the need of the hour.

STRATEGY FOR BUS DEVELOPMENT
The carrying capacity can be maximised by operating the maximum number of seat-kilometers in the required time span. The operation of seats would depend on the number of seats which would be kept moving in a certain period. Such operation of seats would be governed by internal factors such as fleet utilisation obtainable, route planning, bus scheduling, staff scheduling, etc. The fleet utilisation in Bombay, 'the urbs prima in Indis', is as high as 93% and this is probably the highest in the world. Various cities have started thinking in terms of scientific

41

route planning, based on origin destination surveys. Bus scheduling, staff scheduling are also being maximised.

Delhi Bus System till recently severly suffered from a poor routing network developed over the years. The system consisted of a large number of low frequency services circulating through the city and was characterised by substandard operations, uncertain services, long waiting time and highly wasteful carrying capacities.

Additions of routes on piece-meal basis and on regional consideration had made the net-work destination oriented. After a proper study and with a view to rationalize the route plan a revised network of high frequency services converging into a central node from nine traffic focal points on the periphery of the central part of the city was launched in March 1974. A concept of direction oriented travel was thus introduced. This plan proved to be very successful.

The new pattern of operation drew international attention. The New Scientist of London observed:
"By introducing direction-oriented rater than destination-oriented travel, Delhi's buses became able to carry 40 per cent more passengers with only a marginal increase in fleet size. This software rather than hardware solution is a classic instance of the use of appropriate technology, relevant to London and other western cities".

The speed with which the vehicles can move, however, is largely governed by factors such as street congestion, road traffic management etc. The traffic management plays a key role in ensuring optimum utilisation of urban bus transportation. It should be the aim to optimise the speed of buses so that not only the operational costs are minimised but also the carrying capacity of the system is maximised. It has, therefore, been recognised in four jumbo cities in India that it is necessary to give priority to passenger buses on streets, particularly as resources would be limited in the immediate future for powerful modes like a metropolitan railway as the basic system. Against the background of increasing fares, bus priority measures can be identified as one of the first steps forward to a more enlightened transport policy in which public transport operations not only survive economically but regain favour with the travelling public because of improved level of service.

IMPROVEMENT MEASURES

Improvement measures which would require minimum resources and implementation time, can be broadly divided into three inter-related fields:

a. Economical Balance in the use of Transportation Systems.

b. Modal Co-ordination and Management improvements;

c. Relating Urban Form to Transport.

ECONOMICAL BALANCE IN THE USE OF TRANSPORTATION SYSTEMS

It has been accepted in India that extravagant use of road space by private cars means high cost of delay and inconvenience to the vast majority of the other road users like those moving in buses. A start has, therefore, been made to give priority on the streets to the mass transit system like buses in the urban centres. Automobiles are being dissuaded from entering into the C.B.D. during peak hours by the levying of parking charges, etc. A thought is also being given to charging for peak hour use of congested streets similar in principle to the higher charges made in some countries for peak period use of telephones.

It is necessary to prevent cars from going to the congested parts in an urban centre by providing a reliable bus service to the automobile owners as an alternative. In this context a thought is being given to run point-to-point service in Bombay by assuring seats to people at pre-determined hours so that they can reach their workplaces at the appointed time. Such service would also be available in the evenings for returning home.

Bus Priority Measures are generally classified into two categories:

a. Geometric Preferential Measure;

b. Real Time Control Measure.

Bus lane
(Photograph 1)

Geometric Preferential measures range from simple curb radii improvement at an inter-section to construction of exclusive right-of-way for buses. Exclusive bus road-ways on their own right-of-way with complete control on access would provide the higher typer of service. A stage has, however, not come in India for providing bus road-ways on their own right-of-way, as they would be costly and slow to implement. Instead bus lanes (Photograph 1) have been provided in the normal direction of traffic with a view to giving priority to the bus traffic. In a recent experiment in Bombay, it has been found that the introduction of bus lanes has reduced the travel time on the stretch by about 15%, thus improving the carrying capacity of the system.

A wrong way or contraflow bus lanes (Photograph 2) using a portion of the roadways that serve relatively light traffic in the opposite direction has been tried on a large scale in Bombay. They have improved bus flow and at the same time have not reduced the peak directional highway capacity for the other traffic. One such exercise shows on a very congested road in Bombay that late arrivals at termini of buses operating on 11 routes enjoying contraflow facilities were reduced by 65%.

Schemes are also under way for providing a complete separation of cars and buses. Such bus streets not only improve the transit facilities but also create better environments for pedestrians, as it results in a traffic auto free zone. Provision for pedestrian precincts has to be encouraged in countries like India.

Co-ordination of road construction and traffic improvements of bus services will improve street efficiency. Street improvements and removal of bottle-necks will improve bus effectiveness. These improvements include street extensions to increase traffic capacity or bus route continuity, traffic signal improvement such as system co-ordination, inter-section improvements, turn-controls for special permits for buses, bus lay-byes for loading and unloading, longer curb radii, etc.

There are two forms of Bus Priority Real Time Control Measures. The first form deals with strategic measures of optimising the bus operations. These measures hinge on being able to know, within a reasonable degree of accuracy, the location of vehicles within a fleet identification of each vehicle and the status of each vehicle. The second form of Real Time Bus Priority Control Measure deals with technical measures by improving bus operations and are primarily concerned with changing the timings of specific signals to favour bus movements. Certain measures in the first form are adopted in Indian cities with radio communication. In the second form, automatic signals have been introduced but without bus priority measures. More sophisticated equipment as is available in developed countries is not yet available. It has been recognised however, that both classes of priority measures will have to be integrated with a view to obtaining optimum results in the total traffic management system.

MODAL CO-ORDINATION MANAGEMENT IMPROVEMENTS AND RELATING URBAN FORM TO TRANSPORT

The Modal Co-ordination and Management improvements can be attained through a Central high power authority. With such an authority, it should be possible to develop an integrated overall transport system for urban populations. It has also been realised that the land use plan must be so worked out that self sufficient neighbourhoods are established. The land use should be so planned that the trips generated are within the carrying capacity of the overall transportation system. The transport planning must thus be an integral phase of general planning. Equally, it must be comprehensive and encompass all types and modes of transportation, present and future. Transport also is the most powerful tool in city planning, provided transportation is regarded as a total system and as a vital part of the city infrastructure. Transportation must be compounded of different modes serving the many varied purposes it does in an overall metropolitan transport organisation. In this context, Development Authorities have been introduced in the urban centres with a view to co-ordinating the activities of the various agencies like the State Government, Municipal Corporations, State Road Transport Corporations, etc. In Bombay, the State Government has set up the Bombay Metropolitan Region Development Authority for integrating the entire development in the metropolitan area and the transportation would form one of the important functions of this Authority. Such authorities either have been constituted or are being contemplated in other metropolitan cities also.

It should now be possible to carry out an integrated programme for future traffic and transportation projects

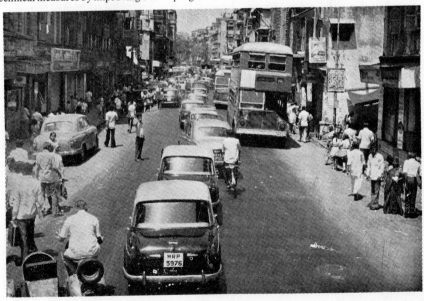

Contra flow
bus lane
(Photograph 2)

and optimisation of the existing ones so as to achieve the maximum benefits at minimum cost for the largest numbers.

VEHICLE CARRYING CAPACITY

Another important factor for improving the carrying capacity of the bus system is the carrying capacity of the vehicle itself. This is particularly important now as the speeds are fast dropping down on account of street congestion. Various measures have been adopted in India for improving the carrying capacity of a vehicle. Some of these measures are (a) use of double-deck buses, (b) use of predominantly 'standee' buses, (c) extension of rear overhang from 50% to 60%, (d) extension in the front so that the entrance is ahead of the front axle and (e) use of road trains.

The use of double-deck buses is not common but in thickly populated areas and in congested areas as the speeds are low, it would be preferable to have vehicles of maximum carrying capacity and in this context, double-deck buses are preferred. During non-peak hours, double-deck buses may become uneconomical because of lower load factor. However, for peak traffic hours these buses are most useful. It is thus clear that what is required in countries like India is the composite fleet comprising of both single and double-deck buses. Normally, double-deckers are about 40% of the total fleet. As far as use of predominantly 'standee' buses is concerned, such vehicles are in operation in some cities but the society is not quite prepared to accept this measure freely as it adversely affects the comfort of commuters and particularly so in a country with a tropical climate. It also increases the workload of conductors considerably. Any such measure is to be accompanied by a suitable system of centralised bus fare collection or by introduction of season tickets. The extension of rear overhang from 50% of the wheel base, which was the case till recently, to 60% is quite common. So also the front extension.

In some cities a bus carrying another bus as a trailer forming a road train is also used on straight and wide roads. The use of such road trains is of course very restricted because of difficulties in manoeuvrability.

DIESEL CONSERVATION

Before I conclude, a special mention has to be made in respect of counter measures that have been taken in response to the increasingly critical need to conserve energy and curtail pollution. Besides, there is an urgent need to economise on its consumption as it amounts to 13% to 15% of the total cost in urban transport. Over 6 million tons of HSD oil is consumed every year in India. This constitutes nearly 30% of India's total consumption of petroleum products. The bulk of it is consumed in the road transport sector.

Studies have been carried in as many as nine State Transport Undertakings in respect to conservation of diesel oil. These studies have established that percentage diesel saving ranging from 10% to 18% can be obtained by simple short and medium term measures like:

a. stricter control over fuel handling-avoiding spillage, leakage, pilferage, etc.,

b. proper machanical maintenance of vehicles.

c. periodic maintenance of fuel injection equipment, proper calibration and derating of fuel injection pumps, checking of nozzle spray patterns, etc.,

d. frequent checks for brake drag and tire pressures;

e. good driving habits like control over maximum speeds, avoiding needless idling, etc.

There is another dimension to this problem that along with simple measures as listed above, effective system of implementation is also required to be devised.

CONCLUSION

I have, in the short time available to me, put before you important aspects of the Indian scene in the field of Urban Mass Transportation. Not only the urban centres are growing in number in India but the urban population in all these centres is exploding. This increase in population in the geometric progression is resulting in continuous increase in traffic demand. There is also constant clamour from the citizens to provide better amenities and travel conditions. The Urban Mass Transportation problem is thus becoming more and more complex in nature. With limited resources, it is becoming difficult for transport planners to satisfy the increasing demand and provide better amenities. I have, therefore, suggested a specific approach to this problem and discussed the various low cost measures to optimise the mass transportation modes, particularly the bus system. Proper discipline and effective co-ordination between various modes will, I am sure, achieve the results.

In the process of tackling the urban mass transportation problems, we in India have developed expertise in various disciplines in this field and this expertise could be made available to other countries facing similar problems. As far as my paper is concerned, I would be too pleased to answer your queries and clarify any point.

I consider it to be a great privilege to have had this opportunity to address this World Conference and I convey to the fellow participants my most sincere thanks for the patient hearing.

REFERENCES

1. The Urban Transportation Problem - J.R. Meyer/J.F. Kain/M. Wohl - Harvard University press, Cambridge, Massachusetts-1965.

2. Special Issue on TRANSPORTATION-April 1968 Institute of Electrical & Electronics Engineers - IEEE.

3. Bus Operation by L.D. Kitchin-Published for "Bus & Coach" by ILIFFEE & SONS LTD.

4. "Organization Structure and Operational Functions of a Single Authority responsible for the co-ordination of all modes of transport in a metropolitan area" London Solution to the Problem. By E.R. Ellen, B.A., A.M., Inst. T.Director of Transportation Planning, London Transport Executive, London, Indian Istitute of Road Transport Monthly Bulletin, Vol. XX No. 10, June 1973.

5. "Urban Pattern" by Arthur B. Gallion And Simon Eisner, Van Nostrand, East West Press.

6. The Metropolitan Transportation Problem by Wilfred Owen. The Brooklings Institution, Wahington D.C. (1956).

7. Report on the Proposed Underground Railway in Bombay City by Japan Consulting Institute-June 1957.

8. Improving & Measuring Productivity in Urban Passenger Surface Transport" by R. Legris, Director General, Compagnie des Transports en Cummun de Nice, Nice, France.

9. Reports of the Study Group (City Services) - Association of State Road Transport Undertakings, New Delhi, July 1971 and June 1972.

10. Report on "Traffic & Transportation Problems in Metropolitan Cities"-Metropolitan Transport Team, Govt. of India, Planning Commission, New Delhi, May 1967.

11. "Master Plan for Mass Transportation in Bombay" by R.N. Joshi, M.S. Nerurkar and P.G. Patankar-Journal of the Institution of Engeneers (India), Vol. XIVIII, No. 11, Pt. CI. 6, July 1968 (special).

12. A Monograph entitled "Some Thoughts on Underground Railway in Bombay" by P.G. Patankar published in 1962.

13. "Urban Transportation" by P.G. Patankar - Journal of the Instution of Engeineers (India), Vol. XLVI, No. 5, Pt. CI 3, January 1966.

14. "Development of Urban Mass Transportation System in India" by P.G. Patankar-Journal of the Institution of Engineers (India), Vol. XLVIII, No. 3, Pt. CI2, November 1967.

15. "Transport in Bombay Costly Omissions" by P.G. Patankar-Paper presented at a lecture meeting of the Indian Institute of Road Transport, held on 2-7-1973. Monthly Bulletin Vol. XX No. 11, July 1973.

Urban transportation policy in Poland

by

WOJCIECH SUCHORZEWSKI

Research Institute on Environmental Development

Warsaw, Poland

1. URBANIZATION AND URBAN AND RE-GIONAL TRANSPORT DEVELOPMENT IN YEARS 1945-1975

In the period between two Great World Wars Poland was an agricultural country where 60% of its population took the living means from farming.

The Second Great World War annihilated circa 38% of permanent productive assets. In the period after the ending of this War the process of an intensive industrialization resulted in a fast increase of the population who found their living means from other occupations.

The industrialization was accompanied by the process of urbanization, the rate of which is illustrated in Table 1. Making use of the possibilities existing in the planned economy it has been endeavored to smooth down unevennesses in the development of the individual country regions. This policy was accompanied by endeavors to slow down the growth rate of the greatest agglomerations.

The physical structure which resulted from such policy is characterized by:
- a relatively more even distribution, arrangement and disposition of the economic potential and the population,
- limited concentration of the population in more than ten already developed, developing or potential agglomerations and in several tens of medium towns; beyond the concentration of the population in the agglomerations the forming of urbanized belts being connected with the technical infrastructure corridors has been stated.

Table 1 – Total population of Poland against the urban Population in the years 1946 - 1975

Year	Population in millions			Percentage of urban population
	total	urban areas	rural areas	
1946	23,9	7,5	16,1	31,8
1950	25,0	9,6	15,0	39,0
1960	29,8	14,2	15,2	48,4
1970	32,6	17,0	15,6	52,3
1975	34,2	18,9	15,3	55,2

The percentage of population basing their living on the non-farming occupations and professions is now higher than the percentage of the urban population. This is the reason for an extensive commuting from rural areas to towns.

Being of an essential importance for the needed capacity of local transport means, taking in total in the passed 30 years, the following phenomenons took place:
- increase of non-farming population
- increase of number of town-dwellers
- socio-economic development which was accompanied by the increasing mobility of urban and rural population,
- transformations in physical structure of towns; such as grouping the industrial plants in ensembles and industrial districts, decreasing density of residential districts, development of green areas etc.;, following in the increase of urban areas extensiveness.

During the last dozen or so years we see also a fast increase of motorization rate. Commencing since 1960 the passenger car number was doubled within five-year periods. At the actual phase of the motorization development we observe the car owner ratio is approaching the number of 100 cars per one thousand inhabitants. It is obvious that during the above period the majority of the transportation needs has been met by the public transport. The scale and the development of this transport are illustrated in Table 2.

The more important conclusions from the presented data are as follows:

1. The scope of the passenger transport service is increasing systematically both in the length of the network and in the utilized rolling stock.

2. The mobility of inhabitants in towns and in suburbs is growing.

3. The greatest development is stated in the suburban and urban municipal bus transport system. The role of the rail transport - railways and tramways - is slightly decreasing at the undecreased number of passengers.

During the last years the participation of the individual transport does not surpass 10 percent of trips.

2. ORGANIZATION AND FINANCING OF PUBLIC TRANSPORT

The public transport is carried out by three groups of carriers:
- Polish State Railways /PKP/,
- State Bus Transport /PKS/,
- urban or regional transport enterprises.

The PKP are servicing primarily the suburban zone of great agglomerations. In Warsaw and Gdansk agglomerations the traffic is carried out on the separated tracks. An exceptionally important role is played by the PKP in servicing the Warsaw agglomeration in which during the 1960s on the diametral line additional tracks were built in the tunnel crossing the City Centre. There are frequent stops on this line in order to shorten the distance to destinations.

The State Bus Transport is servicing the suburban zone and the rural areas. It is also an unique trans-

Table 2 – Passanger transportation in Poland in the years 1965-1975

Specification		In Year			
		1965	%	1975	%
Network					
State railways [1]	thous. of km.	23,3		23,8	
State Bus Transportation [1]/PKS/	– ,, –	73,2		100,5	
Urban transport - street served	– ,, –	6,1		10,6	
buses	– ,, –	5,59		10,28	
streetcars	– ,, –	0,90		0,89	
trolleybuses	– ,, –	0,12		0,05	
Passangers total	mln/year	6577		9630	
State railways [2]	– ,, –	972		1118	
State Bus Transportation /PKS/	– ,, –	784		2219	
Urban transport - total	– ,, –	4821	100	6293	100
buses	– ,, –	1640	34,0	3509	55,8
streetcars	– ,, –	2956	61,3	2694	42,8
trolleybuses	– ,, –	225	4,7	89	1,4
Rolling stock					
Buses - PKS		10275		21176	
Urban transport:					
buses		4743		10404	
streetcars		4350		4600	
trolleybuses		346		106	

1. National network
2. Including long-distance trip /ca 20%/
3. Including long-distance buses

portation means in many small towns which do not belong to agglomerations. The municipal bus transport is servicing mainly the urbanized areas.

An important role in the greatest agglomerations' transport systems is played by the tram. Warsaw is here a particular case, where in the reconstruction of the totally destructed town the tram network has been constructed in 90 percent on the private right-of-way-system. Two wagon trains running at one minute intervals permit to achieve carrying capacity surpassing 12,000 passengers per one hour, in one direction. In result of separation of the tram traffic from vehicular traffic - excluding the one level crossings - no negative impact of vehicular traffic on the tram traffic system is observed so far.

An essential feature of the actual transportation policy in Poland is preserving the low fares in municipal transport. These fares were only once changed (in 1967) during a period of 30 years.

A standard system of fares is applied for single passages (excluding the suburban lines). A preponderant majority of commuters is utilizing the monthly tickets at very low prices for unlimited amount of travel.

In general a "no conductor" honour service is applied.

In result of comparatively low fares there is a deficit of municipal transport enterprises. This deficit is systematically growing in connection with widening service range and introducing a more and more modern rolling stock. At the actual moment the deficit is surpassing 33% of the total running costs of the transport.

This deficit is covered by the State's budget. Moreover from this budget the rolling stock and heavy investments are financed.

This financing of the public transport is done in conformity with the principles of state policy according to which the transport is one of the social services. There is also an opinion that the low fares are counteracting the use of private cars for commuting purposes in densely populated areas.

Great attention is paid also to the coordination of the activity of various carriers who are subordinated to various disposition centres (Polish State Railways and State Bus Transport - to the Ministry of Transport, the municipal transport enterprises - to local authorities who are supervised by the Ministry of Administration, Local Economy and Enviromental Protection). In order to assure this coordination the Regional Groups for Coordintation of Passenger Transport have been appointed.

As an example the range of activity of such a group in the Warsaw Agglomeration includes:
– elaborating the detailed plans and programs of passenger transport development for the region,
– coordination of the actual running operation,
– coordination of a common fare system,
– integrated design of stops and terminals,
– integration of inspection and supervision services,
– coordination in development of depots etc.

This Regional Group consists of directors representing the above mentioned three carriers.

3. URBAN ROADS

Before World War II Poland was known as having proverbial "Polish Roads", i.e. ground roads or the roads made of field stone. Both these two categories of roads included more than 75 percent of the urban roads.

During the last World War about 30% of the pavement and 46% of bridges and viaducts were destructed. In the after-the-war period the entire effort of the country was directed and concentrated to liquidate the effects of the war and then to modernize the roads by constructing improved pavement.

In result of the works, which were accomplished in the years 1950 to 1975, the urban roads length with the improved pavement increased five times from 5 to 25 thousands kilometers, wherein a considerable part of the new streets has the form of two-roadway arteries.

Since the sixties, in consideration of the motorization and road traffic forecasts the process has begun which consists in preparing the urban road systems for the expected increase of traffic. A great effort was made to develop urban transportation planning.

Extensive use was made of the well-known methods of traffic studies and forecasting.

The conclusions following from the transportation studies have been taken into account in the long term physical plans which are elaborated for all towns and agglomerations. These plans are the basis for land reservation for the future roads, intersections are parking facilities. It is worthwhile to emphasize that in the towns which have such plans a rational coordination of all investments being connected with the road corridor is being implemented. For such a corridor a special plan of the location of underground facilities in the road cross-section is elaborated. In this way it is possible to build the individual facilities without any risk of their major interference with future road facilities.

Between the sixties and seventies a decisive acceleration has been achieved in the road construction. In some part it was connected with the dynamic development of housing with related technical infrastructure. At the same time the realization of higher standard roads was begun. The Lazienkowska Highway in Warsaw is an example, being an urban expressway with 2 × 3 lanes of traffic and having the length of about 10 kilimeters. This highway was accomplished during three years. Several other roads of this type were completed and many others are in the course of construction or design.

Dynamic modernization and development of urban roads does not mean that the principle of a full adaptation of the urban transport systems for the needs of mass motorization has been accepted.

Instead of that, a basic assumption has been made, that the freedom of vehicular traffic (in all areas, purposes and at any time) should be differentiated in dependence on the character of the area under consideration. Consequently, in the high intensity areas the car-free streets and zones have been introduced in many towns. Such a position harmonizes with the future transport policy which will be discussed in further points of this paper.

4. PLANS FOR URBAN GROWTH AND MOTORIZATION

In the socio-economic longterm development plans and in the national physical development plan of the country up to 1990 it has been foreseen that the urban population will increase from 19 millions in 1975, to about 25 million inhabitants in 1990.

The distribution concept of this population is described as a "moderate policentric concentration of socio-economic activity". As skeleton of a physical structure the urban agglomerations and the urban centres of growth were taken. The total area of the country has been divided into intensive investment areas (nodes and belts of the system), agricultural areas and areas for recreational purposes.

In total 23 agglomerations have been selected as divided into three groups:
– 10 developed agglomerations,
– 7 developing agglomerations,
– 6 potential agglomerations as expected to be developed after 1990.

The numeric data which characterize the development of towns in the years 1975-1990 are set down in Table 3.

The motorization forecasts are presented in Table 4.

Table 3 – Urban population 1975-1990

Specification	Number	Population in mlns	
		1975	1990
Agglomerations - total	23	11,6	16,6
developed	10	9,1	12,5
developing	7	1,8	2,9
potential	6	0,7	1,2
Urban centers	15	0,9	2,0
Others		4,6	6,2
Total		17,1	24,8

Table 4 – Motorization forecasts

	1975	1990
Private cars/1000 inhabitants	32	142
Private cars in thousands	1078	5300
Trucks/1000 persons	12	35
Trucks in thousands	425	1294
Buses in thousands	52	107
Buses/1000 persons	1,5	2,9
Motorcycles in thousands	1895	600
Motorcycles/1000 persons	55	16

It has been foreseen that in the period up to 1990 a tendency for a faster (than it was up to now) motorization development will come out on the rural and small towns areas. However the motorization index in bigger towns will be higher than the average for the total country.

The transport systems development plans for the agglomerations are based on the assumption that the motorization in 1990 will reach the level of about 200 to 250 cars per one thousand inhabitants.

The consciousness of the problems and difficulties following from such a motorization level in the biggest agglomerations inspired to formulate the principles of the national transport policy which is characterized below as based on a wider background of the urban development planning process.

5. URBAN AND TRANSPORTATION PLANNING PROCES

The history of urban transportation planning in Poland is strictly connected with the history of urban planning, the beginnings of which can be found in the 1920s. An exceptionally fast development of these planning forms commenced after 1945. The Act on "THE PHYSICAL COUNTRY DEVELOPMENT" issued in 1946 has introduced a general three level planning: national, regional and local. The following, consecutive legal Acts and especially the Act on "THE PHYSICAL PLANNING" from 1961, have further reinforced the role of the physical planning.

The transport planning was initially introduced within the frame of the physical planning. The scope of the studial and planistic elaborations was comparatively modest in its beginning. Then in the midst of the fifties a fast development of transport planning began and it achieved a relative autonomy. Consequently a development of methods and techniques of this planning followed, the number and education level of its staff has increased and in the biggest agglomerations the urban transport planning offices have been established as units *independent* of the physical planning. In effect all the agglomerations and the majority of medium and big size towns were granted the long-term transport development plans with their further development guide lines.

As the most essential features of the transportation studies the following can be specified:
– undertaking the Origin (O) and Destination (D) surveys at a larger scale,
– introduction of modern methods in the traffic forecasting; at the moment the known UTPS program systems - elaborated by the US-FHWA and US-UMTA - are being applied; the said systems have been additionally enriched and adapted to the Polish conditions, among others, for taking into account the Polish specifics in the modal split, and partially different objectives,
– elaborating the methods of a rational planning of road networks public transportation,
– among others attempts have been assumed towards introducing the methods of system analysis aiming in a rational structuring of the development of urban transport systems.

The approach has been illustrated in Fig. 1.

The greatest effort towards increasing the efficiency and implementability of the transport planning has been directed however to the process of this planning, and its connection with the socio-economic and physical planning process.

As a starting point the assumption has been accepted that the objective of transport planning does not consist only in elaborating an optimum concept of the urban transport system at a given arrangement of the urban activities but also, and perhaps first of all, in stimulating and inspiring such development of a town which would enable the reduction both in the number and in the length of trips. The planning process recommended at the actual moment is presented in scheme 2.

There are two basic phases of generating the general concept of the land-use-transportation system:
– transportation studies preceding the elaboration of physical development plans; the output of these studies serves as an input to the formulation of the general concept of the physical development,
– works over the plan of the transportation system which corresponds to the selected alternative of the urban physical plan.

The above presented approach to the planning problem imposes on the transport planners a difficult task of choice, selection and adaptation or inventing the methods to create a rational (from the transport point of view) distribution of urban activities.

The above statements visualize a tendency to an accurate interconnection of the transport planning with the physical planning. This tendency found its repercussion in a final embracing of a complete evolutional sequence of the organizational framework of urban and transportation planning.

After the period in which the transport planning was given the autonomy (in sixties) when, as mentioned, the independent urban transport planning agencies started their activity, a nationally unified organizational solution has been reintroduced, in which the urban transportation planning agencies have been combined with urban planning agencies.

The advantages which are following from the integration of various types of planning consist in creating both conditions to take into account the transport factor in development planning and in automatically guaranteeing suitable land reserves for the planned transport facilities.

6. TRANSPORT POLICY IN DEVELOPMENT PLANS FOR TOWNS AND TRANSPORTATION

The principles of long and short term policy for the urban transport have been formulated as based on the results of research and development works, including also the analysis of home and foreign experience from countries with different socio-political systems and different motorization development levels.

The guide lines of the transportation policy, which have been formulated as a result of the above mentioned analyses, are being introduced in practise by the regional authorities.

These guide lines can be summarized as follows.

The urban transport policy should be shaped in consideration of the following circumstances:
– the increasing living standard of the population and its consequent mobility growth,
– development of motorization and its consequences,
– changes in the energy situation,
– environment quality problem.

Of exceptional importance is and will be the development of motorization and the requirements following from the environment protection. The availability of automobiles leads to the resignation from using the public transport. In consequence the traffic volume increases beyond some tolerable limits resulting in traffic congestion and speed reduction to say nothing about the parking problems..

If public transport is not segregated from the individual traffic, the public transport's speed also decreases and consequently its attractiveness. In result the number of public transport passengers is decreasing and economic difficulties of municipal transport enterprises are sharpening.

Attempts to solve the problem first by a better traffic control and then by building better systems of roads and new parkings are giving only partial results. It is known that at a high level of motorization (more than 100-150 cars/1000 inhabitants) no possibilities exist to equip the urban areas of high population density with roads and parkings of such quantity which could enable an unlimited use of the private car (unlimited in any direction, time and travel purpose). The disparity between the demand for roads and parking space and their supply grows along with the increasing density of trip-ends and extensiveness of an area. A relative fluency of vehicular traffic would need so dense a street network in overpopulated urban areas that it is impossible to assure in both, due to the costs and the disposed lend consumption, protection of the existing buildings and human environment.

Consequently, it is reasonable to assume that even at a high motorization level in towns, especially in the large ones, quite a considerable number of travellers will further utilize the public transport, characterized by a better economy of land utilization. Hence the conclusion: it is necessary to promote and develop an efficient and attractive public transportation system.

It is to emphasize that not in every town or in each part of a town a situation exists needing to give the priority to the public transport. In fact even in the biggest agglomerations, beyond the areas on which unrestrained use of car is impossible, there are the areas - as a rule peripherial - which can be equipped with road and parking facilities adapted to the needs.

A rational solution of the problem can be achieved on condition of accepting the well-known three zones concept [1].

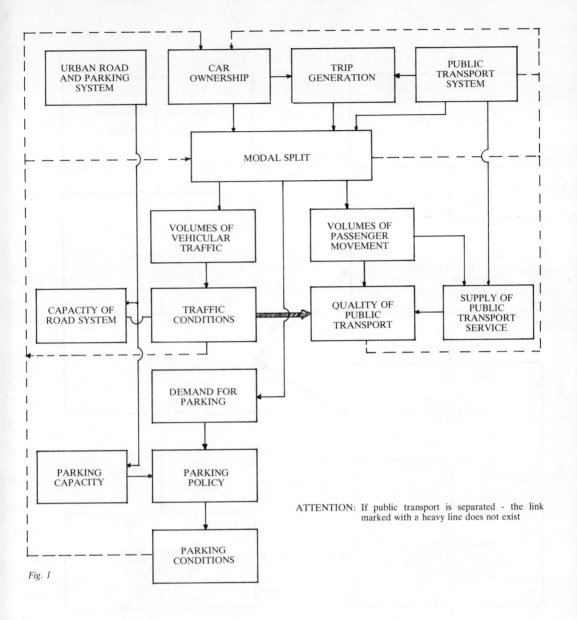

ATTENTION: If public transport is separated - the link marked with a heavy line does not exist

Fig. 1

Table 5 – Transport policy measures in dependence on the zone

Measure	Importance in zone		
	A	B	C
Development of rapid transit	essential	essential in traffic corridors	essential in regional traffic corridors
Priority of tram, bus, trolley-bus transport	essential	recommended	–
Prohibition of car traffic	essential	in some cases	–
Limitation of car traffic	essential	in some cases	–
Parking policy:			
– limited number of spaces	in some cases	–	–
– fares	,,	,,	–
– limited parking time	,,	,,	–
Bicycle traffic system	in some cases	essential	in some cases
Pedestrian passages and areas	essential	in some cases	in some cases
Transfer stations:			
RTS-tramway-bus-trolley-bus	essential	essential	essential
park-and-ride facilities	–	in some cases	,,

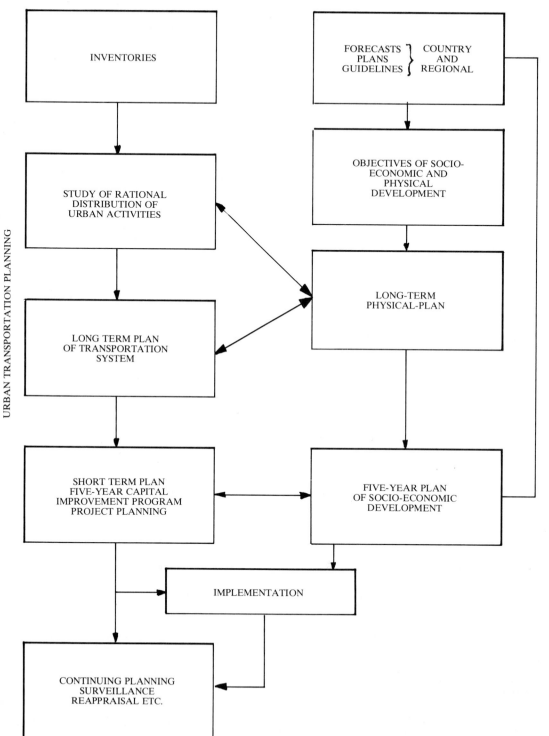

Fig. 2 – Urban transportation planning within the framework of comprehensive socio-economic and physical planning

A practical implementation of this concept would consist in applying a number of planning and organizational measures. They are listed in table 5.

A conscious acceptance of the above presented principles of the transport policy leads to complex solutions characterized by a high level of coordination and *integration* of various measures of a transport system. This integration and coordination are the more important of the larger urban area.

Besides the rational modal split the coordination and integration can be accomplished in practice by:

a. such technical and functional solutions as:

– direct connection between terminals and stops of public transport and passages, and the pedestrian areas;

– forming multimodal nodes of transport (e.g. railway terminal plus metro station plus tram and bus stops plus taxi stops) at which the change of a transport mode can be done in a fast and easy way;

– peripheral railway-bus stops on which the access from train to bus is direct;

– peripheral interchange stops: railway (metro)-private cars (so called park-and-ride);

b. economic and operational solutions such as:

– uniform fares,

– coordinated operation,

– common financing of investments,

– organizational integration.

These general principles of urban transport policy have been used as a base for the formulation of policies for urban areas of various types.

7. PRINCIPLES OF POLICY FOR VARIOUS AREAS

The differentiation of the policy primarily concerns:

– division of tasks among public and individual transport,

– choice of transport means of the public transport,

– range of recommended development of expressways.

Agglomerations

In agglomerations, especially the biggest ones, the problems are unusually difficult. It has been proposed to accept the following principles:

1. the general solution of transport should consist in determining three zones according to the criterion of the urban activity concentration (which density of trip-end depends on);

2. in zone A (the central one) an absolute priority should be given to the public transport and the pedestrian traffic. The use of private cars may and should be constrained, among others by elimination of through-traffic, a suitable parking policy and other means of traffic control. It is therefore not necessary to adjust - for any price - the road network and parking capacity to uncontrolable growing needs;

3. in zone B (the transitional one) a development of public transport and efficient road system is necessary. On the heavy traffic corridors a segregation between the public and individual traffic will be needed. Some parking limitations may also be needed;

4. in zone C (outer one) with a low intensity of trip-ends, the road system should be adapted to the needs in assumption of a free use of car. At the same time these areas should be serviced by the public transport at such a standard level which would assure attractive conditions of travelling to zones B, and especially A;

5. as a result the public transport system should in general consist of:

– on main traffic directions - the railroad transports (regional railroads, metro, tram on private right-of-way, possibly underground tram),

– bus transport.

6. urban expressways (connected with a system of national roads) will penetrate inside the agglomerations;

7. outlet roads system should be adapted to recreational traffic needs;

8. integration of the whole transport system is indispensable.

Towns above 100.000 inhabitants

In this group of towns it is generally possible to create the conditions for relatively unconstrained use of individual private cars, or with some limitations in some parts of town.

Here are some principles concerning this group of towns:

1. Zone A, if it will be necessary, will be a small area (usually the town centre or a part of it);

2. public transport:

– in some cases - tram with private right-of-way,

– generally - bus transport; in zone B it may be purposeful to separate this transport means (e.g. as bus streets or bus - only lanes).

3. connections with rural roads should be solved according to the following principles:

– national roads (especially free-ways) in general will bypass,

– regional roads will penetrate the urban area;

4. urban expressways, in case of their necessity, have to service the external traffic as well as the internal one on the directions of the highest loads.

Towns with 50.000 - 100.000 inhabitants

In this case the following principles are to be followed:

1. The three zones principle will be used only in rare situations. Only in the centre area of the town may it be purposeful to include the pedestrian traffic area and foresee suitable conditions for public transport.

2. As the only means of public transport buses will be used.

3. National roads should bypass the town; efficient connections between them and urban road systems should be assured. Regional roads will, in general, penetrate the urbanized area. In some cases it may be justified to design them as urban expressways.

Towns with up to 50.000 inhabitants

1. Here is no necessity to limit the freedom of vehicle traffic, beyond slight fragments of the centre and the interiors of residential areas.

2. Public transport - exclusively buses.

3. National and regional roads should bypass the town.

The foreseen connection with the urban roads system:

– with regional roads - in any case,

– with national roads - only in case of larger centres.

A brief summary of principles recommended for urban areas of various sizes is presented in table 6.

Concerning the implementation of the above rules - almost the entire postulated approach can be found in lastly eleborated development plans.

8. RESEARCH AND DEVELOPMENT WORKS

Research and development works concerning urban transport problems are being managed in several Polish universities and, at the largest scale, in the Research Institute on Environmental Development - RIED.

The RIED is a state research institute supervised

Table 6 – Policies for various urban areas

	Agglomerations	Towns - thous. of inhabitants		
		> 100	50-100	< 50
Three-zone concept	Essential	Essential	Elements	–
Public transport:				
Regional railway	+	±	–	–
Metro	+	–	–	–
Tramway	+	+	±	–
Bus	+	+	+	+
National roads	Penetrate	By-pass	By-pass	By-pass
Regional roads	Penetrate	Penetrate	Penetrate	By-pas
Urban expressways	+	+	±	–

+ Essential
± In some cases
– Non-applicable

by the Ministry of Administration, Land Economy and Environmental Protection. It employs more than 1200 persons wherein about 800 in research and development, approximately 70 are professors.

This Institute is working out the directions of national environmental development and the development of the elements of human and natural environment.

The scope of works include the following problems: physical planning, housing, environmental protection and technical infrastructure, including the urban transport.

The research works are being financed according to the contracts concluded with the Ministry and regional authorities and other institutions.

The most important program in the range of urban transport in the years 1971-75 was the complex project: "Development of Urban Expressways and Rapid Transit Systems in the Largest Agglomerations". This program included several tasks aimed to:
– the development of methods and techniques of planning,
– solving various technical problems,
– elaboration of the national program of development of rapid transit systems.

As a result of the work, in which the technical universities and regional planning agencies of the individual agglomerations participated as subcontractors, a long-term development program for the eight largest agglomerations has been elaborated.

An analogically complex program for the period 1976-1980 includes the research and development work on "Modernization and Development of Roads and Transport in Towns and Agglomerations" with, among others, the following principal tasks:

1. development of planning methods for urban transport systems in small and medium towns,
2. elaboration of the national development program for urban expressways,
3. development of urban roads construction technology,
4. indication of methods for improvement of existing urban mass transport,
5. specification of direction of development in rolling stock production,
6. elaboration of methods for limiting the negative impact of urban transport and traffic on environment,
7. development methods of urban traffic control.

The above stated tasks only exemplify the range of problems. A complete specification of research and development works to be done is much larger.

We have to underline the fact that in the existing Polish organization and financing system for research and development works, the entire program is ordered to one leading unit who is playing the role of the general executor and coordinator; in this specific case which has been presented such a unit is the RIED.

9. INTERNATIONAL COOPERATION

Although every town, agglomeration, region and country has its specific features, there are some regularities which are common for many countries. Some of these regularities have an universal character. This calls for the exchange of information and cooperation on an international scale.

It is obvious that these regularities are especially numerous in the countries with identical or similar socio-economic systems. This circumstance determines the first step of international cooperation which could be organized in a given group of countries.

In the case of socialistic countries this cooperation has been developing for a long time in the CMEA. The transport problems are being studied by two Commissions: "Standing Transport Commission" and "Standing Building Commission".

Concerning the above discussed problems one of the more important results of the works being managed and carried out within the limits of CMEA was the specification of the general principles of policy for urban development and the urban transport [2].

A still wider framework for the exchange of experience among countries with various political and economic systems has been created by the UN-ECE. The urban transport problems are, since several years, in the focus of common interest of three bodies:
– Committee on Building, Housing and Planning,
– Inland Transport Committee, and
– Senior Governmental Advisors on Environmental Problems.

The results of two seminars on "The Role of Transportation in Urban Planning, Development and Environment" (Munich 1973 and Washington 1976) are well known. Their materials are a rich source of information and precise recommendations.

A number of further valuable materials and recommendations which present the results of the activity of others, beyond the ones discussed, governmental and non-governmental, international organizations, as OECD, UITP, IRF, AIPCR, IFHP etc. can be indicated.

It can be expected that a further development of various forms of international cooperation will contribute to a more effective solving of the urban transport problems in all countries.

If one would have to indicate the form of cooperation which would serve the best to the development and progress then, as the first items, the scientific cooperation is to be exposed. It could consist, first of all, in the exchange of information on directions of research, then, in a wider exchange of information concerning the results of the research, and finally, on managing the common works in bilateral and multi-lateral arrangements.

FOOTNOTES

1. This concept was positively evaluated, among others, on the UN-ECE Seminar On the Role of Transportation in Urban Planning, Development and Environment, Munich 1973.

2. SEV, Aktualnyje Voprosy Razvitija Gradostroitielstvaw Stranach-Czlenach SEV, Sbornik materialov informacii Postojannoj Komissii po Stroitielstvu. No 2/1975. Ch. VI.

Application of Research Works to Metropolitan Transportation Development

by
ZSOLT PÁPAY
Technical University of
Budapest, Hungary

SOME EXPERIENCES AND PROBLEMS IN BUDAPEST TRANSPORT DEVELOPMENT

1. Introduction

Transportation, that is the movement of persons as well as goods through space, is a vital function of the urban organism comparable in its significance to the circulation of blood in the human organism. The welfare of citizens depends considerably on how well and by what technical means transportation problems are solved. The appearance of motor vehicle communication on the scene offered almost unlimited possibilities to serve all urban areas which, in turn, led to their considerable extension, and thus to the agglomeration of hitherto separate settlements. This unlimited possibility has grown, however, into an obstacle to further development since transport service requirements of individual areas have exceeded supply potentials in their present form. These problems are concentrated, fundamentally, on the metropolitan areas and today they represent the key to their future growth.

With the explosive and world-wide growth of metropolitan agglomerations, transportation in the area affected has developed into a problem of cardinal importance also in Budapest.

During the past twenty-five years the population of Budapest increased from

1,3 million in 1950, to

2,02 million in 1975, which represented 20 per cent of the whole population of Hungary. During the same period the number of passengers using the public transport network increased from 2,5 million to 3,6 million per day, and the number of motor vehicles increased from 15,000 to 150,000.

The need for transportation increases steadily and transportation networks, especially in the old historic part of the city, are no longer capable of satisfying many modern transportation needs. Masses of people move between residential quarters, increasingly developed on the fringes of the city, and their places of work or education in the inner part of the city. These flows result in overloaded transportation facilities, risks and other inconveniences.

The problems created by traffic are going to be extremely serious, as in other big towns, in Budapest, too, so that in a short time the city will be unable to fulfil its main functions.

The solution of the organizational, technical and technological problems of the rapid growth has required intensive and broadscale research.

2. The system for the financial support and management of the research works in Budapest

2.1 Development of the system during the past twenty years

After world war II the basic principle in Budapest was the development of the public transport system. Therefore research works concerned mainly the development of a public transport network with a rapid transit railway having an important part in it.

In connection with the development of motorization in Hungary transport research has had greater importance, becoming more and more regular and better organized since the early sixties. When the Government accepted the concept of the progress of motorization, the National Long-term Scientific Research Plan set the most important tasks for transport research. At the same time the need for a comprehensive general transport plan for Budapest has become clear regarding the rapid growth of motorization. The basic principles prepared by the Budapest City Authorities were presented in 1963 as a starting point for planning and research, and a series of research works started. Most of them had been commissioned by the Transport Directorate of the Budapest City Council and that is why a considerable proportion of research pursued practical aims, and served for providing a basis for the transport development plan and for urgent traffic policy decisions.

The provision for a higher motorization level in Hungary particularly needs long-term planning to promote planned development and calls for forecasts ranging further ahead than the usual general town planning period.

The forecasts beyond the end of this century need particularly extensive research. The longer period means greater uncertainty. These, and some other different conditions are the reason why the practice of countries with high-scale motorization could not be accepted without any changes. Particular investigations were needed for providing particular development methods and models. In addition computerization was relatively poor at that time. In spite of the difficulties some good results largely contributed to the augmentation of the financial support for transport development.

2.2 New Conception for Transport Policy

On the basis of the new requirements the Hungarian Government made fundamental transport policy decisions to solve as far as possible the problems referred to above. Taking into account the available resources of the Hungarian national economy, these decisions seek, on the basis of the economic and social requirements of the country and at a national level, to achieve the most economical division of labour among the individual branches of transport in order to encourage the rationalization of transport and communications industry.

In the orientation of this transport policy, as a part of the national economy, a uniform concept is appropriately reflected. As a result of the realization of this concept a national transport system will be created in which the two branches would from a uniform scheme by their integrated relationship.

Urban transport policy is an inherent part of the national level concept. In a summarized form this involves the following main objectives:

– satisfaction of transport requirements within the urban area and, particularly, in the city core, in accordance with the importance and development of the town concerned;

– coordinated development of urban and regional transport systems, with particular regard to their existing connections;

– coordinated development of both public and individual transport with a proper ratio in a rational labour division ensured in this field;

– introduction of correct labour division among individual branches of the urban public transport system within the entire mass communications system;

– development of the urban main road system with provisions for the necessary services to be coordinated for the most appropriate use of available land;

– improvement of the level of urban transport planning, drawing up a planning scheme related to the necessary land use, and a consistent realization of the transport development plans accepted;

– reduction of the harmful environmental effects of urban transport.

On the basis of this conception the Science Research Council of the Ministry of Transport defined the main research programs. Among them there are three programs for urban transport research:

1. Transport network planning on the basis of the interdependencies between land use and transportation demand

2. Development of public transport systems

3. Transport development in Budapest.

Demand for a separate research program for Budapest results from the great differences between Budapest and other Hungarian towns in the structure of the city, in the number of inhabitants, in functions and conditions, in the motorization level etc. and therefore in the solution of the main problems. Despite the differences, part of these research works can be adopted, naturally, for other towns and vice versa. The important task of the Science Research Council is to coordinate, and provide a nation-wide use of the results in planning. The whole system is fully described in the paper prepared for the conference by K. Hegyi.

Transport research in Budapest has been under the direction of the Transport Directorate of Budapest City Council. Much of the research has been supported financially either by this Directorate or by the Ministry of Transport. Research works commissioned by industry, firms or authorities are very few.

Allowance proposed by the Science Research Council for the next fifteen years is shown in table 1.

2.3 The basis of the transport research in Budapest

At the beginning of the progress, in the early sixties, transport research started at the universities, mainly at the Civil Engineering and Transport Engineering Department of the Technical University of Budapest.

Table 1 – Allowance proposed by the Science Research Council
Million forints

Main themes	1976-80	1981-85	1986-90	
Transport demand Investigations	4,0	4,0	5,0	13,0
Transport planning models and methods	5,0	6,0	6,0	17,0
Transport management and control	3,5	3,0	2,0	8,5
Long-term planning requirements	11	15	16	42
Other themes	6,5	10	13	23
Total	30	38	42	110,5

People working on transport research in these places usually took part in preparing the Transport Development Plan of Budapest as consulting planners, they proposed urgent themes for research in several areas of this field and that is why a considerable proportion of research works pursued practical aims and served for providing a good basis for the transport development conception. At the same time the increased research effort at these places has brought important benefits to their teaching work.

As the demand on research quickly increased, the claim to a widened basis became evident. First, a research group was organized within the Communication Planning Company of the City Council and later it became the Research and Long-term Planning Department of the Transportation Directorate.

At the same time universities are keeping on with their research on the main themes and help the City with solving its traffic problems to a large extent.

Although there are many more people working on transport research at the universities and in the Research Department of the City Council than before, and generally the work they are carry out is more relevant and of a higher quality than in the 1960s, further extension is needed in both the personal and the technical field. There is particularly much progress to be made in multi-disciplinary working, in relating transport considerations to those of economy, land use and other aspects of public policy.

3. The main aims of investigations in the last fifteen years

3.1 Development of methods and models for the Budapest transportation planning

– Planning methodology considering the limited computer-technique and the need of a particularly long-term forecast

– Simplified trip generation and distribution models

– Assignment models for road network and for public transport network

– Investigations in the problems of modal split

– The characteristics of long-range plans and plans for the near future, the cost-benefit analysis

– System of data collection and registration in cooperation with the other fields of town planning

– Interrelation between land use and transport demand including persons and goods movement

– Week-end traffic investigations in cooperation with the future development plans of resort places and recreation areas, special generation and distribution model for week-end traffic

3.2 Research in transport management and organization
– Local and overall control systems, regulations and restraint
– Investigations in traffic safety
– Demand, distribution and possibilities of pedestrian movement, control and safety problems
– Parking possibilities, control and restraint, park and ride system
– Goods movement, loading and service, demand and restriction
– Organization and coordination in the integrated public transport system

3.3 Special investigations
– Urban environmental pollution and environmental planning
– Administrative and social problems of the urban transport system
– Regional development problems in the Greater Budapest Region,
and several other themes in addition.

3.4 The main elements of the long-term plan of Budapest on the basis of the research works mentioned above
– To maintain and improve public transport so that it carries as many passengers as can safely, reliably, comfortably and as quickly as possible, and to make the best of public transport's main advantages, that is to carry a large number of people with relatively little environmental nuisance, with economy of space used, and with availability to all
– The extension and development of the road system, principally by the building of high quality primary roads so that a hierarchy of primary, secondary and local roads is formed
– The restraint of the use of cars in central and busy areas at the busiest times where public transport will provide an acceptable alternative
– Restraint and traffic management and control will have to be applied more intensively and extensively to make the best of the present and future road network.
The most difficult task is to achieve an optimal split and division of labour and cooperation between public and private transport.
The degree of freedom for private traffic should vary in different urban areas. The degree of restriction of private traffic should be based upon the road system capacity and parking potential. Restriction of private traffic in certain areas should be carried out if possible in a natural manner through an appropriate design of the control. The balance of parking capacity in certain areas and the traffic capacity of roads which carry traffic to these areas has a crucial meaning. According to the law of critical speed, traffic volume will always stabilize itself on a certain level and will not increase. Public transport operation should not be influenced by vehicular traffic; which means that, in the areas with a restriction of vehicular traffic, a complete segregation of public transport and vehicles should take place.
In the remaining areas a coexistence for both types of transport is quite possible. Public transport should be a coordinated and intergrated system.
Integration means better service for the whole area and increased efficiency. In urban conditions an absolute priority should be given to pedestrian traffic in areas of concentration of traffic (city centre, suburban centres) and in the residential areas as well. This integrated system would be balanced because of the equilibrium which exists between public and private

transport and also between road network capacity and the parking potential.
These ideas are not new, the majority of the elements of this concept may be found in various theoretical and practical works, but they represent a particular problem in the countries where explosion of motorization is expected. The Budapest public transport system consists of suburban rail and underground lines which form the rapid transport system. This system will cooperate with bus, tram and trolleybus transport through improvement and expansion of the feeder lines serving areas adjacent to metro stations.
At main metro stations land is being reserved for parking areas to realize the "park and ride system".
Special attention has been paid to facilities lying close to future underground lines.

4. Main development trends in transport research
4.1 Analysis of traffic demand and circulation
– The system of continous and systematic data collection and registration in land use, socio-economic factors, travel characteristics and volume informations to reduce the expensive and long-term comprehensive survey
– Developing the system of measuring traffic stream characteristics, speed, saturation flow, lost time, etc. in cooperation with the investigations in users' characteristics
– Research in traffic flow characteristics, speed volume-density, use of probabilistic descriptions, car-following models, capacity and level of service
– Characteristics of week-end traffic. Socio-economic and physical aspects of development of recreational areas, origin-destination studies, planning models for week-end traffic distribution and assignment
– Interdependencies between land use patterns, urban structure and travel demand.

4.2 Transport network planning methodology
– Simplified direct demand or general share models to overcome the worst errors of the current models by including economic demand functions, by incorporating levels of transport service as variables and by considering elasticity of demand and urban structure
– Traffic restriction possibilities, parking control, goods movement and other services in the city centre and suburban centres
– Urban and transport network structure of new settlements, secondary road and pedestrian networks, parking systems, environmental elements, relationship between city structure and travel demand.

4.3 Research on transport management
– To develop computer-controlled traffic control system, preparatory examinations, before and after examinations
– Traffic safety studies, accident analysis, relationship between safety and traffic conditions.

4.4. Other research works
– Research on innovative transportation systems, improvement in transport technology, organization and management
– Environmental quality problems, effect of land use and transportation on pollution levels, aesthetics, urban form and space, park and recreation areas and overall quality of life.
The basic condition of these research works is to develop the Research Department of Budapest City Council by inreasing the number of research workers, technicans and equipment in close collaboration

with universities. Investigations should be based on international level cooperation and exchange of views and experiences.

5. Conclusions

5.1 Demand for international cooperation in research activities

Transportation is the most variable and dynamic component of systems of settlement. Decisions on transportation should be oriented primarily towards achieving community development objectives within the framework of comprehensive planning of urban functions. Transportation must be perceived, planned, designed, financed and operated as part of a multi-purpose urban system.

Spatial and economic planning on national and regional schale can contribute to solving the problem of urban transportation, particularly in large agglomerations. This comprehensive approach to planning can be used to control the process of urbanization in order to avoid the nagative consequences of excessive uncontrolled development of metropolitan areas. In many respects, these problems have only recently been fully recognized.

As a basis for rational decision intensive research and exchange of information and ideas in this field, particularly with respect to comprehensive planning of the transportation function in the urban system, is desirable.

The main subjects, in which the international cooperation seem to be particularly promising and fruitful are:

– Comprehensive assessment of various transport modes and systems, so that decisions on alternatives could be taken with full knowledge of their possible economic, social and ecological consequences rather than being imposed by available technology, with greater attention to institutional factors. Studies and research works should offer guidance to the formulation of a number of economic and legal measures that could be employed to promote more efficient use of infrastructure capacity, and should indicate not only new technological alternatives for transport, but also consider new densities, forms and patterns of settlements.

– Studies to investigate interdependencies between land use patterns and travel demands, costs and benefits of the alternative ways for abatement of pollution and noise in urban areas including an evaluation of alternative transportation innovations and improvements, as well as of physical planning measures.

– Investigations into the conditions under which new transport systems may be introduced to replace traditional systems, and space and energy requirements for various systems.

– Research on technical, organizational and other measures in order to integrate different transportation systems.

– Research, not directly in the field of transport, to determine in the planning period the expectations created by the development of increased motorization and of human life itself, to develop different town planning models taking into consideration the features of different countries.

5.2 Main faults and shortcomings of current models

One of the most important tasks for futher research is to develop a new urban transportation planning process to overcome some of the shortcomings of the present model-systems used at many places as well as in Budapest.

Demand for a revision brings different points of view and it is extensively being discussed nowadays. Further follows a very short description of the critique of the conventional metropolitan transportation planning process on the basis of some experiences in Budapest.

The current transportation planning is static rather than dynamic, it is inflexible. It is based upon measurements and estimated relationships from a given point in time, with an assumption that these relationships and estimates will not change with time. Models are calibrated against base year conditions, which inherently implies an assumption that no significant changes in social patterns or behaviour will take place in the design period.

Trip generation models do not take into account either any measure of the economic benefit expected to be derived from a trip or the ability of the network to influence the demand. Models only offer the estimation of total travel demand, and therefore do not allow and specification of the particular transportation system links, which would allow an easy assessment of the accessibility of the zone. So there is no real supply or demand function included in the models.

A trip distribution model - a kind of gravity model in Budapest - does not permit travel time to be included as an explicet variable, therefore an assumption has to be made that the existing relationship between travel times and trip making propensity will remain the same throughout the whole forecast period.

The main problem of modal split and network assignment is, too, that some of the assumptions are unfounded.

The whole planning model, to some extent, is unresponsive and insensitive to many of the questions the decision maker should ask. The whole process is centered around a concept of attemting to produce a plan satisfying a particular demand. There is insufficient attention paid to the question of implementation. Some of the staged implementations that have occured have been in direct response to budgetary and political constraints, and have not been a consequence of a planned implementation strategy.

In addition, the form of planning is so rigid that no possible way is provided by which technological innovations could even be considered, and the existing strategies take little account of effects or wider impacts upon the environment as a whole, and particularly upon the whole spatial organization of urban areas. However the evolution process is beginning to be expanded into the areas of social and environmental consequences.

Another fault of these models is inaccuracy. Errors occur when the model does not take into account all the factors which may affect the output, and simply from sampling. One of the important consequences of this inaccuracy is that the model is suitable only for broad strategy analysis and not for detailed design work.

Last but not least this planning process as practiced currently is too complex and extremely expensive.

5.3 Some possible changes

Although some promising approaches have been taken in the recent years and transportation planning is in a period of change all over the world, the problem has not been solved yet.

The main question to be answered is how we can achieve the transport situation we want in 25 or 30 years in the best way. Alternative transport policies are needed, transport planning must define the best system for the community.

The changes are likely to be in the trip generation distribution and modal split developing general share models or direct demand models, which include explicit economic demand functions and levels of transport service, such as partly suggested in some studies in the United States.

At the same time simplification and reduction of complexity are needed to reduce the data requirements of the model and the interaction between variables, and to reduce the cost of studies. Better balance is needed between short term and long term problems of implementation.

The relationship of research to decisionmaking in intercontinental traffic

by

H. M. ROMOFF

Corporate Development Canadian Pacific Ltd.

Montreal, Canada

INTRODUCTION

The topic which I have been asked to deal with - "The relationship of Research to Decisionmaking in Intercontinental Transport" is not one that I chose myself, and I must say that I had considerable difficulty in trying to respond to it.

The easiest part of the title is clearly "Intercontinental Transport" which seems to limit the scope to long-distance aviation and ocean shipping, putting aside the aberrations of the odd intercontinental railway, highway, inland waterway and even pipeline. I gladly accept this limitation. More specifically, intercontinental transportation naturally breaks down into three modal components - aviation, general cargo shipping and bulk shipping; I distinguish the two shipping modes because of their very different structures and technological development paths.

The more difficult parts of the title are the terms "Research" and "Decisionmaking", and I must say I struggled with these for some considerable time. The definition of research I am most sympathetic to is taken from a well-known definition of economics - "Research is what researchers do". This seemed to describe perfectly my own experience with research and, even more so, researchers. I was recently somewhat disconcerted to come across a definition of research attributed to Wernher Von Braun, most recently of NASA fame, that seemed similar yet was very defferent. His definition was "Research is what I am doing when I do not know what I am doing". The Von Braun definition suggests a useful classification of research into three categories, in increasing order of specification:

a. Non-objective - or abstract non-directed inquiry; the research referred to by Von Braun.

b. Objective non-specific - such as trying to find a means of improving some particular transport vehicle or facility.

c. Objective specific - such as tackling some very specific well defined problem.

This does help in defining my topic further. Transportation research has not been characterized by "mad scientist" types pursuing abstract non-directed inquiry. Furthermore, the objective specific research task - the nuts and bolts of improving a product - which accounts for by far the largest research effort, is too microscopic and detailed for much to be said in this type of presentation. By elimination, I am left with the second category - objective non-specific research - as the focal point of my comments, at least to the extent that they deal with technical research.

This is made all the more complex by the fact that research itself runs the gamut from technical (or engineering) research to market research, to systems research and to socio-economic research, recognizing, of course, the increasing role of interdisciplinary research cutting across traditional lines.

Decisionmaking implies decisionmakers and there are a variety of decisionmakers who are impacted by research. They include:

- Owners/Operators of mobile and fixed systems
- Manufacturers of transport equipment and facilities
- Government officials involved in transport policy
- International agencies and other international groupings involved in intercontinental transport
- Transport users.

I am afraid I will have to deal with all these decisionmakers.

The more I tried to precisely define my topic, the more complex it seemed to become and I did not think it useful to prepare a paper dealing with definitions or taxonomy. Therefore, I have interpreted my topic somewhat broadly and taken as my theme the broad relationships between research and change in long-distance aviation, general cargo shipping and bulk shipping. I was encouraged to do so by the fact that the presentations which follow mine are all mode-specific.

I should like first to deal with the broad macro relationship between research and change over the past two decades in each of the three modes I have identified and to explore the interactions and driving forces. I have concentrated on mobile transport equipment, rather than on fixed facilities, on the theory that fixed facilities tend to respond to perceived needs arising from changed mobile equipment. I would finally like to probe the deficiencies in research performance and explore what the future may hold in store.

THE LAST TWO DECADES

The only way to judge the effectiveness of research is pragmatically - by what is has achieved. It is well and good to publish learned papers, to build impressive research facilities and to appear at prestigious international conferences. But the usefulness of all this is nothing if it does not lead to improvements in transport system. The proof of the pudding is in the eating, not in the recipe or in the cooking.

By this standard, one must conclude that research has served intercontinental transport very well indeed over the past two decades. Those of us who spend our lives working in transport are perhaps too close to the changes to fully notice this. But the progress in the past two decades has been nothing short of remarkable. Any balanced look at the effectiveness of transport research must begin with this in mind. The intercontinental transport system today is a remarkably superior one to that which existed 20 years ago, both with regard to cost and to service. In this most fundamental sense, research has served the industry well.

It is useful to recount briefly the major developments which have occurred.

In long-distance aviation, we have evolved from the DC-7, Constellation and Britannia to the Jumbo and perhaps even the Supersonic. The change in technology, in cost levels and in service standards has been nothing less than remarkable, and the fascination of the story is lost in any short summary. Suffice it to say that the successful development of long-distance aviation will be one of those few basic developments which future historians will attribute to our generation.

With regard to ocean shipping, general cargo handling has evolved from the small, slow multi-purpose general cargo vessel, spending perhaps half its time loading and unloading by methods best characterized as medieval, to the large, fast automated container, Ro-Ro or LASH vessel, capable of being loaded and unloaded in perhaps 24 hours at highly automated ports. Bulk shipping has evolved from the 10-20,000 dwt. tanker or bulker to the flotilla of 250,000 dwt. VLCC's, with some even larger, and 120,000 dwt. dry bulkers, all capable of rapid loading and unloading and literally scraping the bottom in most of the world's traditional ports and channels. These changes are perhaps less dramatic than the changes in international aviation, not only because they are less visible but also because they have not changed the lifestyle of the world as much. But, nonetheless, they are changes which have fundamentally transformed ocean shipping (and hence world commerce) and are certainly the most dramatic since the demise of the sail. Indeed, in comparing the evolution of *inter*continental and *intra*continental transport over the last two decades, it is clear that the changes which have occured in intercontinental transport have been by far the more dramatic and significant. This is by no means intended to disparage developments in automobile, bus, truck, rail, barge, pipeline and short-haul aviation, which have not been insignificant. But in sum total they are certainly overshadowd by developments in intercontinental transport.

HOW HAS THIS HAPPENED

In trying to understand the relationship between research and decisionmaking, it is interesting to explore the mechanism and driving forces whereby dramatic and far-reaching developments occurred in each of the three intercontinental modes. One would be hopeful that some general conclusions could be derived from such a review which might shed some light on what we might expect in the future. I am sorry to report that the only conclusions which emerged were the most general ones and not the least bit surprising - namely that each faced its own set of external and internal pressures and driving forces, and that the developments of each were uniquely related to the specific circumstances of each mode. Expressed more positively, the general theory of the development of intercontinental transport is that there appears to be no general theory. Research responds to pressures, but to a variety of pressures, and progress is the result of the complex interaction of internal pressures, exogenous pressures, technical developments and motivation.

I should like to develop this thought further by considering briefly the developments in each of the three modes, paying particular attention to:
1. The nature of the changed technology
2. The roles of each of the three major players - the manufacturers, the owner/operators, the ultimate users.
3. The driving force for change.
4. The location of the entrepreneurial thrust.
5. The propagation mechanism for the spread of new technology.

Consider first international aviation, the youngest of the modes with an effective birth date after the Second War. Of all the modes, the technological changes in international aviation were the most dramatic, fundamental and far-reaching. But they did not result from dissatisfied users, be they passengers or shippers of cargo, clamouring for better service and/or lower prices, nor from the owner-operators urging the manufacturers to improve their products. Both the users and the owner-operators were too fragmented, too weak financially and too ill-informed technically to have much of an impact.

Rather the driving force for change came from the manufacturing industry - to be more specific, a handful of U.S. aerospace firms - which aggressively packaged the spillover of military R & D into commercial aviation products and then aggressively marketed these products to the owners/operators.

This was clearly the location of the entrepreneurial thrust and drive and remained so even when the spillover effedt from the military side became less important. One is tempted to generalize and say that the pattern whereby the entrepreneurial drive is located at the manufacturing level seems to be true, in general, of the high-technology industries.

The propagation mechanism for spreading the new technology was also interesting. The new products were first purchased by one, or a handful, of airlines and as the advantages in terms of both better service and lower unit costs became obvious, they were followed helter-skelter by the other airlines wishing to maintain their competitive position. It is interesting to note that all *successful* new products featured reduced unit costs,, and the competitive nature of the airline industry took it from there. As an aside, this propagation mechanism explains the waves of re-equipping that have periodically swept the industry and also the persistent oversupply of equipment.

The user of international aviation, both passenger and freight, was an enthusiastic responder to lower real cost coupled with improved service. Indeed, his response was so enthusistic that it added fuel to the flames, furher encouraging the manufacturer to push ahead and the airlines to acquire new products. Only very recently has this process seemed to come to a marked pause. The dismal economics of the Concorde places it out of the mainstream of the story, since all succesful new designs have offered improved economics.

Consider next the developments in general cargo shipping over the past two decades - the so-called container revolution. In total contrast to international aviation, the basic technological changes which were required to make the revolution happen were fairly simplistic, and I have no doubt that a good naval architect working with an equally good production engineer could have put together the basics of today's container handling system in the 1930's, if not the 1920's. The changes were technically simple and in no way pushed against the technological frontier.

When they did finally occur, once again it was not because of pressure from users demanding better service at lower cost; the users were too fragmented and too small individually to initiate change. Nor was change promoted by the manufacturers, the ship-builders, who seemed quite content to carry on producing traditional type vessels forever. Rather the driving thrust for change originated from the owners/operators, faced with dramatically escalating labour costs, particularly at ports, with no scope to improve productivity within the confines of traditional technology. If cargo had to be loaded and unloaded by the traditional methods, port labour costs and port delay could not be reduced.

The driving force for change in this instance was a handful of entrepreneurial ship owner/operators who carried out the research, put together the skeleton of a marine container system and aggressively forced the traditional ship-builders to respond to their needs. And in the first instance, it was not the traditional, well-established owner-operators who developed and promoted the new technology. The lesson in this appears to be that longevity and tradition are poor bedfellows for research and development, and shipping is one of the world's oldest industries.

The propagating mechanism, once the new technology was seen to be remarkably cost-effective and workable, was emulation by the other ship owners-operators, so that within a span of very few years, the entire industry was transformed. The ripple effects of mechanized handling at ports is also interesting: mechanized handling of containers made possible reduced port times which improved the economics of larger and faster ships - all of which could have been built, at least technically - many years before the Container Revolution. Exactly the same is true for the dramatic feedback effects of marine containerization on the inland transport system. Inland transporters responded with a technology that could have been designed in the 1930's or earlier if there had been a need. Fortunately, when marine containerization was being developed, there existed the skeleton of an appropriate inland system in the use of semi-trailers for highway movement and rail piggyback handling.

As in the aviation case, the user of general cargo shipping was an enthusiastic responder to lower real cost coupled with improved service to the point that for many years the only dependable forecast regarding the market penetration of container handling into the general cargo trade was that all existing forecasts would be exceeded.

Finally, consider the case of bulk shipping, the least visible of the three modes under consideration. The technological developments which made possible the 250,000 dwt. tanker and the 120,000 dwt. dry-bulker lie somewhere between the "high" technology of aviation and the "simple" technology of container shipping. Fundamental developments in ship-design and power plants as well as in the strength and fabrication of materials were necessary for the new technology to emerge, but the changes in technology were still an order of magnitude smaller than the changes in aviation technology.

Of all the modes, bulk shipping is the most complex and difficult to understand with regard to identifying the driving force behind the technical change, the entrepreneurial group and the propagating mechanism. This results from the rather unique structure of the industry, with the participants playing multiple roles. Not only are users of bulk-shipping often also owner-operators (the large fleets of the major oil companies and of the iron ore subsidiaries of some major steel companies, for example) but users are often also manufacturers (the ship-building subsidiaries of several Japanese and U.S. steel companies) or closely linked to manufacturers (the Japanese Zaibatsu). All this reflects the fact that in bulk shipping, in direct contrast to aviation and general cargo shipping, the users are few, large, and economically powerful compared with the owner-operators and the manufacturers and there is hence considerable vertical integration.

The closest one can come to a simple and coherent explanation of the driving force and motivation for the change in technology, is to say that it originated in Japan, almost as a national mission. This was a mission with several purposes - to meet and minimize the costs of the country's projected needs for huge imports of raw materials, to maximize the country's manufacturing capabilities, to maximize the country's export capabilities. All these factors came together in a uniquely Japanese way reflecting its role as a user and as a manufacturer. The research and entrepreneurial roles were almost entirely Japanese.

The propagating mechanism, once the Japanese had put together all the pieces and shown that bulk shipping costs could be significantly reduced was a combination of very entrepreneurial owner-operators, responding to pressure from major bulk commodity users, all accelerated by the dramatic increase in international trade in petroleum and dry bulk products, particularly coal and iron ore, resulting from the basic facts of economic geography, and further reinforced by the closure of the Suez Canal. The surge in petroleum trade was exogenous to shipping technology - world shipping would have had to find some way to accommodate to the economic geography of petroleum - while the surge in coal and iron ore traffic was to a major extent a response to the availability of low-cost, long-distance bulk transport.

In summary, I have no difficulty in concluding that, in a macro sense, research has served intercontinental transport well over the past two decades in the sense that the transport product has become very much better and cheaper. But the relationships between research and decisionmaking have been different in all the modes, depending on the complexity of the technology, the economic strength of the various interests and the location of the entrepreneurial thrust. It is an interesting story.

I said before that there was no general theory of the relationship between research and development in intercontinental transport. This was perhaps an exaggeration, because there are a few common threads running through the story. One is that all the successful developments were cost-reducing and service-improving; this is not a very remarkable conclusion. A second is that the very competitive nature of all intercontinental transport modes made available a very effective and rapid propagation mechanism for the developments once they had been perfected. There is hope for those of us who still believe in the effectiveness of the competitive marketplace. A third is that effective research and development requires a dedicated sponsor, prepared to pursue new concepts in a single-minded manner. The sponsor can be the manufacturer - the case of aviation, the owner-operator - the case in general cargo shipping - or some combination of interests - the Japanese coalition of manufacturers and users in the case of bulk shipping.

The final common thread in all of this is that the role of government in the developments which have taken place has been minimal and what role there has been was almost wholly responsive. Government has taken the major role in providing the fixed facilities for the intercontinental modes, but in a responsive manner, reacting to the developing technology of the mobile systems. Government enterprises have been participants in the intercontinental transport scene, in various roles, but generally they have acted as have the private participants; they have not been the driving force, with the possible exception of the Japanese and the well-known difficulty of clearly separating private and public motivations. Government through its regulatory function has had to permit certain commercial developments to take place, but has generally not been a major delaying influence. The key decisions have been made without government involvement and research has impacted private decisionmakers rather than governmental ones. Perhaps this explains some of the dynamism that has taken place.

THE NEXT DECADE

I have discussed developments over the past two decades and, to be consistent, I should use the same time horizon in looking ahead. I am sorry to say that I have not the courage to do this. Two decades is a very long time in terms of technology and the history of technological forecasting over such a timeframe is abysmal. I thus will concentrate my remarks on the time-frame of the next decade.

In looking ahead, there is a natural bias to give excessive weight to the present and to forecast a continuation of present trends. We all know that this is wrong and highly misleading, and that if there is one future certainty, it is that the future will differ from the present. But even acknowledging this bias, my own view is that we seem to have reached a plateau in the development of intercontinental transport, at least in technological developments of the magnitude and importance of those that have occured over the past two decades. Of course, there will be further progress and improvements, but I find it very difficult to believe that they will be as fundamental and farreaching as have occurred over the past two decades.

It is tempting to attribute such a conclusion to overconservatism, to say that any timid person could reach this conclusion at any point of time. But I do not think that this is so. Had I been standing on this platform in the late 1950's, I like to think that I would have been able to predict that dramatic research-based changes were on the horizon for all the intercontinental transport modes, even over a single decade. There was certainly enough work in progress and portents of change. This is simply not the case today. The developments I foresee are more of a filling in, a consolidation, rather than basic new thrusts. I would not mind, and would even welcome, being proved wrong in this prediction.

In intercontinental aviation, aiplanes may become larger, they will certainly become more fuel-efficient and quieter and the present sub-sonic speed standard is most unlikely to change. Costs are unlikely to decrease significantly, if at all, to say nothing of decreasing to the extent they have over the past two decades, given the very large increase in fuel prices that must be met.

General cargo handling seems unlikely to change dramatically. Containerization will continue its spread to lower density routes, new ship configurations may emerge for certain routes, handling equipment will continue to evolve and the actual boxes may become more sophisticated. Ships are unlikely to become much larger, faster or more economic.

Bulk cargo handling also faces no dramatic changes.

Certainly the practical and economic size of vessels seems to have been reached. Further, I see nothing to suggest state-of-the-act changes in ship automation over the next decade. This applies also to general cargo shipping. I do foresee considerable development in the specialized types of shipping, such as transporting LNG or operating in far northern climates, and I will return to this theme later in this paper.

In summary, our expectations for the performance of research over the next decade should be scaled down considerably from the performance over the past two decades. This is not to say that there will be no scope for technical research; rather that the research is likely to be more specific and applied to clearly defined problems rather than to a quantum jump in the overall level of performance.

SOME DEFICIENCIES

I should now like to turn to my second theme - the deficiencies in our research performance to date and how we might deal with them. My comments in this connection will deal more with "soft" research rather than "hard" research; not only is this were I perceive the major deficiencies to be, but it is the area closest to my own interests. Once again, I will deal with each of the three intercontinental modes separately.

With regard to aviation, the success of our technical achievements is only matched by our failure on the commercial side. Structurally, the industry is locked into that very strange and unique organization, IATA. It grew out of the restrictionism in the 1930 and 1940's, and was fashioned in what appears to be increasingly like concrete, but at a time when the airline industry was vastly different from what it is today. It has been described as everything from "a cartel" to "a disaster", but whatever one chooses to call it, there is little doubt that it has very serious shortcomings and, as it presently functions, is not particularly well-suited to the tremendous change and dynamism of the intercontinental aviation industry.

One could write a separate paper explaining the reasons for this. Suffice it to list some of the more serious deficiencies:
- the strange mixture of governmental and commercial interests
- the cumbersome method of decisionmaking
- the veto power
- incomplete coverage of the marketplace.

All of these deficiencies manifest themselves in an inability to deal with change in an aggressive forward-looking manner. I shudder to think how our economy would look if all industries were organized in this matter.

But the basic test again must be pragmatic. International aviation has been one of the classic postwar growth industries, yet the IATA carriers are *not* financially healthy and, have been steadily losing market share. Nor does this seem about to change. The industry has been fortunate in that it was swept along by improved technology, by growth in markets and by large scale government assistance. Commercial success, as we normally understand it, has not been the driving force. One must wonder whether this can continue indefinitely.

This is surely a fertile field for research. Not abstract technical research, nor research done in the ivory tower, but rather policy-orientated practical research of the type that can convince governments and airlines of the world that there must be a better way and that commercial flexibility and viability are in the interests of both users and suppliers.

Another fertile field for useful research is the entire

area of market analysis and research. The market forces governing the demand for aviation services are very far from being understood, to say nothing of being rigorously modelled. The proof of this is that it took the major carriers, their governments and various international organizations at least a decade to understand the growth potential of cheap charter-type transportation. The fact that they had tremendous difficulty in responding to challenge, once they had understood it, is explained by my previous comments on IATA.

It is nothing less than shameful that an industry which has been an acknowledged technological leader is such a laggard in its commercial organization and market understanding. I commend this entire area to those with a serious interest in policy research. I know that many of the relevant decisionmakers would welcome such an effort.

My last comment on aviation has to do with the huge and highly visible commercial disasters which have recently been visited on the industry - and I refer specifically to the Concorde and certain international airports. I suggest these are related to the very large non-transportation impacts that are expected from intercontinental aviation, or aviation generally, and to the very large role played by government in all aspects of the industry. I have seen economic research studies of these projects, done well before the fact, which conclude that they were viable and self-sustaining. Given the well-known outcomes, one can ask whether one should fault the researchers or the decisionmakers. The real answer is probably both. When decisionmakers know in advance what type of answer they want, for reasons only vaguely related to the economics of the project itself, when researchers themselves know what answer the decisionmakers expect, and when major proposals are put forth on the basis of a confused and unquantifiable list of justifications, one has present all the makings of a disaster. This is perhaps the worst type of relationship that can exist between the researcher and the decisionmaker and we should not be the least bit surprised when it produces disasters which discredit everyone in ugly post-mortems.

Given the visibility of aviation projects, their rapidly increasing threshold costs, the high level of non-transportation expectations from such projects, (coupled with the low-level understanding of the propagation mechanism for such effects) and the overly incestuous relationship that can develop between the researcher and the decisionmaker, we must be wary that further disasters are avoided. They do nothing for the integrity of transportation research and decisionmaking, to say nothing about the huge waste of public funds which results.

Turning next to general cargo shipping, the major deficiencies, in my view, once again lie on the software rather than hardware side, and it is there that research effort should be concentrated. For example, the entire documentation, customs clearance and financing aspects of general cargo shipping have yet to adopt themselves to the rationalization which has occured on the physical handling side, and there is still an administrative jungle involved in clearing cargo in nations of the world which should know better. The tools of systems analysis and modern communications/datahandling are at hand and there is need to apply them, for the benefits will be considerable. I am aware that a start has been made at this in many countries and also internationally, but there is still a long way to go.

Another example. Container transport by its very nature is multi-modal transport. It should be more than that, that is to say, integrated transport, with cargo moving on a single waybill, expeditiously transferred between modes where appropriate, with the shipper/consignee fully assured as to responsibility and liability. We are still some distance from that goal and there exists another field for productive policy-orientated research.

Intercontinental transport, particularly for general cargo, is not simply "shore-to-shore" but "door-to-door". The overall test of efficiency must be a total systems test, not simply a modal test. As an example of what can go wrong, I would mention the disasterous port congestion situation in parts of the Middle East and Africa. The problem here has to do both with hardware - the capacity of the port and inland transport systems - and software - the administrative difficulty in clearing cargo.

The difficulty with resolving software problems such as those mentioned, and this applies equally to the software/organizational deficiencies in all intercontinental transport, is the complexity of the decisionmaking process and the plethora of decisionmakers, all with differing interests. Not only are the owners/operators and their customers involved, but a major role is played by various agencies of national governments as well as financial institutions. It will not be an easy task, but there is much scope for interesting and productive research.

Turning finally to bulk shipping, the growing number of maritime mishaps, as more and more ships ply the world's trade routes with environmentally dangerous products, might suggest the need for improved navigation and communication systems, as well as safety standards. I do not think this is the case. Our navigation and communications systems are not deficient. Rather our ability to effectively enforce their use is terribly deficient. The same is true for safety standards. The need is to devise an effective enforcement system, compatible with national sovereignty and freedom of the seas. We are still some way from this - and I commend this area as a most worthwhile one. There is no lack of interested decisionmakers.

The commercial problems of bulk shipping unfortunately do not easily lend themselves to research solutions although those in the industry would welcome solutions from any source. The problems I have reference to can best be seen in the Norwegian fiords where a fleet of VLCC's rides at anchor, or in the fact that almost new ships are being sold at a substantial discount under what it cost to build them 3 or 4 years ago, to say nothing of their present value.

I hardly need elaborate that bulk shipping is the classical boom or bust industry, resulting from the total mobility of its capacity, the exogenous market forces which regularly make themselves felt (e.g. closing of Suez; OPEC) all coupled with a long lead time between ordering new vessels and their delivery. All this is exacerbated by the structure of the industry which results in herd-like swings of over-optimism and over-pessimism, force-fed by competing national subsidy programs which seem to have as their goal the maximization of ship construction in as short a time period as possible. I would be straining the limits of credulity if I were to suggest that research has an answer to these problems or that decisionmakers will change their reaction patterns because of research advice. But we should certainly do the research; perhaps someone will listen and we shall not be condemned to repeat the past.

There are, however, several research areas relating to bulk shipping which are terribly important, and will

63

become increasingly so. One has to do with the entire environmental problem of handling bulk cargo in ports. The problem is a very real one for it does no good to perfect the bulk handling of products by ship if overlapping and confusing port environmental standards, coupled with nervous public reaction resulting from lack of information or misinformation, preclude the construction of appropriate ports where needed. I would not suggest that there are not environmental factors which need full consideration in port planning, but I would maintain that we need as input hard knowledge based on sound and valid environmental research so that the issues can be dealt with rationally rather than emotionally. The research need is physical- what are proper standards and how do they apply - administrative - how do we organize our jurisdictions to apply these standards - and social - how do we communicate the facts to the public. The relationship between the researcher and the decisionmaker, in this instance, is a terribly complex one, but this does not make the problem less important.

A second interesting research area relating to bulk shipping has to do with specialized transport, and I would suggest that more and more maritime research will be devoted to this general area. For example, it is clear that the world energy problem will require dramatically increasing intercontinental shipments of LNG. Indeed, this is now beginning to happen. Ship and shore equipment has responded to the need and presently-produced equipment might be described as second generation. But the complexity and extremely high cost of the equipment remains a major problem. A quantum jump in technology would be a major step forward in meeting energy deficiencies and eliminating wasteful flaring of natural gas. Consumers, producers and owner-operators are all interested clients for such a development.

Another area of specialized transport which must receive increasing attention is marine transport in far-northern areas. This is not simply a Canadian problem, although Canada has a vital interest, but one that impacts most of the world's major countries. Economic pressures are forcing us to develop our far-northern resources and, by necessity, the maritime industry is involved. The research needs are extremely wide-ranging from the design of vessels and power plants, to detailed mapping, to understanding and forecasting ice formations and their movements, and even to attempting to physically control the environment in key areas. As the pressures are not only economic, but also political, the research users will be both private interests and governments.

CONCLUDING COMMENTS

It is the nature of my topic that a simple and clear conclusion is not to be expected. In summary, I have argued that:

1. Over the past two decades, there have been dramatic research-based development of intercontinental transport. Based on results, research has served the industry remarkably well.

2. The interaction between research and decision-making has been different in each of the intercontinental modes. Research responds to pressures and each mode has been subject to different endogenous and exogenous pressures.

3. The development of intercontinental transport seems to have reached a plateau, and the next decade will witness more of a filling in rather than a continuation of the dramatic changes of the past two decades.

4. There remain many interesting and fascinating research problems to be dealt with, with regard to both software and hardware.

If there is any single conclusion, it is that the future will be different from the past, but no less exciting and challenging.

Transport decisions in an age of uncertainty
Trends in port research

by

G. C. MEEUSE

International Cargo Handling Co-ordination Association

PORT MODELS

Preamble

This contribution is greatly determined by the impressions obtained during visits brought by the author and Drs. H.J. Noortman to a great number of ports of various types all over the world.

Also the preliminary studies made by Noortman and Meeuse, published and presented in recent congresses formed bases for this paper. Because of Noortman's role in this world congress a one man presentation was decided upon.

Introduction

Transport has developed rather spectacularly both in intensity and in scale during the past decades. Only in 1962 Peter Drucker stated in his famous publication "The economies dark continent" with regard to distribution that we know little more about enterprise- or manufacturing levels than Napoleon's contemporaries knew about the interior of Africa. They knew it was there and they knew it was big and that was about all. He proved in that study that almost 50 cents out of every dollar the consumer spends on goods, goes to activities occurring after the goods are made. Furthermore he prescribed physical distribution as the last frontier of cost reduction.

In his often cited book "Le grand espoire du vingtième siècle - Great expectations of the twentieth century - Jean Fourastier characterized in 1947 in a wider scope as Peter Drucker did, transport as a service rendering activity. He distinguished three sectors of production. Agriculture as the primary, industrial activities as the secundary and services as the tertiary sector. Among the immense number of services, transport should be reckoned.

Fourastier was not absolute in incorporating transport and communication in the tertiary group. He states that these activities are of a hybride character and that they may not always stay with the tertiary sector. Though he reckons them now to the service rendering group, he admits that because of the degree of mechanisation and of the analogy to industrial activities, transport can easily escape from the tertiary and be taken up in the secundary industrial sector.

This proves the active character of the transport indus-

Fig. 1

development of transport			
period	past	present	future
dominating	craftmanship	technique	technology
movement — appearance / place / time / control	matter [static]	matter energy [dynamic]	matter energy information [cybernatic]
characteristics	manual • manipulation	transport proces	transport system
transport chain	autonomous links	coördinated links	integrated links in industrial chain
consideration directed on	object	function	function + relationship
field of profession	mech. - handling equipment	mech. - handling technique	transport technology

try. It must however be said that, with due respect to the opinion and to the theories presented by Jean Fourastier, the incorporation of transport activities in the tertiary sector has not done much good towards its development, particulary in the direction of integrated systems.

The developments of transport stayed behind those in industry for a long time and despite an acceleration in this development still the two worlds of transportation and of manufacturing, stayed apart or at least they met insufficiently.

The historical development of transport shows the same three steps as industrial history.

First step

Autonomous activities, characterized by craftmanship and manual manipulations performed by individual workers.

During this past - static - period mechanical handling tools and equipment formed the means to support physical labor.

Second step

Coordinated links of transport and production chains could be formed after energy came available. Production and transport became more and more mechanized. The various activities were no longer considered independent.

This present - dynamic - stage can be best characterized by the concept: technique.

Third step

The introduction of information brings systems into sight.

Technologically speaking: the links of the production and transport chains have to be integrated because of their mutual interdependencies.

In this final and futural stage technology offers a cybernetic control of mass, energy and information. The results are product chains consisting of integrated links.

Fig. 2

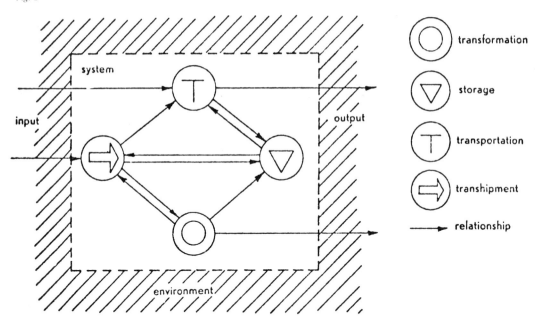

Consequently, technological systems comprise all the activities - both production and transport - necessary to bring products from their origin to their destination, in the right shape, to the demanded place and at the most adapted time.

Together the activities form product chains, in which production and transport are combined and almost alternate.

In fact transport and production should be considered equivalent subsystems of these product chains forming together a technological system. None of the two is subordinated to the other; they are however fully interdependent. In so considering the problems, optimisation can be reached, which is much more advantageous than the usual suboptimae. Nevertheless the problems are of introducing the necessary measures to be taken by various interested parties.

Fig. 3

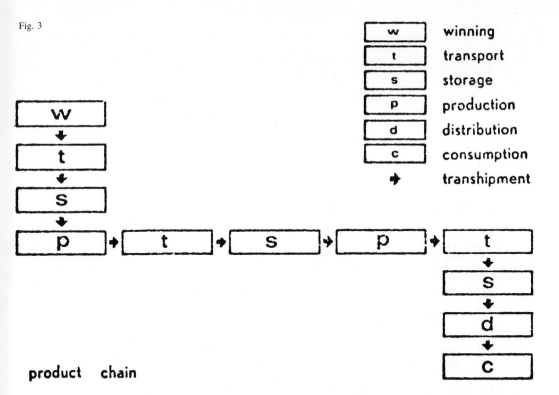

product chain

Ports

Ports seem to receive much interest today, when we look to the number of congresses devoted to terminals and ports. Recently in this same town an international conference titled: "Ports of tomorrow" was held. The interesting question "Must ports lead the evolution or follow it" was dealt with by several speakers. As an introduction to an appraisal of port models in the field of transport research I will give first some observations regarding the rôle and the function of ports taken from my contribution to that conference.

The flows of products pass on their ways from origin to destination several ports, either sea-, inland- or airports, railwaystations or trucking centres. Also the accompanying and synchronised data flows - complementary element of transport processes - have their ports, in which they are transferred, stored and handled.

Observing ports in a helicopter view from various altitudes give a series of impressions. Still on earth one smelled the products handled and saw the silhouettes of carriers and of port equipment. These primary sensory perceptions of port activities indicate some important parameters to be taken into account when studying the phenomenon "port".

After take off first the operational aspects become noticeable, telling something about structure and organization of the field of activities.

Regardless of the equipment used and the methods applied the functions performed are of real importance. This aspect can only be observed after gaining more height, that means more distance.

Functionally speaking a port is but a location where conveyance activities are either completed or where they find their starting point - a terminal of conveyance. For the different types of ports even a specific qualification - a name - was derived from the dominant mode of transport they serve. Such a practice is bound up closely with a restricted, one-sided, view, too often found in ports.

When I urged earlier for an equivalency of activities within technological systems, e.g. production and transport, I now must admit that already in the transport level there is no equilibrium of power. Too often the main mode of transport dominates all others that meet in a particular port.

Consequently the so called "sealag" of a seaport generally is well developed while the "Landleg" still can be improved considerably.

Similar observations can easily be made for airports, railwaystations, etc.

Port Research

The helicopter allows at last, when flying still higher, for a more aggregated picture showing the principles of transport, or better, of technology, on the location under consideration. Such a picture can only be obtained through a system approach of the transport problems.

The description in accordance with such an approach reads: A port is a location in which products are transfered from one stage within a (transport)system to a subsequent one.

Such a location can be called a terminal and a collection of terminals form together a port. The role of such terminals, whatever type we have in mind, can be visualized as an element of the transport- respectively of the product chains. The ports form the cross sections of the different product chains passing them. This implies that terminals and ports also belong to the basic technological systems and therein form elements.

The position of the cross section within a product chain indicates the degree of completion of the technological series of activities a product has to undergo.

Roughly speaking this can be expressed in terms like: raw material stage, semi-manufactured stage, finished stage.

A more accurate way of expressing this could be found in a technological percentage.

Fig. 4

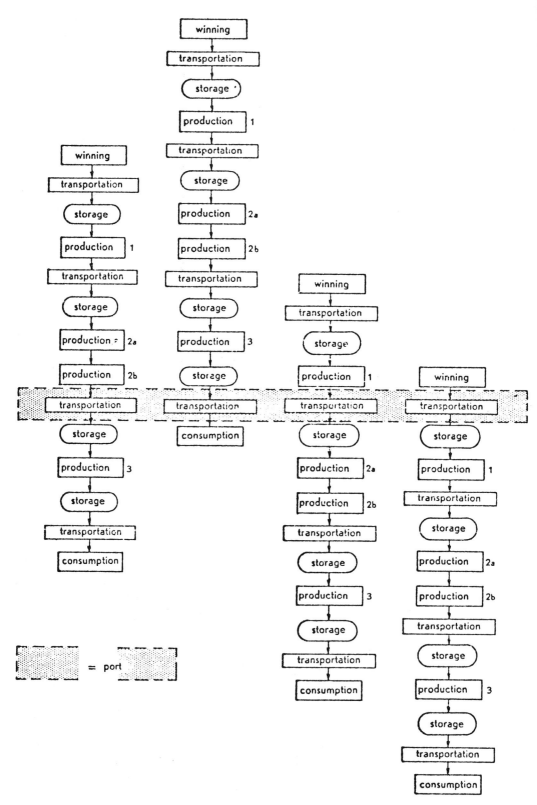

68

Anyway this position should be determined, and particularly changes in that position should be watched carefully.

In the flow of products from less developed areas such shifts, which can occur for a not well prepared observer as a surprise, can be expected.

In a contribution titled "Trends in port development" to the biennial congress of the International Cargo Handling Co-ordination Association held last week in Melbourne, Noortman en Meeuse elaborated this theme much further. In this paper based on the principles of system approach it was strongly emphasized to consider port activities to be part of transport - and finally of technological systems.

The technological completion percentage was there introduced as a magnitude to characterize a port. An other parameter was found in the appearance of the goods, while of course the volumes of the transport flows through the transport chains were given full consideration.

Attention was also paid to the homogeneity of the flows per product and to the geographic location of port activities.

Finally clusters of product chains, for which the ports form a "get togehther" were described.

Similar consideration lead CEPAL - the Economic Commission for Latin America - of the United Nations ECONOMIC and SOCIAL COUNCIL - in February 1977 to a publication titled "The distribution chain as a methodological tool". With the aim "to improve marketing, distribution and transport systems for commodity exports of developing countries, including an increase in their participation in those activities and their earnings from them", some most valuable observations and recommendations have been made.

One of them is the consideration of "transport as part of a broader distribution function, forming a chain in time and space between producer and consumer being an important advance in the methodology of product distribution analysis, because it provides for a comprehensive treatment of all aspects of the process, including physical movement, storage, transformation, brokerage, insurance, banking, regulation and documentation".

A good description of the distribution chain, which I prefer to call a product chain, is useful in a number of ways to aid in achieving the goals.

CEPAL presents a conceptualization of the distribution chain as a methodological tool. Certainly the proposed procedure can serve as "an information organizing scheme which might facilitate the collection and the retrieval of data. As an analytical model it serves as a checklist to assure that important elements, especially those concerning transport and associated services have not been overlooked".

"The model itself is structured in the form of a matrix with eight rows and an undetermined number of columns. Each of the rows - termed "planes" - corresponds to a group of related activities or information in the distribution process between the producer and consumer of a particular product. In turn, each plane is made up of elements, which in the model are called "modules", that form the columns of the matrix".

The eight planes deal subsequently with operations, technology, ownership insurance, credit and payment, regulation and control, documentation and finally process information.

I like on this occasion to complement CEPAL on this important proposition. Further I like to invite interested parties to prove the validity of this proposal through application. Noortman and I will certainly give it full attention and we will record and comment on it in due time.

Systems and models

The three approaches through operations, functions and systems give an increasing level of abstraction.

Speaking on systems and consequently on transport-systems is "in". System-thinking however is more than a common sense approach of every day problems in a modern and rather sophisticated jargon, it is a way of thinking! By applying it a conscious and systematic handling of complex problems it becomes possible, which would present many difficulties if handled by feeling.

In fact system approach is not a recipe, but if offers an expedient to those who acquire it as an attitude. It can be very well trained through application on actual problems derived from industrial circumstances.

In its turn every system taken into consideration is part (=sub) of a bigger whole from which it can be distinguished and separated. The principle keeps off from the earlier mentioned partial treatments, in which relevant qualities are kept invariable.

Quite often it has occurred that technical and technological parameters were in a qualitative sense, kept invariable. The number of tools and implements were thereby taken into account while new methods were neglected. This could result in crooked growth trends in forecastings.

Forecasting and extrapolation are not similar activities. Only to some extent are they connected. Extrapolation forms only an aspect of forecasting but is on its own a rather hazardous activity. Particularly in periods of restricted economical growth, the margin in which corrections can be made are proportionally narrow. Flexibility and being quick at repartee do not help under these circumstances.

To study a system under real conditions and making experiments is mostly impossible. Therefore we have to build models, in which we simplify the complex reality according to our views and aims. Models therefore form an abstraction of the life systems but at the same time through deletion of certain aspects are of a lower level. Consequently modelling includes both profits and losses. This property of models should therefore always be taken into consideration.

The quality of a model is the effectiveness, that is the degree in which the model suits its purpose.

If a model in itself is a system serving to study other more complex systems, it generally will be an aggregation of those systems and therefore will be of a higher level of abstraction.

Prof. in 't Veld gives a survey of models both qualitative and quantitative which can be used, in the circumstances. His ideas are applied on a large scale in the Netherlands and have been published in his book "Analyse van organisatieproblemen". (Analysis of organisational problems). (Figure 5)

The generally expressed preference for dis-aggregated models for decision making purposes - e.g. for real life systems - can only be met if first the coherence of the various elements, their interactions and interdependencies, are considered on a more aggregated level, and from there come down to a zoomed picture through zeroing.

In summing up we must be careful not to take the results of model research too absolutely. Models are but a tool for decision making and too many models have been built already for the sake of modelbuilding only!

Port models

In the congress report of the first international research congress a series of methods are described how to approach port problems.

In my Institution some publicated models have been thoroughly studied. A brief report is presented in annex

Figure 5 - Typology of models

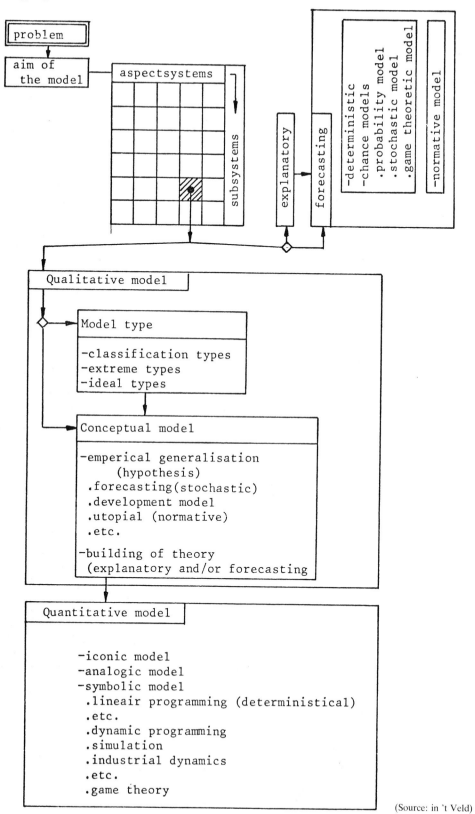

(Source: in 't Veld)

A in terms of goals, structures, methods and fields of application.

When examining these port models it appeared that they reached from static single enterprise models up to dynamic simulation models of regional ports. The level of aggregation is generally low and most models are even of a dis-aggregate type. Only the Dynamo model is of a high aggregation level.

The examined models are not only of differing levels, but are designed for various applications as well. One could put the questions whether still more models have to be built for specific applications or that overall models can be expected to be suitable for most situations.

More and more voices can be heard against the use of large scale models, among those even "A requiem of Large Scale Models". (Mr. Douglas B. Lee Jr., in A.I.P. Journal, May 1975).

Worth mentioning are the ideas of the Netherlands Bureau of Transport presented by Noortman and the author in the earlier mentioned ICHCA-conference (See for schedules Annex B).

These models are discussed at length by Mr. van Es and Mr. van der Wouden in this congress.

Requirements for further modelbuilding for ports

When we consider the trends in port research, it seems that modelbuilders try to broaden the applicability of their models in two ways:

a. by increasing the number of port functions that are taken into consideration, and

b. by enlarging the number of relevant aspects: Technology - economy - ecology.

This form of widening the scopes is of course of great value to the decision-makers that have responsibility for more than one port function and/or aspect.

This way of broadening of the port models leaves however a number of weak points, when evaluating their applicability for policy-making and their properties as policy-orientated models.

In the following these weak points will be considered.

The increase of the number of port functions

Although the relevancy of other functions than the transport function perhaps is understood by modelbuilders, the broadening of the port models in this connection has more the character of parallel running than of integrated efforts. For instance transport and production are considered types of economic activities, that both have significance for the further development of the port areas, but can at the same time be considered competitive with regard to land use. In other words, they are treated in a given geographical port area according their appearance and their characteristics.

A real integrated approach of these two port functions however, asks for a system-approach in which transport and production are seen as equivalent elements of a technological system. Within these technological systems the two mentioned activities add value to the products namely:

– production adds value of shape, whereas
– transport adds values of place and time.

In such an approach for a given port area, transport and production are no longer competitive in asking for land and investment resources. In this approach the port is in the first place a "get together" of a number of product flows, each of which can be depicted as a product-chain. At the moment that these product flows pass a given port, the chains are cross-sectioned at different levels as shown in figure 4.

The integrated approach of transport and production in the first place asks attention for the factors taken into consideration, in the decisionmaking process falling un-

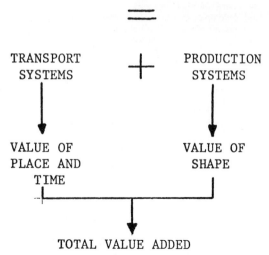

Figure 6

der the heading "business logistics".

In this system all decisions are comprised that deal with the transportation process. It starts with the extraction of raw materials and it ends up in the consumption of finished products.

What priority or emphasis has to be given to specific production or transport activities at a certain moment in a special port, can only be answered - in that context - when transport and production are evaluated phases of product chains. In their actual appearance these links are often much more influenced by exogene variables of the port than by internal variables.

In the total decisionmaking process for product chains, the decision of the port authorities and of port industries are indeed of strategic importance, they form however only one set of decisions, within a much broader scope.

The enlargement of the number of relevant aspects

The earlier port models were in essence orientated at:

– the transport function and
– the handling aspects as such.

By and by the modelbuilding widened towards aspects like economy and later on also ecology.

Here again it appears however that this approach still is confined and focussed on local circumstances. The trade-off between is technological, economic and ecological variables is primarily port-orientated. What relevance do they have however for any particular port?

When we see the ports once again as a "get together" of product flows, the dimensions of the model increase considerably.

The relevance of each of the aspects rather than their weight has to be evaluated for each phase in the total dimensionmaking process; this was earlier condensed in the term "business logistics". In doing so, it becomes clear that an approach via the product chains asks for the introduction of even more aspects than technology, economy and ecology.

Decisionmaking for the main ports of the world asks at least for the additional introduction of the political objective to share the welfare between more and less developed countries.

Given the number of employed people in more developed areas, the structure of the economic pattern in such an area is highly influenced by the stage reached in the distribution of economic activities over developed and developing regions. Each shift in that distribution has consequences for the volume of the product, flows passing the ports as well as for the appearance of the goods within these flows.

The implementation of policy-orientated port models
In the foregoing a further broadening of the port models was suggested. Such a widening has to be realized step by step. From a systematic point of view therefore it seems to make sense to distinguish the main "barriers" that have to be taken:

Figure 7

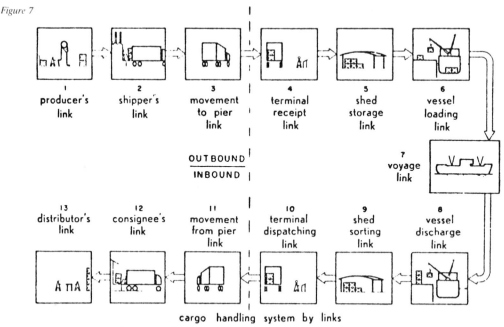

cargo handling system by links

The widening of port models towards (integrated) transportchain models

Port activities generally form a part of transportation clusters. Such clusters consist of several transport activities-storage, conveyance, and transhipment - together comprising transport chains.

Figure 8

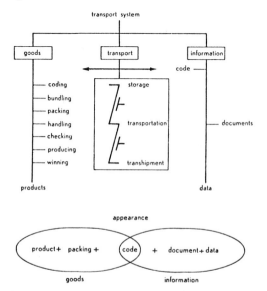

The widening of transportchain models towards transportsystem models
Transport activities as such are not standing alone. They form part of transport systems in which also other elements than transport have to be taken into consideration. Besides the products themselves, the data that accompany their transport should be mentioned.

The widening of transport system models towards technological systems
This step in the widening process of port models is necessary, when we keep in mind that decisionmaking cannot be optimal when it is limited to transport only. This should be only sub-optimization, because the equivalent production activity should not receive the necessary emphasize. The implementation of the results of simulationstechniques on port models can best be achieved via process planning instead of via target (= final stage) planning.

Technological prospects
Technologically speaking the future is hardly uncertain. Todays designs will be realized and applied within a few years. What is on the drawing boards today will be in practice in the eighties. Depending on the complexity and the magnitude of a project it takes a number of years, from two to seven, to build a future.
Consequently, speaking on short terms, the future is already destined today. Though the speed of development is high sometimes, this need not necessarily be dramatised. Even explosions can be kept under control! Combustion engines and explosion suppressions systems

prove that. If one uses a time scale of the same order as the scale of the processes to be governed, solutions are available. One only has to tune in on the existing process speeds. To run after the facts, to be flexible and quick at repartee, used to be good practice but it becomes more and more a stressing and fatigueing attitude.

Following the developments is no longer a lazy man's practice but can easily turn into a loser's fate. These ideas brought me to answer the question whether ports must follow or lead the evolutions. Because, to my way of thinking, ports which follow the evolutions are asking for trouble.

Next to the rather passive way of following, which suits very well the conventional principles of service rendering, there is the more active form of anticipation. Such a disposition asks for an opinion of trends in development based on extrapolations - or at best - on forecasts.

Along such courses quite some ports were developed more or less successfully. Better and in particular more reliable results may be expected from the participation of ports activities in the technological developments.

I prefer the substitution of "anticipation on" by "participation in" technological processes, so expressing the degree of control and of uncertainties.

How can this be done and what are the consequences? For all naïve observers technological changes appear sudden. Still there are signals from which such surprises can be foreseen. It must be granted that such signals are not always obvious because they are often not readily available, and are not lying upon the surface. Still it is worthwhile to trace them because substitution or shifts may, as has been said earlier, have unpleasant effects particularly when they take place unexpectedly.

Such technological accidents can be avoided if one is not frightened by them. Once again: explosions are only swift processes which can be controlled if feedback and steering can be made faster.

As an example of such a surprise the changes in the appearance of cargo is worth mentioning. This "goods-explosion model" shows the trend from "manloads" into unitloads en bulk-products. The historical growth of cargo flows through the port of Rotterdam proves this trend.

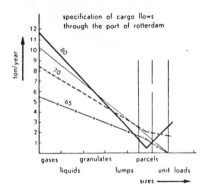

Fig. 10

Ports set up in accordance with the principle of participation have properties deviating from conventional ports.

The application of function analyses and of the principle of disconnection of different functions e.g. transhipment, conveyance and storage, open ways for advanced lay outs. Particularly the location of storage with respect to the quays can change drastically. I do know of some rather exceptional cases, in which ports really gave lead to the evolution. In those cases ports have chosen for some business logistic activities.

Business logistics can be defined as: the process of managing all activities required to strategically move raw materials, parts and finished inventories from vendors, to enterprise facilities and to customers.

Ports keeping stock of certain products chains really can lead the evolution!

The margins of uncertainties

If there are some remaining uncertainties the question arises if these can be quantified and kept between certain known limits. Therefore the transport properties relevant of these factors must be determined and particularly the role they can play in decisionmaking must be known. If one considers the control of transportation activities as an optimizing process, transport forms an element of a technological system. Therein transportation and transformation are of the same order.

On the level of the management of enterprises one enters then the domain of business logistics. Then not only the place of certain functions and ports within an overall technological system is determined.

In the process of decisionmaking this includes the number of variables to be taken into account dependent on the time-span, the time-horizon, that one has to take into consideration at a certain moment. Even the importance of the role of a port depends on the time-horizon.

The longer the period we take into account the greater the number of relevant variables and the more complex will be the model. The closer the time-horizon the more limited the number of degrees of freedom. The more we zero in in terms of time, the more options will be left out and the more the number of relevant variables of decisionmaking is reduced. This does not mean that the decisionmaking process on short term is easier than that for long term.

It is true that for long terms the number of variables to be taken into account is relative large, however most of the variables are very well quantifiable with respect to their relevancy. In preparing decisionmaking on short terms the number of variables to be taken into account might be smaller but they are less quantifiable. This can be caused by the fact that reactions on changed external circumstances can not be sufficiently predicted. This introduces uncertainties-the responses on certain changes-

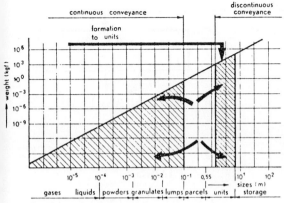

Fig. 9

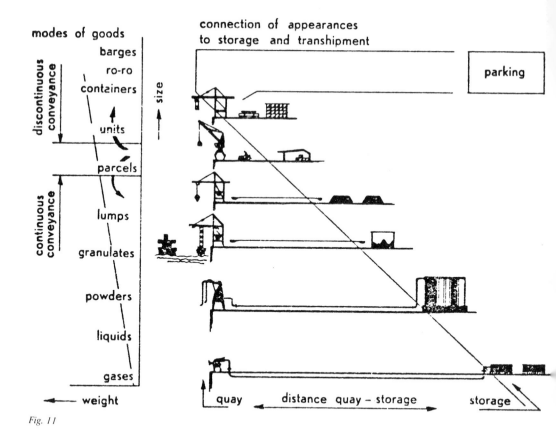

modes of goods

connection of appearances
to storage and transhipment

discontinuous conveyance
- barges
- ro-ro
- containers
- units

continuous conveyance
- parcels
- lumps
- granulates
- powders
- liquids
- gases

size →

← weight

parking

quay — distance quay – storage — storage

Fig. 11

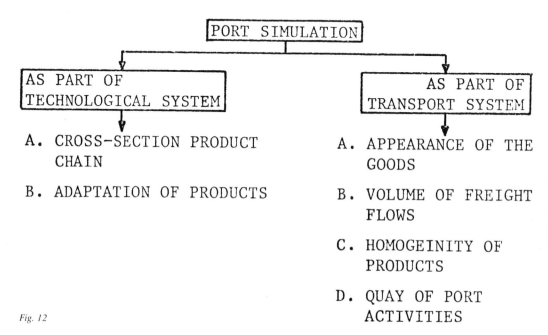

PORT SIMULATION

AS PART OF TECHNOLOGICAL SYSTEM

A. CROSS-SECTION PRODUCT CHAIN

B. ADAPTATION OF PRODUCTS

AS PART OF TRANSPORT SYSTEM

A. APPEARANCE OF THE GOODS

B. VOLUME OF FREIGHT FLOWS

C. HOMOGEINITY OF PRODUCTS

D. QUAY OF PORT ACTIVITIES

Fig. 12

and an element of "gamble" in the decision process. Here the engineer and the economist, preparing transport decision within the scope of wider technological processes, are beginning to feel their uncertainties. They principally based their approach on expected patterns of conduct, which were more or less rational. This supposition appears to be realistic when it concerns a hypothesis for conducts on long terms; on mid-range and short terms such a clinical approach can lead to fully unrealistic results. No matter what the exactness of the calculations, if they are based on a supposed rational pattern of conduct, their results do form an insufficient base for decisionmaking in problems for short- and mid-range planning. For these planning horizons the change in the pattern of conduct between now and the moment on which the rational factors for decisionmaking are dominant again must be taken into account.

This means that for short and mid-range effects important deviations from long range effect must be expected. In this respect time lags should be introduced. We start on the expectation that on long terms the pattern of conduct will adapt itself to the expectations, which can be derived from the calculation based on hard data. The actual conduct shows a deceleration caused by hemming factors with regard to the final expected conduct. These factors are determined by vested interest and these are pure human.

One can speak of psychological resistance to break away from the familiar conducts. Such situations can be elucidated by many examples. An example in the field of transportation, worth mentioning, could be the figure of the loads to be containerized given by the introduction of containerization.

In literature and in discussions two figures were mentioned: the potential containerisable loads and the expected containerized loads in a certain year. Differences between those figures indicate the time lag to be taken into account in the process of decisionmaking, which was dependent on the time horizon under consideration.

Besides the fact that habit and conduct are a second nature to men, the mentioned time lag is caused by the presence of interests, which in turn are a function of our society. These interests are mostly of a financial, economic nature. The decisionmakers in the transportation field may not have the illusion that the corrections to be made on the long term in order to come to short and mid-range decisions can be easily derived through the simple introduction of factors of resistance. In the sphere of transportation we not only have to take into consideration hemming forces, but depending on the geographic relation, also accelerating forces. The latter occurs in transportchains between the developed and the developing countries. The span of time, that can be derived from a simulation model, in which the input is exclusively originating from experiences in developed countries mostly needs corrections. This wil not lead always to decelerations, but on the contrary can easily lead to accelerations in the process of changing over. If vested economic interests work retardingly on the effectuation of change in the pattern of conduct and on changing economic and social relations, considerations of prestige can on the contrary accelerate this process.

It will be clear that a too early start of a new concept is equally dangerous for an enterprise as a late response on exogene changes. Consequently preparation of decisionmaking in the domain of business logistics is certainly more than clinical simulation based on the pattern of conduct of a homo economicus.

It should be studied what the retarding and the acceleration causes are, which act on the reaction pattern depending on the span of time to be taken into consideration and depending on the relevant geographic relations.

I hope that in the above mentioned thoughts it is made sufficiently clear that simulation as a support for decisionmaking cannot be put on a par to the application of a number of calculation rules. The fascinating facts of simulating models might be that we try to predict the pattern of response of human beings behind and against technological processes in a stylised form. In this respect it is important to consider the place of integrated transportsystems within the wider scope of decisionmaking, that is to say transportation being an element of a total technological system.

In the earlier mentioned conference of ICHCA held in Melbourne last week the author and Noortman gave their thoughts on a transport simulation model which suits within the frame of reference just being sketched.

Appraisal

It is the author's firm belief that for the sake of "anticipation on" or better for "participation in" future evolutions, transport systems must be considered an integral part of larger technological systems.

An appraisal of what has been achieved until now can be best given as the report of our helicopter pilot. His views allow for wider horizons and for more neutral evaluation of port research depending on his altitude.

He observed ports as the links in social and economic relations between people with different backgrounds and in differing stages of development.

Though it might not or hardly be possible to change things overnight it certainly is not unrealistic to direct todays decisions towards the presented visions and goals.

Port models tend to be either operationally oriented, e.g. applicable in todays jobs, or they are focussed on vague futureal situations as the crystal ball shows for the year 2000. These two extremes make port planning easily trivial.

What are needed are port simulation models in which feedbacks are supplied between decisions of today without the dollars-budgets that can be spent there, and the long term objectives, based on long term planning without limits set by actual financial barriers.

Thereby we must not pretend to substitute existing procedures drastically but to supplement and to modify them.

New is the train of thoughts leading from autonomy via coordination to integration on as wide a level as possible.

Systems approach does not longer allow for reactive policy but includes new ways towards anticipating policy or better, decisionmaking on the equal basis of participation between transport and all other activities.

This includes a change over from link-to-link decisions towards a worldwide social and economic integration process.

In the outlines of the conference under topic I, four questions have been put. My answers to these questions can be short and I hope clear.

1. What key decision will transport decisionmakers face in the near future?

Answer: Integration through system thinking.

2. What key decisions were faced in the past?

Answer: Coordination through process study.

3. How has research influenced these decisions?

Answer: By the detraction from autonomous activities.

4. How has it failed?

Answer: By the simple extrapolation of trends.

ANNEX A

Survey of four transportmodels

In preparation for this contribution a study was made in my institution of published transport models. In this annex four models are briefly described in terms of goals, structures, methods and fields of application.

1. The deepsea-containerport model
G o a l :

the aim of this simulation model is to estimate the dimensions of an import container stack based on a number of suppositions concerning throughput, and custom operation times. It is assumed that there are no interactions with the export containers. Because a changing throughput is applied, and consequently a changing demand for facilities, this model can be best qualified as a pseudo dynamic optimization model.

T h e m o d e l s t r u c t u r e :

the model is of a low complexity level which can be seen by the number of its components. This is the result of a limitation of the transportation functions taken into consideration. The reduced number of elements is not caused by the aggregation level of the model but more by the fact that a number of parameters have been neglected.

T h e m e t h o d s :

the method used is that of a static simulation model for a single purpose port. Though not explicitly mentioned it is clear that the container traffic between two continents formed the basis of this model. For a certain terminal-capacity the operational costs are determined for a series of throughputs.

T h e f i e l d o f a p p l i c a t i o n :

this model has a rather limited field of application. The model deals only partly with the transport function of a port, viz. the transport of containers. The advantages of this simplification are that the model is rather tangible and that it can lead to applicable conclusions for a container terminal operator.

2. The port simulation model: PORT-SIM
T h e a i m :

the model aims to get hold of the staying, waiting and working times of the various port components in order to describe the port functions. The model is based on a given capacity of goods handled.

T h e s t r u c t u r e :

the model contains a relatively low number of elements. The level of aggregation is low because no efforts are made to cluster the elements. Nevertheless it can not be qualified of a disaggregate level. For that, the model is kept too global and quite a number of details are even not being dealt with.

T h e m e t h o d s :

The model can be best typified as a static simulation model of a multipurpose port.

T h e f i e l d o f a p p l i c a t i o n :

the model is in the first place mentioned to be an expedient to indicate the appropriate port configuration for a given offer of commodities and ships. The model is not suitable for "fine tuning", because too many details of the port operations have been deleted.

3. The UNCTAD-model
T h e a i m :

a. the optimization of methods for transport and commodity handling in ports and hinterlands, in order to obtain the maximum contribution in terms of costs to the growth of the national economy.

b. The elaboration of a research program for the determination of the problems of ports and their hinterland based on a set of statistical data.

c. The elaboration of a set of programs to correct imbalance in the concerning transport system.

The Unctad model consists of a simulation model dealing with the technical aspects and of an optimization model dealing with the economical aspects of a port.

The simulation model aims to specify the handling times for commodities and ships. The optimum to be determined by the

optimization model does not necessarily co-indicate with the technical optimums. The optimum achieved can be best qualified as a dynamic optimum.

T h e s t r u c t u r e :

the Unctad model is a rather complex model, that can be derived not only from the magnitude of the program but also from the number of subsystems to be applied. The activities pilotage and towage, the activities day and shifts, the activities high and season indicate already this complexity. The structure of the Unctad model is quite open, while a number of qualities and properties are determined outside the model. The level of aggregation is that of a dis-aggregate model, because the totality of the port operations is as detailed as possible and no clusters are considered at all.

T h e m e t h o d s :

the Unctad model can be best qualified to be a dynamic simulation model of a multipurpose port.

T h e f i e l d o f a p p l i c a t i o n :

the Unctad model has a wide field of application and can be applied for several situations. One has to keep in mind however when one wishes to take decisions for investments based on this model that the model is restricted to technical and economical aspects only.

The pro and cons of the various other functions such as the living conditions, industrial interaction and quality of life aspects have to be evaluated seperately.

4. The dynamo model
T h e a i m :

a. to simulate and to forecast the developments with respect to three aspect systems (viz. the technological, the economical, and the quality of life system). With regard to four functions of a port (viz. transport, living, service rendering and industry).

b. to consider the relevant interdependencies between the aspect systems and the functions.

c. the influence of the decisions and the supposition on forecast.

Basically this system can be focussed on any goal one wishes.

T h e s t r u c t u r e :

the dynamo model is a very complex model with an open structure. Because of the comprehensiveness this model is highly aggregated.

T h e m e t h o d s :

only this model can be best qualified as a dynamic simulation model, because a connection is made between the industrial growth and the port configuration and because the industrial dynamic methods are applied.

T h e f i e l d o f a p p l i c a t i o n :

in principle this model applies for regions, which are depending on a port and consequently one has to be careful in introducing the necessary restrictions. There are already a number of restrictions and premisses from which the model has been derived of which a number are less realistic under circumstances.

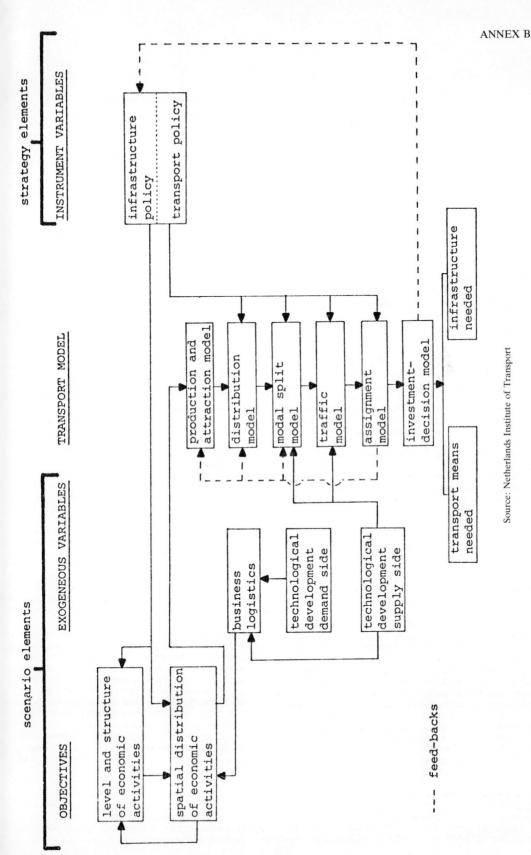

strategy elements

INSTRUMENT VARIABLES

scenario elements

EXOGENEOUS VARIABLES

OBJECTIVES

TRANSPORT MODEL

infrastructure policy

transport policy

production and attraction model

distribution model

modal split model

traffic model

assignment model

investment-decision model

infrastructure needed

transport means needed

business logistics

technological development demand side

technological development supply side

level and structure of economic activities

spatial distribution of economic activities

--- feed-backs

Source: Netherlands Institute of Transport

77

Policy applications of research on the development and evaluation of air fares on the North Atlantic

by

A. KANAFANI

University of California, Berkeley

and

E. C. SPRY

International Air Transport Association

INTRODUCTION

This paper is concerned with the experience in the application of research in policy making in international air transportation. The research deals with fares development and evolution, and the application was within the framework of the operation of the International Air Transport Association, in the setting of fares and the evaluation of fares packages.

In an effort to develop an improved capability for fares development and evaluation, the International Air Transport Association has undertaken a number of research activities. These research activities were specifically aimed at providing insights into the behavior of the air travel market in the North Atlantic, and at developing methodologies suitable for the analysis of this market.

The first effort was aimed at the development of a continuing traffic data acquisition and management system. This activity provided two important components of the data base necessary for a fares development system. One is the traffic and revenue by fare type statistics, normally supplied by carriers, and providing a continuing historic data base upon which to use analysis and projections. The other is an inflight survey from which demographic characteristics of North Atlantic travelers, as well as some indications of their travel habits and preferences, are obtained. Such information is quite helpful in developing traffic analysis procedures for use in fares evaluation.

The second effort was the development of demand analysis procedures, and the construction of traffic forecasting models. This effort provides the central methodological capability in the development of a methodology for fares evaluation. The resulting traffic analysis and forecasting models are used to characterize the response of traffic to changes in fare structure and in the socioeconomic environment. These models have been validated over the past three years and have evolved into a working tool for traffic analysis.

Third, an effort was undertaken to assess consumer behavior and preferences for the various attributes of the air transportation services available in the North Atlantic market. This effort was based on an extensive consumer survey conducted in North America and in Western Europe, and provided a data base intended for predicting market response to major changes in the characteristics of air transport service.

Finally, an effort was made to develop a capability for analyzing the impact of traffic behavior on the operating costs of air transportation in the North Atlantic. It was recognized that cost analysis should provide one valuable input into the process of fares development and evaluation, if fares are to be cost based.

PURPOSE

The research efforts described above provided a number of tools for performing the analyses needed for fares development and evaluation. These techniques have been adapted and validated to varying degrees. However, it became directly clear that in order to increase the usefulness of these techniques a framework was necessary within which to integrate them into a process aimed at fares development and evaluation and to show how each technique fits within this process. It is for this reason that this study was conducted with the following specific objectives:

a. To investigate the feasibility of defining a meaningful framework for integrating the results of the earlier research efforts into a process of fares development and evaluation.

b. If feasible, to develop the integration framework, define the process and the steps involved in it, and

c. To define the role of each methodological activity and to describe it in an operational manner.

RESULT

It was found in this study that integration of the previous research activities into a fares development and evaluation process is indeed possible and feasible. The conceptual and analytical frameworks for this process have been defined and the various analytical methodologies produced by the previous research have integrated into them. The full integration of the demand analysis and the traffic forecasting methods, as well as the data acquisition and management methods has been possible. Consumer research and cost analysis results, on the other hand, have been integrated in a more or less qualitative manner. For consumer research only a limited amount of results have been found compatible with the analytical procedures used in the rest of the process, but there is a potential value of the data base resulting from that research.

Cost analyses remain loosely defined, and while the conceptual framework for their integration has been defined, analytical integration could not be done to the same extent that the other analyses have been integrated. The reasons for this are discussed in greater detail in later sections of this report.

The major conclusion is that the research activities undertaken by the International Air Transport Association can contribute significantly to achieving a rational process for fares development and evaluation, and that such a process is now defined and can be implemented.

CONCEPTUAL FRAMEWORK OF THE RESEARCH

Fares development is defined as a process through which a policy maker, at an industry or carrier level, designs fare packages for an air transportation market, in such a way as to optimize the operation of the system from the standpoint of some objective criterion. Fares evaluation is the complementary process by which a forecast is made of the operation of the air transportation system under a postulated fares structure, in order to generate policy variables useful in evaluating fares development policy. More specifically, a fares system is proposed for evaluation for possible implementation during a one- to two-year period in a particular market. This requires a series of analyses that would permit a forecast of traffic and revenues for the same period, assuming the proposed fares system is implemented. Together with a forecast of capacity and operating costs, this would permit the assessment of the economic feasibility of the proposed fares system (traffic, revenues, profits, etc.) and the technical feasibility (load factors, etc.) of the proposed fares system.

The conceptual framework of this process centers around the idea that fares development and evaluation are policy matters and that the analytical inputs provided by the traffic analysis methodology represent only one input into a policymaking process that must take many other factors into consideration. The process defined in this study deals only with these anlytical inputs to the process, but that should by no means be taken to imply that they alone can provide the answers as to what is an optimal policy for the air transport system.

Figure 1 is used to show the major aspects of the process conceptual framework and its iterative feedback nature. This diagram shows how policy represents the central focus of the process. Policy is influenced by the socioeconomic environment, and by the results of the fares evaluation process. On the other hand, policy guides fares development which in turn affects the traffic environment and the economic environment of the air transport system. Analysis is shown to combine the characteristics of the socio-economic environment and of the air transport service in order to produce the traffic and revenue forecasts needed nor fares evaluation.

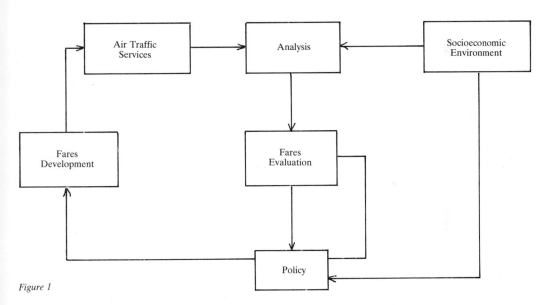

Figure 1

Fares evaluation depends of course on policy, which defines the objectives, and optimization criteria to be used in it whether they be traffic volumes, load factors, revenues, or profits.

With this conceptual framework, it is possible to integrate the various analysis procedures into the process as tools for policymaking. This integration results in the analytical framework discussed next.

ANALYTICAL FRAMEWORK

The integration of the various analytical procedures into the fares development and evaluation process consists of pulling together five major analytical activities aimed at providing the necessary traffic and revenue forecasting capability needed for fares evaluation, and the consumer behavior and socioeconomic information needed for fares development. The five activities are mentioned briefly in this section and then described in detail in following sections.

1. Traffic and socioeconomic data base: This is an activity that deals with the management of a data system to provide information necessary for undertaking the other analytical activities in the process, as well as for influencing policy. It is a continuing activity whereby the data base is updated periodically as more data become available.

2. Consumer research: Using consumer survey data, this activity deals with characterizing consumer travel habits and preferences in an analytical way. It provides inputs to two activities. First, consumer research results may be integrated into the demand analysis methods to increase their scope. Second, these results can be used, albeit in a qualitative manner, to make fares development more responsive to, and compatible with, consumer behavior.

3. Demand analysis: This is the central activity which provides the traffic models necessary to forecast traffic and revenues for any given fares system and socioeconomic environment. Demand analysis is based mainly on historical data and on statistical calibration methods. Therefore, it requires the integration of consumer research results into the traffic models in order to permit them to forecast phenomena on which no historic data exist, such as the market response to novel transport service characteristics.

4. Socioeconomic forecasts: Forecasting the socioeconomic environment for the fares evaluation period is an essential activity. It permits the forecasting of total traffic demand, the forecasting of costs, and it guides policy makers in the process of fares development. For some indicators, such as the macroeconomic indicators, it may be possible to obtain forecasts exogenously made, while for others, such as traffic demand or costs, it is necessary to have a forecasting methodology specific to the process of fares development and evaluation.

5. Costs analysis and forecasting: This activity provides the cost allocation and forecasting inputs to fares development evaluation, expecially in situations where revenue and profit characteristics are important criteria of system performance. Costs forecasts are shown to be influenced by policy. This is because they are strongly affected by the capacity forecast, which is an airline policy matter.

These five activities are integrated in order to provide the necessary inputs to the fares development and evaluation process. Traffic and revenue forecasts are the major analytical input to fares evaluation. They are obtained by combining socioeconomic forecasts with projected fares systems as generated by the fares development activity, and using the traffic models resulting from the demand analysis and consumer research activities. Costs forecasts permit the comparison of revenues and costs in the fares evaluation process.

PROCESS APPLICATION

The process defined here is based on a general framework that is applicable to any air transportation market. As such, the process can be applied in the North Atlantic at an industry level as well as to any segment of the market that is served by one or more air carriers. It can as well be applied to different markets, provided an appropriate data base exists.

The analytical procedures integrated into the fares development and evaluation process have all been constructed and calibrated on the basis of North Atlantic data. However, the procedures themselves are applicable elsewhere. Application of the process to markets other than the North Atlantic would require the construction of a data base similar to that development in this study. This would include traffic and revenue statistics by fare type and season, plus trip purpose information of the type obtained in the North Atlantic Inflight Survey. The demand analysis process can then be applied and models appropriate to the market in question can be constructed. It should be possible to carry out the rest of the process by applying the traffic models without a need for as extensive a consumer research survey as the one conducted for the North Atlantic market. It should be emphasized, however, that the North Atlantic traffic models currently present in the computer system cannot be applied directly to other markets.

The process is also applicable to a segment of a large market such as the North Atlantic. The extent to which such an application is suitable on a one-carrier basis will depend on the extent to which such carrier's operations and market are typical of the segment it serves. For the North Atlantic, origin-destination segments are served by more than one carrier, usually by two. The application of the process to one of the carriers alone would require further data reduction, but more importantly may re-

quire the addition of market share consideration not currently present in the methodologies integrated into the process. This is particularly crucial in markets where high load factors exist during certain periods of the year, when capacity availability becomes an important supply variable affecting the amount of traffic by any one carrier. Therefore, care should be exercised when applying the process on a one-carrier basis.

The International Air Transport Association has validated the choice models for applications to individual carriers in selected segments in the North Atlantic, and given the positive results of this validation, it can be concluded that carrier application of the process is quite feasible. In fact, such an application would have the advantage that cost and demand functions can be assumed more homogeneous, thus permitting a more thorough integration of the cost and demand analysis than is possible at the industry level.

PROCESS LIMITATIONS

The fares development and assessment process defined in this study is based on the integration of a number of analysis techniques into a framework to provide aids in policymaking. The process as defined recognizes the importance of policy inputs other than those generated by the analysis models. Traffic demand forecasting models provide only one input into the process and do not as such provide the answers to all the questions that need to be considered in fares development and evaluation. This is an important limitation of the process, but is one that is inherent to any analysis process dealing with policy matters.

Another strong limitation is the restriction on the applicability of the process that may be caused by lack of appropriate data. It is unlikely that a data base exists for any air travel market that is as extensive as that of the North Atlantic. Having based all the analysis on the North Atlantic studies, they lead to a built-in luxury in data requirements. In many situations the acquisition of appropriate data would be so in time consuming that by the time a data base is ready for analysis policy issues may have changed. By necessity, the application of the process to other markets than the North Atlantic would require making certain assumptions where data are missing. As long as these assumptions are clearly documented and understood, then this limitation is not a severe one.

RESEARCH AND MONITORING NEEDS

The fares development and evaluation process is a dynamic and continuing process. Traffic results in any one year are fed back into the data management system and become historic data in subsequent years. A mechanism is built in the process whereby the traffic analysis and forecasting models are recalibrated and updated as necessary. Therefore, in order to ensure that an updated set of models is always available for the user, the implementation of the process will require a continuous monitoring activity. This involves continuing research into the performance of models, updating the data bases, and conducting the demand analysis activities needed. Methods for checking model validity have been incorporated in the analytic procedure built into the process. The application of these methods, as well as the monitoring of the overall applicability of the process, should be continuing activities.

EXPERIENCE FROM APPLICATION OF FARES MODELS

Having developed and verified the fares models described earlier, the next step in our program, and the one in which we are still actively involved, is to have these models accepted beyond the circle of researchers directly involved in their construction and to have them understood and used by airline industry policy makers. In this second part of the paper, we would like to outline some of the difficulties we have encountered in this respect and to review the experience that has been gained in overcoming them. Since the problems involved have generally been concerned more with matters of communication, acceptance and comprehension than with anything intrinsic to the structure of the models themselves, we believe this experience might also be of some general use and guidance to others similary confronted with the task of straddling research and its policy application.

As was pointed out earlier, the models that have been developed are the product of the efforts of a research team of the University of California and a number of airline research specialists working together in the IATA Commercial Research Committee. The Commercial Research Committee is one of a number of specialist committees within IATA that operate under the direction of the IATA Traffic Conferences, the Traffic Conferences being the forum within which the airline industry negotiates a common fares policy.

It was in direct response to Resolutions passed by the Traffic Conference dealing with air fares on the North Atlantic that these models were first developed. In summary, the Resolutions called for four things. First, the establishment of a more factural industry data base against which fare proposals could be evaluated. Second, a program of industry research into the key factors that affect the way in which the travelling public responds to changes in fare levels and conditions. Third, the development of a means whereby this information could be easily and consistently applied in assessing the likely impact of alternative fare structures - the models which have been described here provide that means. And, finally, application of such models in an attempt to explore ways in which the economic viability of the present fares structure can be improved.

These are admirably rational objectives, and aim to provide the airline Traffic Conference negotiators with a management tool for assembling and applying data and research findings relevant to development of North Atlantic aire fares in a quick and simple fashion, a tool which would introduce an agreed uniform technique for evaluating likely market reactions to changes in the level of fares and thereby facilitate and expedite tariff negotiations between the different airlines involved. With hindsight, however, one can now see certain difficulties hidden in those objectives that were not so apparent when the Resolutions were drafted and first adopted. As we have said, these difficulties relate more to the communication, acceptance and comprehension, terms which have been used earlier this afternoon, of the models by policy makers than to anything intrinsic to the nature of the models themselves. The organizers of this Conference have asked the question: "How can existing research be applied more effectively to policy and planning decisions?". We believe our experience in presenting this research to the airline executives responsible for negotiating the industry fares policy and persuading them to make use of the models derived from it may give some hints on the answer to that question.

In analyzing the difficulties of applying research to policy decision-making, it is necessary to distinguish between situations in which policies are made unilaterally or by some authority with the power to select and arbitrate between competing interests and those situations that involve a genuine dynamic balance of power between a variety of independent and equally sovereign interests. Such a distinction is important because re-

searchers often appear to implicitly assume that the optimal course of developments prescribed by their study findings can be unilaterally pursued by policy makers or soem such all-powerful authority. While, of course, there are situations in which such an authority exists, in most instances this is not the case and, as a consequence, any research built upon such an assumption will quickly be found to be impractical in reality and hence meaningless as applied research in the true sense of the term. In the case of international transportation, such an assumption is clearly inappropriate. International transportation by definition spans more than one jurisdiction and hence involves the interest of more than one independent and sovereign policy maker. Any research related to international transport must take this fact into account if its findings are to be of practical use.

We have been made very aware of such problems by the fact that while the models described here this afternoon were funded on an industry basis and were developed and tested using aggregate industry data, to be truly useful they must be applied on an individual carrier basis. There are at present more than twenty scheduled airlines operating on the North Atlantic; these carriers differ greatly in their objectives and competitive strategies and with respect to the regulatory philosophies to which they are subject; it is unlikely that any single model could take all these factors into account. Agreement between these airlines must therefore as a consequence be a matter of negotiation and compromise. While application of the models on an aggregate basis could produce a theoretically optimal fares structure for the industry treated as a whole, this is of comparative use only. IATA, despite its "monster in the skies" image, is no super-power over the airlines and has no authority to order the pursuit of such an aggregate industry optimum. The only optimum possible is a pragmatic one attained through compromise and negotiation. An IATA fares agreement is optimal in that it reflects an equilibrium between the interests of the various carriers involved. To be of real use in such a situation, research must assist and facilitate that negotiation process - not try to replace it. It is to that end that these models are being found to have their greatest potential.

In application, these models are not used to specify an optimal fares structure for the industry, nor to prescribe any one line of pricing policy development. They are normative only in respect of the logic and methodology they suggest for evaluating the market impact of changes to the fares structure. While the models were initially run using aggregate industry data, this was for development purposes only and is now used mainly for illustration. The nature of each airline's clientele is different, and while the models provide a uniform approach and glossary for negotiations, the assumptions and data to which they are applied must, to be useful, be the prerogative of the airline negotiators themselves. Thus the models provide not only a means for examining the available data in a uniform way, but also offer a discipline for the negotiating process itself and thereby act as an aid to facilitate and expedite such discussions.

We would suggest, therefore, that a part of the answer to the question, "How can existing research be more effectively applied to policy and planning decisions?", lies as much in emphasizing the discipline that a research approach can bring to policy decisionmaking as in any normative guidelines for policy that may be deduced directly from the research findings themselves. Needless to say, this is not so easy in practice. We shall try to explain why.

In all applied research, there is a potential conflict between researcher and policy maker. The essence of policy decisionmaking in any context where there are a large number of independent interests, such as the IATA Traffic Conferences, has to be negotiation and compromise. Negotiation implies a unique, intuitive, nontransferable skill on the part of the negotiator for verbal manoeuver and a flexible and discriminate use of available information. Research models such as those described here and alike all, on the other hand, imply a disciplined, explicit, learnable procedure for applying all available information. Clearly, unless considerable efforts are made by the researcher to ensure that the decisionmaker appreciates how such models can assist him in negotiation, there is a risk that he will interpret the discipline they impose more as an inhibition or constraint to his activities than a help. Under such circumstances, there is little chance for research to have any significant impact on policy decisions. Our application of these fares models again provides an illustration of the kind of problem to which we are referring.

As we have stated earlier, the Traffic Conference negotiators foresaw the need to make greater use of research in determining industry policy on air fares and accordingly established Resolutions calling into effect and funding the research program which has resulted in the fares models being discussed here. It is interesting, however, to trace the cycle through which the reception given by the Traffic Conference negotiators to this work has passed. The program to date has been underway for a little over three years. During the first year to year-and-a-half, when the technical research and data difficulties still loomed dauntingly large, considerable encouragement was given by the Traffic Conference to those working on the research side to continue trying to find a solution. Slowly, however, as such technical difficulties have been overcome and the research models have begun to take on a more coherent form, concern has grown among fares policy makers about possible misinterpretation and misuse to which they may be put, particularly in the sense of there being used in some way to evaluate any policy agreed by the Conferences or to veto any agreement that might be made. A great deal of this concern arose out of a failure on the part of a number of the Traffic Conference negotiators to understand not only the mechanism of the models but also the manner and context in which they are intended to operate. This concern occurred despite the fact that considerable efforts were made during the course of the development of the models to ensure that regular briefings and documentation on the work were given to the Traffic Conferernces. Until about a year ago, a number of policy makers were still thinking of the models as prescriptive and hence, therefore, as some external threat or limit on their negotiating freedom. It was as if the industry research team carrying out this work had in some way been transformed into a group of "Sorcerer's Apprentices" toying with a fearful black box. Only a few policy makers understood from the outset the potential usefulness of such a tool in preparing and evaluating alternative policies prior to a Conference and in developing negotiating strategies. It has taken almost a year to date of airline-by-airline education to bring everyone to the same level of awareness - a process which is still continuing. We are happy to be able to say that now almost all of the major airlines operating in the North Atlantic market are actively working with the models and adapting them to their own company needs. To achieve this state of affairs has, however, required what is virtually a sales program.

Returning again to the question, "How can existing research be applied more effectively to policy and planning decision?", we are obliged to say the obvious. The degree to which research influences policy depends on how well the intentions and results from that research are communicated to those responsible for making policy decisions. This communication effort is imperative and should be planned into any program of applied research.

For some researchers the effort required to effectively disseminate information on their work in a readily comprehensible form seems, however, often to be sadly neglected. To us, this is a strange attitude. Transport research is an applied science. Anyone working in that area must surely then have a potential application in mind whenever they begin a given project? Or do they? "How much research is in fact undertaken without any serious intent that it should find application in policy?" Perhaps implicitly realizing the heavy burden involved in following through any research to a policy stage, many researchers would prefer simply to do what they enjoy doing and to stand back from the grind and sweat of seeking to have their findings implemented in policy. Certainly if the experience we have had in disseminating information on these fares models and encouraging their use in determining fares policy is a good example of the amount of work involved, then we must say we have a certain sympathy with such an attitude. Fortunately, this has not been our case. IATA has had considerable assistance from UCB in these efforts to inform our member airlines about the models and their use. If we may, we should like to briefly mention a few of the lessons we have learned in this respect and the kind of responses which we have met.

First, for such communication to be effective, it is necessary for the researcher to have an understanding of the mentality of the policy maker and of the external factors that will influence his attitude towards the research. For example, we came quickly to realize that those aspects of the fares models that are of most interest to a researcher are not necessarily those that have greatest appeal to policy makers. In presenting them or any findings drawn from them, it has been more important to explain the ease with which the models can be used rather than any advance in techniques which they incorporate. A banal point, we know, but one frequently ignored. The reason for this is easy to see. Airline policy makers, like many others, are confronted with a constant stream of information and documents. To catch and hold the attention of policy makers, research must have an obvious means of application to policy. In our efforts to ensure that the models are truly useful we have, for example, devoted a great deal of time to the adaptation of the original prototype research models into more straightforward management decision tools. This has meant simplification of the computer programs used in the models so that they can be utilized by personnel unfamiliar with the original research efforts made in their development. It has also meant the preparation of considerable amounts of educational material and operating manuals as well as the delivery of a series of presentations and seminars on the subject.

While such efforts may be novel to many reseachers, it has been our experience that the completion of a research study must be considered as the first only of a series of steps in the total progress from theory into practice. We would estimate that between one-third and one-half of the total man-time devoted to the development of these fares models has in fact been concerned with dissemination of information about them. Even now, we still see the need for a continuing effort in this area in order to ensure that in those instances where airlines have begun to try to seriously apply the results from this work, they are not obstructed by others who are still comparatively uninformed and consequently unenthusiastic about this models.

Another area in which we have also found considerable difficulties in application has been the lack of suitable data for use in the models. It was our intention in developing the models to ensure that adequate statistical information was available for their operation and we have, wherever possible, given such information or given guidance as to where it may be obtained. Nevertheless, a number of airlines have experienced some difficulty in assembling the necessary data for their own market areas and, in order that their interest be maintained. we have had to give extensive individual assistance to them in building up the required information base. The problem of lack of data is again one frequently ignored by research· ers and particularly those who choose to work on a purely theoretical plain. If research is to be applied, then it seems obvious that the necessary data for its application must exist as a prerequisite, or if not, steps must be taken to have it gathered subsequently. Knowing that the lack of data frequently prevents the application of research and that this is a situation which can only be fruitlessly repeated many times over unless some attempt is made to initiate the collection of the required information, IATA has also tried to make use of these models as a means of defining the nature of the new statistical collections which are needed. We have established industry data collections that provide a market segmentation that is appropriate for use in these models and have almost all North Atlantic airlines participa-ting in that collection. We are thus ensuring that given the continued willingness of the carriers to try to make use of these models, they will not be prevented from doing so by any future lack of data. It is unlikely that such industry data collections would have been established without the stimulus of these models.

One final point we would like to make concerns the time period required for research to reach a point where it actually influences policy. The researcher is fortunate in that he can work in a relatively unconstrained way. Policy makers are hardly ever able to operate in this way and as a consequence the acceptance of research such as these fares models by an organization as politically complex as the Traffic Conferences must obviously be a long, slow process. We expect that a further three to four years' work is still necessary before the approach to air fares development described becomes normally accepted industry practice. The researcher must have sufficient perseverance and stamina to stay with his research for the necessary period. There is no short-cut. The only comfort that can be offered is that this same conservatism which is delaying the application of his own work will, if it is accepted into policy, eventually come to protect it from any new replacement research approach.

Intercontinental transportation
and
the Marine Container System

by

YOSHIMI NAGAO
Department of Transportation Engineering,
Faculty of Engineering, Kyoto University
and
MICHIHIKO NORITAKE
Department of Civil Eniginering,
Faculty of Engineering, Kansai University

INTRODUCTION

Matters related with transportation are, economically speaking, to be placed in the middle of the junction of the "production" and "consumption". Any improvement in a transportation system gives a significant effect on the production and consumption activities of either a region or nation. There are many cases in the so called developing countries where the improvement of intercontinental marine transportation system had played vital roles for the improvement of the foundation of the national economy, by means of improving ports

and harbours thereby enabling to export their natural resources to other countries. [1]

There are many problems to be overcome for the improvement of intercontinental marine transportation system, because of differences of customs and traditional deed involved in the countries involved. Nevertheless, the remarkable expansion of intercontinental trades can be raised as one of characteristics of the world economy in the latter part of the twentieth century. This will be proved by the fact that the growth rate of world trade had been exceeding the rate of production. [2]

Table 1.1 - Selected Series of World Transport Statistics

Annual	Population (million)	Industrial Production Index of Industrial Production, Total 1963=100 [1]	World Trade Value (FOB) of Exports in U.S. $ 10^6 at 1963 [3]	World Traffic (10^9 net ton km)			Share Rate on this table (%)		
				Rail [1]	Marine [2]	Air [3]	Rail	Marine	Air
1963	3,174	100	135,400	3,793	8,712	2.1	30.3	69.7	0.017
1964	3,234 (1.9)	108 (8.0)	149,100 (10.1)	4,008 (5.7)	9,914 (13.8)	2.4 (15.6)	28.8	71.2	0.018
1965	3,295 (1.9)	115 (6.0)	159,400 (6.9)	4,195 (4.7)	10,832 (9.3)	3.1 (29.4)	27.9	72.1	0.021
1966	3,354 (1.8)	123 (7.0)	172,100 (8.0)	4,346 (3.6)	11,553 (6.7)	3.8 (22.7)	27.3	72.6	0.024
1967	3,421 (2.0)	126 (2.0)	181,700 (5.6)	4,454 (2.5)	13,390 (15.9)	4.4 (15.2)	25.0	75.0	0.025
1968	3,490 (2.0)	135 (7.0)	205,200 (12.9)	4,642 (4.2)	15,505 (15.8)	5.4 (21.7)	23.0	76.9	0.027
1969	3,561 (2.0)	145 (7.0)	227,600 (10.9)	4,813 (3.7)	17,361 (12.0)	7.0 (29.9)	21.7	78.3	0.032
1970	3,610 (1.4)	150 (3.0)	250,000 (9.8)	5,020 (4.3)	19,731 (13.7)	7.7 (9.3)	20.3	79.7	0.031
1971	3,679 (1.9)	156 (4.0)	263,000 (5.2)	5,171 (3.0)	21,722 (10.1)	8.2 (6.2)	19.2	80.7	0.031
1972	3,748 (1.9)	168 (8.0)	288,000 (9.5)	5,397 (4.4)	24,267 (11.7)	9.3 (13.5)	18.2	81.8	0.031
1973	3,818 (1.9)	183 (9.0)	325,500 (13.0)	5,764 (6.8)	28,526 (17.6)	11.0 (18.0)	16.8	83.2	0.032
1974	3,890 (1.9)	191 (4.0)	– –	5,982 (3.8)	30,347 (6.4)	12.2 (11.4)	16.5	83.5	0.034
1975	3,967 (2.0)	186 (Δ 3.0)	– –	5,992 (0.2)	28,452 (Δ 6.2)	– –	–	–	–

Note; This table is made from the following data.
1) Monthly Bulletin of Statistics, published by U.N..
2) Review 1973-1976, published by Fearnley & Egers Chartering CO.LTD..
3) Statistics Yearbook, published by U.N..
4) The figures of Rail traffic relate to the domestic and international traffic.
5) ( ) Annual Rate,Δ Reduce.

In the field of intercontinental transportation, most commodities are transported by sea and rail and a few by air and pipeline. By reason of the time-value of commodities and the comfort of travellers, costly commodities, as well as travellers, will tend to be transported by air in the future. The intercontinental transportation of the great amount of low cost commodities, however, will continue to depend on marine transport, because of its

more economical nature.

The importance of marine transport is most typically shown in the case of Japan. Japan is an island country with few natural resources and all her trading partners located far beyond her shores. Until about one hundred and twenty years ago, Japan was an isolated country with a self-supporting and self-sufficient economy which mainly depended on agriculture. Hence,

84

economic activity, as wel as the general standard of living, was at a low level. In 1854, however, Japan opened her ports to foreign countries and entered the world of international shipping and trade, thus transforming the country from an agricultural nation to an industrial and commercial one. After that, many ports were constructed in Japan, and a number of industrial districts and cities were situated behind them. By means of such advantageous locationing, import and processing of raw materials, as well as export and domestic consumption of manufactured goods, are made cheap and rapid by marine transport; this supports the current national economy in Japan.

INCREASE OF TRADE AND COUNTER MEASURES

Intercontinental marine transportation system can be subdivided into:

1. Domestic cargo transport activity
2. Cargo handling activity at ports
3. Carriage of goods by sea.

Each of such activities is carried out by land transporters, shipping firms, forwarders, port authorities and a great many others. Each of such business activity works under the principle of achieving the best possible benefits with the least possible costs and has been exerting itself for the improvement of the system on which it has to live.

The following five points will be major factors for the decisionmaking for the improvement of such systems:

First is the trend toward a thorough understanding of the intercontinental marine transportation system. In other words, instead of each management authority measuring things purely in terms of his own subsystem, he is now inclined to consider optimization of the total intermodal transportation system. [3] (Fig. 2.1). Recently, management authorities have endeavored to consider also regional environmental preservation and regional economic development within the decisionmaking process.

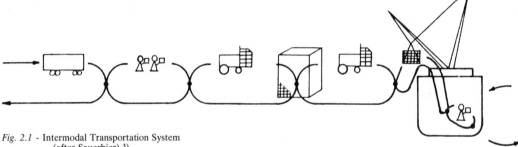

Fig. 2.1 - Intermodal Transportation System
(after Sauerbier) [3]

The second characteristic is specialization of transport methods. The conventional transport system employed liner ships of about 3,000 GT to 10,000 GT in size, but the new transport system which is coming into use employs ships which are specialized according to commodities. The kinds of specialized ships range widely, (e.g.: oil tankers, LPG ships, LNG ships, ore carriers, grain carriers, cement carriers, refrigerator boats, auto carriers, etc.) [4]. (Fig. 2.2). Furthermore, terminal facilities, such as port facilities, have come to be designed in coordination with the specifications (ship type, ship size, etc.) of specialized ships. In this way, the specialized transportation system has enabled a remarkable rise in the efficiency of transportation; the merits of this system are so great that it represents an improvement over the conventional one even when ships return from their voyages empty.

The third development is standardization or unitization of the size of transport commodities. Standardized receptacles, such as container vans and pallets, were devised to facilitate loading or unloading of general cargoes which differed in their shapes. The container transportation system, in particular, using container vans as receptables, made possible great savings in packing costs, which had previously comprised a large percentage of the total cost of shipping. Until about ten years ago, general cargoes used to be handled by mast cranes or wharf cranes, which had a handling ability of about two tons; but containerization made it possible to handle commodities of 20 to 40 tons at one time, thus raising the productivity of transport by some 10 to 20 times. This fact made possible the quick dispatch of container ships in port, and contributed to the decrease of the system's cost.

Fourth is the development of larger and faster ships and transport equipment for use in the intercontinental marine transportation system. In the area of oil tankers, ships of the specifications of 484,337 DW, 15.55 knots have entered service, and with regard to container ships, the Trio Group has put a fleet of ships of the specifications of 58,889 GT (2,200 containers), 26 knots on the line between the Far East and Europe. [5] (Fig. 2.3). Hence the construction of huge berths, the waterway and anchorage with deep depths are necessary at ports which accept the entrance of such large-scale ships.

Fifth is the introduction of automation and comprehensive information into the transportation system. When many management authorities which are concerned with the intercontinental marine transportation system actually make decisions relating to the above mentioned four factors, many risks are involved due to lack of information. In order to minimize and eliminate those risks, methods of collecting, analyzing and transforming large amounts of information concerned with the operation of the transportation system have been developed.

Many studies have been performed at research institutes in various countries for the last ten years, to provide theoretical background and to assist in decisionmaking with regard to the above mentioned developments. The results obtained from these studies have contributed greatly to the site-location and size-determination of ports and inland depots in each country, as well as to the evaluation of alternatives concerning the type or quality of ships and handling equipment on berth. Examples of this will be dealt with briefly in the following section with regard to design of the international marine container transportation system.

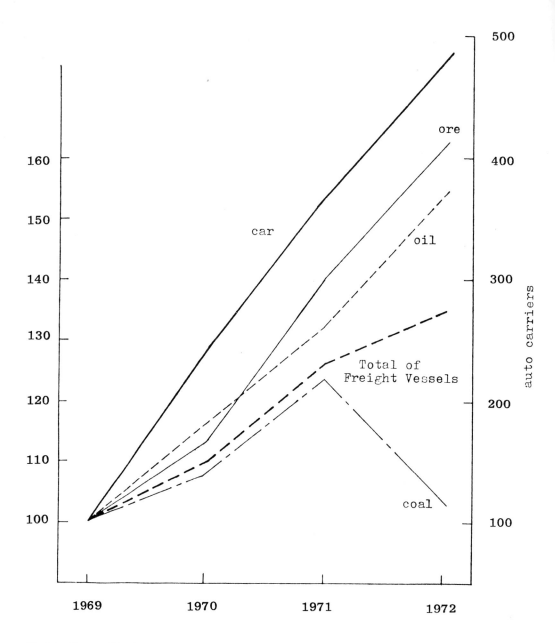

Fig. 2.2 – Changes of Total Tonnage of Specialized Ships

Note; 1) This Figure is made from: "Annual Report", Ministry of Transportation, 1974.
 2) Each Index is fixed to 100 at 1969.

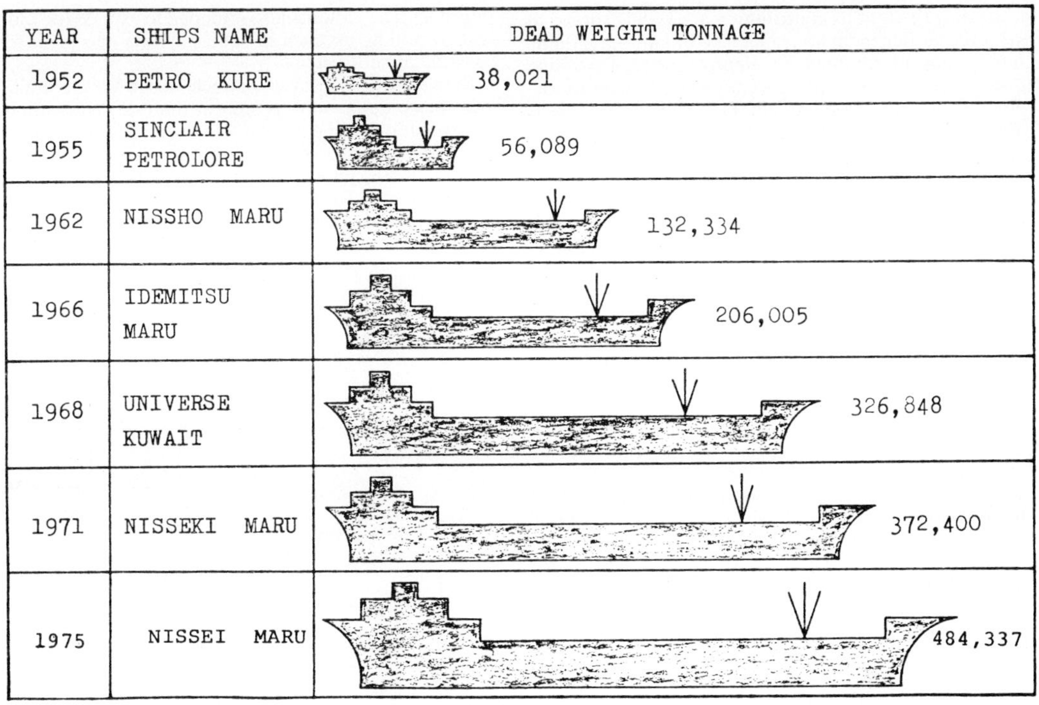

YEAR	SHIPS NAME	DEAD WEIGHT TONNAGE
1952	PETRO KURE	38,021
1955	SINCLAIR PETROLORE	56,089
1962	NISSHO MARU	132,334
1966	IDEMITSU MARU	206,005
1968	UNIVERSE KUWAIT	326,848
1971	NISSEKI MARU	372,400
1975	NISSEI MARU	484,337

Fig. 2.3. – Changes of Ship's Size

DESIGNING OF INTERCONTINENTAL MARINE CONTAINER TRANSPORT SYSTEM

It will be appropriate to note some examples of the contributions derived from such studies for the improvement of intercontinental marine container transport system.

It is a well known fact that the intercontinental marine container transport system was first introduced in 1966 by Sea-Land Services Inc., into the Transatlantic services with a modest fleet of four container ships capable of taking two hundred and twenty-six containers respectively.

Containerization realized the intermodal transport of "door to door" services, and contributed immensely to the economization of costs and labour hours involved in the cargo handling. [6] (Table 3.1).

Table 3.1. – Comparison of Costs between Containerized Transport and Conventional Transport Systems

Cost Item	Cargo Item	Home electric appliances	Frozen tuna	Soy sauce	Furniture	Stainless steel sheet	Toys	Table ware	Machine parts
Cost related to empty containers	Truck loading charge	–	–	–	–	–	–	–	–
	Transport to container packing site	* 1.5	* 0.4	* 5.9	* 6.3	–	* 13.7	–	–
Container packing cost	Material inspection cost, travelling cost	–	* 1.8	–	* 1.6	* 1.7	* 2.8	–	–
	Cargo packing cost	–	* 18.0	–	–	* 5.1	–	* 5.8	–
	Sealing cost	–	–	–	–	–	–	–	–
Inland transport cost	Transportation to the port	0.7	4.2	10.4	6.1	15.9	* 3.9	17.1	0
	Truck unloading charge	–	–	–	–	–	–	–	–
Shipping charges	Customs fee	0	0	0	0	0	0	0	0
	Various shipping expenses	12.5	18.0	18.7	13.3	17.9	12.2	4.0	25.5
Other costs	Packing charges	35.6	–	58.7	3.1	35.1	12.2	0	2.2
	Storage	1.4	26.6	2.9	–	–	–	–	–
Total		48.7	28.6	84.8	14.6	62.1	4.0	15.3	27.7

Note: Figures shown represent the ratio of decrease in cost to the total cost of conventional transport which is 100.
However, figures affixed by * show increase.

Skirting fields of its contribution are widely spread to achieve the dependable availability of cargo handling, stabilization of employment, improvement of working conditions, as well as the prevention of damages to cargo, wetting, rats, dropping pilferage and so on. Effects are not only limited to the improvement of physical aspects but also to social aspects.

However, the system necessitates the vast amount of capital investment for the fulfillment of itself, namely the construction of specialized vessels, the keeping of a numerous number of container vans, acquisition of much space for terminals, provisions for cranes and affiliated mechanical equipment, construction of inland depots etc.

Crucial consideration must be experted to the decision of the size of vessels, because it is a matter of simple calculation that the bigger the vessel size might be, the higher the productivity should be, provided that the very question of how to secure sufficient cargo is out of concern. Also, even a slight congestion in the port or malfunctioning of delivery of vans will cause a bad effect in the economic efficiency of the system as a whole. Location of container terminals, number of vans to be handled, cargo handling capacity and many other factors are under the strains of these conditions.

Improvement works for the facilities as well as the usage of facilities had been sought after by shipping firms, forwarders, intra-port cargo forwarders or by the port authorities respectively and independently for individual benefits. However, improvement of a section or subsystem (might be called a "local optimum") is not the total system, and might even involve the risk of the whole idea of the system collapsing.

Therefore, in order to evaluate the intercontinental marine container system, the wholesome realization of the system must be established; the magnitude of each of consistent subsystems can be placed thereby accordingly. [6]

Fig. 3.1 illustrates, in a net-work model, the components of an intercontinental marine container transport system. [6]

  i: Place of cargo generated
  j: Place of cargo required
  k: Place of container terminal

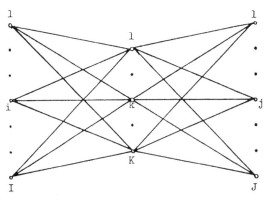

Fig. 3.1 - Network Model of Intercontinental Transportation System

The volume of cargoes estimated at "i" and "j" are to be incorporated into the calculation of transport costs necessary for each route.

Volumes, numbers, capacity, speed of necessary equipment and facilities are to be incorporated accordingly, as variations, thereby to simulate the possible status of the operation of such facilities and equipment. Operation time as well as idle time are to be calculated.

(Fig. 3.2). The model is also intended to express the total cost by adding up each of subtotal costs necessary for constituent sub-systems.

By adjusting the levels of each variation, the model must be so designed to represent the exact situation of the operation of the system. However, there has to be some compromise as to the setting of the reasonable depths of the simulation with providing a permissible allowance in each model, in order to attain a simplification in the model, without which the simulation shall

Fig. 3.2 – Subsystems and Variables of Intercontinental Transportation System

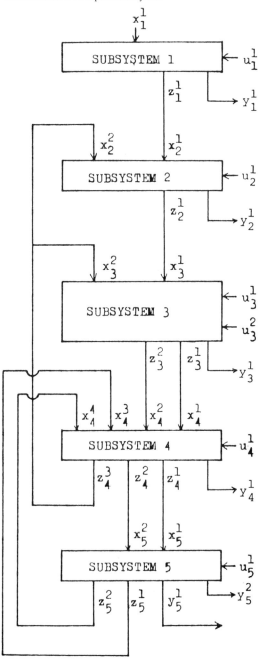

Note; x,u: input variables, and y,z: output variables.

88

be hampered by endless series of calculations or combinations.

Every possible consideration should be provided, utilizing the methods of mathematical divisions and analysis in order to attain possible proper answers.

Many studies under the above principle have been developed to suit the requirements applicable to every component.

Models of the International Marine Container Transportation System

Many models aimed mainly at the economic optimization of the international marine container transportation system have been developed, and they can be divided into four categories. These are:

i) Network Models

Models in this category aim to determine the transportation routes, location of container terminals, and the size of terminal facilities. This type of model is regarded as the applied model of the "Warehouse Location Model" or "Plant Location Model". Mathematical techniques used in modeling the system consist of linear programming or transformed linear programming (mixed integer Programming), which involves fixed costs of terminals. [7],[8] Näslund obtained the optimal ship size, number of ships, number of ports of call, and quantity of commodities handled at each port for the case of integrated marine container transportation system with full ships and fractional ships, between Sweden and the United Kingdom and European Continent. This kind of model is useful for obtaining general information about the international marine container transportation system. [9]

ii) Optimum Size Determination Models of Terminal Facilities

Models in this category aim to analyze the behavior of the arrival of commodities transported from inland regions, and that of ships on sea, and to determine the optimal number of berths in container terminals. This type of study has been used widely as a size determination model of port facilities for many years. [10]-[13] Queuing theories, such as M/M/S or M/E /S types, is often used as a method to analyze the system. Further, a bulk queuing theory has been employed, in which the arrival of container ships in ports is regarded as a bulk arrival. [14] In addition, many simulation models were developed to analyze the behavior of the system in more detail. [15],[16]

iii) Thorough Transportation System Models

Models in this category refer to the "multiple link transportation system". [3] The transportation process from origin to destination is regarded as a multiple link transportation system, which contains in it many links (transport equipment units perform their shuttle activities in links) and nodes (transport equipment units transfer or store the commodities at nodes). (Fig. 2.1).

Hence, if the number of links contained in the transportation system, arrangement of links (parallel or in series), the number of transport equipments operating in each link, operating behavior of transport equipments in each link, relative size of commodities transported at one time by each transport equipment unit, and storage capacity at nodes, are regarded as parameters of the system, it becomes possible to clarify the behavior of the entire transportation system and to quantify the productivity or effectiveness of the transportation system.

These kinds of studies were performed intensively at the University of California in the United States of America, and the influences that each parameter has

upon the productivity and effectiveness of the transportation system were shown through simulation techniques. [17],[18] With regard to handling operations in the container terminals, many studies, which regard the operations as a two-link transportation system, have been carried out, based on the cyclic type of queuing theory, in order to estimate the port time of container ships. [19]

iv) Many other applications of mathematical optimization techniques have been studied, taking note of the characteristics of cost-function and constraints of the marine container transportation system consisting of three principal subsystems, namely, land transport, sea transport, and port interface, and afterward explained positively that the cost-function and constraints of the system are described by posynomials, and obtained ship size, ship speed and terminal capacity by the use of geometric programming. [20] P. Wilmes and E. Frankel regarded the function of ports as a part of the transportation system from origin to destination and presented various type of models. [21] Continuous simulation models were also developed to examine the behavior of the container transportation network under a given demand [22]

Design of the International Marine Container Transportation System in Japan

To design an optimal marine container transportation system between Japan and foreign countries, an analysis based both on the network model shown in Fig. 3.1 and the multiple link transportation model shown in Fig. 3.2 has been performed. [6] Total cost C, of the system is given as

$$C = C_i + C_t + C_o$$

where

C_i: inland transport cost

C_t: terminal cost, and

C_o: cost related to ships and containers.

To calculate actual cost, the total system is divided into many subsystems and the consistency of the entire system is maintained by connecting each subsystem with many intermediate variables. (Fig. 3.3). At the same time, ship size and the port handling system are also determined. Tokyo Bay, Osaka Bay and Ise Bay are adopted as sites proposed for container terminals. As a result of the calculation, the following became evident.

i) Optimum Number of Gantry Cranes

The number of gantry cranes is an indispensable factor for the calculation of terminal cost and it greatly affects the time required for loading and unloading containers, with eventual impact on the marine transport cost. For this reason, it is essential to determine the optimum number of gantry cranes from the standpoint of economic efficiency. Results of a study in this connection are shown in Fig. 3.4. The relative cost shown in the figure includes capital costs on investments for gantry crane and cargo handling equipment in yard and ships at berth, and the operational costs, as well as day charges of container ships.

This figure represents the results to be obtained when the cargo handling method in the yard is to be the straddle carrier system, and the number of carriers is to be three per gantry crane. Based on this chart, the optimum number of gantry cranes form an economic point of view is considered to be two for container ships with a capacity of 700, 1,000 and 1,500 containers, three for ships with a capacity of 1,800 containers and four for ships with a capacity of 2,000 containers.

ii) Terminal Cost

Annual Terminal costs calculated for the Japan-North American Atlantic Coast route are shown in Table 3.2. It is evident that the terminal cost decreases in proportion to the increase in ship size.

iii) Marine Transport Cost (Costs related to ships and number of containers)

Marine transport cost in the case of one port in Japan is shown in Fig. 3.5. The figure shows a case in which the terminal is located in the Tokyo Bay area. From this figure, it is evident that the difference in transport cost depending on ship size is quite clear for the North American Pacific Coast route and European route.

Fig. 3.6 shows the composition of marine transport

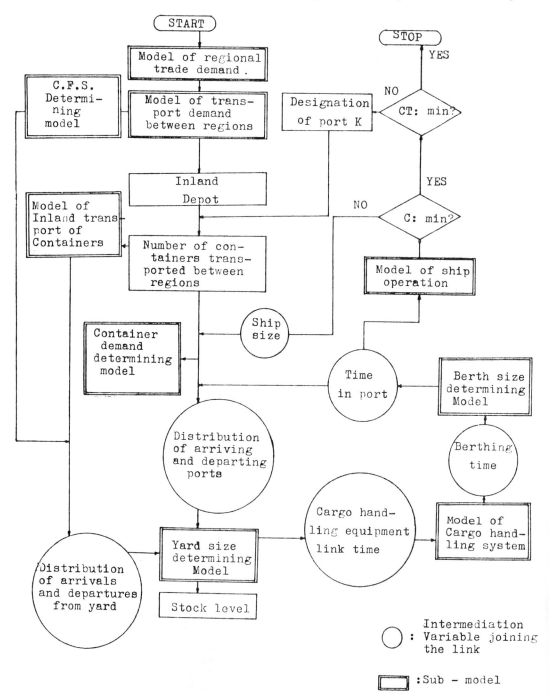

Fig. 3.3 – Flow Chart of the International Marine Container Transportation System

90

costs, by item, for North American Atlantic Coast service. According to this chart the capital cost on investments for ships and container is relatively large, thus suggesting the importance of efficient utilization of ships and containers. As the increase of ship speed results in a sharp increase of fuel expenses, this calculation shows some results which make the merits of larger ships some what doubtful. This is indicative of the need for a thorough study in relation to ship speed in order to fully realize the scale merit.

Table 3.2 – Annual Terminal Cost (100 million yen)

Bale capacity	Facility cost	Equipment cost	Labor cost	Operating cost	Others	Terminal cost
700	36	22.9	6.9	0.8	6.1	71.9
1000	36	22.9	6.9	0.8	6.1	71.9
1500	31.5	11.5	3.5	0.8	3.1	50.3
1800	31.5	8.9	2.7	0.8	2.5	46.4
2000	31.5	11.5	3.5	0.8	3.1	50.3

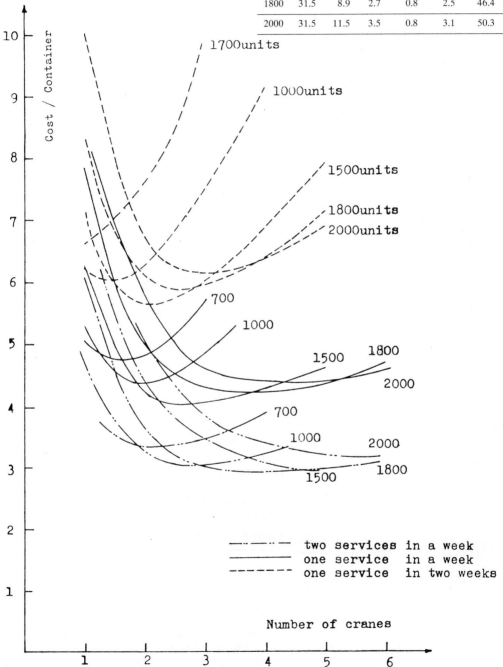

Fig. 3.4 – Physical Distribution Cost in Terminal

91

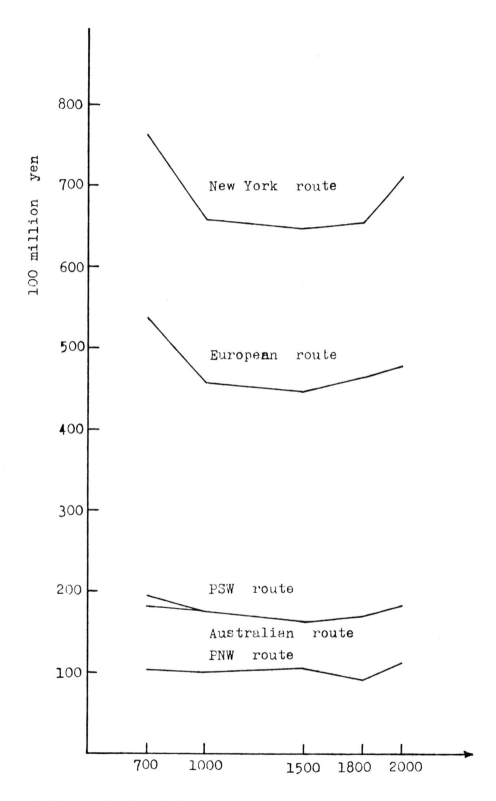

Fig. 3.5 – Annual Costs Related to Ships and Containers

92

From the results of calculation in the above model, it is apparent that if the amount of containerized commodities imported to and exported from Japan is rather small, and only one container port is constructed in Japan, then the development of Nagoya Port, which is located in the middle of Japan, is the most advantageous. On the other hand, if the amount of intercontinental marine container transportation is rather large, the development of Kita-Kyushu and Niigata in southern and northern Japan, respectively, are also needed.

Furthermore, by analysis of the above model, it becomes possible to specify the decision variables, such as number of berths needed in each container port, and number of cranes per berth, quantity of handling equipment in the container yard, and number of ships in each route, when the total cost of the intercontinental marine transportation system is minimized. Due to the efficiency advantage of plural servers (berths), joint use of berths is enforced.

In Japan, in response to the progress of containerization in the intercontinental marine transportation system, Keihin (Tokoy Bay) Port Development Authority and Hanshin (Osaka Bay) Port Development Authority were founded in Tokyo and and Kobe, respectively, in October, 1967. They constructed a number of container

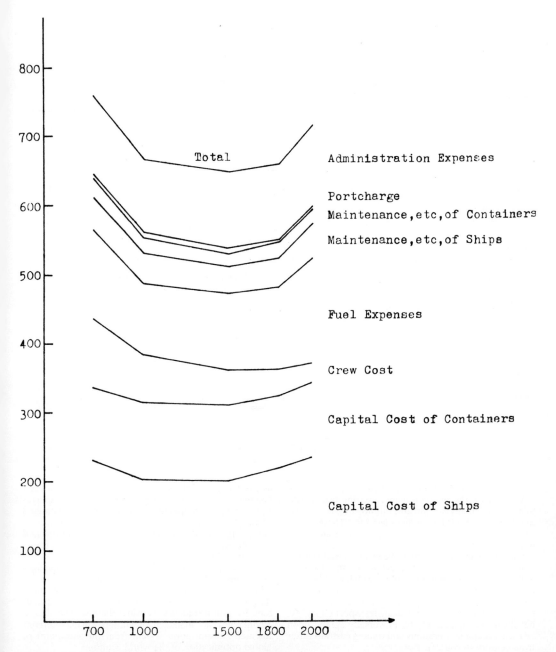

Fig. 3.6 – Composition of Annual Costs Related to Ships and Containers

berths with a depth of 12 m. in Tokyo Bay and Osaka Bay, which had typical Japanese liner ports. At the same time, institutions that manage and administer the operation of ships and the usage of port facilities were introduced. The introduction of these institutions may be regarded as a proper policy when considering the future increase of containerized commodities and the results obtained from the above models.

In fact, construction of container terminals was demanded at Shimizu, Nagoya, and Kita-Kyushu, in addition to the above ports, and this construction was carried out. These ports were constructed as the result of the strong demand in each region, but are also significant as feeder-service ports in Japan.

As of January 1976, 324 full-container ships belonging to 111 shipping companies and having a total capacity of 390,000 containers (20 ft.) have been put on 13 principal intercontinental lines and are involved in intercontinental marine transportation. [23] (Table 3.3).

Table 3.3 – Full-Container Ships in the World (1976. 1.1)

Route	No. of Companies	No. of Ships	G/T	20 ft. Container Capacity	Increase from 1975. 1.1 (*: decrease)		
					No. of Ships	G/T	20 ft. Container Capacity
Far East/ West Coast North America	15	75	1,647,325	88,355	*1	86,669	10,775
Far East/ East Coast North America	12	51	1,147,258	63,803	12	63,803	15,984
Europe/ Far East	15	33	1,470,531	65,359	9	65,359	13,985
Medit./ Far East	6	11	276,361	14,356	*1	14,356	*581
Far East/ Australia	13	18	304,887	15,541	4	15,541	3,814
Europe/ East Coast North America	12	43	813,191	44,453	*3	44,453	2,761
Medit./ East Coast North America	6	28	444,924	25,828	2	25,828	3,514
Gulf/ Europe	2	8	220,453	12,856	0	12,856	730
Europe/ Great Lakes	6	12	127,114	6,120	*1	6,120	*548
Australia/ North America	6	18	306,842	17,803	*4	17,803	2,826
Gulf/ Persian Gulf	–	–	–	–	*1	–	*528
Europe/ West Coast North America	3	4	78,564	4,642	0	4,642	1,202
Europe Australia	15	24	547,273	32,570	2	32,570	2,012
Total	111	324	7,384,723	391,68618	18	424,487	50,294

FUTURE PROBLEMS

To improve the intercontinental marine transportation system, many responsible authorities in various countries have made bold policy-decisions. These developments have been collectively termed a "transportation revolution".

Further, many studies have been promoted for the development of new transport techniques and the planning of new transportation systems, which enable these policies to be put into practice. Standardization of the unit size of commodities, for example, is recognized as a highly useful method for increasing transport efficiency, but it may not necessarily be universally agreed upon because economic conditions and trading customs differ from country to country.

Furthermore, legal and institutional adjustment, such as the revision of the standards of road design of each country to those of the international marine transportation system, coordination of shipping interests with land carriage interests on an international scale, free establishment of feeder-service ports in each country, and amendment of many international stipulations on transport, are all lagging.

The reasons are found in the fact that each management authority in the intercontinental marine transportation system has a different history of progress and has a different view toward the future. It is important, therefore, for future studies to consider the response of each country and each management authority in the intercontinental transportation system from the viewpoint of global optimization of the world economy.

There are some unexplored aspects in the past studies

on the designing of the intercontinental marine transportation system into which further studies are very necessary. They are:

a. Problems of regional community

b. Consideration on the length of time for an estimation of a project

c. Treatment of uncertainty

d. Adjustment of the total evaluation and subdivision

These factors are closely interrelated and some further studies must be made to achieve comprehensive analysis.

As to the problems of regional community, the following questions will be raised:

a. Improvement in the intercontinental marine transportation system will inevitably affect the labour conditions

b. Improvement of economical efficiency cannot be the only reason to justify cooperation from the labourers

c. Innovations or improvement sometimes bring forth the reduction of revenues to a community and discourage the investment to the port

d. Shortage in the funds might cause the provision of preventative measures against traffic congestion on roads, air and water pollution which might lead to the destruction of the environment

e. Acquisition and exclusive use of lands for the system might disturb the possibility of the land utilization by people of the community

f. Sophisticated improvements might not always beneficial to the improvement of social conditions of developing countries or regions.

Therefore, every possible consideration must be taken into account, such as regional specialities, as guidelines for the evaluation of standard or infrastructure. Considerations shall have to be expanded not only from the containerization but also to ro/ro, LASH, SEABEE systems for its combined use.

Secondly, the concept of time in the planning of the transportation system is important. To satisfy a given transportation demand, a huge investment in transportation systems is needed, and the investment, in turn, gives rise to further demand. This fact implies that the concept of "elasticity" in economics is essential for the study of transportation systems. Transportation systems designed over a long period of time are quite different from those designed over a short period of time.

Generally speaking, the former system may easily enjoy the scale merit (the merit of accumulation) of the system in future. Investments aimed at future scale merits, however, often involve risks resulting from the uncertainties involved in estimating future conditions. Hence, except for cases in which the present value of capital is quite lower than its future value, large investments will be made only with considerable hesitation. [24] To resolve this problem, studies concerning the timing of investments are being undertaken. [25,26]

Thirdly, there exists the problem of the evaluation of transportation systems. Formerly, in the evaluation of transportation systems, the economic evaluation method, which is based on cost-benefit analysis, was prominent; but the use of that method alone is not satisfactory. [1,27]/ [29] Some problems referred to in the first item are closely related to the natural and social environments in the port regions.

It is possible to calculate these quantities in terms of economic units (such as dollars) and to include them within the category of economic evaluation (e.g. protection cost and compensation of public nuisance) to a certain extent, but the method has its limits. [30]

Hence, an integrated evaluation method, which estimates the trade offs among multiple objectives aimed at by changes in the transportation system, must be developed. Moreover, a methodology must be sought for the reallocation of benefits derived from changes in the intercontinental transportation system to those who suffer damages as a result of those changes. [31] In this way, people will be able to enjoy fairly the benefits derived from improvement of transportation systems. Those problems will be of utmost importance for many decision makers who manage the intercontinental marine transportation system.

Studies concerned with the above mentioned problems have been undertaken only recently and have not reached the stage of practical application. These problems, however, demand early solutions and those who wish to develop the intercontinental marine transport system must challenge them bravely.

CONCLUSIONS

In the field of intercontinental transportation, the tendency for the greater part of commodities to depend upon marine transportation will not change, even if the share of air transportation continues to grow. In the last ten years, especially, remarkable changes have taken place in marine transportation. The most typical changes are specialization of bulky commodities and containerization of general cargoes. The steps that authorities concerned with intercontinental marine transportation have made to adapt to the changes are as follows: thorough understanding of the total transportation system; specialization of transport method; standardization or unitization of the size of transport commodities; enlargement and speed-up of ships and transport equipment; and the introduction of automation and comprehensive information into the transportation system.

Many studies have been undertaken with regard to the above mentioned aspects of the intercontinental marine transportation system. These studies take a great many approaches, ranging from very large scale ("macro") analyses, to very small scale ("micro") analyses. These studies generally employed the criteria of economic evaluation, based on cost-benefit analysis, and they succeeded in providing much information about the optimum design of the transportation system.

Not all problems contained in the intercontinental marine transportation system, however, have been solved by these studies. The results obtained by these studies proved that many more problems exist for the optimization of the international marine transportation system beyond the situation of each management authority and each country in the world. These problems include not only technical and economical ones, but also socioeconomic conditions, trading customs, and other factors in each country.

Many social and environmental problems have been created, such as those relating to port labor and seamen, [32] the financial problems of port authorities and environmental problems in urban regions. Further, design of the intercontinental marine transportation system requires a huge investment and the decisions with regard to timing are also very important. This problem relates to the investigation and resolution of uncertainties involved in estimating the future merits and demerits of investment.

Finally, the need to establish an integrated evaluation method for transportation systems is apparent in light of the above mentioned factors. The method must be not merely a technical and economic one, but a comprehensive one agreed upon by each country, each region, and each management authority in the world. Furthermore, a methodology on decentralization must be sought for the fair reallocation of benefits derived from improvement in the intercontinental marine transportation system. As the approaches to the study of these kinds of problems have thus far been inadequate, it is hoped that they may be resolved through international, interdisciplinary studies.

If the world is at peace, all countries in the world will desire interdependence with each other, and free and stable trade with other countries will continue. Improvements in the intercontinental marine transportation system will contribute to the betterment of international relations, and produce quantitative and qualitative rises in the production and consumption activities of each country. Japan is one of the countries that can grow only under such international conditions.

REFERENCES

1. Goss, R. O.: **Towards an Economic Appraisal of Port Investments,** Studies in Maritime Economics, Cambridge, 1968, 125-186.

2. United Nations: **Monthly Bulletin of Statistics.**

3. Sauerbier, C. L.: **Marine Cargo Operations,** Wiley, 1956, 512-520.

4. Ministry of Transportation: **Annual Report, 1974.** (in Japanese)

5. Japan Transport Economics Research Center: (in Japanese) **Illustration of Transport Economy, 1976, 93.**

6. Nagao, Y., M. Kinouchi, Y. Nishiyama, and Y. Okuyama: **Consequences of the Rapid Revolution of the Marine Container System on the Layout and Operation of Ports in Japan,** XXIIIrd PIANC, Ottawa, 1973, 97-127

7. Efroymson, M. A., and T. L. Ray: **A Branch-Bound Algorithm for Plant Location,** Operations Research, Vol. 14, No. 3, 1966, 361-368.

8. Gray, P.: **Mixed Integer Programming Algorithms for Site Selection and Other Fixed Charge Problems Having Capacity Constraints,** SED-Special Report, Nov. 1967.

9. Näslund B.: **Combined Sea and Land Transportation,** Operational Research Quarterly, Vol. 21, No. 1, 1970, 47-59.

10. Nagao, Y., and M. Kanai: **A Study on the Method of Port Improvement by Physical Distribution Cost Analysis,** XXIInd International Navigation Congress, Sl-1, 1969.

11. Jones, J. H., and W. R. Blunden: **Ship Turn-Around Time at the Port of Bangkok,** Proc. of ASCE, No. WW2, May 1968, 135-148.

12. Plumlee, C. H.: **Optimum Size Seaport,** Proc. of ASCE, No. WW3, Aug. 1966, 1-24.

13. Nicolaou, S. N.: **Berth Planning by Evaluation of Congestion and Cost,** Proc. of ASCE, No. WW4, Nov. 1967, 107-132.

14. Novaes, A., and E. Frankel: **A Queuing Model for Unitized Cargo Generation,** Operations Research, Vol. 14, No. 1, 1966, 100-132.

15. Murray, L. W., S. Rose, and A. L. Weber: **Simulation of a Maritime Shipping System,** Operations Research, Vol. 16, B-90, 1968.

16. Olson, C. A., E. E. Sorenson, and W. J. Sullivan: **Medium-Range Scheduling for a Freighter Fleet,** Operations Research, Vol. 17, No. 4, 1969, 565-582.

17. O'Neill, R. R.: **Simulation of Cargo-Handling Systems,** Report 56-37, University of California, Sept. 1956.

18. Davis, H., and J. K. Weinstock: **Analysis of Stochastic Model of Cargo Handling,** Report 56-34, University of California, July 1956.

19. Nagao Y., and M. Noritake: **A Consideration on Multiple Link Transportation System,** Proc. of JSCE, No. 212, April 1973, 77-88.

20. Erichsen, S.: **Optimum Capacity of Ships and Port Terminals,** 72-4864 (D-786-1), University of Michigan, 1971.

21. Wilmes, P., and E. Frankel: **Port Analysis and Planning, Proc. of the International Conference of Transportation Research, Transportation Research Forum, June 1973.**

22. **Wilmes, P.: Etude du Comportement d'un Reseau de Distribution Physique de Conteneurs, a l'aide d'un modele de simulation,** University of Louvain, 1973.

23. Keihin Port Development Authority: **General View on Container Terminal Facilities,** 1976. (in Japanese)

24. Gannon, C. A.: **Optimal Intertemporal Supply of a Public Facility under Uncertainty,** Regional and Urban Economics, No. 4, 1974, 25-40.

25. Slettemark, R.: **Optimum Port Investment,** Norweigian Shipping News, No. 18 E, 1970, 25-29.

26. Nagao Y., H. Morisugi, and T. Yoshida: **A Study on Stage Construction under Inelastic Demand,** Proc. of JSCE, No. 250, June 1976, 73-83. (in Japanese)

27. Adler, H. A.: **Economic Appraisal of Transport Project -** A Manual with Case Studies, Indiana University Press, 1971.

28. Vleugels, R.: **The Economic Impact of Ports on the Regions They Serve and the Role of Industrial Development,** Proc. of the 6th Conference IAPH, Melbourne, 1969.

29. Goss, R. O.: **The Turnround of Cargo Lines and its Effects on Sea Transport Cost,** Journal of Transport Economics and Policy, Jan. 1967.

30. Nagao Y., I. Wakai, and K. Hayashi: **A Development Planning Method on the Surrounding Area of the Project with Environmental Impacts,** Proc. of JSCE, No. 243, Nov. 1975, 61-77. (in Japanese)

31. Nagao, Y., H. Morisugi, and T. Yamada: **Method of Terminal Location and Decentralized Decision-Making under External Diseconomy,** Proc. of JSCE, No. 255, Nov. 1976, 93-102. (in Japanese)

32. Wilson D. F.: **Dockers- The Impact of Industrial Change,** Fontana Collins, London, 1972.

The Northeast Corridor:
has research influenced policy?

by
PORTER K. WHEELER
Congressional Budget Office
Congress of the United States, Washington, D.C.

INTRODUCTION

The U.S. government recently initiated a program of high-speed rail passenger improvements along 457 miles of railroad extending from Washington, D.C. in a northeasterly direction through New York, New York to Boston, Massachusetts. This rail route is termed the Northeast Corridor (hereafter NEC). The improvement project and its implementation, now underway, are briefly described in order to define current U.S. policy.

This paper examines the background and development of the NEC improvement project. Proposals for high-speed rail service have been considered from the early 1960s onward. Special attention is given to the legislative history, the underlying research studies, and the experimental service program. The manner in which these factors, combined with the bankruptcy op private eastern railroads and other influences, fed into policy recommendations and the eventual policy decisions are then discussed. Special attention is given to the role of research and analysis as an influence on policy decisions.

THE CURRENT POLICY

In early 1976, the U.S. Congress enacted the Railroad Revitalization and Regulatory Reform (Four-R) Act of 1976. [1] Title VII established the NEC improvement project and authorized funding of $1.6 billion to the Secre-

tary of Transportation for improvements to the main corridor route. An additional $150 million, requiring equal state and local matching funds, was provided for fencing and certain station improvements. Although under the management and supervision of the Department of Transportation (DOT), the actual acquisition of rail properties and equipment and the operation of passenger service was to be undertaken by the National Railroad Passenger Corporation, usually called Amtrak. Amtrak had been created by the Congress in 1970 as a quasi-private but government-sponsored corporation and is now responsible for most intercity passenger service in the U.S. Amtrak had not previously owned its own railroad rights-of-way nor employed engine crews.

Specific goals were set for the improvement project, most importantly the establishment of regularly scheduled and reliable service between Washington and New York with a trip time of two hours and forty minutes and between New York and Boston in three hours and forty minutes, both including intermediate stops. The system performance of proposed service is compared to present service in Table 1. Running time on the Washington-New York segment would be reduced a modest 14 percent relative to present premium service (Metroliners), but trips on both segments would be about one hour shorter than present conventional service.

Table 1 – System Performance

Proposed Service	Washington to New York	New York to Boston
Trip Time (5 Stops)	2:40	3:40
Lateness Allowance	5 Minutes	5 Minutes
On-Time Specifications	Over 95%	Over 95%
Present Premium Service a)		
Trip Time (5 Stops)	3:04	3:56 b)
Lateness Allowance	15 Minutes	15 Minutes
On-Time Performance	63%	66%
Present Conventional Service		
Trip Time	3:50 (6 Stops)	4:30 (5 stops)
Lateness Allowance	15 Minutes	15 Minutes
On-Time Performance	70-80%	70-80%

a) Metroliners/Turbotrains 1st Quarter 1975 Average.
b) No Turbotrain service now operated.
Source: U.S. Department of Transportation, Federal Railroad Administration; "Northeast Corridor Improvement Program, Briefing Notes". December 1976.

The improvements scheduled cover the full range of railroad rehabilitation and construction, but with emphasis on improvement of the existing facility with minimal right-of-way acquisition. Included are track and bridge repair and replacement, roadbed and drainage repairs to tunnels, curve realignment, new or modernized electrification and signalling, gradecrossing elimination, new service facilities, and restored or upgraded stations. Track and bridge work comprise about one-half the total program cost.

The current program should not be viewed as a final policy determination, because the Four-R Act explicitly requires DOT to report to the Congress after two years on the feasibility, both engineering and financial, of further improving service to a two and one-half hour schedule for Washington-New York and a three hour schedule for New York-Boston. However, this faster service level was unsuccessfully proposed during consideration of the Four-R Act, so it could be difficult to get Congressional approval. In addition, annual appropriation of funds, unanticipated inflation, or other vagaries could influence whether the authorized program is in fact implemented over time.

BACKGROUND

In the early 1960s the increasing concentration of population in urbanized areas and the simultaneous shift from central city to suburb was nowhere more evident than in the NEC, the most densely populated region of the U.S. Rapid travel growth was creating highway and airport congestion at peak periods. The bankruptcy of the New Haven Railroad in 1961 caused special concern about intercity travel alternatives north of New York City. As early as 1962, a Public Authority to finance and operate NEC rail passenger service was proposed. [2] A Presidential Task Force was set up, and in 1963 Congress made a special appropriation of funds to officially establish the NEC Transportation Project. After preliminary study, a proposal was submitted and approved in the High-Speed Ground Transportation Act of 1965, with authorized funding of $90 million. [3] It was this legislation that supported the extensive research and analysis of intercity transportation in the corridor and that funded demonstration tests of high-speed rail passenger service over the next few years. These two efforts were the major substantive inputs for the eventual policy decision.

FINDINGS OF THE RESEARCH EFFORT

This section examines the research effort in two phases, first the analytical studies and then the experimental results from demonstration operations in the corridor.

The NEC Transportation Project Report

The research studies examining transportation alternatives in the Corridor resulted in a wide-ranging series of 17 reports describing the NEC transportation network, the analytical methodology employed, the various modal alternatives selected for study and the demand and cost analyses undertaken. These 17 reports were then summarized in a single Project Report which presented and compared nine broadly conceived, multimodal options. [4]

The Northeast Corridor project and accompanying reports in many ways represent an extensive applied experiment in econometric modelling and the model/simulation process in general. Many techniques were developed, refined and often discarded during this research. The term "modal split" and the concept of an "abstract mode", that is, a mode characterized by its service characteristics are examples of concepts closely associated with this project. The Secretary of Transportation in transmitting the Project Report to Congress said "this report breaks significant new ground in the field of comprehensive quantitative analysis of . . . complex long range transportation problems".

The Project Report presented options that were designed to be responsive to a wide range of policy directions, for example, external decisions about the desirability of private versus public investment or about institutional changes that might antedate the actual transportation decisions. In this sense, the research effort was designed to be responsive to broad, unpredicable policy mandates, rather than the reverse. This later proved critical, since bankruptcies among the private railroad carriers in the region provided the impetus for dramatic institutional change and for previously unthinkable forms and levels of government support.

The problem in the Northeast Corridor was broadly identified as one of congested air facilties and congested highway facilities faced with growing demands. This congestion occurred mainly in the large metropolitan areas, but the NEC has several of our largest and oldest metropolitan areas on its route. Hence, the quality of intercity transportation depends not just on line-haul routes but on the ease of circulation through and within the large population centres. An important corollary is that intercity high-speed grounds modes which have terminals in city centers will be most appropriate if cities concentrate on developing radial transportation networks, whereas the development of urban beltways and continued suburbanization has impinged upon decisions and suggests modes oriented towards the periphery.

The Options

The nine passenger transportation options presented in the Projects Report incorporated the existing auto, bus, air, and rail (including rail demonstration improvements) modes, and factored in five new modal possibilities in varying combinations. The four ground modes analyzed were:

– Demonstration Rail (DEMO -- 125 miles per hour top speed, approximately three hour trip time Washington to New York, and three and one-half hours New York to Boston.

– High-Speed Rail "A" (HSRA) -- 150 mph top speed, two and one half-hour trip time Washington to New York, and two and three-quarter hours New York to Boston.

– High-Speed Rail "C" (HSRC) -- 200 mph top speed and two hour or better trip times on both segments.

– Tracked Air Cushion Vehicle (TACV) -- 300 mph top speed and approximately one and one-half hour trip times on both segments.

In addition, two air modes were examined:

– Short Take-Off and Landing (STOL) Air -- 265 mph and multiple landing sites in the downtown areas as well as on the periphery.

– Vertical Take-Off and Landing (VTOL) Air -- 265 mph and multiple landing sites in the downtown areas as well as on the periphery.

The Project Report did not choose among the nine options; that is, no policy recommendation was made. However, a number of general conclusions can be drawn from the document. First, with the exception of DEMO rail, none of the improved ground modes proved commercially viable within 10 to 15 years of start-up and would thus require public support. Both of the new air modes showed ability to attract traffic and produced favorable financial projections (ability to earn a ten percent return on investment). The prime reasons were low access times due to dispersed terminals, their speed advantage on the longer trip stages, and lower immediate capital costs for ground improvements traded-off against higher annual operating costs in future years. Several points favorable to STOL were noted.

Gradations of Railroad Improvement

Because the DEMO rail option showed a positive net revenue impact whereas the higher level ground improvements dit not, ten progressive second-order alternatives were examined for improved rail service ranging from the DEMO level to the HSRA alternative. In fact,

26 specific improvement projects were identified and grouped into these ten intermediate alternatives. [5] The improvement projects showed wide variation in terms of both passenger minutes saved and minutes saved per thousand dollars of improvement costs. The range for passenger minutes saved per day per thousand dollars of improvement was from 10.6 for the most promising projects down to 0.1 on the low end. The highest benefits tended to occur south of New York, primarily because of higher patronage levels on that segment.

The maximum impact on net revenues would be realized by implementing only the first package of improvements (costing $187 million) of the ten examined. This package included DEMO-type equipment (Metroliners) and a relatively small amount of additional right-of-way improvement. Benefits from further roadway improvements tended to be offset by increased costs, so that net revenues would fall as further improvement was undertaken. A middle-ground improvement package, requiring about half the added investment for HSRA, could achieve two and one-half hour times for Washington to New York (identical to HSRA) and three and one-quarter hours for New York to Boston. The remaining improvement north of New York to further reduce the New York to Boston running time would absorb all of the additional funds required to implement HSRA. These supplemental findings, tucked away in a technical appendix, appear to be quite influential in the next stage, the policy recommendations of the Secretary of Transportation.

Metroliner experience to date

Paralleling in time the analytical studies, an operational experiment was underway to implement interim rail improvements described above as DEMO rail. The evidence generated by the Metroliner demonstration should have provided a valuable input into the policy-making process, and the ridership and financial experience is examined in this section. The focus here is on the New York to Washington segment of the NEC, because only one train a day in each direction operated north of New York and because the Turbotrain service between New Haven and Boston has been very spotty and limited in nature. The level of existing ridership also suggests that is it more important to focus on the southern half of the NEC. Traffic on the southern segment totalled about 7.1 million passengers in 1975, whereas total New York to Boston traffic was only about 1.5 million and had fluctuated around that level since 1969. Looking first at overall passenger data for the New York to Washington route, as shown in Table 2, ridership on the Metroliner grew dramatically from its introduction in early 1969 through the end of 1972. Moderate growth continued in 1973 and 1974; part of each of these years reflect gasoline shortages triggered by the Arab oil embargo. The most recent two years, 1975 and 1976, show declines of 8 to 9 percent in Metroliner ridership.

Ridership on conventional trains being operated over the same segment declined in every year from 1969 to 1973 following the introduction of Metroliner service. In 1974 (and in the last months of 1973) conventional

Table 2 – Northeast Corridor Rail Passenger Traffic
(Thousands of Passengers)

Segment/Service	Year							
	1969	*1970*	*1971*	*1972*	*1973*	*1974*	*1975*	*1976* a)
Washington to New York								
Metroliner	605	1,252	1,625	2,153	2,353	2,494	2,266	2,091
Conventional	6,881	5,507	4,848	4,499	4,492	5,067	4,797	4,858
Subtotal	7,486	6,759	6,473	6,652	6,845	7,561	7,062	6,949
New York to Boston b)	1,564	1,177	877	1,188	1,323	1,701	1,535	1,371
Total NEC	8,947	7,936	7,350	7,840	8,168	9,262	8,597	8,320

a) Estimated, figures preliminary and recording basis changed.
b) Includes Turbotrain riders.
Sources: U.S. Department of Transportation, Federal Railroad Administration, *Rail Passenger Statistics in the Northeast Corridor, 1974-1975*, March 1976.

ridership was reserved, primarily attributable to the gasoline shortages and pssible the 55 mph highway speed limit, but declines continued in 1975. The resulting total rail ridership on the southern half of the Northeast Corridor has been remarkable unaffected by the Metroliner service. Prior to the demonstration, total ridership in 1968 was approximately 7.0 million passengers, and the level in 1975 represents only a small increase in passengers. The 1976 estimated totals are actually below 1968

levels. On this score, one can hardly say that the Metroliner demonstration has been an unmitigated success. Indeed, except for high patronage in 1974, few riders have been attracted to rail usage, since Metroliner patronage gains have been matched by declining conventional train ridership. It is only fair to point out that traffic had been declining throughout the 1960s. Also, the quality of conventional trains declined rather sharply in the early 1970s, and has only recently been upgraded by the in-

Table 3 – Estimated Air Passengers, Local Traffic Only, Both Directions, For Selected City-Pairs, 1970-1975,
(Thousands of Passengers) a)

	1970	*1971*	*1972*	*1973*	*1974*	*1975*
Washington to Philadelphia	123	103	117	114	100	22
Washington to New York	1,659	1,355	1,233	1,734	1,673	1,561
Baltimore to New York	245	213	235	202	192	168
New York to Boston	2,045	1,629	1,446	1,913	1,836	1,680

a) Based on 10 percent ticket sample.
Source: U.S. Civil Aeronautics Board, *Origin and Destination Survey of Airline Passenger Traffic, Domestic*, various years.

troduction of the new "Amfleet" equipment. The 1975 data may also reflect a fairly sharp fare increase by Amtrak.

High-speed rail service attempts to compete with the air mode, at least for the longer trip lengths, so selected city-pair data for local air passenger traffic are presented in Table 3 for comparison with the rail traffic experience. The data, based on a ten percent sample, show that the air mode has had very mixed results as well. The large Washington-New York market declined from 1970 to 1972, rose sharply in 1973, and has declined steadily since that time. The remaining city-pairs examined all show falling local ridership between 1973 and 1975. Thus, there is some indication that the NEC passenger market, at least for the high-speed modes, is shrinking overall. In this context, the rail performance looks better, but considerable doubt is created regarding the need for capacity expansion to meet projections of growing demand.

A look at rail city-pair data for sub-segments of this part of the NEC yields some interesting observations. As might be expected, conventional trains are much more popular for short trips where line-haul speed is less important. For example, ridership between New York and Philadelphia amounts to about 72% of the total conventional train ridership. Metroliner dominates for longer trips. Although total conventional passengers are more than twice those using the Metroliner, longer trips such

as between New York or Newark and Baltimore or Washington actually show more passengers on the Metroliner than on conventional trains. Further, the total rail market is substantial relative to air for the longer trips, more than double air for New York-Baltimore and over 60% for New York-Washington. [6]

Is High-Speed Service profitable?

There has been a persistent illusion of profitability for Northeast Corridor operations, and most non-professionals with whom the author has spoken believe that the Metroliner service has been financially successful. This belief appears to stem from a combination of factors including the continued increase in Metroliner ridership, the fact that the early years of the operation were under a demonstration project with costs partly borne by the Penn Central Railroad, and the original method of reporting expenses adopted by Amtrak which did not include many cost items assignable to Metroliner operations. Through 1973, Amtrak reported operating profits on the Northeast Corridor overall with the Metroliner showing quite favorably. A 1974 Department of Transport report pointed out the apparent understatement of operating costs by route. Where Amtrak had projected a NEC operating profit of $6.1 million, DOT estimated a Northeast Corridor deficit of $17.2 million. [7]

Table 4 – Selected Operating Results, By Fiscal Year

	Operating Income (Loss) a) Million of Dollars			Income (Loss) Per Revenue Passenger Mile, Cents ( )		
	1974	1975	1976 b)	1974	1975	1976 b)
Northeast Corridor						
New York to Washington (Metroliner)	$(3.6)	$(4.8)	$(13.8)	(1.0)	(1.4)	(4.3)
New York to Philadelphia (Conventional)	(9.0)	(32.6)	(20.0)	(5.6)	(6.1)	(11.7)
Boston to Washington (Conventional)	(18.4)	(13.1)	(42.8)	(3.2)	(8.1)	(7.5)
Total	(31.0)	(50.5)	(76.6)	(2.8)	(4.9)	(7.2)

a) Includes allocation of most common expenses, but most capital charges not included.
b) Estimated, series discontinued due to accounting change.
Source: National Railroad Passenger Corporation (Amtrak), "Five Year Corporate Plan", September 1976; same document, variously titled, August 1975 and August 1974.

Table 4 shows the annual operation income (loss) and income expressed in cents per revenue passenger mile (rpm) for three recent years. It is evident that the 1974 losses were underestimated by all parties, finally totalling $31 million. However, the deficit solely attributable to Metroliner operations is quite small. When calculated in cents per rpm, the Metroliner service has required federal support of only about one cent per passenger mile, though results worsened considerably in 1976. It is important to note that this loss is very much lower than the overall loss of about 11 cents per rpm experienced on all other rail passenger routes by Amtrak. Clearly, no evidence of operating profits is indicated, but Metroliner service is much closer to that goal than any other rail passenger service in the U.S.

RECOMMENDATIONS -- THE NEXT
STAGE TOWARD POLICY

The NEC Transportation Project Report of 1970 delineated options, but made no recommendations. As the analyses were refined, there were several important intervening developments. These included the bankruptcy of the Penn Central and passage of new federal legislation on airport and airway development, urban transit assistance, highway assistance, and environmental and

air quality standards. Urban and air transport received expanded assistance, at least in part to relieve congestion.

The 1971 recommendations

A new report, *Recommendations for Northeast Corridor Transportation,* was transmitted to the Congress in 1971. [8] This report, often referred to as the recommendations of the Secretary of Transportation, reflected a number of policy decisions and refinements of analysis, some of which were in response to the intervening legislative developments. The 1971 report recommends the implementation of an Improved High-Speed Rail (IHSR) alternative for the NEC, achieving trip times of two and one-half hours for Washington-New York and three and one-quarter hours for New York-Boston. The initial investment required was estimated at $460 million.

The recommended IHSR improvement is essentially the same as the middle-ground project mentioned earlier in the 1970 Project Report, a compromise between DEMO and HSRA. The Project Report had indicated that incremental net revenues would be generated by this improvement. Two noteworthy aspects of this recommendation were the scaled-down goals for the near-term and the relative emphasis on improvements for the Washington-New York segment. Both reflect concern for positive, and high rather than low, financial returns to the capital improvements.

The 1971 report coupled the IHSR recommendation with a program of higway improvements and information systems aimed at reducing congestion experienced by traffic passing through intervening urban areas; this recognized the importance of access and door-to-door times suggested in the research. Serious questions were raised about STOL and VTOL, primarily because of environmental considerations and community opposition, but further research and development toward reducing environmental impacts was recommended. Recognizing the likelihood that improvements beyond IHRS would interfere with freight and commuter service, a plea was made for immediate planning of a new right-of-way along the NEC.

The 1973 recommendations

A new report was issued in 1973, in which basically the same IHSR system are recommend, but new cost estimates and more detailed operating projections were provided. Other modes and options were no longer mentioned. The new document began with an endorsement stronger than that of the NEC project group:
"The Department of Transportation proposes that the Northeast Corridor rail line be upgraded . . . ". [9]

The proposed upgrading would achieve the same non-stop running times as IHSR. The resulting running time with stops for Washington-New York is the same two and one-half hours, but the New York-Boston time has been shaved to three hours, somewhat shorter than before. The new estimate of the initial investment cost is $700 million, including rolling stock but not lease of right-of-way. The fixed-plant improvements are divided by segments of the NEC, showing $285 million for New York-Boston versus only $209 million for the heavily travelled Washington-New York segment.

Reorganization of Bankrupt Railroads

NEC passenger operations were being conducted over the rail properties of the Penn Central and its subsidiaries, though state governments had leased or acquired some right-of-way north of New York. Implementation of improved high-speed rail service was difficult because:
− Railroads had lost interest in passenger service and Amtrak was now responsible for contracting for most operations.
− Penn Central did not have sufficient cash flow to undertake improvements.
− The federal government was unwilling to finance capital improvements for privately-owned right-of-way, primarily because legal precedent suggested that such improvements became the property of the private owner.

The financial difficulties of the Penn Central and the other eastern bankrupts provided the impetus for legislation and an opportunity for change and progress on the Corridor. The Regional Rail Reorganization (Three-R) Act of 1973 provided the goal of "the establishment of improved high-speed rail passenger service, consonant with the recommendations of the Secretary in his report of September 1971, entitled *Recommendations for Northeast Corridor Transportation*". [10] The Three-R Act established a new nonprofit government corporation, the U.S. Railway Association (USRA), responsible for planning the reorganization of the bankrupt eastern railroads. The USRA was originally given obligational authority of $500 million which was intended for the NEC Improvement Project. USRA funds were also

provided for the reorganization and other purposes, and some controversy arose as to the amount of funding available for NEC passenger improvements.

The Three-R Act provided additional legislative instruction regarding NEC improvements. The Secretary of Transportation was instructed to begin the necessary engineering studies and improvements upon enactment. Property arrangements for transfers to Amtrak were discussed, with instructions that the properties should be improved at the earliest practicable date, and USRA was instructed to provide for the necessary coordination between NEC intercity services and freight or commuter services using the facilities. Also, the plan was to identify all short-to-medium distance corridors in densely populated areas where high-speed passenger operations would return substantial public benefits.

USRA Recommendations

In its reorganization plans submitted in 1975, USRA concurred in and made provision for the implementation of the 1971 recommendations, trip times of two and one-half hours for Washington-New York and three hours for New York-Boston. [11] After considering several options, full control of NEC passenger operations was vested in Amtrak.

The USRA recommendations were based in large part on the comprehensive economic and market analyses conducted within the DOT. [12] The trip times were regarded as adequate to achieve substantial ridership increases and to attract a larger share of the total corridor market. However, it was noted that, while revenues were expected to cover operating costs, there was no expectation that rail revenues would be sufficient to cover initial capital costs and/or amortization, so that direct financial support would be necessary.

USRA recommended that high-speed service be limited to the Northeast Corridor in the near future, although 16 other corridors were identified as potential candidates per the goals of the Three-R Act. USRA viewed its role as making certain that rail facilities required for passenger development were indeed available, and proposed a strategy different from that of Amtrak for passenger development outside the NEC. Specifically, USRA proposed that non-NEC expenditures not be concentrated on upgrading a limited route structure, because the major investment required to attract passengers was justified only in the NEC.

This conclusion was based on various DOT corridor studies and existing ridership patterns. The preliminary plan stated:
"In corridors other than the Northeast Corridor, benefit indices are so minimal by comparison that further analysis would be needed before implementation of high-speed service is undertaken".

Having concluded that costly public commitments for high-speed service in other corridors could not be justified, USRA proposed more gradual service improvements to observe whether demand materialized.

Facilities control issue. When facilities are used for more than one operation, desired improvements in curvature, signals, and track standards will vary significantly for high-speed passenger trains versus conventional freight and passenger trains. Further, maintenance must be reconciled. Freight use could deteriorate tract structure and would present a higher probability of operating delays. In order to accomodate projected passenger traffic in ten to twenty years, complete separation of passenger and freight operations was suggested. Private sector ownership of NEC facilities was rejected because of the desirability of pursuing service objectives of high-speed operation and because of the potential burden on the reorganized freight carrier's capital structure.

101

Operating control issue. Operations control is important because of interference between trains causing delays. Priorities for train dispatching can have an important effect on service quality as well as operating expenses. USRA recommended operating control for the passenger operator to insure priority for passenger trains, allowing operations at maximum speeds. The transfer of passenger facilities and operations to an agency whose primary interest was passenger service improvement would recognize and hopefully alleviate the past conflicts between passenger and freight interests.

Financial responsibility issue. USRA recommended that the cost burden of passenger service be borne by the responsible passenger entity. The very low likelihood for profitable passenger operations was recognized, but there was a desire to have the full identifiable cost of passenger service out in the open to assist in more rationale policy making. Cost-sharing principles were proposed wherever NEC passenger operations overlapped with freight or commuter service, attempting to reduce the possibilities for unintended cross-subsidy. It was hoped that an indifferent attitude toward either service could be avoided if costs were properly identified and allocated.

The 1975 recommendations

While USRA was planning the reorganization of bankrupt eastern railroads, the Department of Transportation was undertaking a multi-million dollar update of their NEC analysis, including extensive preliminary engineering which served to better delineate the individual improvement projects needed and their costs. Once more a report containing serveral policy options and a recommendation was prepared, but on this occasion the political nature of policy-making intruded and the report was not publically released nor officially transmitted to the Congress. [13] The options considered in 1975 and the revised cost estimates have since become available and are presented in Table 5. They are very similar to previous options. Rough equivalents of the DEMO option are the low options D and E, except that the Washington-New York time of two hours and forty-five minutes is a better service standard (versus three hours) than previously employed. The high option A is similar to IHSR, formerly recommended in 1971 and 1973, though option A shows 15 minute better trip times for New York-Boston. Thus, the legend in Table 5 which compares each option to the DEMO program reflects somewhat higher standards relative to previous proposals.

The estimated costs escalated dramatically and now range from $1.0 to $3.3 billion. The higher cost estimates can be attributed to several influences including the higher standards, accumulated deferred maintenance, more detailed engineering, and some apparent "goldplating" of the projects. Even these higher costs do

---

Table 5

OPTIONS CONSIDERED IN 1975 RECOMMENDATIONS

Characteristic	Option A	Option B	Option C	Option D	Option E
Trip Time	2:30/3:00 hrs	2:50/3:50 hrs	2:30/3:30 hrs	2:45/3:30 hrs	3:00/4:00 hrs
Maximum Speed 1990 Ridership (Modal Share)	150 mph 30M (23%)	120 mph 26M (20%)	North-120 mph South-150 mph 29 (22%)	120 mph 27M (21%)	105 mph 17 (13%)
Cost a) 1974 Constant $ b) Inflated $ à 7%	$2,4B $3.3B	$1.8B $2.5B	$2.1B $2.9B	$1.8B $2.5B	$0.7B $1.0B
Distinguishing System Characteristic	• Remove Freight • Standards > Metroliner Demo Program	• Freight Remains • Standards = Metroliner Demo Program • No Route Realignment	• Remove Freight South Corridor Only • Metroliner Demo Program -North = -South >	• Freight Remains • Standards = Metroliner Demo Program • Land Purchased for Future Realignment • Route Realignment in South Corridor Only	• Freight Remains • Standards < Metroliner Demo Program • Essentially accomplishes Deferred Maintenance

Source: U.S. Department of Transportation, Federal Railroad Administration, Northeast Corridor Improvement Program, "Briefing Outline", December 1976

---

not include equipment acquisition required for reliable, frequent service.

The unofficial recommendation in the report was for option D, a modest improvement over the original DEMO levels of service. The funds were to be provided as zero-interest loans, with state governments responsible for a 10 percent share. However, the Secretary of Transportation and the Ford Administration did not publically support this recommendation, but rather lobbied for a low spending option of about $1.2 billion, just

above option E in Table 5. This reflected a publically stated disillusionment with rail passenger service, an attempt to hold down the level of Amtrak deficits, and a general low spending posture in a Presidential election year.

POLICY DETERMINATION

The scene now shifts to the legislative arena where a major package of rail legislation was taking shape. The NEC improvements were included as one component of this package that also contained regulatory reforms, federal assistance for the reorganization and consolidation of bankrupt eastern railroads, and rehabilitation and improvement financing for solvent freight railroads nationwide.

Legislative Compromise

Enactment of legislation in the United States sets the overall framework for policy and often provides fairly specific duties and goals for the federal agencies involved. Such legislation invariably involves compromise in order to assemble majority approval and ensure legislative progress. There are two major areas where compromise surfaces publicly in the legislative process. The first is when distinctions or differences arise in the bicameral process between the House of Representatives and the Senate versions of a piece of legislation. The second is when differences arise between the legislation enacted by the Congress and the wishes of the President.

Major differences arose at both stages with regard to the Northeast Corridor legislation. It is impossible to ascertain whether these differences reflected a real divergence of policy or were a result of stategic positioning prior to a final compromise. For example, recognizing the necessity for a final compromise, one or both parties may strategically change their own position on an issue, broadening the middle ground and hoping to effect a compromise closer to their original desired outcome. Thus, the original positions taken are not definitive of policy desires, but are of general interest and usually determine a range which encompasses the final outcome.

The disparities between different positions on NEC policy appeared more extreme than usual. The Senate originally passed a bill (S. 2718) which stipulated improvements leading to the system originally recommended in the 1971 and 1973 reports from the Secretary of Transportation. That improvement would permit service from New York to Washington in two and one-half hours and from New York to Boston in three hours (with stops, faster non-stop service possible). The Senate bill provided $3 billion for improvements, plus funds for takeover of the right-of-way and startup expenses. The House bill originally submitted (H.R. 10979) provided $1.4 billion for Northeast Corridor improvements but, under heavy pressure from the Ford Administration, the House bill as passed contained only $900 million, less than the Administration seemed willing to settle for. This lower amount was said to be required simply to maintain existing levels of service and to increase reliability.

After a conference was held to reconcile the differences between the House and Senate versions, a bill was agreed to by both chambers that contained funding of $2.4 billion for the Corridor in the form of loans plus some supplementary grants for the ownership and operating transition. However, the Administration indicated its intention to veto this bill because the total amount of funds for all rail programs was excessive and because the amount for the Northeast Corridor was unacceptable. In an unusual legislative manoeuver, the bill that was agreed to by both chambers was not sent to the President for approval, as would normally be the case, but was referred back for a new conference.

The second conference, under heavy pressure from the Administration, reported a bill that provided $1.6 billion for Northeast Corridor improvements and a service goal of two hours and forty minutes from Washington to New York and three hours and forty minutes from New York to Boston. Also included were the startup funds and funds for non-operational improvements to stations, the latter requiring state matching funds. These provisions became law in the Four-R Act.

This program for the NEC, this combination of money and service goals, was not one of the official options presented in the Secretary's recommendations of 1971 or 1973, nor can it be identified in the unofficial 1975 Secretary's report. It represents a complex mix of options B, C, and D from Table 5. NEC project personnel fortunately indicate that the funding should be sufficient to obtain the goals specified, although equipment financing will eventually be required. Thus, the decision which determined current policy was premised on the research results, but did not adopt directly any of the recommendations based on that research.

The decision revisited

As the legislative decision neared culmination, there was clearly little stress on empirical evidence and program justification. The weighing of improvement options receded, and running times over major segments came to serve as a proxy in a controversy over the level of budgetary commitment. The policy decision also became embroiled in election-year politics.

The Role of Research

The extensive analytical effort on NEC improvements was instrumental in shaping the eventual policy decision in a number of ways, even though it was not conclusive. Focusing one's perspective on the final days, the legislative process, tends to diminish the role of research. But if a more removed view is taken, the research appears more influential. The original proposal in the early 1960s envisioned very high-speed ground transportation, traversing the entire NEC in four hours or less. The studies and reports investigated this proposal and identified problems in the NEC across the overall passenger transport market. Extensive supporting detail was generated on the need for additional capacity and the costs and service benefits of meeting this need by various improvements in the air, highway, and rail network.

Of course, the results supported a number of actions which have not been implemented. The importance of improved access to terminals, both for its role in door-to-door trip time and in complementary amenities such as parking, has not been adequately reflected in policy decisions. The problems of Washington's Union Station and its conversion to a National Visitors Center are sufficient evidence of this failing. The potential for non-rail solutions such as STOL or improved conventional air has gradually been lost from sight. However, a substantial impact was made in several other decision areas.

Level of improvement. The studies and reports invariably concluded that the benefits of improvements south of New York were much higher because of the larger passenger market and somewhat lower investment costs relative to time saved. Truly, high-speed service northeast of New Haven appeared expensive, maybe even unobtainable on the present right-of-way through Providence along the shore. The policy mandate in the Four-R Act for a higher quality of service from Washington to New York reflects this finding; improvements for the New York to Boston segment are much less ambitious. An alternative route does exist inland via Hartford which appears to have a number of attractive characteristics. However, key political support came from the Rhode Island delegation, and this certainly influenced the route selection. At the other end of the spectrum of options, research showed the more ambitious proposals to be very costly relative to service benefits obainable and projected revenues. Note the disappearance of the TACV and HSRC options that were seriously considered at the outset.

Project selection. Project selection has another aspect, the number of projects to be undertaken. The Northeast

Corridor project represents just one of a large number of potential corridors for high-speed rail improvement. However, it was this specific corridor, its heavy concentrations of population, and its gradual encroachment upon remaining countryside, that inspired the interest in rejuvenated high-speed rail passenger service. This was the first "megopolis", but there are many other regional concentrations in the U.S. The Congress had this in mind in instructing USRA to identify other short-to-medium distance corridors for high-speed passenger operation. USRA did identify 16 additional corridors as candidates for new or improved service, but none had comparable characteristics to the Northeast Corridor. The lower NEC has major traffic submarkets in Newark, Trenton, Philadelphia, and Baltimore, and a high level of white collar business activity. Other corridors tend to be longer and without the major submarkets.

The underlying research substantially influenced USRA's failure to recommend improvement on other corridors and the final legislative outcome that directed only NEC improvement. The research appears critical for two reasons. First, Amtrak has continued to recommend upgrading and high-speed improvements on a number of corridors and in 1974 proposed expenditures of $1.7 billion to upgrade 12 lines. Thus, agency support and a request for funding were in process. Second, focussing a national legislature on a specific project such as the NEC is very difficult indeed and often requires broadening the program to include a number of geographically distributed projects. That this did not happen suggests that the case for improvement on other corridors was simply too weak.

Economic viability. Research considers the economic viability of a proposed investment project for two quite distinct reasons. First, there is the market-test reason, that is, is the project worth undertaking, based on the users willingness to pay? Second, if the project is expected to be a commercial success, than an off-budget source of funding such as a loan or loan guarantee might be found such that direct financial support and appropriations would not be necessary. The legislative task of project approval is much easier in these cases.

Many projects offer promise of being commercially successful, and loan-type funding has been approved for a large number of projects in the U.S. in the past decade. Many have not been commercially successful, creating downstream financial demands on the federal government, for example, the need to liquidate loan guarantees when revenues prove insufficient. One important reason for the passage of the Congressional Budget Act of 1974 that established the Congressional Budget Office was to place constraints on the inappropriate use of this type of funding. Since research showed in unlikely that NEC capital improvements could be financed out of operating revenues, the policy decision was influenced to fund the projects directly.

Are political decisionmakers interested in economic viability? Apart from the differing legislative demands, essentially the need for appropriations, it is not the nature of political decisionmaking to subject every project to a viability test. Economic stimulus, job creation, income redistribution, and many other objectives are important in the policy-making arena. If all federal expenditures were financed by direct use charges, politicians would need a completely new vocabulary. The questions asked by research and those important to the policy decision may diverge on this issue, and, though progress has been made in quantifying non-economic project benefits such as land use, energy, or pollution, in the end it is the legislative process that we use to weigh those factors.

Preconditions for a NEC Decision

Two major preconditions cleared the way for a decisive policy regarding NEC improvements. Research had shown high-speed rail to have considerable, but not overwhelming, promise as a transportation solution for the Corridor, but there were institutional and legislative difficulties impeding further action.

Railroad reorganization. The NEC right-of-way was the property of the Penn Central, a private corporation, and serves as a major freight route south of New York. Passenger improvements were not attractive as a private venture. The institutional and political difficulties of infusing government funds into right-of-way improvements and of coordinating passenger and freight movements seemed insuperable. Little progress had been made since the agreements regarding the Metroliner demonstration in the late 1960s, prior to bankruptcy that further complicated matters. The decision to undertake a government-supported reorganization embodied in the Three-R Act was critical. It created the opportunity to both transfer the right-of-way to a passenger operator and provide for the movement of freight.

The legislative vehicle. NEC improvement was directly supported in the Three-R Act, but still little progress was made. The need for new legislation to complete the reorganization process led to the Four-R Act. That Act served as a legislative vehicle for several rail proposals not directly linked to the reorganization process, including regulatory reform and nationwide assistance for rail rehabilitation. Although all of these proposals had certain merit, it is unlikely that the individual components could have won Congressional approval. This is particularly true of the NEC project, as its benefits were confined to a relatively small though populous region. As a package, a much broader base of support was created.

CONCLUSIONS

Provision of high-speed rail service in the Northeast Corridor is now in the formative stages of implementation. Extensive analysis of the project has been performed over a period of almost 15 years. From an overall perspective, this analysis provided sufficient justification to kindle interest and support. The recommended level and emphasis of the improvements were clearly influenced by the research findings.

From a perspective closer to the actual legislative decisionmaking, the impact of research recedes and other factors predominate. Institutional rigidities had to be overcome as a precondition to implementation, and railroad reorganization became an almost necessary ingredient of the policy. Several policy issues fortuitously coalesced into a viable legislative package.

The policy currently being implemented is not one recommended by the underlying analysis, but it is not far removed from several options brought forward. Budget issues and legislative compromise have intruded, but a positive step has been taken in the recommended direction. This stip will hopefully provide meaningful experimentation with the potentials of the Northeast Corridor. Many problem areas such as terminal access and labor practices wete not successfully addressed. Of course, the current policy is not immutable. Improvement targets could be reduced by budget exigencies or upgraded by favorable experience, but that much is true of any program.

FOOTNOTES

1. Public Law 94-210, approved February 5, 1976, 45 USC 801.

2. Senate Joint Resolution 194, introduced June 1, 1962, by Senator Claiborne Pell. His book, **Megopolis Unbound: The Supercity and the Transportation of Tomorrow** (Praeger, 1966),

contains an interesting history of the NEC project.

3. Public Law 89-220, approved September 30, 1965, 49 USC 1631, subsequently amended in 1968, 1970, and 1972 to extend the Act and provide additional funds.

4. U.S. Department of Transportation, Office of High-Speed Ground Transportation, **Northeast Corridor Transportation Project Report,** April 1970 (NECTP Report No. 209).

5. **Ibid.,** Technical Appendix 5.

6. U.S. Department of Transportation, Federal Railroad Administration, **Rail Passenger Statistics in the Northeast Corridor, 1974-1975,** March 1976.

7. U.S. Department of Transportation, Federal Railroad Administration **Report to the Congress on the Rail Passenger Service Act,** July 1974.

8. U.S. Department of Transportation, Assistant Secretary for Policy and International Affairs, **Recommendations for Northeast Corridor Transportation, Final Report,** September 1971, three volumes. The Secretary's letter of transmittal clearly attributes the recommendations not to himself but to the NEC Transportation Project and indicates that they "are not to be construed as legislative proposals on the part of the Administration".

9. U.S. Department of Transportation, **Improved High-Speed Rail for the Northeast Corridor,** January 1973. The absence of a letter of transmittal from the Secretary to the Congress is an unusual feature of this document.

10. Section 206 (a) (3), Public Law 93-236, approved January 2, 1974, 45 USC 701 **et. seq.**

11. U.S. Railway Association, **Preliminary System Plan,** February 1975, 2 volumes; and **Final System Plan,** July 1975, 2 volumes. The plan is summarized in **Railroad Reorganization: Congressional Action and** Federal Expenditures Related to the Final System Plan of the U.S. **Railway Association,** Congressional Budget Office, January 1976.

12. DOT also influenced the selection of Amtrak as the operator and drew back somewhat from the NEC improvements by insisting on an incremental phasing of improvements which, after restoring the NEC to 1969 DEMO service standards, would implement other phases only "if desirable".

13. U.S. Department of Transportation, **"Recommendations for Rail Passenger Service Improvement to the Northeast Corridor",** September 1975, unpublished.

Intercity passenger transport travel in Egypt, performance and problems

by

ALY F. EL DAGHESTANY

Ministry of Transport, Egypt

INTRODUCTION

The topic of this paper is Intercity Passenger Transport in Egypt, with emphasis on the impact of research and studies on decisionmaking and policy formulation. This subject is particularly appropriate at this time as we have recently embarked on a nation-wide transport study and some preliminary results are now becoming available. In many cases the results tend to confirm what was already known through observation and intuition, but it will now be possible to quantify and clearly demonstrate the points which previously could be made only qualitatively and through judgment. In other cases the results provide new insights into the many aspects of transportation.

The theme of the paper will centre on the complexity of intercity passenger transport. When viewed superficially the provision of such services perhaps seems conceptually simple, but in fact it is a very complex problem when viewed in the context of the whole society and economy. As will be shown, Egypt should provide a relatively uncomplicated example, but even here the situation is exceedingly complex, with many interdependencies, alternative possibilities and complicating factors. Study and research are thus not only desirable but are absolutely essential if decisionmaking and policy formulation are to be undertaken with reasonable confidence.

The format of the paper will be to first describe the geographical and economic environment within which intercity passenger transport operates in Egypt, then to describe the passenger transport facilities provided and the traffic volumes carried. The many factors involved in decisionmaking and policy formulation will then be discussed and plans for further research and study will be outlined.

It is possible that this paper will raise more questions than answers, but in fact we are making good progress if we can first identify and recognize the major problems and possibilities in a systematic way and define the dimensions and many aspects of the problem. Only then can we proceed to the formulation of rational solutions.

THE ENVIRONMENT

Egypt has a population of about 38 million people and a land area of approximately one million square kilometers. However, almost the whole populations lives within the roughly 35,000 square kilometers of the Nile Valley and Delta. The valley and delta are essentially linear in shape and form natural transportation corridors with relatively flat land throughout. The situation in terms of geography and population density is therefore conducive to the low-cost construction and operation of railway and highway transport for both passengers and freight, with the capacity for freight transport further

supplemented by an inland waterway system consisting of the Nile and a number of canals.

The population density in the Nile Valley and Delta is among the highest in the world for areas of comparable size. There is an even higher level of concentration than first appears in that as much as 46 percent of the population lives in urban areas and about 25 percent in the two urban areas of Greater Cairo and Alexandria alone.

With the large urban populations and increasing industrialization there is less subsistence agriculture than in the past but the average per capita income is still relatively low at about U.S. $220 per year. Car ownership is also low at approximately ten cars per thousand persons.

In summary, the situation is well suited to public mass intercity transport with level, natural transport corridors through densely-populated areas connecting large urban areas.

PASSENGER FACILITIES AND TRAFFIC

The major intercity passenger transport facilities consist of the railways and highways. Aviation is not a significant factor in domestic travel in Egypt except for travel associated with tourism.

Railways

Egypt has an extensive rail network with 3,905 route kilometers. In 1975 the system carried 126 million passengers (excluding urban services) and performed over 7,000 million passenger kilometers. The average length of trips is relatively short for intercity rail services at 55 kilometers but this includes branch lines with particularly short trips. Railway passenger capacity is generally adequate with an average load factor of 56 percent on the main and branch lines and passenger traffic has increased fairly consistently since about 1970. However, there is now a shortage of motive power and the policy has been to maintain the passenger service at the expense of a declining freight service.

The railway passenger fleet consists of approximately 1,200 serviceable coaches supplemented by about 350 multiple-unit coaches and 350 diesel railcars, with the first-class coaches being air conditioned and providing a high standard of service.

Highways

The highway system of Egypt consists of approximately 12,000 kilometers of paved roads and 14,000 kilometers of unpaved. Intercity highway transport accounted for about 287 million passengers and 28,000 million passenger kilometers in 1975, with an average length of haul of just under 100 kilometers. This relatively long length of haul is attributable primarily to the high proportion of passenger kilometers performed by taxis on the Cairo-Alexandria route.

The bus fleet in 1974 consisted of approximately 8,700 buses, with about 5,000 for general use and the remainder for special uses such as schools and tourism. Approximately 75 percent of all intercity bus transport is carried out by four Government owned bus companies. The buses have a relatively high average age of almost 7.5 years and tend to be small for intercity buses with an average seating capacity of 36 persons. Capacity is less than adequate with load factors of more than 95 percent.

The limited capacity of the bus fleet and the resulting high load factors has resulted in one of the most notable features of intercity passenger transport in Egypt: the emergence of a substantial intercity taxi fleet. A survey carried out last year indicates that intercity taxis account for about one third of the traffic volume on the main highways and that their average occupancy was more than five persons, excluding driver. The capacity of the taxis is estimated to be slightly more than that of the bus fleet and in 1976 the taxis carried more passengers and performed more passenger kilometers in intercity service that did the buses. In total, taxis accounted for about 42 percent of intercity passenger kilometers, buses for 37 percent and private automobiles for 21 percent.

To summarize to this point, highways account for almost 80 percent of intercity passenger kilometers and railways 20 percent, and 63 percent of the passenger kilometers on the highways are performed by automobiles, either private or taxis. Thus, even in a situation well suited to mass transport and with relatively low incomes, passenger transport tends toward the higher-cost technologies. It is estimated that the economic cost on mainline passenger trains is equivalent to less than one cent (U.S.) per passenger kilometer while the cost by bus is slightly higher when the cost of providing and maintaining roads is included. The cost by intercity taxi is more than double that of buses, and by private automobile about 40 percent higher than by taxi, primarily because of lower vehicle utilization and lower occupancy rates. Apparently, this cost is not the major deciding factor in travellers' decisions. This is further indicated by the fact that the railway passenger tariffs are slightly below the break-even point while the operation of private taxis is apparently profitable, with tariffs somewhat above costs.

Clearly, the task of the analyst is complicated by the fact that, in their selection of methods of transport, passengers consider not only costs but also time, status, comfort, reliability, convenience and other factors, which are often difficult to quantify and which can have greatly different values in the minds of the individual travellers.

The allocation of passenger traffic between road and rail is further complicated in that it cannot be considered in isolation: it must be considered in the context of total traffic, including freight traffic, as this affects both the capacity available for passenger traffic and the costs. Again, there is a somewhat unusual situation in Egypt. There is a temporary shortage of motive power on the railway and for primarily social reasons it has been decided to maintain passenger service as much as possible. As a result, railway freight traffic has declined even though total freight traffic has increased. The inland waterway barge fleet is operating at close to capacity, and the "overflow" traffic has therefore gone almost entirely to highways. Highway capacity is generally adequate to accomodate this traffic, and the vehicle fleet is able to be expanded relatively quickly, but again, it is a question of carrying the traffic by a high-cost rather than a low-cost technology. Highways now carry more than

80 percent of the total freight tonnage, including 85 percent of cereals, 94 percent of sand, gravel, clay and limestone, 93 percent of steel, 98 percent of construction materials and 91 percent of the total tonnage of manufactured fertilizers. Given reasonably efficient rail operation it should be possible to carry such commodities at considerably lower cost by rail than by road. The decision to maintain a given level of passenger service thus has an important impact on freight transport capacity and cost.

This section of the paper, although intended primarily to describe the facilities for intercity passenger transport and the traffic volumes, has already provided some insight into the complexity of the problem. This complexity will become more apparent in the discussion of the factors involved in policy formulation.

FACTORS IN POLICY FORMULATION

In formulating policy regarding intercity passenger transport we should first have one or more objectives in view, but the definition of objectives is itself a difficult task. The mobility of people is not only of economic importance but also affects the whole social fabric of the nation. The prime objective is to have an adequate passenger transport system, but it is difficult to determine what is adequate? A system which meets the requirements at the least real cost to the nation is required. But how is the real cost to be measured? Specialists are far from agreement on these points. In fact, policy formulation generally takes place in an atmosphere of imprecisely defined and often conflicting objectives, which again adds to the complexity of the situation.

Some of the factors to be considered in policy formulation are the same in all countries; some are of greater relevance in developing countries and some are particularly important in Egypt. In considering the various factors, the emphasis will be on the factors which are now of greatest importance to Egypt.

1. A major factor is the appropriate role of the railway in intercity passenger traffic. While railway can be the lowest cost form of intercity passenger service, it is also an efficient carrier of freight, and especially of the bulk commodities which are expected to account for an increasing proportion of the freight traffic in Egypt. There are indications of some degree of preference for intercity travel by highway in Egypt. Under these circumstances perhaps the major role of the railway should be as a carrier of freight, and especially bulk freight. However, the inland waterways can be an even more efficient carrier of bulk freight, and to further complicate the picture, there is considerable excess capacity on the highways so that, in the short and medium term, even the highways can be low-cost freight carriers.

2. As noted previously, incomes in Egypt are relatively low at about U.S. $220 per capita per year. However, the costs of constructing and operating public transport systems are not much lower than in higher income countries, with the major difference being the cost of labour. Even this is offset to some degree by lower labour productivity. Yet, even in high income countries, it is often the case that the passengers are not charged the full cost of providing the services and the services are operated at a loss. Even though railway passenger tariffs, for example, are very low in Egypt, it is socially difficult to impose large increases. We are thus faced with the problem of systems which have costs about the same as those in more developed countries but with much lower revenue possibilities.

3. The land area of Egypt is about one million square kilometers, but only about 35,000 square kilometers, or less than 4 percent, is arable land. There is thus a great deal of population pressure on the land, both for

residence and for agriculture. The use of arable land for transport systems is already a problem, especially in the cases where highway bypasses around urban areas are required. It is now extremely difficult to add to the capacity of the transport system in any way that requires additional right-of-way, unless the capacity can be installed in otherwise unused desert land. This has already been done in some cases, but it is possible only where the points between which added capacity are required can be connected by a desert road or rail line. There are also some indications that, at least in the case of highways, there is a strong preference for roads in the valley or delta and a tendency to avoid desert roads.

4. Egypt, like most countries at this time, is greatly concerned with energy utilization. Even though the country is approximately selfsufficient in oil, its efficient use will allow some export and the earnings of much-needed foreign exchange. The fuel efficiency of the various passenger transport systems is thus very important and must be included in any comparative analysis of the various passenger transport modes and systems.

5. Egypt has become somewhat of a training-ground for the Arab World in that qualified personnel and skilled labour can find employment opportunities in neighbouring countries at much higher pay than is available in Egypt. It is thus often difficult to retain highly-qualified technical and managerial personnel, expecially in the public service where conditions of employment are traditionally less favourable than in the private sector. The degree of technical and managerial skills required is thus a factor in the selection of the appropriate technology. At the same time, employment opportunities must be found for less-skilled workers, and this is also an important factor.

6. Foreign exchange considerations are also important. A number of factors, including the increase in population, reduced surpluses for export, reduced self-sufficiency in food and resulting increased imports, and relatively large defence expenditures have combined to create a difficult balance-of-payments problem. The foreign exchange requirements of the various technological possibilities for intercity passenger transport and the possibility of local manufacture or assembly of equipment or components are thus important considerations.

A number of additional factors could be identified, but these are sufficient to illustrate the main point, which is this: decisionmaking and policy formulation cannot reasonably be based on judgment and intuition, no matter how competent and experienced the people involved. It is simply not possible to weigh all of the factors involved and consistently arrive at rational conclusions by subjective methods alone. It is thus clear that the impact of research and studies on decisionmaking and policy formulation must be an important one, and these functions must be emphasized much more than in the past.

FUTURE PLANNING
The ever-increasing complexity of transport systems,

the many interdependencies within the transport sector and between that sector and the rest of the economy, the increasing choice of technologies and the importance of transportation to economic and social development all indicate an increasing need for a structured, continuing system of transport analysis. This has been recognized by the Egyptian Government, which recently established the Transport Planning Authority to take the lead in systematic transport analysis. A number of studies have been carried out since the formation of the Authority, including the first nation-wide highway origin-destination study to be carried out in Egypt and studies of the cost effectiveness of each mode of transport. However, this is a fairly recent development and further studies are being either planned or executed. Some modifications of the current Five-Year Development Plan for the transport sector are expected as a result of the preliminary studies already completed, and further studies will play a large part in the formulation of the next five-year plan for the period 1981 to 1985. A transportation data bank is to be established and a continuing analytical system, using transport models and computerization as appropriate, is now being planned for implementation over the next two years.

In summary, even though the Egyptian situation seems relatively straightforward in terms of intercity passenger transport, it is in fact exceedingly complicated. It will be very difficult to carry out an analysis which takes account of all the complexities, but it is clearly not possible to have rational decisionmaking and policy formulation without the support of such an analysis, at least to the maximum degree possible. The conclusion is that the decisionmakers will still have to rely on judgement to a considerable degree, but the amount of subjective judgment required will be greatly reduced, and the judgements which are still necessary will be based on the best possible information.

LIST OF TABLES

Railways

Highways

RAILWAYS
Table 1 – E.R. Passenger traffic, 1970-75

Year	Main/Branch Million	Suburban Journeys	Total	Pass. Km (million)	Aver. Trip (Km)
1970/71	91.0	130.2	221.2	6772	30.6
1972	105.2	142.4	247.5	7216	29.2
1973	117.5	164.8	282.2	8258	29.3
1974	125.8	167.2	293.5	8671	29.5
1975	129.2	176.0	305.3	8831	28.9

Table 2 – Seats per train and load factor, 1974

	Main/Secondary Lines	Suburban Lines	Total
Seats Per Train	413	384	410
Load Factor	56%	97%	62%

Table 3 – Seasonal variation in E.R. Passenger traffic (April 1975 - March 1976)

Month	% of Annual	Month	%of Annual
January	7.4	July	8.3
February	7.8	August	8.9
March	7.8	September	7.9
April	8.3	October	9.3
May	8.4	November	8.8
June	8.3	December	8.9

Table 4 – E.R. Daily Passenger trips, 1976

Category	Trips/Day (000)	Percent of All Trips
Suburban Lines	603	55
Other Lines	498	45
Total	1101	100
Of Which:		
Intrazonal	897	81
Interzonal	204	19
Alex-Cairo-Asswan Corridor		
Originating	910	83
Destinating	909	83
Of Which:		
Interzonal	108	10

Table 5 - Egyptian Railway Passenger revenue, 1970 to 1974 (LE million)

Type of Ticket	1970/71	1971/72	1973	1974	Growth Rate 1970/74 % per annum
Main Lines					
First Ordinary	1.54	1.93	2.01	2.01	7.9
Second Ordinary	2.63	2.96	2.92	3.50	8.5
Third Ordinary	7.47	7.67	8.53	8.48	3.7
Total Ordinary	11.64	12.56	13.47	13.99	5.4
Season	0.79	0.84	0.90	1.01	7.3
Kilometric Season	0.38	0.41	0.39	0.37	0.8
Total Main Lines	12.81	13.81	14.75	15.38	5.4
Branch Lines					
Ordinary	1.88	2.33	2.87	3.06	14.9
Season	0.39	0.46	0.48	0.54	9.7
Total Branch Lines	2.27	2.79	3.35	3.60	14.1
Suburban Lines					
Ordinary	1.40	1.75	2.06	2.18	13.5
Season	0.58	0.63	0.71	0.75	7.6
Total Suburban Lines	1.98	2.38	2.77	2.93	11.8
Total Ord. and Season Ticket Revenue	17.06	18.98	20.87	21.91	7.4
Misc. Revenue	7.18	9.21	8.24	9.11	7.0
Total Revenue	24.24	28.19	29.11	31.02	7.3

Table 1 – Road categories

Category	Length	% of Total	Km Paved
Divided Highways	238 Km	1%	238
Main Highways	11,244 Km	42%	10,282
Regional Roads	15,039 Km	57%	1,799
Total	26,521 Km	100%	12,319

Table 2 – Annual average growth of the vehicle fleet
(% per year)

Period	Private Cars	Taxis	Total Pass. Cars	Buses	Trucks	Trailers	Total Trucks, Trail.	Total Fleet
1962-65	11.1	1.4	9.6	9.7	6.8	50.3	8.7	9.4
1965-70	4.9	5.1	5.2	1.5	0.2	20.8	2.3	4.6
1970-74	7.9	20.8	10.0	8.9	9.0	14.1	9.8	9.9
1962-74	6.8	10.0	7.5	5.5	5.7	22.0	7.0	7.3

Table 3 – Passenger and freight transport, 1974

Grouping	No. of Vehicles (000)	Percent
A. Passenger Transport		
Private Autos	138.3	59.9
Taxis	40.1	17.4
Other Autos	5.5	2.4
Buses	8.7	3.8
Subtotal	192.6	83.5
B. Freight Transport		
Trucks	31.5	13.7
Trailers	6.5	2.8
Subtotal	38.0	16.5
C. Grand Total (a)	230.6 (a)	100.0

Table 4 – Characteristics of bus traffic by ownership

	Public Bus Companies	Government and Public Enterprises	Private	Other
Distribution of Number	67.0%	24.7%	6.4%	1.9%
Average No. of seats	42	39	27	40
Load Factor	0.98	0.77	0.81	0.61

Table 5 – Intermodal comparison (ADT)
(1976)

	Private Cars	Taxis	Buses	Total
Total Vehicle Trips	25,654	38,873	4,981	69,508
Average occupancy (persons)	3.60	5.10	37.15	–
Vehicle Km	(38.1%)	(55.2%)	(6.6%)	(100%)
(000)	3,362	4,867	500	8,809
Passenger Km	(20.5%)	(42.2%)	(37.3%)	(100%)
(000)	12,103	24,822	21,902	58,826
Total Passengers	(19,4%)	(41,7%)	(38,9%)	(100%)
Transported	92,354	198,044	185,044	475,650
Average Vehicle Trip Length	131	125	116	–

Conclusions from Action 33

by

J. GREVSMÄHL

Steering Committee of Action 33

Action 33 has been a common study of several interested countries and three international organisations about the future of European intercity passenger transport. The study was terminated in late summer 1976. The reports are being published. Now is the appropriate time to step back and evaluate the whole exercise. What conclusions can be drawn from it?

This paper gives not an official statement of any of the parties taking part in the study but gives the opinion of one member of the national delegations - the German delegation in fact - that had the opportunity to follow the events very closely for about two thirds of the study period. It is thus personal and to a certain extent, of course, also a subjective statement.

STUDY MANDATE AND STUDY RESULTS

The mandate of the study was laid down in the following:

a. to assist the participating member countries in the task of devising long range strategies to meet the growing demand for passenger transport between major metropolitan regions of Western Europe;

b. given the guiding assumption that the development of balanced and compatible transportation facilities is in the common interest of all member countries, to provide the participating countries with an opportunity to consider common solutions and co-ordinated courses of action while respecting their right to pursue diverse approaches to intercity passenger transport problems;

c. to place emphasis on actions which must be taken in the near future to ensure adequate lead time for long term investment decisions during the 1980s.

The study to be conducted in furtherance of this purpose set the following broad objectives:

a. to identify needed improvements in the standard of passenger transportation service between major metropolitan regions of Western Europe, taking into account the likely increases in travel demand, the anticipated patterns of urban growth, regional development and changes in land use, and physical and environmental constraints on location of new transportation facilities;

b. to indicate, after an evaluation of the alternatives, what kind of modification in existing facilities and which of the advanced transportation system concepts now under consideration appear the most promising - with due regard to the goal of achieving a balanced and co-ordinated transportation system;

c. to advise what specific strategies - including research, development, testing and demonstration programmes - would be necessary to bring such concepts to the stage of practical application in the 1980s.

Terms of reference and objectives of the study had been formulated in 1972. Since then, some important changes have occurred in Europe. Generally, expectations of the growth rate for population and the economy seem to be lower than some years ago. At the same time the expected growth rate of cost elements seems to be higher. Consequently the growth of transport demand will be lower in the future than was expected until recently.

Technological research, on which many hopes were placed during 1960-1965, has proved slower and more difficult than expected. In spite of important results obtained, some difficult technological problems, affecting new systems, still remain to be solved.

Therefore transport problems now appear somewhat different from what was expected when the study was initiated. Taking account of the important investment represented by existing infrastructure, the study gives more attention to the improved use of existing facilities and conventional technologies.

At the beginning, interest in new technologies in the field of long distance passenger traffic was one if not the promoting factor of Action 33. But then, the situation has changed and new technologies played only a minor role during the later stages of the project. From this we might draw the conclusion that research projects of the kind as Action 33 should not last for too long a period because otherwise the questions the political decisionmaker asked at the start may no longer be of any relevance at the end!

Let me consider how far the study and its results meet the original study mandate:

– An assistance to the participating member countries in the task of devising, long range strategies has certainly been given. How much the countries eventually will get out of Action 33, however, depends on how seriously they exploit the study for their own purposes.

– The participating countries undoubtedly had the opportunity to consider common solutions and co-ordinated actions. This is quite an important experience and has to some extent contributed to a better mutual understanding, at least on the technical level.

– Emphasis has *not* been placed on actions that must be taken in the near future. On the contrary, Action 33 has become a predominantly long term study. So that point of the terms of reference has not been answered.

– In principle it is possible to identify needed improvements in the standard of passenger transportation services with the help of the study results. However, it should not be overlooked, that Action 33 is a long distance passenger traffic study. Many improvements could be needed because of short distance passenger traffic or because of goods traffic. These two types of traffic are treated only in a summary way and by very simple methods.

– The study results give an indication of what kinds of modifications in existing facilities and which of the advanced transportation system concepts appear the most promising. But the indications on the strategic level are in most cases rather inconclusive and the results on individual links of the networks are not always reliable because methods had to be used that give good results on

111

the strategic level but cannot replace detailed planning studies.

– Finally, advice, what strategies would be necessary to bring advanced transportation system concepts to the stage of practical application in the 1980s, has not been given.

LESSONS FROM THE STUDY ORGANIZATION

Before I turn to some details of the study and its results I want to explain the study organization and make some comments on it.

The Study began in January 1973 and was completed in June 1976. It was co-ordinated by a Steering Committee on which all participating countries and three international organizations were represented. The practical work was carried out by a Project Team based at the OECD, consisting of three scientists. The Project Team was assisted by three Task Forces, appointed by the Steering Committee, with responsibility for demand analysis, transport systems and transport strategies.

To assist the project team in certain specialized fields a number of research contracts were concluded. Not all of these contracts have been equally helpful but at least the contract about computer simulation of traffic behaviour in the networks has been a rather important contribution.

Most of the necessary data input was contributed by the participating countries as is usually the case in international studies. In addition, most of the countries participated in (and financed!) a common household survey that was initiated to improve the data base on long distance passenger transport, which in the event turned out to be quite a decisive piece of information. Five of the participating countries undertook (and most financed) two corridor studies in the corridors Randstad - Rhein/Ruhr - Frankfurt and Genova - Marseille - Barcelona.

By this organization Action 33 did a lot of work and achieved a lot of results both - as you may call it - on the main study line and on several branch lines. Most of this work and these results have gone into the final report, and most of the information that has gone into the final report has been properly analysed. However, some information and perhaps not an unimportant part of it has been lost. This is neither the fault of the project team nor of the participating countries but simply due to the fact that Action 33 had to terminate at a certain date and that at that date the study organization more or less disappeared. Time and manpower did not allow to do everything that perhaps should have been done until that date as is normal in large transportation studies.

The important disadvantage of the study organization was that it was not a permanent body but disappeared at the end of the study time. For instance, the network models can no longer be used. Some countries are making efforts to acquire the models but this has turned out to be a troublesome exercise and to my knowledge until today the network model has nowhere been made to work again. The data of the household survey is no longer readily available. One of the participating countries is trying to collect the results - with variable success. In one case they have found out that the survey results had been thrown away!

I will not hesitate to point out also an important advantage of the Action 33 study organization. By its several committees and sub-committees it enabled the participating countries to follow the study very closely - to see how the project team worked, to comment on the work, to hear the views of the other participants and to comment on those views. These close contacts helped to create close acquaintances and even friendships between the people involved - not an unimportant achievement.

On the other hand, the committees and sub-committees sometimes proved to be a cumbersome organization. The project team prepared papers, which had to be typed and copied and mailed, and then the delegates got them often too late for the meeting. But the work of the project team had continued in the meantime, and the papers were partly out of date.

One last point: the many committees were not a cheap organization. We may estimate an average of ten meetings per year with, say, 15 people taking part. If for one meeting we estimate travel expenses of one delegate at 400 DM and add salary for two working days of also 400 DM then the costs of the meetings only for the national delegation amount for the study period to more than 400.000 DM. A sum which is not negligible.

EXPERIENCE FROM STRATEGY FORMULATION

The main study line of Action 33 may be summarized by the following graph:

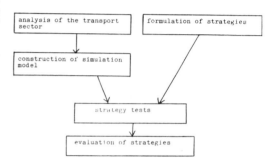

I want to treat the simulation model and the way of performing the strategy tests as a black box. In addition, I assume that the model gives more or less correct and meaningful results. I will say something about strategies and about evaluation.

Transport strategy is defined as the co-ordination of major decisions affecting the transport system in order to achieve relatively long term objectives. Long term objectives considered are of two kinds:

a. transport objectives, such as shorter travel times or greater frequency of service;

b. non-transport objectives, such as regional planning goals or conservation of energy.

The objectives give a general idea for the formulation of strategies. They reappear in the evaluation phase, when the detailed effects of each strategy are evaluated.

A strategy consists of infrastructural and managerial elements. The infrastructural elements are major alternations and additions to the track and terminals including control and propulsion systems. The managerial elements consist of policies influencing price, regulation, operating methods and practices by which transport services are provided on the infrastructure.

The infrastructural elements have been formulated as far as possible by National Delegations. To some extent they have been modified and harmonized by the Project Team. For each mode (rail, air, road) there exist a number of basic network variants. The combination of the network variants (for each of the three modes) is the infrastructural part of a strategy.

The managerial elements have been proposed for the network as a whole by the Project Team. Some important managerial elements are, for example, fares, fuel prices and motorway tolls, speed limits and airport delays.

The following main strategies had been considered in an early stage of the study:

– Status Quo strategy. Assumes that market demand must be met and the resulting problems remedied as far as possible by measures that do not interfere with the market system. In this strategy the growing demand for transport, by all modes, is matched by new roads, airports, etc., in a conventional way as far as the budget allows. Two additional variants of this strategy are a regulated Status Quo strategy (particularly to reduce environmental effects) and a Status Quo V/STOL strategy (to study the possiblities of a V/STOL system).

– Controlled Mode strategy. Assumes that the main problems are caused by excessive demand for car and air and that the basic solution is to find ways of attracting demand from car and air to rail. It implies a smaller road network than the Status Quo strategy and strict anti-nuisance regulations are applied to road vehicles and aircraft. This strategy has two variants: (a) improved railways using conventional technology with only a few new lines; (b) a large network of very fast services requiring new infrastructure.

– Controlled Demand strategy. Assumes that excessive demand for car and air travel cannot in practice be satisfied by other modes and must therefore be restrained directly. A variant of this strategy studies a decentralised air network as a means of reducing the pressure of demand on the major hub airports.

– Planned Demand strategy. Assumes that the problems are largely due to excessive concentration of demand in certain places at certain times. The solution is to disperse demand over time and space, trying in the process to to shorten trip lengths. A variant of this strategy assumes low economic growth together with low growth in investment budgets.

The set of strategies and the way in which different strategies have been tested can be summarised in the following table:

Strategy	Abbrevation	Full network simulation and and evaluation	North Corridor case study	South Corridor case study
1. Base year		X		
2. Reference 1985				
3. Status quo 1985				
4. Status quo 2000	SQ	X	X	X
5. Status quo (regulated) 1985				X
6. Status quo (VTOL) *				
7. Controlled Mode A 2000	CM(A)	X	X	X
8. Controlled Mode B 2000	CM(B)	X	X	
9. Controlled Demand 1985				
10. Controlled Demand 2000	CD	X	X	
11. Controlled Demand (DA) 1985				
12. Planned Demand 2000	PD	X		
13. Planned Demand (low investment) 2000				

* Abandoned

One of the great merits of Action 33 is that it follows a really integrated approach to transport problems. It considers the infrastructure development for three modes together - and not only the infrastructure, but also certain managerial measures. The study gives an example how such an approach can be realized in a study for a large geographical area. To my knowledge this is the only example of this kind. Here we have, I think, the most important contribution of Action 33. It has given a common experience how an integrated transport study for a large geographical area can be done. Of course, there are certain shortcomings, which should not be overlooked:

– Since the infrastructural parts of the strategies were elaborated by the countries, they reflect not so much the idea of a European network but perhaps more a compilation of national ideas of parts of a European network. One curious instance from the process of strategy formulation may be mentioned. Though the consideration of new technologies was an important part of the original study mandate none of the national proposals for the rail networks contained links of niew technology of any importance. A strategy for new technology (CM(B)) more or less had to be invented by the project team.

– Too many strategies have been formulated at the beginning of the study. Eventually less than half of those strategies could be properly tested. It might have been better to formulate and test few - perhaps two or three - strategies and then see how the reality (or the model?) reacts. With the knowledge of the first strategy tests further strategies could have been formulated - probably others than those that actually occur in the study.

– Strategies have been formulated around a central idea as has been described above. This idea has been applied more or less uniformly in the whole study area. However, the starting position is far from equal in all countries. The motorway network, for example, is more developed in Germany and Italy than, say, in France and Spain. A strategy that aims at a certain level of service in the year 2000 will mean something different in the two cases.

– Action 33 developed only strategies with respect to long distance passenger transport and - in accordance with the study mandate - not with respect to short distance passenger transport and goods transport. It is thus of course not an overall integrated study for the whole transport sector in Western Europe. One example to illustrate that this could at least in some cases be a disadvantage: The study found out that the main shortages of road capacity will in future probably exist in the neighbourhood of large cities. It introduced special motorway tolls to ease the problem and then found out that the effect on long distance traffic was rather small. One can of course ask the question if capacity shortage in the road network near large cities is not much more a question of short distance traffic and to reduce road traffic near large cities a detailed short distance traffic study should be made.

EVALUATION RESULTS

The main evaluation results on the strategic level may be summarized in some tables:

Mode	SQ	CM(A)	Strategy CM(B)	CD	PD
(Trips in millions)					
Plane	206	203	198	163	234
Train	375	442	482	407	394
Bus	55	55	55	81	74
Car	1 087	1 024	1 024	1 062	1 089
Total	1 723	1 724	1 759	1 713	1 791
(Status quo = 100)					
Plane	100	98.5	96.1	79.1	113.6
Train	100	117.9	128.5	108.5	105.1
Bus	100	100	100	147.3	134.5
Car	100	94.2	94.2	97.7	100.2
Total	100	100.1	102.1	99.4	103.9

There is some variation in traffic between strategies but in general it is not large. We can notice as significant the increase in rail traffic in the CM(A) and CM(B) strategy, an increase of bus traffic in the CD and PD strategy and a variation of air traffic in the CD and PD strategy.

Investment cost by mode and strategy
1000 Mil. US $

	SQ	CM(A)	CM(B)	CD	PD
Air	6.6	6.2	5.8	4.0	6.3
Rail	25.5	39.2	54.6	25.2	39.2
Road	39.7	23.2	23.2	23.2	39.3
Total	71.8	68.6	83.6	52.7	84.8

Variation in investment cost between strategies is considerable, both for the total and still more for individual modes. However, since most of the air, rail and road networks even of the year 2000 exist already today the variation in the networks as a whole is not as large.

Total traffic cost and total energy consumption by strategy

	SQ	CM(A)	CM(B)	CD	PD
Total traffic cost (1000 mil. US $)	31.75	31.91	30.87	30.56	31.56
Total energy consumption (1000 t)	28,023	28,273	27,915	26,545	28,862

There is no significant variation in total traffic cost and total energy consumption. Also for other evaluation parameters it turned out that differences between strategies were rather small, at least at the strategic level. In individual parts of the networks differences may be larger, for example where new high speed rail links have been introduced. But since Action 33 was aimed to be a strategic study we should look mainly at the strategic results.

The low variation in road traffic obviously is a significant result which explains a lot. As long as there are no severe measures against the private car but "only" relatively light measures and measures to improve the rail services, the private car will remain the predominant mode. Because of this there will be no fundamental variations in global evaluation parameters like total traffic cost and energy consumption.

On the other hand, if we wanted to make any strong effect on the private car in long distance traffic we would have to use very severe measures indeed. Such measures, however, have not veen studied in Action 33.

As to the "rest" of the modes, variations are not so small. Regard, for example, traffic demand, traffic cost and revenue for the train:

Traffic demand (1000 millions of passenger-km)	144.4	176.0	190.2	167.0	164.0
Operating costs (1000 millions of US $)	4.10	4.87	4.63*	4.59	4.53
Receipts (1000 millions Us $)	4.16	5.46	6.39	4.51	5.05

* lower limit; upper limit: 5.39

Whether there is a clear cut case in favour of improved rail services is not certain because the increased surplus of traffic revenues over traffic costs must be weighed against increased investment cost. Both real corridor studies of Action 33 calculated that the increase is not high enough to warrant investment costs. In other relations with even higher traffic density there could perhaps be a better argument in favour of new rail infrastructure.

There is, however, a negative case if we remember that even the SQ strategy represents quite important improvements in railservices quality with quite important investment outlays. For this strategy, traffic costs are just met by traffic revenues. If there was no improvement in the rail sector there would probably be no chance for long distance rail passenger traffic - but such a strategy has also not been studied in Action 33.

There is a further possible conclusion, which I want to present in the form of a question. First an example from the railway sector. If we differentiate by countries we see that some have a surplus of traffic revenues over traffic costs for all strategies, some have a deficit for all strategies, and for some countries this varies. In the light of these results: Was it a good idea to consider uniform strategies for all countries? Perhaps different strategies should have been considered with different economic transport situations and prospects. And perhaps the small variation between strategies can also be explained as the action of averages.

FINAL CONCLUSIONS

Here I will stop my meditation on Action 33. At the end two rather general conclusions:

First, there is something in it. It is worth while, to look into Action 33 and study its merits and its shortcomings. Secondly, it will be useful to make similar studies of similar problems but it is imperative to use a permanent organization so that there can be an accumulation of knowledge and skills in handling the simulation models.

Long distance passenger transport:
The Australian experience

by

G. K. R. REID
Australian Bureau of Transport Economics

INTRODUCTION

T he aim of this paper is to give a short but comprehensive review of the development, current nature and future of long distance passenger transport in Australia. Although the slant of the paper is essentially economic, data limitations for parts of some modes preclude a more technical analysis than the essentially descriptive approach followed. The paper is entitled Long Distance Passenger Transport because in Australia intercity transport is the dominant component of long distance passenger transport.

The paper is divided into six parts. Following this brief introduction, the historical development of Australian intercity transport systems is discussed in order to highlight the unique features of the setting. In part three the current features of the Australian system are reviewed, including the involvement of governments in the provision of transport services. The second last part of the paper considers the outlook and probable future for intercity passenger transport in Australia. The paper ends with a summary and short section of conclusions.

HISTORICAL DEVELOPMENT

Long distance and hence intercity transport development in Australia has essentially been determined over time by the interaction of available technology with the geographical characteristics of the continent. Although Australia is about the same size as the United States of America, it is largely an arid continent. Humid areas are limited to the monsoonal north and narrow coastal strips along the east and south-east coasts, and the south-west of Western Australia. These latter areas are those where initial settlement took place and, to a large extent, has remained.

The early settlements were very widely separated, partially because of a relative lack of good natural harbours along the temperate humid coastlines. They grew into important trading centres and ports, but never became self-sufficient and remained entrepots for one and a half centuries, exporting the produce of and distributing imports to their relatively drier hinterlands. As agricultural and pastoral practices were adapted to the environment this trade grew and the cities with it. In these times coastal shipping services provided virtually all intercity passenger and freight services.

The outcome of this development was the establishment of six independent colonies, essentially widely separate city states with vast sparsely populated hinterlands. Even now, some 60 per cent of all Australians reside in the six State capitals. With few exceptions, cities outside them are small by world standards as shown in Table 1. Despite Australia's image as a rural nation, 86 per cent of Australians lived in urban areas in 1973.

The first railways were constructed by private compa-

nies in the 1850s but were very soon relinquished to the State governments for financial reasons. They gradually extended from each of the colonial capitals into the hinterlands, particularly between 1880 and 1920. For various reasons, alternate States chose different track gauges.

Table 1 - Size of Australian cities as at 30 June 1973

City	Population
Sydney *	2 874 380
Melbourne *	2 583 900
Brisbane *	911 000
Adelaide *	868 000
Perth *	739 200
Newcastle	357 770
Wollongong	205 780
Canberra +	185 000
Hobart *	157 870
Geelong	126 500
Townsville	76 500
Gold Coast	74 500
Rockhampton	50 300

*	State Capital City
+	National Capital City
Source	Australian Bureau of Statistics, **Official Year Book of Australia,** No 60, 1974, pp 143-145

Intercapital city links were not fully established until 1917, when the transcontinental line linked the Western and South Australian systems. Other dates of completion of intercapital links were Sydney-Melbourne 1883, Brisbane-Sydney 1888, and Melbourne-Adelaide 1889.

A journey from Brisbane to Perth, a distance of about 5000 km, took a week and involved six train changes.

Since the Railway Standardization Agreement of 1949, the Commonwealth Government has assisted the State systems to develop standard gauge links by contributing 70 per cent of the cost. Currently all mainland State capitals are linked to the standard gauge system except Adelaine.

Until the 1920s, the road system in Australia was very primitive. With the development of private motor vehicles, demands arose for better roads and the system has gradually been improved with Commonwealth Government assistance to the States since 1926. In 1974 the Commonwealth Government passed the National Roads Act under which it provides 100 per cent funding for the construction of a system of national highways which resulted in all State capitals being linked by sealed roads in 1976. Despite these developments there were only 646 km of dual carriageway in the national highway system of 16,303 km in 1974. [1]

A vigorous air transport industry developed in Austra-

116

lia following the First World War. Initially it principally provided vital links to outback towns and pastoral stations, but has now become the major carrier of intercity passengers. Following World War II, a two airline agreement was initiated which limits interstate flights to two airlines. One is government owned and operated, while the other is a private enterprise. Other smaller airlines operate intrastate services. Air passenger services are a particularly important part of intercity transport in Australia, since the State capital cities are spaced about 1000 km apart.

The history of transport in Australia, therefore, largely revolves about cities acting independently as trade centres. Intercity and long distance passenger transport was initially relatively unimportant and was restricted to the sea mode. It has developed this century as State rail systems linked up, as roads have been improved, and as the airline industry has progressed, in that order. Concomitant with these structural changes has been the demise of intercity sea passenger transport which is now insignificant.

CURRENT SITUATION
The Size of the Task
In Australia, long distance passenger transport really means interstate travel between capital cities. As shown by Table 1, few cities other than State capitals are of significant size. It has already been demonstrated that population is only sparsely distributed outside urban areas. There are high volume flows in the Newcastle-Sydney-Wollongong, Melbourne-Geelong, and Brisban-Gold Coast corridors. These are relatively short and have many of the characteristics of intraurban travel. They will not be considered further in this paper.

An intercapital city corridor also exists between Sydney and Canberra. This corridor has a high density of passenger traffic, being only 300 km in length and joining the nation's largest urban complex to its administrative capital.

This corridor carries about 660,000 private car passengers in total a year, while comparable figures for the other modes are 500,000 for air, 36,000 for rail and 20,000 for express bus. Travel from Canberra to Melbourne by private car, air and rail is much less than half these levels. Compared with other intercapital city links, the Canberra-Sydney route is unique in terms of distance and, as will be shown later, modal split, and for this reason is also not included in this discussion.

Complete data concerning the size of the task of moving passengers by each mode between the major cities is not available. The geatest gap exists in private motoring statistics. Nevertheless, some preliminary estimates from various BTE studies are shown in Appendix Tables A to D.

Intercapital city passenger transport tasks are summarised in Table 2. These figures demonstrate that air is by far the most important of the commercially operated modes. Although figures are not available, private car travel is known to be the next most important carrier. Rail travel is of tertiary importance, but experience suggests that many passengers such as railway employees, school children and welfare recipients travel at concession rates. Express bus and sea intercity transport are insignificant, the latter having declined markedly over time.

Some indication of the possible relative importance of private road travel may be gained from considering the Sydney-Melbourne corridor. A study of this corridor indicates that private car through traffic in both directions per day consists on average of some 273 vehicles, with an average of about 2.0 occupants each. On this basis, the private road passenger task is about 199,000

passengers a year or 178 million passenger kilometers. Comparison with Appendix A to D shows that these levels are less than a quarter of those for the air task between Sydney and Melbourne and are comparable to those for rail.

Table 2 – Size of intercity passenger transport tasks 1972-73

Mode	Passengers	Passenger task
	Intercity	Intercity
	'000	'000,000 km
Domestic air	3 300	3 280
Non urban rail	800	960
Non urban private road vehicles	na	na
Non urban bus	220	150
Coastal sea [1]	28 [2]	47 [2]

[1]   1972
[2]   Includes round trip passengers that were not carried on cruise ships.
        Source: Australian Bureau of Statistics
na   Not available
Source   BTE preliminary estimates

Care should be exercised in applying this relationship to other city pairs. Distances vary and Perth, for example, was not linked across the Nullarbor Plain to the Eastern States by a sealed road until 1976. Furthermore, direct road and rail transport are not possible to Hobart because Tasmania is separated from the mainland by Bass Strait. Nevertheless, there is some indication that the model split is very roughly 60 per cent air, 20 per cent each for road and rail.

Intercapital city movements by air represent 40 per cent of all passengers carried by the domestic airlines and half of their task in terms of passenger kilometers. By contrast, such intercapital city movements only make up small proportions of the tasks of other modes. While intercapital city passengers are about a fifth of all coastal shipping passengers, the trades are overwhelmingly dominated by freight in both bulk and general forms. Apart from air, therefore, intercapital city transport by other modes is only of minor importance.

Market Structure
Previous discussion has emphasised the impact that geographical features have had upon the intercity transport networks of Australia. However, other factors have been and remain influential. Not the least of these is government intervention in Australian transport markets.

The Commonwealth Government of Australia is involved in many forms of activity that influence intercity transport. Governments normally tax, subsidise, regulate and make loans to transport activities but in addition to these functions the Commonwealth of Australia owns and operates large scale transport facilities and services. These include major airports, Trans Australia Airlines, the Australian National Line, air and sea navigation aids and railways in two States (South Australia and Tasmania) and the Commonwealth Territories. The Commonwealth also makes grants for the construction, improvement and maintenance of roads but is not directly concerned with road construction or road operations. It does however levy taxes on fuel and vehicles and encourages cooperation between State governments in matters affecting road use.

The most important mode for intercity passenger transport in Australia has been shown to be air. The Commonwealth controls the *air* mode through powers handed over to it by the States. An important instrument

117

of control is an agreement under which air transport on the major (trunk) routes is divided between two operators. These are the Commonwealth Government owned Trans Australian Airlines and the privately owned Ansett Transport Industries Ltd. The agreement was initiated in 1953 and has been maintained since under the Australian Airline Agreement Act 1958-73. This legislation essentially establishes a government controlled cartel on intercity air routes that is capacity controlled through the licensing of imports of aircraft.

The effects of this agreement are:

a. entry into the industry is effectively prohibited

b. output is held within limits

c. even competition of a non price nature is strictly limited, the difference between the two airlines being insignificant

d. price agreement between the airlines is basically automatic and government sanctioned

e. allocation of routes, flights and times, and hence revenues are also agreed to.

Despite these apparent disadvantages the agreement appears to be acceptable to the public on the basis of consumer protection. It may explain a somewhat higher level of fares than for comparable US services, despite the high load factors achieved in Australia by capacity control.

In Australia, *railways* are owned and operated by State and Commonwealth governments and, in some cases, by private companies. Private railways are mainly ancillary to the operations of mining companies hauling bulk minerals and account for almost half the national rail freight task. The Commonwealth Government operates the Australian National Railways principally in South Australia and Tasmania and the Northern Territory, while each of the mainland States operates its own systems. These regional monopolies are loosely coordinated as Railways of Australia for technical interchange and such matters as striking border transfer charges. Apart from this agreement, they operate separately, although, through the Australian Transport Advisory Council (ATAC), the development and implementation of co-ordinated policies is being pursued. The Commonwealth Government has also made grants to State systems mainly for track standardisation.

Many rail services in Australia run at a loss, often for social or political reasons. Hence, government railways in Australia incur large deficits and new investment is limited. To date deficits have been readily funded by the relevant treasuries and much investment in the form of rebuilding rolling stock and track takes place under the guise of maintenance.

Until recently, railways in Australia were protected to varying degrees from competition with road hauliers by State road taxes and haulage regulations. In Queensland they are still protected by regulation from intrastate shipping. In general, such regulations are being phased out.

Road construction and maintenance is the province of State and local governments. The Commonwealth Government only has the responsibility for a limited length of roads in the Territories. Nevertheless, through its control of taxes and loan and grant monies, the Commonwealth Government has a marked impact on the supply of and demand for road space. The Commonwealth also assumes full financial responsibility for national roads which comprise national highways and declared export and major commercial roads.

Australian State Governments have made various attempts to regulate commercial road transport in an endeavour to protect their railway systems. However, interstate traffic must be able to move unimpeded under Section 92 of the Australian Constitution, even to the extent that vehicle registration fees cannot be levied on vehicles operating interstate. The effects of such regulations are sometimes bizarre. For example, in some instances long distance buses can only pick up in one State or Territory and set down in another. On the whole, regulation of long distance road transport, which has never been particularly restrictive in Australia, is tending to be phased out.

Coastal shipping in Australia is also highly regulated. Australian coastal shipping is heavily protected from competition by ship import and voyage licensing regulations. Unless ships are Australian built and manned, they cannot operate freely in the coastal trades without the approval of the Commonwealth Department of Transport. As mentioned previously, the railways in Queensland are protected by regulation from intrastate shipping. Although coastal shipping is dominated by freight transport mostly in the bulk trades, multipurpose ships ply between Tasmania and the mainland.

In summary therefore, air, rail and sea passenger carriers are all highly regulated or government owned and operated in Australia. The road mode is controlled to a much lesser extent. Only the private motor vehicle moves absolutely freely and only then after paying quite high levels of duty, taxes and fees on vehicles, fuel, accessories and licences. While air and sea are essentially organised as government protected cartels, the railways operate as independent regional monopolies. Only road is truly competitive and even there State regulations and pricing policies have in the past inhibited the growth of intrastate commercial traffic in order to protect the railways. As railway deficits increase, less attention is being given to attempting to protect them by regulation and rather more to the rationalisation of their operations.

There is little doubt that in countries such as Australia with relatively widely separated centres of population leading to fairly modest intercity passenger flows and high per capita incomes, the dominant modes can be expected to be air and the private car. The market shares of the modes with lower fares are distorted by heavy subsidisation of passenger rail services relative to express buses. Because of the distances and low volumes involved, even high speed trains will not compete in the foreseeable future with air travel in Australia on intercapital city links. The future of the various modes appear to be reasonably accurately reflected in their current subsidy levels and market shares.

Factors Affecting Demand for and Supply of Transport

Few studies have been carried out on the markets for transport services in Australia. That work which has been done almost exclusively concentrates on air travel, presumably because a data base is available. Variables which affect the level of demand for transport services may be considered to consist of three groups. These are socioeconomic, level of service and attraction variables.

Socioeconomic variables consist of income levels, age, sex and occupations of travellers, and other user characteristics such as number of motor vehicles per family. Level of service variables include time per journey, costs, fares or charges, frequency and degree of comfort. Attraction variables include population measures, indicators of retail and service employment and distance travelled. Those Australian studies of demand which have been undertaken have used various combinations of these variables.

Studies of Australian intercity air travel have produced results which tend to confirm those obtained by research in other countries. They indicate that the market for air travel is relatively insensitive to changes in the levels of service and costs for other modes. Variations in demand are principally explained by population and income levels and real air fares. In these respects, the demand for air travel by older and higher income persons and business travellers is less sensitive than for younger and non business passengers with lower incomes. These latter distinctions demonstrate that the intercity air travel market is not homogeneous but composed of several strata of travellers with different characteristics. The apparent insensitivity of air travel demand to the costs of rail and road transport in studies undertaken to date may result from a high degree of stability in intermodal fare ratios over time.

The studies on air travel which have been carried out within the BTE returned elasticity estimates which averaged -1.0 for own fares and 2.0 for income. These estimates were based on time series, not cross-sectional analyses, and thus are averaged over income classes. Larger and lesser values would be expected for lower and higher incomes users respectively. Further, most elasticities would also be expected to become smaller over time.

The growth of air travel has averaged 10 per cent annually over the past fifteen years. A setback is currently being experienced and this situation has also occurred in the past. In each instance the drop-off in the rate of increase in demand has arisen in times of recession rather than following increases in the real level of fares. These facts emphasise the importance of the income effect.

The demand for intercapital city passenger transport by either of the other modes has not been investigated fully as yet. Nevertheless, they can be expected to respond in the same way as air with some minor differences. As mentioned previously, train passenger services appear to attract a significant proportion of individuals who simply prefer train travel over other modes. Some of these are entitled to concession fares, and to most of them time is largely immaterial, eg. welfare recipients or overnight or tourist travellers. Others may be fearful of road and or air travel. Intercapital city rail passenger demand should, therefore, be more inelastic with respect to fares and income than its air counterpart. In fact, demand has shown a slight decline in recent years despite rising population and income levels and falling real fares.

The situation with regard to road travel is not as clear due to limited data availability, except for several surveys that are either limited in scope or not very appropriate to the purpose of this paper. Nevertheless, since few single occupant vehicles were observed in these surveys on long trips, it appears that the cost per passenger of private car travel in comparison with that of other modes is an important factor. This contrasts with the results cited for air and postulated for rail. Little can be said about income effects upon the demand for private car travel since they cannot be isolated from those of other factors without econometric analysis. However, statistics indicate that levels of car ownership may approach saturation in the future. This suggests that the income elasticity of demand for this mode is diminishing over time.

The intercapital city sea passenger task is falling rapidly as air travel becomes more popular since it is relatively more expensive in terms of time and money combined. It seems most unlikely that this trend will be reversed.

In summary therefore, much more economic research is required concerning long distance passenger transport in Australia. At present few estimates of demand elasticities exist and these are confined to the air mode. However, before such efforts can be undertaken data must be collected. Because of the past and current nature of transport statistics, this will involve the conduct of continuous surveys of transport users. Plans already exist for the BTE to undertake a national travel survey.

Part 3 of this paper demonstrated that the structure of transport markets in Australia is such that supplies of domestic transport services are very much dependent upon government initiatives. The Commonwealth Government owns and operates all major airports and air navigation aids and limits the import of aircraft under a licensing system. Ports are owned and operated by State government authorities while the Commonwealth owns and operates the sea navigation aids and controls both the import of ships for coastal trades and particular journeys of foreign ships through licensing systems. Passenger carrying railways are all owned and operated by government authorities. Finally, a large part of the cost of motor vehicle purchase and operation consists of taxes while investment in roads, particularly in the national highways that link the cities, are also highly dependent upon federal fiscal initiatives.

Supplies of transport services therefore tend to shift in a once and for all stochastic manner as governments perceive community needs and as budgetary constraints allow. In effect therefore, demand creates its own supply in the government controlled sector of the Australian transport industry.

Investment proposals, particularly those requiring federal finance, are increasingly subject to economic scrutiny. This task has been performed by both the Commonwealth Bureau of Roads and the Bureau of Transport Economics which are currently in the process of being amalgamated. Benefits and costs are weighed against each other and where possible, intangibles are enumerated an their extent documented so that policy decisions are based upon the best possible information. Nevertheless, the analyses undertaken have usually been of a partial nature. A need to resort to more general equilibrium analysis is now being recognised.

THE FUTURE OF INTERCAPITAL CITY PASSENGER TRANSPORT IN AUSTRALIA

Because of the relative lack of analysis of Australian transport markets, the future of the industry cannot be discussed authoritively. Nevertheless, sufficient trends and other information exists to enable an outlook statement to be prepared.

Since 1945 there has been a marked increase in intercity passenger travel in Australia. Rates of growth have been fairly constant and consequently the temptation exists to simply extrapolate these trends into the future. However, due to recent changes in the rate of population growth and in the Australian economy, such a procedure would be untenable.

An intensive study of the Australian population has shown that the rate of growth may fall to only one per cent per annum in the future. From World War II until the late 1960s the Australian economy grew in a very stable fashion and, although income per head is still expected to rise at an average rate of $3^1/2$ per cent per annum, the past six years have seen volatile fluctuations which have not yet been controlled. In the immediate future Australia may therefore experience less consistent growth in GNP than historical precedent suggests.

The costs of transport may be expected to rise at a rate greater than the historical trend. A decrease of one per cent per annum in real terms could well be reversed to a one per cent increase. Such a change will depend particularly upon fuel prices and labour costs. Improving conditions for the Australian workforce can result in falling productivity per man if technology remains constant.

Taking these factors into account and assuming a price demand elasticity of -2.0, total non urban travel is expected to grow at an average rate of 6 per cent over the next decade. In the past, non urban travel has grown at a rate somewhat less than 10 per cent. The forecast therefore implies a reduction in the rate of growth of demand of some 40 per cent. This should also apply to intercapital city passenger transport.

It is expected that the airlines will absorb the bulk of the projected growth in intercity transport as they become more competitive for traffic and introduce more flexible pricing policies. The national highways program will improve intercity road links markedly and should also stimulate private car travel. On the other hand, express buses are only envisaged as holding their current share of the market while intercity rail and sea transport should continue to decline in absolute terms.

On the supply side, governments can be expected to upgrade airports and air facilities as demand increases. It has already been mentioned that considerable investment in intercity roads can be expected as the National Highways program advances. Rising demand for intercity freight should result in the further upgrading intercapital city rail links which will benefit passenger traffic. However, competition from the air and road modes should lead to continued reduction in the numbers of rail passengers on such links. Although further capital investment and expansion of port facilities is anticipated, it is unlikely that these will benefit passenger traffic in any way.

The outlook for intercapital city transport therefore indicates an expansion of passenger movements at a rate of about six per cent per annum, with growth concentrated in the air and private car modes.

SUMMARY AND CONCLUSIONS

Intercity transport in Australia is essentially intercapital city transport. All four major modes - air, rail, sea and road - are involved in the intercapital city passenger transport task. Their relative importance has changed markedly over time with the development of their technologies and investments in transport infrastructure. Currently the air mode dominates with sea and express bus being insignificant.

Transport markets in Australia are characterised by government intervention to the extent that only private car travel is not directly influenced by regulations of some sort, although regulation of road freight and passenger services is limited and tending to decline. As a consequence, the supply of transport services and especially infrastructure is largely dependent upon public as opposed to private investment programs.

Economic research into long distance passenger transport markets is limited and few estimates of demand elasticities exist. There is a need for more research in this area and also for work concerning the effects of regulation.

The outlook for intercity passenger transport in Australia indicates a slackening of growth from less than 10 to 6 per cent, principally as an effect of a lowering of population growth.

The paper demonstrates that transport development has been markedly effected by the geography and governments of Australia. The development of transport systems in the past has demonstrably affected the present. For instance, the adoption of different rail gauges by the colonies last century has had important effects on interstate rail transport.

Because transport services are mainly intermediate goods, the demand for them is derived from that for other goods and services. They are an input to virtually every source of human satisfaction, especially if pede-

strian activity is included as a mode. Non users as well as users benefit from the provision of transport and as such it generates considerable welfare spinoffs to society as a whole. Some examples are the benfits contributed to defence preparedness and emergency services and the enablement of trade. In many respects therefore, transport services resemble public goods.

A further aspect of transport is that, because of geographical differences in income and the varying resource costs of the modes, it has welfare distributional impacts. Finally, because of the massive investment necessary to much transport infrastructure, many undertakings such as railways are effectively natural monopolies.

These features of transport imply that governments will actively intervene in transport markets to avoid excess profit taking, to impose principles such as the user-beneficiary pays and to achieve social welfare goals.

The implications of the Australian experience, particularly for nations developing their transport systems, largely revolves around the need to undertake investment in infrastructure only after considering very long term potential developments. The growth and distribution of population and income are the main factors which will determine future demands and hence supply requirements. Resource costs relative to usage directly influence user charges in the longer term and hence patronage. In Australia changing incomes, shifts in population and technology have caused these ratios for the various modes to change their relative positions over time. The result has been the demise of sea and rail passenger transport to be betterment of air and road travel.

In poorer countries with high population desities, rail and water transport may have resource costs relative to patronage that will ensure their continued viability. However, the Australian case shows that as incomes rise and particularly if population is sparse, private road and air traffic are preferred to the other modes which become limited to long haul freight tasks.

The changes that have occurred in the Australian transport industry demonstrate a need for flexible long term planning by governments in developing transport infrastructure. Australia now has an over-developed inflexible rail system which has become largely redundant and which requires deficit financing to about $A500 million per annum. The degree of rationalisation required to overcome this problem poses considerable institutional and political problems.

Most economists will assert that the market works - in other words, supply tends to adjust towards demand. In transport, because of monopoly effects, scale of investment and government involvement, lags between adjustments can become extremely prolonged. The resulting situation can result in massive waste of resources and reduction of social welfare. Governments can only avoid such circumstances through co-operative flexible planning and policy adaption. Furthermore, development strategies must necessarily be based upon the best information available. There is therefore a need for continual research into transport problems and for increased international co-operation and interchange of information in this field.

FOOTNOTE
1. Commonwealth Bureau of Roads, **Report on Roads in Australia,** 1975, p 153.

City Pair		1972-73		1973-74		1974-75		1975-76	
		m. pass.	m.pass. km. *	m. pass.	m.pass. km. *	m. pass.	m.pass km. *	m. pass.	m.pass. km. *
Sydney	Melbourne	1.1	890	1.3	1020	1.4	1070	1.4	1100
	Brisbane	0.5	450	0.6	480	0.6	490	0.7	510
	Adelaide	0.2	240	0.2	260	0.3	320	0.3	390
	Perth	0.1	360	0.1	380	0.1	410	0.1	440
	Hobart	,,	50	,,	70	,,	60	,,	70
Melbourne	Brisbane	0.1	230	0.2	280	0.2	300	0.2	310
	Adelaide	0.3	220	0.4	260	0.4	270	0.4	290
	Perth	0.1	420	0.2	480	0.2	510	0.2	570
	Hobart	0.2	130	0.3	170	0.3	180	0.3	180
Brisbane	Adelaide	,,	40	,,	50	,,	60	,,	70
	Perth	,,	50	..	60	,,	70	,,	110
	Hobart	,,	10	..	10	,,	10	,,	20
Adelaide	Perth	0.1	170	0.1	210	0.1	230	0.1	280
	Hobart	,,	10	,,	20	,,	20	,,	20
Perth	Hobart	,,	10	,,	20	,,	20	,,	20
Total		3.3	3280	4.0	3780	4.1	4020	4.3	4380

Source: BTE estimates, preliminary figures
* Determined using distances between capital cities as shown in Table No. 157 in ABS, **Transport and Communication** 1971-72, Bulletin, No. 63
,, less than O.lm

City Pair		1972-73		1973-74		1974-75	
		m.pass	m.pass.km*	m.pass.	m.pass.km*	m.pass.	m.pass.km*
Sidney	Melbourne	0.3	280	0.3	310	0.3	270
	Brisbane	0.2	160	0.1	120	0.1	120
	Adelaide	,,	20	,,	70	,,	60
	Perth	,,	120	,,	160	,,	120
	Hobart	n.a.	–	n.a.	–	n.a.	–
Melbourne	Brisbane	,,	90	,,	90	,,	90
	Adelaide	0.1	100	0.2	140	0.2	150
	Perth	,,	130	,,	160	,,	160
	Hobart	n.a.	–	n.a.	–	n.a.	–
Brisbane	Adelaide	,,	10	,,	10	,,	10
	Perth	,,	10	,,	20	,,	20
	Hobart	n.a.	–	n.a.	–	n.a.	–
Adelaide	Perth	,,	40	,,	110	,,	120
	Hobart	n.a.	–	n.a.	–	n.a.	–
Perth	Hobart	n.a.	–	n.a.	–	n.a.	–
Total		0.8	960	0.9	1190	0.9	1120

* Determined using distances between capital cities as shown in Table No. 157 in ABS, **Transport and Communications** 1971-72, Bulletin, No. 63.
,, less than 0.1m.
n.a. not applicable
Source: BTE estimates, preliminary figures.

Appendix Table C - intercapital city passenger movements by express bus: 1975-76

City Pair		'000 passengers	m.pass.km.*
Sydney	Melbourne	60	30
	Brisbane	40	30
	Adelaide	20	20
	Perth	,,	,,
	Hobart	n.a.	–
Melbourne	Brisbane	20	20
	Adelaide	40	20
	Perth	,,	,,
	Hobart	n.a.	–
Brisbane	Adelaide	,,	,,
	Perth	,,	,,
	Hobart	n.a.	–
Adelaide	Perth	20	30
	Hobart	n.a.	–
Perth	Hobart	n.a.	–
Total		220	150

* Determined using distances between capital cities as shown in Table No. 157 in ABS, **Transport and Communications,** 1971-72, Bulletin, No. 63.
,, less than 10,000 passengers, or 10m pass.km.
n.a. not applicable
Source: BTE estimates, preliminary figures.

Appendix Table D - intercapital city passenger transport by sea: 1972 to 1975

City Pair		1972		1973		1974		1975	
		'000 pass.	m.pass. km. *	'000 pass.	m.pass. km. *	'000 pass.	m.pass. km. *	'000 pass.	m.pass. km. *
Sydney	Melbourne	9.4	9.9	5.6	5.9	4.4	4.7	1.9	2.0
	Brisbane	2.7	2.5	4.5	4.1	2.9	2.7	2.5	2.3
	Adelaide	1.0	1.8	0.5	1.0	0.3	0.5	0.2	0.3
	Perth	3.3	13.0	1.8	7.3	1.3	5.3	0.9	3.7
	Hobart	7.3	8.6	7.3	8.5	6.7	7.8	5.8	6.7
Melbourne	Brisbane	1.4	2.7	1.6	3.1	0.6	1.1	0.6	1.1
	Adelaide	0.3	0.3	0.3	0.3	0.4	0.4	0.2	0.2
	Perth	1.9	5.8	0.9	2.9	1.7	5.3	0.8	2.4
	Hobart	0.1	0.1	,,	,,	0.2	0.2	,,	,,
Brisbane	Adelaide	0.1	0.1	,,	,,	,,	,,	,,	,,
	Perth	,,	0.2	,,	0.2	,,	0.1	0.1	0.5
	Hobart	,,	0.1	–	–	,,	0.1	0.1	0.2
Adelaide	Perth	0.6	1.4	0.1	0.2	,,	0.1	0.1	0.3
	Hobart	–	–	0.3	0.4	–	–	,,	,,
Perth	Hobart	,,	,,	,,	,,	,,	,,	,,	0.1
Total		28.1	46.5	22.9	33.9	18.6	28.3	13.3	19.8

Source: BTE estimates, preliminary figures.
* Determined using distances between capital cities as shown in Table No. 157 in ABS, **Transport and Communication** 1971-72, Bulletin, No. 63.

National Traffic Planning in Developed Countries - Taking the Federal Republic of Germany as an Example

by

H. J. HUBER

Federal Ministry of Transport, Federal Republic of Germany

The co-operation among scientists, administrative experts, and politicians in the field of traffic and transport has become increasingly closer during the past decades. The reason for this is, on the one hand, that the science of transport and communications has consolidated and the white patches in its "territory" have become smaller. It is in a better position today to offer practice-related solutions. On the other hand, administration and politics have to deal with much more complex situations than was formerly the case. It does no longer suffice to consider only the individual mode of transport, but the transport system must be looked at in its entirety. In addition to that, the interrelations between the transport sector and other sectors - let me mention as examples only the sectors economy, regional planning, and environment protection - must be given more attention.

This development has in some way formed all those involved in this process. Today administrative experts as well as politicians are much more open-minded vis-à-vis scientific problems than they used to be in the past. In some ways reproaches have even been expressed to the effect that transport-policy decisions were far too much tied to the results of scientific investigations - in the case in hand cost-benefit analyses. On the other hand, science offers nowadays more assistance for the solution of administrative and political questions than formerly.

I will restrict myself in this paper to the co-operation between science and administration in traffic infrastructure planning, more precisely in the planning of long distance traffic routes, which are the direct responsibility of the German Federal Government.

In the Federal Republic of Germany the planning of long distance traffic routes is characterized in the past ten years by progressive integration. It developed from object planning to programme planning for individual modes of transport and from there to comprehensive planning of all traffic routes which the Federal Government is responsible for, the so-called Federal traffic infrastructure planning.

The investive part of the transport budget of the Federal Republic of Germany was, up to the fifties, not much more than the sum of the amounts required for the individual projects together with the considerations justifying these projects. With road construction becoming more and more important, programme planning in the present sense was introduced. The so-called first development plan for the Federal trunk roads was completed in 1959 and covered a period of twelve years.

The necessity of a co-ordination of the traffic route planning of all modes of transport had already been pointed out during the 1950s. As we all know the development of traffic, first in the communal sphere, reached a stage which required planning as well as measures that were not restricted to one mode of transport alone but would cover all modes of transport. The experiences of

the communities led, in connection with the intention of a better harmonization of regional planning and planning in special fields, to the first attempts at master traffic plans at regional level and the level of the Federal Laender. A report of experts on the improvement of transport conditions in cities of 1964 contained the explicit recommendation to draw up master traffic plans for towns, regions, and the Federal Laender.

Today many towns in the Federal Republic of Germany have set up traffic infrastructure plans which comprise all modes of transport. Their methodology meets the high standard which can be expected in developed countries today. At the level of the Federal Laender the master traffic plan of the Land Northrhine-Westphalia, which appeared in 1970, has set up important standards.

A traffic infrastructure plan comprising all traffic routes in the responsibility of the Federal Government was not begun before the end of the sixties, however. Its result was the Federal traffic infrastructure plan first stage submitted to Parliament in 1973.

The four main characteristics of integrated programme planning are the application of uniform *forecasts* and investment *objectives* as well as uniform *assessment* and *financing* of all projects. These requirements have not yet all been fulfilled in the Federal traffic infrastructure plan first stage.

The events in 1973 in the field of energy policy and lasting changes in world economy have strongly affected the growth, the extent, and the structure of overall economic production in the Federal Republic of Germany and in many other parts of the world. A decrease in the population must also be reckoned with in the long run.

Both developments produce consequences for the economy, the finances, and the demand for transport.

For these reasons the Federal traffic infrastructure plan first stage had to be updated during the period 1974-76. This updating did not only take into account the changed demographic and economic development, it even went in its methodology beyond the first stage of the Federal traffic infrastructure plan.

The planning of the traffic routes which the Federal Government is responsible for extends over a period of twenty years. It is subdivided into two periods of five years each and one period of ten years. The four-year planning period of the German financial plan progresses within the two 5-year periods from year to year. It is thus a combined system, consisting of two fixed 5-year programmes and supplemented by a progressing 4-year programme, which is updated annually.

The long-term plan comprises those projects which might be carried out within a period of twenty years. The long time is necessary for the preparation of the project itself, but also communal and regional land use planning require such a long planning period. The inclusion of a project in this plan means that the Government basically intends to realize it; the project may be abandoned, however, if circumstances so require.

The inclusion of a project in one of the two 5-year plans, on the other hand, can already be regarded as a commitment by the Government, even if the realization of these programmes still turns upon the supply of sufficient funds. Such programmes over several years can - from the point of view of the buildings industry or of regional policy - be balanced more easily than annual plans. If the network as a whole is kept in mind, it is possible to create sensible intermediate conditions, so that investments will be of use even if the possibilities of financing deteriorate. Whereas economic reasons are determinant for the inclusion of a project in one of the two 5-year programmes or in the subsequent 10-year plan, it would hardly be sensible to establish an order of the projects contained in a 5-year plan according to their economy, as within such a relatively short period of time the progress of the preliminary work for actual construction work decides in the first place on the sequence in which construction is to begin. These aspects form, therefore, also the basis, when a project is to be included in the German financial plan or in the annual budget.

On account of the urgent problems in connection with the financing and the realization of the development of the traffic infrastructure, it seemed of first importance to establish the two 5-year programmes 1976-80 and 1981-85, when the Federal traffic infrastructure plan first stage was updated. The result was given the name "Koordiniertes Investitionsprogramm für die Bundesverkehrswege bis zum Jahre 1985" [*1]. Statements of the Government concerning projects beyond the year 1985 exist at present only in the sphere of road construction.

The establishment of the co-ordinated investment programme had to solve the task of structuring an investment volume of a total of 110,000 million DM in such a way, that means to select the projects proposed for realization, that they render the greatest possible overall economic benefit. Moreover, the objectives of regional planning and regional policy had to be taken into account. Furthermore, the investments in the railway network of the Deutsche Bundesbahn were intended to reduce the latter's deficit.

The total volume of investment of 110,000 million DM expected to be available had been estimated on the basis of assumptions concerning the development of the gross national product and the Federal budget. This is basically what we might call a "conservative" estimate. The analysis of the costs and benefits of the individual projects showed, however, that this financial volume will suffice for achieving in the transport policy objectives. A catalogue of objectives was set up as a pre-condition of an assessment of the projects proposed for construction. For various reasons the projects were evaluated with the aid of cost-benefit analyses. This means that the significance or the order of the objectives is expressed in the assessment parameters chosen. The establishment of a hierarchy of objectives was, therefore, not absolutely necessary for the achievement of the planning result.

The employment of a system of objectives offers the advantage, however, that certain benefit components can be assessed more easily, that aspects of regional policy or of economy of transfers can be more easily taken into consideration, and that it is easier to give weight to political influences or to control them. I suppose however, that the possibility of expressing one's political will, as it offers itself in the establishment of a system of objectives, is from a political angle just as unsatisfactory as the possibility of influencing the assessment parameters of a cost-benefit analysis.

We decided, despite the afore-mentioned limitations,

to have the bases of a system of objectives and an objective oriented assessment procedure worked out scientifically [2]. The result of the research offers above all possibilities to derive a system of objectives for the transport sector from a system of objectives comprising all sectors of society. The employment of electronic data processing does not only facilitate the establishment of the system of objectives and assessment itself, the result, has moreover, numerous possibilities in its application to demonstrate the influences of alternative political or regional weighting on the order of the projects.

The second step in the planning was the analysis of the existing traffic system in regard to the achievement of the planning objectives. Such explanations occupy much room in many traffic infrastructure plans. Sometimes one cannot help feeling that these extensive analyses serve more the expert's better understanding of the problem than the administration's. When planning is conceived as a continuous process, the scope of such "condition analyses" can be smaller. Just as important as the analysis of the initial state is, in my opinion, the analysis of the change of conditions effected by a project or programme that has been realized, in other words - an ex-post economic analysis. This "ex-post economic analysis" in traffic route construction today mainly consists in stating the length of traffic route built and the amounts spent. We must endeavour to come to such a point, however, and conduct more and more ex-post cost-benefit investigations. Only in this way will we be able to escape the danger of attributing effects to projects, which they do not have, or of overlooking effects that are significant.

The determination of possible measures and the development of strategies for the improvement of the traffic network - which I wish to mention here as the third step in the planning - is often considered to be exclusively the concern of the administration. This has certainly to do with the fact that very often subordinate bodies submit projects to a central planning body or prepare them for the latter. But the backing by research is important also in this planning step, at least as long as the methods of dynamic investment planning have not yet been developed to such a degree as to allow to take the frequently occurring complementary and substitutive effects among the various traffic projects into account at justifiable expenditure. Thus it is necessary to find simplified methods for the practicable definition of projects and the determination of complementary and substitutive effects. The Federal Republic of Germany possesses a dense traffic route network. The purpose of most projects is to improve this network locally. Apart from that there are projects, however, which must be seen in the wider context of a system still to be established. The autobahn network in the Federal Republic had been planned as a system and it really is a system today. The new construction and improvement of railway lines for speeds up to 250 km/h seems to signalize a similar development in the railway sector. Approximately a year ago the Government of the Federal Republic of Germany gave the Deutsche Bundesbahn the green light for the construction of a new line of about 110 km length between Mannheim and Stuttgart. The line is being built with funds from the Federal Government. We must be aware of the fact that the new construction or the improvement of a railway line can bring full advantage only if it is accompanied by a certain improvement in the whole network. Advantages for the users and thus also an increase in the demand due to an enhancement of the attractiveness will occur only after a certain threshold of advantage has been passed. Moreover, the employment of rolling stock suitable for higher speeds will only pay, if the overall demand has reached a certain level. Also in road construction the summation of measures occasions effects which the individual project does not have, e.g. changes in the modal split in passenger and goods transport.

These system effects of some investments make it necessary in the planning to evaluate not only individual projects but also investments strategies. We have carried out such a strategic study in the Federal Republic of Germany, in which a delimitation between rail traffic and domestic air traffic was made [3]. I think it is necessary to increasingly conduct such strategic studies in the future.

The planning of the Federal traffic routes is based on a forecast of the demand for transport of the German Institute for Economic Research [4]. In this forecast the expected traffic distribution in passenger and in goods transport among 79 planning regions within the Federal Republic of Germany and 15 regions abroad have been established for the year 1990. The demand has been subdivided into modes of transport as well as into purposes of travel in passenger transport and into twelve groups of goods in goods transport. This forecast of the demand for transport is founded on an estimate of the development of the population and the economy, which above all takes into account the changes in world economy that have occurred since 1973.

The traffic forecast is based on the assumption that existing development trends will continue - it is thus a status-quo forecast. It was assumed, among other things, that the State will not essentially interfere with the competition among the various modes of transport, that the rate relations among the individual modes of transport will approximately remain as they are, that private transport in city centres is subjected to limited restrictions, and what, owing to environment protection as well as rising oil prices, private transport has to reckon with rising costs. The forecast comes to the result that by 1990 the transport performance in passenger transport will rise by approximately 30% and in goods transport by approximately 40%. This would mean that above all in passenger transport the annual growth rates would be below those during the past 15 years.

Furthermore, the investigation comes to the conclusion that the shares of the individual modes of transport in the total demand will not vary so strongly any more as was the case in the past and that above all the railways will be able to stabilize their share in the market. This is especially true for passenger transport in urban agglomerations, where the supply of rail transport is being improved. For rural areas, on the other hand, a relatively stronger increase in private transport as well as a shift from rail transport to motorcoaches was assumed.

The transport demand of the railways and of shipping could be directly assigned to the railway and waterway networks, since these networks are comparatively widemeshed, so that the calculated volumes of traffic reflect the amount of traffic on railway lines and waterways in passenger trips and goods-tons per year with sufficient accuracy. The construction of new lines and the improvement of existing ones for higher speeds enable us to expect considerable shortening of travel times in long distance travel by rail. This will lead to increased demand of the railways, which has not yet been included in the forecast. The increase was taken account of by adding a certain percentage of traffic. There is considerable uncertainty as regards the estimation of such gains which are due to attractiveness, as no experience has hitherto been made in this field in the Federal Republic of Germany, and it is doubtful whether experiences made in other countries can be transferred to the Federal Republic.

To assess the road construction measures with their effects on for the most part small areas, the rough regional division into 79 regions did not suffice. You know the problem that for the evaluation of planned traffic routes very often forecasts are required which refer to very small regional units, whereas on the other hand such forecasts tend to be increasingly unsharp. For road traffic a forecast very largely disaggregated as to space was set up, which starts out from approximately 1,100 regional units for the Federal territory [5], [6].

It is based as to the number and the regional distribution of the population and gainfully employed persons on the above mentioned forecast of the German Institute for Economic Research [4]. The results of the above rough forecast and those of the regionally more differentiated forecast for road traffic have been adapted to each other. It was not possible, however, to achieve full adaptation, owing to different definitions and delimitations. There are two scientific schools in this field in the Federal Republic of Germany, whose teachings can only be very slowly reconciled. These difficulties of understanding in the scientific sphere have quite concrete effects on the practice of planning.

The central task within the framework of the planning was the evaluation of the proposed measures. The special problem was not only the evaluation by a uniform and comparable standard of the very different measures taken with the individual modes of transport, railways, road, and waterways, but also to deal with the great number of projects in such a short time with only few personnel. In addition to that, the evaluation procedure should be reconstructible. It should take the legal and organizational conditions of the individual modes of transport into account and should apart from results concerning the relative priority of the projects also furnish such with respect to their "absolute" economic efficiency. These demands could largely be met by an evaluation with the aid of simplified cost-benefit analyses. They have the additional advantage that the reference to monetary quantities exerts strong pressure on planners to seek for low-cost solutions.

In view of the great number of road construction measures, the benefits were in the first instance determined by means of a point evaluation process and compared with the costs of the measure represented in terms of money [7]. The point-cost relationships were then converted into benefit-cost relationships. The key for these conversions could be determined from a random sample of projects.

In all projects a difference was made between the benefits of the construction agency concerned and traffic and non-traffic benefits. Traffic benefits were here those savings in operating costs and travel time which are directly connected with the traffic performance, as well as reduced accident costs and environmental nuisances due to noise and exhaust gases. Any effects of the projects on the regional economic structure, regional planning, and economics of water supply and distribution were considered as non-traffic benefits. Jobs that were created or transferred on account of the measures , were counted as benefits only if they were situated in economically weak areas. The objectives of regional planning were taken into account in that way that the benefits brought about by the projects were regionally weighted the higher, the lower was the degree of the development in the field of traffic of the region concerned and its connection with other regions [8].

Such regional weightings are of great significance on the political level, as the territorial bodies naturally endeavour to get as much as possible for their respective area. In the evaluation of road construction measures alternative weightings were therefore applied to those benefit components which contain the contributions of the projects to the improvement of the regional structure and the regional economic structure. The Federal Laender participating in the discussion had thus the opportunity to give their vote for one of the weighting alternatives and in this way to take part in the decision on the extent of the preferential treatment accorded to areas whose development is below average. I think that here a promising possibility has been found to bring pluralistic interests in a planning process to bear. The method to evaluate road construction measures was developed in close co-operation with scientists and specialists of the administration; it would not have been feasible without electronic data processing.

The result of the evaluation was a priority list of most projects of the railways, the waterways, and in road construction. The financial means to be expected were in no way sufficient for the realization of all projects. Besides considerable amounts had to be designated for the completion of projects under construction or which have already been fixed by contract. It had moreover to be taken into account that for existing traffic routes replacement of investments are becoming increasingly necessary. The estimate of the replacement of investments starts out from the previous investment activity which is reflected in the structure of fixed assets according to years; the individual components of the fixed assets, such as earthworks, structures, superstructure, and equipment, were depreciated by the straightline method in accordance with their respective service life [9]. The available financial volume which remains after the deduction of these amounts was compared with the accumulated investment volume of the priority list. The result of this comparison was that only such projects will be realized whose benefit-cost relationship exceeds a certain volume.

As a result of the investigations it was demonstrated that the construction of Federal trunk roads should remain the focal point of investment activity also during the ten years to come, even if its share in the total investment volume will decrease somewhat in favour of railway transport. The share of the Federal waterways in the investments volume will remain approximately the same.

A traffic system is subject to constant change, if it is to adapt itself to changing social requirements. Planning is, therefore, a continuous task. In updating the planning, we will have to take into account not only changed initial conditions and objectives but also improved methods. I had already in the description of the planning process to some extent indicated the necessity of such improvements.

Let me also say some words on the motto of this conference, before I speak about further necessary improvements. You too will, no doubt, have thought about whether there is greater uncertainty in the field of transport today than in earlier decades and what this uncertainty might be. There are doubtless developments nowadays which render planning more difficult than it used to be: the technical development offers us a wider range of possibilities in traffic and transport; the demand for transport performance of the population and the economy have at the same time become more differentiated; the increasing significance of regional policy and environmental protection have on the whole further intensified the insertion of the transport sector in the development of society, and not least the citizen follows the development of the traffic system much more critically than formerly.

I suppose, however, that the intention was to express something else with this motto, namely a certain break in a hitherto fairly steady line of development. The past 25 years were characterized in the Federal Republic of Germany by a steady increase of road traffic. These growth rates will, there can be no doubt, be smaller in the future. We must part with those plans for the development of the road network which were set up in the past and which are to some extent exaggerated. Also the optimistic view that we would be able to fundamentally improve the traffic and environmental situation in our cities by an intensified development of public short-distance passenger transport has disappeared in view of the high deficits of the short-distance transport enterprises.

As far as the energy situatuion is concerned, our forecasts of the demand start out from rising mineral oil prices. We cannot say in how far the latter will not only affect the level but also the structure of the demand for traffic, for we know very little about that.

Road traffic has on the whole proved relatively stable in the economic ups and downs and we can assume that it will remain rather stable if structural changes in the economy occur. Moreover, in road construction even parts of major projects can in most cases be sensibly utilized. The risk in connection with road construction investments is, therefore, comparatively low.

It is different, however, with the railways and with trackbound vehicles of the new technologies. The use of part of a new line is not very promising normally. As I already mentioned, what greatly matters with the railways is the interaction of the elements in a system. This is especially true for an area with a polycentric structure, such as the Federal Republic of Germany. The demand for transport of the railways in passenger transport by rail many times forecast in the Federal Republic of Germany proved to be rather shortlived - apart from local developments. Goods transport by rail is subject to strong economic fluctuations, and it is very difficult to estimate the effects of shorter travel times on the demand for transport. In my opinion, the risk connected with the new construction or the improvement of railway lines is for these reasons higher than that connected with the construction of roads. Nevertheless, I think that the railways will have a chance not only in goods transport but also in passenger transport on the highly frequented lines. In the so-called co-ordinated investment programme for the Federal traffic routes until 1985, we have planned the new construction of two railway lines and the improvement of six other lines.

The work in connection with the Federal traffic infrastructure plan has shown various possibilities and necessities for methodical improvements, part of which concerns the sphere of forecasting. As I think to have observed, forecasts that have been set up to evaluate an individual project often have the drawback that they are not compatible with the development of the traffic in its totality in the country concerned. They tend to over estimate the influence of the project. More general forecasts which are in conformity with the economic and demographic development of the whole country, do à priori not have this disadvantage, but they are in most cases not capable of stating the influence of an individual project on the modal split or on the distribution of traffic. Moreover, they are often not sufficiently well subdivided regionally in order ot allow project-specific statements. Therefore, what we need are methods which make it possible to differentiate demand forecasts of a general type regionally and as to time, and to demonstrate in how far the demand for transport depends upon the project. Such methods are available for short-distance passenger transport. The corresponding methods for longdistance passenger transport are not sufficiently reliable, however, mainly because of inadequate data. The study of the causes of the modal split in long-distance passenger transport is, therefore, an urgent task. The models that have hitherto been developed, are mostly using aggregated data. My impression is that these models have reached a certain limit in their capacity of development. I hope that the elaboration of new models on the basis of disaggregated data will impart new impulses to the investigation in this field. The continuous ascertainment of behavioural patterns in passenger transport, within the framework of which approximately 1 million passenger trips were covered in a sample survey in the whole Federal territory since 1975, provides the data for the calibration of the models. There are also blank spaces in respect of the question of the capacity of railway lines. In road traffic we can rather precisely calculate beforehand how the expenditure in time and operating costs will change with increasing traffic volumes. In rail transport we know only little about the increase in the delay of trains due to an increasing volume of traffic on a line, and the loss of time for passengers and goods as a result of that. We are above all not in a position to quantify the reaction of passengers and shippers in the long term, if they find themselves faced with delayed and overcrowded trains. Although capacity bottlenecks occur only in few places in our railway network, the whole network is affected by them.

Another field of study is the interface between the areas "forecast" and "assessment". The project evaluation can meet today's requirements only through the employment of electronic data processing. This means for the area of forecast that the demand data for the "with" and "without" cases must be made available on data carriers. This is on account of the great number of projects, above all, a problem of quantity and expenditure. Methods must therefore be developed, which enable us to limit within an extensive traffic network the calculation of the distribution of traffic, the modal split, and traffic assignment to those parts of the network which are significantly influenced by the project under consideration. First moves to that effect have already been made.

Great progress has been made in the Federal Republic of Germany during the past years in respect of the question of an evaluation of investments in traffic routes. Now it is important to further standardize, formalize, and automate these methods. The bases of the evaluation must also be further investigated. It will above all be necessary to further examine the effects of new traffic routes on the regional economic structure. The evaluation of time savings should also be further studied, even if it is made in almost every cost-benefit study. With most road construction measures three quarters or even more of the benefits are time savings. The objective economic benefit on account of these time savings must be further analysed just as must the subjective benefit which they produce from the point of view of the road users.

The automation of the evaluation procedures does not take place for the sole purpose of reducing the expenditure in planning. It offers on the contrary new possibilities to let political bodies participate in the planning process. For the planning is to provide bases for decisiontaking and not the decisions themselves. The employment of electronic data processing makes it possible within a short time to demonstrate the effects of alternative evaluation parameters or alternative, regional weightings. It is only in this way that the political bodies are given the possibility to set the most important evaluation parameters according to their objectives.

The investigation of the above questions requires close co-operation between the sectors research, administration, and politics. This has already been practised in the Federal Republic in the past. This is why in this lecture I have mainly spoken of practical problems. Although I have concentrated wholly on the sphere of traffic route planning, I must say that research also plays an important role in regulatory policy. As an example of this I should like to mention a simulation model for the goods transport market in the Federal Republic of Germany, which is intended to reflect the reaction of buyers and suppliers to measures of regulatory policy, e.g. the regulation of capacities and interventions in price or tax policy. Such a model exists already for the sphere of containerizable goods.

Allow me in conclusion to say some words on the international co-operation in the field of traffic research. The Federal Republic of Germany has concluded agreements on the mutual exchange of research results with many countries. In addition to that, there is active multilateral exchange of research results especially within the framework of the ECMT. With the so-called Action 33 the OECD, the ECMT, and the EC jointly worked out a prospective study of European long distance passenger transport for the years 1985 and 2000. A corresponding study for goods transport is being prepared. Such studies meet with considerable data problems, however, since the data of the individual countries are only very rarely comparable with one another. To investigate concrete projects, these demand forecasts must because of the rough regional subdivision be complemented by local studies.

Summing up, it can be said that the consulting traffic research will be faced with a wide range of tasks in the future. Their solution, which in many cases will only be possible through the co-operation between science and the administration, will not always be easy. In any case, however, the fields of research will be of high continuity and they will have a stimulating effect on science and will call for full personal initiative in the elaboration of solutions.

REFERENCES

1. Arnold, Gleissner, Huber: **Koordinierung der Verkehrswegeinvestitionen des Bundes in den Jahren 1976-85** (coordination of traffic infrastructure investments of the Federal Government during the period 1976-85). Internationales Verkehrswesen, No. 5, 1976.

2. Birreck, Klemp, Koelle, Richlmayer, Thieme: **Zielsysteme für die Bundesverkehrswegeplanung** (systems of objectives for Federal traffic infrastructure planning). Research report on behalf of the Federal Ministery of Transport, Berlin 1975.

3. Batelle, Dornier, Treuarbeit: **Untersuchung zur Beurteilung von Investitionen im Fernreiseverkehr der Deutschen Bundesbahn und im Luftverkehr der Bundesrepublik Deutschland bis 1980** (study in regard of the evaluation of investments in long-distance passenger transport of the German Federal Railways and in air transport within the Federal Republic of Germany until 1980). No. 40 of the publications of the Federal Ministry of Transport, 1973.

4. Deutsches Institut für Wirtschaftsforschung (German Institute for Economic Research): **Integrierte Langfristprognose für die Verkehrsnachfrage im Güter- und Personenverkehr in der Bundesrepublik Deutschland bis zum Jahre 1990** (integrated long-term forecast of the demand for transport in goods and passenger transport in the Federal Republic of Germany until 1990), Berlin 1975.

5. Mäcke: **Modellprognose der Entwicklung des Strassenverkehrs** (model forecast of the development of road traffic), 1975 (not yet published).

6. Steierwald: **Trendprognose der Entwicklung der Strassennetzbelastung** (trend forecast of the development of the volumes of traffic on the road network), 1975 (not yet published).

7. Bayer, Eckert, Niemand: **Verfahren und Durchführung der Massnahmenbewertung bei der Überprüfung des bedarfsplanes für die Bundesfernstrassen** (methods for and implementation of the evaluation of measures in reviewing the Federal trunk road requirement plan). Strasse und Autobahn, No. 3, 1976.

8. Fischer, Meyer, Moosmayer: **Vergleichende Bewertung von Verkehrswegeinvestitionen des Bundes** (comparative assessment of traffic infrastructure investments of the Federal Republic of Germany). Internationales Verkehrswesen, No. 1, 1977.

9. Deutsches Institut für Wirtschaftsforschung (German Institute for Economic Research): **Vorausschätzung der Ersatzinvestitionen für die Verkehrsinfrastruktur** (estimate of replacement of investments in the traffic infrastructure), Berlin 1975.

FOOTNOTE

* Co-ordinated investment programme for the traffic routes in the Federal Republic of Germany until 1985.

An equilibrium mode-split model of work trips along a transportation corridor

An equilibrium mode-split model of work trips along a transportation corridor

by

IBRAHIM HASAN

ANTTI TALVITIE

University of California, Berkeley

1. INTRODUCTION

Within the sphere of research associated with transportation planning, the problem of equilibration - one of solving a set of demand and supply (level-of-service) equations - has often been left untouched. This was so primarily because of the conceptual complexity of the problem and secondarily because of the high computational cost of implementing an equilibrium model. Thus, in many applications of transportation demand studies, some kind of supply inelasticity (to travel volumes) assumptions were made. And in those applications where congestion effects were felt to be significant enough to be decisive, the Incremental Assignment technique was invariably used. This technique is computationally quite inexpensive, but is ad hoc and has problems with convergence.

It is in the last decade or so that we begin to see an increased vigor in the development of equilibrium models. The seminal paper of Dafermos and Sparrow [1] can be identified as a turning point and the start of more mathematical analyses of the equilibration problem. For a unified approach to equilibration methodologies, viewed as solutions to an optimization problem, see, for example, the paper by Nguyen [5].

The new generation of iterative equilibrium models are, unfortunately, still quite expensive to use in modeling large transportation systems, and because of their highly aggregate nature, are unsatisfactory from the point of view of behavioral theories of travel demand such as that developed by McFadden [3], [4]. The object of this paper is to suggest a way in which an equilibrium model can be developed, whose components are a set of supply equations and a set of *disaggregate* mode-choice equations. We restrict our attention to the analysis of work-trip mode splits over a *transportation corridor*.

In view of the remarkable success of the applications of Scarf algorithm [6] in computing economic equilibria (see, for example, Shoven and Whalley [8], [9]), we have cast the equilibration problem not as an optimization problem, but as a problem of computing the fixed point of some appropriate mapping.

Section 2 details the components of the model. Section 3 summarizes the key concepts involved in the Scarf algorithm, and its application to the model developed in section 2. In section 4 we indicate briefly our limited experience in applying the model to an actual transportation planning problem.

2. A REFORMULATION OF THE EQUILIBRATION PROBLEM

2.1 Segmentation of the Corridor

Let us begin by reiterating the problem at hand. Given the information on home and work locations; some socioeconomic characteristics which are assumed to completely describe the utility-maximizing workers; the distribution of tastes among these workers; the characteristics of the transportation corridor along which home and work locations are scattered, predict the equilibrium work-trip flow pattern[1] along the corridor. Such a result, being an indispensible prerequisite for any cost-benefit analysis, hardly requires further elaboration as to its importance.

To reduce the number of "markets" where supply and demand have to be equilibrated, we divide the corridor into large segments, each of which consists of several traffic zones. The segment boundaries should be chosen along the most natural geographic lines perpendicular to the "axis" of the corridor (for example, highway intersections might be suitable points through which such boundaries pass). Figure 1 gives a schematic representation of the segmentation of the I-580 corridor in the San Francisco Bay Area.

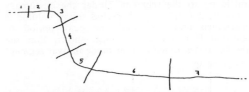

Figure 1 - Schematic Segmentation of the I-580 Corridor in the San Francisco Bay Area

2.2 Travel Demand

Let us assume that each of the workers in our system chooses his mode of transportation to and from work so as to maximize his utility (minimize his discomfort). The individual has a utility function that can be written in the form

$$u(y,t) = v(y,t) + \varepsilon(y,t) \tag{1}$$

where we have assumed that utility depends only on travel time t and an index of socioeconomic characteristics y. This assumption is artificial and is made only for the sake of ease of exposition.

Adding monetary cost of travel and other variables into equation (1) is straight forward, and will have the sole effect of clouding up the structure of the problem. $v(y,t)$ can be interpreted as the "representative" taste of the population, and $\varepsilon(y,t)$ is a stochastic term representing taste variation among individuals. As is usually done in empirical work, we hypothesize a linear dependence of v on y and t:

$$v(y,t) = ay + bt \qquad (2)$$

a and b being coefficients which can be, and have been, we assume in this paper, statistically estimated. Under the assumption that the values $\varepsilon(y,t)$ are independently identically distributed with a Weibull distribution, McFadden [3] has shown that the probability of individual i choosing mode m from a common alternative choice set M is given by the multinomial logit model

$$P_m^i = \frac{\exp(bt_m^i + ay_m^i)}{\sum_{\ell \in M} \exp(bt_\ell^i + ay_\ell^i)} \qquad \begin{array}{l} i=1,\dots,I \\ m=1,\dots,M \end{array} \qquad (3)$$

where I is the total number of individuals in the system, and M denotes both the total number of modes available to any individual, and the alternative choice set which is common to all individuals in the system.

2.3 Supply Equations

Following the convention in transportation literature, we distinguish between two types of supply relations or relations between travel times and volumes over streets and highways: main-mode supply relations and access/egress supply relations. We derive main-mode supply relations for each mode over each *segment* in the corridor, by either extending the single bottleneck formulation of May and Keller [2] and Small [10] to a collection of roads or by an aggregation of individual road performance characteristics, a technique which utilizes Wardrop's [12] first principle and amounts to horizontal (vertical) summation of parallel (consecutive) links' "travel time vs. volume" curves.

To use the technique of May-Keller-Small, we need to identify the "bottleneck" for the segment as a whole and for each main modes of travel. We thus derive a restraining capacity for each segment and main mode which "meters" the traffic on to the segment. Under the customary assumption that the peak period travel volume is distributed uniformly over the peak period of duration P hours, it has been shown that the *average* travel time (x_{jm}) for mode m over segment j is given by:

$$x_{jm} = \max\left[0, \frac{B_{jm}}{C_{jm}} - 1\right] \frac{P}{2} + T_{jm}$$

where $\qquad B_{jm} = \sum_{n=1}^{M} \gamma_n^m D_{jn}$.

B_{jm} is a weighted sum of travel demands D_{jn} of all the M modes in segment j, the weights γ_n^m being the "equivalence" factors of the modes; C_{jm} is restraining capacity of segment j; and T_{jm} is the "free-speed" travel time of mode m in segment j.

As an example, consider the following model with three modes:

$m = 1$: Auto
$m = 2$: Express Bus
$m = 3$: Local Bus

Assume that the modes Auto and Express Bus use freeways and the mode Local Bus uses arterial roads. Then, the travel time for mode 1 over freeway segment j is given by:

$$x_{j1} = \max\left[0, \frac{B_{j1}}{C_{j1}} - 1\right] \frac{P}{2} + T_{j1}$$

where

$$B_{j1} = \gamma_1^1 D_{j1} + \gamma_2^1 D_{j2} + \gamma_3^1 D_{j3}$$

and

$\gamma_1^1 = 1$

$\gamma_2^1 = $ the number of car-equivalents of an Express Bus

$\gamma_3^1 = 0$

γ_3^1 is zero since Local Bus does not use freeways and hence does not affect the travel time on Auto. It should be noted that since Express Bus also uses freeways, the travel time for Express Bus, x_{j2}, is given identically by x_{j1}: [3] $x_{j2} \equiv x_{j1}$.

The second alternative, the aggregation of individual road link supply relations of the segment into a segment relation, is a generalization of the single bottleneck concept of a segment. More realistically, there are more than one bottleneck per segment. Each "road", in fact, has a capacity beyond which travel time shoots up very fast. Thus, we have, for each segment of the corridor, a structure consisting of roads with different supply relations. For example, a segment might have the following structure of roads.

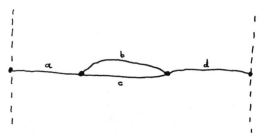

Figure 2. A Segment Made Up of Four Roads a, b, c, d Each Characterized by its Own Time-Volume Curve x_a, x_b, x_c, x_d

Under the assumption that conditional on any chosen mode, a worker will pick the shortest path available, it is easy to see that Wardrop's first principle holds. Thus, two parallel roads characterized by two different supply curves x_a, x_b is equivalent to one road characterized by a supply curve x_c which is a horizontal sum of the supply curves x_a and x_b. Similarly, two roads in sequence is equivalent to a single road whose supply curve is a vertical sum of the two original curves. Figure 3 illustrates these cases.

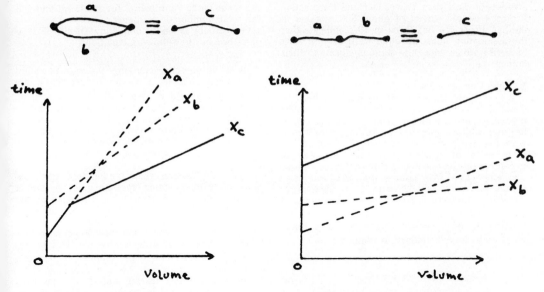

(i) **Parallel Roads**   (ii) **Roads in sequence**

Figure 3 - Note that x characterizes road i

We can apply such simple schemes sequentially and reduce even very complex structures into a single "road" characterized by a single supply relation. In this way, we can derive *segment* supply relations for all segments and modes (the same kind of arguments can be used to construct segment relations for guideway modes). For example, denoting the operation in Figure 3 (i) by $x_a \textcircled{P} x_b = x_c$ and that in Figure 3 (ii) by $x_a \textcircled{S} x_b = x_c$, we derive an expression for the segment supply curve for the segment shown in Figure 2, in terms of its component road supply curves x_a, x_b, x_c, x_d, as follows:

$$x = x_a \textcircled{S} (x_b \textcircled{P} x_c) \textcircled{S} x_d$$

To contrast the two formulations of segment supply functions, consider a segment that consists of two roads in sequence with supply curves x_a and x_b. Now the single-bottleneck approach identifies the restraining capacity which, in this case, happens to be in road b, and assumes that there is no capacity restraint in a. Hence, a is characterized by a constant "freespeed" travel time, T_a, and the segment supply curve is derived by a vertical addition of T_a and x_b. We compare this to the result of the Wardrop scheme of vertically adding x_a and x_b, in Figure 4.

We thus see that in the range of travel volumes from zero to C_a, the single "bottleneck" and "multiple bottleneck" formulations give identical travel times. Beyond C_a the travel times are different, the multiple bottleneck travel time being larger than the single bottleneck travel time. Which one is correct? The answer is not clear. If the two consecutive road links are independent, as in the case of a low volume arterial street governed with unsynchronized traffic signals, then the multiple bottleneck formulation (every signal) is approximately correct. However, if the consecutive links are not independent, as in the case of freeways, then the single bottleneck version is approximately correct. In real world situations both type of cases occur intertwined and it is an empirical question which of the two schemes is better. The single bottleneck formulation is very attractive because of its simplicity and small data requirements. Its success will depend in a large measure on whether the delays in a segment of a corridor are due to congestion or traffic control devices (traffic lights, stop signs, etc.) normally found on arterial streets. Small [10] has used the point bottleneck model to a freeway segment several miles long with apparent success. The prevalence of signals and stop signs and other disturbances on arterials suggest that perhaps a "marriage" between the two methods is the best solution.[4]

An individual's path from home to work (and vice versa) is usually broken down into an access component, a main-mode component and an egress component. We assume that the access[5] part of the trip on any mode will always be from home to the *nearest* "main-mode entrance" (highway entrance, bus station, and so forth) plus the trip from the main-mode exit *nearest* to the work location itself (the trip home from work is dichotomized into access and main-mode in a similar fashion). This assumption eliminates the need to explicitly model each worker's choice probabilities of main-mode entrances available to him. Checks made on

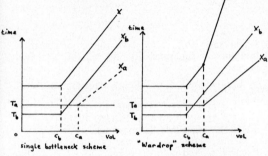

single bottleneck scheme   "Wardrop" scheme

Figure 4

a subset of the Urban Travel Demand Forecasting Project's sample survey of about 800 workers in the San Francisco Bay Area in 1975 indicate that the assumption holds up quite well; around 85% of BART riders chose the stations closest to their homes.

2.4 The Complete Model

We are now almost ready to put together our demand and supply formulations into a complete model. However, note a crucial problem in equilibration: while demand is in terms of individual work-home trip variables, our supply formulation is in terms of segment variables. One way to overcome this inconsistency is to make the following assumption. We assume that the congestion effects due to a vehicle[6] entering a segment of length L_j a distance l_{ij} from the boundary towards which it is going, is equivalent to those due to a fraction δ_{ij} of a vehicle traversing the segment completely from boundary to boundary.

$$\delta_{ij} = \frac{l_{ij}}{L_j} \tag{4}$$

What we are assuming basically is that a lot of congestion over a part of the segment is equivalent to a milder congestion over the whole of the segment. Our assumption enables us to aggregate individual demands for the various modes into segment demands for all modes.

$$D_{jm} = \sum_{i=1}^{I} \delta_{ij} p_m^i \tag{5}$$

Note further that

$$t_m^i = \sum_{j=1}^{J} \delta_{ij} x_{jm} + \bar{x}_m^i \tag{6}$$

where x_{jm} is the travel time over segment j by mode m; $\bar{x}_m^i$ is the access travel time, which depends only on the individual's characteristics (i.e., where his home and work locations are) and

$$p_m^i = \frac{\exp[b(\sum_{j=1}^{J} \delta_{ij} x_{jm} + \bar{x}_m^i) + ay_m^i]}{\sum_{l \in M} \exp[b(\sum_{j=1}^{J} \delta_{ij} x_{jl} + \bar{x}_l^i) + ay_l^i]} \tag{7}$$

$$D_{jm} = \sum_{i=1}^{I} \delta_{ij} p_m^i \tag{5}$$

$$x_{jm} = S_{jm}(D_{j1}, \ldots, D_{jM}; T) \tag{8}$$

$$\bar{x}_m^i = \bar{S}_m(w^i; D_{j_i 1}, \ldots, D_{j_i M}; T) \tag{9}$$

Equations (7), (5), (8), (9) hold for   i=1,...,I
                                       j=1,...,J
                                       m=1,...,M

the main mode "entrances" for mode m; and J is the total number of segments.

Our model is now completely specified. It is described by the following equations.

T is a vector characterizing the transportation system characteristics; j_i denotes the segment where access occurs; and w^i is a variable characterizing the work and home locations of individual i. Equation (8) is a representation of the result of the segment supply derivation in our previous section. Equation (9) can be derived, for example, in a way that parallels the approach of Talvitie-Dehghani [11].

Typically, however, there are hundreds of thousands of workers using the corridor so that a straight individual enumeration, as implied by the above model, becomes too cumbersome to perform. We are forced, therefore, to use only a sample of the whole population. One easy scheme is the following. Sample individuals at a rate Θ from the given trip table. Observe the sampled individual's home and work locations, his socioeconomic characteristics, and the nearest main-mode entrances and exits. From this information, we obtain:

$$\delta_{kj}; \bar{S}_m(w_j^k; \ldots; T); y_m^k \qquad \begin{array}{l} k=1,\ldots,K \\ j=1,\ldots,K \\ m=1,\ldots,M \end{array}$$

where K is the total number of sampled individuals, each of whom is identified with the index k.

Our model is then described by the following equations.

$$D_{jm} = \frac{1}{\Theta} \sum_{k=1}^{K} \delta_{kj} p_m^k \tag{10}$$

$$p_m^k = \frac{\exp[b(\sum_{j=1}^{J} \delta_{kj} x_{jm} + \bar{x}_m^k) + ay_m^k]}{\sum_{l \in M} \exp[b(\sum_{j=1}^{J} \delta_{kj} x_{jl} + \bar{x}_l^k) + ay_l^k]} \qquad \begin{array}{l} k=1,\ldots,K \\ m=1,\ldots,M \end{array} \tag{11}$$

$$x_{jm} = S_{jm}(D_{j1}, \ldots, D_{jM}; T) \tag{8}$$

$$\bar{x}_m^k = \bar{S}_m(w^k; D_{j_k 1}, \ldots, D_{j_k M}; T) \tag{9}$$

Equations (10), (11), (8), (9) hold for k=1,...,K
                                        m=1,...,M
                                        j=1,...,J

Our task now is to solve these non-linear simultaneous equations for the equilibrium flow pattern $\{x_{jm}\}$, $\{\bar{x}_m^k\}$. We will accomplish this task by applying the Fixed Point algorithm of Scarf.

3. ON THE DETERMINATION OF AN APPROXIMATE FIXED POINT

3.1 Scarf Algorithm Summarized

In this section, we will present a restatement of Brouwer's fixed point theorem, and a constructive proof thereof developed by Scarf. The computation

132

of the fixed point in the proof forms the basis of Scarf algorithm so that the reader should get a fairly good idea of the nature of a Scarf algorithm from this exposition.

The relevance of fixed points

Perhaps it would be illuminating to discuss the Walrasian model of pure-exchange economy in order to motivate the use of fixed points.[7] A fixed point of a mapping $y = f(x)$ is a point $\hat{x}$ such that $\hat{x} = f(\hat{x})$, i.e., a point that maps into itself.

Let $x = (x_1, \ldots, x_n)$ represent the (non-negative) prices of commodities $1, \ldots, n$, and let the excess demands at this vector of prices be represented by the continuous functions $g_1(x), \ldots, g_n(x)$ which are assumed to satisfy Walras law, a law derived from a "budget constraint".

$$\sum_{i=1}^{n} x_i g_i(x) = 0$$

A vector $\hat{x}$ is said to be an equilibrium price vector if all excess demands are less than or equal to zero at this price vector, i.e.,

$$g_i(\hat{x}) \leq 0, \quad i=1, \ldots, n$$

The computation of an equilibrium price vector is quite a difficult task to perform. One way of solving the problem is to transpose it into a problem of computing a fixed point, which can then be solved efficiently by the use of a Scarf algorithm. Let us postulate a mapping and show that its fixed point is the equilibrium price vector $\hat{x}$. Consider

$$y_i = \frac{x_i + \max[0, g_i(x)]}{1 + \sum_{l} \max[0, g_l(x)]}$$

We claim that the fixed point of this mapping is the vector $\hat{x}$. [At this point we will not toil over the proof of the existence of such a fixed point. We will simply assume that it exists.] A fixed point x^* of the above mapping satisfies

$$x_i^* = \frac{x_i^* + \max[0, g_i(x^*)]}{1 + \sum_{l} \max[0, g_l(x^*)]}$$

or

$$x_i^* \sum_{l} \max[0, g_l(x^*)] = \max[0, g_i(x^*)]$$

If $\sum_{l} \max[0, g_l(x^*)]$ is in fact greater than zero, the above equation implies that $g_i(x^*) > 0$ for every i with $x_i^* > 0$. Since all $x_i^* \geq 0$ and some are strictly positive, this violates Walras law. We conclude that $\sum_{l} \max[0, g_l(x^*)] = 0$ and therefore,

$g_i(x^*) \leq 0$ $i=1, \ldots, m$ hence x^* is an equilibrium price vector.

Brouwer's fixed point theorem

Let $y = f(x)$ be a continuous mapping of the simplex into itself. Then there exists a fixed point of the mapping, i.e., a vector $\hat{x}$ such that $\hat{x} = f(\hat{x})$.

Before we start the proof of this theorem, the concept of a primitive set needs to be introduced.

Definition

Given any list of vectors $x^{n+1}, \ldots, x^k$ in the simplex S the (n-m) vectors $x^{j_1}, \ldots x^{j_{n-m}}$, along with the m sides $s^{i_1}, \ldots, s^{i_m}$ form a primitive set if no vector $x^{n+1}, \ldots, x^k$ is interior to the simplex defined by $x_{i_1} > 0, \ldots, x_{i_m} \geq 0$ and

$$x_i \geq \min[x_i^{j_1}, \ldots, x_i^{j_{n-m}}] \quad \text{for} \quad i \neq i_1, \ldots, i_m$$

Note that the vectors in the list are indexed $(n+1), \ldots, k$ because the indices $1, \ldots, n$ are reserved for the sides of the simplex S; that is, $x^i, i = 1, \ldots, n$ refers to the ith side of S. We now state an important lemma of Scarf's.

Scarf's lemma [7]

Let each vector in the list $x^1, \ldots, x^{n+1}, \ldots, x^k$ be labeled with one of the first n integers. Let x^j (for $j = 1, \ldots, n$) be given the label j. Then there exists a primitive set each of whose vectors has a different label.

Now recall that a vector x is in the simplex S if

$$x_i \geq 0 \qquad i = 1, \ldots, n \qquad (12)$$

and

$$\sum_{i=1}^{n} x_i = 1 \qquad (13)$$

Thus, the requirement that $y = f(x)$ be a mapping from the simplex into itself implies that

$$\sum_{i=1}^{n} [f_i(x) - x_i] = 0 \qquad (14)$$

It is clear that there is at least one i such that

$$f_i(x) \geq x_i \qquad (15)$$

Label each vector x^j $(j = n+1, \ldots, k)$ in the following manner:

$$\text{label} \ (x^j) = i_j$$
$$\text{where} \ i_j = \min\{l \,|\, f_l(x^j) \geq x_l^j\} \qquad (16)$$

133

The vectors $x^j (j=1,\ldots,n)$ are labeled j. Now, the conditions of Scarf's lemma are satisfied, and hence there exists a primitive set whose labels are all different. That is, there exists a primitive set $(x^{j_1},\ldots,x^{j_n})$ such that

$$f_{i_j}(x^j) \geq x_{i_j} \quad , \quad j=j_1,\ldots,j_n \tag{17}$$

where $i_{j_1},\ldots,i_{j_n}$ are all distinct from each other.

Let us now demonstrate Brouwer's theorem by taking a finer and finer collection of vectors which, in the limit, become everywhere dense on the simplex. Each such collection will determine a geometric subsimplex with the above property. As the vectors are increasingly refined, a convergent subsequence of subsimplices may be found, which tend in the limit to a single vector x^*. From the continuity of the mapping the vector x^* must have the property that

$$f_i(x^*) \geq x_i^* \quad i=1,\ldots,n \tag{18}$$

But (14) holds for any x, and in particular for x^*.

$$\sum_{i=1}^{n} [f_i(x^*) - x_i^*] = 0 \tag{19}$$

(18) and (19) imply that

$$f_i(x^*) = x_i^* \quad \text{for all} \quad i \tag{20}$$

demonstrating Brouwer's theorem.

It is a fact that we cannot really go to the limit in an actual application on a computer. But the final primitive set with distinct labels could be averaged out and the resultant vector becomes an approximation of the true fixed point. Furthermore, we can make the approximation as good as we desire by simply taking a fine enough collection of vectors.

This development is the spirit of Scarf's algorithm for computing approximate fixed points. More specifically, to use Scarf algorithm to compute the fixed point of any continuous mapping from the simplex into itself, we must specify the following:
— A finite list of vectors in the simplex
— A Labeling Procedure
— Replacement Operation
— Final Termination Routine

The algorithm then procedes as follows. Each of the vectors in the list is labeled according to the specified labeling procedure. An initial primitive set is created and a check is made to see if each of the members has a distinct label. If such is not the case, the algorithm constructs a new primitive set in a manner specified in the replacement operation and repeats the check to find out if the new primitive set is "completely-labeled". The process is continued until a completely-labeled primitive set, whose existence is guaranteed by Scarf's lemma, is obtained. The final termination routine then averages out the vectors in the final

primitive set to give a good approximation of the fixed point.

Note that the labeling procedure is determined by what mapping is being considered whereas the creation of the list of vectors, the specification of the replacement operation and the final termination routine rely only peripherally on the specific mapping under investigation.

3.2 Computation of the Equilibrium Flow Pattern - An Example

A seemingly restrictive assumption that needs to be satisfied if we were to apply Scarf algorithm is the condition that $y=f(x)$ be a mapping from a simplex into itself. However, we can define a suitable artificial mapping from the simplex into itself the property that its fixed point corresponds to the desired quantity which, in this case, is the equilibrium flow pattern of a transportation system.

For the sake of exposition, let us, at this point, formulate a simple model. Consider the case where no equilibration needs to be done on the access components. Hence $\bar{x}_m^k$ are fixed constants.

Define

$$\tau_{jm} = \frac{x_{jm}}{MJ\bar{t}_j} \quad j=1,\ldots,J; \ m=1,\ldots,M \tag{21}$$

and

$$\tau_{om} = \frac{1}{M} - \sum_{j=1}^{J} \tau_{jm} \quad m=1,\ldots,M \tag{22}$$

where $\bar{t}_j$ is the upper limit of all x_{jm} :

$$x_{jm} \epsilon [0,\bar{t}_j] \quad j=1,\ldots,J \tag{23}$$

Clearly the "vectors" τ_{jm} are in the simplex:

$$\tau_{jm} \geq 0 \quad j=0,1,\ldots,J ; \ m=1,\ldots,M$$

and

$$\sum_{j=1}^{J} \sum_{m=0}^{M} \tau_{jm} = 1$$

The assumption of no equilibration on access implies that we have determined all variables in the system defined by (8), (9), (10), (11) except for $[x_{jm}]$.

It is easy to verify that the following transformation satisfies the condition of Brouwer's theorem and has a fixed point that corresponds to an equilibrium vector $[x_{jm}]$ for our above example.

$$G_{jm}(\tau) = \frac{1}{MJ\bar{t}_j} S_{jm}(D_{j1}(\tau),\ldots,D_{jM}(\tau)) \tag{24}$$

$$G_{om}(\tau) = \frac{1}{M} - \sum_{j=1}^{J} G_{jm}(\tau)$$

where

$$D_{jm}(\tau) = \frac{1}{\theta} \sum_{k=1}^{K} \delta_{kj} \frac{\exp[b(\sum_{j=1}^{J}\delta_{kj}MJ\bar{t}_j\tau_{jm}) + b\bar{x}_m^k + ay_m^k]}{\sum_{l=1}^{M}\exp[b(\sum_{j=1}^{J}\delta_{kj}MJ\bar{t}_j\tau_{jl}) + b\bar{x}_l^k + ay_l^k]}$$

$$j=1,\ldots,J$$

$$m=1,\ldots,M \tag{25}$$

The fixed point τ^* of the transformation defined by Equations (24) and (25) have the property that

$$G_{jm}(\tau^*) = \tau^*_{jm} \qquad\qquad j=0,\ldots,J \ ; \ m=1,\ldots,M \quad (26)$$

Associated with each τ^*_{jm} is a unique x^*_{jm}

$$x^*_{jm} = \tau^*_{jm} M J \bar{t}_j \qquad\qquad \begin{matrix} j=1,\ldots,J_j \\ m=1,\ldots,M \end{matrix} \quad (27)$$

It should be observed that at segment travel times x^*_{jm}, $j=1,\ldots,J$; $m=1,\ldots,M$, each and every worker in our sample plans his travel in such a way that the segment demands are

$$D_{jm}(x^*) = \frac{1}{6}\sum_{k=1}^{K}\delta_{kj}\frac{\exp[b(\sum_{j=1}^{J}\delta_{kj}x^*_{jm} + b\bar{x}^k_m + ay^k_m]}{\sum_{l=1}^{M}\exp[b(\sum_{j=1}^{J}\delta_{kj}x^*_{jl} + b\bar{x}^k_l + ay^k_l]}$$

$$\begin{matrix} j=1,\ldots,J \\ m=1,\ldots,M \end{matrix}$$

The travel times "supplied" by the transportation system in response to these demands, are, in turn, given by:

$$S_{jm}(D_{j1}(x^*),\ldots,D_{jM}(x^*)) \qquad \begin{matrix} j=1,\ldots,J \\ m-1,\ldots,M \end{matrix}$$

which, in view of Equations (24), (26) and (27), turn out to be exactly

$$x^*_{jm} \qquad\qquad \begin{matrix} j=1,\ldots,J \\ m=1,\ldots,M \end{matrix}$$

Hence, as soon as we have $[\tau^*_{jm}]$, the equilibrium flow pattern $[x^*_{jm}]$ obtains immediately.

Now we apply Scarf's fixed point algorithm to compute $[\tau^*_{jm}]$. By specifying a grid of vectors and utilizing a labeling procedure similar to (16), we get out of the algorithm a final primitive set, each of whose members is "close" to $[\tau^*_{jm}]$. To get a good approximation of $[\tau^*_{jm}]$, we average out the members of the final primitive set in the manner outlined by Shoven in Appendix A of [9]. From the discussion in the preceding section, it is clear that we can get as good an approximation of $[\tau^*_{jm}]$ as we desire by simply making the grid of vectors fine enough. Thus, Scarf algorithm can give us an approximation of the equilibrium flow pattern $[x^*_{jm}]$ which can be made as good as desired.

4. EMPIRICAL APPLICATION

We are currently in tre process of applying our equilibrium model to the I-580 corridor in the San Francisco Bay Area. The I-580 model has the following characteristics:

1. A maximum of 8 modes are available to each worker in the sample.

2. The single-bottleneck formulation is used to characterize the supply equations.

3. There are 9 segments in the corridor.

Although we do not have at hand a final result of this study, initial runs of the model seem very encouraging. Without the Final Termination Routine, it costs less than $ 70 to run the model. Since the Final Termination Routine is basically a Simplex algorithm, we wouldn't expect the cost to go up too much by incorporating it into the model. Far from being conclusive, our experience should nonetheless indicate the magnitude of the cost of implementing our model. We should add that our current programs are by far *not* the most efficient possible, and there is room for further improvements. We will report our final results in a forthcoming paper.

ACKNOWLEDGEMENTS

Dan McFadden originally suggested that we should look into formulating the equilibration of mode choices as an equilibrium rather than a maximization problem and indicated that the economist's experience with Scarf algorithm has been good; he also suggested that in order to reduce the number of "markets" to be equilibrated in a corridor study, the "markets" could be defined as the segments of this corridor rather than the customary zonal interchanges. The present working paper is the result of following up these suggestions.

Research support is gratefully acknowledged from the Alfred P. Sloan Foundation, through grant 74-12-8 to the Department of Economics, University of California, Berkeley, and from the National Science Foundation.

REFERENCES

[1] Dafermos, S. D., and F. T. Sparrow, "The Traffic Assignment Problem for a General Network", **Journal of Research**, National Bureau of Standards, Vol 37-B, No. 2, 1969.

[2] May, A. and H. Keller, "A Deterministic Queueing Model", Transportation Research, p. 117-127, 1967.

[3] McFadden, D., "Conditional Logit Analysis of Qualitative Choice Behavior", in P. Zarembka, editor, **Frontiers in Econometrics**, Academic Press, New York, 1973.

[4] McFadden, D., "The Measurement of Urban Travel Demand", **Journal of Public Economics**, 1974.

[5] Nguyen, S., "A Unified Approach to Equilibrium Methods for Traffic Assignment", paper presented at the International Symposium on Traffic Equilibrium Methods, Montreal, 1974.

[6] Scarf, H., "The Computation of Economic Equilibria", Cowles Foundation Monograph no. 24, 1973.

[7] Scarf, H., "The Approximation of Fixed-Points of a Continuous Mapping", **SIAM Journal of Applied Mathematics**, 15:1328-43, 1967.

[8] Shoven, J. and J. Whalley, "On the Computation of Competitive Equilibrium in International Markets with Tariffs", **Journal of International Economics**, November 1974.

[9] ......, "A General Equilibrium Calculation of the Effects of Differential Taxation of Income From Capital in the US", **Journal of Public Economics**, p. 281-321; 1972.

[10] Small, K., "Bus Priority, Differential Pricing and Investment in Urban Highways", **Working Paper 7613**, Urban Travel Demand Forecasting Project, Institute of Transportation Studies, University of California, Berkeley, 1976.

[11] Talvitie, A. and Y. Dehghani, "Supply Model for Transit Access and Linehaul", **Working Paper 7614**, Urban Travel Demand Forecasting Project, Institute of Transportation Studies, University of California, Berkeley, 1976.

[12] Wardrop, J. G., "Some Theoretical Aspects of Road Traffic Research", **Proceedings of the Institute of Civil Engineers, Part III**, Vol. 1, 1952.

FOOTNOTES

1) By equilibrium flow pattern we mean a complete list of *mode splits* on *all* levels of aggregation. From individual paths up to zonal or segment (a conglomeration of zones) volumes.

2) Actually, since equilibration is done on persons rather than vehicles, in this paper, to be consistent, γ^j_2 should really be "the number of car-equivalents of an Express Bus divided by the number of passengers".

3) The express bus travel time, to be more realistic, must be increased by the time needed for stops. This time is a function of stop spacing and volume entering and exiting the bus. The latter board/alight time is represented as a constant rather than func-

tion, in a present application of the model. Also note that part of the auto volume can be diverted to arterials (assuming Wardrop's principle) without making the model more complex. For simplicity of presentation these details are omitted here.

4) Some of the readers may feel uneasy about such a simple model of highway network performance. They are reminded that the current network algorithms also consider every link independently, "load" the zones in one spot into the network and, thus, differ only marginally from the multiple bottleneck version here.

5) "Access" will, from now on, stand for both access and egress.

6) We should really write "vehicle or person", since in guideway modes persons are the basic units. However, we feel that equilibration will be confined to the highway and not guideway modes. Hence, we describe our model in a way that ignores equilibration on the latter modes. It should be clear, though, that our presumption imposes no restriction on the model's generality.

7) The following example is borrowed from Scarf [6].

The theory and practice of car ownership forecasting *

by
K. J. BUTTON
Department of Economics, University of Loughborough
and
A. D. PEARMAN
School of Economic Studies, University of Leeds

Forecast levels of car ownership play a vital role in the determination of government transportation planning and policy. Both at the urban and inter-urban level, the scale and character of transport provision for the last two decades of this century will be determined to a significant extent by the view taken now about the position of the private car in our society. In the United Kingdom, for example, the British government's recent *Transport Policy* document contained a section specifically devoted to forecasting national car ownership levels. The accuracy of such forecasts has figured importantly in a number of recent controversies in the U.K. surrounding public enquiries into motorway plans. It is clear that well conceived car ownership models are an essential requirement if the uncertainty inherent in the traffic forecasts central to infrastructure investment appraisal is to be minimised.

The first section of this paper is concerned with the theoretical framework within which car ownership decisions may be viewed as being made. It is noticeable, however, that little applied work in car ownership forecasting has endeavoured to incorporate a rigorous theoretical framework of this type. Section 2 discusses a number of the better known types of car ownership forecasting model pointing out some of their strengths and weaknesses and also the frequent inconsistency of their implications, for example, with respect to sensitivity to household income levels, a crucial explanatory variable in many models. Attention is also drawn to the common use of proxy variables and the theoretical and practical difficulties which arise as a result. The final section of the paper summarises the present position in car ownership forecasting and emphasises the need to continue the movement towards behaviourally based models and away from the empiricism which characterised much early work in this area.

THEORETICAL MODELS OF THE CAR OWNERSHIP DECISION

Analysis of the car ownership decision seems to fit most appropriately into the realm of economic theory. In economic terms, the car may be regarded as a consumer durable good. Its purchase represents a medium-term investment of capital which is repaid over the life of the vehicle through the services which its possession provides. However, if the transport planner turns to the literature of economics, either theoretical or applied, for an understanding of this aspect of consumer behaviour, he will get relatively little help. There are a number of reasons for this.

The first problem encountered in specifying an economic model of the demand for cars is to determine who is responsible for the demand. In the main body of neoclassical economic theory it is implicit that the decision maker is the individual consumer. It seems however, that the car ownership decision is far more likely to be a household one, rather than one taken by an individual household member in isolation. The way in which household decisions are reached is a matter which has not received a great deal of attention from economists. The household seems normally to be treated as a single-minded decisionmaking unit, a quasi-individual rather than a collection of individuals. The analytical convenience of such an approach is obvious, given the rich development of theory for individual demand decisions. Its validity is less clear. For some items, where the adult members of the household make similar and approximately equal use of the good concerned, such an aggregation may be justifiable. For something like a car, however, where its use by one member for, say, the journey to work may well deprive other household members of its use altogether, it its harder to justify the ownership decision as a quasi-individual one.

Even if the problem of the nature of the decisionmaking unit is side-stepped, a number of other significant difficulties remain. These involve specifying the good demanded, quantifying the demand and identifying the influences which create the demand and which should, therefore, constitute the explanatory variables in any economic model. Despite the fact that it is normal to discuss the forecasting of demand for cars, this is, to a large extent, a misnoma. The principal demand is for the services of cars, rather than the cars themselves, although, in some kinds of work in this general area, the status symbol aspect of car ownership cannot be overlooked. The importance of the demand for car ownership arises via the demonstrably strong relationship between

* This paper derives from work undertaken as part of a research project carried out under the auspices of a grant from the Social Science Research Council.

ownership and use (see Oi and Shuldiner (1962); Deutschman (1967)) and the implications of use levels for infrastructure policy. Thus the models which are of relevance here are predictors of the total stock of cars and not estimators of new sales per unit of time, as in most economic demand studies. This complicates matters considerably. It means that the second-hand market, with all its complexities and problems of data availability, is involved. It means further that, because the car is a durable consumer good, and one which involves a heavy capital outlay, the variables which explain its purchase may well, in part, be transitory and unavailable for observation in the context of recording of ownership some years after the purchase decision has been made. Alternatively, the opposite problem awaits supporters of Friedman's permanent income hypothesis. In this case, a household with an expectation of an increasing income might well take its car ownership decision on the basis of factors as yet unobserved.

Further, the neoclassical theory of demand is most fully developed in terms of continuous functions and variables. It is not well-suited to the discrete 0,1,2, ... car decision that the household makes. The explanatory variables also cause difficulties. Many of them are likely to be outside the set typically embraced by models of demand, factors like price levels and income. There is stronger interdependence with other economic decisions of the household, particularly job choice and household location. Unlike some other markets, the variation in these factors is so great that aggregative studies of market demand are likely to obscure numerous significant features, matters about which one might well wish to have some insight from a policy point of view. For example, if use of cars is likely to become intolerable given present trends, it might be desired to alter household and job location possibilities as a way of cutting car ownership and hence use. Models which aggregate away the effects of locational decisions are thus of limited value. A final difficulty of specification which may be noted is the widely held belief that many car ownership and use decisions are not justified on the basis of the costs involved. Although other factors may explain this phenomenon, inaccurate perception of costs may also have an influence, and one which would be very difficult to estimate.

Although the preceding paragraphs have only sketched in some of the difficulties likely to be encountered in specifying models of car ownership as an economic decision, they do provide some clue as to why very few economists have been trampled to death in the rush to provide such insights to the transport planner. Probably the best known attempt to explain the car ownership decision, starting from a basis in economic theory, is due to Beckmann et.al. (1973). In outline, the type of approach they adopt is as follows. Without a car, a household's total utility, U^0, at any time is taken to be dependent on its disposable income, Y, its available leisure time, L, and the travel which it undertakes during the specified period. Without a car, the destinations within reach of the household can be defined as D^0 and the total time spent in travel denoted as $\sum_{n \in D^0} r_n^0 T_n^0$,

where T_n^0 represents the number of trips made to destination n and r_n^0 the travel time to reach n. The utility function can then be defined as

$$U^0 = U(Y, L - \sum_{n \in D^0} r_n^0 T_n^0, T_n^0) \qquad (1)$$

The purchase of a car will have several effects. It will immediately reduce the income available to buy other goods by an amount, C, equal to the annual cost of car ownership. It will increase the number of destinations accessible to the household from D^0 to D^1. Finally, it will affect both the travel time it takes to reach each destination and the number of trips likely to be made to each. The total time spent in travel will become

$$\sum_{n \in D^1} r_n^1 T_n^1$$

Consequently, the household's utility with a car can be represented as

$$U^1 = U(Y - C, L - \sum_{n \in D^1} r_n^1 T_n^1, T_n^1) \qquad (2)$$

It now becomes clear that, in general terms, it becomes worthwhile for the household to purchase a car if $U^1 > U^0$. The introduction of additional subscripts enables this simple analysis to be extended to cover decisions about the purchase of a second car, or a better car.

The principal extension of this work is due to Burns et.al. (1975). It takes the form of an empirical test of the general theory using data gathered as part of the Detroit Regional Transportation and Land Use Study. In order to operationalise the theory, a specific functional form for the utility functions has to be assumed and also a model of the interaction between individual household members with respect to car ownership and its effect on total household utility. The detailed nature of these assumptions is certainly open to some criticism. So too is the choice of a sixty-minute time parameter for determining D^0 and D^1 and the use of an attractiveness index for destinations which is independent of household location. Problems of this nature are, however, virtually inevitable in using existing data sources for the preliminary testing of new theoretical approaches. The overall impression is that the multinomial logit model developed on the basis of this theory is a significant step forward in modelling car ownership behaviour.

A second recent American disaggregated behavioural model of car ownership is due to Lerman and Ben-Akiva (1975). Again, a multinomial logit model is used, but the theoretical foundation is given rather less emphasis, with the principal intention being the incorporation of variables which can reflect the full breadth of potential household behaviour with respect to car ownership decisions. Of particular interest is the incorporation of a variable reflecting the position of each household in its life cycle — a measure of household structure. As in the paper by Burns et.al., there are many points of detail which are contentious, but the general approach is a valuable one, deserving further research input.

One respect in which these recent models are open to criticism, in company with many earlier attempts, is their failure to recognise potential dynamic effects. It seems plausible that at least the rate at which society adopts the motor car, if not ultimate saturation levels of ownership, will be influenced by existing ownership rates. This would certainly be the implication of Tanner's work, described in the following section. The appropriate parameters in applying cross-sectional models, in other words, may well be time-dependent, via the effect of ownership rates in intervening periods on behaviour patterns. This matter is discussed further in Section 2 in the context of Bates' work.

If the principal concern in analysing car ownership is to predict its likely course and the outcome of trying to change that course, a fully dynamic model may, therefore, be the most appropriate. Such a model would recognise explicitly the effect of present car ownership rates on future ones. Clearly, introducing a dynamic dimension further complicates an already difficult modelling task. To demonstrate the kind of model which may be relevant to some circumstances, and to draw out some of its implications, a relatively straightforward expository example will be used.

Consider the obverse of the car ownership model, a model forecasting the number of captive public transport users in an urban area consisting of m zones.[1] Although it would be straightforward to disaggregate the model by household type, consider, for simplicity, a zonal level of analysis. Let R_i^o be the percentage of the residents of zone i who are captive users of public transport. Then the utility accruing to this group through their travel behaviour may, for simplicity, be regarded as equal to the difference between the net benefits gained through the trips undertaken and the cost of those trips. For purposes of demonstration it is assumed that all trips have equal unit benefit value, v, and that the costs incurred are a known multiple, p_i, of the percentage of the population who are captive users. Variations in p_i permit the recognition of potentially different cost structures for producing an appropriate level of service in different zones. Thus

$$U_i^o = v \sum_{j=1}^{m} T_{ij}^o - p_i R_i^o \tag{3}$$

Suppose now that the rate of growth (decline) of the percentage of captive public transport users is some constant multiple, k, of utility.

$$\dot{R}_i^o = k U_i^o = k(v \sum_{j=1}^{m} T_{ij}^o - p_i R_i^o)$$

Further, suppose that the number of trips, T_{ij}^o, is estimated using an attraction-constrained entropy maximising model so that

$$T_{ij}^o = \sum_j \frac{O_i D_j e^{-BC_{ij}}}{\sum_i O_i e^{-BC_{ij}}} \tag{4}$$

If we assume that the unconstrained number of public transport trips originating in zone i is a simple linear function, $O_i = k^1 R_i^o$, of the per-

centage of the population captive to public transport, then, by substitution, we have

$$\dot{R}_i^o = kv\sum_j \frac{R_i^o D_j e^{-BC_{ij}}}{\sum_i R_i^o e^{-BC_{ij}}} - kp_i R_i^o \tag{5}$$

$$= \left[kv\sum_j \frac{D_j e^{-BC_{ij}}}{\sum_i R_i^o e^{-BC_{ij}}} - kp_i \right] R_i^o \tag{6}$$

or $\qquad \dot{R}_i^o = M_i (R_1^o \ldots R_m^o) R_i^o \tag{7}$

(6) represents a series of m rather complex simultaneous differential equations. As has been shown, however, by Hirsch and Smale (1974) and by Wilson (1976), some qualitative analysis of this type of equation system is possible.

Following Wilson, the Hirsch and Smale two dimensional analysis generalises to a requirement that three sets of conditions hold with respect to the equation system. If this is the case, then some qualitative conclusions can be reached about the time path of the R_i^o. The conditions which must hold are derived from (6¹):

(a) $\quad \dfrac{\partial M_i}{\partial R_k^o} < 0, \ i \neq k$

$$\frac{\partial M_i}{\partial R_k^o} = - kv\sum_j \frac{D_j e^{-BC_{ij}} e^{-BC_{ik}}}{(\sum_i R_i^o e^{-BC_{ij}})^2} < 0 \text{ if } k \text{ and } v \text{ are} > 0$$

This implies that R_i^o decreases if any other R_k^o increases. This might, for example, occur if there are supply inelasticities in the public transport sector.

(b) $\quad \exists \ K$ such that $M_i \leq 0$ if $R_i^o > K$

As R_i^o is increased, the summed term in the bracket in (6) decreases. It will ultimately become less than kp_i and so the condition is fulfilled.

(c) $\quad \exists \ J_i$ such that $M_i \ (0,0, \ldots R_i^o, 0 \ldots 0) \begin{array}{l} > 0 \text{ for } R_o^i < J_i \\ < 0 \text{ for } R_o^i > J_i \end{array}$

$$M_i \ (0,0 \ldots R_i^o, 0 \ldots 0) = kv\sum_j \frac{D_j e^{-BC_{ij}}}{R_i^o e^{-BC_{ij}}} - kp_i$$

$$= kv\sum_j \frac{D_j}{R_i^o} - kp_i$$

Clearly, by altering the size of R_i^o, M_i may be made either positive or negative, as required. With these three results established, it is now possible to go ahead and analyse the behaviour of the M_i in phase space $(R_1^o, \ldots R_m^o)$. A detailed analysis is not justified for an exploratory model of the type just outlined, nor is it possible without know-

139

ledge of the parameters of the system. However, it is possible to make two points. First, equation sets of this kind can frequently exhibit bifurcation. That is, the equilibrium set of R_i^o to which the system will tend will vary depending upon the initial conditions. An equilibrium with all $R_i^o > 0$ is possible. So is one in which some R_i^o fall to zero. The policy implications are clear. If the current situation corresponds to a point in phase space which leads to an unacceptable equilibrium (say, because it leaves minority groups like the elderly with no public transport provision in certain zones) then an interference with the natural order of things will be required, either to alter the equation system or to change the initial conditions to a set leading to a more acceptable equilibrium. The second point to be made is that, even with the very simplistic model presented here, the complexity of analysis involved in consideration of dynamical systems is clear. Implementation of this type of analysis would not be straightforward. With this in mind, it is interesting now to examine the kind of models which economists and transport planners have tried to implement and to compare them both with each other and with theoretical ideals.

EXISTING MODELS OF CAR OWNERSHIP

In practice there has been little attempt to employ economic models of car ownership for forecasting purposes. Rather, there has been an emphasis on straightforward empirical work, concentrating on techniques which offer a reasonably good statistical explanation of past and current levels of car ownership to predict future growth. Broadly these methods can be divided into two main categories, those employing some form of extrapolation procedure to trace out the past growth in vehicle ownership and to extend this trend into the future and those adopting crude econometric methods, usually, but not exclusively, employing cross-sectional data to determine certain statistical parameters which are then assumed invariant with respect to time. The former method is most widely used at the macro level for national forecasting, while the latter tends to be favoured at the more micro level either for regional or local forecasting.

The extrapolation techniques generally assume that car ownership follows some form of sigmoid growth path through time until ultimate saturation level of ownership has been attained. This is, for example, the standard procedure employed by the Transport and Road Research Laboratory in the U.K. (Tanner (1974)) to draw up their national forecasts. The sigmoid growth path is described by a logistic curve with an exogenously determined saturation level used as an asymptote. Although slightly different methods were used to determine the saturation levels, the logistic curve fitting technique has also been used on Dutch car market (Bos (1970)) and on the U.S. car market (Whorf (1975)). This type of procedure is useful if the only information required is a rough estimate of the car stock at some future date. It has some basic justification in that income is likely to be an important explanatory variable of the car ownership level and that there has been a long term trend for income to increase through time. By relying upon time as the independent variable the logistic curve fitting procedure implicitly circumvents the problem of trying to forecast future income levels.

The detailed method of logistic curve fitting, and in particular, the T.R.R.L. approach, has been subjected to serious criticism in recent years. Although the extrapolation approach removes the need to predict future values for a set of explanatory variables it still requires an estimate of the ultimate saturation level of vehicle ownership, and this is in many ways equally difficult. In the past the T.R.R.L. have attempted to devise an objective statistical method for arriving at this saturation level. They employed cross-sectional information on the annual rate of change in car ownership in each county as the dependent variable in a regression run against the actual ownership level. The ownership level at which the rate of change becomes zero is then used as the saturation level in the logistic curve fitting exercise. Criticisms of this procedure have ranged from the unjustified nature of the orthoganal regression used to determine the saturation level to the T.R.R.L.'s selective use of data in arriving at their final result (Adams (1975)). Even empirically the procedure was unsatisfactory and it became apparent in the early 1970s that the saturation level derived depends crucially upon the year for which the cross-sectional data is taken. There is a tendency for the saturation level to increase over time if successive annual calculations are performed. More recent work at the T.R.R.L. has resulted in the adoption of a much more flexible approach to estimating the saturation level involving a consideration of the eventual number of drivers in the population and a review of trends in other countries. However, it still does not have any underlying theoretical basis to describe the forces working towards this saturation level nor an economic theory of why such a saturation level is inevitable. If we look at the work undertaken in the U.S. by Whorf, we find a similar weakness, he simply runs a series of regressions corresponding to the logistic curve using arbitrary values for a saturation level. The model offering the highest $\overline{R}^2$ is then selected. There is no theoretical justification given for the saturation level finally arrived at, it simply emerges from the data.

For the local planner the logistic curve fitting technique has two fundamental weaknesses. Firstly, the urban transport planner is only indirectly interested in car ownership as such, he is primarily concerned with car use. Car ownership is, therefore, used as an input into a further series of models which forecast travel patterns in the urban area. Aggregate numbers of vehicles are not the important consideration here, travel habits are more strongly influenced by the number of vehicles available to each individual household. Unfortunately, the logistic procedure does not offer information on the number of no car, one car, and two plus car households, only the average ownership level. Secondly, any form of extrapolation implicitly assumes that underlying influences do not alter the *ceteris paribus* conditions — but this is unrealistic at the disaggregated level. Indeed, the transport planner, by modifying the local transport system, will himself disturb these *ceteris paribus* conditions.

In consequence, local car ownership forecasts are distinguished by their use of cross-sectional data in combination with very simply statistical models. A common procedure is to employ category analysis in which a multi-dimensional matrix is defined with each dimension representing an explanatory factor described in discrete categories, for example, households in an area may be categorised by their income group, the number of residents and their social status (Mogridge and Eldridge (1970)). By assuming the average rate of car ownership for each category does not change over time and by forecasting the future number of households falling into each category it is then possible to predict future car ownership rates. The limitations of this approach are clear. It assumes that the average ownership rate in each category is invariant with respect to time, hence it is essentially a static model being used for a dynamic purpose. In addition, there are statistical problems involved in establishing the contribution of each variable to the ownership rate which can only be resolved by messy analysis of variance tests. Finally, category analysis involves expressing certain naturally continuous variables, such as income, in a discrete form which can lead to distortions in the forecasts made.

An alternative to the category analysis approach is the use of multivariate regression techniques. Again the tendency is to employ cross-sectional data from a transportation survey but regression procedures enable continuous variables to be incorporated in their natural form whilst discrete variables can be represented as dichotomous dummy variables taking the values of 0 or 1. Ideally the regressions are performed at the household level to minimise the variation within observations generally encountered using zonal data. This does present certain statistical problems due to the limited range of values the dependent variable can take (ie., 0, 1 or 2+). Only by sacrificing statistical simplicity can this problem be resolved. One method of circumventing the difficulty is to transform the dependent variable into a probability of car ownership, an acceptable way of doing this is to adopt logit analysis. This statistical manoeuvre is not without its own shortcomings, however, and the conventional standard error tests on independent variables cease to be appropriate in the logit formulation.

The logit model has a particular advantage over other forms of micro ownership forecasting in that it does offer a meaningful economic explanation of causal influences resulting in car ownership growing through time (Bates (1971)). If income is used as the sole explanatory variable in the specification

$$P_o = \frac{c}{y^{-b} + c} \qquad (7)$$

(where:- P_o is the probability of not owning a car

Y is income

and b and c are parameters to be estimated) we can see that as Y^{-b} approaches zero, P_o will approach unity, but as Y^{-b} rises so P_o must fall. Transforming this into a logit gives

$$\ln \left(\frac{P_o}{1-P_o} \right) = a + b \log Y \qquad (8)$$

Now we can see that the value of b represents the income elasticity of the odds in favour of a family not owning a car. (Theil (1971)). We can also see that $-\left(\frac{a}{b}\right)$ is the natural logarithm of that income at which the household is as likely or not to own a car. If we examine any changes in the model parameters over a series of cross-sections it is possible to separate the effects of the car market as a whole from other forms of expenditure (if a is held constant, but b is observed to rise over time then there has been a general shift in favour of the car market *vis a vis* other markets) and also to explore the interaction of price and the age of the vehicle stock within the market (with $-\left(\frac{a}{b}\right)$ and held constant a fall in the value of b over time would suggest the spread of ownership was becoming less unequal indicating a probable fall in the price of older cars relative to newer ones).

Subsequent work using this approach has seen the range of explanatory variables employed expand (Fairhurst (1975)) but its use as a forecasting tool is still very limited. In order to produce reliable forecasts from cross-sectional data, the conventional regression analysis approach assumes the model parameters represent long-term elasticities which do not change over time. By its very nature, however, the type of model set out above makes an entirely different assumption, namely that these parameters can vary but that this variation can be given a sensible economic interpretation. To forecast car ownership accurately using such a model requires, therefore, not only estimates of the future magnitudes of a series of independent variables but also some knowledge of how their associated coefficients are going to behave.

Reliance upon empiricism in car ownership forecasting has resulted in two particularly unsatisfactory consequences. Firstly, there is seemingly little consensus about the importance of fundamental economic variables in car ownership regression models. Let us take income as an example. At least two studies (Fishwick (1972) and Bos (1970)) have questioned its importance as an explanatory variable on the grounds of statistical significance. As we observe from Table I the other major studies which do include an estimate of the income elasticity of car ownership seem unable to reach an approximate consensus upon the value of such a parameter. One can perhaps explain away some of the variation in the latter in terms of the type of data employed (time series, cross-sectional, pooled), the level of aggregation adopted (individuals, households or regions), the specification of the model (log-linear, linear or semi-logarithmic) and the other variables included in the regressions but these factors only reinforce the fundamental criticism rather than weaken it. The specifications were accepted on their statistical merits rather than their theoretical soundness and the very multiplicity of results simply illustrates the inadequate theoretical foundations upon which these empirical models are based. Certainly one cannot expect that every attempt to calibrate a model of car ownership decisions will yield identical parameters, but a more solid and rigorous approach to the underlying causal relationships would result in much more consistency and a much narrower dispersion of the parameters obtained.

Secondly, many studies rely for their explanatory powers upon variables which have no readily, identifiable economic rationale. In some cases attempts have been made to justify the use of such variables by adopting the argument that they are acting as proxies or surrogates for influences which are either not immediately quantifiable or for which there is no readily available data. These 'artificial' variables are of three types. Firstly, there are actual variables which may add considerably to the explanatory power of a regression model but which have only an indirect claim to being called explanatory variables. Spatial parameters such as residential density or the percentage of a region's population living in conurbations fall into this category. *Ex post* justifications for their inclusion usually mention their role as proxy for local public transport quality or for accessibility more generally defined. An example of their importance can be seen in the following equation based upon pooled data from English and Welsh standard regions for 1965-72:

$$C = -0.762 + 0.0008Y* - 0.018PD* + 0.027U* + 3.317S* + 0.008H$$

$$\bar{R}^2 = 0.7226 \quad \dots (9)$$

Where
C = Cars per household
Y = Household income net of direct taxes & other deductions
PD = Population density
U = Level of unemployment (%)

B = Employment in basic industries (% of total labour force)
S = Social Economic Group (% in SEGs 1, 2, 3, 4, and 13)
H = Household size
* indicate the variables significant at the 99% level.

One may reject the model in detail because of certain ambiguities in some of the coefficients (e.g., car ownership appears to rise with the level of unemployment) but the P.D. variable is likely to be retained because of its high level of significance and because it would be argued that one would expect car ownership to be lower in regions which are densely populated and likely to have adequate public transport. For forecasting this is not very helpful, however, because the planner is likely to alter the relationship between density and

Table 1

Study	Period Covered by Study	Data Source	Income Elasticity
Evans (a)	1948-64	United States	2.2
Suits (a)	1929-42 & 1948-56	United States	4.2(d)
Cramer (b)	1953	Great Britain	0.69
Kain (b)	1953	United States	0.17(e)
Bennett (b)	1955	United States	1.6
	1956	United States	1.53
	1957	United States	1.67
O'Herlihy (a)	1948-61	Great Britain	1.73-2.48(f)
Kain & Beesley (b)	1960	Leeds	0.72
Smith (b)	1968	United States	0.42-2.04(g)
Sleeman (b)	1968	Less-urbanised British regions	1.76
		More-urbanised British regions	2.89
Buxton & Rhys (b)	1968	English and Welsh regions	1.3
		English regions	1.54
		Less-urbanised English & Welsh counties	0.58
		More-urbanised English & Welsh counties	3.06
	1969	English and Welsh Regions	1.33
		English Regions	2.56
		Less-urbanised English & Welsh counties	0.52
		More-urbanised English & Welsh counties	2.92
Shepherd (a)	1955-71	Sydney	0.347(e)
		Perth	1.032(e)
Pearman & Button (c)	1965-72	English regions	0.3-0.7(h)

Notes
(a) Short run elasticities from time series
(b) Long run elasticities from cross sections
(c) Pooled cross-section and time series data
(d) Relates only to new cars
(e) Calculated from simultaneous models with car ownership treated as an endogenous variable
(f) Sensitive to the rate of vehicle appreciation assumed
(g) Variation between quantities for 1968
(h) Sensitive to the definition of income

Sources: - M. K. Evans; **Macroeconomic Activity, Theory, Forecasting & Control** (Harper & Row) 1969. D. Suits; The Demand for automobiles in the U.S.A. 1929-56 **Review of economics & Statistics** Vol. 40 1958 pp. 273-280. J. S. Cramer; **The Ownership of Major Consumer Durables**, University of Cambridge, Dept. of Applied Economics Monograph 7, 1962. J. F. Kain; A contribution to the urban transportation debate: an econometric model of urban residential and travel behaviour.

Review of Economics & Statistics Vol. 47, 1964, pp. 55-64. W. B. Bennett; Cross-section studies of the consumption of automobiles in the United States **American Economic Review** Vol. 57, 1967, pp. 841-850. C. St. J. O'Herlihy; Demand for cars in Great Britain **Applied Statistics**, Vol. 14, 1967, pp. 162-195. J. F. Kain & M. E. Beesley; Forecasting car ownership and use **Urban Studies**, Vol. 2, 1965, pp. 163-185. R. P. Smith; **consumer Demand for Cars in the U.S.A.** (University of Cambridge, Dept. of Applied Economics Occasional Paper 44) 1975. J. F. Sleeman; A New look at the distribution of private cars in Britain **Scottish Journal of Political Economy,** Vol. 16, 1969, pp. 306-318; M. J. Buxton & D. G. Rhys; The demand for car ownership: a note **Scottish Journal of Political Economy,** Vol. 19. 1972, pp. 175-181; L. E. Shepherd; An econometric approach to the demand for urban passenger transport **Australian Road Research Board Proceedings,** Vol. 6, 1972, pp. 214-245. A. D. Pearman & K. J. Button; Regional variations in car ownership. **Applied Economics** Vol. 8, 1976, pp. 231-233.

public transport as part of the planning exercise.

A further 'artificial' variable is a time trend. This, it is argued, indicates the autonomous growth in car ownership which cannot be explained in terms of economic influences. We can introduce this into the above model very easily:-

$$C = -1.7367 + 0.0003Y^* - 0.066PD - 0.012U + 2.112B^* + 2.790S^* + 0.500H^* + 0.038T^*$$
$$\overline{R}^2 = 0.8605 \quad \ldots (10)$$

where $T = $ A time trend with $1965 = 1$

The introduction of T improves the explanatory power of the model in terms of $\overline{R}^2$ and also results in some of the traditional economic variables, notably unemployment, reverting to a coefficient exhibiting the sign one would anticipate. The limitation for forecasting of this approach is that the time trend must be assumed to continue unchanged in the future. In many ways this is an identical assumption to that underlying the extrapolation techniques discussed above and is open to similar criticisms.

Finally, artificial variables can be in the form of 'dummies' which take the value 1 if the region falls into some specified category and a zero otherwise. Figures I(a) and I(b) show the regional growth paths of car ownership per household and per person. Three groupings emerge: (a) North-West, Yorkshire and Humberside and North, (b) Greater London, East Midlands and West Midlands and (c) South East, South West and East Anglia. For statistical reasons we only use dummy variables for the last two groups. The following regression is obtained

$$C = 0.567 + 0.0003Y^* - 0.011PD^* + 0.025U^* - 0.250B + 0.161S - 0.167H + 0.259D_1^* + 0.155D_2^*$$

$$\overline{R}^2 = 0.8957 \quad \ldots (11)$$

where $D_1 = \begin{cases} 1 \text{ if the observation is in regio-} \\ \text{nal group (c)} \\ 0 \text{ otherwise} \end{cases}$

$D_2 = \begin{cases} 1 \text{ if the observation is in regio-} \\ \text{nal group (b)} \\ 0 \text{ otherwise} \end{cases}$

In purely mechanical terms this equation form is a considerable advance on those preceding it; the $\overline{R}^2$ value is higher, there is less multicollinearity, autocorrelation is considerably reduced and the constant term has a more reasonable positive value. For forecasting purposes, however, one must assume that the parallel growth trends of the three regional groupings will continue with neither any convergence nor divergence and that individual reigons will continue to exhibit the same trends as their parent group. Such assumptions are unlikely to be valid in the longer term but without any theoretical knowledge of why the initial groups occur it is impossible to base forecasts on any other footing.

CONCLUSION

This paper has looked at car ownership forecasting both as a theoretical exercise and as a practical one. Apart from some potential use for time trend extrapolation models at the highest

levels of aggregation, the conclusion reached is that future modelling effort should be concentrated on the development of disaggregated behavioural models with a foundation in economic theory. It is possible to have much more confidence in forecasts derived from an inductive approach of this nature than from the deductive models which have commonly been used in the past. Within this latter set of models there is not only strong empirical evidence of inconsistency, but also the ever present danger, when proxy variables are employed, that statistically significant parameters will be justified on an *ex post* rather than *a priori* basis.

The whole concept of developing and calibrating models using existing experience and existing data as a foundation for long-term forecasts is

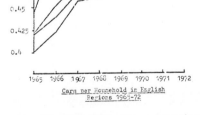

Cars per Household

Fig. 1 (a)

0.85
0.825
0.8
0.775
0.75
0.725
0.7
0.675
0.65
0.625
0.6
0.575
0.55
0.525
0.5
0.475
0.45
0.425
0.4

East Anglia
South-West

South-East

West Midlands
East Midlands

Greater London

North-West

Yorkshire & Humberside

North

1965 1966 1967 1968 1969 1970 1971 1972

Cars per Household in English Regions 1965-72

fraught with difficulties. One whose importance exceeds the brief discussion given to it here is potential dynamic variation in the parameters of a model as a result of levels attained by the dependent variable which are outside current experience. The possibility of a ratchet effect, like that discussed by Duesenberry in consumer theory, should not be overlooked. Data sources with reflect a predominance of decisions to abandon car use are rare. There is some danger in implying that car ownership models calibrated in an environment, say, of generally decreasing public transport provision can automatically be used to predict the effect of a reversal of this trend. New car ownership may be more reliable in this respect, but even here there is the danger of emulation.

Cars per Head
of Population

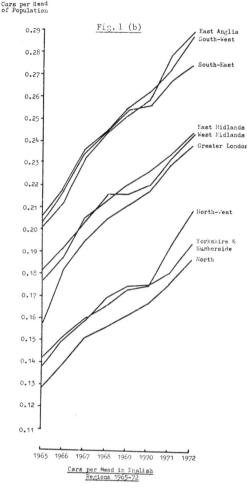

Fig. 1 (b)

East Anglia
South-West

South-East

East Midlands
West Midlands

Greater London

North-West

Yorkshire &
Humberside

North

0.29
0.28
0.27
0.26
0.25
0.24
0.23
0.22
0.21
0.20
0.19
0.18
0.17
0.16
0.15
0.14
0.13
0.12
0.11

1965 1966 1967 1968 1969 1970 1971 1972

Cars per Head in English
Regions 1965-72

Problems of this nature are of long standing. To overcome them is difficult and may be impossible. It is, however, wise to be aware of the dangers. In such circumstances, predictions should at least be tempered with some measure of qualification. It is a well known unwritten law that all economists must quote at least once from J. M. Keynes in every paper they write. We do so in conclusion by way of stating our attitude to what car ownership models should seek to achieve.

"The object of a model is to segregate the semi-permanent or relatively constant factors from those which are transitory or fluctuating so as to develop a logical way of thinking about the latter, and of understanding the time sequences to which they give rise in particular cases."

REFERENCES

J. Adams (1974): Saturation planning. **Town and Country Planning,** December pp. 550-554

J. J. Bates (1971): A hard look at car ownership modelling, **Mathematical Advisory Unit Note 216** (Department of the Environment)

M. J. Beckmann, R. L. Gustafson and T. E. Golob (1973): Locational factors in automobile ownership decisions. **Annals of Regional Science** December pp. 1-12

G. G. J. Bos (1970): **A Logistic Approach to the Demand for Private Cars** (University of Tilburg Press)

L. D. Burns, T. F. Golob and G. C. Nicolaidis (1975): Theory of urban-household automobile-ownership decisions. **Transportation Research Record 569** pp. 56-75.

H. D. Deutschman (1967): Auto-ownership revisited: a review of methods used in estimating and distributing auto-ownership, **Highway Research Record 205,** pp. 31-49.

M. H. Fairhurst (1975): The influence of public transport on car ownership in London, **Journal of Transport Economics and Policy,** September pp. 193-208.

M. W. Hirsch and S. Smale (1974): **Differential Equations, Dynamical Systems and Linear Algebra** (Academic Press).

S. R. Lerner and M. Ben-Akiva (1975): Disaggregate behavioural model of automobile ownership. **Transport Research Record 569,** pp. 34-55.

M. Mogridge and D. Eldridge (1970): **Car Ownership in London** (G. L. C. Research Memorandum 387).

W. Y. Oi and P. W. Shuldiner (1962): **An Analysis of Urban Travel Demands** (Northwestern University Press).

J. C. Tanner (1974): Forecasts of vehicles and traffic in Great Britain. **Transport and Road Research Laboratory Report 650.**

H. Theil (1971): **Principles of Econometrics** (North Holland).

R. P. Whorf (1973): Models of automobile ownership, **Proceedings of International Conference on Transportation Research** (College of Europe/Transportation Research Forum).

A. G. Wilson (1976): Towards models of the evolution and genesis of urban structure, **University of Leeds, School of Geography Working Paper 166.**

FOOTNOTE

1. The model developed here draws significantly from the shopping model analysis contained in Wilson (1976).

Report on investigations of household travel decision making behaviour *)

by

M. C. DIX

Transport Studies Unit, Oxford University

1 INTRODUCTION

The paper reports on a research project "An Investigation of the Travel Decision Process". The rationale for the study acknowledges Ben-Akiva's (1974) cautioning tenet that "In general, it is impossible to determine the correct specification of a model from data analysis. It should be determined from theory or *a priori* knowledge based upon experience with, and understanding of, the phenomenon to be modelled".

This statement reflects the current concern about the "behavioural realism" of alternative trip model structures, which has increased with an awareness of their limited ability to handle research problems posed by recent changes in urban passenger transport policy. Considerable discussion has surrounded questions of which travel choice models correspond more closely to consumer behaviour theory, or show better statistical fits, or are intuitively more reasonable. Here, an initial review of observed responses made by householders confronted with certain contemporary policy measures will lead to the suggestion that the shortcomings of current trip models may be less attributable to empirical features than to the way in which the concept of demand has been applied to the phenomenon of travel behaviour under these conditions.

An alternative framework for the analysis of travel behaviour is described, together with results from exploratory work using this approach towards an "understanding of the phenomenon".

Finally, implications for the development and application of planning models compatible with this characterization of travel are discussed.

2 EFFECTS OF THE NEW POLICIES UPON HOUSEHOLD TRAVEL ORGANISATION

2.1 Urban car restraint

Policy before the sixties was largely a matter of planning for peak demands on road space, and the trip model was developed to forecast the future pattern of work trips, assuming unrestrained car use, together with general conditions of *ceteris paribus*. A subsequent reappraisal of urban transport policy (eg. see OECD, 1975) emphasizes a need to reverse previous trends, using incentives to persuade the public to break existing habits, especially those relating to urban car use.

In the UK, 'new' policies have been pursued within several provincial town centres. During 1976 in Oxford, as a follow-up to a travel survey, some sixty households were interviewed in some depth, in order to assist an understanding of the effects of a comprehensive policy towards "Balanced Transport". The policy package had included escalating parking charges, extinction of on-street parking, closure of some streets, and attempts in general aimed at making public transport a more attractive alternative to the car, through disincentives toward car use.

Drawing from the report by Heggie (1976), and considering for the moment car based shopping journeys, it is apparent that effects of coercive policies, such as restraint on car use, can be both varied and complex. Responses included the following, in order of quantitative importance:

Consolidation of shopping activities. (eg. schopping previously carried out two days per week, now combined within a single journey)

Transfer to another destination (eg. an out-of-town shopping centre. This was often accompanied by transfer of some shopping activities to another household member; eg. 'husband' carrying out specialist shopping in town during his lunch hour).

Transfer to public transport.

Transfer of journey(s) to different times of day, or different days. (eg. shopping switched to day when shops are open during early evenings)

Existing trip modelling procedures could in principle attempt to forecast changes in patterns of modal split, trip distribution and network flows that were involved. However even the most accurate forecasts would fail to account for changes in the timing of trips, and to a large extent changes in the numbers of trips implied by the evidence of what is conventionally termed trip suppression, and release of latent demand. But more significant implications for both research and policy were apparent from inspection of changes in the total daily trip patterns at the household level.

It was clear that changes in the characteristics of trips made by an individual traveller frequently affected both other trips previously made by this person, and trips made by other members of the same household. For example, car-based commuter journeys had frequently involved shopping, errands or visits being made "incidentally" during the journey home; transfer of the main journey to bus apparently then led to special journeys being generated from home during evenings or weekends. Effects upon other members of household were perhaps more complex; the release of the car by a commuter for use by the housewife in off-peak hours (in preference to use of 'park-and-ride') tended to in-

*) This paper is prepared in collaboration with I. G. Heggie and P. M. Jones, for presentation at the World Conference on Transport Research, Rotterdam, April 1977, and is based upon a joint research project sponsored by the Social Science Research Council. The paper may be subject to revision prior to publication in proceedings.

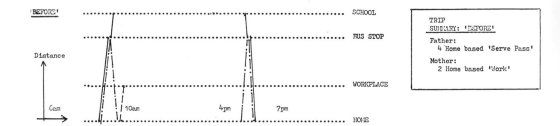

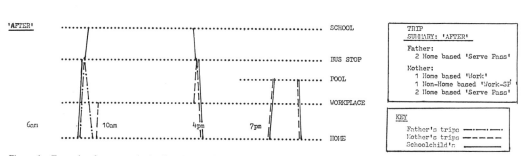

Figure 1 - Example of non-marginal adjustment to household trip pattern
Following changes to school and school bus times

volve substitution of off-peak trips from bus and walk modes. The former of course served to increase the peak loading problem for public transport operators, the latter contributed toward an upsurge in vehicular travel. Similarly, 'doubling-up' of 'serve passenger' trips was reported. For example; to replace a joint shopping activity in town accomplished in one journey, husband would drop wife in town to shop, then return home or drive elsewhere, to collect her and the shopping later in the day.

Secondary effects of policy can therefore be counter-productive if these are not anticipated at the planning stage. They may tend to offset benefits arising from the primary influence. In addition to this, traffic management schemes evidently incur important effects upon family routines, both in and out of the home; yet this is a dimension for the most part inaccessible to current evaluation methodology.

2.2 Other contemporary policy effects

Although some monitoring studies have been carried out into other contemporary policy measures, there is as yet very little detailed information available as to their precise effects. This situation may partly reflect the novelty of the policies, but is also the case that results are often treated in terms of indices, such as a fares elasticity or modal split value, which obscures the identification of response types at a disaggregate level.

Heggie (1977) reviews, in addition to work on car restraint effects, before-and-after studies of 'flexible working hours' introduction (Shapcott, Steadman 1977), and changes to school hours (Jones & Dix 1976). Both were adopted in the U.K., and both were motivated by the aim of spreading peak-hour loadings on road networks and bus systems, respectively. Noting that the 'flexi-hours' study showed that "...only a few people had deliberately altered their travel times so as to avoid the heaviest traffic", but that the opportunity to vary personal working schedules had instead "...enabled staff to get to the shops...in the centre of Reading in their lunch time...", Heggie concludes; "the stereotype of the traveller striving to avoid congested peak hour travel may be misleading. The substitute in this case was

not always travel in the off-peak, but the rescheduling of another linked activity to another time of day, depending on the relationship between home, work and shopping locations, to another destination". The picture is that of the commuter minimizing journey times, perhaps, but only so far as he is allowed by routine commitments over the day, and so far as to allow occasional activities (such as personal business) to be woven into the day's schedule.

The nature of effects from the school hour changes will be described later in the paper, where it is discussed in the context of model development. However an example of one household's response is given in completion of this section (Figure 1) to illustrate a fundamental point; that an apparently marginal change invoked by policy may trigger clearly non-marginal, often dramatic changes in trips recorded before and after the event.

2.3 Implications of responses to new policies for the concept of trip demand

Examination of the foregoing responses to contemporary policy implementation points toward important shortcomings within conventional specifications of trip demand.

At the empirical level, it is observed that general and distinctly non-marginal reorganization of household trip patterns may follow 'forced' changes to specific aspects of travel, such as the timing of journeys to school, or commuter use of cars in town. Under different policy circumstances, trip patterns may alternatively be surprisingly resilient to change, so that for example opportunities to vary times of travel may be foregone despite potential advantage in travel time or 'generalized cost' savings.

Further inspection reveals the presence of strong 'linkage' effects amongst households' patterns of trips; changes to particular trips affecting not only other aspects of given individuals' trips, but also travel arrangements for other members of the same household. Such 'linkage' effects are not embodied within trip demand models; instead, elements of the pattern of trips made over the day by households tend to be isolated, and connecting events obscured.

These two observations, of the non-marginality of responses, and the importance of linkages within household trip patterns, suggest that use of any trip demand model will meet with problems in inferring future travel patterns from the basis of currently revealed demand for trips. The problems will be more or less severe depending upon the particular application, but they cannot be regarded as merely empirical, since the observations raise questions about the appropriateness of a 'consumer demand' paradigm to travel behaviour.

Trip demand models tend to implicitly assume a direct demand for travel, or typically, for various types of trip classified according to purpose (work trips, shopping trips, etc.). This is despite explicit acknowledgement of the indirect nature of travel demand - viz., it is derived from demands to participate in various activities (work, shopping, etc.) which necessitate changes of location being made. The demand for almost any consumer good can of course be interpreted as indirect; the demand for overcoats indirectly reflects, perhaps, a need for warmth. Warmth is a characteristic that the consumer expects from his overcoat, and the distinction does not invalidate overcoat demand analysis since there is a sound conceptual equivalence between this, and analysis of demand for the characteristics of overcoats *per se*. The case of travel demand is less clear cut. A demand for the activity, shopping, may manifest trips to and from shops. Shopping is not however a characteristic of these trips, it is a distinct activity which under given circumstances is carried out in a way that involves a given set of trips. A change to the circumstances may, through the unexplored medium of linkages, be accompanied by changes to the number of trips made, their timing, destinations, origins, modes, and even which person is involved. It is then considerably more appropriate to postulate a demand for shopping than that for shopping trips, since to have any real value 'demand' needs to mean 'relatively stable demand', and whereas a relatively similar amount of household time and money is spent shopping 'before' and 'after', grossly different trip patterns may accompany the activity.

So whilst the failure of trip demand models to account for important linkages withing household travel behaviour may be regarded as an empirical shortcoming, which could be ameliorated by modifications to the structure of the models, to data inputs, and so on, there may alternatively be advantages in adopting some entirely different approach to the analysis of travel behaviour, in order to allow for the demonstrated nature of behavioural responses.

3. AN ALTERNATIVE FRAMEWORK FOR ANALYSIS OF TRAVEL DEMAND BEHAVIOR: EXPLORATORY FOUNDATIONS

3.1 Changing the unit of account in demand analysis

One such alternative is to change the basic unit of account, considering not trips *per se*, but the demand that is expressed over the day for participation in the basic consumer activities themselves (working, shopping, meals, school, TV, and so on) which being location-specific (to degrees) involve the additional activity of travel as a means of shifting location. From this point of view, individuals continuously devote their time to participation in activities, arrangements being subject to choice within constraints (work time and place, shop hours and locations, and so on). There will be a certain flexibility of travel arrangements within limits, whereby some household 'routine' or equilibrium of activity participation can be maintained throughout changes in immediate circumstances, including those determined by transport policy effects.

An approach using human activities as the unit of account has been described by Chapin (1974) within a general planning context, as the basis for investigating quality of life by Hägerstrand (1970), and has long been explicitly and implicitly used in sociology as a means for understanding life styles. Following seminal work by Jones (1974), work in progress at the Transport Studies Unit, Oxford has adopted a "Human Activity Framework" as the basis for "An Investigation of the Travel Decision Process".

Following sections describe research development using this alternative approach.

3.2 The character of individual behaviour in space and time

Simple plotting of individual space-time paths, using the format originating from Lund University (Hägerstrand 1970 et seq., et al) provides a useful means of representation. Using little additional data beyond that embodied in convential trip diary records (Figure 2) the 'backbone' structure of the household-day is given by the information within figure 3.

Individual paths are represented by the three traces for this household in 3(a). Oblique lines represent travel, vertical lines participation in some activity; individuals are always engaged in an activity even if it involves 'doing nothing'. The vertical cylinders represent permanent (short term) constraints; in this case the institutional constraints imposed by fixed work and school times. The local supply network of consumer facilities

	START TIME	ACTIVITY	LOCATION	MODE
	07.30	Wash, dress	Home	–
	07.50	Eat	*Home*	–
	08.10	*Travel*	–	*Car*
	08.40	Work	*Canal St.*	–
	12.45	Lunch	*Canal St.*	–
ACTIVITY DIARY:	13.30	*Work*	*Canal St.*	–
Full set of	*17.00*	*Travel*	–	*Car*
information.	*17.10*	*Shopping*	*George St.*	–
	17.30	*Travel*	–	*Car*
TRAVEL DIARY:	17.55	Prepare meal	*Home*	–
Subset of	18.20	Eat	Home	–
information	18.40	Wash, change	Home	–
which is	19.00	Watch TV	*Home*	–
underlined.	20.00	*Travel*	–	*Walk*
	20.10	*Drink & Social*	*"Dog & Duck"*	–
	22.40	*Travel*	–	*Walk*
	22.55	Prepare for bed	*Home*	–
	23.10	Sleep	Home	–

Figure 2 - Comparison of activity diary with travel diary

147

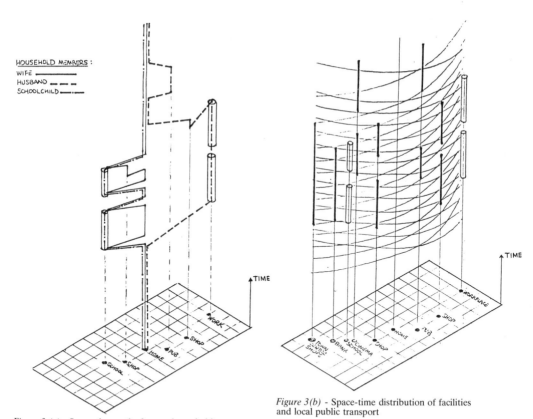

Figure 3 (a) - Space-time paths for one household
After Hagerstrand (1970)

Figure 3(b) - Space-time distribution of facilities and local public transport

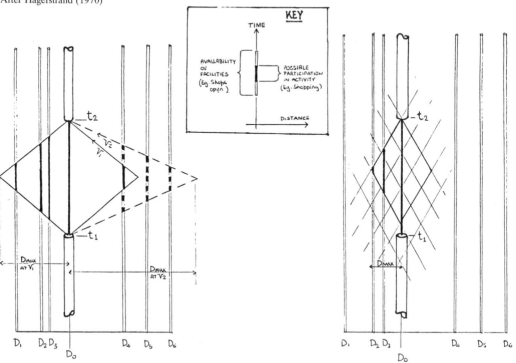

Figures 4 - Physical constraints on action within a 'window' of free time

4(a): Given unrestrained car use   After Hagerstrand (1970)   4(b): Within a bus network

and public transport is schematized in 3(b); this defines all possibilities for public transport use.

During periods of free time, when there is a choice of activity, the nature of the feasible choice set can be inferred from; the length of the block of free time available, the current location, the location and temporal availability of local facilities, and the transport possibilities, Hägerstrand illustrates the effect of these constraints with the concept of time-space prisms; figure 4(a).

Here, the individual has a block of free time (t_2-t_1), which he can fully devote to a chosen activity at his existing location (D_0) or use some of this time to travel to other locations (D_1-D_n) offering alternative activity facilities. The edge of the prism represents his maximum range $(D_{max} = V_1(t_2-t_1)/2)$ using all his time travelling. Increased speed (V_2), or extra facilities within the prism, increase the choice set. The operation of the bus schedule is more constraining (Figure 4b); comparatively few alternative facilities are available.

The choice within these constraints is either intralocational (choice of activity only, location given) or translocational (choice of activity and of destination). The latter would involve a trade-off situation between benefits expected from possible activities, costs of participation among alternative activities, and costs of (return) travel. Since some activity is always being performed, trade-offs must always be involved (for example within a given free-time period, the choice might be between watching TV at home, seeing a film at a local cinema, and seeing part of the film at a more distant cinema).

3.3 Additional constraints upon choice and action

In addition to constraints upon choice and action in space-time imposed by its physical dimensions and by particular configurations of land use, and also by institutional commitments (such as work or school) and physiological necessities (sleeping), the interview surveys identified a considerably larger set of effective constraints generally shared amongst the sample.

Individuals tend to experience a range of quite varied demands on time resources, the more so when functioning in a (family) group which establishes a routine and defines role commitments for its members; being at home "...because I know the dinner is waiting". "...the children will be getting back from school". ". . .my wife needs the car". . . .and so on. The family not only demands the use of individual time, it also tends to regulate when things are done; a "rhythm of urban activities" (Shapcott and Steadman, 1976) is maintained. Whether internal constraints such as these are regarded as determined by personal preference (Chapin 1974) or social commitment (Hägerstrand 1970) does not of course affect the reality of their operations.

Within the common constraints imposed by needs to attend work or school, to observe shop or cinema hours, to spend time sleeping, and preparing and eating meals, and to follow certain sequences of activity (eat and dress before going out), respondents were expected to display considerable variety both day-to-day, and amongst themselves. However, the synchronisation of joint activities (eating together, staying in together in preference to going out independently), through a tendency towards routinization ("you know where you are, then...") acted as a self-imposed constraint. Preconditions for certain optional activities were frequently, as a result, highly time-specific. The coincidence of, for example, 'free' blocks of time in both husband and wife's schedule, availability of the car, and sufficient block of shop opening time, was often restricted to Saturdays only - an extension of shopping hours would increase the choice

set in a predictable way.

Cost constraints operate too, but in a different way. Conceptually, there is a total cost attached to each alternative activity within the choice domain, which includes costs both of participation (cinema ticket) and any travel. Costs are subject to budget constraints. But money, unlike time, can be saved and transferred from one activity to another. Time can be transferred between activities within a given block of uncommitted time, but not beyond it, and the day has to be regarded as a series of separate and constrained time periods. It is unrealistic to regard time as a continuous variable in the functional sense, and this has serious implications both for trip demand models and for evaluations of travel time savings.

An illustration of the extent to which constraints determine the travel decision process is provided by the following 'example'. This is based upon the individual diary given in figure 2.

External constraints (figure 5a) comprise the spatial pattern of land use and the transport characteristics (assumed to comprise walk and car only for simplicity); these have a temporal dimension too since time is taken travelling between locations. Institutional constraints are as per 5b; and some additional time is allocated to physiological constraints; 5c. Internal constraints arising from obligations to joint activities with other household members are ignored.

The broad structure of the day along the time dimension is sketched out in figure 6. Note that from these basic but realistic assumptions, nearly three quarters of the day is taken up with committed activities; this excludes necessary travel time. Three 'windows' of possible choice appear. Firstly, after rising and before work, but the location (home) is effectively fixed. Secondly, during the lunchbreak, if he chooses to spend 15 minutes eating his essential shopping activity is impossible, because travel time plus shopping time exceeds available time. Shopping must instead be done in the free 'window' after work; and of the two shopping locations the more distant is infeasible since this closes at his time of earlies arrival (see figure 7).

Given the needs of this individual, and the constraints affecting him, nearly 80% of his weekday is determined by external factors; and the individual has no choice about the timing, destination, purpose or mode used for the three trips made. Clearly, changes to the pattern of constraints, such as changes to work or shop hours, land use configuration, or network travel times would allow (or force) behaviour to vary in certain respects, which would be predictable.

3.4 Interview surveys: procedures

Initial interview surveys (Dix 1975) were concerned to identify the forces that regulate ongoing patterns of household travel, and which apparently constrain the freedom of travel choice. The concern, as throughout, was with short-term adaptations, that is, residential and employment location decisions are taken as given. In a pre-pilot survey, protracted unstructured interview sessions were carried out among less than thirty multiperson households resident in a commuter village near Oxford. A number of alternative discussion frameworks were introduced into the interviews, the general theme being the conscious planning of travel arrangements. It was found that an interview framework in which household members discussed their sequence of activities over a weekday, and described variations to the plan occurring over the week and longer (including contingencies such as temporary car loss) performed better than one in which attention was implicitly restricted to trips; in the latter, short, incidental, optional and non-vehicular travel was not readily recalled, and explanations were markedly acausal in content. Experience from these interviews was consolidated by:

A pilot survey, which involved all household members from a sample of sixty-six households in Abingdon (Oxfordshire) in personal completion of continuous records of activities carried out over seven days, noting times, locations and travel modes. Unstructured interviews were carried out subsequently.

Following progressive inplementation of policies restraining the use of cars in Oxford, residents were interviewed in depth. (This survey was referred to in the Introduction).

During the most recent and main survey, 1,200 seven-day, activity travel diaries were collected in Banbury, together with full landuse information (including temporal availability of consumer facilities). Diary data is currently at the coding stage, and an additional fifty household follow-up interviews have been completed.

A. *Geographical*

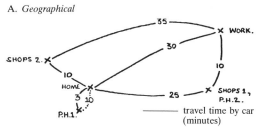

——— travel time by car (minutes)

······· travel time on foot (minutes)

B. *Institutional*

Work hours:	08:45 – 12:45; 13:30 – 17:00
Shop hours:	09:30 – 17:30
Pub hours:	18:00 – 22:30

C. *Physiological and Domestic*

Sleep	At least 8 hours
Meals	3 times a day (minimum 15 minutes plus preparation
Personal care	20 minutes morning; 15 minutes evening
Shopping	20 minutes

No household constraints

Figure 5 - General constraints on action

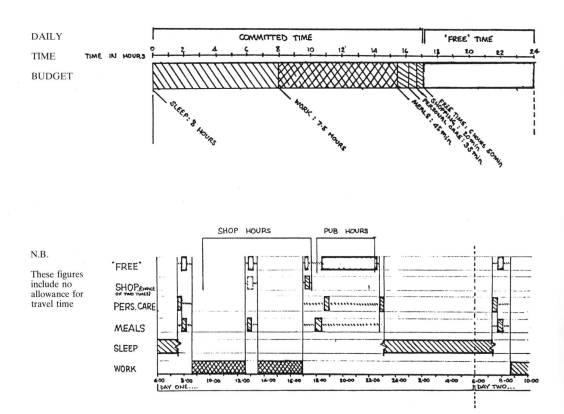

Figure 6 - Temporal scope for arrangement of activities

150

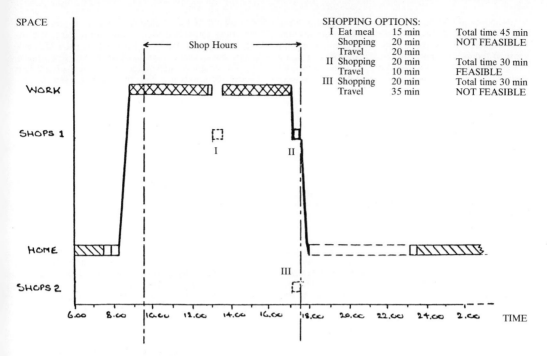

SPACE

SHOPPING OPTIONS:

I	Eat meal	15 min	Total time 45 min
	Shopping	20 min	NOT FEASIBLE
	Travel	20 min	
II	Shopping	20 min	Total time 30 min
	Travel	10 min	FEASIBLE
III	Shopping	20 min	Total time 30 min
	Travel	35 min	NOT FEASIBLE

Shop Hours

WORK

SHOPS 1

I   II

HOME

III

SHOPS 2

6.00 8.00 10.00 12.00 14.00 16.00 18.00 20.00 22.00 24.00 2.00   TIME

Figure 7 - Space-time constraints on action

3.5 The character of preferences and constraints among different types of household

An attempt will be made here to summarise, from the qualitative and quantitative information collected over the course of the investigation, salient differences within the population in terms of travel behaviour but also, more importantly, characteristic differences in preferences and constraints that seem to be causally related to the way travel is organized by identifiably different types of household.

The description is qualitative, tentative and incomplete. It may also only be general to the population of a medium-sized provincial town in the UK. For a somewhat fuller discussion, the reader should refer to Heggie (1977)

Household structure

One of the most striking features about travel behaviour is the apparent importance of stage in the family life cycle. Not only do family circumstances impose constraints on behaviour (eg. families with small children find travelling more difficult than families without), they also impose extra demands on time (eg. children need to be fed and attended to) and create complex problems of inter-personal synchronisation.

The follwing groups seem to represent the main stages in the family life-cycle in an English Provincial town:

Group I: Young adults, whether married or not, without children.

Group II: Families with dependent children, the youngest aged 7 yrs or less.

Group III: Families with dependent children, the youngest aged 12 yrs or less.

Group IV: Families with dependent children, the youngest aged 13 yrs or more.

Group V: Family of adults, all of working age.

Group VI: Elderly

Each group exhibits fairly distinct travel characteristics. They differ markedly between groups and are reasonably consistent within them. Even Group I, which includes both married and unmarried adults, seems to be fairly homogeneous, since the main and most significant change in life-cycle is associated with the arrival of small children. The most difficult division is between Groups III and IV. It is determined by the age at which the youngest child becomes relatively independent. It varies considerably between families, but seems to lie - with some exceptions - between the ages of 10 and 13.

The principal feature of Group I is that they engage in a great deal of discretionary travel. Persons living in or near the neighbourhood in which they grew up have fairly localised travel patterns. People living 'away from home', on the other hand, usually have quite elaborate travel patterns, reflecting the incidence of journeys designed to maintain extended family and friendship ties. This travel (or its end object) is highly valued and does not represent journeys which the individual, or family, would readily give up.

Group II are greatly affected by the presence of dependent children. This takes a variety of forms, but is usually perceived in terms of the physical encumberance itself; less flexibility in the venue and timing of meals; the need to synchronise family activities more closely; together with the increased time needed to prepare food, wash clothes and perform a variety of new household chores. Up to the age of about 5 the child usually has to accompany its mother on most, if not all, journeys and is physically dependent on her. This dependence, which still applies at weekends and during school holidays with older children, continues to be important until the youngest child reaches the age of about 7 years.

Group III are less affected by the physical difficulties associated with small children. Most parents are nevertheless unwilling to leave children of this age at home by themselves, so that they still tend to accompany - and to hamper - adult travel. The most significant phenomenon encountered in this sub-group, relates to the way in which the children stimulate discretionary travel. There

151

is a widespread feeling in this sub-group that free time should be used to "...take the children somewhere nice". Indeed, this becomes a minor preoccupation with most of the group who rationalise it in terms of being "...part of the children's education". It is thus seen as an essential means of broadening the children's learning experience during these particularly formative years. This period is also the time when children's group activities start becoming important with football, swimming, brownies, guides, scouts, etc., as important focal points. This becomes a further motive for engaging in discretionary travel.

The difference in travel patterns between Group III and IV is quite marked. By the time the youngest child reaches the age of about 12, the children (if there are more than one) are becoming relatively independent and both (a) wish to do their 'own thing' and (b) are able to do so because they can make many journeys on their own. The net effect is that parents seem to make fewer discretionary or child-based journeys and do not replace them by many new journeys of their own. Most parents are not willing to leave adolescent children at home by themselves and this restricts discretionary travel during the week, while at weekends the motive for (and child's desire to participate in) quasi-eductional travel is geatly diminished. The adults in such households nevertheless do seem to start recreating a life of their own. This often manifest itself as a desire, on the part of the housewife, to take a temporary job.

Although Group V forms a fairly distinctive category, it is also a little anomalous. Its members are in a state of transition since, although the standard UK Census definition [1] of a household still applies, the unit is really a twin household accompanied by multiple adult employment: one is a potential candidate for Group VI)the elderly); the other is an embryonic 'new' household awaiting reclassification in Group I. The characteristics of this Group are nevertheless not simply an amalgam of Groups I and VI. The embryonic household (the potential member of Group I) faces different constraints and has access to more communal resources while it remains in Group V. Commitments to other household members are also stronger, eg. some discretionary activities are still done on a 'family' basis, while claims on the use of the car are far stronger. A single adult living at home, exercising some claims on use of the family car, will thus make many more car-based discretionary journeys than a comparable Group I household without ready access to the family car.

The parent adults in Group V likewise seem to be more mobile than their counterparts in Group IV. There seems to be a higher incidence of adult group involvement, eg. in P.T.A. activities, church organisations, organised sport, recreation clubs, etc., and this usually involves increased discretionary journeys. Because they are frequently done in groups, however, there tends to be a great deal of car-sharing and use of chartered coaches.

Group VI again exhibits distinctive characteristics; the most obvious being the absence of the work journey. An additional - and quite striking - feature is the generally lower level of travel activity in general. The elderly do not engage in very much discretionary travel, even when they do own a car. Travel involves physical effort and is often thought of as confusing.

Another distinctive feature, is the gradual transformation of the household from an origin of journeys to a destination for them. They may not make many journeys themselves, but this does not mean that they are necessarily deprived of the activity underlying these journeys. The activity goes to them, instead of them going to it.

Stage in the family life cycle is thus an important determinant of travel patterns. Indeed, it seems to be even more important than household income. Income may have some effect (at least within each life-cycle group), but does not seem to be of primary importance. It is the characteristics associated with a progression through the family life-cycle that seem to exert the predominant effect.

Household characteristics

The characteristics of the household, particularly its level of mobility, are another important determinant of travel behaviour. They are a function of a number of factors including car-ownership, the incidence of neighbourhood car-sharing, the ownership of driving licenses, and access to public transport facilities.

The principal differences between car-owning and non-car-owning households lies (a) in the wider range of choice, in both home and workplace locations, available to the former (this usually results in a more complicated work journey) and (b) in the enhanced opportunities they enjoy for discretionary travel, particularly in life-cycle Group III. Non-car-owners are generally constrained to live, work and shop in a more limited physical environment. They are also usually members of life-cycle Groups I and IV; if not they tend to live in areas (particularly when they belong to Groups II and III) where most facilities are accessible on foort.

Neighbourhood car sharing is also associated with stage in the family life-cycle. Passenger journeys made in other people's car represent a large and rapidly expanding mode of travel (in the 1965 National Travel Survey [Dept. of Environment 1967] roughly 25 per cent of passenger journeys by car or van were made in other people's cars). The incidence of this phenomenon varies considerably between the different life cycle groups. It seems to be lowest in Groups II and IV, whilst in Group III it practically explodes. This is the time when children start participating in group activities which, for boys, include such things as: football (watching or playing), fishing, swimming and cubs/scouts. For girls, it includes: brownies/guides, swimming, music and ballet. Typically, one parent in a neighbourhood group provides transport for all the children participating in the activity (whether they come from car-owning households or not). At times the arrangement is formalised and a car-sharing rota is agreed; at others it is more spontaneous and does not necessarily involve a balanced sharing arrangement. Some parents may always take certain children to a common group activity. Car pooling for work also seems to start during this period, although this might reflect the increased demands on use-of-the car associated with the above child journeys. In a sense car sharing relaxes a constraint enabling a joint family asset - the car - to meet increased household demands.

The pattern of licence holding, which affects (or reflects) claims on use of the car, is also importantly dependent on stage in the family life-cycle. Most adult males nowadays acquire a driving licence as soon as possible after reaching the qualifying age. The same pattern is not repeated amongst adult females and a significant proportion do not initially acquire a licence. Once married and bringing up children the mother without a licence furthermore exhibits little desire to acquire a licence, while those with licences do not seem to drive very much. This only lasts until the youngest child reaches the age of about 7 or 8 years. The mothers - or a significant proportion of them - do then acquire a desire to drive and the incidence of driving licences seems to increase. This should be not suprise, since stage in the family life-cycle affects both 'needs' (the move from Group II to Group III coincides with an increase in serve passenger trips) as well as affecting household constraints. It would indeed be surprising if licence holding was not correlated with stage in the family life-cycle.

Access to public transport affects the household in an indirect way. Most non-car-owning households seem to live in areas where most of the necessities of life (shops, work, civic amenities, etc.) are readily accessible on foot, by bicycle, or by means of public transport. They live relatively self-contained lives and often form part of a tightly knit neighbourhood community. Car owning households, on the other hand, generally live in areas that are less accessible and use a combination of car/public transport/cycle/walk to accomplish a much more elaborate set of household activities. Although public transport is not often used, it usually fills a vital gap without which claims on use of the car would become so great that the singel-car owning household would either (a) have to acquire a second car (if they could afford one), or (b) would have to move house to a more accessible place.

It is thus clear that household characteristics have an important effect on travel behaviour. They are nevertheless not entirely independent of stage in the family life-cycle. A number are importantly dependent on it and change - in a quite discrete way - from one stage in the life-cycle to another. Even levels of car ownership are affected by it, although this is an extremely complex phenomenon since some households seem to substitute 'locational' mobility (ie. the choice of where to live), for household mobility (ie. whether or not to own a car).

3.6 Conclusions from exploratory study using the human activity framework

Preceding sections attempted to show how the approach adopted provides a coherent framework within which both quantitative and qualitative information can be integrated towards an understanding of travel behaviour.

The classification of households' preferences for activities by their lifecycle stages, and the description of observed within-group differences associated with additional characteristics such as car and licence ownership, suggests a functional basis for the segmentation of the population. Such a classification may be more appropriate to policy-oriented research than a segmentation carried out with respect to recorded trip-making characteristics. This is because the former is conceptually closer to 'need' for travel than the latter, which is restricted to considering revealed preferences for trips (which may themselves be unstable with respect to the same policy changes that the models may be required to consider). The activity-based classifications has in addition the useful property of closer correspondence to groups that are distinguished in everyday life.

Differences within the population are however subject to those general constraints upon action that were indicated earlier; individual preferences operate within these limits. Furthermore, the general stability of activity time-budgets is indicated by studies carried out internationally (amongst developed countries) which have shown remarkable similarities in terms of time allocated daily to different types of activity (Szalai 1972) despite considerable differences between social, racial, cultural and infrastructural characteristics.

The concern with constraints, largely ignored in the consumer travel choice framework, secures the useful operational advantage that inclusion of additional information reduces the choice set at each decision point.

This property of convergence contrasts with the escalation problem reported in connection with trip model developments; Ben-Akiva (1974) notes that "because of the large number of alternative trips that a traveller (now) faces (in these terms) . . . a simultaneous model can become very complex". In fact household data requirements for the sorts of model described in the following section are little more than those represented by conventional trip diaries; these latter merely happen to be poorly utilized within trip models.

In summary of this descriptive section, it is suggested that explicit consideration of travel as a means of shifting location, in order for participation in activities within space and time, provides a framework offering important conceptual advantages to policy-oriented research. Travel becomes responsive to changes in demand for the activities themselves, whilst the influences of transport supply conditions are themselves explicit. Thus, problems attached to notions of 'trip suppression' or 'latent demand for travel' do not arise, since the question of whether a trip is made is respecified as a trade-off between activity participation in alternative locations. A more realistic basis is also provided for considering questions such as 'travel need', 'minimum transport provision', 'personal mobility', and others, since need is specified in terms of need to be able to participate in certain activities. Appraisal of the opportunities for such participation must then take into account effects of landuse configuration, temporal availability of facilities and transport supply upon possible journey structures, and additionally, non-travel alternatives (such as mobile shop, libraries and deliveries) may be considered.

4. MODEL DEVELOPMENT
4.1 Types of model
Consideration of this characterisation of travel behaviour suggests that a range of models may more appropriately accommodate policy-oriented research needs than a single formulation.

In the first instance, certain mathematical programming approaches lend themselves to the approach, although initially, simplifying assumptions become necessary, so that a fully satisfactory application is regarded as a longer term outcome of the project.

A different alternative is to forego attempts to capture the individual's decision process extrinsically, instead using the individual to participate directly in the predictive exercise. The TSU 'Household Activity-Travel Simulator' realises this concept.

Finally a number of hybrid models can be envisaged, whereby a qualitative understanding of constraints upon action can be used to specify boundary conditions, within which econometric models might then be applied.

The first two developments will be described, beginning with 'HATS'.

4.2 The T.S.U. 'household activity-travel simulator'
The rationale behind HATS [2] is that a sampled group of households, or specifically, their predispositions towards travel decisions, become a functional part of the 'model', replacing any extrinsic system of mathematical proxies.

A number of planning techniques have adopted a similar tactic; for example the Community Priority Evaluator (Hoinville and Prescott-Clarke, 1974) and various Interactive Graphics techniques (egs. Arnstein & Winder, 1975; Rapp et al, 1976) all include the individual in their operational modelling procedures. Their applications are of course different from those of HATS, but a common principle is that a given stimulus provokes a set of tentative responses by the participating individual; a system of logical constraints disallows infeasible responses, and a means of representation feeds back the implications of each response to the participant who then evaluates and decides between alternatives.

Procedure

The HATS equipment, as used by rural Oxfordshire householders to explore responses to changed local school and school bus times before the event, is depicted in Figure 9 and 10. Each household member initially assembled a physical representation of activities and travel over a former termtime day which has previously been recorded on a diary. Figure 11 illustrates how combinations of the 'components' of the day (ten non-travel activity types, each colour-coded, and six alternative modes of travel) are assembled into the given board to provide a record of which activities were performed over the day, where, when, and using which travel links. This assembly is however designed to be readily manipulable, and in the next stage of procedure the necessary changes in external constraints (in this case, changes in times spent at school) are recreated on 'affected' individuals' boards. The immediate result is that the conflict between routines 'before' and the changed commitments 'after' appear as visible inconsistencies on the boards (egs. 'gaps' appear within the day, former transport connections fail to connect, individuals appear in two places at once, and so on; see Figure 12). An iterative process then begins, as household members acting both indivi-

dually and jointly explore their own spontaneous adaptations and what these mean in practice; they reorganize the pattern to produce logically consistent results. The need to account for activities continuously over the day imposes a 'closed system' characteristic, so that reper-

(i) One possible solution, and a certain journey structure

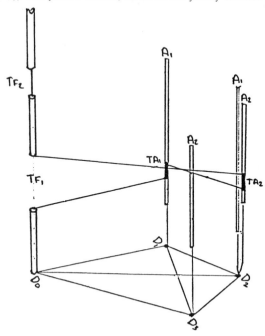

(ii), (iii), (iv); Variations to journey structure resulting from other possible solutions.

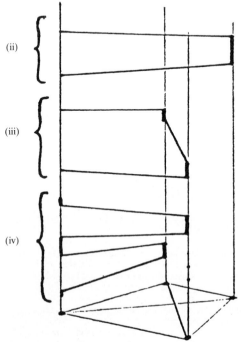

GIVEN:
(1) A home location, D .
(2) A set of non-home locations, D_1 - D_n; each catering for any or all of the non-home activity categories, A_1 - A ; for example . . .

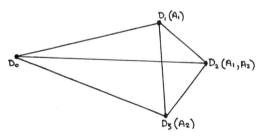

(3) Other network information (see text)
AND GIVEN ALSO:
(4) Constraints on individual schedules (eg. at home) such that the day comprises blocks of free time $T_f \ 1 \ T_{f1} \ldots$
(5) Constraints on availability of non-home facilities, for example . . . . . .

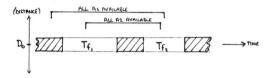

Allocate non-home activities (compulsory, and intitially fixed in duration (T_{A1} - T_{An}) to the supply network, using any or all free time periods (T_f) so as to . . .
(a) Statisfy the criteria (see text)
(b) Minimize travel time, and maximize free time at D_0 (see text)

Fig. 8(a) – Basis of mathematical programming formulation

Fig. 8(b) – Forms of solution to simple case of programming application

154

cussions of a possible primary response are made explicit. The household evaluates alternative possibilities in their own terms; deciding which is most 'convenient', or 'fair' or 'economic', or whatever criterion is normally adopted by the household, before determining the most likely response. The number of alternative feasible outcomes is in practice usually small, which itself reflects the nature of constraints normally operating on a household's day. The whole process, which typically involves an hour's interview time, involves considerable discussion and bargaining, which may be tape recorded for subsequent analysis. The end product is a new set of physical activity-travel diaries, to be coded and translated into the same format as the original diaries for purposes of analysis.

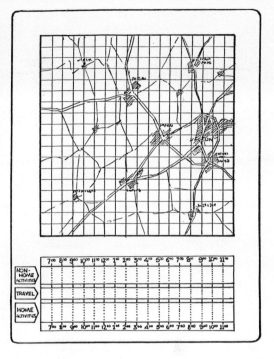

Figure 9 - A 'HATS' board

MAP LOCATIONS	0 SLEEP	1 PERSONAL CARE	2 EATING TEA, COFFEE.	3 HOUSEHOLD CHORES CHILD CARE	4 SHOPPING & SERVICES (e.g Bank, Doctor)	5 EDUCATION HOMEWORK	6 WORK	7 MEETINGS SOCIAL VISITS CHATTING	8 RECREATION SPORTS	9 RELAXATION ENTER- TAINMENT	MAP LOCATIONS
15 mins											15 mins
½ hour											½ hour
1 hour											1 hour
2 hours											2 hours
3 hours											3 hours

	MODE 'J'	MODE 'K'	MODE 'L'	MODE 'X'	MODE 'Y'	MODE 'Z'	MAP LOCATIONS FOR CHANGES OF MODE (Eg. Rail Station)
	10 min	10 min	10 min	10 min	10 min	10 min	
	15 min	15 min	15 min	15 min	15 min	15 min	
	30 min	30 min	30 min	30 min	30 min	30 min	

Figure 10 – Household activity-travel simulator components display box

155

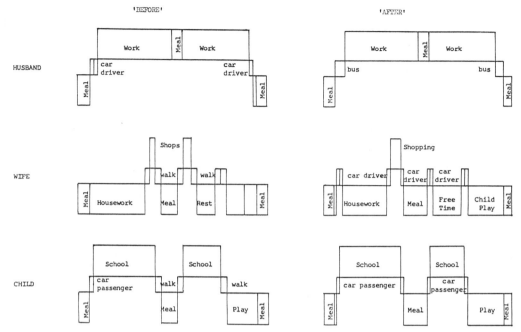

Figure 11 - 'HATS' representations of a household activity-travel pattern, 'before' and 'after' a 'policy change'

THE USE OF 'HATS'. . .

. . reveals the emergence of unaccounted for periods of time and the impossibility of being in two places at once:

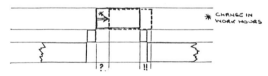

. . shows the repercussions of a change in activity-travel pattern throughout the day:

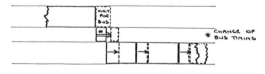

. . and makes explicit the activity trade-offs that lead to trip generation or suppression:

Figure 12 - Logical checks embodied in 'HATS' procedure

Applications

Potential applications of HATS are numerous, the chief limitations on use being: (a) Surveys are necessarily limited in scale to sample sizes typical of depth interview surveys (which in some situations HATS would advantageously replace). (b) Long-term responses to policy are beyond reach, since reliance is upon current knowledge of alternatives, and therefore results of job or residential relocation cannot be anticipated. (c) A financial budget is not explicit. It is implicit to the judgement of alternatives by participants, but money cost changes are not represented physically as are time changes. HATS development is intended to incorporate cost constraints, but the present version would not be suitable for studies of, for example, marginal changes to fares levels.

Within these limitations, HATS can offer hypotheses within areas of policy planning and evaluation that are beyond the scope of current trip models. Its present form was developed specifically for one such application; the school hour changes study.

Some summary results from this study will be presented here, to illustrate the nature of behaviour changes that can be successfully predicted by use of this 'model'. Predictions were gathered from 34 Oxfordshire households with children in attendance at Burford School, prior to introduction of a policy of staggering school transport arrangements, whereby Burford's times were advanced half an hour in the morning, and bus schedules were made more efficient. Predictions were subsequently confirmed by a postal questionnaire survey following the change itself (the only cases where predictions were not borne out involved apparent deviations of actual bus operation from the intended service schedules).

Forms of output

Firstly, HATS was able to expose linkage effects

within individual trip patterns. All school journeys involved changes of timing; for the majority of families, children's arrival home up to an hour earlier led to two kinds of increased trip making. These were in connection with late afternoon activities formerly confined to weekends (mainly social and shopping) or more frequently, evening social and leisure activities. The factor facilitating these arrangements was not a sudden availability of transport, but simply the appearance of a sufficiently 'long' free time 'window' (due to homework being cleared early). This demonstrates the dependence of 'trip generation' upon the temporal scope for return travel *and* activity participation within alternative (non-home) locations.

Secondly, linkage effects between household members' travel arrangements were exposed by HATS, allowing successful predictions of repercussion throughout the entrie household's trip pattern. Examples included cases where earlier return home enabled the family to combine meeting children at the bus stop with another travel generating activity, 'saving' a journey in each case; one household decided to abandon chauffeuring children to two different schools because the phasing would now rule out a round trip, hence children were transferred to buses; and others involved re-routing of a regular journey to work including a chauffeur-to-school role. Cases such as these demonstrate how the concept of 'convenience' of transport (which was raised again and again by participants) is a question of interface between transport supply, and committed household activities both outside and inside home, rather than being an attribute of transport supply *per se* as it is sometimes represented.

A third area in which HATS was able to operate was that of the evaluation of changes incurred to routines within the home. This aspect is dealt with comprehensively in Jones and Dix (1977); a generalization to be noted here being that apparently minor alterations to an in-home schedule (such as a working wife's extra half hour to clear up from the family breakfast before leaving for work) were often considered to represent extremely important benefits from policy. The contrast between the delight expressed towards 'relief of pressure' on normally 'tight schedules', especially associated with 'packing everyone off in the morning', and on the other hand, the potential concern over children returning home before the wife, illustrates that time savings are valued, not absolutely, but in terms of their results. It is their distribution that is important, in a way that has clear objective correlates in analyses of activity diary data.

This outline of results from the trial using HATS shows how results can be expressed at several levels. Forecasts of trip pattern reorganizations can be provided by simple extraction of 'before' and 'after' trip data in conventional terms. Comparison of activity patterns allows for redistributed time savings to be assessed in aggregate between activity groupings, providing a rigorous behavioural basis for valuation of these. In principal, marginal time utilities between activities may also be investigated. Finally, qualitative records of discussion and bargaining provide substantial data for both the investigation of rules by which decisions are made, and the sensitive evaluation of effects from policy changes.

4.3 Applications of mathematical programming

The simplest from of programming model derives from an interest in analysing the possible effects of different landuse configurations upon journey structures. Specific interest is on the timing and sequencing of trips, and the likelihood of multipurpose and multitrip journeys given different patterns of spatial distribution of (in the simple case) local shops and services, and a 'housewife-shopper' with commitments to being 'home' during fixed periods of the day. Specification of different schedules of in-home commitment will simulate characteristic constraints within households of different type, and different home locations selected within the main survey area will simulate characteristically different spatial configurations of local shopping and service facilities with respect to the 'home', base.

The simple problem is set in these terms:

A one-person-day is specified in which given time periods are committed either to 'in-home activities' or 'free time'. A set of non-home activities is also given; each is compulsory and is of specified duration. These latter must be assigned to any of a set of given non-home locations, at any time and in any sequence, provided that (a) the location provides facilities for the activity and (b) these facilities are 'open' for use at the time. Travel and non-home activities must be carried out during a 'free time window' and time for these may be taken from any or all windows. A travel time matrix is constructed, initially, for one mode only. The problem is to establish the optimum timing and route which (a) satisfies the given criteria, (b) minimizes travel time and (c) maximizes continuous free time at home. The problem is set out and explained by Figure 8.

Development into a more sophisticated and general activity-travel model (see Jones and Dempster 1977) will follow in stages, and involves creation of a more detailed supply network, together with more detailed and flexible specifications of 'given' activities over the day. The main data base is to be used as a means of providing data on these input variables, and also for checking results against recorded journey structures as the specification is changed, in a hypothetico-deductive fashion.

Network improvements are to include real times of availability of all facilities; generalized cost matrices for 'all' models by time of day, and attraction ratings across facilities.

Uset representation will also become more realistic by stages. Still at the individual user level, other commitments are specified (work, school, 'logical' sequences). A specification of activity needs for a given type of multi-person household follows, commitments remaining fixed in time, but with joint participation for certain activities appearing as an additional constraint. A move from a given day to a longer period, allowing substitution of activities between different days, would be a further refinement. Ultimately, time duration for certain committed activities would become variable, within limits; this requires both a move towards procedures using optimal control theory, and a specification of marginal utilities of time transfer between certain activities. The use of 'HATS' within semi-experimental situations can, in principle, fulfil the latter requirement.

Objective functions are crucial; experience shows that the nature of these should vary according to the household 'type', and an interesting possibility to be tested is the use of a constant travel time budget in this sense (cf. Zahavi, 1973; Bullock et al, 1974; Goodwin, 1975).

5 CONCLUSIONS

Studies of human activity within the travel research context are in their very early stages, and substantial conceptual and empirical problems remain to be resolved.

Although the potential benefits of such an approach have yet to be widely demonstrated, it would nevertheless appear to offer considerable conceptual advantages over the trip demand framework, and its field of application may be considerably greater.

Further research is to concentrate upon development of increasingly appropriate mathematical models, but the qualitative understanding of the phenomenon of travel behaviour suggests that less formal approaches, including the variants of 'HATS', may have an assured role both for pragmatic planning; and for 'pure' research. In certain applications 'HATS' can produce information about primary and secondary impacts of policy, that can be expected to be both more complete and more reliable than the most accurate output of current 'behavioural' trip models.

6 REFERENCES

Arnstein, S. A., and Winder, J. S. Jnr., 'Discussion of Potential Users of Interactive Computer Graphics in Citizen Participation', **Transpn. Res. Record 553,** Transpn. Res. Board, Washington (1975).

Ben-Akiva, M. E., 'Structure of Alternative Travel Behaviour Structures'. **Transpn. Res. Record 526,** Transpn. Res. Board, Washington (1974).

Bullock, N., Dickens, P., Shapcott, M., and Steadman, P., 'Time Budgets and Models of Urban Activity Patterns', **Social Trends No. 5,** HMSO London (1974)

Chapin, F. S. Jnr., **Human Activity Patterns in the City: Things people do in Time and Space,** John Wiley and Sons (1974)

Dix, M. C., 'Application of In-Depth Interviewing Techniques to the study of Travel Behaviour: some preliminary results' **Transport Studies Unit Working Paper No. 9,** University of Oxford (1975)

Goodwin, P. B., 'Variations in travel between Individuals living in Areas of Different Population Density' **PTRC Paper No. 27,** Annual Meeting, University of Warwick (1975)

Hägestrand, T. 'What about people in regional science?' **Papers and Proceedings, Regional Science Assn.,** Vol 24 (1970)

Heggie, I. G. 'A Pilot Survey of Urban Travel Behaviour in Oxford' **Transport Studies Unit Working Paper No.21,** University of Oxford

.... 'Putting Behaviour into Behavioral Modes of Travel Choice' **Transport Studies Unit Working Paper No.22,** University of Oxford

Hoinville, G., and Prescott-Clarke, P., 'The Priority Evaluation Approach' **Social and Community Planning Reasearch** Reports, London 1974

Jones, P. M., 'An Alternative Approach to Person Trip Modelling', **PTRC Paper N23,** Annual Meeting (1974)

Jones, P. M., **Travel as a Manifestation of Activity Choice: Trip Generation Reinterpreted,** Conference on Urban Transport Planning, University of Leeds (1976)

Jones, P. M. and Dempster, M., **Transport Studies Unit Working Paper;** University of Oxford (forthcoming) (1977)

Jones, P. M. and Dix, M. C., 'Final Report of a Study of changing school hours, using "HATS" **Transport Studies Unit, Working Paper,** University of Oxford (forthcoming) (1977)

O.E.C.D., 'Better Towns with Less Traffic', **Report of OECD Conference,** Paris (1975)

Rapp, M. H., Mattenberger, P., Piguet, C. and Robert-Grandpierre, A., 'Interactive Graphics System for Transit Route Optimisation', **Transpn. Res. Record 559** Transp. Res. Board Washington (1976)

Shapcott, M. and Steadman, P. 'Rhythms of Urban Activity', **Report from the Martin Centre for Architectural and Urban Studies,** Cambridge (1976)

.... 'A Study of the Introduction of Flexible Working Hours in Reading', **Report from the Martin Centre for Architectural and Urban Studies,** Cambridge (1976)

Szalai, A. (Ed.) **The Use of Time,** Mouton, The Hague (1972)

Zahavi, Y., 'The TT-Relationship: a unified approach to transportation planning', **Traffic Engineering and Control,** 15(4/5) (1973)

FOOTNOTES

1. The 'household' includes one or more people sharing common housekeeping

2. The apparatus carries a preliminary patent no.45,433/76 lodged in the names of P. M. Jones and M. C. Dix.

Aggregate forecasting with dissaggregate travel demand models using normally available data

by
FRANK S. KOPPELMAN
Northwestern University Evanston, Illinois

and
MOSHE E. BEN-AKIVA
Massachusetts Institute of Technology Cambridge, Massachusetts

INTRODUCTION

Disaggregate travel choice models have been extensively developed in recent years (CRA, 1972; PMM, 1973; Ben-Akiva, 1973; Richards and Ben-Akiva, 1974; Lerman and Ben-Akiva, 1975; and others). Their development has contributed to the refinement of theories of travel behavior through improved identification of explanatory variables and their relative influence on travel choice behavior. This paper is concerned with the application of disaggregate models to obtain predictions of aggregate travel flows required for transportation systems analysis and planning. In this context prediction is the final step in a sequence of activities which include model development, estimation and prediction (Figure 1). The flow diagram in Figure 1 calls for the use of a prediction procedure which obtains the desired aggregate predictions based on predicted input data and the estimated disaggregate model. The objective of this paper is to identify prediction procedures for use with disaggregate models which (1) use commonly available data or additional data which can be obtained easily, (2) are computationally inexpensive, and (3) provide relatively accurate travel predictions.

Behavioral travel demand theory is postulated at the level ot the decisionmaking or behavioral unit, usually an individual or household. Disaggregate travel choice models are estimated at this level of analysis. The resultant disaggregate model takes the form:

$$P_t = f(X_t, \theta) \tag{1}$$

where
P_t is the probability that individual t selects a given alternative,

X_t is a vector of independent variables for individual t,

θ is a vector of model parameters, and

$f(\ )$ denotes the functional form of the demand relationship.

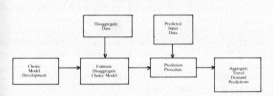

Figure 1 - Model development, estimation and prediction

Aggregate travel demand is the sum of the travel choices of numerous behavioral units making independent decisions. Thus, the aggregate share of travelers choosing an alternative is obtained by averaging the disaggregate choice probabilities over the relevant population so that

$$\bar{D} = \frac{1}{T} \sum_{t=1}^{T} P_t$$
$$= \frac{1}{T} \sum_{t=1}^{T} f(X_t, \theta) \tag{2}$$

where $\bar{D}$ is the share of the population choosing the alternative, and

T is the number of individuals in the population.

This formulation implies that the independent variables for each individual, X_t, must be known or predicted for every member of the population in order to predict aggregate demand. The difficulty of satisfying this requirement motivates the search for alternative aggregation procedures.

An alternative situation exists when the distribution of independent variables is known for the population. The joint distribution of independent variables can be expressed as

$$h(X, \bar{X}, \alpha) \tag{3}$$

where $\bar{X}$ is the vector of mean values for the independent variables, and

α is a vector of other parameters describing the distribution of X.

In this case, aggregate demand is obtained by integrating the individual demand function over the distribution of independent variables so that:

$$\bar{D} = \int_X f(X, \theta) \, h(X, \bar{X}, \alpha) \, dx \tag{4}$$

which can be expressed as an aggregate demand function by [1]

$$\bar{D} = F(\bar{X}, \theta, \alpha) \tag{5}$$

This formulation implies that aggregate demand is determined by the distribution of the independent variables as well as the coefficients of the disaggregate demand function.

159

This definition of aggregate demand shows that, in general, substitution of the mean values of the independent variables in the disaggregate demand function will not equal the aggregate demand function. That is,

$$\bar{D} \neq f(\bar{X}, \theta) \tag{6}$$

since, in general,

$$F(\bar{X}, \theta, \alpha) \neq f(\bar{X}, \theta) \tag{7}$$

The magnitude of the error resulting from substitution of aggregate values in the disaggregate model depends on both the form of the demand function and the shape of the distribution of independent variables. There are two situations for which the substitution does not result in any aggregation error. These are:
- when the aggregate group is homogeneous with respect to the values of the independent variables - that is, every individual has identical values of the variables; or,
- when the disaggregate demand function is linear in the independent variables. [2]

In these two situations only:

$$\bar{D} = f(\bar{X}, \theta) \tag{8}$$

and only information on mean values is required for prediction. However, these two situations are rare in travel demand applications. Thus, in general, the use of average population variable values in the disaggregate choice model (as is normally done in the use of conventional aggregate models) will produce aggregate errors. [3]

Complete elimination of this aggregation error requires detailed information on the distribution of individual variables. Such information is generally either not available or difficult and expensive to obtain. Thus, the basic problem in aggregate prediction is to find a procedure which will reduce this aggregation error using readily available or easily obtained information on the distribution of independent variables.

ALTERNATIVE AGGREGATION PROCEDURES

We can identify a variety of aggregation procedures with different information requirements, different levels of computational complexity and different levels of expected aggregation error. Koppelman (1976a) proposed a taxonomy of aggregation procedures depicted in Figure 2 and described below.

Procedures of enumeration are based on the theoretical relationship between aggregate and disaggregate demand defined in equation 2. Aggregate demand is calculated by averaging individual demands. Complete enumeration is accomplished by averaging individual demand predictions for the entire population and requires values of independent variables for the entire population. Sample enumeration estimates aggregate demand by averaging predictions for a sample of the population only. Sample enumeration requires data only for the sample used, but introduces random variations due to the nature of the sampling process.

Procedures of summation/integration weight the disaggregate demand estimates by the probability density function for the indepentent variables. This is done by integration when the density function is continuous (equation 4), or by summation when the distribution is discrete. The aggregation error of these procedures depends primarily on the accuracy of the distributional representation and secondarily on the computational

procedure used. These procedures may be differentiated by the use of estimated or assumed distributions.

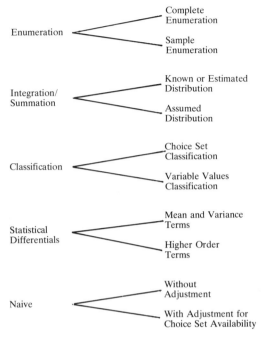

Figure 2 - Taxonomy of aggregation procedures

Procedures of statistical differentials express aggregate demand as a function of the moments of the distribution of independent variables. The aggregate function is obtained by linearizing the disaggregate function by a Taylor series expansion about the mean values and taking expectations (Talvitie, 1973). In practice, the resultant series is always truncated so that aggregate demand is expressed in terms of the means, variances and covariances of the distribution of independent variables.

Procedures of classification assign members of the population to relatively homogeneous groups, use group-average variable values to predict demand for each group using the naive procedure (described below), and compute aggregate demand as the weighted average of group demands. Classification procedures are differentiated by the basis for classification and the number of classes used. An important classification basis in travel choice models is the set of available alternatives (or choice set), which may differ among population subgroups.

The naive procedure uses the mean value of the independent variables in the disaggregate demand function to predict aggregate demand. The naive procedure is a special case of summation/integration procedures (when the distribution is degenerate), statistical differentials procedures (when the series is truncated after the first term) and classification procedures (when only one class is used). It is useful to consider this procedure separately for four reasons. First, the data requirements are the same as those for conventional aggregate models. Second, it is computationally and conceptually simple. Third, it is the method most likely to be used when the aggregation problem (equation 6) is not recognized. Fourth, it establishes a benchmark against which the aggregation error of other procedures may be compared.

The naive procedure can be modified by information on choice set availability when such information exists.

It is useful to identify a smaller set of aggregation procedures which are most likely to satisfy the dual objectives of small aggregation error and minimal requirements for additional information. Sample enumeration is particularly useful for short-range analysis when a prior sample exists. In this procedure, a sample of the population is used for prediction after modifying the variables for each observation to reflect the policy being analyzed (reduce transit fare by X%, impose a parking surcharge of Y dollars, etc.). This procedure has been used in recent studies by CSI (1976), Ben-Akiva and Atherton (1977), and Small (1977). The advantage of this procedure is that it accurately reflects individual or household characteristics when the prediction time-frame is sufficiently short to assume that households remain unchanged except for the effects of the policy imposed.

The sample enumeration is approximated for long-range prediction or when a prior sample does not exist by a Monte Carlo integration procedure which we refer to as the *pseudo-sample enumeration procedure*. In this procedure a pseudo sample is synthesized by taking random drawings from the expected future distribution of independent variables. The development of pseudo samples can be simplified by assuming that the distribution of variables are independent and/or that some variables have no distribution. Procedures for generating a pseudo sample of households using census data or other readily available data have been developed by Duguay *et al.* (1976), and Chatterjee *et al.* (1977), and applied to an area-wide analysis of urban travel by Koppelman *et. al.* (1976).

Naive and classification procedures are suitable for many applications because they require information which is commonly available in existing studies and do not require changes in the basis structure of conventional travel forecasting software. If only the means of the variables are available, the naive procedure must be used. When classifications are available for important variables such as household size, income or automobile availability, these classifications can be used. Classification by the availability of different alternatives, which may be determined by access distance to public transportation alternatives or vehicle ownership for private alternatives, is very effective in reducing aggregation error. Information about the portion of the population which has access to different alternatives also can be used to adjust naive predictions as described in the next section.

Classification using values of level-of-service variables (distance to a transit station) was used in a Dual Mode case study (CSI, 1975). An urban transportation model system developed for the San Francisco Metropolitan Transportation Commission uses a classification scheme based on number of workers in the household, income and automobile ownership (Ruiter and Ben-Akiva, 1977).

Statistical differentials procedures may be used to improve on naive predictions when the spread or variance of the distribution is relatively small. However, when the distribution is wide, statistical differentials with mean and variance terms often produces aggregation errors greater than those of the naive procedure.

Thus, the aggregation procedures most appropriate for general application should be selected from (1) sample enumeration, (2) pseudo-sample enumeration or Monte Carlo integration, (3) classification by alternative availability or variable values, and (4) the naive procedure with or without adjustment for choice-set availability. Each of these procedures provides aggregate predictions based on information which either is commonly available in current forecasting studies or can be developed with reasonable effort.

USE OF CHOICE SET INFORMATION

The choice set adjusted naive procedure modifies prediction by the naive procedure to account for differences in alternative availability. Different adjustment procedures can be used depending on the available information. When the analyst knows the portion of the population which has each set of choices available, the share choosing each alternative within each choice set group is:

$$S_{ig} = \frac{S_i}{\sum_{j \epsilon A_g} S_j} \qquad \text{if } i \epsilon A_g \text{ (if alternative i is available to group g),} \qquad (9a)$$

$$S_{ig} = 0 \qquad \text{otherwise.} \qquad (9b)$$

where
S_{ig} is the share of group g predicted to choose alternative i,

S_i is the naive prediction for choice share i, and

A_g is the set of alternatives available to group g.

That is, the choice shares for alternatives which are not available are set to zero and the choice shares for the remaining alternatives are increased proportionally. The population choice shares are the weighted (by size of choice set group) average of choice shares for each group:

$$S_i^* = \sum_g R_g S_{ig}, \qquad (10)$$

where
S_i^* is the adjusted share prediction, and

R_g is the proportion of the population which has choice set g available.

Consider, for example, a share prediction for three alternatives, two of which are available to the entire population. If R_1 is the proportion of the population which has all three alternatives available and S_1, S_2 and S_3 are the naive predictions, the adjusted shares are:

$$S_1^* = R_1 S_1 \qquad (11a)$$

$$S_2^* = R_1 S_2 + (1 - R_1) \frac{S_2}{S_2 + S_3} = S_2 \left[\frac{1 - R_1 S_1}{1 - S_1} \right] \qquad (11b)$$

$$S_3^* = R_1 S_3 + (1 - R_1) \frac{S_3}{S_2 + S_3} = S_3 \left[\frac{1 - R_1 S_1}{1 - S_1} \right] \qquad (11c)$$

A different situation exists when the analyst knows the portion of the population which has each alternative available but does not know how availability of different alternatives is related. For example, the analyst may know that twenty percent of the population does not have an automobile available and sixty percent does not have commuter rail available, but he might not know which, if any, part of the population does not have either alternative available. In this case the naive prediction is adjusted by:

$$S_i^* = S_i R_i \left[\frac{1 - S_i}{1 - S_i R_i} \right] \cdot \frac{1}{K} \qquad (12a)$$

$$K = \sum_j \left[\frac{1 - S_j}{1 - S_j R_j} \right] S_j R_j \qquad (12b)$$

where
R_i is the proportion of the population with alternative i available, and

K is a normalization factor which assures that the sum of shares equals one.

When only one alternative has partial availability, as in the above example, both adjustment procedures produce identical results.

Classification assigns the population to groups according to the actual choice set available or according to the values of selected variables (the selection of the method of classification in discussed later). Average values of the explanatory variables are determined for each of the population groups. The naive procedure is used to predict choice shares for each group. The overall estimate of choice shares is obtained by weighting the choice shares for each group according to its size:

$$S_i = \sum_g R_g S_{ig}. \qquad (13)$$

where S_i is the predicted share,

R_g is the size of group g, and

S_{ig} is the predicted share for group g.

Classification procedures can be simplified by using population averages for some variables and group average values for other variables based on the differences which they contribute to the choice utility estimates. When only population average variables are used, this procedure is equivalent to the choice set adjusted naive procedure.

EMPIRICAL STUDIES OF AGGREGATION ERROR

Aggregation procedures, other than complete enumeration, introduce aggregation error to aggregate demand predictions. The magnitude of aggregation error depends on the prediction situation. However, Koppelman (1975) has shown that the relative performance of different aggregation procedures is relatively stable over a wide range of prediction situations. The purpose of this section is to describe the results of some empirical analyses of aggregation error. The results of these analyses are indicative of the performance of these aggregation procedures in different situations.

The analysis is based on mode share predictions for the work trip to the Central Business District (CBD) from residence districts in the Washington, D.C. metropolitan area. [4] A disaggregate logit choice model was estimated to predict choice probabilities for drive alone, shared ride and transit. The drive-alone alternative is available only to individuals who have a driver's license and reside in a household which has one or more automobiles. The other alternatives are available to all individuals. The choice model includes variables which describe the household (in terms of income, number of automobiles and number of workers), the level of service by different modes (in terms of travel time and cost), and the existence of incentives (special parking privileges, etc.) to use the shared-ride alternative.

Aggregation errors are determined by comparing the predictions by a selected aggregation procedure to corresponding predictions by the sample enumeration procedure. The aggregation procedures considered are:
– the naive procedure
– the naive procedure with adjustment for choice set availability,
– classification by choice set *and* automobile availability,
– classification by choice set availability *only,* and
– classification by automobile availability *only.*

The aggregation error for each prediction (each mode for each district) is expressed relative to the magnitude of the prediction by

$$E_{md} = \frac{\hat{N}_{md} - N_{md}}{\hat{N}_{md}} \qquad 14)$$

where E_{md} is the relative aggregation error for the prediction of mode m in district d,

N_{md} is the observed number choosing mode m in district d, and

$\hat{N}_{md}$ is the predicted number choosing mode m in district d.

The aggregation errors for each prediction are summarized first by mode in terms of average error, standard deviation of error and root-mean-square error, all weighted by the magnitude of prediction, as follows:

$$AE_m = \sum_d E_{md} \cdot \frac{\hat{N}_{md}}{N_m} \qquad (15a)$$

$$SDE_m = \left[\sum_d (E_{md} - AE_m)^2 \cdot \frac{\hat{N}_{md}}{N_m} \right]^{\frac{1}{2}} \qquad (15b)$$

$$RMSE_m = \left[\sum_d E_{md}^2 \cdot \frac{\hat{N}_{md}}{N_m} \right]^{\frac{1}{2}} \qquad (15c)$$

$$N_m = \sum_d \hat{N}_{md} \qquad (15d)$$

where AE_m is the average error for mode m,

SDE_m is the standard deviation of error for mode m, and

$RMSE_m$ is the root-mean-square error for mode m.

These error measures can be further summarized across modes to obtain overall measures of error by:

$$AE = \left[\sum_m \frac{N_m}{N} (AE_m)^2 \right]^{\frac{1}{2}} \qquad (16a)$$

$$SDE = \left[\sum_m \frac{N_m}{N} (SDE_m)^2 \right]^{\frac{1}{2}} \qquad (16b)$$

$$RMSE = \left[\sum_m \frac{N_m}{N} (RMSE_m)^2 \right]^{\frac{1}{2}} \qquad (16c)$$

$$N = \sum_m N_m \qquad (16d)$$

The average, standard deviation and root-mean-square error terms by mode or overall are related by

$$RMSE^2 = AE^2 + SDE^2. \qquad (17)$$

That is, the root-mean-square error, which is a total error measure, can be disaggregated into average and variational components. [5]

This summarization makes it possible to represent the aggregation error in multiple predictions with a relatively small amount of information. The root-mean-square error for all modes provides a single overall index of aggregation error. Disaggregation into average and standard deviation error or by modes or both provides more detailed information on the types of error and their source. This summary of aggregation error for the naive procedure is given in Table 1. The overall expected aggregation error is 10.5 percent of predicted values. The portion of this error associated with average error is 6.2 percent, and that associated with standard deviation around average error is 8.5 percent. The overall error can also be analyzed in terms of the errors associated with the prediction of each of the modal shares. The observed aggregation errors are substantially larger for the transit-ride alternative than for either the drive-alone or shared-ride alternatives.

Table 1 - Aggregation error by naive procedure summarized across 45 districts

	MODE			
	Drive Alone	Shared Ride	Transit Ride	All Modes
Average error	6.0	0.6	–8.7	6.2
Standard Deviation of Error	7.4	6.6	11.1	8.5
Root Mean Square Error	9.5	6.6	14.1	10.5

Similar summaries of aggregation error by the other procedures have also been developed but will not be reported here. Instead, we compare the aggregation error for all the procedures in terms of the average, standard deviation and root-mean-sqaure error summarized across modes (Table 2). Table 2 indicated the degree to which aggregation error by the naive procedure is reduced by the use of additional information.

The use of alternative information in the naive procedure with adjustment reduces aggregation error by almost 25 percent. This reduction is due to a substantial decrease in the standard deviation of error and a small increase in the average aggregation error. Classification by choice set alone or choice set and automobile avialability alone results in a nominal reduction in aggregation error. The rank order of aggregation error for each procedure is given in Table 3. The corresponding subjective ranking of degree of information and effort required to use each procedure is also given in Table 3. This information provides the basis for selecting procedures which use increasing information to reduce aggregation error. The additional effort of classification using choice set availability compared to adjustment of the naive procedure results from the need to obtain class-specific variable values which are not required for the naive procedure with adjustment.

The rankings for magnitude of aggregation error and information and effort required are generally in reverse order. However, the naive procedure with adjustment for choice set availability is preferable to classification based on automobile availability with respect to both criteria. Thus, we obtain a reduced set of procedures for use when sample enumeration is not feasible. These are (1) the naive procedure, (2) naive procedure with choice set adjustment, (3) classification by choice set availability, and (4) classification by choice set and automobile availability in increasing order of effort and decreasing order of aggregation error.

Table 2 - Aggregation error for five procedures summarized across 45 districts and three modes

	PROCEDURES				
	Naive		Classification		
Error Measure	Without Adjustment	With Adjustment	Choice Set & Auto Avail.	Choice Set	Auto Avail.
Average Error	6.2	6.5	1.2	2.0	7.3
Standard Deviation of Error	8.5	4.8	3.0	4.8	6.6
Root Mean Square Error	10.5	8.1	3.3	5.2	9.9

Table 3 - Comparison of aggregation procedures

	PROCEDURES				
	Naive		Classification		
	Without Adjustment	With Adjustment	Choice Set & Auto Avail.	Choice Set	Auto Avail.
Rank by Minimum Aggregation Error	5	3	1	2	4
Rank by Minimum Information and Effort Required	1	2	5	4	3

This analysis of aggregation error is based on a single set of mode share predictions for 45 groups of individuals (each group living in a common residential district). The representativeness of these results was tested by analyzing the aggregation errors, first for three geographically-defined sets of districts, and second for two different policy changes. In each case the general magnitudes of aggregation error for each procedure were similar and the ordering of different aggregation procedures was unchanged (Koppelman, 1975). Thus, these aggregation errors should be indicative of the errors which might be expected in a variety of situations.

It is useful to compare the aggregation errors to other sources of error in prediction. Using the same prediction situation, errors from other sources were estimated to be 27.8% of the magnitude of prediction. (Note: Errors from other sources are estimated by comparing predictions by the enumeration procedure against the observed shares in the data). Thus, the aggregation error, even by the naive procedure, is small compared to error from other sources.

The empirical analyses indicate that the magnitude of aggregation error by the naive procedure is relatively small compared to errors from other sources. Reduction in these aggregation errors can be obtained by use of alternative procedures based on information which is commonly available or which can be generated with moderate effort. The naive procedure with adjustment, which requires information on availability of alternatives only, reduces aggregation error by about 25%. Classification procedures based on choice set availability, which requires information on the availability of alternatives and class-specific average variable values, reduce aggregation error by more than 50%.

These results indicate the importance of considering differences in choice set availability when they exist. [6] This information can be used either to adjust predictions initially made by the naive procedure or as a basis for classification. Consideration of modal availability will obtain substantial reductions in prediction error. When differences in choice set availability do not exist but wide differences in explanatory variables occur, classification by variable values or pseudo-sample procedures should be used.

PREDICTING CLASSIFICATION GROUPS AND ALTERNATIVE AVAILABILITY

The classification procedures and the naive procedure with adjustment for alternative availability require information about the size of different prediction groups and, for classification procedures, class-specific average variable values. This information is not available in many prediction situations, but often can be generated with a moderate amount of effort. This section describes how this information can be developed.

The criterion for selecting a classification structure is to identify a classification which will obtain significant reduction in aggregation error with a minimal increase in required input data and computational effort. This criterion can best be satisfied by classifying the population according to differences in choice set availability when such differences exist. That is, when different individuals make choices from different sets of alternatives, differences in the choice set provide a powerful basis for classification. Choice set classifications exist for many choice situations. These include mode choice limited by automobile availability or access to public transit, automobile ownership limited by household income and number of drivers, shopping location limited by travel time, etc. Classifications may also be based on differences in the value which members of the population have for selected independent variables. The maximum reduction in aggregation error is obtained by classifying according to the variable which contributes the largest variance to the dependent variable. Recent mode choice studies identify automobile availability, the number of automobiles per licensed driver, as the most important variable for classification. The most powerful classifier for an automobile ownership model is expected to be household income. Powerful classifiers for other models can be obtained by examination of the data for prediction groups and the coefficients of estimated choice models.

Alternative availability information is required for both the naive procedure adjusted for alternative availability and classification by choice set. In the mode choice situation, availability of private alternatives such as drive alone is based on availability in the household of the required vehicle. Availability of public transportation alternatives is based on access to a transit stop.

Prediction of the proportion of households which do not own a vehicle required for a specific mode requires development of a distributional respresentation which relates levels of ownership to the average vehicle ownership of the population. That is, the objective is to transform commonly available information such as the average number of automobiles per household to an estimate of the proportion of households which do not have any automobiles. One method of obtaining the required distribution is to project existing distributions to the future time period. This can be done by grouping districts which have similar average values for vehicle ownership levels as a function of average vehicle ow- which fall in each level of ownership category with particular emphasis on the proportion of households which do not onw any such vehicles. A table of relationships between average values and percent zero ownership can be produced and used to transform predicted average vehicle ownership values to the proportion of households without a vehicle available (Chatterjee et. al., 1977). An alternative approach is to develop a structural model of the distribution of vehicle ownership to predict ownership levels as a function of average vehicle ownership in the district. A more sophisticated procedure for predicting automobile availability, which also has the advantage of producing information on the degree of competition for automobiles within households, is a two-step process which predicts the distribution of household size in terms of number of adults and, conditionally on this distribution, predicts the number of automobiles in each household.

Availability of public transportation is determined by access to the nearest public transportation stop. Estimates of maximum acceptable walk access time are obtained by examining existing data to determine the distance at which choice of the transit mode drops to zero or near zero in a variety of areas. This analysis of reasonable access distance should be undertaken separately for different linehaul transit modes, and should reflect use of different access modes. Past observations suggest that walk access to local transportation service is generally limited to ten to fifteen minutes walk time.

Predicting average values of independent variables for different classification groups requires considerable additional effort. This effort can be reduced by use of simplifying assumptions and simple relationships between class average values and overall average values observed in existing data sets. Variables which have little influence on the dependent variable or do not vary greatly between classification groups can be used at their overall average values. Other class-specific average variable values can be related to overall average variable values by adjustment factors developed from existing data. For example, when classification by drive-alone alternative availability is used, class values of income may be x% below average for the no-auto group and y% above average for the auto-available group. In the special case where classification is based on a selected variable value, the class average value can be derived directly from the classification process. That is, if classification is based on income, class values of income can be taken as the mid-point of the class range.

The pseudo-sample aggregation process requires generation of sample variable values for a set of "individuals". These sample values are obtained by Monte Carlo sampling from the distribution of variables. The procedure requires knowledge of the joint distribution of all variables in the prediction groups. This requirement can be simplified in a variety of ways. Variables which do not have important influence, and which are relatively invariant across the population can be valued at the population average. Variables can be assumed to be independently distributed unless there is strong reason to use joint or conditional distributions. Distributions for the remaining independent variables can be represented by relatively simple density functions. Income can be distributed according to a standard gamma distribution with only one parameter which can be determined from average income. Travel time can be represented by a uniform distribution with mean equal to the predicted average and range proportional to the size of the district. Alternatively, future distributions can be obtained by adjusting empirically estimated existing distributions to fit predicted mean values. For example, the existing distribution may be shifted to increase each value by the increase in the mean values, or the existing distribution may be factored by a constant radio equal to the proportional increase in the mean values.

DISCUSSION AND CONCLUSIONS

The use of disaggregate models has developed rapidly and extensively in recent years. Early research into the development of disaggregate models focused on improved understanding of travel choice behavior. More recent work has been directed at using disaggregate models in the analysis of practical planning issues.

An important advantage of the disaggregate modelling approach over the conventional aggregate models is the reduction in data required for model development. The large-scale home-interview surveys needed to develop aggregate models are not required. Furthermore, disaggregate models can be estimated without increased expense for the development of disaggregate level-of-service data. [7] Thus, substantial savings can be obtained in developing the data base needed for model development.

Even when data are already collected, it is preferable to use disaggregate choice models because of their improved statistical efficiency, transferability, behavioral structure and policy sensitivity. Enhanced behavioral structure and policy sensitivity provide the basis for improved understanding of travel behavior and improved evaluation of transport policy.

The transferability of disaggregate models holds the potential for major savings in data collection and model development costs. These savings result from the ability to "import" a model developed in a different geographic area, subject only to validation testing and adjustment or updating of selected model parameters. Such updating can be accomplished by use of limited data on local-area travel behavior (Atherton and Ben-Akiva, 1976). Corresponding aggregate models cannot be readily transferred between geographic areas because aggregate model parameters implicitly represent the distribution of independent variables in the estimation data. Thus, the aggregate model will not be valid in other areas or future time periods unless the underlying distribution of independent variables is unchanged over time or space.

These advangtages of disaggregate models can be obtained without incurring substantially increased cost or effort in prediction. This paper demonstrates the feasibility of making aggregate predictions using disaggregate models. The aggregation error using the naive procedure, which requires the same data and effort as conventional aggregate models, is likely to be smaller than errors from other sources. Furthermore, this aggregation error can be reduced substantially by use of limited information which can be obtained with little additional effort.

Analysis of alternative aggregation procedures demonstrates the improvements in predictive accuracy which can be obtained by use of information about difference in choice set availability when such differences exist. Alternative procedures for use of this additional information are described and evaluated. Methods to predict this additional information are also described. This material combined with what is already known a-

bout the estimation of disaggregate travel choice models provides a basis for application in a wide variety of policy and planning situations.

ACKNOWLEDGEMENTS
This paper is derived from a report prepared for the Project Bureau for Integral Traffic and Transportation Studies of the Netherlands Ministery of Transport by the authors, working for Cambridge Systematics, Inc. of Cambridge, Massachusetts, U.S.A., under sub-contract to Buro Goudappel en Coffeng B.V. of Deventer, The Netherlands. Earlier research in this area was supported by the U.S. Department of Transportation, Office of the Secretary, under contract DOT-OS-50001 for "Development of An Aggregate Model of Urbanized Area Travel Behavior".

REFERENCES
Atherton, T.J., and M. Ben-Akiva, "Transferability and Updating of Disaggregate Travel Demand Models", **Transportation Research Record,** 1976 (forthcoming).

Ben-Akiva, M.E., **Structure of Passenger Travel Demand Models,** Ph.D. dissertation, Massachusetts Institute of Technology (Civil Engineering), Cambridge, Massachusetts, 1973.

Ben-Akiva, M.E., and T.J. Atherton, "Choice Model Predictions of Carpool Demand: Methods and Results", **Transportation Research Record,** 1977 (forthcoming).

Cambridge Systematics, Inc., **Carpooling Incentives: Analysis of Transportation and Energy Impacts,** Federal Energy Administration, Washington, D.C., 1976.

Cambridge Systematics, Inc., **A Study Design for Dual Mode Transit Planning Case Studies,** Urban Mass Transportation Administration, U.S. Dept. of Transportation, 1975.

Charles River Associates (CRA), **A Disaggregate Behavioral Model of Urban Travel Demand,** Federal Highway Administration, U.S. Department of Transportation, Washington, D.C., 1972.

Chatterjee, A., S. Khasnabis and L.J. Slade, "Household Stratification Models for Travel Estimation", **Transportation Engineering Journal,** Vol. 103, American Society of Civil Engineers, New York, 1977.

Duguay, G., W. Jung and D. McFadden, "SYNSAM: A Methodology for Synthesizing Household Transportation Survey Data", Travel Demand Forecasting Project, Institute of Transportation Studies, University of California, Berkeley, 1976.

Green, H.A.J., **Aggregation in Economic Analysis,** Princeton University Press, Princeton, N.J., 1964.

Kanafani, A., "An Aggregative Model of Trip Making", **Transportation Research,** Vol. 6, 1972.

Koppelman, F.S., "Prediction with Disaggregate Models: The Aggregation Issue", **Transportation Research Record,** Number 527, Transportation Research Board, Washington, D.C., 1974.

Koppelman, F.S., **Travel Prediction with Models of Individual Choice Behavior,** Ph.D. dissertation, Massachusetts Institute of Technology (Civil Engineering), Cambridge, Massachusetts, 1975.

Koppelman, F.S., "Guidelines for Aggregate Travel Prediction Using Disaggregate Choice Models", **55th Annual Meeting,** Transportation Research Board, Washington, D.C., 1976 (a).

Koppelman, F.S., "Methodology for Analysis of Errors in Prediction with Disaggregate Choice Models", **55th Annual Meeting,** Transportation Research Board, Washington, D.C., 1976 (b).

Koppelman, F.S., M.E. Ben-Akiva and T. Watanatada, **Development of an Aggregate Model of Urbanized Area Travel Behavior,** Phase I Report, Assistant Secretary for Policy, Plans and International Affairs and Federal Highway Administration, U.S. Dept. of Transportation, 1976.

Lerman, S.R., and M.E. Ben-Akiva, "A Disaggregate Behavioral Model of Automobile Ownership", Transportation Research Record 569, Transportation Research Board, Washington, D.C., 1975.

Peat, Marwick, Mitchell & Co. (PMM), **Implementation of the N-Dimensional Logit Model: Final Report,** prepared for the Comprehensive Planning Organization, San Diego County, California, 1973.

Richards, M.G., and M.E. Ben-Akiva, **A Disaggregate Travel Demand Model,** D.C. Heath, Lexington, Massachusetts, 1975.

Ruiter, E.R., and M. Ben-Akiva, "A System of Disaggregate Travel Demand Models: Structure, Component Models, and

Application Procedures", Cambridge Systematics, Inc., Cambridge, Mass., 1977.

Small, K.A., "Priority Lanes on Urban Radial Freeways: An Economic Simulation Model", **Transportation Research Record,** Transportation Research Board, Washington, D.C., 1977 (forthcoming).

Talvitie, A.P., "Aggregate Travel Demand Analysis with Disaggregate or Aggregate Travel Demand Models", **Proceedings,** Transportation Research Forum, 1973.

Train, K., "Work Trip Mode Split Models: An Empirical Exploration of Estimate Sensitivity to Model and Data Specification", Working Paper No. 7602, Urban Travel Demand Forecasting Project, Institute of Transportation Studies, University of California, Berkeley, Calif., 1976.

FOOTNOTES

1. Kanafani (1974) provides an example of an aggregate demand function derived using equation (4).

2. This result is shown in detail in Green (1974) and Koppelman (1974)

3. Conventional aggregate models are subject to aggregation error both in the estimation of parameters and the prediction of future demand (Koppelman, 1975).

4. The detailed study is reported by Koppelman (1975).

5. See Koppelman, 1976b, for a discussion of error analysis in prediction.

6. The importance of modal availability is further illustrated in a study of the impact on work mode shares pursuant to the establishment of an auto-restricted zone (ARZ) in the Washington, D.C. central business district. The change in drive-alone mode shares was predicted by the sample enumeration procedure as −2.2%. Corresponding direct incremental share predictions (see Ben-Akiva and Atherton, 1977) were −4.7% by the naive procedure and −2.5% by classification based on modal availability. Thus, the use of modal availability information substantially reduced aggregation error in this case.

7. Train (1976) showed that disaggregate choice models estimated with aggregate (zonal) level-of-service data are not significantly different from those estimated with disaggregate data.

Decision issues and research priorities in intercity freight transportation: a U.S. perspective

A. Scheffer Lang

Association of American Railroads, U.S.A.

INTRODUCTION

The intercity freight transportation system in the United States is characterized by its high degree of development, with respect to both its civil works infrastructure and its technology and operating capabilities. The essential completion of the 43,000-mile system of Interstate and Defense Highways and the rapidly expanding and extensive use of those facilities by all sectors of the motor truck industry has virtually eliminated the differential economic advantage heretofore enjoyed by industries and localities with preferred access to rail freight transportation. With very few exceptions, moreover, the U.S. system of improved navigation facilities has also reached its full, geographic extent; so that there is little further economic advantage to be conferred upon industries and localities with ready access to low-cost water transportation.

Thus, at the end of the second century of U.S. history, the essential issues which we confront in the further articulation of our intercity freight transportation system are no longer ones of economic advantage and economic development, but rather ones merely of economic efficiency. Since most of the resources and virtually all of the operations of this highly-developed system are in the hands of private entrepreneurs, the stimulus of commercial competition for increasing market shares and profits encourages steady improvements in efficiency throughout that system. The inhibitions to such improvements in efficiency lie, directly or indirectly, in the hands of our State and Federal governments. Governments intrude upon the natural workings of the system through the decisions they make regarding the provision of civil works infrastructure and through their regulation of the commercial practices of the private operating companies.

The important research tasks in U.S. freight transportation derive largely from this interaction between government decisionmaking and the steady drive to more and more efficient freight transportation operations.

This paper examines some of the research requirements growing out of these government decision problems. The most important areas of needed research lie in

1) improving our ability to model the workings of the intercity freight market,

2) accounting more carefully for the direct public costs and indirect social costs of freight transportation operations,

3) assessing alternative technological futures, and

4) more carefully structured theoretical and empirical work on the effects of commercial regulation. Overriding most of these research tasks are the special requirements for the development of more comprehensive, continuing programs of data collection on both the characteristics of the intercity freight transport market and the operations which serve it.

THE CHANGED ECONOMICS OF INTERCITY FREIGHT TRANSPORT

All of the developments in intercity freight transportation must be viewed against the background of steady and significant changes in the structure of the intercity freight market. These changes derive from a steady growth in the service sectors of the U.S. economy, as well as from above-average rates of growth in both population and industrial activity in the Southern and Western portions of the continental United States relative to the older, more industrialized Northeastern region. These changes in the market have been extensively reported on in the work of A. L. Morton and others. [1] Their net effect has been to confer steadily increasing market advantage upon the motor truck industry, whose technology is more readily adaptable to service-quality sensitive markets than the railroad technology which is its principal modal competitor.

All things considered, however, the dramatic, long-term improvement in the cost and performance of our intercity motor truck industry has been more important than the changes in market competition which have stimulated its development. A number of factors have contributed to this overall improvement, but none has been more significant than the development of our Interstate Highway System. That system of trunk highways, intended to link all communities of 50,000 population and above, is now essentially complete. Its capability to provide uninterrupted, high-speed truck operations over long distances may one day be recognized as an even more important contribution to the development of our country than its ability to facilitate personal automobile travel. The reductions it has made in the time and cost of line-haul truck operations have permitted high-quality trucking service to penetrate vitually every freight transportation market of any importance.

Less obvious has been the impact of this highway system and of low-cost, high-capacity diesel road tractors upon the relative costs of railroad and truck transportation. The dramatic narrowing of the gap between rail and truck costs has removed the overwhelming competitive advantage enjoyed by railroads in all long-haul markets since that technology was developed to replace the horse and wagon. [2] In the late-19th century U.S. railroads enjoyed a cost advantage over pre-motor truck roadhaulers on the order of one of ten. In the super-highway, diesel tractor era of the 1970's that cost advantage has shrunk to no more than 1 to 1.5 on all but bulk, large-volume commodities, such as coal.

The impact of this shrinking cost advantage on rail-truck competition and on the profit levels of our still privately-owned railroad companies is well-known. What is less appreciated and more important is that this narrowed cost gap has eliminated geographic advantage from the economic landscape of intercity freight transportation, except in the purely length-of-haul dimension. That is, freight transport costs are now determined within a relatively narrow band as a function only of the distance which a commodity must be transported, and not as a function of whether the shipper has convenient access to railroad transportation.

The narrowed cost gap has led to this result not only because of its direct effect upon rail-truck movement alternatives, but also because of its indirect effect upon the rate levels which railroad companies can charge for movements originating or terminating in different regions of the country. The rail-competitive trucking industry, composed as it is of a large number of independent, one-man operations, is characterized by internal competition which keeps rates at generally uniform levels. The gap between these rates and the direct cost of rail transportation is sufficiently small that railroad companies, notwithstanding any regulatory constraints, have little room within which to manipulate rates for the purpose of conferring or maintaining any locational economic advantage.

The picture is similar in rail-water competition for the transportation of bulk commodities, in that the system of navigable waterways in the U.S. is almost fully mature. While bulk shippers who have ready access to water transportation enjoy locational advantage over those who do not (because of the significantly lower cost of modern inland marine operations), there seems litte possibility that this existing pattern of geographic advantage can be altered significantly by any future public or private actions. Again, the economics of the water transport industry are such that extensive intra-modal competition keeps rates at relatively stabel levels determined largely by length-of-haul and the navigation facilities involved. With railroad rate levels constrained within narrow bounds by truck competition, neither private nor public decisions seem likely to perturb the pattern of economic advantage which has already developed.

The U.S. freight transportation system has thus (the out-dated notions of politicians and regulators to the contrary notwithstanding) lost any real usefulness as an instrument of geo-politics and social change. That is, we can no longer promote differential economic growth through the construction of railroads or the exercise of public restraints on the prices charged by freight transportation operating companies. The range of economic impact which can thus be manipulated is simply too narrow. Every one in the continental U.S. has, in effect, equal access to freight transportation whose price and quality are determined almost wholly by the distances over which shipments must be made. These new economic facts of life render unimportant many of the decision issues which have historically occupied the attention of those who study and report on our intercity freight transportation system. Improving the efficiency of this economically and geographically mature system will be the focus of our concerns from this point forward.

THE PAST AND PRESENT ROLES OF GOVERNMENT

Government has played a crucial role since the founding of our country in the evolution of its freight transportation system. This role has taken two forms: (1) the direct and indirect provision of financial assistance for the development of the civil works infrastructure of our system of railroads, highways, and improved waterways (2) the establishment of constraints on the commercial practices of private transportation companies, constraints intended to maximize the availability of freight transportation to all sections of the country and to promote the economic development of those which were otherwise disadvantaged. While state governments have participated extensively in both of these areas, the role of the Federal government has been overriding.

In its role as a provider of financial assistance, government has conferred differential advantage on one type of freight transportation technology or another at various times throughout the 19th and 20th centuries. It has also conferred differential advantage on communities and regions through these same financial assistance policies as applied both to individual modes and technologies and as between modes.

The role of government in providing financial assistance continues today in its ownership and management of the civil works infrastructure of our highway, waterway, and air transportation systems. It has acquired some small share of the U.S. railroad infrastructure, moreover, through the recent purchase by Amtrak (a government-owned corporation) of the Northeast Corridor trackage formerly owned by the Penn Central Transportation Company. In this role as owner and manager of transportation infrastructure, government can affect the efficient allocation of transportation resources (and markets) through its policies for the allocation of cost and assessment of user charges to the transportation companies which make use of those facilities.

In its second role as a regulator of the commercial practices followed by the private operating companies, government has had a profound impact upon the way those operations have developed and thus on the allocation of the intercity freight market to the various modes of transportation competing to serve it. At the Federal level, a pattern of railroad regulation evolved at the turn of the century which was a reflection of the dramatic cost advantage enjoyed by railroad transportation at that time. That pattern of regulation has been applied to a greater or lesser extent to other modes of freight transportation as they have evolved, the very different economic characteristics of those modes and the changing economics of the freight transportation landscape notwithstanding. We thus have a pattern of regulation which was not wholly appropriate when it was fully applied to the intercity freight transportation system by 1940, but one which has also failed to adjust to the different circumstances which have resulted from the recent developments in the intercity motor truck industry discussed above. It is a pattern of regulation, moreover, which was designed importantly to deal with problems of differential economic advantage and not one intended to promote efficiency in freight transportation as our present circumstances dictate.

DECISION ISSUES IN INTERCITY FREIGHT TRANSPORTATION

The important decision issues in intercity freight transportation center around the present and prospective inhibitions to improved efficiency which are created by government in its roles as owner and manager of infrastructure and as regulator of commercial practices. For example, while the highway infrastructure is essentially complete in its geographic dimensions, the growing use of that infrastructure by intercity motor freight operators raises questions about the suitability of both the design of the system and the rules for its use. There has been steady pressure from the trucking industry for increasing the allowable axle and vehicle weights on the system, even as concern has been growing among the state agencies responsible for the highways over rapidly increasing civil works maintenance budgets. These problems raise questions concerning the detailed tradeoffs between construction cost, maintenance costs, truck operating efficiency, safety and equity among the operators of large commercial vehicles on the one hand and automobile users of the highways on the other.

There are also questions about the present schedule of user fees paid by the various classes of highway users. These fees are generally intended to cover the cost of highway construction, maintenance, and management, [1] but there is increasing question as to whether such charges ought not also to defray the social costs of the highway system flowing from such phenomena as noise and air pollution. Furthermore, the allocation of the total of these direct and indirect costs between the various classes of users is a matter of particular importance to the commercial operators of heavy motor trucks. If, as recent studies have suggested, a larger share of these costs might logically be assigned to these heavier vehicles, the ultimate impact upon the overall cost of the intercity trucking could be significant. [3]

At the same time, there are problems with the long-standing government policy of providing improved navigation facilities at no cost to the ships and barges which use them. That policy has its origins in a program designed to develop a modern marine transportation system; but this policy of intentional interference with the market allocation of resources in intercity freight transportation continues long after the basic development of that system has been completed. Indeed, despite theoretical lip service to the need for economically rational decisions on further capital improvements to that system, there continues to be no meaningful commercial test of what is and is not built with government funds. The increasing financial difficulties of the U.S. railroad system have finally called these policies into open question and may yet compel a reform of the decision process associated with both investment in and operation of improved navigation facilities.

Government faces even more difficult decisions in its role as a regulator of the commercial practices of all of the railroad companies, the companies handling about half of the intercity motor freight, and a handfull of the companies handling inland waterway traffic. Here again, policies intended to facilitate the orderly development of a system which is now fully mature and to control the pricing practices of railroad companies are inappropriate to a time when railroad pricing practices have become narrowly constrained by the capabilities of competing technology. Those policies thus stand as obstacles to improved efficiency, while they are no more than monuments to past transportation development goals. The essential question regarding railroad regulation is whether there is any useful purpose in continuing such regulation at all. Increasingly, the existence of such regulation is seen as a major factor in the inability of our railroads to adapt to changing technological and market circumstances and thus a proximate cause of the financial problems which have led to repeated calls for government financial assistance to the railroads.

Current questions regarding the efficacy of continuing to regulate the commercial practices of the roughly fifty percent of our intercity trucking industry also derive from a growing concern that this regulation inhibits economic efficiency and serves little other purpose. The principal counterargument is that continued regulation is necessary to stabilize an industry composed of a very large number of separate companies whose unrestrained entry and exit into markets would threaten a disruption of service, in particular to shippers in small localities. The issue of efficiency has also received additional attention since the energy crisis of three years ago, in as much as present regulations are seen to cause less efficient use of fuel than would be the case if motor truck operators were more free to carry goods without any geographic constraints on their operations.

More generally, government faces a series of questions on reforming its policies relative to railroad trans-

portation. While looking at its policy on financing highway and waterway infrastructure, it must now consider whether and to what extent there is a need to finance railroad infrastructure. It confronts unresolved questions concerning present and future technological capabilities of both the railroads and their competitors, as well as questions about incentives to improved performance of the various modes which might result from a relaxation of regulation.

A FIRST RESEARCH PRIORITY
ESTIMATING DEMAND

Most of the decision issues confronting government turn in one way or another upon an understanding of how the market for intercity freight transportation will respond to changes in the performance of one part of the system or another. It is precisely in this respect that our knowledge is most deficient. For example, virtually all of the possible changes in the existing patterns of government regulation of the commercial practices of transportation companies would have some impact upon both their rates and their service. Depending upon how the market responded to those changes, various groups of operating companies would be advantaged or disadvantaged and, possibly, some groups of freight shippers would be advantaged or disadvantaged. Without some reliable means of estimating market elasticities, these shifts in advantage cannot be assessed, nor can the claims and counter-claims of various interest groups be tested in any explicit way.

Similarly, some of the decision issues confronting government in its role as an owner and manager of civil works infrastructure foreshadow changes in transportation system performance that could produce significant shifts in the use of one mode of transportation vis-a-vis another. For example, the imposition of user fees on the inland waterway system, by increasing the rates charged by inland waterway carriers, will predictably have an impact upon rail-water competition for certain major markets, such as the movement of coal. The extent of that impact is important to government decisions on future investments in the inland waterway infrastructure, as well as to questions of prospective financial aid to railroad companies. Without a more competent set of demand-estimating models, the magnitude and character of such impacts cannot be estimated with any assurance.

Research into the development of competent freight demand models has lagged far behind the highly developed procedures for estimating urban passenger travel. It has only been within the past few years that serious work has begun on this problem, which is in important respects more complex than the passenger demand estimating problem.

Despite the somewhat greater difficulty which seems to attend the problem of estimating demand in a very non-homogenous market such as that for freight transportation, the best work now underway borrows directly from the latest thinking in the passenger demand forecasting area. Specifically, the work of Roberts, Ben-Akiva, et al to develop a disaggregate, behavioral system of freight demand estimating models shows great promise as a procedure to assess the market impacts of government policy options in all areas of intercity freight transportation. [4] That work suffers as all previous work has, however, from an inadequate supply of data describing the movements which take place under existing institutional arrangements.

An important part of this demand-modelling problem lies in the development of better level-of service models for the various modes. These level-of-service characteristics are important explanatory variables in the market response process and have become increasingly so as the overall structure of the market has shifted over the past thirty years.

Leaving the special problem of data aside, much research is needed before we can be comfortable with our ability to explain the present market, let alone predict the response of that market to possible future changes such as those which pending public and private decisions might produce.

A SECOND RESEARCH PRIORITY-
THE ALLOCATION OF PUBLIC COSTS

The direct cost of publicly-provided highway infrastructure and the indirect social cost associated with the use of that infrastructure are fundamental considerations in any rationalization of intercity motor truck operations. That is, a system of highway use charges is needed that will maximize (in all dimensions), the efficiency of our intercity freight transportation system, recognizing that motor truck operations produce about 75% (in value) of all such transportation in the U.S. Our present procedures for estimating social costs and for allocating direct infrastructure costs are not yet competent to give us an adequate basis for structuring such a user charge system.

As for the direct costs, such work as has been done to follow up the findings of the AASHO road tests of the early 1960's has not fully bridged some of the important gaps in our knowledge that must ultimately be filled. In particular, there has been too little empirical work to link the physical degration of highway structures to the cost associated with their design and repair. In part because that work has not been done, there has been too little work on the explicit optimization of highway design for various classes of highway use, lacking which work options with regard to vehicle size and use regulations can be only imperfectly assessed.

With the grwong recognition that heavy truck operations are taking an increasing share of the traffic necessary to provide adequate financial support for our still-extensive system of freight-carrying railroads, the question of truck sizes and the proper assessment against those trucks of their reasonably-allocable share of direct infrastructure cost has become a matter of importance. If the overall efficiency of the intercity freight transportation system can be improved through the more extensive use of heavy truck operations, even when those operations are made to bear their full share of infrastructure cost, then present policy support for the rehabilitation and modernization of the freight-carrying railroad system needs careful review.

In all of this, the procedures used for allocating the largely-common costs of a highway infrastructure used by passenger as well as freight-carrying vehicles poses a difficult and unresolved set of conceptual and analytical issues. The current level of research into this difficult set of problems is inadequate to support the decisions confronting both state and Federal governments in this area.

Research into the related problem of the unrecouped social cost of highway operations has also lagged behind the developing importance of that problem as perceived by the public. Research is needed into both the estimation of these costs and into administratively-feasible and equitable procedures for the assessment of such costs against the highway users themselves.

A THIRD RESEARCH PRIORITY-
COMMERCIAL REGULATION

The literature on the pros and cons of the commercial regulation of our intercity freight transportation companies is voluminous. Starting with the landmark work by Meyer, Peck, Stenason, & Zwick, a whole series of transportation economists has examined the classical theories of freight transport regulation in a new methodological framework. [5] Despite this extensive body of work, much remains to be done.

This work has been flawed most importantly because of its failure to confront the changing character and economics of the intercity motor truck industry. This failure has been partly the result of a lack of adequate data on this sprawling and atomistic industry. For reasons discussed earlier in this paper, however, the dramatic changes in this industry have necessarily put the question of regulation in a new light. In particular, the cost and performance of the unregulated sectors of this industry have received too little attention. As a result (other methodological shortcomings notwithstanding), the extensive efforts to estimate the economic dead loss associated with the inefficiencies introduced by regulatory constraints is largely worthless. Lacking any competent means to estimate market response to changes in the efficiency of various types of motor truck operations, moreover, the ultimate effects of any amended regulatory policy cannot be reliably estimated.

At the same time, the potential effects of significant changes in the regulation of railroad commercial practices cannot be assessed rationally on the basis of any of the analytical work done to date. This inadequacy is compounded by changes in the internal economics of railway operations undetected by these same economic researchers. Work to analyze the more competent data sets on railroad markets and operations which are now available has only just begun, and it is work which will inevitably lead to a reformulation of questions posed by the U.S. Congress in its omnibus railroad legislation of a year ago.

All in all, the new era in transport regulatory economics ushered in by the work of Meyer et al must now give way to yet another body of work which is only in its beginning stages. Much research is needed before this new body of work can be given its appropriate direction.

A FOURTH RESEARCH PRIORITY-
TECHNOLOGICAL CAPABILITIES

Despite extensive studies of inland freight transportation technology conducted by various government agencies and outside research groups over the past few years, there remain lingering uncertainties regarding the future technological capabilities and possibilities for various modes of intercity freight transportation. With specific respect to the U.S. railroad industry, the Congress has mandated a number of studies which are only now getting underway. These studies will look at questions regarding the possiblility for improved railroad operating efficiency through restructuring of railroad network operations, through improvements in performance of railroad terminals, through improvements in the utilization of railroad freight equipment, and other related questions. These studies, however, still promise to leave unanswered questions regarding the possibilities for significantly different railroad freight vehicle technology, as well as the reconfiguration of railroad operations which might be facilitated by major changes in the structure of existing railroad labor contracts.

Important questions regarding the possibilities for technological change which would improve the performance of the intercity motor truck industry also require further research. Our ability to do that research is constrained by both the lack of adequate data on the industry and the lack of supporting work on the economics of the highway infrastructure which have already been mentioned. Possibilities for improved energy efficiency in this industry are of particular interest, but have received only preliminary attention, thus far.

The possibilities for the transportation of solids by pipeline are also important. While much research has been done into this relatively new technology (and some solids pipelines installation are already in operation), the ultimate usefulness of such technology is still unclear. Government already faces important decisions concerning legal steps to facilitate the development of this technology, decisions which call for a more credible assessment of the economics of such technology.

Beyond questions relating to the technology of individual modes of transportation there lies a more general set of questions concerning the technological tradeoffs associated with the steadily increasing cost of energy. These call into question, for example, the possibilities for improving the technology of trailer and container on flatcar transportation, a mixed mode of transportation which can potentially reduce the overall energy requirement for some part of the freight transportation job. Similarly, there is increasing interest in the economics of railroad electrification and the extent to which a program of investment (not heretofore justified by relative energy costs and the better-than-average performance of North American diesel locomotives) could assist in reducing the requirement for petroleum-based fuels.

THE SPECIAL PROBLEM OF DATA

Overhanging most intercity freight transportation research questions are long-standing problems of inadequate data. The data collection programs of Federal and state governments relating to both the demand and supply sides of this system are fragmentary, unduly constrained by present statutory and administrative restrictions, and inadequately funded. While some additional data are available to the private operating companies in various sectors of the system, the proprietary nature of these data has precluded their availability to those who are researching questions essential to the public decision issues discussed above.

On the demand side, data describing past and present intercity freight traffic flows are simply incomplete. As has been suggested above, this deficiency derives most importantly from a general lack of such information for the traffic being handled by the unregulated sectors of the motor truck industry which account for 35% to 40% of the transportation value produced in the entire intercity freight system. Surveys conducted once every five years by the U.S. Bureau of the Census provide some fragmentary data on these traffic flows, but at a level of detail insufficient to support demand-estimating models competent to deal with the characteristics of specific markets and the competition for those markets between various modes and types of freight transportation operations. Much of the demand-related data that is available lacks important dimensions, moreover, such as that of the actual freight charges paid by shippers whose traffic flows are otherwise reported on. Again, the lack of these dimensions inhibits the development of competent demand models; but it also renders incomplete any assessment of the overall economics of freight transportation such as that essential to many important decision issues.

On the supply side, and not unrelated to the demand side, existing data sets do not provide an adequate profile of the cost and performance of many sectors of the freight transportation business. Again, data on unregulated trucking are virtually non-existent. Such data as we do have often lacks important dimensions, such as the service quality dimension (e.g., transit time and transit time reliability) of the transportation being produced by all modes. As to the modes, themselves, our data on rail transportation are most nearly complete and our data on unregulated truck transportation the most incomplete.

The need for greatly improved and expanded programs of data collection poses significant research issues in its own right. The scale and complexity of the intercity freight transportation business is an important barrier to its development. Research is needed into more automated and reliable data collection techniques. Research is also needed to develop more carefully structured samples which can adequately describe the universe of transportation activities at reasonable cost.

Politics has also played a role in delaying the development of better data collection programs, the need for which has been pointed out repeatedly by transportation researchers over the past twenty years. Because of the cost and complexity of the data collection job and the need for explicit research in this area, the time constants for such a program are very long. Responsible government officials have been less enthusiastic about major government expenditures on projects whose value to those officials is prospectively low, concerned as they are with issues that lie largely in the present and the immediate future.

All in all, this data collection requirement is the most important problem which confronts intercity freight transportation research in the U.S. While much can be done in the important research areas outlined above, and while the quality of the decisions which we confront can be improved by work already underway, the lack of adequate data has seriously affected both the quality and quantity of research done in the past few years. There are many in the U.S. who feel that the most exciting and important research in transport problems turns on the availability of data which we could have but have not yet started to collect. Perhaps the important missing dimension of this problem has been inadequate research into the data collection problem, itself. Fortunately, some new initiatives are being discussed in this area, but too much remains to be done.

FOOTNOTES

1. See especially, A. L. Morton, "Freight Demand" unpublished Ph. D. dissertation, Harvard University, January 1973.
2. See D. D. Wyckoff and D. H. Maister, **The Owner-Operator: Independent Trucker** (1975).
3. See, for example, K. Bhatt, R. McGillirray, M. Beesley, and K. Neels, "Congressional Intent and Road Payments", The Urban Institute, Washington, D.C. (1977).
4. See P.O. Roberts, Jr., "Forecasting Freight Flows Using a Disaggregate Freight Demand Model", paper presented at the 56th Annual Meeting of the Transportation Research Board (1977).
5. See J. R. Meyer, M. J. Peck, J. Stenasen, and C. J. Zwick, **The Economics of Competition in the Transportation Industries** (1958). See also work by Friedlaeder, Moore, and others.

Transport policy and regional policy in the European Communities

by
W. A. G. BLONK

European Economic Community

I have the honour to speak to you for a few minutes about "Transport Policy and Regional Policy in the European Communities". As I guess you are especially interested in the interrelationship between the Community's transport policy on the one hand and the regional policy and land-use-planning on the other hand I will limit myself to the links between those two policies as we see it in Brussels.

As a matter of fact the European Communities have already developed some activities in this context. As the most important I should like to mention the following ones:

– in 1972 a memorandum was drawn up on transport as an instrument of regional policy and land-use-planning in the Community. The main assumptions contained in it still apply. I will come back on this later.

– one year later, in 1973, the Commission published its new approach to the common transport policy and stated that transport infrastructure is an essential basis for the development of structural policies, particularly regional policy and planning.

– in order to give substance to the link between transport and regional policy, the Advisory Committee on Transport, set up under article 83 of the Treaty, was instructed to examine this question and reported early in 1975.

– the Economic and Social Committee payed also attention to this subject and published its report at the end of 1975.

– finally the consultation of a number of university professors as regards the regional impact of a set of Commission's proposals to the functioning of the transport market should be mentioned.

These activities have enabled the services of the Commission to set clear priorities, resulting in a number of more general bases which are taken into account in the common transport policy and in the Community's regional policy. What follows deals exclusively with these general bases. Before starting with this, it is useful to make one preliminary and fundamental remark. That is to say that the Commission believes that transport is only one of the means of acting in solving regional policy problems; there are others which, often are even more important and helpful.

The Commission's memorandum of 1972 set out two bases which still fully apply:

– regional policy and land-use-planning measures must not impinge upon the management independence and financial balance of transport operators. If the authorities decide to impose public service obligations, then the operator must be given appropriate financial compensation.

– regional policy and land-use-planning measures must not rule out competition within a mode of transport or between modes.

Both these principles reveal clearly that the Commission subscribes to the opinion that there can be no question of transport being subordinated to the aims of regional policy and land-use-planning. This does not of course mean to say that transport cannot make a contribution to the achievement of these aims. In fact, transport policy and regional policy should contribute in a coherent and non-contradictory way to the fundamental objectives of the Community.

After these introductory remarks, let us now try to answer the question how transport can be used to help achieve regional policy objectives. The Commission in Brussels is distinguishing here between three types of transport policy instruments: transport infrastructure, support tariffs and the imposition of public service obligations. It is worthwhile to deal with them separately.

As regards the first item "transport infrastructure" a distinction once again between three aspects should be made, e.g. the expansion of transport infrastructure, the financing of the creation of new infrastructure and, when the infrastructure is available, the charging for the use of it. Transport infrastructure has to be taken in the largest sense of the word, e.g. land transport, ports, airports, but also the telecommunications.

It is obvious that there can be no transport when no transport infrastructure is available. This also implies that the basic prerequisite for developing a specific region is an adequate infrastructure for the raw materials to be brought in and semi-finished and finished products to be moved to, from and within the region as well as for a satisfactory passenger transport. But the view in Brussels is that the transport infrastructure's development function should not be overrated. As things stand in the Community at present, perhaps with an exception for Greenland, it appears that practically every place can be reached in some way or another. It is far more a matter of the existence of a desequilibrium in the quality of the various transport infrastructures. Improving the quality and not the quantity of the existing infrastructure is therefore what counts in the first place. When carrying out such specific infrastructure projects it is advisable to take account of the extent to which they really complement or replace existing or planned infrastructure networks; otherwise there is the risk that new imbalances may result. The E.C. Commission believes therefore, that an attempt should be made to achieve integrated and coordinated infrastructure planning both within a mode of transport and between modes, thereby taking into account the various characteristics of the regions concerned.

It is true that the improvement of transport infrastructure has in fact the same effect as decreasing transport prices in both directions. In fact the existing competition position of industries located in those regions, will be improved: the same is however true for the industries located in the concentration areas. If therefore, from the regional policy point of view, a transport infrastructure project is carried out without other measures being taken outside the transport sector, for example in the field of industrial projects, there might conceivably be the danger that the outcome could be the reverse of that desired. Cases are known in the Community of, for instance, a motorway built to an underdeveloped area without any accompanying measures; instead of boosting the area in question, this has resulted in a vacuum. In this context, the Commission believes therefore that it is sensible to carry out transport infrastructure projects only if they form an integral part of a regional development programme. This point was in fact expressed very clearly when the Regional Fund was set up.

On this point the Commission is urging the Member States to attract, as far as possible, industries which are not too capital intensive and those who are not very sensitive to transport costs to the regions in need of development.

At this very moment, little practical information is available about the effects of transport infrastructure projects as such on regional policy, especially as regards defining their extent. The Commission is therefore considering the possibility of ordering a study to provide insight into the regional effects of transport infrastructure projects from both the economic and political angles. We think that special attention should be paid to the structural effects of projects of this type.

As regards the financing of the creation of transport infrastructure, the European Communities currently dispose of two possibilities, a third possibility has been proposed last year to the Council of Ministers. Let us see what this is all about.

Under article 129 of the treaty of Rome a European Investment Bank was set up with the task to contribute to the balanced and steady development of the common market. In practice, projects for developing less-developed regions, amount to 75% of all loans. The majority of these loans - 85% - are for infrastructure projects, the remaining 15% for typical industrial projects. Transport infrastructure projects play a leading role, accounting for 15-20% of the total; this increases to 35-40% if loans for telecommunications projects are included.

In March 1975 the Regional Fund, the second possibility, was established officially for a period of three years with funds of 1.300 millions U.C. in total. The Regional Policy Committee, set up at the same time, was not able to reach a unanimous decision on whether or not transport infrastructure projects qualify for financing for projects of this type. As a result of this attitude transport infrastructure projects account for about 10% of all financing approved till now. It should be pointed out that this figure concerns only the transport infrastructure projects pure and simple; finance is also provided for transport infrastructure as part of more comprehensive projects, in particular, road building in industrial estates and access to the public road network. It is, however, not statistically possible to show separately the share accounted for by these transport infrastructure projects.

Apart from these two resources of finance, the Commission sent the Council a proposal in mid-1976 on the establishment at Community level of a system of financial support for projects of Community interest in transport infrastructure. It will not be possible to fix detailed rules for this financing system until the Council approves this proposal. Among projects coming into consideration there will be those who link areas between two Member States, which may have important implications for the frontier regions of the Community.

The third and last aspect of the item "transport infra-structure" concerns the charging of infrastructure costs. As things stand at present in the various Member States, a charge is made for the utilisation of the infrastructure by means of a tax on motor vehicles and fuel; in some cases tolls are also imposed, e.g. on motorways in France and Italy. These tolls apart, the user of the infrastructure pays just as much (or just as little!) wherever he is based and irrespective of where the journeys take place. In other words, the current charging system does not take account of the special circumstances in various regions. This state of affairs must obviously be considered unsatisfactory from the point of view of "making whoever originates costs pay them". Apart from a certain link between this principle and tax on motor fuel, infrastructure costs are not passed on directly to the actual users of this infrastructure.

One of the principles behind the Commission's ideas on the common transport policy is the charging of infrastructure costs. In 1971 a proposal was submitted to the Council of Ministers for a Community solution to this problem. The system proposed is based on the principle of marginal social costs, coupled with the need to cover budgetary costs. As regards the marginal social costs, it is proposed that the road-user should pay not only costs directly caused by him, e.g. wear and tear - but also the indirect or external costs. The latter include, in particular, congestion costs, external costs caused by air pollution and noise and the costs connected with road safety. As it would be a pure coincidence if revenue from charges, on the basis of marginal social costs, were to equal expenditure on the building of infrastructure projects over a certain period, the requirement for the meeting of budgetary costs is brought in. In case it appears in a given year that revenue from the marginal social costs is not sufficient to cover expenditure on infrastructure projects, the users of the infrastructure will have to be charged an additional charge.

Although opinion inside the services of the Commission is not unanimous to this point, I nevertheless should like to mention the possibility of promoting regional policy objectives by means of this system. To illustrate this, it is necessary to examine the situation in a highly developed or densely populated region and in a backward region. The marginal social costs will be high in a highly developed or densely populated region. But because the demand for transport services in this area is also very high, the revenue from the charging system will also be high; it may even be assumed that the point of equilibrium where the marginal revenue is equal to the marginal cost will in this case be above the average total cost curve, suggesting a surplus over expenditure and ruling out the problem of a balancing budgetary outlays. The level of marginal social costs is usually appreciably lower in a less developed region. As demand for transport services is normally very low in such regions, it is extremely probable that the point of equilibrium where marginal reveneue is equal to marginal cost will also be appreciably lower because of the low revenue from charges based on marginal social costs. It may also be assumed that this point will lie actually beneath the average total cost curve, which implies that the revenue from charges is not sufficient to cover expenditure; a deficit will therefore result.

Implementation on a regional basis of the Commission's proposal for a system of marginal social costs plus cost-covering could thus plainly lead to high user charges in the less-developed regions while infrastructure users in the densely-populated areas would pay lower charges. The situation nevertheless, and this is very important, changes completely if the proposed system is applied not on a regional basis but for a whole country or even for the whole Community. In this case the surplus on charges in the densely-populated areas could be used to cover all or some of the deficits in other areas. This qould lead to so called "spatial equalization" as it were. It must however be borne in mind that if this method is employed, i.e. if the system of charges is used to pursue regional policy objectives, there can no longer be any question of charging infrastructure costs purely on the principle that the originator of costs pays them. But not too much attention should be paid to this objection since in practice a number of arbitrary distribution scales have in any case to be used so that the originator will not pay in fact the exact costs that he causes; he may pay too little or too much.

The "Leitmotiv" of the EEC Treaty is the creation of a common market based on freedom of competition, a fact that once again has clearly been confirmed in the communication of October 1973. . . In principle, therefore, there is no place in this framework for support tariffs which, by definition, encroach upon freedom of competition. Specific support tariffs are compatible with the aims of the Treaty only in those cases defined in Article 92 (2) and (3). The Commission therefore considers that support tariffs in the transport sector in fact should be abolished. It believes that, through transport, a number of basic disadvantages are inherent in support tariffs:

– They prevent undertakings from gaining an accurate picture of their actual position as they artificially reduce the disadvantage of their remote siting, thereby causing wrong sitings, or make it harder to perceive what changes are needed in the long term; in other words, they may give rise to incorrect siting.

– they prevent society at large and the public authorities from realizing the exact importance of their financial assistance to the recipient undertakings; it is also difficult to assess precisely their real effectiveness and their impact on competition and trade.

– the public authorities may modify or even completely abolish a support tariff from one day to the next, which may have considerable impact on firms' continuity i.e. survival.

– anyone, irrespective of need, can take advantage of support tariffs in transport. In other words, even sound undertakings have a right to the reduced tariff.

The Commission considers therefore that direct support measures (support tariffs in transport are indirect support measures) are generally more effective and often less expensive as well. This means to say that in many cases it would be better to award the support directly to those concerned so that they are able to spend the funds put at their disposal as best suits their position. This opinion is shared also by the Advisory Committee on Transport. However, it must not be denied that the system of direct support has a number of disadvantages, chiefly:

– from the administrative viewpoint, direct support measures are more difficult and complicated as the amount has to be determined in each case;

– post-facto supervision is also more difficult. There must be a check on whether the funds made available were actually used for the stated purpose.

Apart from these pros and cons specific limits however are set, in the Treaty itself, on the abolition of existing support tariffs or steps to block the introduction of new support tariffs in transport by the Commission.

Article 80 (2) states that the Commission shall, when examining these rates take "account in particular of the requirements of an appropriate regional economic policy, the needs of underdeveloped areas and the problems of areas seriously affected by political circumstances".

This final aspect is stressed in respect of the Federal Republic of Germany in Article 82 which states that this country may take measures "to the extent that they are required in order to compensate for the economic disad-

vantages caused by the division of Germany to the economy of certain areas of the Federal Republic affected by that division".

Hitherto the Commission has applied the provision of Article 82 (2) in such a way that support tariffs in transport may be approved when other forms of action appear inadequate for resolving the difficulty. These support tariffs are permitted only for a clearly specified period, during which they must be degressive. The purpose is to show recipients clearly from the very beginning that they must adjust their operations in such a way that they become competitive again in the longer term.

As already indicated, the Commission considers that when the public authorities decide to impose public service obligations (tariff obligation, the obligation to operate and the obligation to carry) they must also compensate the transport undertakings for the financial disadvantages which may arise. The Council of Ministers has accepted this in priniple by adopting Regulation No 1191/69 [1]. It was agreed that the general objective should be the removal of public service obligations, though where their imposition is necessary in order to ensure the provision of adequate transport services the burdens should be subject to the compensation made in accordance with common procedures. At the same time the scope of the Regulation was restricted to the national Railways while the Regulation was made nonapplicable to undertakings in the other modes of transport (road and inland waterway) which mainly provide transport services of a local or regional character. The Commission has repeatedly tried to extend the scope of this Regulation to other railway companies and to road transport undertakings more particularly engaged in regional operations. But up to now these attempts have not met with success. It may be assumed that the Member States fear a considerable increase in the financial burdens.

The Commission attaches great value to the possibility of pursuing general political objectives by imposing public-service obligations; regional policy objectives will definitely be one of the maor priorities. It may also be automatically assumed that this whole question will become more topical when closures of uneconomic railway lines are under discussion.

Let us try to come to a conclusion! The Commision is of the opinion that transport should be considered as one of several methods of boosting less-developed regions. In particular, consultation with the academics in 1975 clearly revealed that the effects of measures taken in the transport sector for this purpose emerged only in the medium, or even long term. Short-term effects are rare. This fact is of importance if it is proposed to close an uneconomic railway line, for instance, without taking any compensatory measures (e.g. by means of road transport); the adverse effects of such a policy on the area in question only emerge in the long term.

It should also be mentioned that it is very difficult to make universally valid statements as general and specific siting factors vary from region to region, as regards both quality and the possible combinations of factors. It is for instance possible that a specific measure may give ideal results in one region and have an unfavourable effect in another. The Commission therefore considers it inadvisable to formulate a detailed policy that is to be applied in every respect; it is much better to set up a general framework which allows sufficient latitude for taking account in practice of the specific circumstances which may occur in a particular situation.

It is therefore a question of framing a policy under which it should be possible to reach pragmatic solutions and, above all, the optimum one in each case. This implies that the Commission should restrict itself to drawing up guidelines which allow the Member States so much latitude at both national and regional level that specific regional factors may be taken into consideration.

FOOTNOTE

1. Regulation (EEC) No 1191/69 of the Council of 26 June 1969 on action by Member States concerning the obligations inherent in the concept of a public service in transport by rail, road and inland waterway. OJ No L 156 of 28 June 1969.

Planning for inland navigation in Western Europe

by

G. GORT

Economic Bureau for Road and Water Transport, The Netherlands

The possibilities for inland navigation are quite different in the various countries of Western Europe. Especially where originally natural waterways were found these were used from ancient times for transportation. On the western european continent notably Germany, the Netherlands, Belgium and to a lesser degree France are the countries where inland navigation plays a large role. For that reason most of the figures mentioned in this paper will be confined to these four countries. *Table 1* gives a rough impression of the part played by inland navigation.

Of the total in- and export flows of commodities in tons carried by the three modes of transportation i.e. road, rail and water, 49% was transported by water. Especially for the Netherlands with over 70% and Ger-

many with almost 50% the importance of inland navigation is very obvious. It would seem to make sense to pay first some attention to the problem of planning for the so-called "Wet infrastructure". With this we do not mean that it will be sufficient to think only of the planning of the necessary infrastructure. Also the development of the so-called institutional framework - that is the sum total of legal reulations and the implementation of the legal possibilities on behalf of the regulations of the branch by the industry itself - which the individual transport entrepreneur has to take into account for his own policy, should be organized in such a way that the individual transport entrepreneur can make his plans accordingly based on reliable data.

Table 1 - The share of 3 inland transport-modes in the total im- and export commodity-flows between 4 countries of the common market in 1974

Country	Inland transport-mode				
	Rail	Water	Road	Total	
				%	Millions of tons carried
Belgium	31	38	31	100	150
France	39	26	35	100	154
Germany	27	49	24	100	302
The Netherlands	8	74	18	100	194
Total	26	49	26	100	799

When we now first pay attention to the problem of infrastructure we can distinguish two main aspects. In the first place the supply of necessary waterways and secondly the design and equipment of the harbours, both seaports and the inland loading and unloading places alike.

THE WATERWAYS

When we nowadays in our part of the world speak about planning of infrastructure for inland navigation the thinking starts mostly from the existing waterwaysystem.

What does this system comprise. (see figure 1). As said the development started centuries ago with natural waterways, especially rivers. These original natural waterways have by training, regulation and also by canalisation been modified to modern waterways. As exemples of these original natural waterways we mention the Elbe, the Weser, the Rhone, the Seine, the Meuse, the Schelde and of course as backbone the Rhine, with its tributaries Moselle, Neckar and Main and the dutch outlets of the Rhine as Waal, Lek and IJssel.

In addition to these natural waterways a network of

Table 2 - The share of the 4 different capacity-classes of the waterwaysystem of the 4 countries in 1974

Cap. classes In tons of vessels	Belgium	France	Germany	The Neth.	Total	
					%	Length in kms in 1974
50–250	1	13	7	21	13	2268
250–650	59	56	9	27	37	6629
650–1350	0	5	20	4	8	1464
1350– and more	40	26	64	48	42	7579
	100	100	100	100	100	17940

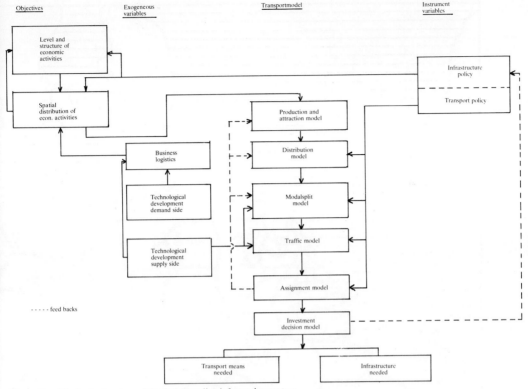

Objectives   Exogeneous variables   Transportmodel   Instrument variables

Figure 2 - The basic structure of the freight policy information system

canals were built. Here we should mention the canals from Amsterdam and from Antwerp to the Rhine, the canals from Ruhrort to Dortmund and on to the German North Sea harbours and the canals in Belgium to Bruxelles and Gent and from Antwerp to Liège, as from Duinkerken to Lille/Valenciennes. Also the approaches to the seas were improved. Thus was constructed an inter-connected system of navigable waterways. The total length of the regularly used waterways in the four countries Belgium, France, Germany and the Netherlands, is about 18.000 km. This total length can be divided into different categories depending on the size and the loading capacity of the vessels that can pass. *(table 2)*

Table 3 - The development in the waterwaysystem of the 4 countries to higher capacity-classes in the period 1960 to 1974; 1960 = 100

Cap. classes in tons of vessels	Belgium	France	Germany	The Neth.	Total
50– 250	24	57	44	38	45
250– 650	85	84	61	95	84
650–1350	0	179	119	113	119
1350– and more	152	173	120	102	125

Table 4 - Classification of European inland waterways and standard dimensions of vessels

Class of Waterway	Conventional navigation					Pusher navigation Barges		Classes defined by the
	General Description	Characterist. Tonnage (Tons)	Length (M)	Beam (M)	Draught (M)	Length (M)	Beam (M)	ECE (Geneva) deadweight capac. (tons)
1	2	3	4	5	6	7	8	9
1	Barge	300	38.50	5.00	2.20			250– 400
2	Campine barge	600	50.00	6.60	2.50			400– 650
3	Dortmund-Emskanal type	1000	67.00	8.20	2.50			650–1000
4	Rhein-Herne-kanal type	1350	80.00	9.50	2.50	70	9.50	1000–1500
5	Large Rhine barge	2000	95.00	11.50	2.70			1500–3000
6	Pushed convoy	10000	185.00	22.80	3.85	76.50	11.40	3000 and over

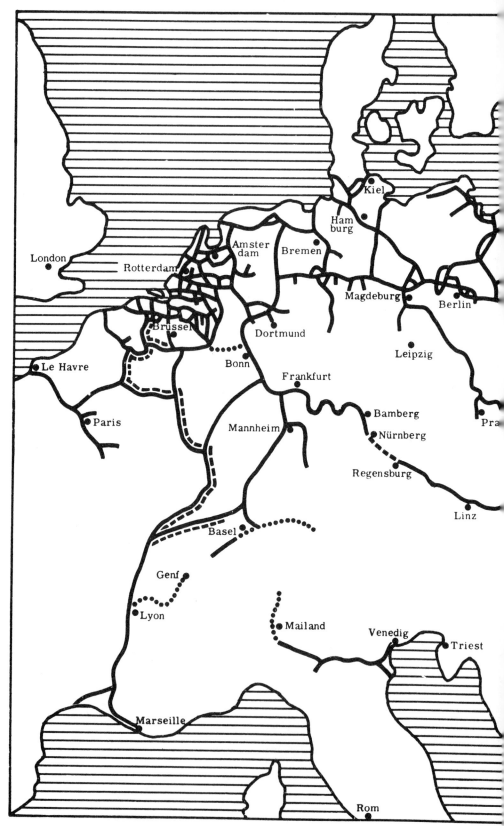

Figure 1

London
Rotterdam
Amster dam
Bremen
Kiel
Ham burg
Magdeburg
Berlin
Le Havre
Brüssel
Dortmund
Bonn
Leipzig
Frankfurt
Paris
Mannheim
Bamberg
Nürnberg
Pra
Regensburg
Basel
Linz
Genf
Lyon
Mailand
Venedig
Triest
Marseille
Rom

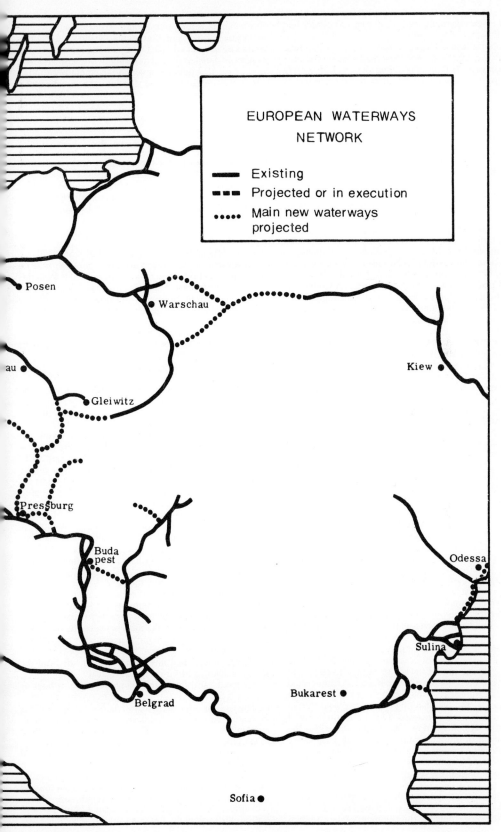

EUROPEAN WATERWAYS
NETWORK

——	Existing
▬ ▬ ▬	Projected or in execution
••••	Main new waterways projected

Posen

Warschau

Kiew

au

Gleiwitz

Pressburg

Buda
pest

Odessa

Sulina

Belgrad

Bukarest

Sofia

The total length of the waterways that exclusively can be used by vessels smaller than 250 tons has diminished to less than half since 1960.

The ability to use bigger vessels has primarily come about by widening and improving the substandard existing waterways. This process of improvement of existing waterways has taken place in all of the four countries mentioned *(table 3)*. Expansion of the network of waterways in the various countries was prompted primarily by the extensive traffic on the main artery of the western european waterway system: the Rhine. At the Treaty of Paris in 1815 the foundations were laid of a supranational policy with respect to this so very important waterway.

It is the Central Rhine Commission at Strassbourg who promoted and still promotes the improvement of this river as a navigable waterway. The possibilities to the transport industry that arise from the activities of improving the Rhine navigation have also their direct impact on the design of the, nowadays mostly with the Rhine interlinked, infrastructure of waterways. The process of growth since 1815 and 1868 (Act of Mannheim) and the closer international relationship, especially after the second world war, led to more formal standardization of planning goals. Thus the European Council of Ministers of Transport adopted in 1954 a report by a Group of Experts on standards for waterways of international importance, classifying these into five categories *(table 4)*.

Basis for the classification were the dimensions, especially the length and the beam of 5 different types of vessels that were selected out of a great number of types existing in the different countries at that time. The Economic Commission for Europe of the U.N., to which all european countries and USA belong, followed the E.C.M.T. initiative. Finally after many years of discussions also the E.C.E. Commission agreed, as E.C.M.T. did earlier, to accept class IV as waterway of international importance. So the vessel of 1350 tons (length 80 m, beam 9,50 m) "Rhine-Herne Canal type" set the minimum effective dimensions of locks. This size vessel came to be known as the Europe type vessel.

With the coming into being of the Common Market by the Treaty of Rome in 1958, besides Strassbourg also Bruxelles became of importance to the realisation of the transport and infrastructure policy. For an adequate planning of the needed infrastructure also of waterways it is essential to ensure compliance with the other governmental policies and to act in this respect in an integrated way.

The Dutch situation presents a good illustration of the various coherent laws and regulations affecting the planning of waterways, with issue by public authorities of so-called 'Vaarwegennota' and a 'Struktuurschema vaarwegen". The structure scheme is meant as an instrument to plan land use to enable future construction and improvement of big infrastructure projects. Emphasis is here on the long term policy (up to the year 2000). The aim is to prevent that the decisionmaking with respect to separate projects gets an ad hoc character. An integrated planning of waterways, which also means improvement of waterways, and the planning of land use on different governmental levels is needed. For the Netherlands it looks as though this is now being done while also the development of the international commodity flows are taken into account; an integrated European approach however would of course be a better starting point for what is now basically a set up along national considerations.

What are the perspectives in this respect? Well, in Oktober 1973 the European Commission issued a Communication concerning the development of the common transport policy. According to this communication the European transport policy would no longer as in the past mainly be shaped by market regulation but should aim as well to be subject and part of a planned infrastructure.

A more detailed specification about the action relative to the infrastructure was given in the communication of June 1976. A first modest step into the direction of a more European approach of the infrastructure policy is made herewith. How can scientific transport research be subservient to the realization of an infrastructure policy that harmoniously fits into the whole of governmental responsibilities with respect to the various policy grounds that are connected with this infrastructure? It might be interesting for the answer to this question to pay some attention to the NEA-transport [1] model as it was in the first instance developed and implemented for the Dutch situation and as it is being made operational for the E.G. countries and some other European countries affiliated with the E.C.M.T.

THE NEA FREIGHT TRANSPORT MODEL

As regards its basic structure the model can best be shown in its entirety as in *figure 2*. It is obvious from this chart that the transport model in a narrower sense is part of a larger system, the policy information system. The transport computer model in its narrower sense is fed by three categories of data, i.e.:
– the general objectives of government
– the economic and technological variables exogenous to the transport sector
– the instrumental variables

Furthermore, the feedback from the transport model to the three categories of data is explicitly shown in the chart. This feedback possibility is extremely important. In planning it will be necessary to take into account the dynamic relationship existing between the transportation of commodities and land use planning. Well, the NEA model offers the opportunity to simulate the consequences of alternative starting points with respect to the regional distribution of the transport production.

It should be taken into consideration that a transport model divided as it is in a number of submodels is based on the so-called production and attraction model. In this submodel one has to explain the total volume of incoming and outgoing transport per region including the interregional and international transport. The distribution model is used to calculate the transport volume per origin/destination pair and has as determining factors the transport times, transport costs and -distances per relation weighted. Within the *modal split model* the shares of the different modes on each transport relation are determined. The determinants can be the total volume of transport (i.e. the total per relation calculated in the distribution model), the ratio between the times and costs of transport for each mode and quality of available infrastructure. The cost and time of transport by each mode are determined inter alia by the quality and the size of existing and future infrastructure.

Per mode, also for inland navigation, the *traffic production* model converts the flows of transport (tons carried by various origin destination pairs) into movements of vessels and barges. Similarly the number of empty movements is determined. The *assignment model* is used to load the infrastructure network. So given the forecast of the number of vessel movements in 1980, 1990, 2000 and the traffic technological characteristics of the dutch waterway system it was possible by using the model to forecast the traffic intensities per link of the waterway system for each of the future years mentioned.

Considering the specific characteristics of inland navigation the originally for road traffic developed assignment techniques had to be adjusted and completed before they could be applied. As specific characteristics of inland navigation we mention:

a) varying restrictions with regard to the loading capacity of the vessels on the various waterways
b) speed differences between vessels with varying loading capacities depending on the class of the waterway
c) the occurrence of overlay times at locks and bridges.

Crucial in the assignment model are the route choices by the masters of the vessels, as these determine the ultimate traffic intensity per link of the waterway system.

In this connection our basis was the assumption that always the route with the lowest transport costs will be chosen. The transport costs in inland navigation are depending on the factors travel time and distance which thus are the ultimate determinants of the route choice. In view of the just mentioned navigability restrictions and the apparent speed differences we had to assume that the choice of route for vessels of various loading capacities may differ. The traffic movements that had to be assigned were for that reason differentiated into a number of loading capacity classes. For every loading capacity class a representative standard vessel was chosen with known technical characteristics as length, width, draught, enginepower and so on. The traffic assignment model was built in such a way, that the vessel movement could be put into the network separately per loading capacity class on base of the characteristics of the respective standard vessels. The model was fitted for two assignment techniques:

a) all or nothing assignment
b) capacity restrained assignment

In an all or nothing assignment the travel times for the various links of the network are calculated on a base of so-called free - no capacity restrained - waterways, i.e. no overlay times at locks and bridges, and no negative impact of a certain traffic intensity on the speed of the vessels. For every origin and destination pair and for the respective loading capacity classes one route was defined namely the one with the lowest costs. All traffic is further in accordance with these routes assigned to the model.

The all or nothing method gives in certain cases a good picture of the traffic performance; if however the traffic intensity (I/C-ratio) gets so high that a certain traffic congestion results, it will be likely that a part of the traffic will switch to alternative routes when available.

The method of capacity restrained assignment is based on the mutual interdependencies that exist between the route choices of the participators in the traffic. The traffic time per link is then no longer an unchangeable datum, but becomes to be an endogenous variable which is dependent on the intensity/capacity ratio. The method aims at a balanced distribution of the traffic over the alternative routes, that means a distribution in such a way that taking another route would not be advantageous to any traffic participant. The results of the assignment model deal with many aspects of the traffic performance. Besides the data about the traffic intensity per link of the waterway, the chosen routes, transport costs, transport time and - distance per transport relation per loading capacity - class are defined.

So the use of the model provides an insight into the future use by the transport industry of the various links of the waterway system. Bottle-necks that may arise can be foreseen, while the assignment model also offers the opportunity to show the consequences on the traffic intensities on the waterwaysystem as a result of changes in parts of the system.

Table 5 - The share of loading- and unloading time in the turn-around-time of dry-cargo motor vessels in inland navigation in the Netherlands

Phases of turn-around-time	200–300	300-400	400-600	600-1000
	In % of turn-around-time			
Loading time	15	17	16	17
Unload. time	32	36	38	42
Total	47	53	54	59

THE IMPACT OF PLANNING AND DESIGN OF HARBOURS ON INLAND NAVIGATION

Besides planning of waterways much attention is devoted to designing and planning of ports especially seaports and also inland ports. This work has tremendous impact on the operational possibilities of inland navigation. If e.g. in Rotterdam a seaport can be planned where the admission of inland vessels is prohibited it significantly affects the modal split possibilities. But also the complete separation of inland navigation and sea going transport has its impact on the operational possibilities of the inland transport industry. The same can be said of the loading and unloading facilities in the inland ports. That for the economy of inland navigation the loading and unloading facilities are of major importance can be seen from the break-down of the average turn around time of the inland vessel as shown in *table 5*.

We only mention these themes here very briefly, but in the planning of inland navigation much thought should be given in an integrated overall approach of the total transport chain to these items. The available models might be very useful in this respect.

As we saw the first agreements on dimensions aimed at the Europe type vessel of 1350 tons and somewhat later the for Europe new technique of push barge operations raised the standards required for international waterways. In harbours the technological developments increased the loading- and unloading capacities in tons per hour enormously. Most of these investments in waterways and harbours was done both by local as well as national and even international authorities. In general the transport industry had to cope with these developments on its own. In the transport research it is necessary to pay attention to the development of the transport industry itself.

This kind of research is done by the Economic Bureau for Road and Water transport. In this field three types of research can be distinguished:
– basic research, to get an insight into the structure of a certain branch of industry
– research that enables following the developments of a certain branch
– cost price research to find i.e. a base for the fixing of a tariff foundation.

As example of basic research as far as inland navigation is concerned can be mentioned an investigation into the structure of the Dutch transport industry as far as dry cargo was concerned.

Other examples would be a similar investigation of the Dutch tanker vessel operations. An investigation into the structure of the fleets of Belgium, France, Germany and the Netherlands and an inquiry into the needs of the shippers with regard to inland navigation in these four countries.

With regard to research as far as the developments in certain branches are concerned we mention:
– monitoring the profitability of the transport firms concerned
– investigation into the relations between water levels in the Rhine, loading depth of the vessels and freight rates as well as seasonal fluctuations and fluctuations in waiting times of empty vessels before rechartering

The cooperation of the Netherlands Institute of Transport and the Economic Bureau for Road and Water transport has proven to be very effective, many of the data about inland navigation and road haulage that are made available by the research program of the Economic Bureau for Road and Water transport are of great value in an aggregated way as input in the transport model.

At the moment the existing NEA transportmodel is provided with a cost price simulation model. This model enables creating a tariff structure for the Dutch inland navigation with which it will be possible to keep the future tariff structure up to date.

Many other applications of the NEA model with regard to inland navigation can be mentioned:
– calculating consequences of imposing user charges
– delivering basic information needed for cost/benefit analysis with regard to certain infrastructure projects
– predictions about the size and composition of the fleets needed in the future. Confrontation of these sizes and compositions with the available capacities gives information with regard to investment of desinvestment plans.

So in the cooperation between the institutes with the model a unique instrument has become available to the authorities and the industry as well setting policies relative to planning inland navigation. An instrument which has proven and still will prove to be of great value.

FOOTNOTE
1. NEA: The Netherlands Institute of Transport; Economic Bureau for Road and Water Transport; Administration and Computer Centre for Professional Transport.

Passenger travel demand forecasting:
applications of disaggregate models and directions for research

by
MOSHE BEN-AKIVA
Massachusetts Institute of Technology
Cambridge, Massachusetts

1. INTRODUCTION

The Williamsburg Conference on Urban Travel Demand Forecasting held in 1972 observed that:

"The confidence in that approach (conventional aggregate travel demand models) has been shaken and significant changes must be made to restore it" *(Transportation Research Board Special Report 143, page 11)*

The conference concluded that:

"Travel demand forecasting is entering into a new era in which are emerging a stronger behavioral basis for travel demand models, a coherence and unity of directions of current work, and the potential for major improvements in practical capabilities for forecasting future travel in the context of today's urban transportation decisionmaking needs" *(Page 207)*

The purpose of this paper is to provide an overview of a body of research and practical applications of urban travel demand models since the Williamsburg Conference. Two major observations are made:

— The disaggregate choice models which were viewed then as "emerging techniques" have been developed into a flexible forecasting approach which addresses the shortcomings of the conventional models. The feasibility and validity of the approach has been demonstrated in several empirical studies and practical planning applications.

— The progress in the implementation of disaggregate travel demand models in recent years has opened many directions for further research which will bring further improvements in aspects of traveler response prediction that are important for transportation policy evaluation.

The most significant theoretical and practical characteristics of the applications of disaggregate travel demand models are as follows:

1) **Policy relevant** - The models that have been developed are capable of more accurate travel response predictions to a wider range of operating and construction options.

2) **Explicit theory of individuals' choice behavior** - The models are based upon explicit hypotheses about individuals' travel behavior. Travel demand is viewed as a process arising directly from individual decision maker's choices. Every observed trip is the result of a selection made by an individual traveller from some set of feasible choices.

3) **Explicit structure of all relevant travel related decisions** - The models are based on an explicit theory of choice which includes the entire set of relevant decisions (unlike simple mode-choice models). Thus, the models are derived from a theory which includes employment location, residential location, housing choice, automobile ownership, mode to work, and frequency, destination, mode, time of day, and route choice for various non-work travel purposes. This structure provides a basic working hypothesis within which the various models operate. It includes interdepencies among related decisions and among individuals in the same household.

4) **Valid statistical estimation** - The models, primarily based on the multinomial logit form, are statistically estimated using the methods of maximum likelihood and least squares. Disaggregate survey data is used directly for estimation. This reduces the data requirements needed to develop the models and fully exploits the information available from a given survey data set. In contrast, aggregate modelling approaches lose a great deal of the variability inherent in existing data by grouping observations at the zonal level. Disaggregate estimation also reduces the potential of biases in estimated model coefficients due to the existence of the simultaneous link from travel demand to level-of-service attributes.

5) **Explicit aggregation** - The disaggregate models are employed to produce aggregate forecasts based on available aggregate input data. A variety of procedures for aggregating geographic areas and socioeconomic market segments have been developed and applied.

6) **Equilibration of travel demand and transportation system performance** - The models have been applied together with efficient iterative network equilibration techniques.

7) **Variety of application procedures for different planning contexts** - The models have been applied in a variety of planning situations including long- and short-range predictions, sub-area and are wide analysis, as well as in a conventional urban transportation study framework. The wide range of applications is demonstrated by the following list of transportation policy options that have recently been analyzed in the U.S. using the disaggregate models:
— carpooling incentives
— pollution control strategies
— auto restricted zones

183

— parking restrictions
— downtown circulation system
— feeder bus service to rail stations
— public transportation system in suburban communities
  — demand-responsive transit
  — dual mode/transit feasibility
  — bridge tolls
  — transit fare structure
  — ramp metering and preferential lanes
  — effect of highway supply on vehicle-miles of travel (VMT)

The remainder of this paper is divided into three parts. Section 2 provides a brief summary of the theoretical aspects of the disaggregate modelling approach. Section 3 reviews systems of models and application procedures. Finally, Section 4 presents a discussion of current and future areas of research.

2. THE DISAGGREGATE TRAVEL DEMAND MODELLING APPROACH

Choice Models[1]

Conventional consumer demand models are not suitable to the qualitative and discrete nature of travel-related decisions such as mode of travel and automobile ownership. Therefore, the approach is based on qualitative choice models. The individual behavioral unit is faced with a feasible set of alternative travel options from which one is selected. Denote the choice set of individual t as

$$C_t = \{1, 2, \ldots, i, \ldots, J_t\}$$

where J_t is the number of available alternatives. The choice process is analytically modelled using the concept of utility maximization. Denote the utility of alternative i to individual t as U_{it}; alternative i will be selected if and only if

$$U_{it} \geq U_{jt}, \qquad j = 1, \ldots, J_t$$

For predictive purposes the relative values of the utilities must be related to observed variables as follows:

$$U_{it} = V(Z_{it}, S_t) + \varepsilon_{it}$$

where
Z_{it} = a vector of attributes of alternative i faced by individual t;
S_t = a vector of socio-economic characteristics of individual t; and
ε_{it} = an unobservable random component of the utility of alternative i to individual t.

The random utilities are due to omission of unobservable variables, measurement errors and other possible source of errors in the specification of the utility functions (Manski, 1973). Thus, only choice probabilities can be predicted, as follows:

$$P(i|C_t) = \text{Prob } [U_{it} \geq U_{jt}, \quad j = 1, \ldots, J_t]$$

$$= \text{Prob } [\varepsilon_{jt} - \varepsilon_{it} \leq V(Z_{it}, S_t) - V(Z_{jt}, S_t),$$
$$j = 1, \ldots, J_t]$$

where $P(i|C_t)$ denotes the probability of individual t faced with a choice set C_t selecting alternative i.

A probabilistic choice model is derived by assuming a specific joint distribution of the random

utilities $(\varepsilon_{1t}, \ldots, \varepsilon_{J_t})$ for given values of the observable variables. Assuming that the random components are independently and identically Weibull distributed results in the following multinomial logit model (McFadden, 1974):

$$P(i|C_t) = \frac{e^{V(Z_{it}, S_t)}}{\sum\limits_{j=1}^{J_t} e^{V(Z_{jt}, S_t)}}$$

The utility of the choice to the individual denoted as U_t is the value of the utility of the chosen alternative as follows:

$$U_t = \text{Max } (U_{1t}, \ldots, U_{J_t})$$

Since the utilities are random, the maximum utility is also an unobservable random variable. However, its expected value can be determined. For example, the distribution assumption of the logit model results in[2]:

$$E [U_t] = \ln \sum\limits_{j=1}^{J_t} e^{V(Z_{jt}, S_t)}$$

A measure of consumer benefits is obtained as the difference of the expected utilities from before and after the change.

The parameters of the systematic utilities functions, $V(Z_{it}, S_t)$ are estimated using a random sample with the following information:

$$[c_t, C_t, S_t, (Z_{jt}, j=1, \ldots, J_t)], t=1, \ldots, T$$

where
T = number of observations in the sample; and
c_t = the chosen alternative by individual t.
Maximum likelihood with linear in the parameters utility functions is the method of estimation used most frequently.

Choice Sets

The summary presentation above of choice models treats the choice sets available to individuals, C_t, as given. Traditional models of consumer behavior usually consider income and time constraints. However, the set of feasible travel alternatives is also determined by a variety of other factors. An example would be a trip to a location which is not served by transit; the use of transit to this location is not a feasible alternative. Socio-economic characteristics, other than income, also influence the available alternatives. For example, a person without a driver's license does not have "auto driver" as an available mode. Empirical tests have shown the importance of information on availability of travel modes for accurate forecasts (Koppelman and Ben-Akiva, 1977). Thus, the determination of the set of feasible alternatives is a key element in any application of disaggregate choice models to travel related decisions.

Aggregate Forecasting

Aggregate demand is by definition a sum of disaggregate demands as follows:

$$T_i = \sum\limits_{t=1}^{T} P(i|C_t)$$

where
T_i = the expected number of individuals selecting alternative i; and

184

T = the number of individuals in the aggregate group.

In addition, it is often necessary, particularly in application of location choice models; to aggregate over alternatives.[3]

Since detailed data is not available, aggregation must be based on limited information about the distributions of socio-economic characteristics and attributes of the alternatives. Several aggregation procedures that have been developed are evaluated in Koppelman (1975) and their applications in travel demand forecasting will be reviewed in the following section of this paper.

3. APPLICATIONS OF DISAGGREGATE TRAVEL DEMAND MODELS

Estimated Models

The development and applications of disaggregate travel demand models are described in two recent books by Domencich and McFadden (1975) and Richards and Ben-Akiva (1975), a recently completed report by Spear (1977), and a survey paper by Ben-Akiva, Lerman and Manheim (1976).

The initial transportation applications of disaggregate modelling techniques were made for the

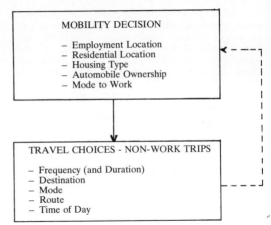

MOBILITY DECISION

 – Employment Location
 – Residential Location
 – Housing Type
 – Automobile Ownership
 – Mode to Work

TRAVEL CHOICES - NON-WORK TRIPS

 – Frequency (and Duration)
 – Destination
 – Mode
 – Route
 – Time of Day

Figure 1 - A simple choice hierarchy

choice of travel mode (e.g. Warner, 1962; Lisco, 1967; Lave, 1969; McGillivray, 1972; and Peat, Marwick and Mitchell, 1973). A large number of researchers have investigated the performance of mode choice models for work trips. Atherton and

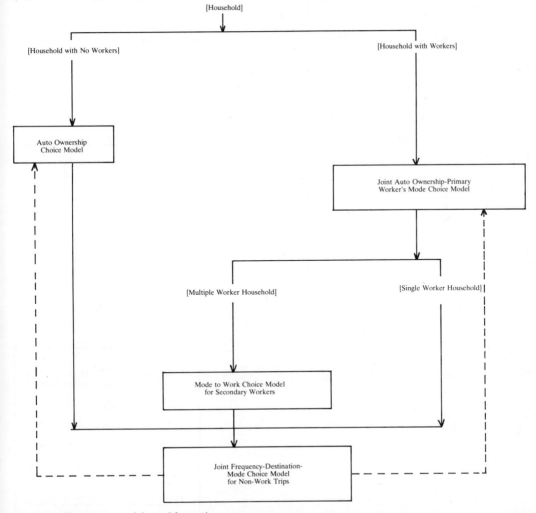

Figure 2 - Short range travel demand forecasting system

Ben-Akiva (1976) used data from widely different urban areas and obtained remarkably similar estimates of model coefficients. Ben-Akiva and Richards (1975) have successfully tested a work mode choice model with six modes using data from the Netherlands. Parody (1976) and Train (1976) showed that the inclusion of socio-economic variables in a work mode choice improves significantly the forecast accuracy. Several disaggregate work mode choice models were estimated and incorporated in existing systems of aggregate models (e.g., Cambridge Systematics, 1975; Richards, 1975; Pratt and DTM, 1976).

The first extension of disaggregate models to a multi-dimensional choice situation was made in a study by Charles River Associates (1972). In this study, the choices of frequency, destination and mode for shopping travel were modelled with reasonable results. However, each choice was modelled separately and in an arbitrarily-assumed

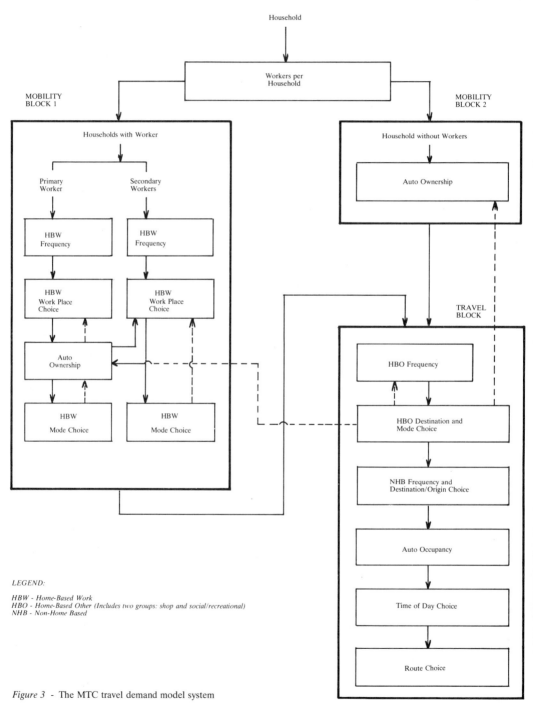

Figure 3 - The MTC travel demand model system

sequence, thereby imposing a strong, and statistically-unsupported structure on the travel decisions.

Ben-Akiva (1973) demonstrated the differences among alternative model structures in terms of behavioral assumptions and statistical estimation properties. For this reason, Ben-Akiva (1973 and 1974), Adler and Ben-Akiva (1975) and Richards and Ben-Akiva (1974) extended this work by applying disaggregate choice models to a set of non-work travel choices in a joint structure. This work also extended by Lerman and Ben-Akiva (1975) and Lerman (1975) to the joint modelling of mobility choices including residential location, automobile ownership and mode of travel to work.

These models follow the hierarchical choice structure suggested by Ben-Akiva (1973) for modelling two classes of choices — mobility choices and travel choices — as shown in Figure 1. The arrows indicate the direction of conditionality and the feedback of expected utilities (defined in the previous section) from lower-level choices, affecting higher-level choices.

Two examples of travel demand model systems that were used in several policy and planning studies are shown in Figures 2 and 3. The short range travel demand forecasting system was used in a study of the effects of alternative carpooling incentive programs (Ben-Akiva and Atherton, 1977; and Cambridge Systematics, 1976) and the MTC model system was designed for conventional urban transportation study applications in the San Francisco region (Ruiter and Ben-Akiva, 1977). These are systems of inter-related disaggregate models which proceed through a set of hierarchically-structured household travelrelated choices as shown. The specific models are described in detail in the references.

Application Procedures

The same set of disaggregate models can be used as the basis for a range of aggregate forecasting procedures:

1) Manual calculations using elasticities or the incremental logit form (Ben-Akiva and Atherton, 1977) for crude predictions of the effects of changes in transportation level of service attributes.

2) Sample enumeration procedure in which a random sample of households is used to represent the aggregate population of interest. Forecasts are made by applying the models to each household individually using revised values of the independent variables. These disaggregate predictions are expanded to obtain the required aggregate predictions. This procedure was used in several studies, focused primarily on pricing policies and low capital options (Cambridge Systematics, 1976 and Small, 1976). An existing sample could be updated, based on available or forecasted aggregate socioeconomic data, using the procedure described in Duguay, et al., (1976) and used by Cosslett, et al., (1977) to generate a sample for the San Franciso Bay Area from Census data.

3) Monte Carlo simulation using available aggregate data to synthesize a sample of households (and a sample of locations if aggregation of spatial alternatives is also required). This approach was employed by Watanatada and Ben-Akiva (1977) for an area-wide sketch planning procedure. It is a simplified procedure that requires limited input data and provides quick turn-around. It is suitable for applications at a high level of geographic aggregation.

4) Network analysis system with market segmentation using available software such as the Urban Transportation Planning System (UMTA, 1976). An experimental system developed at MIT was used to demonstrate the feasibility of this approach and differences among alternative models (Ben-Akiva, et al., 1977). The MTC system, shown in Figure 3, was also implemented in a forecasting system compatible with UTPS (Cambridge Systematics, 1977). It is being used by the regional transportation planning agency for ongoing studies.

Applications in Policy and Planning Studies

Clearly, one of the most important advantages of the disaggregate models that have been developed is their sensitivity to a wide range of transportation service changes as well as urban area characteristics and socio-economic attributes. In addition, as was shown above, the models can be applied to aggregate forecasting in a variety of ways ranging in level of detail and data requirements from detailled subarea analysis and conventional network-based simulations, to a highly-aggregate sketch planning procedure based on a small number of market segments. Some of the recent applications in policy and planning studies are summarized below to demonstrate the models' wide range of applicability and to emphasize the fact that disaggregate models are "practical" analysis tools. They are no longer the "research frontier", but are "production" methods.

The models have been used for:

— A policy study, for the U.S. Federal Energy Administration, on the effects of alternative programs of incentives to carpool (shared use of autos for work trips). Washington, D.C. and Birmingham, Alabama were used as prototype cities. The Sample Enumeration method was used (Cambridge Systematics, 1976).

— Planning studies of auto-restricted zones, for the U.S. Urban Mass Transportation Administration. The models were used to predict the effects of various auto-restricted zone concepts in selected cities, as part of the process of selecting sites and implementation strategies for a federally-sponsored demonstration program (Alan M. Voorhees, et al., 1976).

— A planning study of anticipated guideway transit strategies for Milwaukee for the U.S. Urban Mass Transportation Administration. The models were used in conjunction with UTPS in both sketchplanning and detailed-network analysis approaches (Cambridge Systematics, 1975).

— For the agency planning a "people-mover" system for internal circulation within the Los Angeles central business district, models have been developed for predicting, for peak-period trips, choice of parking lot and egress mode (travel from parking to destination), if arrival by auto, and egress mode if arrival by transit; and for noon-hour trips, frequency destination and mode of within-CBD trips (modes include walk, minibus, and people-mover systems.) (Barton-Aschman, et al., 1976).

Many other applications, primarily of mode choice models, have been performed (e.g., Difiglio and Reed, 1975; Liou, et al., 1975; Train, 1976; Small, 1976; and Dunbar, 1976). A detailed review of several applications is given by Spear (1977). Thus, disaggregate methods are being used for a variety of practical policy and planning applications.

Discussion

The preceding summary has indicated, in very general terms, the progress made on travel forecasting improvements since the Williamsburg Conference. During the intervening period, as would be expected, the research needs have changed somewhat. The application experience has demonstrated the substantial advantages of well-specified disaggregate travel demand models. Disaggregate models can be estimated using less data than equivalent aggregate models, potentially have better transferability properties, and can be applied at any level of geographic aggregation. In the case study comparisons conducted at MIT by Ben-Akiva, *et al.*, (1977), the importance of a complete specification was demonstrated; omission of level-of-service effects on trip generation and of specific elements of level-of-service (e.g., auto operating costs) resulted in significant underpredictions of the changes in travel due to transportation policies. Since the effect on travel demand of many short-range, low capital options is small to begin with, this underprediction can be very significant in the evaluation of such options.

Thus, travel demand modelling approaches which were viewed by the Williamsburg Conference as "emerging techniques" have now been demonstrated to be both feasible and desirable. While the improved modelling methodology has several shortcomings that require further research as discussed in the next section, it can be immediately applied to produce more accurate and more useful predictions than those available from conventional travel forecasting procedures.

4. DIRECTIONS FOR RESEARCH

The work described in this paper is part of a rapidly evolving body of knowledge. Extensions of existing models, new applications to policy questions, and new methodological developments are underway. While the feasibility and usefulness of the disaggregate modelling approach has been demonstrated in previous work, there are several areas which are being or need to be addressed in further research. These are classified into the following five major areas:
— improved model specification;
— spatial choice modelling;
— sketch planning procedures;
— extensions to other transportation planning contexts; and
— alternative choice models.

Improved Model Specification

Travel demand models are developed to analyze a variety of future scenarios which almost always require prediction outside the range of current data. The likelihood of a successful extrapolation will increase with greater variability of both the dependent and the independent variables in data sets which are used for model estimation. Improvements can be achieved by using data from several geographical areas and several points in time. In addition to transferability tests, the models' predictive validity could be improved by applying the models in situations where data exists before and after a change in transportation services.

However, the basic problem of extrapolating beyond the range of existing data remains and requires the use of behaviorally credible models. The most important step in achieving this objective is a complete description of consumer response which serves at the basis for the specification of the dependent variables of travel behavior models. Examples of significant phenomena of consumer response which have been observed over time but are excluded from some existing models are: consolidation of travel by trip chaining; changes in time allocation to various home and non-home activities; and substitutions among residential and employment location choices, automobile ownership levels and travel choices.

The range of independent variables must also be expanded and should not be restricted to those that can easily be forecast. The importance of a full set of socioeconomic and demographic variables in travel behavior models has been demonstrated in several recent studies. The before-and-after studies conducted by Parody (1976) and Train (1976) showed how a model with a larger set of socioeconomic variables was better able to predict changes in mode choice. Thus, there is a need to expand the scope of the dependent and independent variables in travel behavior models.

The logit model has been critized for its "independence from irrelevant alternatives property." However, since alternative formulations such as multinomial probit are still significantly more expensive to apply, the logit model will continue to be the most commonly-used choice model. Therefore, it is important to apply tests of the logit specification with multiple data sets as described above as well as the statistical tests of the "independence" assumption described by McFadden, Tye and Train (1977).

Spatial Choice Modelling

Most of the research in behavioral travel demand models has been focused on short-run mode choice decisions, and knowledge of behavioral mechanisms of other relevant impacts is still limited. It should be extended to include other transportation-related choices, especially spatial choices. The key research problems in this area are the joint modelling of the longrun household choices including residential location, automobile ownership and travel to work, and the modelling of trip chaining or tour formation.

These two modelling efforts share a set of common methodological questions. The most critical of these issues are discussed below, with possible approaches to their resolutions.

1) *Definition and Aggregation of Spatial Alternatives*-Spatial choices differ from mode choices in that there is no natural definition of the alternatives. In some spatial choice situations it is possible to define an *elemental alternative* such tha any spatial alternative is a grouped alternative consisting of one or more elemental alternatives and each elemental alternative is included in one and only one grouped alternative. Stores and dwelling units are two examples of such elemental alternatives.

Unfortunately, in most real-world applications the number of possible elemental alternatives is far too large to be of any practical use. Therefore, some form of *aggregation of elemental alternatives* must be performed in spatial choice models.

Two basic approaches can be used to perform such an aggregation: (1) assuming a behavioral choice hierarchy; and (2) explicitly aggregating elemental alternatives. In the first approach, different levels of aggregation of elemental alternatives represent sequential steps in an assumed choice hierarchy. An example would be the aggregation of dwelling units into neighborhoods, communities, sectors of the metropolitan area, etc., where the decisionmaker is assumed to first select the sector in which he wants to reside, then he selects a community, followed by a choice of neighborhood, and finally a choice of an actual dwelling unit. This procedure is commonly employed in mode choice studies when various transit alternatives are treated as one mode and the mode choice model is followed by a transit sub-modal choice procedure. The problem in this approach is that no single hierarchy applies to all individuals and there is no empirical or theoretical evidence to suggest an appropriate hierarchy.

The second approach is to use a theoretically-consistent procedure for the aggregation over elemental alternatives. Such an approach can be based on the concept that the utility of a group of alternatives is the utility of the best member of the group, since only the best will be selected. Lerman (1975) employed this approach in developing a residential location model. An alternative approach is to assume a continuous spatial choice density function that can be integrated over zones using numerical integration methods (Watanatada and Ben-Akiva, 1977; and McFadden, 1976).

2) *Choice Set Generating Process*-The large number of potential spatial alternatives makes the computational requirements of a choice model prohibitively expensive in many applications. But, more fundamentally, the use of very large choice sets to represent individuals' choice processes would appear to be behaviorally unrealistic. In a model of residential location, for example, not all dwelling units in the urban area are feasible alternatives for a given household. Some dwelling units are simply too expensive, others may not be feasible if they are not served by transit and the household members cannot drive, and so on. Yet, even if an alternative is feasible according to these types of constraints it may still not be considered by some consumers due to lack of information. The effect of advertising on consumer behavior can be partially attributed to the fact that an alternative which has been previously unknown has been introduced into consumers' choice sets. Since for behavioral, practical and efficiency considerations we must define feasible subsets of alternatives, it is necessary to further investigate potential constraints for the feasibility of spatial alternatives.

3) *Activity Time Allocation*-In searching for more powerful constraints for determining the feasibility of spatial alternatives the most obvious measure that comes to mind is that of a *time budget*. If it was known how much time is allocated by a consumer for the performance of a given non-home activity, one could subtract from it a minimal activity duration (which could be zero) and use the result as an upper limit on travel time. This will exclude a significant number of potential destinations.

The concept of time allocation is different from "travel time budget" which has been proposed by some researchers (e.g., Zahavi, 1974; and Goodwin, 1976). Travel is an intermediate good that is only rarely being consumed for its own sake. Travel time and travel costs are inputs required to participate in non-home activities, not anything which people budget without reference to the value of those activities.

This indicates that the allocation of time is a key element in modelling spatial decisions. Explicit time allocation modelling is likely to improve the existing specifications of travel and mobility models. More important, it can be extremely powerful in delineating spatial choice sets. An exploratory study of modelling activity choice and time allocation by Bain (1976) indicates the feasibility of this approach.

4) *Trip Chaining*-The choice set of alternative trip destinations is further complicated by the consideration of trip chaining. A large percentage of urban travel is comprised of multiple-stop tours, where the choices of the destinations visited on a tour are interdependent.

Since much of the short-run response to transportation policy changes now under consideration seems to involve increased trip chaining, it is important that models which explicitly represent such decisions be developed. Exploratory research in this direction by Adler (1976) and Horowitz (1976) provides significant insights into the biases of existing link-based models. This information will be useful in determining the most appropriate simplifying assumptions that are required in order to make trip chaining models feasible.

Sketch Planning Procedures

Sketch planning procedures are designed to perform a quick examination of a large number of alternative policies. Such analysis tools have been or are being developed over the past few years for different planning purposes which range from the study of national urban transportation resource allocation (Weiner, et al., 1973) to the preliminary screening of alternative transportation system configurations at a sub-area level (Dial, 1973). Urban transportation sketch planning packages can generally be characterized by a high degree of geographic aggregation and network abstraction, limited information requirements, ease of input data preparation and fast response times. Reviews of recent research efforts in sketch planning methodologies are given in Landau (1976) and Watanatada (1977).

In achieving these needed capabilities, the incorporation of disaggregate models can significantly increase the validity and policy-sensitivity of impact predictions. The contrasts between disaggregate travel demand models and sketch planning tools are striking. The former require the representation of socioeconomic characteristics, transportation level-of-service and locational attributes at the level of individual behavioral units, while the latter must be capable of operating on highly aggregate, readily available input data.

A promising two-pronged approach to this incompatibility problem is, first, to represent the distributions of the independent variables as parametric functions of readily obtainable aggregate data, and, second, to empoy Monte Carlo simulation methods in forecasting aggregate travel demand. This approach has been used for an urbanized area travel demand prediction model developed by Watanatada and Ben-Akiva (1977). Monte Carlo methods are employed in two stages of sampling. The first stage generates a sample of households distributed over the urban area. The second stage samples a set of potential destinations by trip purpose for each household in the sample; travel forecasts for each household are then computed based on these potential destinations.

The Monte Carlo simulation approach has three important advantages. First, it is not restricted to any type of mathematical presentation. Second, its prediction errors do not suffer from aggregation bias and can be easily controlled. And, third, it has been found from computational experience to be relatively inexpensive to produce the kind of forecasting precision required for most urban transportation planning purposes.

One of the most difficult issues in applying disaggregate travel demand models to sketch planning is the problem of developing concomitant transportation supply and traffic assignment models for different levels of geographic aggregation. One fundamental modelling difficulty is that since a transportation network is not just a direct summation of the individual links, the problem of network aggregation becomes analytically intractable. Because no consistent theory exists for network-abstract supply modelling, past researchers have developed relationships based on experimental results or highly simplified assumptions on transportation supply characteristics. For a given zone pair, the supply models should predict the distribution of level-of-service attributes as a function of travel demand and network capacity.

Because of the extremely wide range of geographic aggregation employed in sketch planning, transportation supply and traffic assignment models should be developed in integrated network and network-abstract forms. Network supply models represent transportation facilities, mostly of major types, as network links. Network-abstract supply models represent transportation facilities, mostly of ubiquitous nature, as aggregate transportation systems defined by mode, facility type and geographic unit. A network-abstract model can be developed to relate parametrically the aggregate performance measures of a system to its transportation supply characteristics and traffic loads. Network-abstract supply models can be developed for both access and linehaul travel. Talvitie, et al., have developed network abstract supply models for the access portion of a trip (Talvitie and Hilson, 1974; Talvitie and Leung, 1976).

Network traffic assignment models for sketch planning can be developed based largely on existing knowledge. Network-abstract traffic assignment models can be developed to allocate traffic, not to routes, but to aggregate transportation systems (Creighton and Hamburg, 1971).

Extensions to Other Transportation Planning Contexts

Some preliminary efforts have been made in applying disaggregate choice models to transportation planning contexts other than urban passenger transportation. In intercity freight transportation, Antle and Haynes (1971) and Hartwig and Linton (1974) estimated disaggregate mode choice models based on data from individual shipments. Antle and Haynes attempted to aggregate their data across commodities and re-estimate the model. The results were significantly poorer. Terziev (1976) formulated a joint mode-shipment size model and estimated the model with available Census data.

In air passenger transportation, Kanafani, et al., (1974) estimated a joint fare type-season choice model based on aggregate data. Fares were the only level-of-service variable employed. This and other attempts to estimate intercity and international models resulted in a limited specification that was attributed to the poor quality of the available aggregate data. Therefore, it appears that a new survey to collect disaggregate data would permit a broader range of policy variables to be incorporated. The cost of data collection is not expected to be excessive. For example, Hartwig and Linton (1974) estimated their freight mode choice model with statistically significant results using a sample of 1,213 waybills.

In terms of forecasting, the Monte Carlo approach, which has been found feasible and relatively economical in urban transportation planning applications, could be extended to other transportation planning contexts. Roberts (1976) has developed a Monte Carlo simulation procedure for forecasting freight traffic flows based on the generation of individual firms of varying sizes as the basic behavioral units. The sum of commodity demand forecasts for the firms generated in the sample are then expanded to obtain freight traffic volumes.

Alternative Choice Models

The choice model which has been used in almost all travel demand applications involving more than two alternatives is multinomial logit. The properties of the model, including its derivation from the theory of individual utility maximization, are given in McFadden (1974). The property of "independence from irrelevant alternatives" (IIA) is the basic deficiency of the logit model. Its key advantage is mathematical simplicity or ease of implementation. However, due to the IIA property, the validity of the model in many travel demand applications has been questioned, particularly in complex choice situations where different degrees of similarities exist among alternatives.

Two recently developed models do not have this "independence property" and explicitly incorporate different degrees of interdependencies among alternatives. The first is the multinomial probit model which is based on the multivariate normal distribution. Recently, feasible probit estimation procedures have been developed by Hausman and Wise (1976) (for up to four alternatives only) and by Daganzo, et al., (1976) and Manski, et al., (1977). The probit model can be used to directly estimate the correlations among utilities, or similarities among alternatives.

The second development is the derivation by McFadden (1977) of a model which is based on a multivariable extreme value distribution. This Generalized Extreme Value (GEV) model is expressed as follows:

$$P_i = \frac{e^{V_i} G_i(e^{V_1}, \ldots, e^{V_J})}{G(e^{V_1}, \ldots, e^{V_J})}$$

where

P_i is the choice probability of alternative i;

V_i is the systematic utility of alternative i;

$G(e^{V_1}, \ldots, e^{V_J})$ is a function which satisfies certain conditions described in McFadden (1977, pp. 6-9); and

$G_i(e^{V_1}, \ldots, e^{V_J})$ is the derivative of the function with respect to its ith argument.

The special case

$$G(e^{V_1}, \ldots, e^{V_J}) = \sum_{i=1}^{J} e^{V_i}$$

yields the multinomial logit model:

$$P_i = \frac{e^{V_i}}{\sum_{j=1}^{J} e^{V_j}}$$

An important class of special cases of the GEV models is based on partitioning a choice set into subsets of similar alternatives. Consider, for example, a choice set where i denotes a subset of similar alternatives and V_{ij} is the representative utility of the jth alternative in subset i. In the following function:

$$G(e^{V_{11}}, \ldots, e^{V_{ij}}, \ldots, e^{V_{IJ}})$$

$$= \sum_{i} a_i (\sum_{j} e^{V_{ij}/\delta_i})^{\delta_i}$$

the parameter δ_i is an index of the similarity of the alternatives in subset i. This function results in the following choice model:

$$P_{ij} = \frac{e^{V_{ij}/\delta_i}}{\sum_{j} e^{V_{ij}/\delta_i}} \cdot \frac{e^{\delta_i \ln \sum_{j} e^{V_{ij}/\delta_i + \ln a_i}}}{\sum_{i} e^{\delta_i \ln \sum_{j} e^{V_{ij}/\delta_i + \ln a_i}}}$$

$$= P_{j|i} \cdot P_i$$

where P_{ij} is the joint possibility of selecting alternative ij, $P_{j|i}$ is the conditional probability of selecting alternative ij given that the choice lies within subset i, and P_i is the marginal probability that the choice lies within subset i. If all the similarity parameters are equal to one we get a joint logit model as follows:

$$P_{ij} = \frac{e^{V_{ij} + \ln a_i}}{\sum_{i} \sum_{j} e^{V_{ij} + \ln a_i}}$$

If we assume that

$$\delta_i = \delta \text{ for all } i$$

and

$$V_{ij} = \delta \alpha Z_{ij} + \beta Z_i$$

where
Z_{ij} is a vector of attributes which are specific to both i and j,
Z_i is a vector of attributes specific only to i and
α, β are vectors of coefficients

we get

$$P_{j|i} = \frac{e^{\alpha Z_{ij}}}{\sum_{j} e^{\alpha Z_{ij}}}$$

and

$$P_i = \frac{e^{\beta Z_i + \ln a_i + \delta LS_i}}{\sum_{i} e^{\beta Z_i + \ln a_i + \delta LS_i}}$$

where

$$LS_i = \ln \sum_{j} e^{\alpha Z_{ij}}$$

This special class of the GEV model is a sequence of multinomial logit models that could be estimated sequentially using existing logit estimation packages. This procedure has been applied for special cases in several existing urban travel demand models (e.g., Ben-Akiva, 1973; Daly, 1977; and Ruiter and Ben-Akiva, 1977) and can be used to test alternative partitioning of complex choice sets.

The parameter δ must be between 0 and 1, for the model to be consistent with its basic assumption.[4] However, in estimation the value is not constrained. An estimated value outside the range will indicate an error, either in the specification of the utility functions or in the partitions of the choice set. A value of δ greater than one indicates that the sequence should be changed to $P_j \cdot P_{i|j}$. If the estimated value of δ is not significantly different from one, then a joint logit model is appropriate and more efficient.

ACKNOWLEDGEMENTS

I would like the thank my colleagues, Marvin Manheim, Thawat Watanatada, Steven Lerman, Thomas Adler and Jesse Jacobson, for their valuable assistance in the preparation of this paper.

REFERENCES*

Adler, T. J., **Modelling Non-Work Travel Patterns,** Ph. D. Thesis, Transportation Systems Division, Department of Civil Engineering, MIT, Cambridge, Massachusetts, 1976.

Adler, T. J. and M. Ben- Akiva, "A Joint-Choice Model for Frequency, Destination and Travel Mode for Shopping Trips," **TRR 569,** 1975.

Alan M. Voorhees and Associates, Inc. and Cambridge Systematics, Inc., **Auto Restricted Zones: Background and Visibility,** Phase I Report, UMTA, 1976.

Antle, L. and R. Haynes, **An Application of Discriminant Analysis to the Division of Traffic Between Transport Modes,** Report 71-72, U.S. Army Eng. Institute for Water Resources, 1971.

Atherton, T. and M. Ben-Akiva, "Transferability and Updating of Disaggregate Travel Demand Models," **TRR 610,** 1976.

Bain, J. H., **Activity Choice Analysis, Time Allocation and Disaggregate Travel Demand Modelling,** S. M. Thesis, Dept. of C.E., MIT, Cambridge, Mass., 1976.

Barton-Aschman Associates and Cambridge Systematics, Inc., **Los Angeles Central Business District: Internal Travel Demand Modelling,** prepared for Community Redevelopment Agency, Los Angeles, California, 1976.

Ben-Akiva, M., **Structure of Passenger Travel Demand Models,** Ph. D. Thesis, Dept. of C.E., MIT, Cambridge, Ma., 1973.

Ben-Akiva, M., "Structure of Passenger Travel Demand Models," **TRR 526, 1974.**

* See key to abbreviations at end of references.

191

Ben-Akiva, M., T. J. Adler, J. Jacobson, M. Manheim, **Experiments to Clarify Priorities in Urban Travel Forecasting Research and Development,** Summary Report (draft), U.S. DOT, Feb. 1977.

Ben-Akiva, M. and T. Atherton, "Methodology for Short Range Travel Demand Predictions: Analysis of Carpooling Incentives," in forthcoming **Journal of Transport Economics and Policy,** 1977.

Ben-Akiva M. and S. Lerman, "Disaggregate Travel and Mobility Choice Models and Measures of Accessibility," in forthcoming Proceedings of The 3rd Internat'l Conf. on Behavioural Travel Modelling, Australia, 1977.

Ben-Akiva, M., S. Lerman and M. Manheim, "Disaggregate Models: An Overview of Some Recent Research Results and Practical Applications," **Proceedings of the PTRC Summer Mtg.,** 1976.

Ben-Akiva, M. and M. Richards, "Disaggregate Multimodal Model for Work Trips in the Netherlands," **TRR 569,** 1975.

Brand, D. and M. Manheim, eds., "Urban Travel Demand Forecasting," **HRB Special Report** 143, 1973.

Cambridge Systematics, Inc., **The Development of a Disaggregate Behavioural Work Mode Choice Model for the Los Angeles Metropolitan Area,** prepared for the Los Angeles Regional Study and the Southern California Association of Governors, 1975.

Cambridge Systematics, Inc., **A Study Design for Dual Mode Transit Planning case Studies,** prepared for UMTA, DOT, 1975.

Cambridge Systematics, Inc., Travel Model Development Project: Project Memos, Prepared for the Metropolitan Transportation Commission, Berkeley, Cal., 1977.

Cambridge Systematics, Inc. and A. M. Voorhees and Associates, Inc., **Carpool Incentives: Analysis of Transportation and Energy Impacts,** Final Report, FEA, June 1976.

Charles River Associates, **A Disaggregate Behavioural Model of Urban Travel Demand,** prepared for the FHWA, U.S. DOT, 1972.

Cosslet, S., G. Duguay, W. S. Jung and D. McFadden, "Synthesis of Household Transportation Survey Data: The SYNSAM Methodology," UTDFP Working Paper, Inst. of Transportation Studies, Univ. of Cal., Berkeley, 1977.

Creighton, Hamburg, Inc., **Freeway-Surface Arterial Splitter,** prepared for FHWA, U.S. DOT, July 1971.

Daganzo, C., F. Bouthelier and Y. Sheffi, "an Efficient Approach to Estimate and Predict with Multinomial Probit Models," draft paper, Dept. of Civil Eng., MIT, Cambridge, Ma., 1976.

Daly, A. J., "Some Developments in Transport Demand Modelling," Paper presented at the 3rd Internat'l Conf. on Behavioural Travel Modelling, Australia, 1977.

Dial, R. B., "A Procedure for Long Range Transportation (Sketch) Planning," Proceedings of the Internat'l Conf. on Transportation Research, **Transportation Research Forum,** Bruges, Belgium June 1973.

Difiglo, C. and R. F. Reed, Jr., "Transit Sketch Planning Procedures," **TRR 569,** 1975.

Duguay, G., W. Jung, and D. McFadden, "SYNSAM: A Methodology for Synthesizing Household Transportation Survey Data", W.P. no. 7618, UTDFP, Inst. of Trans. Studies, U. of Cal., Berkeley, Sept. 1976.

Domencich, T. and D. McFadden, **Urban Travel Demand: A Behavioural Analysis,** North Holland, Amsterdam, 1975.

Dunbar, F. C., "Quick Policy Evaluation with Behavioural Demand Models," Paper presented at 55th TRB Mtg., 1976.

Goodwin, P. B., "Travel Choice and Time Budgets," prepared for the PTRC Summer Annual Meeting, University of Warwick, England, July 1976.

Hartwig, J. and W. Linton, **Disaggregate Mode Choice Models of Intercity Freight Movement,** S. M. Thesis, The Transp. Ctr., Northwestern Univ., Evanston, Il., 1974.

Hausman, J. and D. Wise, "A Conditional Probit Model for Qualitive Choice: Discrete Decisions Recognizing Interdependence and Heterogeneous Preferences," W.P. 173, Dept. of Econ., MIT, Cambridge, Ma., 1976.

Horowitz, J., "Effects of Travel Time and Cost on the Frequency and Structure of Automobile Travel," **TRR 592,** 1976.

Kanafani, A., E. Sadoulet and E. C. Sullivan, **Demand Analysis for North Atlantic Air Travel,** Special Report, The Institute of Transportation and Traffic Eng., University of California, Berkeley, April 1974.

Koppelman, F.S., **Travel Prediction with Models of Individual Travel Behaviour,** Ph. D. Thesis, Dept. of C.E., MIT, Cambridge, Ma., 1975.

Koppelman, F. S. and M. Ben-Akiva, "Aggregate forecasting with Disaggregate Travel Demand Models Using Normally Available Data," prepared for presentation at the World Conf. on Transport Research, Rotterdam, Apr. 1977.

Landau, U., **Sketch Planning Models in Transportation Systems,** Ph. D. Thesis, Dept. of Civil Eng., MIT, Cambridge, Ma., 1976.

Lave, C. H., "A Behavioural Approach to Model Split Forecasting," **Transportation Research,** Vol. 3, No. 4, 1969.

Lerman, S. R., **A Disaggregate Behavioural Model of Urban Mobility Decisions,** Ph. D. Thesis, Dept. of Civil Eng., MIT, Ma., 1975.

Lerman, S. R. and M. Ben-Akiva, "A Disaggregate Behavioral Modal of Auto Ownership," **TRR 569,** 1975.

Liou, P. S., G. S. Cohen, and D. Hartgen, "Application of Disaggregate Modal-Choice Models of Travel Demand Forecasting for Urban Transit Systems," **TRR 534,** 1975.

Lisco, T. E., **The Value of Commuters' Travel Time: A Study in Urban Transportation,** Ph. D. Thesis, Dept. of Econ., Univ. of Chicago, 1967.

Luce, R. D. and P. Suppes, "Preference, Utility and Subjective Probability," in **Handbook of Mathematical Psychology,** Vol. III, Luce, Bush, and Galanter (eds.), John Wiley, N.Y., 1965.

Manski, C. F., **The Analysis of Qualitative Choice,** Ph. D. Thesis, Dept of Econ., MIT, Cambridge, Ma., June 1973.

Manski, C., S. R. Lerman and R. L. Albright, Series of Technical Memos for ongoing project entitled "An Estimator for the Generalized Multinomial Probit Model," Cambridge Systematics, Inc., 1977.

McFadden, D., "Conditional Logit Analysis of Qualitative Choice Behavior," in Zarembka, P. (ed.), **Frontiers in Econometrics,** N.Y. Academic Press, 1974.

McFadden, D., "The Mathematical Theory fo Demand Models," in **Behavioral Travel-Demand Models,** (Stopher and Meyburg, eds.), Lexington Books, Lexington, Ma., 1976.

McFadden, Daniel, "Quantitative Methods for Analyzing Travel Behavior of Individuals: Some Recent Developments," paper presented at the Third Internat'l Conf. on Behavior Travel Modelling, Australia, April 1977.

McFadden, D., W. Tye and K. Train, "Diagnostic Test for Independence-from-Irrelevant-Alternatives Property of Multinomial Logit Models," Presented at the 56th Mtg. of the TRB, 1977.

McGillivray, R. G., "Binary Choice of Urban Transport Mode in the San Francisco Bay Region," **Econometrica,** Vol. 40, No. 5, 1972.

Parody, T. E., **A Disaggregate Prediction Analysis of Mode Choice,** Ph. D. Thesis, Dept. of Civil Eng., Univ. of Massachusetts, Amherst, Ma., 1976.

Peat, Marwick and Mitchell & Co., **Implementation of the n-Dimensional Logit Model,** prepared for Comprehensive Planning Organization, San Diego County, Ca., 1973.

R. H. Pratt Associates, Inc., and DTM, Inc., **Development and Calibration of Mode Choice Models for the Twin City Area,** Prepared for the Metropolitan Council, 1976.

Richards, M., "Application of Disaggregate Modelling Techniques to Transportation Planning Studies," Prepared for the PTRC Summer Annual Mtg., Univ. of Warwick, July 1975.

Richards, M. G. and M. Ben-Akiva, **A Disaggregate Travel Demand Model,** Saxon House, D. C. Health, Ltd., England, 1975.

Richards, M. and M. Ben-Akiva, "A Simultaneous Destination and Mode Choice Model for Shopping Trips," **Transportation,** Vol. III, No. 4, Dec., 1974.

Roberts, P., "Forecasting Freight Flows Using a Disaggregate Freight Demand Model," Ctr. for Trans. Studies, Report No. 76-1, MIT, Cambridge, Ma., 1976.

Ruiter, E. R. and M. Ben-Akiva, "A System of Disaggregate Travel Demand Models: Structure, Component Models and Application Procedure," Paper presented at 56th Mtg. of the TRB, 1977.

Small, K., "Bus Priority, Differential Pricing, and Investment in Urban Highways," W. P. no. 7613, UTDFP, Inst. of Trans. Studies, U. of Cal., Berkeley, 1976.

Spear, B. D., **A Study of Individual Choice Models: Applications of New Travel Demand Forecasting Techniques to Transportation Planning,** U.S. DOT, FHWA, Office of Highway Planning, 1977.

Talvitie, A. and N. Hilsen, "An Aggregate Access Supply Model," **Trans. Research Forum Proceedings,** Vol. 15, No. 1, 1974.

Talvitie, A. and T. Leung, "Parametric Access Network Model," **TTR no. 592,** 1976.

Terziev, M., **Modelling the Demand for Freight Transportation,** S. M. Thesis, MIT, Cambridge, Ma., 1976.

Train, K., "Work Trip Mode Split Models: An Empirical Exploration of Estimate Sensitivity to Model and Data Specification," W. P. no. 7602, UTDFP, Inst. of transp. Studies, U. of Cal., Berkeley, 1976.

Urban Mass Transportation Administration, **Urban Transportation Planning System: Reference Manual,** Washington, D.C. 1976.

Warner, S. L., **Stochastic Choice of Mode in Urban Travel: A Stduy in Binary Choice,** Northwestern Univ. Press, Evanston, Ill., 1962.

Watanatada, T., **Application of disaggregate Choice Models to Urban Transportation Sketch Planning,** Ph. D. Thesis, Dept. of C.E., MIT, Cambridge, Ma., June 1977.

Watanatada, T. and M. Ben-Akiva, **Development of an Aggregate Model of Urbanized Area Travel Behavior, Final Report,** Prepared for U.S. DOT and the Fed. Highway Admin., July 1977.

Weiner, E., H. Kassoff and D. Gendell, "Multimodal Nat'l Urban Transportation Policy Planning Model," **HRR 458,** 1973.

Williams, H. C. W. L., "On the Formation of Travel Demand Models and Economic Evaluation Measures of User Benefit," **Environment and Planning A,** Vol. 9, pp. 285-344, 1977.

Zahavi, Y., **Traveltime Budgets and Mobility in Urban Areas,** Final Report, FHWA PL-8183, U.S. DOT, Washington, D.C., May 1974.

ABREVIATIONS

C.E.	=	Civil Engineering
DOT	=	Department of Transportation
FEA	=	Federal Energy Administration
FHWA	=	Federal Highway Administration
HRB	=	Highway Research Board
MIT	=	Massachusetts Institute of Technology
TRB	=	Transportation Research Board
TRR	=	Transportation Research Record
UMTA	=	Urban Mass Transportation Administration
UTDFP	=	Urban Travel Demand Forecasting Project

FOOTNOTES

1. For more detail see Luce and Suppes (1965), McFadden (1974) Domencich and McFadden (1975) and Richards and Ben-Akiva (1975).

2. For more detail see Williams (1977) and Ben-Akiva and Lerman (1977).

3. A detailed discussion of this definition is given in Watanatada and Ben-Akiva (1977).

4. This is explained in McFadden (1977), Ben-Akiva and Lerman (1977) and Daly (1977).

Equilibrium between travel demand system supply and urban structure

by

YACOV ZAHAVI

World Bank

INTRODUCTION

While techniques for urban travel-demand modeling have reached high levels of sophistication, basic understanding of the travel process still lags behind. This paper tries to close the gap, by suggesting an approach which, though is in some disagreement with current models, appears to unify the isolated components of travel under a unified process, consistent with basic economic concepts. More specifically, it seems to both describe and explain the interactions between travel demand, transportation system supply and urban structure.

This paper is based on on-going research conducted for the Urban Projects Department of the World Bank, and the US Department of Transportation, FHWA, [2]. It should, however, be noted that

(i) the results are preliminary, and

(ii) the views expressed in this paper are those of the author and not necessarily those of either of the above two organizations.

Since the subjects of urban travel are too numerous and complex to be covered in one paper, the presentation in this paper is short, telegraphic in style, with the belief that a perspective view of the concepts is preferable at this stage to a detailed, micro scrutinization of only a limited number of issues.

The first part of the paper describes the Unified Mechanism of Travel (UMOT), while the second part suggests several possible implications of the UMOT to the understanding of, and models for, urban travel.

Travel demand models should preferably be based on behavioral travel phenomena which tend to be stable both cross-sectionally, within and between cities, and over time. For instance, trips, which are currently regarded as the building blocks of travel demand, do not meet such a criterion; consider a car driver who used to make 6 trips per day in his small hometown, but after moving to a large city reduced it to 3 trips per day; did his travel demand change? Did his mobility decrease?

Figure 1 shows how the trip rate changes with city size, as one parameter of many, in a selection of cities in one country (App.1).

It may, therefore, be inferred that models which are based on trips are not fully transferable between cities and, as such, have to be carefully calibrated to local conditions in each city separately. But if they are not fully transferable between two cities during the same period, how can we be certain that they are transferable over time for one city, especially when this city is planned to undergo substantial expansion in the future? While this problem may not be serious in relatively stable cities in developed countries, it could become critical in rapidly expanding cities in developing countries, some of which double their population every decade.

The problem facing us, therefore, is to find the stable behavioral travel phenomena upon which demand models can be based with a high level of assurance and reliability.

Another subject discussed in this paper is the a-priori assumption that travel demand, system supply and urban structure are in equilibrium. This approach is mainly dictated by the structure of the current models, which have to be calibrated by the observed daily trips. Furthermore, an equilibrium condition must always be reached at the conclusion of the converging iterations, whether of trip distributions or traffic assignments. Thus, travel demand is portrayed on a daily basis, always under equilibrium conditions with supply, and latent demand is reflected, if at all, implicity only.

It will be suggested here that travel demand, in the general sense (including latent demand), may be in disequilibrium with system supply, and that this disequilibrium is one of the major forces that can change urban structure.

It was already suggested by many researchers that the money and time allocated by travelers (or their households) for travel act as constraints within which travel benefits (utilities) are maximized [3],[4]. While the concept was basically correct, its application suffered from two difficulties: (i) the daily money and time constraints are mostly applied in the early stages of model formulation, to appear later in the combined 'genera-

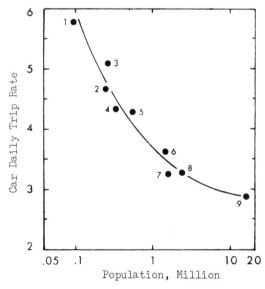

Fig. 1 - Car Daily Trip Rate vs. City Size in a selection of Cities in the US.

lized-cost' as relative measures affecting single trips only, and (ii) such models still need calibration on the same trips that they are expected to produce as outputs, thus they tend to be self-fulfilling.

Although the UMOT starts with the same basic concepts of travel money and time budgets, it applies them in a different way, thus arriving at conclusions which diverge from the current beliefs and techniques. It considers the travelers - and not their trips - as the building blocks, the indivisible units, of travel demand models. Furthermore, it is shown that only then are the two travel budgets found to be stable both cross-sectionally and over time, as detailed in the following sections.

THE TRAVEL TIME BUDGET

Since the resources of time and money available to travelers are limited, they have to allocate them sparingly to their daily activities, in accordance with their perceived values of each.

The available evidence indicated that the daily door-to-door travel time per traveler, including access time, tends to be stable, at about 1.1 hrs., both cross-sectionally and over time, even when speeds increase by over 30 percent, as can be seen in Table 1. This daily travel time per traveler is defined as the travel time budget, or TT-budget for short.

Table 1 - The TT-budget and other travel characteristics of car
and transit travelers in a selection of cities in the US

| City | Year | CAR TRAVELERS | | | | TRANSIT TRAVELERS | | | |
		TT,hr.	v,kph.	R	D,km.	TT,hr.	v,kph.	R	D,km.
Washington	1955	1.09	18.8	3.07	20.48	(1.27)	10.7	2.31	13.60
Washington	1968	1.11	23.3	3.16	25.91	(1.42)	10.0	2.12	14.35
Twin Cities	1958	1.14	21.5	3.62	24.48	1.05	12.0	2.12	12.58
Twin Cities	1970	1.13	28.5	3.84	32.26	1.15	12.1	2.09	13.87
Whole US	1970	1.06	47.4	3.33	50.47	0.99	24.6	2.03	24.33

Hence, while travelers may save time on single trips when speeds increase, they appear to trade it off for more travel. In Washington, D.C. and Twin Cities most of the time savings went into longer trip distances, which are not represented at all in the travel demand models.

It may be added that trip rates were hardly affected, which suggests that models based on trip rates are not sensitive to system supply, nor to urban size and structure. Furthermore, the apparent stability of trip rates over time - a strong argument for their use for travel demand, forecasting - actually does not reflect travel demand in the general sense. For instance, a 33 percent increase in speed in Twin Cities during 1958-1970 resulted in a corresponding increase in the daily travel distance, but in only a marginal increase in the trip rate.

It should also be noted that if travel speeds fall below a critical level, of about 11 kph., travelers appear to spend additional time in order to make the minimum number of just 2 trips per day, as was the case in Washington, D.C. in both 1955 and 1968. Namely, under US conditions it seems that only when the daily travel time is above 1.1 hrs., can be there the real savings in time if speeds increase.

In conclusion, although the TT-budget may differ widely between different travelers from day to day, it appears to be a stable behavioral phenomenon, at least as a controlling total, thus it can be used as a basis for describing and explaining travel demand and patterns.

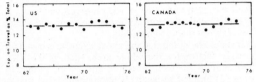

Fig. 2 - Expenditure on Travel vs. Total Consumer
Expenditure, US 1963-1975 and Canada 1963-1974

THE TRAVEL MONEY BUDGET

The concept of the travel money budget, TM-budget for short, is similar to the TT-budget, in the sense that the money resources available to a household are limited and, therefore, have to be divided between different activities in accordance with their perceived value.

The TM-budget tends to be stable over time, similar to the TT-budget, as can be seen in Figure 2. (The proportions may be different between countries, depending on local definitions and living habits).

The TM-budget tends to be a stable proportion of income also when analyzed cross-sectionally. Figure 3 shows the daily expenditures on travel by households who made all their travel by cars versus their annual income, in Washington, D.C. and Twin Cities.

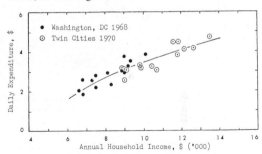

Fig. 3 - Household Daily Expenditure on Travel vs.
Annual Income (when all travel was by car only)

The relationship can be expressed, within the range of observations, by:

$$\text{Exp.}/_{\text{HH}} , \$ = -28.95 + 3.52 \text{ In Inc.}; (r^2 = 0.807); (1)$$

It then becomes evident that the expenditure on travel, as a proportion of income, is very stable at about 10.5 percent *at all income levels,* as can be seen in Figure 4. This figure also shows the same trend in the whole UK (although at a different level, depending on the definitions).

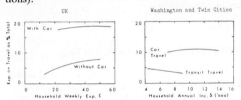

Fig. 4 - Household Expenditure on Travel vs. Total
Household Expenditure, UK 1972; and vs. Household
Income, Washington D.C. 1968 and Twin Cities 1970

195

Figure 4 also shows the proportions of expenditure on travel by households that made all their travel by transit, where it becomes evident that a wide gap exists between the two categories of households, a crucial gap that will be discussed later.

In conclusion, it appears that travelers are constrained in their daily travel by their individual TT-budgets and by their households' TM-budget.

APPLICATION OF THE TT-BUDGET FOR TRAVEL DEMAND ESTIMATION

Before going on any further, let us first examine the meaning and possible application of the TM-budget for travel demand estimation. The following exercise is based on data from the studies in Washington, D.C. 1968 and Twin Cities 1970.

Figure 5 shows the daily travel distance per household, by district, versus income for households who made all their travel by car. The relationship can be expressed by:

$$D/_{HH}, km. = 1.8(10-6)Inc.^{1.869} ; (r^2 = 0.885); (2)$$

(Data on a disaggregated basis result in even a better relationship, $r^2 = 0.943$).

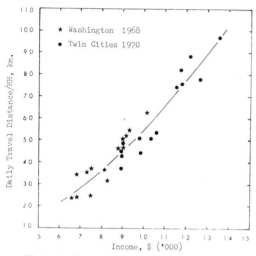

Fig. 5 - Daily Travel Distance per Household vs. Annual Income (all travel by car only)

It can also be shown that the daily door-to-door travel speed of households is strongly related to the income level, and can be expressed for the above case by:

$$v, kph. = -2.72 + 0.0029 Inc. (r^2 = 0.833); (3)$$

The car travel cost per unit distance depends on the speed of travel, as can be seen in Figure 6 for the travel conditions in the US in 1967-68 for a standard size car. This figure is based on the conventional operating costs by speed, while the standing costs are related to the car TT-budget, and within the range of speeds in urban areas it can be expressed by:

$$c = 1.494 v^{-0.75} ; (4)$$

where c is in US ¢ and the speed is in kph.

Table 2 summarizes the estimation of travel distance by income groups for households who made all their travel by car in Washington, D.C. 1968 and Twin Cities 1970, according to the following steps:
1) Income group, by district;
2) The road travel speed, derived form Eq. 3 and

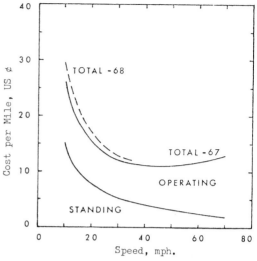

Fig. 6 - The cost per mile vs. Speed for standardsize Car in the US, 1967-1968

multiplied by 1.58, the factor which transfers door-to-door speeds to network speeds;
3) The cost per unit distance at the above speed, according to Eq. 4;
4) Income per weekday = Annual Income/312 days;
5) The TM-budget per household, at 10.5 percent of the daily income;
6) The daily travel distance per household, derived as the quotient of TM over c and multiplied by 1.5, the car average occupancy rate;
7) The observed daily travel distance per household, as derived from Eq. 2.

Table 2 - Estimated vs. observed daily travel distance by car per household, by income, Washington D.C. 1968 and Twin Cities 1970

(1) Inc.	(2) vxl. 58	(3) c	(4) Inc/day	(5) TM	(6) Dxl. 5	(7) Dobs.
7,000	27.78	0.123	22.44	2.36	28.7	28.15
8,000	32.36	0.110	25.64	2.69	36.7	36.13
9,000	36.94	0.100	28.85	3.03	45.4	45.02
10,000	41.52	0.091	32.05	3.37	55.5	54.82
11,000	46.10	0.084	35.26	3.70	66.1	65.51
12,000	50.69	0.079	38.46	4.04	76.7	77.08
13,000	55.27	0.074	41.67	4.38	88.7	89.52
14,000	59.85	0.069	44.87	4.71	102.4	102.82

The comparison between the estimated and the observed values is shown in Figure 7, where the curve represents the best-fit line of the observed values, as in Figure 5, while the dots represent the estimated values for each discrete income group.

It should be noted that the above exercise is based on average factors for the whole area, such as the TM-budget at 10.5 percent, and 1.58 and 1.5 mentioned in steps (2) and (6) respectively. Nonetheless, the match between the estimated and the observed values can be regarded as fully satisfactory.

Two conclusions may be inferred at this stage:
1) The daily travel distance appears to be a better representation of travel demand than the trip rate because:
(i) it is a direct derivation from the TM-budget, which is a stable behavioral phenomenon;
(ii) it interacts with system supply through speed; and

196

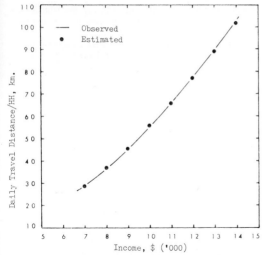

Fig. 7 - Estimated vs. Observed Daily Travel Distance per household vs. Household Annual Income, Washington, D.C. 1968 and Twin Cities 1970

(iii) it does not need calibration and, therefore, is fully transferable both within and between cities;

2) Income alone is a sufficient descriptor of the amount of travel generated by households and their travelers, when related to the cost of travel.

It is of interst to note that while the daily travel distance is the *final* output from the current lengthy models, it can now be derived as the *first phase* directly from the TM-budget and the speeds available from system supply. Furthermore, the same results shown in Figure 7 can also be derived from the TT-budget. The question on how does the TM-budget interact with the TT-budget is discussed in the following section.

THE FUNDAMENTAL TRAVEL EQUATION

The fundamental travel demand equation is:

$$\frac{M}{T} = \bar{v}\bar{c} \qquad ; \qquad (5)$$

where M is the TM-budget, T is the TT-budget, $\bar{v}$ is the daily mean speed and $\bar{c}$ is the cost per unit distance traveled at this speed.

While the left hand side represents travel demand, as expressed by the travelers willingness to allocate money and time for travel, the right hand size represents the product that they would like to purchase from the system supply, in terms of the system's performance and the price of using it.

When substituting Eq. 4 for c in Eq. 5 and applying the fundamental travel equation to the available observations from Washington, DC 1968 and Twin Cities 1970, it becomes evident that households at increasing incomes tend to travel at increasing speeds, as can be seen in Figure 8.

These observations are consistent with the hypothesis that households would tend to locate their residence and travel to such places that will enable them to maximize their daily travel distance (namely, maximize their spatial opportunities) within the constraints of the two travel budgets and the speeds obtainable from the transport system.

The stability of the two travel budgets also suggests that there is a negligible amount of substitution between the money and the time budgets on a daily basis [5]. Thus, while the current understanding of travel behavior is based on the observation of single trips, where some

travelers are found to exchange money for saved travel time, it becomes evident that they often do so in order to travel more during the day.

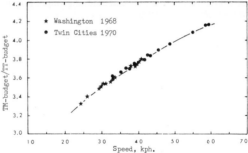

Fig. 8 - The Demand for Speed with increasing Household Incomes, as expressed by their Two Travel Budgets

It may, therefore, be concluded that the 'generalized cost' concept, where the two stable travel budgets are combined with full substitution between them, does not seem to be helpful when applied on a daily basis. In other words, applying the generalized cost to single trips and then aggregating all the trips over the day, could lead to erroneous results. (This brings into mind the known problem of 'the one and the many' where the rules that govern the behavior of the sum of trips could be on a different level from the rules that govern the behavior of single trips).

Another interesting aspect of the fundamental travel equation is whether the right hand side of it, representing the product that the household would like to purchase from the system supply, can actually be realized. Namely, must travel demand always be in equilibrium with system supply? ('Equilibrium' is defined as the state in which both budgets are just satisfied).

Let us consider first a household that increases its income. At low incomes it will be able to purchase only the low speeds, that can be supplied by transit. However, as its income increases, it will search actively for the higher speeds that can be supplied only by cars and, hence, the household will tend to purchase a car after crossing a certain income threshold. This process can explain the rapid increase in motorization after incomes cross such thresholds (which depend on the cost of owning and operating a car).

Referring back to Figures 6 and 5, it becomes evident that there is a very strong incentive to travel at higher speeds, since a stable proportion of a TM-budget at increasing incomes results in accelerated increases in the daily travel distance per household. Namely, the daily travel distance per household vs. income is significanly elastic (at 1.87, as seen in Eq. 2).

Households that do not, or cannot purchase a car and have to rely on buses only, are then found to exhaust their TT-budget on the slow buses much before they expend even half of the TM-budget; they are in a 'disequilibrium' condition, in the sense that they would be prepared to spend more on travel than they actually do.

At this stage one might raise the argument that such a household may prefer to allocate less money for travel, thus remaining in an equilibrium condition between their travel demand and system supply. There are, however, several indirect indications to suggest that generally this is not so. The first indication, of course, is the rapid increase of motorization with income. The second is that households owning and not owning cars tend to expend the same proportion of their income on housing, at least in the UK, although there is a wide gap between their expenditures on travel. For instance, the same basic data upon which the diagram for the UK in Figure 4 is based, also supplies information on household expenditures on housing, and as can be seen in Figure 9, there is no marked difference between the two groups along the major range of incomes [6].

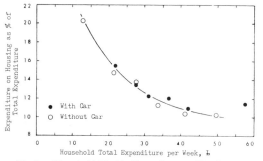

Fig. 9 - Household Weekly Expenditure on Housing as Percentage of Total Weekly Expenditure, by Car Availability, All UK 1971

In conclusion, it is suggested that travelers, within their own TT-budget and their household's TM-budget, tend to maximize their daily spatial opportunities. If, however, the system supply and/or urban structure do not allow them the freedom of choice in the short run, their travel demand is in disequilibrium with system supply and urban structure, thus generating forces that may change urban structure in the long run.

All current models are based on the concepts and techniques of equilibrium between travel demand and system supply. This may be so in the short run, on a daily basis. If, however, travel demand is based on the two behavioral travel budgets, it becomes more fruitful to measure the amount of disequilibrium, and dissatisfaction, as an aid to forecasting changes in motorization and/or urban structure.

One indication should, however, be emphasized again: the door-to-door travel speed appears to be the key to a better transportation system, whether car or transit. This is especially true for transit, where travel is found to be inelastic to fares.

THE TRAVEL COMPONENTS

Almost all current models regard most of the travel components in isolation. For instance, trip rates are generated as the first phase, while trip distances are produced as incidental outputs from the distribution of trips between zones at a later and independent phase. Even when all phases are conducted simultaneously, they are still independent, in the sense that they are rigidly calibrated to observations with no explicit feed back mechanism between the various travel components, such as between the trip rate and the trip distance. Another example is the treatment of trip purposes, where a trip generation equation is calibrated for each purpose separately.

As already mentioned above, it appears that travelers strive to maximize their daily travel distance within their TT-budgets and their household's TM-budgets. Each traveler then has to decide how to allocate his daily travel distance between the trip rate and the trip distance. It was shown above that travelers tend to use their 'saved' time for longer trips rather than for more trips. In other words, they tend to value their spatial opportunities over more trips as long as the trip rate is still above a critical value.

Travelers are found to rank their trip purposes by their perceived values. Hence, all trip purposes are interlinked within their daily trip rate. The proportions of trip

purposes by the trip rate, for both car and transit travelers in Twin Cities 1958 and 1970, can be seen in Figure 10.

It is also indicated that the perceived value of the trip rate increases with the trip rate at decreasing rates, thus following the expected decreasing marginal utility [7]. Namely, the addition of one trip to a daily trip rate of 2 is valued more than the addition of one trip to a daily trip rate of 6.

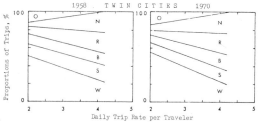

Fig. 10 - The Proportions of Trip Purposes vs. the Daily Trip Rate per Traveler, in the Car and Transit Modes W - HB to Work; S - HB to Shopping; B - HB to Business; R - HB to Recreation/Social; O - HB to Other; N - Non Home Based.

The daily trip is inversely related to both the trip distance and the trip time, as can be seen in Table 3.

Table 3 - Car travel characteristics in two cities in the UK

Characteristic	Hull	London
Year	1967	1961
Population	344,890	8,826,620
Car trip rate	6.25	3.27
Car trip distance, km.	4.2	7.9
Daily travel distance	26.3	25.8
Trip time, min.	6.9	13.7
Daily car TT-budget, hr.	0.72	0.75

As can be seen, although the daily travel distance and the daily travel time are practically identical in the two cities, the trip rates are entirely different, and related inversely to both the trip distance and the trip time.

Since the inverse relationship holds true both within and between cities, it is also suggested that the trip time frequency distributions can be tied up with all other travel components, as an integral part of travel behavior, without having to calibrate them in each city separately.

There is strong evidence that the difference between the mean distances of the population and the job spatial distributions to the city center approximates very closely the daily mean trip distance, thus suggesting a link between travel characteristics and urban structure, and explaining changes in urban structure, such as the change of mono-nucleated cities into multi-nucleated ones [8]. Expansion of a city, dispersion of households by income, and the shift of jobs from the center outwards, can all be explained as part and parcel of the behavioral mechanism of travel.

When only two travel modes are considered, such as cars and transit, modal splits by travel distance can be solved directly by the equations of the two travel budgets, of time and of money. However, when more than two modes are considered (such as the addition of a rapid transit system) the travel utility functions have to be established first. It is of interest to note that the formulation of the two travel budgets allows the derivation of the structure of the utility functions directly from observations, without having to assume them a-priori.

Preliminary estimates of modal splits with 2 and

3-mode conditions have produced very encouraging results.

In conclusion, all travel components, such as the daily travel distance, trip rate, trip distance, trip time, proportions of trip purposes and modal splits, can be unified in a consistent way within one mechanism, with interactions between them. The same mechanism also appears to unify the interactions between travel demand, system supply and urban structure.

POSSIBLE IMPLICATIONS OF THE UMOT TO TRAVEL MODELING

Current models, both aggregated and disaggregated, start with trip generation and conclude with the daily travel distance of travelers and vehicles. It now appears that the models should be turned upside down, by starting with the daily travel distance, as constrained by the two travel budgets, and conclude with the trip rates.

It is indicated that no calibrations should be made to the same outputs that the models are expected to produce, and certainly not for each travel component separately. If the model is to be a behavioral one, all the isolated travel characteristics observed should be explained by one behavioral mechanism.

It is indicated that the 'generalized cost' should be split back into its two constituents, especially when the daily travel is considered.

Accessibility indices are currently calibrated and allocated to zones on the basis of incidentally observed travel conditions. It is indicated that a preferable procedure would be to define 'travel demand' descriptors on the one hand, and 'system supply' and 'urban supply' descriptors on the other hand. The spatial distribution of travel (and the observed 'accessibility' indices) would then be the result of the interaction between demand and supply, at least in the short run, on the basis that travelers strive to maximize their daily travel distance within their budget constraints. Thus, the distribution and assignment phases can be combined into one process, with feed back sensitivity with all other travel components.

Mobility should be expressed by the daily travel distance weighted by the travelers' perceived values and preferences of trip distance vs. trip rate. Thus, travelling, say, 30 km. per day, at either 6 trips of 5 km, each or 3 trips of 10 km. each, could result in different levels and values of mobility.

An approach based on the two separate travel budgets allow the analyst to evaluate the possible effects of policy options on travel, such as changes in the components of travel cost (e.g., operating or standing costs), road pricing, free transit, car pooling, and so on. The important part to note is that different options will have different effects on different income groups. For example, and referring back to Figure 6, it becomes evident that increasing either the standing costs or the operating costs will have different effects at different speeds, thus affecting households at different income levels in different ways.

The economic evaluation of urban transport improvements is assisted by the UMOT process in that design year conditions can be assessed 'with' and 'without' proposed investments or policy changes under realistic conditions. The concept of the TM-budget to estimate travel demand, including latent demand, is particularly useful for the analysis of the travel of specified income groups - such as those with low incomes - which might be of special concern.

IN CONCLUSION

In closing, it should be noted that although this paper presents examples and relationships from cities in developed countries, the same principles seem also to apply in cities of developing countries, only under much more adverse conditions. For instance, there is an urgent need to define the thresholds under which travelers cannot afford even a bus fare. Furthermore, in fast developing cities the poor live farthest from jobs, thus aggravating their conditions and forcing them to expend higher proportions of both money and time on travel for less spatial opportunities.

As can be seen from the indications in this paper, and they are only indications at this stage, much search and research are still needed before we can close the gap between the highly sophisticated techniques currently available for analyzing each travel component separately and the basic understanding of travel behavior.

It may come as a surprise to many that simple questions about travel are still unanswered. For instance: How do we measure the benefits of mobility? Is mobility beneficial, to be encouraged? Or is it a luxury that should be suppressed? And if mobility increases with increasing incomes, will a decrease in mobility also decrease income? Namely, what is cause and what is effect in travel behavior? Surprisingly enough, there is no operational model that can answer such questions. And they are crucial questions especially now, when we are faced with continuously increasing shortages of energy and available funds for transportation improvements.

Hence, the message of this paper is that more attention should be given now to the neglected basic issues of travel demand, and its interactions with system supply, urban structure, and economic development.

ACKNOWLEDGEMENTS

I am grateful to Mr. E. V. K. Jaycox, Director, Urban Projects Department, the World Bank, and to Mr. D. S. Gendell, Chief, Technical Support Branch, US Department of Transportation, FHWA, for the permission to refer in this paper to results from on-going studies conducted for their organizations. However, the views expressed in this paper are those of the author and not necessarily those of the two organizations.

Appendix 1 - Car Daily Trip Rate vs. Population Size in a selection of US Cities (Figure 1)

No.	City	Year	Population	Trip Rate
1	Monroe	1965	96,530	5.79
2	Baton Rouge	1965	245,076	4.66
3	Peoria	1964	260,826	5.10
4	Orlando	1965	355,619	4.33
5	Springfield	1965	532,188	4.30
6	Cincinnati	1965	1,391,869	3.63
7	Baltimore	1962	1,607,980	3.26
8	Washington, DC	1968	2,562,025	3.28
9	Tri-State	1964	16,303,000	2.89

FOOTNOTES

1. The UMOT - a Policy Sensitive Model. In preparation for the Urban Projects Department, the World Bank, Washington, D.C.

2. Travel over time. In preparation for the US Department of Transportation, FHWA, Washington, D.C.

3. Entropy in urban and regional modelling. A. G. Wilson. Lion Ltd., London, 1970.

4. A critique of entropy and gravity in travel forecasting. M. J. Beckmann and T. F. Golob. Proceedings of the Fifth International Symposium on the Theory of Traffic Flow and Transportation. American Elsevier Publishing Co., Inc., 1972.

5. This may reflect the relatively low charges payable for the use of roads in cities. Evidence on the effect of the Singapore Area Road Pricing scheme is not yet available.

6. Family Expenditure Survey for 1971, Tables 28-29, HMSO, UK.

7. Travel characteristics in cities of developing and developed countries. World Bank Staff Working Paper No. 230, March 1976, pages 56-61.

8. The effects of transportation systems on the spatial distribution of population and jobs. Y. Zahavi, Joint National Meeting of ORSA/TIMS, 1976.

Personal travel in towns:
the development of models that reflect the real world

by

M. G. LANGDON and C. G. B. MITCHELL

Transport and Road Research Laboratory

Crowthorne, England

INTRODUCTION

In studies of personal travel in towns, recourse is frequently made to transport models. A transport model can be defined as an approximate representation of some aspects of the real world, usually by a set of mathematical equations but sometimes by a set of intuitive non-quantitative statements. This paper is concerned with the development of demand models for personal travel that accurately reflect our increasing knowledge of travel patterns in urban areas, and which can be used as an aid to answering some of the increasingly complex questions raised by policy issues that cover transport, land use, and social factors.

The fundamental purpose of these demand models is to predict how travel patterns will alter in response to changes in land-use patterns and in the supply of transport, or changes in other relevant factors such as levels of car ownership, working hours or schooling arrangements. There are several ways in which this predictive task can be approached. One method is to consider in detail the travel decision process for individuals or small groups of people, and then estimate the travel demands for larger groups of people by an aggregation process from the predected behaviour of many small groups. This is the basic concept of disaggregated modelling. A very different method is to observe empirical relationships (such as the variation in the total travel time per person per day with age, income or employment category) and patterns of movement that appear to be relatively stabel over time and which are constant or predictable between different communities and different social groups. The conventional method, used in the great majority of transport modelling to date, is not unlike the first method, except that disaggregation is not taken very far. The population is disaggregated geographically into a set of zones, and socially into a few very broad categories (for example into car-owning and non car-owning households, and possibly into a few income bands). The behaviour of each category is accounted for by a simple semi-empirical model, usually only containing a rate of exchange between the time and money costs of travel. The model is calibrated on average data, often aggregated over whole zones, before being used to make predictions.

This conventional type of model has been used, in various forms differing only in detail, to plan most almost all recent large British transport projects and in some respects constitutes a satisfactory predictive tool. It effectively provides an extrapolation of existing experience, and is suitable when the proposed transport or other changes are not very great and when prediction is required for the reasonably near future. However, as more information on urban movement is accumulated it is becoming clear that in some respects these models can be improved; on the one hand to reflect the more detailed knowledge of the travel decision process provided by the disaggregate type of model, and on the other to take account of increasing knowledge of the broad relationships and movement patterns already mentioned.

Some typical examples of these relationships and patterns will be described in detail immediately after the initial section of the paper, which sets out the requirements for transport models. These examples use data from travel surveys in specific British cities and from the (British) National Travel Survey. It has been found that the existing transport models have problems both in representing these patterns and in predicting the behaviour of particular groups of people; some of the improved techniques that are being studied or developed are described later in this paper. Mention is also made of some of the problems of long term forecasting and planning, and of the interaction between transport investment and land use.

THE REQUIREMENT FOR MODELS

Transport models are required to provide an input to planning the development of transport systems, and indeed, of urban areas. In the field of strict transport modelling, they are needed for three different purposes, which are:

(i) To predict the future traffic flows and to indicate whether it will be necessary to do something to avoid problems forecast to arise in the future.

(ii) To predict the changes in traffic flows that would be caused by different policy decisions.

(iii) To estimate the costs and benefits of different projects, so that alternatives can be ranked and decisions taken on whether a project is worth carrying out.

It is well known that the emphasis of transport modelling has shifted from predicting flows of vehicles to predicting flows of people on public and private transport, to enable complete transport systems to be evaluated. The greater attention that is now being paid to the social effects of transport and planning decisions is leading to a continuation of this change of emphasis to include all travel in an urban area, particularly those journeys made on foot. In addition, transport studies are increasingly considering the travel of different groups of people and the opportunities for access to different activities available to people of different social groups. The consideration of measures of accessibility is becoming more important as urban areas become more diffuse and as the differences between the opportunities accessible to car-users and non-users increase.

A further class of models should also be considered, which provides the necessary inputs to the transport models. The most important of these is the forecasting model used to predict future levels of car ownership. There are also important inputs from planning models, to provide estimates of factors such as population and employment.

URBAN MOVEMENT IN THE REAL WORLD

In the earliest studies of urban movement in Britian, made using models of the conventional type described above, it was assumed or deduced that people travel more when they get cars, that private and public transport are alternatives between which travellers can be switched by changes of costs and level of service, and that all members of car owning households have the choice of car travel when they need it. More recent studies of urban travel and transport experiments are suggesting that these early concepts were not wholly correct, and that they could lead to transport investment decisions that would not achieve the results desired.

Number of trips

There is growing evidence that provided all trips are counted, including short walks, then the number of trips per person per day is stable over time and is only slightly affected by car ownership. It is, however, influenced by the employment category (employed, retired, house-wife, student) of the persons concerned.

For example, Figure 1 shows the variations of house-hold home-based trip rates with household size and car ownership, based on surveys in the town of Reading in 1962 and 1971 [1]. Trip rates have changed little with time, are almost linear with household size and only vary by about 2 to 3 trips/day between no-car households and multi-car households.

Similarly, Table 1 gives the variations with car owner-ship of the total number of journey stages [1] per day by all modes by different groups of people. It can be seen that the rate is almost invarient with car ownership for employed persons, but not for retired people, house-wives and "others". The number of journey stages per person per day (about 4) is rather higher than the num-ber of trips implied by Figure 1 (about 3). This difference is due to differences of definitions and the inclusion of non-home-based journey stages in Table 1.

Table 1 - Total number of journey stages per day per person by all modes (including walking)

Cars	Employment category	Full Time	Part Time	Retired	Housewife	Other	Total Population
0		4.87	4.34	2.21	2.43	3.50	3.58
1		4.76	4.35	3.09	3.02	4.12	4.24
2		4.89	4.29	2.83	3.76	4.66	4.55
3+		5.10	4.69	2.88	3.55	5.33	4.75
All Car owning		4.79	4.34	3.06	3.13	4.27	4.30
TOTAL		4.82	4.34	2.43	2.76	3.88	3.98

(Source, National Travel Survey 1972/3)

Goodwin has shown that the number of stages per day does not vary much with the population density of the travellers home area (Fig 2), but the variations in the number of stages by each mode and total distance travel-led are significant and systematic [2]. The lower the densi-ty, the more cars are used and the greater the total distance travelled.

Travel time budgets

There is some evidence that the total time a person from a particular employment category (employed man, housewife, retired) is prepared to spend travelling each day is rather constant. Zahavi has shown this for vehicu-lar travel in the USA [3], and Bullock has found that in a British town travel time was relatively unaffected by car ownership (see Table 2), although in this instance car ownership did affect the number of trips [4].

Table 2 - Total time per day spent in travel (survey in Reading, 1973) (hours)

	Men	Employed women	Housewives
With car	1.59	1.47	0.81
Without car	1.51	1.42	0.93

In Britain the total travel time per day does not vary much with the population density of the traveller's home area, but an analysis by Goodwin of National Travel Survey data does suggest that travel time is a little higher for car owners than non-car owners, and that it increases with increasing income up to an income of about £ 1500 per person per year (Fig 3). There is some variation with age, but this appears to be largely due to variation with age in the distribution of employment categories [2].

There is some evidence also that people choose the distance that they are willing to travel on the basis of the time it takes using the most convenient mode available to them. The travel time to different activities is more con-stant than is the travel distance, and travel distances by different modes appear to be adjusted to keep the travel time approximately the same (Fig 4) [5].

Trips by different modes and for different purposes

When all trips, including short walks, are recorded it is found that walking accounts for some 41 per cent of all journeys in Britain [5]. When the modes used for different trip purposes are compared it is found that trips to work and for social purposes are most likely to be made by car, while trips to school, to shopping and for day trip/play are most likely to be made on foot (Table 3). This is not surprising - most of these latter journeys are made by women and children who are relatively unlikely to have

Table 3 - Modal Split for Each Trip Purpose (per cent)

Modal Split / Trip Purpose	Train/ Tube	Bus	Car	Bicycle	Walk	Motor-cycle	Total	Proportion of *all* trip purposes
Work	4.5	20.4	45.3	5.4	22.0	2.5	100	20.8
In course work	1.8	4.5	79.6	0.8	12.8	0.4	100	3.8
Education	1.1	18.0	10.2	3.1	67.4	0.2	100	9.9
Shop	0.5	13.7	27.4	2.2	55.8	0.3	100	10.2
Personal business	0.8	10.9	44.3	2.0	41.4	0.4	100	7.8
Eat/drink	0.7	7.1	41.5	0.4	49.7	0.7	100	4.1
Entertainment	1.1	16.7	46.0	1.6	33.6	0.9	100	4.6
Social	0.9	11.5	51.8	2.6	32.3	0.9	100	14.2
Day trip/Play	1.0	3.5	28.1	2.7	64.5	0.3	100	5.9
Escort	0.4	3.2	66.2	0.4	29.6	0.3	100	5.9
Other	2.0	9.9	52.6	3.9	31.1	0.5	100	2.8
All purposes	1.6	13.2	40.7	2.8	40.9	0.9	100	100.0

Source: National Travel Survey 1972/3

the use of a car. The journey purpose for which the bus is most likely to be used is work, but even for this it only carries 20 per cent of all trips. The three modes, bus, car and walk, together carry over 94 per cent of all trips in Britain. The majority of trips are short, with 50 per cent less than 3 km, 70 per cent less than 6 km and 90 per cent shorter than 16 km. As would be expected, shopping and education trips are shorter in distance than work and social trips, though the difference in travel time was not large (Figure 5).

Availability of private cars

In Britain at the present time there are 0.25 cars per person, or 0.34 cars per person old enough to hold a driving licence. 45 per cent of households do not own a car, 45 per cent own one and 10 per cent own two or more cars. Ownership varies markedly with income and socio-economic group; the probability of the households of managers or professional workers owning a car is about twice that of the households of semi- and un-skilled manual workers. About 63 per cent of adult males held a driving licence in 1972, compared to 21 per cent of adult females. Within each sex the numbers hol-ding driving licences varies considerably with age (Table 4) and also with the socio-economic group of the house-hold. Overall there are about 1.3 driving licences per car. When cars are available they tend to be used by male members of the households, and to be used for work journeys and for social purposes rather than for school or shopping trips. There is thus a number of identifiable groups of people who either do not have the use of a car at all, or do not have one without making complicated arrangements. The travel needs of these groups are largely met by the use of buses and walking; Table 5 shows that lifts in non-household cars only account for some 6 per cent of all journeys by people in non-car owning households.

Table 4 - Driving Licence-holding by age and sex

Age group	Per cent holding licence in	
	1965	1972/73
Male		
17-20	29	35
21-29	60	72
30-39	68	79
40-49	62	74
50-59	54	68
60-64	41	60
65-	19	31
All 17 or over	50	63
Female		
17-20	6	13
21-29	15	32
30-39	18	34
40-49	13	27
50-59	9	19
60-64	6	10
65-	2	4
All 17 or over	10	21

Notes 1. National Travel Survey data
2. Data refer to full licences for driving cars

Table 5 - Travel by bus, as a car passenger, and on foot. Percentage of journey stages made by each mode. (NTS 1972/73 seventh day - short walks included)

Household cars	Local Bus			Passenger in Non-Household car			Passenger in Household car			Walk		
	Men	Women	Child.	Men	Women	Children	Men	Women	Children	Men	Women	Children
0	17	19	13	6	7	4	0	0	0	60	69	77
1	4	9	6	3	5	4	2	17	19	33	52	61
2	1	5	6	3	5	4	3	14	29	27	36	49
3+	2	4	0	3	9	7	3	13	36	24	39	43
All Car owning	3	9	6	3	5	4	2	17	21	32	49	59
TOTAL	8	13	9	4	6	4	1	9	13	42	58	66

Choice between public and private road transport

It appears that, except in the larger cities, very few people use buses from choice, and many do not use them at all. Table 6 shows the proportions of people of differ-ent socio-economie groups [2] who did not use a bus during the week of the 1972/73 National Travel Survey. Overall, 58 per cent of the population did not use a bus even once during the week.

Table 6 - Percentage of each SEG who did not use a local bus during the week of the NTS 1972/73 survey

SEG category	Men	Women	Children	Adult total	Total
A (Senior non-manual)	80.0	61.7	67.5	70.9	70.0
B (Junior non-manual)	70.1	46.1	60.8	56.7	57.5
C (Skilled manual)	65.9	44.7	60.8	55.5	56.9
D (Unskilled manual)	56.9	37.1	53.2	47.0	48.4
Total	67.8	46.9	60.8	57.2	58.0

Table 7 - Diversion from car to bus

Service	Percentage of car occupants diverting to bus	
	Car drivers	Car passengers
Dial-a-bus (Harlow)	0.5%	2.3%
Dial-a-bus (Dorridge & Knowle)	0.7%	2.3%
Subscription service (Stevenage)	3.0%**	9.0%**
Subsidised conventional service (Stevenage)	8.0%**	20.0%**
Park and Ride (Oxford)	5% (7% in peak hour)	
	Diversion from complete car trip	Diversion from car previously used for access to station
Rail feeder (Formby)	0.9%*	9%*

* Work trips only.

** Work trips only. Percentage is given in terms of car trips to same destination as that served by bus.

Several experimental bus services have been provided in Britain in recent years to determine the potential for attracting passengers to public transport. These experi-ments have covered subsidised, high-frequency, conven-tional services; dial-a-bus; rail feeder services; park and ride services from peripheral car parks and subscription services to employment centres. In addition, one New Town has a segregated bus-way along which houses are clustered. This allows the provision of an exceptionally high level of service.

One of the conclusions from these experiments is that although it is possible to attract passengers on to new bus services, very few of these use the bus instead of a car. The two dial-a-bus experiments each attracted about ½ per cent of the car driver trips and 2½ per cent of the car passenger trips that potentially could have transferred to bus. Other experiments using subsidised conventional services and park-and-ride services attracted a few per cent of the potentially transferable car trips (Table 7). The reason for this inability of buses to attract passen-gers from cars is almost certainly that on any measure - travel time, generalised cost, or even marginal money cost - the best practicable bus services are much less attractive than the private car.

Other factors

People are extremely good at modifying their travel to make the best use of the opportunities available to them. Thus if congestion occurs, then the times at which some journeys are made will be shifted to less congested times. Journey times are also shifted to allow car-sharing, and journeys for different purposes are combined into multi-purpose, multi-leg trips. Destinations may be changed, and in the long term people will move home, if travel on journeys which must be made regularly be-comes too difficult. These complex effects are not cover-ed to any significant extent by transport models at present in use.

TRANSPORT MODELS AND THE REAL WORLD
Definition of a model

The word "model" is used to describe an approximate representation of a part of the real world by a set of mathematical equations. These equations require an in-put in the form of various descriptive parameters of the part of the world being examined; in a transport model these would normally be quantities such as travel costs and times, levels of car ownership, and the distribution of population and activities. Some of these input parame-ters, such as future levels of car ownership, may in turn have been derived from the output of other kinds of model. The outputs from the equations that comprise the models are of two types; those that are, in principle, directly observable and which therefore can be checked experimentally, and derived results which are intrinsically not directly observable and so can only be estimated by the use of a model. Examples of the first type are trip numbers between various places and modal split; and example of the second type is the estimation of benefits resulting from a change in the provision of transport.

The word "model" has frequently been used to refer simply to the set of mathematical equations, but it is felt that this usage is too narrow and that the definition of a model should include a description of its overall concept. An important practical point is to keep a transport model as simple as possible in order to reduce the computational effort required to obtain the desired outputs. It is of course pointless to strive for apparent accuracy which is better than that of the input data. Simplicity is also desirable so that it is possible to retain a clear view of the fundamental concepts on which the model is based, and to ensure that all the implicit assumptions and approximations remain valid in any particular application.

Calibration

With current knowledge it is not yet realistic to construct a transport model entirely from theoretical considerations. All models therefore contain a number of arbitrary constants, the value of which must be found by a calibration process. In practice the mechanics of this are usually complex and involve much statistical theory, but in principle the process consists of adjusting the various constants in the model until, when values for the input parameters which represent the existing situations are inserted, it produces results that agree closely with the conditions known to exist.

There is a natural tendency to equate goodness of fit with goodness of model, but the aim of the model is not to describe an existing situation, which can be done adequately by a survey without any need for a model. The aim is to predict what will happen in some future situation when the input parameters are changed. A complex model may well calibrate to describe an existing situation, but totally fail to predict; experience in other fields suggests that the more complex the model the more likely is this to be the case. An important practical point in model design is that the input parameters should be confined to items for which the values can reasonably be forecast for as far into the future as predictions will be required. Many of these difficulties could be reduced or avoided if calibration could make use of time series data; in practice to date transport studies have used a single survey and calibrated their models on cross-sectional differences.

Philosophy of predictive modelling

In the Introduction a broad distinction was drawn between transport models based on the decision processes of individuals or small groups of people, and models based on broad empirical relationships which appear to be stable over time, and constant or predictable between different communities. Most conventional transport models are related to the first method, but use data aggregated and averaged over fairly large groups. Category analysis trip generation models belong to the second group.

The other major division in modelling concepts is between those using empirical curve fitting methods and those based on behavioural hypotheses. The empirical method (various forms of regression or classification analysis) effectively takes the input parameters which could reasonably be expected to have an influence on the output results, postulates some functional relationship between input and output, and then carries out a multiple regression or classification analysis in order to evaluate the arbitrary constants in the functions and determine the relative importance of the various input parameters. The method has been used successfully when predicitions have involved relatively minor changes in the input parameters, but cannot always be considered reliable where major changes in the scenario are involved.

The behavioural hypothesis method involves certain assumptions about human behaviour, and using these as a foundation on which to build up a theoretical structure until a complete transport model evolves. The behavioural constants of the model will stil require calibrating, but the potential advantage of the method is that once evidence has accumulated that the initial assumptions or theories appear to fit the real world, then a model developed in this way can be extrapolated to new and untested situations with much more confidence than one developed by empirical methods. The method has not been used much in practice, though recently it has been used successfully in the development of new modal split models to deal with the problems presented by the existence of more than two main modes.

As in many fields of science, the empirical projection of observations is being succeeded by theories that attempt to represent mathematically the pattern of the observed data. There is as yet little sign of progress in the further stage of determining the physical or psychological laws that are the actual cause of the observed patterns. (In the field of astronomy, for example, the fitting of a complex set of circles and epi-cycles to planetary orbits was succeeded by the appreciation that they were actually ellipses. This in turn was succeeded by the theoretical prediction of orbits using Newtonian mechanics and the law of gravity). If progress in the direction of greater fundamental understanding is possible, it should initially reduce the amount of data needed to build a model and increase the transferability of a model from one place to another; ultimately it could permit the construction of transport models on theoretical grounds alone.

It is not suggested that the behaviour of human beings can be explained by laws as simple as the inverse square law of gravitation. Any behavioural law must be statistical and be limited to predicting the average behaviour of a large number of people, since there is no suggestion that it will ever be possible to predict the behaviour of a particular individual. A statistical method has already been applied with some success to problems of modal split and trip distribution. In these applications it has been possible to draw conclusions on traveller's behaviour by making very simple assumptions about their decision making processes, and about the variability in their perception of travel costs. The step that has not yet been taken is to link assumptions on behaviour with observations of broad empirical relationships which are relatively invariant with time or location.

Current experience of predictive modelling

Since 1962 some 100 transport studies have been made in Britain for areas with populations between 10,000 and 8,800,000. It is only now that sufficient time has elapsed to allow an assessment to be made of the predictive accuracy of the earliest studies, and in practice comprehensive assessments of complete studies have not yet been made. The accuracy of parts of the transport modelling process have been checked individually by TRRL, and some of these are mentioned below. Similarly, some examination of the results of studies for complete urban areas have been made by the local authorities concerned (notably the Greater London Council), but these examinations have been largely for their own use and have not been published. Inevitably, repeat surveys tend to be used to update transport plans rather than to look back to previous studies.

The TRRL forecasts of car ownership that were based on data up to 1960 have to date been justified by events (Figure 6). Forecasts issued in the mid- to late- 1960s tended to overestimate the actual growth of car ownership. The most recent forecasts, [8] issued in 1975 and based on data up to 1972, predict a range of levels of car ownership within which current levels still lie.

A study has been made of the stability and forecasting ability of trip generation models [1]. An initial travel survey of the town of Reading in 1962 was followed by a repeat survey in 1971. The results of the 1962 survey were used to predict zonal trip generations in 1971, and the estimates were then compared with the actual measurements. Good agreement was obtained, demonstrating that the trip generation model was stable with time, at least over a nine year period. It was also demonstrated that trip generation was not sensitive to the location of a household within the town.

The accuracy of a conventional modal split model has been tested by using it to predict the patronage on an experimental dial-a-bus service in Harlow. The actual effects of the bus service were measured by comprehensive surveys, and were compared with the predictions [6]. Considerable care was taken to make the model represent the real world as accurately as possible, and the results were surprisingly good in terms of the number of trips predicted for different times of day and different purposes. However, the total ridership (by travellers included in the model) was overestimated by about 30 per cent, and the proportion of trips diverted from existing car use was also overestimated. Another comparison of the predicted and measured patronage of a bus service has been made by Papoulias and Heggie for a park-and-ride service in Oxford [7]. Again, the prediction overestimated the actual patronage by between 20 and 30 per cent, while achieving a reasonable representation of the distributions of trip purposes.

TECHNICAL PROBLEMS OF CURRENT MODELS

In this section of the paper a range of current problems in transport modelling is discussed. Although these are of necessity considered as a number of separate topics (not necessarily in order of importance), it should be understood that in practice many of the problems are related and may be part of the same fundamental difficulties.

Trip generation

From a theoretical standpoint the trip generation sub-model using disaggregated household data can be considered as one of the most satisfactory components of current transport models, though one in which many detailed developments are still being made. As already indicated earlier total trip generation rates appear to be stable with time and to be almost invariant to household data other than employment status. It must be stressed that this only applies when walk trips are included in the total, and that the split between different modes can vary markedly with circumstances.

The practical problems of trip generation modelling are concerned with the form and structure of the disaggregated model, and the difficulty of forecasting the planning inputs to the model. With regard to data handling, for example, it is still not clear whether it is better to base the model on households or individual persons. Recent work suggests that it should be possible to reduce considerably the size of survey required to estimate trip generation rates. The problem of forecasting planning inputs in terms of the future number of households in an area and the distribution of household types is a serious

one, as errors in the predicted total number of trips made is directly proportional to errors in predicting the number of persons available to make trips. Further consideration of this problem is outside the scope of this paper.

Interaction between modal split and trip distribution

As well as the problem of trip generation (shall I go somewhere?), transport models are concerned with questions of trip distribution (where shall I go?) and modal split (by what mode shall I travel?). Some models treat these last two problems sequentially, while others carry out both calculations in a single stage. Both methods give rise to problems, and it is doubtful whether either is a very good representation of the actual decision making process of individual travellers. One of the complexities of the real world is that this is not necessarily even the same for different types of trip. For trips to work the distribution pattern can be considered as fixed, at least in the short term, and the only choice open to the traveller is the selection of travel mode. For non-work trips, on the other hand, the choice of mode may well be restricted, but there may be a wide choice both of destinations and of times at which the trip can be made.

One current suggestion [2] is that in many travel situations choice of mode may be more restricted than it is represented to be in most transport models, and that the apparent modal split seen in the real world is in fact simply the effect of overlapping trip distribution patterns of several different populations of travellers, each of which is constrained to using a single specific mode. Another possibility is that trip destinations are selected on the basis of the door to door travel time by the quickest mode that is economically available to the traveller. [5]

The practical effect of this may be very significant when an attempt is made to influence modal split by deliberately altering the characteristics of one or more modes. If modal choice and trip distribution are linked, as appears to be the case for many trip purposes, then either the actual change in modal split will be less than that predicted by most models, or associated changes in trip destinations will occur.

Red bus/blue bus - the multi-mode problem

Various methods have been devised to extrapolate the well established two mode modal split model to cater for more than two modes. Unfortunately these mostly fail to overcome the red bus/blue bus anomaly. This is the colloquial description of a defect of multi-mode models which causes them to give results which vary as the way in which the competing modes are described varies. For example, consider a particular journey for which a conventional model predicts that the two modes, train and bus, each attract half the travellers. If the front doors of the buses are painted red and the rear doors blue, and the buses are regarded as two modes (red bus and blue bus, depending on which door is used), then the same conventional modal split models applied to the three modes would predict the bus patronage as 2/3 of the travellers (1/3 red bus, 1/3 blue bus) and the rail patronage as 1/3 of the total. This superficially trivial example shows one way in which the results from conventional modal split models can be altered by factors which in reality would have no effect on modal choice. Indeed, it is only a specific example of the more general difficulty, that the results from these models are sensitive to rather detailed assumptions, such as whether the choices between several modes are made simultaneously or sequentially, and if sequentially, in what order. Recent work has clarified the cause of the red bus/blue bus problem and has produced models which successfully overcome the anomaly [9,10,11].

Availibility of different modes

As described in section 5.2 above, evidence is growing that the choice of modes available to a traveller is probably not as wide as is usually assumed. It is now known, for example, that knowledge of whether or not a traveller lives in a car owning household is a poor guide as to whether the car mode is actually an available choice for any particular trips. Similarly, bus travel is not realistically available to some motorists because of lack of knowledge of routes and time-tables. There are many other complex interactions between different travellers and different activities that can affect the availability of travel modes to any specific individual.

Walk and cycle modes

Until recently walk and cycle trips have generally been omitted from transport studies. This has been partly because of their presumed lack of importance, either as a section of the transport system or as a determinant of road capacity, and partly because of the difficulty of including them within the existing modelling framework (because of the multi-mode problem). It is now realised that they make up a very significant part of the total urban movement pattern, and that for short distance trips they are important competitors with public transport. For example, diversions to or from the bus mode following changes in service levels or in fares are likely to be mainly with walk or cycle trips, with very little diversion from or to the car mode.

The value of time

This appears in models in two ways. The first is the "behavioural" value of time, and represents the trade off that an individual is prepared to make between time and money costs of travel, while the second is the "social" value used in benefit evalution, which represents society's valuation of time saving in money terms. There are considerable doubts about how one should measure the behavioural value, how constant it is for any particular individual under different circumstances, and whether the spread of time values for different individuals is important and should be included as a modelling parameter [12]. In any case, it appears that the behavioural value of time derived from the calibrations of actual transport models is a proxy for a complex set of factors, so it is not surprising that the values deduced from simplified observations vary considerably.

The connection between the behavioural value perceived by the traveller and the social value poses difficult questions of equity, and in the end must be based on political judgement. Different organisations have taken different views on this.

Compatability of demand and benefit estimation models

As mentioned briefly above, a major problem in estimating the value of benefits arising from transport changes is that these cannot be actually measured on the ground; they can only be estimated in terms of the output from some form of model. It is much less easy to check that the model is producing the right result than it is for an output such as trip distribution or modal split which can at least be checked by comparison with observations of the real world at the model calibration stage.

It is therefore particularly important to ensure that the model is internally consistent, so that the benefit estimation process is, as far as possible, consistent with the methods used to estimate trip distribution and modal split. This has not always been the case with models used in the past.

It is also important to check whether, in any particular case, the estimation of benefits is sensitive to details of the methods of calculation used. Some calculations have been found to produce estimates of benefits (which cannot be checked) which are much more sensitive to small changes of assumptions or methodology than are the outputs such as patronage.

Interaction between transport supply and land use

When a traditional transport model is used for the prediction of future traffic levels it is usual to assume a certain pattern of future land use which is fixed regardless of the transport supply. This is in fact very different from the real world situation, where land use and transport supply interact closely with each other. In order to study the social and economic effects of various land use and transport policies, it is desirable to develop a dynamic transport/land use model which includes the effects of these interactions. Although several such models are in use in the USA, they have not yet been applied to any significant extent in Britain.

Spatial and temporal stability of models

The use of transport models for predicting future travel patterns involves an implicit assumption that the basic model and its calibration constants are stable with time. There is no reason to suppose that this assumption is untrue, but apart from the work on stability of trip generation models already referred to, there does not seem to have been much work done to investigate the matter.

The question of spatial stability is significant for both practical and theoretical reasons. In Britain almost every transport study carried out to date has involved an independent survey and calibration. Several different transport models have been used, which makes it difficult to compare the calibration from different areas. Even in cases where the same models have been used the calibration constants have been different between areas. In only a few studies (aspects of the West Yorkshire study, for example) has it proved possible to use calibrations from one area in models for another area. Spatial stability and potential transferability does appear to occur for trip generation, but has not yet been demonstrated for trip distribution. Some modal split expressions have been transferred from one model to another, usually when local data have not been available. There is at present little indication of whether the apparent variation of calibration constants reflects real differences between geographical areas or simply differences, between studies, of the model details and the choices of zone sizes and zone patterns.

The development of models that could be transferred from one area to another would be an important practical step towards cheaper and quicker transport studies. Such a development would also greatly increase confidence in the predictive abilities of models, for if they could be transferred successfully from one area to another it would be much more likely that their calibrations would still apply to the area being modelled when it has experienced the changes that the passage of time brings.

FUTURE IMPROVEMENTS IN MODELLING
Possible approaches to improvement

In this paper three possible ways of improving the art of transport modelling have been identified. The first is to take the existing conventional transport model as a basis and improve it to remove some of the current problems. The second is to extend the conventional model to enable it to answer new types of question, such as the interaction between land use and transport and the overall effect of changing long term policy in either field. The third is to take a completely new look at the problem, to see whether the conventional model provides the best method of providing information to aid policy decisions, or whether some radical new approach to modelling might be preferable.

These different approaches need not necessarily be viewed as exclusive alternatives. While the third approach may be a desirable long term objective, work on the first two is undoubtedly necessary to give immediate improvement to our forecasting methodology, and probably also forms an essential input to a proper appreciation of how to develop the necessary items to make the third approach practicable.

Improvements to the conventional model

(i) *Modal split models.* Understanding of the problems of estimating modal split between more than two modes has been improved by recent work at TRRL [9],[10] and LGORU [11]. This has led to a new concept of multi-mode modal split models which fundamentally eliminates the red bus/blue bus anomaly. It has also provided further insight into the relationship between trip demand modelling and benefit estimation. The new model is based on consideration of the distribution of perceived costs (time and money, for travel by each mode) among different potential travellers, and the assumption that each traveller chooses the mode which, in his perception, provides the cheapest journey. The method originally developed at TRRL involved quite complex mathematics and lengthy computation, but it was subsequently shown that a very close approximation could be obtained by a relatively simple modification of the conventional logistic modal split model. The two-mode modal split model used in most conventional transport models is in fact a special case of this new, more general model.

Work is in progress on further developments of the concept to include the effect of distributed perceived values of time and other effects. It is hoped that this will help to solve problems occuring in the inclusion of walk mode in transport models, and in situations where two classes of travel are provided in a single vehicle.

(ii) *Combined modal split and distribution models.* It may be possible to extend the concept of models based on the distribution of perceived costs, to produce a combined modal split and trip distribution model. Cochrane [13] has already demonstrated a derivation of the conventional "gravity" trip distribution model using the concept, and Goodwin [2] has produced new ideas on trip distribution using the same basic concept, though not yet in a form usable in practical models.

(iii) *Estimation of car avialability.* It now appears that this is a major factor in the estimation of modal split between car and other modes. The Telford Transportation Study is an example of a recent attempt to include a better method of estimating car availability [14], with promising results. Interesting work in this field has also been carried out at the Cranfield Institute of Technology [15] and at the Transport Studies Unit of Oxford University (not yet published). It is clearly time to put major effort into this problem, and also into investigating practical problems of availability, or lack of avaiility, for other modes; for example, is bus a practical mode for a mother shopping with young children?

Further uses for the "conventional" model

Various attempts have been made to bring land use effects into transport modelling, but much more work is needed before it will be possible to model the dynamic interactions between land use and transport supply [16],[17]. The difficulties are both theoretical and practical. On the theoretical side the problem is the scale and complexity of the interacting systems which have to be considered, while on the practical side there is a shortage of data covering the time span required to calibrate and verify a dynamic model. Results in this field are mostly produced

either on the basis of a step-by-step approach in which various sub-systems are developed in detail before the overall synthesis is attempted, or on the basis of using very simplified models of sub-systems, which in some cases may be thought to lack plausibility. In view of the tentative nature of work at present in progress in Britain it is not proposed to comment further in this paper.

Another obvious extension of the use of conventional transport modelling is to examine the transport energy and other resource implications of various transport and land use policies.

New approaches to transport modelling

A recent development is the extension of the use of disaggregated data from the modelling of trip generation to the modelling of trip distribution and modal split. Such a model uses data at an individual or household level directly in the calibration process. This preserves the inherent variability of the data within a zone, which is lost when the zonal data is aggregated in conventional models.

Although disaggregated data has been used for model calibrations, when the model is used for predictive purposes this is usually done on a zonal basis, and input data for the model is supplied in aggregated form. Since the model calibration was made with disaggregated data, the variability within the zone of the input data has to be included in the prediction process. Where this intrazonal variability is important it can be represented by a statement of the statistical variation to be associated with the mean values of the inputs.

As well as allowing the modeller to get closer to the decision processes of individual travellers and so, hopefully, to produce a more accurate model, the use of disaggregated techniques is claimed to considerably reduce the amount of data needed for model calibration. It is not yet known whether the use of disaggregated techniques will produce model calibration constants which have less variability than those from conventional models. A thorough examination of the relationships between disaggregated and zonal models might well lead to a better understanding of the effects on calibration constants of changing zone size and distribution.

A disappointing feature of all current transport models, which the current disaggregated approach appears to have changed only in the case of trip generation, is that they neither predict nor make use of the invariant factors in actual travel patterns [3]. Any new form of transport model should take greater account of the various constraints which face real travellers than has been done in existing models. To achieve this it may well be necessary to break away completely from the traditional modelling framework, and make a fresh start. If it proves possible to develop the necessary mathematical tools to build such a new model, it is likely that under some circumstances its numerical predictions would closely approximate those produced by the current models. Indeed, one of the values of a model that accurately represents many aspects of the real world is to indicate which studies require sophisticated modelling and for which the simpler conventional models would be satisfactory. Eventually, it may become possible for much of the calibration to be done on a theoretical basis with only a limited requirement for local surveys: an interim stage would be to develop models which can be transferred from one area to another.

CONCLUSION

This paper has described the sort of trip patterns observed in the real world, and discussed some of the problems of transport models in both reproducing the current real world situation, and predicting future changes in personal movement. It is concluded that, while there are various problems in the existing models, they can in many cases usefully be used for prediction, provided that the changes between present and future are not too great.

However, deficiencies have been revealed in some areas, such as in the predicted substitutability of bus for car when car restraint is applied. Also, due to the lack of a solid theoretical basis, the reliability of prediction into the long term future must be suspect. A further cause for concern is that the models neither use nor predict some of the invariant factors in real world trip patterns, described in this paper, though a model under development at TRRL is using a fixed total number of trips.

Worthwhile improvements in the traditional type of transport model are currently being made, with the introduction of models using disaggregated data, and of new ideas for modal split modelling. However, even these innovations are to some extent only patching the existing model structures at the expense of added complications, and it is suggested that the time may be coming for more radical new approaches to modelling. These should be based on two concepts. The first is a mathematical approach on the traveller's decision making processes, including all the real world constraints applied to individuals; the second is the incorporation of the invariant factors in trip patterns, discovered by suitable analysis of survey data. There is probably a close connection between these two concepts, which the new models should try to exploit. Within the broad framework fixed by these concepts, an attempt should be made to tailor transport models more precisely to answer the questions actually posed by transport planners, without wasting time and effort on unnecessary complexity, irrelevant to current problems.

ACKNOWLEDGEMENTS
The work described in this paper forms part of the programme of the Transport and Road Research Laboratory and the paper is published by permission of the Director.

Crown Copyright. Any views expressed in this paper are not necessarily those of the Department of the Environment or the Department of Transport. Extracts from the test may be reproduced, except for commercial purposes, provided the source is acknowledged.

REFERENCES
1. Downes J. D. and L. Gyenes, **Temporal stability and forecasting ability of trip generation models in Reading.** Department of the Environment. Transport and Road Research Laboratory Report LR 726, 1976.
2. Goodwin P. B., **Travel choice and time budgets** (and addendum). PTRC Summer Annual Meeting 1976.
3. Zahavi Y., **Traveltime budgets and mobility in urban areas,** Us Department of Transportation, Report FHWA PL 8183, May 1974.
4. Bullock, N, et al., **Time budgets and models of urban activity patterns.** Social Trends, No. 5, pp 45-63 London HMSO 1974.
5. Mitchell, C. G. B. and S. W. Town., **Accessibility of various social groups to different activities.** Department of the Environment, Transport and Road Research Laboratory Report SR 258, 1977.
6. Martin P. H., **The Harlow dial-a-bus experiment: Predicted and observed patronage.** Department of the Environment. Transport and Road Research Laboratory Report SR 256, 1977.
7. Papoulias D. and I.G. Heggie., **A comparative evaluation of forecast and use of park-and-ride in Oxford.** University of Oxford, Transport Studies Unit. Working Paper 12, 1976.
8. Tanner J. C., **Forecasts of vehicles and traffic in Great Britain, 1974 revision.** Department of the Environment. Transport and Road Research Laboratory Report LR 650, 1975.
9. Andrews R. D. and M. G. Langdon, **An individual cost minimising method of determinig modal split between three travel modes.** Department of the Environment. Tranport and Road Research Laboratory Report LR 698, 1976.
10. Langdon M., **Modal split models for more than two modes.** Paper for PTRC Annual Summer Meeting 1976.
11. Daly A. J. and S. Zachary, **Improved Multiple Choice Models.** Paper for PTRC Summer Annual Meeting 1976.
12. Goodwin P. B., **Human effort and the value of travel time.** Journal of Transport Economics and Policy, Vol X, No 1. January 1976.
13. Cochrane R. A., **An economic basis for the gravity model.** Journal of Transport Economics and Policy, Vol IX, No 1. January 1975.
14. Lawson G. P. and P. Mullen, **The use of disaggregated modelling techniques in the Telford Transportation Study.** PTRC Summer Annual Meeting 1976.
15. Lucarotti P. S. K., **Car availability, the fundamental modal split.** Transportation Planning and Technology, 1977 (in press).
16. Mackett, R. L., **Modifications to a transportation model to include land use.** Paper presented at the PTRC Annual Meeting, Warwick University, 1976.
17. Echenique, M., **An integrated land use and transport model.** Unpublished paper. The Martin Centre for Architectural and Urban Studies, Cambridge. 1976.

FOOTNOTES
[1] Different surveys use different definitions of units of travel, and this can affect the numerical values of results. The definitions used in the surveys quoted above are:
National Travel Survey: Journey - Any travel for a single main purpose Journey Stage - A sub-division of journey required for each change in the mode of travel or each new ticket needed.
Reading Surveys: Trip - any travel for a single purpose.
[2] Socio-economic group is a classification based largely on the occupation of the head of the household.
Category A - SEG groups 1,2,3,4,13. Employers, managers, professional workers.
Category B - SEG groups 5,6,7. Intermediate & junior non-manual, service workers.
Category C - SEG groups 8,9,12,14. Foremen, skilled manual, self-employed manual.
Category D - SEG groups 10,11,15. Semi- and un-skilled manual, agricultural.
[3] A model under development at TRRL by Webster includes an invariant number of trips.

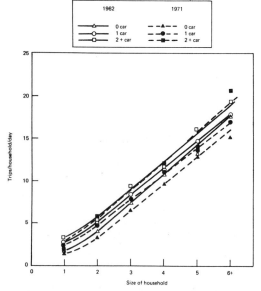

Fig. 1 - Household mean daily trip rates for all purposes by all modes (including walking)

(Source - Travel Surveys in Reading, 1962 and 1971)

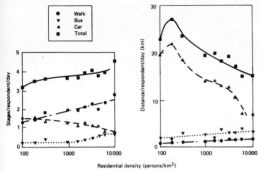

Fig. 2 - Variation of travel with residential density
(National Travel Survey 1972/3)

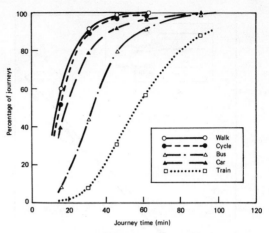

Fig. 4 - Cumulative distribution of travel distance and time
for journeys to and from work
(National Travel Survey 1972/3)

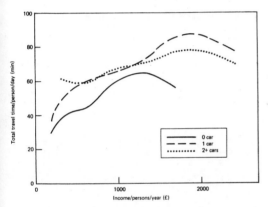

Fig. 3 - Variation of total time spent travelling with income and
car ownership
(National Travel Survey 1972/3)

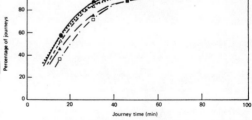

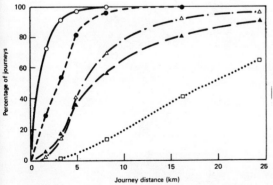

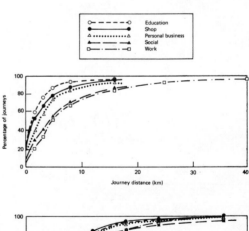

Fig. 5 - Cumulative distribution of travel distance and time
for several journey purposes
(National Travel Survey 1972/3)

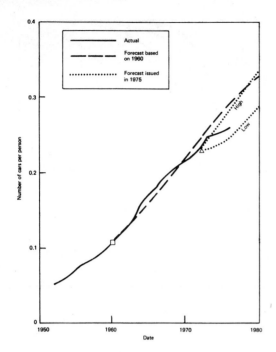

Fig. 6 - Comparison of forecast and actual numbers of cars per person in Britain

European Passenger Travel Demand
Analysis and Strategy Responsive Forecast

by

D. WILKEN

German Aerospace Research Establishment, Federal Republic of Germany

INTRODUCTION

The paper reports of the first comprehensive attempt to analyse and forecast long distance passenger travel in Europe under different hypotheses of future transport supply development. It is based on the work which has been pursued in the OECD Programme on European Intercity Passenger Transport Requirements. The OECD, together with the ECMT and the EEC, had been asked by 12 European governments to carry out a prospective study, the objective of which was to assist Member Countries in the task of devising long-range strategies to meet the growing demand for passenger transport between metropolitan regions of Western Europe.

From this, five working objectives were derived:
- description and analysis of the intercity transport system;
- analysis of factors affecting future demand;
- analysis of possible new modes and improvements to existing services;
- formulation of possible, European transport strategies;
- examination of the possible consequences and impacts of alternative strategies on passengers, carriers and the community.

In the following, emphasis is put on the description of the characteristics of European passenger travel, the model formulation and calibration, and the simulation and forecast of travel.

OBJECTIVES OF THE FORECAST

The question to be answered was not: What will be the magnitude and structure of the European travel demand in 30 years from now? But rather: What could be the future demand under status quo conditions and how could the demand be affected by different transport policy measures intended to bring a change to the status quo development.

To study the consequences of possible future courses of action in transport policy, a strategy approach was adopted. A transport strategy is defined as the co-ordination of major decisions affecting the transport system in order to achieve long-term objectives. They are of transport internal nature, like shorter travel times and lower costs, or external nature, like regional planning or industrial policy, and may be conflicting. One main aim of strategy is undoubtedly to reduce the objectional characteristics of today's transport modes.

The strategy options, i.e. individual policies and programmes, which permit a choice of strategy fall into three broad categories:
- management, like pricing or regulation;
- infrastructure, like new facilities;
- research and development.

Too numerous are the possibilities of formulating options in a quantitative way and combining them to transport policy alternatives.

Four main strategies were chosen for study, based on four alternative philosophies towards the fundamental problem of how to deal with the growing demand for transport:
- *Status Quo Strategy:* The basic thesis underlying this strategy is that market demand must be met by providing sufficient capacity. This strategy was intended to represent a continuation of transport policies of the sixties. The growing demand is to be matched by new roads and airports.
- *Controlled Mode Strategy:* The hypothesis is, that the main problems are caused by excessive demand for car and air, and the solution must be found in attracting demand to a greatly improved rail system. This implies a rather modest road building programme and major service improvements, i.e. higher speeds, in the European intercity rail network. One variant of this strategy was the superposition of a very high speed rail network of new infrastructure to the existing network.
- *Controlled Demand Strategy:* Assumes that excessive demand for car and air travel connot in practice be satisfied by rail and must therefore be restrained directly by introducing taxes at the largest airports and motorway tolls around the largest cities.
- *Planned Demand Strategy:* The basic thesis is that the problems are largely due to excessive concentration of demand in certain places at certain times. The solution is to disperse demand over time and space. This strategy calls into question land use planning, which the other strategies accept as given.

These strategies were interpreted in terms of structural additions to the road, rail and air networks in each country, so that different networks with different service characteristics were derived for each strategy. The objective of the demand forecast was to produce an estimate of the mode specific passenger flows for each transport situation as defined by the strategies and thus, give a quantitative idea of the impact of strategy on demand. It was clear that this task for a study area with around 350 million inhabitants and a transport network, which comprises around 350.000 Kms of highway, 45.000 Kms of railway and 105 international airports, could be solved only - if at all - by means of a demand - supply model.

ANALYSIS OF PAST AND PRESENT DEMAND
Recent Developments of Long Distance Travel

Although good statistics of long distance passenger traffic in Europe are scare it is well known that the demand particularly for car and air travel, has evolved dramatically since the War, mainly as a consequence of population and economic growth and technological advance. Nine-tenths of the present motorway network were built, and nearly all Europe's airports were built or rebuilt, during this period. Between 1950 and 1973 the car population expanded from 5,6 million to 75 million and the annual number of passengers by air grew from 4 million to 91 million. Intercity rail passenger traffic grew much slower, however increased by an estimated 75-100%, despite the enormous new competition from road and air.

While the traffic on intercity roads multiplied around six times between 1950 and 1970 in some central European countries, international road traffic grew much faster. In only ten years, the number of frontier crossing cars increased by 7 times. This traffic, however being international, constitutes only a very small part of the total road traffic. The international portion of rail traffic has also been growing, at a rate of 2,6% p.a. in the last ten years.

In 1950 European air transport was in its infancy and the growth rate was naturally higher. During the 1960s, air traffic in Europe increased by 15-20% p.a., mainly because of the charter traffic, and the international part grew from 17 million passengers in 1960 to 90 million in 1973. In the same time the international rail traffic grew from 28 million to 38 million. The rail share of total international rail and air traffic decreased thus from 62% to 30%.

Socio-economic as well as supply factors have strongly influenced the growth of travel. Whereas the total population rose only by 17% (from 290 million in 1950 to 340 million in 1970), the urban population, which is responsible for much long-distance travel, rose by 34% and the number of urban households probably rose by about 50%. Employment shifted from the primary to the secondary and, more important, to the tertiary sector, thus causing an increase in business travel. The intersectoral movement of labour was associated with a big increase in national income, and a new life style, which again contributed to more travel.

A large part of long-distance travel is leisure travel undertaken in the course of holidays or weekend trips. Since 1950, holiday allowances for employees have increased from two weeks to four, whereas weekly working hours have come down to normally 40 within a 5-day week.

With higher incomes, more and more people became car owners. At the same time, costs of transport decreased. In real terms, the family car became not only cheaper to buy, but also to run. Air travel too became cheaper at least until 1973. Thus, lower costs combined with greater and denser networks and faster and more frequent services contributed on the supply side to the strong growth in European passenger travel.

Characteristics of Todays' Travel
Household Surveys
Because of a severe lack of passenger transport statistics information of the magnitude and structure of demand for long-distance travel was almost non-existent. In order to understand the demand and to predict with some confidence how it will respond, either to changing socio-economic conditions or to alterations in the quality and price of transport, it is necessary to know about the people who travel or do not travel, why they travel (or not), what sort of places they come from and go to, and what factors determine their choice of mode. To get information of this kind, household surveys were conducted in 9 European countries.

About 5.200 households with over 15.000 members were questioned about all their long-distance trips during the preceding year. Information of the following characteristics of all trips with a minimum distance of 80 Kms during the year was obtained:

- trip purpose
- travel mode
- distance
- destination type and size and nationality
- season
- type of accommodation
- party size.

In addition, characteristics of the household, like size age structure, occupation of employed members, income, car ownership, etc. were asked.

Not all results of the survey were representative for Europe, like the total number of trips generated or the split between national and international trips, nor could some of them be used directly for calibrating a demand model, because they were only of descriptive nature, like the information on business travel. It became therefore necessary to identify and structure the information in such a way as to reveal causal or typical relationships, which then could be applied for the whole of Europe.

Trip Generation
The analysis revealed details of today's trip making of Europeans, that were unknown before. The average European undertook in 1973 less than two journeys with a one-way distance of more than 80 Kms. A few people travelled much more often than others: 5% of the population made 33% of all journeys, while 30% didn't travel at all and 25% made only one journey. This means that more than half of the population did not travel or travelled only once a year.

There are three principal reasons why people travel: Some 25% of the trips were for business, another 25% for holidays, 45% were for weekend recreation and 5% were for other personal reasons. For analytical purposes the latter two groups were combined as "short stay personal" trips. Thus the travel market consists of three clear divisions, business, holidays and short stay personal, in which the motivations are so different that it is necessary to separate all demand analysis into these three parts.

Unlike business trips, which are generated by the need of the working place, personal trips are largely generated by the needs, desires and resources of the household. Three household characteristics have been identified as main factors influencing trip generation: income, age structure, and car ownership. The number of trips per household rises considerably as income rises. Whereas this relationship is of pure descriptive value in the case of business trips, it is presumed to be a causal one for personal trips. The relationship should, however, not be exaggerated: household income has to increase by the factor eight, before the trip generation rate (trips per household per year) doubles.

The impact of car ownership is striking on short stay trips but not on holiday trips. The possession of a car induces households to make nearly three times as many weekend trips, compared with non-car-owning households of the same type and income: but is is not a major factor in determining whether or not they go on holiday. Obviously, as incomes rise, households tend to move from non-car-owning to car-owning households.

Families have the lowest trip generation as compared with young and old adult households, given the possession or non-possession of a car, and the young adults have the highest trip generation. With one exception: old adults, who own a car, make more holidays than the other household types.

Trip Length and Attraction
The average trip lengths (air distance) in the survey were around 480 Kms for holidays, 260 Kms for busi-

ness, 150 Kms for short stay personal trips, and 260 Kms for all trips. The trip length distribution by trip purpose is shown in Fig. 1. More than 50% of all trips with a minimum distance of 80 Kms were shorter than 150 Kms and 75% shorter than 300 Kms. Only 10% of all trips exceeded trip lengths of 500 Kms. The distribution is quite different for holiday trips, which are on average much longer. Less than 50% of them are shorter than 300 Kms and almost 10% are longer than 1200 Kms.

The comparison of average trip lengths by purpose is somewhat misleading since only trips of over 80 Kms are considered. As can be seen in Fig. 1 there are in fact far more short stay personal and business trips below the 80 Km limit than above it; whereas there are not many holiday trips of less than 80 Kms. The survey showed that income affects trip distance, however, only of holidays. Higher income groups tend to go farther for holidays but not for weekend trips.

Whereas the typical destination of business trips is the town and the city, it is the rural area and the small town for personal trips. Less than 20% of all long-distance trips are "intercity", i.e. have both ends in towns of over 100.000 inhabitants. More than 50% are urban rural trips and the remaining 25% are purely rural. Since public modes offer in general their best services in intercity transport they cater only for a small part of the market. The survey proved in fact that the car is also for long-distance travel the mostly used mode.

Modal Split

Under today's circumstances, over three-quarters of all trips over 80 Kms are done by car. It takes roughly two-thirds of business and holiday trips and nearly eight-ninths of short stay trips. Nearly 15% of all travellers chose the train, but over 20% of business travellers did so. More business travellers took the train than others, because business trips concentrate rather more on intercity relations. In contrast only 8% of the weekend travellers took this mode. The air is negligable for short stay trips but takes about 10% of business trips and a little less of holidays, about 40% of the holi-day air passengers went by charter. The bus was chosen by less than 4% of all travellers, mainly for personal reasons.

One of the principal determinants of modal choice is the length of the trip. Fig. 2 shows the modal distri-bution by trip length. As can be seen modal split varies greatly with distance. The car takes most of the short trips, while the plane takes most of the trips over 1200 Kms. The share of the train exceeds at no distance that of the car or the plane and rises to a maximum of around 30% between 500 and 600 Kms. The bus takes a steady 3 to 4% of the market at most distances.

Trip length, however, is only one factor which influ-ences model choice. The presence of other factors is indicated if one compares the modal distribution of each trip purpose, for car-owning and non-car-owning house-holds separately, as shown in Figs. 3, 4, and 5. Most business travellers choose the plane from distances of 600 Kms upward, but some prefer to go by air already on trips with more than 200 Kms (air distance).

Whereas the plane plays an important role in holiday travel for car-owning as well as non-car-owning house-holds, it is as yet unimportant for short stay personal trips. Clearly, the train takes over a major part of the travel of non-car-owning households, particularly for holidays. A striking fact is, however, that in those households the car is the principal mode over the shorter distances, both for holidays and short stay personal trips. This suggests that non-car-owners often travel in other people's cars for leisure purposes.

DEMAND MODEL

General

It was felt that only a network study could reveal or take account of the important interactions between dif-ferent parts of the network, which occur as consequences of different, regionally limited developments of trans-port infrastructure or socio-economic factors. The means for accomplishing this was a fairly elaborate de-mand - supply model by which all the main demand and supply factors affecting the future development of travel and traffic can be taken into account.

Nevertheless the model is only a tool designed to give broad answers to simplified questions its purpose is to make some big and laborious calculations in order to help the analyst to come to some conclusions. The results need careful interpretation, with a full understanding of the model and its weaknesses. One weak point in the model is the treatment of goods and short-distance traf-fic using the same network as long-distance passenger traffic. Only crude forecasts could be made of their vol-umes on the intercity network.

The model was used to predict future traffic move-ments and costs on the European network, on the basis of numerous assumptions or judgements, including alternative transport strategies. By using a model the analyst is forced to assemble in a coherent and inter-nally consistent manner the many known facts and rela-tionships which determine the volumes of traffic by each mode on every link of the network. This has to be done in a way which facilitates the substitution of different data to represent the future, i.e. 2000. It must permit the substitution of alternative data, to represent alterna-tive socio-economic developments and alternative trans-port strategies.

Models are no better than the data with which they are built. The amount of data available on European traffic is small, although information on the infrastruc-ture is rather good. The model was built primarily on the basis of the household survey results and some national and international surveys, and was calibrated against surveys and statistics, which existed in some countries and international organisations.

The model consists of two parts: supply and demand. The supply part consists of a detailed, quantitative description of the transport system and the services it offers, including prices. The demand model consists of all the main factors determining decisions to travel, including the transport services and prices on offer. The demand model thus reacts to supply, in that effective demand must be consistent with the services offered, but the supply model does not react to the demand, because that would have entailed an iterative model beyond the resources of the study. In addition, the level of detail in the simulation of the traffic conditions was not fine enough as to justify the development effort. A planning study, but not necessarily a strategy study should aim at simulating equilibrium conditions. Never-theless, the model results must be checked in this re-spect before they can be accepted.

The spatial unit of the demand analysis is the zone, of which there are 109 in the study area (see Fig. 6). On average, three million people live in a zone, which measures 24.000 Kms² in size. Travel flows were cal-culated between the 109 zones by the three trip pur-poses: business, holiday and short stay personal. These purpose categories are the main components of long-distance travel. Although purpose specific statistics did not exist, it was felt necessary to distinguish between these purposes, since the factors which underly travel decisions, and their importance vary considerably with trip purpose.

Fig. 7 shows the structure of the demand model. As

can be seen it follows the conventional subdivision into trip generation, spatial and modal distribution, and assignment. This process is however, again subdivided into many behaviourally based categories and the model phases are combined differently by trip purpose.

The models for the two personal travel groups are conceptually similar, treating trip generation, distribution, and modal split as separate phases, whereas the business trip model is a combination of direct demand and modal split.

Personal Travel
Trip Generation
As a result of the long-distance travel survey, trip generation rates for holiday and short stay personal trips were found for 30 household categories, which are combinations of three household types, two car-ownership classes and five income classes. The income classes relate to the declared household income in nine predetermined classes. The following table gives the trip generation rates (trip/person/year) as found in the survey:

| Income class | Household Category | | | | | |
| | Non-Car Owning HHs | | | Car-Owning HHs | | |
	Young Adults	Old Adults	Families	Young Adults	Old Adults	Families
			1) Holiday Trips			
A	2,9	1,2	0,8	3,1	1,4	0,6
B	1,6	1,3	1,0	2,4	2,0	1,5
C	2,2	2,0	1,0	2,4	4,2	1,8
D	1,95	1,95	1,7	2,9	2,7	1,95
E	2,4	1,85	4,4	3,1	4,8	2,7
			2) Short Stay Personal Trips			
A	2,8	1,0	1,1	5,7	4,0	3,3
B	2,7	1,1	1,2	9,5	2,4	3,5
C	2,3	4,4	1,4	5,7	5,6	3,8
D	2,4	1,6	1,2	4,1	7,1	4,6
E	3,4	4,9	0,9	6,6	3,3	6,0

As one can see some variation of trip rates remained, which cannot be explained by the three factors forming the categories. It was found that a further stratification of factors would improve the description of reality, but not necessarily the forecast, given today's data situation in European zones.

Based on the hypothesis that income, age structure and car-ownership determine personal trip making, the trip rates were applied on the assumption that they would not change in the future. Changes in trip generation could therefore arise solely as a result of changes of these factors. The application of trip generation rates by category required a knowledge of the number of households and persons in each category, for each zone and each year under consideration.

The following variables were therefore predicted for each zone:
– the proportions of the three household types;
– the distribution of households by income;
– the proportion of households with and without a car by type and income class;
– the average household size by type.

These variables were derived from relationships with more basic data, which were predicted beforehand:
– population;
– GRP per head;
– number of households;
– average size of households;
– degree of motorization;
– percentage of households with cars;
– degree of urbanization.

The result of the estimation process was a matrix of the number of households and persons by category. The number of trips generated in each zone is given by multiplying the trip rate matrix with the household and person matrix.

Changes in the transport system affect the generation of personal trips only via the car-ownership. The analysis of the long-distance travel survey did not yield a conclusive relationship between differences in trip making and interregional accessibility in addition to the relationship with the three factors mentioned. While this may be true for holiday trips - changes in transport services affect more the distribution and modal split than the generation of holidays - it is believed not to be true for weekend trips. A new motorway or cheap charter air services attract not only travellers from other modes but also new travellers who would not otherwise have made the journey at all or would have made a short-distance journey. By means of a comparison of distance distribution curves under different strategies the number of newly generated long-distance short stay personal trips was estimated. More research will be needed to improve the forecasting method in this respect.

Trip Distribution
Trips generated by residents in zone i were distributed to all other zones by means of a gravity type function (see Fig. 7). Since no data existed on the number of tourists attracted by different zones, a special analysis was carried out to develop, for each zone, attraction factors for holidays and weekend trips. These attraction factors should be a measure of the inherent power of the zone to attract tourists, i.e. they should reflect the proportion of all tourists in the study area who would be attracted to the zone if all zones were equally accessible. In the model they stand for the relative importance of attractions in the destination zones.

The study area was subdivided into around 1200 cells, the land use of which with respect to tourism was identified, e.g. resort area or urban area. Then each cell was graded according to the intensity of the land use and was given in a third step two weights, one for holiday attractiveness, the other for weekend attractiveness. This stage involved a considerable amount of judgement. To make the decisions as objective as possible, some controles were introduced. First, the average weighting of each of the land use types was made to agree with the actual distribution of trips as known from the survey. Secondly, the range of weighting in each type was determined by reference to tourist data from the Channel Tunnel survey. Thus each cell was eventually weighted and the cellular weights were added up to zonal weights, which were used as attraction factors in the model. These values were held constant for all transport strategies.

The impedance function should include variables which measure differences in travel resistance. To account for the varying marginal utility of money to travellers with different incomes, generalised time (Tij *) was taken as the impedance measure. This factor varies both with the type of traveller and the mode of transport. Travel times and costs between zones were derived for each mode and type of traveller (i.e. by purpose and income) in each strategy as a result of the network analysis.

The perceived value of time of the traveller (λ^1) was assumed to be related to his declared household income, for holiday travel it was taken as 50% of the declared income per employed person of the household, and for short stay personal travel, 100%.

The distribution function was estimated from the survey results as a power function of the generalised time (Tij *). Since Tij * is a mode specific variable there are, for each ti to be distributed to zone j, as many values of Tij * as there are modes offered. The value applied in the distribution function was the minimum value per traveller type. The elasticity of demand with respect to travel impedance was derived from the trip distance distribution as revealed in the survey. For short stay personal trips, the elasticity was found $\propto$ = 3,9 for car-owning and non-car-owning households and over all income ranges. For holiday travel, the value is lower and varies between $1,9 \leq \propto \leq 2,1$, depending on the income of the household.

In the calibration process of holiday trips the calculated country-to-country flows were compared with national statistics from some countries, and some significant differences were noted.

It could be shown that the presence of an international frontier invariably had a great effect in reducing the volume of personal travel. As a result of the calibration a matrix of country-to-country time penalties was therefore calculated to reproduce the frontier resistances.

Modal Split

Travel flows between zones by trip purpose and household category, for each strategy, were modally split by means of a combination of category analysis and diversion curves. As part of the analysis of the long-distance travel survey each trip, which had been reported, was analysed with respect to modal choice criteria and alternatives. It was found that the factors which influence modal choice can be classified into three groups related to the traveller, the trip and the transport system. Age, income, car-ownership and party size pertain to the traveller; trip purpose, destination and duration to the trip; travel time, cost reliability, safety and convenience pertain to the transport system. One can assume that each traveller will weigh up the relative importance of these various factors and will decide on the mode which suits him best. His decision is thereby governed by a limited knowledge of the alternatives and their characteristics. For simulation purposes one should take account of a large number of factors, for long

term forecasting one must concentrate on those which are significant and can be forecast without great problems. As a result of the analysis the following factors have been isolated:
  – traveller's car availability and income;
  – party size;
  – trip purpose;
  – trip destination;
  – trip distance;
  – travel time and cost.

The combined effect of these factors has been accounted for by placing trips in one of a number of categories and then considering the modal choice case in each category. The categories consist of specific groups of travellers making similar trips in similar circumstances. They are distinguished by traveller and trip related factors. The modal choice is then determined within a particular category by transport service variables, i.e. travel time and cost, whereby an attempt was made, to reflect the perceived values of these factors.

18 Categories have been identified for holiday and short stay personal travel, which are shown in Fig. 8. The cases, where there is little or no real modal choice have been separated from those where there is an important modal split, and the latter have been divided between those with bimodal and multimodal choices. Diversion curves were then derived for the modal choice cases which describe the probability of choosing mode m_1 from modes m_1 and m_2 as a function of the ratio of the generalized times Tij * of the two modes. The function has been found to be of a logistic type and its form varies considerably with the modal split case, indicating the varying importance of the generalised times and of other factors not explicitly included in the analysis. Some diversion curves have rather flat slopes, which means, that other factors besides travel time and cost influence the modal choice.

One can conclude from the modal split analysis of the survey that the majority of weekend trips were undertaken without modal choice considerations. They were mode specifically generated, in most cases car generated trips. In contrast, for most of the business trips there were modal choice situations.

The technique of estimating the modal split by a category analysis simplifies the analysis and gives a higher accuracy in each category, it may create, however, a forecasting problem of allocating flows to certain categories. It was therefore necessary not to create too many categories.

Business Travel
Direct Demand

Contrary to personal travel, business trip attractions can be described by the same variables as the generations, the spatial distribution of trips is determined by the locations of business contacts, factories, branch offices, clients, etc. In contrast with personal travel, too, the decision to make a business trip usually includes the decisions about the destination, so that for modelling one can combine the two phases, trip generation and distribution. A gravity function has been taken by which the total number of business travellers on an origin-destination link was directly estimated, using regression analysis for calibration. Generation and attraction variables are the same and are the product of the gross regional product (GRP) of the origin and destination zones. The GRP has been chosen as a measure well describing the economic output, given the poor availability of economic data of European zones.

The impedance factor was rather well described by the travel time. This confirms what has been found in former studies of business travel, namely that business travellers seek to minimize journey time rather than journey costs. If one employs travel time only as the impedance variable, in a model which simulates the flow on all modes, it is not sufficient to take the travel time of one mode only. The modally weighted travel time was therefore applied as a measure of total impedance. This required the modal split phase before the generation-distribution phase.

The coefficients were calibrated using two sets of data business flows between zones in the United Kingdom and the Continent, for international travel, and between selected zones in Germany for domestic travel. Other data on business travel were not available. Since both situations were not typical for all European domestic and international flows, national correction factors had to be introduced.

Since the model employs GRP directly as a generation and attraction factor, national currencies had to be converted into some common unit. For simplicity the U.S. dollar had been adopted, but account was taken of the fact that market exchange rates do not and did not give a true comparison of the international purchasing power of different currencies.

Modal Split

The modal split of business trips was estimated by means of the same method and on the basis of the same data (from the survey) as for personal trips. Generalised time was taken as the modal split variable because of future changes in the tariff structure in some strategies. Nevertheless, the costs play only a minor role since the value of time of business travellers is more than twice as high as of personal travellers. The inclusion of generalized time required a stratification of travel flows by travellers' income.

For the modal split analysis business trips were placed in four categories:
− trips of less than 250 Kms to rural areas → car trips;
− trips of less than 250 Kms to towns and cities → car and train trips;
− trips of between 250 Kms and 1200 Kms → car, train, and air trips;
− trips of more than 1200 Kms → air trips.
The first and last category are predominantly unimodal, whereas the second offers a bimodal and the third a trimodal choice. Clearly, most of the business trips can be found in the modal choice categories.

MODEL RESULTS AND DISCUSSION

The demand boom of 1950-1973 is certainly not fully spent, though in some respects it is slowing down. On the assumption of the central forecast that
− population grows from 340 million to about 400 million in the year 2000 with more people living in urban areas,
− the gross national products multiply by 2,1 - 3,1 (2,5% - 3,8% per annum) in the 11 countries with relatively developed economies and by 4,3 - 5,0 (5,0% - 5,5% per annum) in the other five, the precise amounts depending on population growth, and
− car-ownership rises from 60 million to around 150 million and the number of car-owning households from 47 million to around 115 million,
and on many hypotheses regarding the development of costs, transport services, and relationships in the demand functions one may expect that - under Status Quo conditions - long-distance travel will double between 1970 and 2000, with the strongest growth in air travel (by the factor 3,75) and lowest growth in bus travel (by the factor 1,3). The 70% predicted growth of rail traffic consists largely of business passengers and is quite critically

dependent on the improved level of service assumed (at investments outlays of 25 billion US $).

The impact on rail traffic of a much faster rail network, together with a somewhat worse road network than in the Status Quo (Controlled Mode strategy), is substantial: high speed trains with maximum crusing speeds of 250 Km/h in a European network, raise the number of rail trips by nearly 20%, with 350 Km/h by additional 10%. The Controlled Demand strategy, restraining traffic directly by low investments and charging motorway tolls and airport taxes, proved remarkably ineffectual in reducing road traffic, but much more successful in reducing air traffic.

The Planned Demand strategy generates more traffic than the other strategies because the decentralisation of population and employment away from the biggest cities leads to the substitution of intercity trips for intracity trips. It is, however, the only strategy which significantly relieves the problem of road congestion near the largest cities. Only by actually reducing the population of these cities and with it the number of cars, does it seem possible to make any real impression on this problem.

How reliable are these forecasts? Clearly, they are subject to numerous uncertainties. Having studied the many assumptions involved and the sensitivity of the conclusions to errors in the assumptions, one must issue certain warnings. The business travel forecast could easily be too high, because the technique used was rather weak, due to lack of data. The holiday forecast could well prove to be rather low if a change of fashion should occur in favour of second and third holidays. Equally, the forecast of personal travel by air may be wrong, because air traffic is sensitive to price and incomes and one cannot easily forecast future consessionary price schemes, nor the numbers of people in the highest income group, which is primarily responsible for air travel.

The travel forecasts depend on three types of input variables of the model:
− forecasts of demand factors, e.g. income;
− hypotheses of supply factors (i.e. strategies), e.g. costs,
− functional relationships between demand and supply.
There is always a degree of uncertainty about the accuracy of the values chosen for the horizon year; indeed the analysis year values are sometimes open to question. As transport planner, one has to accept more or less the uncertainties in the forecasts of demand factors, i.e. socio-economic factors, because these forecasts often have an official character. They have been prepared (and revised) by government agencies and form a base for other sectors of politics.

The development of the transport system has a long term aspect in its infrastructural part and a short term aspect in its regulatory or management part. These characteristics can be treated as alternatives and formulated in a quantitative way rather easily by the transport planner.

The greatest problem lies in the formulation and verification of demand - supply relationships, because they have not been researched in sufficient detail and over sufficiently long periods, particularly with respect to interregional passenger travel. It seems that the efforts in research and development of the technology of new transport systems are more successful and more advanced than those which try to find out the demand for these systems. It is a clear fact, that we need better data of people's travel behaviour, the travel structure, and factors influencing travel. The transport planner has then - and not before! - the task and the responsability

216

to establish causal relationships between travel demand and demand and supply factors, in a way which permits them to be used as forecasting tools. It is hoped that the description of the model, which has been used for strategic forecasting of European travel, has not only given an idea of its complexity but also its deficiencies, from which the need and the direction of further research should be deduced.

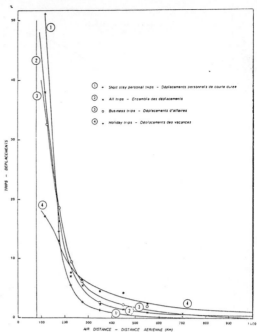

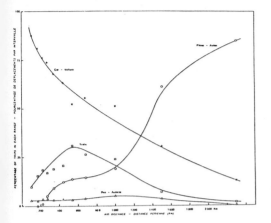

Fig. 2 - Modal distribution of trips by trip length
(household survey data: air distance)

Fig. 1 - Trip length distribution

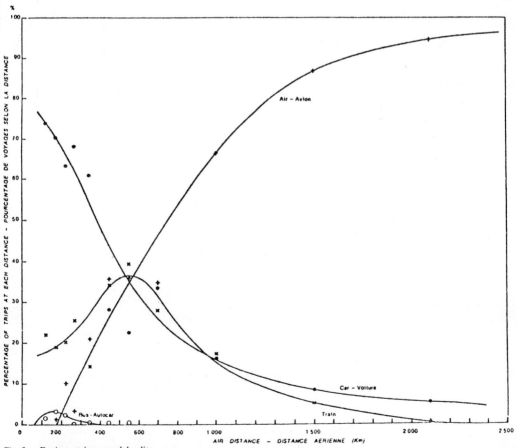

Fig. 3 - Business trips - modal split

217

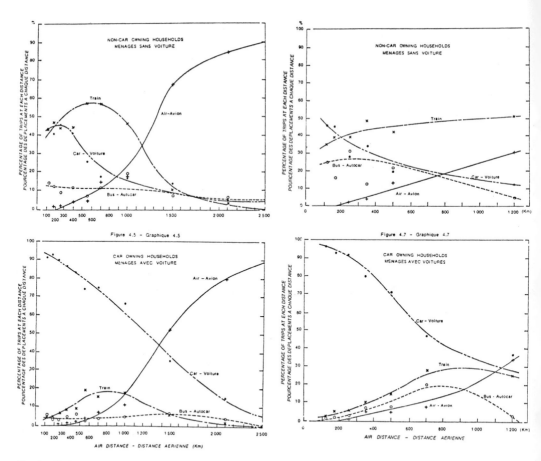

Fig. 4 - Holiday trips - modal split

Fig. 5 - Short stay personal trips - modal split

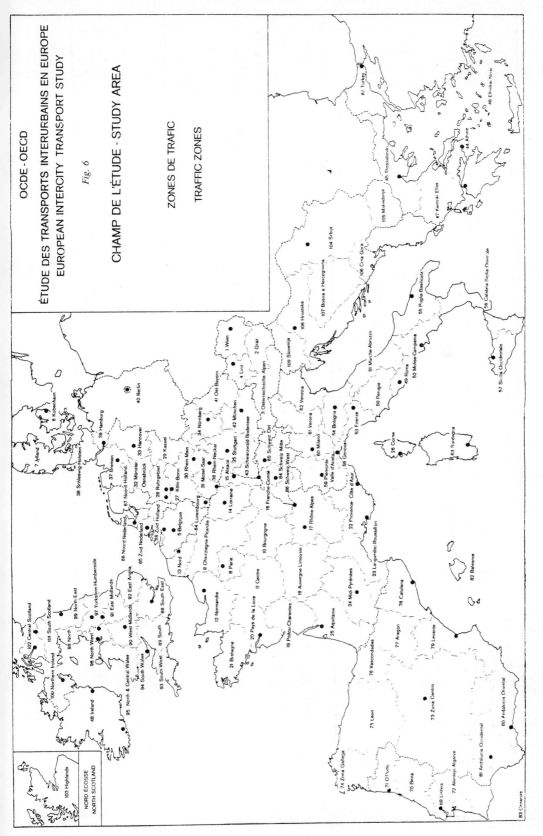

OCDE - OECD

ÉTUDE DES TRANSPORTS INTERURBAINS EN EUROPE
EUROPEAN INTERCITY TRANSPORT STUDY

Fig. 6

CHAMP DE L'ÉTUDE - STUDY AREA

ZONES DE TRAFIC

TRAFFIC ZONES

NORD ÉCOSSE
NORTH SCOTLAND

Trip purpose / Model Phase	Personal trips		Business trips
	Holiday	Short stay personal	
Trip generation ($t_i = \sum_{\bar{j}} t_{i\bar{j}}$)	Category analysis: $$t_i = f(ST, I, CO)$$ Categories: household structure (ST) household income (I) car ownership (CO)		Gravity function: $$t_{ij} = \alpha \left(GRP_i \cdot GRP_j\right)^{\beta} \cdot \bar{T}_{ij}^{\delta}$$ Measures of generation and attraction zonal income, GRP Travel impedance: function of modally weighted travel time (Tij)
Trip distribution ($t_{i\bar{j}} = \sum_m t_{i\bar{j},m}$)	Gravity function: $$t_{i\bar{j},I} = k_i \cdot t_{i,I} \cdot A_j \cdot TI_{i\bar{j},I}$$ Zonal attraction (Aj): attraction weight Travel impedance ($TI_{i\bar{j},I}$): function of min. generalised travel time ($T_{i\bar{j},I}^*$) $$(T_{i\bar{j},I}^* = T_{ij} + C_{ij}/\lambda_I)$$		
Modal Split ($t_{i\bar{j},m}$)	Category analysis: Categories: unimodal, bimodal, multimodal } Modal split function: diversion curves with $P(t_{i\bar{j},m}) = f\left(\dfrac{T_{i\bar{j},m}^*}{T_{i\bar{j},m+1}^*}\right)$		
Trip Assignment	Route assignment (for each $t_{i\bar{j},m}$) → Link and corridor volumes by network		

Fig. 7 - Structure of the demand model

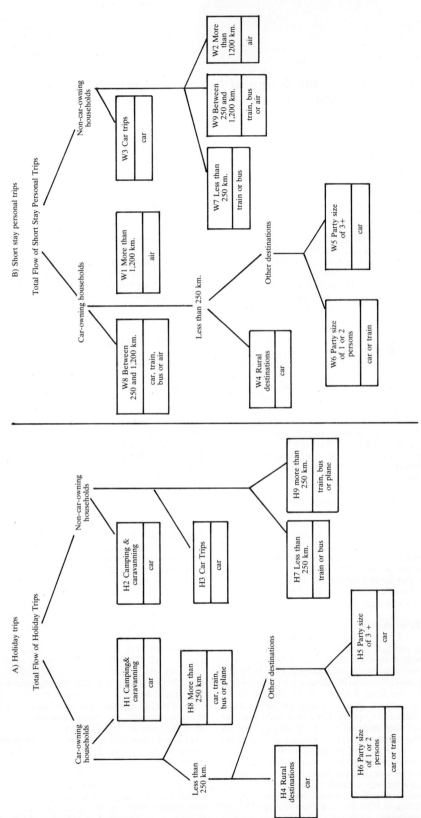

Fig. 8 - Modal split categories of personal trips

221

Considerations on the design of behavioural orientated models from the point of view of empirical social research

WERNER BRÖG

and

WILFRIED SCHWERDTFEGER

Sozialforschung Brög, Federal Republic of Germany

TRANSPORT USER BEHAVIOUR AS RESULTING FROM SITUATIONAL CIRCUMSTANCES AND INDIVIDUAL ATTITUDES

Transportation planning was recently defined as the "totality of systematic activities through which future measures are studied and laid down in advance for the purpose of changing specific conditions in the transportation sector in line with planning goals". [1]

What do we understand by "conditions in the transportation sector?" They are certainly not only momentary traffic patterns obtained for example from statistics on the volume of traffic. On the contrary, we must proceed further, particularly if future conditions are to be anticipated, and examine the causers of traffic phenomena and their reactions to changes in their environment in the broadest sense of the word, i.e. study individual persons and their actual transportation behaviour. Measures initially affect only the constraints of behaviour and therefore changed conditions in transportation result only from the summation of subjective changes in the behaviour of individuals on those changed constraints.

Accordingly, reliable prognosis is only possible when individual behaviour is inferable, i.e. explained from given situations. If the determinants of the subjective assimilation of environmental influences are known, it can be assessed how specific users will react to modified conditions in which way. The clarification of such operating mechanisms should therefore be an important task of basic research in the transportation sector. This paper attempts to stimulate efforts in this direction from the viewpoint of social science.

BASIC APPROACHES TO TRANSPORTATION PLANNING MODELS

Without claiming to be exhaustive, the following section will briefly review several historical lines of development in the conceptions of transportation planning models. This would seem to be necessary for several reasons. On the one hand, some of these lines of development have - so to speak - taken an autonomous course, i.e. they have been refined and elaborated to such a degree that discussion of their internal partial problems largely only takes place within a narrow circle of "initiated" experts, with the result that frequently a critical examination of the basic assumptions of these conceptions is no longer undertaken. Many pronounced mathematical approaches, be they of econometric origin or developments of traffic engineers, are particularly exposed to this danger. This detailed discussion shall be left out of our considerations because - as will be established

later - it can be partly viewed as irrelevant to the goals of transportation planning.

On the other hand - and this is considered to be more important - a development could be observed in recent years which seemed to make a positive effort to include the social sciences, notably sociology and psychology, in transportation planning models. Key words here are disaggregate and attitudinal models, which - as Heggie [2] aptly observes - are currently shooting up like mushrooms. But viewed against the background of the following attempt to adopt an approach actually orientated to the real behaviour of individuals, in several cases the suspicion can not be dispelled that it is a question of misunderstanding or mere fashionable terminology when long established approaches are furnished with additional components or exponents and suddenly renamed "behavioural models". It must therefore be made clear what demands are to be fulfilled by models which not only describe but also explain individual behaviour, thereby opening the way for prognoses.

The decisive points of this necessarily abridged discussion of transportation planning models are the type and number of variables, the operation mechanism and the structure of the models.

Initially, strictly descriptive approaches were developed by using means of spatial aggregates as independent variables in regression analysis. These approaches based solely on the empirical proof of more or less even covariation of traffic and land use data. Proceeding analogically from physical-mechanical laws (gravitation, entropy, etc), such approaches were also given the status of "laws", but their basis was generally formed only by common-sense assumptions (e.g. the role of distances) instead of theoretically based validity investigations of the influence factors and operating mechanisms employed.

It was not long, however, before the constructors of these models also began to express a feeling of uneasiness over results that were often not really appropriate, which led to at least a verbal demand that more attention should be paid to the actual causer of observable flows of traffic - namely to the individual. This happened at a time when the concentration of urban and transportation planning on motorised private traffic was felt to be abandoned. Accordingly, it was no longer tenable to use motorisation as the virtually exclusive and decisive variable in the models.

At this point in the development a massive engagement of the social sciences should and could have resulted, for the analysis of fundamental determinants of human behaviour and the development of methods for the empirical acquisition of behavioural data clearly lies within the scope of sociology. The (small) circle of professional transportation planners who realized this and tried to obtain appropriate support were often just as disappointed as the (few) sociologists who wanted to take an active interest in the problems of transportation planning. The engineers made hurried demands for handy and exact prognoses of human behaviour over extended periods of time, whereas the social scientists began by stressing the necessity of developing a sociological theory of traffic behaviour, and for scientific reasons rejected the "muddling through" of the engineers. There are still considerable difficulties of communication between the two disciplines.

Subsequently, a relatively indiscriminate search set in for factors which, due to diverse opinion surveys or the personal convictions of individual researchers, were thought to influence the traffic behaviour of individuals.

This resulted, for instance, in the development of a category of models on an econometric basis whose basic assumption was a rationally behaving, completely informed individual primarily orientated to economic criteria. By means of various combinations of numerous variables utility functions were formed, which, for example, were intended to depict individual preference with respect to alternative transport facilities. By using the utility functions in logit - or probit - approaches, it is then possible to calculate individual probabilities relating to the occurence of journeys, modal choice, and the spatial distribution of the journeys.

A basically different approach was taken in the Federal Republic of Germany by Kutter. [3] Starting from the basic needs of people, he used a schema adopted from sociological theory for the causal explanation of behaviour patterns. According to this schema, a person's sociodemographic characteristics determine his status, and from this a specific role behaviour with specific activity patterns can be tracted. This concept led to "homogeneous behavioural groups" which were also able to be proved by empirical-inductive method. Höttler [4] has quite rightly noted that new ground was broken here to the extent that an attempt was made to classify individuals according to their respective environmental situation and to explain their patterns of behaviour in the context of these situations. Thus, whereas, there is a danger of the (roughly described) econometric models chasing after an artefact with their basic assumption of a "homo oeconomicus" and a considerable expenditure of mathematical effort, Kutter's models based on homogeneous behavioural groups arrive at their statements via strictly deterministic lines. It would appear doubtful, however, whether the alleged stringency of the chain demography - status - role - acivity pattern - transportation pattern corresponds to real conditions. This implies quite clearly an overtaxing of the role theory. Kutter has partly noticed these limitations himself and qualified the validity of his model with respect to chronological and spatial applicability.

If we look for the reasons for the shortcomings exhibited (to a very varying extent) by previous models, the following can be observed:

– The constructors of models have frequently submitted far too readily to the pressure exerted by users of transportation planning models for quantitative prognoses. Even in cases where specification of the scope (of possible behaviour patterns or of traffic volumes) would be totally adequate, it is attempted to dispel all doubt about the effectivity of the model employed by emphasising a would-be accuracy.

– A relatively "blind" application of methods developed in natural sciences and economy to causal social phenomena avoids the necessity of having to grapple with complicated facts which are difficult to express in mathematical-formalistic terms, and are found to be infinitely variable and hardly susceptible to systematization.

– The fascination held by "exact" methods in connection with large computer capacities, encourages the neglect of all variables that can not be quantified at all or only with difficulty, and occasionally leads to the fading-out of entire segments of reality. Accordingly, highly complex model systems with an extremely high degree of descriptive accuracy are designed without checking their *explanatory value.*

– The lack of an easy-to-use, directly applicable sociological theory of transport behaviour encourages the disregard of relevant psychological and sociological research findings.

– A general approach to transportation behaviour as a mass phenomenon loses sight of the individual who acts from within his social context. Behaviour patterns in traffic (as in other spheres of life) are, however, neither solely the result of rational utilitarian considerations nor the product of wholly determined behavioural roles.

This is, of course, a simplified representation and has been partly superseded in several new approaches. As far as we can see, however, general practice is still based to a very large extent on the inadequate assumptions described above.

EMPERICAL FINDINGS
Empirical examination of the assumptions entailed in the models

To avoid constantly new - artificial - impasses in the search for practicable transportation behaviour models, it is therefore imperative to reflect back on the causers of traffic.

In order to be able to recognize the "goodness" of a model approach, it is thus necessary to establish if this approach is capable of explaining individual decision and behavioural sequences. In many cases, the simplest empirical examination suffices to show that this requirement is not met and that functional relations are implied in the model which can not be proved empirically.

Before briefly discussing several selected empirical data, we should at least mention at this point that the problems of "empirical methodology" - to a large extent neglected in discussions among transportation research scientists - plays an essential role here. We shall return to this question later on.

For a number of reasons, this brief degression into the subject of relevant empirical findings shall concentrate on a small selection of essential results. A detailed discussion of the abundant material available is beyond the scope of this paper. We also feel that a precise analysis of all the demonstrated errors of measurement is not necessary to substantiate our hypotheses. We base the discussion of the importance of travelling times and costs - as the most common variables in transportation models - on the results of a pilot study on modal choice in commuter traffic. First of all, 300 gainfully employed persons who travel to work by private car or by means of public transport were surveyed in depth; the results of this survey were fully confirmed by a later survey of 1.200 heads of households in urban areas in the Federal Republic of Germany [1].

Importance attached to travelling costs

If an investigation is made of the awareness of costs incurred by the respective journeys to and from work, the first thing to be observed is that in neither of the two cases - use of private car and use of public transport - a clearly quantifiable result can be obtained. The reason for this is that in calculating the private car costs it is by no means clear what items - apart from the cost of petrol

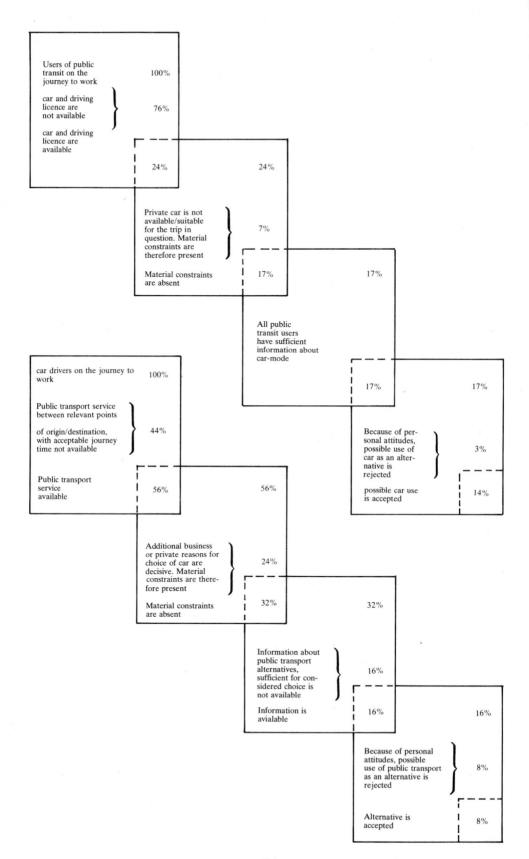

Users of public transit on the journey to work   100%

car and driving licence are not available   76%

car and driving licence are available   24%   24%

Private car is not available/suitable for the trip in question. Material constraints are therefore present   7%

Material constraints are absent   17%   17%

All public transit users have sufficient information about car-mode   17%   17%

Because of personal attitudes, possible use of car as an alternative is rejected   3%

possible car use is accepted   14%

car drivers on the journey to work   100%

Public transport service between relevant points of origin/destination, with acceptable journey time not available   44%

Public transport service available   56%   56%

Additional business or private reasons for choice of car are decisive. Material constraints are therefore present   24%

Material constraints are absent   32%   32%

Information about public transport alternatives, sufficient for considered choice is not available   16%

Information is avialable   16%   16%

Because of personal attitudes, possible use of public transport as an alternative is rejected   8%

Alternative is accepted   8%

used - should be entered into the calculation, and in ascertaining public transport fares the varied possibilities of daily, weekly or monthly tickets has to be taken into account. Thus, while the results obtained do not furnish an exact insight into the individual's precise *knowledge* of costs, this is furnished with respect to his *awareness* of costs (and its role in modal choice) which is, however, quite sufficient for our purposes - the examination of the relevance of "economized" model assumptions.

For example, a good half of the car users surveyed were unable to supply an answer to the question of what their car costs them per kilometre; a similarly large proportion had never even considered what costs were incurred in driving their car to work.

The figures supplied by the rest of the drivers surveyed are systematically too low; the supposition that by no means all of the relevant cost variables had been taken into account only partially explains this phenomenon. It can be directly concluded from this that the real costs can only influence modal choice of transport in very rare cases, or - in other words - there is no proof of a cost-utility decision on the factor travelling costs.

This statement gains considerable support when we include the knowledge of the costs of the (real) alternative of public transport. Only about half of the car users surveyed could accurately state the price of at least one type of fare; only one in ten knew the costs of weekly and monthly tickets, which are relevant to commuter journeys. A similar picture results from the investigation of public transport users (who, per random sample definition, could also use a car if they wished): on an average they knew the costs of at least two of the four possible types of fare in public transport, but only one in four could state the per kilometre cost of his own car. This proportion increases in the case of the question of the real cost of a journey by private car *to work*. Analogous to the car users, about every second public transport user supplied a cost estimate, but - in contrast to the car users this information shows a considerable overestimation of the costs actually incurred. This means that an economic functional relations - assumed in many models - can not be proved, and also that the real awareness of the individual is so emotionally and irrationally distorted that it counteracts the considerations assumed in the models.

Estimation of travelling times

Quite similar results are obtained in the subjective estimation of real travelling times: the subjectively estimated travelling times tend rather to express justification for the chosen mode of transport than to indicate that preference has been given to one mode of transport on the basis of rational consideration of alternatives. For example, car users systematically underestimate the actual travelling time by car and systematically overestimate the times of alternative journeys by public transport; the share of estimates that are approximately correct is remarkably low, accounting for only one third; about every seventh car user has given no thought whatsoever to the real time he takes to drive to work. The information supplied by public transport users is just as remarkable: they overestimated the travelling time of their "own" mode of transport by a good quarter - although they use it daily.

These results illustrate quite vividly that the individual transport user can not be credited with making rational decisions based in time and cost considerations. The variables control individual behaviour at the most indirectly and by no means always rationally - which is naturally specially important when designing planning measures.

Accordingly, quite obsolete results can be expected if,

for instance, information on travelling times is expressed in terms of cost variables, as done in many cost-utility studies. Since this involves systematic, non-random false estimates, accumulations of errors result.

"Complete" information

With this, we have touched upon a further important prerequisite of economic models, one which partly proves to be an unwarranted assumption: the assumption that the individual is fully informed about the concrete system of his environment.

In the investigations referred to above, we stated that only those car users were surveyed, who could also travel to work - in comparable time - by means of public transport. Just under half of these car users were totally unaware or very scarcely informed of this possibility. Frequently, car users are as unaware of routes as of stops, and in many cases there is even a total ignorance of public transport connections which are more convenient with respect to time than the journey by car. This means, however, that in the few cases in which time/cost considerations are taken into account it can by no means be assumed that this is done on the bases of the variables offered by the objective environment; on the contrary, this environment is first filtered through the subjective information - a process which in any case would have to be accounted for in a corresponding model approach.

Influence factors relevant to behaviour

This observation, however, takes us back to the beginning of our considerations, back to the requirement that observed behaviour has to be explained first before it is represented in model form and prognosticated.

This step becomes possible when a theoretical concept and a set of methods are available for its empirical realization. Both prerequisites will be discussed in greater detail in the following sections. Nevertheless, we should like to refer in advance to the finding "explanation of modal choice in commuter traffic", in this section on "Empirical findings", for two reasons. Firstly, it can be shown that it is actually possible to establish empirical explanations for behaviour. On the other hand, an impressive demonstration can be given of how many well-known transport behaviour models (necessarily) ignore simple and perceptive relations and what possibilities of explanation and prognosis they lose in doing so.

If we consider the above mentioned representative survey of households in urban areas, the following picture is obtained: (see page 224).

It is obvious that this is still a rough classification which could be refined further, but it is equally evident that it offers explanations which are convincing and actually determine human behaviour. The key to these explanations is evidently the respective individual situation on the basis of which behavioural choice is made. This conceptual approach will be taken up in the next section and considered in greater depth on the basis of several sociological considerations.

SOCIOLOGICAL DIGRESSION

In the historical development of sociology we find many attempts to comprehend the "social complex society" theoretically as a whole. Such attempts, made, for example, in the theories of functionalism, or - more generally - in the systems approach, are characterized by the fact that their propositions have to be made in a kind of generality that is no longer commensurate with individual subsystems.

This theoretical direction has been significantly enriched by Herbert Spencer, who defined modern society as a social organism in analogy to biological systems. This strictly "biological" thinking was soon abandoned, but not the system thinking per se [1]), which among other aspects returns in various theories about roles and role behaviour in refined form. Parsons' structural-functional theory of society must be placed in this category, which endeavored to establish a logically integrated theoretical system of principles, concepts and laws in order to be able to describe and explain the functional connections of certain segments of society with reference to empirical elements.

Even though these system theories were improved and refined in many respects, they were able only to deal with overall problems of the whole, but could not make any detailed statements concerning its parts [5]. But the whole is different from the sum of its parts, as the ancient philosophers already told us.

Other parallel theories in sociology defined behaviour as the resultant of the entire individual habitat. They are based on philosophers like Georg Simmel, who understood the individual as an intersection of overlapping circles, whose spheres of influence determine his behaviour and thinking.

The continuation of this line of thinking [6] is characterized by the effort not to deduce social relationships from a model of the entire society (regardless of the nature of this model), but to conclude quasi inductively from individual situations to typical behaviour patterns. The total social structure of society is then the result of a generalisation of individual behaviour.

By interpreting each specific individual as an actor in a specific situation, it is possible - in contrast to system thinking styles - to consider also informal or formally not established processes.

On the other hand this approach requests to regard individual behaviour patterns only in the context with others and with the environment generating them. The situation in which the person finds himself, is defined as the entirety of the factors influencing his behavioural reaction.

This entirety is determined first of all by variables of the material environment and the overall social situation, but also by factors determining the individual himself. Accordingly, "the overall situation always contains more or less subjective factors, and the behaviour reaction can therefore only be studied in the general context, i.e. both the existing situation (as it can be objectively examined), as well as the situation as it is regarded by the person concerned, must be investigated" [7].

From this theoretical viewpoint the real causes for human behaviour with their specific individual complexity and also the changes in behaviour can be estimated. They take place whenever the parameters determining the individual situation are replaced by new ones.

This idea has been even further differentiated by the authors cited above. Without stepping into greater details on these (in some cases important) refinements here, three essential advantages - particularly with respect to its transfer to planning models - remain to be noted:

1. It proceeds from a simplified cause-effect relationship and asks: in what situations do individuals react with which behaviour?
2. It designates the variables of behaviour by studying behaviour patterns in various situations.
3. It demonstrates the necessity of comparison groups in order to be able to measure the significance of single parameters by comparing the behaviour of different individuals in varying situations.

This means that future model constructions must get away from thinking in terms of aggregates, because otherwise important individually oriented parameters of the decision process will be neglected in favor of the theoretical assumptions constituting the specific system concerned.

A SOCIOLOGICALLY-ORIENTATED APPROACH TO EXPLANATION OF MODAL CHOICE BEHAVIOUR

An attempt is made in this section to incorporate the basic concept of thinking described above in a model of behaviour in modal choice of transport. There can be no question at present of obtaining an absolutely flawless, directly applicable model. Before a final formulation is possible, a series of fundamental investigations are still necessary, which partly have already got underway. There are several results available, however, which not only serve to illustrate the path taken here but can also provide evidence for the practicability of the approach.

As we have shown, the prerequisite for this type of model is a thorough knowledge of the individual situation which leads to the respective mode of behaviour.

The example treated here - modal choice between private car and public transport in commuter traffic - has already indicated that a situation of option can be essentially determined with three basic dimensions:
- supply of transportation alternatives
- socio-demographic determinants
- subjective attitudes

The individual situation of option is defined by various factors from these basic dimensions according to their form and combination. Under supply of transportation alternatives we understand both the availability of public transport (for travel from home to work) and individual transport facilities (possession of driving licence and car).

On the other hand, the socio-demographic determinants - represented here by so-called material constraints - frequently limit an objectively existent situation of option. Examples of material constraints for the use of private car for journeys to work are:
- the necessity of using the private car at work; in this case, it is the car that is "transported" to the place of work and not the driver. The most striking examples are persons who need their car as a "tool of their trade", or who are not tied to one particular place of work;
- irregular working hours at the place of work which either prevent or make use of public transport difficult; this applies in particular to weekend, night and shift workers;
- The necessity of performing extra activities at work or on the journey to and from work; this is typical for households located in an area with a lock of infrastructural facilities, as well as for gainfully employed persons who for family reasons are obliged to reduce the hours spent away from home to a minimum;
- the need to take along additional members of the family on the way to and from work, in particular when children are driven to schools or to kindergartens and adult members of the family to their places of work;
- health reasons, especially physical disabilities which make use of public transport very difficult or impossible.

The two main material constraints making for the use of public transport are:
- the (in principle available) family car is already being used by other members of the family;
- there are no suitable parking facilities at the place of work [2].

It is obvious that these material constraints are not all of the same importance. "Hard" material constraints which are impossible or extremely difficult to evade are to be distinguished from "soft" material constraints which allow freedom of action to be gained by making new arrangements within the household. Attempts are currently being made to incorporate such a differentiation

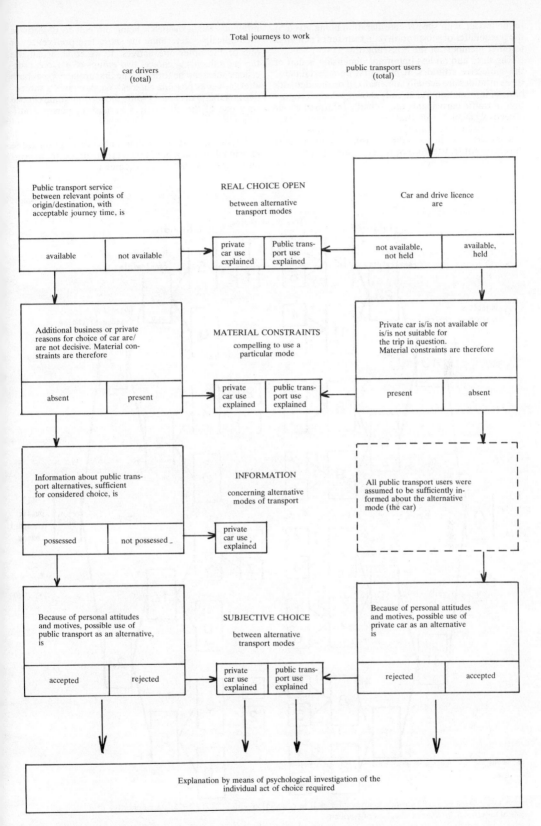

Figure 1 - Explanation of modal choice by reference to individual situations of option

in the model, with special consideration being given to the possibilities of substitution (e.g. transfer of activities to other members of the household).

The third and no less important dimension is that of the subjective attitudes. It must first be ascertained if these attitudes are actually materialized on an adequate basis of information. As already shown, a large proportion of traffic participants are so badly informed about objectively available alternatives that a subjective situation of choice does not exist for these individuals.

Knowledge of the available transport alternatives is thus a constituent feature of the situation of option. A role is also played in this dimension of course by the influence factors which - being difficult to objectivize methodically - determine the subjective preference for one or the other alternatives. If we combine all the factors influencing choice, two groups of persons exercising choice can be formed. The first group regards both alternatives as possible choices - i.e. perceives a subjective possibility of choice - while the second would choose only one of the alternatives because of personal attitudes.

To sum up, this means that for the description of the individual situation of option it is thus necessary to establish for every individual whether it

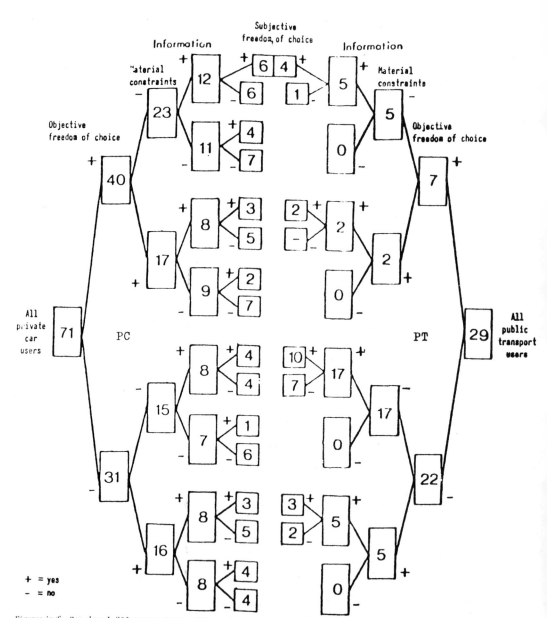

Figures in %. Based on 1.200 answers to an opinion poll in connection with KONTIV 1975. Representative of heads of households in urbanised regions of Germany.

Figure 2 - Model of situations of modal choice: quantitative form

228

- has an objective possibility of choice,
- is subject to material constraints,
- is adequately informed about the objectively available alternatives, and
- considers all alternatives to be subjective possibilities of choice or not.

Figure 1 represents this system for modal choice between private car and public transport in diagrammatic form.

This system was initially conceived as an explanatory model for the genesis of modal split - modal split being considered as the result of decisions taken in the various individual situations of option.

In the combination of the situation of option defined by objective and subjective constraints, two partial structures - mirror images of each other - emerge for car drivers and users of public transport which enable every individual decision to be assigned to the corresponding situation of option. This presupposes, however, that the corresponding objective (e.g. transportation facilities, travel times, household structure) and subjective (amount of information, personal preferences) parameters have been individually surveyed using adequate methods.

Figure 1 clearly shows that causal explanations for the modal choice of certain individuals can already be detected in every stage of the decision making process: situative conditions act as a constraint for the use of a specific mode of transport. The individuals concerned are consequently no longer responsive to planning measures which do not aim at these limiting conditions exactly. For instance, reductions of fares or travelling times in public transport are irrelevant for those individuals who don't have any public transport facilities on their origin/destination route, or who are dependent on the use of their car at work due to professional material constraints.

On the other hand, it now can be determined which individuals gain new options if certain planning measures take place. Then it is possible to conclude by analogy from persons already having been in such a situation of option to the changes of behaviour of those people, who are new in this situation.

This is an important step towards the formation of a policy-sensitive model, and which in our view fulfils an essential requirement in such models, namely easy application and maximum clarity.

In Figure 2 the model approach is drawn up in quantitative form on the basis of the results obtained from the study of commuter traffic mentioned above. Each individual person was analysed in his respective situation and assigned to a group so that the groups affected by specific measures, for example, can be easily identified.

Obviously, this is a simplified conputation; as yet only parts of the work have been carried out on an exact formulation, which is conceivable in a number of ways. Moreover, it will be necessary to make a closer examination of differentiations, feedback and dependencies in the system of the model planes.

What can be shown, however, is not a finished prognosis model but a fundamental mode of thinking. this mode of thinking finds expression, for instance, in the fact that anticipated changes in behaviour are not read off a function for aggregates but the actual process of decision is "recreated" by addition of each of the individual changes in behaviour. This is possible because the model preserves the homogeneity of the individuals and takes account of the scope of action determined by formal and informal, objective and subjective factors. A conceptual approach of this type is consistent with the sociological considerations outlined. It is limited merely by the possibilities of acquiring sufficient empirical data.

METHODICAL INSTRUMENTS OF EMPIRICAL SOCIAL SCIENCE

Empirical data requirements

Models which are orientated to individual behaviour and the individual situation impose other demands on the respective initial data and in consequence on the methods of empirical social research as usual in the transportation field.

Contrary to the general view, a number of these requirements can be fulfilled if the empirical survey methods are conceived to be an integral component of a scientific discipline (sociology) in just the same way as chemical experiments are in chemistry.

These considerations, however, must focus on the individual as an indispensable source of data. Accordingly, it is primarily a question of employing survey instruments that are attuned to the individual.

The set of instruments, therefore, should not be determined predominantly by the technical demands - whatever form they might take - of a theoretical-formalistic mechanism of reproduction of reality; empirical survey methods should be determined by research conceptions and not vice-versa.

It should be quiet clear that in a scientific discipline as young as empirical social science by no means every methodical possibility has been developed and tested. Accordingly, the development of suitable models in transport research will also be determined by a readiness to engage in basic empirical research. Transport research scientists, who constantly employ empirical data, could perform a decisive initiating function in this context.

Two fundamental aspects should be considered when discussing methods:

- the problem concerned
- the methodical procedure

The first aspect involves the question whether - proceeding from the consideration that an "all-embracing" survey method does not exist - the respective procedure is adequate for the problem to be investigated. The second aspect concerns the practical realization within the process of research, which is generally discussed under the concepts of validity, reliability and objectivity.

As a rule, discussions of method tend to focus on instrumental questions, i.e. they are orientated to the second aspect. It is, however, of fundamental importance for the survey method to be properly orientated to the problem concerned, as this simple consideration shows: According to the comments in the previous sections, a given mode of behaviour is determined by a quite specific constellation of variables: the respective individual situation. This situation is experienced subjectively by an individual and constrains the freedom of action and decisionmaking sequences. An empirical determination of this situation thus requires - in simplified terms - data relating to the material environment, the demographic structure of the individual and his household, and subjective attitudes and evaluations - which are determined by society and its reference groups, as well as by the individual personality structure.

Generally, it is inconceivable that all these data can be acquired via a single empirical measurement. It is still more inconceivable, however, that a demographic enquiry into these data can supply an exact picture of all these variables, for the demographic enquiry serves to determine subjective opinions. In our example it determines, at the most, the individually experienced but not the actually existing situation.

This is not to say that it would not be important to determine this subjective description of the situation, but it should only be taken as one form of information among several others; otherwise, a realistic analysis is not possible.

As a rule, therefore, a problem-orientated empirical procedure will not manage without different, strictly co-ordinated, survey stages. It must always be borne in mind that not all the required data can be directly surveyed.

In the case in question, it is certainly not (yet) possible to comprehensively measure the actual cause of behaviour - the individual decision. Accordingly, it is necessary to survey as accurately as possible the actual behaviour as the direct result of individual decision, and to put these data in the original context of the respective individual situation.

In addition to a survey of the individual behaviour, it is necessary to acquire
— "secondary statistical" data on the infrastructural environment
— demographic data of the most diverse type
— dimensions of subjective attitudes.

Methodical problems arise here mainly with respect to the measurement of the individual behaviour and the dimensions of subjective attitude. While the importance of the second sphere is often overestimated - as shown such variables only take effect in a small section of the individuals - the problems involved in the first are often underrated.

As we are unable to do more than just touch on a few important problems here, we shall report briefly on our efforts to develop better instruments for measuring individual behaviour. Our work is based on many years of basic research, which will published in detail elsewhere.

Reflections on the measurement of transportation behaviour

No scientific measuring procedure is able to reproduce an absolutely true picture of reality. This applies in particular to empirical social research, above all because it is frequently dependent on verbal information from individuals surveyed and thus fully exposed to the problem of subjective distortion.

It is mainly the question, therefore, to reduce inaccuracies in measurement as far as possible. This means that in the case in hand it is necessary to make the target group into "recorders" and not into "reporters" of their behaviour. It can be proved, namely, that behaviour patterns described in an interview situation partly deviate quite substantially from reality, whereas the informations recorded in diary form possess a relatively high degree of accuracy.

Some of the most important reasons for this are:
— The enquiry into behaviour is always an inquiry into the subjective appraisal of behaviour, an effect which can be minimized in the case of diary usage.
— The survey situation "interview" creates special situative factors which influence the responses. The persons being interviewed report - unconsciously (memory problems) and consciously (a "stranger" vis-à-vis the interviewer) - significantly less activities (ca. 10% - 15%) than they are willing to record in diaries.
— The interviewer is not the "soulless being" he often attemps to be, but an elementary component of the act of communication. This influence is considerable and has been proved in a large number of - largely social-psychological - experiments.

If, in line with these considerations, we decide in favour of a written survey we can expect to encounter two frequently mentioned difficulties:
— The problem of observation of answering instructions
— The problem of the readiness to answer

Today it can be shown in both cases that the misgivings often expressed in the relevant technical literature are unfounded or quite false.

For instance, the advantages of the written survey for the target persons are so considerable (e.g. choice of the most convenient time for completing the questionnaire) that the instructions for filling in are mostly kept concise. Two examples serve to illustrate this:
— In a survey addressed to only one *specific* person in each of the households covered, this instruction was correctly observed in over 90% of the cases.
— Set day surveys were also filled in correctly on the day specified in over 90% of the cases.

In both cases, the results would more than do justice to a (verbal) interview survey.

The one-sided orientation of the relevant literature is even more obvious with respect to the problem of readiness to answer. Whereas in the social sciences one reckons with a rate of return of 30-40% in written surveys, and while some transport research scientists recommend to be satisfied at a rate of 25%, we regularly obtain a return between 70% und 80% (with a current total of ca. 300.000 cases!). These figures are higher than those generally obtained in comparable verbal surveys. This also indicates that adaquate orientation of the survey methods to the problem involved is appreciated by the target group of persons.

This is, however, only possible - and we emphasize this - if the measuring instrument, the questionnaire, is designed with the utmost skill. This brings us to an aspect of survey activity which is still badly neglected today. One must bear in mind that pure variations in the questionnaire design (with identical survey topic) can cause differences in returns of up to 40%, and different questionnaire lay-outs can double the number of wrong entries. This demonstrates the extent to which the quality of empirical research depends on the insight that questionnaires are scientific measuring instruments, and as such can only be properly used by trained and experienced scientists.

However, since properly filled in questionnaires and above all high returns can only be achieved by extensive flanking measures, one is often temptect in an effort to save costs to accept lower - but in comparison still high - returns. Such considerations are just as irresponsible as they are dangerous. They forget for instance, that the random sample theory mostly applied in empirical research projects is only valid when information is actually available on every selected individual.

The fact that this requirement is practically never fulfilled should not, however, lead to an uncritical attitude towards the question of returns. It can be proved that returns, particularly under the 50% mark, often furnish such distorted results that it would actually be better to dispense with such data.

At the same time, considerations of the non-response problem are frequently only orientated to data relating to demographic structure. It can be shown, however, that transportation mobility in particular is generally falsely reproduced by incomplete returns even when the demographic structure, which can be checked against secondary statistics, is "correct". Thus, according to our current findings, we must still reckon with an excessive mobility of ca. 3% with a return of ca. 75% and *after* correction of demographic distortions (!). In cases of lower returns these distortions arise in the region of 10% or above, a circumstance which can seriously mislead a planning project.

A number of experimental investigations is still needed in order to bring the development of suitable instruments in this sector to a provisional conclusion. It has been demonstrated particularly in this field, however, that social research - conducted according to scientific rules - is fully capable of keeping up with the theoretical - conceptual development.

OUTSTANDING PROBLEMS AND RECENT RESEARCH APPROACHES TO SOLVE THEM

A different situation prevails in the field of empirical measurement of dimensions of subjective attitudes. Public opinion research has just set off on a number of wrong tracks, taken on the basis of - hitherto nonprovable - assumptions of a direct relation between opinions and behaviour.

Accordingly, it is also necessary to search for new possibilities and paths in this field, which is only being undertaken in a few isolated cases.

The basic objective here is to make an area of subjective attitudes accessible to measurement which is actually relevant for concrete behaviour.

Promising in this connection appear to be procedures that simulate specific situations which are as real as possible together with the individual. Their importance - and this can not be emphasized enough - does not lie in the production of simulated results which can be directly used for prognosis, however, but in the possibility of discovering mechanisms and attitudes in the simulated situation which actually determine the respective behaviour.

An important work in this field seems to be the "Household Activity Travel Simulator" (HATS) developed by Jones and Dix, which comes close to meeting the requirements needed in a realistic model as laid down by Heggie. [8] Starting from the actual household situation, the procedure acts out changes in the concrete system of the environment primarily with respect to their effects on the time budget of all the household members.

We are currently pursuing a similar approach using a "Grandma-game" which we developed to discover the reactions to restrictions imposed on a household's financial resources. The game starts with an allocation of the household's total income to 18 different budget items. By means of a step-by-step reduction of the total income the members of the household are forced to reconsider and to redistribute their individual items of spending.

This leads to intensive discussion among the participants, which occasionally results in the development of completely new activity patterns on the part of certain household members. The reactions extend from the simple forgoing of weekend excursions, selling the car, to persons hitherto unemployed taking on extra work, and to a change of dwelling place or job. A game leader draws up a detailed record of the proceedings and tapes them for subsequent evaluation.

The records, and the detailed written and verbal surveys which we carried out with the game leaders at the end of a first stage of one hundred household games, show that the participants take the proceedings quite seriously. In some cases, the household members discuss their budget down to the last penny, and come to a decision only after long and careful consideration. It was again conspicuous that a substantial number of households initially possessed no information whatsoever on how the monthly income was allocated to the individual budget items. This fact often created an additional game motivation - the persons concerned now wanted "to find out exactly what was going on themselves".

No individual result can be passed on at the moment as the final evaluations have not been concluded. It seems certain, however that this instrument can be used to obtain extensive information on attitudes and opinions relevant for behaviour, within the context of defined situations.

We must emphasize again, however, that we do not intend to use the results of the games for direct prognoses of modes of behaviour resulting from changes in the household budget. In this respect, we differ from the Oxford group around Heggie, who consider it possible and meaningful to replace comprehensive survey by game simulations in a relatively small group of households.

The experimental method described here is only one example of how to acquire "difficult" data. The approach of a situation-orientated behaviour analysis can also be successfully adapted for application in other fields; for example, for the analysis of migration processes or for user behaviour with respect to infrastructural facilities in the broadest sense of the term. Ivestigations have already started or are scheduled to be carried out in this field of research. Once the basic structure of these processes has been recognized, an attempt can be made to describe them and make them computable by means of mathematical-statistical methods. At this stage, the use of formal methods is quite justified.

REFERENCES

[1] Baron, P.: **Einheitliche Begriffsbestimmungen im Verkehrswesen,** Internationales Verkehrswesen (28) 1977, 1, p. 35

[2] Heggie, I. E.: **Putting Behaviour into Behaviour Models of Travel Choice,** p. 2, University of Oxford, Transport Studies Unit, Working Paper No. 22, 1977

[3] Kutter, E.: **Demografische Determinanten städtischen Personenverkehrs - Veröffentlichung des Instituts für Stadtbauwesen,** TU Braunschweig, Braunschweig 1972

[4] Höttler, R.: **Soziologische Verkehrstypologie,** Thesis, TU Berlin, Berlin 1975

[5] See Bühl, W. L.: **Verstehende Soziologie;** München 1972, and Bühl, W. L.: Reduktionismus; München 1973

[6] See on this, for example, the works of Peter L. Berger, Thomas Luckmann, George H. Mead, William F. Ogburn, William J. Thomas.

[7] Thomas, W. L.: **Person und Sozialverhalten;** Neuwied/Berlin 1965; p. 114

[8] Heggie, I. G.: **Putting Behaviour into Behavioural Models of Travel Choice** p. 28/29. University of Oxford, Transport Studies Unit, Working Paper No. 22; 1977

FOOTNOTES

1. Both surveys covered target groups which were in a real situation of option, i.e. who could use a car for the journey to work as well as public transport.

2. In view of unfavourable parking facilities at the place of work, use of public transport is also dependent on socio-demographic variables (e.g. no senior position in firm, otherwise right to parking place or rented space in a multi-storey car park).

Transport demand models and policy
A Comparative Analysis

URI ZOHAR

Faculty of Administrative Studies, York University, Toronto

KONRAD W. STUDNICKI-GIZBERT

Canadian Transport Commission, Ottawa

GOALS, OBJECTIVES AND POLICY INSTRUMENTS

A necessary condition for a policy proposition to be valid is the prevalence of consistency among goals, objectives and policy instruments.[1] The intent of this paper, therefore, is to suggest a rational sequence of steps in structuring a set of policy guidelines consistent with a macro framework from which forecasts are derived. Since the transportation sector is a part of such macro framework, it becomes immediately obvious that any given forecast and/or policy proposition must be consistent with the overall structure and objectives of the economy. This means that a sectoral analysis is considered valid, if and only if, it is derived from a consistent macro structure. A case in point is the sequence and the substance of a Strategic Planning Guidelines[2] for the transport sector.

The first step in formulating such document is to explicitly state an attainable choice-set of socio economic goals and objectives, which are relevant to transport planning. Transportation infrastructure is indeed the "nervous-centre" of any market economy, and thus, it contributes to and affected by (directly and indirectly), most of society's goals and objectives. More specifically, goals relating to an increase in society's welfare through:

a. a resource and product mobility
b. income distribution and transfers
c. urban and rural development
d. increased capacity of market diversification
e. technological applications to industrial development resulting in relocation of plant and markets;

are predicated on an existence of a well developed transport and communications infrastructure. It is just natural, therefore, that a cornerstone of the Document would be a consistent set of the economy's goals and objectives from which priorities are to be derived. Such a statement would constitute the first section of the Document, and as such, should set the "ground-rules" for the entire subsequent parts of it. Once the Document is ordered in such a way it lends itself to the derivation of operational policy instructions and instruments at the Ministerial level.

Once a set of national goals is established on the federal level, a corresponding subset of objectives is derived from it. Objectives thus, are operational statements designed to aid the attainment of the national goals. It is interesting to note that an objective defined by the Federal Government becomes immediately a goal to be attained by a particular ministry. Such an objective thus becomes a *policy directive* in an operational sense for the respective ministry. Policy instructions are then derived by the Ministry, and the proper instruments are assigned for the execution of these policy instructions.

The assignment of policy instruments motivates a multi-stage process of monitoring re-examination and reconciliation within the operating ministry. First comes the function of monitoring on-going programs concurrently with bottlenecks which arise within the ministry and relating them to general goals and objectives. Resolution of this stage leads to a completion of the Planning Document draft with a high probability of consistency between goals and objectives, and possibly minimal operational conflicts between the on-going set of programs and the proposed undertakings. The re-examination stage comes next. This stage consists of preliminary budget submission which inevitably presents the planners with a new series of trade-offs and conflicts of choice. Specific analyses and forecasts on the commodity level are required at this stage in order to fully comprehend all probable technical and financial conflicts. A final reconciliation stage occurs at the budget level, where policy directives "from above" (translated into operational departamental objectives) *plus* the effects of monitoring current problems, are formulated as a set of programs with price-tags attached for the final review and approval of the cabinet, via the Treasury Board.

Such multi-stage process results in an approved set of programs, and a final draft of the Planning Document is then considered as a Plan-of-Operation for the operating ministry. The time horizon of the Document determines how detailed such Plan-of-Operation would be, for operationality must be concurrent with budget allocation decisions.

For the sake of clarity and for illustrative purposes, let us develop a logical chain from the national goal level down to the level of Transport Ministry's relevant instruments. Suppose a stated national goal is an improved income distribution in the country, through increased employment. The Federal Government objectives become immediately:

a) to increase income of the poor by x% during the next five years converging gradually to the long run income distribution goal.

b) increase mobility of people and economic activities within and across regions in order to maximize employment opportunities.

Government's instruments to increase income distribution and to induce industrial development and relocation, would be derived from fiscal and monetary policies.

The Federal Government objective (b) becomes however, a proper given goal for its Transport Ministry. It views its derived objective as the removal of infrastructure obstacles due to locational factors. Policy instructions to the Transport Ministry might include:

a) improvement of services to relatively poor regions;

b) an instruction to pursue with shared road programs subject to budget limitations;

c) develop subsidy or grant aid program to facilitate movements of commodities between given origins and destinations.

The Ministry might select the following instruments to execute its policy instructions:

a) monitoring incidents of user charges to examine efficiency vs. income distribution effects

b) monitoring incidents of subsidies

c) allocation of investment programs

Once a rigorours flow from goals to policy instruments is established, we can rationalize the contribution of any given instrument towards an attainment of an upper level objective and goal. Summing up the total effect (results) of the instruments on an assigned goal, we are in a position to assess the contribution of the Ministry to the attainment of national goals and objectives.

Similarly, when we wish to forecast (or estimate) the parameters of a given sector, say transportation, they must be derived from a consistent macro structure or model. In the event that the above procedure is not rigorously thought through there exists a high probability of overlapping and/or contradictory objectives, with some that are irrelevant insofar as they are not capable of generating objectives and policy measures for which policy instruments exist. The role of economic forecast is that one of the inputs — although an important one to the overall planning process. The relevant questions which the forecasting activities would answer are:

a) What is the likely state of the general economic environment which affects the short term trade-offs between long term objectives, and the ability of a department to advance towards the objectives and thus set concrete targets?

b) What are the likely developments of specific transport demands to be dealt with by specific programs?

Clearly, macro-economic forecasts are the relevant tool for answering the first set of questions; specific demand forecasts both at the sectoral (i.e. transportation) level and specific transport demand level require transport sector forecasting model further disaggregated into specific transport markets (i.e. commodity movements) forecasts.

Obviously, there must be internally consistent and sectoral or market forecasts must be derived from a consistent macro-model. If a direct linkage between the sectoral and market (commodity) forecasts and a general macro-model does not exist (as in the case at present), a formal linkage between the macro-model and transport model must be developed preserving the consistency of the assumptions of the macro-model. It should be noted, however, that in reality this ideal state of heirarchial modeling is yet to be attained. That is, in order to construct a transport planning model fully consistent with all other sectors of the economy and the variables within these sectors; all of which are consistent with a national macro model, we must have a set of models gradually disaggregated from a national level to a regional level down to the commodity level. Specifically, this means that as long as the national macro model (in our case CANDIDE) does not contain sub-systems of adequate and consistent regional and commodity disaggregations, we ought to ling our transport model to proxy variables of CANDIDE and rely on some market forecasts where such proxy variables do not exist. Thise introduces a serious obstacle to the model builder, for the consistency of the transport model with the main aggregates of the economy must be maintained at all times. The next sections will deal with the rationale of the development, the use and problems inherent in the employment of the forecasting work insofar as it affects the planning activity.

ECONOMIC INPUTS TO THE PLANNING DOCUMENT

This section entertains a central problem confronting planners in the preparation of the Document. Such a problem is the choice of the most desirable forecasting model, from which results are likely to be considered reliable as inputs to the Document. Since the purpose of this paper is not purely theoretical, we would like the reader to accept a priori that the formulation and the estimation of a valid economic model is based upon sound economic and statistical theories respectively.

Historically, the development of the theory of quantitative economic policy laid down by Jan Tinbergen [1] led to the formulation of the first large-scale economic models[3]. These developments provide the foundations for the application of the theory to practical policy making. The development of these models received its principal impetus in the "Keynesian revolution" in economics during the post-war years. The Keynesians focused on the study of the dynamics of the economic system, mainly from the short-term point of view. Although these models have found important uses in the area of short-term economic forecasting, detailed investigation of the structural characteristics of the economic system has also provided us with sophisticated models for use in quantitative economic policy. Three ancillary developments have helped in the construction of large and increasingly sophisticated models of the economy. First, the development of national income statistics and the collection of many other types of economic data, have provided the raw material for macro models. Second, estimation methods developed earlier, most for application to experimental data, have been adapted and refined to deal with more complex and interdependent data in the social sciences and particularly in economics. Third, the computational problems of dealing with large interdependent systems have been facilitated by the rapid development of computers and computer programs.

The type of model that results from the theoretical specification of the equations has important implications for both the ease of estimation and the efficiency of the parameter estimates to predict and form a policy. The benefit from using forecasting model for planning purposes is that it provides a coherent view of the economic environment, and it is capable of tracing changes in the economy during the forecasting period; while maintaining relative consistency among the various elements of the economy. The preceding exposition leads us now to consider the suitable type of model from which results may be obtained for the Planning Document.

In general, there are three different types of models all of which generate quantitative information as inputs to a planning Document. It is thus vital to differentiate among them and to briefly assess their usefulness in terms of the quality of their output.

Purely Projection Models

Purely projection models are the "curve-fitting" type models. They generally contain a set of relationships which have "bound together" different variables. The validity of the specification of such models is no more and no less than that of any linear transformation of the same. In practice such models may be useful for predicting but for obvious reaons they are not a useful tool for economic policy making. The specification in this case does not necessarily indicate the direction of causation, nor the direction of influence among the variables. The dominant assertion in such models is merely a proposition of functional relationship among variables which seem to correlate with one another. More often than not, the variables which are repeatedly seen in such models as independent variables are Gross National Product, Population series and Time; all of which appear to be highly correlated with a continuously increasing dependent variable. It is obvious that we strongly advise planners to avoid the use of results from purely projective model (i.e. time trend forecasts) as reliable inputs to Planning Document. It would obviously lead to an inconsistent set of projections and consequently to misleading policy recommendations.

Structural Models

In structural or explanatory models the specification must be such as to indicate the direction of the influence among the variables. The model builder is asserting more than a merely functional relationship among the variables. Causality is therefore infered in terms of stimulus-response mechanisms; thus causal relationships are asymmetrical and irreversible except in special cases. In probability terms, the distribution of "y" is causally conditional on the realization "x", but not vice versa. In this definition of causality we have in mind the implication of control. Thus, "y" is causally dependent on "x" if the probability distribution of "y" can be controlled by specifying a value for "x". This explanation of causal-

ity is in somewhat pragmatic terms and based on controllability, and can be carried over with great effect into the interpretation of recursive systems. A recursive system may be written in the form:

$$B_{y'} + G_{z'} = u'$$

where

$$B = \begin{bmatrix} 1 & \beta_{12} & \beta_{13} & \cdots & \beta_{1g} \\ 0 & 1 & \beta_{23} & \cdots & \beta_{2g} \\ 0 & 0 & 1 & \cdots & \beta_{3g} \\ , & , & , & , & , \\ , & , & , & , & , \\ , & , & , & , & , \\ 0 & 0 & 0 & 0 & 1 & \beta_{g-1,g} \\ 0 & 0 & 0 & 0 & 0 & 1 \end{bmatrix}$$

$$G = \begin{bmatrix} \gamma_{11} & \gamma_{12} & \cdots & \gamma_{1k} \\ \gamma_{21} & \gamma_{22} & \cdots & \gamma_{2k} \\ \gamma_{31} & \gamma_{32} & \cdots & \gamma_{3k} \\ , & , & \cdots & , \\ , & , & \cdots & , \\ , & , & \cdots & , \\ \gamma_{g1} & \gamma_{g2} & \cdots & \gamma_{gk} \end{bmatrix}$$

and

$$y = (y_1, y_2, \ldots, y_g);$$
$$z = (z_1, z_2, \ldots, z_k);$$
$$u = (u_1, u_2, \ldots, u_g)$$

where the y's are causally dependent variables, the z's are the predetermined variables, and the u's are stochastic variables which are statistically independent. Each error u_j is assumed to be statistically independent of y_{j+1}, y_{j+2}, ..., y_g. The variables with unit coefficients are regarded as the resultant variables and the other y's and z's are regarded as causal variables. If it is actually possible to control a variable y_j through the manipulation of the other y's appearing in the jth equation, all that is necessary is to strike out this equation and reclassify y_j as a predetermined variable rather than as a dependent variable. The coefficients of y_j in the other equations remain the same as before.

This is the causal interpretation of the β's in the recursive system. Thus the values of the coefficients describe the influence of the causal variables on the resultant irrespective of whether the former are dependent or predetermined. No such causal interpretation is possible in the general interdependent system. In a certain sense, the vector z may be said to cause the vector y. This is immediately seen from the reduced form:

$$y' = -B^{-1}Gz' + B^{-1}u'$$

but the reduced form tells us nothing about the inter-relationships among the y's. For purposes of prediction this model is useful, since it enables us to predict the effect on y of controlled variations in the predetermined variables.

It may, however, be possible to partition y into subsets such that a conformal partitioning of B results in a block-triangular matrix:

$$y' = (y_1 \ y_2 \ y_3)'$$

and

$$B = \begin{bmatrix} B_{11} & B_{12} & B_{13} \\ 0 & B_{22} & B_{23} \\ 0 & 0 & B_{33} \end{bmatrix}$$

In this case, y_2 is caused by y_3, and y_1 is caused by y_2 and y_3 together. However, since the relations within the subsets are not recursive, no causal explanation within subsets is possible. This extension of causal systems by Herbert Simon [2] advances the mode of causal interpretation from macroeconomic models much further, because block-triangular structures are more likely to occur than purely triangular ones [3].

Since we are committed to examine the usefulness of structural models to the process of economic planning and in particular to transport planning, we ought to pursue the discussion one step further. It is clear at this point that a structural model is a representation of economic behavior which is based on economic theory, the outgrowth from such theory (or theories) is a set of hypothese to be tested statistically, from which conclusion of validity or nulification of such hypotheses are drawn. The most important element in structural models is that the dependent variables (y's), are always explained by economic variables (x's) and policy variables for we seek an explanation of causation rather than correlation, as projection model do. This leads us to an in-depth understanding of the interdependence relations in the economy, and only then we may decide whether or not to accept our forecasts as reliable input to policy planning.

Suppose a structural model has satisfied all the conditions posted above, how can we utilize it in transport planning? An answer to such question is relatively straigthforward, a proper forecast of transport variables while capturing the interrelationships of transportation with the rest of the economy, could be performed *only* with the aid of an integrated hierarchial set of structural models. We shall thus term such hierarchial structure as a Forecasting Framework or as the already coined name to it a Forecasting Program[4]. Such Forecasting Program should involve three major elements which must evolve one another.

1. A consistent analysis of the economy and a forecast of probable range of its development.

2. A detailed set of sectoral forecasts which carry significant impact on the use of transport services.

3. A forecast of transport demand generated by the change in sectors of particular significance to transport.

The problem now becomes how to order logically and effectively the available building blocks of forecasting to coincide planning steps, and this is the subject of our next section. In closing, we strongly endorse the use of structural models for policy planning for their results are defendable on more solid grounds than any other type of forecasting models.

Intuitive or Descriptive Models

These models are generally offered by "experts" in particular industry or of particular commodity. Results from such models are often a consequence of simple extrapolations, or based on "personal feelings" or experience. Since it is a partial judgement relating to specific sub-sector or commodity, consistency with the rest of the economy is practically impossible. We therefore suggest that only at the extreme case of unavailable data such approximations be considered as inputs for planning.

A Digression on The Nature of Structural Econometric Models [5]

Whether for use of forecasting or for policy analysis, the structural models we employ are complete systems of equations; that is, they consist of as many equations as there are endogenous variables. Each endogenous variable must occur in its current or unlagged form in at least one equation, and the structure specified by the complete set of structural equations must be uniquely identifiable. For this reason, alle the parameters of each structural equation must be uniquely dentified within the model specified; that is, the parameter must have the same value for all equivalent structures contained in the model. When all parameters have been identified, the model is ready for use.

The necessary condition for the identifiability of a structural equation within a given linear model of N-equation is that the number of endogenous variables excluded from the equation must be at least one less than the number of equations. If the coefficients of these excluded variables in the other N-1 equations of the system form at least one non-vanishing determinant of order N-1, we then have the necessary and sufficient conditions of identifiability. Given the conditions, the system of equations can be solved for the values of the endogenous variables in terms of the predetermined variables, both the exogenous and the lagged endogenous variables. The coefficients of these reduced-form equations are always identifiable, being parameters of the joint distribution of the observations. In certain cases an originally unidentifiable system can be rendered identifiable by the introduction of specific explanatory variables, but these must be specified on the basis of valid economic theories and not merely to apply available tools of statistical analysis. An example of this is Ezekiel's [4] estimation of an investment schedule by partitioning investment into four components and introducing as two new exogenous variables (1) the cyclical component of housing investment and (2) the exogenous component of net contribution from foreign trade and the government budget as explanatory variables.

MACRO ECONOMIC FORECASTS

Two points should be emphasized at the outset of this section:

a. Macro forecasts should not be used as inputs to the Document *unless* the underlying macro model from which these results were derived is completely consistent with the official set of National Income Acounting System, and it contains all the sectors of the economy[6].

b. One must keep in mind that a "super-model"

which is constructed to solve *all* economic planning problems does not exist: that is, each model is built with the intent to focus on a particular set of problems, i.e., international trade, monetary questions, growth and others.

An awareness of (a) and (b) leads us immediately to the most important "don't-do" rule for planners which is, "if you want your set of forecasts to be consistent and reliable ingredient of your Document, do not 'assemble' it from a number of different models". That is the macro model which in view of the users is most suitable for their purposes should be selected and only its results should be used as a basis for the macro analysis. The available macro models in Canada are CANDIDE, TRACE and the various versions of RDX. Each of these econometric models has certain strengths and weaknesses [5] with respect to its sensitiveness to economic changes, disaggregative abilities to sectors and industries, and its focal point of forecasts.

The Bank of Canada RDX, for instance, was designed to concentrate primarily on the monetary aspects of the economy. It would then be a mistake to use RDX for the analysis of the production sector of the economy.

CANDIDE and TRACE are basically structural models encompassing all the sectors of the economy. CANDIDE is the larger model of the two, and furthermore, it was designed to be disaggregated at most to industry forecast level. It is imperative therefore, to study carefully the advantages and the shortcomings of these (and possibly others to come) macro models prior to the use of their various forecasts.

Since CANDIDE is an intra-governmental project and it was designed to produced medium-term forecasts, it is reasonable to consider its results as *macro* inputs for the Planning Document. Some of the shortcomings of using CANDIDE to "drive" our Transport Forecasting Model (TFM) are discussed in the next section of this paper.

THE TRANSPORTATION FORECASTING PROGRAM

If one wishes to forecast the demand for transport on a commodity group level, the problem becomes one of model integration. This means a creation of a scheme where micro level could be forecasted while accounting for all possible macro impacts.

In order that TFM would constitute a continuous sub-structure of CANDIDE, there are at least three conditions which should be satisfied: a) there must exist a correspondence between those endogenous variables of CANDIDE which appear as exogenous ones in TFM; b) a correspondence between the degree of regional disaggregation in TFM and CANDIDE must exist if the values of the latter are to be used in the first; c) a broad commodity breakdown should exist in CANDIDE, as to provide a feasible link with TFM's more detailed commodity groups (by close proxy).

Condition a) is satisfied and implemented in TFM for the last two years. This, of course, provides the conditions to obtain sectorial forecasts of TFM while preserving the internal consistency of the economy's structure via CANDIDE.

Condition b) is not yet fulfielled for it calls for a proper regional disaggregation of CANDIDE.

Such a project is on its way for the last two years (CANDIDE R), and hopefully would be operational in the near future.

Ultimately, however, a transport model which intends to generate forecasts on a regional level should be "driven" by or linked with a proper regional development macro model. The benefits from such a link are far reaching and beyond the scope of this paper.

Condition c) is not yet satisfied for CANDIDE's disaggregation does not extend beyond the sectorial level.

A short description of the CTC[7] Transport Forecasting Program might illuminate some of the problems which are related to the attainment of such macro-micro continuum (i.e., a complete mapping from CANDIDE into TFM). It will also expose the reader to certain plausible "second-best" solutions which we have attempted in order to overcome inevitable gaps in such continuum.

By way of illustration let us pose the following set of questions that TFM as a sectorial model could satisfy.

1. To what extent there exists a correspondence between the demand for commodities and sectors (and thus derived demand for transportation), and the existing differential rates and patterns of regional growth in the country?

2. What are the major determinants of derived demand for transport within a given region, given variations in economic activities within the region?

3. What is the interactive nature of certain commodity groups and different transport modes? That is, the complementary, substitution or competetive relations which exist in the economy, and the implications derived from them to a realistic planning of infrastructure for different modes. Here elasticities and cross-elasticies of derived demand are instrumental to a better understanding of such planning problems.

4. To what extent transport cost policies be effective in increasing commodity flows among regions, and thus affect employment opportunities in such regions.

In order to relate to such questions (or problems) while showing the way in which we overcome some of the discontinuities between CANDIDE and TFM, we should point out how these two models interact in the actual process of estimation.

The structure of the CTC model fulfills the conditions put forth in the previous section of this paper. It is a structural forecasting model where causality in it is well defined. Moreover, it was built as a satellite model of CANDIDE in order to maintain at all times consistency with the economy's major aggregates.

The CTC model (TFM) is a multi-model medium term econometric model. It contains 23 groups of equations each of which represents a commodity group and designed to forecast its demand of freight flows across regions in Canada, as well as imports and exports to and from the rest of the world.

These forecasts are disaggregated into five domestic regions and to Canada's major trading countries, (each country represents a region). It thus becomes obvious that one TFM's focal points is to identify regional differences of commodity flows and to provide a structural explanation for it [6].

The basic structure of the model incorporates three modes, rail, marine and trucking, although the last mode has not yet been empirically tested due to data limitations.

The model is based on the assumption that flow of goods from a region of origin "i" to a region of destination "j" is determined by identifiable economic factors. Thus we explain commodity flows among regions, on the supply side, by excess production or "push" variables (EP_i), and on the demand side, by excess consumption or "pull" variables (EC_j). In addition to these economic variables we use transport rate as a "friction variable", for it either induces or impedes traffic flows along various links.

The general form of the model
$$T_{ij} = f(EP_i, EC_j, R_{ij}) \tag{1}$$
where

T_{ij} denotes transport flows in tons for a given commodity along the link, with origin i and destination j.

EP_i and EC_j represent vectors of "push" and "pull" variables respectively, and R_{ij} is a vector of rates along various links. For any given link with origin i and destination j we have
$$T_{ijt} = \alpha_{ij} + \beta_{ij}EP_{it} + \gamma_{ij}EC_{jt} + \delta_{ij}R_{ijt} \tag{2}$$
where the "push" and the "pull" variables are vectors and the R_{ij}(rate) is a variable.

For a given commodity, where all links are estimated simultaneously we have the following
$$T_{ijt} = \Sigma\Sigma \alpha_{ij} + \Sigma\Sigma \beta_{ij}EP_{it}$$
$$+ \Sigma\Sigma \gamma_{ij}EC_{jt} + \Sigma\Sigma \delta_{ij}R_{ijt} \tag{3}$$
which becomes our system of equations over all the transport links. In practice, such an unconstrained model is unmanageable due to (a) the number of parameters to be estimated in a combined time series — cross sectional analysis; and (b) due to the short time series available to allow adequate degrees of freedom in order to obtain stable estimates for each link in the system. We then constrain

$\beta_{ij} = \beta_i$ for all j

$\gamma_{ij} = \gamma_j$ for all i

$\delta_{ij} = \delta$ for all i and j

assuming that if our "pull", "push" and rate variable generate similar effects on both points of origin and destination, shippers and receivers of goods are indifferent with respect to their points of destination and origin respectively.

The system of equations (3) thus becomes
$$T_{ijt} = \Sigma \alpha_{ij} + EP_{it} + EC_{jt} + \delta R_{ijt} \tag{4}$$
which is far more manageable form to be estimated. The interdependence among the different modes is accomplished in the following way:

Let

TR_{ij} denote a rail link from i to j

θ denote "push" and "pull" variables

TR_{lk} denote interdependent rail movement

TM_{lk} denote interdependent marine movement

TT_{lk} denote interdependent truck movement

and l, k range over all modes.

We specify a rail movement from i to j to be
$$TR_{ij} = f(\theta, TR_{lk}, TM_{lk}, TT_{lk}) \tag{5}$$

A marine movement from i to j is
$$TM_{ij} = g(\theta, TR_{lk}, TM_{lk}, TT_{lk}) \tag{6}$$
and for truck movement from i to j we write
$$TT_{ij} = h(\theta, TR_{lk}, TM_{lk}, TT_{lk}) \tag{7}$$
Interdependent movements result generally in one of the following relations:

a. substitutes where $\dfrac{\delta L_1}{\delta L_2} < 0$

b. complements where $\dfrac{\delta L_1}{\delta L_2} > 0$ (8)

c. independent where $\dfrac{\delta L_1}{\delta L_2} = 0$

where L_1 and L_2 represent two links.

We thus introduce into our multi-model system the possibility of either complementarity or competitiveness. The final form of our Transport Model becomes now
$$T_{gijmt} = \alpha_{gijm} + \beta_{gim}EP_{git} + \gamma_{gim}EC_{git}$$
$$+ \delta_{gm}R_{gijmt} + \underset{i',j',m'}{\Sigma} \psi_{gijm} V_{gi'j'm't} \tag{9}$$

$g = 1, \ldots G; \quad i = 1, \ldots, I_g; \quad j = 1, \ldots, J_g;$
$m = 1, \ldots M_{gij}$

and the Σ is over all relevant complementary or competing origins i', destinations j', and modes m'.

We have $N = \overset{G}{\underset{g=1}{\Sigma}} \overset{I_g}{\underset{i=1}{\Sigma}} \overset{J_g}{\underset{j=1}{\Sigma}} M_{gij}$ equations in (9), where G is the total number of commodities, I_g is the total number of origins for commodity g, J_g is the total number of destinations for commodity g, M_{gij} is the total number of modes for commodity g, origin i and destination j.

To satisfy the constraints β, γ, δ we must pool data over different origins and destinations, and thus we work with time-series — cross-sectional data.

Most of TFM's exogenous variables, however, are endogenous in CANDIDE. It becomes obviously clear that the most logical linkage between TFM and CANDIDE would be through the integration of TFM exogenous variables.

What has been done for the last two years and seems to work well is the following procedure:

a. A scenario of the major aggregates which are relevant to TFM is selected and processed (run) through CANDIDE structure. The process leading to a selection of a given scenario involves a thorough examination of several 5-10 years optimal scenarios offered by CANDIDE. Such options vary considerably in the annual rates of growth of the economy's aggregates, ranging from very optimistic to pessimistic states of the economy in years to come.

b. The resulting forecasts of the selected scenario which are fully consistent with the set of national accounts, are being used as inputs into TFM. This simply means that instead of assigning arbitrarily linear rates of growth to TFM exogenous variables, they are being estimated endogenously in CANDIDE, accounting for domestic and international impacts on each and every variable. These variables become the "mo-vers" of the TFM model maintaining sectoral and macro consistency with final demand of the economy.

c. Each of these forecasted variables is then linked with TFM by the use of proper function which establishes a direct transformation of the variables from CANDIDE into TFM. Once such a link is executed TFM becomes a micro extention of a macro model (CANDIDE in this case) and this is wat internal consistency is all about.

So far we have satisfied a condition of a sound continuity between national and the sectorial models. The element of a "second-best" solution lies in the fact that not all TFM's exogenous variables have exact counterparts in CANDIDE. In such cases the transformation function uses the closest proxy variable in CANDIDE which seems to be highly correlated to that of TFM.

By completing the above task of consistency and having on our hands a causally integrated transport model for two modes (Rail and Marine), we can see that answers to question (3) can readily be generated by TFM for planning purposes.

In the absence of an operational regional model we have derived answers to question (1) by proxy. That is, our model contains a set of production, consumption and income variables (personal disposable income) of each of the model's regions. On the supply side production variables are generally used as a point of origin variables, where on the demand side consumption and income variables are used as a point of destination ones.

Assumptions regarding the expected rate of growth of such variables are then drawn by the Forecasting Team. Such assumptions are based on market judgements, interviews conducted by team member in the various governments, and Statistics Canada data analysis. Such assumptions are then imposed on TFM and simulated, without disturbing the overall model consistency.

So far the results are far better than other "ball-park guesses" available on the market, and for a simple reason. Our results are reflecting probable changes in all other variables of the model for the total is always maintained in accordance with the final demand figures. In short, none of the "independent forecasts" are as consistent as ours with the rest of the economy.

Our method will be much improved when a set of regional accounts coupled with regional economic models will be available to "drive" our transport demand model.

ALTERNATIVE APPROACHES TO TRANSPORT DEMAND MODELS (FREIGHT)

1. The essence of an economic model is the simplification of the complex reality. This does not imply that models cannot be highly complex — however, regardles how complex a model is, it still is simpler than the reality it attempts to represent. Every simplification produces its own set of distortions; every model can be attacked on the grounds that it "distorts the reality", but such a general criticism is meaningless. The sensible problem statement clearly is: does the model in question preserve the essential features of the reality which are of interest to the prospective user? This does not preclude the indirect,

potential usefulness of general explanatory models, where no specific user is considered. Such models may indeed provide the essential general overview of the pattern of relationships, which later have to be studied in greater depth from a specific point of view, for a specific purpose.

2. From that general statement, a general taxonomy of demand models according to objectives perceived can be derived; an approach to such general taxonomy of transport models is given below:
1. General transport demand models
   1. Analysis of generalized relationships in "qualitative" terms.
   2. Quantitative analysis of basic relationships affecting demand for transport.
2. Specific purpose transport demand models
   1. Transport demand models forming a part of transport (investments) planning models
   2. Transport demand models timed at the examination of *effects of the use of* specific "policy instruments", e.g.
      (a) Pricing policies — rate regulation; user charges; operating subsidies
      (b) Policies affecting the supply of facilities (infrastructure) and/or investments in equipment (equipment subsidies)
      (c) Policies affecting competitive position of carriers or modes through licencing, restrictions, etc.

3. An alternative manner of classifying models in the area of transport demand analysis is in terms of *approach*. Two extreme ways of approaching the problem are:
1. The basic intellectual "building block" is the analysis of *individual* transport decisions, i.e. decisions:
   (a) to ship or not to ship? and/or how much to ship and at what cost?
   b) How to ship? i.e. modal choice
2. The basic unit of observation and analysis are the existing commodity, place and mode (carrier) specific flows. The questions asked are: what are the factors responsible for the existence of observed flows? and — this leads us to the realm of conditional or structural forecasting — if the factors responsible are changed, how will the flows be affected?

Clearly, a number of intermediate approaches is possible.

4. A comprehensive survey of transport demand models would be an enterprise of very considerable scope. In view of the fact that most of the empirical work was sponsored by governmental or international agencies to deal with specific problems, not all of the experience thus gained is directly transferable, and in many cases, not even documented in a manner adequate for professional discussion by outsiders. This is especially true in the case of work done "inside" of governmental offices or done by consulting firms (in the latter case, the "proprietary" interests of model builders were not necessarily conducive to the full description of the work performed). Furthermore, the range, the scope and the number of projects would make a full survey either too long or too superficial.

Thus the practical approach, adopted here, is to apply high selectivity and to concentrate on the key methodological issues.

5. To a very large extent, serious development

of large scale transport demand models was affected by the planning of transport systems in less developed nations. The reasons for that were:

(a) Transport systems in developed countries *appeared* to be more mature and thus an incremental approach more acceptable.

(b) International lending and development agencies have quite early insisted on preparation of comprehensive economic plans both at the national and sectoral level.

The pressure for comprehensive planning arose from the desillusionment with specific, individual project evaluation approach,

"A more integrated and comprehensive approach to transportation planning and analysis is aimed at three principal deficiencies in the present project approach:
1. Total system effects are not considered in the evaluation of single projects.
2. The transportation plan is not related to the overall economic plan.
3. Different effects of alternative pricing policies are not considered in conjunction with investment decisions". [7]

This development has not been restricted to the transport sector. A recent thoughtful article on demographic working models contains the following observations which are directly relevant to the present discussion —

"Aims of the Models
"Wat do these models [large scale economic-demographic computer models] do? Their primary purpose, as seen by model builders, is to aid planners in policy evaluation. This aim is expressed differently in each model, but it is common to all. . . .
"Other aims are occasionally stated - for example, to help maintain consistency of planning in different sectors and to point up areas where further research and data are needed. The main purpose, however, remains that of 'policy evaluation'."
"Model builders justify the use of expensive computer models in policy evaluation by arguing that development processes are too dynamic and complex for the unaided mind to foresee with any degree of confidence. . . .
"It will be useful for our purpose to split 'policy evaluation' into two related but distinct parts: qualitative and numerical evaluation. Qualitatively, simulation models aim to spell out the sequence of events that follow particular policy choices and make planners more aware of subtle and unforeseen implications. Their function is to illuminate discussion on policy choice, serving, for any particular issue, as a framework for debate. Numerically, models add to policy evaluation precise figures on the outcome of particular strategies. When budgetary trade-offs are involved. . . this aspect becomes particularly important." [8]

6. One of the most influential attempts to develop a comprehensive transportation model was the Harvard Transportation and Economic Development Program initiated under the direction of John R. Meyer and financed by a research grant from The Brookings Institution. It must be noted that a number of models emerged from this project or were inspired by the original "Harvard Model" methodology which were developed by analytical groups outside of the original project, thus the common usage often confuses the "Harvard Model — proper", i.e. the model which initially emerged from the project (sometimes referred to as "The Brookings Model"), and a number of mutations which claim their direct descendence from the Harvard model.

The basic structure of the Harvard model consists of the following interrelated parts:

(i) the transportation model (or submodel) "which determines inter-regional flows, the actual level of transport facility usage, real (social) costs of providing the transport service, as well as the realized total cost to the user of the transport system"

(ii) the general economic model aimed at explaining the factors which ultimately determine transport flows. It "interrelates general economic variables like prices, incomes, consumption, savings, investments and profits, and specifies the appropriate regional or industry location. All activities, including resource extraction, intermediate goods processing and the production of final goods are included in this general model"

(iii) policy variables, i.e. explicit statement of variables assumed to be under control of the policy maker which affect directly, or indirectly, demand for transport

(iv) the relationship between the transport sector and the "general economy" is twofold:

(a) "Transport charges and congestion costs (e.g. inventory costs to overcome time delays and interest charges on loans to cover goods in transit) are reflected in the industry production costs and in the prices of final and intermediate goods. Also . . . the availability of transport facilities . . . or the existence of regional differences in transport costs, can make one region more competitive than another in particular markets thus leading to regional differences in growth" [9].

(b) Investment in the transportation sector require specific inputs (material, services, labour) which affects the demand for such goods and employment levels. (It sould be noted that the regional distribution of such demands need not correspond to the location of transport investments[8]. For diagramatic presentation of the working of the Harvard model, see fig. 1.

A different view of the Harvard model is:

(a) A general macroeconomic model is used for the forecasting of inter-regional flows.

(b) The macroeconomic model is directly connected with network optimization and investment optimization models.

(c) The model is "partially opened", i.e. "policy variables" are independently specified and they react both on "transport" and "general economic" parts of the model.

Thus the understood "Harvard model" provides a general framework for policy evaluation analysis — and thus is a "normative" rather than "descriptive" or "positive" model. It is not *per se* a forecasting model, but forecasting of traffic flows is the key part of the apparatus, and, by exposing the interrelationship between "general economic" and "transport" variables, the model provides also a framework for demand forecasting program.

7. As it was already noted, the "Harvard Model" produced a number of specific mutations. In general, the reasons for the mutations related to the gluttonous data requirements which were not satisfiable in practice. For example, the "Dahomey model" developed by N.D. Lea and Lamarre-Valois for the IBRD sponsored project in Dahomey, used the following analytical sequence:

(a) Demand for transport was derived from specific projection of key exports and imports, allocated to specific areas.

(b) Projected sectoral demands were used as inputs into network and investment optimization models.

8. Applications of this type of model to trans-

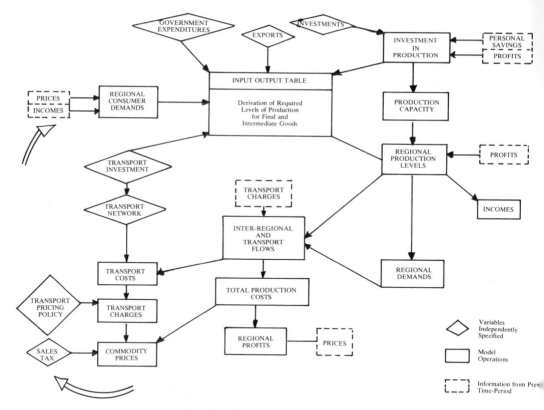

Figure 1 - Major Phases of Model Operation

port planning in an advanced and complex area involves another set of difficulties:

(a) Capacities of the transport system are extremely difficult to define, let alone measure.

(b) Given the widespread existence of joint and common costs, as well as differences in cost structure and supply objectives in different sectors of the system;[9] from the users point of view, the relevant costs are "tariff rates" and "user charges" which may or may not reflect "real costs", and which are by themselves the manifestation of investment and pricing strategies of different decision making units.

In short, the complexities of modelling the supply side — which affect the *observable* level of traffic flows — introduce new difficulties both for the construction of demand models and policy evaluation models[10].

9. Let us now turn to a basically different set of transport demand models, which were inspired by classical location theories. The questions asked by location theorists are of two types:

(i) What determines the location of economic activity (or its rate of growth) at a particular point or in a particular area?

(ii) What are economic consequences of location of economic activity or of growth of economic activity at a specific point or a specific area?

This leads to more specific transport questions:

(a) If we want to develop economic activity (or accelerate its development) at a specific point or in a specific area, can this development be affected by transport policies, and if so to what degree, at what cost and what mix of transport and non transport development instruments is most effective?

These issues can be narrowed down to a more specific analytical question: what is the role of transport in the development of economic activity in a specific location?

(b) What are the transport consequences of developing certain activity (or set of activities) at a specific location? In the econometric terms, the function to be estimated is

$$\text{Demand for transport TO or FROM x} = f \left(\begin{array}{c} \text{Growth of activity(ies)} \\ y_1, y_2 \ldots \text{at x} \end{array} \right)$$

In practice, this leads to two sets of demand problems, viz.

(i) transport demand related to the expansion (in volume and/or geographical extent of the trading area) of production at x. ("Market area" problem)

or (ii) transport demand related to the growth of consumption (including local production) at x — ("Supply area" problem).

Transport demand analysis (or analyses) in this context is essentially partial, and difficult to integrate with network analysis.

However, some interesting results may be obtained from that type of analysis. In fact, very specific transport demand models can be viewed as members of this "analytical family" (e.g. models aimed at estimating automotive traffic generated by shopping centres, models aimed at estimating transport requirements of "new", remote mining communities. Furthermore, "transport demand models" geared to the analysis and fore-casting of traffic at a terminal point (be it a point of origin or destination) have considerable utility in themselves, since a number of transport investment decisions relate to terminal facilities problems.

10. It appears to be useful, at this stage, to consider briefly the manner in which "location effect models" are constructed. Only general con-siderations, rather than specifics of model con-struction are considered.

The simplest formulation of the location effect model is as follows:

$$T_{dx} = f_x (c_1, c_2, \ldots c_i; p_1, p_2, p_3 \cdots p_i;$$
$$s_1, s_2, \ldots s_i)$$
$$T_{ox} = g_x (p_1, p_2, \ldots p_i; s_1, s_2, \ldots s_i)$$

Where Td and To are respectively traffic flows destined to and originating at the location studied; x is a commodity or a group of commodities which is being investigated.

$c_1, c_2, \ldots c_i$ are the consumption activities, or characteristics determining consumption levels (by commodities).

$p_1, p_2, \ldots p_i$ are the production activities or characteristics determining production levels (by commodities)

$s_1, s_2, \ldots s_i$ are the stock levels.

A moment of reflection reveals that the above formulations do not include any transport var-iables — such as transport costs, congestion costs, etc. and that, in fact, such variables cannot be directly introduced without further elaboration of the model. For example, let us assume that x is the commodity group "foodstuffs" then var-iables $c_1, c_2, \ldots c_i$ in function

$$T_{d(foodstuffs)} = F_{(foodstuffs)} (c_1, c_2, \ldots c_i, p_k, s_1)$$

can be population, income per head, average price of food, etc., p_k is production and s_1 is storage of foodstuffs. After estimating the values for the specified variables, we can estimate the elasticities of demand for transport with respect to population, income, etc. but not the effects of changes of transport rates, except to the extent they influence the price level of foods. The rea-son for that is that without specification of points of supply, transport costs are not determinable. A possible way out is to define commodities in such a way as to distinguish explicitly their point of origin, e.g. commodity x would not be "coal", but "coal produced in Alberta". Once this re-formulation is admitted, a much more interesting model can be derived.

For example, we are interested in transport implication of the establishment of industry pro-ducing widgets at a point P. The generalized pro-duction for widgets[1] production at P is

$$P(x_1, x_2, x_3, \ldots x_n; y_1, y_2, \ldots y_n; \pi_1, \pi_2, \cdots \pi_n)$$

where $x, \ldots x_n$ are inputs and $y_1, \ldots y_n$ are outputs. Inputs are defined as being location of supply specifically i.e. physically the same inputs coming from different points are de-fined as different inputs. $\pi_1, \pi_2, \ldots \pi_n$ are input prices, including transport costs.

In this formulation, price of an input coming from "outside", π_k, can be decomposed $\pi_k = \pi_{k(0)} + \pi_t$, i.e. price at the origin and transport costs.

If adequate information is available to estimate this production function, it could provide us with interesting information on substitution both be-tween inputs and points of origin.

Similarly, we can write the demand function for a consumption good y at point p as follows:
$$Q_{yp} = Q(\pi_y, \pi_{yk}, i, u_r)$$
where π_y is price of a consumption good y, π_{yk} are prices of "competitive" consumption goods $(k = 1 \ldots n)$; i — income, and u_r $(r = 1 \ldots n)$ — other relevant socio-economic factors.

Obviously, in the case of an "imported" con-sumption good $\pi_{y(p)} = \pi_{y(0)} + t$ — i.e. price at P equal price at point of origin plus t — transport and related costs. For reasons of analyt-ical convenience, goods produced at different points of origin are treated as "different goods", whether the consumer perceives such goods as "identical" or perfect substitutes is reflected in demand cross-elasticities. If goods are perceived, the distribution of supplies by different points of origin will depend on relative supply elasticities and transport costs.

11. These formulations, set within a restrictive framework of "location effects models" lead us to a more general investigation of the problem of more rigorous derivation of transport demand.

A possible approach to the problem is illus-trated in the following diagram derived from a monograph by Terziev, Ben-Akiva and Roberts [10].

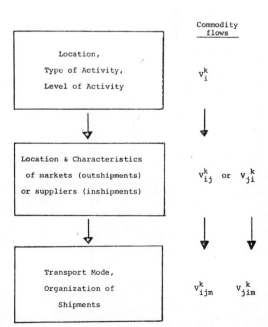

291

This diagram can be extended and the framework re-formulated as follows:

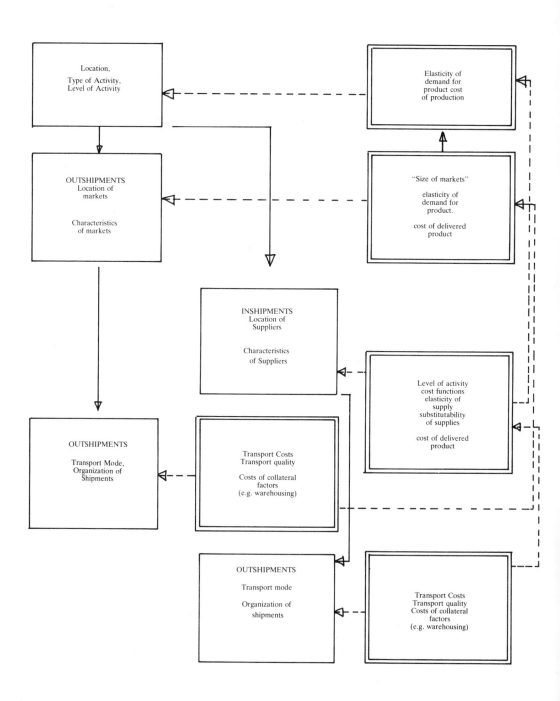

The difference between the two approaches is quite basic and illustrative of important decisions which must be made in transport demand modelling which is: should transport and trade (i.e. economic determination of flows of commodities) analyses be integrated in a model *jointly* or treated separately (sequentially)?

A. If transport and trade considerations are to be treated as interdependent, then, the transport demand model must be commodity (or commodity group) specific; demand for transport is treated as a demand from the demand for a commodity produced at a specific location, and there is no demand for an "abstract commodity" from which transport demand can be derived. Thus commodity aggregation must be related primarily to demand characteristics of the commodity in question, and not to its transport characteristics.

B. If, on the other hand, transport and trade considerations are to be treated sequentially[11], then shipment attributes (not necessarily commodity specific) and service attributes (not necessarily mode or carrier specific) determine the modal choice (as well as 'no shipment to market j' option).

The types of questions the two approaches are expected to answer are:

(i) Assuming a level of economic activity (locationally) determined, what is the expected demand for carriage of a given commodity from a specific origin to a specific destination? (formulation A.)

(ii) Assuming changes in transport relative quality price mix, or assuming changes in production or marketing methods which affect shipping/receiving/warehousing[12] pattern, how will the choice of transport mode change?

12. The recent empirical work in the area of freight forecasting is varied both in terms of approaches selected and its scope. As a starting point of this brief review, a study by Brian T. Bayliss is presented [11]. Bayliss starts his review by going back to a standard demand function with the dynamic elements (change over time) taken care of through a distributed lag formulation. However, his review of current work, characteristically enough, relates only marginally to the theoretical demand model. The results given for the freight forecasting model use a simple formulation $T = aP^b$ (where T is traffic volume in ton-miles, $P - GNP$, a and b constants). The results of estimates made for different countries are reproduced below:[13]

Country	Period	Results	R^2
U.K.	1952-67	$T = 0.66\,P^{0.76}$	0.96
U.S.A.	1947-63	$T = 0.21\,P^{0.62}$	0.99
W. Germany	1950-60	$T = 2.76\,P^{0.70}$	0.94
U.K.	1952-60	$T = 0.54\,P^{0.56}$	0.90
U.K.	1960-67	$T = 0.38\,P^{0.96}$	0.93
U.S.A.	1947-57	$T = 0.28\,P^{0.74}$	0.86
U.S.A.	1956-63	$T = 0.14\,P^{0.51}$	0.63

13. More recently, the Port of New York Authority engaged in econometric forecasting work; the model was based on a two phase estimating procedure: (i) U.S. simple trade model was estimated, then (ii) these results were used to estimate the share of the Port of New York.

The model formulation was as follows: [12]

a) Exports (general cargo) - X_{usg}

$X_{usg} = f(Y_w, P)$ where Y_w - World income
                                     P - Relative prices

$X_{usg} = 12.84 + 0.489\,Y_w - 26.38$
$$(R^2 = 0.963;\ DW = 1.38)$$

(b) Imports (general cargo) — M_{usg}

$M = f(Y_{us}, P)$ where Y_{us} - US income (GNP)
                                     P - Relative prices

$M_{usg} = -10.4 + 1.79\,Y_{us} - 0.074\,P$
$$(R^2 = 0.955;\ DW = 1.67)$$

(c) Ports share — Exports

The port's share was assumed to be dependent on commodity mix — i.e. it was assumed (quite reasonably) that specific commodity groups follow a certain stable traffic dispatch pattern — 'trading partner mix' and production distribution of exports ('Domestic Market Effect'). The the functional formulation is:

$$\frac{X_{nyg}}{X_{usg}} = S\,(S,\ D,\ T)$$

where $\dfrac{X_{nyg}}{X_{usg}}$ is New York share of US exports

         C — 'Commodity Effect'
         D — 'Domestic Market Effect'
         T — 'Trading Partner Effect'

$\dfrac{X_{nyg}}{X_{usg}} = -0.035 + 2.312\,C + 0.146\,D + 0.043\,T$
$$(R^2 = 0.986)$$

A similar method was used to estimate New York's share of U.S. Import Trade, where the independent variables used were income in the port's hinterland (D), 'Commodity Effect' (C) and 'trading partner effect' (T), where Japan/U.S.-Europe exports ratio was used as the measure. The results obtained were

$S_{nyg} = 0.931 + 0.448\,C + 1.836\,D - 0.108\,T$
$$(\overline{R}^2 = 0.942)$$

The third phase of that forecasting project related to the estimate of model market shares, relating to penetration of new modes to physical characteristics of the commodities.

The model is described here with some detail for the following reasons: (i) it represents an attempt to link trade and transportation models; (ii) it tuses rather broad aggregates (thus it represents a continuation of the tradition reported by Bayliss); (iii) is moves towards 'transport' estimates by stages; (iv) the approach is really orthodox with no special theoretical underpinnings (in contrast with abstract mode/abstract commodity approach; (v) time series analysis and proxy series are used as appropriate.

14. Another serious line of investigation was to attrack directly the problem of modal split. The possible lines of approach are:

(i) modal split estimates to be obtained as the last phase of transport model building;

(ii) modal split estimates to the based on the changes in production levels of sectors of the economy which are more-or-less linked with specific transport modes;

(iii) the use of demand and supply characteristics ('abstract mode-abstract commodity');

(iv) direct shippers' survey.

Two distinct methodologies relating to shippers' surveys can be identified:

(i) asking the shippers to rank the importance of the factors involved in the choice of carriers (thus leading to abstract mode formulation), and

(ii) direct observation of the choice of the mode selected.

Bayliss offers the following comments on those alternatives:

(i) Asking the shipper to identify and rank factors determining his choice. "This method is in many respects problematic. Firstly, when the performance of two or more carriers is not explicitly compared (as is usually the case) the obtained information relates only to general transport requirements and not on the value of a factor in the choice whether to use one or the other carrier. For example, if speed is an important consideration, but both carriers offer the choice carriers." Secondly, the preparation of lists which would be acceptable to the respondent and yet capture the complexity of different situations is an extremely difficult task. "Thirdly, such inquiries had considered the factors independently and not their simultaneous interaction." (This is also a serious and valid criticism of abstract mode or abstract mode-abstract commodity approaches.) "Lastly, there is always a businessman who wants to appear efficient and assigns precise values to factors which before he never took into account." [13]

(ii) Attempts to deduce the model choice from the actual shipments. This method has been attempted in the extensive studies conducted in the U.K. in the late sixties [14].

The analysis has been limited to the processing industries, since in the case of their shipments, there exists the greatest substitutability between the carriers. The businessmen were asked to provide specific waybills (or bills of lading) which *i.a.* contain information on the carrier, type of traffic, weight, destination and rate. This information can be obtained from the records of many firms, but as it was necessary also to ask questions on the so called "special characteristics" of shipments, the waybills had to be complete as at the time of movement and not retrospectively. Questions regarding "special characteristics" relate to the use of containers and special vehicles as well as to the regularity and urgency of shipments. By means of a postcard which the shipper sent at the time of despatch it was possible to obtain information on the damage and speed of delivery and by means of a questionnaire following the inquiry one could obtain data on the lost shipments. An important information not contained in the waybill are the costs which would have been incurred if other transport media were used. Two aspects of this problem can be considered: one can either use the *actual* costs or the *expected* costs of the alternative. In a perfect market system there is no difference between the both approaches, but in an imperfect one, as it exists in reality, the shipper can have either false or no perception of the alternative costs. Since the demand research attempts to obtain the subjective estimate of the shippers which lead to the modal choice, the second method was chosen. The completed waybills were thus returned to the shipper so that the expected costs for every shipment if the alternative mode was used could be given. The measuring of the subjective vs. objective factors for the choice of mode also applied to other factors than costs. E.g., the expected transport time and the expected damage or loss and not the actual transport time or loss. While one used sample data of this type, the market was also analysed *ex post*. When the shipper considers the damage as an important factor in his choice of carriers, then he will try to find a carrier who is likely to transport the commodity in question without damage. Hence the individual carriers will obtain business carrying goods which they are likely not to damage and thus the results of different carriers with respect to damages *ex post* will not vary.

In different words, the *ex post* analysis of a situation will

indicate the specialization of carriers with respect to different types of traffic, but it will not bring into focus the possibility that these results followed the wishes of the shipper.

In order to overcome these problems, the shipper was asked about his personal assessment of the importance of speed, accessibility, damage and loss in his choice of carriers.

In addition to the factors such as information on the objective shipping conditions and subjective evaluation by the shipper there exist also enterprise factors which have an effect on the choice of carrier. Often the state of transport facilities to which the enterprise has an immediate access, such as own vehicles or vehicles under contract, private railway siding or location on a canal as well as the location and size of the enterprise, exercise an influence on the choice of a transport medium.

Altogether there are three main groups of factors which influence choice of the carrier, namely factors relating to shipment, plant or enterprise characteristics and the subjective evaluation.

A rather different approach to the problem of modal choice was reported by Atsushi Komatsu of Nittu Research Center in Japan [15]. This approach involved the analysis of common characteristics affecting modal choice but grouped by industry. The common factors considered were: (1) location, (2) point of delivery, (3) traffic volume, (4) duration (time) of movements, (5) number of employees, (6) area of plant, (7) dispatching facilities, (e.g. railway sidings), (8) receiving facilities.

Leaving the first approach aside, the problems arising can be summarized as follows:

(a) The use of relatoinships between the producing industry (commodity type, location) and consumption activities (economic determinants of consumption, location), on one hand, and specific transport modes is adequate where such relationships are reasonably stable and either one mode predominates or an inter-model competition pattern is firmly set. Such conditions exist (in general) in bulk commodity production, but not in the more advanced parts of the manufacturing sector.

(b) Modal split models based on the demand and supply characteristics. These have been discussed in the context of the abstract mode. Remarkably, the costs of transport were not included, which may be explained by local difficulty in getting these types of data. This approach attempts to link observable industrial distribution characteristics such as the dispatching and receiving facilities with industry structure information. Properly carried through, this approach may provide a useful elaboration and extension of traffic forecasting based on the changes in production levels.

15. A comprehensive attempt to deal with all the facets of transport demand modelling based — let us add — on superb and comprehensive statistical information, was the model developed by the Netherlands Institute of Transportation [16].

The model developed consists of a number of sub-models:

a) The production and attraction model to determine the incoming and outgoing traffic flows per region and per commodity group.

b) The distribution model to determine the geographical distribution pattern for each commodity group distinguished.

c) The modal split model to determine the volume of the freight transport per transport relation, per commodity group for each mode of transport.

d) The traffic production model to determine

244

the number of traffic movements per transport relation, per commodity group and per mode of transport.

e) The assignment model to determine the future traffic volume in relation to the capacity of the future traffic infrastructure per mode of transport.

... the various sub-models do not operate as one simultaneous process but that the determination of the volume of the traffic and transport flows take place interactively [17].

For the details of this work, the reader is referred to the quoted source. The following observations can be made:

(a) The model was based on firm theoretical foundations.

(b) Alternative formulations of estimating techniques have been considered and adopted or rejected on the basis of comprehensive testing.

(c) A superb statistical base both relating to transport industries and production/consumption activities existed.

(d) This excellent base was *further* supplemented by a large scale sample survey of shippers which provided information on individual consignments (time, cost, size, traffic volume, loading and unloading facilities, size of the firm). Based on extensive information collected (and high quality collection system in place) extensive tests on homogeneity of groups of commodities have been made.

It is important to keep in mind the data base advantages which Dutch model builders enjoyed as well as compactness and centralization of the country and the tradition of government-industry-research co-operation. These conditions are rarely duplicated in other environments, which forces the realistic model builders to proceed in a less ambitious manner.

16. At this stage, the Canadian traffic forecasting model can be briefly introduced. The model referred to is the CTC freight demand forecasting model; since extensive descriptions of the model are available only most general methodological considerations need to be noted. At the very earliest stage of the model building, the following desiderata were stated as follows [18].

– Forecasting activity is necessarily a service function - its only aim is to improve decisionmaking. Thus the assessment of the usefulness and adequacy of a program is necessarily a pragmatic one.
– Forecasting may be viewed as a bridge between the *available* quantitative material . . . and forward planning.
– Theoretically a consistent general interdependence model is obviously desirable. In practice, the success of such an approach is made difficult by the demand such an approach curtails for consistent and detailed data . . . data requirements [for a comprehensive model] are likely to exceed the potential - let alone actual - capacity of our statistics collection system.
– For many (most?) purposes, specific sub-models will have to be developed.

Specific problems foreseen in model construction referred not only to data problems, but also to linkages with macroeconomic or regional models and aggregation (disaggregation) problems. Modal split and peak measurement and forecasting issues were noted as the important *further* stages in program development.

The actual model development has indeed proceeded in stages, individual stages were regional trade[14] pattern/traffic by a specific transport mode, and subsequent linking of specific commodity models. Modal split, analysis of the influence of supply conditions on the observable traffic patterns, peak analysis and finer regional disaggregations still remain to be considered. In effect, a more comprehensive approach noted in the previous section has been stretched out and phased over a longer period of time to exploit fully data availability. This approach, adopted by necessity, has had an advantage of permitting "learning by doing".

REFERENCES

[1] Jan Tinbergen, **On the Theory of Economic Policy,** North Holland Publishing Company, Amsterdam, 1966.
[2] Simon, Herbert, "Causal Ordering and Identifiability" in Wm. C. Hood and T.C. Koopmans (eds.) **Studies in Econometric Methods,** Wiley and Sons, 1953.
[3] R. H. Strotz, H. O. Wold, "Recursive versus Nonrecursive Systems: An Attempt at Synthesis", **Econometrica,** Vol. 28, 1960, pp. 417-427.
[4] M. Ezekiel, "The Statistical Determination of the Investment Schedule", **Econometrica,** Vol. 12, (January, 1944): 89-90.
[5] For comparison between CANDIDE and TRACE see an unpublished CTC paper by Can D. Le.
[6] For detailed description of TFM and its econometric structure see G. Hariton, R. Lee, U. Zohar, **Econometric Forecasting Model Demand for Freight Transport in Canada,** ch.2, Canadian Transport Commission, Ottawa, June 1976. G. Hariton, U. Zohar, C. D. Le, R. S. H. Lee, "Demand for Freight Transport in Canada", **International Journal of Transport Economics,** Vol. III, No. 2, August 1976.
[7] Brian V. Martin and Chas. B. Warden, "Transportation Planning in Developing Countries", **Traffic Quarterly,** Vol. 19, 1965, p. 61.
[8] W. Brian Arthur and Geoffrey McNicoll, "Large-Scale Simulation Models in Population and Development: What Use to Planners?", **Population and Development Review,** Vol. 1, 1975, pp. 253-254.
[9] Martin and Warden, **op. cit.,** pp. 65-66.
[10] M. Terziev, M. Ben-Akiva, P. O. Roberts, **Freight Demand Modelling: A Policy Sensitive Approach,** Cambridge, Mass: Massachussetts Institute of Technology, Centre for Transportation Studies, CTS Report 75-6, 1975.
[11] Brian T. Bayliss, **Methodische Probleme von Verkehrsprognosen** [Methodological Problems of Traffic Forecasting], Gottingen: Vandehoeck Ruprecht, 1970. At that time, Bayliss was Professor of Economics, University of Sussex (England), and had been responsible for the major U.K. traffic survey.
[12] J. Gilbert, Nai-Ching Sun, A. Ilan and M. C. Bunamo, "The Foreign Trade Econometric Model", Transportation Research Forum, **Proceedings - Fifteenth Annual Meeting,** vol. XV, No. 1, 1974, pp. 115-124.
[13] Bayliss, **op. cit.** Translation from German text.
[14] B. T. Bayliss and S. L. Edwards, **Transport for Industry,** London: H.M.S.O., 1968 and B. T. Bayliss and S. L. Edwards, **Industrial Demand for Transport,** H.M.S.O., 1970.
[15] "Factors Influencing Freight Mode Choice", College d'Europe and Transportation Research Forum, **Proceedings of the International Conference on Transportation Research,** (Bruges 1973), Oxford, Indiana: R. B. Cross Co., 1974, pp. 599-606.
[16] J. van Es and C. J. Ruijgrok, "Modal Choice in Freight Transport", College d'Europe and Transportation Research Forum, **op. cit.** pp. 585-598.
[17] **ibid.** p. 587.
[18] K. W. Studnicki-Gizbert, "Conceptual Problems in Forecasting Inter-regional Traffic Movements", College d'Europe and Transportation Research Forum, **op. cit.** pp. 580-584. Statements quoted reflect the preliminary thinking on the development and scope of the program.

FOOTNOTES

1. For the sake of clarity we offer the following difinitions:
a) A goal is an ultimate desire of a society to be attained at some given time horizon;
b) an objective represents a short-run preference between alternative states of the economy, and it is expressed in a form

of a set of targets to be attained subject to socio-economic constraints. Short-run refers to a period within which resource constraints are absolute and cannot be altered. Casual empiricism suggests any period up to five years;

c) instruments are these policy tools at the government's disposal which it can impose on the system to attain objectives and advance society toward the attainment of its goals. Such tools are (among others) monetary and fiscal policies.

2. Will be termed as the "Document" hereafter.

3. It was Jan Tinbergen who constructed and estimated the first large scale econometric model of the Netherlands (in 1936).

4. The CTC Forecasting Program follows such logic.

5. This section may be omitted without loss of continuity. We think it is desirable to include it in this paper, for it summarizes in a compact way the properties of causality in structural models.

6. This is in addition to the model's internal consistency requirements discussed in preceding paragraphs.

7. CTC stands for Canadian Transport Commission

8. The "natural extension" of this line of analysis, is to trace the macroeconomic effects of transport investments, either in the context of cyclical fluctuations (see J. Beare's article in K. W. Studnicki-Gizbert (ed), **Issues in Canadian Transport Policy** or in the context of long term pressure on the available investment resources.

9. E.g. objectives and capital costs differ between the "public sector" of transport which is responsible for the supply of infrastructure in road, air and water transport and the "private sector".

10. This is a general problem in demand analysis: "Unless strong assumptions are made about supply conditions, the estimation of **demand** equations is impossible; instead the function estimated may be a supply curve or mixture of the two". A. Brown and A. Deaton, "Models of Consumer Behavior", in Royal Economic Society, **Surveys of Applied Economics,** Vol. I, London: Macmillan, 1973, p. 220. Unfortunately, in transport "strong supply assumptions" (prices are fixed by producers; supply is forthcoming at that price) violate some observable "real life" conditions (especially that 'adequate' supply is forthcoming at a price fixed by producers).

11. It should be noted that Terziev et al explicitly noted that "these decisions [production and consumption, distribution and modal split] are often determined jointly and are interdependent in a way that makes a specific sequence arbitrary". **op. cit.** p. 43.

12. There exists a strong relationship of "abstract commodity - model split determination model" and "inventory theory" models of transport demand (see e.g. W. J. Baumol and H. D. Vinod, "An Inventory Theoretic Model of Freight Transport Demand", **Management Science,** vol. 10, 1970. The authors describe their model as an "abstract mode-abstract commodity model" **op. cit.** p. 413). However, not all "abstract commodity" models aimed at the explanation of modal split take inventory theoretic approach.

13. **ibid.**

14. As reflected by production and consumption of major commodities by regions.

Forecasting freight demand

by

PAUL O. ROBERTS

Massachusetts Institute of Technology, Massachusetts

FREIGHT FORECASTING:
A NEGLECTED AREA

Freight forecasting is an area that appears to have received considerably less attention than it deserves. The literature available describes a range of techniques that have been applied over the years, none of which seems to have worked extremely well. There are no routinely accepted and applied approaches. Even the "gravity model", which is the closest thing to a standard technique, is used either out of total naivety or complete frustration over the lack of suitable alternatives. One is forced to conclude that quantitative forecasting techniques for freight are not well developed, at least operationally, in comparison to those used for urban transportation planning.

Two possible reasons for this lack of development can be advanced. The first is the complexity of dealing with freight rather than passengers. The second is the lack of a consistent and comprehensive data base for use in development. Let us briefly examine the arguments for each.

In some ways, freight is more complex to deal with theoretically than passengers. Freight has a wider range of "choice-influencing attributes" (i.e. density, value, shelf-life, etc.) and is less discrete in terms of the size of an individual shipment (i.e. 50 pounds, 5000 pounds or a full truck-load). It should, however, move under more "rational grounds than do passengers. After all, the only motivation for moving freight is an economic one.

The availability of data, however, is another question. A variety of data is typically gathered and published. However, there are invariably problems with it. On the one hand, a complete and consistent set of origin to destination flows by commodity and mode does exist for most countries. Published data almost always lacks the desired detail spatially, modally or in terms of commodity disaggregation. On the other hand, a representative sample of individual shipments from which estimates of the origin to destination flows could be prepared either does not exist or the holder of such data is reluctant to release it because its disclosure might reveal the operations of individual firms.

Why this data gap has been allowed to exist is hard to explain. Obviously, everyone's data needs are not the same. Developing a complete and consistent set of origin to destination flows at a level of detail that would be generally satisfactory might well be considered to be too expensive for most government agency planning budgets. Another explanation for this lack of data in the U.S., could be due to the fact that much of the freight planning in the past has been done in the private sector. Government has tended to take a "hands-off" attitude. This is unfortunate since most small private forms cannot afford to undertake major research efforts. Obviously, there have been corporate planners who have developed the data needed to support specific decisions they considered to be crucial to the company's well-being such as regulatory proceedings, acquisitions, planning in support of new facilities or services, etc. But the effort required typically exceeds the resources of all but the largest firms on all but the most important problems. In the U.S., we are therefore left with neither the origin-destination flow figures needed for planning nor the data required to develop proper forecasting techniques.

SOME IMPORTANT DISTINCTIONS

It is useful to sharpen the distinctions between the actual shipments which take place in the real world, representative samples of these shipments, aggregated estimates of total flows and forecasts of future flows. See Figure 1. Actual shipments

  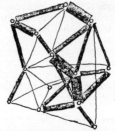 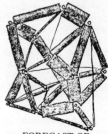

| SHIPMENTS IN THE REAL WORLD | REPRESENTATIVE SAMPLES OF THESE SHIPMENTS | AGGREGATED ESTIMATES OF TOTAL FLOWS | FORECAST OF FUTURE FLOWS |

Figure 1 - Four types of shipment information

can never be known without some kind of sample. There may, in any particular case, be more than one sample. Samples are typically summed and expanded by an appropriate factor to produce an aggregate estimate of total flows. Aggregate estimates can be further aggregated to provide summary demand statistics. For example, total ton-miles for the U.S. as a whole is one such super-aggregated statistic. Aggregate estimates then, have their origins in disaggregate samples. It is relatively easy to sum disaggregate samples to obtain aggregate estimates of the whole. It is much more difficult to "disaggregate" an aggregate estimate since information has actually been given up in the process of aggregation.

Forecasts of future demand are different in several important ways from estimates of existing origin to destination flows. There is only one past. It is a matter of certain historical record, if the record was saved. By contrast, there are literally an infinitude of possible futures. The one that will occur is more or less uncertain. It depends, in part, on the chance occurences that make up the environment within which the transport system is located and in part on the choices which an individual decision maker exercises. Forecasting future flows always involves the use of a model which incorporates these chance and choice elements. The model may be either quantitative or qualitative. It could involve simple extrapolation or more complex causal relationships. It may be assumed to be either determinstic or probablistic. It may involve digital or analog computation or no computation at all. However, there is always a model either explicitly or implicitly involved since the future, if it is interesting at all, always involves changes from the present.

Since we are concerned here with forecasting freight demand we must, as a consequence, be concerned with the nature of various models for accomplishing this purpose. We must also be concerned with the status of the data both disaggregate and aggregate since it serves both as a starting point for estimates of future flows and as the only source of quantitative information on causal responses to changes in the process. Thus, models and data are closely tied. Ultimately, one cannot know whether a model performs properly without comparing its predictions against observed changes in the data.

FACTORS AFFECTING MODELS OF FREIGHT DEMAND

Freight demand forecasting has a wide variety of uses, ranging from providing estimates of future inputs to the transport sector to determining the volume of flow on a particular link as a function of price. The exact uses will depend importantly on who the user is and what he is using the forecast for. For some uses, the precision required is not great. For others, as much accuracy is desired as can be obtained. Obviously, the type of model to be used will depend upon such factors as degree of aggregation, policy responsiveness and requirements for accuracy.

1) **Aggregation** — There are at least four important dimensions over which aggregation can be performed. These are: time, space, commodities and modes. See Figure 2. Most models deal with time only in the most basic way. That is, demand

is expressed as a rate per unit of time. Time is not explicitly considered as a separate variable as it is, for example, in a Monte Carlo simulation of a time dependent process such as queuing. It could be treated but for most demand forecasts, the average rate of flow per day, per week, or per year is satisfactory. Where seasonality of flow is important, a separate estimate can be made by seasons. However, this is a complication that is difficult to handle in existing models.

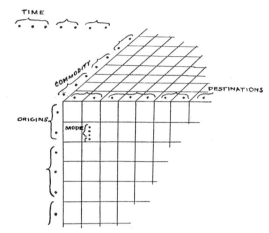

Figure 2 - Common dimensions of aggregation

Spatial aggregation is also common in demand forecasting though the need to preserve spatial detail is widely recognized. Where the origin and destination areas are large, there is also a question on the inclusion of intra-regional flows in addition to the interregional flow. The ability to preserve spatial detail in the forecasts depends importantly on the spatial detail which exists in the base data used in developing the model and the availability of values for independent variables in compatible detail. In the U.S., some data for independent variables are available from published statistics at various levels ranging progressively from the county, SMSA, state and region to the nation as a whole. Unfortunately, agregate flow statistics are available between only a selected set of major metropolitan areas and then for only a portion of the commodities in the total economy in relatively aggregate form.

The most pervasive aggregation occurs over commodities. The great diversity in attributes between commodities, even those within rather detailed commodity categories, and the importance of these attributes for the selection of mode tend to make even moderate aggregation unfortunate. There are a great many commodity coding systems in use throughout the world. In the U.S., the Standard Industrial Classification (SIC) and the compatible Standard Transportation Commodity Classification (STCC) are widely used. Establishments tend to be classified at 4 digits, particular commodities at 5 digits and commodities in various forms of packaging at 6 and 7 digits. Since freight rates tend to be quoted at the 6 and 7 digit level, significant disaggregation must exist if the ability to make a modal choice is to be preserved.

Aggregation over modes is less common probably because of the rather large distinctions between the costs and the services rendered. Rarely, for example, does one see a single figure for ton-miles over the whole economy while ton-miles by rail, by truck, or by air are common. There is, however, considerable aggregation over sub modes. Piggyback is frequently undistinguished from rail carload, which is also typically not differentiated from rail unit train. Likewise, the various categories of private and forhire trucking are frequently combined. A major distinction between various modal service offerings is the minimum shipment size required to qualify for a specific set of tariff charges. For example, LTL truck shipments are almost a different mode from truckload shipments.

A great many of the differences found in the various models and modelling approaches can be accounted for by different levels and types of aggregation. Depending on the level of detail required for addressing the questions of interest, the models at higher level of aggregation may not be useful at all.

2) **Policy Responsiveness** — A second major factor of interest in developing models of freight demand is policy responsiveness. Policy responsiveness becomes important whenever the choices open to a decision maker become important. By contrast, the chance elements are not of particular interest unless particular choices are impacted differentially. Obviously, the policy responsiveness of a particular model is affected by the variables incorporated into the model. It would, for example be difficult for the demand for high speed service to be forecast by a model unless the model incorporates travel time for each of the modes. Each policy to be evaluated by the model must be expressed in terms of the variables in the model. This would become almost impossibly complicated if it were not that almost all transport policy can be expressed in terms of a relatively small set of level of service variables. For freight, this set might typically consist of:

waiting time (or schedule frequency)
trip time
time reliability
probability of loss and damage
minimum shipment size
transport charges
other costs

Factors such as availability of special handling, expediting, environmental controls, transit privileges, enroute tracing, facilitated claims processing, etc. could also be important, but they are not as general as the list above.

The policy responsiveness of the models can be enhanced by proper model design. That is, some model features work in favor of policy responsiveness, others against it. Clearly, what is desired is a model which for a variety of decision makers and/or types of decisions can reflect the choices that would be exercised by the decision maker as he faces different level of service combinations reflecting the policies of interest.

3) **Accuracy** — Model acuracy is the third major factor. Clearly, if policy responsiveness is important, the accuracy required is that necessary to discriminate between policies. This will vary depending upon the nature of the policy. It could require more or less aggregation over time, space, commodities or modes. If sampling techniques are used, explicit criteria could be developed to produce confidence limts for any forecast. The modelling methodology will also be important. This will be discussed in greater detail below.

CAN GENERAL PURPOSE MODELS BE DEVELOPED

So far, we have not described a particular model or class of models, but have rather described factors affecting all models regardless or who was using them or the questions that were being addressed. There is some question as to how long maintaining this generality is useful. Is it possible, for example, to design a general purpose freight demand model that can be used by all parties on all types of problems? The answer is probably no, but the degree to which generality can be built into any model will obviously govern its usefulness.

The purpose of a freight travel demand model is clearly to allow the forecasting of the volume of travel of a particular commodity that will move between a given origin and destination by a given modal service offering over a given interval of time. A demand model does not take a particular point of view. There is no inherent difference between the demand model used by a carrier to determine the volume of travel that would take place if a specific change in service offering were made and the demand model used by the federal government to understand the same problem. Thus, one demand model should work for all types of users.

The same question arises as to issues. Can all types of policy questions be asked and answered with the same model? The answer is probably mode dependent on the factors of aggregation, policy responsiveness and accuracy mentioned above than it is on the issues to be addressed. There is no inherent reason why issues concerning labor, technology, pricing, regulation, capital investment, equipment utilization, or the like cannot be addressed using the same demand model as long as the issue depends upon the estimates of demand for a particular commodity or set of commodities between given origins and destinations by individual modal service offerings over a given interval of time. Some issues could require an ability to discriminate between impacts by type of shipper, but this depends on the features of the modelling approach. It is possible to select modelling approaches that can handle this routinely. If so, it would appear that a more or less general purpose model could be developed which was broadly policy responsive subject to the factors of aggregation and accuracy.

DESIRABLE MODEL FEATURES

A careful review of the literature, such as that performed by Terziev [1], reveals a series of models developed over the years at different levels of aggregation and accuracy. The models reviewed were not very policy responsive and for the most part performed poorly, even for their stated purpose. The question, of course, is whether this is an inherent property of all freight travel demand models or whether the problems lie with the features of the models constructed to date.

Our hypothesis is that the problems lie with the features of previous modelling approaches and that the adoption of a set of carefully thought out modelling features could greatly improve the generality as well as the utility of present approaches. These features then can be stated as criteria for constructing the desired travel demand models. These criteria are:

1. Work at a disaggregate level.
2. Model the behaviour of individual decision making units.
3. Use the shipment as the basic element to be modelled.
4. Base the model at the destination.
5. Determine model parameters empirically.
6. Formulate the model to use generalized attributes.
7. Base the computation scheme on forecastable data sources.

Each will be discussed in more detail in the sections which follow.

1) **Work at a Disaggregate Level** — Since most forecasts must be reported and used at an aggregate level, a model that works at an equivalent level of aggregation would appear to be the simplest to use. This is undoubtedly true, but a model formulated at a higher level of aggregation is not usable at a more disaggregate level. For example, a model for the United States of ton-miles of transportation by truck as a function of GNP is simpler to use than a model of state-to-state truck flows based on state-level economic indicators. However, the state-to-state model can be used to generate ton-miles between specific states, ton-miles by region, and ton-miles by state of origin or destination. Importantly, the results can also be summed to produce total ton-miles by truck for the United States as a whole. The more disaggregate model is, therefore, more flexible and can be used for purposes which the higher level model cannot be used. This generality is gained at the expense of being slightly more difficult to use.

In general, models formulated at lower levels of aggregation have more general utility, since they can be combined in more ways. The results can always be aggregated to obtain the same results as those of the more aggregate models. By summing the disaggregate units, the information content inherent in the disaggregate units is not lost.

Another feature of using the mode disaggregate models is their increased policy sensitivity. Policies which apply differentially to the individual sub-units can be analyzed. Changes in the environment which impact the sub-units differentially can also be handled. Thus, a policy such as the imposition of differential user charges in the various states could be handled by the disaggregated state-to-state model described above, whereas the aggregated U.S. model could not incorporate such a change.

The disadvantages of a more disaggregate model are that there are more inputs to be dealt with, there is more computation to obtain disaggregate forecasts, and there must be a scheme for aggregation, which in some instances might be quite complicated. In general, however, the advantages of using more disaggregate approaches seem to outweigh the disadvantages. The models are more flexible. That is, they can handle a wider range of policies and a wider range of environmental change. It is not necessary to know at the time the model is being developed the

exact policies or exact environments as carefully as it is for a more aggregated model. The ability to reaggregate according to a new aggregation scheme is an extremely valuable asset to a set of models since it automatically increases their generality.

2) **Model the Behavior of Individual Decision Making Units** — If an individual decision making unit can be identified, it is much easier to understand this individual's point of view. In many cases, it will be possible to understand his objectives and to identify the choice variables which he can exercise. For freight modelling, this individual will be either a shipper or a receiver of freight. It should be possible, therefore, to understand the costs which he faces, and to hypothesize a cost function in general terms which approximates his view of the world. This should greatly improve freight demand models, because it removes ambiguity from the shipping process. Instead of a generalized cost function representing impedence crudely defined, we can have a cost function which incorporates those elements typically faced by the decision maker.

Likewise, the choices that are available to the decision maker can be more easily identified. By knowing the choices that are available and if the costs can be developed for each, a model of the decision making process can be formulated. There is now a theoretical basis using consumer theory for formulating a utility, or cost function, and the theory of consumer choice can be applied in the formulation of appropriate models. It should no longer be necessary to fall back on the gravity model because there is nothing better.

There are some disadvantages to attempting to model the individual decision making units. It may no longer be possible to simply sum the component parts, as it was in the case of state-to-state flows, to obtain the national flow. We must now have an explicit scheme for aggregation. We may, for example, want to use a representative sample of the population as a whole in which the choices made by each individual are recorded, and the final results factored up to represent the total universe.

Working with individual decision making units carries with it one major advantage. The advantage is "transferability". This means that once a model is available for one part of the country, it can be used in other parts as well. A model that works for any decision making unit can be transferred from place to place as long as the individual decision making units do not change in character; that is, where the changes can be described by inputs to the model. For this to be the case, a model must be based on attributes of the individual, and not the individuals themselves. There are, obviously, considerable economies in calibrating such a model once and for all.

Another extremely important feature of the use of individual decisionmaking units as the basis for modelling is the ability to determine the impacts of a specific policy on certain definable groups of individuals. For example, if various individuals can be identified as belonging to a particular group, i.e. a given industry, firm size, region, etc., then the impacts on this particular group can be determined by merely isolating the individual observations and observing their behavior before and after the policy application. This feature is extremely important in issue-oriented questions. There is frequently a need for determining the groups that will be impacted as a result of a specific policy-changes in user taxes, pollution, etc. Models based on the behavior of individual decision making units are amenable to tracing the impacts characteristic of issue-oriented policies. Aggregation tends to lose this ability.

3) **Use the Shipment as the Basic Element to be Modelled** — Standard practice in passenger demand modelling is to use the person-trip as the element to be modelled. In the case of freight, there are a number of possible choices for the basic element to be modelled. These include vehicle trips by mode, ton miles by mode, tons irrespective of mode and shipments. Commodity type may or may not be explicitly considered. The arguments for one as opposed to the other must be developed in more detail for the advantages of using shipments to be apparent.

Modelling truck trips, barge trips, rail trips or air trips directly is filled with problems. Train length and barge tows can vary in size. Equipment with different playloads can be used. Imbalances in flows can lead to different load factors in different directions which cannot be represented easily. Intermodal trips cannot be handled without special treatment. Commodity distinctions are also difficult, if not impossible. In spite of these apparent disadvantages some models, such as those used in urban transportation planning, still work with vehicle trips. This is probably because

vehicles are the aggregate unit which is most directly related to the policy questions of interest, such as capacity, noise, pollution, etc.

Working with tons is better. Individual commodities can be identified. Imbalances in flow by direction can be handled. Different types of equipment can be used and train lengths and barge flows are no longer a problem. There is, however, a fundamental problem with shipment size. The problem results from the fact that shipments of different sizes pay different transport charges even where all other aspects of the shipment are identical (i.e. commodity, origin and destination). The freight charges per unit can drop to one half, one third, one quarter or less as the size of the shipment rendered increases. Using tons as the basic element ignores this factor.

By working directly with a shipment as the basic element, the size problem can be addressed directly as one of the explicit choices to be made by the decision making unit. The interrelationships between the annual flow of a commodity by an establishment, the frequency of shipment and the shipment size should also be noted. If the annual flow rate is known, as it could be if the individual decision unit is identified, then the choice of shipment size will also result in knowing the frequency of shipment.

4) **Base the Model at the Destination** — If we are to model the behaviour of individual decision making units, then the unit to be addressed will be either the shipper or the receiver. It cannot be both, because to do so would involve double

ORIGIN BASED MODEL

DECISION UNIT IS THE SUPPLIER (SHIPPER)

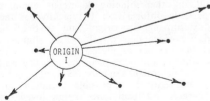

DESTINATION BASED MODEL

DECISION UNIT IS THE CONSUMER (RECEIVER)

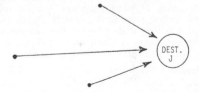

> SUPPLIERS TYPICALLY MAKE DECISIONS ON PRICE AND PRICING POLICY (F.O.B., C.I.F.)

> A SUPPLIER TENDS TO PRODUCE ONLY A FEW PRODUCTS

> SUPPLIERS SHIP OUTPUT TO MANY DIFFERENT CONSUMERS IN MANY DIFFERENT CITIES

> COMPETITION BETWEEN PRODUCERS IS DIFFICULT TO REPRESENT WITHOUT MANY TO MODEL

> DIFFICULT TO IDENTIFY DECISIONS AND ATTACH BEHAVIORAL SIGNIFICANCE

> DIFFICULT TO SPECIFY AND ESTIMATE MODEL BECAUSE OF THE LARGE NUMBER OF DESTINATIONS, THE DIFFICULTY WITH DECISIONS, ETC.

> CONSUMERS TYPICALLY MAKE DECISIONS ON CHOICE OF SUPPLIER, QUANTITY TO PURCHASE, FREQUENCY OF PURCHASE AND CHOICE OF MODE IN FOB PRICING (70% OF CASES)

> A CONSUMER OBTAINS VARIETY OF INPUTS FROM ONLY A FEW SUPPLIERS IN FEW LOCATIONS

> COMPETITION BETWEEN SUPPLIERS CAN BE EASILY INCORPORATED INTO A SINGLE MODEL

> DECISIONS ARE EASILY IDENTIFIED AND HAVE A CLEAR BEHAVIORAL INTERPRETATION

> RELATIVELY EASIER TO SPECIFY AND ESTIMATE MODEL SINCE THERE ARE FEW SUPPLIERS AND DECISIONS ARE MORE EXPLICIT

CONCLUSION: DESTINATION BASED MODEL IS SUPERIOR

Figure 3 - Comparison of origin and destination based models

counting. We could presumably sample existing distributions of industry and population to get the individuals to be examined. There are a number of reasons why the receiver of commodities, rather than the shipper, is the appropriate decision making unit to sample in the general case. There are obviously cases in the real world where the shipper is actually making the decisions and it should be possible to modify the models to reflect this difference in point of view where it is appropriate. However, it is necessary to base the model either at the origin or the destination end of the shipment and our contention here is that the more appropriate place is the destination, for a variety of reasons. These reasons are summarized in Figure 3.

First, the decisions made by suppliers concern themselves primarily with price, and pricing policy. This may include whether the commodity is to be priced on an FOB factory price or CIF delivered price basis. By contrast, consumers typically make decisiosn of the choice of supplier, the quantity to purchase, the frequency of purchase, and the choice of mode in those cases where the price is quoted FOB. Since in some 70% of the cases prices are given FOB factory, the bulk of the travel/demand related decisions are made by the consumer rather than the supplier.

Another point of contrast has to do with the easier modelling approach which can be adopted on a destination based model. By and large, a supplier tends to produce only a few products, and to ship these products to many consumers in many different cities. A consumer, on the other hand, typically uses as input a large number of products, each from only a few suppliers in a few locations. Thus, if we work with a single commodity at a time, it is easier to work on the consumer side than the supply side, since competition between suppliers can be relatively easily incorporated into a simple choice model at the destination end, whereas the competition between producers is much more difficult to represent without a many-to-many model.

Another argument for the destination-based model is that travel-related decisions are more easily identified, and have a clearer behavioral interpretation, whereas, on the origin side it is much more difficult to identify the decisions and to attach behavioral significance. For example, the decisions identified above on the part of the consumer as choice of supplier, quantity and frequency of purchase, and choice of mode are understandable choices faced by the decision maker given the price of the product at each origin and the transport level of service available to the destination. On the supply side, the decisions are harder to interpret, however. There is no reason, for example, why the supplier does not ship to every destination, except that he has not been asked to do so by the consumer. Thus, in the final analysis, the consumer makes the decisions about where his supplies will be obtained.

This all adds up to a situation in which it is ultimately easier to specify and estimate a destination-based model, since there are fewer suppliers to deal with in the choice, and the decisions are more explicit. By working with the full distribution of industries, including agriculture, mining, manufacturing, wholesale and retail trade services, and those final-demand elements, such as pop-

ulation, government, investment, inventories, and exports, all receiving elements can be covered.

Our conclusion is that a destination-based model is easier to develop and easier to use than an origin-based model, and there are no corresponding disadvantages to working at the destination end.

5) **Determine Model Parameters Empirically** — The advantages of an empirically determined model are clear. One does not have to guess at the values which a shipper places on time, on loss or damage in transit, or on any of the other attributes associated with transport of the shipment. There is some question, however, as to how this can be done. Value of time, for example, cannot be observed directly—they must be inferred from choices made by the receiver. To do this, a situation must be identified in which choices involving different tradeoffs between cost and time can be observed. This is, in fact, not difficult to do, since each shipment made in the real world is proof of some choice. There is no dirth of choices. There is a problem, however, in determining the choice set actually faced by the shipper. The dependent variable in this case is either a zero or a one. Only that item chosen out of the set of possible choices would receive a one; the remainder are indicated by a zero. The relative frequency of a given choice could be developed for those choices with similar attributes. This suggests that a probability model might be useful. Consumer choice theory could then be used to infer values of the unknown parameters in the utility function.

Since each shipment involves a choice on the part of the decision maker, transportation waybills are the paper transaction proof of this choice. A waybill, or other shipping document, contains all the pertinent information. It typically has the commodity moving, its origin and destination, the mode by which it is travelling, the shipment size, and the number of pieces. From the name of the consignor and consignee, the industry and firm size of the establishments involved can be inferred. Ordinarily, it is possible to obtain the freight charges, and from time to time, even the transit time from a waybill. Also, from the using firm's industry and size, it is even possible to infer the annual use rate of a given commodity, though this would require some economic sleuthing. By obtaining samples of the waybills for given shipments at the destination-end, the receiver of the goods is well known, and pertinent information can be developed concerning him. Also, the sample of input commodities should be quite robust, since most firms use far more items as input than they produce as output.

There is, therefore, an obvious empirical base for the determination of freight-demand models— literally millions of waybills are produced daily. If these waybills could be obtained and used in the estimation procedures, an empirically-based model could be developed. These same procedures will also work for shipments by private carriers (i.e., private truck, pipe-line, barge), since in almost every case, there is some shipping document. The key question is the ability to capture this document and to supplement it with other information concerning the establishment making the shipment decisions.

6) **Formulate the Model to Use Generalized Attributes** — The use of generalized attributes to describe the commodities, the modal service offerings, the market or suppliers and the receivers is crucial to producing an economical and usable model. There is no area in which this is more true than with the different commodities. If it were necessary to formulate and calibrate a separate model for each commodity, the utility of the entire effort is in question. If, on the other hand, one generalized model can be built for a wide range of different commodities, with the individual commodities described by their attributes, then a much more workable approach is possible. Even if it becomes necessary to segregate into broad classes of commodities, such as bulk goods, particulates, liquids, packaged goods, etc., the number of classes can be workable. Commodity attributes for practically any level of commodity detail are available. The MIT Freight Transport Research Group has prepared a commodity attribute file for commodities at a 5-digit STCC level [2]. This commodity attribute file contains information on the value per pound, density, shelf life, state, and environmental protection requirements for approximately 1200 commodities. Thus, the use of generalized commodity attributes allows the development of a single set of commodity abstract freight demand models that can subsequently be used for a wide range of commodities, even those never before observed.

Generalized attributes can also be used to describe the level of service variables for the modal service offerings, as mentioned before. The models developed may then be either generic or mode specific, but since there are only a few modes in comparison to the large number of commodities, it is possible to estimate mode specific models if this proves to be more desirable. The use of generalized supplier and receiver attributes allows the models to be specified generally, so that they may be used for a wide range of industries and firm sizes. Same care must be taken to keep the attributes general, rather than industry-specific, so that a generalized set of models can result.

7) **Base the Aggregation Scheme on Forecastable Data Sources** — If a disaggregate behavioral model is used, then it will ultimately be necessary to develop an aggregation scheme for use in forecasting. The forecasting scheme does not actually have to be developed at the time the model is developed, since the aggregation scheme is more directly related to the policy questions being addressed. If, for example, a national level forecast of mode choice is desired, it may be unnecessary to develop the flows state-by-state. Instead, a representative sample of receivers can be developed with observations from a wide range of geographical regions, industry types and commodities, and the model results for the sample can be aggregated directly and expanded to produce the national estimates. If, on the other hand, state-to-state estimates were required, then the sample used would have to include sufficient observations to be able to develop the additional detail needed state-by-state.

It is possible to work with small homogenous groups rather than a representative disaggregate sample. If small groups are used, the group means for each of the groups can be used in the forecast and the results summed over all groups to produce the overall forecast.

Regardless of which scheme of aggregation is used for the U.S., the future population industry and firm-size distribution use in forecasting can be developed from the very large data sets provided by the Census Bureau, by the BEA, and by the Bureau of Labor Statistics. The BEA regions in particular have forecasts to several future years already prepared by the issuing agency. These forecasts could be used in developing the sample used in the model.

Another possible source of observations are the Dunn and Bradstreet files. These files contain information on more than three million commercial establishments in the United States. There are also more than 300,000 Canadian establishments recorded. More than 367,000 establishments are reported for the state of California alone, covering all of the industry sectors—agriculture, forestry and fisheries, mining, contract construction, manufacturing, transportation, communication and public utilities, wholetrade, retail trade, finance, insurance, and real estate and services. These files are continuously updated to record only the existing population.

Both of these basic sources—the Census data and Dunn and Bradstreet—can be used to develop a sample of establishments in any area of the country. They could serve, therefore, as the forecastable data source upon which future freight demands can be developed.

CURRENT STATUS OF FREIGHT DEMAND MODELLING

At present, the principle barrier to the development of a set of policy-sensitive, disaggregate behavioral demand models for freight is the existence of an appropriate disaggregate data set for use in estimating such a set of models. The U.S. Department of Transportation has recently entered into a contract with the MIT Center for Transportation Studies to gather the required data and to develop a set of models for the United States. Explorations of the status of existing data are currently underway, and preliminary model specification has already been performed. Current thinking as to the specification of these models is included as Appendix B to this paper. The models described are formulated with simultaneous choice of point of origin, choice of shipment size and mode. They embody all of the desirable attributes described above.

Work on the models will proceed in three phases: Phase I includes model specification and pilot data collection. Phase 2 involves full-scale data collection, and Phase 3 involves model calibration and testing.

The models developed will be disaggregate at the level of the individual decision maker. They will, therefore, be extremely flexible. They could be used either individually to predict the choices made by an individual establishment for the transport of an individual commodity, or they could be used in aggregated form either embodying a disaggregate random sample or some more elaborate aggregation scheme. It is anticipated that the results will surpass those of other models developed to date. The literature review described in Appendix A tends to support this contention.

APPENDIX A

Literature Review

Relatively little work has been done in the area of freight demand modeling in comparison to the extensive body of literature on modelling the demand for passenger transportation. Nevertheless, a fairly large number of studies of freight demand have appeared in the transportation and economics literature during the past ten years.

In reviewing freight demand models, primary consideration should be placed on the policy sensitivity and completeness of each model. One measure of a model's policy sensitivity is the extent to which it includes transportation level of service variables which are under the control of carriers and regulators. As described earlier, the list of level of service variables includes rate, mean travel time, and travel time reliability.

The second criteria is completeness. One aspect of completeness relates to the range of decisions addressed by a model. Models which predict only the choice of mode are less complete and less useful in policy analysis than models which cover the mode, shipment size and O-D choices. Another aspect of completeness relates to the range of situations in which a model can be applied. Some models can be used to forecast flows only for the commodities represented in the estimation data set, while other models can be applied to any commodity. Also, some models can be used to study the demand in only one region, while other models are transferable to any region. Hence, the completeness criteria is a measure of the applicability of a model to a wide range of demand related freight transportation problems.

Table A. 1 - Summary of Freight Demand Models

Type of Model	Modeler	Level of Service Variables	Commodity Descriptors	Other Variables	Functional Form	Principal Data Sources
Aggregate-Volume by Mode	Sloss, 58	rate		economic activity measure	log linear	19
	Perle, 51	rate	dummy variables, (stratification)	regional dummy variables	log linear	1,4
	Miller, 43	change in rate		production index	linear	1
	Black, 12	distance	(stratification)	regional consumption and production	gravity	2a, 2c
	Morton, 44	rate	(stratification)	production indices	log linear	5,7
	Wang, 60	rate		production indices	log linear	7,8
	Tihansky			GNP, production indices, modal shares	linear log linear	7
Aggregate-Systems	Mathematica, 39 Volume 2	rate, travel time	value, size distribution	GRP, population, sales, employment, area	linear	2, 9, 10
	A. D. little, 1	distance, circulty index	value, bulk dummy, seasonality dummy	population, employment, production and consumption factors	linear, special	1, 2b, 6
	Swerdloff, 61	distance	(stratification)	population, employment	share model	1, 2, 6
	Krosge, 36	rate, travel time, time variability, L&D	cost factor for LOS variables	consumption, investment, exports, production	linear program, min. cost	11
Aggregate-Modal Shares	Herendeen, 29	rate, travel time	(stratification)		log linear	1, 2a
	Perle, 51	rate	dummy variables, (stratification)	regional dummy variables	log linear	1,4
	Miller, 43	rate, stratification by distance	stratification by size	percent of firms with rail siding	linear	1, 2a
	Surti, 60	distance	size, (stratification)		linear	2
	Boeing, 13	rate		GNP	log linear	12
	Mathematica, 39 Vol. 3, p. 24	rate, travel time	value, (stratification)	annual volume	(special)	2, 20
	Mathematica, 39 Vol. 3, p. 30	rate, travel time	value, (stratification)	annual volume	(special)	2, 20
	Kullman	rate, travel time reliability, distance	value	annual volume	logit	1, 2, 13
	Roberts, 54	rate, travel time reliability, L&D	value, perishability packaging cost	stockout cost, variability of usage, cost of capital	linear	—
	Mathematica, 39 Vol. 1	rate, travel time, time reliability	value	frequency of orders variability of usage	(special)	—
	American Airlines, 3	rate, distance, pickup charge	value, density packaging cost	inventory, safety stock, cost of capital	linear	—
	Miklius, 42	distance	size, (stratification)	employment at the origin firm	linear discriminator	2
Disaggregate-Mode Choice	Miklius, 42	distance	size, (stratification)		linear	2
	Antle, Haynes, 5	distance, travel time, rate, handling cost	size, (stratification)	annual volume of shipments	linear discriminator	14
	Army, 30	distance, travel time, rate, handling cost	size, (stratification)	annual volume of shipments	linear discriminator	16
	Beuthe, 11	rates, fixed costs	size, (stratification)			15, 20
	Hartwig, Linton, 28	rate, travel time	value, (stratification)		logit, probit, linear discriminator	17
	Ruijgrok, 56	rate, travel time	dummy variables for state	outgoing dummy, industry variables	logit	18

Note: The number after the modeler's name refer to the bibliography
Note: Due to space limitations, it is impossible to list all co-authors, variables and data sources.

254

Table A.1
Key to Data Sources

1. *Carload Waybill Statistics.*
2. *Census of Transportation.*
   a. Volume 3, Part 1 Shipper Groups
   b. Volume 3, Part 1 Geographic Areas
   c. Volume 3, Part 1 Commodity Groups
3. *Freight Commodity Statistics, Motor Carriers of Property.*
4. *Freight Commodity Statistics, Class I Railroads.*
5. *Waterborne Commerce of the United States*, Part 5.
6. *Transportation Facts and Trends.*
7. *Survey of Current Business.*
8. *County and City Data Book.*
9. *Federal Reserve Statistical Release.*
10. Reports from the Columbian Ministry of Transport.
11. Civil Aeronautics Board Form 41.
12. *Census of Manufacturers.*
13. Survey of 63 Firms in the Ohio River Valley.
14. Reports from the Chicago Board of Trade on Grain Shipments.
15. Survey of 97 Firms in the Arkansas River Valley.
16. A Sample of 1213 Waybills from a Midwestern Shipper.
17. Mail Survey of Shippers made by Dutch Ministry of Transport.
18. Reports from Canadian Dominion Bureau of Statistics, and Principal Counterparts.
19. Carrier's Tariffs.

Demand models can be separated into two general groups: aggregate and disaggregate. Furthermore, the aggregate and disaggregate models can be grouped according to their dependent variable. A summary of previous freight demand modelling studies is given in Table A.1.

Aggregate Models of Intercity Freight Demand

Most of the freight demand studies done to date have utilized aggregate data from government sources. However, empirical work with the *Census of Transportation* and other similar data sets has brought to light several serious problems arising from the use of aggregate data.

The results of most aggregate freight demand studies have been disappointing. In particular, those models which encompass several choices are reportedly more difficult to estimate than single choice models (such as mode split models). However, this does not imply that single choice models are superior. These results simply imply that better data is required for the estimation of a complete system of models.

Aggregate Mode Choice Models

One of the best known studies of freight demand was conducted by Perle (1964). Perle postulted a model of mode split between common carrier truck and rail as a function of the rates. The data used in this study came from the *Carload Waybill Statistics — State to State Summary* and the ICC *Motor Carrier Freight Commodity Statistics*. The data were aggregated into five commodity groups: products of agriculture, animals, mining, forestry, and manufacturing. The data were also aggregated into the nine geographic regions used by the ICC in reporting the truck data. A time series of five years of this type of data was prepared.

The model split used as the dependent variable in Perle's model was computed on the basis of tons of shipments. The explanatory variables, rates were computed as total revenue divided by total tons. Perle's model is of the following form:

$$\log(V_{m1}/V_{n2}) = \beta_0 + \beta_1 \log(r_{m1}/r_{m2}) +$$

$$+ \sum_{i=1}^{9} c_i R_i + \sum_{i=1}^{5} d_i y_k + \sum_{k=1}^{5} f_k c_k$$

where

V_{m1}	=	volume carried by truck
V_{m2}	=	volume carried by rail
r_{m1}	=	average revenue/ton on truck shipments
r_{m2}	=	average revenue/ton on rail shipments
R_i	=	(1 for region i, 0 otherwise)
Y_i	=	(1 for year i, 0 otherwise)
C_k	=	(1 for commodity k, 0 otherwise)

Perle estimates this model using ordinary least squared regression. The commodity dummy variables were found to be the most powerful explanatory variables. The regional variables had some impact, but the time variables were all insignificant. Perle concluded that the explanatory power of the rate term was minimal.

In an effort to improve the fit of this model, Perle stratified the data by commodity, by region and by both region and commodity. Models were then estimated on each subset of the data using the appropriate dummy variables in each case. The results of his work were very mixed. Some models fit very well, while others had large residuals and insignificant coefficients. Estimates of the price elasticities varied widely depending on the level of aggregation. In general, the effects of the commodity and region dummy variables were more significant than the effect of the rate term.

The results reported by Perle are not surprising. The dummy variables used for commodities are correlated with many of the important commodity attributes and transport level of service attributes. In particular, the commodity variables acted as a proxy for value per pound. And since value is correlated with rates, the commodity variables are correlated with rates. Furthermore, the regional dummy variables acted as a proxy for travel time reliability, loss and damage, and other level of service variables which vary significantly between regions (especially for rail transport).

Several conclusions can be drawn from Perle's work. First even simple mode split models require a more complete set of commodity and level of service variables. Secondly, the problem of aggregation bias in the values of the coefficients can be quite severe. Thirdly, aggregate level of service variables are neither good explanatory variables, nor good policy variables. The rate variable turned out to be very weak in all of perle's models. And in terms of policy analysis, the average revenue per ton is too vague to be of much use because it includes such a wide range of commodities and lengths of haul. Thus is can be concluded from Perle's study that the use of more level of service attributes, more commodity attributes, and more disaggregate data is desirable.

The conclusions drawn from Perle's study are reinforced by a study conducted by Miller (1972). Miller proposed a model of the rail market share as a function of the rates and a measure of rail availability. The rail market share was computed for each weight-mileage block in each of the 85 shipper classes included in the 1967 *Census of Transportation*. An average rail rate corresponding

255

to each weight-mileage block in each shipper group was computed from a special tabulation of the 1965 *Carload Waybill Statistics*. No suitable source of truck rates could be located and therefore the truck rate variable was dropped from the model. Rail availabilitiy was measured as the percentage of plants with rail sidings, using data from the 1967 *Census of Manufacturers*.

The general form of Miller's model is the following:

$$(V_{ml} / _m V_m) = \beta_0 + \beta_1 (r_{ml}) + \beta_2 \text{ (rail availability)}$$

where

V_{ml} = volume carried by rail

r_{ml} = average rate on rail shipments

A separate model was estimated for each weight-mileage block. In general, the results were poor. In most cases the availability term had a significant coefficient, but the rate variable did not. Miller tried aggregating the data over weight blocks and estimating a model using only the rate variable. As expected, the rate variable had a significant coefficient in this second version of the model. However, when the availability variable was put back into the model and a third estimation was attempted, the rate variable was again insignificant.

These results are not surprising. The influence of rail rates on modal shares is largely a function of the rates on the competing modes. Thus the lack of a truck rate variable in this model makes the rail rate variable difficult to interpret. It should also be noted that rail availability is one outcome of the plant location decision. The plant location decision is influenced by the transport level of service attributes, even though this strategic choice is not very sensitive to short-run fluctuations in the level of service. Therefore, the rail availability variable captured part of the influence of travel time, reliabilty, loss and damage, as well as the rates. The problems with the model could have been mitigated by using these level of service variables explicitly in the model. It is also evident that a greater disaggregation of data is needed to allow a more precise definition of the level of service variables (including rates) which influence demand in particular market segments.

Another study of modal split was conducted by Surti and Ebrahimi (1972). These researchers estimated a model of truck-rail mode split using the data on the tons of shipments in each weight-mileage block of the 24 shipper groups in the 1963 *Census of Transportation*. A separate model was estimated for each shipper group. The length of haul was used as a proxy for the level of service variables and shipment size was used as a proxy for other logistics costs. The data on both of these independent variables were also taken from the Census.

The most successful version of their model is of the following form:

$$v_{ml}^k / (v_{ml}^k + v_{m2}^k) = \beta_0 + \beta_1 \text{(dist)} + \beta_2 \text{(q)}$$

where

V_{ml}^k = volume of commodity k carried by truck

V_{m2}^k = volume of commodity k carried by rail

q = shipment size

This model fits most shipper groups fairly well.

All estimated coefficients have significant t statistics and all r^2 statistics are above 0.80. Note that these results are better than one might expect based on the experience of Miller (1972). The reason for this is a subtle difference in the specifications of these two models. Because of his stratification scheme, Miller actually estimated a model of mode choice conditional on shipment size and distance, but not commodity type. Since Miller's model lacked commodity attributes, the variation in commodities undermined his results. In contrast, Surti and Ebrahimi stratified their data so that their model represents the mode split conditional on the type of commodity. Therefore the lack of commodity attributes in the Sutri/ Ebrahimi model caused no major problems. Furthermore, since the mode and shipment size choices are made jointly, shipment size should be a good explanatory variable of mode choice. However, the usefulness of the Surti/Ebrahimi model is limited because of the lack of level of service variables. Rates and travel times are policy sensitive, but distance is not.

A somewhat wider variety of variables was included in a rail-barge mode split study conducted by A. D. Little Inc. (1974). The data for this study came from the 1967 *Census of Transportation*, the 1966 *Waterborne Commerce of the United States*, and the 1966 *Carload Waybill Statistics*. The variables used in this model are:

V_{ij}^k = volume of commodity k shipped from i to j

v = value/ton of commodity k

d = distance from origin i to destination j by rail

c = circuity index = (water distance/rail distance)

S = (1 for seasonal goods, 0 otherwise)

B = (1 for bulk goods, 0 otherwise)

L = percentage of production facilities located on the water at the origin plus the percentage of consuming facilities located on the water at the destination.

Note that the variable L is similar to the availability measure used in Miller's study. Also, distances are used as a proxy for rates as in the Surti and Ebrahimi study. However, this study includes some different variables as well. Three commodity attributes (v, S, and B) are used, in addition to a market attribute (V_{ij}).

The functional form of the A. D. Little model is the following:

$$\sin^{-1} \sqrt{V_{ij,m1}^k / (V_{ij,m1}^k + V_{ij,m2}^k)}$$
$$= \beta_0 + \beta_1 \log (V_{ij}^k) + \beta_2 \log (v) + \beta_3 \log (d) + \beta_4 \log (L) + \beta_5 \log (C) + \beta_6 (B) + \beta_7 (S)$$

where

$V_{ij,m1}^k$ = volume of k carried from i to j by barge

and

$V_{ij,m2}^k$ = volume of k carried from i to j by rail

This model was estimated for each of five geographic regions. Within each region, modal shares were computed for flows between BEA zones of 17 commodity groups (including raw materials and finished products).

The results from estimating this model were mixed. The r^2 statistic varied from 0.2 to 0.64. All of the coefficients had the expected sign and most were significant, except for the coefficient of the variable L. Note that the problem with the variable L is similar to the problem with the availability variable in Miller's model. Both studies indicate that the correlation between long run decisions such as plant location and various level of service and commodity variables is strong enough to force some key variables to have insignificant coefficients. However, this does not imply that plant location should be excluded from mode split models when level of service attributes and commodity attributes are used. Often the long run decisions are sub-optimal with respect to the current situation. Uunder these circumstances, the correlation between the long run decision variables and the level of service attributes will be lower, and terms like L will tend to add a significant amount of explanatory power to the model.

Several researchers have attempted to specify aggregate mode split models in which the mechanism for decision making is somewhat more apparent in the model structure. One such model was proposed by the consulting firm Mathematica (1969). The model that was proposed is the following:

$$V_{ij,m1}^k / (V_{ij,m1}^k + V_{ij,m2}^k) = 1 / [1 + (AVC_{m2} / AVC_{m1})^{\beta 1}]$$

The important feature of this model is that the variable AVC has been defined in the following manner:

$$AVC_m = rate_m + \beta_2 (time_m * value) * \beta_3 / [V_{ij}^k]^{0.5}$$

The first term of this expression represents the out-of-pocket transport cost and the second term represents the in-transit carrying cost. The third term is designed to reflect the inventory carrying cost. Together these three terms add up to an approximation of the average variable cost of using mode m to transport commodity k from origin i to destination j. The advantage of this kind of specification is that it incorporates a comparison of the logistics cost of the shipment alternatives. It should be noted that this model addresses freight demand at a more disaggregate level than the models previously discussed. This allows variables such as rates, transit time and commodity value to be more precisely defined.

The Mathematica model was estimated for each of 15 commodity groups using data from the 1963 Census of Transportation on rail, truck, and air shipments. Rates were estimated for all three modes using models developed for this study. Crude procedures for estimating travel times for each mode were also developed. In general the estimation results were good. Most coefficients in the set of estimated models were significant and many of the r statistics were above 0.80. These encouraging results tend to support the opinion that this Mathematica model was a step in the right direction.

In the same paper which was discussed in the previous review, Mathematica (1969) proposed another model. This second model does not make use of logistics cost variables. Instead, ratios of the level of service variables are used to compare the two competing modes. The form of this model is the following:

$$V_{ij,m1}^k / (V_{ij,m1}^k + V_{ij,m2}^k) = 1/(1 + w)$$

where:

$$w = [(t_{m1}/t_{m2})^{bc}{}_{m1} (c_{m1}/c_{m2})^{bt}{}_{m1} (c_{m1}^{\ln(t_{m1})} / c_{m2}^{\ln(t_{m2})})^{b}]u$$

$u = [b*\ln(v) + b*v] [b*\ln(V_{ij}^k) + b*(V_{ij}^k)]$

$t_m =$ mean travel time from i to j by mode m

$c_m =$ tariff on mode m for shipment of k from i to j

$v =$ value of commodity k

$V_{ijm}^k =$ volume of commodity k sent from i to j by mode m

This model performed about as well as the other Mathematica model. But this second model suffers from the drawback that its parameters are much harder to interpret than the parameters of the first model.

Kullman (1974) also tried to develop a mode split model with a clear interpretation. Kullman assumed that the cost of shipping by a given mode could be expressed as a linear function of the level of service attributes, commodity attributes and market attributes. The independent variables used in this model include high-way distance, annual tonnage, commodity value, rates, mean travel times and a measure of the variation in travel times. These variables were used in a logit form model of the rail-truck mode split.

$$\log (V_{m1}^k / V_{m2}^k) = \beta_0 + \Sigma_i \beta_i x_i$$

where x_i is an explanatory variable, and

$V_{m1}^k =$ volume of commodity k carried by rail

$V_{m2}^k =$ volume of commodity k carried by truck

Unlike the first Mathematica model, the independent variables used by Kullman are not estimates of logistics costs. He simply substituted rates, travel times and other independent variables for the x's used in the formula shown above. Kullman experimented with three sets of flow data which came from the 1967 Census of Transportation. The first includes national level mode splits for 2, 3, 4 and 5 digit commodities. The second data set contains mode splits for 2, 3, 4 and 5 digit commodities which were shipped between Production Areas and Market Areas. The third data set is a special preparation of the Census data. It includes mode splits on flows between counties of high, medium and low value goods.

The empirical results from Kullman's study were disappointing. The r² statistics were low and there were many insignificant coefficients in the models that were estimated. One conclusion that can be drawn from this study is that data without geographic detail *and* commodity detail *and* market/firm detail is not adequate. This study reinforces the conclusion that a model which is sensitive to the full set of level of service variables must be estimated with disaggregate data.

Aggregate Systems of Models

Several attempts have been made to build systems of aggregate models which are capable of covering the full range of freight shipment decisions. Typically these systems consist of a series of one decision models organized along the lines of the Urban Transportation Model System. A sequential model system is acceptable if it includes feedback from short run decisions to long-run decisions. However, this has not been adequately modeled in the systems which have been developed to date.

Systems of aggregate models suffer from the same problems that plague individual aggregate models. They may not be transferable in space or time because the estimates of the coefficients depend (in an unknown way) on how the data has been aggregated. Also, systems of aggregate models may not contain some policy variables because the aggregation of data tends to reduce the explanatory power of key variables such as travel time reliability. Nevertheless, the demand modeling systems currently available do offer a simple methodology for doing comprehensive freight planning.

The A.D. Little mode split model discussed earlier in this chapter has been used as part of a system of models developed by this firm (A.D. Little, 1976). The mode split model was reviewed separately because it has several particularly interesting features. The other elements in this system of models will not be reviewed here, although they are referred to in the summary table.

One aggregate model system of interest was developed by the consulting firm Mathematica (1969) as part of the Northeast Corridor Transportation Project. This system is composed of four stages. The first stage involves a projection of the total production in each of 16 commodity groups. The projections are made with a separate regression equation for each group. The independent variables in these regressions include a time variable and projections of various segments of the GNP. The GNP projections must be provided from an outside source.

The second stage involves a projection of the regional share of originating and terminating tonnage in each commodity group. In the final version of the model, it was assumed that the regional shares of originating tonnage remain unchanged. The regional demand for each commodity is predicted using a regression model. The independent variables in this model include population, retail sales, per capita income and regional income. Projections of these independent variables must be provided from other sources.

In the third stage, a distribution model is used to predict interregional flows. An initial guess is provided by a regression model which uses the following independent variables: production at the origin, consumption at the destination, distance, and various socio-economic variables such as population and employment at the destination. But when flows are predicted in this manner, the total flow in and out of each region will not match the totals predicted in the second stage. Therefore, a flow adjustment algorithm was developed using Lagrange multipliers. The objective of the Lagrangian is to minimize the flow of adjustments subject to the constraints on the total flow in and out of each region.

The final stage in the system involves the modal split of the inter-regional flows. A separate market share regression model was used for rail, common carrier truck, private truck, air, water and "other". The independent variables used in these models

include the fraction of shipments falling into each of five weight groups, the fraction of shipments falling into each of eight distance groups, commodity value and average gross revenue per ton. Note that when these mode split models are used, the shares must be normalized so that they total to 100 percent.

Mathematica's system of models was calibrated with data from the 1963 *Census of Transportation*. The data base included flows in 16 shipper groups between 25 Production and Market Areas. Supporting data came from the *City and County Data Book* (Bureau of the Census), "Business Statistics" (Dept. of Commerce), and the "Federal Reserve Statistical Release". Unfortunately, information on the performances of the complete system was not included in the report.

Another system of sequential aggregate models has been developed by the Office of Systems Analysis (1970) in the Department of Transportation. The data base for this study was built around a 506 zone system that covers the entire country. Networks connecting these zones were constructed for rail, truck, water, air refined product pipelines and crude pipelines. In this model system, flows are classified as being petroleum or non-petroleum. Non-petroleum flows are subdivided into large and small shipments. Both large and small shipments are further divided into three value classes. Petroleum products are divided into crude and refined.

The first step in this study was to build base year inter-zonal flow tables for each commodity group. Air flows were estimated using CAB data on the commodity flows in and out of all major airports. A gravity model was used for flow distribution. Barge flows came from a special preparation of *Waterborne Commerce*. Pipeline flows were estimated by applying a linear programming model to data on the production and consumption of crude and refined petroleum in various zones. Truck flows were estimated from an inter-county motor vehicle trip table prepared from data collected by the Bureau of Public Roads. In preparing the truck flows, auto trips were "factored out" of vehicle trips and then average truck load factors were applied to the remaining highway volumes.

Projections of inter-zonal flows are made using the Fratar model which was developed as part of the Urban Transportation Model System. The Fratar model has been used to adjust interzonal flows so that they will be consistent with the zonal in-flows and out-flows projected in the previous step. The independent variables in this model are the changes in zonal population and employment.

Adjustments in model split are made using a share model of the following form:

$$V_{ij,m1}^k / {}_m V_{ijm}^k = (\beta_{1,m1}\, t_{m1}^{\beta_{2,m1}}\, r_{m1}^{\beta_{3,m1}}) /$$
$$({}_m \beta_{1,m}\, t_m^{\beta_{2,m}}\, r_m^{\beta_{3,m}})$$

where

t_m = mean travel time from i to j by mode m

c_m = tariff on shipments from i to j by mode m

The time and rate variables used in this study were derived from the minimum path distances in each of the model networks. Regression equations relating distance to rate were estimated using I.C.C. data on the costs and revenues of each mode.

This model system has been tested with a number of policy scenarios. The results were reportedly reasonable. However, the details on the system have not been widely publicized.

Aggregate, Joint Demand Models

Single choice models can be assembled into sequential model systems which address the full range of freight shipment decisions. However, there are two drawbacks to this approach. The first is that some choices (such as mode choice) are made jointly with other choices (such as shipment size). Secondly, even when two decisions are not made jointly, there is feedback from short-run decisions to long-run decisions. Neither of these two aspects of freight demand are adequately represented in sequential model systems.

The problems with sequential model systems have given rise to joint or direct, aggregate demand models. The advantage of this approach is that several choices are modeled in the same equation. In theory, the independent variables can be structured in such a way as to reflect the combined effect of a set of decisions. The independent variables could represent the interactions between choices and the model coefficients would then reflect the importance of various interactions. In practice, this approach has not been used to its full advantage. Most applications of aggregate joint demand models have involved a combination of the trip generation and mode split elements of the sequential model systems. However, the level of production and mode of shipment are usually not chosen jointly. This makes it difficult to specify independent variables which reflect the interaction of these two choices. Consequently, most aggregate, joint demand models have been constructed around two separate sets of variables: the mode choice variables and the volume of production variables. In this respect, these models are more like two separate models contained in the same equation. Whatever interaction effects are represented in the model, they are imbedded in the coefficients.

A joint aggregate demand model was estimated as part of Perle's (1964) study which was described earlier. The data set used to estimate this model is the same as the one described before. It includes truck and rail flows in five commodity groups, in nine regions, during each of five years.

The model used by Perle is of the following form:

$$\log(V_{m1}) = \beta_0 + \beta_1 \log(r_{m1}) + \beta_2 \log(r_{m2}) + \sum_{i=1}^{9} c_i R_i + \sum_{i=1}^{5} d_i Y_i + \sum_{k=1}^{5} f_k C_k$$

where

V_{m1} = volume of traffic carried by mode m1
r_{m1} = average revenue/ton on mode m1
r_{m2} = average revenue/ton on mode m2
R_i = (1 for region i, 0 otherwise)
Y_i = (1 for year i, 0 otherwise)
C_k = (1 for commodity k, 0 otherwise)

Perle estimated a truck model and a rail model of this form. In general his results were very poor.

In all cases, the results from this model had poorer r^2 and t statistics than Perle's aggregate mode split model.

These results are to be expected. The dependent variable in the joint model includes the choice of a level of production as well as the choice of a mode. In contrast, the Perle model previously described covers only the choice of mode. Obviously the joint model taxes the explanatory power of the data more heavily than the mode split model. However this does not entirely explain the difference in results.

The most crucial flaw in the joint model is that it does not reflect the fact that the demand for transportation is derived from the demand for commodities. The dependent variable includes the volume of transportation, but none of the independent variables explain the demand for the commodities being transported. It is true that the price of transportation is a component in the sales price of a good, which in turn determines the demand for that good. However if this rationale is to be used, then the appropriate variable to put in the model is the sum of the cost of transportation and all other costs associated with the production of a good. But where all commodities are aggregated into a small number of groups, the average cost of production for each group is almost meaningless. On the other hand, it is impractical to estimate a separate demand model for each commodity. As will be shown, other researchers have found methods of using proxy variables to represent the demand for commodities. Nevertheless, Perle's study does reinforce the conclusion that aggregate models are inherently difficult to specify properly.

Another important study in this area was conducted by Sloss (1971). Sloss postulated a model for the volume of truck traffic as a function of the average truck rate, the average rail rate and a proxy variable used to represent the demand for commodities.

One unique aspect of this work is that Canadian rather than U.S. data were used. The dependent variable was defined as the annual tons of freight carried in intra-provincial, interprovincial and international hauls by trucks registered in each province. The sources of information on this variable are the "Motor Transport Traffic: National Estimates" published by the Dominion Bureau of Statistics, and the provincial counterparts of this report. These same reports were used to collect data on the average revenue per ton for truck hauls, which were used to estimate average truck rates. The average rail rates were measured in terms of the average revenue per ton for intra-regional FCL shipments of selected commodities. Data on this variable came from the "Waybill Analysis" published by the Canadian Board of Transport Commissioners.

Unlike Perle, Sloss used a measure of economic activity in his model to represent the demand for commodities. This variable was defined as the sum of farm cash income, the value of new building permits and the value of shipments of manufactured goods in each province. Data on this variable came from the "Canadian Statistical Review" and the *Canada Yearbook*.

Data were collected for eight provinces for the years 1958 through 1963. Then ordinary least squares was used to fit the following model:

$$\log(V_{m1}) = \beta_0 + \beta_1 \log(r_{m1}) +$$
$$\beta_2 \log(r_{m2}) + \beta_3 \log(E)$$

where

V_{m1} = volume of truck traffic

r_{m1} = average revenue/ton on truck

r_{m2} = average revenue per ton on rail

E = economic activity variable

The results of Sloss' work indicate demand elasticities of nearly unity with respect to each of the three independent variables. Although the r^2 statistic was quite high, the estimation results are not conclusive. The reason for this skepticism is that the data used in this study was so highly aggregated that almost all variability was lost. This implies that very different results might be reported if this model was estimated using data on much smaller geographic units. Unfortunately, this is a problem which plagues all aggregate models to some degree.

Alexander Morton (1969) has conducted a demand modeling study using data similar to Perle's and the same model specification as Sloss. The data on rail volumes was taken from "Freight Commodity Statistics for Class 1 Railroads" which is published by the ICC. The 242 commodities listed in this report were aggregated into five groups: products of agriculture, animals, forestry, mining and manufactures. Truck volumes were taken from the American Trucking Association pamphlet titled "Transportation Facts and Trends". Using data from the same source, truck rates where calculated as total revenue divided by total ton-miles. Rail rates were calculated from the RI-1 index of relative rates, which was published as part of the I.C.C. "Rail Waybill Study". The data were gathered for the years 1947 through 1966, for the nation as a whole and selected regions. The economic activity variable used in this study was GNP for the nation and gross regional product for regions.

Morton estimated the model for truck and rail, using various subsets of the data. He also estimated a similar model in which the truck and rail rates were replaced by the average rate on both modes, and the ratio of truck and rail rates. The results of this work varied considerably with the level of geographic and commodity aggregation. Due to the aggregation of data, the r^2 statistics were fairly high, ranging from 0.58 to 0.94. However, over one-quarter of all coefficients estimated in this study had the wrong sign. Morton attributed part of the problem to the historical shift from rail to truck caused by level of service factors other than rates. This demonstrates once again how the exclusion of key variables can undermine a model.

Disaggregate Models

For purposes of policy analysis, a demand model must be able to forecast aggregate patterns of freight movements. In theory, this can be accomplished by aggregating the data on the independent variables before they are used in the model, or by using disaggregate data in the model and then aggregating the results. It was shown in the preceding section that the aggregation of the data on the independent variables has led to major problems in many studies. These problems can be avoided if the model is estimated using disaggregate data.

The advantages of disaggregate models are numerous. One of the most important points is their efficient use of data. Since the data is not averaged, there is no loss in the variability (i.e., explanatory power) of the independent variables. This means that reliable estimates of the model coefficients can be obtained from relatively small data sets. Furthermore, disaggregate models often contain significant coefficients for variables that usually have insignificant coefficients in aggregate models. This is particularly true of policy sensitive variables such as travel time reliability.

A second important feature of disaggregate models is that they are potentially transferable. This means that an estimated disaggregate model which is properly specified can be applied to a wide range of commodities and markets.

Another feature of this kind of model is that forecasts can be prepared for any level of aggregation. Hence it is not necessary to have separate sets of models for local, regional and national planning.

One point that should be emphasized is that disaggregate models require data on the atributes of all of the available freight shipment options, both the chosen and unchosen. Although the collection of this kind of data may seem like a nuisance, it does allow the modeler to view the shipment process from the point of view of the decision maker. All of which means that the independent variables can be defined clearly and concisely, and the coefficients can be interpreted unambiguously. Furthermore, any a priori knowledge of the manner in which decision makers evaluate alternatives can be incorporated into the specification of the model.

Because of the lack of data, very few disaggregate freight demand studies have been conducted. To date, there have been no attempts to estimate a joint choice model, although several mode choice models have been estimated.

A disaggregate mode choice model was estimated by Antle and Havens (1971) at the Institute for Water Resources. The independent variables used in this study are the following:

x_1 = shipper's annual volume of shipments of given commodity between given O-D pair

x_2 = length of haul

x_3 = average travel time

x_4 = average shipment size

x_5 = rate on chosen mode

x_6 = difference in rates between chosen and alternative mode

x_7 = handling cost on the selected mode

This data was collected for coal, coke, and petroleum shipments in the Ohio River Valley. The dependent variable was defined as having the value 1 if barge was chosen and 0 if rail was chosen.

The modeling technique used in this study is known as discriminant analysis. The form of the model is the following:

$$Z = \sum_{i-1}^{7} \beta_i \, x_i$$

When using the model, if the computed value of X exceeds a critical value, then the model predicts that barge will be chosen, otherwise the model predicts that rail will be chosen.

The results from the estimation of this model are fairly good. All of the coefficients came out with the expected sign and most were significant, although the distance, annual volume and rate variables were weaker than expected.

Antle and Haynes also tried aggregating their data across all commodities and then re-estimating the model. The results were significantly poorer. This supports the claim made earlier that disaggregate models use data more efficiently than aggregate models.

The latest attempt at estimating a disaggregate mode split model is described in a thesis written by Hartwig and Linton (1974). These two researchers collected 1213 waybills from one shipper of consumer durables. Using the data from the waybills, they calculated the rate, mean travel time and variance in travel time for the full truckload and full rail carload alternatives. Commodity value was also included as an independent variable.

Hartwig and Linton used this data to estimate logit, probit and discriminant analysis models. Although the logit and probit models performed quite well, the travel time variable was insignificant in most of the specifications which were estimated. Nevertheless, this study is important because it provides further evidence of the practicality of estimating disaggregate freight demand models.

The first attempts at estimating disaggregate freight demand models are encouraging. However, the problem of building a joint choice model and including a wider range of independent variables has yet to be tackled.

APPENDIX B
Formulation of Disaggregate Freight Demand Model [3]

This section develops a general specification for a disaggregate freight demand model. This model can then be specialized for the case of the urban/regional planner or for the case of the national transportation policy planner.

The impetus for a disaggregate approach to freight demand modelling originated in the urban passenger transport field, where recent breakthroughs in the modelling of individual travel behaviour have occurred. Urban transportation researchers, after years of frustration with aggregate models of travel behavior, concluded that the choice of transport mode is intertwined with choices of workplace, residential location, and auto ownership, as well as household characteristics such as family size, income, and number of workers. The response to this condition was to develop models (or model systems) that would make, for the individual household, probability estimates of choosing each of the possible combinations of mode to work, workplace, residential location, etc., based on household characteristics and transport levels of service.

In the freight field, a similar situation exists. The shipper must make three simultaneous choices: where to buy, how much to ship, and by what mode (or carrier), based on annual requirements for a commodity, storage, ordering and other costs, the levels of service offered by competing modes, the price of the commodity quoted at different origins, and characteristics of the commodity (shelf life, value, packaging, special handling requirements, etc.). As in the passenger transport field, it

is conceptually appropriate to formulate a choice model which assigns probabilities to combinations of shipper alternatives (origin, shipment size, and mode) based on shipper, transport mode and commodity attributes. [4]

The mathematical form most frequently specified for disaggregate choice models are multinomial logit functions of the form:

$$P((\underline{X}|\underline{A}) = \frac{e^{U(\underline{A})}}{\sum e^{U(\underline{A})}}$$

$\underline{X}$ = vector of choice combinations

$\underline{A}$ = vector of attributes

P = probability of choosing a particular combination $\underline{X}^*$

U = utility function based on all the attributes

For the case of freight demand prediction, this general form specializes as follows:

$$p^k(i,mq|ALTS) = \frac{e^{U(T,C,M,R)}}{\sum e^{U(T,C,M,R)}}$$

where

$U(T,C,M,R)$ = the utility function of the receiver
k = commodity index
i = supply (origin) point
mq = mode/shipment size combination
$ALTS$ = alternatives avaible to the receiver
U = utility function
T = transport attributes
C = commodity attributes
M = market attributes
R = receiver attributes

Figure 1 defines the T, C, M and R variables that could enter the utility function.

Transport Attributes
W = wait time (days)
T = transit time (days)
R = reliability (days)
L = loss and damage (unitless, $0 \le L \le 1$)
$\$$ = freightrate ($/1b)
C = special charges ($/1b)

Market Attributes
P = relative price (unitless)
O = ownership (binary 0-1)

Commodity Attributes
V = value ($/1b)
D = density (1b/ft³)
S = shelf life (days)

Receiver Attributes
A = annual use rate (1bs/year)
M = mixed order (unitless, $0 \le M \le 1$)
S^1 = seasonal purchase (unitless, $0 \le S^1 \le 1$)
Q = shipment size (1bs)
U = reliability of use rate (days)
G = guarantee of availability (unitless %)

Figure 1 - Variables that can Enter a Utility Function

The task of the freight transportation analyst is quite clearly the *specification* and *estimation* of the utility function U(T,C,M,R). While several specifications for U(T,C,M,R) are possible, they are all estimated using maximum likelihood techniques.

Specifying the utility function of the receiver

can be done in light of the logistics process he/she is trying to manage. Basically, total costs consist of purchase costs plus logistics costs, as follows [5].

Total Costs = purchase cost + order and handling cost + transport cost + capital carrying and storage cost + stockout cost

The utility function of the shipper is developed by combining the variables previously specified with appropriate parameters. See Figure 2. By careful specification, the parameters can be presented in such a way that they can be interpreted as constants, interest rates, elasticities or dimensionless. This would allow the estimated models to be checked for reasonableness and extended to other environments where estimation is not practical. It would even allow the model to be used without estimation should that be necessary.

The utility function in Figure 2 is based on the "classic" calculation of logistics costs, with parameters taking on values that represent various aspects of a shipper's/receiver's cost structure. The equation is constructed to yield a disutility measure in units of $/lb., i.e., the *total* cost of the commodity from time of purchase until time of consumption. Each cost element in Figure 2 is discussed below:

Purchase Cost — P, the relative price at each origin, is multiplied by V, the value per pound delivered, to obtain a local price. Both P and α_1 are dimensionless, and α_1 should be equal to unity.

$U (T,C,M,R,)$ = purchase cost + order and handling cost + transport cost + capital carrying and storage cost + stockout cost

Purchase Cost

cost to buyer

$\alpha_1 P \cdot V$

Order & Handling Cost

set up charge

$\alpha_2 \, 1/Q \cdot M$

Transport Cost

capital cost in transit   loss & damage   perishability   transport charges

$\alpha_3 \frac{W+T}{365} \cdot P \cdot V \cdot 0 + \alpha_4 (L \cdot P \cdot V) 0 + \alpha_5 (\frac{W+T}{S})^n \cdot P \cdot V \cdot 0 + \alpha_6 (\$+C) \, 0 \cdot M /Q$

Capital Carrying Cost & Storage Cost

$\alpha_7 (\frac{Q}{2A} + \frac{R+U}{365}) \cdot V \cdot P \cdot S^1 + \alpha_8 (\frac{Q}{2A} + \frac{R+U}{365}) \cdot S^1 /D$

Stockout Cost

stockout

$\alpha_9 (1-G) \cdot (1/Q)$

Figure 2 - Specification of the Utility Function

Order and Handling Cost — the cost of the personnel and paperwork required to order each shipment, where $1/Q = F/A$. The term M varies from 0 to 1.0 and is the percent by weight of this commodity in a mixed shipment. Mixed shipments, in which more than one commodity is involved but where the sum of all commodities is less than a full truckload, are transported under the freight rate applicable to be highest rated commodity applied to the combined shipment weight. Both transport costs (see α_6 below) and order costs must be apportioned over all items in the ship-

ment. The term α_2 will be the cost of placing each order.

Transport Cost — the first term represents the capital carrying costs of the goods while in transit; 0 is a 0-1 variable which signifies ownership. If the receiver is buying the goods f.o.b. the origin, 0 takes on the value 1. If the receiver is buying f.o.b. the destination, the shipper bears these charges and $0 = 0$. The parameter α_3 is simply the cost of capital for the receiver.

The loss and damage term hinges on the transport attribute L which is derived from a separate model and represents the fraction of units totally destroyed. The cost of damaged units is subsumed in L. The parameter α_3 should calibrate to unity.

The perishability term has the units of $/lb., and α_5 is consequently expected to calibrate to unity. The parameter n on the term $[(W + T)/S]^n$ is designed to modify the influence of this term and must be specified exogenous to the model. For example, if the commodity is fresh fruit, n may lie in the range $0 \leq n \leq 1$ to reflect the fact that as W + T approaches S, there will be a significant los due to spoilage. Alternatively, if the commodity does have a finite shelf life but does not lose value until W + T is very close to S, then n will take on a positive value greater than 1. The determination of a proper value for n will be left to analyst judgment and the experience of the traffic managers who assist in data preparation.

Transport charges are the freight rate per pound times the binary variables 0 to indicate who pays the freight and the mixed shipment variable M described above. Dividing by Q distributes the freight charges on a per pound basis. The parameter α_6 should calibrate to unity.

Capital Carrying & Storage Cost — the first term is the cost of the merchandise while in the receiver's warehouse prior to consumption. The term Q/2 is the average level of stock on hand (exclusive of safety stock) and the term (R + U)/365 represents the safety stock required to protect from transit time unreliability and usage rate unreliability. The variable R is the number of days beyond the mean transit time in which there is a probability G that the shipment will arrive, given a constant rate of daily commodity use. The variable U represents the variation in the rate of use of stock and is measured by the standard deviation of the (presumed normally distributed) use rate. The term S^1 represents the influence of seasonality and is the fraction of the year that the item is held in inventory. Hence, $0 \leq S^1 \leq 1$. Note that for an item which is special ordered as needed (i.e., is not held in inventory), $S^1 = 0$ as would be expected. For an item used for a production run which lasts only four months, $S^1 = .33$. The parameter α_7 should calibrate to the cost of capital.

The second term is an expression for the costs of warehousing and represents the average amount of goods on hand $[Q/2A + (R + U)/365] \cdot S^1$ times the reciprocal of the density. This expression is valid for either bulk or packaged commodities. The term α_8 will be the cost of storage per *cubic* foot. (Note that warehouse costs are normally calculated on a per square foot basis so that the stacking height of cartons becomes key. However,

262

it is too difficult to generalize about this variable, so it was not put in the model). Thus, the parameter α_8 for packaged commodities will pick up the influence of both warehouse costs per square foot and stacking height which will increase the variance of this parameter estimate.

Stockout Costs — the final term is a representation of the cost per pound of stocking out, which occurs with probability 1-G each time there is a shipment (F times per year) and is distributed over the annual use A, where $F/A = 1/Q$. The parameter α_9 is a measure of the cost of each incidence of stockout. The variable G is measured in terms of the probability that the shipment arrives in time to prevent a stockout and will typically range from .90 to 1.0.

This brief discussion of logistics costs is in no way intended to substitute for a careful reading of any of the available texts on physical distribution management. It is intended only to provide an overview of the way that logistics terms might enter the model. In a given situation the regional planner would likely have to add, delete, or modify terms to meet local data requirements.

The four attribute vectors (T,C,M,R) can be developed in the following way. *Receiver attributes* are determined through exercise of the industry firm size table and input/output model coefficients

$$A_{IND, SIZE}^K = a_{K,IND} \cdot \hat{X}_{IND, SIZE}$$

where:

$A_{IND, SIZE}^K$ = annual usage rate of commodity K by firm of size class SIZE in industry IND

$a_{K, IND}$ = input-output coefficients

$\hat{X}_{IND, SIZE}$ = average output of all firms of industry IND and size class SIZE

Note that the annual usage rate developed by this procedure will only be as detailed as the input-output table used. It is possible that regional planners may have access to input-output tables that differ in degree of detail from national tables which are typically at the 3-4 digit SIC. Also, the result is in dollars. To convert to physical units the result must be divided by the value per pound, using the commodity attribute described below. Other receiver attributes, such as available facilities, whether the commodity is used as an intermediate or final good and whether the receiver uses mixed orders are a function of the receiving industry. Once the receiving industry is known, these inputs can be quickly determined.

Transport level of service variables can be developed for a given situation using three separate classes of level of service models by mode. These models, developed by the Freight Transportation Group at MIT are: [6]

1) Waiting and Transit Time and Reliability Models
2) Loss and Damage Models
3) Freight Rate Estimation Models

Each is described in detail in the references; however, a brief description of each is given below.

The waiting and transit time and reliability models predict time distributions for waiting plus transit from origin to destination as a function of number and type of terminals and the line haul distance, speed and frequency of service between terminals for each of the modes. See Figure 3. Since the principle cause of delay in the system is that which occurs at terminals this approach has produced very good comparisons with observed travel time disributions measured in the real world [7]. The probability of delay at a given type of terminal is represented by a cumulative function of the time available between arrival and the next regularly scheduled departure.

Loss and damage by mode is a function of the commodity attributes and the particular transport mode under consideration. The models used are simple regression models based on the experience record of the mode.

Freight rate estimation using a model is essential because of the complexity of the commodity rate structure and its huge size (more than 3 trillion separate commodity tariff rates are on file in the U.S.). The model uses as input the various commodity attributes (i.e., density, value per pound, shelf life, etc.) and the distance and shipment size by mode. The regression models have been developed using actual waybill or freight bill information for the various modes. Though point estimates of the freight rate are produced, it is possible, using the error distribution produced by the regression, to predict the distribution of likely freight rates if this becomes desirable.

The commodity attributes, the third class of variables, are available for 1200, 5-digit STCC commodities from the MIT Commodity Attribute File [8]. This file uses the Standard Transportation Commodity Classification (STCC) code at the five digit level to record the following information in machine readable form:

Waiting & Transit Time & Reliability Model

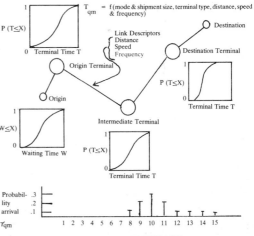

T_{qm} = f(mode & shipment size, terminal type, distance, speed & frequency)

TRANSIT TIME IN DAYS

Loss and Damage Model

L_{mq}^k = f(Mode & Shipment Size, Commodity Attributes)

Freight Rate Estimation Model

R_{mq}^k = f(Transport Attributes, Commodity Attributes, Mode & Shipment Size, Distance)

Figure 3 - Features of the Level of Service Models

1) STCC Code No.
2) 35 digits of Description
3) Wholesale Value per pound ($/lb)
4) Density (lbs/ft³)
5) Shelf Life (weeks)
6) State (solid, liquid, gas, particulate)
7) Environmental protection required (frozen, temperature, pressure, shock)

Given the commodity, this information can be made quickly available.

Market attributes are more difficult to secure. The most important is price. The price variable is designed as a *relative price*, which when multiplied by the wholesale value per pound becomes a local price. Using relative price enables differential model prices to reflect the spatial distribution in prices in the input. Even wholesale and retail markups can be simulated. Price and availability information can be obtained from the Office of Business Economics, the Agricultural Marketing Service, and the Bureau of Mines of the U.S. Government. Or, this data may be furnished by a macro-economic model used in conjunction with the study. Data on ownership and facilities is normally a function of the industry from which the commodity of interest is drawn. For example, the food industry normally sells its products with CIF delivered prices and has rail sidings available for loading rail cars.

Model Outputs

The output of the model is the probability that a particular receiving firm located in the region will secure its input from origin i in shipment size q by mode m. When this probability is multiplied by the annual use rate, $A^k_{IND, SIZE}$ calculated from the industry/firm size analysis previously described, the result is the commodity k moving from each of the known producing regions to the mode choice/shipment size for each region for the firm under consideration.

$$V^k_{i, qm, IND, SIZE} = p^k(qm|i) \cdot A^k_{IND, SIZE} \qquad (8)$$

where:

$p^k(qm|i)$ = probability of shipping commodity k by mode m at shipment size q from origin i

$A^k_{IND, SIZE}$ = annual use rate of commodity k by industry IND of size SIZE

When summed over all firms and firm sizes in the region, the results can be stored in a single three-dimensioned table. See Figure 4. If the commodity moving is of no particular interest, then the result should be presented using only two dimensions.

$$V_{i, qm} = \sum_k v^k_{i, qm} \qquad (9)$$

A third possible approach is to summarize flows by major commodity grouping or segment. In this case:

$$V^{kseg}_{i, qm} = \sum_{k \in kseg} v^k_{i, qm} \qquad (10)$$

kseg = aggregation of individual commodities k

This minimizes the extent of the third dimension to some reasonable size from the full size used for the analysis (k at 5 digits) would be approximately 1200).

Obviously, the computations to be performed are voluminous if the number of commodities is large and the number of origin regions is extensive. The process described above is, in fact, merely an enumeration over all decision makers. This number of computations can be reduced by sampling instead of using total enumeration. The best dimensions for sampling appear to be those concerning industry, IND, and firm size, SIZE. However, the commodity, k, also looks like it should be sampled, particularly because of its size. On the other hand, the dimension i, covering each origin region is a good choice for enumeration since there is considerable reason to preserve spatial detail.

A random sampling process can be set up for selecting the representative sample so that the commodity k to be used is selected based on the relative size of the Kth row of the input-output table. Finally, a firm size is selected based on the relative size of the appropriate row in the industry/firm size matrix. Each such randomly selected point is used for computation until a sufficiently large sample is available that the total, by mode and shipment size, from the different supply points can be adjusted up to equal the total volume flowing.

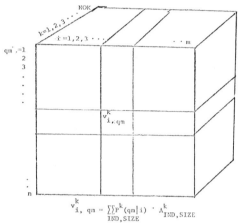

Figure 4 - The Output of the Model

REFERENCES

[1] Marc N. Terziev, Chapter 4 of "Modeling the Demand for Freight Transportation", (unpublished Master's dissertation, Department of Civil Engineering, Massachusetts Institute of Technology, September, 1976).

[2] Ralph D. Samuelson and Paul O. Roberts, "A Commodity Attribute Data File for Use in Freight Transportation Studies", MIT Center for Transportation Studies Report 75-20, November, 1975.

[3] This section was taken from The Resource Paper prepared by Paul O. Roberts and Brian C. Kullman for Presentation to the Workshop on Goods Movement at the Third International Conference on Behavioral travel Modelling, April, 1977, Adelaide, Australia.

[4] P. O. Roberts, "Forecasting Freight Flows Using a Disaggregate Freight Demand Model, MIT Center for Transportation Studies, CTS Report 76-1, January 1976.

[5] Roberts, Paul, **The Logistics Management Process as a Model of Freight Traffic Demand**, International Symposium on Freight Traffic Models, May 1971, Amsterdam, Holland.

[6] Roberts, Paul O., **Transport in Intercity Markets: An Overwiew of the Physical Distribution System**, Task II report, CTS no. 75-17, October, 1975.

[7] Martland, Carl D., **Improving Railroad Reliability: A Case Study of the Southern Railway, Volume 10, Appendix B**, MIT, 1975.

[8] Samuelson, Ralph and Paul O. Roberts, **A Commodity Attribute File for Use in Freight Transportation Studies**, CTS Report no. 75-20, November, 1975.

Management - a potential source of improved long-term demand forecasts in aviation and shipping

by

M. S. BRADBURY

Department of Industry, England

INTRODUCTION

For the purposes of this paper long-term demand forecasts are distinguished from more immediate predictions, by their need to allow sufficient time for major investment projects to be evaluated, implemented, and in many instances generate sufficient net benefits to fully remunerate the capital devoted to them.

It is widely accepted that better long-term demand forecasts are likely result from the use of improved data and more sophisticated econometric techniques. The central theme of this paper is that an additional source of improvement is to be found in the better management of the working environment within which such forecasts are prepared. Though of potentially wider application, I have chosen to illustrate my theme by reference to some aviation and shipping problems which have arisen during my work as a Civil Servant. Consequently, I must stress that what follows is a personal view, which should not be imputed to the Department of Industry.

STATE OF THE ARTS

In common with other areas of forecasting, long-term demand predictions in aviation and shipping are tending to place less reliance on the crude projection of the previous decade or so's broad aggregate data and are increasingly based on disaggregated economic models with parameters derived via econometric techniques. However, useful surveys of the current state of forecasting methodologies applied to aviation and shipping problems are available elsewhere [1]. Consequently, I have confined my discussion of the 'state of the arts', to commenting on a few apparent differences between long-term demand forecasts in aviation and shipping, and to illustrating the need for substantial improvements in their quality.

Subject to obvious exceptions long-term demand forecasts tend to focus on passengers in aviation and freight in shipping. However, whilst this apparently attractive physical distinction rightly influences working procedures, it is of limited importance when considering long-term demand forecasting methodology. Ignoring unimportant exceptions, transport demand is derived rather than final. Thus for example the demand for non-business international passenger travel by air is largely derived from the demand for overseas holidays and visits to friends and relatives. Likewise, the demand for iron ore transport by sea is derived from the demand for products made from iron and steel. Ultimately the demand for both aviation and shipping services can be analysed by resort to a common conceptual framework, ie. the economic theory of consumer behavior. Economists usually regard the market demand for a final product as being the sum of the effective demands of individual consumers. In turn, individual demand is usually viewed as a function of such basic variables as product price, the prices of substitute and complementary goods, disposable income, net worth, tastes and expectations, where long-term demand forecasts in aviation and shipping do sometimes differ, is in the extent to which they attempt to analyse basic variables directly, rather than assume a stable relationship between basic variables and intermediate or proxy variables. For example, many aviation non-business passenger forecasts use relatively close proxies to individual consumers incomes such as consumption per capita, whilst a forecast of seaborne trade in steel may rely on more remote relationships say between steel output and gross domestic product, and between the stage of the economic cycle and international trade in steel. Although in principle the use of basic variables is preferable to reliance on intermediate or proxy variables, data deficiencies and/or working-time constraints usually determinie which variables are to be used.

Long-term demand forecasts in aviation and shipping are primarily used to aid decisionmaking on the acquisition of aircraft and ships and the provision of infrastructure. Whilst it is quite common for aircraft manufacturers to forecast their market 15-20 years ahead, it is rare to see shipbuilding demand projections looking more than 5-10 years into the future [2]. This situation can be explained by differing relationships between technology and capital costs in aviation and shipping. A new aircraft design is often formulated at the frontiers of technology and may involve several years of research and development before production starts. Consequently, the decision to launch a new aircraft often involves a major investment which must be recovered from high volume sales in the relatively distant future [3]. Conversely, although some specialised tonnage involves expensive research and development, the majority of ships incorporate existing technology and are built on a 'one off' or small batch basis. Major expansions of both airports and seaports often involve relatively long *minimum* timescales. In part, this reflects the technical need to evaluate the external effects of such projects on, for example, inland transport facilities, housing, the environment and land use planning in general. Increasingly, however, the timescale also reflects the time needed for related administrative and political processes to operate.

Lastly, although fluctuations in the world business cycle influence the demand for both aviation and ship-

---

Crown Copyright. Any views expressed in this paper are not necessarily those of the Department of the Environment or the Department of Transport. Extracts from the text may be reproduced, except for commercial purposes, provided the source is acknowledged.

ping services, it can be argued that bulk shipping services are particularly prone to cyclical influences. Thus freight rates, ship prices, orders for new tonnage and lay-up/scrapping of tonnage can fluctuate by several orders of magnitude on numerous occasions within the physical life of a ship. In such circumstances the timing of a ship purchase, sale or charter becomes critical to financial success or failure. Consequently, shipowners, shippers, shipbuilders and bankers all have an interest in predicting turning points in shipping markets. Despite such interest and much effort, it has to be admitted that progress to date leaves much to be desired [1].

There is an old English saying that 'the proof of the pudding is in the eating'. Applying this test there seems little doubt that very considerable improvements are still required in the quality of long-term demand forecasts in aviation and shipping. The two examples which follow illustrate this point all too clearly.

The first example is taken from the official reappraisal of the Maplin project for a Third London Airport [4]. Table 1 below shows air passenger demand at London airports in 1972 and 1973 (actual) and 1990 (forecast). The forecasts for 1990 were derived from a disaggregated economic model which was considered to be an improvement on earlier work by the Roskill Commission [5]. The high forecast incorporated a combination of assumptions which would tend towards a high level of passenger demand and the low forecast a combination which would tend towards a low level of demand. Given uncertainty, single values were taken for the price of oil and some elasticities and further tests of sensitivity applied. The point of this example is not whether the forecasts are 'right' or 'wrong', but the policy uncertainties implicit in the range between high and low forecasts. Although not large as a percentage of the mid point between the high and low forecasts, the absolute magnitude of uncertainty significantly exceeds actual 1973 terminal throughput. Put another way, it was not possible in 1974 to say whether a substantial current terminal investment programme would need supplementing in the 1980s by a further programme costing several hundred million pounds.

Table 1 - Air passenger demand London airports

million passengers

1972	1973	1990 (Forecast)			
		Without Channel Tunnel		With Channel Tunnel	
27	29	High	114	High	106
		Low	78	Low	73

Source: *Maplin: Review of Airport Project*, p.4.

The second example relates to shipping and shipbuilding. It is tempting to argue that current excess capacity in both the tanker market and shipbuilding shows clearly the need for better long-term demand forecasting, particularly as the tanker order boom contined for several months after oil prices had risen. However, it should be recalled that in the summer of 1973 some forecasters were predicting a tanker surplus even at the pre-increase oil prices then prevailing. The implication is that even where forecasts were subsequently vindicated by reality, there must have existed a credibility gap which led many decisionmakers to prefer other judgements of the future. It is not difficult to see why such a credibility gap exists. Within the past year technically respectable forecasts have appeared suggesting restoration of equilibrium in the tanker market at almost any date between

1979 and the mid 1980s [6]. For many decisionmaking purposes this is clearly an excessive margin of uncertainty.

The examples quoted above were not selected for dramatic effect, a wide range of similar instances could be listed by almost anybody involved in such forecasting exercise. What the examples do show very clearly, is that measured against the needs of decisionmakers, substantial improvements are still needed in long-term demand forecasts for aviation and shipping.

THE NEED FOR FORECASTERS TO CONSIDER A WIDER RANGE OF ISSUES THAN HITHERTO

'Demand analysis should not be conceived as confined to the estimation of the influence of income and prices, but should seek to draw upon as complete an understanding as possible of the whole complex of factors influencing consumption'.
Report of the Informal Consultation of Experts on Demand Analysis, Geneva, June 1957. FAO/ECE Agric, p. 5 [7].

How are much needed improvements in the quality of long-term aviation and demand forecasts to be obtained? At this point I want to briefly consider three possible sources of improved forecasts:

a) Better statistics

b) Greater use of sophisticated econometric techniques

c) Consideration by forecasters of a wider range of issues than hitherto.

The frequent caveats about data deficiencies to be found in almost all long-term demand forecasts could be taken to imply that all would be well if only better statistics were available. Indeed, I have no doubt that better statistics *of the right sort* would lead to much improved forecasts, particularly in shipping, where in my experience internationally available statistics fall short of those available in many other industries. However, better statistics are not only expensive to obtain but of limited value if the methodological framework within which they are to be used is unsound, or perhaps more likely, imperfectly understood. For example, a few years ago it was quite common for long-term forecasts of tanker demand to be based on correlations between the oil consumption of leading industrial countries and changes in gross domestic product. Even assuming stable real oil prices and reliable oil consumption and gross domestic product statistics, such forecasts underpredicted demand because they ignored the spatial dimension, ie. the tendency for demand for tanker ton miles to expand faster than tonnage demand because of the trend towards longer voyages.

Another potential source of improved long-term demand forecasts in aviation and shipping is the greater use of more sophisticated econometric techniques. It would be foolish to deny that in many circumstances worthwhile improvements can be obtained in this way. However, as with statistics, better econometric techniques will not *of their own account* guarantee better results if the underlying conceptual framework is suspect or misused. There is of course also the danger that more sophisticated techniques will create further communication barriers between forecasters and their customers. On this point I am more optimistic. The proposition that all decisionmakers are innumerate is just as suspect as the proposition that all forecasters are illiterate. Indeed, on balance understanding between forecasters and their customers might be improved if greater stress were given in final reports to the results of statistical significance tests. All to often there is little more than a nod in the direction of R^2.

I have already argued that long-term demand forecasts in aviation and shipping share a common conceptual framework, ie. the economic theory of consumer behavior. To the extent that the economic theory of consumer behavior is unsatisfactory so too will forecasts based thereon. It is clear from recent work [8] that the economy theory of consumer behavior is much more complex than the simplistic distillations given in most first year undergraduate textbooks. In particular, dealing with quality changes raises severe technical difficulties, whilst the behavioral assumptions used are often simplistic. It does not follow that forecasters should search for a new conceptual framework. However, it does imply that forecasters should pay more attention than hitherto to the strengths and limitations of their conceptual framework. The two examples which follow serve to illustrate my belief that this end will best be served by forecasters considering a wider range of issues than hitherto.

THE APPROACH TO SATURATION LEVELS OF LEISURE PASSENGER DEMAND FOR INTERNATIONAL FLIGHTS [9]

The figures in Table 2 have been produced purely to illustrate an argument in this paper and cannot be treated as a serious forecast of international passenger traffic at United Kingdom airports in 1990 [10]. The figures show a projection to 1990 of pre-oil crisis traffic growth rates using 1975 as a base year and making the assumption that the market environment and causal relationships which prevailed between 1962 and 1973 continued to operate during 1975-90. On the basis that a trip involves two passenger movements (out and return), the implication of the 1990 projection is that on average every inhabitant of the United Kingdom will take an overseas holiday by air in 1990. If we allow for some people not taking a holiday at all, domestic holidays and seaborne overseas holidays, such a prediction loses all credibility. In short, future growth rates of international

Table 2 - Crude projections of international passenger movements at United Kindom Airports in 1990

	1975 (Actual- Millions)	% Charge Per Annum (Average 1962-73)	Growth Factor 15 Years	1990 Projection (Millions)	
United Kingdom Inclusive Tour	6.65	20.2	15.797	105.05	) Total United Kingdom) Leisure 133.7m
Other United Kingdom Short Haul Leisure	2.27	6.3	2.5	5.675	)
Other United Kingdom Long Haul Leisure	1.61	19.4	14.291	23.01	)
Foreign Leisure Short Haul	2.83	15.5	8.684	24.58	) Total Foreign) Leisure 60.5m
Foreign Leisure Long Haul	4.59	14.7	7.824	35.91	)
United Kingdom Business Short Haul	1.91	10.1	4.235	8.09	) Total Business) Travel 27.1m
United Kingdom Business Long Haul	0.58	16.0	9.266	5.37	)
Foreign Business Short Haul	1.66	12.4	5.774	9.58	)
Foreign Business Long Haul	0.99	9.9	4.12	4.08	)
TOTAL	23.09			221.35	

NOTE: These projections are derived from the International Passenger Survey (IPS); the results of which are published in *Business Monitor M6: Overseas Travel and Tourism,* Department of Industry Business Statistics Office, H.M.S.O. The IPS excluded about 7 million international passenger movements in 1975.

leisure passengers originating in the United Kingdom are likely to be below those experienced during the past decade and simple extrapolations such as those given in Table 2 can be highly misleading. The forecasting problem is to get some feel for the path demand will take between a known present and a saturation point whose magnitude and timing is unknown, and to identify ways in which this path will differ from growth in the recent past.

Given the limited length of the main data series (13-15 years) and the need to retain a reasonable number of degrees of freedom in the estimation, one is effectively limited in any econometric analysis to a small number of explanatory variables - say 3 or 4 - if one is to derive useful results. In practice, experience shows that in economic models of the demand for international air travel by leisure passengers only price and income usually emerge as significant explanatory variables. Total population, relative fares for other modes, flight time reductions etc. all tending to add little to the explanatory power of forecasting equations. Even when constant price and income elasticities have been derived for the past in this way, there remains the problem that elasticities can be expected to change in the future. Income elasticity in particular can be expected to decline as income rises - a pattern for which there is both theoretical and empirical backing. In addition, the luxury nature of air travel and its position as a relatively new

commodity is likely to be related to high price elasticities in the leisure market. Over time, as air travel takes an increasingly well established place in consumption patterns and comes to be regarded as less of a luxury and more of an essential then price sensitivity will also decline.

At this point the forecaster is left in a rather unsatisfactory position. Factors other than price and income, which a priori ought to be significant fail to merit individual inclusion in the forecasting equations, whilst considerable scope for judgement exists in selecting future price and income elasticities. One potential route which is now being explored in the United Kingdom has evolved from taking a wider viewpoint than hitherto. Leisure passengers on international flights do not demand air travel as a final product. The final product is a holiday, which in turn may compete with other outlets for leisure time and expenditure. At present in Britain about 60% of the population take a holiday and about 13% take a holiday abroad. Table 3 shows the propensity of Great Britain residents to travel in 1975, by age and socio-economic groups. Clearly, Table 3 casts considerable doubt on the 1990 trend projections in Table 2; it also suggests potentially useful lines of further work. For example, do people over the age of 65 travel less because of custom (which may not occur when the next generation reaches this age), or because of medical constraints?

Table 3 - Propensity to travel - 1975 - GB residents

% *in group*

		Domestic holiday	Overseas holiday	Any holiday
Age group	16–24	43	16	55
	25–34	54	12	62
	35–54	54	15	66
	55–64	53	18	66
	65+	46	6	51
Socio-economic group	AB	61	30	81
	C1	54	19	67
	C2	53	10	60
	DE	40	6	46

Source: British National Travel Survey

To conclude this example, it is worth considering the 1990 projections of foreign tourists visiting the United Kingdom by air (Table 2 refers). Even using the economic modelling techniques described above rather than the simple extrapolations of Table 2, forecasts of a substantial inflow of tourists emerge for 1990. At this point it is essential not to lose sight of the basic economic concept of market clearance via an inter-action between supply and demand. Only if supply were perfectly elastic could such a surge in demand occur without, for example, a rise in hotel prices. To the extent that higher hotel prices are needed to stimulate investment or to ration capacity, there will be a reaction on demand, ie. some incoming tourists will be deterred by higher hotel prices. Narrowly based forecasts which ignore such potential constraints run obvious risks.

PORT CHOICE FOR GENERAL CARGO WHEN PORT HINTERLANDS OVERLAP

For many purposes seaborne cargo can conveniently be divided into bulk and non-bulk or general cargo. In this example we are not concerned with bulk cargo, ie. single shipload consignments. Instead our interest is in general cargo, ie. consignments of diverse goods which require aggregation to obtain a shipload. The forecasting problem with which we are concerned is one faced by decisionmakers considering proposals for investment in major extensions of port facilities for general cargo - if port hinterlands overlap, which ports will cargo be shipped through and what types of ship will be used.

The problems of forecasting the volume, commodity composition and geographical spread of seaborne trade have been studied extensively in the United Kingdom by the National Ports Council [11]. Although such forecasts involve substantial problems they are not our concern in this paper. Instead, the results of such exercises will be regarded as an input to further analysis. Until the late 1960s the problem of predicting which ports would be used by general cargo in the United Kingdom was less difficult than is now the case. Inland transport costs were such that most goods would not move more than about 30 miles from the quayside and hence for all but expensive/low bulk items hinterland overlaps were limited. However, with the growth of containerisation, other forms of unitisation, freightliner and improved roads, the shippers' choice of port has widened considerably. Further, whilst in the mid 1960s it was usually safe to assume that general cargo would be shipped by general cargo vessels of conventional design, a much wider range of possibilities now exists, eg. cellular containership, ro-ro modernised conventional cargo ship. To the extent that such ships require different purpose built port facilities an extra dimension has been added to the forecasting problem.

Again, I would argue that useful insights into this type of forecasting problem can be obtained by forecasters taking into account a wider range of considerations than hitherto. For example, recent studies from the Marine Transport Centre of Liverpool University [12] cast serious doubt, at least in respect of the North Atlantic, on the widely held belief that containerisation reduces the range of ports served in a given trade. Likewise, another recent study from the same source [13] gives important insights into the choice of vessel type. In the absence of such studies, there is a danger that past trends will be extrapolated without asking searching questions, eg. facilities may be built for giant vessels which may not materialize.

MANAGEMENT IMPLICATIONS

Before concluding the paper by commenting on the implications of my arguments for research management, there remains one general point which can most usefully be made at this stage. I referred earlier to three possible ways of getting better long-term demand forecasts in aviation and shipping, without defining what was meant by 'better' in this context. In an ideal decision-makers world 'better' might be thought to mean more accurate forecasts of the future subject to narrower bands of uncertainty than are now normal. However, in practice the future is usually very uncertain, consequently 'better' forecasts may sometimes encompass a wider rather than a narrower range of uncertainty. Forecasters do not serve the best interests of decision makers by predicting certainty where it does not exist.

Throughout this paper I have stressed the need for forecasters to counter the limitations of the economic theory of consumer behaviour, by taking a wider view than has hitherto been normal. I wish to stress the following important implications of such an approach for the management of forecasters:

a) Forecasters are unlikely to be able to take a wider view unless they work in an open intellectual climate in which purposeful contact with other researchers, both business and academic, is encouraged.

b) To gain insights into the weak points of forecasting methodology there is a case for re-running forecasting equations *after* the forecasting period is over and using correct data at each point so as to identify problem areas. Although I know of no published examples of such work, I have seen very useful unpublished consultants post-mortems of shipbuilding demand forecasts.

c) Given the pressure of other work and staff mobility there is a danger that successive forecasting teams will merely re-discover the problems which earlier forecasters failed to solve. If progress is to be made a conscious management decision to commit scarce resources to research, which will not produce results until beyond the next forecasting round, is required.

d) At appropriate stages during the evolution of a forecast, the methodology and results should be exposed to constructive criticism from people with a different but related interest, eg. long-term forecasts of leisure passenger traffic by air can usefully be discussed with tourism as well as aviation interests.

REFERENCES

1] D. C. Garvett and N. K. Taneja, **New Directions for Forecasting Air Travel Passenger Demand,** Department of Aeronautics and Astronautics, Massachusetts Institute of Technology, July 1974. P. Lorange and V. Norman (editors) **Shipping Management,** Institute for Shipping Management, Bergen and Maritime Research Centre, the Hague, 1973 (see 'forecasts and Their Use').

2] Contrast for example the Boeing forecast cited in 'Making

Fuel Go Further', **Flight International,** 29 January 1977, with almost any shipbuilding forecast.

3] See page 7 of the **Report of the Committee of Inquiry into The Aircraft Industry** (Plowden Report), Cmnd 2853, HMSO, London 1965, for an illustration of this point.

4] **Maplin: Review of Airport Project,** Department of Trade, HMSO, London 1974.

5] **Report of the Commission on the Third London Airport,** HMSO, London 1971.

6] Examples include **An Outlook for World Tankers 1976 to 1979,** Terminal Operators Limited, London January 1976 and Chapter 5, **Maritime Transport 1975,** OECD, Paris 1976.

7] I owe this quotation to Chapter 6 of D. S. Ironmonger **New Commodities and Consumer Behaviour,** Cambridge University Press, Cambridge 1972.

8] See Ironmonger op at.

9] This section has benefit considerably from discussion with my colleague Mr.J.H.T.Green. The author is alone responsible for any views expressed or errors remaining.

10] More sophisticated forecasts than those used for illustrative purposes in Table 2 can be found in [4], and **Airport Strategy for Great Britain Part 1: The London Area - A Consultation Document,** Department of Trade, HMSO, London 1975.

11] **UK International Trade 1980-85,** National Ports Council, London 1976.

12] E. D. Edmunds and R. P. Maggs, 'Container Ship Turnaround Times at UK Ports', **Maritime Policy and Management,** July 1976. S. Gilman, R. P. Maggs, and S. C. Ryder **Containerisation on the North Atlantic: An Economic Analysis of Ships and Routes,** Marine Transport Centre, Liverpool University, February 1977.

13] S. Gilman, 'Shipping Technologies for Developing Countries', **Journal of Transport Economics and Policy,** January 1977.

Reflexions sur la situation et les objectifs de la recherce dans le domaine des transports de marchandises

par

W. Schwanhäusser

Technical University Aachen, Federal Republic of Germany

Les prognostics établis à partir du volume des prestations de transport pour déterminer l'importance des courants de trafic en ce qui concerne les différents modes et systèmes de transport constituent la base de toute planification d'infrastructure des transports. Pour le trafic voyageurs on a, dans une très large mesure, mis au point des modèles de prognostics concernant le volume, les courants et la répartition (modal split) des transports. Pour le trafic marchandises par contre, la mise au point de modèles n'en est encore qu'à ses débuts du fait que, par rapport au trafic voyageurs qui a connu une très grande expansion grâce au rapide développement de l'automobile, le trafic marchandises a d'abord eu une importance tout à fait secondaire pour la mise en place de l'infrastructure et, surtout, la détermination de la coupe transversale des routes. On se contentait jusqu'ici d'intégrer le trafic marchandises dans la planification en ajoutant des volumes plus ou moins forfaitaires à ceux du trafic voyageurs.

Si l'on songe que, dans la seule République fédérale d'Allemagne, le trafic marchandises routier à longue distance a augmenté de 42% entre 1970 et 1975, il devient évident qu'il est nécessaire de développer des méthodes de planification permettant de quantifier au moyen d'algorithmes le trafic marchandises en fonction de son importance.

Le trafic voyageurs peut être décrit à l'aide de modèles relativement simples du fait de l'uniformité du comportement humain, et ceci avec beaucoup d'exactitude. La situation dans le trafic marchandises est au contraire plus complexe car le nombre des facteurs qui entrent en jeu de façon déterminante dans le trafic marchandises est beaucoup plus important. Le grand nombre des sortes de marchandises d'une part, leur nature d'autre part, qui les prédispose plus ou moins pour certains moyens de transport, font que les modèles mis au point pour la description du trafic voyageurs ne peuvent pas être tout simplement appliqués au trafic marchandises. En outre, tandis que, dans le domaine du trafic voyageurs, plus les facteurs dissuasifs sont nombreux, moins l'envie de les surmonter est grande, dans le trafic marchandises au contraire, décider s'il y aura ou non transport dans une certain relation dépend en premier lieu des coûts de revient de la marchandise à son lieu de destination (possibilité de substitution de la marchandise transportée).

Si une différence de niveau des coûts de fabrication ou de transport a pour raison une variation des coûts de revient, la marchandise la moins coûteuse sera celle qui trouvera la première acquéreur; ce n'est qu'ensuite que naîtra un trafic dans les relations ou peuvent être acheminées les marchandises les mieux placées après du point de vue coûts. Pour qu'il y ait transport, il faut faire entrer en ligne de compte non seulement la demande enregistrée pour ladite marchandise mais encore la somme résultant des coûts de fabrication, de manutention, de transport auxquels s'ajoutent les charges fiscales

(douanes, impôts, etc).

Notre méthode de travail part d'un modèle fondamental qui sera présenté et discuté sur base d'un exemple. Nous soulignons que ce modèle n'existe qu'en hypothèse et que son fonctionnement n'a pas encore été démontré par des tests.

Comme d'habitude on divise le domaine étudié en cellules. Pour chaque cellule on définit les masses M_i des marchandises de différents types de produits qui y sont produits ou consommés, masses déduites de données statistiques. Les marchandises peuvent avoir à chaque endroit des prix différents qui reflètent les frais différents ou la saturation des besoins.

Le modèle doit receler trois dimensions: la distance entre les cellules, la masse des marchandises et le prix des marchandises par unité de poids. Par exemple (fig. 1): à l'endroit c pendant le temps de référence T (l'année) et la phase de production 0 750 t d'un produit premier seront produites et mises en vente sur le marché de la cellule c à un prix de P_{co}. Dans la cellule c le produit premier peut être transformé à un prix de P_{c_1} en un produit fini ou un produit plus raffiné. A la phase 1, 250 t du produit seront consommées dans la cellule pendant le temps T.

Dans l'exemple on suppose en outre, que les frais de transport de c aux autres cellules augmentent linéairement avec un angle τ_0 pour la matière première du produit en question. A l'échelle du trafic mondial les frais de transports ne seraient cependant que par pur hasard identiques pour des distances et des masses égales.

500 t de la matière première nécessaires au produit considéré sont également extraites dans la cellule b. A cause de l'extraction plus difficile, le prix de cette matière première devrait être dans la cellule b trois fois et demie plus éleve que celui de la cellule c. Dans la cellule b 1250 t de la matière première seront transformées en 1250 t du produit considéré. 500 t peuvent être offertes à 16 \$ par tonne et 750 t à 12 \$ par tonne. L'analyse du marché montre que le produit est vendu dans la cellule b à un prix moyen P_{b_1} de 13,6 \$.

On voudrait bien vendre le produit fini dans les cellules a et c (fig. 2). On aura des frais de transport τ_1 [\$ par km] à considérer. Dans la cellule c le prix moyen atteint facilement et se trouve même en-dessous du prix du marché, tandis qu-il serait moins cher dans la cellule a d'obtenir la matière première de c et de la raffiner à un produit de la phase 1 en a à un prix de P_{a_1}.

Il se pose la question, si l'on transporte à cause de cette disposition du marché 750 t de la matière première de c vers a ou 750 t de la matière première de c vers b et 750 t du produit de b vers a.

Comme on utilise en général lors de ce genre de transports, d'autres chemins et souvent aussi d'autres moyens de transport, il faut également essayer de reproduire dans le modèle les processus d'une décision. Un reflet ou une estimation du transport des marchandises se désinera au moment où on reconstruit pour chaque sorte de produit dans chaque cellule la manière d'agir des services d'expédition (pour les entreprises à haute production il faut entreprendre des études particulières) et où l'on superpose ces décisions particulières.

Le producteur dans la cellule b va analyser le marché dans la cellule a et va constater qu'il peut proposer 750 t à un prix tel qu'en ajoutant les frais de transport $T_{ba}Y$ (fig. 3) de b vers a il reste en dessous du prix qui résulte de la production du produit dans la cellule a. Quand aux 250 t restantes qui sont nécessaires en a, sa position est plus intéressante, parce que c ne peut fournir les matières premières nécessaires. Il faut se demander, à quel prix des producteurs de cellules autres que celles considérées peuvent offrir le produit. Si ce prix est plus elevé que le prix en b résultant de $P_{bo} + P_{b1}$ et des frais de transport $T_{ba}Y$ de b vers a, on peut obtenir partout des prix couvrant les frais.

A long terme, le prix du produit en a va s'établir à $P_{co} + T_{cao} + P_{a1}$. La détermination de ce prix est une des choses fondamentales dans la collecte des données du modèle.

Si ce prix est trouvé pour le produit en a, on refait un calcul du prix en b en supposant qu'en c le produit sera encore disponible sous le prix $P_{co} + P_{c1}$. La partie des frais non couverts en a est inclus dans cette offre.

Cet exemple montre qu'il y a une multitude de décisions possibles pour l'expéditeur. Ces décisions ont des conséquences très différentes pour l'exécution du transport et le choix du moyen de transport.

L'expéditeur prend sa décision aussi suivant les critères: rapidité, fiabilité, disponibilité, accessibilité et facilité. Il leur donne des poids qui dans leur somme peuvent adoucir ou accentuer certaines différences des tarifs. Il faut fixer ces poids pour le modèle et les transcrire en prix. Pour la résolution de ce problème on peut prendre le procédé de la ,,Nutzwertanalyse'', dans laquelle il faut représenter ces poids sans forme de différences de tarif.

Sur un marché avec un rapport fixe entre tarifs pour le transport de marchandises par route et par chemin de fer, la division du trafic entre les deux moyens de transport concurrentiels va jouer en faveur de l'un ou l'autre des deux. Ceci joue surtout, si ce rapport a été fixé à un moment où ces poids avaient une importance moins grave à cause d'une règlementation des temps de travail très large p.ex, ou d'exigences moins poussées des clients quant à la fraîcheur des produits ou l'importance du stockage par rapport aux différences des tarifs.

Comme ces aspects, qui sont resumés ici sous le terme de qualité de transport, doivent être considérés en tout cas pour le modèle, on peut les utiliser pour les prévisions comme paramètre de la même manière que les différences de tarif. Il sera alors possible d'estimer combien du trafic passera d'un moyen de transport à l'autre si la fiabilité ou la disponibilité de l'un baisse d'une certaine quantité. La qualité de transport peut être rendue objective au moment où l'on sait mesurer les différents aspects de cette qualité.

Ainsi la rapidité peut être mesurée par le temps nécessité entre la fin de la production et le lieu de l'activité suivante (vente, début de la production). La fiabilité peut être exprimée par la probabilité avec laquelle les contrats de transport ont été remplis dans les temps prévus.

Même la sécurité peut être exprimé par la probabilité avec laquelle le bien arrive intact à son destinataire. Il sera plus difficile de mesurer la bienveillance dans le règlement des dommages et la facilité du déroulement du transport pour l'expéditeur.

Les acheteurs d'une cellule vont donc choisir dans le cas d'un marché suffisamment transparent parmi des produits équivalent d'un même type la marchandise offerte au prix le plus bas. Connaissant ce phénomène l'offreur va tenir compte dans son offre des prix qui sont pratiqués et il va considérer comme bénéfice la différence entre les prix du marché et le prix minimum auquel il pourrait faire son offre. En tout cas le transport intervient dans cette relation. Le plus intéressant est donc de choisir comme critère de distribution le rapport entre prix de marché dans la cellule j et prix de marché dans la cellule i inclus les frais de transport pondérés et ceci pour chaque type de produits et chaque cellule. Le transport des quantités demandées interviendra d'abord dans la relation là où ce rapport sera le plus grand.

Par l'introduction de ce rapport comme grandeur scalaire les qualifications par unité de monnaie déviennent à la fin superflues dans le modèle. Même les écartements entre les cellules i et j, qui sont représentés dans la présentation graphique des relations fondamentales comme une distance, sont également superflus dans le modèle, parce qu'on les représente comme prix pondéré du transport.

On entend ici par prix de transport la somme de tous les frais qui interviennent entre expéditeur et destinateur et qui seront multipliés par un facteur de pondération déduit de la qualité du transport.

Pour les transports des marchandises à l'intérieur des cellules, les frais de transport ont une importance moins importante par rapport aux autres critères. Il est donc possible de décrire d'une facon suffisamment précise le transport de marchandise à courte distance par les modèles connus.

Les modèles complétants le modèle de base doivent en outre tenir compte des transformations éventuelles de structure du trafic marchandises consécutives à des modifications dans le processus de production, dans les rapports commerciaux sur le plan national et international, et dans les techniques de transport.

La structure des modèles doit être telle que ceux-ci permettent de concrétiser des objectifs relevant de la politique des transports sous la forme de mesures de planification concernant les différents systèmes de transport. Sans prétendre les nommer tous, ces objectifs peuvent être les suivants:

— emploi plus parcimonieux des ressources de l'économie nationale (travail, sol, capital, énergie) grâce au progrès technique,

— suppression de goulots d'étranglement et meilleure exploitation des capacités inutilisées,

— augmentation des capacités de l'infrastructure des transports déjà existante,

— diminution des moyens financiers accordés par les budgets des pouvoirs publics,

— augmentation de la productivité de l'économie nationale au moyen de décisions d'investissements prises sur la base de critères coûts-bénéfices,

— diminution des effets négatifs du trafic sur l'environnement (bruit, pollution de l'air),

— encouragement du potentiel de développement des régions faibles sur le plan de l'économie et des structures entre autres.

Les problèms liés à l'élaboration de ces modèles apparaissent clairement quand on confronte les différents objectifs de politique en matière de transports aux situations de départ dans chaque domaine concerné.

Le poids des différents facteurs varie suivant qu'on examine le transport marchandises dans les relations urbaines, nationales, internationales continentales ou intercontinentales. Il faut à ce sujet accorder une attention toute particulière aux blocs économiques (C.E.E., A.E.L.E., Comecon, etc.).

Pour une partie des problèmes mentionnés, des solutions ou des débuts de solutions sont connus ou en cours d'examen. En ce qui concerne le trafic marchandises routier à courte distance, on dispose de modèles de production qui s'appuient sur ceux du trafic voyageurs. L'analyse du trafic marchandises routier à longue distance en vue de son intégration explicite dans des processus de planification dans le domaine des transports est aussi en cours d'élaboration, cette planification étant basée sur des modèles qui traitent de la naissance de trafics et de leurs courants.

Pour le trafic aérien et maritime à longue distance, des modèles éprouvés existent déjà. Les répercussions de l'augmentation du prix de l'énergie sur les coûts des différents modes de transport ont déjà été analysées. L'utilisation de trains rapides urbains pour le trafic marchandises en vue de décongestionner les transports de surface dans les grandes agglomérations fait l'objet d'un travail de recherche actuellement en cours dans mon institut.

Les efforts entrepris par les administrations ferroviaires dans le domaine de l'automatisation de l'exploitation (cibernétisation des transports) et de la concentration sont de plus en plus couronnés de succès. De nouvelles technologies de manutention (manutention horizontale) font l'objet de recherches dans différents pays. Il faut à ce sujet mentionner aussi le développement de trains à très grande vitesse et à grande capacité. Comme dans les chemins de fer, les progrès techniques sont constants dans le domaine de la navigation fluviale, maritime et aérienne.

Bien qu'on ait entrepris dans certains cas des analyses méticuleuses sur la rentabilité et, par voie de conséquence, la possibilité de commercialisation d'une innovation technique, on n'est cependant pas encore en mesure d'évaluer et de chiffrer ces influences de façon à pouvoir les intégrer dans un ensemble logique. Etant donné le caractère de plus en plus international du trafic marchandises par suite des échanges croissant entre les pays, il faudrait intensifier les recherches en matière de

trafic marchandises sur le plan international. D'après une analyse des résultats obtenus dans ce domaine, il serait nécessaire de mettre sur pied un ,,plan de recherches pour le trafic marchandises''.

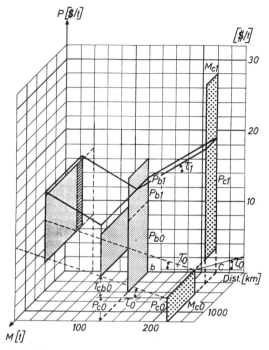

Figure 2

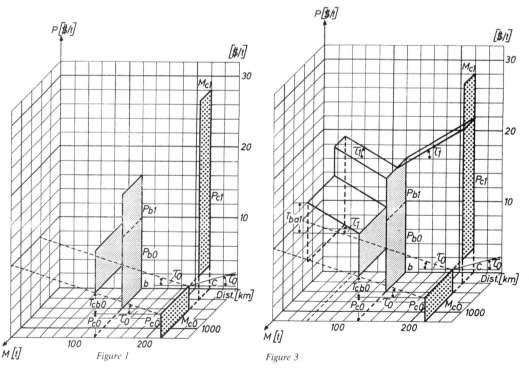

Figure 1

Figure 3

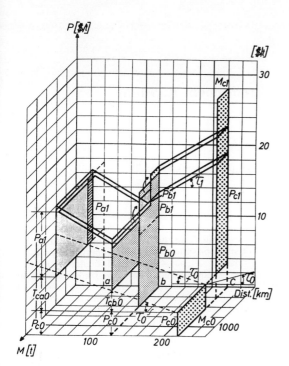

Figure 4

Bus acquisition and retirement decisions

ERZA HAUER

EZRA HAUER

Department of Civil Engineering, University of Toronto

INTRODUCTION

Bus fleet planning is part and parcel of orderly management of a bus transit property. Budgetary provisions need to be made for the future acquisitions of new buses; maintenance programs tailored to the upcoming retirement of old ones; subsidies requested, orders placed etc. It is not uncommon to prepare Strategic Acquisition and Retirement Programs several years into the future for internal planning or as a part of request for subsidies towards the purchase of new equipment, or for both.

The managerial and technical content of the process leading to the formulation of such acquisition and retirement programs seems to be less than well documented. A recent servey of four transit properties in Ontario revealed a predictable variability in practice. One property follows the general guideline that " . . .a vehicle is retired when it starts to cost more in depreciation, operation and maintenance than the costs associated with the acquisition and operation of a new bus"; another property attempts to replace buses after 15 years of service; elsewhere, buses are candidates for resale already at the early age of ten years provided the selling price is right; others aim to obtain an average fleet age of 6-7.5 years through an appropriate acquisition and retirement program.

Documented studies of bus fleet planning seem to be few. Those which came to our attention are faulty in concept and therefore in their conclusions. One study [1] postulates that " . . .the optimum economic age of a bus occurs just prior to the occurrence of the first major maintenance repair . . .". This leads to the baseless conclusion " . . .the optimum economic life of a bus can be identified as eight years . . .". Another study [2] disregards the fact that annual mileage varies with vehicle age (from 60,000 miles/annum for new buses to 10,000 miles/annum for old ones). Thus, the author concludes that a bus making 30,000 miles per annum in Cleveland should be replaced at the age of 20 years, whereas in Chicago it should be retired after 11 years.

In summary, the preparation of bus acquisition and retirement programs by transit properties is guided by a variety of rationales and is largely qualitative in method. The aforementioned quantitative studies are not applicable to real situations. The need exists to forge a tool which can deal effectively with the more quantitative aspects of bus acquisition and retirement to aid management in bus fleet planning.

PROBLEM DEFINITION AND DESCRIPTION

It appears that the process leading to the acquisition of new buses and to the resale of some old vehicles is complex and involves many people at different levels of management. However, a certain hierarchical structure is apparent in the larger properties. A strategic program for several years into the future is prepared. This program merely specifies the number of vehicles to be acquired and retired during each of the budgetary periods throughout the program. The Five-Year Program for the London (Ontario) Transportation Commission illustrates the concept (Table I). The guidelines incorporated in this strategic program are later made specific, determining which vehicles will be retired, what type of vehicle purchased etc. All this in accordance with the conditions prevailing at the time decisions are made. Application procedures for subsidies make the preparation of similar strategic programs mandatory also for the smaller bus transit properties.

Discussion in this paper will focus on the generation of Strategic Acquisition and Retirement Programs to be denoted (for brevity) SARP.

Selection of the phrase "acquisition and retirement" instead of the more customary term "replacement" is deliberate. Firstly, when an old bus is retired from service, its task is not assigned to the new vehicle joining the fleet. Rather, the next oldest vehicle remaining in the

Research supported by National Research Council Canada Grant A8158.

Table I – Five Year Program of Replacements and Additions (Adapted from Schedule "B" June 11, 1974, The London Transportation Commission)

Year	Proposed Purchases	Proposed Retirements	Net Addition	Buses in Fleet at year end
1974				126
1975	25	7	18	144
1976	15	7	8	152
1977	14	11	3	155
1978	12	8	4	159
1979	11	5	6	165

fleet assumes the task of the retiring bus and is called into service only during periods of peak vehicle utilization. The incoming new bus, on the other hand, will be used as much as possible. Consequently acquisition and retirements cause a shift in the tasks performed by all vehicles in the fleet. Therefore, the concept of "replacement" is misleading. Secondly, buses are acquired and retired in face of changing demand conditions often without any reference to "replacement". It is impossible, therefore, to discuss the bus acquisition and retirement problem in terms of a "one for one" substitute or comparison. That is, the prototype model of substituting a new (low maintenance cost) item for an old (high maintenance cost) piece of equipment does not apply. Indeed, the following factors should influence SARPs (Strategic Acquisition and Retirement Programs):

1. Number of buses needed in the fleet in future years and their utilization.
2. Budget and subsidy considerations.
3. Operating and maintenance cost characteristics of *all* vehicles in the fleet as well as their reliability performance.
4. Purchase and resale prices of buses.

Missing in the group of factors is the less tangible but not less important consideration of desirability of riding new vehicles both as passengers and as drivers. As will become evident later the evaluation procedure allows for management judgement in this respect.

The objective of modelling then, is to formulate a limited number of SARPs to be presented for consideration to management. All alternatives must comply with constraints specified by 1 and 2 and be presented parsimoniously in terms of the implications in 3 and 4.

FACTS AND FIGURES

In concept it is not difficult to see that the number of buses acquired and retired during a particular budgetary period should be such that neither the operating cost budget, nor the budget for purchase of capital equipment are exceeded while at the same time the fleet is large enough to satisfy demand for service, and the resulting fleet age profile is a good base for the next period. The difficulty resides in the quantification of the exact relationships which determine how many miles per year, which bus is being used, and what is the associated variable cost of operation and maintenance and how this would change if more (or less) buses are bought and retired etc. Clarification of some of these basic ingredients is the subject matter of the present section.

Preparation of forecasts of a wide variety is part of routine planning activity by transit properties. Forecasting methods may differ in sophistication from naive trend projections to elaborate econometric models. Whichever method is used, formulation of a SARP requires estimates of:
a. Number of buses needed in future periods. (See, e.g., column 5 in Table I);
b. Total annual vehicle miles of travel for future periods, (See, e.g., Figure 1).

Estimates of the costs associated with operation, maintenance and reliability as a function of fleet composition are more difficult to come by. It is commonly assumed that vehicle age has little to do with costs of operation which do not fall into the "maintenance" category. (Fuel comsumption, driver wages, etc.). The dependence of maintenance cost on vehicle age and mileage will be discussed in the next section. The influence of age and accumulated mileage on vehicle reliability is to our knowledge not documented. Thus costs associated with reliability (towing, vehicle reserve, service disruption etc.) can not at present be accounted for. Research in this area is continuing.

Bus Maintenance Costs

Some costs associated with the maintenance of a bus fleet are largely independent of the fleet age profile and the details of fleet utilization. (e.g. allocated costs, cleaning, tyre grooving etc.). This component of maintenance cost should exert no influence on the formulation of bus acquisition and retirement programs. Thus, in what follows, only those items of maintenance are considered which vary with vehicle age.

Detailed accounting information on such maintenance costs was obtained from the Toronto Transit Commission, the Ottawa-Carleton Regional Transit Commission and the Guelph Transportation Commission. On its basis estimation equations for components of maintenance costs were derived. These are illustrated (Equations 1-4) for a specific vehicle type (GMC bus, Model 5303, seating 41 passengers).

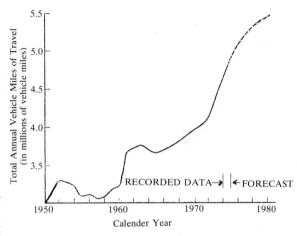

Figure 1 - Annual Vehicle Miles of Travel. Recorded Data Based on: Annual Report 1974, London Transportation Commission.

Let

TC_{ijk} be the annual cost of bus maintenance during calendar year i when the age of the vehicle is j and its annual mileage is k.

ELH   Number of Labour Hours spent annually on Engine maintenance of an (average) bus.

BLH   Number of Labour Hours spent annually on Body maintenance of an (average) bus.

EM   The cost of parts and Materials spent annually on the maintenance of the Engine of an (average) bus estimated in 1972 dollars.

BM   The cost of parts and Materials spent annually on the maintenance of the Body of an average bus estimated in 1972 dollars.

AGE   Age of vehicle (years after purchase) at end of year for which information on annual basis is given.

ANN. MILEAGE   Annual number of vehicle miles averaged over vehicles of a group.

Then,

TC_{ijk} = [(ELH(AGE=j, ANNUAL MILEAGE= k) + BLH(AGE = j)] x (Wage Rate for Year i) + [EM(AGE =j, ANNUAL MILEAGE =k) + BM (AGE = j)] x (Material Cost Index for Year i)

275

$$[(ELJ(AGE=j, ANNUAL\ MILEAGE=k) + BLH(AGE=j))] \times (Wage\ Rate\ for\ Year\ i) +$$
$$[EM(AGE=j, ANNUAL\ MILEAGE=k) + BM(AGE=j))] \times (Material\ Cost\ Index\ for\ Year\ i)$$

$86 + 38.05\ (AGE)$	for AGE < 6 years
$24 + 0.009224\ (ANN.\ MILEAGE)$	Otherwise ... 1

$$22 - 9.4\ (AGE-0.5) + 6.75(AGE-0.5)^2 - 0.3528\ (AGE-0.5)^3 \quad \text{for AGE < 13 years}$$
$$156 \qquad \text{Otherwise} \qquad ...2$$

$136 + 201.87\ (AGE)$	for AGE < 6 years
$771 + 0.004955\ (ANN.\ MILEAGE)$	Otherwise ... 3

$$26 + 27.3\ (AGE-0.5) + 4.02\ (AGE-0.5)^2 - 0.3700\ (AGE-0.5)^3 \quad \text{for AGE < 13 years}$$
$$365 \qquad \text{Otherwise} \qquad ...4$$

proportion of fleet in service for that duration of time.

2. Allocate annual fleet miles to vehicles using the equivalent graph from (1) and assuming that normally younger vehicles are assigned longer hours of service.

3. Calculate the cost of maintenance for each age group of vehicles.

4. Aggregate the maintenance costs over all age groups.

Information on different vehicle types as well as other details are given in reference 3. Figure 2 serves to illustrate the association of the average annual vehicle mileage with vehicle age and also the variation of the total maintenance cost per vehicle with age for the given average annual mileage.

Determination of Annual Vehicle Mileage

It appears that the cost of maintenance of a bus depends on its utilization which is in turn measured by "annual vehicle mileage". The annual mileage of a specific vehicle is dictated by two factors. Firstly, by the diurnal pattern by which vehicles are inserted into and removed from service. (See e.g., Figure 3). Secondly, on

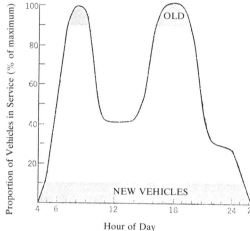

Figure 3 - T.T.C. Daily Bus Utilization (April - May, 1972).

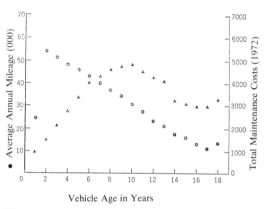

Figure 2 - Maintenance costs and Average Annual Mileage for a "Fleet Average" vehicle (Toronto Transit Commission)

the prevailing fleet composition which determines largely when the specific vehicle will be called on and how long it will remain in the shift.

The concept is best illustrated by example. Consider the vehicle utilization pattern for the Toronto Transit Commission depicted in Figure 3. Normally, the shiny new vehicles will serve the bottom part of the bus requirement graph whereas the veteran buses will be called on to cover the peaks. The shaded portions of the graph represent the share of the service burden carried by the youngest and the oldest 10% of the fleet. Thus, derived from the daily utilization pattern (Figure 3) is the relationship between the proportion of fleet miles performed and different segments of the fleet, as shown in Figure 4. As may be seen, the 10% of the fleet composed of the newest vehicles performs some 18% of the total annual mileage whereas the 10% of the fleet containing the oldest vehicles perform only some 3% of the total annual mileage.

Fleet Maintenance Cost Estimation

Thus, to obtain a sensible estimate of the fleet maintenance cost for a certain period,

1. Convert the applicable daily utilization pattern into an equivalent graph, showing duration of service vs.

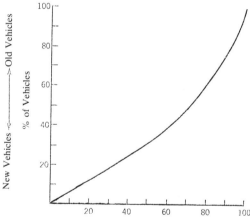

Figure 4 - Proportion of Annual Fleet Miles Performed by Proportions of the Fleet.

Consider, e.g., the fleet age profile in column 2 of Table II. (This will be shown to be the fleet age profile prevailing during 1975 in an example used in the later part of this paper). The annual fleet vehicle miles for 1975 are 4,850,000 (Figure 1). Using the proportions of vehicles by age group given in column 3 and Figure 4, the proportion of annual fleet miles assigned to each age group is determined. Using now the annual mileage of an average vehicle by age group as determined in column 5, the average annual cost of maintenance can be calculated from Equations 1-4. Multiplied by the number of vehicles in each age group (column 7) the sum represents the total fleet maintenance cost for 1975.

It appears then that a tool for the estimation of fleet maintenance costs has been forged. It remains to specify the machinery by which all sensible acquisition and retirement options can be examined and evaluated.

THE BUS ACQUISITION AND RETIREMENT MODEL

Consider the bus requirements specified in Table I. During, say, 1975, a total of 18 buses need to be added to the fleet. This could be accomplished by acquiring just 18 new buses and no retirements. Alternatively, one

could purchase 19 new buses and retire one old vehicle; or buy 20 and sell 2 etc. The entire range of options is conveniently represented in tabular form. In Table III, line 1 represents the SARP in which no buses are retired throughout the duration of the program. The shaded entries correspond to the SARP embodied in Table I.

The total number of SARPs which can be formulated is given by the number of lines in Table III raised to the power of the number of periods for which the SARP is being prepared. When represented in this manner, the computational problems associated with the search for a set of good SARPs do not appear formidable. Even explicit enumeration by brute force appears feasible. As

Table II - Fleet Maintenance Cost Estimation

1	2	3	4	5	6	7
Age Group (Years)	Number of Vehicles In Group	Proportion of Vehicles in Group	Proportion of Fleet Miles Assigned to Group	Annual Mileage of on Vehicle (Miles)	Average Annual Cost of Maintenance per Vehicle $	Average Cost of Maintenance for Group $
0- 1	20.000	0.148	0.255	61770.	937.512	18750.240
1- 2	11.000	0.081	0.135	59305.	1442.640	15869.030
2- 3	7.500	0.056	0.083	53424.	2012.036	15090.260
3- 4	7.000	0.052	0.070	48402.	2631.080	18417.550
4- 5	7.000	0.052	0.063	43668.	3285.156	22996.080
5- 6	9.000	0.067	0.072	38629.	3959.641	35636.760
6- 7	10.000	0.074	0.069	33270.	4124.426	41244.250
7- 8	10.000	0.074	0.059	28388.	4062.414	40624.130
8- 9	8.500	0.063	0.043	24515.	4035.786	34304.170
9-10	7.000	0.052	0.031	21702.	4032.838	28229.860
10-11	3.500	0.026	0.014	19992.	4041.444	14145.050
11-12	2.500	0.019	0.010	19084.	4029.510	10073.770
12-13	2.500	0.019	0.009	18364.	3946.541	9866.348
13-14	5.000	0.037	0.018	17342.	3342.646	16713.220
14-15	7.500	0.056	0.024	15777.	3251.454	24385.890
15-16	5.500	0.041	0.016	14305.	3165.719	17411.450
16-17	5.500	0.041	0.015	13182.	3100.288	17051.580
17-18	2.500	0.019	0.006	12423.	3056.122	7640.305
18-19	0.000	0.000	0.000		2332.399	0.000
19-20	0.000	0.000	0.000		2332.399	0.000
20-21	2.500	0.019	0.006	11976.	3030.081	7575.199
21-22	1.000	0.007	0.002	11674.	3012.436	3012.436
22-23	0.000	0.000	0.000		2332.399	0.000
23-24	0.000	0.000	0.000		2332.399	0.000

Fleet Maintenance Cost $ 399,037.

Table III - Representation of Acquisition and Retirement Options

	(1)		(2)		(3)		(4)		(5)	
Year	1975		1976		1977		1978		1979	
Net Additions	18		8		3		4		6	
	A	R	A	R	A	R	A	R	A	R
1	18	0	8	0	3	0	4	0	6	0
2	19	1	9	1	4	1	5	1	7	1
3	20	2	10	2	5	2	6	2	8	2
4	21	3	11	3	6	3	7	3	9	3
5	22	4	12	4	7	4	8	4	10	4
6	23	5	13	5	8	5	9	5	11	5
7	24	6	14	6	9	6	10	6	12	6
8	25	7	15	7	10	7	11	7	13	7
9	26	8	16	8	11	8	12	8	14	8
10	27	9	17	9	12	9	13	9	15	9
11	28	10	18	10	13	10	14	10	16	10
12	29	11	19	11	14	11	15	11	17	11

A – Acquisitions

R – Retirements

will become evident, significant computational shortcuts are available.

Each of the many SARPs represented by Table III is associated with a unique fleet composition (assuming that the oldest vehicles are retired first). Column I of Table IV represents the fleet age profile for the London Transportation Commission prevailing at the end of 1974. The proposed acquisitions and retirements embodied in Table I yields for the period 1975-79 the fleet composition given in columns 2-6 of Table IV. The first line always contains the newly acquired buses; the re-maining groups are shifted one line down for each year; the oldest buses are retired.

Selection of a specific SARP from Table III has the following consequences:

1. It determines the fleet age profile for all periods of the program.

2. It implies a stream of expenditures for acquisition of new buses as well as a stream of receipts from the resale of old ones.

3. It determines the cost of fleet maintenance as influenced by the fleet age profile prevailing during the periods of the program.

Table IV - Fleet Age Profiles

Number of Vehicles in Age Group at the end of

Age Group (Years)	(1) 1974	(2) 1975	(3) 1976	(4) 1977	(5) 1978	(6) 1979
0- 1	15	25	15	14	12	11
1- 2	7	15	25	15	14	12
2- 3	8	7	15	25	15	14
3- 4	6	8	7	15	25	15
4- 5	8	6	8	7	15	25
5- 6	10	8	6	8	7	15
6- 7	10	10	8	6	8	7
7- 8	10	10	10	8	6	8
8- 9	7	10	10	10	8	6
9-10	7	7	10	10	10	8
10-11	0	7	7	10	10	10
11-12	5	0	7	7	10	10
12-13	0	5	0	7	7	10
13-14	10	0	5	0	7	7
14-15	5	10	0	5	0	7
15-16	6	5	10	0	5	0
16-17	5	6	5	8	0	0
17-18	0	5	4	0	0	0
18-19	0	0	0	0	0	0
19-20	0	0	0	0	0	0
20-21	5	0	0	0	0	0
21-22	2	0	0	0	0	0

All the aforementioned consequences can be quantified by methods described in this paper. However, as each of the very many SARPs is now characterized by a long string of measures of performance, the need exists to separate the wheat from the chaff.

Constraints

Constraints arising out of practical consideration serve the useful purpose of eliminating from further analysis alternatives which can not be implemented. Two constraints will be considered.

1. The cost of acquisition of new vehicles during any period contained in the program can not exceed the budget allotment for purchase of capital equipment. (The same constraint can be used to introduce limitations on availability of equipment etc.).

2. The cost of fleet maintenance can not exceed the budgetary allotment for that purpose during any of the periods contained in the program.

In some situations additional constraints may be applicable. The aforementioned two, however, seem to capture the most common concerns.

The first constraint is easy to comply with. If, e.g., the maximum number of buses that could be considered for acquisition during 1975 is 26, no SARPs containing more than 26 buses are feasible. Thus, column 1 of Table III can be terminated at the heavy line. The heavy line in Table III indicates that the largest number of acquisi-tions to be considered throughout the program are 26, 17, 14, 15 and 14.

The second constraint sets limits to the cost of fleet maintenance. Consider, e.g., the SARP indicated by the shading in Table III. Assume that the fleet maintenance cost associated with it does nog exceed the limits in any period. The next SARP to be considered in the search is one which retains the same entries in all columns, save column 5. Here the number of acquisitions is changed from 11 to 10. Assume that now the fleet maintenance cost limit for 1979 is exceeded. Surely, all SARPs which have in 1979 even less acquisitions that 10 (while retaining unchanged entries in all other columns) need not be considered. Two conclusions follow. First, that the enumeration search should commence at the lower boundary of Table III. Second, that the systematic search proceed in the upward direction till the maintenance cost limit is violated.

Narrowing the Choice

Ordinarily, in spite of the constraints, admissible options are many. Consequently, additional criteria must be invoked to narrow the choice.

The period by period information on fleet maintenance costs, cost of acquisitions and receipts from bus resale are easily converted to present values and aggregated. The only other relevant aspect of the choice of a SARP is the fleet age profile at the end of the program.

The younger the fleet at that point in time, the better the heritage for future programs.

It is easy to envision what form the relationship between the present value of the aggregate cost and the fleet age profile at the end of the program will take. As more new buses are acquired, the present cost of new acquisitions (less resale) increases, the present cost of fleet maintenance drops and the fleet delivered at the end of the program is generally younger. (Figure 5). Obviously, options to the right of point 1 are inferior on two counts. Firstly, they have a higher aggregate cost than the alternative represented by point 1.

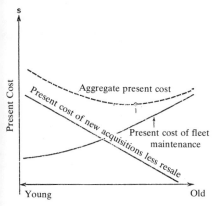

Figure 5 - Relationship between Aggregate Cost and Fleet Age Profile at End of Program.

Second, they deliver a generally older fleet at the end of the program. This observation translates into the algorithmic search procedure as follows: The search begins with the youngest feasible fleet. This corresponds to the extreme left in Figure 5 and to the lower boundary of Table III (as before). The search will be discontinued when the aggregate present cost commences to increase while the fleet age profile continues to deteriorate.

The range of choice is now narrowed to options which are to the left of point 1 in figure 5. Some of the options contained in this range may again be shown to be inferior to others. Towards this end, a compact characterization of the fleet age profile is needed. Management would most likely prefer "average fleet age" as a measure of fleet age profile quality. Alternatively, "annual cost of fleet maintenance" or "fleet resale value" could be used. In the following, "average fleet age" will serve as a proxy for the quality of the fleet age profile at the end of the program.

Each of the remaining SARPs can then be described by two numbers:
1. Average Fleet Age at end of program,
2. Aggregate present cost.

The complete set of options can be represented as in Figure 6. Evidently, SARPs labelled 1-6 dominate the other options. Thus, only the labelled options need to be considered by management.

ILLUSTRATION

It remains to bring the illustrations used throughout this paper to their conclusion. The objective is to generate a set of SARPs for the period 1975-1979 for the initial fleet age profile shown in column 1 of Table IV and using the cost and limit information of Table V.

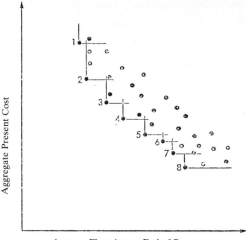

Figure 6 - Cost-Effectiveness

Alternative 1, being the least restricted by allowable acquisititions and maintenance costs represents a broad range of options. Point A, e.g., will yield an average fleet age of 7.5 years at the end of 1979. The present cost of maintenance, acquisition and resale of this alternative is $5.492 million. The SARP is implemented by acquisition of 18, 9, 12, 13, 13 new buses during the corresponding years of the program. The associated number of retirements is 0, 1, 9, 9, 7. As during the third and fourth period of the program the maximum number of acquisitions is reached, relaxation of this constraint could be considered in order to reduce cost. Point B in Figure 7 implies an average fleet age of 8.0 years at the end of 1979. The present aggregate cost of this alternative is $5.257 million. It can be implemented by acquiring 18, 8, 11, 7 and 15 new buses during the corresponding years of the program.

Alternative 2 has a lower maintenance cost limit and thus SARPs with terminal average age higher than 7.3 years can not be attained. Alternative 3 is also restricted by the same low maintenance budget. Simultaneously, budget limitations for the acquisition of new buses are also in effect. This limits the left hand branch of the cost effectiveness curve for alternative 3.

DISCUSSION

A quantitative tool for the formulation of Strategic Acquisition and Retirement Programs has been developed. It is sufficiently versatile to allow exploration of a fairly wide range of options and assess the sensitivity of the solutions to various budgetary constraints.

The major shortcoming of the method at present resides in the lack of quantitative information on the costs associated with fleet reliability and the functional relationship between reliability and fleet age profile.

REFERENCES

1. The Cleveland Transit System: **Optimum Bus Age Study.** W.C. Gilman Inc., Cleveland, Ohio, September 1970.
2. W.B. Tye: **The Economic Costs of the Urban Mass Transportation Capital Grant Program,** Ph.D. Thesis, Department of Economics, Harvard University, October 1969.
3. E. Hauer: **Maintenance Cost of Buses for Economic Life Studies,** Ontario Ministry of Transportation and Communications, O.J.T. & C. Research Project T-31, October 1974.

Table V - Input Data for the Generation of SARPs

Period number (1)	Net additions (2)	Max. no. of acquisitions (3)	Annual fleet miles (4)	wage rate (5)	Material cost index (6)	Maintenance cost limit (7)	Cost of new bus (8)
1	18		4850000.	5.70	1.15		57000.
2	8		5020000.	6.05	1.20		62000.
3	3		5160000.	6.40	1.25		68000.
4	4		5280000.	6.75	1.30		75000.
5	6		5360000.	7.10	1.35		82000.

Columns 3 and 7 of Table V are left blank intentionally as the following alternatives will be tried out.

Alternative number	Max. no. of acquisitions (3)	Maintenance cost limit (7)
1	27	500000.
	17	550000.
	12	600000.
	13	650000.
	15	700000.
2	27	500000.
	17	550000.
	12	600000.
	13	600000.
	15	600000.
3	26	500000.
	16	550000.
	11	600000.
	12	600000.
	14	600000.
4	26	500000.
	16	550000.
	11	600000.
	12	650000.
	14	700000.

The corresponding cost-effectiveness curves are shown in Figure 7.

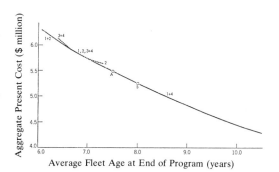

Figure 7 - Cost effectiveness curves for alternatives 1 - 4.

The Uncertainty of Decisionmaking in a Direct Democracy

by

HANS B. BARBE, Barbe A. G., Switzerland

THE DELEGATION OF POWERS IN DECISIONMAKING

Democracy means government by the people, direct or representative. Most western countries are in fact ruled by the people – some more directly, some less. Perhaps the most direct democracy in existence has been developped in Switzerland. The following notes may give some indications what this means with regard to the decisionmaking in the field of traffic and transport.

The Swiss direct democracy means that the government has mainly an administrative function. Unlike in the United States – whose constitution was a strong guideline for the creation of the Swiss federal constitution of 12th September 1848 – the president has no special powers at all. He is considered "primus inter pares", which means that he is Chairman of the Board running Switzerland like a huge industrial enterprise, but with no powers beyond those of his colleagues among whom he was elected for a one-year term. In this respect, incidentally, it is interesting that the most direct democracy of the world does not elect its president directly by a public vote. The reason is that his election does not mean the adoption of a certain political strategy and that, within this framework, the presedent would be free to decide as he sees fit for the best of the country.

Also the federal councilors are mainly administrators. Although a "magic formula" has been developped over the years, ensuring that each party, each minority and each national language is duly and in good proportion represented by the seven federal councilors, they do not have any special powers, are not elected directly by the people but by the parliament, and can remain in office as long as they live or until they resign. These councilors – the equivalent to ministers in other countries – thus form a government which cannot be overthrown. They only execute what they are ordered to do by the federal parliament; usually this results in a referendum which can be either accepted or rejected by the people. If rejected, however, this is not a vote of distrust to the government and no reason that a minister should resign. This whole construction may sound curious to citizens of other countries but it has certainly contributed toward a unique stability of government. It is up to the people to decide in all important matters, and if they do not like a government proposal, there are no hard feelings from either side.

The real power is with the federal parliament, consisting of the Senate (upper house), representing the cantons (states), and a Congress (lower house), representing the population in proportion to numbers. Together, these two houses represent the United Federal Congress, the highest power in the government which, among other duties, has to appoint the federal councilors. The president of the National Council (the Congress) is actually the "first man" in Switzerland; he ranks higher than the federal president.

It may sound paradox that this construction which was designed to provide an extreme stability of government and administration, at the same time has built-in the germ of a deadly paralysis on the decision level. Firstly, the government does not have to produce success in order to fight for survival. Secondly, the responsibility finally remains with the people; if something goes wrong because a vote was rejected, only the voters could be blamed.

When the constitution was drafted in 1848, things were still straight-forward, simple and comprehensible also for the average citizen. To entrust him with the final decision in many matters of utmost importance was, therefore, not too much of a risk. The first little railroad had just been constructed, the main problems were religion, alcohol and similar items. It should be borne in mind that the Swiss democracy is basically very decentralized, the federation principally doing only what cannot be done on a cantonal basis. This entails mainly foreign policy, the monetary system, the postal service, military questions and the like. All states – the cantons – have their own constitutions with quite a strong autonomy. So, most decisions of importance are being taken on this level. Since 1848, of course, there were many changes. In 1874 the constitution was completely revised, and since this date more than seventy amendments were added or articles exchanged.

TRANSPORT REQUIRES CENTRALIZED PLANNING

Right from the beginning of the present constitution (revised in 1874), the federal government retained the right to retain legislative authority on railway transport. Article 26 states bluntly that "legislation concerning construction and operation of railways is a federal matter". This does not mean that the public is excluded from the decisionmaking in this field; all it means is that railways are not a cantonal matter as the highways were and still are. All laws concerning railway traffic had to be submitted to the people, including the proposal to nationalize most of the Swiss railways around the turn of the century (which now, incidentally, accounts for one fourth of our national deficit). Quite early, however, the federal government has taken advantage of this legal situation – and also of the fact that more and more it had to subsidize the federal railway system – by building up a legislative structure which virtually excludes the public from any decisions of importance. Also being a very convinced democrat, one has to concede that this is the only feasible way to run our rail transport.

A few issues which, by constitution or otherwise, remained in the power of decision by the people, have been subject to discussions for decades. Particularism and local interests make it virtually impossible to find solutions of national importance and so most of these questions just remain unsolved. This can be seen most clearly in the question of a new alpine tunnel, but to a lesser degree also in minor problems like a national scheme for removal of at-grade railway crossings, the redesign of the main station in Zurich and others.

That Federalism and direct democracy tend to paralize technical developments of such a scale, was most evidently seen in the development of highway traffic. Wedged in between the cantons of Basel and Zurich there is the canton of Aargau. Of the approximately 90 kilometers between Basel and Zurich, more than 70 are in this unfortunate canton of Aargau because both the cantons of Zurich and Basel happen to have their boundaries just beyond the suburbs of these main traffic generators. Why should the canton of Aargau build more than 75 percent of this communication which is of vital interest to Basel and Zurich but of a much lesser interest to the Aargovians? This canton, again, has other road problems which absorb its financial capacity. There are many examples like this and they led to a situation where the need for some superimposed, transcantonal planning was felt. In 1958, two amendments to article 36 of the constitution were accepted in a nation-wide vote, authorizing the federation to build and maintain a national motorway system and to collect additional import duties on fuels for its financing. These amendments (articles 36 bis and ter) constitute quite a unique situation in respect to the powers of the federal government. In fact, the people entrusted its voting power with regard to a national highway system to the government, based on a proposed system of more than 1600 kilometers. It was later said that the people had been tricked into committing this political castration. However, there was never any doubt about what this amendment implied and also what the reason for this centralistic exception was. Without it, probably not a single kilometer would have been constructed to date. Now, at least we have more than 50 percent of this system completed.

This windfall was only possible because motorists were fed up with the existing chaos on the Swiss highway system which consisted of a conglomerate of local connections. I think it was quite evident for all those who accepted this amendment to the constitution that something ought to be done now. That this was the only way to obtain any reasonable results, can easily be seen on the local level. The cantons, agian, only concern themselves with those matters which cannot be solved on a community level. On the communal level most issues come up automatically for voting when they exceed a certain amount of expenditure. Since most modern technological proposals are of financial consequences which far exceed these limits, this means that every main road construction, each metro system, each airport or even extension of runways have to be voted upon.

In the city of Zurich, which, including its suburbs, has close to 1 million population, all major issues in the last 15 years were rejected. The reasons are hard to grasp; in an analysis which we have carried out a few years ago, it became evident that there are so many parameters involved that no rules can be found why certain issues are rejected and other accepted. The only more or less consistent correlation which could be found was with the construction of new parking garages: there the percentage of negative votes increased roughly in proportion to the price per unit parking stall. Apart from this, however, people seem to behave erratic and irrational. Many highway proposals were rejected, for instance, with the reasoning that now we should stop spending money in road traffic and rather improve public transport. When, however, a few months later improvements for the tramway, a new financial basis for the public transport authority or even a proposal for an underground metro system were put up for voting, the result again was negative.

Decision making, under these circumstances, is any-thing but easy. The long life expectancy of modern transport facilities and constructions, combined with the tremendous investments required, call for long-range decision making based on underlaying tools or plans allowing to assess possible future developments and the consequences of alternative options. The public, however, is not at all concerned about such long-range outlooks; their decisions arise from momentary problems or feelings and are likely to change within no time. It may happen, therefore, that for instance two or three sections of an urban inner ring road system are accepted in public votes, whereas a few years later additional sections are rejected and the whole system cannot be completed.

A curious example to this effect is Zurich International Airport where the first requests for funds to extend the runways were rejected by the public. After many years, even the public became aware that the present situation was impossible, and finally the runway extension came up for voting once again. Now, however, considering the heavy inflation in these boom years, the new issue, costing about as much as the old one, contained only about half as much. Further amendments were required in subsequent votes. Finally, less was achieved for much more money.

THE PRICE OF DEMOCRACY

This may be the price of democracy. There is another price, however, which may weigh heavier. The Swiss democratic system contains, among others, the right of a number of voters to submit an "initiative" requesting a referendum on a certain issue. The necessary number of signatures having been established a century ago, it is now quite easy to assemble the required number of supporters for almost any initiative. Thus, a real inflation in initiatives has resulted. They all tend, basically, to restrict the powers of central government rather than to enhance them.

Quite recently, on March 13, 1977, an initiative with the nice name "Democracy in Road Construction" was submitted to the voters in the canton of Zurich and – was accepted! This law establishes the compulsory obligation of the state government to submit any constructions beyond 20 million Swiss francs to public vote, while the public can, on request with another initiative, vote on road constructions from as little as 3 million Swiss francs. It remains to be seen whether with this new law further major roads will be constructed in the state of Zurich. This law, incidentally, creates a curious conflict of objectives. On one hand, certain funds from vehicle registrations fees and fuel custom duties must be used for county road constructions. On the other hand, the same constructions must be submitted to voting. It may well happen that eventually quite some funds will accumulate which cannot be spent. This, in actual fact, has already happened in the city of Zurich itself where a special fund has been created using the revenues from parking meters and reserved for the construction of new parking garages. However, since all projects for parking garages were rejected in public votes during the last years, 24 million Swiss francs have now been assembled on this fund and cannot be used. Already an initiative is under way, requesting that this money should also be made available for other purposes.

Finally, a source of uncertainty in the decisionmaking process of our direct democracy are those citizens who deliberately misuse these liberties for other objectives. Arbitrariness, malice or even professional trouble making tries to use the direct democracy to bring about its own end. The abolishment of war as an outlet of frustration and violence has led many minorities to noisy actions, aimed at the destruction of our existing social, if not political structures. The deliberate and intentional character of this attitude makes any reasonable and rational approach futile. The creators of these difficulties want to render decisionmaking impossible; only then can they later point out that the existing "establishment" has not been able to solve society's problems.

Not all of these destructive groups, however, are actually malevolent. Sometimes, they are indeed guided by idealistic intentions but, in their missionary zeal and enthusiasm, they tend to see only one singular aspect and to overlook interdependencies and interactions with other activities required by our level of civilization. In their eagerness to provide a better environment, for instance, they earnestly propose to abandon motor traffic entirely, although the loss of quality of life resulting from such a measure would, most probably, be considered unbearable by most citizens.

Many efforts have been undertaken to please all groups – whether benevolent or malevolent – having themselves appointed as advocates of public health and happiness. Advocacy planning, public participation, voting and long discussions with "anti-groups" have been the result of a desire to please even small minorities who are certainly not representing the "silent majority". Mostly the results of these efforts have been disappointingly negative. The malevolent groups do not want to be convinced; the benevolent groups, if succeeding with one demand, proceed immediately to the next action. A typical example, again from Zurich may illustrate the difficulties of the desire to please everybody.

In 1970, a four-lane viaduct was constructed to relieve the adjacent streets, many of them in densely populated areas, from motor traffic. This viaduct was, incidentally, the result of an overwhelming acceptance in a public vote. In the submission to the contractors, emphasis was laid on the fastest possible procedure, not on the cheapest solution. When this bridge was almost completed in 1972, a second vote had to take place in order to provide an access ramp. Meanwhile, public sentiment had changed considerably and this ramp was – rejected! So, after having pushed the contractors into making costly overtime to complete the bridge as early as possible, it remained closed after completion! With a provisional ramp it was made accessible for a bus line, probably one of the most expensive separate busways in the world!

Evidently, this situation was impossible and the authorities tried to redesign the access ramp in such a way that it would pass the second public vote. Therefore, a highly sophisticated procedure was lined up, combining public participation with advocacy planning, incorporating representatives of all minority groups and even professional troublemakers (the latter in order to prevent that they would later claim not to have had a chance to participate). This giant committee, reinforced by several public hearings, has now – five years after completion of the bridge – finally come up with a solution. And, surprisingly, the best and most acceptable alternative turned out to be the original one! In order to make it more acceptable in the next vote, it was somewhat reduced and had to undergo a low-calorie diet, but in principle we are back to the original solution. A deplorable result for such many years of expensive "open planning". Maybe this is the price of democracy?

ALTERNATIVES

Would there be any other or better possibilities? Indeed, if looking at the last example, one might ask why not the whole bridge, including its access ramps, were submitted to voting in the first place. The reason is that, according to the present law, any project brought to a referendum must be consisting of completed contract drawings including a most accurate cost estimate, because the vote also (or mainly) concerns the budget available for the construction.

In the attached Scheme 1, this present procedure can be seen quite clearly. A lot of work has to be completed before the actual voting takes place, and the basic principle – the underlying scheme – is not part of the referendum. So the voter can decide only on its consequences; hence the high degree of uncertainty.

If, however, the procedure could be changed over to a system as outlined in Scheme 2, the citizens would have a real chance to accept or reject the principle and to leave its implementation to the authorities appointed for this purpose. Most probably, this would be more democratic than the present procedure, but there would be a long way to change the law to this effect. At present, the trend points exactly the other way, to more "participation" in the detail stages.

The involvement of the public at the end rather than in the beginning of the planning procedure makes reasonable decisionmaking in this direct democratic system so adventurous. Many decisions happen "by chance" – the administration then has to make the best out of it and sometimes must turn the course around by 180 degrees. Under these circumstances, many investments have been lost or not been used to their best possible efficiency.

CONCLUSIONS

It could be concluded from the above considerations that a technocratic and autocratic policy may still be the best and easiest way to serve the public's needs. This conclusion, however, may be misleading.

Firstly, the public is certainly entitled to get what it wants. This may not be the best or the cheapest solution. But, as Frederik the Great use to say, "everybody should be happy according to his own fashion". Obviously, in the case of the rejected bridge access, the impact of the bridge traffic on the (mostly industrial adjacent landuse) was considered a bad trade-off against the noise and air pollution in the densely populated areas which had to bear a considerable through-traffic for many years longer.

Secondly, also technocrats may be wrong. Traffic planners, just to name one example, were taught to design a balanced network according to the projected needs. The general public, however, seems to prefer* a "bottle-neck philosophy", keeping the total traffic volume under control by restrictions in the capacities for inflowing traffic. This is less comfortable in that it enforces a modal split which is not necessarily to everybody's taste; it certainly is a more economical solution, however, and deserves serious recognition by specialists even though it conflicts with the accepted state of the art.

Thirdly, other criteria may really be more important. The environmental quality or the availability of resources is indeed of paramount importance. This, however, does not necessarily mean that new constructions should just be avoided. Sometimes, the do-nothing method is not the most economical and advantageous one with regard to environment and resources.

One example may be the strong sentiment building up all over the world against nuclear power plants, stimulated by people whose real interests are on a different level. The fact that for heating purposes atomic energy may be more compatible with environmental requirements than the burning of fossil fuels, is readily overlooked. Similar mis-proportions can be observed in the complex discussions of mobility versus environment and energy.

Fourthly, there is always hope that eventually – although sometimes with considerable delay – the public will understand the advance warnings of technocrats. For many years, specialists have warned that fossil fuels are being depleted at a terrific rate of speed, that alternative developments should be started and that considerable financial means would be required for research in this field. Nothing, however, happened as long as oil and electricity were so cheap that there was no viable economic alternative to be expected. After the so-called "energy crisis" in 1973 the public mind suddenly became aware of this problem (mainly, though, because of the increasing fuel prices). Now, of course, it is very fashionable to design new modes of transport, even if they are most unrealistic.

As a guide-line for decision making, planners and economists have certainly learned from these developments that there can be no "this-is-it-solution". All forecasts are based on assumptions which, owing to exogenous constraints, are beyond our control, let alone the influence of benevolent and malevolent pressure groups. So, the "scenario philosophy" has been developed, reducing all forecasts and proposals to an "if-then" system. The decision maker should obtain information as to what will happen if this decision is not taken – the do-nothing alternative. The assessment of all feasible alternatives, including the do-nothing solution, should serve as a tool for the decision maker to make up his mind.

Sometimes conditions are more complex. The assessment of the consequences of any decision may be beyond the grasp of the decision maker himself. New methodologies have been developed for this purpose. The Technological Assessment, for instance, is one effort to evaluate the positive and negative consequences of a given technical decision, also in fields which seem hardly related to the original problem. Another method is the cost/benefit-analysis, providing a more economic approach to the evaluation of decision consequences.

A further requirement to any economic or technological decision is that it should contain a maximum of built-in flexibility. A Metro system, once started, should be completed even if it takes half e century. If, however, for any reason, second thoughts prevent the completion of such a system, each completed section should for itself be fully operational and selfsupporting. Not only is it uncertain how later generations will feel about our present-day philosophies; moreover it is entirely beyond our control how later politicians, authorities or voters may decide. It would be unfair to design a system in such a way that for all times people will be forced to implement it even against their better convictions.

Finally, all specialists, consultants and advisers should always be aware of the fact that they can only supply the tools, never the decisions themselves. Decisions are always of a political nature; but politicians have frequently tried to transfer the burden of decision to the technical level because the problem was too complex for them to decide. Such a misuse of the technocrates is dangerous; if for any reason – and as we have seen, there are many – the public sentiment will change within a short time, it will always be the technocrate who is blamed for "wrong" developments. If, however, the decision was right and the construction succesful, he will hardly ever get the credit for it.

FOOTNOTE

* presently, at least.

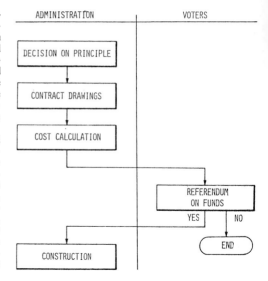

Scheme 1 - Present procedure for voting and implementation of road constructions in Switzerland. Before a project can be submitted to the referendum, a long and costly preliminary working phase is required. If the voters reject the proposal, these efforts are lost, including the time required for their preparation.

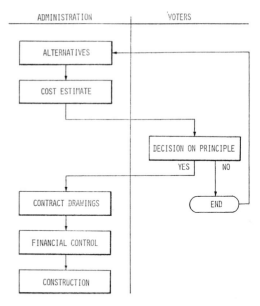

Scheme 2 – Possible flow diagram for an improved voting procedure. Without sacrificing the principle of the direct democracy, such a procedure would considerably reduce the preparatory phase and transfer the voter's decision to a much earlier period of time.

The Inseparability of Operational Control Policy Analysis and Strategic Planning: An Experience With U.S. Airports

by

DAVID G. SMITH

U.S. Department of Transportation, Office of the Secretary
The University of Virginia, McIntire School of Commerce

DANIEL P. MAXFIELD

U.S. Energy Research and Development Administration, Division of Transportation

STAN FROMOVITZ

The University Maryland
College of Business and Management, Department of Management Science

INTRODUCTION

Transportation planning research appears to be proceeding along two distinct and seemingly divergent methodological paths. The analytical developments of shorter range operational control methodology seems to be incompatible with analytical techniques being developed to evaluate long range transportation policies and plans. Yet these operational control policies are causing significant changes in the cost structure of transportation. In this paper we
  1. define the analytical difficulties encountered in simultaneous consideration of long range capital investment planning and short range operational control policy.
  2. describe our methodology for combined short and long analysis in airport investment planning.
  3. summarize our findings in analysis of sixty-eight U.S. airports.
  4. demonstrate the potential benefits that may result from continued research in this area.
  5. indicate future research directions and areas of application.

Our methodology, at this point has been developed for the particular problem of airport system planning and applied to the sixty-eight largest airports of the United States. Selected results of these applications have been reported in the *1974 National Transportation Report* [1] and in the long range planning document *National Transportation: Trends and Choices*[2] for the Office of the Secretary, U.S. Department of Transportation. The existence of trade-offs between operational policy that affects the demand for capacity and strategic investment policy that affects the future supply of capacity is established. A method is described that approximates long run marginal costs of capacity that are defined in terms of the appropriate short run marginal cost functions. In the case of airports, short run marginal cost approximation

involves the solution of a peak load pricing problem where peak period activity may substitute off-peak capacity until the marginal cost of this substitution just equals the incremental cost of a new capacity increasing project. The short run operational problem is inseparable from the longer run investment problem. We show that these are the costs appropriate to strategic investment and facility planning.

Our experience in airport system planning suggests that when the inseparability of short and long range planning is explicitly recognized and dealt with in the planning methodology, requirements for future capacity are significantly reduced. When the two are separated, long range plans tend to perpetuate operational inefficiencies. We summarize our findings in support of this observation.

THE SHORT RUN: OPERATIONAL CONTROL POLICY ANALYSIS

For many years, economists have recognized the inseparability of short and long run analysis. The economist's long run cost functions required for investment decisions are developed by collecting the short run cost functions for alternative investments. The problem encountered is in the specification of the appropriate short run cost functions. The economic paradigm assumes that a productive facility is managed optimally with respect to input factors leaving price and quantity to be determined. In reality there are additional managerial dimensions to short run costs. In fact, some of these dimensions are substitutes for investment in increased capacity.

Skirting the semantics of what is the short and what is the long, these management options must be associated with short run cost functions in the same fashion as are investment alternatives. However, this demands that all of the variables that are controllable in the short run must also be controlled in the long. A difficult problem results.

New techniques emerging for optimal control of transport systems offer great potential for altering short run costs. This is especially true for management of transient conditions such as peak loads at airports or congestion on urban road networks. These new techniques have greatly enlarged the number of manageable variables but in doing so has restricted scope to analysis at a single point in time for all practical purposes. Examples of this result abound in transportation planning. The examples here are from the airport system planning area where investment and operational control decisions are to be made in anticipation of future traffic growth.

The analysis of short run airport costs typically begins with an average cost related to airport utilization and a direct cost related to congestion delays. Aircraft operations (arrivals or departures) are considered to be the output of the airport. Figure 1 shows the cost structure facing an aircraft of a particular weight classification at a U.S. airport.

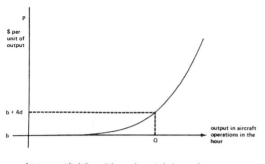

b = average cost (including capital cost and operating/maintenance)
d = cost per minute of delay to an operation (aircraft and passenger)
Q = capacity in operations per hour such that the expected delay is 4 minutes

Figure 1 - Short Run Cost Curve

For simplicity, airport capacity is shown as constant, although it is somewhat variable even in the short run. Knowledge of the types of aircraft and the distribution of activity over time (hourly, daily, weekly, monthly, etc) results in a simple arithmetic operation to determine the annual cost to users of a given airport at its existing capacity.

To compute values required for Figure 1, the method of Warskow, et.al. [3] has been refined. The procedure (Delay Algorithm) determines the delay incurred in shifting all aircraft scheduled in excess of capacity to a later time. To demonstrate this delay computation, let

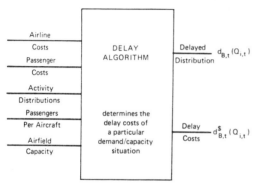

Figure 2 - Delay Algorithm Input-Output Diagram.

$d_{B,t}(Q_{i,t})$ = total daily delay for the busy day in year t as a function of the capacity of the i-th configuration (see Figure 3.17) if implemented in year t, as a function of system capacity ($Q_{i,t}$).

$d_{A,t}(Q_{i,t})$ = total daily delay for the average day in year t as a function of $Q_{i,t}$.

Where

$Q_{i,t}$ = capacity of configuration i in year t.
$d\$(Q_{i,t})$ = delay cost associated with having configuration i in place in year t.

The method assumes that the three classes of aircraft are uniformly mixed in order within the hour. Figure 3 shows a typical distribution, where the profile obtained shows for hour h, the summation

$$\sum_{c=1}^{3} D_{B,h,t}^{c}$$

In the figure, only the portion of the distribution in which delays occur are shown.

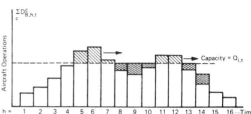

Figure 3 - Typical Hourly Distribution of Aircraft Operations and the Effect of Delay Procedure

The shaded area above the $Q_{i,t}$ capacity line represents over capacity operations at the airport. In calculation of delay by this method, all of the aircraft above the capacity line in hour 4 and all aircraft to the right up through hour 11 must be shifted (delayed) to the right such that the resultant distribution is everywhere below the capacity line.

Given the input for the average day, the average day delay and costs are also computed using the Delay algorithm. These must be combined to allow approximation of the annual costs. Experience with the Delay algorithm suggests that the delay $[d_{x,t}(x;Q_{i,t})]$ as a function of the peak hour demand magnitude x is approximately exponential in process. Given $d_{B,t}$ and $d_{A,t}$ with knowledge of the maximum over h of both $d_{B,h,t}^{c}$ and $D_{E,h,t}^{c}$ at time t, the function

$$\delta(x) = \alpha e^{\beta x}$$

can be fit by regression techniques. With this average delay function, the total delay lost function can be derived.

Now let,

$P_t(x)$ = the proportion of the 365 days of the year when peak magnitude is x.

Then

$$d_t(Q_{i,t}) = \sum_{x=0}^{\infty} P_t(x)\,\delta(x)$$

Of course infinity can be replaced by the peak magnitude of the busiest day distribution. Finally, $d\$(Q_{i,t})$ is approximated in a similar fashion using the total user costs components. The following equations define the average cost per minute of delay to an aircraft operation and an aircraft passenger.

286

$$\lambda A = \sum_{C=1}^{3} C_{A,t}^c \frac{\sum_{h=1}^{24} D_{B,h,t}^c}{\sum_{C=1}^{3}\sum_{h=1}^{24} D_{B,h,t}^c}$$

$$\lambda p = \sum_{C=1}^{3} C_{P,t}^c P_t^c \frac{\sum_{h=1}^{24} D_{B,h,t}^c}{\sum_{C=1}^{3}\sum_{h=1}^{24} D_{B,h,t}^c}$$

where

$C_{A,t}^c$ = cost per minute of delay to aircraft of type c in year t.

$C_{P,t}^c$ = cost per minute of delay to passengers on aircraft of type c in year t.

$D_{B,h,t}^c$ = hourly distribution of aircraft operations of type c for hours (h= 1,2,...24) on the busiest day of year t.

P_t^c = average number of passengers per aircraft of type c in year t.

Then using the total minutes delay for the average and busy day, the average and busy day costs are computed by

$$d_{B,t}\,(Q_{i,t})\quad(\lambda A + \lambda p)$$

$$d_{A,t}\,(Q_{i,t})\quad(\lambda A + \lambda p)$$

and ultimately used to calculate an annual user cost,

$$d_t^\$(Q_{i,t}) = \sum_{x=0}^{\infty} P_t(x)\,\delta(x)\,(\lambda A + \lambda p)$$

To obtain an approximation of marginal delay costs, the original average delay curve

$$\delta(x) = \alpha e^{x}$$

would be converted to a cost function by use of λA and λp. Hence total delay cost as a function of x would be approximately

$$\delta^*(x) = \alpha e^{\beta x}(\lambda A + \lambda p)\quad x$$

The approximate short run marginal delay cost is then

$$\frac{d\delta^*(x)}{dx} = \alpha(\lambda A + \lambda p)\,e^{\beta x}(\beta x + 1)$$

This can become quite high in relation to marginal capacity cost and, as will be shown later, is responsible for much of the perceived airport capacity investments in the future. However, the use of this cost relation ignores the substitution of off-peak capacity at a cost lower than the cost of additional capacity.

In the short run scenario, with no expansion in output capacity, it is possible to modify this cost structure. An approach that has been suggested [4,5] would institute a pricing policy that would charge the incremental unit of output with the incremental change in costs incurred by all others, ie. a variant of the marginal cost price. Observing Figure 1, it is clear that an additional aircraft operation during a congested period increases the delay cost incurred by all other aircraft operating in that period. Even here the cost arithmetic is simple employing the above short run marginal delay cost function approximation. The problem lies in predicting the response of demand to the increased charge. To the extent that there is any price elasticity of demand, there will be a decrease in activity during the peak period.

Faced with the increased cost, an aircraft operator will either pay the price or seek a substitute. In the short run, substitutes include a shift to an off-peak period or a shift to a different airport. An airline engaged in multiple flight markets may reduce frequency. A non-scheduled flight may be cancelled entirely. Of course, purchase of an increase in capacity may be the choice in the long run.

With little information about price elasticity and practically no information about time elasticity, a model of the substitution process became a necessary replacement for time variant demand functions. The short run model [6] begins with the hourly distribution of aircraft and seeks to redistribute the activity at minimum cost. It spreads the peak periods to attain a more uniform utilization of the airport. The assumption is that the aircraft operator will seek the least cost substitute. In the case of carriers competing in the same market at low load factors, it is assumed that the airport authority will enforce a suitable compromise.

The analytical procedure (Peak Spreading Algorithm) calculates the cost of rescheduling the demand such that no hour contains scheduled demand in excess of existing capacity. Figure 4 shows the concept.

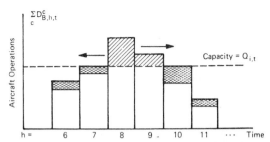

Figure 4 - Typical Hourly Distribution of Aircraft Operations and the Effect of the Peak Spreading Procedure

The diagram shows over capacity operations being rescheduled to the left and right of the peak period. This is in contrast to the delay procedure shown in Figure 3.

The Peak Spread Algorithm requires the same inputs as the Delay Algorithm. Its output is a measurement of the magnitude of passenger time and aircraft operating cost losses due to rescheduling and a monetary evaluation of these. Figure 5 displays the inputs and outputs of the procedure where the output activity distributions are constructed by type of aircraft.

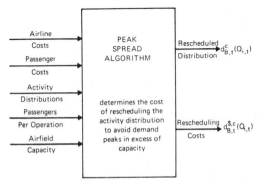

Figure 5 - Peak Spreading Algorithm Input-Output Diagram

Rescheduling is accomplished under a discipline which orders aircraft with priorities
1) Air Carrier Aircraft
2) Commuter Aircraft
3) General Aviation Aircraft

This represents the generalization that, with respect to airport system public productivity, social value of the flight types are ranked in this order.

The algorithm begins by solving the rescheduling problem for the air carrier distribution. Having solved this problem, it then adds (by horizontal summation) the commuter distribution to the original air carrier distribution and a second solution is obtained. The general aviation distribution is then added to the first two input distribution and a third solution is obtained. Costs are assigned to each aircraft type as the added cost of successive solutions; e.g., air carriers are assigned the cost of the first solution, commuters the difference between the second solution and the first, general aviation the difference between the third and the second. This is shown in the flow diagram of Figure 6.

In solving the rescheduling problem, the Peak Spreading Algorithm operates as follows: (see Figure 7)

1. Searches the input distribution locating *chains* (or sequences) of hours of activity that define peak and off-peak periods.

2. Establishes the *central points* (mean, mode) of each chain and determines the number of aircraft involved in the peak periods (chain value).

3. Assesses off-peak periods for their ability to *absorb* aircraft operations being rescheduled.

4. Locates the *weighted center* of each peak period. These centers depend upon the steepness of the peaks and valleys of the activity distribution. Aircraft in a peak period are rescheduled to the right and left (in time) of the weighted center of each peak.

5. Employing empirically derived probability functions, the location (in time) of unused capacity during off-peak periods is determined by Monte Carlo procedures. This reflects the observed preferences of airline schedulers for certain times within the hour.

6. At this point, each peak period is treated independently. Before rescheduling can begin, a search must be made to locate off-peak chains that are to receive a greater number of aircraft than can be accomodated. This can occur when two peaks are close together. When it does happen, the two peaks (chains) are said to *intersect*.

7. If chain intersections exist, then an iterative procedure is executed that adjusts the assignments until a feasible allocation occurs.

8. Assignments are completed producing the rescheduled distribution.

9. The time duration of aircraft rescheduling is computed.

10. Costs are computed.

11. At this point, the peak spreading is either complete, requires another iteration to resolve intersecting peaks or there is not enough off-peak capacity available to reasonably apply the procedure. Reasonableness is defined in terms of rescheduling time in step 9. This usually occurs when total daily demand is in excess of 80% of total daily capacity.

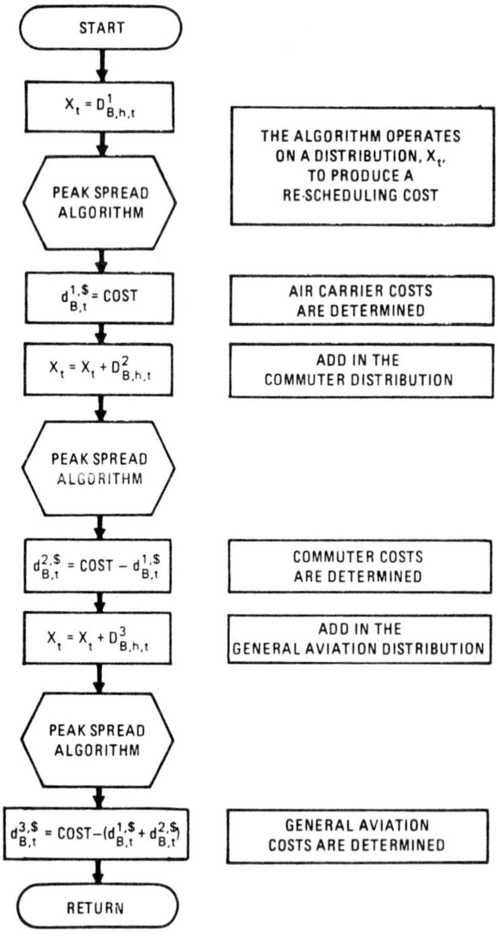

Using the Peak Spreading Algorithm, the value of off-peak substitution is established.

THE LONG RUN ANALYSIS: STRATEGIC INVESTMENT PLANNING

The short run model considers the systematic substitution of off-peak capacity for peak capacity. In the long run, construction programs can be implemented that increase the physical capacity of the airport. Figure 8 shows a segment of the long run cost curve for airport expansion along two airfield expansion paths. The solid short run curves define average incremental costs of capacity and delay to individual operations in peak periods. Expansion possibilities are arranged in a tree structure [7]. Each path has a long run cost curve associated with it. The appropriate path, and hence cost curve depends upon the demand for additional capacity. Movement along a path represents the investment of successive increments of capital in airfield and passenger facilities. Extending the analysis to the long run brings an additional option to the aircraft operator faced with the relatively high marginal cost based charges. This additional option associated with an increase in peak period capacity completes the components of the cross-elasticity of demand between peak and off-peak periods.

Recall that the first component of the cross-elasticity is the value differential between peak period airport use and off-peak use as measured by the differences between the cost of rescheduling to an off-peak period and not doing so. The aircraft operator has the option of having his effective price increased by congestion delay during peak periods or reexamining his preferences and perhaps reschedule to an off-peak time. This cost differential, over all levels of output, defines one component of the cross-elasticity.

The long run option is a contribution to the purchase of additional capacity. A capacity increasing project may be selected that will insure sufficient capacity to eliminate certain congestion costs. The fundamental criterion for this selection is cost minimization. However, the existence of this alternative affects the magnitude of the

Figure 6 - Peak Spreading Cost Computation Flow Diagram

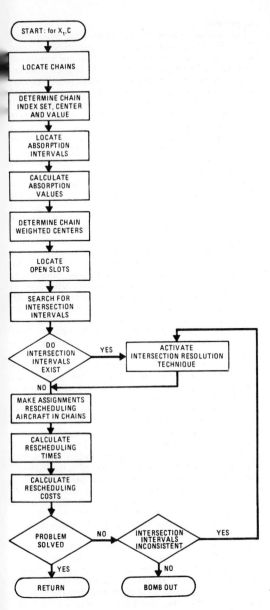

Figure 7 - Peak Spreading Algorithm Procedural Flow Diagram

D(Q_1) to zero. Because capacity increments can only be purchased in large blocks, the cross-elasticity is discontinuous.

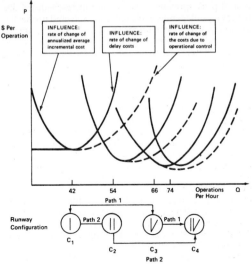

Figure 8 - A Segment of the Long Run Cost Curve

From here, a standard construction sizing and staging procedure can be applied to develop a strategic investment plan. For example, discrete variable dynamic programming procedures were employed in the study described. below. A severe problem arises, however, in that the short run cost structure is not simply a function of hourly output but of a complete distribution of interrelated demands over the time of day. As a result, the Peak Spreading Algorithm must be executed for every state variable-stage combination in the enumeration. Computation time can become excessive depending upon distributional characteristics. By any standard, the expense is too great for effective sensitivity analysis typically demanded of a planning methodology.

The short run operational policy analysis for the airport strategic planning problem employs a heuristic technique. The procedure recognizes certain characteristics of daily demand distributions, produces expected first cross-elasticity component and conversely, the economic attractiveness of the project is affected by the potential for a shift in the timing of demand. Thus, the second component of the cross-elasticity is the effect that capacity increasing projects, i.e., their present valued cash flows, have on the first component.

Figure 9 depicts the situation where peak period price (P_1) is equal to short run marginal cost (SRMC) which is constant and equal to to (b) for peak period demand (Q_1) up to capacity (Q_c). For demand in excess of (Q_c), the SRMC increases by a congestion component cost expressed functionally as D(Q_1). (P_1) is determined by the congestion component as a function of (Q_1). Peak/off-peak cross-elasticity can be written as the partial derivative ($\partial Q_2/\partial Q_1$) and plotted as a function of (Q_1). The rate increases from (Q_c) as a function of D(Q_1) up to the point (Q_c^* ,r) where a capacity increasing project of size (Q_c^*) is cost justified and reduces

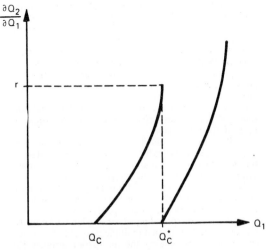

Figure 9 - Peak/off-peak Cross-elasticity

289

schedules and proceeds iteratively toward an optimal redistribution of that demand. A natural possibility for reducing computational expense is the development of an approximation method. Dependent variables are the cost of peak spreading and the output rescheduled distribution. Independent variables are selected properties of input activity distributions and certain search parameters of the Peak Spreading Algorithm. Using the results of Peak Spreading Algorithm applications on several representative demand distributions, a set of linear statistical models were developed.

Current use of these models is restricted to a relatively small range of independent variable values. Outside of this range, the Peak Spread Algorithm is used. This has resulted in a computer cost reduction in the 50 to 80 percent range. One observation bearing note is that due to the very large cost of even minimal capacity increasing projects, the pattern of project selection and staging is not highly sensitive to moderate approximation errors. The poorest statistical model in use has coefficients significant at the 20 percent level based on standard t-tests but produced long run analytical results that compare reasonably well with results using the Peak Spread Algorithm. These models are probably not acceptable for detailed short run analysis of energy consumption and pollution. They do, however, capture the significant effects of short run operational policy upon long run costs.

Our plan for modification of the relationship between the linear models and the Peak Spreading Algorithm is to implement a statistical model building subroutine. This subroutine will maintain a data base independently of any particular application. Depending upon the characteristics of the demand distribution being operated upon, the subroutine will select, revise or build models based upon predefined conditions or will execute the Peak Spreading Algorithm as necessary and append the results to the data base.

ANALYSIS OF THE POTENTIAL OF SHORT RUN OPERATIONAL CONTROL POLICIES TO REDUCE INVESTMENT IN AIRPORT CAPACITY

Air carrier airports can be described as being in one of several activity categories that define the levels and types of congestion present. An airport will typically track through these categories in succession as air carrier traffic increases:

1. High peaking and a high percentage of general aviation (HP-HG).

2. Moderate peaking and a high percentage of general aviation (MP-HG), as general aviation begins to avoid the air carrier peaks and spreads itself into the off-peak hours.

3. Moderate peaking and a low percentage of general aviation (MP-LG), general aviation begins to decrease as a percentage of total operations and eventually in absolute terms as much of this demand will shift to other airports.

4. Low peaking and a low percentage of general aviation (LP-LG), as air carrier peaks begin to spread to other parts of the day.

5. Pressure is applied for the construction of a new airport. The tendency is for a previously congested situation with low peaking and a low percentage of general aviation to result in two highly peaked airports.

The alternatives analyzed for management of this cycle and to reduce investment requirements include various combinations of reducing general aviation activity in peak periods, spreading of air carrier peaks by rescheduling and, in certain multiple airport hubs, reallocating the traffic among the air carrier airports. [8]. These alternatives are each variants of the peak spread-

ing process.

The sixty-eight airports were analyzed in two groups. [9,10]. The first group consists of the twenty-seven large hub airports that each represent at least one percent of the total enplaned passengers at U.S. airports. The remaining forty-one airports are the medium hub air carrier airports. The large hub results are best summarized by consolidation into three distinct situations:

A. Airports in the high peaking categories where a new airport is not actively being planned.

B. Airports in the medium or low peaking categories where a new airport is not being planned.

C. Airports in hubs where a new airport is actively being planned.

For airports in the first situation, the analysis has shown that reducing general aviation demand in the peak periods is generally more effective than either the construction of additional capacity or the spreading of air carrier peak demands. Reducing peak period general aviation activity would result in reductions in peak hour capacity requirements ranging from 43 operations per hour to 95 operations per hour between 1974 and 1990. Congestion delay cost savings would range from 5% to 90% for airports in these high peaking situations. It should be noted that high peaking is almost always accompanied by high general aviation percentages except in the cases of multiple airports.

For seven of the airports in situation A, there would be no capacity related airfield investments required if the operational control policy reducing peak period general aviation were applied. For two of these airports, there is no problem of capacitation. For all but one of the remaining airports of situation A, a combined reduction of peak period general aviation traffic and the spreading of air carrier peaks, would eliminate the need for capacity related investments through 1990. The State of Colorado reports that the remaining one airport (Denver) is planning a policy of general aviation diversion to other airports. The data reflects this and indeed no further application of the policies were indicated in the analysis. The combined plans reported by the States include a total of $717 million in airfield investment through 1990 at the large hub airports in situation A. Our analysis indicates that the implementaion of operational control policies and the elimination of nearly all of this capacity related investment is economically justified.

For four of the medium to low peaking airports in situation B, the analysis has indicated that no capacity related airfield investments would be justified through 1990 if peak period general aviation reduction and air carrier peak spreading were combined. For the remaining two airports it was found that the investments planned for the period prior to 1980 could be postponed to the period between 1980 and 1990. These airports reported a total of $558 million in capacity increasing projects was planned. About 75% of this investment could be justifiably replaced by the implementation of the operational control policies.

For the airports located in hubs where new airports are under active consideration, it was found that the use operational control policies and capital investment at the existing airport could satisfy the demands on capacity through 1990. Some redistribution of air carrier traffic to reliever airports would be required. One exception was Chicago, where forecast demand could not be satisfied there even with maximum investment. Midway would offer some relief through 1985 but after that time only a new airport or a major reorientation of connecting traffic flow would satisfy the forecast demand. Los Angeles was found unable to handle the forecast traffic at the present site. Rescheduling of activity could not be accomplished realistically. Inspection of neighboring suburban airports suggests that enough capacity exists to relieve Los Angeles International through the 1990 period. In the New York hub, sufficient capacity appears available without the new airport at Stewart Field. This would require fuller utilization of Newark together with diversion of general aviation and implementation of air carrier peak spreading at all three airports. In the large hubs that have new airports under consideration, the overall cost of these airports has been estimated at about 4.4. billion dollars, of which 1.3 billion would be for airfield construction. If these new airports (except at Chicago) were not built by 1990, further increases in existing airfield capacity would be required at a cost of about $680 million even when operational control policies are employed. Existing terminal facilities would need to be expanded as well. It is clear that major cost savings in new airport construction are possible through the more efficient use of existing capacity.

Terminal area capacity requirements are affected by the short run operational policies, particularly the gate processing facilities and airport access systems. For airports in the high peaking and high general aviation activity situations, reduction of peak period general aviation activity will increase the airfield capacity available to air carriers in their peak period. The increase in peak period passengers that results may produce a need for more terminal capacity. It is estimated that a reduction in peak period general aviation could lead to required new terminal capacity of from 10 to 40 percent. On the other hand, air carrier peak spreading will reduce terminal area capacity requirements. For airports in the moderate peaking situations, a decrease in new terminal capacity requirements in the range of from 6 to 40 percent would result from implementation of the operational control policies.

The study indicates that, for major airports in large hubs, the economically justified level of investment is small in comparison with the investment levels being planned. This is the case because of the potential savings attributable to operational control policies for making better use of existing capacity in the short run.

Of the forty-one medium hubs studied, twenty-seven were planning no additional capacity, nor were they found to be in need of new capacity using our methodology. For the remaining fourteen medium hubs where major capacity additions are being planned, the composition of peak period demand is highly concentrated with general aviation. Spreading these general aviation peaks enables a reduction in capacity requirements of between 10 and 60 percent. The average reduction is about 35 percent. This reduction in general aviation traffic during peak periods was found to permit higher concentration of air carrier activity in peaks. As in the analysis of large hub airports, this tended to produce increases in the requirements for terminal capacity.

CONCLUSION

Potential results are significant for continued planning research recognizing the inseparable relationship between operational control policy and strategic planning. Terminal and link congestion problems that force capa-

city increasing investment exist in all modes of transport. Our methodology for airport system planning is directly applicable to other transport systems characterized by a high proportion of scheduled service or systems with predominant investment in terminal facilities, eg., water ports and rail yards. Applications in urban systems and on other problems where network structures are being analyzed probably will require methods of a different nature. The ability to incorporate the effects of operational control policy into long range planning analysis techniques will be essential.

In addition to the involvement of the U.S. Department of Transportation in investment planning research, several other agencies of the U.S. Government are interested in the energy and environmental impacts of operational control policies in the airport work. Short run inefficiencies often are responsible for resource waste having significant proportion. In reducing congestion delay and concentrations of activity, the operational control policies reduce fuel consumption and the level of engine emissions. The environmental impact of construction projects is often great. As we have seen, the operational control policies can be substitutes for capacity increasing projects. Their environmental impacts are certainly less, although their economic and political impacts may be strong. In guiding the process of transport planning, the application of operational control policy analysis should be encouraged. Techniques to implement this analysis must be developed and made available.

REFERENCES
[1] U.S. Department of Transportation, **The 1974 National Transportation Report,** Office of the Secretary (July 1975).
[2] U.S. Department of Transportation, **National Transportation: Trends and Choices,** Office of the Secretary (January 1977).
[3] Warskow, M.A. and I.S. Wisepart, "Capacity of Airport Systems in Metropolitan Areas: Methodology of Analysis". Deer Park, Long Island, New York: Airbourne Instruments Laboratory (January 1964).
[4] Douglas, George and James C. Miller, III, **Economic Regulation of Domestic Air Transport: Theory and Policy.** Washington, D.C.: The Brookings Institution, 1974.
[5] Warford, Jeremy, **Public Policy Toward General Aviation.** Washington, D.C.: The Brookings Institution, 1971.
[6] D.G. Smith, et. al., **The Airport Investment Model - A Methodology for Airport Investment Planning,** U.S. Department of Transportation, Office of the Secretary (February 1977).
[7] Velona, Walter D., "Determination of Airport Costs." U.S. Department of Transportation, Office of the Secretary, Washington, D.C., 1969. Unpublished Working Paper. (Also in reference 6).
[8] Smith, David G. and Stanley Fromovitz, "Resource Allocation in the Multiple Airport Hub." Presented at the ORSA-TIMS Joint Meeting, Atlantic City, New Jersey (October 1972).
[9] D.G. Smith, et. al., **An Analysis of the Financial Impacts of Non-Capital Alternatives at the Large Air Transportation Hubs of the United States.** U.S. Department of Transportation, Office of the Secretary (February 1977).
[10] D.G. Smith, et. al., **An Analysis of the Financial Impacts of Non-Capital Alternatives at the Medium Air Transportation Hubs of the United States,** (Working Paper), U.S. Department of Transportation, Office of the Secretary (September 1976).

Operational requirements for new transit technology

by

RICHARD M. SOBERMAN

and

GEORGE CLARK

Planning Services Urban Transportation Development Corporation Ltd., Canada

INTRODUCTION

Urban planning in North American cities over the last 5 to 10 years has been characterized by a strong interest in improving the quality of public transportation. This renewal of interest in public transit reflects changes in both community and governmental attitudes toward the increasing dependence on the private automobile that dominated urban planning in the postwar era. As a consequence, proposals have been produced in many North American cities for substantial investment in more extensive networks of high quality transit. In many cases, these proposals are intended to achieve land use objectives and influence the pattern of urban growth, rather than simply respond to a projected transportation problem.

Interest in public transit has been paralleled by increasing recognition of the financial difficulty of providing expanded transit service in lower density areas and in providing adequate service in high- and medium-density travel corridors. This is particularly true where new transit facilities are proposed in order to support land use objectives, but where demand levels fall below those that have traditionally been served by rapid transit.

The need for improved coverage of the urban area and for a high standard of transit service in medium-density corridors suggests a range of travel volumes that cannot be served adequately by surface bus or streetcar or economically by underground rapid transit. This has led to renewed interest in Light Rail Transit and busways and to the concept of Intermediate Capacity Transit Systems (ICTS), designed to provide a higher level of transit service than is possible with surface systems, but at costs that are substantially lower than conventional subways. Most new development work in the transit field in the last several years has been in this area of mediumcapacity transit systems. Perhaps the most difficult design requirement of these systems is the need for exclusive right-of-way in developed areas. Development of new systems in the medium-capacity range is severely constrained by the fact that they must be acceptable from visual, environmental, and social points-of-view, a fact which has not been given priority by developers of many new systems.

Application of medium-capacity transit in major metropolitan centres involves networks of high-quality service on "trunk" lines or on feeder routes to higher capacity, conventional subway lines. For smaller communities where demand levels do not justify subway construction, these services may serve as the backbone of the transit system. In addition, mediumcapacity transit can serve a special-purpose function such as ensuring high levels of accessibility to major activity centres such as airports or new regional sub-centres.

Another important application may be the use of parallel facilities or services to provide capacity comparable to that of a single subway line at similar total cost. For example, two parallel lines may provide better overall coverage and lower access times and distribution costs than a single, conventional rapid transit line. The lower costs of individual medium-capacity lines would be achieved through less stringent right-of-way and guideway requirements.

In summary, most new developments in medium-capacity transit have been in response to a perceived need for high-quality transit services in a capacity range that matches land use objectives, and at costs that are significantly lower than those of conventional rapid transit systems. These developments must be acceptable from a community point-of-view, and must offer economical operation over a range of demand that cannot be economically handled by conventional rapid transit, or adequately handled by existing surface systems. In Canada, the cities of Toronto, Ottawa, Hamilton, Calgary, Edmonton and Vancouver are now in the process of responding to or planning for requirements in this range.

Much of the recent interest in technological innovation in the urban transit field has centred on medium-capacity transit. However, there have been few successful applications of new systems and the thesis which this paper proposes is that transit technology to meet current development objectives in urban areas will be successful only if a clear statement of performance requirements is defined from the perspective of a transit operator and urban planner, rather than a system engineer or system designer.

PROBLEMS IN TECHNOLOGICAL INNOVATION

The current interest in improved public transit has generated considerable activity in the field of technological innovation. Most development work has been directly, or indirectly, sponsored by government agencies in Europe, the United States, and Canada. In spite of extensive development effort there has been very limited implementation of new types of transit systems. Unlike other fields requiring technological innovation, such as the military, space research, or process control, most transit research programs have concentrated on technical solutions, with little emphasis on careful definition of the operating problem. Consequently, many new concepts for transit improvement have emerged which have achieved little or no market acceptability among the municipal officials and transit operators who would ultimately implement and operate them.

There are several reasons for this. First, technological innovation in the transportation field has tended to occur only when there has been a profit incentive. As a result, in marine transportation we have seen the advent of containerization, and larger, more specialized ships, because it made economic sense to move in that direction; in the field of aviation, we have seen technological innovation because of the commercial viability and marketability of particular advances.

By contrast, technological innovation in railway passenger services and urban transit has been almost non-existent because there is little or no profit incentive to be derived from services that are generally characterized by deficit operation and are extended or re-equipped rather infrequently.

As a result, much of the so-called innovation has occured outside the traditional sources of equipment supply for the transit industry and much of it at government request or sponsorship. In most cases, the product simply has not responded to any real requirement of urban planners and transit operators and has not accounted for the realities of operating conditions, consumer preferences and community values. In fact, many unsuccessful development efforts have involved entire transit systems designed around a novel idea for suspension, propulsion, control or passenger service without sufficient consideration of the viability of these ideas in the transit market-place. Ideas or designs searching for an application are rarely an ideal match to any existing need. For example, during the "heady" atmosphere that characterized support for technological innovation during the 1960's, proposals for elevated "mono-rail" systems abounded; these proposals almost totally ignored one of the most fundamental concerns of transit operators — namely, the evacuation of passengers in case of emergency or break-down.

Second, many of the attempts to develop new urban transit technology have failed to understand the political and institutional constraints which impede technological innovation in the public arena.

At the general level, there may be considerable interest in development of new systems, but once proposals are made for specific applications, almost everyone is afraid to make the first mistake. Most elected officials and transit operators would rather be safe than daring. In the end, given a choice, they will almost always decide against major technological innovation in favour of more conventional, incremental solutions on grounds of system compatibility and "proven" reliability.

A third problem relates to the tendency amongst innovative "systems designers" to display more interest in sophisticated solutions (due to their presumption of high service standards) and less interest in some rather simple things that imply modest performance, but are relatively easy to achieve and could go a long way to improving the low quality of public transit service that now exists in suburban areas. In fact, because so much of the recent history of urban transportation is littered with the wreckage of ill-conceived transport technology, a back-lash

against innovative, system solutions has led to renewed interest in technology that is basically "off-the-shelf". In many North American cities, for example, there is now considerable enthusiasm for new Light Rail Transit lines which emerged from disillusionment with air cushion vehicles, magnetic levitation, linear induction propulsion and highly automated, small-vehicle technology which characterized the personal rapid transit (PRT) era. Even in the case of interurban services and after years of assessing technology that included gravity vacuum tubes and tracked air cushion vehicles, it was finally concluded that it just might be "best" to run conventional railway equipment between Boston and New York at speeds slightly higher than the 40 miles per hour that is characteristic of the present service.

In short, many proposals for technological innovation in the urban transit field have never been implemented because some interesting or innovative engineering feature that formed the basis for the new system simply was not beneficial to transit operators and municipal planning agencies responsible for providing transit services. To succeed, therefore, the need for new systems or technological innovation in urban transit must first be defined in terms that are responsive to requirements or objectives of urban planners and transit operating agencies. This definition of need is referred to as an Operational Requirement.

THE SYSTEM CONCEPT

The Urban Transportation Development Corporation is now developing an ICTS system. Production of an Operational Requirement was one of the primary elements of the initial stages of system development, and that Operational Requirement is now a major determinant of system design.

The origins of the basic ICTS concept are illustrated in Figure 1. Transportation planning studies in several Canadian cities had identified a need for new transit facilities in a range of site and operating conditions which were not ideally suited to existing transit systems. These studies and their land use implications, together with the objectives of municipalities and local communities, suggested the need for intermediate levels of capacity that would support medium development densities but without creating pressures for rapid redevelopment to high densities. In many cases, these proposed transit corridors pass through already established communities that are sensitive to new transportation facilities and any disruption that they might generate. On the other hand, plans and objectives raised the need for high levels of service in terms of reliability, average speed and frequency, which could only be achieved with some form of separated right-of-way.

Separate right-of-way can be achieved through the use of underground facilities, or, where conditions permit, by at-grade or elevated facilities. Underground facilities, of course, introduce high capital costs; at-grade facilities have lower costs, but opportunities for separate at-grade alignment are extremely limited in already-established urban areas.

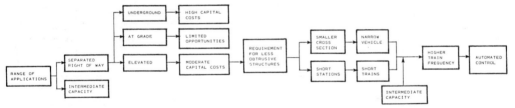

Figure 1 - Principal characteristics of ICTS

293

established urban areas. Elevated facilities have the advantage of lower capital costs but, for obvious reasons, may be considerably less acceptable from the community standpoint, particularly with regard to visual intrusion.

In order to achieve the requirements of intermediate capacity, separated right-of-way, and lower capital costs, it is essential that a guideway structure be developed that has a low level of visual and environmental intrusion. In fact, this has become a major aspect of the ICTS development program.

Achieving less obtrusive elevated structures involves both reducing the apparent massiveness of the structure itself and, more importantly, reducing the size of stations. The minimum cross-sectional area of the structure is determined by suspension design, stability and the limited capacity of narrow vehicles, while the objective of reducing station length imposes a requirement for short train lengths. Achieving capacity requirements with this combination of narrow vehicles and short trains forces higher operating frequency than is traditional in the transit industry.

Thus, the characteristics of possible applications of new transit systems led to a system concept, responsive to capacity, level of service and cost targets, and characterized by high-frequency service involving short trains that operate on elevated guideways wherever feasible.

DEVELOPMENT OF THE OPERATIONAL REQUIREMENT

The process of developing an Operational Requirement involved three basic elements:

1. It was prepared with inputs from municipal planning and transit operating agencies so as to arrive at an accepted set of requirements for intermediate capacity transit systems. In other words, the ultimate users of the new system have been asked to define its performance requirements and ultimately to endorse the specifications of a particular technical solution.

2. The Operational Requirement was based on several applications studies involving typical corridors in a number of North American cities. These potential applications helped to define the geometric and performance requirements of the system, including grade-climbing

ability, track curvature, capacity requirements, acceleration/deceleration rates and maximum speed.

3. Development of the Operational Requirement was an iterative process, involving continuous trade-off among operator and community requirements for economy, capacity, frequency of service and minimum impact on the community and environment.

At the outset, the program was proceeding along "traditional" lines, building on an operating concept and an assessment of available technologies and leading toward a preliminary system design. However, it was recognized at a early stage in the design process that non-engineering inputs were essential if the program was to be successful and, in fact, that the system concept might change substantially as a result of those inputs. The result has been an iterative process in the general form of Figure 2, but without the formality and structure implied by Figure 2. In fact, the development of operational requirements has involved continuous "give and take" between program management, design engineers, equipment manufacturers, transportation planners, planning agencies, transit operators, architects and cost analysts. The process has generally been one of constructive debate, sometimes of joint study and often of conflict between different points of view.

This process of debate, analysis and refinement extended to the point where there was substantial agreement on the Operational Requirement, as the basis for a "Model Specification" around which the system design would be developed. As the design has progressed, the Operational Requirement has been under continuous review as further information is produced on the projected cost, reliability and performance or the system.

Development of the Operational Requirement produced substantial changes in the initial system concept. At the start of the program in 1975, the system concept was presumed to have the following form:

– small vehicles carrying 10 to 20 passengers

– operating as single cars or in trains

– complex operating strategies, including skip-stop and express services with multi-platform stations

– extensive networking with direct transfer of vehicles or trains between lines through interchanges

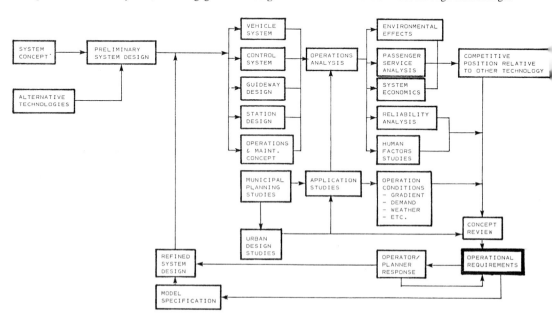

Figure 2-Operational requirements and the design process

– elevated guideway and stations over the full length of most applications
– direct service to low-density suburban areas
– demand-responsive service.

Preparation of the Operational Requirement forced consideration of this concept in respect of all of the factors listed in Table 1. In the process, engineering, economic and planning studies, together with input from planning agencies and transit operators, produced the following concept, representing a substantial departure from the initial concept:

– vehicles with a capacity of 50 to 70 passengers, and a minimum of 2 cars per train
– a system "optimized" for line-haul operation, but capable of extension to accommodate complex strategies
– concentration on single lines with branching capability
– elevated structures wherever possible with extensive design effort to produce acceptable structures, but with the overall system designed for efficient, economic operation at-grade, elevated or underground
– service confined to medium-density corridors of 5,000 to 20,000 pphpd
– scheduled service.

These examples illustrate the most fundamental changes in the Operational Requirement and system design that have occurred at this point in the development program. In addition, there have been many changes in areas such as train control, station operation, grade climbing capability, passenger evacuation, fleet management and maintenance concepts. Rather surprisingly, engineering analysis has initiated very few of these changes; and this appears to be a key factor. Transit development programs

Table 1-Principal elements of the operational requirement

1. *Level of Service*
   Service strategies
   Headway
   Speed/Acceleration/Deceleration
   Hours of Operation
   Comfort Criteria
   Interior noise, vibration and air conditioning

2. *System Performance*
   Line capacity
   Station capacity
   Directionality
   Grade capability
   Turning radii
   Switching performance
   Exterior noise, vibration and appearance
   Performance in adverse weather
   Reliability
   Safety and security
      structural integrity
      fire protection
      passenger evacuation
      operations control
   Passenger/system interface
   Passenger information

3. *Guideway Design*

4. *Station Design and Operation*

5. *Operation*
   Maintenance operations and maintainability
   Operation procedures

that have failed in the past have tended to be approached as an engineering problem, in isolation from other disciplines or other points of view. The Operational Requirement and the involvement of several disciplines and outside interests in its development is designed to avoid this pitfall.

The experience and objectives of transit operators and municipal planning agencies was a major factor in changes in ICTS concept that occurred as the Operational Requirement was developed. However, systems analysis that concentrated on the application of the system, and the costs, public acceptance, service quality and performance of the system, was the major influence on the Operational Requirement. For example, the shift in vehicle size is an outcome of transportation planning studies that included, as one consideration, the capital cost of the proposed ICTS system. Initially these studies were based on small-vehicle systems in the entire range of applications that had been proposed by municipal planning agencies, extending from closely-spaced lines in suburban areas to heavily-travelled radial or cross-town routes. By comparison with other modes – private and public – and considering cost, service and community effects, it became evident that the fixed-guideway concept was feasible only on the more heavily-travelled applications and, in fact, that its performance in these applications would be improved by increasing vehicle size. The process was repeated with alternative vehicle size, finally arriving at a vehicle size that is a good match to potential applications. It is worth noting that, at the outset of this process, some of the participants were convinced that the very small vehicle was the obvious route to take, that a small vehicle was central to the ICTS concept, and that any upward shift in vehicle size would lead to a system design that violated basic objectives of high service standard, low cost and high public acceptance. Others felt, equally strongly, that without larger vehicles the concept was not viable and would not be applied at competitive or acceptable costs. The Operational Requirements and the design process adopted for the ICTS program forced analysis and conclusion on this issue. In other circumstances, the debate over vehicle size might never have emerged or, in a design process that was closed to non-engineering input, the design might have proceeded without regard to a view that a different vehicle size might strengthen the concept.

A similar process has been applied to all of the principal system characteristics and, in fact, will extend throughout the entire design process. It is a process that relies on constructive conflict between disciplines or interests within the design agency and between the design group and "client" or public interests.

In the case of the ICTS program, the Operational Requirement has provided a focus for several different perspectives that might otherwise have been overlooked, and produced a system concept that is responsive to conditions, concerns and requirements in developing urban areas.

The U.S. Owner-Operator Trucker:
A Transportation Policy Based on Personal Bankruptcy

by

D. DARYL WYCKOFF

Harvard University, Massachusetts *

A large, highly productive, and vital segment of the U.S. intercity freight transportation capacity is subject to violent and, at times, disruptive convulsions as a buffer to absorbing shifts in transportation demand. I am referring to that group of single-truck fleet, independent operators known in the United States as "owner-operators." It has been estimated that some 100,000 such persons own and operate their own trucks without Interstate Commerce Commission (ICC) authority and provide approximately 25 to 40 percent of the intercity truck transportation in the United States. Until recently this segment of the U.S. transportation industry received little attention. Certainly there was no concern for the welfare of this group of independent small businesses that were ignored by the government and the larger competitors.

Two events have brought these carriers greater attention. First, during the fuel shortages of 1973 and 1974 these operators found themselves to be without fuel allocations. This led to a national shutdown of the owner-operators with serious reprocuions. Second, during the economic down turns of the U.S. economy in recent months a large number of the owneroperators went bankrupt, and there is little rush to replenish the ranks als the economy has begun to pick up.

These unregulated carriers are the elastic that permits expansion and contraction of the U.S. capacity. The behavior of these owner-operators hold many lessons for governments contemplating regulatory policy for transportation.

U.S. TRUCKING INDUSTRY
REGULATORY STRUCTURE

To understand the role of the owner-operator in the U.S. trucking industry it is necessary to understand his position within the U.S. regulatory framework. Exhibit 1 provides a general structure for the U.S. industry. The private carriers are not regulated by the ICC. The for-hire carriers are divided into those who operate entirely within one state and those who transport goods across state lines. Each state exercises its unique forms of regulation on the intrastate carriers. The interstate carriers are regulated by the ICC unless exempt commodities are carried (such as fish and unprocessed agricultural products).

Carriers under ICC jurisdiction must comply with restrictions on certification, routes or areas served, commodities handled, rates charged, finance, mergers, and acquisitions. Unlike some other national transportation

* *This paper is based on the research of D. Daryl Wyckoff of Harvard University and David H. Maister of the University of British Columbia.*

regulators, the ICC does not regulate the number of trucks a carrier may operate. So, by regulating entry and exit the number of competitors is controlled but the capacity is not.

Common carriers must secure "certificates of public convenience and necessity," and they must make certain services available to all shippers without discrimination. Contract carriers are required to obtain a "permit" to provide prescribed types of contract services to a small number of shippers (usually no more than 10). It is generally considered difficult for new common carriers to enter and for existing firms to extend their authorities without purchasing the existing rights of other companies. Even such a transfer of rights requires the permission of the ICC.

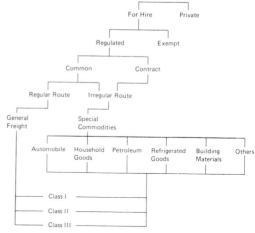

Exhibit 1 - The structure of the motor carrier industry

Owner-operators usually do not have the resources to secure an operating authority from the ICC nor purchase existing operating rights from other carriers. Because of this, the owner-operator has three options available, all of which are exercised: transport exempt commodities (directly or through a broker), act as a subcontractor (usually called a lessee) to a regulated carrier, or transport regulated goods illegally. ICC regulations permit an owner-operator to "lease" himself and his equipment to a regulated carrier on a "permanent" (30-day notice to cancel) lease. He may also "trip lease" to return to his base of operations, but he is prohibited to originate a trip on this basis. It is easy to see how such a provision might invite abuse. The 3-day permanent leases are not particularly successful in creating long-term relationships between owner-operators and the regulated carriers. Since the regulated carrier is not usually required to provide an owner-operator with any specified amount of work, the owner-operators often drift between the regulated, and exempt sectors. In fact, such situations are often well understood and expected by the regulated carriers when an owner-operator is contracted for.

The arrangement between the regulated carrier and the owner-operator usually calls for the former to pay the latter a fixed percentage of the revenue from a load carried. If the owner-operator provides the truck and trailer, this amounts to approximately 75 percent. In some respects it might be argued that the 25 percent retained by the regulated carrier who holds the certificate is charging the owner-operator a toll for the privilege to operate under ICC regulation. However, the regulated carrier may be providing the owner-operator with a variety of services including arranging highway permits, licenses, health and welfare benefits, and, not the least, selling. Since rates for exempt commodities are usually substantially below the rates for regulated commodities, there is substantial temptation for an owner-operator to bypass the regulated carrier to deal illegally with the shipper. It is difficult to estimate precisely the volume of regulated traffic which moves illegally each year. My own field interviews indicate that roughly 10 percent of the traffic of the owner-operators sampled was in this category. It is so common that the regulators tend not to even bother to investigate but the most blatant violators.

THE OWNER-OPERATOR'S ROLE IN THE INDUSTRY

The main operating characteristic of the owner-operator is that he is basically a truckload (TL) carrier. This is a very important feature to recognize as it explains a great deal about his role in the trucking industry. A truckload operation requires no investment in terminals (or depots); no employees for loading, sorting, and unloading; no consolidation (one shipper per truckload); and relatively little administrative control. The truckload operation is essentially very simple: loading at the shipper's dock (bank), driving to the consignee, and unloading. This simplicity, lower investment, and freedom from fixed base and route operation implied in a consolidation operation, are obviously very attractive, if not essential, to the owner operator.

General commodities carriers are most frequently identified as consolidators and carriers of less than truckload (LTL).[1] But, as seen in Exhibits 2 and 3 there have been a number of subcontract operators providing services to these carriers. In general these general commodities carriers do not use owner-operators for LTL movements. In some respects this is because of the method of pay to owner-operators (it would be difficult to determine an equitable pay system for LTL shipments which are rated to include consolidation and handling expenses appropriate to the size of the shipment). Also, most of the labor contracts do not provide for the use of owner-operators in this operation. Here is the first hint of the systematic discrimination of these drivers by the labor unions and truckline managers. Finally, most managers are unwilling to "trust" their highly-valued LTL freight to owner-operators. There is no question that this is discrimination. In practice, many general commodities carriers see the use of owner-operators as a means for rapid expansion to take incremental, marginal business at little cost and nominal risk. A number of general commodities carriers have established separate "special commodities" divisions which utilize owner-operators. Here the term special commodities does not refer so much to unique handling characteristics as much as a list of commodities agreed to by management and the

Teamsters as being of such a low rate that the carrier would not handle them with the conventional union payscale. In exchange for this Teamster agreement, the carrier must limit this operation to the commodities and contribute monthly to the Teamsters' health and welfare fund for each driver. This comes from the 25 percent, described earlier, retained by the company. Few of the owner-operators ever receive benefits from this fund. Most owner-operators greatly resent but accept this practice with resignation.

Exhibit 2 - Number of power units rented with driver by class I and II regulated motor carriers, 1957-1973

	General commodity carriers	Special commodity carriers	Local carriers	Total
1957	5,575	15,516	284	21,375
1959	6,815	22,392	285	29,492
1961	4,884	23,566	229	28,679
1963	7,656	24,832	560	33,048
1965	9,433	29,033	211	38,677
1966	7,395	32,666	351	40,412
1967	7,777	34,380	261	42,418
1968	7,436	38,695	407	46,538
1969	8,139	39,804	284	48,227
1970	8,153	40,796	191	49,140
1971	8,481	44,095	214	52,790
1972	8,959	49,096	191	58,246
1973	9,169	50,150	186	59,505

Source: TRINCS Blue Book of the Trucking Industry, various years.

Exhibit 3 - Percentage of total power units rented with drivers, by all class I carriers of general commodities, 1957-1973

Year	% power units rented with driver
1957	7.57
1959	8.81
1961	6.33
1963	9.70
1965	10.64
1966	8.27
1967	8.62
1968	8.59
1969	8.51
1970	8.43
1971	8.71
1972	9.16
1973	9.00

Source: TRINCS Blue Book of the Trucking Industry, various years.

Exhibit 4 - Number of power units rented with drivers by class I and II special commodity carriers, by commodity group 1973

	Power units rented with drivers	Miles rented with drivers (000)	% all miles
1. Household Goods (intercity)	17,178	657,238	84
2. Petroleum Products	4,241	317,385	23
3. Refrigerated Products	4,239	522,213	54
4. Agricultural Products	969	89,369	30
5. Motor Vehicles	603	42,591	5
6. Building Materials	2,170	156,945	31
7. Other Special Commodities	21,200	1,561,882	39

Source: TRINCS Blue Book of the Trucking Industry, 1974.

The larger use owner-operators by ICC regulated carriers is by the special commodities carriers, as of the types listed in Exhibit 4. The greatest use of owner-operators is in the household goods (removals) industry. Most household goods carriers are, in fact, an alliance of agents that provide pickup, delivery, local movement, and goods storage within a restricted area. The organization provides services to the member agents to or from points outside their areas. These agents may move customers to any area of the United States. Since the owner-operator will travel almost anywhere for a load, they are well suited for the seasonal and directional imbalances of such traffic. So, owner-operators are added or eliminated from the rolls of the household goods carriers as the traffic demands.

The agricultural and refrigerated products (including perishable products such as fresh fruits and vegetables, fish, meat, and frozen goods) are typically seasonal and move over changing routes depending on availability of produce and market demands during the year. The actual number of owner-operators employed in such service depends on the crop volume, availability of railroad capacity, and aggressiveness of railroad pricing. Again, the owner-operator's participation is primarily controlled by forces and institutions outside of his control.

The building materials category, which includes dump trucking (tipping) is a very cyclical and seasonal business responding to a demand derived from the generally unstable construction industry. The demand for owner-operators by the trucking companies is intense over relatively short periods of time, but the time between demands may be quite long.

Similar patterns are seen in the owner-operator's participation in the other commodities listed in Exhibit 4. From this description it is relatively easy to deduce the plight of the owner-operator roaming from one market or operation to another following seasons and promises of work. The owner-operator is the capacity employed by unexpected demands or temporary displacements, but he is also the first to be eliminated when peak demands contract to base levels. The only hope of these itinerant subcontractors is that the downturn in one market will be offset by an upturn in another market. Unfortunately this is not always true.

Exhibit 5 - Estimated owner-operator expenses, 1974

	Low Estimate	Average	High Estimate
(A) Fixed Annual Expenses			
Tractor Depreciation	$ 2,813	$ 3,375	$ 3,938
Trailer Depreciation	429	536	643
Finance Charges	1,575	2,109	2,640
Insurance	1,700	1,850	2,000
Licenses and Permits	900	1,350	1,800
(B) Variable (Per Mile) Expenses			
Maintenance and Tires	$ .050	$ .065	$ .080
Fuel and fuel taxes	.078	.106	.143
(C) Required Driver Payment	$15,100	$19,125	$23,150
(D) Overhead*			
(1) Lease Basis	25 %	33 %	43 %
(2) Brokers	5.3%	11.1%	17.6%

* Overhead calculated as a percentage of all other expenses, including driver's payment.

Source: Field Interviews

OWNER-OPERATOR ECONOMICS

Since there are no reliable published data on owner-operator costs, estimates based on extensive interviews were made. These estimates are shown in Exhibit 5. [2]

The item "required driver's return" in section (c) of Exhibit 5 is the net cash flow that was considered necessary to keep the driver willing to stay in the business. The figures given (which include on-the-road living expenses) are actually slightly less than the wage a Teamster driver would receive under the union contract. Interviews and other investigations indicated that owner-operators were willing to accept this lower income as a price of his independence. This point will be discussed further later in this paper.

The item identified as "overhead" in section (d) of Exhibit 5 reflects that part of the revenue paid to an ICC regulated carrier or to a load broker. The 20 to 30 percent of revenue paid converts to 25 to 43 percent of all other expenses.

To compare these expense figures with those of other modes of transport it is necessary to convert these figures to a cost per ton-mile. Interviews with owner-operators indicate that they often drive 100,000 revenue miles per year. Some were able to achieve productivity as high as 150,000 miles per year. This contrasts with an average of 65,000 miles per power unit per year recorded by the regulated carrier fleets. Assuming an average payload of 40,000 pounds, the typical owner-operator has the potential of producing 2 million ton-miles per year.

Combining these figures with the data in Exhibit 5, it is possible to estimate the earnings of an owner-operator as shown in Exhibit 6. If an owner-operator were fully employed at a rate of 3 cents per ton mile, his earnings might range from $9,000 tot $45,000 per year. The problem is whether the owner-operator can expect to be fully employed.

Exhibit 6 - Earnings potential of an owner-operator

Miles Travelled per year	Level of Expenses	Amount Charged Shippers (in cents per ton-mile)			
		2.0	2.5	3.0	3.5

I
Owner operator working on a subcontract to a regulated carrier (lease basis)

Miles Travelled per year	Level of Expenses	Approximate Annual Earnings			
100,00	High	($5,000)	$2,000	$9,000	$16,000
150,000		($2,000)	8,000	18,000	28,000
100,000	Low	12,000	20,000	28,000	36,000
150,000		21,000	33,000	45,000	57,000

II
Owner operator hauling exempt commodities and utilizing a broker

Miles Travelled per year	Level of Expenses	Approximate annual Earnings			
100,000	High	$1,000	$9,000	$17,000	$25,000
150,000		7,000	19,000	31,000	43,000
100,000	Low	18,000	27,000	36,000	45,000
150,000		31,000	45,000	59,000	73,000

Source: Calculations based on Exhibit 5.

OWNER-OPERATOR'S BEHAVIOR

Exhibits 5 and 6 explain part of the owner-operator behavior. If a nominal salary to himself is viewed as part of the fixed cost, he has an annual fixed cost of $28,345 against a variable cost of $0.171/mile. Roughly $0.106 of this variable cost is a direct out-of-pocket cost in the very short term.

The owner-operator is at the extreme end of a series of derived demands and peak sharing decisions to expand or contract capacity. The owner-operator is viewed by the shipper of exempt commodities and the ICC regulated carrier as a variable cost. In fact, the owner-operator as a transportation enterprise is a relatively high fixed cost operator who has often speculated his entire personal savings on the down payment for the purchase of a truck and trailer.

Owner-operators as a group appear to be relatively unsophisticated managers. Being cash oriented, they tend to maximize cash flow. When demand is low they will cut their charges too close to out-of-pocket costs. When demand is high, the regulated carriers will hold the owner-operators to 75 percent of the rates on the low rated "special commodities." Being unsophisticated, most owner-operators fail to reserve funds for emergencies, periodic maintenance, and salary and bank payments during periods of low demand.

A second part of the owner-operator behavior that must be understood is the importance of independence, or the perception of independence. As mentioned earlier, most owner-operators will receive an annual income that is lower than they would receive for equivalent work if they were driving as an employee for a trucking company with a Teamster union contract. This economic inequity is further exacerbated when it is observed that the calculation in Exhibit 5 does not include any opportunity cost on the owner-operator's investment in the down payment in equipment and working capital. At a nominal 5 percent risk free investment alternative (in federally insured savings banks in the U.S.) it is reasonable that the owner-operator might except a premium of

approximately $750 per year over what his Teamster equivalent would earn.

Is the owner-operator simply economically irrational or ill-informed? The answer appears to be complex. First, many of the owner-operators are ill informed when they enter the market. Obviously most owner-operators enter when business is vigorous, and they are rudely surprised to find that they are suddenly considered redundant by the shippers or carriers they served faithfully. Second, some owner-operators are confused by cash flow and net earnings after fully allocated expenses and reserves. Putting these points together with a substantial optimistic but naive view of the situation, most owner-operators enter with expectations of great financial success.

Why do owner-operators stay in the business if the economics are so unattractive? In fact, many do exit through sale of equipment, or bankruptcy or repossession of equipment. Analysis of the records of several financers of owner-operator equipment indicated an average of 15 percent repossession rate (primarily during the first 6 months and months 13 to 24 of the period of the loan). During periods of reduced demand investigations indicated repossession rates of up to 50 percent. Under most circumstances the owner-operator loses most of his equity in the unit in a repossession, which indicates a distressed exit. The reasons for continuing are often as complex. First, many are trapped. If they are unable to find a buyer for the equipment they may lose a substantial portion of their life savings. Second, the optimism that led them to the business originally may sustain their hopes for eventual success. Third, some owner-operators see their driving activities as second incomes after primary occupations (such as farming) that do not require their full time throughout the year.

The major feature that holds owner-operators in the business, based on several hundred field interviews, is independence. Many of the owner-operators demonstrated an antipathy to rules and regulations, sensitivity to bureaucracy, and resentment of routine and authority that were well beyond the natural rebellion experienced among workers in other situations.

It is ironic that an individual would remain an owner-operator on this basis, given the economic penalty he pays for this privilege. The independence he values as an owner-operator is more a matter of his perception than a reality. In most cases he has simply exchanged the authority of a dispatcher for the monthly demands of a bank or finance company. While the owner-operator is generally not directly economically regulated by the ICC, he is required to conform to a number of safety regulations of the U.S. Department of Transportation. First, he is restricted in the number of hours he may drive, which seriously hampers his productivity on which his profitability depends. Second, he is restricted on size and weight. These restrictions not only appear to be arbitrarily limiting his productivity, but they are often quite irritably inconsistent between various states. Third, the owner-operator working for another company may be subject to the rules of that company. Finally, the income received for a load may depend on market forces or ICC rates that are outside of the hands, and possibly comprehension, of the owner-operator. This hardly describes the desired environment of a "free spirit" who is willing to make an economic tradeoff for independence.

Most of the features of the behavior described above were demonstrated by the owner-operators in the national shut down in 1973 and 1974. As a result of the fuel crisis in the United States prices for diesel fuel rose from $.31 per gallon in May of 1973 to as high as $.55 in December. The owner-operators, dependent on productivity for their livelihood found they were spending significant portions of their time waiting in lines at fuel stops. The federal government made arrangements to allocate fuel to users based on a pro-rata portion of their proven consumption the previous year. Owner-operators were left out of this allocation. The larger carriers, for whom many owner-operators worked, simply cut these subcontractors from their fleets to conserve fuel for company-owned trucks. On December 3, 1973 three drivers blockaded Interstate Highway 84 at the New York-Connecticut line. On the same day spontaneous blockades were established on Interstate Highway 80 in Pennsylvania. These blockades spread to highways in Ohio. The owner-operators, usually very independent of each other were willing to act in unity because the lack of fuel meant that there was no opportunity cost for not operating. Also, a little known communications revolution was well under way as the result of a major technological innovation that had largely been unobserved by the outside world. The citizen's band (CB) radio had been installed in their trucks by most owner-operators. These limited-range, two-way radios provided the communication system for organizing the shutdown as well as means of frustrating the efforts of law-enforcement officers to open blockades. The shutdown led to a major adjustment in ICC rates to permit recovery of the additional costs of fuel being experienced by the owner-operators. More importantly, it forced the government to release fuel to owner-operators. The owner-operators also learned the value of organized action. But, once the specific shortterm objectives of this effort were achieved, the independence of the owner-operators ruled again. None of the owner-operator organizations created during that crisis have been sustained. As the American economy turned down, the owner-operators were cast off by the regulated carriers to preserve traffic for their own trucks and employees.

FOOTNOTES

1. Less than truckload is generally defined as shipments under 10,000 pounds. While this is not a physical truckload in modern equipment, it is the weight break used historically for setting rates by the ICC.

2. A more complete explanation of the methodology used to develop these estimates is included in: D. Daryl Wyckoff and David H. Maister, **The Owner-Operator: Independent Trucker** (Lexington, Mass.: Lexington Books, D.C. Heath and Company, 1975).

A System Analysis of Effectiveness of Energy Saving Measures in Transport

by

HIDEO NAKAMURA
University of Tokyo

TAKEO UEMURA
Ministry of Transport, Japan

TATEO NISHII
Japan Transport Economics Research Center

NORIHIRO SHIOMI
Mitsui Jyoho Kaihatsu, Japan

ENERGY SAVING MEASURES IN PASSENGER TRANSPORT

Studies on the energy saving measures in Japan have been motivated by the so called "oil crisis" which occured in the end of 1973, under the grave realization that there was a limit in the energy resources. In particular, the transportation field in general have to rely on the petroleum energy as much as 90% or more, and therefore, the transport is one of the most important sectors where the energy saving is inevitable.

This paper is a brief report of an analysis on effectiveness of some energy saving measures in passenger transport. The analysis is done by two different approaches, the first is to estimate amount of energy saving by some measures which could be practicable in near future and the second is to evaluate dynamic impact by several measures which could be applied in an emergency of energy shortage, such as last "energy crisis".

1. Energy Saving Measures in the Passenger Transport Sector

Discussion was made among some twenty experts from various fields by means of so called brain storming, to derive some one hundred measures for the energy saving. These measures were sorted out under the criteria of (a) purpose and method (b) field of application and (c) mode of transport, and the following 15 measures were selected for detailed analysis of the effectiveness, from the viewpoints of the practicability and the expected effectiveness:

1) Lightening of railway vehicles
2) Utilization of electric regenerative braking system with thyristor chopper
3) Lightening of automobiles
4) Recommendation for radial tires
5) Speed limit on expressway
6) Speed limit for express railway (Shinkansen)
7) Increase of exclusive lane for commuter buses
8) Limitation of entry of private cars into center of cities

9) Increase of gasoline tax
10) Increase of tax rate for automobile registration and weight
11) Increase of air fares
12) Expansion of the express railway (Shinkansen) network
13) Cutting down some air routes replaceable by rail
14) Introduction of the zone control system of traffic signals
15) Replacement by wide-bodied aircraft

2. Effect of Energy Saving Measures

Energy consumption in passenger transport is represented as,

$$E = \frac{Q_c}{P_c}1_c + \frac{Q_b}{P_b}1_b + \frac{Q_r}{P_r}1_r + \frac{Q_a}{P_a}1_a + \text{---}$$

E: whole energy consumption in passenger transport
Q: traffic volume   (Kcal)
l: average energy consumption (Person. Km)
p: load factor   (Kcal/Km. Vehicle)
c: automobile   (Person/Vehicle)
b: bus
r: rail
a: aircraft

Therefore, energy saving can be achieved by the following three processes:

1) Improvement in the energy consumption of vehicles or carriers
2) Increase of load factors of the vehicles or carriers
3) Shifting of passenger to the energy saving-type modes.

The amount of the energy saving caused by these measures is estimated according to the flow-diagram as shown hereunder:

For the estimation, three major types of model are applied, namely

(1) Estimation model of split by modes and types of vehicles
(2) model of traffic conditions

(3) model of energy consumption of vehicles.

(1) model of split by modes and types of vehicles.
This model is comprised of three submodels of (a) modal split model for short distance trips (b) modal split model for long distance trips (c) model for share of types of private cars. The changes of shares in the modes and types of vehicles which are resulted from change in cost and time for travelling caused by application of the energy saving measures are estimated by this model.

(2) traffic conditions model.
This model describes traffic conditions such as conges-

tion of highways, cruising speed, load factors, etc. These traffic conditions are derived from the transport demand, modal split and existing traffic facilities and equipment.

(3) energy consumption model.
This model describes the energy consumption of various types of vehicles of each mode in reference to weight of vehicles, passenger capacity, engine power, etc. under various conditions of running, such as cruising speed, frequency of stopping.

Table 1 shows amount of saved energy estimated by applying the above mentioned models.

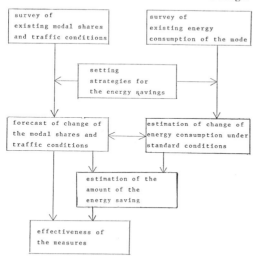

3. Practicability of each saving measure

Each of the afore-mentioned energy saving measures is not free from causing some impacts in the society and its economy and is sometimes causing some difficulties of institutional, technical nature and financial burden involved for the actual application. These varying factors cannot be discussed in minute detail in each of energy saving measure, practicability of each measure was assessed from comments and opinions expressed by experts engaged in the field of transportation by means of enquete.

The enquete contained the items of (a) Impacts on the traffic users, environment, economy and others to be caused by measures for energy saving, (b) Costs and time to be involved, and (c) Other problems and their solutions, and asked for evaluation as well as the free expression of comments.

The Table 1 also shows the results of assessment thus obtained.

Table 1: Results of the estimation and points to be raised

Measure	Assumptions and conditions	Results			Background and problematic points
		Energy to be saved 10⁹ kcal	Ratio of savings within specific mode of transport (%)	Ratio of savings within the whole transport (%)	
1) **Lightening of railway vehicles** weight saving 22.1% by aluminum body Energy for production of vehicles + operation	Ratio of lightening is the actual one obtained by "Rapid Transit Corp." life of wagon is set in accordance with pertinent law * Electric cars 13yrs * Diesel cars 11yrs * Passenger cars 20yrs	1,245	8.6	0.70	* Availability of aluminum & electricity * Lessening of profitability due to higher cost * Safety problems
2) **Utilization of electric regenerative braking system with thyristor chopper** Electric cars and locomotives	* Ratio of regeneration is set at 27.8% which was obtained by "Rapid Transit Corp." by experimental running	1,998	12.6	1.11	* Problems of induction wave disturbance * Lessening of profitability by higher cost * Applicability or selection of routes * Adopted by several lines
3) **Lightening of automobiles** Reduction of 10% of the weight of whole automobiles	* Energy for production of aluminum is counted for the energy for production of bodies * Life is set at 6 years	6,729	6.2	3.74	* Technically, it is difficult to put off more of weight * Some problems in safety and endurability * Contradictory to air pollution control * Availability of aluminum & electricity is questionable
4) **Application of radial tyres** Lessening of rolling friction (all vehicles) at 20% 30%		 2,258 3,349	 1.5 2.2	 1.25 1.86	* Lessening of riding comfort and increase of noise

No.	Measure	Method / Assumptions				Remarks
5)	**Speed limit on expressways**	* Assumed 20 km/h speed down * Average speed is obtained by experimental running * Checked at Tomei (Tokyo-Nagoya), Meishin (Nagoya-Kobe) and Chuo (Tokyo-Nagoya via Matsumoto) express-ways	3,568	21.4	0.43	* Practicable execution of speed control will be difficult * May cause a traffic congestion * Effects on over-all traffic will be rather small because the high speed transit volume is not so great
6)	**Speed limit for Shinkansen** * 20 km/h slow down * Shifting to air is counted	* Apply to Tokyo-Osaka-Okayama section * Increase of energy efficiency is estimated from energy consumption model for railway * Shifting to air is estimated by modal split model for air/railways	1,448	38.3	0.80	
7)	**Increase of exclusive lanes for commuter buses**	* Peripheral effects on traffic in surrounding areas are placed out of investigation * Effects on the traffic of private cars are counted as increase of waiting time due to traffic congestion and the modal shifting rate is derived from the modal split model * Lessening of energy efficiency of private cars is counted as the increase of idle time	−412	−9.0	−0.2	Effects on the general traffic in particular cargo traffic should be further studied
8)	**Limitation of entry of private cars into the city centre** * Surcharge ¥ 500 per entry ¥1,000 per entry	* Change of modal split is counted by means of modal split model of private car vs. public transport	853 1.456	4.5 7.6	0.47 0.81	* Practicable execution is rather questionable ° Collection of surcharge ° Selection of objective cars (chargeable or nonchargeable) * Increase of congestion in public transport medias
9)	**Increase of Gasoline Tax** increase by 50% increase by 100%	Basic price is set at the price of March 1973 (¥ 65) per lit.) Share of private cars is estimated by the modal split model of private cars vs. public transport	6,512 11,118	5.7 9.7	3.62 6.18	* Non-selective increase of tax will be questionable * Some consideration onto freight transport & public transport should be made * Objectives of investment from the increased tax revenue shall have to be carefully selected
10)	**Increase of Automobile Tax for registration an weight** Registration Tax by two times	Same as above	719	0.6	0.40	Effective to encourage the trend of compact cars
	Increase of Weight Tax 4 times greater than the tax rate of 1972 (¥ 10,000 per 0.5 tons)	Total volume of traffic by private cars is assumed at constant	397	0.3	0.22	Effect will not be so great
11)	**Increase of air fares** * 10% increase * 50% increase	* Shifting to rail is estimated by the modal split model for rail vs. air * Deduction of number of flight frequency is estimated to be proportionale to the decrease of traffic	392 322	3.8 12.9	0.22 0.73	* Consideration on the route where there is no alternative * May generate decrease of noise problems in the areas adjacent to airports
12)	**Expansion of the express railway network** * 2,800 km. lines in Kyushu, Jyoetsu and Hokkaido areas	* Shifting from air due to shortening of travelling time is estimated from the model * Consumption of energy for construction of basic facility and equipment is estimated from actual case of the existing lines	2,476 −57,428	13.3	1.38	* Problems of noise and vibration * Energy consumed for newly generated traffic demand will be enormous * When energy consumption for the construction of the facilities is taken into account, it will hardly be a saving measure
13)	**Abolishment of some air routes which are replaceable by alternatives** * Where the difference of travelling time is within 1 hour		1,023	10.0	0.57	* Selection or justification of such routes is difficult * Decrease of noise problems in airport areas
14)	**Introduction of the zone control system of traffic signals** Applied in 50% of whole urban area	Cruising speed and frequency of stopping are estimated refering the existing systems in the CBD of Tokyo	7,064	10.7	3.91	Good effect on environment No negative effect
15)	**Replacement by wide-bodied sized aircraft** Introduction of jumbo aircraft to 10 trunk routes (Load-factor is estimated at 65%)	B-747 and L-1011	754	13.1	0.42	Decrease in the Load-factor must carefully be avoided Deduction of flight frequency and selections of routes should be carefully agreed upon

303

4. Emergency measures for energy saving against "oil crisis" and analysis of the effects

1) Outline of model structure

In order to assess the energy saving measures against a short range oil crisis, the system dynamics model (referring to the transport and the petroleum supply) is developed. And it is used to evaluate the efficiency of each countermeasure.

The model is comprised of two sectors, namely, "Economic" and "Transport" and is to be sub-divided as shown in the following figure (Figure 2).

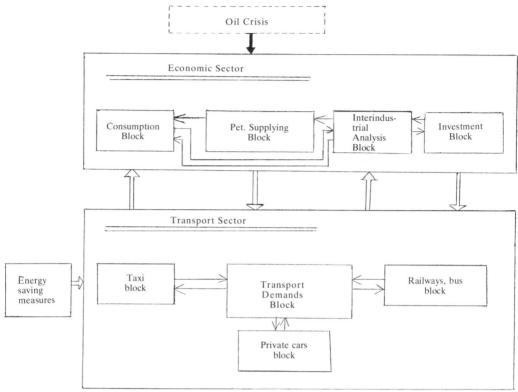

Figure 2

Petroleum supplying block describes relationship between amount of oil import, stock, and supply in every month. The price of petroleum is resulted from these conditions. In the *consumption block,* final demand of domestic consumption which are caused by consumer price, is estimated. On the other hand, the *investment block* shows relationship between economic growth rate and demand for private investment. The final demand which is owing to final consumption and the investment is input to the *interindustrial block* and gross national product is estimated by input-output model. The total amounts of petroleum which are needed in every industry to maintain this economic equilibrium are estimated from this model. Thus the change of petroleum demand caused by the restriction of oil supply is estimated by these models.

Three blocks in the *Transport Sector* are in a position to reflect how the fuel price (Gasoline, LPG, light oil and electricity) and some energy saving measures affect the transport demand in each of transport-mode, and shows how the reduction in the demands eases off the supply and results new equilibrium stage of demand and supply.

Applying this system model, the traffic demands of each mode which are affected by economic activities under the restriction of petroleum supply and also energy saving measures in transport are macroscopically forecast, and a procedure of approaching to a new balanced state in transport modal shares and economic activi-

ties will be shown, so that it could be applicable to find out some suitable measures in oil crisis which will not cause much disturbance of the socio-economic activities of the country.

2) Results of simulation

Simulation was conducted under the assumption that the oil crisis occurred in the end of 1973 had lasted until June of 1974 and that the oil supply capacity was suppressed down to 75% of the total demand, and the following five countermeasures were studied of their effects.

(1) Control or regulation over the fuel supply at service stations

(2) Limitation of speed on expressways

(3) Increase of petroleum tax

(4) Adjustment of train and bus fares

(5) Petroleum supply control policy over transport modes

As the result, the following points were observed:

(1) Economic Activities (Fig. 3)

(a) Decrease of oil consumption is delayed in rate and time than that of oil supply. Therefore, the amount of oil stock is going to decline very quickly.

(b) The final demand follows to the decrease of oil supply, but in a smaller rate.

(c) The consumer price is rising up inversely proportionally to the oil stock and levels off in the highest level.

(d) Traffic volume of taxis and private cars decreases

304

violently, so that the demand of gasoline is balanced with the supply.

(e) The traffic volume of mass transportation does not decline and light oil will be in short supply.

Supply and demand of oil

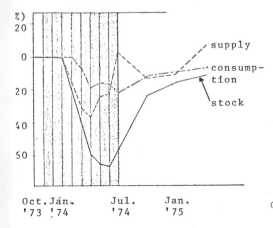

Economic index

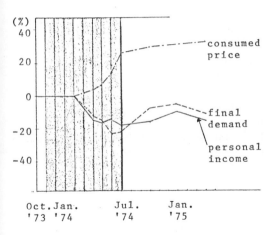

Traffic volume

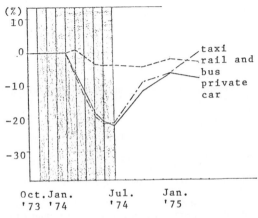

Figure 3

(2) The effects of the energy saving measures in transport (Fig. 4)

(a) Restriction of fuel supply at service station has the most effect on the energy saving in passenger transport.

(b) When the restriction of supply at service station, limitation speed in expressways, adjustment of mass transport fares and increase of petroleum tax are applied, consumption of gasoline will be reduced in 10%, though light oil will be consumed slightly more.

(c) One year after the end of the shortage of oil supply, fluctuation of modal share will be stabilized and the share of private cars will be reduced at 3%, though that of mass transit will increase at 2%.

ACKNOWLEDGEMENT

This study was carried out by a study group organized by Japan Transport Economics Research Center. The authors wish to thank the members of the group for their contribution in this study.

Amount of saved energy by each measure

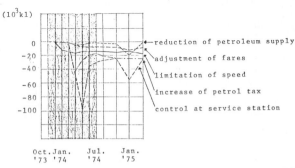

Amount of saved energy by composite measure

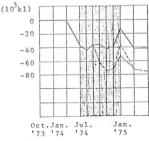

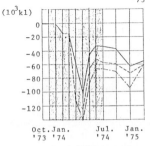

——————— control at service station + limitation of speed
— — — — — control at service station + limitation of speed
  + adjustment of fares
—·—·—·— control at service station + limitation of speed
  + adjustment of fares
  + reduction of petroleum supply

Figure 4

305

Aspects of governmental research and development funding programmes for ground transportation systems

Federal Ministry for Research and Technology,
Federal Republic of Germany

MOTIVATION AND OBJECTIVES OF GOVERNMENT PROMOTION

Transport and traffic services are essential components of the infrastructure in every country; of an infrastructure guaranteeing that the social and economic demands made on both the mobility of the population and on the exchange of goods and commodities are being met. The efficiency of this infrastructure is a yardstick for the individual's quality of life as well as for positive overall national accounts.

Transport and traffic systems in advanced industrialized countries are characterized by a high degree of mechanization and by complex organizational structures. In most cases, the interlacement of the different sub-systems to become an integrated or combined transport and traffic system optimized throughout is, however, poor and insufficient. The difficulties with which we are already confronted today and which we must expect to increase in future, have been caused by the concentration of the population in conurbations, by an increase in the production of goods as well as in the transportation of goods and services at European and international level, and by an increase in transport and traffic due to leisuretime activities. At the same time, the demands made on the quality of available services have increased, above all with a view to safety, profitableness, energy utilization, environmental protection, speed and comfort.

The rapid increase in traffic during the past, as well as the high share of private vehicles in the traffic system, and increasing deficits in nearly all sectors of public transport, are particular problems we have to solve.

If we want to avoid a critical intensification and accumulation of problems already existing within the field of transport and traffic, we must – apart from improving investments and organisation – try to develop and implement technical improvements and establish better links between the different sub-systems.

Structural planning and regional development, road planning and road building, provision of traffic and transport services, as well as the organization of the overall transport system, have always been tasks which must undoubtedly be fulfilled by the government. Thus it goes without saying that the government has an increased obligation to open up and implement new technical possibilities for fulfilling the above tasks. It is to be feared that – without direct government measures to promote technological developments in the transport field – those technical innovations which are either required or, at least, desirable during the next few decades will either not be available at all or not in due time, and that they will not be available to a sufficient extent.

Furthermore, we would not be able to take sufficient account of the fact that means of transportation should be accident-proof and reliable in operation, and that they should take account of environmental protection. We could further not expect a long-term improvement in the cost structure of public transport companies; and we will not be able to exhaust the possibilities for achieving economical energy and other resources utilization for the overall system quickly enough.

The following are the main objectives of government measures to support research and development in the field of transport developments (Fig. 1):

Saveguarding of Material Resources
●
Saving/Raising of the Ability of Industrial Competition
●
Improvement of Human Life Quality
●
Reconfiguration And Improvement of Infrastructure and Service
●
Basic Research

Objects of Fundings by BMFT

BMFT
522

Figure 1

– Provision and maintenance of efficient transport and traffic services, as well as of infrastructures in the transport sector, above all within and between the individual conurbations;
– reduction of the total costs for means of transportation and, at the same time, improvement of the economic situation of the transport companies;
– increase in the reliability, safety, rational energy utilization and low pollution of all technical systems and their components;
– guarantee of the long-term competitiveness of the transport companies and the export industry at international level.

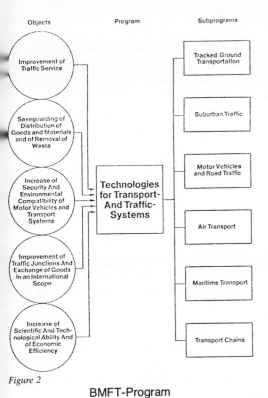

Objects — Program — Subprograms

Improvement of Traffic Service

Safeguarding of Distribution of Goods and Materials and of Removal of Waste

Increase of Security And Environmental Compatibility of Motor Vehicles and Transport Systems

Improvement of Traffic Junctions And Exchange of Goods in an International Scope

Increase of Scientific And Technological Ability And of Economic Efficiency

Technologies for Transport- And Traffic- Systems

Tracked Ground Transportation

Suburban Traffic

Motor Vehicles and Road Traffic

Air Transport

Maritime Transport

Transport Chains

Figure 2

BMFT-Program
Technologies for Transport-
and Traffic-Systems

TASKS TO BE FULFILLED (Fig. 2)

The following are the main tasks to be fulfilled with a view to the above objectives – limited to the field of surface transport and traffic:

– the technical and organisational improvement of conventional, as well as the development of new, means of urban mass transportation until they are ready for commercial use;

– the development of conventional railway techniques or of new contact-free vehicles as an integral part of a future European transport network;

– the improvement of traffic safety, of energy utilization and reduction of environmental pollution by all means of transportation, in particular, however, of motor vehicles, by developing and introducing appropriate technical auxiliary means; and

– the examination and, possibly, development of new technical transport systems for raw materials, goods and wastes, taking into account the criteria of economy, safety and environmental protection.

E.g. more than 10 percent of annual governmental budgets are spent for transportation and traffic purposes with effects strongly influencing the situation in future decades. Therefore long termed planning and far reaching technical problem solving attempts are needed.

As a result of the support given to selected projects, the responsible persons and authorities shall be given comprehensive and expert information, as well as a list of clearly-defined technical solutions, so that they will be able to select and introduce those systems best suited for future tasks in the field of transport and traffic.

PROMOTION PRIORITIES

The following sub-programmes are supported by the Federal Ministry for Research and Technology in the field of surface transport and traffic systems:

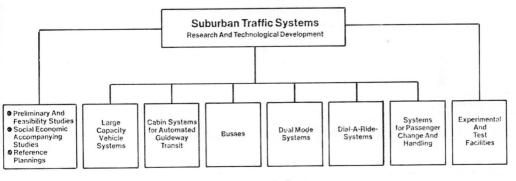

Suburban Traffic Systems
Research And Technological Development

● Preliminary And Feasibility Studies ● Social Economic Accompanying Studies ● Reference Plannings

Large Capacity Vehicle Systems

Cabin Systems for Automated Guideway Transit

Busses

Dual Mode Systems

Dial-A-Ride-Systems

Systems for Passenger Change And Handling

Experimental And Test Facilities

Figure 3

BMFT-Research-Program
Suburban Traffic

Public systems of urban mass transportation (Fig. 3)

If we want and in the future inevitably have to improve the ratio between private and public transport and – in the long run – want to make this ratio a reasonable one, then we must – in addition to existing means of urban mass transportation which are being further improved – develop and demonstrate those technical systems and transport concepts which are better suited to meet the requirements of users, operators and the environment.

The following are the technical development lines, partly including new structural and operational concepts, which are being promoted:

– urban mass transportation systems using large-capacity vehicles (light rail systems, underground)

– urban mass transportation systems using small and medium sized cabins,

– bus systems suited for future needs,

– systems which can be used in several modes of operation (dual mode systems),

– demand-oriented systems of urban mass transportation (demand bus, dial-a-ride),
including

– new technical systems for passenger transport and the transhipment of goods and commodities,
as well as

– traffic lane and station construction techniques.

307

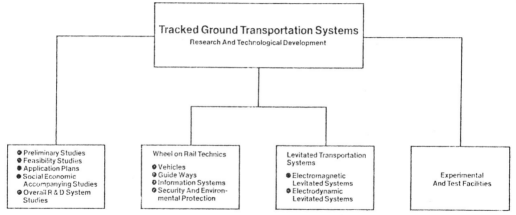

Figure 4

BMFT-Research-Program
Tracked Ground Transportation Systems

Tracked ground transportation systems (Fig. 4)

By a promotion programme in this field, we wanted to establish a basis for rail systems, the technical and operational design of which would be adapted to future needs. Under the sub-programme

– steelwheel-on-steelrail technologies (RS)

methods for an improvement of the railroad system are being elaborated, in order to open up the reserves in technology as well as economy.

Apart from advanced wheel-on-rail concepts,

– magnetic levitation techniques (MS)

with linear motor propulsion system are being studied for future generations of rail systems, i.e. new high-speed transportation network. In this field, the Federal Republic of Germany has been able to take a good position.

The following systems are still being examined in order to select the very best one:

– the system of electromagnetic levitation (by attraction) (EMS),

and the

– system of electrodynamic levitation (by repulsion) (EDS),

whereas the studies on the air cushion system have been dropped.

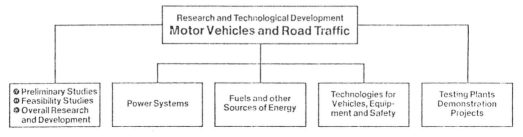

Figure 5

BMFT-Research-Program
Motor Vehicles And Road Traffic

Motor vehicle engineering and road traffic techniques (Fig. 5)

Today, as well as within the nearer foreseeable future, a major share of traffic and transport services will be borne by the motorcar. Technically advanced systems may contribute to a reduction of environmental pollution, safety risks, energy consumption and disturbances in the traffic flow. Therefore, support mainly concentrates on

– propulsion systems,
– unconventional fuels,
– undercarriage and body construction,
– technical auxiliary means in the field of road traffic,
– systems to control the traffic flow,
– safety technologies.

Transport chains (Fig. 6)

Individual households, local communities, as well as industrial enterprises, are increasingly dependent on a centralized supply and exchange of raw materials and both industrial and consumer goods. A lot of technical and especially organizational problems have to be solved to guarantee the quality of life as well as a sound basis for industry.

IMPLEMENTATION OF PROMOTION
MEASURES

The giving of advice, holding of objective discussions and performance of expert work for the Federal Ministry for Research and Technology in connection with the management, control and efficiency control of sub-programmes and individual projects are tasks for the following bodies in particular (Fig. 7):

– ad hoc panels of experts,
– project advisers,
– project committees,
– annual status seminars.

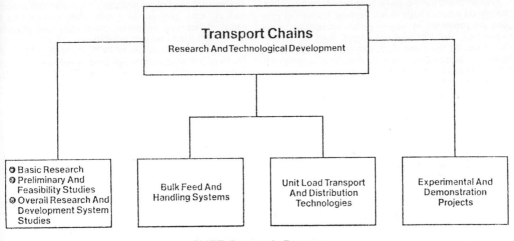

Figure 6

BMFT-Research-Program
Transport Chains

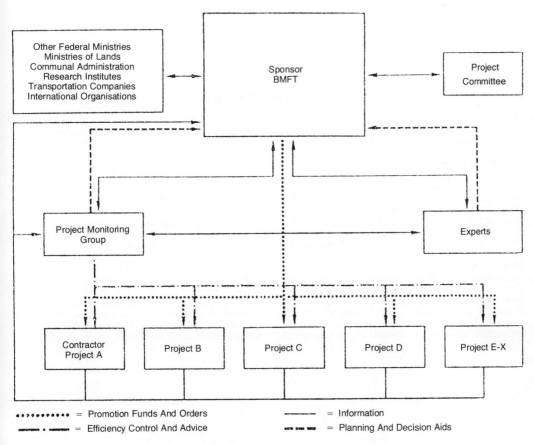

•••••••••• = Promotion Funds And Orders   ——— = Information

━━━ • ━━━ = Efficiency Control And Advice   ━ ━ ━ = Planning And Decision Aids

Organisation of Fundings

Figure 7

Priority promotion is given to selected projects. Promotion on a broad scale is not desired. Individual projects are promoted by way of grants amounting to between 50% and 100% of the overall costs incurred in each case. At the same time, enterprises in trade and industry are themselves required to make an appropriate contribution. Contracts may be awarded in special cases. Systems analyses, socioscientific studies and cost-benefit analyses are carried out both in advance and also accompanying each project. As a rule, close cooperation is required between industrie, universities and government-supported research institutions.

From 1969 up to the end of 1976, the Federal Minister for Research and Technology made funds available for promotion to the amount of 485 million DM (Fig. 8).

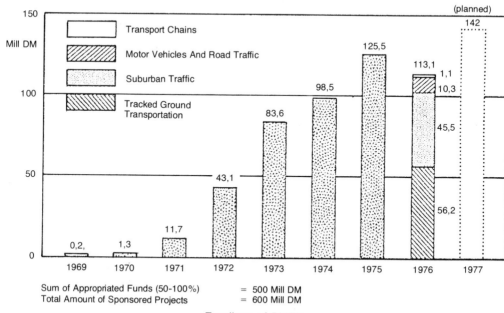

Sum of Appropriated Funds (50-100%) = 500 Mill DM
Total Amount of Sponsored Projects = 600 Mill DM

Figure 8

Fundings of BMFT
for Transportation R & D

FUTURE PROSPECTS

Many countries are actively engaged in seeking solutions to the problems posed by the tasks devolving on us in the future in the sector of transport and traffic. Intensive research and development work is being carried out for the greater part with considerable by support governments. The technical development lines being pursued vary to a great extent, and the stage reached in development also varies in each case. Up to now, the course taken by studies carried out in the Federal Republic was mostly very promising, rapid and relatively inexpensive, with the result that the next development phases could be commenced. Good results, however, do not in themselves ensure the success of most projects. They merely constitute a few initial steps along a path which will be laborious, difficult and – even in the most favourable circumstances – not without setbacks. We cannot yet be certain whether our suppositions and plans are correct, whether the demand as forecast for the coming decades will actually occur, whether it will be possible to arrive at a competitive price/product or price/service ratio and thus achieve real profitability, and – last, but not least – whether the general economic situation creates fairly favourable prerequisites. There is no patent solution to the problems raised by urban mass transportation systems and motor vehicles. Market demand will determine the choice of the systems ultimately selected. A high-speed surface rail transportation system cannot, however, be introduced on a national scale in our country. It must be considered in a greater context, e.g. a uniform system of this type should be designed for use in Europe. The advantages of such a system can only be fully appreciated if it is introduced on such a scale, ignoring the borders of countries. This specific instance – and the same holds for the other fields of development – demonstrates the necessity for international cooperation, which is possible, being of obvious use and therefore of benefit to all concerned.

A road transport investment model for developing countries

by

J. N. Bulman

and

R. Robinson

Transport and Road Research Laboratory

Crowthorn, England

INTRODUCTION

In developing countries investment in rural and inter-urban roads continues to represent a large part of national development programmes. It is therefore important that decisions about such investments are made on the basis of the best possible information. The economic consequences of building roads to particular geometric and structural standards are rarely adequately investigated at project appraisal stage, largely because knowledge of the interaction between the various factors involved is very limited. Usually a set of geometric and structural standards for a road is adopted arbitrarily, and little attention is given to the effect on vehicle operating costs that the choice of alternative design standards would have.

In 1968 the World Bank wishing to improve the quality of investment decisions in the roads sector in developing countries, invited the United Kingdom Transport and Road Research Laboratory (TRRL) to participate in a co-operative research effort to investigate the inter-relationships between road construction costs, vehicle operating costs, and road maintenance costs in developing countries. These relationships were to be incorporated in a computer model that would enable road planners and designers to determine with ease the sum of these costs for a particular road investment proposal.

TRRL readily agreed to co-operate in the proposed research because much of its work for developing countries is concerned with these issues.

As a first step the World Bank awarded a contract to a research group at the Massachusetts Institute of Technology to construct a model on the basis of existing published knowledge that would relate road construction and maintenance costs to the cumulative cost of vehicle operation over the design life of a road. [1] [2] This "highway cost model" was a considerable advance on existing methods of road investment appraisal for developing countries, and it identified quite clearly the areas where knowledge about the relationships between important parameters of road and vehicle behaviour in tropical developing countries was inadequate. In particular it was clear that better information was needed on the rate and characteristics of road pavement deterioration, and the influence of road maintenance on pavement deterioration. Equally importantly the model showed that vehicle operating costs were likely to be very sensitive to vehicle type, road geometry, and road surface condition, and yet knowledge of the relationships between these factors was very limited.

Accordingly a research programme was jointly planned by the World Bank and the TRRL with the objective of improving knowledge of these relationships through field experimentation and survey in a developing country. This research programme, which included the production of a revised model, was undertaken by the TRRL in the period 1971 to 1974. During this period a wide-ranging study of road deterioration and vehicle operating costs was undertaken in Kenya to determine relationships for incorporation in the revised model more appropriate to the physical and economic conditions of developing countries. The new computer model, which has been called the Road Transport Investment Model (RTIM), calculates for any road project the sum of the construction costs, the road maintenance costs, and the vehicle operating costs over the "design life" of the project. There is considerable interaction between these costs; vehicle operating costs are a function of the volume and composition of the traffic, the geometric design standards of the road and its surface condition; road maintenance costs are influenced by the condition of the road surface, which is in turn dependent on the initial construction standard, the environment, the volume and character of the traffic.

The model therefore permits the designer to minimise the sum of construction costs, maintenance costs, and vehicle operating costs by enabling him to select the optimum choice of geometric standard and road type, either earth, gravel or bituminous surfaced.

Clearly there are many reasons for investing in roads in developing countries other than to acquire the benefits of savings in vehicle operating costs and road maintenance costs. In the case of low-volume roads in rural areas vehicle operating costs are usually a relatively insignificant factor in influencing investment decisions. Much more important factors in such situations are the provision of basic access in order to allow agricultural development projects to be instituted, or health and education services to be improved, or the general social well-being of rural populations to be enhanced.

Nevertheless at vehicle flows of more than about 100 vehicles per day, savings in vehicle operating costs and road maintenance costs are usually the predominant economic benefits that are identified as accruing from non-urban road investments in developing countries, and the greater part of the funds allocated to road construction in developing countries in recent decades has been invested on this basis. The growing interest of Third World governments and aid donors in stimulating rural development in developing countries will clearly place more emphasis on the provision of low-volume rural roads in the future, but even so, investment in the construction or upgrading of more heavily trafficked roads is unlikely to diminish.

THE FIELD RESEARCH

The field research in Kenya consisted of three distinct studies:

a) A study of the rate of deterioration of paved and unpaved roads, taking into account the influences of initial standard of construction and subsequent road maintenance on deterioration rates.

b) A study of the effect of road geometry and surface condition on vehicle speeds and vehicle fuel consumption.

c) A survey of typical vehicle operators to obtain information on the components of vehicle operating cost other than fuel.

These studies have been fully described earlier. [3] [4]

In the first two studies a programme of detailed measurements of road deterioration, vehicle fuel consumption and vehicle speed were made on selected 2 km-long sections of normally-constructed road. These test sections were selected so that the effects of road geometry, pavement type, rainfall and maintenance input could be studied. The sampling frame included three levels of vertical and horizontal road geometry, two levels of an-

Table 1 Classification of paved road test sections

Geometric Classification		Low rainfall < 1000mm/year			High rainfall > 1000mm/year		
	Vertical	Flat <1.5%	Intermediate >1.5% <3.5%	Steep >3.5%	Flat	Intermediate	Steep
	Horizontal						
Old surface-dressed roads (OB)	Low <30°/km	OB17* OB18	OB20* OB24	OB21 —	OB7* OB10	OB5 OB11*	OB2 OB3*
	Medium >30°/km <90°/km	OB23* OB25	OB19* OB22	— —	OB8* OB9	OB13 —	OB1* OB4 OB14 OB16
	High >90°/km	— —	— —	— —	— —	OB6 —	OB12 OB15*
New surface-dressed roads (NB)	Low	NB10	NB12	NB13	NB2	NB4	NB3
	Medium	—	NB11	NB14	NB1	NB9	NB8
	High	—	—	—	NB5	NB6	NB7
Premix surfaced roads (P)	Low	P8	—	—	P2	P7	P6
	Medium	P10	—	—	P3	P1	P4
	High	—	P9	—	—	—	P5

Note: The asterisk* indicates a nil maintenance section.

Table 2 – Classification of gravel and earth road test sections

Geometric Classification		Low rainfall ≤1000mm/year			Hig rainfall >1000mm/year		
	Vertical	Flat ≤1.5%	Intermediate >1.5% <3.5%	Steep ≥3.5%	Flat ≤1.5%	Intermediate >1.5% <3.5%	Steep ≥3.5%
	Horizontal						
Gravel sections (G)	Low <30°/km	G22(N) G28(I) G29(Z) G41(N)	G21(N) G26(N) G31(I) G32(Z)	G24(N) G33(N) G35(I) G36(Z)	G4(I) G8(Z) G9(N)	G5(I) G7(N)	G12(N) G13(I) E2(N)**
	Medium >30°/km <90°/km	G30(N) G42(Z)	G34(N) G38(I)	G20(N) G25(I)	G1(I) G2(N)	G3(I) G10(Z) G11(N)	G6(N)
	High >90°/km	G40(N)	G16(N)	G23(N)	—	G17(I)	G18(I) G19(Z)
Earth sections (E)	Low <30°/km	G27(N)* —		—	—	E1(N) E3(I) E4(Z)	
	Medium >30°/km <90°/km	G37(I)* G39(N)*	G15(I)* —	—	—		—
	High >90°/km	—	—	G14(N)* —	—	—	—

Notes:
- (N) Normal maintenance level
- (I) Intermediate maintenance level
- (Z) Nil Maintenance level
- * These sections were originally gravel sections but were reclassified as earth sections because the particle size distribution was poor.
- ** This section was originally an earth section but was reclassified as a gravel section.

nual rainfall and four road types as follows:

    (i) gravel-surfaced roads;

    (ii) recently built roads with cement-stabilised bases and bituminous surface treatments;

    (iii) older roads with cement-stabilised and bituminous surface treatments; and

    (iv) roads with crushed stone bases and asphaltic concrete surfacings.

This frame provided 72 cells, many of which were sub-divided into two or three different levels of maintenance, to allow the effect of road maintenance on deterioration to be studied.

In practice it proved impossible to find sections of road to fill every cell, and the experiment actually embraced 95 test sections of road, 49 of which were paved and 46 unpaved. Tables 1 and 2 show the sample frames for the paved and unpaved roads.

On each of the test sections measurements were made of the strength, grading, moisture content and thickness of the pavement layers, the surface irregularity (roughness), the depth of rutting and the rainfall. On unsurfaced roads the looseness and rate of loss of the gravel surface were also measured. In addition the volume and composition of the traffic, the average vehicle speeds, the weights of vehicles and their axle loads, were recorded. Finally the fuel comsumption of specially instrumented vehicles was measured as they traversed the test sections at different speeds. All these measurements were repeated at regular intervals over a period of three years, during which time the condition of many of the test sections deteriorated significantly.

The methods of measurement used were kept as simple as possible. [5] Standard tests were used for the pavement evaluations, such as the CBR test, deflection tests and standard soil tests. Surface irregularity was measured, both with a standard BRR roughometer [6] (or '5th wheel bump integrator') and a simple vehicle-mounted bump integrator. On the gravel road sections gravel loss was recorded by levelling surveys and the looseness of the gravel was measured by recording the quantity of loose material that could be swept up by hand from a given area. Vehicle flows were recorded with simple automatic traffic counters and vehicle speeds were measured using two synchronised stopwatches operated by observers stationed at each end of the test sections. Vehicles were weighed using a portable weighing unit specially developed by TRRL for use in roadside axle-load surveys in developing countries. [7] Fuel consumption was measured by a simple volumetric displacement device fitted to the three test vehicles that were used for the series of controlled fuel consumption experiments.

The highest average daily traffic encountered on any of the test sections was less than 1500 vehicles per day, hence at all sites free-flow traffic conditions prevailed.

The survey of vehicle operators was conducted to gather information on those elements of vehicle operating cost that cannot be satisfactorily investigated by measuring experimentally the operating characteristics of a small number of instrumented vehicles. These are vehicle maintenance costs, tyre costs, vehicle depreciation costs, crew wage costs and the cost of lubricants consumed. Information on these costs was collected from a variety of vehicle operators, ranging from one-vehicle owners to companies operating a large number of vehicles. Detailed information was collected on nearly 300 individual vehicles ranging from motor cars to 26-ton lorry/trailer combinations, whose ages ranged from new vehicles to some that had covered over one million kilometres. In addition information was collected about the routes on which these vehicles normally

ran. The geometric characteristics of these routes were measured from large-scale maps, and the road surface roughness of the routes was estimated from sample measurements with a 5th wheel bump integrator.

Subsequent to the field research in Kenya, further research into vehicle operating costs has been untertaken in Ethiopia, [8] Scotland and Ghana to extend certain of the relationships and to investigate their validity in other environments.

THE MODEL

On the basis of the field studies a series of relationships were derived that enable the construction costs, road maintenance costs, and vehicle operating costs for a specified road to be calculated, taking account of the very considerable interaction that exist between these costs.

The relationships were incorporated in a model, called the Road Transport Investment Model (RTIM)[9], which calculates these costs for each year of a road's "design life", adds them together and discounts them back to a base year at a given discount rate. For a given road project the model can calculate this "total transport cost" over an analysis period of up to 24 years.

The model operates in terms of physical quantities to which any desired system of costs and prices may be applied. Costs can thus be presented in terms of any desired currency, provided the unit rates are input in the same currency.

The model also has the facility of analysing the cost consequences of a variety of stage construction policies. Many options can be examined, such as upgrading an earth road to a gravel or paved road either on an existing or on a new alignment, the widening or overlaying of a road pavement, or the complete reconstruction of a pavement.

The model is designed to operate with the same sort of basic input information as is normally collected by a team of engineers and economists undertaking a feasibility study for a non-urban road project in a developing country. The model is thus conceived essentially as being a tool to assist and improve the quality of the execution of such feasibility studies.

The basic inputs required to operate the model are as follows:

    a) route location;

    b) road design standards;

    c) terrain information;

    d) properties of construction materials;

    e) construction unit costs;

    f) environmental factors;

    g) unit costs of vehicle operation;

    h) traffic volumes;

    i) traffic composition;

    j) vehicle loads;

    k) road maintenance policy; and

    l) road maintenance unit costs.

An outline flow diagram of the model is shown in Figure 1. A typical run of the model begins with construction. In each year in which construction or reconstruction occurs, the model calculates the quantities and hence the costs of earthworks, pavement, drainage and site clearance. The deterioration of the road surface is then estimated as a function of the initial construction standard, the maintenance policy selected, the rainfall and the traffic flow. An estimation of the average speeds of different vehicle types is then made, based on the previously estimated road surface condition and the geometric characteristics of the road.

Fuel consumption, tyre wear, vehicle maintenance and depreciation costs are then calculated and applied to the traffic forecasts to produce the total vehicle operat-

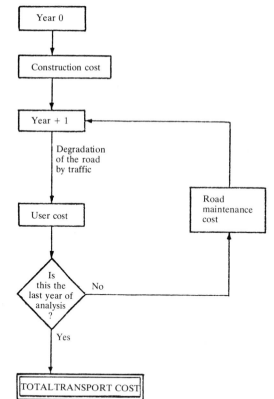

```
        ┌──────────────┐
        │    Year 0    │
        └──────┬───────┘
               │
        ┌──────┴───────┐
        │ Construction cost │
        └──────┬───────┘
               │
        ┌──────┴───────┐
        │   Year + 1   │◄──────────────────┐
        └──────┬───────┘                   │
               │                           │
          Degradation                      │
          of the road              ┌───────┴──────┐
          by traffic               │     Road     │
               │                   │  maintenance │
        ┌──────┴───────┐           │     cost     │
        │  User cost   │           └───────┬──────┘
        └──────┬───────┘                   │
               │                           │
            ╱──┴──╲                        │
          ╱   Is    ╲    No                │
        ╱  this the   ╲─────────────────────┘
        ╲ last year of ╱
          ╲ analysis  ╱
            ╲   ?   ╱
               │
              Yes
               │
        ┌──────┴──────────────┐
        │TOTAL TRANSPORT COST │
        └─────────────────────┘
```

Fig. 1 - Framework for determining total road transport cost

ing costs for the year in question. An option is available to calculate time costs based on values of time that must be input into the model. Road maintenance costs also depend on the condition of the road and thus they are also estimated for each year of the analysis period on the basis of the predicted road surface condition.

At the end of each year the road condition and the traffic volumes are compared with the values set by the User as being those at which upgrading or reconstruction should take place. If required these operations are costed and the condition of the upgraded or new road thus specified is taken into account in the subsequent year-by-year analysis. Figure 2 is a flow diagram showing the upgrading and maintenance options available in the model.

If desired parts of the model can be used independently. For example it is possible to calculate construction quantities and costs for a new scheme without considering vehicle operating costs or road maintenance costs. Similarly the model can be used to analyse the pavement deterioration, user cost, and maintenance cost of an existing road, without activating the construction cost sub-model: this is very useful for analysing the consequences of upgrading an existing road.

The model does not attempt to calculate any of the benefits that might accrue from a road investment other than those that derive from vehicle operating cost or road maintenance cost savings. Hence in undertaking a feasibility study other benefits, such as increases in agricultural production or other quantifiable increases in economic activity, must be estimated separately. The model also does not calculate the commonly used indicators of economic viability, such as net present value, benefit/cost ratio, internal rage of return etc. However,

the output is in such a form that the information from each separate run can easily be used to calculate these indicators. Similarly, when the introduction of a new or improved road leads to induced traffic, the output from a "do nothing" run and a "do something" run can easily be combined to calculate the benefits for this type of traffic. The model does not optimise in the strict sense of the term, it simply determines the total transport cost of a series of options that must be specified by the User. It was felt desirable to retain this dependence on User/model interaction for seeking the minimum cost solution so that the road designer maintains adequate control of the selection of options that are investigated.

METHOD OF OPERATION
Vehicle and traffic input data

The model can consider separately up to eight classes of vehicle, passenger cars, light commercial vehicles, buses and up to five classes of heavy commercial vehicles. In the case of the heavy vehicles, the degree of loading and axle load equivalence factors for the five classes are required to be input to the model, and if desired the loading and axle load equivalence factors can be different for the traffic travelling in each direction. Traffic growth forecasts must be made for each vehicle class over an analysis period of up to 24 years. The vehicle speed relationships in the model assume "free flow" conditions, and hence if traffic growth is such that speed reductions caused by congestion begin to occur during the analysis period, a warning message is printed in the output to inform the User that a separate analysis outside the model will be required.

Geometric design and ground input data

The vertical alignment can be specified in terms of the intersection points of tangent lines and the vertical curves that connect the tangents. If no vertical alignment has been designed the model will produce a design using a method based on that of program VENUS. [10] The required standards for maximum gradient and minimum radius of vertical curvature must be input into the model. If these standards are violated the model will automatically adjust the vertical alignment to ensure that it complies with the required design standards.

Ground information is specified to the model in terms of centre line levels and crossfalls at stations along the centre line. Alternatively grounds levels may be given at two offsets at each station. If only contour maps are available stations may be specified whenever the centre-line crosses a contour.

The vertical alignment and ground data are of course used by the model to calculate earthworks quantities, but the model also uses the vertical alignment to predict vehicle speeds and fuel consumption and the rate of loss of surface material from unsurfaced roads.

Horizontal alignment is specified in terms of the average degree of curvature per kilometre, and this is used only for the prediction of vehicle speed.

The road cross-section is defined in terms of the width and crossfall of the running surface, the width and crossfall of the shoulders, the angle of cut and fill slopes, and the ditch details. (See Figure 3) When the alignment traverses ground that slopes steeply across the roadline the model can calculate the earthworks cost on the basis that retaining walls will be used, the cost of the walls themselves being included in the calculation. The side-slope at which retaining walls become necessary must be input to the model, together with standard dimensions for the walls expressed as a function of wall height.

Construction costs

Earthworks volumes are calculated by the average-

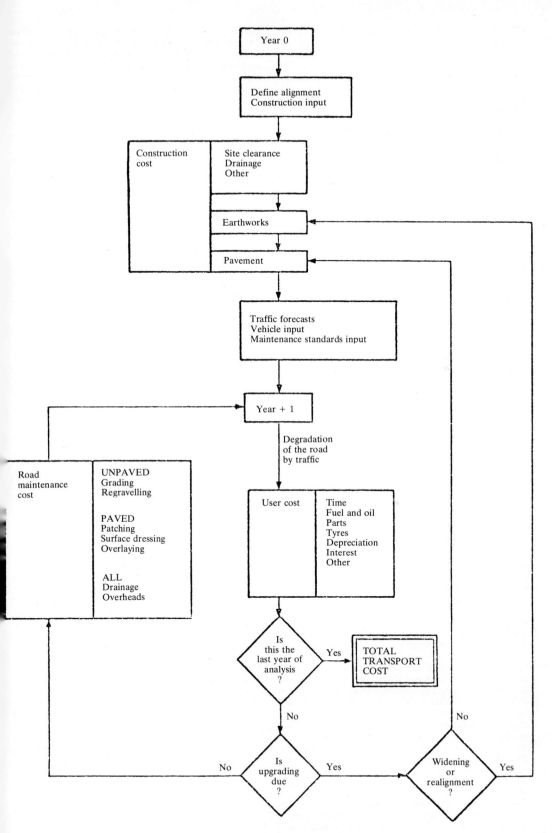

Fig. 2 - Flow chart of road transport investment model showing costs and upgrading

end-area method, cut and fill being considered separately. The unit costs of excavation, filling, hauling, borrowing and spoiling must be input to the model. The model calculates the maximum haul distance beyound which it is cheaper to borrow or spoil material rather than haul it, and then it constructs a mass-haul diagram with the balance lines so positioned that the material within the balance loops is that which can be economically hauled and the rest of the material is either spoiled or borrowed. The model calculates site clearance costs from the width of clearance specified and unit rates for clearing different types of vegetation that must be input to the model.

Pavement costs are calculated on a layer by layer basis, up to six pavement being considered by the model if required. For gravel roads only one pavement layer is considered and for earth roads none. Each layer must be specified in terms of its thickness, the type of material, and the strength of the material. The strength of sub-base material is expressed in terms of its California Bear-ing Ratio (CBR), base material in terms of CBR or unconfined compressive strength, and asphaltic materials in terms of strength coefficients. [11] The cost of each material per square metre or cubic metre must be input.

The shoulders, which may be earth, gravel or paved, are specified in the same way as the road pavement itself.

Three elements of drainage cost are considered by the model; the cost of cross-flow culverts for the transfer of water from one side ditch to the other, the cost of culverts for carrying streams and small rivers under the road, and the cost of bridges for larger water crossings. The cost of the latter must be specified directly, but the model will calculate the size and the cost of culverts for stream crossings provided that data on catchment areas, rainfall and unit costs of construction are input. The required spacing and size of the crossflow culverts must also be input to the model.

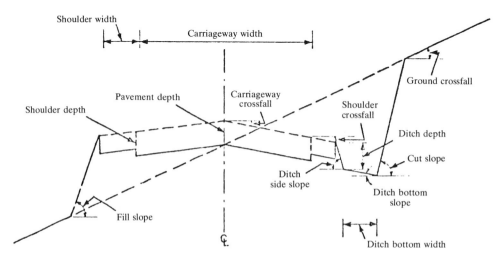

Fig. 3 - Road cross-section

Road deterioration

The model predicts the amount of deterioration of the road surface that will occur due to trafficking on a year-by-year basis. For earth and gravel roads deterioration is defined in terms of roughness, rutting, looseness of the surface, and in the case of gravel roads only, the loss of gravel. The factors that the model considers in calculating the rate of deterioration of unpaved roads are the volume of traffic, the type of surfacing material, the rainfall and the road gradient.

Paved road deterioration is defined in terms of roughness and the amount of cracking. These are functions of the pavement strength and the cumulative axle loading expressed in terms of equivalent standard axles [12] (of 8.2. tons). Using the input data on the strength and thickness of the pavement layers, the model calculates a "modified structural number" as an index of pavement strength. The model then predicts the deterioration of the road surface in each year that the road is trafficked. The deterioration relationships used by the model for both paved and unpaved roads were derived from the results of the studies in Kenya. They represent a considerable advance in knowledge about the rate of deterioration of roads in environments similar to that of East Africa, but they cannot be used with the same degree of confidence in very different tropical environments, such as those with very high or very low rainfall.

Road user costs

The sum of time costs and vehicle operating costs is determined for each year that the road is open to traffic. Time costs are calculated by multiplying the value of passenger's time by journey time. The value of passenger's time must be input to the model, but journey time is calculated within the model from the road length and the average vehicle speed.

Vehicle speed is calculated for each class of vehicle. For paved roads it is a function of the rise and fall of the road, its horizontal curvature, its width and its altitude. Similarly on unpaved roads vehicle speed is a function of road geometry, but the roughness of the road surface, its moisture content and the depth of ruts, are also significant factors.

The fuel consumption of the spectrum of vehicles that will traverse the road is calculated for each class of vehicle. On paved roads fuel consumption is a function of the distance travelled, the speed, the rise and fall of the road, and in the case of heavy vehicles, the gross weights and power-to-weight ratios. On unpaved roads the same factors are significant with the addition of the road surface roughness and surface looseness. The cost of fuel must be input to the model.

The costs of tyre consumption, spare parts and lubricating oil are also calculated for each vehicle class, all three costs being related to vehicle type and the distance travelled. Tyre costs are additionally related to the roughness of the road surface, and for heavy vehicles, to gross vehicle weight. Spares costs are related to road surface roughness and the distance covered by vehicles since manufacture, and oil costs are related to road surface type. The unit costs of new tyres, vehicles and lubricating oil must be input to the model.

The depreciation cost of vehicles is calculated on the basis of vehicle age, an initial age spectrum being assumed which is modified each year by growth and wastage of the vehicle population.

The model also calculates vehicles' crew costs, interest charges and standing costs for the vehicle population using the road under consideration. Values of crew wage rates and interest rates must be input to the model.

All road user costs may be expressed in both economic and market terms, separate accounts of these costs being kept within the model, thus enabling the User to analyse a project in either terms.

Road maintenance costs

Road maintenance costs are analysed by the model in some detail. In the case of paved roads the operations of patching, surface dressing and overlaying are considered. On unpaved roads the operations considered are grading and regravelling. Additionally on both types of road shoulder maintenance and ditch clearance are considered. The model predicts the amount of maintenance required annually on the basis of the amount of traffic the road carries. The cost of the maintenance is then calculated using unit rates that are input to the model.

Stage construction

When either the condition of the road deteriorates below a given standard, or the level of traffic grows to a "threshold" value set by the User, it may be necessary to upgrade a road. For example an earth road may need to be upgraded to a gravel road, a gravel road may need to be paved, or a paved road may need to be overlaid. The model can consider any of these stages, taking into account the costs of any widening or re-alignment that may be required in addition to the pavement costs. The effects of the upgrading on vehicle operating costs and road maintenance costs are of course allowed for in calculating the cost streams subsequent to the upgrading operation. A number of different stage-construction strategies can be evaluated by the model, thus allowing the User to investigate many possible options.

APPLICATIONS OF THE MODEL

The model has already been used to evaluate several road projects in developing countries.

Initially it was applied in retrospect to a recently completed road project in Kenya to test the functioning of the model, and to compare its estimate of construction cost with the actual contract costs. In addition the sensitivity of discounted costs to variations in the assumptions made about discount rates and traffic growth rates were examined. Good agreement was obtained between the construction costs calculated by the model and the actual contracts costs. Also at a first year average daily traffic of 400 vehicles per day, the discounted road user costs over ten years were two and a half times the cost of construction, and discounted road maintenance costs were less than one per cent of total transport costs. Total discounted transport costs were found to be very sensitive to traffic growth assumptions but relatively insensitive to road construction and maintenance costs, whatever discount rate was assumed. This case is typical of many non-urban roads in developing countries and demonstrates the value of adopting a stage-construction strategy when traffic prediction is uncertain, and the wisdom

of undertaking effective road maintenance since its cost is relatively minor and its effect on the major cost of vehicle operation is substantial.

The model has also been used to evaluate road projects in Belize, Thailand, Lesotho and the Central African Republic (CAR). In each case the model proved its worth and enabled the relevant features of widely differing types of road project to be examined more thoroughly than otherwise would have been possible. For instance in the Belize project alternative routes with similar geometric standards were compared, in the CAR project the effects on total transport cost of various vertical alignment standards were investigated, and in the Lesotho project the upgrading of an existing gravel road was examined.

In use the model has been found to be easy to operate and its data requirements easy to satisfy. Some of the lessons that have been learnt from these applications are:

a) on roads carrying more than about 100 vehicles per day the total transport cost is very sensitive to road length, hence it may be worth incurring extra construction costs if the road can be shortened by so doing;

b) on gravel roads carrying more than 100 or so vehicles per day total transport cost is sensitive to the estimates made of road surface roughness; as a consequence in such cases it may not be possible to estimate total transport costs to closer than plus or minus 20 per cent for this reason alone;

c) on all but very low-volume roads total transport costs are very sensitive to the estimates of future traffic; and

d) there is a need to extend the vehicle operating cost relationships to cover roads with more extreme geometric characteristics and surface roughness, to encompass a wider range of gravel types, and to test all the relationships in other climatic and economic environments.

CURRENT DEVELOPMENT

As has been mentioned, further field research has been undertaken, subsequent to the main study in Kenya, to improve and extend several of the relationships within the model.

In Ethiopia a study of the speeds and the weights of commercial vehicles [8] has enabled the speed estimating equations for medium and heavy goods vehicles to be improved. These improved equations have been incorporated into the model, together with improved pavement performance equations. [11]

A study has been made of the fuel consumption of heavy vehicles on mountain roads in Scotland as a first stage of a programme of research planned to extend the vehicle operating cost relationships to cover roads with more severe geometric characteristics than those of Kenya.

Research on pavement deterioration and road strengthening is being continued in Kenya, the results of which will be incorporated into the model as they become available.

In parallel with this research being undertaken by TRRL, a major study of the inter-relationships between the costs of highway construction, maintenance and vehicle operation is in progress in Brazil, and a study of vehicle operating costs is being started in India. The World Bank played a key role in initiating both of these studies, the conceptions of which are very similar to that of the Kenya study. In due course it can be expected that these studies will result in models very similar to RTIM, and that they will produce relationships that may improve, complement, or extend some of the relationships currently incorporated in RTIM.

ACKNOWLEDGEMENTS

The work described in this paper forms part of the programme of the Transport and Road Research Laboratory and the paper is published by permission of the Director.

Dr. C.G. Harral of the World Bank was a major contributor to both the original concept of the model, and to the design of the experimental study in Kenya. His contribution is gratefully acknowledged.

Professor F. Moavenzadeh was the architect of the prototype model, which was the foundation on which the Kenya study and RTIM were built.

The co-operation of Halcrow and Partners, Roughton and Partners and T.P.O'Sullivan and Partners, in testing the model, is gratefully acknowledged.

We are indebted to the Government of Kenya for permitting the conduct of experiments on the public roads of Kenya. Particular thanks are due to the Ministry of Works and Mr. F. Nderitu, the Deputy Permanent Secretary.

Many colleagues in the Overseas Unit of TRRL contributed to the work described in this paper.

REFERENCES

1] Moavenzadeh, F., J.H. Stafford, J.H. Suhrbier and J. Alexander. Highway design study phase 1: the model. **International Bank for Reconstruction, Economics Department Working Paper** No 96. Washington DC, 1971 (unpublished).

2] Moavenzadeh, F., Investment strategies for developing areas: analytical model for choices of strategies in highway transportation. **Department of Civil Engineering, Research Report** No 72-62. Cambridge, Mass, 1972 (Massachusetts Institute of Technology).

3] Hide, H., S.W. Abaynayaka, I.A. Sayer and R. Wyatt. The Kenya Road Transport Cost Study: research on vehicle operating costs. **Department of the Environment, TRRL Report** LR 672. Crowthorne, 1975 (Transport and Road Research Laboratory).

4] Hodges, J.W., J. Rolt and T.E. Jones. The Kenya Road Transport Cost Study: research on road deterioration. **Department of the Environment, TRRL Report** LR 673. Crowthorne 1975 (Transport and Road Research Laboratory).

5] Abaynayaka, S.W., Some techniques for measuring vehicle operating cost and road deterioration parameters – with particular reference to developing countries. **Department of the Environment, TRRL Supplementary Report** SR 193. Crowthorne 1976 (Transport and Road Research Laboratory).

6] Potocki, F.P., A portable wheel-weighing unit and data recorder. **Department of the Environment. RRL Report** LR 391. Crowthorne 1971 (Road Research Laboratory).

7] Hudson, W.R. and R.C. Hain. Calibration and use of BPR roughmeter at the AASHO road test. **AASHO Road Test Technical Staff Papers, Highway Research Board Special Report** 66. Washington DC, 1961 (National Research Council).

8] Abaynayaka, S.W., H. Morosiuk and H. Hide. The effect of vehicle and road characteristics on commercial vehicle speeds in Ethiopia. **Department of the Environment, TRRL, Supplementary Report** SR 271. Crowthorne 1977 (Transport and Road Research Laboratory).

9] Robinson, R., H. Hide, J.W. Hodges, S.W. Abaynayaka and J. Rolt. A road transport investment model for developing countries. **Department of the Environment,** TRRL Report LR 674. Crowthorne 1975 (Transport and Road Research Laboratory).

10] Robinson, R., A further computer method for designing the vertical alignment of a road: program VENUS II. **Department of the Environment, TRRL Report** LR 458. Crowthorne 1972 (Transport and Road Research Laboratory)

11] Rolt. J. and S.W. Abaynayaka. Revision 1 of the Road Transport Investment Model. **Department of the Environment, TRRL Supplementary Report** SR 246. Crowthorne 1976 (Transport and Road Research Laboratory).

12] Liddle, W.J., Application of AASHO road test results to the design of flexible pavement structures. **Proc. of the International Conference on the Structural Design of Asphalt Pavements held at the University of Michigan, Ann Arbor. 1963** (University of Michigan). pp 42-51.

Fondements techniques et économiques du transport ferroviaire des voyageurs à grande vitesse

par

D. MONNET

Société Nationale des Chemins de Fer Français, France

La politique de développement des transports ferroviaires de voyageurs à grande vitesse (250/300 km/h) sur des lignes nouvelles, dans laquelle la SNCF s'est engagée depuis près d'une dizaines d'années, repose principalement sur les idées ou constatations suivantes:

Les besoins de déplacement des voyageurs, à moyenne et longue distance (200 à 800 km), augmentent rapidement, plus vite que l'accroissement des revenus, et la SNCF a acquis la certitude qu'elle pouvait offrir un service compétitif, en qualité de service et en prix, vis-à-vis du recours à la voiture particulière ou au transport aérien.

Les études, recherches et expérimentations, qu'elle a poursuivies depuis une trentaine d'années dans le domaine des grandes vitesses, lui permettent d'assurer que, dans la gamme de vitesses visée ci-dessus, tous les problèmes techniques sont résolus, depuis la motorisation, le freinage, la captation du courant électrique, jusqu'à la sécurité des circulations, notamment en ce qui concerne la stabilité, et le confort des passagers. Elle peut affirmer que, non seulement ces problèmes sont résolus sur le plan technique, mais, également, que les solutions apportées, recourant à des moyens éprouvés et bien souvent classiques, le sont à un coût acceptable, notamment en ce qui concerne la maintenance, tant du matériel que des installations.

Sur le plan de l'exploitation, la double option prise, concernant à la fois la spécialisation des lignes nouvelles au trafic voyageurs et leur compatibilité avec le réseau existant, permet, tout en réduisant le coût de construction de l'infrastructure en rase campagne et en évitant d'avoir à créer de nouvelles pénétrations urbaines, d'amener le transport à grande vitesse au coeur des villes, d'offrir une desserte directe, sans rupture de charge, à des agglomérations situées en dehors de la ligne à grande vitesse et de réserver les infrastructures existantes, parallèles aux lignes nouvelles, pour les besoins du développement du trafic marchandises. Cette spécialisation conduit, en effet, à tirer un meilleur parti de l'ensemble des installations.

Ainsi, la création de lignes nouvelles, en nombre limité, sur quelques axes lourds convenablement choisis, greffées sur le réseau existant, traduit-elle une politique ferroviaire globale, permettant à la fois une amélioration très marquante de la qualité du service voyageurs et le développement du trafic marchandises, en éliminant les freins constitués par des sections du réseau en voie de saturation. Ce double avantage permet de rentabiliser les projets de lignes nouvelles grâce à l'apport du trafic supplémentaire qui en résulte, à la réduction de certaines dépenses d'exploitation, et au fait d'éviter des investissements de renforcement de la capacité sur les itinéraires existants; le poids relatif de ces avantages variant, évi-demment, selon l'importance des axes de transport intéressés, les situations de concurrence, et le degré de saturation des lignes existantes. Le premier projet de ligne nouvelle, en cours de réalisation, entre PARIS et LYON, sur l'axe Paris – Sud-Est, permet d'illustrer ces considérations générales développées en introduction.

Au passage, seront évoquées les conclusions dégagées par la SNCF au double plan de l'analyse de la demande voyageurs, et de l'impact du TGV sur ce marché, ainsi que les connaissances acquises dans le domaine technologique et technico-économique, garantissant la viabilité, sur le plan des coûts, des nouvelles exploitations envisagées.

L'ANALYSE DE LA DEMANDE: L'APPORT DE L'ECONOMETRIE
Position du problème

L'analyse de la demande transport est une démarche préalable, indispensable à la recherche du type de service à offrir pour répondre aux besoins réels des usagers, et définir le compromis optimum entre les facteurs de qualité du service et le coût de production, dans le cadre d'une contrainte de rentabilité financière. Elle constitue l'outil de base indispensable à l'étude des projets d'amélioration des systèmes existants ou de mise en place de systèmes entièrement nouveaux, ainsi que des stratégies tarifaires qui les complètent sur le plan économique.

Dans le domaine du transport terrestre des voyageurs à grande vitesse, son objet propre est de répondre à la question suivante:

Quelle est l'influence du prix de transport et des paramètres de qualité du service sur le volume et la structure du trafic empruntant le service à grande vitesse ainsi que sur le trafic des modes de transport en situation de concurrence?

La réponse à cette question doit être apportée de façon différenciée:

– sur le plan géographique, les situations de concurrence varient, en effet, sensiblement selon les données de la géographie humaine

– sur le plan temporel, les situations de concurrence se déforment au cours du temps en fonction de l'élévation du niveau de vie par exemple ou des changements de l'offre des modes concurrents

Pour un flux élémentaire de trafic donné entre deux zones, la demande de transport pour un mode déterminé dépendra ainsi, à une époque donnée:

– des tarifs du mode

– des facteurs de qualité du service de la desserte envisagée: vitesse, fréquence, confort, sécurité et, à un degré moindre, régularité et „garantie" du service

– des tarifs et des qualités de service de modes concurrents

Par ailleurs, cette demande évoluera au cours du

temps en raison de l'évolution temporelle, à la fois des éléments précédents, et des caractéristiques des zones considérées: démographie, structure d'activités, élévation du niveau des revenus, modification des comportements, etc.

Diversité des situations de concurrence

Les études menées par la SNCF dans ce domaine reposent essentiellement sur deux types d'informations:
– des éléments statistiques relatifs aux flux de transport ferroviaires ou aériens, la route étant malheureusement fort déficiente en ce domaine,
– des éléments obtenus au cours d'enquêtes effectuées, soit à domicile, soit en cours de déplacements, concernant les divers modes.

Par ailleurs, ces études tendent à distinguer:
– les déplacements à caractère urbain,
– les déplacements à courte distance dans un domaine où les migrations journalières restent possibles,
– les déplacements à moyenne distance caractérisés essentiellement par la concurrence train – voiture dans une gamme de temps de parcours permettant l'aller et retour dans la journée ou la demi-journée,
– les déplacements à longue distance (400 - 800 km) où l'avion apparaît dans le champ de la concurrence,
– les déplacements plus longs encore où la formule du train de nuit devient la seule valable pour concurrencer efficacement l'avion.

De même, d'autres éléments de distinction apparaissent très importants:
– le motif et la durée d'absence du domicile, (affaires, déplacements personnels, vacances et tourisme)
– la situation des origines et destinations vis-à-vis de PARIS est également essentielle dans la situation française (déplacements ,,radiaux'' intéressant PARIS, déplacements ,,transversaux'' ou déplacements ,,passe-PARIS'')
– la taille du groupe qui se déplace simultanément.

Je m'étendrai sur les résultats obtenus plus particulièrement dans 2 domaines:

– déplacements radiaux à moyenne distance,
– concurrence train – avion sur les relations radiales à longue distance.

Les déplacements radiaux à moyenne distance

Dans ce domaine caractérisé par la concurrence train – voiture, les études menées par la SNCF se sont attachées à la construction de modèles explicatifs des niveaux observés pour le trafic ferroviaire en fonction des caractéristiques des relations (populations desservies, distances) et des paramètres d'offre du transport ferroviaire (prix, vitesse, fréquence, confort, services directs) avec cette circonstance particulièrement malheureuse à savoir, la quasi-proportionnalité du prix du transport ferroviaire avec la distance du fait de la structure tarifaire.

Dans ce domaine, les séries temporelles homogènes faisant défaut, la seule approche qui semble praticable est d'utiliser des méthodes de régression sur une coupe géographique instantanée.

Ces méthodes ont commencé à être utilisées systématiquement en 1967 sur la base d'estimations de trafics annuels gare à gare obtenus par voie de sondage statistique, et elles ont conduit à développer deux types de modèles:
– des modèles de régression à élasticités constantes par rapport aux variables explicatives,
– des modèles à coûts généralisés, d'inspiration gravitaire.

Modèles à élasticités constantes

Ils ont été ajustés séparément pour expliquer les trafics en 1ère classe et en 2ème classe et j'en donnerai pour exemple les résultats obtenus sur un ensemble de 56 liaisons centrées sur PARIS en 1963, se situant dans une gamme de distances d'environ 100 à 300 km, qui se présentent comme suit, lorsque l'on prend comme variables explicatives les 4 variables: population (P) distance (D) temps de parcours (T) et l'intervalle moyen entre les trains (I) (voisin de l'inverse de la fréquence).

		P	D	T	I	Valeur de R (1)
1ère classe	Elasticité	0,98	+0,79	−1,50	−0,38	0,945
	Ecart type d'estimation	0,08	0,39	0,46	0,14	
2ème classe	Elasticité	0,61	− 0,72	−0,26	−0,56	0,954
	Ecart type d'estimation	0,05	0,25	0,28	0,12	

(1) Coefficient de corrélation multiple

Ces résultats font ressortir évidemment une valeur explicative très forte de la population qui explique à elle seule une part notable de la variance avec le résultat un peu inattendu, mais cependant interprétable, d'une élasticité du trafic de 2ème classe nettement inférieure à 1.

Le deuxième résultat marquant est le caractère assez significatif des élasticités relatives à l'intervalle moyen, la plus faible valeur trouvée en 1ere semblant en partie s'expliquer par le fait que la fréquence de desserte est en général plus forte en 1ère qu'en 2ème classe, l'élasticité ayant tendance à décroître assez rapidement lorsque la fréquence augmente.

La différence de signe entre les élasticités distance de la 1ère classe et de la 2ème classe reflète la différence de comportement de ces deux groupes vis-à-vis du prix du voyage et surtout l'impact de la concurrence train/voiture particulière en ce qui concerne la 1ère classe. Alors qu'en 1ère classe, le voyageur est sensible au gain de

temps que lui procure le train (gain de temps qui s'accroit avec la distance) et relativement moins sensible au prix, en 2ème classe l'effet du prix l'emporte sur toute autre considération.

En conclusion, il semble bien que les modèles ainsi ajustés ne peuvent par être utilisés comme fonctions de demande sans précautions. Dans ce souci, on est orienté vers la recherche de formes utilisant la notion de coût généralisé pour l'usager.

Modèles à coût généralisé

La démarche est simple: elle tend à assimiler aux coûts monétaires les désutilités entraînées pour l'usager par la durée du transport et l'intervalle moyen entre les trains en incluant les dépenses et sujétions imposées par les parcours terminaux.

La demande apparaît alors comme une fonction de la forme:

$$N = \frac{P^\alpha}{(C_o + cD + hT + h'l)^\beta}$$

Dans les conditions économiques actuelles, par exemple la valeur du temps associé aux voyageurs de 2ème classe s'établit à 16 F environ.

L'élasticité β est de l'ordre de 2.

La valeur de la constante, représentative du coût et des sujétions terminales de transport s'établit à 35 F (pour des déplacements ayant une extrémité à Paris).

Une telle formulation permet notamment, outre de calculer les élasticités, vis-à-vis des variables d'offre dans une situation déterminée, d'avoir une idée de leur variation avec la distance, par exemple.

En conclusion, je voudrais également citer le rôle important d'autres paramètres qui ne figurent pas dans les exemples précédents donnés à titre illustratif: il en est notamment ainsi des ruptures de charge qui en elles-mêmes provoquent une chute de trafic importante.

Enfin, il ne faut pas se dissimuler que la formulation actuelle restera très imparfaite tant que l'on aura des difficultés à intégrer explicitement la concurrence de la voiture particulière; ce point fait actuellement l'objet de recherches qui pourraient peut-être aboutir à la conclusion que le trafic par voiture particulière est moins captif qu'on ne le pense généralement, tout au moins pour certains types de déplacements.

La concurrence train – avion:
le modèle ,,Prix-temps"

Ce modèle se propose de décrire la répartition entre l'avion et le transport de surface.

Tout voyageur qui choisit entre le train et l'avion arbitre (au moins implicitement) un gain de temps de transport contre une dépense moindre. Cet arbitrage peut être interprété comme la comparaison entre le prix que le voyageur est prêt à payer pour l'heure de trajet économisée et le prix que l'heure lui coûte effectivement sur la relation considérée.

Le modèle utilisé suppose que la valeur horaire attribuée au temps de trajet économisé est répartie au sein de la population des voyages suivant une loi de distribution pour laquelle il est naturel de prendre la loi log normale qui représente bien la distribution du principal facteur explicatif: la répartition des revenus.

Le modèle peut se formuler par une intégrale donnant la part F du trafic fer:

$$F = \frac{1}{2\,\mu\sigma} \int_o^x e^{-\frac{(Ly - L\mu)^2}{2\,\sigma^2}} \frac{dy}{y}$$

où
– x est le coût horaire du temps sur la relation considérée c'est-à-dire le rapport entre la différence des prix et la différence des temps du fer et de l'avion.
– μ est la médiane de la valeur du temps dans la population des voyages
– σ caractérise la dispersion de la valeur du temps dans la population.

Les valeurs ajustées de μ et σ dépendent essentiellement de la distribution des revenus, mais aussi des différences entre les situations de choix pour les voyages (temps terminaux, réduction, etc..) et des différences de comportement individuel.

Ce modèle a été ajusté sur des données de trafic commercial fer 1ère classe et avion pour les années 1965 - 1967 - 1969 - 1972. Ces clientèles sont en effet à peu près homogènes du point de vue du motif de voyage et des catégories socioprofessionnelles.

Divers ajustements effectués ont montré que les meilleurs facteurs explicatifs étaient:
le temps de trajet par les services les plus rapides y compris les temps terminaux comptés à partir du centre des agglomérations,
les perceptions moyennes effectives en y incluant pour le fer les suppléments train rapide.

On a obtenu les résultats suivants sur 10 relations où la concurrence est déjà ancienne qui sont représentées en coordonnées gausso-logarithmiques dans la planche 1 (année 1967):
– coefficient de corrélation (R): 0,930
– médiane de la valeur du temps (μ): 14,3 F
– écart-type de la distribution (σ): 0,79

La valeur médiane du temps évolue en Francs constants de la manière suivante (Francs de 1965):

Année	1965	1967	1969	1972
Valeur de μ (F 1965)	11,7	12,9	22,4	27,3

On voit que la période 1967 - 1969 est caractérisée par une forte croissance de μ (31,8% par an en moyenne), alors que les périodes encadrantes font apparaître des taux plus faibles (5% entre 1965 en 1967; 6,8 entre 1969 et 1972). C'est en effet au cours de cette période qu'Air Inter a intensifié la diffusion du transport aérien intérieur en France. Il semble qu'à l'avenir la croissance des valeurs du temps devrait se stabiliser et être plus directement liée à la croissance des revenus.

Ce modèle peut être utilisé de deux manières:
– sur la situation actuelle pour étudier la substitution entre modes en fonction de la modification de l'offre,
– dans des conditions d'offre données pour prévoir l'évolution du marché au fur et à mesure que les valeurs attribuées au temps s'accroissent.

Dans la situation actuelle il est par exemple possible de déterminer des élasticités de substitution directes et croisées en fonction du prix et du temps de parcours. Pour les obtenir, il suffit de faire varier marginalement le prix ou le temps de transport, de calculer le coût de l'heure qui en résulte et d'en déduire la nouvelle répartition de marché.

Ainsi sur la relation Paris-Lyon, dans les conditions de 1967, les élasticités de substitution directes et croisées pour le trafic 1ère classe par fer et pour le trafic aérien pouvaient s'évaluer comme suit, par rapport aux principales variables d'offre:

	Temps fer	Prix fer	Prix avion
Trafic Fer 1ère	– 1	– 0.7	+ 1.8
Trafic Avion	+ 2	+ 1.4	+ 3.7

Ces élasticités varient suivant les relations, ainsi à plus courte distance on observe des élasticités – prix du trafic fer 1ère classe par rapport au prix du fer nettement plus faibles (–0.3 pour Paris – Nantes par exemple).

Conséquences pour la politique commerciale de la SNCF

Les modèles présentés ci-dessus montrent que, à qualités de confort et de sécurité respectives données, le marché des transports interurbains de voyageurs à moyenne distance (400 à 800 km) est sensible aux trois paramètres prix-temps de parcours-fréquence. Suivant le segment de marché auquel on a affaire, le paramètre prépondérant sera tantôt le prix (marchés 2ème classe fer – voiture particulière), tantôt le temps porte à porte

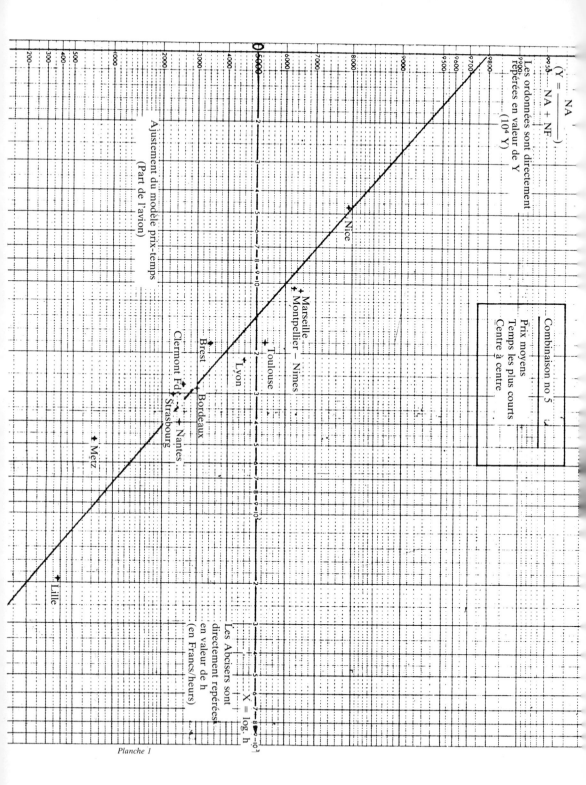

Planche 1

322

(marchés 1ère classe fer – avion), la paramètre fréquence jouant sur tous les marchés un rôle secondaire quoiqu'important.

Les conclusions ont orienté la SNCF vers le développement des services rapides et fréquents en tirant parti au maximum des possibilités techniques du matériel et des infrastructures ferroviaires existantes. Ces dernières sont généralement loin d'être saturées, ce qui permet d'augmenter les fréquences sur un grand nombre de relations, au prix d'un accroissement modéré des coûts d'exploitation. C'est ce qui a pu être fait sur Paris – Lille et Paris – Le Havre par exemple.

L'augmentation de la vitesse peut être obtenue par l'utilisation de matériels plus performants, sans modification de l'infrastructure. Mais le gain ainsi obtenu reste faible en général. Pourtant dans certains cas particuliers, cette méthode peut conduire à des résultats substantiels, comme par exemple sur la ligne Paris – Cherbourg où grâce aux turbotrains de la première génération il a été possible d'obtenir en 1970 un gain de temps d'environ 20% sur le meilleur train antérieur. Sur cette ligne, on a procédé simultanément à un doublement de la fréquence.

Une augmentation plus grande de la vitesse nécessite une rectification des courbes, une modification de la signalisation, et éventuellement un renforcement des installations fixes de traction électrique, plus ou moins importants selon le niveau de vitesse visé. Le niveau maximum de vitesse économiquement praticable de cette manière, éminemment variable en fonction des caractéristiques de tracé, se situe dans la gamme 160 – 200 km/h. C'est ainsi que des relèvements de vitesse échelonnés ont été pratiqués, par exemple depuis 1967 sur la ligne Paris – Toulouse, avec la mise en marche du Capitole (200 km/h sur la section Les Aubrais – Vierzon) et depuis 1973 sur Paris – Bordeaux, la longueur cumulée des sections de voies aptes à 200 km/h atteignant ajourd'hui 780 km, et procurant un gain de temps de 10 à 12% sur les meilleurs trains antérieurs.

Pour gagner davantage de temps encore, il est nécessaire de construire des lignes nouvelles, mais il se pose alors le problème du choix de la meilleure technique qu'il convient de développer.

LES POSSIBILITES TECHNIQUES DES SYSTEMES
Les systèmes étudiés
Dès lors que des voies nouvelles doivent être construites pour dépasser significativement la vitesse de 200 km/h, il n'y a pas à priori de raison fondamentale à fixer un objectif de vitesse plutôt qu'un autre, une technique de transport plutôt qu'une autre. Il convient donc d'ouvrir aussi largement que possible l'éventail des solutions envisageables; le choix entre ces solutions devant s'effectuer suivant des critères à la fois techniques (faisabilités, sécurité, fiabilité, nuisances) et économiques (capacité, consommation des ressources rares, rentabilité).

Le système ferroviaire
Le chemin de fer constitue une solution satisfaisante au regard de ces critères. En effet, il y a maintenant près de 20 ans qu'a été démontrée la possibilité de réaliser des vitesses supérieures à 330 km/h avec le matériel commercial de l'époque sur des voies non aménagées du réseau existant. Les essais systématiques effectués avec les prototypes expérimentaux à turbines d'une part (TGV 001), électrique d'autre part (Z 7001) ont confirmé que ces vitesses étaient réalisables en toute sécurité en service continu sur des voies ordinaires, pourvu que les rayons en plan et profil soient adaptés. Par ailleurs les composants utilisés sont de technologie connue, ce qui permet d'assurer leur fiabilité et d'estimer leurs coûts (en capital, entretien, consommations) avec une bonne approximation. Enfin l'utilisation de voies à écartement standard permet de profiter de la continuité de passage des lignes nouvelles sur les lignes existantes, ce qui est source d'avantages importants: cela permet d'éviter les ruptures de charges pour les voyageurs qui doivent poursuivre leur voyage au-delà des extrémités de la ligne nouvelle, cela permet également en utilisant les terminaux et les pénétrantes existantes d'aboutir au coeur des villes sans avoir à engager de coûteux investissements.

Les calculs effectués par la SNCF ont montré par ailleurs que les coûts d'exploitation (charges de capital du matériel, coûts d'entretien, d'énergie, de personnel, frais généraux et commerciaux) pouvaient être non seulement du même ordre de grandeur, mais inférieurs à ceux des trains classiques, grâce à la réduction des distances et à l'augmentation de productivité procurée par la vitesse (amélioration des rotations). La seule condition économique à la construction de lignes nouvelles est que celles-ci drainent un trafic suffisamment important pour assurer la rentabilité de l'investissement d'infrastructure. L'utilisation des modèles de demande évoqués au chapitre précédent a montré que cette condition était très largement réalisée dès aujourd'hui sur la ligne Paris – Lyon, et que d'autres lignes pouvaient devenir rentables, sous certaines conditions, dans un avenir plus ou moins proche: Paris – Lille et triangle Paris – Bruxelles – Calais (sous condition de réalisation du tunnel sous la Manche), Paris – Le Mans – Tours notamment, en visant la gamme des vitesses situées entre 250 et 300 km/h.

Les techniques non conventionnelles
Si le chemin de fer constitue une bonne solution pour cette gamme de vitesse, on peut se demander si des objectifs plus élevés, de l'ordre de 400 à 500 km/h, ne permettraient pas de fournir une solution meilleure encore.

Tour d'abord il n'est pas exclu que le chemin de fer puisse y parvenir. En effet, des essais récents aux Etats-Unis ont permis de dépasser la vitesse de 400 km/h sur rails, classiques pour la sustentation et le guidage, la propulsion étant assurée par un moteur linéaire chevauchant une plaque de réaction placée dans l'axe de la voie, ce qui permet de s'affranchir de l'adhérence.

Bien que la limite de vitesse réalisable par le moyen de cette adhérence ne soit pas connu, on s'accorde généralement à la situer aux environs de 400 km/h. Si donc nous devons encore aujourd'hui confesser notre ignorance sur cette limite technique du chemin de fer, nous ne pouvons pas conclure à son inadaptation à des vitesses comprises entre 300 et 400 km/h. Les recherches menées dans ce domaine par les réseaux devraient permettre de fournir dans quelque temps une réponse moins évasive.

La difficulté principale à résoudre pour assurer la sustentation et le guidage à grande vitesse par le système roue/rail réside dans le maintien de la stabilité. En effet, les irrégularités de la voie appliquant sur les roues des perturbations d'intensité croissante avec la vitesse, plus la vitesse augmente, plus il est nécessaire, soit de réduire les tolérances de la voie, soit de compliquer les organes de suspension des bogies.

Pour surmonter ces difficultés, les techniciens ont imaginé des systèmes évitant tout contact entre la voie et le véhicule. Ce sont les techniques dites non conventionnelles, qu'on peut classer en fonction de la nature physique des forces mises en oeuvre (procédés pneumatiques ou électromagnétiques) et de leur signe (attraction ou répulsion).

L'absence de contact voie/véhicule impose d'avoir recours pour la propulsion à un procédé affranchi de l'adhérence. Deux classes de propulseurs ont été expérimentés: les propulseurs thermiques (turbo-moteurs entraînant une hêlice, turbo-réacteurs) associés exclusivement à la technique ,,coussin d'air'', et les propulseurs électriques (moteur linéaire, dont la partie active peut être placée dans la voie ou sur le véhicule) qui peuvent être du type asynchrone on synchrone et peuvent être associés à tous les types de sustentation – guidage expérimentés à ce jour.

Indépendamment des difficultés de mise au point des composantes et des incertitudes qui en résultent pour les systèmes, quant aux délais de mise au point jusqu'à la phase opérationnelle, et aux coûts qu'il est possible d'envisager, ces systèmes ont par définition le handicap important d'avoir une infrastructure non compatible avec le réseau ferroviaire existant, ce qui les empêche de bénéficier des avantages évoqués plus haut.

Intérêt des différents créneaux de vitesse

Les niveaux de vitesse que permettent d'atteindre les systèmes ferroviaires d'une part, les systèmes non conventionnels d'autre part, étant supposés par hypothèse d'un ordre de grandeur différent, soit par exemple 350 et 500 km/h respectivement, il convient de s'interroger sur leurs avantages et éventuellement leurs inconvénients.

Influence de la vitesse sur le temps de parcours

Il est intéressant de comparer les ordres de grandeur des temps de parcours sur une distance moyenne (600 km par exemple) pour des vitesses moyennes de plus en plus grandes dans la gamme envisagée. On obtient le tableau suivant:

Vitesse moyenne (km/h)	150	200	250	300	400	500
Temps de parcours (minutes)		240	180	144	120	90	72
Gain de temps procuré par un supplément de vitesse de 100 km/h (minutes)		96	60	41	30	18	12

Le gain de temps procuré par un accroissement constant de vitesse (ici 100 km/h) s'amenuise donc très rapidement lorsque la vitesse initiale augmente.

Influence de la vitesse sur la puissance et l'énergie consommée.

Par ailleurs, la puissance nécessaire pour vaincre la résistance de l'air au niveau du sol augmente considérablement avec la vitesse, comme le montre le tableau ci-après, calculé pour une rame de 300 places au gabarit ferroviaire:

Vitesse maximale (km/h)	200	300	400	500
Puissance de propulsion (kW)	1600	5500	12000	23000

L'installation de ces puissances à partir de 400 km/h, soulève des problèmes considérables de poids (moteurs et convertisseurs électriques) et d'encombrement (volume de ces équipements). Or les expériences récentes effectuées sur les systèmes à sustentation électro-magnétique ou électro-dynamique montrent qu'à ces vitesses, les traînées électro-magnétiques de sustentation atteignent des valeurs d'un ordre de grandeur comparable à celles de la traînée aérodynamique. C'est donc une puissance double de la puissance de propulsion qu'il conviendrait d'envisager, ou même triple de celle-ci

pour les systèmes à mauvais rendement électrique.

Il y a donc là, à performances égales, un handicap important pour les techniques à sustentation électromagnétique.

Par ailleurs tous les coûts et consommations liés à la puissance augmentent avec la vitesse; c'est le cas en particulier de l'énergie, dont les modes non conventionnels sont fort peu économes. En se limitant au contraire à des vitesses de l'ordre de 300 km/h, on reste dans le domaine des moteurs rotatifs classiques à bon rendement, et avec le système ferroviaire on fait bien évidemment l'économie des consommations d'énergie pour réaliser les fonctions de sustentation et de guidage.

C'est ainsi que pour réaliser le temps de trajet en 2 heures sur les 425 km de la ligne nouvelle Paris – Lyon la consommation d'énergie électrique par siège kilomètre offert, s'établit à 11 grammes d'équivalent pétrole, soit environ 0,05 kWh.

Conclusion

Indépendamment des problèmes techniques rapidement évoqués ci-dessus on peut schématiser la comparaison entre TGV et systèmes non conventionnels (SNC) selon deux cas de figures différents:

– soit en restant dans le domaine des vitesses accessibles aux techniques ferroviaires, c'est-à-dire jusque 350 km/h environ. Dans ce cas, la concurrence entre SNC et TGV peut s'apprécier principalement sur le plan des coûts. Les SNC sont plus chers que les TGV sur 3 postes au moins: investissements d'infrastructures en zones urbaines, puissance de sustentation-guidage (traînées induites), consommations d'énergie. Par ailleurs, les frais de personnel et les frais généraux sont du même ordre de grandeur dans les deux systèmes, puisque la qualité de service est comparable. Les SNC ne peuvent présenter d'intérêt que si sur d'autres postes de dépenses, leurs coûts sont notablement plus bas que ceux des TGV: investissements d'infrastructures en rase campagne, entretien de la voie et des véhicules. Or, si cela est effectivement probable pour les coûts d'entretien, il est douteux qu'il en soit de même à caractéristique de tracé identique, pour le coût d'établissement de l'infrastructure,

– soit en supposant que la SNC offrirait une qualité de service, en terme de vitesse, très supérieure à celle du TGV, dans la gamme de 400 à 500 km/h de vitesse moyenne. De tels niveaux de vitesse exigent des caractéristiques de tracé coûteuses et des puissances très importantes, qui impliquent probablement le recours à des techniques de voie active; les coûts supplémentaires correspondants sont à mettre en regard de la fraction du marché qui requiert un tel niveau de qualité.

Il semble qu'une telle fraction soit relativement faible et on peut s'interroger sur le fait de savoir si elle justifie à elle seule les coûts correspondants.

Par ailleurs, la non compatibilité constitue pour la SNC un handicap important, qui peut cependant être résolu dans certains cas.

Cependant si, en raison des éléments évoqués ci-dessus, il paraît illusoire d'escompter des développements commerciaux de SNC à court et moyen terme, les recherches correspondantes peuvent présenter un intérêt éventuel pour le grand avenir.

EVALUATION DES COUTS DU SYSTEME
FERROVIAIRE À GRANDE VITESSE

Si l'augmentation de la vitesse (et de la fréquence) a une influence largement positive sur les niveaux de trafic interurbain de voyageurs, et si la réalisation de vitesses comprises entre 300 et 350 km/h en service commercial est possible dans un avenir très proche, en recourant à la technique ferroviaire, il reste à s'assurer que les coûts correspondants restent dans les limites tels qu'ils conduisent à une rentabilité suffisante des capitaux à investir.

Structure des coûts: méthodologie

Certains éléments de coût sont parfaitement calculables, car les phénomènes qui leur donnent naissance sont identiques dans le chemin de fer traditionnel. C'est le cas en particulier des coûts variables en fonction du temps d'utilisation: main d'oeuvre (conduite et accompagnement des trains notamment), nettoyage et entretien des aménagements intérieurs des voitures (propreté, entretien des sièges et revêtements des sols et parois, équipements d'éclairage et de climatisation), entretien des appareillages fixes ou suspendus (réservoirs, robinetterie, équipements pneumatiques et électriques sur caisse, automatismes divers).

D'autres éléments sont connus au niveau du coût unitaire. C'est le cas par exemple de l'énergie. Il convient alors d'en évaluer les consommations. On peut classer dans cette catégorie les coûts d'entretien de la voie, des équipements non suspendus des trains (organes de roulement, équipements sur bogies, freins, pantographes), des équipements de liaison (suspensions, transmissions mécaniques, attelages), ainsi que les parties extérieures des caisses (peintures, glaces, joints, appareillages extérieurs). Pour ces équipements en effet, il existe un coût unitaire d'intervention connu, mais il est nécessaire de procéder à des expérimentations en service réel afin d'évaluer la fréquence et l'importance de ces interventions.

Avant de procéder à de telles expérimentations qui pourraient se révéler inutilement onéreuses en cas d'insuccès, il convient néanmoins de procéder à des évaluations préalables pour lesquelles la participation de techniciens expérimentés est absolument nécessaire. Grâce à une telle expertise, qui doit être conduite avec prudence et réalisme, il a été possible d'évaluer un ordre de grandeur raisonnable des coûts.

Ultérieurement, après avoir acquis la conviction par cette approche que les ordres de grandeur ainsi dégagés étaient raisonnables, la SNCF s'est engagée dans la construction de prototypes et dans un programme d'expérimentation à grandes vitesses pour confirmer et préciser ces premières évaluations.

Modèle de coûts: vitesse optimale

On distingue trois types de coûts: les coûts de construction de la ligne, les coûts d'exploitation, et les coûts annexes du transport.

Coût de construction de la ligne

Ce coût est fonction essentiellement des caractéristiques géométriques en plan, en profil et en travers de la voie. Celles-ci dépendent non seulement de la vitesse maximale envisagée, mais aussi de la disparité des trafics. Ainsi, une voie construite pour acheminer simultanément des trains de voyageurs à 300 km/h et des trains lourds de marchandises à 120 km/h devra avoir des courbes de grand rayon (car les devers qui pourraient être acceptés sur les rayons plus faibles par le matériel voyageur à grande vitesse ne conviendraient pas au matériel marchandises) et des déclivités faibles (5 à 8%) déterminées par les limites de traction en rampe des locomotives remorquant les trains les plus lourds. Une telle voie sera d'autant plus difficile à inscrire dans le relief que celui-ci sera plus accidenté: la proportion d'ouvrages d'art (tunnel, viaducs) de déblais et de remblais deviendra vite très importante et pèsera lourdement sur le coût de construction de la ligne.

Si au contraire on spécialise la ligne au trafic des voyageurs à grande vitesse, on peut tracer des rayons plus courts en compensant la force centrifuge par un

devers acceptable, et des déclivités plus fortes (35‰) autorisées par le taux important de motorisation des essieux. Il en résulte un abaissement considérable des frais de terrassements et d'ouvrages d'art. Par ailleurs, ces caractéristiques géométriques sont voisines de celles des autoroutes, ce qui permet le jumelage des deux infrastructures et procure d'intéressantes possibilités de réduction des coûts. Enfin, cette option facilite l'évaluation des coûtes et leur contrôle.

Le coût d'une voie ferrée double ayant les caractéristiques précédentes, comprenant: acquisitions de terrain, terrassements et ouvrages d'art, voie sur traverses en béton (rail de 60 kg/m), installations de sécurité, d'électrification, d'entretien et de voierie de service, clôture complète (pas de passages à niveau) se situe à environ 8 MF/km (hors TVA) dans les conditions économiques actuelles, et dans les conditions françaises sur le plan de la topographie et de la densité d'habitat.

Coûts directs d'exploitation

Ce sont les coûts liés au matériel roulant et à son exploitation. Ils comprennent:
– des coûts annuels fixes qui ne dépendent que du volume du parc nécessaire à l'exploitation,
– des coûts dépendant de l'utilisation, appréciée sur une base temporelle ou kilométrique.

Coûts annexes

On regroupe sous ce vocable l'ensemble des coûts occasionnés par le trafic, mais qui ne sont pas liés directement au matériel roulant et à son utilisation.

Il est possible, grâce aux lois de variation de ces diverses natures de coûts, d'établir un modèle mathématique permettant de calculer une vitesse optimale en fonction de paramètres techniques ou de paramètres relatifs à la demande et de coûts unitaires spécifiques.

L'un de ces paramètres de la demande joue un rôle fondamental: la valeur du temps. Grâce à celle-ci, on peut tester l'adaption de tel ou tel mode à tel ou tel segment du marché des voyages. Par exemple, il est possible de constater que la vitesse de 500 km/h est optimale pour une valeur du temps très élevée – ce qui signifie que, avec la distribution actuelle des valeurs du temps, le segment de marché intéressé est très étroit.

Le modèle a été exploité pour le TGV, et pour les valeurs moyennes du temps de l'ensemble de la clientèle ferroviaire et aérienne. On a pu ainsi établir que la vitesse moyenne optimale à l'horizon 1980 – 2000 évoluerait entre 250 et 300 km/h avec une dispersion allant de 230 km/h environ pour le voyageur de 2ème classe à 350 km/h pour le voyageur de 1ère classe. Ces ordres de grandeur ont été confirmés par des études semblables faites par l'UIC.

Expérimentations

Pour conforter ses évaluations concernant les coûts, la SNCF a passé commande, en juillet 1969, d'une rame expérimentale à turbines, le TGV 001. Cette rame, livrée en 1972, a effectué en trois ans plus de 320.000 km à des vitesses supérieures à 200 km/h, la vitesse de 300 km/h ayant été dépassée au cours de 156 marches d'essais. En 1974 et 1975, une automotrice électrique, la Z 7001, venait compléter ces essais pour étudier un nouveau bogie et une nouvelle transmission. Elle a effectué en 2 ans près de 275.000 km, dont 39 marches à des vitesses supérieures à 300 km/h. C'est donc une expérience portant sur 600.000 km parcourus à une vitesse supérieure à 200 km/h, qui a été menée à bien au cours des quatre années précédentes.

Ces essais avaient d'ailleurs été précédés, avant la mise en service du Capitole à 200 km/h, de nombreux essais de stabilité et de captation de courant à la vitesse de 230 km/h sur du matériel moteur et remorqué de série. De même, avant la mise en service en mars 1970 de la première génération du turbotrain ETC sur la ligne Paris - Cherbourg, le turbotrain expérimental TGS avait permis d'explorer le domaine des vitesses jusqu'à 250 km/h. Enfin un programme d'essais allant jusqu'à 250 km/h s'est déroulé avec la rame RTG 01 simultanément au programme TGV 001.

Programme d'essais du TGV 001
Les objectifs

Le but poursuivi était d'accumuler très rapidement les enseignements nécessaires à la mise au point des rames de série, en poussant jusqu'aux limites l'étude du comportement des organes essentiels afin de procéder au choix des options fondamentales.

Par ailleurs, ces essais devaient permettre de confronter à la réalité les prévisions des études théoriques antérieures, portant sur l'aérodynamisme, la stabilité, les transmissions, l'équipement électrique et le freinage.

La rame expérimentale devait donc permettre de procéder aisément à des réglages progressifs dans une gamme étendue pour un grand nombre de paramètres permettant d'assurer en toute sécurité les fonctions principales: mise en marche et régulation des groupes propulseurs, captation d'air, stabilité du roulement, suspension, transmissions, liaisons caisses-bogies, freinage.

Elle devait également, après mise au point des domaines de sécurité pour l'ensemble des paramètres, permettre de rechercher la combinaison optimale sur le plan de l'endurance compatible avec les performances maximales de vitesse.

Les essais

Ceux-ci se sont déroulés en trois phases:
1 – vérification de bon fonctionnement des composants et réglages à poste fixe ou à faible vitesse,
2 – montée progressive en vitesse (jusqu'à 200 km/h) et amélioration des réglages,
3 – exploration aux limites et essais d'endurance.

C'est évidemment cette dernière phase qui présente le plus d'intérêt. L'exploration aux limites concerne:
– les performances de stabilité, freinage, vitesse, adhérence
– le comportement des groupes propulseurs et des organes de sécurité (boîtes d'essieux, transmissions, liaisons caisse-bogies, organes de suspension, etc.).

Des essais particulièrement approfondis ont porté sur les éléments suivants:
– la stabilité (mesure des efforts transversaux en courbes de différents rayons, aux franchissements d'aiguilles, sur chantiers de nivellement, etc.)
– le freinage (avec toutes les combinaisons permises par les équipements)
– l'adhérence (dans les conditions climatiques les plus diverses).
– l'aérodynamique (écoulements sur les différentes parties de la rame, couche limite, effet de souffle, résistance à l'avancement).

Performances

La vitesse maximale de 318 km/h a été atteinte le 8 décembre 1972. Ce résultat met en évidence les excellentes caractéristiques aérodynamiques de la rame, qui se sont révélées plus favorables que prévu. Il en résulte un gain d'environ 30 km/h par rapport à la vitesse maximale envisagée. Les consommations d'énergie seront donc inférieures à ce qui avait été prévu, ce qui constitue un facteur important d'économie sur le coût d'exploitation.

La stabilité ne constitue pas une qualité constante, mais évolue en fonction de l'usure des tables de roulement. Aussi, après avoir procédé aux réglages initiaux (conicité de 1/40, empattement du bogie, rigidité de la suspension, amortissement anti-lacet, charges non suspendues) et constaté qu'ils ne conduisaient pas à des instabilités importantes dans la gamme des vitesses envisagées, il y avait lieu d'étudier leur évolution dans le temps, au cours des essais d'endurance. Ceux-ci se sont montrés satisfaisants, mais ils ont fait apparaître l'importance de paramètres que le TGV 001 ne permettait pas d'explorer dans une gamme suffisamment large: la masse suspendue du bogie, son empattement, la rigidité des liaisons entre essieux et châssis de bogie. Aussi a-t-il été décidé d'explorer ces paramètres sur un nouvel engin expérimental, la Z 7001.

Le freinage s'est également révélé excellent, permettant une décélération moyenne allant de 0,91 m/s² à 300 km/h, à 1 m/s² à 220 km/h; grâce à un ensemble de 4 types de freins pouvant fonctionner suivant toutes les combinaisons: frein rhéostatique, frein rotatif à courants de Foucault, patins électromagnétiques, frein pneumatique à sabots, sans provoquer d'échauffements dangereux pour les tables de roulement. On a pu observer que l'adhérence ne constituait pas, dans la limite des vitesses pratiquées, un obstacle à une progression plus importante de la vitesse.

Dans le domaine des nuisances, le bruit a fait l'objet d'études approfondies, qui permettent d'affirmer que les normes sont respectées en toutes circonstances: le TGV 001 apparaît plus silencieux à 300 km/h qu'un train classique à 200 km/h.

On a pu également constater le bon comportement des organes mettant en jeu la sécurité: outre les bogies, les liaisons entre caisses, les attaches d'amortisseurs, etc.

Programme d'essais de la Z 7001

Comme il a été dit ci-dessus, le programme d'essais de la Z 7001 visait essentiellement l'étude du comportement d'un bogie de plus grand empattement, plus léger et mieux découplé de la caisse, afin de réduire son agressivité par rapport à la voie, d'améliorer sa stabilité, et si possible le confort des voyageurs comme le laissaient pressentir les modèles mathématiques et les expériences antérieures.

Par ailleurs, dans le domaine du freinage, il y avait lieu de poursuivre l'expérimentaion d'un nouveau système de frein linéaire à courants de Foucault sans contact avec le rail, susceptible de développer une puissance de freinage deux fois plus élevée par unité de longueur que celle du patin électromagnétique équipant le TGV 001 (lequel prend appui sur le rail).

Enfin s'ajoutait à ces objectifs de comportement aux limites l'étude habituelle relative à l'endurance des organes dont dépendent la sécurité et le bon fonctionnement du véhicule, ainsi que la recherche de la technologie optimale pour une utilisation commerciale.

Les essais se sont déroulés en trois phases, comme pour le TGV 001. Ils ont permis d'obtenir une stabilité latérale de caisse très satisfaisante aux très grandes vitesses, par simple réglage des amortisseurs transversaux, après avoir élucidé les lois de variations de la vitesse critique en fonction du parcours d'usure des tables de roulement (paramètre imputable au seul véhicule), de la conicité équivalente (paramètre intégrant en plus les caractéristiques de pose de la voie: écartement et angle de pose) et du couple d'amortissement anti-lacet.

Compte tenu de ces bons résultats, il a été décidé de poursuivre les essais du TGV 001 en dotant celui-ci de bogies identiques à ceux de la Z 7001.

L'ensemble des essais a permis de définir les caractéristiques de deux rames de pré-série qui seront pratiquement identiques au matériel retenu en définition pour l'exploitation commerciale.

LA LIGNE NOUVELLE PARIS – LYON

L'ensemble des considérations qui précèdent a été utilisé pour définir ce que serait l'impact sur la demande de transport, de la création d'une ligne nouvelle entre Paris et Lyon utilisant, ainsi qu'il a été dit, les pénétrations urbaines existantes, de façon à définir les caractéristiques optimales du service sur cette ligne et à évaluer la rentabilité d'un tel projet. De façon plus précise, l'ensemble des études économiques a été mené selon une démarche qui peut se synthétiser selon le schéma de la *planche 2* qui met en évidence les principales interactions entre les divers éléments pris en compte.

Les prévisions de trafic

Les flux élémentaires de trafic intéressés par le projet peuvent se regrouper en fonction des données de géographie humaine de l'implantation de la ligne nouvelle et des lignes existantes selon trois ,,axes":

– Paris – Lyon,
– Paris – Savoie,
– Paris – Bourgogne.

Le premier regroupe l'ensemble des courants de trafic qui pourraient emprunter la totalité de la ligne nouvelle, le second ceux qui l'emprunteraient sur le tronçon Paris – Mâcon, le troisième est relatif au tronçon Paris –

St-Florentin. Une excellente visualisation de ces trois axes est fournie par ce que nous appelons ,,l'arbre à boules" (planche 3).

En nombre de voyageurs par fer, l'importance relative des 3 axes se situe comme suit:

Axe Paris – Lyon	: 60%
Axe Paris – Savoie	: 17%
Axe Paris – Bourgogne	: 23%

Pour les études, on a défini une ,,situation de référence" sans ligne nouvelle qui repose sur une projection tendancielle de la qualité de service des modes existants (vitesse, fréquence, temps d'acrès), de leurs prix de vente et de la valeur du temps ainsi que des trafics en cause, à l'horizon de la date de mise en service de la ligne nouvelle, prévue pour 1982-1983.

Après avoir ainsi défini la situation de référence, pour chaque mode (fer 1ère classe, fer 2ème classe, avion, route), on détermine, à l'aide des modèles économétriques, les répercussions de la mise en service de la ligne nouvelle:

– reports de trafics ferroviaires de l'ancienne ligne sur la nouvelle,
– reports de l'avion sur le train,
– reports de la route sur le train,
– induction de trafics nouveaux.

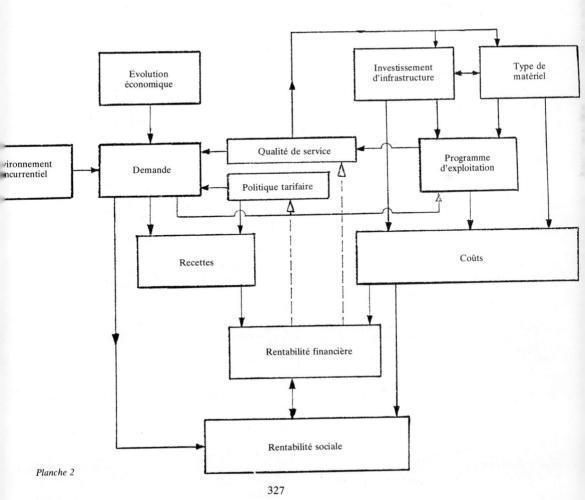

Planche 2

327

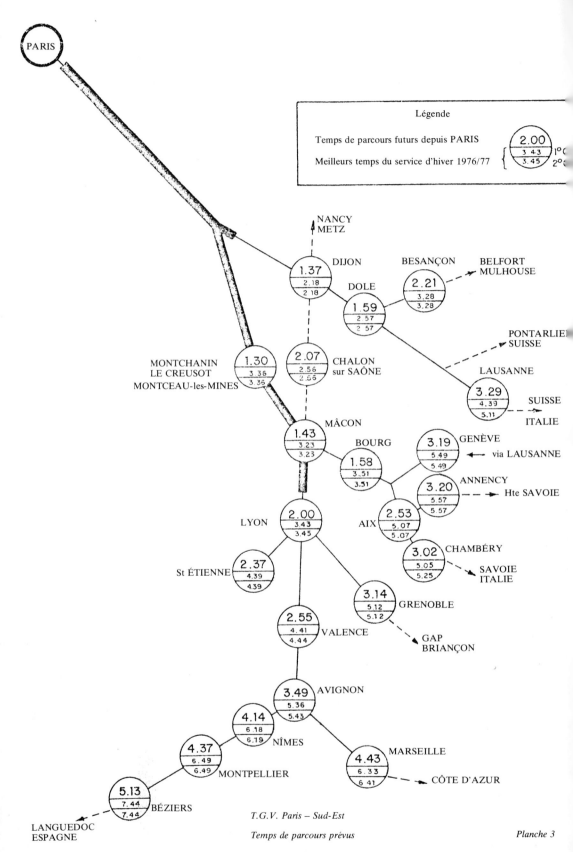

PARIS

NANCY
METZ

DIJON
$\begin{array}{c} 1.37 \\ \hline 2.18 \\ \hline 2.18 \end{array}$

BESANÇON
$\begin{array}{c} 2.21 \\ \hline 3.28 \\ \hline 3.28 \end{array}$

BELFORT
MULHOUSE

DOLE
$\begin{array}{c} 1.59 \\ \hline 2.57 \\ \hline 2.57 \end{array}$

PONTARLIER
SUISSE

MONTCHANIN
LE CREUSOT
MONTCEAU-les-MINES
$\begin{array}{c} 1.30 \\ \hline 3.36 \\ \hline 3.36 \end{array}$

$\begin{array}{c} 2.07 \\ \hline 2.56 \\ \hline 2.56 \end{array}$
CHALON
sur SAÔNE

LAUSANNE
$\begin{array}{c} 3.29 \\ \hline 4.39 \\ \hline 5.11 \end{array}$
SUISSE
ITALIE

MÂCON
$\begin{array}{c} 1.43 \\ \hline 3.23 \\ \hline 3.23 \end{array}$

BOURG
$\begin{array}{c} 1.58 \\ \hline 3.51 \\ \hline 3.51 \end{array}$

$\begin{array}{c} 3.19 \\ \hline 5.49 \\ \hline 5.49 \end{array}$
GENÈVE
← via LAUSANNE

$\begin{array}{c} 3.20 \\ \hline 5.57 \\ \hline 5.57 \end{array}$
ANNENCY
Hte SAVOIE

LYON
$\begin{array}{c} 2.00 \\ \hline 3.43 \\ \hline 3.45 \end{array}$

AIX
$\begin{array}{c} 2.53 \\ \hline 5.07 \\ \hline 5.07 \end{array}$

$\begin{array}{c} 3.02 \\ \hline 5.05 \\ \hline 5.25 \end{array}$
CHAMBÉRY
SAVOIE
ITALIE

St ÉTIENNE
$\begin{array}{c} 2.37 \\ \hline 4.39 \\ \hline 4.39 \end{array}$

$\begin{array}{c} 3.14 \\ \hline 5.12 \\ \hline 5.12 \end{array}$
GRENOBLE

$\begin{array}{c} 2.55 \\ \hline 4.41 \\ \hline 4.44 \end{array}$
VALENCE

GAP
BRIANÇON

$\begin{array}{c} 3.49 \\ \hline 5.36 \\ \hline 5.43 \end{array}$
AVIGNON

$\begin{array}{c} 4.14 \\ \hline 6.18 \\ \hline 6.19 \end{array}$
NÎMES

$\begin{array}{c} 4.37 \\ \hline 6.49 \\ \hline 6.49 \end{array}$
MONTPELLIER

MARSEILLE
$\begin{array}{c} 4.43 \\ \hline 6.33 \\ \hline 6.41 \end{array}$
CÔTE D'AZUR

$\begin{array}{c} 5.13 \\ \hline 7.44 \\ \hline 7.44 \end{array}$
BÉZIERS

LANGUEDOC
ESPAGNE

T.G.V. Paris – Sud-Est

Temps de parcours prévus

Planche 3

Les résultats de ces projections conduisent aux prévisions de trafic suivantes:

Situation de référence

	Trafics observés[1]			Trafic projeté[1] en situation de référence
	1969	1972	1975	1982-1983
Fer 1ère classe	2.533	2.839	3.350	3.992
Fer 2ème classe	7.948	8.662	9.950	11.513
Avion	1.942	2.779	3.502	6.218
Total	12.423	14.280	16.802	21.723

Situation avec ligne nouvelle

	Trafics en 1982-1983[1]
Fer 1ère classe sur ligne nouvelle	6.060
Fer 1ère classe sur ligne ancienne	870
Fer 2ème sur ligne nouvelle	10.840
Fer 2ème classe sur ligne ancienne	3.800
Total général FER	21.570
Total Fer ligne nouvelle	16.900
Avion résiduel	4.490
Avion détourné	1.730
Avion antérieur	6.220
Total fer + avion	26.060

La répartition du trafic de la ligne nouvelle se ferait de la manière suivante:

	Trafics en 1982-1983[1]
Trafioc reporté de l'ancienne ligne	
1ère classe	3.130
2ème classe	7.710
Trafic reporté de l'avion	
1ère classe	1.730
Trafic reporté de la route et trafic induit par la ligne nouvelle	
1ère classe	1.200
2ème classe	3.130
Total	16.900

[1] en milliers de voyageurs par an.

Simultanément, le report de 70% environ du trafic voyageurs de l'ancienne ligne sur la ligne nouvelle permettra de résoudre le problème de la saturation de la ligne actuelle, qui se traduit par une détérioration du service non seulement des voyageurs, mais surtout des marchandises et pour ces dernières, par des augmentations de coûts importantes résultant de la nécessité de recourir à des itinéraires de détournements plus longs et moins bien équipés.

Programme d'exploitation

Les études de trafic global annuel par classe et par relation ont été complétées par l'étude de la distribution temporelle du trafic par mois, semaine, jour de la semaine, et à l'intérieur de la journée, par tranches horaires, afin de déterminer avec suffisamment de précision les moyens d'exploitation à mettre en oeuvre, compte tenu des performances réalisables.

On a ensuite bâti un programme d'exploitation permettant de satisfaire la demande, qui donne à la fois l'importance du parc nécessaire et les éléments de pro-

ductivité moyenne (nombre de kilomètres, d'heures, de parcours effectués annuellement par rame) qui permettent de calculer les coûts d'exploitation ainsi que la qualité de la desserte en termes de fréquence.

Les coûts du projet
L'infrastructure
A l'exclusion des investissements liés aux installations terminales, le coût de construction de la ligne nouvelle s'élève, dans les conditions économiques du 1.01.1976 à 3 317 MF soit 8,5 MF/km, frais généraux et taxes incluses.

La décompositon de ce coût en ses principales composantes, est la suivante, en pourcentage:

Acquisition de terrains	: 5,8%
Retablissement des voiries traversées	: 6,0%
Plate-forme (terrassements)	: 28,7%
Ouvrages d'art	: 22,0%
Superstructures (voie, signalisation)	: 27,3%
Electrification	: 10,2%

Le matériel roulant
Le matériel roulant sera constitué par des rames automotrices articulées composées chacune de 2 motrices aux extrémités et de 8 remorques, et comportant 13 bogies dont 6 moteurs, capables de circuler à la fois en courant continu 1500 volts et en courant alternatif 25000 volts Hz.

Leur capacité totale sera de 384 places pour une masse de 380 tonnes à vide et leur puissance, de 6.300 kW, leur permettra de circuler à une vitesse de 260 km/h.

Leur coût, résultant d'un marché passé, est de 22,2 MF, hors taxes, dans les conditions du 1.01.1976, soit environ 58.000 F/place offerte.

Coût d'exploitation des rames
On se bornera à indiquer les postes essentiels du coût d'exploitation des rames; pour un parcours annuel prévu de 380.000 km effectué à la fois sur la ligne nouvelle et sur le réseau existant, ils se situent aux niveaux suivants, par rame-km:
énergie: 2,5 F/km
entretien: 7,3 F/km

Rentabilité du projet
La rentabilité du projet trouve son origine dans trois sources différentes:
– la réduction des coûts d'acheminement du trafic ferroviaire préexistant à la ligne nouvelle et reporté sur celle-ci,
– l'apport de trafic nouveau, en provenance des autres modes, ou engendré par l'amélioration des conditions de desserte,
– la réduction des coûts d'acheminement du trafic marchandises obtenue en allégeant la ligne actuelle de la majeure partie de son trafic voyageurs.

Au total, la rentabilité immédiate d'un tel projet se situe approximativement à 15% et si les échéances prévues à l'heure actuelle pour sa mise en service sont respectées, l'ensemble des investissements engagés sera récupéré avant 1990, en termes de comptabilité d'entreprise.

Sur le plan collectif, l'intérêt en est également considérable; compte tenu des avantages monétaires ou des avantages de temps apportés aux usagers, la rentabilité sociale du projet, en valeur actualisée sur 20 ans dépasse largement 30%.

Research issues in rail transport operations

by

CHARLES E. TAYLOR

Association of American Railroads

INTRODUCTION

This paper will examine some current research issues in North American rail transport operations and some on-going and anticipated research activities related to those issues. The specific research activities examined were selected to illustrate some issues associated with research priorities, approach, data requirements and analytic methodology.

A convenient framework for structuring a review of some of these issues and research activities is the so-called car cycle. Car cycle, as used here, refers to the sequence of communication, decision and physical activities which is repeated each time freight is transported by a rail vehicle. A typical load-to-load car cycle begins with a shipper's order for an empty car, includes such intermediate cycle elements as the assignment of an empty car to fill the order, placement of the car at the shipper's rail siding, release of the loaded car by the shipper, followed by the initial, intermediate and final terminal and line haul handling of the car over one or more railroads and the placement of the car at the receiver's siding. The cycle is completed when the car is unloaded, released back to the rail carrier and, finally, reassigned to a new shipper car order (see Exhibit 1).

This car cycle framework is particularly appropriate in light of the growing recognition of the need for more

Exhibit 1 – Sequence of a typical load-to-load freight car cycle
1. Shipper orders empty car for loading
2. Railroad assigns empty car to shipper's order
3. Railroad delivers empty to shipper's siding
4. Shipper loads car
5. Shipper notifies railroad car is loaded and ready to move
6. Railroad pulls loaded car from shipper's siding, moves it to (origin) terminal
7. Car is processed for outbound movement from origin terminal
8. Car is hauled to intermediate yard by road train
9. Car is processed for outbound movement from intermediate terminal
10. Car is hauled to next terminal where it is interchanged with connecting railroad
11. Connecting railroad hauls car to destination terminal
12. Car is delivered to receiver's siding
13. Receiver unloads car
14. Receiver notifies delivering railroad car is unloaded and ready to move
15. Railroad assigns destination to empty car
16. Railroad pulls empty car from receiver's siding
17. Railroad delivers empty to new shipper for loading

attention, and research, directed to the disposition of the individual freight car as it moves through the rail network, both loaded and empty. Too frequently, past attention was directed almost exclusively to optimization of train operations, to the neglect of the physical and economic utilization of individual freight cars and the closely related dock-to-dock service provided to rail customers.

Dramatic increases in the costs of freight car ownership and operation, combined with increased loss of business to competing modes, have resulted in a signifi-

cant shift in research emphasis to the physical and economic utilization of the freight car as it cycles from load to load throughout its lifespan. An important example of this new emphasis was the establishment, in 1975, of the Freight Car Utilization Program. This Program, which is jointly supported by North American railroads, shippers, labor, and government, is conducting research in such areas as the definition and measurement of utilization, the design and development of a system to collect and analyze car cycle data, improved freight car information and control systems, the effects of car service loading restrictions on utilization, and the relationship between car utilization and service reliability. [1] [2]

CAR CYCLE ANALYSIS

An initial of the Freight Car Utilization Program is the development of a system to continuously capture and analyze data on a sample of freight cars as they move throughout the rail network. A primary objective of this system is to provide the identification and quantification of transport operation problems associated with the movement cycles of selected homogeneous car groups. The system will thereby provide a quantitative basis for the identification of research needs and priorities. The system will also support analyses of specific research experiments designed to correct or minimize such problems, by providing a measurement system to determine the effects of experimental changes on car cycles.

Movement data on some 8,500 cars have been reported to this system since March, 1976. This system will collect, edit and logically sequence car movement data to create complete load-to-load car cycles for each car in the sample fleet. For a typical load-to-load cycle record for a car in the sample, the location data would be recorded for each of the cycle events described in Exhibit 1. Thus, the complete load-to-load cycle could be examined to determine the amount of time the car spent under shipper control, how long the car was in the origin terminal, in each intermediate terminal, how long the consignee took to unload the car, and how long the empty car then took to move to its next loading point.

The sample of some 8,500 cars was selected to provide statistically significant cycle data for specified subsets of the freight car fleet. The freight car characteristics used to partition the freight car fleet for subsample studies were car type, car age, and type of service. Type of service was defined by both commodity carried and by the degree of carrier and shipper control over car movement by partitioning the fleet into three groups: free-running, assigned and private cars. Thus, for selected combinations of car type, car age, car assignment and commodity, analysis of the distributions of overall load-to-load cycle times or specific cycle event times can provide valuable insight for the identification of car movement and utilization problems. Equally important, the same system can be used to evaluate the effects of **changes** introduced into the transportation system which were designed to improve cycle times.

The attention and resources that are being devoted to this car cycle analysis system are in response to a growing appreciation of the complexity of the rail transport system and the attendant need for a more comprehensive and quantitative approach to the analysis of the operations of that system. The judgement of those capable and experienced in rail operations and analysis is an essential ingredient to this research, however, the complexity of the rail operating network demands that the researchers also have available data systems designed to identify the source and magnitude of network operating problems, and to measure the total system effects of changes designed to reduce those problems.

Some preliminary analyses of such car cycle data have helped document the need for further research in such areas as empty car distribution, and rail yard and terminal operations. The remainder of this paper willl discuss some of the on-going research and perceived research needs in these two major areas on the premise that, collectively, they contain a fairly representative mixture of some of the more important research issues related to rail transportation operations.

EMPTY CAR DISTRIBUTION

Car cycle data frequently reveal inefficient handling during the empty portion of the cycle. A major source of this inefficiency is lack of adequate information and techniques for the efficient matching of empty cars to shipper car orders. Examination of this process has led to the identification of research needs in three areas:

1. Forecasting of shipper demand for empty cars,
2. Forecasting of the supply of empty cars, and
3. Efficient decision rules and assignment algorithms to match supply and demand.

Research to date has concentrated primarily on the first and third needs.

Demand Forecasting

A current project, supported jointly by the Federal Railroad Administration (FRA) of the U.S. Department of Transportation, and the Association of American Railroads, has provided valuable insights into the problems associated with shipper demand information and forecasting, and has resulted in the development of a car demand forecasting model which has significantly advanced the state of the art. [3]

The analysis of the data collected for this research, combined with discussions with rail shippers and railroad personnel, led to the following conclusions:

1. Most railroad forecasts of shipper demand for empty cars are based on historical car loading data. Such forecasts typically understate demand, since the percentage of demand not filled is ignored. Such data is also misleading since it ignores substitution of equipment, i.e., it describes equipment loaded rather than equipment requested. These observations led to a recommendation to record historical shipper car order data in addition to historical car loading data.

2. Analysis of shipper car order data indicated that shipper demand is highly variable and lead time on orders extremely short. Analysis of sample data collected on two major railroads for this project revealed fluctuations in demand ranging from plus or minus 50% of the average, and the average lead time for the order data was only 1.5 days. This combination of widely fluctuating demand and short lead time makes it extremely difficult for rail carriers to efficiently distribute equipment.

3. Since most areas unload either more or less cars than they load, railroads must maintain large inventories of empty cars at loading points and continously move empty cars from surplus to deficit areas.

4. The size and impact of the time lag to recognize and react to changes in demand patterns can be reduced if potential surplus and deficit areas can be forecasted and car flows adjusted to reduce imbalances before they occur.

As a result of this research, a forecasting system was developed which was designed to be used as part of the freight car allocation and distribution process of major railroads. The forecasting system objectives included accuracy sufficient to aid empty car distribution, information requirements consistent with the capabilities of rail information systems, and simplicity and robustness sufficient to require only infrequent maintenance and updating of the estimation and forecasting algorithms imbedded in the information system.

The forecasting model developed provides one, two, and three-week ahead forecasts of empty car demand, by car type. The model utilizes three sources of information:

1. Historical car loadings,
2. Historical car orders, and
3. A subjective order forecast by the local railroad agent.

More specifically, the demand forecast is produced by a linear composite model using as input variables, (1) a loading forecast based on previous loadings, (2) an order forecast based on previous orders, and (3) the local railroad agent's subjective forecast of orders. The first two forecasts are developed using discrete linear stochastic models, often referred to as Box-Jenkins Models. The model is of the form:

$$O_t = W_0 + W_1 \hat{L}_t + W_2 \hat{O}_t + W_3 A\hat{O}_t$$

where:

$O_t =$ the number of cars of a given type ordered during week t

$\hat{L}_t =$ the forecast of loadings during week t given by a loadings forecasting model using actual loading data

$\hat{O}_t =$ the forecast of car orders during week t given by an orders forecasting model using actual order data

$A\hat{O}_t =$ the subjective agent order forecast for week t

W_0, W_1, W_2, W_3 are coefficients estimated by regression analysis.

This composite model has the logical advantage of using predictor variables which are subject to somewhat offsetting biases. Loadings tend to be biased downward as they neglect unfilled demand, whereas orders tend to be biased upward as shippers overorder to protect their requirements. Additionally, the local railroad agent is in a unique postion to assess the probable effects of irregular occurrences such as strikes and severe weather conditons. (The mean absolute forecast error for the study sample of 27 region-car type combinations was 11.77% of the mean weekly car orders.)

Interestingly, for the 12 car types operating in six geographic regions examined during this research study, an autoregressive model of order 1 [AR(1)] provided the best all-around forecast model for both the loadings forecast ($\hat{L}_t$) and the orders forecast ($\hat{O}_t$).

Plans are currently under development to install a linear composite forecasting model of the type described herein on one or more North American systems for demonstration and further development.

A critical limitation of existing rail information systems to the implementation of any such forecasting models is the lack of current and historical car order data. For the model described, data on both loadings and car orders are required for the previous 26-week period. Such data are usually recorded for car loadings. Car orders typically enter the rail system at the local level. However, these orders are usually transmitted to the central data system only if the order cannot be filled by an empty car available in the local area. Even the orders reported to the central system are purged once they have been acted upon. Historically, car orders have not been considered accurate measures of demand, and this attitude has been carried into the design of most rail information systems.

Supply Forecasting

There is a recognized need for improved techniques to forecast the supply of empty rail cars for more efficient distribution and to minimize empty car inventory requirements at terminal loading points. Empty cars are moved to loading points to fill anticipated demand whenever local car availability is estimated to be inadequate. Too frequently, such moves are inefficient because, subsequent to their initiation, unpredicted changes occur in supply or demand. As an example, a railroad may assign and begin transporting more empty cars to a terminal than will ultimately be required because predictions of cars received in interchange from connecting railroads, or cars released empty by local rail customers were too low. Since techniques currently employed to forecast both supply and demand are imprecise, most railroads tends to protect their customers by maintaining unnecessarily large empty car inventories at terminal loading points. With the average purchase price of freight cars now in excess of $25,000, there is strong economic incentive to develop more efficient methods to forecast car supply as well as demand, in order to improve the utilization of such equipment.

A car supply forecasting system would likely be a composite model with input from such sources as:

1. real-time terminal inventory of empties on hand,
2. cars estimated to be released from local cleaning and repair facilities,
3. estimates of empty cars to be released by local customers,
4. estimated arrivals of empties enroute to a terminal from points within a railroad, and
5. estimated arrivals of empty cars from connecting railroads.

A task to develop an empty car supply forecasting procedure which can be widely used with existing or planned railroad data is currently under consideration for the next phase of the Freight Car Utilization Research Program.

Empty Car Assignment

The distribution of empty cars on most North American railroads is based on variations of the "flow-rule" concept. Flow rules are essentially a set of instructions which specify the disposition of empty cars for every terminal point on a rail system. These rules are now based on best available estimates of the location and magnitude of empty car surpluses and empty car deficits, i.e., terminal-specific supply and demand estimates or forecasts. These rules also attempt to minimize total empty car distribution costs using techniques which range from fairly fixed sets of empirically derived distribution rules which designate preferred supply points for each demand point, to frequent updates of the rules using linear programming techniques. Some railroads have operating control systems which permit flow rule adjustments one or more times per day, whereas other roads make such adjustments on a weekly or monthly basis.

At present, most of these flow rules are based on experience and rough estimates of average terminal area supply and demand by car type.

There has been considerable research and development devoted to improve empty car decision rules and

assignment algorithms. [4] The major constraints to the further development and implementation of such systems appear to be more related to the availability of data necessary for supply and demand forecasting than to the availability of the necessary analytic techniques or operating information and control systems technology.

The functional requirements and specifications of a viable empty car assignment algorithm must take proper account of such factors as:

1. current and anticipated accuracy of supply and demand information and forecasting systems,
2. response time of the rail system to assignments and assignment changes,
3. comparison of costs to maintain local inventories of empty cars with costs to move cars from supply points elsewhere in the rail system, and
4. efficiency requirements of assignment algorithms (computer operating costs).

Proposed research to examine relationships between current and anticipated supply and demand forecasts and allocation logic requirements is currently under consideration by AAR and FRA. Preliminary investigations may include rail network simulations designed to examine the efficiency of various empty car assignment algorithms beginning with assumptions of perfect supply and demand information and progressively degrading forecast quality. Such research would help determine what distribution logic is best suited for various assumptions of uncertainty. A research objective would be the development of heuristics for desensitizing assignment models to avoid unnecessary empty car moves intended to satisfy spurious demand caused by forecast errors.

The assignment algorithms currently available are batch processors. Car orders and location and status data on empty cars may be accumulated for a 24-hour period. The algorithm is then run to generate car assignments. This batch procedure often leads to inefficiencies due to the continuous nature of this process. More frequent iterations of such algorithms would avoid inefficient assignments caused by out-dated empty car supply and demand information. Obviously, the optimum frequency of iterations for assignment algorithms is closely related to achievable levels of forecast accuracy. Thus, requirements for frequent iterations of the empty car assignment process provides incentive for the development of efficient algorithms which require minimum computer processing time.

YARD AND TERMINAL OPERATIONS

Analyses of car cycle data consistently point to yards and terminals as major sources of delay to both loaded and empty car movements. These delays have been identified as the primary cause of transit time unreliability, a major source of complaints by rail transport users. Preliminary examinations have revealed that two of the sources for such delay and unreliability are (1) the management of operations within a classification yard, and (2) the coordination and control of car movements over two or more railroads within a multi-road interchange terminal.

Classification Yards

Considerable research and development have been directed at the operation of classification yards. The emphasis of most of this research and development has been in such areas as improved information and process-control systems. Modern classification yard systems, for example, now have the capability to automatically generate switch lists from verified train consists, to automatically control locomotives engaged in classification switching, and to automatically line switches and control car velocity to insure cars are switched into the correct classification tracks and that they couple to the standing cars in those tracks at the proper velocity. In addition, these systems can monitor cars pulled from the classification track for train makeup and automatically maintain a real-time inventory of the location of every car within the yard. While these systems have contributed significantly to the efficiency of yard operations, substantial opportunities for productivity improvements remain in even the most modern of these automated yards. A major source of this improvement potential derives from the fact that most of the work planning and scheduling, and much of the real-time monitoring of work progress is still performed manually in even the most modern yards. Recognition of this potential has led to plans for research in such areas as computer-based decision systems for the advanced planning and scheduling of yard work.

The productivity of classification yards is extremely sensitive to the human ability of individual supervisors to plan, schedule and monitor yard tasks. These tasks typically include switching cars from receiving tracks to classification tracks, pulling cars from classification tracks to assemble outbound trains, and inspection and repairs of cars and locomotives. Great variability has been observed between individual yard supervisors, with differences of over 30% in the number of cars handled per eight-hour shift not uncommon. These observations confirm the need for research which would examine the types of decisions these supervisors are required to make, the information available upon which to base those decisions, and comparisons of decisions made by the more productive supervisors with those of the less productive. This significant relationship between the "human factor" and productivity suggests opportunities for improved planning and decision aids. The more productive supervisor may be the one who has greater natural ability to mentally visualize, organize and recall the key elements of his yard operation. Once these ability requirements and decision processes are documented and analyzed, it should be possible to develop information and analysis systems to support the management process. Such a management support system could contain current information on yard configuration, locomotive and car inventory, arriving and departing trains, and available work resources such as yard engines and mechanical inspection and repair crews. The system could evaluate work scheduling plans proposed by yard supervisors by simulating them in advance of execution and developing estimates of the results. A more advanced system could actually develop an optimum solution to the yard work planning problems and recommend a sequence of work tasks for consideration by the yard supervisor.

A management support system for yard operations could provide supervisors with continuous monitoring of all important work events, and prompt them whenever new decisions or updated work plans are required. Such a system could also be used for training yard supervisors and as a planning and research tool to evaluate proposed yard system changes.

Terminals

Car and train movements between yards, to and from local rail customers, and between two or more railroads within multi-road interchange terminals are receiving increasing attention by rail researchers. The justification for this growing attention also derives from analysis of car cycles, which consistently point to operations within these large terminal complexes as major sources of delay. A major industry response to these terminal problems has been developed by the Labor-Management Task Force on Rail Transportation, comprised of representatives from railroad labor and management and supported jointly by labor, management and government. This Task Force has established project teams in several large multi-road terminals. These terminal project teams are identifying the sources of delays to car and train movements within these terminals.

Once these sources have been identified, the project teams, working with local rail management and labor, identify the underlying causes of the delays. Specific experiments designed to correct these problems are then developed and proposed. If approved by all affected parties, the experiments are conducted under closely controlled conditions and the effects are carefully measured and analyzed.

This research approach has proven to be very successful. Several terminal project experiments have already resulted in permanent changes in labor agreements and operations which have resulted in substantial reductions in delays and improved service to rail customers. As an example, the average time a car spent in the St. Louis Terminal on the Missouri Pacific Railroad decreased by nearly 25% in the six-month period from March to October, 1975 as a result of this research approach. [5] The St. Louis project on the Missouri Pacific Railroad was the first of these terminal projects. Further testimony to the success of this approach to rail transport research is the recent installation of project teams in the terminals in Chicago, Illinois and Houston, Texas.

The initial requirement for each of these terminal projects is a data analysis system for the evaluation of car movements within the terminal. The experience of the first project team on the Missouri Pacific Railroad in St. Louis established the need for such a data system as essential to both the identification of specific car movement problems and the evaluation of experiments. The system design is oriented to our old friend the car movement cycle. The car cycle within the terminal can begin either when the car arrives at the terminal on a road train or is released by a local customer within the terminal. Intermediate terminal cycle events can include arrivals to and departures from yards within the terminal, and delivery of the car to other rail carriers that also operate within the terminal. The terminal cycle can close with either delivery of the car to a customer within the terminal or its departure from the terminal on a road train.

The AAR currently has under development a data collection and analysis system designed to support the Labor-Management teams in Chicago, St. Louis and Houston. The system will be designed to support project teams in additional terminals as they come on line. The railroads that operate in these terminals will create a weekly magnetic tape record of all car movements on their rails within those terminals from their master car movement data files. These tapes will then be sent to the AAR where they will be loaded into a program that will chronologically sequence the individual cycle elements of each car as it moves through the terminal. Thus, the terminal cycle for a car that moved over more than one railroad within a terminal will be created by merging the cycle event data for that car from each carrier that participated in the movement, in chronological sequence. This terminal cycle data base can then be used to generate reports designed to identify specific car movement problems. The system will provide weekly reports on the movements of car groups which should move through the terminal in the same manner, receiving identical handling. These weekly reports can provide statistics on the distributions of time for the overall terminal cycle and for the individual cycle elements for each homogeneous group of cars. The system will also be designed to generate special reports and support special analyses. Thus, by inputting specific parameter values, the termi-

333

nal project teams can call statistical reports on any one or combination of terminal car movements.

This data collection and analysis system will not only provide for the identification of specific terminal car movement problems, but will also provide insights and quantitative assessments essential to the establishment of research priorities. Once the preliminary problems and priorities have been established, the next step is for the terminal project team, working closely with terminal labor and operating management, to identify the specific characteristics and underlying causes of the high priority research problems that have been identified. Specific experiments to correct or improve these problems are then designed. If all parties that would be affected by the experimental change are willing to proceed with, and participate in, the experiment, and the Labor-Management Task Force on Rail Transportation authorizes the experiment, it is conducted. The effects of the experiment on the total terminal rail network will be measured using the data collection and analysis system. Some experiments may require supplemental data collection and analysis using either the data systems of the participating railroads or manual data collection.

Experiments to date have included both temporary changes in operating procedures, and temporary relaxation of labor agreements. Many of the experiments involved yard-to-yard movements of cars. Cars handled by more than one yard within a terminal frequently experience excessive delay and are not moved consistently. For example, temporary relaxation of labor agreements, which permit more flexible use of terminal switching crews and road train crews for the transfer of cars between yards have proven very successful in reducing the time cars spend in yards. Additional experiments either underway or under consideration involve changes in schedules for intra-terminal movements, revisions in procedures for processing arriving road trains, and the addition of switch engine assignments. All of these experiments are in response to problems initially identified through analysis of the terminal car cycles of specific car groups.

At the completion of each experiment, the data are analyzed to assess the impact of the change on car and train movements. A final report is prepared for review by the Task Force and all directly affected parties. It is then up to local railroad management and labor to review the findings and determine whether permanent changes to operating practices and labor agreements are in everyones' best interest. As mentioned previously, this research approach has already resulted in permanent changes with significant improvements in operations and service to rail customers.

CONCLUSIONS

The research activities and associated problems discussed in this paper were selected to illustrate some of the more important research issues in North American rail transport operations. Among these is the need for more systematic approaches to the identification of research needs and the quantification of those needs to enable the rational establishment of priorities. Too frequently research has been based on the judgement of individuals whose knowledge encompassed only a subset of an overall problem. At best, such projects consume scarce resources that could have earned much higher returns if invested in research more carefully conceived. At worst, they reduce or correct subset problems at the expense of the rest of the system. The complexity of rail operating networks requires a system for the collection and analysis of operations data to monitor the performance of transport operations, identify undesirable performance, and thereby direct the intelligent allocation of research resources.

A related issue is the need to measure the total system effects of changes introduced into the rail operating network. Complex network interactions often make it impossible for even the most knowledgeable operations and research personnel to predict where and how the system will respond to change. The introduction of operational changes often results in secondary system responses which are difficult or impossible to anticipate. Thus, data collection and analysis systems are necessary to identify the location and magnitude of the response of the overall system to experimental changes in operations.

It was not until transportation researchers began examining individual car movements that some of the really significant rail transport problems and associated research needs were identified. Until recently, however, most computer information and control systems for rail transport operations in North America were not designed to provide the data necessary for such examinations. Fortunately, there is increasing recognition of the need for such evaluation and analysis, and many railroads are now providing for this capability in their information and control systems.

The development of this data and analytic capability by individual railroads must be complemented by a similar industry-level capability to provide data for the evaluation and analysis of multi-road car movements. Recognition of this need formed the basis for the development of the car cycle analysis and terminal car movement systems previously described.

Thus, the real challenges facing researchers in rail operations derive from the need for better information with which to describe those operations. The analytic methodologies required for such research are, for the most part, within the present state of the art. The challenge is to develop systems and procedures to capture data to monitor rail transport operations, identify problems and support research analysis.

REFERENCES

[1] Shaffer, Frank E.; Taking Car Utilization To Task; **Modern Railroads;** July, 1975, p 56.

[2] Car Utilization Final Task Force Report, Recommended Research Program; **Association of American Railroads;** July, 1974.

[3] Freight Car Demand Information and Forecasting Research Project, Phase I Final Report; **Federal Railroad Administration, U.S. Department of Transportation;** March, 1975.

[4] Development and Evaluation of a Computer-Based Model For Optimal Railroad Freight Car Distribution: Final Report; **Federal Railroad Administration, U. S. Department of Transportation;** July, 1975.

[5] A Cooperative Program of Experiments Involving Changes in Railroad Operations: St. Louis Project 1975 Progress Report; **Association of American Railroads,** April, 1976.

Advanced Airline Planning Models as a Tool for Developing Regulatory Policy

by

ROBERT W. SIMPSON

Flight Transportation Laboratory, Cambridge, Mass. U.S.A.

INTRODUCTION

This paper introduces a much more detailed economic theory of the firm for carriers who supply transportation services over a network of markets. Three levels of analysis are defined for transportation economics – a system level, a market level, and a network level. One particular airline model for analysis at the network level is introduced, and then applied to a study of a potential liberalization of route authority for Continental Airlines – a medium sized U.S. airline presently restricted to routes generally in the south-western portions of the U.S.A.

ECONOMICS OF THE TRANSPORTATION FIRM

Let us define three levels of economic analysis for public tranportation systems: a system level, a market level, and a network level. In our view, it is essential to a valid understanding of transportation economics that we work at the network level even though this will lead us to the use of rather complex computer based analytical tools. In this section, we will describe the three levels of analysis, and explain the reasons for this viewpoint.

System Level Economics

At the system level, the transportation firm is studied in terms of aggregate measures of input and output over some time period. The analyst is forced to assume as system output a homogeneous good called a passenger-mile (or seat-mile or ton-mile) which is produced in some ill defined, general market. System consumption of input factors in the form of labor, fuel, and transportation facilities is expressed in terms of total system expenditures, and then unit costs for output are expressed in terms of dollars per passenger-mile.

At this macro-level of aggregation, many ideas essential to the understanding of transportation economics cannot be expressed. The basic error is to assume that buyers are purchasing an economic good called a passenger-mile. They actually purchase a quantity of transportation service of a specific kind in an individual market well defined by its origin and destination. The service purchased in one such market is not substitutable in any other market. The quantity of services purchased is best measured simply by passengers in each market. It is necessary to describe the quality of services purchased in its various dimensions of trip time, trip frequency, punctuality, onboard comfort or class of service, etc. Ton-miles, passenger-miles, or seat-miles are measures of the amount of work required to deliver the service, not a measure of the quantity or quality of the service itself. For most issues in transportation economics, treating the transportation firm as a factory which **produces** passenger-miles is grossly inadequate.

Market Level Economics

Since we can see that buyers are purchasing transportation services in a market defined by an origin and destination, the next level of analysis is to study demand and supply in such a market. In particular, the theory of transportation demand requires that demand functions be defined in such markets. Models of market demand have been developed which present the daily demand measured in passenger-departures per day or per week averaged over some longer time period as a function of price, quality of service variables (such as trip time, service frequency, punctuality, etc.), and demographic descriptors of the regions represented by origin and destination points. As well we may know something about the cyclic variations of this expected market demand value, and the stochastic variations around it.

Market Demand (Passenger-Departures)

Let us denote such an average value by D^{mc}, the average passenger-departures per day expected in market m using a class of service, c. (We can extend the index c to cover demand for cargo, mail, etc. if carried simultaneously as in the airline case.) A model of market demand for D^{mc} would normally be a function of the complete set of prices for the different classes of service, and some of the qualities of service variables for each class. In particular, for the study of U.S. airline firms where competitive services exist in most markets, it is important to introduce the carrier frequency of service in the market, n^m, as a demand variable. The market share of demand obtained by an airline is strongly dependent

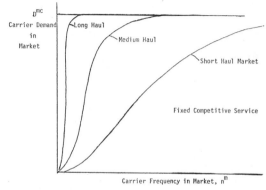

Figure 1 – Typical Traffic-Frequency Curves for a Market

upon its frequency share. For fixed competitive conditions, there exists a "Traffic-Frequency" curve of the form shown in Figure 1 which is derived from demand models and market share models. Notice that these curves saturate as increasing frequency is offered. The saturation point is a function of competitive frequencies, and length of haul for the market.

Network Level Economics

In contrast to the demand function which is defined for each city-pair market, the supply function is defined on a network. Only in the case where the complete network is one single, isolated market can we define the supply function for a market. In the usual case, vehicles move along multistop routes in a network and provide service simultaneously to groups of markets. If we have such a network system, we must perform our analysis at the network level. For the U.S. domestic airline system only one third of the flights are non-stop, and the traffic from other markets usually exceeds the local demand for any non-stop portion of a flight.

Let us define some new terminology. We shall define a route r as a series of consecutive links in a network followed by a vehicle trip (or "Flight" in airline terms). There is a large set of possible routes, denoted $\underline{R}$, which exist under the route authority granted to a carrier by some regulatory agency. There are a set of markets associated with each route. Similarly, we define a path p as a series of consecutive portions of vehicle routes followed by demand in a network travelling from its origin to its destination. In this paper, we shall denote such paths by the index r to simplify our notation. Finally, we define a segment, l, as a link in the network, or as a non-stop portion of a vehicle route. Segment l has a variety of vehicle routes, passenger paths, and markets which traverse it.

a) Market Demand on a Network

As before we define D^{mc} as the daily demand of class c in market m, but now we split this demand into portions which follow path r in the network, D_r^{mc}. If we define the set of paths r which demand in market m may follow as $\underline{R}^m$; then

$$D^{mc} = \sum_{r \in \underline{R}^m} D_r^{mc}$$

We now can denote the totality of traffic of a given class which flows over a segment by D^{lc}. We need to indentify the set of markets which use link l of a route r, $\underline{M}_r^l$, and the set of routes which contain link l, $\underline{R}^l$, then

$$D^{lc} = \sum_{r \in \underline{R}^l} \sum_{m \in \underline{M}_r^l} D_r^{mc}$$

This segment traffic, D^{lc} consists of *"local demand"* from the market of the link l, and *"non-local demand"* from all other markets which use link l. For example, if the link l goes from A to B, the local demand originates in A and terminates in B: The non-local demand consists of two types; 1) demand which transits station A or B on board a vehicle whose route includes the segment, 2) demand which connects at A or B from one vehicle route to another. (Because of this traffic, even a non-stop flight will have non-local demand on board.)

If non-local demand flows are small over the network, we can perform market level analysis for each segment of the network. As stated above, this is not true of the U.S. domestic airline system. In this case, there are roughly 500 cities served and therefore roughly 125,000 markets. Only 1250 segments exist, or about 1% of the total markets get non-stop service. However, these are major markets which produce roughly 75% of the passenger demand. The remaining 25% of passengers come from the other 99% of the nation's markets and must traverse two, three, or more segments. They do so in such a way that they outnumber the local passengers - on these 1250 segments local demand averages only 43% of the total segment flow.[1]

b) Supply on a Network

Where before the supply decision variable n_v^m the daily frequency by vehicle type v in the isolated market m, now it becomes n_{vr}, the daily frequency by vehicle type v along the route r which serves multiple markets.

i) Vehicle Departures

The number of vehicle departures in a market is still determinate. Let us define n_r, the *frequency of single vehicle,* or *through service on a route.*

$$n_r = \sum_v n_{vr}$$

Then, we can find n^m, the *frequency of single vehicle service in a market.*

$$n^m = \sum_{r \in \underline{R}^m} n_r$$

where $\underline{R}^m$ is the set of vehicle routes which serve market m. But now n^m consists of services with multiple stops. If we define $\underline{R}^{ms}$ as the set of routes which serve market m in exactly s stops, then we can define *frequency of s d stop service in a market,* n^{ms}

$$n^{ms} = \sum_{r \in \underline{R}^{ms}} n_r$$

If desired, we can also find the "through" services by vehicle type (n_v^m and n_v^{ms}). However, it is impossible to count the frequency of connecting services in a market. Although we know the frequency of service on portions of vehicle routes which make up a connecting demand path, we will not know the number of connections (or connection times) until the timetable is constructed.

We can also find n^l, the *frequency of service over a segment*

$$n^l = \sum_{r \in \underline{R}^l} n_r$$

Thus, while the supply decision variable is n_{vr}, we can derive the frequency of single vehicle services for a market, segment, or route from it.

ii) Seat Departures

Similarly, we can count the number of seats (or space) offered on a given route to a given class of demand, q_r^c.

$$q_r^c = \sum_v S_v^c \cdot n_{vr}$$

But we cannot count the number of seats (or space) offered to a given market of the network. Even for a given class of service, the space on board a vehicle following a non-stop or multistop route is being offered to several route markets and many connecting markets simultaneously, usually under an indeterminate first come- first served policy. We cannot decouple this sharing of the quantity of supply offered to multiple markets.

This is a very important result in the analysis of transportation systems at the network level. Let us repeat it for emphasis. *We cannot determine the quantity of seats (space) being supplied to a market embedded in a network of services.* Thus, we cannot compare market supply and demand, or market revenues and costs.

We can count the supply of seats (space) for any demand class traversing any segment of the network, q^{lc};

$$q^{lc} = \sum_{r\in R^l} \sum_v S_v^c \cdot n_{vr}$$

where R^l is the set of routes containing segment l. Note that in the case of a single link network, this quantity reduces to the market supply and we perform market level analysis.

c) Demand/Supply Rations on a Network

In the network, it is the segment supply of seats (space), q^{lc}, which must exceed the average segment traffic, D^{lc}, for a given class of demand and every segment of the network;

$$q^{lc} > D^{lc} \quad \text{for all l, all c}$$

Thus, we can define a segment average load factor, $\overline{LF}^{lc}$

$$\overline{LF}^{lc} = \frac{D^{lc}}{q^{lc}} \quad \text{for a segment l, class c}$$

We cannot find the load factor for a market since q^{mc} is indeterminate. We cannot find the load factor for a route except by weighing the route segment load factors by the segment distance. Thus, we define the average load factor for a route, LF^{rc}

$$LF^{rc} = \sum_{l\in r} \frac{D^{lc}\cdot d^l}{q^{lc}\cdot d^l} \left(= \frac{RPM^r}{ASM^r}\right) \text{for a route r, class c}$$

where RPM^r = average revenue passenger miles for the route
ASM^r = available seat miles flown on the route.

For complete carrier systems, this ratio of demand-miles to space-miles is commonly used to compute a system average load factors.

d) Supply Costs on a Network

i) Vehicle Operating Costs – we can determine the costs, c_{lv}^l operate a vehicle type v over a segment l given its distance or trip time. By summing over the segments of a route, we obtain the costs, C_{vr} to operate vehicle type v over route r.

ii) Station Operating Costs – The costs per passenger (class c) can be determined for each passenger route for demand of class c in market m, c_r^{mc} This value would be the sum of station loading/unloading operations along the route. These costs can also be made a function of the level of station demand operations if desired.

iii) System Fixed Costs – As in the market level analysis, there may be fixed costs, FC, for the system which do not vary directly with supply and demand variables in the short term.

From the above, we express the total supply costs for the network as,

$$TC = \sum_r \sum_v c_{vr}\cdot n_{vr} + \sum_c \sum_r \sum_m c_r^{mc}\cdot D_r^{mc} + FC$$

By associating the station loading and unloading costs with a segment, we can determine the total variable costs for a segment, TVC^l, and for a route, TVC_r. We cannot determine the variable costs for a market since multiple markets share the vehicle operating costs.

When we turn to average costs per seat, we again have difficulties with an arbitrary allocation unless we assume there is only one demand class. Even then, since there are fixed costs for the whole system, we cannot find any average costs per seat unless we make some arbitrary allocation of fixed costs to routes, segments, or markets.

For a single class of demand, we can find the average variable costs per seat for a segment or route since we have shown that we can determine (TVC^l, q^{lc}) and (TVC$_r$, q_r^c). For a market, we cannot determine either of these quantities. *Average variable cost per seat cannot be found for a market imbedded in a network even if there is only one class of service.*

For marginal costs per seat, we have the same difficulties with the discreteness of seat supply discussed in the market level analysis. *No true marginal costs per seat can be determined for a segment, route, or market.* However, we can determine the incremental costs of adding a frequency and its block of seats to a segment or route. We cannot find the incremental costs per seat added to a market since the seats are shared by multiple markets, but we can find the costs of adding one more market frequency with a specified number of stops, $\frac{\Delta TC}{\Delta n_{ms}}$

Notice how this would be accomplished on the network. If we require one more frequency in a market, all of the routes and vehicle frequencies can be re-examined with a view to changing vehicle size, vehicle routes, and demand paths. We would not necessarily add one more service non-stop, or along the shortest route available in the market because this would normally be expensive. Instead we would rearrange the pattern of service in the surrounding portion of the network to achieve this increase at perhaps zero cost, or at least some small fraction of the cost of simply adding another frequency in the market.

Similarly, if we ask for one more frequency across a segment, n_l, the incremental costs $\frac{\Delta TC}{\Delta n_l}$ would be minimized by rearranging the patterns of service in adjacent portions of the network. For a segment, we can also ask for the incremental cost of adding more seats, $\frac{\Delta TC}{\Delta q_{lc}}$, when only one class of service exists. *To find the incremental costs of adding a frequency of service to a segment or market, or of adding seats to a segment we need to re-route the pattern of services in the network. We must work at the network level to find incremental costs.*

This capability of rerouting can give a large network carrier a competitive advantage over local carriers on a segment. Because of "feed" or non-local demand, the large carrier may offer a high frequency of service and many seats whether or not any local demand is carried. Its incremental costs of adding a frequency or more seats may be quite low. In the absence of pricing policies which require fairness across merkets, the large carrier has significant discretionary powers to reduce price in any individual market of its network down to the level of its incremental costs.

e) Revenues and Profitability on a Network

The current fare structure for U.S. domestic airline service makes the price for service in each market depend upon a terminal charge plus the distance between origin and destination along the shortest authorized routing (which generally is non-stop, great circle distance). Is is not the sum of the local fares along the segments of the demand path, and consequently we cannot associate revenues with a segment. Also, since demand paths will connect portions of more than one vehicle route, we cannot associate revenues with an aircraft route.

Thus while we can find the variable operating costs for a segment or route as described in the previous section, we cannot determine their revenues, and hence their contribution to system fixed costs. On the other hand, we can determine the revenues from each market, but cannot determine the operating costs for the market.

337

Thus, we cannot determine the contribution to system overhead for a segment, a route, or a market in a transportation system which operates on a network.

This is a remarkable conclusion. We cannot look at any part of the pattern of services on a network and make a statement as to its profitability. Of course, this has not deterred analysts from making arbitrary allocations of costs and revenues in order to obtain arbitrary values of profitability for a segment, route, or market.

We can determine the revenues, costs, and profitability for the complete system;

$$REV = \sum_m \sum_c Y^{mc} \cdot D^{mc} (n^m)$$

$$\pi = \sum_m \sum_c (Y^{mc} - c^{mc}) \cdot \overset{mc}{D(n^m)} - \sum_r \sum_v c_{vr} \cdot n_{vr}^{-Fc}$$

As in our market analysis, we have made the market demand a function of market frequency of service, n^m. Since this depends on n_{vr}, the profit π is optimized by finding the best set of decision variables, $\underline{n}_{vr\ opt}$. If we could express D^{mc} as a function of price and service frequency in which case the profit would be maximized by finding the best set of decision variables, $\underline{Y}^{mc}$ and $\underline{n}_{vr\ opt}$. The set of optimal market prices would depend in a rather complex way upon the network structure, cost and demand functions, and available aircraft.

Notice that suppliers will be optimizing over their network of services, and will not be optimizing in each market independently. Each supplier in a market will behave differently depending upon his surrounding network. Even if their supply costs are similar, a different network would lead competitive suppliers in a market to serve it differently, and choose different prices in absence of competition. It is difficult to perceive any market equilibrium in the case where supplier networks only partially overlap and there is an absense of regulation over prices and entry. Remember that marginal costs for a market are indeterminate, so we cannot find a normative standard to guide regulatory pricing policies aimed at achieving economic efficieny.

At present, U.S. airline regulatory practice posts prices across all markets in the nation, and closely controls the route authority of each carrier. Given a set of prices, $\underline{Y}^m$, and a route authority, $\underline{R}$, each airline has to make a decision on the set of supply variables, $\underline{n}_{vr}$. In the longer term, the carriers select vehicle types and make decisions about applying for new route authority to optimize their individual system profitability. If the Civil Aeronautics Board changes the posted prices in different markets, $\underline{Y}^m$, or the route authorities, $\underline{R}_a$ for different airlines, the carriers will react by rearranging their patterns of service, and purchasing different aircraft in the longer term.

Adding a single segment to a route authority will affect many markets besides the local market. Adding it to different route authorities will have varying impacts- for some carriers the new segment will greatly improve profitability even if the traffic and revenues from the local market are negligible; for other carriers, the segment may be only valuable for its local market.

If we wish to study the effects of changing fare structures, or route structures on an airline we need to use the network level of economic analysis. In the next section, we present a particular network model for the airline firm which we shall subsequently use to study the impacts of freeing regulation over entry and market prices.

A MODEL FOR THE AIRLINE FIRM

In this section, we will describe a computer model for an airline firm which works at the network level of economic analysis. It consists of a series of equations which we can solve to find a profit maximizing set of supply

decisions for an individual carrier using techniques from mathematical programming. It is one of several such models developed in the flight Transportation Laboratory at M.I.T. in recent years. The model is designated FA-4, and optimizes system profit by choosing $\underline{n}_{vr}$ given a set of market prices and a set of Traffic-Frequency curves which presume fixed competitive conditions in all markets.

For the analyst, the input information concerning market prices, traffic-frequency curves, available aircraft, operating costs, station capacities, minimum required levels of service, route authorities is easily entered into preprocessor computer programs which set up the mathematical problem. This is then solved using a standard mathematical programming code (in our case, MPSX from IBM). The solution is then presented to the analyst by a post-processor program which tabulates the data into a comprehensible summary format. Sensitivity to changes in various input data such as route authority, market prices, new aircraft, etc. can quickly and easily be obtained. In effect, he has a computer tool for economic analysis of a given airline system operating over a network of routes.

MODEL FA-4, AN AIRLINE FLEET ASSIGNMENT MODEL

Objective Function

Find the optimal set of supply decisions, $\underline{n}_{vr}$, which maximizes operating income, given a set of demand functions for each market of the system which depend upon the frequency of services offered, and subject to various operating constraints.

$$\text{Maximize } \pi_{op} = \sum_r \sum_m \sum_c (Y_r^{mc} - c_r^{mc}) \cdot D_r^{mc} - \sum_r \sum_v c_{vr} \cdot n_{vr}$$

where π_{op} is operating income. The first term represents net revenues from all markets. The second represents vehicle operating costs. Since D_r^{mc} is a function of n^m, which in turn is a function of n_{vr}, we are seeking to find an optimal set of n_{vr} values.

Constraints

1a) Market Demand depends on Market Frequency of Service

For each market, we may construct a linearized traffic frequency curve as a function of a weighted frequency of service, n^{-m} which discounts one stop, two stop, and connecting services relative to non-stop service;

$$\bar{n}^m = \sum_s w^s \cdot n^{ms} \quad \text{for any markte, m}$$

Then, the non-linear relationship between demand and service is represented by a series of linear terms;

$$D^{mc} = \sum_i d_i^{mc} \cdot n_i^m \quad \text{for any market m, class c}$$

$$\bar{n}^m = \sum_i n_i^m \quad \text{for any market m}$$

where n_i^m is a frequency variable for each term. d_i^{mc} is the slope representing the rate of demand increase with frequency term i.

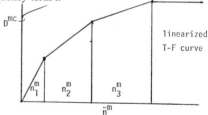

Figure 2

338

1b) Market Demand is served over a set of routes, $\underline{R}^m$

We allow the demand in a market to follow a set of paths in the network; i.e. D_r^{mc} is an output variable showing how demand class,c, in a market is served;

$$\sum_{r \in \underline{R}^m} D_r^{mc} \leqslant D^{mc} \text{ for all markets in all classes,c}$$

Note we do not insist that all market demand must be served. In certain cases we may not be able to supply sufficient vehicle capacity to the system and be forced to refuse potential demand from certain markets of classes.

2) Sufficient Capacity must be Supplied to each Segment

For each <u>segment</u> the maximum allowable average load factor, LF_{max}^{lc} for each demand class, must be determined so that peak loads will exceed capacity offered only on a small percentage of days;

$$\pi^{lc} \leqslant \overline{LF}_{max}^{lc} \cdot q^{lc} \text{ for all segments,l all classes,c.}$$

where D^{lc} is defined previously as average segment traffic of class c.

q^{lc} is defined previously as segment space capacity for class c.

3) Sufficient Station Capacity must exist for Vehicles and Demands

a) Vehicle Departures

For any station k, the number of vehicle departures, N_k, may be restricted by an upper limit NU_k.

$$N_k = \sum_{r \in \underline{R}^k} \sum_v n_{vr} \leqslant NU_k \text{ for any k}$$

At stations where there may be limits on daily operations due to ATC or gate capacities, the upper limit on aircraft operations may be applied. Also, constraints may be placed on maximum daily operations by vehicle type at the station.

b) Demand Departures

Although not usually needed for today's airline terminals, it is possible to include a limit on station loading operations for any demand class, DU_k^c;

$$D_k^c = \sum_{m \in \underline{M}_k} \sum_r D_r^{mc} \leqslant DU_k^c \quad \text{for any station k, any class c}$$

where $\underline{M}_k$ is the set of markets which use path r to originate or connect at station k.

4) Sufficient Flight Hours must be available from each Vehicle Fleet

Generally, the airline has a limited number of flying hours available for each type of aircraft. The assignment of an aircraft, type v to fly a route r will use U_{vr} available block hours of flight time. There is an upper limit to the hours of average daily utilization, U_v, for each fleet of vehicle types. Thus,

$$\sum_r U_{vr} \cdot n_{vr} \leqslant U_v \text{ for all aircraft types, v}$$

For longer term studies, additional fleet can be leased or purchased, and present vehicles can be sold at forecast used market prices. Financial constraints for the airline can be included over a series of future planning periods and the model is extended to become a corporate financial and operations planning model.

5) Specified Minimum Levels of Service

While economic criteria may indicate otherwise, there may be policy or political reasons to maintain a minimum level of service in certain markets or at certain stations.

a) Market Minimum Service

We may wish to specify a minimum daily frequency of service of s-stops in market, N^{ms};

$$n^{ms} \geqslant N^{ms} \text{ for any market in any number of stops,s}$$

Alternatively, we can specify a minimum daily frequency of S-stops or less, NS^m;

$$\sum_{s = 0, S} n^{ms} \geqslant NS^m \text{ for any market m}$$

Both of these constraints can be written for a particular vehicle type if desired

b) Station Minimum Service

We may wish to specify a minimum daily frequency of station departures at stations of low demand generation. Thus, there may be a lower bound, NL_k, on station operations at such stations similar to the upper bound for busy stations specified in 3a).

$$N_k = \sum_{r \in \underline{P}_k} \sum_v n_{vr} \geqslant NL_k \text{ for any station k}$$

Again, there may be some desire to have a lower bound specified for any given type of vehicle.

AN APPLICATION TO AIRLINE REGULATORY POLICY ANALYSIS

For the past few years, there has been some interest in relaxing the economic regulation of domestic air transportation in the U.S.A. Proponents of "regulatory reform" have argued that with freer entry to markets, airline competition (or the threat of competition) would move market prices to values which would increase the "economic efficiency" of the air transportation system. Opponents have countered that free competition would lead to abandonment of the less lucrative markets and an unstable destructive competition in price and service in the major markets. There have been several legislative proposals for new policies to govern the economic regulation as administered by the Civil Aeronautics board. Although these proposals are always accompanied by glowing descriptions of the benefits they will bring, it is difficult, perhaps impossible, to evaluate their impact in any credible fashion.

In this section we will describe an application of the network model FA-4 to examine in a general way to the issues of relaxed entry controls. It is a case study of Continental Airlines as it existed in the domestic air transportation system in 1974. We remove all restrictions from within its present route authority, and extend a small set of new segments to New York. We assume, unrealistically, that all other airlines remain passive at their 1974 patterns of service, and ask a series of questions – "If Continental Airlines had this expanded route authority, what would its new pattern of service look like? What markets and cities would it abandon? What new markets would it enter at the existing levels of competition? If we lowered prices in these new markets by 10% or 20% would Continental still enter them? Would Continental acquire new aircraft and expand its service?"

The general issue to be addressed with such network analysis is whether or not the potential exists for a radical restructuring of the current airline networks. Is has been claimed that the present structure of airline competitive services is more or less in equilibrium, and that under relaxed entry controls one can expect only minor changes by the management of each airline. As we shall see, our case study of Continental Airlines indicates that this not true.

Continental Airlines Case Study

Using data for the calendar year 1974, we have esta-

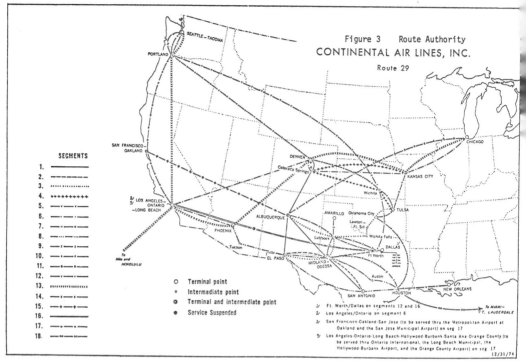

Figure 3   Route Authority
CONTINENTAL AIR LINES, INC.
Route 29

SEGMENTS
1. ————————
2. — — — — — —
3. ••••• •••••••••••
4. +++++++++
5. —v—v—v—
6. —||—||—||—
7. —|—||—|—
8. —•||—|||—
9. —||—I—I—
10. —I—I—I—
11. —•—•—•—
12. ————————
13. ×××××××××××
14. —I—I—I—
15. —•—•—•—
16. ————————
17. —•—•—•—
18. —••——••——

○   Terminal point
∘   Intermediate point
⊙   Terminal and intermediate point
●   Service Suspended

1/ Ft. Worth/Dallas on segments 12 and 16
2/ Los Angeles-Ontario on segment 6
3/ San Francisco-Oakland-San Jose (to be served thru the Metropolitan Airport at Oakland and the San Jose Municipal Airport) on seg. 17
4/ Los Angeles-Ontario-Long Beach-Hollywood-Burbank-Santa Ana-Orange County (to be served thru Ontario International, the Long Beach Municipal, the Hollywood-Burbank Airport, and the Orange County Airport) on seg. 17

12/31/74

blished a network model of Continental Airlines, a medium sized trunk airline which serves cities in the southwest area of U.S.A. A list of cities served by Continental and their three letter airline code are given in Table II.

However, Continental is not free to supply service between any pair of these cities. Its route authority consists of 18 routes added to their original authority at various times in the past thirty years. Figure 4 shows a map taken from CAB documents which gives some indication of its pattern of service. A full reading of the route authority is required to understand the various restrictions specified. Continental has been aggressive in seeking new route authority and willing to accept restrictions as a strategy in overcoming objections from other airlines. At a later date, it can try to remove the restrictions placed on an original award.

For example, it has a route authority, segment 13 which goes from Hawaii to Los Angeles, then splits to go on to Portland/Seattle and across the continent to Phoenix, Denver, Kansas City, and Chicago. Normally such an authority would allow non-stop service between any of the listed cities. But in this case, the award was part of an expansion of service of Hawaii and segment 13 restricts Continental to carrying only Hawaiian passengers, i.e. it is a "closed door" restriction to passengers in other markets. As a result Continental does not fly at present between Phoenix and Denver, Kansas City, or Chicago or between Seattle and Phoenix, Chicago, or Kansas City. We assume that such restrictions on service between cities already on the Continental system would be removed.

The demand data is taken from the CAB Airline O & D data for the year June 1973 - June 1974. This data provides information on the traffic flow on a given airline under the pattern of services offered. We obtain the annual average passengers per day for each carrier in a city pair market less any interline traffic data. (For markets where this interline data is significant, we may include it). We know the frequency of services by each carrier and by Continental, and using a simple "market-

share equals frequency share" model we construct a traffic-frequency curve for present and prospective markets.

The aircraft operating costs and other data are given in Table 1 for the Continental Fleet as it existed in June, 1974. Aircraft variable operating costs are expressed in terms of segment distance. The assumed average yield, sales costs, passenger service costs, and traffic servicing costs are given in Table 2. This results in a net revenue value for a passenger in each market. The data supporting these tables is taken from CAB reports for Continental Airlines in the calendar year 1974.

With these data assembled, the first run was a "base case" run to establish that the model reproduced the pattern of service offered by Continental under the 1974 route authority, i.e. we should see the same aircraft flying the same routings and frequencies, the same market shares, revenues and operating costs.

Initial base case runs indicated that traffic on Continental's Hawaiian routes was too low and the model selected the smaller B720B over the DC-10 aircraft even though its costs per seat were much higher. In view of Continental's recent acquisition of these DC-10 aircraft and the use of similar widebody aircraft by competitors in these markets, we prevented the use of B720-B aircraft on these routes. The base case then used DC-10 aircraft at a frequency of service below the actual Continental service for 1974. The B720-B aircraft remained ineligible for Hawaii service in all subsequent study cases.

A comparison of actual and base case system values is given in Table 3. A detailed comparison of the nonstop and multistop service frequencies for all markets of the 1974 Continental system can be made using Table 7 (Compare actual service NS/MS with Case 1, base case).

It is necessary to select a strategy for expansion of the route authority which management might follow under a scenario of liberalized entry controls. Here we shall show only one such strategy which is based upon adding New York city to the system. It is called the JFK Case study,

340

although due to lack of airport gates at JFK the service might be based at Newark airport which is currently underutilized. From New York there are 12 new segments added to cities already served by Continental. These are listed in Table 4 along with an associated set of 45 new possible multistop routings for aircraft as service is continued within the Continental system. There are 17 new markets from New York associated with these 12 segments (See Table 8).

As well, the elimination of the present restrictions on Continental route authority will add 34 new markets which are also contained in the set of 45 JFK routings. No new routings besides those JFK routings were selected, although this would be possible when the restrictions are eliminated. So a total of 51 new markets accompanies the 12 new segments and 45 new routings. This is a small subset of the strategies which the management of Continental might persue.

Given this expanded route authority, a series of computer cases were run under varying assumptions. Case 1 is the base case representing the 1974 actual patterns of service by Continental. Case 2 introduces this new route authority at normal market prices using the 1974 aircraft fleet. Case 3 presumes that in the new markets added, Continental would have to match price reductions of 10% by incumbent carriers. Prices in other markets remained at normal levels. Case 4 further presumes that Continental could purchase or lease additional DC-10, DC-9, and B-727-200 aircraft whose operating costs now include their ownership costs. Case 5 then extends the price reductions to 20% in the new markets with the assumption that the fleet could be expanded.

Results from the New York Case Studies

The impact of expanding the Continental network to New York with the normal fleet and prices is indicated by the results of Case 2. In general terms, the short haul mid-continent services in Texas and New Mexico are abandoned and the fleet is used in highly competitive long haul markets, predominantly from New York. Notice that the short haul services are profitable in the base case, and that the restricted fleet availability causes them to be abandoned when more profitable markets and routes are possible. Most of these markets will return when more aircraft can be obtained in later cases.

The service along the new routings out of JFK (New York) for Case 2 are shown in Table 5. The segment New York-Chicage is flown 10 times per day with a variety of routings to points like Los Angeles, Kansas City, Denver, New Orleans, and Seattle. Notice that New York-Chicage as a non-stop routing is not flown. The DC-10 and B-727-200 aircraft are both used on these routes. The next segment is New York-Denver which is flown 4 times per day, followed by New York to Dallas twice per day, continuing to Houston and San Francisco. Then, we see that the model places Continental strongly into the transcontinental markets New York to Los Angeles, and San Francisco with non-stop flights per day each. These probably would be other new competitors entering these two markets which would reduce its attractiveness. We have assumed that all other carriers remain passive while Continental restructures its system.

Table 6 shows the service levels in all 17 new markets from New York. Notice that the model places Continental strongly into the New York-Miami market with 10 flights per day. Again, it is unrealistic to assume that only Continental decides to enter this market.

A summary of new markets entered is given in Table 7. Of the 51 new markets available under this expanded route authority, only 20 are entered in Case 2. Of these, only one is presently a monopoly, single carrier market. Most of them (12) are presently two carrier markets,

while six are three carrier markets, and one is a four carrier market. The larger markets already have competitive service while any monopoly market is probably very small.

Table 7 also categorizes the pattern of markets abandoned. Of the 119 markets on the Continental system, 32 are monopoly markets, and 19 of these are abandoned in Case 2. In fact, Case 2 abandons service in 76, or 64% of Continental's present markets. Interestingly, the percentage abandoned is lowest for the three competitor markets where only one out of four is abandoned.

The top ten monopoly markets of Continental are examined in Table 8. In seven of these, service is abandoned. One receives reduced service while in the last two, service is actually improved. Finally, out of the pattern of market abandonment, several cities are completely abandoned as listed in Table 9.

In Table 10, we see the summary of system results. For Case 2, revenues increase from 418,000 \$/day to 503,000 \$/day, and the contribution to overhead increases from 129,000 \$/day to 182,000 \$/day. Notice that passengers boarded actually decreases by 10% while revenue passenger miles increases from 14 million to 17.5 million per day. The average passenger trip length has increased from 1033 miles to 1475 miles, and the average aircraft stage length from 735 to 1329 miles. There is a switch to longer haul markets, and longer stage length service pattern.

In Case 3 we assume that there is price competition which reduces the level of prices by 10% in the new markets. This decreases their attractiveness to the model which is seeking a profit optimal pattern of service. We can see the reduction of service in the new markets and routes by comparing Case 3 with Case 2 in most of the Tables 5-11. For example, the New York-Chicago and beyond routes we halved to a level of 5 flights per day; New York-Los Angelos is reduced from 7 to 2 flights/day; New York-Miami is reduced from 10 to 3 flights per day.

Similarly, service in existing markets is restored in Case 3. From Table 10 there was service is only 35% of the existing markets in Case 2, but in Case 3, service is offered in 62% of them. For example, services from Denver to Albuquerque, Colorado Springs, and Houston, and from Houston to Midland/Odessa, Miami, Oklahoma City and Tulsa are resumed. Remember once again that prices in these markets remain at their normal levels since we assume no competitive entry by other airlines.

From Table 10, we see that system revenues and contribution to overhead are reduced in Case 3. Passengers per day and their average length of haul remain constant but aircraft stage lengths decrease as the older shorter haul markets are re-entered. The increases in system revenues and contribution to overhead are only half the increases of Case 2 over Case 1.

From the results of Cases 2 and 3, it was obvious that the limited fleet available was a major constraint on the amount of service offered by the system. Cases 4 and 5 remove this constraint with the general result that the system triples in size in Case 4, and still doubles in size in Case 5 where fares are further reduced 20% in the new markets. In these cases, most of the existing markets are served (92%), plus a major entry is made into the new and newly unrestricted markets made available to the system by this case study.

In Case 4, the system acquires 29 DC-10 and 57 B-727-200 aircraft. All 15 of the available B-720B aircraft are placed in service even though they are relatively expensive. System revenues, revenue passenger miles, and passengers almost triple. Contribution to overhead more than doubles, but, ofcourse, we cannot expect

341

overhead costs to remain constant with such large charge. Now all of the new segments are strongly entered as gateways into the existing Continental system.

The reduction of fares in new markets moderates this system expansion in Case 5. Only 16 new DC-10 and 53 new B727-200 aircraft are acquired, and the B720B fleet is grounded. Now system revenues, and contribution are only doubled, but passengers and revenue passenger miles are still tripled. Passenger trip length increases further to an average of 1592 miles.

These last two cases give some indication of the potential for competitive entry which exists in the present airline network. Here we have held the other airlines constant, and allowed Continental to acquire aircraft and enter a set of new markets along a few gateway segments from New York. In a sense we might say that Continental puts all the additional service into these markets that the other airlines plus Continental would provide in a more realistic scenario. Normally, market share results depend upon the number of competitors as well as their frequencies of service. Two new competitors offering 5 flights/day each against two old competitors with 5 flights/day each will obtain equal shares in the market for everyone with a tendency for head to head, simultaneous departures of four aircraft. If there is only one new competitor with 10 fights/day, he will obtain more than 50% of the markets and will be scheduling an extra five departure times throughout the day. This "S-shaped" market share curve has not been used in this case study. Continental's markets shares would have been higher and more profitable if it had been used. As a result, the market expansion gives an indication more representative of equal share, industry entry.

Table 1 – Aircraft Operating Data – Continental Airlines, 1974

Aircraft	Number	Utilization		Operating Cost	
		hrs/day	Seats	$/hour	$/mile
DC10	11	10.2	200	1194	118 + 2.27d
7275	30	9.7	124	728	576 + 1.44d
720B	15	9.5	106	959	738 + 1.83d
DC9S	7	6.0	71	595	384 + 1.25d

Source – Aircraft Operating Cost and Performance, CAB (Redbook), 1974

Table 2 – Passenger Yield and Ground Operating Costs – Continental Airlines, 1974

1. Revenue Yield
    For 1974, yield = $13.60 + .056d
    where d = market distance
2. Promotion and Sales Costs
    Assume 12% of revenues from above yield
3. Passenger Service
    Assume 2 $/boarding + .005d
4. Traffic Servicing
    Assume 2 $/boarding + (100 $/departure + 1.5 $/100C GW) The last two erms are added to aircraft costs.

From above, Y^m = ompetitors. (13.6 + .056d) x 0.88

$$= 11.97 + .49d$$
$$C^m = 4 + .005d$$
$$Y^m - c^m = 7.97 + .044d$$

Source – CAB Form 41

Table 3 – Base Case Comparison with Actual Continental System

	Continental Actual 1974	Base Case
[1]Passengers Carried (000)	5,053	4,849
Revenue Passenger Miles (10)	5,645	5,008
[2]Revenues $ (000)	348,790	346,878
[3]Operating Expenses $ (000)	297,951	272,781
Flying Operations	152,320	131,405
Passenger Service	44,760	34,736
Aircraft & Traffic Servicing	59,358	65,015
Promotion & Sales	41,513	41,625
Total Variable	297,951	272,781
Depreciation (Flight Equipment)	34,799	27,126
General & Administration	22,686	21,822 (estimate)
Total Fix	57,485	48,948
Interest Expense	27,356	?
Average Stage Length (miles)	551	735
Average Passenger Trip Length (miles)	869	1,033

[1] On line Origin-Destination Passengers.
[2] Schedule Passenger Revenues Only.
[3] Depreciation Expenses and General & Administration Expenses omitted.
[4] 8% of all costs except depreciation.

Table 4 – New Aircraft Routes – JFK Case Study

1. JFK-ORD
    continuing to DEN, MCI, DFW, LAX, MSY, SEA, SFO
    continuing to LAX-HNL, PHX-LAX, MCI-DEN, IAH-SAT, PHX-SFO
2. JFK-MCI
    continuing to DFW, LAX, PHX
    continuing to DEN-SEA
3. JFK-DFW
    continuing to IAH, LAX, SAT, SFO
    continuing to LAX-HNL, TUS-PHX
4. JFK-TUL
    continuing to OKD-DFW, OKC- LAX
5. JFK-MSY
    continuing to IAH, IAH-SAT
6. JFK-DEN
    continuing to LAX, PHX, SFO
7. JFK-PDX
    continuing to SEA
8. JFK-SFO
    continuing to LAX, SEA, HNL
9. JFK-LAX
    continuing to LAX, SEA, HNL
9. JFK-LAX
    continuing to HNL
10. JFK-MIA
11. JFK-IAH
12. JFK-SEA

Table 5 – Continental Daily Frequency by Aircraft Routing – JFK Case Study

JFK ROUTES

A) ORD Gateway Routes

	Cases 1	2	3	4	5
1. JFK-ORD	0	0	0	0	4
2. JFK-ORD-DEN	0	1	0	0	0
3. JFK-ORD-MCI	0	0	0	0	0
4. JFK-ORD-MCI-DEN	0	1	0	0	0
5. JFK-ORD-DFW	0	1	0	1	1
6. JFK-ORD-LAX	0	4	4	7	8
7. JFK-ORD-PHX-LAX	0	0	0	3	2
8. JFK-ORD-LAX-HNL	0	0	0	0	0 ·
9. JFK-ORD-MSY	0	1	0	1	0
10. JFK-ORD-SFO	0	0	0	0	0
11. JFK-ORD-PHX-SFO	0	0	0	1	0
12. JFK-ORD-IAH-SAT	0	0	0	2	0
13. JFK-ORD-SEA	0	2	1	5	5
Total	0	10	5	20	20

b) DEN Gateway Routes

1. JFK-DEN	0	3	4	1	2
2. JFK-DEN-PHX	0	0	0	2	0
3. JFK-DEN-SFO	0	1	0	6	10
4. JFK-DEN-LAX	0	0	0	1	2
Total	0	4	4	10	14

c) DFW Gateway Routes

1. JFK-DFW	0	0	0	0	0
2. JFK-DFW-IAH	0	1	1	1	1
3. JFK-DFW-LAX	0	0	0	4	0
4. JFK-DFW-SAT	0	0	0	0	0
5. JFK-DFW-SFO	0	1	0	3	3
6. JFK-DFW-LAX-HNL	0	0	0	0	0
7. JFK-DFW-TUS-PHX	0	0	0	0	0
Total	0	2	1	8	4

d) LAX Gateway Routes

1. JFK-LAX	0	7	1	0	0
2. JFK-LAX-HNL	0	0	1	6	8
Total	0	7	2	6	8

JFK ROUTES   *TOTAL DAILY FREQUENCY*

e) SFO Gateway Routes

	Cases 1	2	3	4	5
1. JFK-SFO	0	7	5	0	0
2. JFK-SFO-HNL	0	0	0	9	0
3. JFK-SFO-SFA	0	0	0	0	0
4. JFK-SFO-LAX	0	0	0	0	0
Total	0	7	5	9	0

f) MSY Gateway Routes

1. JFK-MSY	0	1	0	9	1
2. JFK-MSY-IAH	0	0	1	2	0
3. JFK-MSY-IAH-SAI	0	0	0	1	1
Total	0	1	1	12	2

Table 6 – Competition and Level of Service in New JFK City-Pair Markets

City	Pairs	No. of Carriers	NS/MS	Case 2	Case 3	Case 4	Case 5
JFK	DEN	2; UA, TW	6/3	4/1	4/0	5/1	13/1
JFK	DFW	2; AA, BN	14/4	2/2	1/0	8/1	5/1
JFK	HNL	2; UA, AA	1/1	0/2	0/1	0/15	0/8
JFK	IAH	3; DL, EA, BN	7/10	0/2	0/2	1/6	0/2
JFK	LAX	3; AA, TW, UA	13/8	8/5	2/4	6/15	8/10
JFK	MCI	2; TW, UA	2/5	1/1	0/0	7/0	8/0
JFK	MIA	3; EA, NA, DL	30/6	10/0	3/0	10/0	10/0
JFK	MSY	2; DL, EA	6/6	1/1	0/0	4/1	1/0
JFK	OKC	3; TW, AA, Bn	1/4	0/0	0/0	0/1	0/0
JFK	ORD	3; AA, UA, TW	49/15	10/0	4/0	20/0	20/0
JFK	PDX	2; UA, NW	0/4	0/0	0/0	1/0	0/0
JFK	PHX	2; AA, TW	3/5	1/1	0/0	0/8	0/5
JFK	SAT	3; BN, EA, AA	0/10	0/0	0/0	0/3	0/1
JFK	SEA	2; UA, NW	3/2	1/2	0/1	0/6	0/6
JFK	SFO	3; AA, TW, UA	9/14	7/1	5/0	8/9	0/13
JFK	TUL.	3; AA, TW, BN	1/5	0/0	0/0	1/0	0/0
JFK	TUS	2; AA, TW 0/8	0/0	0/0	0/0	0/0	0/0

Header row for Table 6: City | Pairs | Competitive Service (No. of Carriers) | Continental Service (NS/MS, Case 2, Case 3, Case 4, Case 5)

343

Table 7 – Entry and Exit in Continental's Markets

Entry – New Markets Entered in JFK Case Study

	CASE	1	2	4	5
One-Competitor Market		1	0	1	0
Two-Competitor Market		12	7	23	15
Three-Competitor Market		6	5	9	8
Four-Competitor Market		1	0	2	0
Total New Markets		20	12	35	23

Exit – Abandonment of Continental's Existing Markets, JFK Case 2
Continental Markets

	%	Number	Abandoned Case %	
Monopoly Markets	27%	32	19	60%
1 Competitor Market	52%	62	42	68%
2 Competitor Market	18%	21	14	67%
3 Competitor Market	3%	4	1	33%
Total	100%	119	76	64%

Table 9 – Cities Abandoned in JFK Case Study – Flights/Day

	Case	2	3	4	5
AMA	Amarillo	0	0	0	0
LBB	Lubbock	0	0	3	3
MAF	Midland-Odessa	0	2	4	2
OKC	Oklahoma City	0	1	6	6
TUL	Tulsa	0	1	3	2
SJC	San Jose, Calif.	0	3	4	3
ICT	Wichita	0	1	2	3
LAW	Lawton-Fort Sill	0	0	0	0
SPS	Wichita Falls	0	0	0	0
AUS	Austin	1	0	1	1

Table 8 – Top Ten Monopoly Markets of Continental in Terms of Passengers, 1974

Market		Case 2 Service	Daily On-line O-D Passengers	Distance in Miles	Carrier Share (%)
Denver	Wichita	*	310	428	1.00
Colorado Springs	Chicago	+	228	918	0.99
Denver	Tulsa	*	214	549	0.96
Seattle	San Jose	*	198	695	1.00
Portland	San Jose	*	170	566	1.00
El Paso	Houston	*	142	673	1.00
Colorado Springs	Los Angeles	+	118	822	1.00
Houston	Phoenix	*	110	1015	1.00
Burbank	Portland	*	90	818	1.00
Burbank	Seattle	–	84	941	1.00

* Abandoned	in JFK Case 2 Study
– Reduced Service	,,
+ Improved Service	,,

Table 10 – System Results, New York Case Studies

	Case 1 BASE	Case 2 (1)+NEW MARKETS	Case 3 (2)+NEW MARKET FARES x0.9	Case 4 (3)+ EXPANDED FLEET	Case 5 (4)+NEW MARKET FARES x0.8
FLEET SIZE					
DC-10	10	11	11	11 + 29	11 + 16
B727	30	30	30	30 + 57	30 + 53
B720B	0	7	7	15	1
DC-9	7	7	7	7	7
System Rev/Day	$418,130	502,800	479,200	1,263,200	994,634
Contribution to Overhead	$129,200	182,400	156,683	423,407	331,178
Pax/Day	13,284	11,859	11,559	32,346	31,415
RPM/Day	$13.7x10^6$	$17.5x10^6$	$17.3x10^6$	$51.2x10^6$	$50.0x10^6$
Avg. a/c stage (miles)	735	1,329	1,196	1,029	1,041
Avg. pax trip length	1,033	1,475	1,493	1,583	1,592
No. of markets abandoned	—	76	45	23	22
% of original markets served	100%	35%	62%	92%	92%
No. of new markets entry	—	35	26	49	38

Table 11 – Code Names for Stations on Continental Airlines Route Map, 1974

Code	Station	Code	Station
ABQ	ALBUQUERQUE, N. MEX.	MIA	MIAMI, FLA.
AMA	AMARILLO, TEX.	MSY	NEW ORLEANS, LA.
AUS	AUSTIN, TEX.	OKC	OKLAHOMA CITY, OKLA.
BUR	BURBANK, CALIF.	ONT	ONTARIO, CALIF.
CAS	COLORADO SPRINGS, COLO.	ORD	CHICAGO, ILL.
DEN	DENVER, COLO.	PDX	PORTLAND, OREG.
DFW	DALLAS-FORT WORTH, TEX.	PHX	PHOENIX, ARIZ.
ELP	EL PASO, TEX.	SAT	SAN ANTONIO, TEX.
HNL	HONOLULU, HAWAII	SEA	SEATTLE-TACOMA, WASH.
IAH	HOUSTON, TEX.	SFO	SAN FRANCISCO, CALIF.
ICT	WICHITA, KANS.	SJC	SAN JOSE, CALIF.
ITO	HILO, HAWAII	SPS	WICHITA FALLS, TEX.
¹JFK	NEW YORK CITY, NEW YORK	TUL	TULSA, OKLA
LAW	LAWTON-FORT SILL, OKLA	TUS	TUCSON, ARIZ.
LAX	LOS ANGELES, CALIF.		
LBB	LUBBOCK, TEX.		
MAF	MIDLAND-ODESSA, TEX.		
MCI	KANSAS CITY, MO.		

¹JFK is added in accordance with the study. Traffic data used is inclusive of Kennedy, Neward and La Guardia Airports so that JFK really represents New York City region.

CONCLUSIONS

1. There are three levels of economic analysis of transportation systems - a system level, a market level, and a network level. If the transportation firm is supplying services over a network of markets, it is essential to work at the network level in studying its behavior. We can construct and apply computer models for the transportation firm, (at least for airline systems) which should be useful to the planner or policymaker on certain issues.

2. At the network level;

a) we cannot determine the quantity of seats (space) being supplied to a market imbedded in a network of services.

b) average variable cost per seat cannot be found for a market imbedded in a network.

c) marginal costs per seat cannot be found for a route, segment, or market in a network.

d) we cannot determine the contribution or profit for a route, segment, or market in a transportation system which operates on a network.

3. Extending the analysis of a firm to the analysis of the industry may not be possible. Is is not clear that there is any network equilibria when the networks for individual firms only partially overlap. As a result, we may not be able to study the economic behavior of competitive firms, even for a given segment of the network.

4. A potential for a major restructuring of the existing airline networks exists under conditions of free entry.

5. Adding a major new city to an airline system introduces profitable new service opportunities even in the face of existing competitors and lowered fares. Linking one new segment into an airline network may bring several new markets.

6. Due to limited resources in the form of aircraft and crews, an individual airline system will drop existing profitable markets, routes, and cities in order to enter more profitable ones even though they face competition in the form of multiple competitors, high frequency of service, and lowered prices.

7. In the longer term, there are indications that individual airline systems will find it profitable to acquire more aircraft of smaller capacity which allow them to expand their route system such that they enter major markets as additional competitors. If this produces a viable economic equilibrium, the increased use of smaller aircraft means higher operating costs, increased fuel consumption, and increased noise impact on the communities around airports.

FOOTNOTE

1. The Domestic Route System – Analysis and Policy Recommendations, A Staff Study by the Bureau of Operating Rights, Civil Aeronautics Board, U.S.A. October 1974, (see Tables 5, 6, 7 based on 1972 data).

Aspects économiques de la propulsion nucléaire civile

par

S. RUEL

Ministère de l'Economie et des Finances, France

INTRODUCTION

Au cours du XIXème siècle, la machine à vapeur s'est développée et a progressivement supplanté la voile, s'imposant en premier lieu aux bâtiments de commerce, car les Marines Militaires l'estimaient trop dangereuse sur les navires de guerre de l'époque, construits en bois lors de son apparition.

Le XXème siècle a vu les hydrocarbures supplanter le charbon, la turbine éliminer la machine alternative, tandis que le moteur diesel, plus économe en combustible que l'ensemble chaudière-turbine, s'imposait pour les puissances faibles et moyennes.

L'apparition de l'énergie nucléaire dans la propulsion navale date de la mise en service, en septembre 1954, du sous-marin ,,Nautilus''.

Depuis, une certitude est acquise, celle de la faisabilité technique et de la fiabilité dont font foi plus de deux cents bâtiments militaires, qui à quelques exceptions près sont des sous-marins équipés d'un seul réacteur du type PWR, ils totalisent depuis 1954 plus de mille années/ réacteurs de fonctionnement sans incident grave lié au caractère nucléaire de la propulsion.

La première mise en oeuvre de cette nouvelle technologie dans le secteur non militaire ne tarda pas puisque, dès 1956, l'U.R.S.S. mettait en chantier le ,,Lénine'', brise-glace de 44 000 ch. auquel la propulsion nucléaire donnait une autonomie illimitée à l'échelle de l'hiver, ce qui lui conférait une efficacité compensant largement le surcroît d'investissement. Deux autres ont été mis en service: ,,L'Artika'' et le ,,Sibir'', ce dernier le 23 février 1976. Trois autres réalisations civiles ont vu le jour. Il s'agit de petits navires expérimentaux de faible puissance: la ,,Savannah'', américain, de 22 000 ch mis sur cale en 1958; l',,Otto-Hahn'', allemand, de 10 000 ch., mis sur cale en 1963, et le ,,Mutsu'', japonais, de 10 000 ch., mis sur cale en 1968. Ces bâtiments sans prétention à la rentabilité sont l'équivalent du Prototype à Terre (P.a.t) que la Marine Nationale mit en place à Cadarache aux débuts du programme militaire français.

En permanence à l'ordre du jour depuis 1954, le développement de la propulsion nucléaire reste au point mort en ce qui concerne les flottes marchandes malgré son brillant succès dans le domaine des marines nationales.

Pourquoi ce retard?

Indépendamment des réticences à caractére psychologiques qui s'expriment devant la perspective d'une application de l'énergie nucléaire quelle qu'elle soit, les raisons en sont de deux ordres: En premier lieu, un accord mondial sur les aspects réglementaires et juridiques constitue un préalable obligé à toute exploitation commerciale régulière, tant en ce qui concerne les règlements de sûreté et les modalités d'autorisation d'accès dans les ports, que les limitations de responsabilité, notamment le seuil au-delà duquel l'Etat du pavillon couvre la responsabilité des opérateurs; La valeur de ce seuil est un paramètre important du prix des assurances.

C'est sur ces aspects réglementaires et juridiques que se déploie actuellement la plus grande activité internationale; si un consensus général n'a pas encore été atteint, on peut raisonnablement escompter que le développement de la propulsion nucléaire, s'il en a souffert, n'en soit pas bloqué à terme dans la mesure oú l'acceptation du fait nucléaire n'aura pas regressé dans l'opinion publique.

La seconde résidait dans la faiblesse du prix du pétrole; on sait que les transports maritimes consomment 7% de la production mondiale de pétrole. Aussi l'intérêt général s'est-il vivement animé, donnant naissance à de nombreux projets, devant les hausses de fin 1973 qui laissaient entrevoir un regain de compétitivité économique tout en épargnant les hydrocarbures.

Une conférence tenue à New York a fait le point en juin 1975. On peut en retenir pour l'essentiel:

– une rechute de l'enthousiasme suscité l'année précédente par la hausse du prix du pétrole,

– un consensus général sur la certitude, à long terme, du développement de la propulsion nucléaire sur certains types de navires,

– une certaine dispersion des estimations des valeurs des paramétres gouvernant la rentabilité de la propulsion nucléaire.

Depuis ce sursaut d'intérêt, en effet, l'évolution de la conjoncture dans le transport maritime, tout particulièrement pétrolier, et dans la construction navale vers une situation de crise aigue a calmé les esprits: malgré l'aspect positif de l'expérience des marines militaires et des brise-glace soviétiques, aucune réalisation n'est en cours. Seuls existent des programmes d'études, ou des projets sur lesquels aucune décision ne paraît encore avoir été prise, abstraction faite d'un projet canadien de brise glace qui a fait l'objet d'appels d'offre.

Les perspectives actuelles de développement de la propulsion nucléaire civile sont donc dépendantes de l'évolution de la construction navale et du marché de fret, et dans l'hypothèse où cette évolution serait satisfaisante, de sa rentabilité économique qui dépend des coûts et performances comparées des propulsions classique et nucléaire, en fonction notamment de l'évolution prévisible des prix de l'énergie.

C'est le sujet de la présente communication, consacrée aux aspects économiques du développement de la propulsion nucléaire.

GÉNÉRALITÉS

L'aspect économique que nous abordons maintenant est primordial puisque la rentabilité est une condition nécessaire à la substitution de la propulsion nucléaire à la propulsion classique. Cette rentabilité est gouvernée par de nombreux paramètres dont les principaux sont le prix des soutes, 1e prix du cycle du combustible fissile et le supplément d'investissement propre à la propulsion nucléaire.[1]

Nous examinerons ces paramètres en premier.

Ensuite, notre démarche sera la suivante:

– Considérant des navires aux caractéristiques identiques (puissance et vitesse notamment), nous examinerons à partir de quel niveau de puissance, compte tenu du coefficient de charge de l'appareil propulsif, l'économie réalisée sur les combustibles permet d'amortir le supplément d'investissement dû à la propulsion nucléaire.

– Considérant le système de transport constitué par le bâtiment, compte tenu de la ligne et des conditions d'exploitation, nous chercherons à minimiser le prix de revient de l'unité de charge transportée en faisant varier la vitesse de croisière, et donc la puissance, pour deux types de navires: un pétrolier de 550 000 tonnes de port en lourd, sur le trajet Golfe Persique – Le Havre (calcul du prix de revient à la tonne transportée (Prtt); un méthanier de 130 000 m³ sur différents trajets (calcul du prix de revient de la thermie transportée). Nous n'aborderons pas ici le cas du navire porte-conteneurs, dans lequel interviennent des considérations commerciales difficiles à quantifier, mais qui paraissent constituer en réalité le domaine d'élection de l'apparition de la propulsion nucléaire.

– Nous examinerons enfin quelles économies d'hydrocarbures seraient permises par le développement de la propulsion nucléaire, critère susceptible de présenter de l'intérêt pour le décideur.

Dans cette étude économique, les hypothèses économiques de base, en particulier sur les suppléments d'investissement, sont assez floues. Aussi l'intérêt réside-t-il essentiellement dans les ordres de grandeur, les classements, les sensibilités aux hypothèses, plutôt que dans les valeurs brutes des résultats.

LE PRIX DES SOUTES

Dans la gamme des puissances pour lesquelles nous verrons ci-dessous que la substitution de l'énergie nucléaire est rentable, ou du moins neutre sur le plan économique, les appareils propulsifs sont à vapeur, et consomment 220 grammes de fuel lourd parchevalheure. L'évolution du prix des soutes est donc liée à celle du prix du pétrole brut et de la décote du fuel lourd par rapport au pétrole brut.

Le prix du pétrole brut

Indépendamment de toute réflexion politique, on peut s'interroger d'abord sur le sens du niveau actuel du prix du pétrole. Une étude récente[2], appuyée sur un modèle simple d'allocation des ressources, justifie l'existence d'une rente pétrolière: la minimisation du coût actualisé d'extraction implique d'épuiser les gisements dans l'ordre des coûts d'exploitation croissants tandis que le prix du pétrole doit différer du coût d'extraction d'une certaine quantité, de façon à expliciter l'anticipation de la croissance future du coût de production et à faire apparaître la nécessité d'éviter le gaspillage d'une ressource à coût croissant.

Un calcul simple, basé sur le coût d'extraction quasi nul des pétroles arabes, conduit à estimer la rente des producteurs à environ 3 dollars par baril, nettement inférieure à la rente existante, de l'ordre de la dizaine de dollars. Très théorique, cette approche ne permet pas de dégager un concept de prix optimal, car le prix réel résulte d'un jeu complexe.

Or son évolution à moyen terme constitue un élément important d'appréciation pour les décideurs qui envisagent des investissements destinés à développer de nouvelles ressources énergétiques ou à pro mouvoir des techniques génératrices d'économies. Ils calculent en effet la rentabilité de ces derniers en se fixant un prix directeur de l'énergie qui est le reflet de l'idée qu'ils se font de l'évolution du prix du pétrole au cours de la durée de vie de leur investissement.

De nombreux scénarios d'évolution peuvent certes être imaginés:

– La forte rigidité de la demande des pays développés donne une marge de manoeuvre importante à l'OPEP; son volume d'exportations semble devoir conserver un rythme élevé.

– La croissance de la part des importations des USA, que vise à réduire le recent plan Carter, est un élément de tension sur les prix;

– A l'inverse, les degrés de liberté réels ou supposés dont ils disposent sont des éléments de detente susceptibles d'entamer la stabilité de la position de l'OPEP.

– La persistance de l'état déprimé des économies des pays développés crée une situation relativement fragile à court terme, de nature à inciter les pays de l'OPEP à mener une politique de prix modérée, notamment sous la pression de l'Arabir Saoudite, ainsi qu'il en est aujourd'hui.

Dans l'ensemble, l'hypothèse sur laquelle s'accordent les observateurs est celle d'un maintien jusque vers 1985 à un niveau relativement élevé, quoique peut-être inférieur à celui atteint en 1974, compris à l'intérieur d'une fourchette de onze à quatorze dollars le baril (valeur 1977).

A plus long terme, une évolution haussiére apparait comme justifiée:

– Les coûts d'extraction du pétrole iront croîssants;

– La mise en oeuvre des énergies alternatives se révèle aujourd'hui moins aisée et plus coûteuse qu'on ne l'avait prévu il y a deux ou trois ans;

– Le prix actuel est insuffisant à assurer la rentabilité des énergies de substitution ou des techniques d'économies relativement capitalistiques, ainsi qu'à inciter les agents économiques à contenir leur consommation d'hydrocarbures en deça des capacités de production aujourd'hui prévisibles d'ici à quelques années.

Si l'on tient compte en outre du risque politique, la probabilité de fortes tensions sur les prix, dans la ligne de la revendication déja exprimée par Sarkis d'un niveau de 20 dollars le baril – contre 13 actuellement –, apparaît donc comme élevée.

Le prix du fuel lourd

Le prix du fuel lourd bénéficie d'une décote par rapport à celui du pétrole brut. La valeur de cette décote est variable selon l'adéquation de la structure de la demande de produits pétroliers à celle du raffinage et de considérations commerciales.

La valeur actuelle de l'ordre de 150 F/T de la décote du fuel lourd sur le marché français paraît liée à des raisons commerciales et conjoncturelles.

Néanmoins, le maintien de la décote à un niveau notable, quoique inférieur, peut être justifié par l'évolution de la structure de la demande dans laquelle, au moins dans les pays industrialisés, et tout particulièrement en France, la part des produits blancs croît.

En France notamment, l'accélération du programme nucléaire justifiera prochainement la conversion de quantités notables de fuel lourd, et une décote notable.

On est donc conduit à retenir plusieurs valeurs possibles de la décote, en fonction du marché local.

Les diverses combinaisons possibles encadrent une plage moyenne de 300 à 350 F/Tonne qui constituera l'hypothèse centrale de prix des soutes dans notre étude.

LE PRIX DU COMBUSTIBLE FISSILE

L'ensemble des operations d'extraction et de mise en oeuvre de l'uranium avant irradiation, de retraitement après, constitue le „cycle combustible", dont l'annexe O decrit et évalue les principales operations.

Le coût du cheval-heure s'établit dans une fourchette de 2,0 à 2,8 centimes; les hypothéses de base etant les suivantes:

Uranium: 200 à 250 F/Kg.;
UTS: 350 à 410 F/Kg.;
Fabrication: 1000 à 1500 F/Kg.;
Retraitement: 600 à 800 F/Kg.;
Plutonium: 40 à 50 F/g;
Taux d'irradiation: 30 000 MWj/t;

Outre ces facteurs, la taille du coeur, la durée et le taux d'irradiation, la fréquence et les modalités des renouvellements, constituent à puissance donnée des paramètres plus ou moins influents du coût du cycle qui ont un effet sur la fréquence optimale des rechargements, de l'ordre de un à quatre ans, tandis que sur les bâtiments militaires, les contraintes opérationnelles conduisent à une durée du cycle du combustible de l'ordre de 10 à 15 ans qui n'est pas économiquement optimale. Les résultats obtenus sont compris dans une fourchette de l'ordre de 2,0 à 2,8 c/ch.h., sans que les calculs qui précèdent reposent sur des hypothèses parfaitement fermes.

En effet, les valeurs numériques restent sujettes à caution. Ainsi, de même que le pétrole, l'uranium est une ressource naturelle, à coût d'extraction croissant, dont il existe des millions de tonnes disponibles à moins de 200 francs le kilo, mais dont les reserves, à l'inverse du pétrole, sont dispersées à travers le monde. Si la constitution d'un cartel de producteurs apparaît improbable, l'évolution de la situation pétroliére a permis la prise de rentes, puisque le prix de la livre d'oxyde U_3O_8 est rapidement passé, pour des contracts à long terme d'à peine 15 à une trentaine de dollars.

Il semble donc que le prix de l'uranium doive évoluer de façon semblable à celui du pétrole, quelques pointes près sur le marché spot; le fait que des réserves importantes soient détenues par des pays developpes en voie de disposer d'équipements nucléaires notables constitue a priori un élément de modération.

Le service d'enrichissement de l'uranium tend également à la hausse: cotée en 1975 à 350 francs, l'UTS est évaluée à 450 vers 1985.

Un élément incertain est le coût du retraitement, dont l'évaluation croît continuellement; son impact est à vrai dire mineur puisque viennent en déduction les crédits corrélatifs d'enrichissement et de plutonium; il est d'autant plus incertain que l'on n'est pas sûr qu'existent dans l'avenir des capacités de retraitement suffisantes. Peut-être donc ne serat-il pas réalisé.

Les coûts de fabrication du combustible, enfin, peuvent varier dans des fourchettes relativement larges et constituent l'élément essentiel d'incertitude dans une comparaison, tous prix précédents égaux, du coût du cheval-heure de propulsion nucléaire avec celui du Kwh produit par les centrales qu'E.D.F. construit actuellement, seule référence disponible à ce jour. En effet, bien que constitué d'oxyde d'uranium enrichi à un taux comparable ou légèrement supérieur à celui du combustible des centrales électrogènes, le combustible de propulsion navale civile ferait l'objet d'une fabrication particulière, en relativement petites séries, qu'il s'agisse d'éléments à crayons, adaptés du combustible des centrales terrestres, ou à plaques, dérivés de celui des sous-marins préconisé en France par Technicatome pour des raisons tenant essentiellement à l'accroissement de la sûreté de fonctionnement. De plus, les perspectives d'évolution du marché sont mal prévisibles. On pourrait s'attendre que sur un marché stabilisé, la différence de prix reste au moins de 30%.

SUPPLEMENT D'INVESTISSEMENT PROPRE A LA PROPULSION NUCLEAIRE

L'évaluation du supplément d'investissement propre à la propulsion nucléaire est délicate actuellement, car il n'existe pas de réalisation récente de référence. Ce supplément résulte de plusieurs éléments, tels que la substitution de la chaufferie nucléaire à la chaufferie classique, les renforcements de structure au droit de la chaufferie, les modifications éventuelles liées à des règlements de sécurité, les modifications de formes dues à l'augmentation éventuelle de la vitesse et, en sens inverse, la suppression des soutes à mazout, etc.

Ne pouvant faire une étude précise, nous signalerons que des évaluations approchées ont été tentées par divers auteurs; ceux-ci ont observé dans les centrales terrestres une élasticité du coût à la puissance de l'ordre de 0,45. Le supplement d'investissement correspondant à l'installation d'un appareil propusif nucléaire est peu different du coût propre de ce dernier.

On peut donc considérer comme vraisemblable l'évaluation suivante proposée par une étude relativement récente donnant une élasticité de 0,5, et aboutissant à la formule:

$\Delta = 0,3\ P^{1/2}$ en millions de francs 1972, intérêts intercalaires compris, dans laquelle Δ représente le surcoût d'investissement, et P la puissance de l'appareil propulsif.

Une estimation française plus récente prise comme hypothèse de travail dans une étude non publiée, atteignait 120 MF 74 pour 80 000/100 000 ch.

Sans doute les études américaines citées au cours de la conférence de New York font-elles état de montants supérieurs: 60 M$ par exemple pour un méthanier de 120 000 ch. par rapport au navire conventionnel de 105 000 ch., dont 34,5 M$ pour le générateur de vapeur; mais on doit rappeler que les évaluations américaines des coûts des centrales terrestres sont souvent de l'ordre du double de celles d'E.D.F.; car elles incluent le prix de la première charge et sont exprimées en dollars courants, alors que les évaluations françaises, exprimées en monuase constante, excluent la première charge.

Dans l'intervalle 60 000/150 000 ch., et dans le cas d'une fabrication en série par l'industrie française, première charge exclue, il nous est apparu raisonnable de tabler comme hypothèse de calcul sur

$\Delta = 0,5\ \sqrt{P}$ MF

Dans ces conditions, le surcoût annuel par cheval peut être évalué à $\dfrac{77\ 000\ F}{\sqrt{P}}$ avec un amortissement à 10% sur quinze ans et un coût d'assurance de 2,3% (valeur moyenne). La figure 1 donne l'allure de la courbe représentative de ce surcoût par cheval.

PREMIERE APPROCHE DE LA COMPETITIVITE DE LA PROPULSION NUCLEAIRE

En fonctionnement continu, un appareil propulsif marin à vapeur consomme environ 220 g de fuel lourd par cheval.heure, soit près de 2 tonnes/an/cheval.

Si les coûts de combustible sont désignés par:

− π francs la tonne de fuel lourd
− γ francs le cheval.heure nucléaire et si λ est le coefficient d'utilisation annuelle de l'appareil propulsif, l'économie annuelle par cheval de puissance installée résultant de la substitution du combustible nucléaire au fuel lourd est égale à $8\ 760\ \lambda\ [0,220\ 10^{-3}\pi - \gamma]$

Une variation de 50 F du prix de la tonne de fuel lourd équivaut à une variation de 1,1 cF du coût du combustible nucléaire. La figure 2 présente de façon graphique cette économie annuelle par cheval en fonction de λ pour $\gamma = 2,2$ cF/ch.h. et pour π variant par 50 F de 150 F à 400 F/tonne.

Economie annuelle par cv de puissance installée

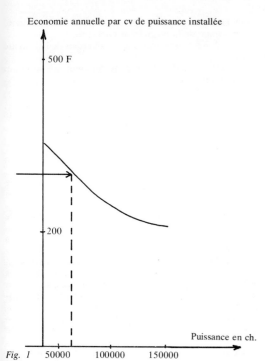

Fig. 1

Surcoût annuel d'amortissement et d'assurance par cheval dû à la propulsion nucléaire:
– Amortissement: 10% sur 15 ans
  Assurance: 2,3% par an

A partir des figures 1 et 2, on peut construire les courbes d'indifférence de la figure 3, qui pour un couple de valeurs du prix des soutes et du coût du cycle du combustible, donne en fonction du coefficient d'utilisation de la puissance propulsive le seuil de puissance pour lequel l'économie résultant de la substitution du combustible nucléaire au combustible fossile suffit à l'amortissement du surinvestissement lié à la propulsion nucléaire.

La figure 3 peut se lire de deux façons: à prix constant du combustible nucléaire (2,2 cF/ch.h) et prix des soutes variable de 250 à 400 F/T; à prix constant des soutes (350 F/T) et prix du combustible nucléaire variable de 1,1 à 4,4 c/ch.h. D'après cette figure, la compétitivité de l'énergie nucléaire apparaîtrait par exemple pour une utilisation annuelle supérieure à 62% d'une puissance de 70 000 ch lorsque les prix de l'énergie sont 350 F/T de fuel lourd et 2,2 c/ch.h nucléaire.

Pour ces niveaux de prix, une puissance de 100 000 ch est rentable à partir de 52% d'utilisation, mais une puissance de 50 000 ch à partir de 72% seulement. Une baisse du prix du fuel lourd de 50 F/T déplace ces seuils à 77% pour 70 000 ch, 64% pour 100 000 ch, mais 95% pour 50 000 ch; une hausse du combustible nucléaire de 1,1 cF pour 350 F/T a le même effet.

La compétitivité de la propulsion nucléaire apparaît ici plus sensible aux variations en valeur relative du prix du fuel lourd que du combustible nucléaire, mais plus encore à celle du coefficient de charge.

En prenant un coefficient de charge de 66%, un prix des soutes de 300 F et un prix de combustible de 3,3 cF/ch.h, la compétitivité de la propulsion nucléaire apparaîtrait au niveau de 90.000 ch.

Si les hypothèses précédentes ne sont pas optimistes, on peut cependant retenir cette valeur comme ordre de grandeur raisonnable de la puissance de base du navire nucléaire.

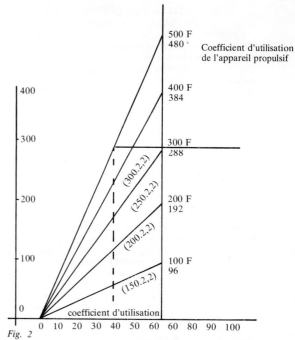

Fig. 2

Economie annuelle résultant de la substitution de combustible nucléaire au fuel lourd par cheval de puissance installée pour différents couples de valeurs:
– prix du fuel en francs/tonne;
– prix du combustible nucléaire en centimes/ch.ch

On peut utiliser l'ensemble des figures 1 et 2 en abaque pour estimer la compétitivité de la propulsion nucléaire en fonction des divers paramètres. (figure 3)

L'abaque se lit:
en A: à prix constant du combustible finile (2,2c/ch.h) et prix des soutes variable (250 à 400 F/T)
en B: à prix constant des sortes (350 F/T) et prix du combustible fissile variable: (1,1 à 4,4 c/ch.h)

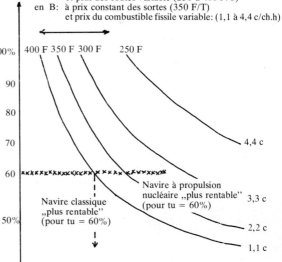

Fig. 5

Figure 3

Seuil de puissance en fonction du taux d'utilisation, qui rend l'économie résultant de la substitution du combustible nucléaire au combustible fossile égale à l'amortissement du surinvestissement lie' à la propulsion nucléaire (courbes construites à partir des figures 1 et 3)

349

COMPARAISON DES COÛTS À L'UNITÉ DE CHARGE TRANSPORTÉE

Quoique relativement sommaire, le raisonnement précédent a le mérite d'illustrer simplement les conditions de compétitivité économique de la propulsion nucléaire en fonction de quatre paramètres essentiels: le surcoût de la propulsion nucléaire, les prix des combustibles fossile et fissile, le coefficient de charge de l'appareil propulsif; il nous a permis d'obtenir une évaluation de la puissance raisonnable d'un navire nucléaire, soit 90 000 ch.

Une approche plus globale, qui se prête à une étude de sensibilité, consiste à considérer l'économie globale du système de transport et à rechercher la minimisation du prix de revient à l'unité de fret transportée, tonne de pétrole ou thermie de gaz (Prtt), compte tenu des paramètres économiques et de la vitesse de croisière du bâtiment, le navire étant optimisé en fonction de cette dernière. Le lecteur trouvera en annexe les grandes lignes du calcul de Prtt pour un pétrolier de 550 000 tonnes de port en lourd sur le trajet Le Havre-Golfe Persique (11 200 milles nautiques) et les résultats obtenus pour un transporteur de gaz naturel liquéfié (méthanier) de 130 000 m³ sur différents trajets.

Dans le cas du pétrolier, la figure 4 illustre les résultats sous la forme de courbes représentant les variations de l'indice du Prtt en fonction de la vitesse dans les deux hypothèses: propulsion classique et propulsion nucléaire, pour deux valeurs du prix du combustible dans chaque hypothèse. Le caractère très plat de l'optimum du Prtt du bâtiment à propulsion nucléaire, situé entre 20 et 25 noeuds, ne justifie pas d'envisager de relever la vitesse au-delà des 19 à 20 noeuds qui paraissent constituer la limite technologique imposée à moyen terme par les hélices pour des bâtiments de cette taille à deux lignes d'arbres à rotation lente. On observe que le Prtt, pris égal à 100 pour le bâtiment conventionnel navigant à 16 noeuds (1) s'abaisse vers 92 à 98 pour le bâtiment à propulsion nucléaire navigant entre 19 et 20 noeuds.

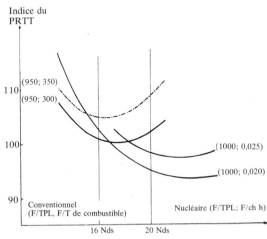

Figure 4 - Variations du PRTT

La valeur intrinsèque de ces résultats bruts n'est autre que celle des hypothèses faites; aussi l'attention ne doit-elle pas se porter sur ces valeurs numériques, mais sur la sensibilité des valeurs du Prtt et des vitesses optimales aux variations des paramètres économiques, résultat qui nous semble de prime abord le plus intéressant, susceptible de faciliter la réponse aux questions qui peuvent être posées sur les perspectives de compétitivité économique de la propulsion nucléaire.

Ainsi, on a obtenu quelques évaluations de l'élasticité du Prtt:
— dans le cas du navire conventionnel, à l'optimum (vers 16 noeuds):
0,3 au prix du combustible;
0,6 au prix de la coque.
— dans le cas du navire à propulsion nucléaire (vers 19/20 noeuds):
0,6 à 0,7 au coefficient „amortissement + assurances;
0,11 au coût du combustible nucléaire;
0,10 au surcoût propre au caractère nucléaire de la propulsion.

Dans les deux cas, l'élasticité au prix de la coque est de l'ordre de 0,6.

Ainsi le Prtt est-il trois fois moins sensible à l'évolution du combustible nucléaire qu'à celle du combustible fossile. De plus, l'incidence de l'évolution des composants du coût du cycle combustible nucléaire est très modérée: le doublement du prix de l'uranium n'augmenterait le Prtt que de 3,5% environ, celvi de l'UTS de 4%, celvi du coût de frabrication de 4% environ. Dans les hypothèses de coût de retraitement choisies, soit 600 à 800 francs par Kilogramme, et pour un prix du plutonium de 40 à 50 F/g, l'exécution du retraitement diminuerait le Prtt de 1%; le doublement de son prix en annulerait le crédit, laissant ainsi le coût du cycle, et donc le Prtt inchangé.

De la même façon, l'incidence du surcoût d'investissement proprement nucléaire apparait limité; en definitive, les facteurs les plus influents sont le prix de la coque elle-même, et les conditions d'amortissement et d'assurance.

Dans le cas d'un méthanier de 130 000 m³, sur un trajet court du type Algérie – Manche/Mer du Nord, les prix de revient à la thermie transportée sont équivalents, tandis que sur un trajet long, du type Iran – U.S.A., la propulsion nucléaire peut apporter un gain de l'ordre de 15% sur un bâtiment plus rapide (27 à 28 noeuds).

ECONOMIE D'HYDROCARBURES LIÉE À LA PROPULSION NUCLÉAIRE

Un facteur peut-être mieux susceptible d'emporter la décision de certains responsables en faveur de la propulsion nucléaire est celui de l'économie d'hydrocarbures. On sait en effet qu'un navire de 280 000 tonnes de port en lourd (TPL) consomme sur le trajet précité 40 kg de fuel par tonne de pétrole transportée et par rotation, soit 4% de sa cargaison. Plus économe, un navire de 550 000 tonnes optimisé pour seize noeuds se contente de 30 kg par tonne.

On observe ainsi que si la moitié de la flotte assurant l'acheminement de l'approvisionnement français était nucléaire, l'économie de soutes réalisée se chiffrerait à prés de 2,5 millions de tonnes, soit un milliard de devises.

L'investissement par tonne de capacité annuelle du système de transport est de l'ordre de 160 francs dans le cas du navire classique, et supérieur de moins de 10% dans le cas du navire nucléaire. A supposer que l'on considère que le surinvestissement lié à la propulsion nucléaire comme exlusivement affecté à la réalisation de l'économie d'hydrocarbures, il s'avère que par tonne d'équivalent pétrole économisée annuellement il reste inférieur à 500 F. On peut porter une appréciation sur la valeur de ce montant en notant que les industriels ont en France tendance à réaliser spontanément, c'est à dire sans subvention; des investissements économisant l'énergie dont le coût est de cet ordre; on considére par ailleurs qu'un coût inférieur à 2000 F est acceptable pour la collectivité. Enfin, le coût correspondant pour des opérations de géothermie atteint 5000 F par tonne économisée; il évolue de 5000 à 25000 F dans les opérations portant sur l'énergie solaire.

CONCLUSION

L'exploitation de navires marchands à propulsion nucléaire semble recevoir, pour une partie non négligeable du transport maritime, une justification économique, qui est plus évidente si elle est appréciée du point de vue collectif que du point de vue de l'armateur.

Certes, les évaluations sont sujettes à un certain nombre d'aléas, qui affectent les coûts d'investissement, d'exploitation d'assurance, de prix du combustible, et qui tiennent à l'absence de toute réalisation de référence. Le maintien du prix du pétrole à un niveau élevé constitue par ailleurs une condition nécessaire de compétitivité de la propulsion nucléaire, tandis que le prix de l'uranium naturel et celui de l'UTS sont également des paramètres non dénués d'influence sur le prix du combustible nucléaire.

Trois types de bâtiments sont susceptibles de remplir les conditions de rentabilité de l'exploitation d'un navire marchand à propulsion nucléaire:
— puissance importante et vitesse élevée, de façon que l'économie réalisée sur le combustible soit sensible;
— coût élevé d'investissement du bâtiment conventionnel, de façon que le surcoût nucléaire soit faible en valeur relative;
— coefficient d'utilisation de la puissance propulsive élevé, comme dans le cas de tout équipement;
— valeur de la cargaison élevée, de façon que les frais d'immobilisation de la cargaison, plus faibles si le navire est plus rapide, puissent intervenir.

Ces bâtiments sont:
— les transporteurs de gaz liquéfiés,
— les porte-conteneurs,
— les pétroliers géants.

Dans le cas des transporteurs de gaz liquéfiés, la conclusion n'est pas encore apparue très positive à la conférence de New York. Les résultats que nous avons obtenus, quoique approximatifs, recoupent ceux avancés à cette conférence: un avantage n'apparaît que pour de longues distances, supérieures à celles que parcourent les méthaniers concourant à l'approvisionnement de la France. On ne doit donc pas escompter voir un armateur français envisager de se doter de transporteurs de gaz liquéfié à propulsion nucléaire pour le service de l'approvisionnement français; inversement, le marché étranger (très étendu puisque l'O.C.D.E. envisage une capacité totale de transport de l'ordre de 7.10^6 m^3 en 1980, et près du double en 1985, dont l'essentiel en service sur des liaisons à très long cours) pourrait être largement ouvert à la propulsion nucléaire, d'autant que, dans ce cas, la valorisation de l'économie d'hydrocarbures est supérieure, puisque le gaz qui s'évapore chaque jour est reliquéfié au lieu d'être brûlé par les chaudières, ce qui, de plus, augmente ipso facto la capacité de transport du navire. En raison de la forte position de certains chantiers français sur le marché de ce type de bâtiments, le développement de la propulsion nucléaire serait de nature à consolider leur situation qui constitue un sujet de préoccupation à moyen terme.

Dans le cas des porte-conteneurs, l'équivalence économique pour un bâtiment de 120 000 ch à 30 nds se situerait vers 7 $ le baril pour un combustible à 2,5 millls/ch.h [3] (conférence de New York); l'hypotèse de 2,5 mills paraît très optimiste. A notre avis, il faut compter 4 à 5 mills/ch.h, ce qui remonte le prix d'équivalence du pétrole vers 8,5 à 9 $/baril, valeur nettement inférieure au prix actuellement pratiqué. Nous n'avons pas fait d'étude précise dans ce cas, compte tenu du caractère, très délicat de la prise en compte de certains aspects commerciaux. Il semblerait que ce soit sur des bâtiments

de ce type, qui est celui exploité par le Consortium Soa Land, que la propulsion nucléaire civile puisse le plus facilement percer.

Enfin, dans le cas des pétroliers géants, la propulsion nucléaire se présente différemment selon que l'on se place du point de vue de l'armateur ou de celui de la collectivité française. Du point de vue de l'armateur, le recours à la propulsion nucléaire apparaît en effet sans intérêt majeur puisque, si l'investissement à consentir pour une même capacité de transport n'est que peu supérieur, il ne procure qu'une faible économie sur le Prtt, le bilan actualisé à la tonne restant peu sensible au mode de propulsion. Par contre, du point de vue de la collectivité nationale ce recours presente un interet certain au plan des échanges exterieurs. En résumé, le navire porte-conteneurs apparaîtrait comme le mieux placé, dans la mesure où les U.S.A. concrétiseront leurs projets sur ce type de bâtiments, tandis que la compétitivité des transporteurs de gaz liquéfiés ne se dégagerait que pour des liaison du type Iran-Côte Ouest des U.S.A. et qu'à capacité de transport donnée, le bilan actualisé des coûts d'investissement et d'exploitation d'une flotte pétrolière semblerait peu sensible au mode de propulsion.

Si diverses estimations évaluent à près d'une cinquantaine le nombre de navires nucléarisables dans la production annuelle durant décennie 1980-1990, il faut noter

Annexe 0

LE PRIX DU COMBUSTIBLE FISSILE

L'ensemble des opérations d'extraction et de mise en oeuvre de l'uranium, avant irradiation, de retraitement après, constitue le cycle combustible, dont le schéma ci-dessous décrit les opérations essentielles.

Ce schéma retrace les flux de matières combustibles, rapportés à un kilogramme d'uranium mis en pile, dans le cas d'un enrichissement à 4,5% en isotope U 235.

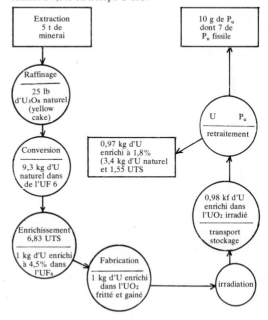

Le tableau 1 donne les principaux éléments de son coût avec des hypothèses moyennes sur le prix de l'uranium, de l'enrichissement, de la fabrication des éléments combustibles et du retraitement.

Le Tableau 2 donne les valeurs extrêmes du coût de cycle déduites des coûts unitaires précédents. Taux d'irradiation: 30 000 MWj/tonne. Rendement thermodynamique de l'appareil propulsif: 30%. Charges financières: 20%.

qu'en raison des délais de réalisateur, la mise en sevice du premier navire à propulsion ne saurait être envisagée pour une date antérieure à 1982; ceci permet d'escompter que d'ici là les problèmes juridiques et réglementaires aient trouvé des solutions et que le niveau de la demande de transport maritimes soit redevenu suffisant pour assurer des conditions d'exploitation commerciale satisfaisantes. Mais l'incertitude conjoncturelle au moyen terme hypotheque le démarrage: Indépendamment des aspects juridiques, réglementaires, écologiques et psychologiques, le creux de la construction navale qui se profile pour le courant du VII° Plan n'est pas de nature à inciter les chantiers à investir dans son développement, à moins que ceux-ci n'y voient un axe privilégié d'extension de leur activité, et que la longueur du délai de réalisation des chaufferies nucléaires, de l'ordre de quatre à cinq ans, est nettement supérieure à celle de la construction des navires conventionnels, peut dissuader un armateur à se lancer aujourd'hui dans cette innovation.

Tableau 1

Opérations	Coûts * unitaires	Application des prix aux quantités	Remarques
Obtention de 9,3 kg d'U nat.	200 à 250 F/kg	1 860 à 2 325 F	—
Fluoration	15 à 18 F	140 à 170 F	
Enrichissement: 6,83 UTS à	350 à 410 F	2 390 à 2 800 F	—
Fabrication de 1 kg de combustible	1000 à 1 500 F	1 000 à 1 500 F	—
Ratraitement	600 à 800 F	600 à 800 F	valeurs actualisées à 5 ans: 370 à 500 F
Crédits: 0,97 kg d'U à 1,8% équivalent à:			Valeurs actualisées à 5 ans:
3,4 kg d'U naturel	200 F à 250 F	680 à 850 F	420 à 530 F
1,55 UTS	350 à 410 F	540 à 635 F	335 à 395 F
7 g Pu fissile	40 à 50 F	280 à 350 F	175 à 220 F

Tableau 2

	Coût du cycle pour 1 kg (F)		Coût du cheval-heure (cF)	
	Min	Max	Min	Max
Avec retraitement	4 970	6 495	2,03	2,65
Sans retraitement	5 390	6 795	2,20	2,78

* Ces coûts, exprimés en fleues 1 p + 5, sont ceux de repoque.

Annexe 1

EXEMPLE DE CALCUL DU PRIX DE REVIENT COMPARE DE LA TONNE TRANSPORTEE PAR PETROLIERS DE 550 000 TPL A PROPULSION CONVENTIONNELLE OU NUCLEAIRE

Notations:
Puissance P en chevaux;
Vitesse de croisière V en noeuds;
Prix du bâtiment par tonne de port en lourd: pN en francs
Amortissement + assurances: fraction λ du total de l'investissement;
Prix des soutes: π francs la tonne;
Prix du combustible fissile: γ centimes le cheval-heure.

Les principaux paramètres économiques du Prtt sont le prix de base du navire par tonne de port en lourd, le surcoût d'investissement du navire nucléaire, l'hypothèse d'amortissement, le coût du combustible nucléaire, celui du combustible fossile.

Surcoût d'investissement lié à la propulsion nucléaire:
La puissance propulsive croît comme le cube de la vitesse; pour le pétrolier de 550 000 TPL P et V sont liés par la relation P = 13,7 V³.

Le bâtiment est supposé optimisé pour chaque vitesse de croisière. Ses formes, et donc pN, en dépendent donc. On admet les valeurs suivantes dans le calcul de base:
pN = 950 F pour le bâtiment conventionnel (16 noeuds);
pN = 1 000 F pour le bâtiment nucléaire navigant vers 19/20 noeuds, hors le surcoût purement nucléaire évalué à 0,5 √P, soit 1,85 10⁶ V³²

L'exactitude de ces coûts de construction par TPL ne présente que peu d'importance pour l'interprétation des calculs effectués, dont l'intérêt est surtout d'évaluer un ordre de grandeur et une sensibilité à l'incertitude sur les dits coûts, ainsi qu'à classer les résultats du navire nucléaire par rapport au navire conventionnel.

Coûts de combustible:

	Immobilisation pour carenage	Séjours au port et au mouillage	Consommations de fuel	Coûts de combustible γ le ch.h nucléaire π F la tonne de fuel
Conventionnel . . .	15 j	30 j	220 g fuel/ch.h	24,66 π V³
Nucléaire . . .	20 j	40 j	—	109 200 V³ γ

Nombre de rotations annuelles:

Le nombre annuel de rotations sur le trajet Le Havre-Golfe Persique (11 200 milles). est de

Nucléaire	Conventionnel
345	(ou 350)

$$\frac{11\ 200}{12\ V} + 6$$

En prenant les frais fixes d'exploitation égaux à 10 MF/an dans les deux cas, le prix de revient de la tonne transportée s'établit comme suit:

$$\text{Prtt conv} = \frac{550\ 000\ pN \bullet \lambda + 24,66\ V^3\ \pi + 10^7}{550\ 000\ \dfrac{350\ V}{933 + 6\ V}}$$

$$\text{Prtt nucl} = \frac{(550\ 000\ pN + 1,85 \bullet 10^6\ V^{3/2})\ \gamma + 109\ 200\ V^3\gamma + 10^7}{550\ 000\ \dfrac{345\ V}{933 + 6\ V}}$$

Annexe 2

EXEMPLES DE CALCUL DES COUTS COMPARES DU TRANSPORT DE GAZ NATUREL PAR METHANIERS DE 130 000 M3 A PROPULSION CONVENTIONNELLE OU NUCLEAIRE

Les caractéristiques principales des navires en cause sont les suivantes:

– volume des cuves de cargaison: 130 000 m3;
– port en lourd en service: 64 340 T;
– vitesse aux essais: 20 noeuds;
– puissance correspondante: 38 000 ch;
– P max continue de l'appareil propulsif: 45 000 ch;
– volume de fuel-oil des soutes: 4 400 m3;
– la relation entre P et V est: P = 4,75 V³.
Le coût actuel d'investissement de ces navires est de l'ordre de 5 000 F/m3 de Gnl. Un mètre cube de Gnl représente environ 600 m3 de gaz aux conditions normales de température et de

pression. Le méthanier de 130 000 m3, chargé à 98%, transporte environ 77 10[6] m3 de gaz, soit environ 700 millions de thermies, ou l'équivalent de 70 000 Tep.

L'isolation thermique des cuves est assez poussée pour réduire l'évaporation à environ 0,25% par jour, soit 320 m3 et l'équivalent de 175 Tep. Le Gnl évaporé est consommé dans les chaudières, mélangé à 10% au moins de fuel-oil et permet donc d'alimenter l'appareil propulsif développant quelque 36 000 ch, soit une puissance proche de celle qui correspond à la vitesse de 20 noeuds. Ainsi donc, la chaufferie consomme le Gnl évaporé et un appoint de fuel relativement faible; lorsque le navire navigue à vide (sur ballasts), il consomme uniquement du fuel dont ses soutes contiennent 4 400 m3.

La propulsion nucléaire permet d'augmenter la charge utile en rendant disponible l'espace occupé par les cuves à mazout et en facilitant la reliquéfaction du boil-off. On peut donc admettre que la capacité de transport effective du navire doit augmenter d'environ 10 000 m3, toutes choses étant égales par ailleurs, sur des liaisons longues (trois semaines), sans augmentation sensible du coût total du navire, abstraction faite du surcoût propre à la chaufferie nucléaire [4].

Bien que le navire consomme une quantité notable de gaz comme combustible, on ne tient pas compte du prix de départ de celui-ci dans le calcul comparé des prix de revient du transport de la thermie, car il faut considérer que toute thermie de gaz consommée au cours du transport doit être compensée par une thermie de pétrole. Les coûts de combustible fossile devraient donc être pris égaux au coût de la thermie de pétrole.

On admet que les délais d'escale sont de deux jours par rotation, les opérations de manutention du gaz pouvant s'effectuer en 12 heures environ, que les délais annuels de carénage sont de 15 jours, que la fraction ,,amortissement + assurances" est de 13,5% [5] et que les frais d'exploitation sont de 10 millions par an.

Deux trajets-types ont été retenus:

Le trajet A est soit Rotterdam-Golfe Persique, soit Golfe Persique-Los Angeles (de l'ordre de 11 500 milles parcourus à 20 noeuds).

Le trajet B est Algérie-Mancher/Mer du Nord (2 600 milles).

Pour chaque trajet, on a considéré les trois hypothèses suivantes:

– bâtiment conventionnel navigant à 20 noeuds;
– bâtiment nucléaire navigant à 20 noeuds (surcoût nucléaire de 150 MF);
– bâtiment nucléaire navigant à 27,5 noeuds (surcoût nucléaire de 200 MF).

Il est en effet intuitif que la vitesse économique du méthanier nucléaire est nettement supérieure à 20 noeuds. Un calcul approché indique que cette vitesse est de l'ordre de 35 à 40 noeuds, valeur déraisonnable sur le plan technique, compte tenu notamment de la platitude de l'optimum et de la valeur élevée de la puissance correspondante, de l'ordre de 250 000 chevaux.

On a donc recherché le Prtt pour un navire à deux lignes d'arbres transmettant chacune 50 000 ch à la vitesse de croisière; celle-ci est de l'ordre de 27,5 noeuds.

Les résultats sont les suivants (cF/th):

	Trajet A (long)	Trajet B (court)
Conventionnel . . .	2,60	0,57
Nucléaire à 20 noeuds	2,51	0,60
Nucléaire à 27,5 noeuds	2,27	0,56

NOTES EN BAS DE PAGES

1. Sauf mention contraire: évaluations en francs 1975
2. Nota: Hausse du prix du pétrole et choix économique. Statistiques études financières, 1976 21
3. mill: millième de dollar U.S.
4. Dans la réalité, le navire de 130 000 m3 à propulsion nucléaire aurait un port en lourd inférieur d'environ 3 500 tonnes et serait plus fin.
5. Amortissement à 10% sur 20 ans + 1,8% d'assurances.

Interaction of costs and technological developments in the shipping industry

by

N. Dijkshoorn

Netherlands Maritime Institute,

University of Technology, Delft, Department of Shipbuilding and Shipping

NO-THROUGH ROADS

The above mentioned topic requires a more detailed explanation. Hidden within the subject-matter are conflicting elements which can only be in harmony with each other after a suitable synthesis has been found. Part of my work consists of giving lectures in the following two fields, Marine Engineering and Shipping. The days on which the lectures on shipping take place begins by taking a critical attitude towards all technologists, especially marine engineers who, armed with facts concluded from optimisation-procedures, are determined to improve shipping. At such a moment the boundary conditions within which shipping must find itself present themselves. There are many conditions: trace balance, investment restrictions, solvency, risks, market trends, price developments, changes in transport methods etc. The interests of a country or those of an individual shipowner should, within the context of international boundaries, be served. The room for manoeuvring is relatively small and is more than often marginal; the space for new concepts is bound by a multitude of rules. As the door of the university opens the first proposition is put in words: "Discussion of Technological Developments approached solely from a technical point of view is, with respect to the other interests at stake, of no avail". Bearing this in mind any direct effect which may be the benefit of a new concept is put into second place. A second proposition supports this: "Technological Developments are not directly, and quite naturally so, responsible for changes in income and expenditure". Due to these propositions technical progress has been moved to second place. It is now quite clear that in order to join the two main elements of this topic an extension of the horizon must be realised. This horizon must be found by using further analysis and the supposition can already be offered that insight and penetration will be gained when the technological aspects are placed in the complete life-pattern of shipping; this pattern includes the people involved and the countries in which they reside. This aspect is considered to fill the first place. Both ways of thinking however, that of the second as well as the first place, call upon caution to be exercised. On the days when lectures on marine engineering take place a critical attitude is then exercised towards all "shipping-people", these being almost completely immune to any technical progress. From of old, when it comes to introducing changes, shipping has been reticent. This being said with the exclusion of recklessness and on-purpose acceptance of risks, whilst thinking in terms of a decently kept ship sailed by a competent crew in all respects. The sea, when indulged in her game of forces with a ship, is without pity and poor visibility or bad weather is of no excuse when accidents occur. The sea answers to no one for her deeds.

The risks of a technical-breakdown also include the threats of high costs and operational damages. These effects have left their mark on the character of shipping.

The introduction of important technical developments, being attached to long periods of testing and gaining of experience, leads inevitably to high investment costs. The abundance of boundary conditions relating to a ship however almost always result in doubts concerning the application of laboratory test-results on board without first-hand ship experience.

Both ways of thinking, that of the shipowner as well as that of the technologist, also calls for caution. The first of these two creates false perspectives due to his inclination towards isolation when faced with progress or new concepts, the second however forms false perspectives concerning the demands of the sea or even the complete world of shipping itself.

Should both proceed to exist apart from each other, then the inevitable outcome will be that both shall walk their own separate roads during the span of their lifetime.

The following analysis is aimed at finding some "facts of interest" which will prevent the taking of these "hypothetical no-through roads".

ANALYSIS OF THE SHIPPING SYSTEM

By taking the factors which already fill the first place a form of presentation can be found that represents an integrated shipping-system. The total system comprises of all the elements that govern the behaviour of shipping. For the sake of clarity and supervision the size of the system must not be too large. It must therefore be simplified, be it with the aid of depreciating abstraction or the method of alternating abstraction. Having reduced the size of the system the role played by typical influencing factors will still be noticeable whilst, with the aid of sensitivity analysis, less important factors can be dispensed of.

Within the system shipping one finds the sub-system ship. The conflicts resulting from demands and possibilities are related to the typical influencing factors within the system, from this a dynamic compromise can be arrived at and numerically fixed.

These qualities can be found in the report "U.S. Ocean Shipping Technology Forecast and Assessment"[1], which deals with the future developments of shipping in U.S.A. analysed on the same bases as mentioned above.

The basic-relations diagram can, after suitable remoulding, be used as starting point for shipping under different conditions.

Figure 1 shows the diagram of relation in which governments play an important part. Figure 2 represents

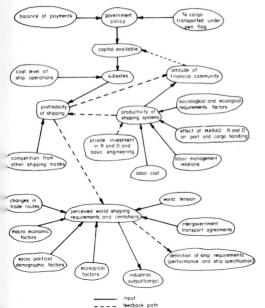

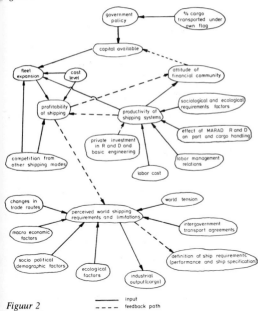

input   input
- - - -   feedback path

Figuur 1

input   input
- - - -   feedback path

Figuur 2

Productivity of shipping systems is related to:

input:
- labor costs
- labor managements relations
- effect of government sponsored research and development on port and cargo handling
- sociological and ecological requirements factors

feedback: + private investment in research and development and basic engineering

Profitability of shipping is related to:
= world shipping requirements and limitations
= productivity of shipping systems

input:
- competition from other shipping modes
- subsidies

Attitude of financial community is related to:
= profitability of shipping
= productivity of shipping systems

input:
- cost level of ship operations
- balance of payments
- % cargo transported under own flag
- government policy
- capital available

When governments play a decisive role the cost level of ship operations, as mentioned under attitude of financial community, is directly related to the office granting subsidy; the latter also regulating influence and monitoring with the government as sponsor.

By free enterprise, without government intervention, changes occur in the system. Fleet expansion is then a result of profit and capital availability.

The sponsoring of research and development remains intact and only the interaction between costs and technological development is apparent.

Via a number of indirect influences technological developments can be freely handled within a combined shipping and economical system of a country. In a way one can see this happening in underdeveloped countries which start with simple, not completely new ships. In these cases the available ships are run on general basic experience resulting in little research requirement.

On the other hand, in countries where priority is given to advanced transport systems which only become profitable after a long introduction period, research may be found to occupy a dominant position. This type of priority is aimed at obtaining a guarantee regarding transportation of a prognosticated cargo-quota by ships sailing under her own flag. The thought of an advantage results in the acceptance of high risks and in the providing of large capital amounts. Seeing as how limited an undeveloped country is in making up deficiencies in her daily exploitation costs, a matter where extreme caution should be exercised even for a developed country, susceptibility for useful and costsaving developments can be strongly felt.

The independant undertaker knows of no subsidy and is entirely committed to the results of technological developments in order to increase his profits.

The three afore-mentioned possibilities are grouped together in table 1.

Table 1 – Control of developments
CD1 no noticible change in low cost developments
CD2 high level of developments sponsored by government investments
CD3 medium level of developments, directly related to short term advantages

the same type of diagram for free enterprise.

The main elements are:
– perceived world shipping requirements and limitations
– productivity of shipping systems
– profitability of shipping
– attitudes of financial community

Perceived world shipping is related to:

input:
- macro economic factors
- production levels per country
- world tension
- intergovernment transport agreements
- socio, political and demographic factors
- ecological factors

feedback: + definition of ship requirements, with regard to capacities and performances

355

These three systems do not tend towards a state of equilibrium. By a change in one of the three uncertainty appears by the other two . Since research and development are both connected to their surroundings, their manifestations will have to be looked into in order to make a more accurate analysis.

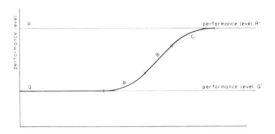

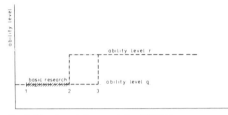

Fig. 3 Time based characteristics (TBC 1)

MANIFESTATIONS OF TECHNOLOGICAL DEVELOPMENTS

In a simple diagram actual situations and the different phases therein can be drawn up for research in shipping, Figures 3 and 4 show two possibilities.

In figure 3 two lines draw attention, that of ability level and that of performance level. These are both time-based.

At time-point 1 a basic-research program is started and at time-point 2 has reached such a stage that it can be wholly or partly applied. The application possibilities are accepted, or the circumstances are favourable, for the first time at time-point 3.

During application of the newly found know-how or learning the performance curve moves through three different phases, namely A, B and C.

In the first phase A research is directed at finding ways and methods to realise application. It bears the mark of a slow starting period in which each success or small advancement leads to encouragement. With few means an increase in performance level is obtained.

In the second phase B application on a larger scale has presented itself and becomes even larger. Owing to distribution to an abundant number of users a more rapid increase is seen in the performance curve. There is little attention payed to detail improvement, at this stage all effort being concentrated on the advancement itself and there are no unfavourable influences felt because large application has not yet given any feed-back.

In the third phase C feed-back takes an active part in slowing down application as well as introducing itself. Sociological and ecological arguments start to take part in further developments and in this stage also negative effects are recognised and play a part in detail developments. This given picture is of course a strongly simplified one, however it gives us the opportunity to find connecting-points with which we can approach given real situations.

Figure 4 shows a different configuration. In the period A 1 development has begun without any previous basic-research. Some results are gained thus showing the need

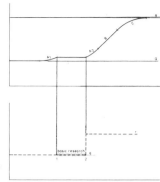

Fig. 4 - Time based characteristics (TBC 2)

for further research which in it's turn leads yet again to an increase in results. The remaining part of the performance lines conform with those of figure 3.

To find a suitable way for application in the Shipping Industry a selection must be made of the most important State Variables. Table 2 shows some of these important factors. A further analysis will have to take place in order to be able to apply and appreciate the dependence of these state variables on each other. The time-relationship of these variables must also be taken into consideration.

In the following, examples will be given showing past developments and the different stages therein. As restriction however, it may already be stated that in these examples only new ideas, one could call them boundary rectifying, are used. Phase B only deals with partial improvements. An example of this is the container-crane. In phase A the crane is realized and purchased by cargo-handling companies. In phase B research studies are made to increase speeds. The elements which arise out of this are well known techniques, increase of power, application and learning of kinematics, electronic control and the fitting out of a feed-back mechanism in order to correct the followed path via actual readings.

These developments belong to the types of gradual changes which are always taking place in industry and will proceed to do so until eternity.

Table 2 - State Variables

Un certainty
Costs
Technological developments
Interactions
Control of developments
Time based characteristics

PAST DEVELOPMENTS

Around the year 1950 the change was made to heavy fuel 3000 sec. R.I. for ships main engines.

The decision to make this experiment was so abrupt that it is now difficult to know whether ship costs gave the first impulse, or technical curiosity, or the persistence of the oil producers to boost the sale of this fuel type.

Without any preliminary research on board of ships at all, trials were taken and the involved risks were accepted. Indeed these risks turned out to be rather nasty. Consequently basic research was set up and after a few years the main problem of high cylinder wear belonged to the past. In fact as far as technical knowledge was concerned there was a sufficient amount of this available at the time of initiating the use of heavy fuels on board of ships.

However there was a boundary condition in force which made high demands on the ship's officers at the same time.

Bearing this in mind the table of state variables (table 2) can now be filled in:

Uncertainty	Negligible
Influence on costs	Positive
Technological developments	Favourable
Interaction	Indifferent
Control of developments	CD3 (table 1)
Time based characteristics	TBC 2 (figure 4)

Figure 5 shows the interrelationships.

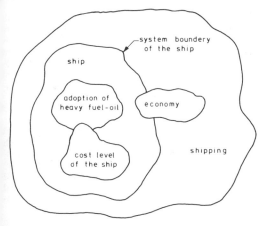

Figuur 5   — developed technology

Ten years later, around 1960, a far greater and far more spectacular development began to play a role. This development is well known under the name of automation.

This name is a collective term for many intermingling conceptions. In this case the basis mechanisms are otherwise orientated than in the foregoing. Here cost influencing is one of the main aims. Which expenditures can the shipowner cut down?

The choice of the ship follows from an optimization procedure, the capital costs result from the building costs, subsidies, investment decisions and replacement procedures. Insurance is a factor which can be reduced to a minimum by good crew policy and the same can be said for cargo claims. Fuel costs result from the choice of ship.

As a result the most prominent variables with which the total casts can be directly influenced are crew and maintenance costs.

Around 1960 the freight market trend and the in between time strongly increased wage sum resulted in powerful economical pressure to reduce expenditures. Meanwhile, by increasing the dependability of the engines and machines and their production methods while also continuing research in analysing breakdowns, overal increase in reliability of the whole plant was realized. Both of these were stimulated as it happens by competition of the companies involved.

Due to the already mentioned economical pressure a reduction of the crew number became feasible and was put into practice. In fact a remarkable occurance took place because in spite of no research having been carried out automation presented itself as a sort of by-product of knowledge and learning already available. Combined under the word control, conditon monitoring, regulating and automatic operating systems were built up out of the already available arsenal of pieces of apparatus and added to the same.

Characteristic for this phase is that technology was added on and not built in. The period of extremely sober equipment now belonged to the past and this chance did

not go unnoticed, resulting in the manufacture of some very fine control desks.

Indeed these developments resulted in feed backs which in turn, via discussions, interpretations of working experiences and further research, lead to a reliability increase for instruments as well as other parts.

There where economics puts the pressure on technology, the way in which the required levels of quality and knowledge adjust themselves can only be apparant after feasibility has been reached. A parallel to this can be found in the construction of the first big container ships.

Following transport model operational analysis a new means for transport presents itself. The fact that many of the large ships of the first generations had cracks in their decks and heavy vibrations were present resulted once again in feed back which in turn initiated further study and research out of which an adequate scientific approach to the problems was found. During these transitional periods risks are accepted but no time delays. Exactly the same is happening in the offshore industry.

To-day, as a result of automation, ships are sailing with unmanned engine rooms at night time and during the weekend.

The table of State Variables (table 2) can now be filled in:

Uncertainty	Considerable
Influence on costs	Positive
Technological developments	Insufficient
Interactions	Extensive
Control of developments	CD 3 (table 1)
Time based characteristics	TBC 2 (table 4)

Figure 6 shows the interrelationships.

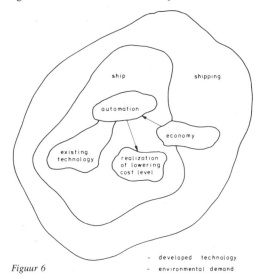

Figuur 6   — developed technology
                    — environmental demand

A new time era has presented itself. Taking into account the time delay which seems to be intrinsically necessary for ships, this previously mentioned in the introduction, one can expect to see noticeable application from 1980, nominally speaking.

The structure of shipping is changing. Internationally regulated distrubution of cargo has already been a topic of discussion in the UNCTAD.

There are no objections against placing such forms of progress against a background of uncertainties. However future changes themselves are not completely prone to clarity. Never the less uncertainties must not be weighed too much, rational relations carry on.

Indeed speaking from a structural point of view these

357

changes are both complicated and comprehensive. One can summarize the essential point with the following well known term: Introduction of Systems Engineering.

Before a more thorough analysis is made of this, differences with past development phases are brought forward.

In 1960 technique lagged behind. In 1980 technique has taken up a foreground position.

In 1960 economical impulse took up a foreground position, 1980 finds economical aspects separately represented in a field built up of all different types of branches.

Interaction, until 1960, had the form of an explicit function, in 1980 it is an implicit one. In 1960 research on application came afterwards. 1980 starts with it. A question mark may be placed when considering where costs belong, do they remain of primary importance or become secondary.

Why should shipping, a small part of an economical system, have the nerve to think that she alone can answer this.

The table of State Variables (table 2) can now be filled in:

Uncertainty	Considerable
Influence of costs	Derived Function
Technological developments	Initiative
Interactions	Extensive
Control of development	CD 2 (table 1)
Time based characteristics	TBC 1 (figure 3)

Figure 7 shows the interrelationships.

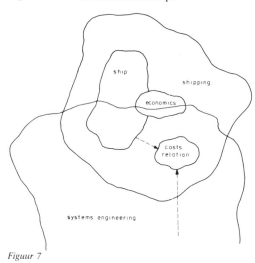

Figuur 7

SYSTEMS AND COMMUNICATIONS

For quite some time now the want for more principle changes in the structures of shipping and ships, economy and technique, world and transport, have been in the air. While this process is taking place the memories of the slide-rule and simple adding machines are still fresh in our minds.

The computer, having arrived only a short while ago, is already awe inspiring in its performance, the limits of which are still unknown. By the application of the computer in shipping, elementary thinking must take place.

Lines of communication reach out further than before and are more wide-spread. Large numbers of happenings can be numerically expressed and combined together under one number or parameter.

Learning to think in areas much larger than beforehand acknowledges interactions which initiates the pos-

sibility to relate different branches of science together while solving daily problems.

As a result of this, thinking is transformed into a more homogeneous form. Laws of physics appear to have the same form of appearance in different branches of science. Sections are taken from these branches and all appear to make up the different elements of a single problem after which their structures and places are rearranged in such a way that a solution to the problem i found.

Time-sensitive happenings can now be described with the aid of interactions based on a wide range of factors which was in past years unthinkable. The fact that this resulted in a long change-over period has already been brought forward and discussed by many people. Problems and procedures are of the heuristic type when viewed from directly social-bound economy and technique.

The reasons, acknowledgement of achievements and their perspectives, resulted in the search by pure science to find suitable connections. The outcome, Management Sciences and Operations Research, now passes through a time of disappointment because out of all the impressive possibilities only a minimum appear to be feasible.

However, such extreme specializations may well be used in small parts of a process but must not be allowed to form unrestrained ties between the different subsystems which make up that process.

Having become conscious of great possibilities, at the same time a boundary sets itself up due to the inability with respect to the system-formulation when the terrain gets too large. Risks are felt even more and the feeling of uncertainty increases.

These rules of conduct for economics, as mentioned up to now, must be critically assessed through and by the system of rational thinking.

Both striking and remarkable is the realisation that a small change, interpreted as an impulse, can be the cause of such a big un-balance, which in its turn lies outside the sphere of quasi-static thinking.

Quasi-static thinking, interpreted statically, resulted in an over increase in the use of energy in the technological plane and in an overproduction in shipbuilding. The excess of tankers is well known in shipping. Model-building in this sector is difficult and hardly worth thinking about without large concentration of research. One should be alert for new equilibrium-disturbers. Especially the cry for new means of transportation and other ships receive easily to much attention, thus opening shipping to new disturbing impulses.

Shipping being governed by technological developments results ultimately in clashes with its boundaries, The use of energy is one of these, high speeds are eliminated by costs, another is pollution of sea and harbour.

A third one is safety because often cargo is carried which is a danger to both crew and the sea. A fourth one is the increase in size of ship which in the light of threatening danger requires an almost faultless crew. The joint action of man, machine and handling is already a subject of mathematical study because faultless is a meaningless term.

Some of these named boundaries are inclined to increase costs and therefore threathen the position of the costs priority. Within system-regulations this can be accepted, without these regulations however uncertainty becomes dynamically amplified. This can be shown by the fact that in the present unstable situation as a result of a change in cargo quota, loss of equilibrium in ships-tonnage or fleet expansion can overcome any country. The dynamic amplification becomes greater as the independently influenceable part of the fleet or market becomes smaller.

Even though the necessity of system-formulation is evident there is a lack of sufficient documents and forecasts. This means that, apart from the pure economical side and the surroundings of shipping, technology must function in a certain area and remain functioning there. In this view accepted risks and costs must not change too much or too quickly until the function of the system is thought out, formulated and controlled numerically. Opposing this conclusion are the attitude of unemployment fighting governments with an unlimited volume of production and their almost unlimited financial resources in which only a weak feed back is to be found. The difference between Shipping Pattern and Operations Research is shown in figure 8.

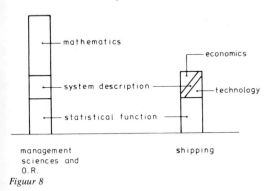

management   shipping
sciences and
O.R.

Figuur 8

ANALYSIS OF SHIPPING- AND SHIPSRESEARCH

In the earlier mentioned report from the U.S. Department of Commerce, Maritime Administration [1] a flow diagram of their research methods is given. This diagram can be found in figure 9. According to this, research is carried out into the situation of shipping and shipbuilding for the year 2000. By the collection of a large number of elements and variables which participate in present and future happenings and possibilities an enormous list of interactions and procedures is evolved.

This mixed list is re-arranged by having it judged by different workgroups, checked out against the company's policies, industrial needs, and supply and demand of cargo transport.

As a result of this a number of factors fall out while others, the weighted average values having been decided upon, are re-arranged and put into ranking order. External impulses, if necessary, are detected. By the confrontation with non-economical factors it is plain to see that the idea behind the system itself has not been neglected. Supply and demand of cargo to and from this nation is so large the system boundary "rest of the world" can be omitted.

As part of the conclusions a list of research topics, importance in order of presentation, are shown:

1 – General pollution
Definition of appropriate maritime environmental and pollution control criteria along with a program of research into the technologies needed for meeting these standards.
2 – Pollution loading and discharging
Development of offshore cargo feeder systems for liquid bulk.
3 – Pollution, oil spill
Development of effective, economical oil spillage prevention and cleanup systems.
4 – Safety of the ship
Development of low-cost, highly accurate and reliable marine collision avoidance systems for ocean and harbour use.

5 – Technology
Accelerated research on gas turbines directed at reductions in specific fuel consumptions and the ability of gas turbines to operate with low-grade fuels.
6 – Technology
Development of low-specific fuel consumption, high horsepower/weight power plants (especially for ocean express cargo systems)

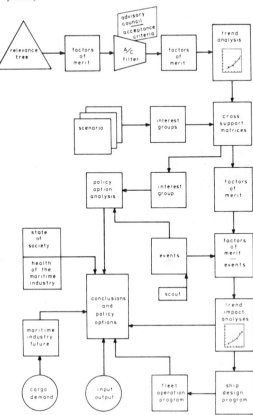

Figuur 9

After the high priority "Anti Pollution" measures technological aspects occupy the 5th and 6th places. Despite of the subjective starting point of this method and that interpretation also plays a role, a picture is still shown which is in agreement with causal expectations of the near future.

Pollution contesting, as a necessity for human life, receives great attention. Systematic approach has at last resulted in the appreciation of the interaction between life and waste productivity. Disturbances do not allow themselves to be graphically formulated but require calculations on the influences of impulses. In the working out of this system at least the word people has once again come forward.

The next named is safety and here the conclusions tend towards the automation of processes where risks for people are involved.

Between these indications on system techniques and the future lies an enormous piece of research. The element of costs is not directly connected here, so therefore the question smaller ship versus other means does not arise.

The last two points, the gas turbine and the low-fuel consumption low weight plants, are aimed at an important development area which is beginning to gain even

359

more attention. With this, starting points for further developments requiring separate attention have been fixed.

GAS TURBINE TECHNOLOGY

The meaning of gas turbine technology as a development project alone is not a very clear one. One can say that the U.S.A. is more used to rotating engines while Europe more to diesel engines. The heart of the matter remains unaffected by this. The following contains a number of facts concerning the usual types of engines found on board from which preference for gas turbine technology is to be rejected or confirmed.

A number of three demands can be put forward concerning the main engines:
1 – Reproduction of the physical and mechanical processes per revolution.
2 – Registrationable debugging period.
3 – Minimum number of auxiliaries and auxiliary systems.
A ship without engineers requires that the main engines keep running for a guaranteed time and that deficiencies can be foretold.
The analysis is made for each engine type.
The number of revolutions by ships application for a complete debugging is approx. 10^9 revs. Some load variations require a smaller amount, slower processes such as creep and corrosion of materials require a longer amount.

- Low-speed diesel engine
  Debugging period — 30 years
  Reproduceability — Nihil, piston rings rotate, injection volume varies dynamically
  Auxiliaries — Many
- Medium speed diesel engine
  Debugging period — 6 years
  As above
- High speed diesel engine
  Debugging period — $2^1/_2$ years
  As above
- Steam turbine
  Debugging period — 1.2 years
  Reproduceability — good
  Auxiliaries — boiler required

- Gas turbine
  Debugging period — 1 year
  Reproduceability — good
  Auxiliaries — few, but expensive

The gas turbine appears to be intrinsically the best engine for an unmanned engine room.

Despite the marked advances made with lined blades fuel consumption is still too high. Principally the view still remains that the gas turbine knows of no other efficiency boundary than that which is understood to be found in the maximum temperature of the gases.
The diesel motor, by increasing the compression ratio of the supercharger, finally changes into a gas generator and therefore becomes a gas turbine.

Dynamic monitoring in the running condition is in its first stages for diesel engines because not all the parameters are understood yet. [3] and [4].
One cannot speak of a forecasting function yet. Only after a long debugging period can the monitoring parameters be found and thus allow programming.

Although hints have been given and many questions remain unanswered, the impression is still given that the rotating engine meets the requirements of the programmed running condition thus making an unmanned engine room and even an unmanned ship possible.
The situation at present is presented against a proposition of priorities. As a result of this the threat is imminent that the in the engine built high reliability, gained through both processed experience and continued research, will be under-estimated. The prediction of failures however still requires understanding of the parameters involved from which the necessary priorities will follow in sequence.

PLANT OF HIGH HORSEPOWER/WEIGHT RATIO AND LOW SPECIFIC FUEL CONSUMPTION

To elaborate this here, without further research, is difficult. Systems engineering must place a number of different possibilities beside each other. A break-through in this direction may only be expected if a second virtual problem has been solved. After reducing the risks in engines and machines a step can be taken towards reducing the number of auxiliaries, finally leading to the abolishment of spare sets.
The condition for each part must be numerically known for this case. This technique still requires much research. To start with, one must return to the basic design idea of the machines and check all the known measurement methods and their validity ranges.
As such, the 1960 phase threatens to return. The detour, via the low frequency monitoring, has already been taken by many and is almost without perspective. In fact there is an explanation for this. The low frequency range was already being monitored by engineers with normal feeling senses. This did not result in condition monitoring and condition forecasting.
The monitoring of low frequency vibrations is up to a certain point necessary for safety purposes, such as the prevention of vibrations due to a broken turbine blade or due to the unbalance of separators. As a criterium for quality this is insufficient, the same being said for the present, 1960 phase, instrument measured parameters.
The 1960 phase ended with a trustworthy engine room plant which met the requirements set at that time: unwatched engine room at night and during the weekends.
Advanced research transforms the shipsofficer into "interpretation officer" and places him as universal officer on the bridge with a numerically monitored plant which at least 100 hours before faults occur gives signals to that effect. Into this same picture fits point 4 of the U.S.A. research program: "low costs, highly accurate and reliable marine collision avoidance system for ocean and harbour use". At the same time together with this, as idea and experiment too early in the 1960 phase, the interpretations officer can now be introduced.
Now the advanced research itself must be analysed in more finer detail. The perspectives of further research lie in the sectors dealing with the control of high frequency side-effects. Here understanding is poor and incomplete.
Due to this lack of understanding too much is being installed and invested and thus the cost price remains too high. There are indications that along these lines remarkable technological developments may yet take place.
These thoughts are induced by systemthinking and result in confrontations with boundary conditions which were earlier ignored or left out of the picture.

EXTERNAL BOUNDARY CONDITIONS

Two conditions are important. In the first place life on board. One cannot reduce the number of crew indefinitely and keep the same living conditions. On top of this, education, daily chores and responsibility must remain in equilibrium with each other.

One of the ways of increasing living conditions is by creating the possibility for all the personnel to meet together at the same time. This means that at one time, or even more, the whole crew must have no specific work to do. This supports the demand that the ship be run by instruments and that these instruments take over the human functions.

Each following step in the development requires higher demands. This corresponds to the C phase of figures 3 and 4. The 1960 phase was started by hard work by one of the groups involved, extensive and expensive research are the requirements for the 1980 phase.

In the 1960 phase one could go his own way, in the 1980 phase a number of boundaries come into sight.

As well as this the set problems, from a technological point of view, are not so simple anymore.

A second condition is that of normalization.

This is based on the following two reasons. High quality products are far mor expensive, even when spare sets have been bannished.

When constructing thinking in terms of reliability is taken as starting point in a similar way as this is done when aircraft modules are calculated.

If the thought of producing in series is allowed then a reduction in the total costs may be feasible.

The second reason originates from the shipsofficer. Due to the extension of his plane of work more types of specializations are required and the boundary, one speciality per instrument, will have to be set up. Changing over to another ship or installation will have to take place via renewed education and training, just as in the airlines industry. Shipping is not used to these conditions. The comparison of purchasing costs play a large part in determining the choice of the manufacturer.

Slowly but surely a point is reached where advancement can be seen in perspective but feasibility remains a function of a number of conditions.

The difference here with 1950 and 1960 is that it is now no longer the individual who takes the next step but that the decision must be taken by the community. Not one factor decides but a series of factors taken from different walks of life. The earlier mentioned explicit costs aspect thereby disappears as one of the system elements.

DIFFERENTIATION

The main lines have been explained, via computer to the system ship, a part of the system shipping.

The followed line of thought is no final target for all shipping. Not all ways in which the target is reached will be the same, as in the past there will be differentiations made.

The advantage of a well formulated system build-up is the possibility of finding several probable solutions, each one itself intrinsically life-like. However these must be placed in the surroundings which adopted them in the first place.

Countries with high crew costs will accept the 1980 phase and make research money available in order to keep a hold on competitive means of transport.

Through this they will accept that ships sail without delay, time for repairs are reduced to a minimum, and that cargo handling is regular and quick.

Countries having a large transport volume of their own may also go through this development, their fleet is a large one and series effect has large financial advantage. In such a case the system shipping shall be both centrally and strictly run.

Then again other countries, with more unfavourable conditions but having a high level of quality, can take on forms of specialized transport methods.

The third countries have little money and not so very highly educated personnel. But the wages are low and shipping is attractive to keep down unemployment and as a means of obtaining foreign currency.

The conclusion must be that the 1950, 1960 and 1980 phases remain together in existence. Each phase accumulating that piece of the transport market which is best suited to itself. Simple cargo for simple ships, expensive cargo for expensive ships.

Technology can react to demands of safety and put a brake on transportation risks. Technology can also react to price levels but not to uncertainty. The latter is done by the system transport and the system shipping, the ship remains a subsystem.

The most important perspective that technology can offer to the specific costs aspect is an important contribution in the formulation of the systemthinking and the application of this for the computer. In the handling of physical and dynamical phenomena and in the struggle to get force and energy to serve mankind, the power lies mainly in the overwinning of uncertainties which the designer must achieve in order to make a functional piece of machinery possible.

This points towards a synthesis, made up out of many branches of science, so that finally with numerical support uncertainties may be limited.

LITERATURE
[1] Dr. A. Wade Blackman a.o., **U.S. Ocean Shipping Technology Forecast and Assessment,** United Aircraft Research Laboratories, Report M - 971623 - 16,
U.S. Department of Commerce, Maritime Administration, Contract 3 - 36204, Vol. 1-5 1974.
[2] Sh. Masson et J. Roget, **Un nouveau moyen de contrôle non destructif: la détection de l'émission acoustique,** Association Technique Maritime et Aéronautique, Session 1976.
[3] Ir. W. de Jong, **Condition Monitoring, trend analysis and maintenance prediction of ship's machinery,** Netherlands Ship Research Centre T.N.O., Report 190 M, 1974.
[4] M. Langballe, L. Tonning and T. Wiborg, **Condition monitoring of diesel engines,** Norwegian Maritime Research, No. 3, Vol. 3, 1975.
[5] KLTZ A.C. Pijcke and Ir. C.A.J. Tromp, **Trillingsonderzoek aan roterende werktuigen aan het Koninklijk Instituut voor de Marine,** Royal Netherlands Navy, Report WE 100 - 1975
[6] R.A. Collacott C. Eng, **Mechanical fault diagnosis,** Journal of Ship Repair and Maintenance. March, 1976

Uncertainties in airport cost analysis

by

Tore Knudsen

Technical University of Norway

INTRODUCTION

Uncertainty in View of the History of Decisionmaking

The ultimate goal for all planning is to generate sound alternatives and to supply enough information about their performance for the decisionmakers to be able to make a decision.

In the past, choice among transportation alternatives was made more or less on basis of the alternatives economic performances which were supplied to the decisionmakers by the planners as for example "internal rate of return", "benefit-cost-ratios" or "net-present-worth-values". This can be classified as a one-dimensional information about the alternatives since all information supplied were measured in monetary values.

This technique has later been extended to take into account other attributes such as for example travel-time and traffic accidents, but then transforming the new attribute measurements into monetary values to make them compatible with the other data or information. Thus, the one-dimensional structure is kept.

In recent years the planners and the decisionmakers have acknowledged the loss of information resulting from transforming the data to a common scale and aggregating the information in an early stage of the planning process. As a result, the planners started to supply information about the alternatives as attribute measurements along their original scales, that is, travel time measured in minutes, noise measured in dBA or in number of people or houses inside an area with noise-level above certain dBA-limits etc. As shown, such attributes are not at all measurable along the same common scale without making assumptions about the trade-off values. In the broadest sense one can imagine that information about transportation alternatives is given on different nominal, ordinal, interval and ratio scales. This kind of information requires a multi-attribute or multi-dimensional evaluation and decisionprocess.

While in the earlier work of multi-attribute evaluation, the information given was regarded as being exact, the recent development in this field of decisionmaking [2, 3, 4, 5] is to look upon the multi-attribute measurements only as estimates of random variables. However, so far their probability distributions, or uncertainty distributions as they may be called, are unknown in most cases. This leads up to a fundamental question which is considered to be the main objective for this type or research:

– What is the impact of uncertainties in attribute measurements on the decisions to be made?

However, on basis of this fundamental question, new problems arise:

– What is the nature of the uncertainties and shapes of the uncertainty distributions for different attributes?
– How is it possible to generate probability models to describe these uncertainties?

The Scope of the Research

In order to go into some depth of the problem and in particular to provide some empirical data and results, it is necessary to limit the scope of the work. The first limitation consists of choosing one particular transportation planning problem. In this case, the problem of site selection for a new major airport in an area presently served by airports with capacity- and environmental problems, is chosen.

Although this is, as will be shown later, undoubtedly a multidimensional decision problem, in this research only one attribute, the capital cost incurred by the airport operator, is analysed. However, by doing so, variables having an effect on the cost attribute, such as air transportation demand and capacity of airports will be dealt with to some extent. This represents the second limitation of this work compared to the basic questions already raised.

In order to utilize certain available data, and to apply the results to a realistic problem, it was decided to perform the research with a view towards a specific case study: "Location of a New Major Airport for the Oslo-Region in Norway".

With respect to the basic questions raised in the first section and the limitations of this particular study described in this section, one can rephrase the objective for this particular research:

– What is the nature of the uncertainty distribution for capital costs of a major airport and how can an estimate for this distribution be derived?

Developing a Hypothesis

So far the questions posed do not indicate any specific direction for the research to be performed. Although the historic development of decisionmaking points to the area of uncertainties and uncertainty distributions as academically interesting topics, it is yet to come to establish the need for and the importance of knowing the nature of the uncertainty distributions for capital costs of a major airport and to develop a hypothesis of the possible effect of the uncertainties on the site selection problem.

As a starting point, uncertainty distributions for capital costs of a major airport are assumed to exist. That is, it is possible to describe the uncertainty of capital costs for different airport sites by probability distributions. These distributions, which are still unknown, may have different shapes and both the mean value and the magnitude of the uncertainty expressed for example by the variance of the distributions may vary from one site to another.

However, the need for knowing these probability distributions is not generated by pure academic interest, but these distributions are assumed to be of vital importance when evaluating different airport sites.

So far, cost estimates[1] have been used when evaluating

the capital costs of the airport related to alternatives sites, and the differences in costs between the sites have more or less automatically been considered significant. By introducing the concept of uncertainty and analysing the nature of the uncertainty distributions, a statistical treatment of whether or not differences in estimated costs are significant may be possible. Further will knowledge about uncertainty distributions also provide information about confidence limits for the actual costs, and probabilities of exceeding certain cost limits can be calculated. By facing this more complex information, the decisionmakers may come out with decisions different from the ones based on the use of only cost estimates. At least two effects will be of some importance.

First, the use of uncertainty distributions will tend to reduce the significance of the differences in cost estimates, thus also reducing the importance of cost differences in the multi-dimensional evaluation and decision process.

Second, if the dicisionmakers are increasingly averse to high costs (that is "risk averse" in decision theoretic terminology), and capital costs are expressed as probability distributions, alternatives with little uncertainty (small variances in the probability distributions) will come better out compared with high uncertainty alternatives (large variances) than would be the case if only cost estimates were used.

All these statements, although mostly not proven so far, lead up to the hypothesis that information about uncertainties in cost estimates may be of vital importance for the decisionmakers when evaluating different sites for location of the major airport.

STRUCTURING THE RESEARCH
The Case Study: "Location of New Major Airport for the Oslo-Region in Norway"

The Oslo-region in Norway is the most densely populated area in the country with a population of approximately 1 million in the area to be served by the airport. Thus, it is also the single most important origin/destination for both domestic and international flights. Presently the region is served by Fornebu Airport located 8 km (5 miles) south-west of Oslo city center. Due to aircraft noise, night operations are limited by a curfew, and one is also experiencing capacity problems. To relieve the situation, most of the international charter traffic in 1973 was transferred to Gardemoen Airport which is located 35 km (22 miles) north-northeast of Oslo city center.

At Fornebu both runway capacity and passenger- and freight terminal capacities are expected to be exceeded in very near future. Besides, both runways (fig. 1) are, with respect to length (2200 m and 1750 m) considered inadequate for todays air traffic operations. However, there is strong local opposition against extending runways and expanding passenger- and freight-terminal buildings at Fornebu because of the effect of aircraft noise on nearby areas.

The present situation at Gardemoen is that both the strength of the pavement and the runway length are inadequate (fig. 2), thus limiting the aircraft types and the take-off weights. The terminal building is expected to suffice for a few more years.

The airport problem in this area is considered a federal problem thus giving the National Assembly of Norway the decisionmaking power. Several governmental committees, research organisations, and consulting firms have dealt with the problem more of less continuously the last seven years. So far no final decision is reached, but the basic questions appear to be:

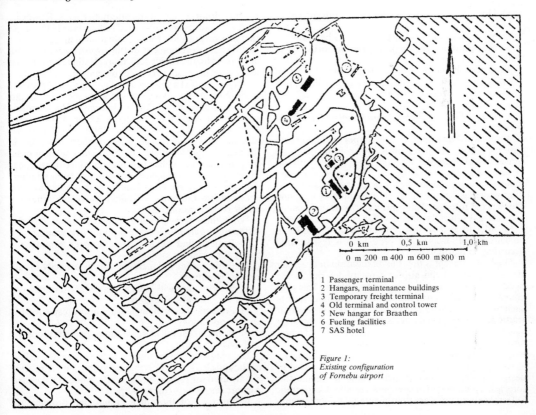

0 km   0,5 km   1,0 km

0 m 200 m 400 m 600 m 800 m

1 Passenger terminal
2 Hangars, maintenance buildings
3 Temporary freight terminal
4 Old terminal and control tower
5 New hangar for Braathen
6 Fueling facilities
7 SAS hotel

Figure 1:
Existing configuration
of Fornebu airport

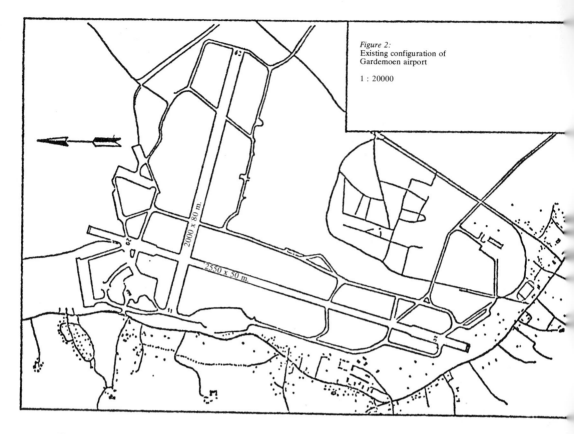

Figure 2:
Existing configuration of
Gardemoen airport

1 : 20000

1) Does the Oslo area need a new major airport?
In case:

2) When does the new airport have to be ready?

3) What airport size is expected for the horizon year, 2000?

4) Where should the new major airport be located?

5) What will be the consequences of building a new airport with respect to costs and other attributes?

The Airport Planning Process and the Structure of this Research

A simplified description of the airport planning process used in the Oslo-region is shown in figure 3. As already mentioned, this research deals mainly with uncertainties in the cost attribute. The figure, however, indicates the dependency between the cost, of an airport alternative, as one of the resulting consequences, and the demand forecast. Thus uncertainties in the demand forecast may affect the uncertainties in the actual costs.

In order to analyse this problem of uncertainties in actual costs of airports, the problem was restructured according to figure 4.

The basic concept is that the relationship between air transport demand and airport capacity determines the need for airport expansion or a new airport. This is of course a simplification of the problem since other factors such as length and strength of runways, regularity of air traffic or environmental effects may also affect the decision whether or not to expand an existing or build a new airport. However, at least some of these considerations may be transformed to a question of airport capacity.

As shown in figure 3, the demand forecast is used to design an airport model which is able to handle the forecasted number of passengers (terminal capacity). Different alternatives are then generated by implement-

ing this airport model at the alternative sites. However, such alternatives are considered rather static in the sense that they do not allow for an evaluation of more stepwise and flexible development of the airport system for the area. In order to provide for a more flexible and dynamic use of alternatives, the concept of strategies is introduced. In this context a strategy is defined as a list of projects to be implemented at a given site when the need for the projects is determined. This is determined by comparison of the demand for and capacity of the airports serving the area. The complete list of projects may be identical to what earlier is called an alternative, that is the airport model, but one alternative may serve as basis for generating more than one strategy, since operational differences may distinguish one strategy from another. This gives the possibility of analysing not only different sites, but also different operational strategies for the sites under consideration.

When these principles are applied to the case study, different airport projects are put into five groups:

1) Projects that will increase passenger terminal capacity for airline passengers.

2) Projects that will increase runway capacity for air carrier operations.

3) Projects that will increase passenger terminal capacity for charter passengers.

4) Projects that will increase runway capacity for charter operations.

5) Projects that will increase runway capacity for general aviation traffic.

The reason for distinguishing between regular airline traffic and charter traffic is that today Fornebu Airport is mainly used for regular airline traffic while Gardemoen Airport serves as a charter airport.

Within each of these five groups, the projects are

364

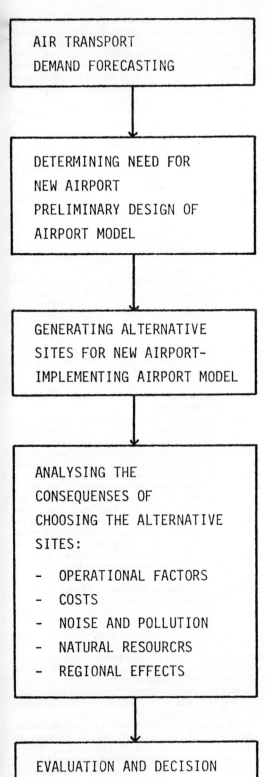

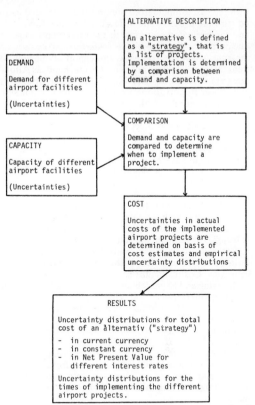

AIR TRANSPORT
DEMAND FORECASTING

DETERMINING NEED FOR
NEW AIRPORT
PRELIMINARY DESIGN OF
AIRPORT MODEL

GENERATING ALTERNATIVE
SITES FOR NEW AIRPORT-
IMPLEMENTING AIRPORT MODEL

ANALYSING THE
CONSEQUENSES OF
CHOOSING THE ALTERNATIVE
SITES:

- OPERATIONAL FACTORS
- COSTS
- NOISE AND POLLUTION
- NATURAL RESOURCRS
- REGIONAL EFFECTS

EVALUATION AND DECISION

Fig. 3 – Simplified Description of the Airport Planning Process used in the Oslo-Region

ALTERNATIVE DESCRIPTION

An alternative is defined as a "strategy", that is a list of projects. Implementation is determined by a comparison between demand and capacity.

DEMAND

Demand for different airport facilities

(Uncertainties)

CAPACITY

Capacity of different airport facilities

(Uncertainties)

COMPARISON

Demand and capacity are compared to determine when to implement a project.

COST

Uncertainties in actual costs of the implemented airport projects are determined on basis of cost estimates and empericial uncertainty distributions

RESULTS

Uncertainty distributions for total cost of an àlternativ ("strategy")

- in current currency
- in constant currency
- in Net Present Value for different interest rates

Uncertainty distributions for the times of implementing the different airport projects.

Fig. 4 – Diagram showing how the Problem is structured and expected Results.

ranked according to a specified order of implementation. This feature, together with methods of comparing demand and capacity, give the possibility of analysing both alternative sites and different operational procedures.

By comparing the demand forecasts for different years and the capacity of the existing airport(s), the need for additional capacity is determined. However, since both the demand forecast and airport capacity are assumed having uncertainty distributions, the times for implementing the different airport projects will also have its uncertainty distributions. For each project a cost estimate is assumed to exist. However, the actual costs are not known. By deriving uncertainty distributions for cost of airport projects on basis of empirical data, it is possible to utilize these distributions to calculate uncertainty distributions for actual costs of the airport projects to be implemented.

As results from this analysis, one expects to derive uncertainty distributions for total cost of a strategy (sum of all projects which are implemented), where cost is measured in both constant and current currency and where net present values are calculated for different interest rates. In order to derive these distributions, computer simulation was used. However, as it appears in figure 4, necessary inputs to this simulation process are uncertainty distributions for air traffic demand, capacities and costs of airport projects. In this paper the demand and the cost studies are described.

THE COST STUDY
Reasons for Uncertainty in Actual Cost of Airport Projects

Final cost figures from construction projects often reveals that the actual cost of a project does not coincide with the cost estimate from the time it was decided to go on with the project. The difference between the actual and the estimated cost most of the time seems to go in one particular direction, that is cost overruns seems to be the rule. However, complete agreement about how to treat this problem does not exist. On one hand, as Altouney [6] quotes from "The June 1955 Water Resources and Power Report to the Congress by the Commission on Organisation of the Executive Branch of the Government":

"If the cost of a project is underestimated when it is presented to the Congress, obviously the benefits and justifications upon which the Congress made its decision have been misleading."

However, on the other hand, as Zimmerman and Merewitz [7] state:

"Should we seek better cost estimates? Not necessarily. The effort to make more accurate cost estimates may result in higher total costs for projects than would otherwise have been the case. Perhaps an "unrealistic" cost estimate operates as a restraining factor."

These two opinions indicate the nature of the cost estimation problem, that is the "dual purpose" of cost estimates. Cost estimates serve both as basis for decisionmaking and as guidelines or restraining factors during the construction period. This "duality" also explains some of the cost overruns which are observed. In order to get a project accepted, a deliberately low cost estimate is submitted to the decisionmakers. This, however, will of course lead to cost overruns, in spite of the fact that the low cost estimate will work as a restraining factor. The degree of underestimation may vary from project to project and does not consistently imply unrealistically low cost figures from those responsible for the cost estimation.

What is mentioned above may be classified as political or tactical reasons for uncertainty in a specific direction, that is underestimation. Such reasons are believed to exist and to be important, but equally or more important in most cases are other factors which are not tactically motivated and which are to a certain extent characterized by some randomness.

One such factor is "specification completeness". At the estimation stage it is easier to forget to include cost components than it is to include more costs than actually will occur.

Another factor is "quantity and price accuracy". It is difficult to establish the exact quantities of work that has to be done, and materials and equipment needed at a preliminary stage. In addition come uncertainties in unit prices and wages which increase with the length of time until completion of the project.

This again points to yet another factor, "the uncertainty of time". "Time" in this context may be interpreted in two different ways. First, it may mean "construction time", and uncertainty in construction time will again affect the cost of the project. Secound, time may be understood as the time when the whole project is completed. If part of the project, for example one or more sections of the terminal buildings or one or more runways, are intended completed at a later stage, uncertainty in these time estimates will affect the cost, especially combined with other factors mentioned in this section.

"Unpredicted natural causes" is also a factor to be considered. These natural causes often are related to weather conditions or to geotechnical conditions on the construction site. Geotechnical conditions may be either better or worse than expected, but the uncertainty is strongly related to more or less insufficient, preliminary investigations.

A more deterministic cause for what is called uncer-

tainty, is change of design, although the reason for the change may be of random nature. Conceptually, change of design can work to both decrease and increase in actual cost. At an early stage of the project planning, change of design may be used to find cheaper solutions. Later on, however, design changes are mostly made in order to satisfy change in demand and such changes tend to increase the cost of the project.

The last factor to be mentioned is "technological uncertainty". Cost estimates are most of the time based on previous experience, that is "yesterday's technology". In addition one anticipates what kind of new technology will be available before construction starts and what effect it will have on the construction cost. Technology is in this context given a very wide interpretation, since not only construction technology, but also technological development affecting air transportation demand and airport capacity is included. Thus technological uncertainty may result in uncertainty in cost both through construction technology and through change of design or change of time for implementing part of the project due to unpredicted technological development affecting demand and capacity.

The different factors which may give reasons for uncertainty in actual cost of projects are here listed independently. However, as indicated for some of them, they are all strongly interrelated and the resulting uncertainty in actual cost is hard to evaluate. One would expect, however, on basis of this list of factors, both the tactical, political, psychological and the more technical factors, and their most common effects, that cost overruns will be the rule rather than the exception.

Probability Structure for Statistical Treatment of Uncertainties in Actual Costs.

In the preceeding section reasons for uncertainty in actual cost of construction projects were discussed. So far "uncertainty" or "uncertainty distributions" have not been properly defined but uncertainty has implicitly been interpreted as having to do with the relationship between actual and estimated cost. Although there is great uncertainty about the actual cost of an airport project when the cost has not been estimated, in this context the terms "uncertainty" and "uncertainty distributions" refer only to situations when a cost estimate for the project exists. The cost estimate is used as a reference point for measuring the uncertainty. Thus, it is only relevant to talk about an uncertainty distribution during a time period when the cost estimate is known, but the actual cost is unknown. Then, the actual cost can be regarded as a random variable being affected by all the factors mentioned and having a probability density, $f_e(c)$. This probability density shows the distribution of the actual cost. C, given the cost estimate, E. The distribution of C is thus a conditional distribution, it depends on E. Nothing is so far said about the shape of the distribution, $f_e(c)$. It is only assumed to exist, as was also done in the first section. From the conclusions arrived at in the third section it may be assumed that the estimated cost, E, is not equal to the expected value of the actual cost, C. This, however, will be discussed later in the context of the results from the empirical cost study.

In this work, the main objective is to study the uncertainties in actual costs of airport projects. Altouney [6] and Merewitz [8, 9] have studied uncertainties in cost estimates for other types of projects, and they found it useful to study the ratio, R, of actual cost to estimated cost.

$$R = \frac{C}{E}$$

This relationship can also be written:

$$C = E \cdot R$$

It is already stated that the uncertainty is only defined when E is known. In such a case, E can be considered a constant, E = e. This implies that the actual cost, C, will have the same distribution as the ratio, R, but with a different scale factor which is known through the knowledge of e. By studying the variations of R for different airport projects, a measure of the uncertainty in the actual costs can be derived. Mathematically this can be expressed:

$$P(C<c|E = e) = P(R<\frac{c}{e})$$

Thus:

$$f_e(c) = \frac{1}{e} \, g\left(\frac{c}{e}\right)$$

or:

$$f_e(c) = \frac{1}{e} \, g(r)$$

where: $f_e(c)$ is the density function of C given E = e expressing the uncertainty in actual cost.
$g(r)$ is the density function of the ratio R, given E = e, where

$$R = \frac{C}{E}$$

When studying the distribution of R and assuming that

$$(C|E = e) \stackrel{\mathcal{L}}{=} (e \cdot R \,|\, E = e)$$

one implicitly also makes the assumption that the cost estimate, E, is arrived at through the same procedure for each project, that is, the distribution of R represents the uncertainty with respect to this estimation procedure as well as C. This is rather serious assumption, but for this research it was found necessary. However, the possibility exists that when observing r, the variations observed are not only randomness in the actual cost, C, but also include more or less systematic variations in the estimation procedure.

Analysis of Empirical Cost Data
Introduction
The main objective for this study of empirical cost data is to investigate the relationship between actual costs and estimated costs for different airport projects according to the probability structure defined in the preceding section.

This relationship is also considered the single most important component of this research as described through figure 4. The approach is to use historical data for both estimated and actual costs in order to derive the distribution of the ratio:

$$R = \frac{\text{Actual Cost}}{\text{Estimated Cost}}$$

Some additional questions to be answered by the analysis of the empirical data are:
1) Do cost estimates appear to be biased in any direction?
2) Is there any relationship between the size of a project and the uncertainty in actual cost of the project?
3) Is there any relationship between "the completion time"[2] and the uncertainty in actual cost of a project?
4) Are there any differences in the uncertainties for different types of projects within the airport?

One fact should probably be made clear on this initial stage of the cost study. This particular research does not intend to further explain the causal relationship for the uncertainties in cost estimation as for example it is attempted in [7], [9]. Neither will the underlying assumptions for the probability structure as described in the previous section be tested. The purpose of this study is merely to observe historical facts in order to recognize the uncertainties in the relationship between actual and estimated costs. The resulting distribution will both

serve as an independent tool for evaluating actual costs of specific airport projects and as input to the simulation model described in figure 4. Finally, the uncertainty distributions will be applied to the case study, both as an independent tool and as part of the simulation model.

Data collection
The district offices of the Federal Aviation Administration (FAA) keep records of estimated costs and final costs for different airport projects. Part of the data for this research are acquired from the FAA Regional Office in Burlingame, California and refers to different airport projects in Northern California. The rest of the data were collected from journals and magazines covering news in the airport and construction field.

In order to derive an uncertainty distribution as described in the preceding sections, the ratios actual costs to estimated costs were calculated. These ratios were named "original ratios". Besides "corrected ratios" were calculated, that is ratios calculated on basis of constant dollars, were the correction was made according to the "Construction Cost Index"[3].

A detailed analysis of these cost data is performed in [1]. In this section a summary of the most interesting results are given.

For each airport project the following information existed:
i) Estimated cost
ii) Actual cost in current dollars
iii) Actual cost in constant dollars (corrected by construction cost index)
iv) Original cost ratio
v) Corrected cost ratio
vi) Completion time
vii) Type of project.
The projects are classified in three groups:
I: Runway projects
II; Terminal building projects
III: Land acquisition
Based on this information some of the most interesting relationships are analysed.

Results from the Cost Study
Relationship between the Cost Ratio and the Size of a Project
Altouney [6] investigated the relationship between the size of a project expressed as final cost and the cost ratio, but he did not find any such relationship. Merewitz [8] postulates: "One hypothesis arising from earlier work is that the ratio of actual to estimated cost, R, is larger on bigger projects". However, Merewitz did not test this hypothesis.

In figure 5 corrected cost ratios and actual cost data

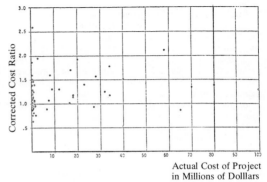

Actual Cost of Project in Millions of Dolllars

Figure 5 – Plot of the relationship between actual cost and corrected cost ratios.

are plotted for different airport projects. The figure does not reveal any relationship between the two variables investigated.

Relationship between the Cost Ratio and the Completion Time

From the beginning of this study, the completion time, that is the time from when a cost estimate is made and until the project is finished, has been assumed to affect the cost ratio. In figure 6 the corrected cost ratios are plotted against the completion times. The figure does not reveal any relationship between the two variables investigated.

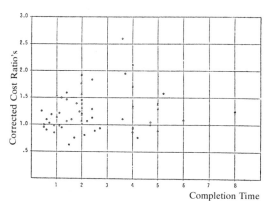

Figure 6 – Corrected Cost Ratios Plotted Against Completion Time

Comparison Between Different Types of Projects

Although the number of observations in the data set is rather small and the possibility for errors is large, it is tempting to look at the data separately for two of the project-types (for land acquisition, type III, the number of observations is definitely insufficient). In this case only projects exclusively classified in one group are included. Tables 1a and b show the most important properties for the two project types. The difference of the mean values of the original ratios is considered less important in this case since it can be explained by the difference in completion times. (A t-test shows that the means are significantly different on the 99% confidence level). More important is the observed difference in the corrected ratios. A t-test performed on the mean values yields a t-value of only 0.8883, which is below any reasonable critical t-value [10]. However, a difference in the mean values is observed although the statistical proof is lacking.

Another feature which seems to be different for the two project types is the skewness. However, the coefficient of skewness, calculated as a function of the second and third central moments, is very sensitive to small variations in the data, especially the occurence of a few rather extreme values. In order to test if the observed difference in the coefficient of skewness also indicates a significant difference in the shape of the two distributions, the hypothesis that the two distribution functions are equal is tested:

H₀ : $F_I(x) = F_{II}(x)$

The Smirnov Test [11] was used and the conclusion was that the hypothesis of the two distributions being equal cannot be rejected at any reasonable significance level. The results from both these tests show that although differences are observed in the distributional properties of the two types of projects, the differences are not significant from a statistical point of view. How-

Table 1 a) and b) - Properties of cost ratios for type I and type II projects

Projects type I	Original Ratios	Corrected Ratios
Mean value	1.3295	1.2224
Standard error or the mean	.0762	.0721
Standard deviation	.3492	.3304
Coefficient of Variation	.2627	.2703
Coefficient of Skewness	.5663	.7538
Average completion time	2.1905	2.1905
Number of observations	21	21

Projects type II	Original Ratios	Corrected Ratios
Mean value	1.6705	1.3220
Standard error or the mean	.1219	.0864
Standard deviation	.5453	.3866
Coefficient of Variation	.3264	.2924
Coefficient of Skewness	1.5199	1.6857
Average completion time	3.300	3.300
Number of observations	20	20

ever, in spite of the lack of statistical proof of the possible differences, additional support can be found by comparing these results with similar results from other areas. Merewitz [8] presents several tables of raw data comparable to those used in this research for different types of projects. Since these data are what here is called original ratios, that is ratios based on actual costs which are not corrected for price increase, they will be compared with similar data from this study.

In table 2 the different project types are arranged in order of increasing mean values.

Table 2 – Cost Ratios for Different Types of Projects

Project Type	Original Ratios Mean Values	Average Completion Time
Highway Projects	1.2633	4.6541
Airport Projects Type I	1.3295	2.1905
Water Resource Projects	1.3774	10.0200
Urban Rapid Transit	1.5447	6.1679
Buildings	1.6272	3.0833
Airport Projects Type II	1.6705	3.3000
Ad Hoc Public Works	2.1447	4.9333

Conceptually, this ordering makes sense with highly experienced, state or federal agencies on the top of the list. However, that such an argument is not consistent is documented by Altouney's [6] results.

He found average, uncorrected ratio for water resource projects to be 2.63, far above all the results reported by Merewitz and the airport data collected for this study.

If the results from the airport projects are compared with other types of projects, the runway projects (type I) came out very close to the highway projects. The other type (type II) consisting mainly of terminal buildings and internal transit systems came close to "Urban Rapid Transit" and "Building"-projects. Without being able to prove statistically the difference between the different project types within the airport by use the airport data, this comparison is another indication that such a difference may exist.

Properties of the Complete Data set and the Resulting Uncertainty Distribution

The main reason for collecting these data and deriving their distributional properties, was to get information about the size and shape of the uncertainty distribution associated with cost estimation of airport projects. With this objective in mind, it was decided to gather all the collected data in one data set and analyse its distributional properties. The results of the numerical calculations are shown in table 3.

Table 3 – Major properties of the complete dataset

Project Type	Original Ratios	Corrected Ratios
Mean value	1.4351	1.2330
Standard error of the mean	.0605	.0464
Standard deviation	.4724	.3623
Coefficient of Variation	.3292	.2938
Coefficient of Skewness	1.4622	1.2689
Average completion time	2.6328	2.6328
Number of observations	61	61

In the further analysis the corrected ratios are chosen as data base for deriving the uncertainty distribution.

In order to derive the density function for the corrected cost ratios, the observations can be plotted as a histogram. However, here is used a modified density estimate (e.g. Bickel and Doksum [12] which is continuous and consistent at every point. An existing computer program which utilizes this technique was modified and used to produce a plotter output of the resulting density function, figure 7. As a comparison, a gamma- and a log-normal distribution calibrated by the method of moments are plotted.

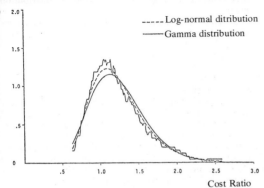

Figure 7 – Density Function for Corrected Cost Ratios

This distribution is accepted as an uncertainty distribution for the fatio R for airport projects and it will be used according to the probability structure described to calculate the uncertainty in actual costs for airport projects of some interest for the case study. This will be shown in a further section.

THE DEMAND STUDY

Introduction

When analysing air traffic demand, the airport facilities are grouped in following two groups:

1) *Passenger facilities* such as terminal buildings with their ticketing, baggage handling and internal transportation systems, parking areas and ground transportation.

2) *Aircraft facilities* such as runways, taxiways, apron, gate positions, fuel supply and maintenance facilities, landing instrumentation and airport and air-traffic control.

Less aggregation is of course possible, but for this project, the grouping above is considered sufficiently detailed. Besides, it corresponds to the aggregation of projects made in the cost study. It is also necessary to stratify demand according to type of operations, that is air carrier, charter, and general aviation to mention the most important categories. In this case the annual number of passengers is chosen to represent the demand for passenger facilities while peak hour aircraft operations represent the demand for aircraft facilities. Since the underlying case in this research is an airport which mainly will serve commercial air transportation, it was decided to limit the studies of uncertainties in demand to "annual number of airline passengers" and "peak hour air carrier movements". In order to perform this analysis, it was necessary to recognize the dependency between these two demands and identify their relationship. In this case, the annual number of airline passengers is considered the basic demand for air transportation. From this basic demand, first the annual number of air carrier movements, and then the peak hour movements are derived.

As was done when analysing uncertainties in cost of airport projects, historical data will be analysed. However, in the cost study, engineering reasons for bias and uncertainties could be found and it was assumed that the knowledge acquired could be used to make better estimates in the future. In demand forecasting this is not exactly the situation. Bias observed in old forecasts cannot be utilized to a large extent when dealing with future years since there is no a priori reason to believe that the forecasts are biased in any particular direction. But in spite of this limitation in the use of historical data when dealing with forecasting, it still may be possible to learn something about the uncertainties of forecasting by comparing old forecasts with what actually happened.

When dealing with demand, expressed as "annual number of airline passengers", one would expect to get a fairly accurate statistical material for different airport for past years. However, when informations from two different sources covering the same airport are compared, one discovers small and large differences, some of them impossible to explain although some sources of possible errors are known. Transit passengers, for example, are not counted identically all the time. Sometimes they are counted twice, other times once, and in some statistics transit passengers are not included at all. Another problem occurs when an airport accommodates international and domestic charter, airtaxi, commuter traffic and helicopter routes. Treatment of the passengers on these types of flights obviously varies and gives reasons for uncertainty with respect to what kind of traffic is reported in a particular statistic. The last source of uncertainty in the data-material to be mentioned here, is the treatment of general aviation passengers for types of flights not mentioned above, which also obviously varies.

Uncertainties of these and similar types, make it to a certain extent difficult to compare demand forecasts with actual traffic data. An old set of forecasts for 107 US airports made in 1953 by "Air Transport Association" and which appeared in "American Aviation" in November 1953, could not be evaluated because the base year data (1953 F.Y.) could not be verified by available statistical data. FAA's 1953 data for those airports were not at all similar to the data used as basis for the forecast. The general impression of these forecasts was that annual number of passengers and movements for year 1970 were underestimated by a factor of 2 – 8, that is actual traffic was 2 – 8 times estimated traffic volumes.

Probability Structure for Statistical Treatmant of Uncertainties in Demand

As was the case in the cost problem, uncertainty in demand is connected to the relationship between actual and forecasted values. That is, in this case the relationship between actual demand, T, and forecasted demand, F. Further, uncertainty is only defined when a demand forecast is known. Thus, actual demand, T, is considered a random variable, and the distribution of T is considered conditional on the forecast, F.

Again the ratio: $M = \dfrac{T}{F}$

is of considerable interest. It is already stated that the uncertainty is only defined when the forecast F is known. In such a case, F can be considered a constant, F = f. This implies that the actual demand, T, where

T = f · M

will have the same distribution as the ratio, M, but with a scale factor given by the value of F = f. By studying the variations of M for different airtraffic forecasts, a measure of the uncertainty in the actual demand, given a forecast, can be derived. This is very similar to the probability structure for the cost study and thus the resulting mathematical expression will be

$$f_f(t) = \frac{1}{f} h(m)$$

where $f_f(t)$ is the density function of T given F = f expressing the uncertainty in actual demand
h(m) is the density function of the ratio M given F = f, where $M = \frac{T}{F}$ f is the known demand forecast

As in the cost study, one should, also when dealing with demand, be aware of the fact that by assuming:

$$(T|F = f) \stackrel{c}{=} (f \cdot M|F = f)$$

one implicitly also make the assumption that the forecast, F = f, is arrived at through approximately the same forecasting procedure and with the same a priori accuracy for each forecast. This, is a rather serious assumption, but necessary in order to make some progress toward realizing the nature of uncertainty in demand.

Observed Uncertainties in Annual Number of Passengers

Uncertainties in annual number of passengers will be analysed according to the probability structure described in the previous section, that is by studying the ratio, M, of actual to forecasted demand for different airports.

In 1968 FAA made forecasts for all airports in the United States classified as medium hubs [13] both for annual number of passengers and annual number of aircarrier movements. Actual traffic data were found in [14, 15, 16]. In figures 8 and 9 are shown the distribution of the ratios: actual traffic/forecasted traffic for both categories and for different ages of the forecasts. Although the distributions are based on 33 observations, these cannot be regarded as independent since they all probably are subordinated in a national forecast. For both passengers and air carrier movements an almost consistent overestimation seems to exist. This implies that the distribution of ratios is biased. In order to measure the uncertainty, the following two measurements are used.

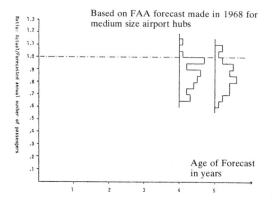

Figure 8 – Distribution of ratios: Actual/Forecasted number of passengers.

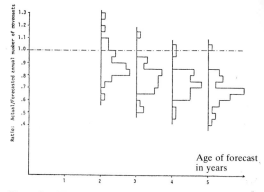

Figure 9 – Distribution of ratios: Actual/Forecasted annual number of movements.

1) The variance (and standard deviation) of the observed distribution, s_r^2 (and s_r) around the distribution mean, $\bar{r}$.

2) The mean square error (M.S.E.) (and its square root, the root mean square error, R.M.S.E.) around the value, $\bar{r} = 1,0$, (unbiased mean) s_b^2) and s_b).

It can easily be shown that:
$s_b^2 = s_r^2 + (bias)^2 = s_r^2 + (\bar{r}- 1.0)^2$
and thus:
$s_b = s_r^2 + (\bar{r} - 1.0)^2$

Numerical results from this study are given in table 4 and show a considerable bias for both passengers and aircarrier movements, .1574 and .2960 after five years respectively. Compared to figures 8 and 9, the root mean square error, s_b, seems to reflect the increasing uncertainty over time in a satisfactory manner, increasing from .1639 for two years old forecasts of aircarrier movements to .3159 for five years old forecasts.

The Washington D.C. airports, two of them owned and operated by the Federal authorities, have been given special attention by the FAA. Forecasts for these airports were made by the FAA in 1962, 1968, 1969 and 1971 [17, 18, 19, 20], and the forecasts were compared with actual data. In figures 10 and 11 are shown how the different forecasts compare with the actual development. For the Washington D.C. area forecasts were also made for each of the two federal airports. Figure 12 shows the comparison with actual data.

For San Francisco International Airport there also exist forecasts made at different points in time, but contrary to the data for the Washington D.C. airports, these forecasts are made by different agencies and research organizations. FAA District Office in Oakland, 1957, Stanford Research Institute, 1965, and Association of Bay Area Governments, 1969 and revised in 1970 - 71, have made the forecasts which are compared with actual data, both absolutely in figure 13 and relatively, figure 14.

At this point it is time to look back and consider what kind of conclusions can be drawn on basis of the knowledge acquired through the analysis of these data.

Most planners probably have to admit that uncertainties in forecasting as they appear in figures 8-14 and table 4 are greater than what has so far been realized. From the results it seems reasonable to assume RMSE around unbiased mean, $\bar{r} = 1.0$, that is s_b of the magnitude, $s_b = .20$ for 5 years old forecasts, $s_b = .30 - .40$ after 10 years, and probably $s_b > .50$ for 20 years old forecasts.

Table 4 – Numerical results from the statistical analysis of the FAA forecasts made in 1968

Age of forecast in years	Passengers			Movements		
	– 4 –	– 5 –	– 2 –	– 3 –	– 4 –	– 5 –
Mean ($\bar{r}$)	.8655	.8426	.9020	.7708	.7303	.7040
Standard error of the mean	.0199	.0208	.0229	.0209	.0174	.0192
Uncertainty measurements:						
Standard deviation (s_r)	.1107	.1158	.1314	.1198	.1074	.1104
RMSE around $\bar{r} = 1.0$ (s_b)	.1742	.1954	.1639	.2590	.2903	.3159
Coefficient of Variation	.1279	.1374	.1457	.1554	.1470	.1568
Coefficient of Skewness	.0882	.0549	.7341	.4391	.5508	.6243
Number of observations	31	31	33	33	33	33

It is also apparent from the Washington D.C. data that when an area is served by two or more airports the uncertainties of the individual forecasts, figure 12, are larger than the uncertainties of the aggregated forecast for all airports, figure 10 and 11. But in this case the individual forecasts seem to improve over time.

With respect to the shape of the uncertainty distribution, there are at least two indications that we may expect a positively skewed distribution.

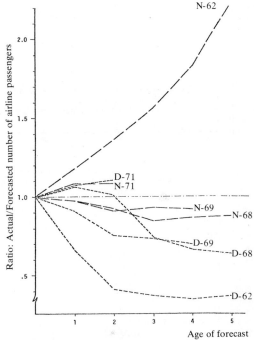

Figure 12 – Comparison of different forecasts for Dulles and Washington National Airports.

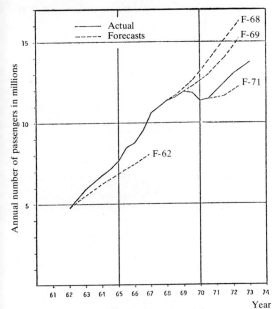

Figure 10: – 1962, 1968, 1969 and 1971 forecasts compared to actual annual number of airline passengers for Dulles and Washington National Airports.

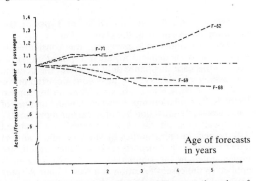

Figure 11 – Comparison of ratios: Actual/Forecasted number of annual passengers for 1962, 1968, 1969 and 1971 forecasts for Dulles and Washington National Airports.

Ratios arrived at by dividing two positive variables, always have a lower limit equal to zero, but not necessarily any upper limit, thus indicating a density function skewed to the right.

The development of annual number of passengers over time can be described by the following model:

$$T_{an} = T_0 \prod_{t=1}^{n} (1 + a(t))$$

where T_{an} – actual demand in year n
    T_0 – base year demand
    $a(t)$ – actual growth factors for each year t
    n – horizon (number of years)

However, at the forecasting stage, the actual growth factors, $a(t)$, are not known, but estimated (forecasted) values, $\bar{a}(t)$, are used.

The forecasting model will then be:

$$T_{en} = T_0 \prod_{t} (1 + \bar{a}(t))$$

where T_{en} is estimated (forecasted) demand in year n

Once the $\bar{a}(t)$-values are determined, the estimated demand, T_{en}, is calculated and can from then on be regarded as a constant. The uncertainty is now tied to what actually will happen, that is $a(t)$. At the forecasting

371

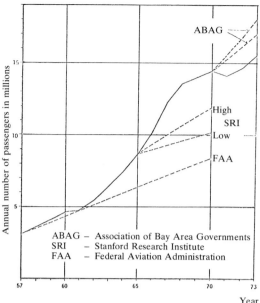

Based on the assumption that the actual growth factors are random variables having density functions with non-negative skewness, the density function for M will be skewed to the right, for example similar to a gamma-, log-normal- or an F-distribution. Its standard deviation (RMSE) increased with the age of the forecast. In figure 15 are shown examples of M for $s_b = 0.2$ (5 years old forecasts) $s_b = 0.4$ (10 years old forecasts), $s_b = 0.5$ (20 years old forecasts) and $s_b = 0.6$ (30 years old forecasts). It should be evident that these distributions represent a very crude estimate of the nature of the uncertainty connected to demand forecasting. However, if true, they do imply some interesting consequences:

– Due to the assumption made and the resulting skewness, actual demand is more likely to be less than the forecasted demand, that is, overestimation is more likely than underestimation.

– The 95% confidence interval for a 5 years forecast given an estimated demand of $T_{en} = 5$ million is approximately:
3.4 mill. $< T_{an} < 7.2$ mill.

– The 95% confidence interval for a 10 years forecast given an estimated demand of $T_{en} = 5$ million is approximately:
2.6 mill. $< T_{an} < 9.7$ mill.

Figure 13 – 1957, 1965 and 1970 forecasts compared to actual number of airline passengers for San Francisco International Airport

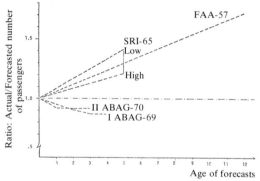

Figure 14 – Comparison of ratios: Actual/Forecasted number of annual passengers for different forecasts for San Francisco International Airport.

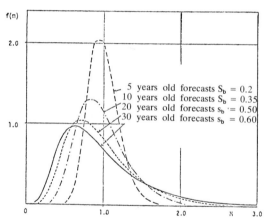

Figure 15 – Uncertainty in the variable M as a function of the age of the forecasts

stage growth factors are expected to be chosen such that the RMSEs are minimized which again lead to unbiased $\bar{a}(t)$-values. The $a(t)$'s can then be considered random variables coming from distributions with $\bar{a}(t)$ as expected values. In [1] is shown that when multiplying two variables, X and Y, each having symmetrical or positively skewed distribution, the resulting variable, Z, will be positively skewed.

$$Z = X \cdot Y$$

Applying this result to the demand model described above, one would expect the distribution of T_{an} to be positively skewed because of the multiplicative model.

Based on these theoretical considerations and the analysis of the historical data, the conclusion is that when dealing with demand forecasting for air transportation, uncertainties can be expressed as the density function of the variable M, where:

$$M = \frac{T_{an}}{T_{en}}$$

Uncertainty Distributions for Different Types of Demand for the Airports in the Oslo-region

"Annual number of passengers" was considered to express the basic demand for air transportation. However, in this case this figure only expresses the demand for passenger facilities while "peak hour aircarrier movements" was chosen to express the demand for runway facilities. The relationships between "annual number of passengers", "annual number of aircarrier movements" and "peak hour air carrier movements" are analysed with respect to uncertainties by study of actual airport data for a number of airports [1] and all these results are implemented in the simulation model which again is applied to the case: "Location at a New Major Airport for the Oslo-region". The resulting simulated uncertainty distributions for demand are given in figures 16, 17 and 18.

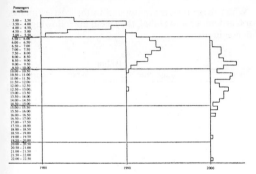

Figure 16 – Uncertainty distributions for annual number of passengers for 1980, 1990 and 2000

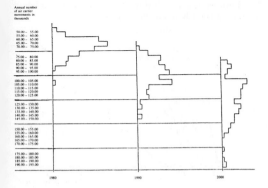

Figure 17 – Uncertainty distributions for annual number of air carrier movements for 1980, 1990 and 2000

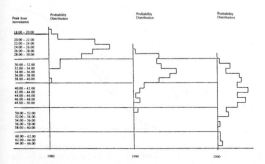

Figure 18 – Uncertainty distributions for peak hour air carrier movements for 1980, 1990 and 2000

The calculations are based on existing forecasts for the demand for air transportation in the Oslo-region and the figures are drawn on basis of 100 simulation runs. Keeping in mind the importance of the demand forecast when designing the airport model (figure 3), the knowledge of these rather large uncertainties may have a significant effect on the decisions to be made. This problem, however, is not analysed in detail in this work, but should be given considerable attention in the future.

APPLICATIONS AND CONCLUSIONS

Introduction

The purpose of this final chapter is to demonstrate the effect of the uncertainty distributions developed in the third and fourth sections. This is done by applying the results to the case study described briefly in the second section. In order to minimize the computations and to make the presentation more clear, only two of the alternative sites for a new airport are considered. The two sites chosen are Gardemoen and Hobøl which represent the low and the high values for the estimates of construction costs. The cost estimates for two-stage development of the two alternatives are given in table 5.

Uncertainties in Actual Costs Based Only on Uncertainty Distribution for the Cost Ratio

As a first application of the research results the uncertainty distribution for the cost ratios is applied to the cost estimates for the alternatives, table 5. Recalling the basic model:

$$R = \frac{C}{E}$$

or:

$$C = E \cdot R$$

where

R – the ratio of actual to estimated cost
C – the actual cost
E – the estimated cost

When E is known, that is $E = e$, the expression can be written: $C = e \cdot R$

The cost ratio, R, which is considered a random variable, was found to have an approximate log-normal distribution. Better fit to the observed data was however obtained by considering the variable $R^1 = R - 0.3$ which was approximately log-normal distributed with parameters

u = 0.1385
o = 0.3719

This yields the following properties for the distribution of R.

Mean	1.2330
Standard of deviation	0.3623
Coefficient of variation	0.2938
Coefficient of skewness	1.2125

Table 6 – Properties for the distribution of R

	Gardemoen		Hobøl	
	1. stage	2. stage	1. stage	2. stage
Runway costs (includes land acquisition)	1062	383	1141	403
Terminal costs	515	350	515	350
Ground transportation costs	44	—	129	—
Sub-total	1621	733	1785	753
Total airport cost		2354		2538
Cost of general aviation facilities		90		127

All costs in mill. N. Kr. (1970)

Table 5 – Cost Estimates for two-stage development of new airport at Gardemoen and Hobøl

373

Confidence limits for the actual cost, C, will then be:
95% level: $.72 \cdot e < C < 2.10 \cdot e$
90% level: $.77 \cdot e < C < 1.91 \cdot e$
50% level: $.98 \cdot e < C < 1.42 \cdot e$

When these results are applied to the cost estimates for Gardemoen and Hobøl, they yield the following confidence limits:

| | Gardemoen | | Hobøl | |
	Stage one	Whole Airport	Stage one	Whole Airport
95% level	1167 – 3405	1695 – 4943	1285 – 3749	1827 – 5330
90% level	1248 – 3096	1813 – 4496	1374 – 3409	1954 – 4848
50% level	1589 – 2302	2307 – 3343	1749 – 2535	2487 – 3604

Cost in mill. N. Kr. (1970)
General Aviation facilities not included

Table 7 – Confidence intervals for actual costs for Gardemoen and Hobøl

The resulting distributions are shown in figure 19.

As it appears when applied to the case study, this method has its limitations. The method cannot be used to analyse the effect of a two or multiple stage development of the airport, and it is not possible to assign different uncertainties to different groups of projects. Finally, this approach does not reflect the uncertainties in demand and capacity, and the method cannot be used for analyzing different operational strategies. However, such analysis does provide some useful information about the uncertainties in actual costs of airport projects and represents an "easy to use" tool for both planners and decisionmakers.

port. By use of a simulation model, demand and capacity values are simulated for each year up to year 2000 while uncertainties in actual costs are calculated according to their uncertainty distribution. The resulting uncertainty distributions based on 100 simulation runs are shown in figures 20 (Gardemoen) and 21 (Hobøl).

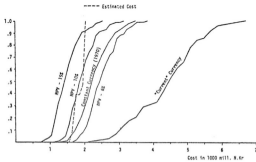

Figure 20 – Uncertainty distributions for Gardemoen derived by the simulation model

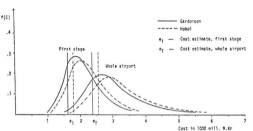

Figure 19 – Uncertainty distributions for Gardemoen and Hobøl derived by use of the empirical uncertainty distribution for the cost ratio, R

Uncertainties in Actual Cost Based on Uncertainties in Costs, Capacity and Demand
Application of the Research Results to the Alternatives Gardemoen and Hobøl

The two alternatives, Gardemoen and Hobøl, are both described as two-stage developments. The first stage, that is the first main runway and terminal facilities to accomodate up to 9 million passengers, is to be implemented when air carrier demand exceeds either the terminal or runway capacity of the existing Fornebu Air-

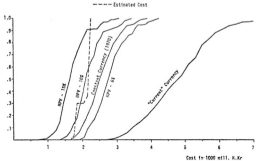

Figure 21 – Uncertainty distributions for Hobøl derived by the simulation model

Table 8 – Some of the properties of the different cost distributions for Gardemoen and Hobøl

| | Net Present Values | | | Actual Cost | |
GARDEMOEN	6%	10%	15%	Constant Currency	Current Currency
Mean	2564 mill	1981 mill	1526 mill	2380 mill	4473 mill
Standard deviation	449 mill	379 mill	358 mill	449 mill	960 mill
Coeff. of variation	0.175	0.191	0.234	0.189	0.210
Coeff. of skewness	0.516	0.692	0.728	0.428	−0.108
HOBØL					
Mean	2860 mill	2235 mill	1743 mill	2652 mill	4882 mill
Standard deviation	501 mill	456 mill	439 mill	462 mill	923 mill
Coeff. of variation	0.175	0.204	0.252	0.174	0.189
Coeff. of skewness	0.486	0.774	0.866	0.332	−0.064

The fact that even the estimated cost has a distribution indicates that the number of projects to be implemented before the horizon, year 2000, is not the same in all simulation runs.

The simulation results also include numerical information about some of the properties of the different distributions. These are given in table 8.

As information to the decisionmakers, all these distributions and their properties may turn out to be rather confusing, but as basis for a discussion of the properties of the different cost distributions and their use in the decision process, such information is considered valuable.

Cost information in terms of net present values are commonly used in economic evaluation of construction projects. The interest rate is usually determined on basis of economic considerations in the country where the project is to be realized. However, it is worth noticing that higher interest rates, in this case exemplified by 15%, tend to decrease the absolute uncertainty expressed as the standard deviation, while the relative uncertainty, that is the coefficient of variation, and the skewness are increased.

The simulation program also gives information about what projects are implemented in each simulation run (table 9).

Table 9 – Projects implemented in each simulation run; excerpt from computer output

PROJECTS IMPLEMENTED

1RUN	11	21	51	12
2RUN	11	21	51	12
3RUN	11	21	51	12
4RUN	11	21	51	12
5RUN	11	21	51	
6RUN	11	21	12	51
7RUN	11	21	51	
8RUN	11	21	12	
9RUN	11	21	51	12
10RUN	11	21	51	12
11RUN	11	21	12	51
12RUN	11	21	12	51
13RUN	11	21	51	12
14RUN	11	21		
15RUN	11	21	51	12
16RUN	11	21	51	12
17RUN	11	21	51	
18RUN	11	21	51	
19RUN	11	21	51	12
20RUN	11	21	51	12
21RUN	11	21	12	51
22RUN	11	21	12	51
23RUN	11	21	51	12
24RUN	11	21	51	
25RUN	11	21	51	12

Projects: 11 – Terminal facilities at new airport
 1. stage – Capacity: 9 mill. passengers
 21 – First main runway at new airport
 51 – General aviation runway at new airport
 12 – Terminal facilities at new airport
 2. stage – Capacity: 18 mill. passengers
The sequence 11-21 indicates that new airport is needed because of demand for terminal facilities.

Based on this information the probabilities of the different projects being implemented before year 2000 can be calculated. These results are shown in table 10.

Additional information about when the first stage of the new airport is needed is also given by the simulation program.

Figure 22 shows the resulting distribution of years when stage 1 of the new airport has to be completed.

Table 10 – Probabilities of Inplementation of Different Projects Before Year 2000

Project Description	Probability of Implementation Before Year 2000
Terminal facilities at new airport 1. stage – Capacity: 9 mill pass.	1.00
First main runway at new airport	1.00
General aviation runway at new airport	0.86
Terminal facilities at new airport 2. stage – Capacity: 18 mill. pass.	0.66
Second main runway at new airport	0.00

As shown in table 9, the project sequence 11 - 21 indicates that the critical facility at the existing airport is the passenger terminal. This conclusion is not at all surprising since the terminal facilities at Fornebu are now being improved.

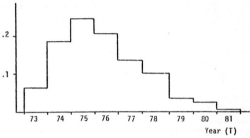

Figure 22 – Distribution of years when stage 1 of new airport has to be completed

Extensions in the Use of the Simulation Model

The results discussed in the preceding section were based on the use of the simulation model on two of the alternative sites for a new airport. However, the use of the model can be extended in several ways.

The simulation model gives, in addition to the results already discussed, information to the planner about forecasted demand, stratified according to air carrier demand for terminal facilities and runways, charter traffic demand for terminal facilities and runway, and general aviation demand for runways. This information also includes uncertainty measurements for the forecasts as already shown. Based on this information the planner can discover the most critical parts of the airport system with respect to capacities, and thus generate new solutions for these particular problems. For example, as shown in table 9, two of the most important problems for the airport system in the Oslo region, seem to be:

1) Capacity of the terminal facilities for air carrier traffic
2) General aviation runway capacity

Although the quality of the existing runways at Forneby Airport may represent a problem (figure 1), there is no immediate runway capacity problem if the general aviation demand for runway capacity can be taken care of.

However, the noise problem has resulted in severe constraints on the operational procedures. Due to these constraints, no plans or cost estimates for major improvements of Forneby have been made public. If adequate cost and capacity data were available for such major improvements of Fornebu Airport, the economic impacts of the operational constraints could be analysed by the simulation model. This points to another possible use of this approach, that is; analysing different operational procedures for the airport system.

General Conclusions and Suggestions for Further Research

Based on empirical data, uncertainty distributions are estimated for actual cost of airport projects and for air transportation demand. The magnitude of the uncertainties is likely to be considerably larger than most planners and decisionmakers expect. The shape of the uncertainty distributions is found to be approximately log-normal for the actual cost of airport projects. For air transportation demand, reasons are given for expecting a distribution slightly skewed to the right (positive coefficient of skewness).

The effect of uncertainties in actual costs on decisionmaking is hard to analyse since cost is only one factor in a multidimensional evaluation and decision process. The importance of cost of projects as basis for decisions has decreased in recent years due to the introduction of a number of other attributes into the decision process.

By realizing the rather large uncertainties in actual costs, differences in cost estimates between different projects may be even less important in years to come.

Since this research represents one of the first attempts to gather and analyse information about uncertainties in the attribute measurements for transportation facilities which planners supply to the decisionmakers, the whole area is open for research. Within the field of air transportation, the most urgent projects seem to be to analyse the nature of the uncertainties in other attribute measurements. Since noise obviously is of major importance, uncertainty analysis of noise measurements should be given high priority, but also attributes such as operating costs, ground transportation costs and regional effects should be dealt with.

Within the specific areas treated in this work, additional research should be performed both with respect to costs and to demand. As for the uncertainties in actual cost of projects, a crucial point is the assumptions of complete independence or dependence between projects within one airport and between alternative airport sites. These problems seem to be of great importance in order to extend the statistical treatment of the uncertainty distributions. However, additional research is also needed in order to verify or adjust the distributions as they were found in this work.

As for the uncertainties in air carrier demand forecasts, the problem should also be analysed by going more deeply into the individual forecasting models and deriving uncertainties on basis of the structure of the models and the uncertainties in the input to the models.

So far only airport problems are considered. Of course, other modes of transportation and their transportation facilities can be analysed in similar ways.

ACKNOWLEDGEMENT

This paper is based on a Ph.D. dissertation [1] submitted to the University of California, Berkeley in 1976. The research was performed under the guidance of Professor Adib Kanafani, and financial support was provided by the University of Trondheim, Norway and The Norwegian Council for Scientific and Industrial Research.

The author is now an associate professor at The Division of Transportation Engineering, The University of Trondheim, Norway.

REFERENCES

[1] Knudsen, T. **Uncertainties in Airport Cost Analysis and Their Effect on Site Selection.** Ph. D. Dissertation University of California, Berkeley 1976.

[2] Hutchinson, B.G. Stucturing Urban Transportation Planning Decisions: The Use of Statistical Decision Theory. **Environmental Planning,** Vol. 1. 1969.

[3] Khan, Ata M. Transport Policy Decision Analysis: A Decision-Theoretic Framework. **Socio-Economic Planning Sciences, Vol. 5,** No. 2, April 1971.

[4] Mac Crimmon, K.R. **Decisionmaking among Multiple-Attribute Alternatives: A Survey and Consolidated Approach.** The Rand Corporation, RM-4823-ARPA, December 1968.

[5] Manheim, Marvin, L. Decision Theories in Transportation Planning. **HRB-Special Report 108,** Highway Research Board, Washington D.C., 1970.

[6] Altouney, Edward A. **The Role of Uncertainties in the Economic Evaluation of Water Resources Projects.** Institute of Engineering – Economic Systems. Stanford University, 1963.

[7] Zimmerman, J. and Merewitz, L. **The Effects of Uncertainty and Conscious Underbidding on Cost Overruns: The BART Experience.** University of California, Berkeley, 1974. Unpublished.

[8] Merewitz, Leonard. How Do Urban Rapid Transit Projects Compare in Cost Estimating Experience? **Proceedings of the International Conference on Transportation Research First Conference, Bruges, Belgium.**

[9] Merewitz, Leonard. Cost Overruns in Public Works. Niskanen, W. (ed) **Benefit Cost and Policy Analysis.** Chicago, Aldine, 1973.

[10] Selby, S.M. (ed) **Standard Mathematical Tables Fourteenth Edition.** The Chemical Co. Ohio, 1965.

[11] Conover, W. **Practical Nonparametric Statistics.** John Wiley & Sons, New York, 1971.

[12] Bickel, P.J. and Doksum, K. A. **A Course in Mathematical Statistics.** Holden Day, San Francisco, 1976.

[13] Federal Aviation Administration. **Aviation Demand and Airport Facility Requirement Forecast for Medium Air Transportation Hubs Through 1980.** Washington D.C., 1968.

[14] U S Federal Aviation Administration. **Air Traffic Activity.** 1965 - 1972.

[15] U S Federal Aviation Administration. **FAA Statistical Handbook of Aviation.** 1965 - 1973.

[16] U S Civil Aeoronautes Board. U S Federal Aviation Administration. **Airport Activity Statistics of Certificated Route Air Carriers.** 1971 - 1974.

[17] Federal Aviation Agency. **Aviation Forecasts for Dulles International Airport and Washington National Airport.** Calendar years 1963 - 1967. Washington D.C., 1962.

[18] Federal Aviation Administration. **Washington National and Dulles International Airport Forecasts.** Fiscal Years 1969 - 1980. Washington D.C., 1969.

[19] U S Federal Aviation Administration. **Washington National and Dulles International Airport Forecasts.** Fiscal Years 1970 - 1981. Washington D.C., 1969.

[20] U S Federal Aviation Administration. **Washington National and Dulles International Airport Forecasts.** Fiscal Years 1972 - 1983. Washington D.C., 1971.

FOOTNOTES

1. The term "estimate" is in this context not used according to its statistical interpretation, but as a synonym to "forecast" which is the way it is used in the references dealing with cost-oriented problems.

2. Completion time is here defined as the length of time from when a cost estimate is made and till the project is completed.

3. Construction Cost Index is published monthly in Engineering News Record and annual averages are calculated and published annually.

Safety at sea and related research

by

J. A. H. PAFFETT

National Maritime Institute, England

SUMMARY

This paper deals with mishaps to ships, their consequences and prevention. It is argued that present world accident rates are still higher than they need be, and that the causes are mainly human rather than material. Current research related to ship safety is reviewed in general terms.

ACCIDENTS AT SEA

Safety, like health, is conveniently defined in terms of its opposite; health is the absence of sickness, and safety is achieved if accidents do not happen. We can think of accidents as being of two sorts; injuries ot men, whether or not the ship is damaged; and damage to the ship, or the loss of the ship, whether or not people are hurt.

INJURIES

People are hurt and killed aboard ships, as in any other transport system or industry. The incidence, though regrettable, is not exceptionally serious by general industrial standards. Table 1 shows some figures for deaths in the British registered fleet over a recent period; when

Table 1 - Deaths among crews of UK registered merchant ships

Cause of death	Average 1934-38	Average 1964-68	Average 1969-73	Year 1974
Casualties to vessels	82	33	31	13
Other accidents	227	95	71	75
Disease, homicide or suicide	492	181	161	142
Totals	801	309	263	230

Breakdown for 1974

Cause of death	Total
Foundering of ship	7
Explosion or fire	6
Accidents on board	35
Accidents ashore	29
Homicide	7
Suicide	17
Missing at Sea	11
Disease	118
Total	230

The above total of 230 relates to an estimated total of 78,000 men at risk, representing a death rate of 2.9 per thousand seamen at risk. The rate has varied between 2.5 and 3.6 during the period 1964 to 74.
The total of 13 due to casualties to vessels represents a death rate of one man per 6000 at risk.
The above figures have been extracted from ref. 1.

deaths due to suicide, sickness and so on are discounted, those due to injury are relatively few. No doubt similar figures could be produced by other shipping nations.

An important exception to this favourable picture lies in the fishing fleets, where the figures for injury and death are much worse. Such injuries are typically associated with accidents on deck during the fishing process - handling nets, working with wires and so on - and suggest that some benefit could be expected from research into the ergonomics of fish-catching. However,

fishing is not a transport process, and so the matter of fishing safety - as of safety aboard oil rigs and offshore servicing vessels - will not be considered further in this paper.

MISHAPS TO SHIPS

We shall consider a mishap (usually referred to by marine specialists as a "casualty") as an incident which leads to the damage or loss of a ship, whether or not people are hurt or killed. A convenient crude measure of casualty rates is provided by the over-all figure for ships lost each year, expressed as a percentage of the total number of ships at risk over the same period.

Alternatively this can be set out as gross tonnage lost in relation to tonnage at risk. The figures in Table 2 show

Table 2 - Annual World Merchant Ship Losses Expressed at a Percentage of Gross Tonnage at Risk

Year		Percentage lost
1891	Sailing ships	3.7
1891	Steam ships	1.7
1913	Sailing ships	3.7
1913	Steam ships	1.0
1949	All ships	0.30
1959	All ships	0.23
1966	All ships	0.48
1975	All ships	0.29

Figs are from Ref. 1.
(1949 and 1975 from Ref. 2)

377

how this rate has fallen over the past century. The falling trend from the days of sailing ships and no radio is only to be expected. However, closer examination of the figures shows that the curve does not reach the zero level, or even approach it asymptotically; over recent years the loss rate has hovered uncertainly, and some interpreters even see signs of an increase. Table 3, abstracted with the author's permission from the so-far unpublished text of ref. 2, shows the indeterminate fluctuation over the last few years. Too much should not be read into these swings, the loss of a single large modern ship can distort the short-term figures; the "Olympic Bravery" for instance at 126,622 tons gross representing over one-third of the world losses for the first quarter of 1976. However, one firm conclusion can be drawn: the steady improvement evident up to the 1950's has been checked, and it may even have been reversed.

Is this any cause for concern? The loss of life due to ship casualties is very small, microscopic in fact in relation to the rate of deaths in road transport. The rate of loss of cargoes and vehicles, though not negligible, is reasonably small in relation to the total at risk. It can plausibly be argued that things are very well as they are, that the sea will always impose an unavoidable minimum of hazard to any vessel which ventures out of harbour, and that any research devoted to reducing loss rates further will not be cost-effective.

THE CAUSES FOR CONCERN

There are two good reasons for not accepting this let-it-go argument. The first is that the ocean is not expanding in width and depth to suit the large modern ships; as vessels grow in speed and size, above all in draught, they are increasingly confined to narrow channels and fairways which cramp their motions, degrade their steering and lessen the scope for collision-avoidance manoeuvres. The risks of grounding and collision, in fact, seem bound to grow with the number, speed and size of ships operating in the finite ocean. If losses are not to get worse, some positive action is called for to prevent such groundings and collisions from happening.

The second reason lies in the size and physical nature of many cargoes now being carried. A generation ago the sinking of a cargo ship meant a loss to the owners and the underwriters, and possibly distress to the crew and passengers, but the community at large was not affected. Now, however, we are carrying enormous quantities of obnoxious substances by sea, in particular oil, gas and chemicals, and an accident can have widespread effects far more unpleasant and actively harmful than could have resulted from any conceivable mishap with the cargo ships of past years. The effects and cost of oil pollution are familiar enough to need no elaboration (though it should be borne in mind the Torrey Canyon was a relatively small tanker by present standards). Apart from the sheer scale and cost, the new factor here is the involvement of innocent third parties; members of the public remote from the scene and unconnected with the shipping business can suffer. In this context it is not only chemical pollution we should worry about; one can point to the private householders ashore in south-east England who had their windows broken by the blast from a foreign tanker blowing up in 1971, in waters which were then regarded as international. More recently a Liberian tanker has exploded in Los Angeles harbour, breaking windows ashore up to 21 miles away. A notable number of private citizens live within 21 miles radius of the world's main oil terminals.

Since, then, the community at large can now suffer loss from the activities of the marine transport industries, the community is entitled to take an interest in the conduct of those industries, and if necessary to impose regula-

tions to minimize such loss. In such activities Governments individually, and collectively as IMCO, act on behalf of their citizens.

The really serious accidents, however, are those which have not so far happened at all, outside science fiction stories. The one usually quoted is the collision between a liquid gas carrier and a cross-Channel ferry. There is nothing inherently impossible about such an occurrence, indeed it seems less unlikely than a head-on encounter between two air-liners at 10,000 metres altitude. The ships move in only two dimensions, and these can be crowded in places as the Dover Straits radar plot will show at any time (see fig 1).

ANALYSIS OF STATISTICS

The loss figures compiled by Lloyd's lend themselves to breaking down in various ways - by nationality, by cause of loss, by type and size of ship, by age of ship and so on - and a fascinating set of such figures will shortly appear in ref. 2. It is proposed here to comment briefly on only two features of these figures; the type of loss, and the effect of nationality.

The world figures broken down into broad categories of accident - Grounding, Collision, Burnt and so on - show considerable fluctuations, but there seems to be a slight decrease in groundings since 1960 balanced by an increase in Burnt (which include explosions) and founderings (ie sinking due to weather damage or capsizing). The Burnt category includes the various tankers affected by ballast tank explosions.

The nationality subdivision shows a quite remarkable scatter of loss rates, (see Table 3). The wide discrepancy

Table 3 - Shipping losses of some of the principal flags, expressed as a percentage of the total gross tonnage at risk, over the period 1967 to 1975

	%
Lebanon	4.72
Philippines	2.23
Cyprus	1.96
Korea	1.66
Somali Rep.	1.57
Singapore	1.32
Panama	1.11
Greece	0.90
Netherlands	0.56
Liberia	0.46
Spain	0.41
Italy	0.38
Canada	0.37
Denmark	0.26
U.S.A.	0.21
Norway	0.18
Japan	0.17
Sweden	0.16
Germany FR	0.14
United Kingdom	0.11
France	0.09

The figures are extracted from ref. 2.

in loss rates between the best and the worst shipowning nations has been pointed out time and again in the marine press (E.g., in ref. 8). The causes can lie to only a small extent in the ships themselves, as even in the worst fleets these are for the most part still classed by reputable classification societies and thus mechanically adequate for safe operation. The causes must be sought rather in the way in which the ships are operated, in the standards of officer qualification and of inspection. (A detailed study of ship loss causes among the flags of convenience would make a fascinating research project if one could only come by accurate information for each loss). The spread of loss rates between flags suggests that human factors may have an important bearing upon marine safety.

THE CAUSES OF SHIP CASUALTIES

It is easy enough to list casualties under types - grounding, collision and so on - but far harder to establish exactly why each grounding etc. did occur. Press reports are usually uninformative on the subject, for understandable reasons where officers' careers and reputations are at stake. However, in a small sample of cases one can delve further. If a shipping accident involving British registered ships involves significant loss of life, or attracts public concern for some other reason, then the UK Department of Trade sets up a Court of Inquiry to conduct a formal legal investigation, and the reports of a number of such inquiries are available. For the cases so investigated over a period of some 14 years, it will be found that in roughly 2 cases out of 3 the accident could be put down to human error of one sort or another, rather than to material failure.

This sample is not of course large or random, and the 2/3 ratio cannot be assumed to apply to all shipping at all times. However, other studies carried out quite independently on different samples still show the preponderance of this human factor. For instance, the US Coast Guard reported in 1963 that over the period 1957-59 in 199 collisions involving 398 vessels there was mechanical failure in 6 vessels and "personal failure" in 289 vessels. (Ref. 3). Other observers have estimated "human causes" as 9 out of 10.

Evidently, therefore, if we wish to reduce further the present loss rate we should look first to the human element rather than to the material engineering of our vehicles. This is not to say that ships cannot be improved mechanically, but mechanical performance and reliability are already well researched and further effort will lead to only marginal gains, whereas the human field is so far little explored and moderate effort may lead to major gains.

THE NATURE OF HUMAN FAILURE

Consider first the part of the human in groundings and collisions, which together account for something near a half of all losses of ships, and an even higher proportion of damaging casualties short of total loss. A grounding or a collision results from the ship being in the wrong place, ie. from a navigational error of some sort. In steering or navigating a ship the man is provided with information, through his own eyes or via sensors such as radar sets.

On the strength of this information, and drawing upon his training and experience and local knowledge he takes various decisions. He gives effect to these decisions by giving orders or operating various control knobs. What can happen to lead to a wrong navigational act?

Following the chain of events through, we can group errors into four categories. First there is the error of perception, where the man fails to see another ship in his path, or sees it but wrongly interprets its aspect. A commonly quoted instance arises when the masthead lights at the two ends of a long ship are wrongly thought to belong to two separate small ships; in trying to steer between them the navigator rams the tanker amidships. Similar but more subtle errors occur in interpreting the radar display or echo-sounder chart. The slippage in fact occurs at the interface between the world and the man's senses.

The second sort of error happens inside the man's head. He acquires the right information, but through ignorance or bad training or downright incompetence he takes the wrong decision.

The third kind happens when the man has the right facts and makes the right decision, but gives orders which are misunderstood or operates a control wrongly. The error again happens at the interface between the man and his surroundings.

The fourth kind of error happens when the man knows axactly what he ought to do and how to do it, but deliberately does something different. An example might be when he fails to reduce speed in bad visibility in order to save a tide, or when he enters a shallow harbour with less than the under-keel clearance prescribed by the local harbour master. Such actions are conveniently called errors of malfeasance.

At one time all these human manifestations were regarded as outside the world of the engineer; fit matters for discussion perhaps between the officer and his Owner and the underwriters and the Marine Administration, but not amenable to treatment by research. In recent years this view has been revised, and there is now research going on in a number of countries aimed at reducing the incidence of human failure. The remaining sections of this paper are mainly devoted to reviewing this work.

BRIDGE ERGONOMICS

Errors of the first and third categories outlined above happen at the interface between the man and the "world", meaning in this case mainly the equipment and instruments on the ship's bridge. The study of the relationship between man and his working environment is known as ergonomics, which is now a respectable branch of science with established techniques and principles. Ergonomic studies have long played a part in the design of aircraft cockpits, and even of automobiles. How do modern ships' bridges stand up to an ergonomic examination?

The answer is, pretty poorly. A classic study by Wilkinson in 1971 (Ref. 4) showed that merchant ships were ripe, ideed over-ripe, for the ergonomists' attention. A field study carried out by a UK firm under contract to the Department of Industry confirmed this view, and in a long series of visits to ships a collection of cases was built up illustrating in a multitude of ways "how not to do it" in designing or laying out instruments. One could list a multitude of petty instances - inaccessible switches, confusing labelling and dial markings on instruments, windows which could not be cleaned, indicator lamps causing dazzle at night, slippery decks and absence of hand-grips; mostly small points, but adding up sometimes to what looked like a deliberate effort to make the officers' job difficult and confusing.

Concurrently with this project, similar studies have been under way in Holland, Germany, Norway and Sweden. The emphases of the various national programmes are different; the British effort has depended mainly upon watching the seaman at work, the Continental programmes have placed more reliance upon questionnaires addressed to practising mariners. However, an important point to note is this: the marine ergonomics teams in these countries are in touch with one another, and with the US Coastguard too, and there is a fruitful interchange of ideas and information. In the UK the study has produced a draft "Code of Practice for the design of ships' bridges", the text of which is now under discussion with the marine industries. Parts of the document read largely like a platitudinous recitation of the obvious, but the need for it is apparent in the numerous bridges which fall short of some of the most elementary ergonomic requirements.

Apart from the physical design of the ship's bridge, there are physiological aspects of the man-ship match which deserve investigation; for instance, the deterioration in human performance caused by noise, vibration, heat, fatigue and seasickness. Some spin-off from military work in these fields could benefit civil studies.

EXTERNAL ERGONOMICS

This refers to the functioning of the interface between the man and the external world, as distinct from the shipborne environment of bridge instruments and controls. Here the main matching requirement lies in the need for the man to be able to judge the tactical situation correctly with his own unaided senses, and in particular to be able to assess another ship's movements simply by looking at her, and by listening to her whistle signals. In daylight and good visibility there is little difficulty, but at night or in fog visual problems can arise from the difficulty of interpreting the appearance of the ordinary navigation lights. By international agreement all large ships carry five navigational lights, laid out in a specified manner - two masthead lights, a stern light and the red and green side lights. These serve to indicate the presence of a ship, but not her size, speed, aspect angle (except in very approximate manner) or intentions. The lighting standard was based upon oil lamps and was adequate for the days of sail and slow steamers. Now however the availability of modern electric lighting techniques suggests that a great deal more information could be conveyed at modest cost, in particular by using the ability to modulate or flash the navigation lights so as to make them stand out from accommodation lights, shore lights or other sources with which they might be confused. Collision studies suggest that an indication of intent or helm action - eg. "I am putting my rudder to starboard" - could be valuable to other ships in the area; such an intent could conveniently be signalled by, eg. flashing or occulting the starboard side light. A study of marine optical perception in relation to various lighting schemes is being planned in UK.

Regarding audible perception, whistle signals still have a part to play in closequarters situations, in harbour or in fog. A difficulty sometimes arises in deciding which of several visible ships is the one emitting a perceived noise. In the days of steam this was conveniently indicated by the white plume issuing from the funnel responsible, but the air whistle of the diesel ship or tug offers no such clue. A proposal has been made that the operation of such a whistle should also trigger a bright all-round flashing light. This would show identity in clear weather, and also bearing and range (from the time delay) in poor visibility.

TRAINING

The second sort of human error discussed above is that which arises from incompetence, ignorance or inadequate training. In this context the training concerned is that involved in ship handling, navigational decision making and emergency procedures. At one time the necessary skills could be picked up on the job, largely by trial and error, and this may still be feasible in small ships. In large modern vessels however the trial and error process is ruled out by the cost and danger; it is simply not practical, for instance, to let a pilot learn how to con a VLCC into Rotterdam by experimenting with a loaded vessel.

The air transport industry has long faced a similar problem, and air pilots are now regularly trained on flight simulators, machines which reproduce faithfully the reactions of the vehicle and present a realistic "machine interface" to the man. It was a logical step to apply the simulation technique to the training of seamen, and a number of training simulators are now in operation in europe and USA. Those known to the author are listed with outline particulars in Table 4.

It is not claimed by any simulator operator that the simulator can take the place of sea experience. It is

Table 4 - Ship training simulators in commission

	Country	Place	Operator	Optical display
1.	France	Grenoble	Sogreah	Manned ship models in lake
2.	Holland	Delft	TNO	Shadowgraph
3.	Holland	Wageningen	NSMB	Shadowgraph
4.	Germany	Bremen	School of Navigation	Slide projector
5.	Sweden	Goteborg	SSPA	Multiple CRT screens
6.	UK	Warsash	School of Navigation	Point light projectors (nocturnal view)
7.	USA	King's Point	MARAD	Multiple projection TV (mainly research facility)
8.	Japan	Hiroshima	University	Projection TV
9.	Japan	Tokyo	University	Projection TV

however claimed that, for a certain range of instructional topics, it is far more cost effective and safe. Moreover, the simulator enables some things to be done which could not be done at all at sea, even if the cost and time could be afforded; in particular the simulator enables exercise conditions to be repeated exactly, time and again. This is useful for testing purposes, for comparing students, for weeding out the basically imcompetent and those with no aptitude for seamanship, and even for examinations. Further, exercises can be carried through to the point of actual collision or grounding if necessary. Time is saved because the desired environment and weather conditions can be laid on immediately the machine is switched on - there is no time lost in steaming to the exercise area and waiting for the right conditions of daylight and weather.

As in ergonomics, there are different emphases in the various national approaches. First in the simulator field were the Dutch with their shadowgraph machines at Delft and Wageningen. These were specifically for train-

ing in ship handling in currents and shallow water; no other ships were involved and so collision avoidance could not be exercised. The lighting conditions represent subdued daylight. The French approach is to use manned models in a lake. The German simulator at Bremen uses a daylight scene made up from a multiplicity of slide projections, and again is primarily for ship handling. The British simulator at Warsash is entirely nocturnal, ships and buoys being shown only by points of light. This machine can be used for handling, but it is intended mainly for exercises involving up to four "other ships" controlled by the instructor. The American CAORF machine at King's Point is vastly more elaborate and expensive than any of these, using colour television projections of daylight or nocturnal scenes, including other ships; this machine however is intended for research purposes rather than training.

With this diversity of approaches the art of marine simulation should make rapid progress. While simulator construction is a matter of development rather than research, the research world has a crucial contribution to make in the formulation of the mathematical models which, fed into the computer, represent the behaviour of "own ship" in the response of the simulator to the man's orders. These models are far from simple, because they have to take into account not only hull and engine characteristics of the ship, but also the sea depth (which seriously affects steering behaviour), current, wind, tug forces and so on. An un-representative model is at once detected by an experienced ship handler, who knows what response to expect from a given change in helm angle or propeller revolutions.

Making a simulator and filling it with officers under training is not enough. Follow up studies are required to assess just how effectively the simulator is in fact doing its job, to detect any weaknesses in the procedure and to devise improvements. This involves the objective measurement of human capability in seamanship, a far from simple matter. Human measurement of this sort has been common enough in some fields ashore; marine scientists now have to learn the techniques and apply them to the mariner.

The simulators referred to so far are for ship handling and navigational decision making generally - they represent in effect the bridge. There is however scope for simulation techniques in several other aspects of ship operation, notably in main engine control, cargo working and so on. Engine control room simulators are already in use, particularly for complex installations involving, eg. combinations of gas turbines and diesels. One could contemplate the possibility of linking a bridge and an engine simulator together, for exercising jointly deck and engineer officers. This could, incidentally be done for a new ship before the construction of the actual ship; for exercising entry to a harbour before the construction of the harbour.

MALFEASANCE

This is what happens when the man possesses all the correct information, knows the right thing to and and quite deliberately does something different. It is not peculiar to any one mode of transport, and quite possibly some members of this Conference will have malfeasantly exceeded the road speed limits on the way to this session.

It can be argued that action of this sort is as old and as incurable as sin itself, and that any transport system will have to accept a certain amount of wrong-doing by its practitioners as long decisionmaking is left in human hands. In some transport modes we can replace the driver by a computer, and we can program the computer to be completely without sin, but the unmanned ship is a long way off yet and we are left with the mariner and his sinful ways. Can anything be done to incline the seaman towards virtue?

History suggests that exhortation unsupported by enforcement is likely to make no more impression upon the seaman than it does upon the ordinary motorist. Driving behaviour on the roads, however, does improve when the traffic police are visible and active, even though the actual number of prosecutions may be small. There is evidence that marine traffic responds in a similar way, and here it is appropriate to cite experience over the last few years with shipping in the Straits of Dover area.

The narrow seas between Dover and Calais carry one of the most dense concentrations of shipping in the world. Up till 1967 ships were left to pick their own routes through the Straits, but in that year a "Routing scheme" was introduced by IMCO under which preferred paths were set out on the charts, laid out in such a way that ships travelling into the North Sea would keep to the French side and those leaving the North Sea to the English side. "Inshore Zones" adjacent to the two coasts were reserved for local and coastal traffic. All seaman were exhorted to comply with the scheme, but there was no legal enforcement.

In 1972 a survey was carried out by the National Physical Laboratory on behalf of the UK Department of Trade to ascertain the extent of compliance with the routing scheme. Over a sample period it was found that no less than 12% of the traffic in the main lanes was travelling in the reverse direction, and that a considerable proportion of the traffic in the inshore zones was on international passages not calling at UK ports and so ought not to have been in these zones.

Following these surveys, the Channel Navigation Information Service was set up by the UK and French Governments in collaboration. This organization includes radar stations ashore on both sides of the Channel by means of which Coastguards observe all shipping movements, and a VHF radio service over which shipping is advised of local conditions, any special hazards and so on, and in particular ships in general are warned about "rogues", ie. individual ships seen to be moving the wrong way in the main lanes. Further, when conditions permit such rogues are identified by aircraft and their behaviour is reported to their owners.

The effect of this surveillance upon shipping behaviour has been marked. During a special survey of shipping carried out over a sample period of 3 days in August 1976, the proportion of ships travelling the wrong way in the main lanes had fallen to 6%, and of these some were minor fishing vessels. The proportion of ships on international passages improperly using the English inshore zone had fallen from around one-third to about 10%. More detailed information is in Refs. 5 and 9.

Since 1972 certain countries have made compliance with the IMCO routing scheme mandatory upon ships of their own flag. In July 1977, by international agreement, compliance will be made mandatory upon ships of all IMCO members-ie. of all the major shipowning nations. There are many routing schemes throughout the world; compliance generally cannot be predicted, but in the Dover Straits scheme it can be expected that compliance will be virtually complete because this scheme is effectively policed, it is seen to be policed, and there have already been procecutions against certain British seamen detected in transgression. (The UK Government was one of those which made the scheme mandatory upon UK ships in anticipation of the international agreement on routing). Such prosecutions do not need to be particularly numerous or drastic to convey the message: Coastguard can see you.

This brief account of one result of the Channel Navigation Information Service suggests that, in resisting the temptation to commit an act of malfeasance, the wavering seaman's conscience can be remarkably stiffened by the knowledge that an impartial outside agency can observe his movements, and if necessary identify him and call him to account. At the same time it shows up an area where the policing action could be made more effective by some suitable research; this is in the field of ship identification. Existing radar sensors are very effective in detecting and locating ships and plotting their movements, but to a radar set one echo is just like another; to achieve positive identification it is at present still necessary to send out an observer in a patrol ship or aircraft to apply the human eye - preferably backed up by a camera if prosecution is contemplated. Patrol activities of this sort are expensive and can be hazardous in bad weather, and a positive method of identification by remote means would be invaluable. Admittedly the technology already exists to do this by means of radar transponders, but these argue a target ship willing to purchase, fit, maintain and operate the device properly at all times; in the long term this may be achieved by international agreement, but in the short term some device to provide information without active participation by the target ship would be welcome; even partial information - such as size and type of ship - would be useful.

In the absence of patrol identification, a certain amount of detective activity is possible using the photographic records which are kept at all times of the Coastguard radar. For example, in the retrospective examination of a reported collision incident, it proved possible to identify one of the ships involved by analysis of her speed and course, as traced back through the radar photographs, in conjunction with the information on arrivals and departures in European ports chronicled daily in Lloyd's List. However, such studies can take days; for an identification procedure to be useful operationally it must produce results while things are still happening at sea. If cmmercial shipping data are to be consulted, this would call for on-line access to a constantly updated computer bank of commercial data.

THE RULES

In discussing human failures we have so far assumed that there is available somewhere a body of rules by observing which a seaman can keep out of danger, or at least avoid colliding with other ships. In relation to the latter hazard there are the internationally-agreed "Rules for preventing collisions", which do in fact tell the seaman just what he should do in the way of changing course and speed where he meets another ship. The rules however cannot cater for every possible eventuality; most importantly, they provide no clear-cut guidance to the seaman who is confronted with not one but two or more on-coming ships, a common enough situation. Unfortunately opinion among seamen themselves is far from clear-cut on what the rules should say in such cases, or even whether it is really practical for the rules to say anything at all. In theory an experiment could be mounted by devising alternative sets of rules and setting sample populations of ships to follow them to see if collisions increased or decreased. Although manifestly impossible in the real world, such an operation is still feasible by computer if we can devise a mathematical model of how a ship's master will behave in various situations when constrained by an appropriate set of rules. Ideally one should also introduce the random element inseparable from human participation, and this means introducing a real man working in real time. There is clearly scope in this area for operational research workers using simulation techniques. The mass of data recorded on films taken over five years radar observations of shipping in the Dover Straits are available to provide real-life tactical situations for input to such studies.

SHIP ENHANCEMENT

So far we have considered how best to enable the seaman to operate safely with the conventional merchant ship as at present conceived. Is it possible however that by making material changes or additions to the fabric of the ship we could enable the seaman to do his job better?

We have already discussed sensors and controls under the heading of ergonomics; there is always room for improvement here. As regards the ship itself, it is often argued that the risk of collision and grounding can be reduced by improving the stopping ability and manoeuvrability, on the reasoning that the more quickly a ship can decelerate and turn, the less likely she is to run into something.

The stopping requirement is one which appeals to the public imagination, and braking devices for slowing down big ships are invented and re-invented with tedious regularity. As can be predicted from basic mechanics,

such devices will work, but if they are effective they are too large and heavy to be practical; if they are small enough to be feasible they give so poor a deceleration that they are not worth fitting. The water parachute has in fact been demonstrated on the full scale in Japan for slowing down a ship, but the operational hazards of this device seem likely to exceed those which its stopping power is supposed to avoid.

With manoeuvring devices we are on more promising ground. A variety of thrusters are becoming available which can be used to impel the ship in various directions, notably sideways, and special rudders are available which greatly improve ship handling, in particular at low and zero speed. Examples are the Pleuger, Becker and Schilling rudders and the Rotating Cylinder Rudder. Specialised propellers, notably the Voith-Schneider and Schottel propellers, can generate thrust in any desired direction. Oddly enough, however, none of these devices seems to have demonstrated any particular virtue in preventing major collisions. In ref. 6 Dr. Gardenier of the US Coast Guard office of Research and Development argues that improved manoeuvrability does not necessarily help in avoiding collisions, and that in certain cases it can in fact even increase the net collision risk. The main virtue of the devices discussed appears to be in harbour manoeuvring and docking, where they undoubtedly minimise minor incidents of the sort discussed below. The prospect for reduction of major collisions and groundings by the operation of manoeuvring devices, however, appears small.

If the manoeuvring device can be thought of as a means of strengthening the seaman's arm, then there are various black boxes becoming available which correspondingly strengthen his brain power. These include the various kinds of shipboard computer, and in particular the different makes of "collision avoidance radars" (CARs). These will analyse the radar echoes, label them, predict their likely future movements and advise the ship's officers of the predicted outcome of any contemplated manoeuvre. Nevertheless, too much should not be expected. In a retrospective study the US Coast Guard examined the records of collisions occurring to ships over 10,000 tons gross over a period of five years. Analysis showed that "something between 9.6 and 13.1% of the collisions could possibly be prevented by such a system" (ie, a CAR system; ref. 6 again).

Thus, while there are undoubtedly some benefits to be obtained from enhancing the ship so as to provide the master with more muscle power and more brain power, it seems generally true that the prospects of reducing major accidents by hardware additions alone appear disappointing. It still seems that major accidents by hardware additions alone appear disappointing. It still seems that major accidents are more likely to be reduced by attention to the man himself and to his interface with his equipment, than by an equal effort devoted to inventing new hardware. Indeed, in some circumstances sophisticated hardware could even be actively pernicious - eg. a manoeuvring device which makes it possible to execute violent turns not expected by other ships' officers. Sending such machinery to sea would be of no service to the sailor.

MINOR INCIDENTS

The whole of the paper to this point has been concerned with serious incidents - those likely to result in the loss of the ship or severe damage, and to pollution of the environment. It is the duty of Governments to protect their citizens from such incidents and the consequences of them, regardless of economic factors; hence the attention devoted by the UK and other Governments to the prevention of collisions and groundings.

However, from the shipowner's point of view total losses of ships are relatively unimportant; far greater total sums of money are involved each year in what the insurance industry call "partial losses", ie. incidents which involve damage falling short of total loss of the ship, and extending right down to the trivial level, such as dented side plates, bent guard rails and so on. Also included are damage and breakdowns in ships' machinery and equipment. Very few of these incidents involve human injury or death, and so Governments take less interest. Nevertheless the total cost of "partial losses" to the insurers, and hence to the shipowners via premium payments, is very large; one approximate estimate suggests that over a recent one-year period "partial losses" cost the UK shipowners about 16 times as much as total losses. There is thus a substantial economic incentive for cutting down on the partial loss rate.

Of the incidents other than machinery breakdowns, by far the most common are those occuring in port and variously described as contact, impact or striking - ie. the contact between the moving ship's hull and a stationary object such as a dock, pier, moored ship or buoy. Many such contacts occur during berthing, particularly when the wind is strong. Of a sample of contact incidents examined at NMI, two-thirds occurred in winds exceeding 30 knots. The ship damage is not always the whole story; impacts frequently necessitate expensive civil engineering repairs to fixed structures as well.

The sums of money involved in partial loss repairs suggest that research in this field could be economically effective. Much of the incentive for the development of the various manoeuvring devices referred to above has come from consideration of the movement of ships in harbour. The berthing phase in particular still demands attention. The effect of wind has been mentioned. Modern container ships, and tankers when unloaded, present enormous side areas to the wind and the aerodynamic forces can be very large. Indeed with tankers at oil terminals the risks extend well beyond the minor category. To the detached observer it would appear that berthing techniques, and in particular the method of using tugs, would merit close examination. The conventional tug with a single screw propeller has severe limitations in putting large ships through complex manoeuvres, indeed the tug itself can on occasion be in danger, as the occasional "girding" or capsizing of a tug by the pull in its own tow rope shows. Improved flexibility can be obtained by replacing the screw propeller by one of the vectorable thrusting devices referred to above, but these have limited power. Perhaps we should drop completely the concept of a tug - the very name of which implies a device for pulling on a rope - and replace it by the idea of a moveable thrusting machine, a device which can be floated out and secured to the ship for use during berthing under the pilots direct control. There is scope here for considerable ingenuity.

SUMMING UP

Safety at sea is a complex matter and this wide review has unavoidably been somewhat superficial. However some general conclusions can be drawn.

First, ships are subject to a large number of minor accidents. These cost the owners a considerable amount of money. They happen mostly in harbour, often in berthing, but involve very little injury or loss of life. There is some economic incentive for research and development work, particularly in connection with harbour movement and berthing.

Secondly, the number of major incidents such as ship sinkings is relatively small, though the incidence varies markedly from one national flag to another. The cost in human life and injury is not at present very large, but there is potential for very serious loss, not only by the seafarers directly involved but also by unconnected third parties. There is also potential for serious pollution of the environment.

Thirdly, there are indications that major incidents are mainly due to human failure of various sorts, from which it follows that research is needed into the causes of human failures and the development of means to make such failure less likely. In particular there is scope for improvement in the methods and equipment used for training mariners. There is also a great need for the worst-trained mariners to be brought up to the standard of the best; this calls for political action and international negotation rather than research.

Finally, it is repeated that the safety of sea transport, as of land and air transport, depends in a large degree on the human element. As the years go by, bigger and bigger disasters become possible through simple human error or misjudgement. Such errors may never become completely impossible, but research is making available techniques for rendering them less likely. The extent to which these techniques are actually applied in practice depends upon the will and the money.

FOOTNOTE

The view expressed in this paper are entirely those of the author. The paper does not necessarily represent official policy or the views of the National Maritime Institute or the U.K. Department of Industry.

REFERENCES

1] United Kingdom Department of Trade, **"Casulties to Vessels and Accidents to men - Returns for 1973 and 1974"**, H.M.S.O. London, 1976.

2] Cashman, J.P., **"Analysis of World Merchant Ship Losses, 1967-75"**, West European Conference on Marine Technology, Royal Institution of Naval Architects, 1977.

3] Committee on Tanker Hazards, **"Final report to the Secretary of Treasury"**, U.S. Coast Guard, 1963.

4] Wilkinson, G.R., **"Wheelhouse and Bridge Design - A Shipbuilder's Appraisal"**, Transactions of the Royal Institution of Naval Architects, 1971.

5] Cash, R.F. and Marcus, N.G., **"Ship identification in the Dover Strait using Helicopters"**, National Physical Laboratory Mar Sci Report R 104, Dec 1972.

6] Gardenier, J.S., **"Towards a Science of Marine Safety"**, Schiff und Hafen, Heft 7/1976, 28.

7] Beer, W.J., **"Analysis of World Merchant Ship Losses"**, Transactions of the Royal Institution of Naval Architects, 1969.

8] Doganis, R.S. and Loree, P.J., **"Safety Standards and the Convenience Flag Debate"**, Conference "In Search of Safety", SEATRADE, Colchester, England, 1976.

9] Batchelor, K.S., **"Comparative Study of Marine Traffic using the English Inshore Zone and near Westbound Lane, 1972, and 1976"**, National Maritime Institute Report No 9, Feb 1977.

Pedestrian safety:
the role of research

by

H. TAYLOR

Transport and Road Research Laboratory
Crowthorn, England

INTRODUCTION

In nearly every country people are grappling with the many problems of motorization which increasingly dominate their lives. In some 70 years the transport scene has been revolutionized and the desire for unrestricted personal mobility expressed by the growing ownership of private transport has brought with it many problems not least of which is road safety. Because road accidents have grown up in a transport context they tend to be regarded as inevitable penalty of personal freedom and their dispersal into many incidents each with only a few casualties tends to diminish public appreciation of their overall magnitude. Throughout the world some 1 million people die every 4 years in road accidents and for the young adult road accidents are the major cause of death in many countries; road accidents rank therefore as a public health problem of epidemic proportions. The vast majority of road accidents stem from human failure but the consequences of these failures can be prevented or mitigated by various means; by education and training, by better highway design, by safer operational techniques and by improving vehicle safety.

Historically, mechanically powered road vehicles began primarily as public transport, to be followed as roads improved by smaller private vehicles owned initially by wealthy citizens. Throughout these early days the road user on foot became more and more disadvantaged; the introduction of private powered vehicles reinforced the difference in status between vehicles borne road users and those on foot. Duff [1] has reminded us that the conflict between pedestrians and road traffic is not new. 250 years ago the pedestrians of London were in trouble. Swift in 1710 wrote in the Tatler:

"We are very glad to watch an opportunity to whisk across a passage, very thankful that we are not run over for interrupting the machine that carries in it a person neither more handsome, wise, nor valiant than the meanest of us".

When hackney carriages first appeared there were many accidents because pedestrians refused to give way to them. As the flow of vehicles became greater and

more dangerous pedestrians had to give way but occasionally their anger would get the better of them and they would overturn a coach and break its wheels. Not only were pedestrians impeded in their passage along the streets, they were often killed or injured by being crushed against the houses.

It is also interesting that the most modern concepts of providing for pedestrian safety in towns, shopping precincts, elevated pedestrian walkways and subways are amongst the oldest. In 1500 Leonardo da Vinci proposed a scheme for ground level pedestrian ways with the vehicular traffic running in tunnels. A sketch of his proposal is in the British Museum. In the same year The Rows in Chester, an upper level pedestrian market with shops in arcades, was completed. The seventeenth century Pantiles in Tunbridge Wells is an early example of a pedestrian precinct.

During the first half of the twentieth century few concessions were made to the road user on foot except for those that interfered only slightly with the flow of vehicular traffic or were needed to deal with various major problems; it is presumably not a coincidence that 'pedestrian' in the English language also means 'prosaic', 'dull', 'uninspired'.

Over the last 25 years in the well-developed countries increasing attention has been given to pedestrian safety but the idea of the pedestrian as a second-class citizen has lingered on both in general attitudes and in road user behaviour. This is so notwithstanding the fact that a substantial proportion of people today are both users of private vehicles and pedestrians.

Attempts to derive a basis for striking a balance between vehicle users and pedestrians have been generally unsatisfactory; the comparitive value of time delays during a journey on foot or in a vehicle has been assessed, but the significance of interactive delays overall in economic or social terms has hardly been touched. Outstanding and consistent over recent years has been the high proportion of road casualties that are pedestrians with fatalities approaching half of the total in certain countries and perhaps 80,000 in number annually, worldwide. It is encouraging that in some countries pedestrian casualties have not increased pro rata with the increase in motorization but the problem remains a major one and there is no obvious reason why the situation should change radically unless fresh initiatives are taken.

In most well-developed countries the pedestrian safety problem is predominantly an urban one but there is nevertheless concern for the safety of pedestrians on rural roads. Of the various age groups children and elderly people are over-represented in pedestrian accidents and therefore merit special consideration.

Another major group of road accident casualties is that of car occupants. Their future safety has received considerable attention through the international car safety programme piloted by the United States of America [2] and the nature of the countermeasures is such that substantial reductions in casualties can be forecast with confidence provided these measures are incorporated and used in future passenger cars. The international nature of trade in, and usage of, cars is such that in practical terms these measures can be implemented only by international regulations, most of them at government level. In the vehicles field in Europe considerable progress has been and is being made to establish uniformity of standards, primarily to facilitate trade but with improvement in safety well to the fore [3].

Greater safety for pedestrians is not so readily described either in terms of effective countermeasures or in the incentives for concerted international action. It is perhaps partly for these reasons and partly for those mentioned earlier that improvements in pedestrian safety are hard-won and sometimes seem to be disappointing. It has often been said that there has been little research into pedestrian safety, but this statement could be misleading. Substantial reviews under the auspices of the Organisation for Economic Co-operation and Development (OECD) [4] and NATO Committee on the Challenges of Modern Society (CCMS) [5] have quoted many references to research studies carried out in various countries. Just recently the International Conference on Pedestrian Safety [6] held in Israel discussed a wealth of research into pedestrian safety which has been carried out worldwide or is currently in progress. It would therefore be more appropriate to say that despite the pedestrian safety work already carried out, a great deal more effort is required if a substantial impact is to be made on the problem.

Turgel has described the involvement of international bodies in the road safety field [7]. Since 1968, the Road Research Programme of the OECD has been concerned with providing a substantive scientific and technological basis for governmental decisionmaking on the most urgent road transport problems. Of particular interest are the efforts of the Road Research Programme toward the formulation, planning, and implemention of common strategies for road safety. Various groups of experts have been assembled and symposia have been held to provide a broad and thorough assessment of the options available for combating road accidents. The options studied include an array of specific measures and techniques regarding accident prevention and victim protection.

The creation of the OECD Road Research Programme came about as a result of the similarity of the main problem areas encountered by each of the Member countries [1] during an era of expanding road transport facility development and increasing user demand for these facilities. The programme is aimed at assembling and interpreting, on an international basis, road research results which are often fragmentary and, to a certain extent, diffuse. It is also enables practices and techniques proven successful in one country to be brought to the attention of other countries.

Government policymakers have to strive for a road transport policy which takes into account economic growth factors and the contribution of technology in general while maintaining a balance relative to the negative side effects of roads and traffic, such as accidents, congestion, and deterioration of the environment, and the consumption of limited natural resources. The Road Research Programme strives to provide a mechanism to ensure the rational use of the participating countries' research potential in view of the international dimension and similarity of road transport problems, and the need to optimize scarce natural road research resources.

In 1975 a combined OECD-ECMT group on pedestrian safety research was set up to study research needs in the field of pedestrian safety in relation to the policy orientation defined by the ECMT and other responsible international bodies; to recommend desirable research projects; to co-ordinate research activities between Member countries and exchange appropriate information; and to submit the results of this research to the OECD Steering Committee for Road Research and in due course to the ECMT Road Safety Committee and other interested international organisations.

Apart from basic research, which it would like to see intensified, particularly with regard to methodological questions and those relating to the cost/benfit analysis of the various political or administrative measures, the joint Group is concentrating on the following priority areas for international co-operative research:

(i) technical improvements to the pedestrian's road environment (pedestrian crossings: location, form, signs, signals and markings, lighting, etc.);

(ii) road safety education;

(iii) information and education campaigns on the theme of pedestrian safety using the mass media.

The aim of the group was to identify as soon as possible pedestrian safety measures which had been scientifically validated and could be implemented quickly, and to identify research needs in pedestrian safety which could lead to early implementation of measures for the reduction of accidents and casualties to pedestrians.

The work of the Group to-date has been published in the form of a summary report and three sub-group reports [8]. The work of this Group excluded areas that were the subject of other major activities such as the influence of alcohol and drugs or of vehicle measures for pedestrian safety. Considerable use has been made of the work of the Group in preparing this paper.

A FRAMEWORK FOR CONSIDERATION OF PEDESTRIAN SAFETY

One of the complexities of road safety is that the problems to be solved are usually multi-factored and thus rarely susceptible to simple single answers. On the other hand they often involve interactions between road users which can be used to advantage in the interests of greater safety. Errors or difficulties of one road user can often be countered and an accident avoided, by compensating actions on the part of other road users or by compensating features of the highway system.

It is important therefore to recognise that the best chances of improving pedestrian safety do not depend solely on pedestrians alone; other road users, the road environment, various educational and social factors are all of crucial significance to pedestrian safety as are their interactions.

The main principles of a framework for road travel may appear to be similar to those applicable to other forms of transport for example to rail travel. Similarities exist in that the system hardware, including vehicles, is subject to regulation to ensure minimum standards of standards of safety and conformity in essential respects [4] (Table 1). But the road situation is very different from the other major modes of travel in that they employ a high proportion of professional 'drivers' and at most critical points there is external surveillance and control of vehicle movements. Considerable progress has been made in recent years towards this approach in the road situation in order to define priorities at conflict points more precisely and to regulate the occupancy of road space more rigorously. Nevertheless the bulk of road

Table 1 - Framework for pedestrian safety

Field		Conflicts			
		Separation of conflicting elements	Improvement of conflict situation	Crash	Post crash
Road and Traffic		Space segregation e.g. pedestrian precincts Time segregation e.g. predestrian crossing facilities	road furniture crossings signs lighting speed control of vehicles	design and location of road furniture	
Human	Rider or Driver	Selection and licensing of drivers	Training & education Legislation and Enforcement		emergency warning and aid
	Pedestrian	Regulation of pedestrian movements	Propaganda techniques Conspicuous clothing for pedestrians		
Vehicle		Modification or elimination of certain vehicles or vehicle features	Speed restraint Vehicle conspicuity	Redesign of vehicles for greater compatibility in pedestrian impacts	

users in this context are non-professional and there are in any case many conflict situations where priorities cannot be defined with any clarity. This is particularly so in the case of pedestrians and they are extremely vulnerable when in conflict with vehicles.

A consequence of the scale and non-professional character of most road movements is that breaches of road traffic law occur frequently and this situation is compounded by the inescapable fact that these breaches rarely involve the transgressor in an accident. As a Transport Minister once observed [9]:

"For most people and for most of the time, road safety is a matter of regulation, restriction and advice observed at least as much from fear of being caught as from any possible desire to be safe.

For relatively few there comes a moment of horror when the thing which "only happens to other people never to me" breaks into their lives, bringing with it death and injury, pain and misery".

In formulating road safety policy, in making international comparisons and in carrying out research it is essential to recognise the realities of the road situation and to maintain close links with what actually happens in practice.

The next part of this paper is concerned with these realities and how situations may be improved. Following the framework for pedestrian safety the road and traffic environment, the human component and the vehicle are considered in turn.

THE PEDESTRIAN'S ROAD ENVIRONMENT

Changes in the environment are the oldest form of pedestrian countermeasure to road accidents. For many years these were the only countermeasures, and are still by far the most important in terms of allocation of resources. Traditionally, environmental measures have fallen within the domain of the traffic engineer, but in recent years the influence of urban planning has been increasingly felt. Environmental measures are now used in a wider context, as there has been a move from the installation of isolated facilities to the consideration of entire schemes for pedestrian safety integrated within the urban framework. This latter has been termed the systems approach. Two manifestations of the contribution of urban planning to pedestrian safety are the rapid safety are the rapid growth in the numbers of pedestrianisation schemes in city centres, and the move towards designing residential areas with the needs and safety of pedestrians in mind.

It is possible to identify three philosophies or approaches to pedestrian safety which have been developed over the years. First is the traditional traffic engineering approach already referred to. The second is segregation, where the objective is to keep pedestrians and vehicles apart. The third, and most recent is the integration approach, where pedestrians and vehicles share common areas, whether in city centres under the so-called pedestrian priority or space sharing system, or else in residential districts.

The aim of all environmental countermeasures for pedestrians is to prevent injurious contact between pedestrians and vehicles, and each of the three philosophies attempts to achieve this in different ways. The traffic engineering approach aims to separate pedestrians and vehicles either in space, for example by providing adequate footways and installing refuges and guardrails as well as grade separated crossings, or in time, by means of controlled or uncontrolled crossings at grade. The segration philosophy sets out to provide systems within which pedestrians and vehicles have separate routes, and where the possibility of contact between the two is reduced to a minimum by planning and design. The third approach that of the integration philosophy, is quite different. Here the basic principle is to make pedestrians and drivers more aware of each others presence and to stimulate neighbourhood activities, whilst minimising conflicts and accidents by various design measures.

It is important to emphasize that the three approaches are not opposing alternatives, but should instead be regarded as complementary. There is no best option in absolute terms; the most satisfactory is the one which is most appropriate in the total context. It must also be acknowledged that the choice of option is often influenced or determined by factors other than safety; even with small schemes a balance must often be found between safety and amenity. Thus is it crucial that planners and others who influence the shape of the urban environment should be fully aware of the importance of pedestrian safety and of the measures which can be taken to improve it without detracting from amenity.

A further point which should be made is that as the different philosophies have evolved, there has not been an accompanying increase in knowledge. Thus most is known about the effects of traffic engineering measures, and least about the effects of the integration approach. This comes about for two reasons. Firstly, the object of many city centre schemes has been the improvement of amenity and the general quality of the environment; the evaluation of safety considerations has often been accorded only low priority. Secondly, residential areas generally have low accident rates, and changes are difficult to detect in the short term. The implication of this is that there is a need for both new research techniques, and for research on a wider scale than has usually been the case in the past if the new approaches to pedestrian safety are to be properly evaluated within an acceptable time scale.

Complete segregation

Urban planning can greatly reduce the number and nature of conflicts between pedestrians and motor vehicles.

The most obvious urban planning measure is the physical segregation of traffic categories, the environment being designed so that conflicts between pedestrians and other traffic are practically eliminated. Enforcement is minimised, for there is a clear comprehensible system determined by its design. In other words, physical design determines and encourages certain traffic behaviour patterns.

Two types of segregated areas may be defined where vehicles are not allowed. These are (i) pedestrian precincts and pedestrian streets which have a local interest and are often small in size due to access problems and (ii) pedestrian routes or networks which give access to various town or neighbourhood services or points of interest.

The basic principle of pedestrian schemes is that they should be designed to be more attractive than other parts of the system. In this way pedestrian usage will be maximised, and the overall level of safety thereby improved.

Pedestrian priority areas

Where complete segregation is not practicable areas may be defined where the needs of pedestrians are given priority, but where vehicles are allowed to enter under certain conditions. Dalby [10] has described a project in Oxford where vehicles and pedestrians share space on two of the city's main shopping streets, Queen Street and Cornmarket Street. At the time of the investigations traffic flow was of the order of 80-160 vehicle/h, of which about 70-80 were buses.

The speeds of buses were related to the concentrations of pedestrians in the area through which they were shortly to pass.

Table 2 - Accident statistics for Queen Street and Cornmarket Street

	QUEEN STREET			CORNMARKET STREET		
	Serious	Slight	Involving pedestrians	Serious	Slight	Involving pedestrians
1968	1	5	3	..	..	..
1969	4	1	4	4	10	13
	0	1	0			
1970 April -				4	18	16
	0	0	0			
1971	0	0	0	7	6	11
1972	0	1	1	1	4	4
	0	0	0	0	0	0
1973 August ***** ***** *****			January - - - - - - - - - - - - - - -			
	0	0	0	0	1	1
1974	0	0	0	0	0	0
				0	0	0
1975	0	0	0	February ***** ***** *****		
				0	1	1

- - - - introduction of access limitation during month stated
***** completion of kerbless surfacing during month stated
Source: *Thames Valley Police.*

Because of the pattern of behaviour there is produced around the moving vehicle a 'pedestrian-free space' with shape and dimensions related to the vehicle speed. The shapes and dimensions of the pedestrian-free spaces associated with the 3 speed ranges 5-8, 8-11 and 11-14 km/h, at the time when the street had a surface of 2-ft square paving slabs overall are shown in Fig. 1. The indications of 'emergency' and 'comfortable' stopping points (0.5 g and 0.15 g decelerations respectively) include an allowance for decision time. The location of 'comfortable' and 'emergency' stopping points well within the pedestrian-free spaces suggests the interaction between pedestrians and vehicles is such that

a driver should have ample time to take action where a person in front of his vehicle fails to get out of the way for any reason.

The continual breakage of paving slabs under the wheels of the buses and goods vehicles led the Oxford City Council in 1975 to reconstruct that part of the public right-of-way originally the carriageway, and to provide it with a fine asphalt surface (Plates 1 and 2). The surveys already made were then repeated. It was found that there had been a modification to the pattern of pedestrian distribution in all but the most crowded conditions.

In times of less crowding, such as was found on days

other than Saturdays, and when there was no vehicle
for some considerable distance down the street, pedestrians walked in the middle of the road as before. However, the presence of even a stationary bus led them to
take avoiding action a good deal earlier than had previously been observed. The introduction of a contrasting
section of surface had led to an increase in maximum
bus speeds and a reduction in the numbers of people
using the middle of the street when vehicles were nearby.
It seems reasonable to deduce from this that the removal
of apparent boundaries is desirable if there is to be improved space-sharing by pedestrians and vehicles. Thus
it is advisable that any space-sharing scheme should have
footways and carriageway at the same level.

There appear to be few problems in pedestrian priority areas where there are larger numbers of pedestrians but the position is not so clear in streets with few
pedestrians. Such circumstances can occur in pedestrian
priority streets designated as play areas for children.
Where pedestrian numbers are likely to be small, the
installation of items of road furniture, speed control
humps, or modification of sight lines are all options
available to prevent the free passage of vehicles.

In general, legislation to accord legal priority to pedestrians has been found to be neither feasible nor necessary
in most countries, and the achievement of self enforcement through design features is the usual objective.

Integration of mixed traffic

In residential areas, the principle of segregation can
again impose limitations on the numerous activities and
contacts for which these environments are normally
used. Thus, a need has arisen for a new approach to
road safety in residential areas, based on integration

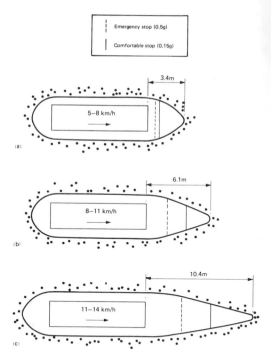

Fig. 1 - Distribution of pedestrian - free space around
buses moving in a space sharing situation - Queen Street, Oxford

PLATE 1: Queen Street, Oxford, showing the original wall-to-wall surfacing, with paving slabs overall.

PLATE 2: Queen Street, Oxford, showing the modified central section

of mixed traffic. The benefits of physical segregation can also be built into such an integrated system.

A number of cities have made small-scale attempts to integrate traffic in a limited number of residential streets. Some larger scale applications are now being introduced, both in new developments, and as part of renovation schemes for old established areas; the examples of Delft and Emmen [11] in the Netherlands may be quoted.

The basic unit of such schemes is what is known as the residential court or yard. The function of a residential yard differs from that of a traditional street in that the same paved area can be and is used for various activities such as driving, playing, cycling, walking, and parking, but does not cater for through traffic.

The characteristics of a residential yard are that it is open to traffic, but in the absence of kerbs and pavements there is no demarcation of space in the traditional way between pedestrians and vehicles. Various design features are provided to slow traffic entering the area in order to protect pedestrians. The underlying principle is that the design and layout of the area should encourage traffic behaviour patterns which are optimal for safety.

While integration schemes are being considered or introduced in many countries, it should be noted that there has not yet been any full evaluation of the safety benefits of such schemes.

Pedestrian crossings

A pedestrian crossing at a particular location on the road gives the pedestrian a certain measure of legal and physical protection. Particular care needs to be taken with the design and location of the facility to ensure that pedestrians use it. The safest way to cross a road is by using a grade-separated facility such as a subway or footbridge.

At-grade crossings either of the zebra crossing type or light controlled also significantly reduce the risk of road crossing. However, the presence of the facility also introduces a more dangerous zone in its immediate vicinity. In the vicinity - say 20 m from the crossing - it is advisable to ban parking of vehicles, ban overtaking by drivers, and to discourage or restrict pedestrians from crossing. This applies to crossings away from junctions, but it would also seem useful to apply this recommendation to all crossings. Such areas should be clearly marked to road users and these markings may also be useful as guides to motorists that they should reduce speed on approach to the crossing. It may also be particularly useful in the case of zebra crossings as a guide to the pedestrian who may place not only himself but also vehicular traffic at risk if he steps on the crossing when the approaching vehicle is within this zone.

One of the major factors responsible for the good safety record of pedestrian crossings is the high usage rate. Potential safety benefits can therefore be increased if the particular crossing facilities form part of a pedestrian crossing elsewhere.

Light controlled crossings are the safest form of at-grade facility. In order to obtain a high level of usage, it is important that pedestrian waiting times are not too long. It is also desirable that there should be uniformity in the light control systems used.

Special provision is often made to protect children crossing roads near schools. Where there is heavy traffic on such roads adult wardens should be employed. Care is recommended in their recruitment and training. The use of older school children as wardens should be confined to traffic conditions where adequate gaps occur, and it is important that drivers should have been alerted to the presence of the patrol. Pedestrian actuated signal crossings should be supervised.

Other pedestrian facilities

A wide range of measures is available to improve pedestrian safety apart from crossing facilities. Little evaluation has been made of the precise effectiveness of these measures, but it is clear that many of them are capable of making a considerable contribution to the pedestrian safety problem in urban areas.

A basic distinction can be made between technical measures and regulatory measures. In the first category, measures affecting pedestrians include the provision of adequate and well maintained pavements and footways. Some countries have drawn up guidelines for this purpose. The proper use of urban furniture is important to pedestrian safety, and the installation on wide streets of central refuges and reserves is a desirable measure. The reduction of vehicles speeds is another objective; this can be achieved either by modification of the street layout, particularly at intersections, or by the placing of obstacles to prevent the rapid passage of vehicles. Traffic control measures can have an influence on pedestrian safety, and the general level of lighting of the road system in another factor which must be considered.

The effects of regulatory measures have also been examined. Several studies have shown that one way streets are beneficial to pedestrian safety. Parking regulations are particularly relevant to the problem of child pedestrian safety. Speed limits in urban areas, both general and local, can play an important part in protecting pedestrians.

In most well-developed countries the pedestrian safety problem is an urban one. But on rural roads vehicle speeds are often high thus making the judgement of gaps in the traffic difficult and allowing little time for detecting pedestrians by drivers, or oncoming vehicles by pedestrians. Where possible separate space should be provided for pedestrians but when this is not possible they should be encouraged to walk facing oncoming traffic and to make themselves as conspicuous as possible especially at night; the provision of roadside lighting and well-lit crossings can greatly aid the safety of pedestrians at night where the scale of the problem merits it.

ROAD SAFETY EDUCATION

It is attractive to hypothesize but less easy to obtain rigorous proof that road safety can be improved by road safety education, i.e. that by gaining acceptance of the teaching in practical terms behaviour will be favourably influenced in critical situations which may otherwise develop into accidents. For this approach to have prospects of success it is necessary to know what constitutes safe behaviour and how it may best be taught.

Reference has already been made to the special problems of rural roads which have no footpaths but the major problem relates to situations beginning with the pedestrian walking on a footpath or pavement. Conflicts with vehicles occur when the pedestrian attempts to cross the road or steps into the road for some reason. In road safety it is essential to distinguish between behaviour that people normally do, behaviour that may be achievable by various means and behaviour that exceeds the innate abilities of many people or of critical groups such as young children. Far too often it has been assumed that young children should be trained to use adult techniques and that this can be achieved by

using educational material suitable for adults. It is also evident that parents tend to overestimate the ability of their children, especially very young children, to cope with vehicular traffic. Since it is possible to influence the safety of very young children only through their parents, informative campaigns are needed for parents telling them why children are not able to perform as adults in traffic and also what they can do to increase the safety of their children on the roads both by supervision and training. Information needs to be given for example about children's limited vision and audition, and their limited ability to anticipate and predict future events.

Theoretical training given to children needs to be reinforced by practical training exercises in real traffic conditions. This practical training should be carried out by both parents and teachers. Traffic clubs as used in Scandinavian countries are an effective way of integrating both theoretical and practical training and of involving parents. Adequate training in road safety for teachers is required e.g. by courses, journals, conferences and seminars, and suitable material for teaching purposes must be developed. The training of children should be frequent and continuous. It is important that teachers should be given regular encouragement. One way to do this is to distribute at frequent intervals, material that is designed to be of interest to both children and teachers e.g. road safety journals, and road safety calendars for use in the classroom. School crossing patrols (both children and adults) are an effective way of protecting children on routes to and from school and merit consideration for use on a larger scale.

A conceptual framework of road safety education is given in Fig. 2. A considerable amount of work has al-

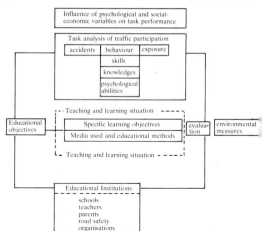

Fig. 2 - Conceptual framework of road safety education

ready been carried out on various aspects of this framework and studies of the problems facing children on roads generally fall into one of three classes; analysis of accident statistics, studies of the social background or personality characteristics of accident involved children, such as those by Backett and Johnston [12[and, less commonly, direct observation and experiments on children typified by the work of Sandels [13[.

Accident statistics are not in themselves indicative of the relative risk for children of a particular age group when making a road crossing. This is because such data do not take account of the number of road crossings made and the lack of a reliable measure of this leads to difficulties. The social, environmental and individual factors which affect the likelihood of a child being on the roadway are also little understood.

If behaviour leading up to the accident is to be analysed special studies are needed. Such a study was carried out in 1972 with the co-operation of the Hampshire Constabulary [14]. However, detailed studies of behaviour are also needed in order to identify and formulate educational objectives.

Video tape recording of childrens' road crossings and interview data have been used in a mathematical framework to relate accident statistics to the mean number of roads crossed per day by children of various ages in Nottingham [15].

It would seem that risk of accident during a road crossing decreases with age from 5 to 11 for both boys and girls and that the accident statistics may underestimate the greater risks run by younger children in road crossings. The limited data available also indicate that the greater number of accidents to boys aged 5 to 7 years may not be due to their greater exposure at least as far as purposeful crossings are concerned. Reasons must therefore lie in differences in behaviour, skills, exposure during play and perhaps behavioural changes during play near roads.

Time lapse photography was used by Grayson [16] at sites near four schools, two primary and two secondary, to obtain records of 1790 road crossings by children and adults. The results showed that children differed from adults not only on individual items of behaviour, but also in the crossing strategies they displayed. Adults tended to make their assessment of the road situation before reaching the kerb with the apparent aim of eliminating or minimising delay at the kerb. Their behaviour was often far from satisfactory (in some respects the opposite of what children are taught) which could influence some children to copy them and consequently be endangered since the children would be less able to cope with the resulting situation. Examples of this are that adults were more likely than children to start to cross before the road was clear and were more likely to cross at an angle.

Other studies aimed at elderly pedestrians have shown that their behaviour is similar in some respects to that of children, ie. they are more likely to stop at the kerb, they have longer delays, and they make more head movements than do younger adults.

Behavioural studies are valuable in that they can identify aspects of behaviour which may need to be improved and such improvements can be taken as indicative of the success of educational measures.

Without doubt, the ultimate goal of road safety education is the reduction of accidents, and most intermediate objectives have been derived from this point of view. Nevertheless, educators sometimes specify objectives concerning road user education in a broader sense. Examples of such objectives are: traffic participation without fear, compliance with traffic rules that are not necessarily related to traffic safety and traffic participation as an example of good citizenship. Many international conferences have been held that have given recommendations about the specification of educational objectives including the ECMT, Council of Europe and the Group of Experts on Road Traffic Safety of UNESCO [17]. The latter have made the following recommendations:

"To be effective, road safety education must be provided on a systematic and continuing basis in pre-school establishments and primary and secondary schools and knowledge must be built up step by step".

It is essential that the methods used for road safety instruction should be the same as those used for other subjects on the school curriculum.

Road safety instruction should not be treated separately, but should be an integral part of a child's education, so that it continues to have the maximum educational impact instead of remaining at the level of purely formal teaching of the rules of the highway code.

Road safety instruction should therefore also be included in other branches of study e.g. technical subjects and natural sciences; ethics and the social sciences; and also physical education. It would be useful to refer for this purpose to the example provided by the Czechoslovak authorities.

These considerations should not dissuade school authorities from providing road safety instruction as a subject on its own for a certain number of hours".

Printed material on road safety education for teachers in the form of posters, journals, manuals and booklets are produced in many member countries but little research has been carried out to discover what effect this has had on teachers attitudes to, knowledge about, amount done, and methods used, for teaching road safety.

In the UK two types of road safety curricula are currently being evaluated. One is concerned only with road safety, the second combines road safety with other aspects of health education to form a general curriculum on health education. Both schemes are currently being piloted, and data on teachers' attitudes, usage of materials, and amounts of teaching done and what the children learn are being collected.

In general, printed material seems to be an effective method of informing teachers about and encouraging them to do road safety teaching particularly if it is distributed regularly to teachers. In some countries this is done, e.g. United Kingdom - a safety journal and pictorial learning aids, Austria - a road safety calender, Netherlands - two illustrated road safety journals for children with teachers' notes.

MASS MEDIA COMMUNICATIONS FOR PEDESTRIAN SAFETY

There are many different channels for mass media communications: newspapers, radio, television, magazines, books, audiotapes, films, pamphlets, brochures, posters, stickers, and even personalized mail if it is forwarded in bulk.

The development, as well as evaluation of any mass media communications programma may be succintly described by means of a flow diagram described in an OECD report (Fig. 3).

In contradistinction to the period up to approximately the late 1960's, recent developments in mass media communications for safety have shown a marked increase in the number of programmes which are evaluated on their effects [18]. There is at present much more widespread awareness that running unevaluated programmes for the promotion of road safety is useless from the point of view of building expertise in accident prevention, whether they save lives or not. Although such campaigns might seem to serve other purposes, for instance of a public relations nature, it is obvious that accident prevention measures ought to be examined on their ability to prevent accidents.

The OECD report on road safety campaigns [19] had this to say about the need for scientific evaluation of mass media communication efforts:

"From the available literature it becomes readily evident that the amount of scientific information on safety communications is rather limited indeed and that it contrasts sharply with the social importance of the issues involved as well as with the total number of campaigns launched in various countries at different times. However, if there is one thing that emanates clearly from the experience hitherto obtained, it is that the area is characterised by many serious problems, both with regard to the design

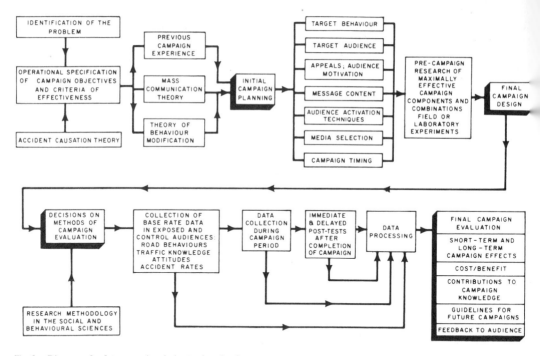

Fig. 3 – Diagram of safety campaign design and evaluation

of safety publicity campaigns, as well as concerning the accompanying research efforts dealing with the assessment of campaign effectiveness.

Perhaps one of the most likely and blatant blunders made in the evaluation of traffic safety campaigns is to mistake the amount of public and official interest generated by the campaign for its true effectiveness. The success of a safety campaign cannot be assessed by the number or magnitude of newspaper articles, letters to the editor, comments in parliament or small-talk between friends and neighbours and similar forms of public or official reactions triggered by the campaign efforts, nor by the flattering congratulations extended to those who organized campaigns for their commendable efforts. The energy of a fire does indeed depend upon the fire, not upon the amount of smoke. The true effectiveness of a safety campaign is its power to actually reduce accident tolls and to increase the frequency of those road behaviours which are compatible with safety.

That changes in behaviour on the road and reductions in accident rates are the only meaningful criteria for campaign success may appear obvious enough, if one is truly interested in the promotion of traffic safety rather than in curtains of smoke which cover up the real issues. And yet, in the recent past many a safety campaign has been evaluated in ways which betray this fundamental conceptual error".

Thirty different mass communication efforts aimed at the promotion of pedestrian safety have been reviewed [20]. Mass publicity was accompanied by changes in enforcement in six of these, and by both enforcement and physical changes in two cases.

Behavioural measures of effect appear to be the most commonly applied. These were used in seventeen of the twenty-two programmes involving mass media publicity only, and in all seven of the programmes combining mass media and enforcement activity. Dependent variables taking the form of extent of message recall was

used only once, changes in knowledge four times and changes in attitudes twice. Very few studies involved more than one type of measure of effect.

The studies involving mass media only and using behavioural indices as a measure of effect showed significant influence upon behaviour with few exceptions. Thus, there can be no question that mass media communication is capable of modifying pedestrian and driver behaviour.

Changes in accident rates were examined in less than one-third of all studies reviewed. Two of the three mass media only programmes, which were evaluated on their ability to reduce accidents, showed clear and positive results. One of these reduced pedestrian accident rates, namely the British Green Cross Code [21]. This programme embodied very careful and detailed preparatory research, which was conducted to give the Green Cross Code its eventual format.

The Green Cross Code replaced the so-called 'kerb drill', a behavioural routine for crossing the road. The priorities of safe behaviour were determined, the new instructions were lengthier and hopefully would be used to convey principles of safety instead of rote learning of a behaviour repertoire. They were intended for children seven years or older and aimed at teaching children to *judge* when it is safe to go across. The Green Cross Code contains the following instructions:

1. first find a safe place to cross, then stop
2. stand on the pavement (sidewalk) near the kerb
3. look all round for traffic and listen
4. if traffic is coming let is pass, look all round again
5. when there is no traffic near, walk straight across the road
6. keep looking and listening for traffic while you cross.

These instructions were primarily intended for children over 7 years old, but it was felt that it could be useful also to youngsters between 5 and 7, provided

392

that a special teaching effort were made. Some seven million brochures explaining the Code were distributed. The total media expenditure was £570,000 covering television, procedures, posters, and announcements in movie theatres. It was calculated that the average member of the audience had five opportunities to see the publicitiy on television and fourteen opportunities in the press.

Effect evaluation took place on three levels, roadside observations, knowledge and accident reductions. All showed the success of the Code. Applying conservative criteria, an eleven per cent drop in accident rate was arrived at, with a chance probability smaller than .01. The greatest reductions in accidents was observed between the ages of 5 and 9, the target audience, but decrements in adult pedestrian casualties were also identified.

It is important to note that the Green Cross Code programme showed a positive return, even if the effects had dwindled or extinguished after completion of the programme proper.

THE INFLUENCE OF ALCOHOL IN PEDESTRIAN ACCIDENTS

The risk of a driver being involved in an accident increases with the level of alcohol in the driver's blood (BAC) and rises dramatically at the higher levels of impairment. Early studies demonstrated impairment of task performance and later studies demonstrated the causal link with risk of involvement and with the higher severities of accident.

A great deal of the data apart from the classical research of Borkenstein has come from drivers involved in accidents or from post-mortem data on road users who have died from their injuries. These data generally show high levels of blood alcohol in young drivers and generally high levels in the late evening, but they provide no information on the levels of blood alcohol present in drivers generally. This wider information is necessary if effective countermeasures are to be designed and implemented and random surveys of drivers have been carried out in several countries to provide this information.

In the case of pedestrians there has to date been little firm evidence about the significance of blood alcohol in respect of accident involvement though there is information of the levels for those killed in road accidents. In recent years the proportion of fatalities above 200 mg alcohol/100 ml of blood was similar for driver and pedestrian fatalities but at the lower levels of proportion of pedestrians at each level was less than that of drivers.

Just recently a study has been completed in the UK [22] which determined the blood alcohol distribution of adult pedestrian fatalities in a large urban area and by comparing it with the BAC distribution of a control sample of non-accident-involved pedestrians, established the role of alcohol in the aetiology of such fatalities.

The accident sample comprised all fatal adult pedestrian accidents that occurred within the West Midlands Metropolitan County (population 2.8M) during the period 1 January 1969 to 31 December 1975. Data on the BACs of adults ($\geq$ 15 years) who died within 12 hours of the accident were obtained from coroners' records. Further data on the pedestrian and the accident were obtained from police records.

The control sample was matched in terms of the location, time of day, and day of week of the accident and the sex of the pedestrian. Accidents which occurred during the period 1 January 1969 to 31 December 1973 constituted the retrospective sample and were visited on the same day of the week nearest to the anniversary of the accident. Fatalities which occurred during the period of the fieldwork (1 January 1974 - 31 December 1975) were controlled within a month, again on the same day of the week as the accident.

Pedestrians obviously engaged is essential services, such as policemen, postmen, milkmen, etc, were not approached. No such people were involved in fatal accidents.

During the period 1 January 1969 to 31 December 1975, 794 adult pedestrians died as a result of traffic accidents in the West Midlands Metropolitan County. They comprised 5.1 per cent of the national total during that period.

Out of the total, there were 344 cases in which the BAC of the accident victim was known and at least one corresponding control interview was obtained. Of the remaining fatalities, 319 died more than 12 hours after the accident and there were 69 cases in which the BAC of the accident victim was not measured despite his dying within 12 hours. A further 62 cases were not controlled mainly because of the absence of pedestrians passing the site at the appropriate time.

A total of 1,118 pedestrians were interviewed, a mean of 2.9 interviews per site visited. The gross refusal rate was 18.4 per cent but that figure included many people who were genuinely in a hurry. In the vast majority of cases, once a pedestrian had stopped, he or she completed the interview and provided a breath sample.

Alcohol-related accidents, particularly those involving high BACs, tended to occur mainly in the late evening. The highest incidence was in the 2300-0259 hours period when 70.2 per cent of the accident group had BACs $\geq$ 80 mg/100 ml and 50.9 per cent had BACs in excess of 150 mg/100 ml. The comparable figures for the control group were 18.8 per cent and 3.1 per cent respectively. During the day, the incidence of alcohol amongst both the accident and control groups was comparatively low (Fig. 4).

The BAC distributions of both the male accident and control groups were significantly higher than those for the females (p < 0.001). For males 47.4 per cent of the accident group had been drinking (BAC $\geq$ 10 mg/100 ml) and 28.9 per cent had BACs in excess of 100 mg/100 ml, compared with 14.7 per cent and 7.3 per cent respectively for the females.

In the male control group, 33.1 per cent had been drinking and 6.9 per cent had BACs in excess of 100 mg/100 ml. For the female control group, the corresponding figures were 6.6 per cent and 0.2 per cent respectively.

Alcohol has a major role in fatal pedestrian accidents. The study showed that at BACs above 120 mg/100 ml, the relative risk of accident-involvement increases rapidly. The data suggested that the effects of alcohol upon male pedestrian accident experience were not significant below 120 mg/100 ml. At 120-159 mg/100 ml, the relative risk of accident was over three times that of a sober pedestrian and, at higher BACs, the risk was fourteen times greater. A similar analysis for female pedestrians established that the relative accident risk for the 120 + mg/100 ml group was over 36 times that of a sober female pedestrian.

Alcohol is undoubtely one of the most serious problems in relation to road safety and the impairment of drivers is a major threat to pedestrian safety, quite apart from the risk to pedestrians who are themselves impaired. The major beneficial effect that can be produced by legislation directed at drivers who drive after drinking has been demonstrated in several countries; unfortunately the initial benefits tend to decline as the perceived risk of detection by police is found to be less than expected and as publicity related to the legislation declines. In the case of pedestrians legislation of similar severity to that imposed on drivers cannot be readily adopted. Its deterrent effect would in any event be small since a much greater deterrent is the high risk of death or serious injury to any pedestrian involved in a road accident. But some pedestrians under treatment for their physical injuries might with advantage be referred for treatment of drinking problems.

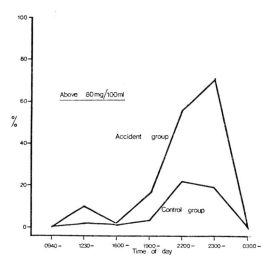

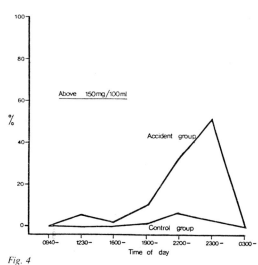

Fig. 4

BAC distributions by time of day for males and females combined

VEHICLE DESIGN TO ENHANCE PEDESTRIAN SAFETY

The majority of pedestrian injuries are inflicted by cars and apart from regulations preventing sharp projections on the exterior of them, little attempt has been made until recently to mitigate pedestrian injuries by vehicle re-design.

Over the last five years growing attention has been given to the problem [2], [23], [24], [25], [26] and [27]. It is now evident that valuable improvements in pedestrian safety can be gained by adopting suitable frontal designs. The two major objectives are to prevent the pedestrian being seriously injured in the primary collision with the car and to prevent the pedestrian being flung down into the road by the initial impact or subse-

quently. This can be achieved by retaining the pedestrian on the bonnet of the car [28] (Plate 3). It has been shown that it is much more difficult to meet these objectives for a child than for an adult and that the problem becomes rapidly more difficult at the higher impact speeds. This emphasizes the need to limit vehicle speeds in areas of high pedestrian concentration and to plan the road environment so that drivers have the maximum opportunity of slowing down before striking a pedestrian when this is unavoidable.

Harris [29] has suggested that pedestrian accident injury may be reduced by cars that are designed to satisfy the following conditions:

1. The severity of primary impact is reduced by matching the collapse characteristics of the front of the car to the appropriate human tolerance loads.

2. An adult pedestrian should be picked up and retained on the bonnet over as wide a range of impact speeds as possible without being projected over the roof or wings to the ground.

3. A child should be picked up into the bonnet or bonnet front rather than knocked forward to the ground.

4. The head should impact a suitably designed energy absorbing bonnet top rather than the more rigid windscreen surround. Some features of vehicles design that contribute to these conditions are:

A low mounted energy absorbing bumper with a yield of at least 100 mm; this also ameliorates lower limb injury, moving the impact to below the adult knee.

An energy absorbing bonnet leading edge with a yield of at least 150 mm and preferably much more.

Bonnet and wings with controlled vertical collapse characteristics.

The height of the leading edge of the bonnet has conflicting requirements, it needs a low bonnet front for projecting a child on to the bonnet and a high bonnet front for reducing the frequency of adult head impact with the windscreen surround. A long bonnet also reduced this latter possibility.

It may no longer be appropriate to talk of the bumper as an independent component of the car but rather to consider an overall frontal design of vehicle which has the necessary characteristics to satisfy impact requirements in both car-to-car and car-to-pedestrian collisions.

Compatible designs cannot be fully exploited by individual manufacturers and new international vehicle regulations will be needed for harmonisation of the future vehicle fleet.

RESEARCH NEEDS

Pedestrian safety research is carried out in many countries but it has not often been possible to identify with precision the benefits obtained from specific safety measures. This is because of the difficulty of carrying out evaluation in terms of accident or casualty savings. When similar measures are applied in different countries the results frequently seem to differ due to the difficulty of making valid comparisons and to differences in the background against which the measures are applied. One notable difference lies in the different legislative frameworks that exist.

There is therefore urgent need to develop internationally accepted techniques for the assessment of pedestrian safety schemes and to identify the legislative differences between countries and their influence on particular safety measures.

Older and Grayson [30] have recently published a comparison of pedestrian and vehicle flows and pedestrian casualties collected from busy streets in the cities of Vienna, Copenhagen, London and Tel Aviv.

There was no evidence in the data presented in this

PLATE 3: Experimental front-end No. 2b retaining adult on bonnet at 16 km/h.

PLATE 4: Experimental front-end No. 2a picking up child at 16 km/h.

paper of any large overall differences in risk to pedestrians crossing busy roads in each of the four cities, the differences within cities being far greater than those between cities. In fact it is a little surprising that, with the differences in detail in the ways in which some of the data were collected, the four comparable risk values on common sections lie within a range of ± 11 per cent of a common value. It might appear that, at least in the conditions studied, no city was markedly better than the others in its handling of the pedestrian safety problem.

However, it is important to note that this conclusion is based on a comparison of risks in the sections of road common to all cities. While the risks on these sections were similar, the four cities differed in the proportions of their total pedestrian flow found on the common sections, as follows:

Vienna 52%, Copenhagen 47%, London 70%, Tel Aviv 23%.

It should also be remembered that the common sections did not include signalized crossings with pedestrian signals near intersections which proved to have the lowest relative risk in those cities which had such crossing facilities.

While differences between the common sections of the four cities were relatively small, greater variability was found when all sections of the road were considered. A possible explanation of this can be found in relating the amount of pedestrian flow to various sections of the roads.

The low level of overall risk in Tel Aviv can largely be attributed to the heavy concentration of pedestrian flow on to the low risk signalized crossings. Although the usage of crossings in Vienna was low, this was offset by lower risk levels in the vicinities of crossings. Copenhagen and London both had high risk measures near crossings compared with the other two cities.

As far as relative risk is concerned, a detailed comparison of the risk of crossing at recognised crossing places and near road intersections showed more similarity than difference between the cities. The pattern of low risk on crossing places with high risk on the adjacent sections was common to all four cities and the relative risk levels on crossings were similar.

Due to the variability of the data it is difficult to clearly rank the crossings with respect to safety but there is a trend indicating that the order of crossings (from safe to less safe) was:

1. Crossings with pedestrian signals at signalized intersections.
2. Crossings without pedestrian signals at signalized intersections.
3. Crossings with pedestrian signals at non-signalized intersections.
4. Crossings without pedestrian signals away from intersections.

Pedestrian crossing facilities at signalized intersections maintained an overall benefit to safety even when the adjacent high risk areas were combined with them, that is, they contributed to safer lengths of road. Crossings where there was no signal control only produced a marginal improvement in safety in most cities over the length of road including the adjacent sections. In the latter case presumably an improvement would occur if pedestrians were persuaded or forced to use the facility rather than cross the adjacent lengths of road.

This leads on to a consideration of whether the use made of crossings in the four cities is a reflection of the legal regulations governing such use. Austria has a law requiring pedestrians to use crossings if there is one within 25 m. Denmark has a law requiring use of the crossing if it is nearby and there is sufficient traffic present. No specific distance is mentioned. In the United Kingdom there is no law requiring pedestrians to use crossings, or to observe light signals. In Israel the responsibilities of the pedestrian are set out in detail, including an obligation to use crossings where these are provided.

The regulations in force in Austria were not reflected in the proportion of pedestrians using crossings in Vienna, which was in fact the lowest of the four cities even when the immediate effect of number of crossings was allowed for. Under similar conditions it would appear that more use was made of the Copenhagen crossings than those in London which may be partly due to the difference in regulatory measures. It would also appear that the strict regulations controlling pedestrian behaviour in Israel were much more effective in encouraging use of signalized than of unsignalized crossings.

The OECD Special Research Group [8] has identified detailed research needs under the headings of the pedestrian's road environment, road safety education and the mass media (Appendix).

DEVELOPING COUNTRIES

This paper has mainly discussed the situation obtaining in Europe and North America but much of the material is applicable to the urban areas of less well-developed countries and certain countries with multiracial societies. However there are important differences and these differences may well require different approaches and solutions.

Jacobs has studied the general road accident situation in developing countries [31], [32], [33], [34] and Oldendaal [35] has studied pedestrian behaviour in the heterogeneous society of the Republic of South Africa where there are four main population groups with widely differing cultural backgrounds, socio-economic structures, degrees of literacy, beliefs, values, etc. These differences are not only confined to the four groups, but also exist within each of the particular groups.

Uken [36] has pointed out that in 1975, 44 per cent of all road fatalities on South African roads were pedestrians. Out of these some 55 per cent were Black males. Unlike most developed countries where the young and the aged are overpresented in pedestrian accidents, one is here faced with the middle-aged group. The 18 to 49 year age group, in fact, constitutes 72 per cent of Black male pedestrian fatalities. Put differently, the Black male pedestrian of the 18 to 49 year age group, constitutes about one-fifth of all South Afican road deaths.

It is evident that considerably more effort is required to tackle the pedestrian problem in developing countries if it is to be at all comparable to the scale that is being deployed in the developed countries.

CONCLUDING NOTE

Pedestrian safety is today a matter for concern in most countries on account of the relatively high level of casualties and the difficulty in identifying worthwhile measures that have the prospect of making substantial improvements in the situation.

It is not for lack of government attention or of research in the well-developed countries that this situation exists but rather that the problem is one of great complexity and the more effective of available measures are costly to implement or not generally acceptable. Road safety is a major public health problem and as the numbers of deaths from disease and illness falls the proportion of those due to road transport becomes of increasing significance suggesting that it merits a greater share of national resources.

Unfortunately, the knowledge of effectiveness that could have been derived from the wealth of pedestrian safety schemes which have been applied, has not been fully realized. However, current international activities which link research more closely to policy formulation in the pedestrian safety field show promise of improving the effectiveness of international endeavours.

Greater prominence needs to be given to pedestrian safety in the planning and redevelopment of urban areas. There is a continuing need to clarify the shape and significance of the various legislative frameworks that apply in different countries because these may profoundly affect the general suitability and success of individual safety measures that have been sucessful in some countries.

Above all there is a need to carry out rigorous scientific assessments (in terms of accidents and casualties) of the benefits of new pedestrian safety measures as they are applied.

Most of the pedestrian safety research carried out to date has taken place in well-developed countries but most of the findings are applicable also to less well-developed countries. There are however, some important differences that emphasize the need for pedestrian safety research in these countries to deal with the special problems that arise.

REFERENCES

[1] Duff, J. T., **Warrants for and design of pedestrian facilities,** Eleventh OTA/PIARC study week, Brussels 1972.

[2] **Proceedings of International Technical Conferences on Experimental Safety Conferences from 1971** - NHTSA Department of Transportation. USA

[3] Taylor, H., **Structural strength and compatibility of vehicles in the event of impact, potential hazard to other means of transport and to pedestrians.** European Motor-Vehicles Symposium, Brussels 1975.

[4] OECD. **Pedestrian safety.** OECD, Paris 1969.

[5] Committee on the Challenges of Modern Society. **Pedestrian safety project.** CCMS Report No. 27. US Department of Transportation, Washington 1974.

[6] Hakkert, A. S. (Ed). **Proceedings of the International Conference on Pedestrian Safety,** Technion, Haifa 1976.

[7] Turgel, J. The OECD Research Programme. **Proceedings of the International Conference on Pedestrian Safety.** Haifa 1976.

[8] Special Research Group on Pedestrian Safety. **Chairman's report and reports of the sub-groups.** (In press).

[9] Peyton, J. **Proceedings of the National Road Safety Congress,** RoSPA. Southport 1972.

[10] Dalby, E. **Space-sharing by pedestrians and vehicles.** TRRL Report LR 743. Transport and Road Research Laboratory, Crowthorne 1976.

[11] Kraay, J. H. **Urban planning, pedestrians, and road safety.** Proceedings of the International Conference on Pedestrian Safety, Haifa 1976.

[12] Backett, E. M. and A. M. Johnston. **Social patterns of road accidents to children.** British Medical Journal, 1959 **1,** 409-413.

[13] Sandels, S. **Children in traffic.** Elek. London 1975.

[14] Grayson, G. B. **The Hampshire child pedestrian accident study.** TRRL Report LR 668, Transport and Road Research Laboratory, Crowthorne 1975.

[15] Howarth, C. I., D. A. Routledge and R. Repetto-Wright. **Analysis of road accidents involving child pedestrians.** Ergonomics 1974, **17,** 319-330.

[16] Grayson, G. B. **Observations of pedestrian behaviour at four sites.** TRRL Report LR 670. Transport and Road Research Laboratory, Crowthorne 1975.

[17] Unesco. **Economic Commission for Europe Inland Transport Committee; groups of experts on road traffic safety.** Geneva, 1975.

[18] Wilde, G. J. S., L. J. Cake and R. LeBrasseur. **Mass media safety campaigns:** annotated bibliography 1970-1973. US Department of Transportation, 1974.

[19] OECD. **Road Safety campaigns: design and evaluation.** OECD, Paris 1971.

[20] Special Research Group on Pedestrian Safety. **Mass media communications for pedestrian safety.** Report of Sub-Group III. (In press).

[21] Sargent, K. J. and D. Sheppard. **The development of the Green Cross Code.** TRRL Report LR 605, Transport and Road Research Laboratory Crowthorne, 1974.

[22] Clayton, A. B., A. C. Booth and P. E. McCarthy. **A controlled study of the role of alcohol in fatal adult pedestrian accidents.** 7th International Conference on Alcohol, Drugs, and Traffic Safety, Melbourne, Australia.

[23] Stcherbatcheff, G., C. Tarriere, P. Duclos, A. Fayon, C. Got and A. Patel. **Simulation of collisions between pedestrians and vehicles using adult and child dummies.** Proceedings of Nineteenth Stapp Car Crash Conference, San Diego, Calif. November 1975.

[24] Pritz, H. B. **A preliminary assessment of the pedestrian injury reduction performance of the Calspan RSV.** Battelle Columbus Laboratories Paper. September 1976.

[25] Bacon, D. G. C. and M. R. Wilson. **Bumper characteristics for improved pedestrian safety.** Proceedings of Twentieth Stapp Car Crash Conference, Deaborn, Michigan, October 1976

[26] Sturtz, G., E.G. Suren, L. Gotzen, S. Behrens and K. Richter. **Biomechanics of real child pedestrian accidents.** Proceedings of Twentieth Stapp Car Crash Conference, Dearborn, Michigan, October 1976.

[27] Hall, R. R., R. G. Vaughan and A. J. Fischer. **Pedestrian crash trauma and vehicle design in New South Wales, Australia.** 3rd International Congress on Aut. Safety. San Francisco, July 1974.

[28] Jehu, V. J. and L. C. Pearson. **The trajectories of pedestrian dummies struck by cars of conventional and modified frontal designs.** TRRL Report LR 718, Transport and Road Research Laboratory, Crowthorne, 1976.

[29] Harris, J. **Research and development towards improved protection for pedestrians struck by cars.** Sixth International Technical Conference on Experimental Safety Vehicles, Washington 1976.

[30] Older, S. J. and G. B. Grayson. **An international comparison of pedestrian risk in four cities.** Proceedings of the International Conference on Pedestrian Safety, Haifa 1976.

[31] Jacobs, D. G. and P. Hutchinson. **A study of accident rates in developing countries.** TRRL Report LR 546. Transport and Road Research Laboratory 1973.

[32] Jacobs, G. D. **A study of accident rates on rural roads in developing countries.** TRRL Report LR 732. Transport and Road Research Laboratory 1976.

[33] Jacobs, D. G. and P. R. Fouracre. **Further research on road accident rates in developing countries.** TRRL Report SR 270. Transport and Road Research Laboratory. Crowthorne 1977.

[34] Jacobs, D. G. and Marguerite N. Bardsley. **Road accidents as a cause of death in developing countries.** TRRL Report SR 277. Transport and Road Research Laboratory, Crowthorne 1977.

[35] Odendaal, J. R. **Traffic law enforcement and the pedestrian.** Proceedings of the International Conference on Pedestrian Safety, Haifa 1976.

[36] Uken, E. A. **Pedestrian training programmes for developing nations.** Proceedings of the International Conference on Pedestrian Safety, Haifa 1976.

FOOTNOTE
1. Austria, Belgium, Canada, Denmark, Finland. France, the Federal Republic of Germany, Greece, Iceland, Ireland, Italy, Japan, Luxembourg, the Netherlands, Norway, Portugal, Spain, Sweden, Switzerland, Turkey, the United Kingdom and the United States.

APPENDIX: DETAILED RESEARCH NEEDS (OECD SPECIAL GROUP)
The OECD Special Research Group has identified detailed research needs under the headings of the pedestrian's road environment, road safety education and the mass media.

The pedestrian's road environment

(i) Research is recommend on the needs of pedestrians in urban areas, and particularly into the factors which influence their choice of routes.

Aim: better location and assessment of policy and design, for pedestrian precincts and networks.

(ii) Research is recommended to determine the risks to pedestrian at different parts of the road networks in urban areas.

Aim: assessment of overall levels of risks and the rational design of traffic management countermeasures; monitoring of pedestrian safety.

(iii) More research is needed on criteria to be used in the

implementation of pedestrian segregated areas, pedestrian networks and space sharing schemes.

Aim: to produce guidelines for engineers and planners.

(iv) Research on design measures aimed at reducing vehicle speeds, both in pedestrian zones and in residential areas.

Aim: identification of optimal and acceptable features to avoid proliferation of measures and the introduction of possibly hazardous ones.

Road Safety education

(i) Further research is needed to define the requirements of safe pedestrian behaviour through task analysis for children of different ages.

Aim: to identify and define training objectives which are appropriate for children at different stages of development.

(ii) Research is needed to determine the best methods by which training objectives can be attained, and also on the optimal amount and frequency of training.

Aim: to achieve the most efficient use of educational resources.

(iii) More research is require on the best way of integrating the training efforts of parents and teachers.

Aim: to develop more specific and effective educational countermeasures.

Mass Media

(i) Research is recommended on the rationalisation and evaluation of the legal responsibilities of drivers and pedestrians in Member countries.

Aim: to enable mass media programmes to be based on clearly defined requirements for behaviour.

(ii) Further research is needed into the design features of mass media campaigns, and evaluation must be an integral part of all such programmes.

Aim: to increase the effectiveness of mass media campaigns.

(iii) More extensive and informative data on pedestrian accidents is needed in all Member countries.

Aim: to increase understanding of the pedestrian safety problem; to assist in the rational selection of target audiences and target behaviours.

Some observations on evaluation methods pertinent to selection of a public urban transport system

Y. Yashoshima
Department of Civil Engineering,
University of Tokyo

A. Takeishi
Ministry of Transport, Japan

N. Sugino
Mitsubishi Research Institute, Japan

FOCUS OF THE STUDY

Recent problems of urban transport are a combination of various factors such as accidents, road congestion, and air and noise pollution, as well as demands for much more sophisticated services which acknowledge the needs of users, society and the operators. Problems no longer are confined to system management and carrying capacity improvement.

Therefore, at the time of selection or development of a new urban transport system, every possible factor shall have to be taken into consideration, not only the exact estimation of future needs but also the interrelationship among users, society and the operators. A new system cannot be satisfied with only an evaluation of technical feasibility but must be assessed systematically in reference to society and the economy.

For assessment of society and the economy in the selection of a new system, enough consideration should be given to the financial situation of the users or society involved, their sentiment, and their historical or traditional tendencies. In addition, assessing what the users and inhabitants expect from a system is necessary to estimate possible traffic demands.

Furthermore, it is necessary to develop a theory for the quantitative analysis of the items for evaluation, and to develop methods for the quantitative analysis of the correlativity between the social situation for the users and their preference in transport modes.

This paper, in recognition of such necessity, will discuss the "Utility Function" method users in quantitative analysis pertaining to selection of a public urban transport system, and the applicability of the "Utility Function", by means of some case studies.

ITEMS FOR EVALUATION

In conjunction with the above, the establishment of newly created items for evaluation was planned with an emphasis on simplifying recognition in relation to the study of a methodology. At the same time, it was acknowledged that coverage under the new items for evaluation would have to accommodate many diverse aspects.

In defining the 'interest group' in evaluation of the transport system (as groups categorized in reference to the interests involved), it will be composed mainly of the 'users', 'society', and 'operators'. Items for evaluation on each of these parties were made as follows:

A. Items to be evaluated by "USERS"

Rapidity
　Rapidity

Convenience
　Punctuality
　Operation reliability
　Entrance and exit simplicity
　Walking distance
　Waiting time
　Train and line transfer simplicity
　Sheltered station availability
　Early morning services
　Late night services

Riding comfort
　Internal car noise
　Vibration
　Views from the windows
　Insurance of privacy
　Degree of congestion
　Seating capacity and adequacy
　Air conditioning

B. Items to be evaluated by "SOCIETY"
　Noise
　Air Pollution
　Structure occupancy capacity (above surface)
　Degree of intrusion into privacy
　Physical and social division of community

C. Items to be evaluated by "OPERATORS"

Construction costs
　Laying of rails
　Construction of stations and relevant structures
　Aerial or ground wiring provisions
　Provisions for car yards
　Transformer substations construction
　Provisions for train control systems
　Inspection and administration

Operational costs
　Personnel expense
　Maintenance of cars and vehicles
　Maintenance of rails
　Maintenance of aerial or ground wiring
　Electric supply expense
　Administrative expense

In general, items for the users are categorized by five factors; namely passenger fare, rapidity, safety, convenience and comfort. But, in the case of Japan, rail fares cannot be decided by independent action, the public railroad enterprise being overseen and subsidized by the government. Accordingly, passenger fares for the operators have been excluded from corresponding items in lists "A" and "C".

In respect to safety, it is assumed that there are no safety differences between the transport systems, with the understanding that the safety of any public transport system would have to exceed a regulation standard. Therefore, the cost of safety was included in the operational costs.

Regional societies concerned here are, by the development and installation of the new system, to take advantage of an improvement in economic and social status, while at the same time assuming the disadvantages of being exposed to environmental air and noise problems as well as the inevitable physical and social separation of the society.

The potential involved in this area is the greatest of all. It can be subdivided into categories of 'health', 'right-of-way' (right to compensation from society separation), 'effects on the economy', 'effects on city deformation', and 'effects on politics and the society'.

Since establishing the quantitative analysis method was the major requirement, the number of items concerning the evaluation of regional societies were simplified to the smallest practical number.

Therefore, it would appear that evaluation of the regional society in this study emphasized the disadvantageous aspects but it should also be considered that the advantages of regional and other economies would be considerable.

Concerning the evaluation of the operators, only major items relative to profitability were considered. Consequently, the comparison of expenses was incorporated, but revenue determination was excluded, due to the differences explained before.

Generally, considerations as to the degree of difficulties of construction and securing of experienced workers, as well as the consistency and discretion of the management, were incorporated.

METHOD OF EVALUATION

Assessment was made on the users' evaluation and preference toward each of the items of a transport system, after which the results were incorporated in a summary of system comparisons.

"Preference" is an expression of the users', psychological judgement based upon their value opinions, the quantitative value of which is designated as "Utility". "Utility Function", therefore, represents the situation where the users' attitude toward each item would be reflected by means of individual review and replies to a questionnaire.

"Weight of importance" among the items was set in conjunction with the "Utility Function", thus the 'total utility' was determined as the sum total of all items, as shown in Formula - 1, hereunder:

$$U = \sum_{i=1}^{n} W_i \times U_i \qquad (1)$$

where,

U	:	Utility for user
i	:	Item of evaluation by user
n	:	Number of items evaluated by user
U_i	:	Utility Function of item 'i'
W_i	:	Weight of importance of item 'i'

This formula is applicable to the assessment of the utility for an individual person. For the assessment of the utility for a group of people, it can be determined by adding up each individual value of 'U' which in turn is obtained by applying each variable to the function 'U_i' in accordance with the values estimated on each type of trip by individuals (such as origin and destination, time of trip, distance to the station, etcetera).

The "Utility Function" on the evaluation of the society is almost equivalent to that for users. However, it should be noted that each item of evaluation has its own range of coverage, or expressed alternatively, the range of people to be involved in the evaluation differs from item to item.

Thus, the "Utility Function" for the society evaluation is to replace 'i' in the formula - 1 by the item 'j' of the items in the society evaluation. Thereupon the degree of regional largeness and the population density shall be taken into consideration for the calculation of 'U_j'.

Expenses will only be items for operator evaluation. Therefore, it would not be necessary to convert "expenses" into "utility" but to compare the extent of expenses in a direct way, in order to make an independent evaluation of each of the three parties involved.

The "evaluation function" is therefore to discuss the 'annual costs' as shown in Formula - 2, hereunder:

$$TC = CC + OC$$

$$CC = \sum_{k=1}^{m} \frac{I(1+I)^{Y_k}}{(1+I)^{Y_k} - 1} \times C_k \qquad (2)$$

where,

TC	:	Annual costs
CC	:	Annual capital costs
OC	:	Annual operational costs
k	:	Item of construction costs
m	:	Number of items of construction cost
C_k	:	Construction cost of Item 'k'
Y_k	:	Life of 'k' facility
I	:	Interest rates

The execution of 'systematic evaluation' is deceptive in that the parties, namely the users, society and the operators, could take positions opposed to each other. Therefore, it would be preferable to consider that the overall or eventual evaluation, including the processing of evaluation values on the peripheral situations, should be removed from the quantitative analysis and placed in a superior field for judgement.

In conformity with this thinking, the results of the evaluation have incorporated an illustrative example to augment this study. While the illustration includes each of the three parties, summation of the information is not analytic but descriptive in nature.

CASE STUDIES OF URBAN TRANSPORT SYSTEMS

A series of case studies were conducted on urban transport systems with the application of quantitative analysis by "Utility Function". The situation where new transport systems could be introduced was categorized into seven patterns according to factors of origin and destination, trip distances and others.

To manage the population concentration in the big cities and the consequent shortage of living space, many new towns (bed towns) were developed in suburban areas of large cities in this country.

The following is an example of one study conducted for the evaluation of an urban transport system linking a medium-sized new town with an adjacent railway station.

For provision of transport between this new town and an adjacent railway station on a trunk line, it was found imperative to develop and introduce a new kind of transport system. This was necessary because the construction of a new rail line would be too expensive for uncertain transport demands while bus transport ability was termed inadequate.

Assuming the situation that a new town of about 50,000 population located approximately five kilometers from the nearest railway station on a trunk line, an evaluation was made for the possible choices of connecting transport. But services and the introduction of a "medium traffic rail transport" system (which is being developed in this country) were compared.

Three types of bus services were considered;
1) bus service given an exclusive express lane,
2) bus service on an exclusive, elevated road and
3) dual-mode urban electric bus service.

Following is an illustrated representation of the systems analysis results in reference to evaluations of the three parties involved - the users, society and the operators.

Outward direction of each axis represents the negative effect as well as the scale of monetary investments involved, setting the standard on the development of the system by the aforementioned "medium traffic rail transport".

Deducible from the situation is the conspicuous relationship between the society and the operator where the situation of "trading off" (too good for one is too bad for the other) is apparent. This will show the applicability of the evaluation analysis by "Utility Function" to the extent evaluation of public transport would be satisfied.

CONCLUSION

This study for the development of a method of evaluation for the selection of a public urban transport system seems to be valuable in its basic concept, but it should be emphasized that further studies are necessary to increase the range of applicability.

ACKNOWLEGDMENTS

This study was made at Japan Transport Economics Research Center, with the sponsorship of the Japan Shipbuild Industry Foundations.

The authors wish to thank many individuals who contributed to the development of the Project, in particular, the members of the Research Committee organized by Japan Transport Economics Research Center, without whom the research and development reported here would not have been possible.

Adverse effects on the users

_____ Medium traffic rail system
_ . _ Exclusive, elevated bus road system
· · · · · Exclusive lane bus system
_ _ _ Dual-mode electric bus system

Costs to the operators

Adverse effects on the society

SUPPLEMENT

FIG 1
APPLICATIONS OF NEW TRANSPORT SYSTEMS
(Examples)

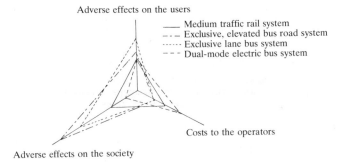

Pattern Of Transport \ System Concept	Railway System	· Non-Railway System	· Dual-Mode System	· Continuous System
1. Suburbs — Center	Fast Intraurban Transit (FIT) Monorail	———	Dual-Mode Bus (DMB)	———
2. Airport — Center	FIT Monorail	———	DMB	———
3. New Town	Intermediate-Capacity Transit (ICT) Monorail	Dial-a-Bus	DMB	———
4. Central Business District	Personal Rapid Transit (PRT)	Minibus City Car	———	Moving Way High-Speed Continuous System (HSCS)
5. Airport Or Terminal	ICT	———	———	Moving Way HSCS
6. Access (in the suburbs)	ICT Monorail PRT	Dial-a-Bus Minibus City Car	DMB	———

①

401

FIG 2
AREA OF THE CASE STUDY

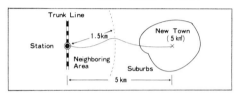

- ●Population
  - Residents ·················· 50,000
  - (Commuters ··············· 20,000)

- ●Density of Population
  - New Town ················· 10,000/km²
  - Suburbs ·················· 2,000/km²
  - Neighboring Area ·········· 8,000/km²

- ●Demand
  - Peak (4 hours, one way) ·········· 7,500/hour·line
  - Off·peak (14 hours, both ways) ··· < 375/hour·line

- ●Modal Split
  - Transit System ··············· 75%
  - Other Systems ··············· 25%

②

FIG 3
ROUTE AND CHARACTERISTICS OF THE INTERMEDIATE-CAPACITY TRANSIT (ICT)

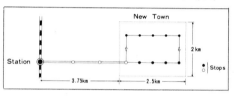

- ●Location Of Stops:
  - Access Time In the New Town ·········· 5.5min. (Mean)
  - Changing Time At the Station ·········· 2min.

- ●Vehicle And Guideway:
  - Capacity Of a Car ····················· 30 (11 Seats)
  - Support ········· Air Tire On a Concrete Surface
  - Drive ·········· Rotary Electric Motor
  - Air Conditioning ········ Both Heating And Cooling
  - Guideway ········Elevated (5 m) Concrete Way

- ●Operation:
  - Service Time ·········· From 6:00A.M. Till 12:00 P.M.
  - Headway At a Peak Time ······· 1.5min./3.0min./5.0min.
  - Overcrowding At a Peak Time ······· 100%/150%
  - Delay ·········· About 5 min., Once a Month
  - Speed ·········· 40km/h / 50km/h / 60km/h

③

FIG 4·1
AN INTERMEDIATE-CAPACITY TRANSIT IN A NEW TOWN

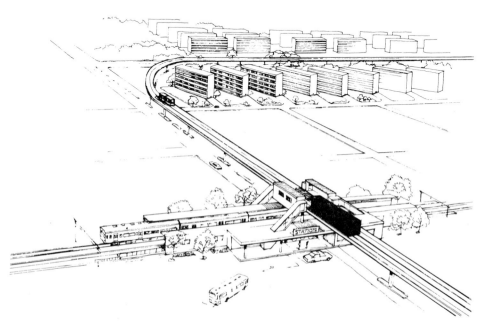

④

FIG 4-2
**VIEWS OF AN INTERMEDIATE-CAPACITY
TRANSIT**

(A)   **(B)**

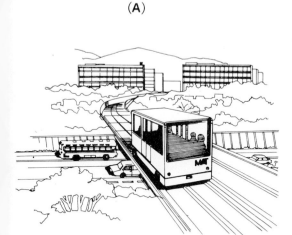

⑤

FIG 5
ROUTE AND CHARACTERISTICS OF
THE EXCLUSIVE-LANE／ROAD BUS (ELB/ERB)

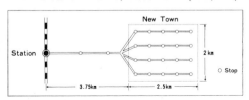

● Location Of Stops:
    Access Time In the New Town ············· 3.1 min. (Mean)
    Changing Time At the Station ············· 4 min.

● Vehicle And Guideway:
    Capacity Of a Car ············· 80 (40 Seats)
    Support ············· Air Tire On a Road Surface
    Drive ············· Diesel Engine
    Air Conditioning ············· Heating Only
    Guideway (Out Of the New Town)
        ELB ······ Exclusive Lane (Ground Level)
        ERB ······ Elevated Exclusive Road

● Operation:
    Service Time ······ From 6:00 AM. Till 12:00 P.M.
    Headway At a Peak Time ······· 2 min./2.5 min./3 min.
    Overcrowding At a Peak Time ······· 100%
    Delay   ELB ······ About 10 min., 4 Times a Month
          ERB ······ About 7 min., 3 Times a Month
    Speed (Out Of the New Town) ELB ······ 20 km/h
                           ERB ······ 40 km/h
    Operator ············· One-Man System

⑥

FIG 6
ROUTE AND CHARACTERISTICS OF
THE DUAL-MODE BUS (DMB)

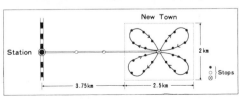

● Location Of Stops:
    Access Time In the New Town ············· 3.1 min. (Mean)
    Changing Time At the Station ············· 2 min.

● Vehicle And Guideway:
    Capacity Of a Car ············· 30 (11 Seats)
    Support ············· Air Tire On a Concrete Surface
    Drive ············· Rotary Electric Motor
    Air Conditioning ······ Both Heating And Cooling
    Guideway (Out Of the New Town) ······ Elevated Electric-
                                Supplied Way
    Power (In the New Town) ······ Storage Battery

● Operation:
    Service Time ······ From 6:00 A.M. Till 12:00 P.M.
    Headway At a Peak Time ······ 2 min./3 min./5 min.
    Overcrowding At a Peak Time ······ 100%/150%
    Delay ············· About 7 min., Twice a Month
    Speed (Out Of the New Town) ············· 40 km/h
    Operator In the New Town ······ One-Man System
              Out Of the New Town ··· Automatic System

⑦

FIG 7

ITEMS TO BE EVALUATED BY USERS

Rapidity
- Rapidity (Travel Time)

Convenience
- Punctuality
- Operation Reliability
- Entrance And Exit Simplicity
- Walking Distance (Time)
- Waiting Time
- Train And Line Transfer Simplicity
- Sheltered Station Availability
- Early Morning Service
- Late Night Service

Riding Comfort
- Internal Car Noise
- Vibration
- Views From the Windows
- Insurance Of Privacy
- Degree Of Congestion (Overcrowding)
- Seating Capacity And Adequacy
- Air Conditioning Availability

⑧

FIG 8

EVALUATING FUNCTION FOR USERS

$$U = \sum_{k=1}^{N} \sum_{j=1}^{n} W_j \cdot U_j \ (X_j \ (k)) \ \dots\dots\dots\dots\dots\dots\dots\dots \ (1)$$

Where, U : Total Utility For Users

j : Item Of Evaluation By Users

n : Number Of Items Evaluated By Users

k : Individual User

N : Number Of Users

W_j : Weight Of Importance Of Item "j"

U_j : Utility Function Of Item "j"

$X_j \ (k)$: Characteristics Of the System Pertinent To Item "j" And Individual User "k"

⑨

FIG 9-1

UTILITY FUNCTIONS FOR USERS

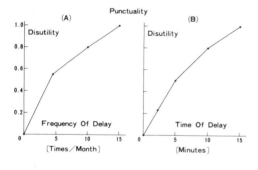

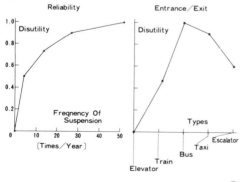

⑩

FIG 9-2

UTILITY FUNCTIONS FOR USERS (Continued)

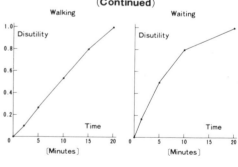

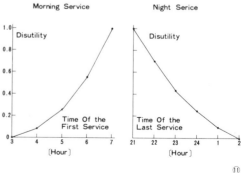

⑪

FIG 9-3

UTILITY FUNCTIONS FOR
USERS (Continued)

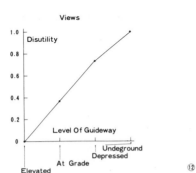

Noise / Vibration / Views

FIG 9-4

UTILITY FUNCTIONS FOR
USERS (Continued)

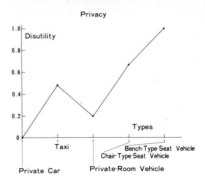

Privacy

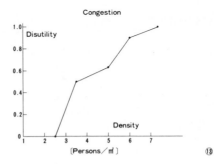

Congestion

⑫   ⑬

FIG 10

WEIGHTS OF IMPORTANCE OF ITEMS
TO BE EVALUATED BY USERS

Items	Weights		Improvements Of a System
	To Attend	To Return	
Rapidity (Time)	·164	·146	60 min → 45 min
Punctuality	·178	·132	15 min×2/w → No Delay
Reliability	·156	·133	Once a Month → Once a Year
Entrance / Exit	·085	·083	Bus → Elevator
Walking	·128	·125	15 min → 5 min
Waiting	·155	·151	15 min → 2 min
Transfer	·126	·123	1 → 0
Shelter	·119	·116	No → Equipped
Morning Service	·078	—	7:00A. M. → 4:00A. M.
Night Service	—	·140	9:00P. M. → 2:00A. M.
Noise	·125	·130	Sudway → Not Felt
Vibration	·128	·134	Bus On a Bad Road → Not Felt
Views	·096	·100	Underground → Elevated
Privacy	·084	·088	Bench-Type-Seat Vehicle → Private Car
Congestion	·142	·149	Jammed → Straps Occupied
Seating	·157	·165	Standing → Seated
Air Conditioning	·139	·145	Only Heating → Heating & Cooling

⑭

FIG 11

ITEMS TO BE EVALUATED BY SOCIETY

- Noise

- Air Pollution

- Structure Occupancy Capacity (Above Surface)

- Intrusion Into Privacy

- Physical And Social Division of Community

⑮

FIG 12

EVALUATING FUNCTION FOR SOCIETY

$$U = \sum_{j=1}^{n} W_j \cdot \iint U_j \left(X_j (x, y) \right) \cdot P (x, y) \, dx \, dy \quad \cdots\cdots\cdots\cdots (2)$$

Where, U : Utility For Society

j : Item Of Evaluation By Society

n : Number Of Items Evaluated By Society

W_j : Weight Of Importance Of Item "j"

U_j : Utility Function Of Item "j"

$X_j (x, y)$: Characteristics Of the System Pertinent To Item "j" And Spot (x, y)

P (x, y) : Density Of Population Pertinent To Spot (x, y)

⑯

FIG 13·1

EVALUATING FUNCTIONS FOR SOCIETY

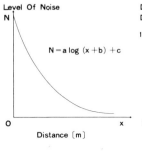

Level Of Noise

$$N = a \log (x + b) + c$$

Distance [m]

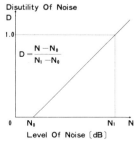

Disutility Of Noise

$$D = \frac{N - N_0}{N_1 - N_0}$$

Level Of Noise [dB]

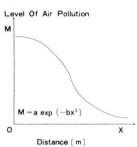

Level Of Air Pollution

$$M = a \exp (-bx^2)$$

Distance [m]

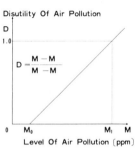

Disutility Of Air Pollution

$$D = \frac{M - M_0}{M_1 - M_0}$$

Level Of Air Pollution [ppm]

⑰

FIG 13-2

EVALUATING FUNCTIONS FOR SOCIETY (Continued)

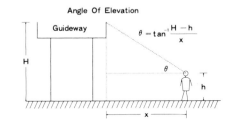

Angle Of Elevation

Guideway

$$\theta = \tan^{-1} \frac{H - h}{x}$$

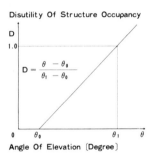

Disutility Of Structure Occupancy

$$D = \frac{\theta - \theta_0}{\theta_1 - \theta_0}$$

Angle Of Elevation [Degree]

⑱

FIG 13·3

EVALUATING FUNCTIONS FOR SOCIETY (Continued)

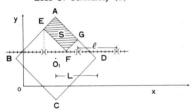

Loss Of Community (S)

L: Extent Of Community ℓ: Interval Of Crossings

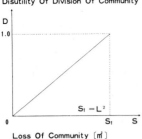

Disutility Of Division Of Community

$S_1 = L^2$

Loss Of Community $[\text{m}^2]$

FIG 14

WEIGHTS OF IMPORTANCE OF ITEMS TO BE EVALUATED BY SOCIETY

Items	Weights
Noise	·245
Air Pollution	·241
Structure Occupancy Capacity	·198
Intrusion Into Privacy	·176
Division Of Community	·140

⑳

FIG 15

ITEMS TO BE EVALUATED BY OPERATORS

Construction Costs
- Laying Of Rails
- Construction Of Stations And Relevant Structures
- Aerial And Ground Wiring Provisions
- Provisions For Cars And Vehicles
- Provisions For Caryards
- Transformer Substations Construction
- Provisions For Train Control Systems
- Inspection And Administration

Operatioral Costs
- Personnel Expense
- Maintenance Of Cars And Vehicles
- Mairtenance Of Rails
- Mairtenance Of Aerial And Ground Wiring
- Power Expense
- Administrative Expense

㉑

FIG 16

EVALUATING FUNCTION FOR OPERATORS

$$TC = CC + OC \quad \cdots\cdots\cdots\cdots\cdots\cdots\cdots\cdots\cdots\cdots \quad (3)$$

$$CC = \sum_{j=1}^{n} \frac{I\,(1+I)^{Y_j}}{(1+I)^{Y_j}-1} \cdot CC_j \quad \cdots\cdots\cdots\cdots\cdots \quad (4)$$

$$OC = \sum_{k=1}^{m} OC_k \quad \cdots\cdots\cdots\cdots\cdots\cdots\cdots\cdots\cdots \quad (5)$$

Where,   TC : Annual Total Costs

       CC : Annual Capital Costs

       OC : Annual Operational Costs

       j   : Item Of Construction Costs

       n   : Number Of Items Of Construction Costs

       CC_j : Construction Cost Of Item "j"

       Y_j : Life Of "j" Facility

       I   : Rate Of Interest

       k   : Item Of Operational Costs

       m   : Number Of Items Of Operational Costs

       OC_k : Operational Cost Of Item "k"

㉒

FIG 17

EVALUATIONS OF USERS AND OPERATORS

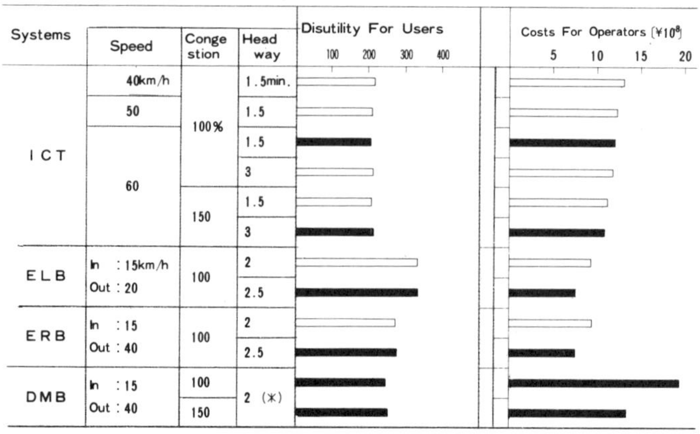

Systems	Speed	Conge stion	Head way	Disutility For Users	Costs For Operators (¥10⁶)
ICT	40km/h	100%	1.5min.		
	50		1.5		
	60		1.5		
			3		
		150	1.5		
			3		
ELB	In : 15km/h / Out : 20	100	2		
			2.5		
ERB	In : 15 / Out : 40	100	2		
			2.5		
DMB	In : 15 / Out : 40	100	2 (✻)		
		150			

Disutility For Users scale: 100 200 300 400
Costs For Operators (¥10⁶) scale: 5 10 15 20

(✻) Stop Skipping Service

㉓

FIG 18

EVALUATION OF SOCIETY

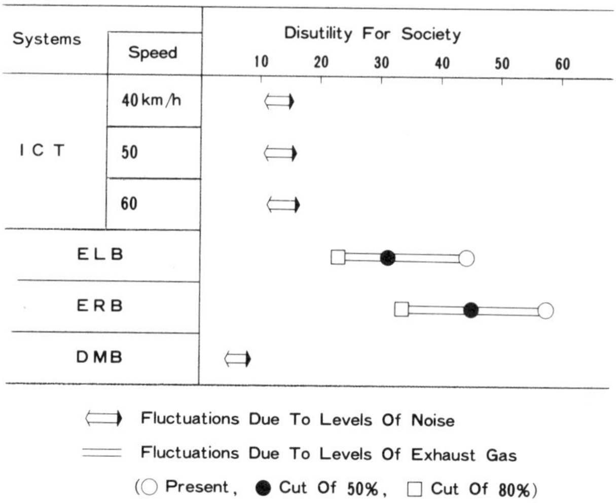

Systems	Speed	Disutility For Society
ICT	40 km/h	
	50	
	60	
ELB		
ERB		
DMB		

Disutility For Society scale: 10 20 30 40 50 60

⟸⟶ Fluctuations Due To Levels Of Noise

═══ Fluctuations Due To Levels Of Exhaust Gas

(○ Present , ● Cut Of 50% , □ Cut Of 80%)

㉔

FIG 19

CHARACTERISTICS OF TRANSPORT SYSTEMS FOR

"TRADE-OFF" ANALYSES

Systems	Headway [min]	Congestion [%]	Skipped Stops	Routes	Speed [km/h]	Noise / Air Pollution
ICT (A)	1.5	100	0	1	60	N : High
ICT (B)	3.0	150	0	1	60	N : High
ELB	2.5	100	0	4	20	A : 50%Cut
ERB	2.5	100	0	4	40	A : 50%Cut
DMB (A)	2.0	100	2	4	40	N : High
DMB (B)	2.0	150	1	4	40	N : High

㉕

408

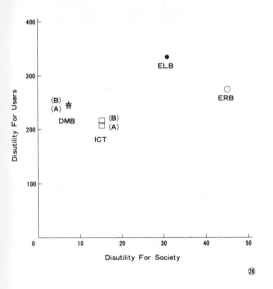

FIG 20

"TRADE-OFF" BETWEEN
USERS AND SOCIETY

㉖

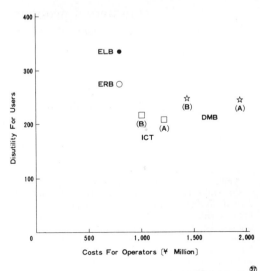

FIG 21

"TRADE-OFF" BETWEEN
USERS AND OPERATORS

㉗

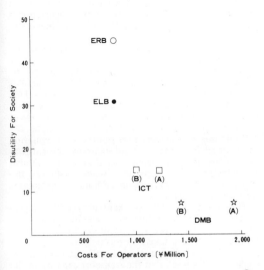

FIG 22

"TRADE-OFF" BETWEEN
SOCIETY AND OPERATORS

㉘

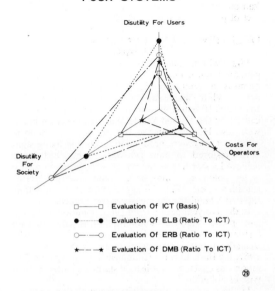

FIG 23

"TRIANGLES" OF EVALUATION OF
FOUR SYSTEMS

□——□ Evaluation Of ICT (Basis)

●┈┈┈● Evaluation Of ELB (Ratio To ICT)

○—·—○ Evaluation Of ERB (Ratio To ICT)

★——★ Evaluation Of DMB (Ratio To ICT)

㉙

Environmental problems related to railways in Japan
(Special Reference to the Shinkansen)

by

H. YOSHIMURA

Environmental Preservation Dept.

Japanese National Railways

INTRODUCTION

Japan is an island country consisting of Honshu, Hokkaido, Shikoku and Kyushu. Of its total surface of 370,000 square kilometers, 70 percent is mountainous with the result that most of the population, exceeding 100 million, is confined to a few small plains. Nonetheless, in 1976, business activities resulted in a Gross National Product of US $ 550 billion. With this situation, environmental problems have developed into a major national issue.

Severe public criticism arose over the pollution of the atmosphere, the rivers and the seas that has accompanied the development of heavy and chemical industries, and lately increasing attention is being paid to pollution problems created by transport systems. Among these are exhaust gas emissions, noise, and vibration caused by automobile traffic, problems Japan shares with numerous other countries. In Japan, however, railway traffic is also often cited as a cause for the deterioration of the environment. This has created yet another difficult problem for the railway industry which is already saddled with heavy deficits.

I therefore propose to examine the environmental problems facing Japanese National Railways and the measures being taken to cope with them, with particular reference to noise and virbration problems of the Shinkansen super-express trains, which have been the subject of particularly severe criticism.

OVERVIEW OF ENVIRONMENT PROBLEMS IN JAPAN

First I wish to touch upon environmental problems in general in our country. The development of these problems is analyzed chronologically in the following manner in a White Paper issued by the Environment Agency. In the first 10 years following the widespread destruction caused by the Second World War, pollution problems were few. However, in the 10 subsequent years up to 1965, not only were production levels and living standards restored to their pre-war heights, but Japan achieved a startling economic growth, bringing with it water pollution, atmospheric contamination, ground subsidence, etc. With the aggravation of the situation, the first administrative measures were taken.

In the five-year period from 1965, pollution worsened and spread. Vigorous countermeasures, coupled with legislative steps, were undertaken to create a systematized administrative framework to deal with pollution. In 1967, the Basic Law for Countermeasures Against Pollution was enacted, establishing statutory curbs on each type of pollution.

In the five years after 1970, the pollution problem became a major social and political issue. In particular, severe criticism was directed at pollution caused by public undertakings such as the operation of airports, highways, railways and land reclamation and refuse disposal projects. The conservation of nature was given unusually heavy emphasis, with the pollution problem being discussed not in isolation but as part of this broader issue.

While industry and commerce developed as the result of an exceptionally high economic growth rate over a long period, the stresses caused by this rapid pace gave rise to numerous pollution problems. With increased material affluence in their daily lives, the people's sense of priorities underwent a change so that beginning in 1970 their criticism of pollution, including that caused by the railways, reached new heights.

THE SITUATION OF THE RAILWAYS IN JAPAN AND THE CONSTRUCTION OF THE SHINKANSEN

Because of geographical conditions such as the scarcity of land that can be effectively utilized, railways play an important role in land transportation in our country. This is particularly so in passenger transportation, where dependence on railways is high because they meet the requirements for mass transportation of a dense population with a highly concentrated mobility. In this respect, Japan, where railways have more than 30 percent share in the total volume of domestic transportation in terms of man-kilometers, is markedly different from other countries.

This railway transportation is mostly provided by Japanese National Railways, with the exception of private railway services available in a number of urban centers. With a history of more than a century, JNR now operates 1.9 million passenger and freight train-kilometers daily over the 21,000 kilometer traditional network of 1,067 mm narrow-gauge tracks to transport a daily average of 19 million passengers and 400,000 tons of freight.

While this railway transport system is encountering competition from road and air transport, measures to meet future needs are being taken through quantitative increases in its transport capacity and qualitative improvement of its services, in addition to promoting modernization policies.

The construction of the Shinkansen was undertaken as a part of this program for the strengthening and improvement of the railways. It constitutes the most important largescale step taken for this purpose.

This line was built as a solution to the problem various studies had forecast, that the transport capacity of the original Tokaido main line- the most important rail link in the JNR connecting Japan's two major cities, Tokyo and Osaka- would soon reach its limit.

This project was the result of considerable research. It would increase transportation capacity for both passengers and freight to the maximum by using a standard-gauge, highspeed line in addition to the traditional lines, allowing transfers between them at important stations. Construction of the new line could thus adopt the latest technology and the sytem could be simplified without being constrained by existing lines. The plan was adopted because it embodied these advantages, far superior to any other method.

Work on the 515.4-kilometer-long Shinkansen was started in April 1959 and the line went into operation in October 1964. In 1972 it was extended westward to Okayama and further extended to Hakata in March 1975. Today, it operates over 1,070 kilometers.

The number of passengers using this line has increased dramatically year by year, reaching a total of over of 1,000 million by May 1976 in the twelve years since it started operating, and it has now won high praise as a public transportation system.

THE PROBLEMS OF NOISE AND VIBRATION OF THE SHINKANSEN

In the planning stage of the Shinkansen, before its construction was started in 1959, technical studies were made on a wide variety of subjects such as safety, riding comfort and maintenance, required for the creation of what was to become the fastest railway line in the world. The problems of noise and vibration that could create external nuisances were also borne in mind.

With the set objective of keeping noise and vibration down to the level of existing lines, various steps were adopted. These included the use of long rails, double elastic fastenings and movable nose rail frogs for track material, and the structural lightening of carriages, which were equipped with air springs. These measures were principally aimed at achieving good riding comfort and reducing track maintenance manpower requirements, but since they also proved to serve in reducing noise and vibration they were incorporated into construction standards. Running tests carried out 18 months before operation showed that these objectives had been attained on the basis of external noise and vibration measurements.

When the Shinkansen began operating between Tokyo and Osaka in October 1964, however, complaints came from some areas. Although noise of about a 90-phon level created by the use of ballastless steel girders was admittedly a problem, it became a source of complaint in built-up urban zones that the Shinkansen entered even though it was of approximately the same level as the noise and vibration caused by the old lines.

Thus public dissatisfaction can be attributed to the fact that pollution problems were no longer measured simply in terms of physical quantity but were influenced by the psychological impact they made on the inhabitants living alongside the railway tracks. Furthermore, it shows a condition in which the background of the public attitude towards pollution cannot be ignored.

Representative examples of noise values after the Shinkansen began operating are shown in Table 1.

Table 1 - Shinkansen Noise Levels

Structure	Roadbed	Sidewalls	Noise Level - dB (A)			
			70	80	90	100
embankment	with ballast	none			•——•—•	
		1.9 m		•——•—•		
viaduct	with ballast	none			•—•—•	
		1.9 m		•——•——•		
steel girder bridge	with ballast	none			⊢————⊣	
		1.9 m		⊢———⊣		
	without ballast	none			⊢————⊣	
		with sound insulation		⊢————⊣		

Notes:
1. Measurements were taken outdoors 25 m from the center of the track at a height of 1.2 m from the ground.
2. Actual measurements were made of trains with speeds over 160 km/h and adjusted to represent the levels at 200 km/h.
3. ——— represents 90% of the range of measured noise levels.
   —•— represents the mean of this 90%.
   - - - represents the total range of measured noise levels (used where the total number of measurements was low).

In the construction of the 164.4-kilometer-long extension from Osaka to Okayama, a reduction in noise and vibration was sought by a drastic improvement in structural design, taking into account experience gained in the Tokyo-Osaka section. For this, the steel girders without ballast were eliminated and replaced by reinforced concrete or prestressed concrete girders with ballast. The sectional dimension of reinforced-concrete viaduct structural members was enlarged to the extent that it did not result in uneconomical design, and the existing sidewalls were heightened to the extent where they served to dampen noise. As a result, the noise level was reduced to about 80 phons at a distance of 25 meters, except under exceptional conditions.

However, in view of complaints that arose after this section went into operation in 1972, sound barrier walls

411

with an overhang were adopted in the 397.9 kilometer extension between Okayama and Hakata as an additional countermeasure, while the route itself was located so as to avoid urban areas by the use of tunnels.

The ratio of tunnel length to the total length of the Shinkansen line is 13 percent between Tokyo and Osaka, but has grown to 35 percent in the Shin-Osaka to Okayama section, and to 56 percent between Okayama and Hakata.

Obtaining approval from inhabitants for construction work became increasingly difficult each year as popular consciousness of pollution grew to an excessively high level during the period when the line was being built.

Moreover, the delay in responding quickly to complaints on sections that had begun operating because of technical and administrative difficulties had the effect of fanning the fires of criticism.

THE ENACTMENT OF LEGAL CONTROLS ON NOISE AND VIBRATION OF THE SHINKANSEN

The Environment Agency in Japan formulates the basic policies concerning pollution in accordance with the Basic Law for Countermeasures Against Pollution, and environmental standards are promulgated and legislation enacted on the recommendations of the Central Consultative Council on Pollution.

As the noise and vibration caused by the Shinkansen tended to become a social issue, the Environment Agency recommended temporary guidelines to the Minister of Transportation in 1972 by which it should endeavor to contain the noise to 80 phons. In the event that the noise level exceeded 85 phons, noise-proofing and other noise-abatement measures for affected housing should be utilized. Japanese National Railways took steps along these lines but was unable to achieve adequate results at an early date.

In July 1975, the Environment Agency promulgated the "Environmental Standards For Noise Levels of the Shinkansen", shown in Tables 2 and 3. These environmental standards are based on Art. 9 of the Basic Law on Pollution which specifies "objectives for administrative efforts laid down by the government as being desirable for the protection of health and the preservation of the environment". Their standard values consequently differ somewhat from, for instance, the regulatory levels established concerning poisons harmful to health. Moreover, they contain an element of ambiguity in what they refer to as "desirable objectives". Thus reaction to these standards ranges from the opinion that they ought to be taken as the ideal but are difficult to attain to the view that they should be taken as a realistic and practical target.

Table 2 - Environmental Standards For Noise Levels of the Shinkansen

Area type	Noise standard
I	under 70 phons
II	under 75 phons

Notes: I represents residential districts; II commercial and industrial districts and others not covered by I where the normal quality of life needs to be protected.

In any case, when looked at from the inhabitants' position, the railways are clearly defined targets for action in that their responsible owners and operators are much easier to determine than in cases involving highways and automobiles.

The base for the values laid down in these environmental standards was established through two surveys of reactions carried out among those living alongside the Shinkansen. The base line was drawn at the level where 30 percent of the respondents said it was noisy.

The Environment Agency in March 1976 also adopted a provisional policy regarding vibration on the grounds that it was desirable to enact the noise countermeasures comprehensively with aid for those living alongside the tracks who suffered from the vibration. This policy calls for "efforts to control the vibration level to 70 dB and to take countermeasures, combined with those against noise, in cases where this level is exceeded".

NOISE AND VIBRATION COUNTERMEASURES FOR THE SHINKANSEN

In view of these strengthened administrative measures taken for the protection of the environment, Japanese National Railways carried out research into pollution countermeasures and has put them into effect.

These steps can be roughly divided into countermeasures against the sources of vibration and noise, and countermeasures relating to nuisance prevention for houses along the right-of-way.

The former deal with improvements and additions to railway structures near the source of noise and vibration, and the latter concern the measures for noise-abatement and anti-vibration on houses adjacent to the tracks where former measures have proven to be insufficient. On occasion, the affected residents are moved to another location.

Table 3   Shinkansen Noise-Prevention Targets

Shinkansen wayside regions		Target achievement periods		
		Period of existing Shinkansen lines	Period for Shinkansen lines under construction	Period for new Shinkansen lines
a	Region of 80 phons or higher	Within 3 years	At time of opening	
b	Region of 75 to under 80 phons	i	Within 7 years	Within 3 years from opening	At time of opening
		ii	Within 10 years		
c	Region of 70 to under 75 phons	Within 10 years	Within 5 years from opening	

Among the measures taken against sources of noise are the strengthening of sound-barrier walls in viaduct and embankment sections. From Shin-Osaka westward, vertical reinforced-concrete walls 10 to 15 centimeters thick and 1.9 to 2.4 meters high were constructed, together with other types of sound-barrier walls. Between Tokyo and Osaka, the strength of the existing constructions proved insufficient to support such walls, so frameworks of H-shaped steel pillars and beams were erected and covered both inside and out with cement-asbestos panels. Sound-barrier walls have the effect of reducing noise by 7 to 10 phons.

Another method is covering the steel girders without ballast. This consists of affixing noise-insulating plates suspended with cushions under and on the sides of the main plate girders and truss girders, reducing by 15 to 20 phons noise that had reached a near-100-phon level. Noise abatement studies related to the track and wheels are also being made. The results of these measures are shown in Table 1.

The first step in nuisance prevention for houses situated along the right-of-way is to subsidize and execute the installation of noise-abatement devices for homeowners. Because of Japan's humid temperate climate, most houses are of wooden construction and of a traditional open design that makes it difficult to soundproof them or make them resistant to vibration. These conditions call for the replacement of walls and ceilings with soundproofing materials and the fitting of double-pane, glass windows in aluminum sashes. These steps result in hermetically sealed houses, which in turn require the installation of air-conditioning equipment. While the normal insulation capacity of a traditional Japanese house against noise is about 10 to 20 phons, such improvements can generally heighten this capacity to about 30 phons. When such changes cannot be expected to reduce the in-house noise level to less than 60 phons or when vibration is very strong, the owners are urged to move, with JNR buying their property.

JNR estimates that the number of households where the noise level exceeds 80 phons and which require these measures to be completed within the next three years is 18,000. If the 70-to-75 phon standard must be met, this number reaches some 130,000.

THE EFFECTS AND PROBLEMS OF ENVIRON-MENTAL PRESERVATION ALONG THE SHINKANSEN

Inasmuch as the preservation of the environment is a most reasonable aspiration, JNR does not begrudge its efforts in this direction. But it cannot be denied that the imposition of too hasty measures for this purpose leads, in effect, to unnecessary confusion.

Those who dwell alongside a railway line like the Shinkansen, which is not utilized daily like commuter lines and whose stations are 30 kilometers apart, do not develop a sense of familiarity with such a facility. The imposition of various control measures based on changeable, emotional factors such as complaints from residents with only a few surveys as a guide is therefore open to question.

Even conceding that, as a matter of principle, it is the polluter who should pay, the resulting burdens are beyond the capacity of the railways to bear in the light of their present financial condition as well as in consideration of the colossal amount of work required to carry out countermeasures designed to meet the large number of demands. Many are concerned by the manner in which controls have taken priority over administrative capacity without a sufficient prior investigation of this capacity being carried out. Moreover, such policies cannot be effective unless they are adopted in an integrated manner together with other policies such as those related to land utilization, building regulations and the construction of suitable private and public buildings and facilities alongside the tracks. While proposals have been made to this effect, they are far from being implemented.

Consequently, further studies must be carried out before the remaining problems of environmental preservation along the Shinkansen can be solved.

OTHER PROBLEMS

Cited above are the major environmental problems concerning the Shinkansen - namely noise and vibration. Some other existing problems concern interference with television reception, the creation of shaded areas that prevent the penetration of sunlight, and the noise from pressure waves in tunnels.

The TV interference problem is being solved by the erection of common transmission antennas connected to affected homes by cable.

As to the sunlight problem, we have established a set of rules for compensation to homeowners in keeping with similar measures adopted by other public bodies.

Pressure waves radiating from tunnel exits are created when a train enters a tunnel, where slabs tracks are used, traveling at a high rate of speed. These waves travel at sonic speed and emerge from the opposite end of the tunnel. The consequent minor variation in atmospheric pressure has a boom effect like that of a cannon being fired that is heard in neighboring houses. We have succeeded in eliminating this nuisance by installing experimental damping hoods at the entrance to the tunnels to absorb the variation in atmospheric pressure. We intend to apply this process to other tunnels where such effects have been reported.

Environmental impact assessment and transport facilities

by

A. Alexandre

and

C. Avérous

Organization for Economic Co-operation and Development

INTRODUCTION

Since four or five years the context of transport policies has been evolving very profoundly in developed countries.

Firstly, *uncertainty about the future of the general economic situation* leads to long-term options being kept open and to operation within a shorter horizon for analysis and action. This leads to the difficult question of inserting heavy investment choices into more adaptive processes of decision and transport planning.

Secondly, the diversification of both individual and collective values and the *uncertainty concerning the future value changes,* coupled with the more active role that individuals and groups of citizens are taking in decision-making processes, lead to questions of *arbitrage among the interests of various groups, between local and national interests and questions of solidarity between generations.* These questions are at the heart of environmental and quality of life concerns.

The irreversible character and the role played by major transport infrastructure in spatial and economic development seem a priori hard to integrate within this double context of uncertainty about the economic future and trends in social values. But studies of environmental impact assessments of major transport infrastructures testify to a new *effort to respond to this dilemma inherent in major transport facilities namely to reconcile irreversibility and changing needs.*

We will attempt now to *evaluate the environmental impact assessments* and more precisely on one hand the methods and on the other hand the processes of environmental impact assessment presently used. We shall stress the *impact of infrastructures.* However, it must be underlined that environmental impact assessment apply also to transport "products" such as supersonic planes, VSTOL, electric cars, oil tankers, etc. and that these latter environmental impact assessments can have important international implications, in particular if they are used as non-tariff barriers to trade.

EVALUATION OF METHODS OF ENVIRONMENTAL IMPACT ASSESSMENTS

The methods of evaluation used within environmental impact assessment are not by nature fundamentally different from the analysis of other impacts. We can distinguish in particular:

i) the expert meeting, or more broadly the use of informed judgement;

ii) the analysis of cost-damages and cost-benefits;

iii) the analysis using multiple objectives (multiple criteria); and

iv) the analysis of technology assessment.

On the basis of this experience, it is possible to draw the following lessons.

1. Environmental impact assessment contributed to the analysis of the impacts either in quantitative and non-monetary terms, or in qualitative terms. It is however clear that a monetary analysis of damages concerning the environment can constitute a useful complement. In particular one can ask whether such analysis of damages should only follow the decisions of courts about the compensation to be accorded to victims (as it has been the case for safety) or whether they could not come before court decisions and provide the foundation of such decisions. For instance the British Land Compensation Act of 1973 obliges the dwellings exposed to level of noise exceeding 68 dBA (expressed in L_{10}) on exterior walls to be sound proofed at 100% level, as well as making obligatory compensation for a loss of property value due to noise or pollution. The additional cost of freeways due to this concern is usually estimated at 10 to 15%. It is important that research be made in this field to provide better foundations for the compensation decisions.

2. Environmental impact assessments contributed to widening the set of choice criteria and therefore to reducing the importance of cost-benefit analysis and cost damage analysis and to making more explicit and in a more disaggregated way the necessary choices among criteria. By increasing the heterogeneity of the set of criteria, *evaluation and assessment is no longer the selection of the best alternative but information to be fed into a wider decision process.*

Thus, it becomes possible to present in a better way the effects on different groups, and to improve analysis of the conflicts among criteria. Evaluation is thus conceived as a tool for decisionmaking and not as the decision itself. This is a necessary condition for any technical study in a democratic process, if we want these studies to have credibility for decision takers, for professionals and for citizens in general.

3. These environmental impact assessments can however be improved. First, they often deal with a *spectrum of alternatives* which has not enough contrast. For instance, not only alternatives about the characteristics of a certain infrastructure, but also about its location as well as alternatives using other modes including the solution of not doing anything, should be part of the scope of such studies.

4. Second, environmental impact assessment should also consider a wider *spectrum of criteria:*

(i) Indeed the environment does not equate annoyance or pollution. It is also *quality* of life. In this wider sense the impact of transport facilities on the environment *can be positive* and is not solely negative. As we can all see in the Netherlands, the environment is already transformed by man, and is already integrated in his culture. The negative character of the word "impact" is

414

n that sense to be regretted: any new transformation is not necessarily negative.

(ii) Impact assessments must consider the *various aspects of the project:* the impacts of its construction, of its physical existence, of its use, as well as its indirect effects.

(iii) The analysed impacts must be local as well as regional, national, and international.

5. It is thirdly important to distinguish clearly between a descriptive analysis of impacts and a normative analysis of impacts. In that sense, it is appropriate to avoid the confusion between factual information and personal views.

6. Moreover, the foundations of the technical analysis of the effects on the environment have often to be handled with caution for two reasons: on the one hand, knowledge is not sufficient in this area; and *research is needed;* on the other hand, the *dissemination* of available knowledge is not sufficient either - for instance we know a reasonable amount about the question of noise, but this knowledge is not sufficiently widespread. It is *information and training* in the professional milieux and of the public which are called for here.

EVALUATION OF PROCEDURES OF ENVIRONMENTAL IMPACT ASSESSMENT PRESENTLY IN USE

The appropriate insertion of impact studies into decision processes is necessary for impact studies to have a *concrete* effect, in other terms *for impact studies to have an impact.*

The Major Types of Procedures

The United States law on the national environmental policy introduced in 1969 the requirement of an *environmental impact statement* for any Federal action having an effect on the quality of man's environment. The *creation of a specific procedure for environmental impact assessment* was an innovation. Similar types of procedures have later been defined in a number of states of the United States (sometimes for public as well as private projects) and in other countries such as Canada, Australia, France. A law is in preparation in Japan. The experience of these countries - United States, Canada, Australia (the implementation ordinances are not yet available for the French law of 1976) provide the basis for a first review of the advantages as well as the limits of this procedure.

It is important to distinguish the approach of the United States from a second approach exemplified by the choice made by the Department of the Environment in United Kingdom, which considers that the *assessment of environmental impacts must be inserted explicitly within existing planning mechanisms* and thus *do not require any specific procedure.*

Finally, a third approach considers that the usual planning mechanisms are sufficient to treat environmental concerns. There is no need to establish either *a specific procedure* or an explicit mechanism. Such an approach can be justified in countries where the environmental "consciousness" is traditionally high and where land-use planning is already rigorous. . .or on the contrary in countries where such environmental concerns are considered secondary.

Lessons to be learned from Environmental Impact Statements

The experience acquired from environmental impact statements allows us to draw a certain number of conclusions, firstly negative ones.

1. It seems that such environmental impact statements may imply additional *costs and additional delays* for the implementation of projects. However, such a judgment must be qualified to take into account opportunity costs and delays (by comparing to a situation without environmental impact statements). The example of sections of motorways missing in larger networks such as the "embarcadero" freeway in San Francisco, or the example of the Narita airport (Tokyo) are significant in that respect. This new international airport of Tokyo was originally planned to open in 1971 and is not yet open to traffic because of the opposition of local populations (particularly of farmers) and the cost of a day's delay in the opening is currently estimated at 60,000 dollars.

2. The creation of an additional procedure may appear as a heavy bureaucratic requirement, particularly if problems arise such as coordination with other existing procedures, or, let us say, of harmonisation of the actions of different administrations. In the United States context, the importance of the courts often leads to more emphasis on the satisfaction of court's procedural requirements and less analysis of the environmental concerns themselves.

3. The effect of environmental impact statements on the definition and the implementation of the project can be nil if the statement comes too late and if it is done by a group without power over the orientation of the project. On the contrary the effect can be to simply stop the project in the case where the study is useless, or situation of conflict develops sometimes with the arbitrage of courts as this may happen in the United States context. However, these impact statements have three major positive effects of *education,* of *prevention* and of *concertation.*

4. The impact statements by contributing to the integration of environmental concerns have a *pedagogic effect on the public* (through participation in decision processes), on the *administrations* which propose and/or control the project and the *consulting firms* (which usually do the impact statements and sometimes allocate to these studies an important part of their activities).

5. As far as they have an effect on the content of the project the impact statements have *a major preventive role.* It is sometimes better to modify the route in advance than to create ex-post under local pressure an expensive barrier against noise. This *preventive* aspect is essential since the environmental policies, like health policies, cannot restrict themselves to being mainly curative as this would imply much higher costs and lower efficiency.

6. The Environmental impact statements have finally an effect on the decisionmaking process by establishing a consultation mechanism among administrations, politicians and the various publics. It makes explicit the necessity of a political mechanism to integrate the concerns of different groups. It seems that such instruments could be viewed as contributing in a positive way to the search for a consensus and for the solution of conflicts through dialogue rather than through arbitrage. They can, if they are efficient, become precious tools to improve *local democracy* and to lead everyone to take more into account other people's concerns.

Environmental impact assessment of transport facilities are still too recent to allow a definite judgement. They are a good example of the need for both qualitative and quantitative research, both on methods and on decision processes. If they can contribute to a better understanding between people, if they can lead to a satisfactory balance between local interests and collective interests, impact assessments will surely be a useful tool since preventive analysis and action will always be preferable to costly curative solutions.

REFERENCES

OECD (1973): **"Environmental Implications of Options in Urban Mobility",** Paris

OECD (1974): **Recommendation of the Council on the Analysis of the Environmental Consequences of Significant Public and Private Projects,** C(74)216, Paris

OECD (1974): **"Environmental Damage Costs",** Environment Directorate, Paris

OECD (1975): **"Airports and the Environment",** Environment Directorate, Paris

OECD (1976): **"Analysis of the Environmental Consequen-** ces of Significant Public and Private Projects' (ENV/URB/76.7/3.2), Environment Directorate, Paris

OECD (1976): **"Evaluation of Traffic Policies for the Improvement of the Urban Environment",** Environment Directorate, Paris

OECD (1976): **"Social Cost of Noise",** Environment Directorate, Paris

FOOTNOTE

The opinions expressed in this document are those of the author and do not necessarily reflect those of OECD.

Measuring the impacts of Singapore's area license scheme

EDWARD P. HOLLAND

PETER L. WATSON

Urban Projects Department, World Bank

INTRODUCTION

Research on transport policy suffers from the impracticality of setting up closely controlled laboratory experiments with and without whatever policy measure is to be investigated. Comparisons between different countries or (in urban transport) different cities with or without some specific policy are confounded by differences in many factors other than the one to be studied. Before-and-after studies in one city are usually hampered by a lack of advance knowledge that would permit gathering an adequate data base before the policy change takes place.

One of the rare exceptions to the last statement was the case of the Area License Scheme instituted in Singapore in 1975. With more than a year's advance notice, members of the World Bank's Transport Research Division, in cooperation with the Government of Singapore and with support from the United Nations Environment Programme and the United States Department of Transportation, were able to design and carry out an extensive program of empirical data collection before the Scheme went into effect and a follow-up program afterward. This made before-and-after comparisons possible on many different impacts of the measures.

At the most general level of impact monitoring, one might say that the only requirement is to measure vehicle flows -- distinguishing types, time of day, location, and the occupancy of cars. This would be more than enough information to show whether the target, set in terms of reduced entries into the central part of the city, is being met. However, a more basic purpose underlying the target was a reduction in congestion. Hence it is desirable also to measure vehicle speeds as a measure of how freely the traffic moves or how much it is slowed by congestion. Beyond simply monitoring the effectiveness of the policy measures, the Bank's research program was intended to learn the differential impacts on different groups of people, to do some elementary evaluation of these impacts, and to gather and analyze information on underlying relationships that would help in designing and assessing the merits of restraint schemes for other cities. For these broader purposes, travel behavior interviews were conducted at several thousand households, interview surveys were made of business conditions and public opinion, and observations were made on pedestrian movements and air pollution.

SINGAPORE - BACKGROUND INFORMATION

The main island of Singapore is situated about 150 kilometers north of the equator at the tip of the Malay Peninsula. It is diamond-shaped, measuring 42 km from east to west and 22 km from north to south with an area of about 584 square km. The City of Singapore is located on the southern coast of this island and approximately 70% of the island's population and 70% of jobs can be found within a radius of 8 km around the central area. The population of Singapore is about 2.25 million, of whom about 74% are Chinese, 14% Malay, and 8% Indian. Singapore's strategic position in Southeast Asia has given it considerable importance. Its port is the fourth busiest in the world and an active industrialization policy has resulted in rapid economic growth.

At the end of 1975, 280,378 motor vehicles were registered in Singapore. 143,155 were private cars - a ratio of one car to 16 persons. 4,585 were buses, 41,391 were goods vehicles, and 83,145 were motorcycles or scooters. From 1962 to 1973 the average annual growth rate of private cars had been 8.8% per annum. In more recent years, government efforts to limit the growth of ownership of private cars through heavy taxation have stabilized the fleet at around 143,000 cars.

Two major transport studies were carried out in Singapore between 1967 and 1974. The first was a comprehensive land use and transportation study and the second was the first phase of a study which involved a more detailed examination of Singapore's public transport requirements. Both studies independently reached the conclusion that restraints on both car ownership and car usage would be necessary before 1992. This implied radical changes in terms of both the policies of the Government and the attitudes of individuals toward car ownership and usage. Both would have to be re-oriented towards a more widespread use of public transportation. Against this background, a transportation strategy for Singapore emerged. The measures adopted included:

a) land use development strategies to minimize the need to travel,

b) the implementation of a modest road construction program,

c) traffic management measures to promote better utilization of existing road capacity,

d) rationalization and improvement of existing public bus services, including expansion of the bus fleet, improved maintenance, and the introduction of 14 km of reserved bus lanes in the central area,

e) the provision of supplementary bus services during peak hours by using the school bus fleet and other private buses to carry commuters,

f) increases in the various taxes on private car ownership,

g) revision of regulations on car parking within the central area, to discourage commuter traffic while catering to the needs of business and shopping for short time parking,

---

The views expressed in this paper are those of the authors and not necessarily those of the World Bank.

h) prohibition of all large vehicles with three or more axles within the central area during peak hours, and

i) a national campaign to promote and encourage staggered work hours and car pooling.

A high level, interministerial Road Transport Action Committee was set up to coordinate the transport planning measures and to formulate future policies. Early in 1974, the committee considered the problem of growing traffic congestion in the central area and concluded that it would be appropriate to introduce restraints on the use of private cars in the central area as soon as possible.

THE TRAFFIC RESTRAINT SCHEME

The Singapore Government set itself the specific goal of designing a scheme to reduce peak-hour traffic by 25 to 30 per cent. It was estimated that this reduction would restore reasonably good traffic conditions equivalent to those found during off-peak hours. At the same time, several constraints were recognized. First, accessibility to and mobility within the central area should be maintained to protect the economic vitality of the area. Thus, efficient and reliable alternative modes of transport should be available to those commuters who would be discouraged from driving into the central area. Second, the mobility of the private car should be recognized as a benefit, and restrictions should apply only when and where they are needed to combat local congestion. Third, the scheme should be easy to administer and enforce. Fourth, it should not require a subsidy.

Several alternative policies were considered. General fiscal measures, such as import duties or gasoline taxes, do not discourage the use of cars at specific times or in specific areas; vehicle metering requires the use of special equipment that is not currently available in quantity; applying tolls to city streets requires collection facilities that take up too much urban space and themselves contribute to congestion. The Government rejected these alternatives and based its traffic restraint scheme primarily on area licensing supplemented by increased parking fees, combined with a park-and-ride scheme to provide motorists with an attractive alternative mode of transport. The Government was confident that it could deal with the problems of administering and enforcing these measures.

In the Singapore context, the key concept underlying the area license scheme is that a special, supplementary license must be obtained and displayed if a motorist wishes to enter a designated restricted area within which congestion is to be reduced.

The Restricted Zone

The Restricted Zone includes the areas with congestion problems, leaves diversion routes for motorists who do not have destinations in the zone, minimizes the number of entry points that have to be monitored, and takes advantage of existing facilities for use as fringe car parks. The zone covers about 500 hectares and has 22 entry points.

The License

The Government had no previous experience to guide it in setting the license fee. Thus, it was necessary to set the fee by judgment. Licenses were initially sold for S$60 (US$26) a month or S$3 (US$1.30) a day. They have since been raised to S$80 a month and S$4 a day.

Categories of Vehicles

The requirement to display an area license does not apply to buses or commercial vehicles, in order to favor public transport and maintain commercial activity. To encourage higher vehicle occupancy and more efficient use of road space, car pools (defined as cars carrying at least four persons) are also exempt from the license requirements, as are motorcycles. These exemptions also counter objections that driving into the center becomes a luxury only the rich can afford; others can also do it if they form car pools or ride motorcycles. Taxis are not exempt.

Restricted Times

The aim of the Singapore Government was to reduce the congestion arising during the peak hour, and it was thought that applying restrictions during the morning peak would significantly reduce traffic both then and in the evening peak. Therefore, the scheme was designed to operate from 7:30 a.m. to 9:30 a.m. After implementation, congestion developed after 9:30 and the time period was extended to 10:15 a.m.

The Park-and Ride Scheme

In order to provide an alternative mode of transport for motorists who had become accustomed to driving into the central area, a park-and-ride scheme was designed to complement the Area License Scheme. Ten thousand spaces in car parks around the periphery of the restricted zone were opened to commuters, and special shuttle buses were introduced to carry commuters from the fringe car parks to the central area. The shuttle bus routes had limited stops, and only seated passengers were carried in an attempt to provide a fast, comfortable alternative to the car. The combined monthly cost of parking and using the shuttle was set at S$30(US$13). This service attracted very few patrons.

Parking policy

The third element of the scheme was an increase of about 100 per cent in parking charges at public car parks within the restricted zone. Previously, there had generally been a flat rate of S$0.40 (US$0.18) an hour. The new rates are higher and are designed to reflect the geographical distribution of congestion and to favor short-term as opposed to all-day parking. In the most congested part of the Restricted Zone, the rates are:

1st hour	S$0.50 (US$0.22)
2nd hour	S$1.00 (US$0.44)
Each subsequent 1/2 hour	S$1.00 (US$0.44)

The monthly rate for all-day parking in the central area has also been increased from S$40-60 to S$50-80.

MONITORING THE DIRECT IMPACTS

Traffic Flow Measurements

The Singapore Public Works Department scheduled extensive measurements of traffic volumes, composition, and occupancy. Therefore, the Bank undertook no flow measurements except those that came as a byproduct of the speed measurements described below. The Government's program started about three months before introduction of the Area License Scheme and was continued on a monthly basis for about six months afterward, and then on a quarterly basis. Some of the traffic counts were done by observers, who recorded the types of vehicles and on some occasions, the occupancy of cars. Other counts were made by automatic machines, which record only the total numbers of vehicles without distinguishing types. The primary focus of the monitoring was on morning traffic entering the Restricted Zone, but some data were also collected in the afternoon, mainly on outbound traffic.

These measurements showed that the number of cars entering the Restricted Zone between 7:30 and 10:15 a.m. fell by 73 per cent from 42,790 in March to an average of 11,363 in September and Oktober 1975. The volume of cars entering during the half hour before 7:30 a.m. rose by 23 per cent as people started their trips earlier to avoid paying the Area License fee. The exemption from the license requirement for cars with four or more occupants ("car pools") induced a large increase in occupancy during the restricted hours. The absolute number of car pools entering during the 7:30 - 10:15 period increased by about 60 per cent at the same time that the total number of cars including car pools was falling by 73 per cent. The proportion of car pools thus jumped from less than 7 to 37 per cent for those hours.

Before these changes, cars had constituted about 60 per cent of all motor vehicles entering the area during these hours, the other 40 per cent being taxis, goods vehicles, buses, motorcycles, and scooters. Taxis were at first exempt from the license requirement, and the number of them entering the Restricted Zone during restricted hours increased dramatically. Three weeks later, their exemption was rescinded, and the number entering between 7:30 and 9:30 a.m. fell to 17 per cent of the level before the scheme began. By September and October, during the extended restricted hours, the number of taxis entering seemed to have stabilized at 35 per cent of its original level. Flows of other vehicle types either increased or decreased by much smaller proportions, and the net result was a 44 per cent reduction in total traffic during the 7:30 to 10:15 restricted period.

A surprising finding from the flow counts was that traffic flows in the evening peak (4:00 to 7:00 p.m.) changed very little. It had been expected that reductions in the morning peak flows would be reflected by a sizeable reduction in the evening. It was assumed that much of the reduction in flow in the morning would be the result of commuters using other modes of travel and leaving their cars home. These cars, then, would not be available for the homebound trip after work. When the flow data showed only a 6 per cent decline in the evening peak, it could not be explained until a detailed analysis of the home interview data gave enough clues to piece together the explanation.

The main factors were "trans-Restricted-Zone trips", trip scheduling and taxi trips. The term "trans-Restricted-Zone" refers to trips with an origin on one side of the zone and destination on the other. It was found that many car drivers making work trips of this type used the ring road to bypass the zone in the morning but returned home through the zone in the evening when the restrictions were not in effect. Another group of commuters, with work places in the Restricted Zone, took to driving in before 7:30 a.m, thus contributing to the reduction in traffic during the restricted hours, but still drove home during the evening peak. Taxis, as mentioned earlier, entered the zone in greatly reduced numbers in the restricted period, but of course the logic that suggests a reflection in the evening of reduced morning commuting traffic does not apply to taxis. In fact, it seems that the number of taxis operating during the evening peak may have increased markedly. This is not known with certainty, since the data on evening flows before the license scheme started do not distinguish vehicles by types, having been obtained from mechanical counters.

Vehicle Speed Measurements

An important indicator of performance of the traffic system is mean vehicle speed. The speed, of course, depends on the level of congestion, and one of the purposes of congestion-reducing measures is to allow traffic to move faster. It should be recognized that there are other purposes, including reduction in annoyance and frustration of vehicle-users, improvement in pedestrian conditions, in air quality, and in the general ambience of the city. Nevertheless, the expected increase in traffic speed was one of the important effects to measure.

In order to measure mean speeds with confidence and to obtain a measure of the distribution around the mean, we decided that relatively large numbers of observations should be obtained on any road link at any time. To accomplish this, we adapted a method of license plate matching which has previously been used mainly on uninterrupted stretches of highway. Several observers at each end of a segment read license numbers and occasional time signals into hand-held cassette tape recorders. Observations were made for ten minutes out of each quarter hour, continuing for an hour or sometimes longer.

Afterward, the information on the tapes was used in a computer process which related the license observations to the time signals and calculated the average speed of each vehicle whose license number was recorded at the successive stations. The computer program also screened out implausible values that sometimes resulted from errors in recording or coding and computed mean speeds and standard deviations for each vehicle type in each ten-minute period on a particular road segment.

Obviously, reliable results from this procedure depend on accurate recording of time, including the establishment of a common time scale for observers at different locations. The procedure that was eventually developed made use of several digital electric watches. The watches were synchronized within less than half a second before each observation session, and one was issued to each group of two or three observers stationed on the same corner of any intersection. In this way, the problem of the common time scale was solved. The use of digital watches also practically eliminated error in reading the time, which had evidently occurred rather frequently in earlier operations using either conventional stop-watches or sweep-second-hand watches.

Unfortunately, this procedure was not perfected until after the Area License Scheme was in effect. Data collected before that time proved unusable because of many errors in time recording and in determining the corrections necessary for synchronizing time scales. Thus, before-and-after comparisons were not possible. However, in the later period reliable data were obtained at different times of day, so that comparisons could be made between restrained and unrestrained conditions.

Because of the earlier problems, we decided in the final survey to conduct moving-car observations at the same time as the license recording, so that results from the two methods could be compared. Eight moving-car circuits (loops) were laid out so that they covered a sample of routes within the Restricted Zone, along radial roads, and along part of the ring road. Each circuit included segments selected as suitable for license-matching observations. The operations were scheduled so that whenever licenses were being matched on a given segment, the moving car was surveying the loop that included it.

In general, the speeds from the two methods were scattered over the same range for each segment, although the number of moving-car runs accomplished during an hour of observations was usually only three or four. There was no systematic bias between the mean speeds from the two methods.

From comparisons between restrained and unrestrained conditions, inferences have been drawn about changes due to the Area License Scheme. Mean speeds within the Restricted Zone were 22 per cent higher during the restricted hours than during the evening peak (33 kilometers per hour compared to 27). It seems plausible that the speed during the morning peak before the Area License Scheme was about the same as that in the evening, and therefore that there has been a 22 per cent improvement within the zone during the restricted hours. On the ring road, speeds were 20 per cent lower in the morning restricted period than in the evening peak, and this is taken to imply a 20 per cent slowdown in the morning due to the Area License Scheme. On inbound radial roads in the morning, the flow with the License Scheme in effect is relatively uncongested and travels at almost the same speed as in the evening. It is assumed that before the License Scheme was instituted the speed inbound in the morning was approximately the same as that observed on the outbound radials in the evening. On the basis of this assumption there was a 10 per cent increase in speed on inbound radials during the restricted hours, from 29 kph to 32 kph. Presumably, the speeds on outbound radials were not affected by the scheme, inasmuch as outbound flow volumes diminished only slightly.

Travel Behavior Impacts

The direct impact of the traffic restraint scheme on travel behavior falls on those car owners who formerly drove into the Restricted Zone. However, many other groups - bus riders, pedestrians, as well as other motorists - are also affected to some degree. Changes in the travel behavior of those directly impacted by the scheme have widespread ramifications on other groups of travelers. For example, traffic diverted away from the central area cause congestion on peripheral streets.

Thus, to provide an overall picture of the impact of the traffic restrain scheme on travel behavior, it was necessary to obtain information on the characteristics of trips by users of all modes traveling into, through, or outside the Restricted Zone before and after implementation. It was also necessary to obtain data on the characteristics of the travelers in order to be able to classify impacts by socio-economic groups.

A household survey program was carried out to obtain this information. A sample of 2,053 households was selected, made up of 1,554 vehicle-owning households and 449 non-vehicle-owning households. The former contained households selected at random from the data files of the Registrar of Vehicles and supplemented by a sample selected at random from households owning cars that were observed crossing the Restricted Zone cordon before the Area License Scheme was introduced. The supplementary sample was added to ensure adequate representation for the primary impact group -- households whose members drive cars into the Restricted Zone. The non-vehicle-owning households were selected at random from a local sample frame. Each household was interviewed once before the introduction of the Area License Scheme and again four to six months later. A household informant provided information on the household and each person was then interviewed to obtain personal information as a detailed record of all trips made on the day preceding the interview.

The data were analyzed at two levels. The first was at the macro-level; this is convenient for examining the overall changes in the proportions of people making different decisions, for example, the proportion of people traveling by bus before and after the introduction of the Area License Scheme. Analysis at the second, or micro-level, was carried out on a sub-sample of 719 people who made home-to-work trips to the Restricted Zone both before and after the introduction of the scheme. The micro-level analysis makes it possible to observe the complex and sometimes opposing changes in individual behavior that underlie the global results.

Impacts on People Making Work Trips

The most important impacts in this category were expected to be on the choice of mode and on travel times of people who traveled to work in the Restricted Zone.

For these people, the monthly cost of commuting by car rose from S$153 (US$65) to S$228 (US$97). In response, the proportion of trips that members of vehicle-owning households made by car fell from 56 per cent to 46 per cent while the bus share rose from 33 per cent to 46 per cent. Within the declining car mode, the car pool share rose by a factor of three, from 14 to 41 per cent of all car trips. In addition to the modal changes, there was an important change towards earlier starting times. The proportion of work trips that were started befor 7:30 a.m. rose from 27 to 40 per cent for car drivers and from 17 to 28 per cent for car passengers. The data indicate that about the same numbers of people from vehicle-owning households chose the options of changing to the bus, joining or forming car pools, and making the trip at a different time. People form non-vehicle-owning households did not change their behavior -- 90 per cent of them traveled by bus both before and after the introduction of the Area License Scheme.

The changes in travel time for travelers who did not change mode were very small. Car drivers, on average, took about one minute longer; bus riders from vehicle-owning households reported taking, on average, half a minute longer. However, bus riders from non-vehicle-owning households, who constitute the vast majority of bus riders in Singapore, reported taking, on average, about one minute less. Car drivers who changed to the bus took an average of nine minutes longer, and bus riders who changed to the car took an average of nine minutes less.

The second group to be significantly affected were travelers who traveled to work through the Restricted Zone to destinations on the other side of the city. For these people, the proportion of trips made by car fell from 53.5 per cent to 50 per cent, but the proportion of car trips made in car pools rose from 9 to 28 per cent. The proportion of trips started before 7:30 a.m. rose from 50 to 60 per cent. Of course these travelers had the additional option of detouring around the Restricted Zone. Before the introduction of the scheme, 88 per cent of trips passed through the zone. Afterwards, only 66 per cent of them drove through the zone, and of these, only 13 per cent drove through during the restricted hours. The remainder changed time to avoid the fee.

Impacts on People Making Shopping Trips

The number of shopping trips made to destinations in the Restricted Zone fell by 34 per cent, but not all of this can be attributed to the Area License Scheme, since the number of shopping trips outside the zone also fell by 14 per cent. The information gathered in the business survey indicates that the remaining 20 per cent is due to recession, decentralization of jobs and residences, and the increased parking charges associated with the Area License Scheme. It seems unlikely that the contribution of the increased parking charges could account for more than about 5 per cent.

Impacts on People Traveling Outside the Restricted Zone

It is useful at this point to note that over 70 per cent of all trips and over 60 per cent of work trips are made outside the Restricted Zone. The majority of trips to work outside the Restricted Zone are made by bus, and the majority of shopping trips are made on foot. The people making these trips have been unaffected by the Area License Scheme. Those motorists who use the ring road have been adversely affected by the increased congestion and reduced speeds.

LESS DIRECT EFFECTS

Flow counts, speed measurements, and household interviews provided the data on the changes in traffic performance and the changes in people's travel behavior underlying the traffic effects. For a general evaluation of the scheme, research was also conducted on some other effects.

Impacts on Business

Many people have expressed concern that a scheme like Singapore's would hurt business in the central area of the city. After exploring the possibilities of collecting before-and-after data on retail sales and other business transactions or on physical indicators of activity, we concluded that the available data in Singapore were not sufficiently comprehensive to yield a direct measure of business conditions, and that it would be too costly to design and carry out a reliable quantitative survey of transactions. Instead, in-depth interviews were conducted with selected leaders in the business community, including store managers, bankers, wholesalers, and property agents. Members of this group generally agreed that the Area License Scheme had not had an adverse impact on the business climate. It was believed that the increased parking charges had further depressed central area retail sales that were already suffering from recession and decentralization. It was also believed that the restrictions on car travel to the center were accelerating the existing trend towards decentralization. In both cases, the Area License Scheme and the increase in parking charges were viewed as adding to existing problems and not creating new ones.

Certain industries and business have been specifically affected. Some companies have been involved in additional expenses to buy licenses for company cars. Taxi operators report that business is now very poor during the morning shift. They are not able to recoup their losses later in the day. Wholesalers and retailers, on the other hand, report that they have benefited from easier movement of goods in the central area during the morning when many deliveries are made. The bus company also enjoys higher revenues and improved conditions in which to operate. They claim to be able to meet schedules better and avoid delays as a result.

Effects on Pedestrians

In order to assess the effects of the traffic restraint policies on conditions for pedestrians, observations of pedestrian movements at various times of day were made by time lapse photography at a number of different locations within the Restricted Zone. It was originally expected that reduced traffic would result in reduced delays to pedestrians trying to cross busy streets and that measuring crossing times before and after the traffic restraints were imposed would yield a measure of any improvement in conditions. Results in these terms proved inconclusive, and a careful study of the films indicated that, with less traffic, many people were crossing in more leisurely fashion, so that longer crossing times did not necessarily mean delays due to traffic or indicate worse conditions. Analysis of the films in terms of the frequency with which pedestrians had to change pace or back up in response to challenges by motor vehicles showed that the ease of crossing streets had clearly improved. One of the advantages of using time lapse photography was the feasibility of re-examining the films in terms of different criteria than had originally been thought adequate.

Air Pollution

Although air pollution had not been considered a problem, the Singapore Government's Anti-Pollution Unit made measurements of air pollutants at several downtown locations before and after inauguration of the Area License Scheme. The most clearcut result was the not surprising fact that carbon monoxide levels varied through the day in much the same way as traffic flows. The level during restricted hours, which had formerly been a peak, was reduced below that in the middle of the day. All-day average levels were also lower.

Public Opinion

One of the ultimate objectives, but a somewhat intangible one, was to improve the quality of the central city for the people who worked, lived, shopped, and did business in it. To probe this dimension as well as to find out whether the policies viewed as fair or unfair to particular groups, opinions were solicited from people in on-street interviews carried out in the central area and on the outskirts thereof.

The public opinion survey revealed that Singaporeans believed that the Area License Scheme had relieved congestion and improved conditions in central Singapore. Pedestrians, bus riders, taxi riders, and motorcyclists believed that they personally were better off as a result of the scheme. Central area residents reported that it was easier and safer to cross roads, that general conditions in the Restricted Zone had improved, and that the amount of fumes had been reduced. Motorists reported that they were worse off but not greatly so. All, including the motorists, believed that the effect on Singapore as a city was favorable.

EVALUATION AND CONCLUSIONS

The various impacts of Singapore's Area License Scheme are set forth above in terms of a wide variety of variables measured on different scales or, in some instances, assessed qualitatively. The increased ease of crossing streets for pedestrians, cleaner air, and people's perceptions that downtown Singapore has been improved are important benefits, but do not lend themselves to evaluation in economic terms without strong and arbitrary assumptions. The impact of the scheme on business was identified only qualitatively, not only because of a lack of statistics but perhaps even more importantly because the impact of the Area License Scheme could not be quantitatively separated from the effects of the general recession or from the existing trend toward decentralization.

Because of interest in having some portion of the evaluation done in economic terms even if many important elements were omitted, a calculation was made of the value of net time savings to trip-makers. It must be stressed that the debate over the value of small time savings is unresolved. It is the view of the authors that time savings such as those derived from the household survey are too small (a) to be perceived by the travelers and (b) to be considered of value in an economic evaluation. Nevertheless, for the purpose of arriving at a figure comparable to those resulting from analyses of other sorts of projects, all time savings and losses, no matter how small, were valued at the same rate. Like all value-of-time analysis, this one also involves a value judgement about the social value to society of time saved by individuals. For the present analysis, this was assumed to be independent of individual income levels. Thus all time savings and losses were valued at one Singapore dollar per hour, which is between 25 and 30 per cent of the average wage rate. Based on these assumptions, the investment expenditures for fringe car parks, shuttle bus facilities (but not buses), signs, and ticket booths, the minimum estimate of the rate of return in the first year was 15 per cent. This counts only net travel time savings as benefits, omitting savings in fuel and other vehicle operating costs as well as the other benefits that are even less easily converted into economic terms. Moreover, the benefits will increase each year, since, without the traffic

421

restraints, congestion would have continued to get worse. Thus, without putting a precise figure on it, we may conclude that the economic rate of return is more than adequate to justify the investment. Had it been possible to foresee the actual demand for space in the fringe car parks, about three-quarters of the investment cost could have been saved, thus multiplying the rate of return by a factor of four. (In fact, some of the initial cost has already been recovered by converting car parks to other uses).

The economic rate of return based on the value of time savings may seem rather abstract. Public officials are more likely to be interested in cash costs and revenues. In these terms, the revenues from license sales exceed operating costs (including special police for enforcement, and the printing and distribution of licenses) by about S$500,000 per month or S$6,000,000 a year, which amounts to an annual cash return to the Government of more than 90 per cent of the total capital cost.

Rather than either economic or cash flow considerations, it was the more general objective of changing people's attitudes toward the use of cars for commuting that motivated the planners of the Area License Scheme. The aim was to prevent the existing moderate congestion from growing progressively worse. The penalties of congestion were described by Singapore's Road Transport Action Committee in these words:

"Daily traffic congestion results in delay and frustration to motorists, bus commuters, goods and emergency vehicles, and poses danger to pedestrians and other road users. It also causes deterioration to the environment through noise, air pollution, and visual blight".

To solve the problem, the planners perceived that they had to, first, explain the rationale behind the need for more widespread use of public transport and other high occupancy vehicles, and second, induce motorists to review and fundamentally change their attitudes towards the ownership and use of cars. This revision of motorist's attitudes and, hence, behavior was expected both to reduce the problem caused by congestion and at the same time create an environment in which public transport services could be improved.

In order to translate this objective into practical and measurable terms, a target was set at a 25 to 30 per cent reduction in traffic entering the central area in the morning peak. This target was more than achieved. Therefore, it is clear that the Area License Scheme has forced motorists to modify their behavior, at least in the short run. The Area Licefe Scheme has reduced congestion in the central area, largely by inducing a shift towards public transport and car pools. Whether these are simply short-term behavior modifications or whether they represent fundamental changes in the attitudes of motorists cannot be determined at this point. It seems likely, however, that the continued use of such measures will result in a more widespread acceptance (rather than tolerance) of public transport and car pooling in the long run.

The benefits of meeting these general objectives cannot be valued in money terms. However, the creation of a breathing space and of a high probability that both the streets and the economic life of central Singapore can be prevented from being completely choked by automobiles is clearly an important and valuable achievement.

Transportation systems management;
Alternatives to capital investment in a period of uncertainty

by
Stein G. Jahnsen
Alberta Transportation, Canada
and
John F. Morrall
The University of Calgary, Canada

Transportation Systems Management alternatives are considered to be those options that relate to improving the utilization and efficiency of existing transportation facilities to accommodate demand, as against supplying more transportation facility capacity to accommodate demand.

INTRODUCTION

At a time when numerous future uncertainties are facing the transportation industry, such as energy and its availability, requirements and policy directions; introduction of new or improved technology; a lack of co-ordination in policymaking between different departments and levels of governments; a shortage of and competing demand for capital in the face of substantial new investment requirements for transport all over the world; and the role of the public transport modes vis-a-vis the automobile, it is important for government and operators to know when *not* to make a decision involving large capital investments.

Rather, until the nature of these and other uncertainties are better understood, or until they are reduced, interim measures to maintain and improve the efficiency of existing systems should be undertaken in order to avoid sub-optimal investments. As such, Transportation Systems Management alternatives are much less risky and a more viable strategy than Capital Investments at this highly uncertain state in the history of transportation. As well as being alternatives to capital investment, Transportation Systems Management alternatives can also be used in a multi-modal fashion to support and enhance capital investment in a particular mode of transport. One advantage of considering Transportation Systems Management is that the analysis will indicate for how long the investment decision can be delayed, thus giving the decisionmaker a much better perspective of the overall situation, including how to treat the uncertainties.

In this paper, the evaluation and use of Transportation Systems Management alternatives are undertaken at a multi-modal level for passenger transportation in the low-to-medium density Edmonton-Calgary corridor, and are based on work performed in the recently completed Edmonton-Calgary Corridor Transportation Study. The analysis is directed towards the key issues, strategic choices and policy problems that will prevail or surface in various time periods in the study area. Before discussing in detail the TSM alternatives that were considered, a description of the study area and the issues will be presented.

THE CORRIDOR SETTING AND THE PRESENT TRANSPORTATION SYSTEM

The Edmonton-Calgary Corridor is situated in the Province of Alberta in Western Canada (see Figure 1). The Corridor Study Region boundaries define a rectangular area of about 300 km by 160 km. Within these 48 000 km², or 7% of Alberta's surface area, are located six of Alberta's ten cities. The central axis of this study area is the major north-south highway, a four lane rural expressway. The corridor or Corridor Spine is immediately adjacent to this route and contains most of the major communities in the region. The Corridor Spine also contains a single track rail line which links a number of corridor communities with transcontinental rail lines which pass through Edmonton and Calgary. The populations of the communities in the study area vary widely, with Edmonton and Calgary each approaching one half million while the next largest community Red Deer, has approximately 28 000. The combined Edmonton and Calgary population accounts for 82% of Corridor Region population of 1,1 million, which in turn accounts for 68% of the provincial total. This distribution is rapidly changing as Edmonton and Calgary account for almost all new growth while the rural population is declining. This trend suggests even further concentration in the two main metropolitan areas, which would imply even more investment in intercity transportation services and facilities.

THE PRESENT TRANSPORTATION SYSTEM

The four modes of travel available in the Corridor Region - rail, bus, air and automobile - offer a variety of both regional services and express services, the latter being non-stop service between Edmonton and Calgary. Of the total Edmonton/Calgary travel, 24% consists of intercity travel with the remainder intercentre travel, or trips from other corridor communities to Edmonton and Calgary. The automobile captures the predominant share of the *total* travel market accounting for 93% of the travel. Bus contributed 3%, air 4% and rail less than 1% of the total. The modal split for Edmonton-Calgary *intercity* trips is 66% automobile, 21% air, 12% bus and less than 1% rail. If no changes are made in the system, the intercity market shares are expected to be 59% automobile, 29% air, 12% bus, and less than 1% rail by 1983.

The present rail service in the Corridor caters to intercity, intercentre, and short local trips. Four runs are made every weekday between Edmonton and Calgary making four intermediate stops. The rail diesel cars cover the 314 track kilometres in 3 hours and 25 minutes at an average speed of 92 km/h. The present service is uneconomic and unattractive for a number of reasons. Low quality service is offered, travel times are longer than for any other mode, fares relatively high and only two departures a day provided in each direction. In addition, the equipment used is old, generally not attractive and does not take advantage of the express capa-

bilities that rail is usually assumed to have. The net result is low demand, in turn resulting in high per-passenger system costs, high per-passenger energy consumption and high levels of direct federal subsidies approximately Can. $700 000 in 1974.

There is fairly extensive bus service in the Corridor Region, with both regional and express services offered. Eighteen Edmonton-Calgary express runs and twelve intercentre express runs are provided per day with travel times slightly lower than rail. In addition, the regional bus routes provide service to most of the communities in the Corridor Region. In all cases the bus provides the user with a low-cost mode of transportation, and from society's point of view, is a mode of transportation that has low system cost, requiring no subsidy. As a conse-

Figure 1 - The Edmonton-Calgary Corridor Region: National and Provincial Setting

quence of being the least comfortable mode with fairly long travel times it is generally used by low-income, non-business travellers, although some business travel does occur on the bus.

The Airbus between Edmonton and Calgary is a highly successful service providng thirty flights eack weekday and caters to over 1 600 passengers per day who are mainly high-income business travellers. Use is made of a downtown airport in Edmonton rather than the international airport, resulting in a relatively fast CBD-CBD total travel time of 1 hour and 35 minutes, of which 35 minutes represent the actual air line haul. The airbus is profitable for the operator, but indirect subsidies of approximately Can. $5.5 million are being paid to the service.

With over 93% of all Edmonton/Calgary travel, the automobile is by far the major mode of travel in the Corridor Region. The high use of the automobile is due to its many attractive features. The highway network covers all parts of the Corridor Region and hence provides access between all communities and for many, but not all users, it is a very inexpensive mode of travel. In addition the auto is the most flexible of all modes offering maximum convenience for departure times and maximum privacy when travelling. The high use of the auto is also attributed to the fact that there are many travellers who are captive to the automobile. This includes those who have no alternative, those for whom travel by common carrier is too expensive in terms of time or money, and those who require the use of their cars at the destination end. The auto mode requires little or no subsidy, with fuel taxes and licence fees covering the auto share of highway infrastructure costs. It is the fastest of all the surface modes, completing the CBD-CBD intercity trip in 3 hours and 20 minutes

In summary the intercity traveller has the best choice of modes available and the best choice of service levels; from the slower but inexpensive bus service to the very fast and much more expensive air service. The air traveller (mainly expense account travellers) make up the bulk of the common-carrier express passengers. While receiving the best level of service and paying consequently the highest fares, the air travellers also receives the bulk of the transportation subsidy that is paid to travellers in the Corridor Region. The regional travellers, on the other hand, have little or no choice of mode, particularly away from the Corridor Spine. Furthermore, the service offered is the lowest in terms of comfort, frequency, and reliability. Finally, it is the regional traveller (who is particularly conscious of the cost of travelling) who receives little or no subsidy and hence pays for most of his travel costs.

THE ISSUES FACING TRANSPORT DECISION MAKERS

The issues facing transport decisionmakers in the Corridor Region are related to general questions concerning land use, development policies, environmental factors, equity in transportation services, level of service, economic efficiency, multi-modal planning and future uncertainties. In order to allow transportation planners and decisionmakers focus on both short-term operational management decisions as well as middle range planning decisions the future was divided into three time periods on a functional basis as follows:

(i) Immediate Period (1976-1977) - a two-year period, when management and operational decisions involving non-capital investment can be implemented.

(ii) Planning Period (1978-1983) - the period during which decisionmakers should be in a position to commit new funds and implement new systems and during which the trend future is likely to hold.

(iii) Long Range Period (1984 and beyond) - characterized by uncertain forecasts, limited knowledge of the effects of new technologies, and incomplete information on which to base transportation planning decisions.

It is particularly for the Planning Period that Transportation System Management (TSM) alternatives can be most beneficial and used to good advantage, in order to reduce uncertainty and not to preclude any option that may become viable in the early and mid-1980's.

The major issues, modal opportunities, and the TSM and investment alternatives in the corridor region are listed in Table I for the Planning and Long Range Period. The general future uncertainties to which these issues are related are given in Table II. The issues in Table I are only a partial list of those uncovered in the Edmonton-Calgary Corridor Transportation Study, and only a few of these will be selected for detailed discussion in this paper.

As noted earlier, the automobile is the most heavily used and the most flexible of all modes, and because of its popularity tampering with it entails some risk for governments. Still, the decision must be faced in the relatively near future of whether to encourage and make auto travel more efficient, or to discourage auto travel and place more emhasis on common carriers. Since any improved common carrier service depends upon drawing from the automobile for additional patronage, detailed TSM measures to discourage auto travel must accompany any such improvements. On the other hand, considerable system improvements are possible by making auto travel more efficient, without necessarily adding more highway infrastructure.

Rail is the transportation mode where the most obvious problems exist. First, there are the high costs and subsidies involved in providing the service to only about 16 000 travellers per year. Second, there are access problems related to the Edmonton station because of its poor location. Additional problems with this mode include a lack of incentive for the operator to improve service, the high number of grade crossings between Edmonton and Calgary, and a failure to achieve economies in energy because of low load factors.

While the regional bus service could be more extensive and more frequent than at present, it is noted that it is currently operating at a loss, being cross-subsidized by the operator from the profitable intercity express service. Thus, any improvement in regional services would require government subsidies to be implemented. Other problems are related to productivity because of restrictions in vehicle length and urban traffic congestion in Edmonton and Calgary.

Problems with the intercity air service concern the substantial indirect subsidy given to high-income business travellers, and alternative uses of the downtown Edmonton airport land. As well, questions of noise and safety arise.

Closely related to the transportation issues in the planning period are likely growth patterns that will emerge and solidify in the long range period. Whereas the Alberta Government has general policy statements espousing regional development, growth and decentralization, these must be much more clearly defined before any firm infrastructure and service planning can be undertaken.

TRANSPORTATION SYSTEM MANAGEMENT ALTERNATIVES TO REDUCE UNCERTAINTY

The TSM alternatives will be discussed in terms of the uncertainties in Table II, and reference will be made as to how they will affect the issues described in Table I.

Table 1 - Selected list of issues, modal opportunities and alternatives by time period

	Main issues	Modal opportunities	TSM and investment alternatives
Planning Period (1978-1983)	**1. Private transportation** **(a) Automobile** Auto Efficiency, energy consumption, roadway requirements, What is the role of the automobile in the region?	Ai: Encourage auto travel, but make it more efficient Aii: Discourage auto travel	Ai: **TSM**: Increase auto occupancy rate, auto sharing programs, Aii: **TSM**: Impose 90 km/h speed limit, road user taxes, congestion costs, gasoline and licence price increase
	2. Private transportation vs. the common carrier **(a)** Can patronage be shifted from the auto to common carrier? What benefits can be gained from such a shift? What are the consequences for the common carriers if the shift from auto is too rapid, i.e. equipment shortages, service levels, etc? **(b) Intercity Market** Which mode should capture what share of the intercity market	A. Define modal roles for a "planned" multi-modal intercity transportation system.	A. **TSM** and/or **CAPITAL**: Dependent upon the specific roles that will be defined.
	3. Common carriers **(a) Rail** What is the purpose of rail service? What market segment should this mode be designed to capture? Is the improved service worth the large expenditures involved? What are the benefits of passenger rail service? Would the loss of rail service be unacceptable?	A. **Rail** i: Discontinue rail services ii: Upgrade present rail service	Ai. **TSM**: discontinue present rail service ii: **CAPITAL** – 145 km/h conventional service - Can. $10,1 million – 145 km/h Improved service - Can. $17,9 million – 200 km/h improved service - Can. $37,9 million with supporting **TSM**: Peak or premium fares on air and bus, 90 km/h. speed limit, road user tax, gasoline and licence price increases, congestion costs, restrict landings at Edmonton downtown airport
	(b) Bus Should this mode be encouraged to continue to offer low cost service? Would improved rail adversely affect regional and/or express bus service? Should regional bus service be subsidized?	B. **Bus** i: Subsidize regional bus services	Bi: **CAPITAL**: Subsidy payments to bus operator
	(c) Air Should the air mode continue to receive large indirect subsidies? A substantial increase of jet flights into the downtown Edmonton Industrial airport which is really what makes the intercity air service successful might not be allowed. Would moving the service out to the International airport (32 km. distance) hurt the air market share?	C. **Air** i: continue present service ii: Pricing of present service iii: Continue present service but restrict landings at Edmonton downtown airport iv: Move present service to Edmonton International airport and continue using present equipment (Boeing 737) v: Continue using the down-town Edmonton airport, but buy RTOL (A300) equipment vi: Discontinue present service and replace with downtown-downtown STOL service	Cii, iii: **CAPITAL**: Rail investment alternatives 145 km/h conventional, improved or 200 km/h improved with supporting TSM as for Rail **or CAPITAL**: Upgrade spine highway to 6 lane divided Civ, vi: **TSM**: Impose 90 km/h Speed limit and **do not** implement any rail improvement
	4. Highway congestion congestion is experienced on highways within the 40 km. commuter shed of Edmonton and Calgary	Alleviate peaking problems in morning and afternoon rush hours	TSM: Activity rescheduling such as; staggered work hours, flex time four-day work week to change travel patterns, car pooling. and/or **CAPITAL**: Implement subsidized commuter bus services
Long Range Period (1984 and beyond)	**5. Development patterns and policies** **(a)** Growth concentrated in Edmonton and Calgary	A. Greatly improved common carrier intercity system **or** Increased importance of automobile	A. High-speed rail, CTOL, RTOL, or VTOL air services with supporting **TSM** to restrict auto travel, **or** Upgrade spine highway from 4 to 6 lane divided standard.
	(b) Growth concentrated in linear spine between Edmonton and Calgary	B. Improved common carrier system **or** Increased importance of automobile	B. Improved rail, bus, and/or STOL air service with **TSM** to restrict auto travel, **or** Upgrade spine highway from 4 to 6 lane divided standard
	(c) Regional and/or New Corridor Growth	C. Increased dependence upon automobile with some scope for limited common carrier improvements	C. New corridor highways to the east and west of the spine, and regional bus services and STOL air services.

426

Table II - Selected future uncertainties

Selected uncertainties	Time frame in which a strategic choice is required	Issue(s) in Table I to which it is related	Nature of uncertainties	Strategic choice facing decisionmaker
Rail Passenger Service	1977 - 1983	1a, 2a & b; 3a, b & c	National rail passenger policy uncertain; Purpose of rail service uncertain; Market segment designed to capture uncertain; Benefits of improved rail service are unknown; Uncertainty surrounding termination of the present service	Terminate the service, *or*, improve the service at a cost of $2 million or more per year
Future of Airbus Service	1980 - 1984	3a, c; 5a	Uncertainty as to number of landings and take-offs that will be allowed at downtown airport; Alternative uses of scarce downtown land; Safety and pollution aspects of jet service over downtown area	Continue present service but use larger equipment (A300), *or*, relocate to International airport, *or* implement improved rail alternatives
Role of the automobile	1980 - 1985	1a; 2a & b; 3a, b, c; 5a, b & c	Uncertain as to the minimum level of service acceptable and public reaction to schemes to discourage auto usage; Ultimate technological and management efficiencies are unknown; The importance of the automobile in shaping growth patterns	To encourage or discourage auto travel. Decisions are required to conduct TSM experiments related to energy savings, level of service and potential diversion factors - both to get more out of the existing highway system as well as making the common carriers more viable
Energy	1976 - 1980	1a; 2a & b; 3a, b & c	Uncertain Supply situation; Unclear government positions; Energy priorities undefined; Type of energy mix for future transportation system uncertain; New energy sources uncertain	Take interim measures to delay investment decisions until the energy picture has clarified, and at the same time take whatever action is necessary to maintain a full range of future options
Technology	1977 - 1983	1a; 3a & c; 5a	Several new or improved technologies emerging; No single new technology has been proven operationally; Relationship between new technology and energy; Suitability of new technology to various demand levels; Timing of new technology and government industrial strategies	Invest in conventional equipment, or, invest in technology showing the most promise, or, delay decision and take interim measures until a proven new technology is introduced
Need for Future Transportation Corridors	1977 - 1980	5a, b & c	Transportation systems/corridors required to support land-use/development policies - both are unknown	Reserve right-of-ways for highways and high speed ground transportation system
Transport-related Government Policies	1977 - 1980	5a, b & c	Most government policies directly and indirectly related to Corridor transportation are very vague and often working at cross-purposes	Government development and transportation policies need to be clearly defined and co-ordinated

Table III - Summary of energy savings through automobile strategies for intercity trips
Edmonton-Calgary Corridor Region, Planning Period

Strategy	Annual Energy Savings, 1980 [1] Absolute (Litres/Year) x 10 [6]	As a % of Intercity Consumption Indicated by Trend	Resulting Delay in Growth of Intercity Auto Traffic	Investment Associated with Each Strategy	Risk Associated with Each Strategy
Imposition of a 90 km/h Speed Limit [1]	4,860	8,7%	–	Very low	Little
Doubling Present/ Automobile Occupancy [2]	15,165	27,3%	12 years	Very low	Risky
Utilization of Full Automobile Capacity	17,595	31,6%	15 years	Very low	Risky
10% Shift from Automobile to Bus	2,340	4,2%	2 years	Moderate	Risky

[1] Using an 8 km/litre average for the automobile
[2] Present occupancy is 2.1 persons per auto

Energy

There is substantial scope for improvement in total energy consumption of the transportation system in the corridor. For demonstration purposes, only one year, 1980, will be selected rather than presenting a time series. In that year, assuming trend forecasts and no significant changes in travel patterns, total energy (gasoline) consumption will be 55,6 million liters for all intercity travel. Since automobile is the dominant mode in the corridor, it is also there that the largest savings can be effected. Table III depicts the savings possible through various auto strategies.

Imposing a 90 km/h speed limit (the present speed limit is 112 km/h) will result in a savinf of 4,86 million litres per year, or 8,7% of total intercity consumption. Other than changing highway signs, there is hardly any investment or expenditures associated with this strategy, and politically it is virtually a non-risk situation, having already been proven elsewhere. Since auto travel time would still be the lowest of all the surface modes, no changes in travel patterns would be likely to occur.

Doubling present average auto occupancy from 2,1 to 4,2 persons per auto gives even better results, with a maximum saving of 15,165 million litres per year, or 27,3% of the annual total consumption. This strategy would have the additional benefit of delaying highway growth for 12 years. This is particularly important because large sections of the Highway 2 corridor spine will be congested by 1983 and the government will have to make an upgrading decision by about 1980. If this TSM alternative was implemented, energy savings would be substantial, and the upgrading decision could probably be delayed to about 1990. By that time, the whole energy picture, as well as the role of the automobile should be clarified. There are several ways such as strategy of doubling auto occupancy can be implemented. Official hitch-hiking centres can be established, as well as "trip registration centres" where passengers and drivers with similar trip origins and destinations can register. Depending upon how important the program was deemed to be, some kind of policing system could be established with automatic fines imposed on a driver with less than a predetermined number of people in his automobile.

Again, the investment required would be quite minor, but the political risk could be quite major. Basically, the government would be imposing travel restrictions on anybody using the automobile and restrict somewhat the freedom to chose from available modes. This strategy might also divert some travel to the common carriers, because the convenience of the automobile would be somewhat curtailed.

The potential effects of this strategy are very complex, in that a shift to common carriers is a possible result, and depending upon the magnitude of such a shift, potential savings in energy consumption may be considerably less than those expected. Because of potential adverse public reaction, extreme caution must be exercised in implementing this strategy.

The greatest energy saving can be affected by a TSM that is probably unattainable, that of achieving full auto occupancy. This would save 17,595 million litres per year, or 31,6% of total system consumption. However, this is probably more utopia than anything that can realistically be expected.

The best energy saving measure by shifting people from auto to a common carrier was found to be a 10% shift from auto to bus. However, this would only result in a saving of 2,34 million litres per year, or 4,2% of total consumption, which is much inferior to any pure automobile TSM strategy. Moreover, highway growth would only be delayed for two years, and the highway upgrading decision would still have to be made. A wide range of TSM measures would likely be required to affect such a shift, including a 90 km/h speed limit for autos only, substantial road user charges, gasoline and license price increases. Such extensive measures would surely meet with adverse reactions from most, if not all, auto owners, and could thus be classified as politically risky in an auto-oriented society.

The investment required by such a shift would be mostly for additional buses, since the shift would mean a 52% increase in bus patronage.

Rail is generally contended to be very energy intensive. However, in the Edmonton-Calgary corridor region a shift from auto to either the present rail service or some of the suggested new rail services would result in an actual increase in total consumption.

In conclusion, if energy savings are desired, the best strategy is to implement TSM alternatives that affect the automobile only.

Upgraded Rail Passenger Service

If the rail passenger service is to be improved, multi-modal TSM alternatives to support the capital investment are essential. For the rail alternatives discussed here to break even, a 60% average load factor is required. Because of the low total demand in the corridor, this is probably unattainable. However, if it is implemented it would be for societal reasons rather than a profit motive, i.e. rail is more efficient than air in that it uses less total resources, and multi-modal TSM can help it achieve a respectable demand level.

The 145 km/h conventional rail service will not be discussed here, since even extensive use of multi-modal TSM will not help it to achieve a reasonable level of demand.

145 km/h. Improved Rail Service

This alternative involves a total investment of Can. $17,9 million (1974 dollars), of which $11,1 million is infrastructure and $6,8 million for locomotive hauled tilting coach trains with a top speed of 200 km/h. Club and coach car services would be offered, with airline-type on-board services. Ten runs per day would be offered and the ticket prices would be $12 for coach car and $18 for club car service, which would allow the service to break even at a 60% load factor. CBD-CBD travel time for this alternative would be 3 hours and 05 minutes at an average of 102 km/h. The line haul travel time would be 2 hours and 25 minutes at an average speed of 130 km/h. One intermediate stop is assumed at Red Deer, and the start-up year is 1983.

The following TSM support strategies are used to enhance rail's viability; 90 km/h highway speed limit, restricted landings at the downtown Edmonton airport, peak or premium fares for the air service. As well, it should be mentioned that the new Calgary air terminal will be located further away from the city, adding about 10 minutes to the air travel time. With the TSM in place, comparable BD-CBD travel times will be 1 hour and 45 minutes air, 3 hours and 05 minutes rail, 3 hours and 50 minutes auto and 4 hours and 25 minutes bus. It should be noted that the rail travel time is still somewhat excessive (for making a daily return business trip), but at least there is potential for picking up one direction of the trip.

Even though bus is still cheaper than the improved rail by about $4, it can be assumed that the savings in travel time (1 hr. 20 min.) and improved on-board services will cause all bus business travellers to switch to rail. Bus business travel is currently 18% of total bus demand, and by 1983 this would represent 73 000 intercity and 22 000 Red Deer trips, for a total diversion of 94 500 bus business trips. It is very unlikely that any other bus travellers will switch to rail, because the majority of them have very low incomes, 53% making less than $5 000 per year, and 76% making less than $10 000 per year.

Assuming that the number of landings and take-offs at the Edmonton downtown airport is restricted to its present level, the airbus will run with a 100% load factor on all its flights in 1983. Presently the load factor is close to 100% for the morning and afternoon peak periods, but the average for the service is only 50%. In practice this means that patrons are turned away and are probably flying mid-morning and in the evening. Presently 73% of total demand is represented by high-income business travellers and 10% are making connecting flights for holidays. About 43% of all air users earn more than $20 000/ year, and 62% make more than $15 000. Only 30% are making a daily round trip, leaving 70% staying over for at least a day.

In terms of why people use air, surveys have indicated that a total of 83% use it because of either convenient schedules, best connections, fastest way to destination or the only mode suitable to the travel circumstances. Since rail would be inferior on all those counts, it is assumed that these people (at least for this rail alternative) are captive to air. Thus, the potential for an air to rail switch is a maximum of 17% of total air demand.

The TSM premium air fare is assumed here to be $36 (in 1974 dollars) or three times the cost of the coach car rail service. If the 17% potential shift to rail is made up of non-business travellers, and it is assumed that the great majority of these are staying over for at least a day, then the conversion to rail should be quite high. Whereas the Edmonton-Calgary Corridor Study did not determine exactly how many would switch, additional work now being performed within Alberta Transportation indicates that about half of the 17% would switch. This gives a conversion rate from air to rail of about 8,5%, representing 84 000 persons in 1983.

These TSM strategies result in a total conversion from other common carriers to the 145 km/h improved rail service of 194 000 people, including users of the present rail service.

The total auto intercity demand will be about 2 million person trips in 1983. Of these, 700 000, or 35% are business auto trips. The most important reasons why auto business trips are undertaken are convenience of schedule, door-to-door travel time, and, to a lesser extent, the convenience of having an automobile at the destination. Thus, cost is not a factor for the business auto user. For non-business trips, the most important reason for going by car are convenience of schedule, door-to-door travel time and cost. The actual cost of going by automobile is $23 per vehicle, but the percived cost (oil and gas only) is only $14 per vehicle. Thus, with anything more than one person per automobile, the actual cost of taking the trip by car will be less than the rail fare. The door-to-door travel time for auto, as mentioned earlier, is 45 minutes slower than rail if the 90 km/h limit is imposed. However, it is very likely that as costs increase in the future, travel cost will become an extremely important factor in making a modal choice (at least for non-business group travel), and consequently little if any diversion from non-business auto to rail can be expected. Because the improved rail service offer a more convenient schedule, and its door-to-door travel time is faster, it was estimated that 1% of non-business auto, or 13 000 person trips would be diverted.

For the business auto user, the 145 km/h improved rail service can be said to be an extremely attractive offering. The rail schedule is much improved, offering 5 departures from each city daily, and the door-to-door travel time is greatly reduced. One will still not have an auto at the destination, but the Calgary terminal is in the heart of downtown, so an auto would probably not be required on one end of the trip for those persons who do business in the downtown areas. As well, even buying the comfort and servic of the club car one would be paying less than for auto, and substantially less than for air. Additional work now being undertaken by Alberta Transportation indicates that the shift from business auto would be in the order of 15% of all intercity auto business trips, at least initially. Nothing is known about whether this would be a novelty effect, or if the diversion would be stable at that level. The 15% diversion represents 105 000 person trips. Including the non-business switch, the total diversion from auto would be 118 000 person trips per year, which represent 6% of total intercity auto travel.

The total diversion to the 145 km/h improved rail service would thus be 312 000 trips per year, which works out to an average load factor of 38%. At such a load factor the rail service would still require substantial subsidies, with losses running at slightly more than $1 million/year. Even so, the implementation of this rail service will result in a more balanced corridor transportation system, the market shares being changed to 55% auto, 26% air, 9% rail, and 9% bus. If a larger diversion is desired, then TSM alternatives such as road user taxes, gasoline and license price increases, and congestion costs (increased travel times and costs) could be gradually introduced to effect a larger transfer from the automobile mode. The congestion cost alternative is particularly appropriate, in that the spine highway will experience congestion by 1983, and the 6% total diversion from auto to rail will only delay growth in auto traffic for one year.

There are two main advantages to implementing the 145 km/h improved rail alternative. First, it provides an intermediate level of service in terms of cost and travel times, and an acceptable alternative mode is available if the present air service should be curtailed or relocated. Secondly, since the 145 km/h equipment is the same as for the 200 km/h alternative, the rail service can be upgraded in the future if conditions and demand are conducive to such a strategy. It must be kept in mind, however, that TSM is an indispensable support tool to capital investment, especially in low-to-medium density corridors with a limited total demand from which to draw.

On some of the other issues listed in Table I, such as regional services, air services, and high-speed ground transportation systems, decisions need not be made soon, but they must always be taken into account in the planning and decision making process. The main action required now is the selection and reservation of a right-of-way for a high-speed ground transportation system and future highways. This can very easily be done by using a TSM alternative such as classifying the areas where these systems are most likely to be located as Restricted Development Areas, where only those developments compatible with transportation land use would be allowed. To a limited extent, this technique is already being employed by the Government of Alberta.

DISCUSSION

It has been demonstrated, through two specific examples, how TSM alternatives can be used in isolation to effect efficiencies in the transportation system and delay decision horizons, and how, coupled with a capital investment, they can be used (in this case) to reduce the risks of such investments. Many more examples can be selected from Table I, but hopefully the use of TSM has already been amply demonstrated.

In working the various alternatives listed in Table I, the authors have come to realize that the information requirements for using TSM and getting meaningful results, are much higher than what has traditionally been collected for multi-modal transportation planning. A detailed market segmentation analysis is essential, the first step being a breakdown between modal captives and those who can make a choice, and whether or not there are specific situations which make them captive for any particular trip purpose. To complement and enhance this information, knowledge about public attitudes towards the various modes, why the various modes are used for particular trip purposes and how often, perceived modal improvements that would increase demand, and travel patterns and behavior is extremely useful. This is very expensive to obtain, since extensive public attitude surveys are required, but such information will greatly contribute to the successful use of Transportation Systems Management alternatives. Furthermore, since TSM is involved with effecting efficiencies and "fine tuning" in a specific system, general attitude information is often not applicable to the area being studied.

Undoubtedly, TSM is most valuable in areas where limited demand must cover a wide range of services, particularly in supporting investment decisions. However, TSM should also be very useful for high-density corridors with high total demand, particularly in making the existing system more efficient by exploiting its capacity. This was demonstrated earlier by the fact that if auto occupancy rates were improved, not only would energy consumption improve, but a multi-million dollar decision of whether or not to upgrade the spine highway could be delayed for as much as ten years. By that time, the decision may be redundant if the energy picture, the future role of the automobile, and new technology availability have been clarified.

THE FUTURE OF TSM

As capital resources become more scarce, Transportation Systems Management alternatives should become increasingly more important tools for transportation planners. Ever-increasing operating costs for the various modes also dictate that systems effeciency measures are of paramount importance for existing services.

A substantial amount of work is still required to determine systems-wide effects of multi-modal Transportation Systems Management alternatives. There is perhaps a requirement for experimentation with existing systems to get a detailed understanding of these effects, particularly as they affect the auto mode. This requires substantial understanding and good-will on the part of governments, operators and the general public, because temporary disruptions in the system would certainly occur. However, the potential pay-offs should be well worth the effort, in that considerable capital may be saved and planners would gain superior knowledge of the systems for which they are responsible.

On a more detailed, level, there seems to be considerable scope for TSM analysis of the effects of travel substitutes, particularly new communication technology such as audio-visual communication, fascimile transmission, remote commuter centres and various cable-based systems. Some work has already been done in this area, but our understanding of the issue is extremely limited. However, it is a distinct possibility that total travel (especially business travel) could decrease substantially when a mass-introduction of this technology occurs. I that is the case, and in view of the numerous other uncertainties that remain unsolved, we may even today be over-investing in our present and new transportation systems.

ACKNOWLEDGEMENTS

The authors would like to thank the Planning and Services Division of Alberta Transportation and the Transportation Systems Branch of the Transportation Development Agency, co-sponsors of the Edmonton-Calgary Corridor Transportation Study, for permission to prepare this paper. The opinions expressed and conclusions reached in this paper are those of the authors, and do not necessarily reflect the opinions and conclusions of Alberta Transportation and the Transportation Development Agency.

REFERENCES

Alberta Transportation ; **Edmonton-Calgary Corridor Transportation Study,** Final Report, Edmonton, Alberta 1976.

Alberta Transportation ; Edmonton-Calgary Corridor Transportation, Technical Report No. 2: **Transportation Demand Analysis** (unpublished)

Alberta Transportation ; Edmonton-Calgary Corridor Transportation Study, Technical Report No. 3: **Rail Passenger Services Analysis** (unpublished)

Alberta Transportation ; **Alberta Rural Passenger and Express Study** (unpublished)

Uncertainty and the transport investment decision

A. D. PEARMAN
School of Economic Studies,
University of Leeds, England

INTRODUCTION

Uncertainty pervades virtually all aspects of life. It is not to be expected that transportation would be an exception in this respect and, as the title of this conference implies, it is indeed not. Despite the inevitability of uncertainty in the circumstances surrounding transport decisions, it is still a potentially valuable exercise to ask some quite basic questions. How seriously does uncertainty affect transport decisions? To what extent are its potential effects recognised? Is such recognition a matter of both theory and practice? What techniques exist for analysing uncertainty? Are available techniques regularly applied? If not, why not?

The purpose of this paper is to look briefly at these points in the context of transport investment appraisal. It will be argued that there has been a significant failure to take proper account of the potential importance of uncertainty in transport investment appraisal as a whole. Such an omission can certainly affect the correctness of individual decisions and, it will be shown, can unjustifiably favour certain types of investment proposal of a kind, moreover, which may be subject to particularly strong public opposition. It will be further argued that the level of theoretical understanding of problems in this area is reasonably high, and that the principal difficulty lies in the development of operational methods. As a step in this direction, two techniques are described which are appropriate to the preliminary stages of the evaluation of investment strategies in the presence of uncertainty.

THE IMPORTANCE OF UNCERTAINTY IN TRANSPORT INVESTMENT APPRAISAL

What is the correct transport investment strategy in any situation will depend upon future events, or states of nature, which cannot be predicted with certainty. Furthermore, many such decisions involve infrastructure investments which are, by their very nature, particularly inflexible. They are likely to be long-term, suited to a sigle use only and to be fixed both in location and size. It is frequently difficult to adjust the level of their performance once construction is completed. Marginal changes in capacity are likely to be particularly difficult to achieve and demand may not be price-elastic, either naturally or because of constraints of a social, political or institutional nature.

Infrastructure investments in transport, therefore, may have to operate in any one of a number of quite distinct future states of nature in a situation where both supply and demand may exhibit significant inelasticities, especially in the short and medium terms. In such circumstances, the proper recognition of uncertainty at the appraisal stage is of special importance. It is, therefore, rather surprising to learn from the literature that the treatment of uncertainty in the appraisal of transport investment projects is by no means adequate. "A number of decision rules are available but, so far as is known, these have not been used in decision making in the transport sector." (Gwilliam and Mackie (1975), p. 125). Similar comments are made elsewhere, for example, in Meyer and Straszheim (1971), chapter 13 and Heggie (1972), chapter 9.

When the analysis of a topic first moves from the qualitative to the quantitative, it is natural that early techniques should be of a simple kind. They are likely to be deterministic or, if a stochastic element is introduced, it may well not go beyond analysis in terms of expected values, or some simple sensitivity tests. Once quantitative modelling in transport passed the basic stage, the predominant demand, not unreasonably from many points of view, was for models which were wider in scope, both spatially and in terms of the complexities of interdependent behaviour patterns which they sought to analyse. The success with which investment strategies based on such models might cope with sets of circumstances other than the predictions upon which they were founded has been the subject of relatively little attention. Given the computer time demands of many such models and the need for multiple runs of programme suites if different future states of nature were to be considered, the reticence to pay great attention to the analysis of uncertainty is scarcely surprising.

At this juncture, however, when computer technology has reached a stage when quite sophisticated planning models can be run with relative ease, it might well be appropriate to devote future increases in computer power to more thorough consideration of uncertainty, rather than to further modelling advances *per se*. Moreover, it seems that transport is becoming subject to more and more uncertainty, for example through the likely existence of energy shortages within the time horizon of many current investment appraisals, through the increasing doubts about the desirability of living in large conurbations and generally through the increasing importance of transport in the political arena. It may also be added that, when the effects of the provision or nonprovision of transport can impose themselves so heavily on certain small sections of the community, for example, countrydwellers, the elderly, etc., then this possibility of gross social inequity if transport fails to react flexibly to changing circumstances must also be fully recognised.

One significant reason, then, for bringing the analysis of uncertainty in transport investment decisions more sharply into focus is the likelihood that variations in the ability of alternative strategies to deal flexibly with a number of different future states of nature are likely to be increasingly important. Uncertainty in demand is also of potential importance. There are a number of theoretical papers in economics which treat problems of this type. For example, Weisbrod (1964) has shown that, where there is uncertainty in the demand for a publicly provided good, there may be an "option value" benefit to the individual in addition to the conventional consumer surplus. Cicchetti and Freeman (1971) have extended this analysis and further work on this still contentious subject has appeared recently, viz., Schmalensee (1972; 1975) and Bohm (1975). Another dimension of the problem has been highlighted by Arrow and Lind (1970). They argue that, in social investment accounting, different rates of discount (by implication, a different evaluation of risk), should be applied depending upon whether the risks associated with the cost and benefit streams are publicly or privately borne. A further aspect of this question is that, even if this latter policy is adopted, the differential social and spatial effects of a public investment such as one in transport are such as to make important some recognition of the distributional implications of different strategies and how these might vary in different states of nature.

A second reason why the transport analyst should give increased attention to the importance of uncertainty stems from a very interesting point which has arisen recently in the economic literature, namely the treatment of irreversible decisions in project appraisal in the face of uncertainty. This has been discussed by Arrow and Fisher (1974) from the point of view of environmental preservation and, in a more theoretical paper by Henry (1974). The argument which Henry puts forward is that if, in a dynamic decision making environment where knowledge increases over time, irreversible projects with uncertain streams of returns are compared in terms only of their expected values as viewed at the present, there will be a significant tendency for such irreversible decisions to be taken prematurely. Indeed, they may be taken quite unnecessarily in circumstances where an explicit recognition of the full spectrum of possible outcomes would suggest some alternative time path of decisions.

Henry's interest in this theoretical problem was originally sparked by considering the official attitude to the appraisal of a ring road system around Paris which threatened to spoil a number of famous parks on the fringe of the conurbation, in a way which was, for all intents and purposes, irreversible. Clearly, this is not a problem which has affected Paris alone. Many, if not all, major transport improvement schemes tend to involve severe and effectively irreversible dislocation of their immediate environment. Many of the most controversial public enquiries into proposed road extentions in the United Kingdom have had at their heart decisions of this general type. It is thus a matter of some concern when theoretical results such as Henry's come to light. Furthermore, not only does the failure to give proper weight to uncertainty imply that irreversible decisions may have been wrongly taken, but it seems plausible that a similar analysis might reveal that investment schemes which were merely relatively inflexible rather than totally irreversible might similarly be given undue favour by analysis in terms of expected values alone.

PRESENT TECHNIQUES OF INVESTMENT
APPRAISAL IN THE PRESENCE OF
UNCERTAINTY

Given that transport investment decisions are likely in practice to be taken more and more in circumstances of significant uncertainty, and having mentioned briefly that project appraisal in the presence of uncertainty has received a good deal of attention from theoretical economists, it is appropriate to look briefly at the ways in which uncertainty has typically been taken into account in transport investment appraisal. This question has

been reviewed in rather more detail in Pearman (1976), where it is pointed out that, very often, no account of uncertainty is taken at all.

In theoretical discussions of decision making, a fundamental distinction is usually made, following Knight (1921), between decision making under risk and decision making under uncertainty. This distinction was not rigorously adhered to in the first two introductory sections of this paper, but will be from now on. In the former case it is assumed that future states of nature can be identified, and that the probability of occurrence of each alternative can be estimated. In the latter case, it is assumed that no such probability estimates can be made. Objective estimates of probabilities of future states of nature are virtually impossible in the circumstances of most transport investment appraisals. Models of decision making under uncertainty seem, therefore, to be the more relevant of the two theoretical extremes.

For decision making under uncertainty, three principal approaches have been adopted. The first, and most common, is implicit or explicit conservatism. Where doubts are felt about the future, cost elements tend to be biased upward and benefit elements downward in ways which are more or less arbitrary. This will obviously have the desired effect of militating against those strategies which are felt to be less capable of handling an uncertain future. What it fails to do however, is to provide any rational basis for implanting the correct degree of bias against such projects. Some may be cut back far too harshly, others by not enough.

A second approach to appraisal in the presence of uncertainty has been to convert an uncertain environment into one of risk (in the technical sense described earlier) by making some type of objective estimate of the probabilities of the future states of nature, after which an expected value maximisation approach is adopted. Some potential dangers in analysis in terms of expected values alone were mentioned at the end of the previous section, but the approach is a very common one. Its main weakness is that, although the probability estimates may appear objective at one level, they usually have to be calculated from the probabilities of more fundamental events which in turn require a priori estimation of probabilities. If these are truly objective, then the problem was never really one of uncertainty in the first place. If not, then the real problem has been obscured rather than solved.

The third category of techniques for handling decisions under uncertainty are termed "complete ignorance" methods, since they assume no knowledge of the probabilities of future states of nature. In the context of road investment appraisal, for example, Quarmby (1967), pp. 1–4, has pointed out the highly volatile nature of the demand component of road use and hence the difficulty of making accurate net benefit assessments over a time horizon of twenty or thirty years. In circumstances such as these where the probabilities of different future states of nature would be virtually impossible to estimate, the application of complete ignorance methods may, on occasions, be appropriate.

Complete ignorance decision making rules – maximax, maximin, the Hurwicz α criterion, minimax regret – are a well established part of most undergraduate courses in economics. Their practical implementation is less common. The reasons for this may be readily demonstrated using the following example. Consider three different investment strategies, A, B and C which will have to operate, it is believed, in one of six future states of nature. The payoffs, measured as net present values (n.p.v.) in millions of pounds of the benefits accruing to each of the eighteen possible strategy/state of nature combinations, are shown in Figure 1.

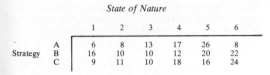

		State of Nature					
		1	2	3	4	5	6
	A	6	8	13	17	26	8
Strategy	B	16	10	10	12	20	22
	C	9	11	10	18	16	24

Figure 1

The strategies which would be selected by the four different complete ignorance criteria are as follows:

1) Maximax: Strategy A on the basis of state of nature 5. An optimist's approach, maximax selects the strategy which would give the maximum possible return if the right state of nature occurs.

2) Maximin: Strategy B on the basis of states of nature 2 or 3. A pessimist's approach, maximin selects the strategy which would give the highest minimum payoff, assuming the least favourable state of nature for that strategy were to occur.

3) Hurwicz α Criterion (α = ¹/₂): Strategy C. The Hurwicz criterion is merely a weighted average of the maximin and maximax payoffs. The weighting is arbitrary, reflecting only the importance which the decision maker gives to each extreme. Here, equal weights of one half were chosen for each, leading to scores for the three strategies of:
A = 16 (¹/₂[6 + 26]);
B = 16 (¹/₂[10 + 22]);
C = 16¹/₂ (¹/₂[9 + 24]).

4) Minimax Regret: Strategy B on the basis of state of nature 5. For this calculation, an opportunity cost or regret matrix is first calculated, representing, for each state of nature, the absolute value of the difference between the best outcome from any strategy and the actual outcome. The regret matrix is shown in Figure 2.

		State of Nature					
		1	2	3	4	5	6
	A	10	3	0	1	0	16
Strategy	B	0	1	3	6	6	2
	C	7	0	3	0	10	0

Figure 2

The principal weakness of the first three of these techniques is that their decision is based on only a very small subset of all possible outcomes. For each strategy, all intermediate states of nature are ignored. This is particularly serious if a large number of potential states of nature are identified. Minimax regret partially avoids this criticism by going through the intermediate step of calculating opportunity costs, which will tend to have a neutralising effect, but one which is by no means complete. Established complete ignorance criteria, then, overlook a great deal of potentially valuable information and, furthermore, may very reasonably be criticised on the grounds that they are too crude for application to real problems. There is also no real guidance as to which of the complete ignorance criteria is likely to be the most appropriate. The risk averting maximin model is often favoured for the private sector. The case for risk aversion is less persuasive for the public sector, except insofar as it may help to avoid very poor outcomes for certain sections of the community.

In summary, the evidence on current practice in appraising transport investment projects is this. The most common practice of all seems to be to ignore uncertainty altogether. Also relatively common, and rather more justifiable, is to use expected values, but the first moment of the probability distribution cannot be expected to encapsulate all that might be of relevance in an appraisal. If uncertainty is explicitly recognised, then this recognition is most likely to take the form of using conservative estimates throughout. These are potentially arbitrary. Converting from uncertainty to risk seems likely to give more the illusion of dealing with the problem than actually providing a solution. The complete ignorance methods are theoretically sound, depending upon the attitude to risk of the decision maker, but lack the subtlety required for applied work in the transport sector.

EXTREME EXPECTED PAYOFFS AND VARIANCES

This section describes an approach to decision making which represents a compromise between the classical extremes of decision making under uncertainty and decision making under risk. Further details of the development are available in Cannon and Kmietowicz (1974) and Kmietowicz and Pearman (1976). The technique is based on the assumption that, while it is unreasonable to expect decision makers to calculate precise probabilities of future states of nature and so calculate expected values under risk, it is plausible that they should be able to rank the probabilities of different states of nature. The ranking will reflect both objective information available and the decision maker's subjective views. Moreover, such information must frequently be available and, *ceteris paribus*, to ignore it can only lead to poorer decisions.

The technique to be described provides a simple analytical method of determining the maximum and minimum expected payoffs of any strategy consistent with a probability ranking of states of nature and also the maximum variance of payoff. It is these figures which are then used as a basis for decision making, rather than the crude extrema normally used by the complete ignorance methods. Suppose there exist m alternative investment strategies (i = 1 . . . m) and that the decision maker identifies n (j = 1 . . . n) possible future states of nature in which a given transport investment may have to operate. The states of nature are assumed to be mutually exclusive and exhaustive. Suppose also that a payoff matrix has been constructed with elements X_{ij} which correspond to the n.p.v. of investment strategy i should state of nature j occur. In addition, it is assumed that the decision maker has ranked the n states of nature such that $P_j \geq P_{j+1}$ [j = 1 . . . (n-l)].

Given this foundation, minimum and maximum expected payoffs may be computed for each strategy. Dropping the i subscript for simplicity of notation gives the following linear programming problem for each strategy:

$$\text{Maximise or Minimise} \quad E(S) = \sum_{j=1}^{n} P_j X_j$$

$$\text{Subject to} \quad \sum_{j=1}^{n} P_j = 1 \quad \text{(I)}$$

$$P_j - P_{j+1} \geq 0 \ [j=1 . . .(n-1)] \quad \text{(II)}$$

$$P_j \geq 0 \ [j=1 . . .n] \quad \text{(III)}$$

The problem may be greatly simplified by the application of the following transformations:

(i) Let $Q_j = P_j - P_{j+1}$ [j = 1 . . .(n-1)]

(ii) Let $Y_j = \sum_{k=1}^{j} X_k$ [j = 1 . . .n]

This leads to the following re-expression of the original problem:

433

$$\text{Maximise or Minimise} \quad E\ (S)\ =\ \sum_{j=1}^{n}\ Q_j\ Y_j$$

$$\text{Subject to} \qquad\qquad \sum_{j=1}^{n}\ j\ Q_j\ =\ 1 \qquad\qquad \text{(IV)}$$

$$Q_j\ \geqslant 0 \qquad\qquad \text{(V)}$$

Because it has only one functional constraint, a linear programming problem of this type will have an optimal solution with only one of the decision variables, Q_j, positive and the rest zero. From constraint (IV), if only one Q_j is non-zero, it must equal $1/j$. Thus it is clear that the objective function will be maximised when $Y_j/_j$ is maximised and minimised when $Y_j/_j$ is minimised.

The extreme expected payoffs of any investment strategy can thus be found by computing the n partial averages.

$$\frac{1}{j}\ Y_j\ =\ \frac{1}{j}\ \sum_{k=1}^{j}\ X_k$$

The largest such partial average will be the maximum expected payoff and the smallest will be the minimum.

In choosing between alternative investment strategies, it is probable that, in addition to minimum and maximum expected payoff, the decision maker may wish to have some information about the likely dispersion of outcomes around these mean values. In some cases, it is possible that the decision maker's attitude would favour trading off some loss in expected returns in order to obtain a greater probability of an actual outcome close to that expectation. It follows that any judgement which can be made about likely variance of payoff is potentially valuable. As is shown in Kmietowicz and Pearman (1976), it is possible to calculate minimum and maximum variances in a similar way to that in which extreme expected values were calculated. It transpires that minimum variance will be zero for all strategies and is there-

fore of no value for purposes of discrimination. Maximum variance, however, varies from strategy to strategy and is found by computing n partial variances

$$\text{Var}\ (S)\ =\ \frac{1}{j}\ \sum_{k=1}^{j}\ X_k^2\ -\ (\frac{1}{j}\ \sum_{k=1}^{j}\ X_k)^2$$

for $j = 1 \ldots n$. The largest of these partial variances gives the maximum variance.

The computation of the partial averages and variances is straightforward. For example, for Strategy A of the example given in the third section, the first three partial averages and variances are shown below:

$$\overline{X}_A^1\ =\ 1\ (6)\ =\ 6$$

$$\overline{X}_A^2\ =\ 1/2\ (6\ +\ 8)\ =\ 7$$

$$\overline{X}_A^3\ =\ 1/3\ (6\ +\ 8\ +\ 13)\ =\ 9$$

$$V_A^1\ =\ \frac{1}{1}\ (6^2)\ -\ [-\ (6)]^2\ =\ 0$$

$$V_A^2\ =\ 1/2\ (6^2\ +\ 8^2)\ -\ [1/2\ (6\ +\ 8)]^2\ =\ 1$$

$$V_A^3\ =\ 1/3\ (6^2\ +\ 8^2\ +\ 13^2)\ -\ [1/3\ (6\ +\ 8\ +\ 13)]^2\ =\ 8\,2/3$$

Complete results for all strategies are given in Figure 3.

	Partial Average						Partial Variance					
	1	2	3	4	5	6	1	2	3	4	5	6
Strategy A	6	7	9	11	14	13	0	1	8.7	18.5	50.8	47.3
Strategy B	16	13	12	12	13.6	15	0	9	8	6	15	22.3
Strategy C	9	10	10	12	12.8	14.7	0	1	0.7	12.5	12.6	27.9

Figure 3

Similar calculations may also be undertaken in terms of the regret matrix.

If now the conventional complete ignorance criteria are applied to the extreme expected values rather than the crude extrema, it is clear that Strategy B will be favoured by the maximin, maximax and Hurwicz rules. It also has the lowest maximum variance. Such unanimous support would be relatively rare, even using the expected value approach. It serves to emphasise, however, that by taking into account the extra information implicit in the probability ranking, a very different light can be thrown upon a decision making problem.

The techniques just described are potentially valuable when decision making must take place in the face of only partial knowledge about future states of nature. They enable all available information to be used to reduce the range of uncertainty within which the strategy choice decision must be made. In addition to these basic results, various sensitivity tests are available, relating both to potential changes in the decision maker's ranking of the probabilities of future states of nature and to alterations

in the values placed on the payoffs, X_{ij}. [See Pearman and Kmietowicz (1976)]. Circumstances in which the use of these methods is likely to be preferable to the alternative of conventional complete ignorance criteria are explained in detail in Pearman (1976). The principal requirements are that there should be a number of separate decisions over which it is possible to trade off payoffs. The relative improvement will be especially high if a large number of potential states of nature is identified. Where these criteria are not obeyed, or where policies such as maximin, minimax regret, etc. are thought to be too simplistic, the expected value techniques can still form a useful alternative to be considered as one of a range of criteria to be entered into a multiattribute decision making process. One of these attributes might well be the maximum variance of payoff described earlier.

A SECOND APPROACH TO THE CALCULATION OF EXTREME EXPECTED VALUES

This section describes a second technique for delimit-

434

ing a range of expected values for a given strategy. It is appropriate to planning problems specified at about the same level of detail as those discussed in the previous section. Its philosophy, however, is one of estimating the probability of success or failure of a given strategy on the basis of the success or failure of independent component parts of the strategy, and then combining this information with the anticipated outcome of the strategy should it be successful as a whole. The method is most easily demonstrated by example.

Suppose a local authority is considering the introduction of an urban mass transit scheme. For its successful operation, a given minimum level of demand is required. Excess demand can be stifled by appropriate pricing policies. In order to achieve this minimum demand level target, the authority has certain policy instruments at its disposal and there are, additionally, exogenous influences beyond its control. It is assumed that, within the context of the strategy under evaluation, each one of the exogenous variables and instruments can take values which correspond to "success" or "failure". A success may stem from a deliberate policy decision in which case the variable I_j, corresponding to the jth policy instru-

ment, takes the value of one. Failure to implement the right policy from the point of view of this strategy causes I_j to take the value zero. On the basis of the general political environment and the pressure which may be exerted by the need to force I_j to zero or one as a result of policy conflicts in other areas of administration, assume that a probability, P_{Ij} may be estimated giving the chance that $I_j = 1$. Similarly, assume that $E_k = 1$ corresponds to a successful outcome in respect of the kth. exogenous variable and that the corresponding probability is P_{Ek}. It is assumed that the I_j and E_k can reasonably be taken as being statistically independent of each other.

Suppose now that it is possible to identify certain minimum combinations of "success" with the policy instruments and exogenous variables which will achieve the desired level of transit demand while, by implication, all others which do not contain at least one of the minimum combinations as a subset will result in failure to achieve the target. For example, suppose that the six combinations shown in Figure 4 are regarded as the only minima which will guarantee circumstances sufficiently favourable to mass transit for the required target level to be achievable.

Acceptable Combinations

	I	II	III	IV	V	VI		
I_1	X	X				X	Parking	
I_2	X		X				Urban Planning	Policy
I_3	X			X		X	Rate levy for mass transit	instruments
E_1		X				X	Import controls on cars	
E_2		X			X		No home-based mass prodn. of small cars	Exogenous
E_3				X	X		High petrol tax	variables
E_4			X				No alternative fuel to petrol	
E_5				X		X	Government grant to mass transit	

Figure 4

An alternative and illuminating way of presenting the information contained in Figure 4 is to construct a network, as shown in Figure 5. The implication of the network is that, provided there exists at least one path from the start node to the finish node made up of the links which correspond to the policy instruments and nous variables of Figure 4, then it will be possibl.... achieve the desired level of transit use. Furthermore, using this visual insight, it is straightforward to develop an expression for the probability that the required level of mass transit demand be attainable:

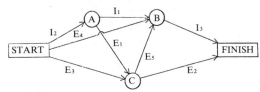

Figure 5

P [Demand level is attainable)
= P [There is at least one path through the network from Start to Finish]
= 1 − P [There is no path through the network from Start to Finish]
= $1 - P[(I = 0) \Omega (II = 0) \Omega (III = 0) \Omega (IV = 0) \Omega (V = 0) \Omega (VI = 0)]$

In the final row of this expression, $I = 0$ implies that the path Start − A − B − Finish is broken by having at least one link missing. Equivalently, this requires $I_1 I_2 I_3 = 0$ where the I_j are binary variables taking the value one if a "success" is recorded for the policy in question and zero

otherwise. Interpreting the remainder of the expression similarly leads to the relation:

P [Demand level is attainable]

$$= 1 - P[(I_1 I_2 I_3 = 0) \Omega (I_1 E_1 E_2 = 0) \Omega (I_2 E_4 = 0) \Omega$$

$$(I_3 E_3 E_5 = 0) \Omega (E_2 E_3 = 0) \Omega (I_1 I_3 E_1 E_5 = 0)]$$

In principle, the above probability may be calculated, given that the P_{Ij} and P_{Ek} are known. However, the individual parts of the probability statement are strongly interdependent and the computation would be complex, even for a small example such as this one. More promising, therefore, is the possibility of calculating upper and lower bounds on the probability, which is possible by taking advantage of the following theorem concerning binary random variables:

Theorem: if $X_1 \ldots \ldots X_n$ are independent $(0, 1)$ random variables and $Y_i = j \in J j = X_j$ $(i = 1 \ldots r)$ where the J_i are any subsets of the integers $1 \ldots \ldots n$, then

$$P[(Y_1 = 0) \Omega (Y_2 = 0) \Omega \ldots \ldots (Y_{r6} 0)] > P(Y_1 = 0).$$
$$P(Y_2 = 0) \ldots P(Y_r = 0)$$

Applying this theorem, an upper bound may immediately be obtained:

P [Demand level is attainable]

$$\leq 1 - P(I_1 I_2 I_3 = 0). P(I_1 E_1 E_2 = 0). P(I_2 E_4 = 0). P(I_3 E_3 E_5 = 0). P(E_2 E_3 = 0). P(I_1 I_3 E_1 E_5 = 0)$$

435

$$= 1 - (1 - P_{I_1} P_{I_2} P_{I_3}) (1 - P_{I_1} P_{E_1} P_{E_2}) (1 - P_{I_2} P_{E_4})$$

$$(1 - P_{I_3} P_{E_3} P_{E_5}) (1 - P_{E_2} P_{E_3}) (1 - P_{I_1} P_{I_3} P_{E_1} P_{E_5})$$

Returning to the network representation of the problem, it can be seen that the required level of demand can be regarded as attainable provided that at least one of the policy instruments of exogenous variables in each cut of the network is recorded as a "success" (see Wagner (1975), p. 597 for the definition of a cut in this context). In this example, this implies
P [Demand level is attainable]

$= $ P [(at least one of $I_1, E_4, E_3 = 1$) Ω (at least one of I_2, $E_4, E_1, E_3 = 1$) Ω

(at least one of $I_1, E_4, E_5, E_2 = 1$) Ω (at least one of $I_2, E_4, E_5, E_2 = 1$) Ω

(at least one of $E_2, I_3 = 1$)Ω (at least one of $E_1, E_3, I_3 = 1$)]

$= $ P $[(1 - (1 - I_1) (1 - E_4) (1 - E_3) = 1) \Omega (1 - (1 - I_2) (1 - E_4) (1 - E_1) (1 - E_3) = 1) \Omega$

$(1 - (1 - I_1) (1 - E_4) (1 - E_5) (1 - E_2) = 1) \Omega (1 - (1 - I_2) (1 - E_4) (1 - E_5) (1 - E_2) = 1) \Omega$

$(1 - (1 - E_2) (1 - I_3) = 1) \Omega (1 - (1 - E_1) (1 - E_3) (1 - I_3) = 1]$

$= $ P $[((1 - I_1) (1 - E_4) (1 - E_3) = 0) \Omega ((1 - I_2) (1 - E_4) (1 - E_1) (1 - E_3) = 0) \Omega$

$((1 - I_1) (1 - E_4) (1 - E_5) (1 - E_2) = 0) \Omega ((1 - I_2) (1 - E_4) (1 - E_5) (1 - E_2) = 0) \Omega$

$((1 - E_2) (1 - I_3) = 0) \Omega ((1 - E_1) (1 - E_3) (1 - I_3) = 0)]$

Now the $(1 - E_k)$ and $(1 - I_j)$ are independent binary variables, so the previously quoted theorem may be applied again:

P [Demand level is attainable]

$\geq$ P $[(1 - I_1) (1 - E_4) (1 - E_3) = 0]$. P $[(1 - I_2) (1 - E_4) (1 - E_1) (1 - E_3) = 0]$.

P $[(1 - I_1) (1 - E_4) (1 - E_5) (1 - E_2) = 0]$. P $[(1 - I_2) (1 - E_4) (1 - E_5) (1 - E_2) = 0]$.

P $[(1 - E_2) (1 - I_3) = 0]$. P $[(1 - E_1) (1 - E_3) (1 - I_3) = 0]$

$= [1 - (1 - P_{I_1}) (1 - P_{E_4}) (1 - P_{E_3})] [1 - (1 - P_{I_2}) (1 - P_{E_4}) (1 - P_{E_1}) (1 - P_{E_3})]$

$[1 - (1 - P_{I_1}) (1 - P_{E_4}) (1 - P_{E_5}) (1 - P_{E_2})] [1 - (1 - P_{I_2}) (1 - P_{E_4}) (1 - P_{E_5}) (1 - P_{E_2})]$

$[1 - (1 - P_{E_2}) (1 - P_{I_3})] [1 - (1 - P_{E_1}) (1 - P_{E_3}) (1 - P_{I_3})]$

This expression constitutes a lower bound on the probability that the required demand level is reached.

By way of numerical illustration, suppose that the demand level specified is 200,000 trips per day, that each exogenous variable has a probability of 0.3 as being recorded as a success and that the equivalent figure for the policy instruments is 0.7. By substituting into the expressions given for the upper and lower bounds, it may be shown that a demand level of 200,000 can be met with a probability lying between 41.50% and 60.36%.

This basic analysis may readily be extended in at least two directions. Firstly, the probability limits may be subjected to sensitivity tests in response to marginal changes in various P_{Ij} and P_{Ek} terms. Secondly, supposing that opinions differ as to the demand level required adequately to support an urban mass transit system, it would be possible to re-run the whole analysis with a different target figure, different combinations of required policy decisions and exogenous outcomes (indeed different variables, if necessary) and so obtain a series of probability limits, which might be illustrated graphically in the manner shown in Figure 6.

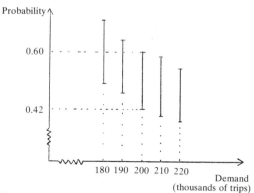

Figure 6

It should be noted that the reason the minimum probability levels associated with the five demand levels 180…220 sum to more than one is basically that the corresponding events are not mutually exclusive.

CONCLUSIONS

This paper has sought to achieve two main goals, one largely by assertion, the other by demonstration. The first concerns the attitude towards uncertainty typically found in the transport sector. Uncertainty has not been adequately taken into consideration in the past. Now, however, not only is there good reason to believe that its presence is likely to be felt more and more often in transport decisions, but also there is increasing evidence from the theoretical literature, that proper recognition of uncertainty will not only affect individual decisions, but, more importantly, may have a real qualitative effect on the type of investments which are undertaken. In particular, flexibility in the face of uncertainty may well have a significant value in its own right which ought to appear in the cost-benefit analyses which normally form the basis for major transport investment decisions. In addition to potential bias within the transport sector, there also exists the possibility of inter-sectoral distortions if, say, health service investments are less prone to uncertainty than projects in transport.

The second goal of the paper has been to demonstrate the existence of a sizeable gulf between theoretical understanding of uncertainty and the practical tools for taking it into account. Although both the proposed methods discussed in the later part of the paper are very simplistic, they do demonstrate that workable analytical tools can be devised appropriate to at least some types of problem in the transport sector. Equally, their limitations should serve to emphasize how great is the need for further research effort on this particular interface between theory and practice.

REFERENCES

Arrow, K.J. and A.C. Fisher (1974) Environmental Preservation, Uncertainty and Irreversibility, **Quarterly Journal of Economics,** Vol, 88, pp. 312-319.

Arrow, K.J. and R.C. Lind (1970) Uncertainty and the Evaluation of Public Investment Decisions, **American Economic Review,** Vol. 60, pp. 364-378.

Bohm, P. (1975) Option Demand and Consumer's Surplus: Comment, **American Economic Review,** Vol. 65, pp. 733-736.

Cannon, C.M. and Z.W. Kmietowicz (1974) Decision Theory and Incomplete Knowledge, **Journal of Management Studies,** Vol. 11, pp. 224-232.

Cicchetti, C.J. and A.M. Freeman III, Option Demand and Consumer Surplus: Further Comment, **Quarterly Journal of Economics,** Vol. 85, pp. 528-539.

Gwilliam, K.M. and P.J. Mackie (1975) **Economics and Transport Policy,** Allen and Unwin, London.

Heggie, I.G. (1972) **Transport Engineering Economics,** McGraw-Hill, London.

Henry, C. (1974) Investment Decisions Under Uncertainty: the "Irreversibility Effect", **American Economic Review,** Vol. 64, pp. 1006-1012.

Kmietowicz, Z.W. and A.D. Pearman (1976) Decision Theory and Incomplete Knowledge: Maximum Variance, **Journal of Management Studies,** Vol. 13, pp. 164-174.

Knight, F.H. (1921) **Risk, Uncertainty and Profit,** Hart, Schaffner and Marx, New York.

Meyer, J.R. and M.R. Straszheim (1971) **Techniques of Transport Planning,** Vol. 1, Pricing and Project Evaluation, Brookings Institution, Washington D.C.

Pearman, A.D. (1976) Transport Investment Appraisal in the Presence of Uncertainty, **Transportation Research,** Vol. 10, pp. 331-338.

Pearman, A.D. and Z.W. Kmietowicz (1976) Decision Theory and Incomplete Knowledge: Sensitivity Analysis, **School of Economic Studies Discussion Paper No. 40,** University of Leeds.

Quarmby, D.A. (1967) The Road Programme – Uncertainty in Investment Appraisal, **Mathematical Advisory Unit Note No. 25,** Ministry of Transport, London.

Schmalensee, R. (1972) Option Demand and Consumer's Surplus: Valuing Price Changes under Uncertainty, **American Economic Review,** Vol. 62, pp. 813-824.

Schmalensee, R. (1975) Option Demand and Consumer's Surplus: Reply, **American Economic Review,** Vol. 65, pp. 737-739.

Wagner, H.M. (1975) **Principles of Operations Research with Applications to Managerial Decisions** (2nd edition), Prentice-Hall International, London.

Weisbrod, B.A. (1964) Collective-Consumption Services and Individual-Consumption Goods, **Quarterly Journal of Economics,** Vol. 78, pp. 471-477.

A predictive model of highway interchange land use development: A decision tool for planning

by
RAYMOND W. EYERLY
RICHARD D. TWARK
RICHARD B. NASSI
The Pennsylvania State University, Pennsylvania

INTRODUCTION

The most extensive highway construction program ever attempted in the United States of America is the National System of Interstate and Defense Highway which, when completed, will comprise over 42,000 miles of multi-lane divided highway. This system will link together more than 90 percent of the cities of the United States having populations of 50,000 or more.[1]

Incorporated into the program (Federal-Aid Highway Act of 1956) authorizing the construction of the Interstate System are provisions which prohibit roadside development of user oriented facilities such as gasoline stations, restaurants and motels within the rights-of-way of the Interstate System. The controls, in effect, force users to exit the system for services. In addition, the Act also limits the number of access and egress points to grade-separated interchanges with connecting highways. Interchanges are designed with approach and exit ramps so as to channel traffic to and from the Interstate System, without hindering the free and save movement of traffic upon the system or the connecting highways. It is estimated that there could be as many as 14,000 of these interchanges on the completed Interstate System.[2]

The fact that traffic to and from the Interstate System must be channeled through an interchange makes the neighborhood area uniquely favorable for economic development. Users traveling long distances do not ordinarily desire to go far from an interchange in search of gasoline, food, or lodging, and hence, the vicinity of an interchange is advantageous for the construction of highway oriented establishments such as service stations, restaurants and motels.

Just as many present trade centers, towns, and cities can trace their origins to the existence of transportation crossroads (e.g., river junctions or railroad connections) which provided improved linkages between local land uses and distant land uses, the interchange area also offers opportunity for community development by reason of improved access between land uses. The development of commercial or industrial establishments, recreational facilities, residential units, and the above mentioned highway oriented establishments at an interchange stimulates general business activity, creates new jobs, increases income, and expands the tax base of the community.

Many of the completed interchanges have already become focal points for economic development and are likely to become more so in the future. However, not all interchange areas have the same potential for economic development. This is supported by the fact that some interchanges have grown considerably in a very short period while others have shown no development even after a lapse of several years. A problem of economic importance is the determination of the reasons for such differences in development.

OBJECTIVE OF THE STUDY

The primary concern of this investigation is to develop a method for predicting the economic development that is likely to occur at a given interchange site. The goal is to identify the interrelationships among the important factors leading to interchange development and to provide planners with a guide to estimating the potential development of non-urban interchange areas. Knowing the probable level of interchange area development, State and local planners can then prepare a reasonable land use plan for the interchange. Design engineers can, in turn, proceed to determine the highway capacity requirements, geometric configurations and traffic control needs according to the land use plan framework. With an accurate development forecast, the highway design and land use plan can be coordinated to encourage desirable and efficient development, while at the same time facilitating both traffic flow and safety and reducing the probability of premature obsolescence. In cases where premature obsolescence of the interchange facility has occurred, knowledge of future growth potential can be incorporated in the redesign and reconstruction of the interchange.

Many problems are involved in attempting to develop a means of predicting economic development at interchange areas. Some of the initial points to be established involve proper definition of

1) the interchange area or "interchange community," and

2) the economic development or "economic growth" of an interchange community. Another type of problem arises in quantifying the various factors which cause differences in the economic growth of interchange communities.

AN ECONOMETRIC GROWTH MODEL

The spontaneous economic development of a community is a complex phenomenon which involves balancing the rates of growth of the various segments that together form the community. There is, however, considerable variety in community types (residential, commercial, industrial etc.), and the balanced growth of one type of community will differ from that of another.

The pattern of development for a particular community will often depend upon circumstances that are unique to that community. For example, the speculative withholding of land from the market may delay the growth of the community, whereas the establishment of a new industrial plant close to a residential area may substantially promote its growth.

Since the economic growth of a community is such a complex phenomenon, to describe the state or level of development for a given community must involve measurement of the many characteristics of that community. The population of the community, number of persons employed in the community, capital investment in service facilities, number of housing units and the like, are all examples of variables that may be used to describe the level of economic development for a given community.

In order to predict the development of the community as a whole, each variable (which measures a particular characteristic or segment of the community) would have to be predicted. On account of the interrelationships of these variables, each one affects the "growth" of the community, and is, in turn, affected by the growth that takes place. For example, as a residential community grows, a need for service facilities such as grocery stores, gasoline stations for automobiles, variety and drug stores etc. develops. Consequently, this development encourages further residential expansion.

Similarly, a large flow of traffic on the crossroad at an interchange area may lead to more intense development of service facilities such as service stations, restaurants and motels at the interchange. As a result, this development may cause additional traffic on the crossroad.

Factors of this type which affect one or more other factors and, in turn, are influenced by them, are called *endogenous* variables. In short, these are the variables whose values the model seeks to explain.

In addition to the endogenous variables described, there are other factors that affect the level of economic development or growth of an interchange community; these factors, however, are generally not affected by the growth that takes place. These factors are called *exogenous* variables. For example, the variables which describe the geographical or physical environment of an interchange community are generally not influenced by economic development, although they do affect the degree of development that may be expected to occur.

Exogenous factors affecting the growth of an interchange community may include distances from nearby urban centers, topographic characteristics of the interchange area, access, zoning etc. Briefly, these are the variables which are determined apart from development at an interchange area. They are predetermined and may be regarded as given for purposes of explaining the values of the endogenous variables.

The classification of a variable as exogenous or endogenous depends upon the nature and objectives of the model. A variable classified as exogenous in one model may be considered as endogenous in another. The criterion to be used in classifying a variable is to regard as exogenous to a specified system those variables which influence the remaining (endogenous) variables but are not, as a result, affected.[3]

ASSUMPTIONS OF THE MODEL

It will be assumed that the entire model can be presented as a system of simultaneous linear equations [4] where each equation describes the way in which a particular aspect of economic development (endogenous variable) is determined by other relevant endogenous and exogenous variables. Such an equation describes a particular "structure" of the economic community and is called a structural equation of the model.

Any one of the structural equations in the model will have the same mathematical appearance as that of an ordinary multiple regression equation. However, the parameters of a structural equation in a system of equations cannot (in general) be derived by ordinary regression techniques. Other suitable methods have been developed.[5] One of these should be used.

In addition to the endogenous and exogenous variables in the model, it is assumed that each equation contains a stochastic variable called a disturbance (or shock) term which represents the aggregate effects of the unspecified variables for each relation.

An exceedingly large number of variables may influence the economic development of an interchange community. Many of these may have very slight effects, others are not quantifiable. Still, others may be unique for a given area. It is not practical to include all of these variables in a model. Hence, the model specifies only the variables thought to be most important. The net effect of the excluded variables for each equation is then represented by a disturbance term.

It will be assumed, for purposes of estimating the parameters of the model, that each of the disturbance terms behaves as a random variable having an expectation of zero, constant variance, and zero covariance with each other disturbance term.

Besides assuming linear structural equations for the model, we shall assume that no errors of observation have been made in measuring the endogenous and exogenous variables.

LIMITATIONS OF THE MODEL

It is assumed that the entire model can be presented as a system of simultaneous linear equations, in which a separate equation is used to describe the level of economic development of each of the segments of the interchange community in terms of the levels of development of the other segments (endogenous variables) and in terms of the characteristics of the environment itself (exogenous variables). The actual relationships among the variables of the model, however, may be more complex than the linear form assumed, in which case misleading estimates of the influence of the variables may result.

There may be unique or peculiar characteristics associated with specific interchanges which the model (being of a general nature) will not take into account, except as they may be represented as a part of the stochastic term. For example, the speculative withholding of land from the market may delay the growth of an interchange area. Similarly, intangible factors (e.g., aesthetic considerations) or other non-economic factors which might have a profound influence upon the degree to which a given interchange develops may be unaccounted for by the model.

The model developed is of a static nature. That is, it describes the equilibrium state of economic development in the neighborhood of a given interchange. It cannot, however, predict the *course* of economic development.

Since the model will be designed to predict economic development at interchange areas, the problem of properly defining the interchange area or "interchange community" arises. The area to be included or the boundary of the interchange community is not easily determined.

Some authors have used the term "interchange area" rather loosely to cover the entire vicinity in which the existence of the interchange may stimulate intensive uses of land that would not, otherwise have located there.[6] Others have used the term "area of influence" to mean the area within the vicinity of the interchange that is affected by the facility.[7]

Various studies have found that for non-urban interchanges, the majority of new economic development occurs within one-half mile of the interchange.[8] For this reason, the model will consider the "interchange community" as the area located within one-half mile of the interchange. Some arbitrary limitation of the interchange community is necessary and the one chosen will have some adverse effects on the applicability of the model to some interchanges, where exceptional geographic or topographic conditions lead to important developments more than one-half mile from the interchange.

Another very practical as well as important consideration is that the model be designed such that it can be implemented easily using secondary data. Although a model that requires an extensive primary data collection effort may have greater predictability for a specific location, it would have very limited general value.

DEVELOPMENT OF THE SIMULTANEOUS EQUATIONS MODEL

The development of a particular structure of the general model that reasonably may be expected to describe and predict development of an interchange community is itself a complex matter. Firstly, the relevant variables have to be identified and measured. These variables must be classified into the endogenous and exogenous categories.

The next step is the construction of the equations of the model. Involved in this is the problem of determining the form of the equations that best describes the nature of the relationships among the variables. Also there is the problem of determining which of the many variables that belong to the complete system should be included in (or excluded from) a particular equation. An incorrect inclusion or exclusion of a variable constitutes what is known as an error of specification and may have serious effects on the estimates of the parameters of the model.[9]

After the variables of the model have been defined and the equations constructed, the next step is the statistical estimation of the parameters of the structural equations of the system. An essential prerequisite to the statistical estimation of the parameters of the model is to verify that each equation in the model is unique in the sense that it is not a linear combination of the other equations in the model.

The method of estimation to be used in this research endeavor is a form of the so-called two-stage least squares technique. [10] The set of equations that constitutes the structure contain both exogenous and endogenous variables as mentioned earlier. There are as many endogenous variables as there are equations - since each equation "explains" the level of a particular measure of development (an endogenous variable) in terms of the levels of all other variables (endogenous and exogenous). This set of equations may be solved so as to obtain for each endogenous variable an expression relating the level of that endogenous variable to the values of all the exogenous variables.

For example, the first of the structural equations will be of the form $y_1 = f_1 (y_2,...,y_n, x_1,...,x_m)$ where the y's are endogenous variables and the x's are exogenous variables. There will be "n" such structural equations. This set of equations may then be solved for the y's in terms of the x's. The solution will yield a set of equations, the first of which will be of the form: $y_1 = g_1 (x_1,...,x_m)$. There will be "n" of these latter equations. This derived set of equations is called the reduced form of the structure.

Each of the reduced form equations explains the level of one factor of development of an interchange (one of the y's) at a given time in terms of levels of the exogenous variables (the x's) alone. Further, the exogenous vari-

ables (x's) are predetermined in the sense that they are either fixed characteristics of the site and neighborhood of the interchange or they are determined by influences outside the structure. It follows that for a given interchange, the levels of the relevant x's may be known and used to predict the values of the y's. In other words the levels of development that may be expected to occur at any given interchange may be estimated by means of the reduced form equations. It follows from the above that the estimates derived from the reduced form equations may be interpreted as the "potential" for economic development of the given interchange.

The two-stage least squares technique involves obtaining the estimated values of the y's from the reduced form equations and substituting these estimates for the actual y's on the right hand side of the structural equations. The y to the left of the equal sign is then regressed on the estimated y's and the relevant x's. The first structural equation in this way modified to the following form:
$y_1 = f_1 (\hat{y}_2,...,\hat{y}_n; x_1,..., x_m)$
where $\hat{y}_i$ is the estimated value of y_i obtained from the estimated reduced form equation:
$\hat{y}_i = \hat{g}_i (x_1,...,x_m)$.
The estimates of the parameters of the structural equations obtained by this technique are asymptotically unbiased.

The importance of the structural equations may be illustrated by their ability to estimate the marginal effect on different types of development at an interchange when the level of some other type of development has been determined at a level different from that predicted by the reduced form equation. For example, the reduced form equations may estimate the economic "potential" of some particular interchange to be very small. However, if for any reason the site should be selected for a large motel, this fact would change the "potential" of the interchange and the structural equations could be used to estimate the effect of this on the further development of the interchange, e.g., the likely appearance of service stations and restaurants.

By appropriate definitions the *system* of structural equations may be represented by the following matrix form:
$YA = XB + e$
The solution of this system of equations would be:
$Y = XBa^{-1} + eA^{-1}$
which may be written:
$Y = XC + u$
where $C = BA^{-1}$ and $u = eA^{-1}$
The above solution is the matrix representation of the "reduced" form of the structure.

PRELIMINARY DATA ANALYSIS

Data describing traffic flow, economic activity, and geographic and demographic characteristics for 144 non-urban Pennsylvania interchanges have been collected annually by The Pennsylvania State University. The approach will be to use these data to design a model for forecasting interchange development.

The analysis presented in this section is of a preliminary nature. The purpose of the analysis is to provide insight for the construction of a specific structure of the model for predicting economic growth at non-urban interchange areas and to investigate whether the observed relationships among selected variables are in agreement with *a priori* considerations.

The data collected for each of the 144 interchanges in the sample were analyzed by means of appropriate classifications as well as simple and multiple correlation analysis. Some of the more important findings are presented here.

As a first step in the analysis, the various types of new

440

economic development observed at the interchanges were classified as highway or non-highway oriented commercial, industrial, residential, or public. New economic developments were defined to be those developments that had taken place since the opening of the interchange. The interchanges studied were divided into two basic categories, "Complete access interchanges", which provided access to abutting lands along the cross route from all directions and "Incomplete access interchanges," which limited or totally prohibited access to one or more quadrants of the interchange.

Interchange area land development and interchange highway design are highly related. As the highway design restricts access to adjacent land, the potential for certain types of land development is sharply reduced.

For example, Table 1 shows the impact of the highway design upon land use. Of all the interchanges where access to adjoining land was limited, 44 percent of the

interchange sites had no new development from their opening date to 1975. In contrast, only 4 percent of the interchanges which provided for complete access to adjoining land failed to attract any new development. The comparable figures for 1970 were 63 and 25 percent, respectively.

Commercial development was the most common form of new development occurring at 91 percent of the complete interchanges and 31 percent of the incomplete access interchanges by 1975. Perhaps of greater significance is the fact that 89 percent of the complete interchanges had highway oriented commercial development, while only 6 percent of the incomplete access interchanges had such development.

Some new industrial development occurred at 13 percent of the complete interchanges and 0 percent of the incomplete interchanges by 1970 while increasing to 25 and 6 percent, respectively by 1975. On a relative basis,

Table 1 - Types of new economic development and percentage of interchanges with each type

Type	N= 128 Complete Access Interchanges (%)		N= 16 Incomplete Access Interchanges (%)	
	1970*	1975**	1970*	1975**
NO NEW DEVELOPMENT	25	4	63	44
SOME NEW DEVELOPMENT	75	96	38	56
EXCLUDING RESIDENTIAL	73	94	38	50
COMMERCIAL DEVELOPMENT	70	91	31	31
HIGHWAY ORIENTED	67	89	12	6
NON-HIGHWAY ORIENTED	30	59	31	31
RESIDENTIAL DEVELOPMENT	19	35	6	19
SCATTERED	13	24	0	6
PLANNED	6	11	6	13
INDUSTRIAL DEVELOPMENT	13	25	0	6
PUBLIC DEVELOPMENT	9	13	13	25

* The ages of the interchanges in 1970 ranged from 1 to 15 years with an average age of 7.9 years for the complete and 8.0 for the incomplete access interchanges.
** The ages of the interchanges in 1975 ranged from 6 to 20 years with an average age of 12.9 years for the complete and 13.0 for the incomplete access interchanges.

Table 2 - Endogenous variables and their 1975 mean level of intensity per interchange, standard deviation and range at the 128 complete non-urban interchanges

Endogenous Variable	Mean	Standard Deviation	Range
SERVICE STATION DEVELOPMENTS			
Y_1 Number of Stations	2.1	1.5	0 to 7
Y_2 Number of Gas Pumps	13.5	11.4	0 to 54
RESTAURANT DEVELOPMENTS			
Y_3 Number of Restaurants	0.9	1.0	0 to 5
Y_4 Number of Seats	154	270	0 to 1434
MOTEL DEVELOPMENTS			
Y_5 Number of Motels	0.5	0.8	0 to 4
Y_6 Number of Rooms	38	79	0 to 455
TOTAL HIGHWAY ORIENTED SERVICES			
Y_7 Highway Oriented Developments	3.8	3.2	0 to 16
NON-HIGHWAY ORIENTED DEVELOPMENT			
Y_8 Public Developments	0.2	0.4	0 to 2
Y_9 Industrial Developments	0.5	1.1	0 to 6
Y_{10} Other Commercial Establishments	1.6	2.5	0 to 15
TOTAL NON-HIGHWAY ORIENTED DEVELOPMENT			
Y_{11} Non-Highway Developments (Sum of Y_8, Y_9, Y_{10})	2.3	3.1	0 to 18
TOTAL DEVELOPMENT			
Y_{12} Highway and Non-Highway Oriented (Sum of Y_7 and Y_{11})	6.1	5.0	0 to 26

Table 3 - Exogenous variables and their 1975 mean level of intensity per interchange, standard deviation and range at the 128 complete non-urban interchanges

	Exogenous Variable	Mean	Standard Deviation	Range
X_1	Average Daily Traffic Cross Route (vehicles)	3.366	2,596	133 to 13,304
X_2	Average Daily Traffic Interstate (vehicles)	12,550	4,623	5,400 to 29,690
X_3	Community Zoning	0.59	0.49	0 or 1
X_4	Age of Interchange (years)	13	4	6 to 20 years
X_5	Distance to Nearest Urban Area (miles)	12.3	7.8	1 to 43 miles
X_6	Population Density-Local Community	157	232	10 to 2,010
X_7	Population Density Change – Local Community	24	69	−330 to 523
X_8	Market Value of Real Estate Per Capita – Local Community	$4,410	$3,710	$1,513 to $30,657
X_9	Change in Market Value Per Sq. Mile – Local Community (in 000's of dollars)	$423	$1,584	$–170 to $3,815
X_{10}	County Population Density	228	153	25 to 734
X_{11}	County Population Density Change	12	18	−17 to 78
X_{12}	County Market Value of Real Estate Per Sq. Mile (in 000's of dollars)	$890	$627	$73 to $2,977

public development occurred more frequently at the incomplete than complete interchanges. This may be due, in part, to the fact that highway oriented commercial development which usually competes for land around interchanges was not present to any appreciable degree at the incomplete access interchanges.

Due to the small number of incomplete access interchanges and the vast differences between developments at the complete and incomplete interchanges, further preliminary analysis is limited to the 128 complete interchanges.

Table 2 gives an indication of the endogenous variables considered for inclusion in a forecasting model as well as the average intensity and range in development at the 128 complete interchanges for year 1975.

Average total development (excluding residential) was six establishments per interchange and ranged from no development at a few of the interchanges to 26 units at one of the interchanges. The average number of highway oriented establishments (e.g., service stations, restaurants, motels, truck garages) was 3.8 units, while non-highway development such as industrial, public and other commercial establishments averaged 2.3 units per interchange.

As expected at the non-urban interchanges, gas stations were the most frequent form of new highway oriented development followed by restaurants and motels, respectively. For the non-highway oriented category, other commercial establishments such as those found in small shopping centers were most common, followed by industrial and public developments.

The exogenous variables considered for inclusion in the model together with their mean, standard deviation and range per interchange for the 128 complete interchanges are given in Table 3. The first two variables consisted of average daily traffic (ADT) volumes on the interstate highway and intersecting cross routes for the year 1970. Traffic data were obtained from traffic log books supplied by the Pennsylvania Department of Transportation.

The population per square mile of the local township or borough containing the interchange was also for the year 1970 and is simply referred to as population density – local community. In instances where more than one township contained the interchange, the populations of both townships were combined and an average density figure was computed.

Population density data for the county containing the interchange and all market value of real estate data were also for the year 1970, while all changes in population and market value from 1960 to 1970.

It should be noted that some of the variables that were classified as exogenous in this particular study are often classified as endogenous variables. For example, the population of an interchange community is usually of an endogenous nature in that it affects the growth of the community and is, in turn, affected by the growth that takes place. Annual population data are not readily available, hence, the population variables, being of a lagged or predetermined nature, are classified as exogenous

Similarly, the volume of traffic on the crossroad at the interchange will tend to influence the degree of development of service facilities such as gasoline stations, restaurants and the like. Consequently, these developments will create additional traffic. However, variation in the ADT will be related to the characteristics of a much larger geographic area than the immediate neighborhood of the interchange itself. The factors that determine the character of the larger area are often dominant in the explanation of the traffic flow. These factors may not be included in, or related to the exogenous variables explicit in the model, but they tend to describe the peculiar characteristics of the interchange area. Since variations in the ADT may largely be due to characteristics peculiar to the various interchanges, the ADT can be considered exogenous for it and serve as an aggregate measure of the unique characteristics of the interchange otherwise not included in the model.

It can also be noted that some of the endogenous variables in Table 2 are different measures of the same type of development. For example, service station development per interchange is measured by the actual number of gasoline stations and also by the number of gasoline pumps. In addition, service station development is included in the number of highway oriented establishments which is the sum of the numbers of gasoline stations, truck garages, restaurants, and motels at the interchange. Similarly, restaurant and motel development are measured in different ways. These different measures can give rise to several different models.

Simple correlations for each of the 12 exogenous variables with each of the 12 endogenous variables were obtained in order to get a "feel for the data." Table 4 shows the simple correlations with Y_7 through Y_{12}.

As can be seen from Table 4, among all 12 exogenous variables, ADT on the cross route correlated highest with highway oriented development (.327) and total development (.421), while population density change and change in market value of real estate of the local community had the two highest correlations with non-highway oriented development (.446 and .459, respectively). These coefficients are all statistically significant at the one percent level.

Table 4 - Simple correlation coefficients for each of the 12 exogenous variables with each of the six endogenous variables (Y_7, Y_8, Y_9, Y_{10}, Y_{11}, Y_{12}), 1975 data level

	Exogenous Variable	Endogenous Variable					
		Y_7 Highway Oriented	Y_8 Public	Y_9 Industrial	Y_{10} Other Commercial	Y_{11} Non-Highway oriented	Y_{12} Total Development
X_1	Average Daily Traffic - Cross Route	.327**	.172	.253**	.294**	.348**	.421**
X_2	Average Daily Traffic – Interstate	.016	.069	.453**	.340**	.443**	.282**
X_3	Community Zoning	.101	−.006	.089	.075	.091	.120
X_4	Age of Interchange	−.087	.060	.320**	.223*	.300**	.129
X_5	Distance to Nearest Urban Area	−.100	−.093	−.167	−.210*	−.245	−.211*
X_6	Population Density – Local Community	−.021	.061	.297**	.199*	.273**	.154
X_7	Population Density Change – Local Community	.047	.127	.359**	.374**	.446**	.303**
X_8	Market Value of Real Estate Per Capita – Local Community	.070	−.021	.024	.049	.046	.073
X_9	Change in Market Value Per Sq. Mi. – Local Community	.081	.138	.402**	.370**	.459**	.333**
X_{10}	County Population Density	−.111	.079	.313**	.128	.224*	.066
X_{11}	County Population Density Change	−.168	.214*	.174*	.125	.189**	.009
X_{12}	County Market Value of Real Estate Per Sq. Mi.	−.083	.105	.344*	.206*	.301*	.132

* Coefficient is statistically significant at the 5% level.
** Coefficient is statistically significant at the 1% level.

It is also interesting to note that the age of interchange had virtually no correlation with highway oriented development, but did correlate significantly with non-highway oriented development (.300). Perhaps this is explainable by the fact that the minimum age of the interchanges using the 1975 data is six years with much of the highway oriented development occurring sooner and more rapidly than the public, industrial and other commercial developments. If recently constructed interchanges had been part of the study, one normally would have expected the age of the interchange to also correlate with highway oriented developments.

The highest and only significant correlation with public development was county population density change. Industrial development correlated significantly with 9 of the 12 exogenous variables, the two highest of which were average daily traffic on the interstate (.453) and market value of real estate per capita of the local community (.402). Other significant variables included population density change - local community age of interchange, county market value and county population density. Other commercial development was signifi-

cantly correlated with 8 of the 12 variables; the highest correlation was with population density change in the local community (.374). As expected, the only negative correlation involved distance to the nearest urban center. This coefficient, (−.210), was not very high but did indicate an inverse relationship between the two variables and was statistically significant at the five percent level.

Tables similar to Table 4 were also constructed for the highway oriented endogenous variables Y_1, Y_2,...,Y_6 but are not presented here for the sake of brevity. The results closely followed those of Y_7 (total highway oriented development) with ADT on the cross route being the most highly significant variable in each case.

For each endogenous variable in Table 4, the 12 simple correlation coefficients were ranked in order of magnitude. The results are presented in Table 5. Some variables ranked consistently high or low depending upon whether highway orientated or non-highway oriented development was considered (e.g. population density change and market value per square mile of the local community, community zoning, and county population density).

Table 5 - The simple correlation coefficients in Table 4 ranked for each endogenous variable, 1975 data levels

	Exogenous Variable	Endogenous Variable					
		Y_7 Highway Oriented	Y_8 Public	Y_9 Industrial	Y_{10} Other Commercial	Y_{11} Non-Highway Oriented	Y_{12} Total Development
X_1	Average Daily Traffic – Cross Route	1	2	8	4	4	1
X_2	Average Daily Traffic – Interstate	12	8	1	3	3	4
X_3	Community Zoning	4	12	11	11	11	9
X_4	Age of Interchange	6	10	5	5	6	8
X_5	Distance to Nearest Urban Area	5	6	10	6	8	5
X_6	Population Density – Local Community	11	9	7	8	7	6
X_7	Population Density Change – Local Community	10	4	3	1	2	3
X_8	Market Value of Real Estate Per Capita – Local Community	9	11	12	12	12	10
X_9	Change in Market Value Per Sq. Mi. – Local Community	8	3	2	2	1	2
X_{10}	County Population Density	3	7	6	9	9	11
X_{11}	County Population Density Change	2	1	9	10	10	12
X_{12}	County Market Value of Real Estate Per Sq. mi.	7	5	4	7	5	7

443

Table 6 - Simple correlation coefficients for each of 3 exogenous variables with each of the 6 endogenous variables 1970 and 1975 data levels

Endogenous Variable		X_1 ADT-Cross route		X_2 ADT-Interstate		X_4 Age of Interchange	
		1975	1970	1975	1970	1975	1970
Y_7	Highway Oriented	.33**	.25**	.02	.22**	−.09	.40**
Y_8	Public	.17*	.09	.07	.09	.06	.14
Y_9	Industrial	.25**	.17*	.45**	.41**	.32**	.35**
Y_{10}	Other Commercial	.29**	.23**	.34**	.34**	.22*	.33**
Y_{11}	Total Non-Highway	.35**	.26**	.44**	.47**	.30**	.43**
Y_{12}	Total Development	.42**	.31**	.28**	.40**	.13	.50**

* Coefficient is statistically significant at the 5% level.
** Coefficient is statistically significant at the 1% level.

A few variables ranked relatively consistent across all categories of development (e.g. county market value of real estate square mile, distance to the nearest urban center, and market value per capita of the local community). Still other variables such as ADT on the cross route and ADT on the interstate highway were less predictable. While it was not surprising to find that average daily traffic on the cross route correlated highest with highway oriented development, it was somewhat unexpected to find that average daily traffic on the interstate correlated the least among the 12 exogenous variables.

In order to see the extent to which the simple correlation coefficients and subsequent rankings would differ over time, additional preliminary analysis was conducted involving data levels for the year 1970. Remarkably, most of the coefficients and rankings remained consistent from 1970 to 1975. Three notable exceptions were the age of interchange, ADT on the interstate, and ADT on the cross route. Table 6 gives the simple correlations of these exogenous variables with each of the 6 endogenous variables (Y_7 through Y_{12}) for 1970 and 1975 data levels.

As can be seen from Table 6, all correlations with average daily traffic on the cross route were less in 1970 than in 1975. This caused the rankings for this variable to slip somewhat using 1970 data (see Table 7). The most notable changes were a drop in rank from 1 to 2 in the correlation with highway oriented development, and from 1 to 4 when correlated with total development.

Average daily traffic on the interstate highway, on the other hand, improved its position on both an absolute and relative basis when compared to 1970 data. The correlation of this variable with highway oriented development in 1970 was r = .22 as compared with r = .02 in 1975, thus moving from its rank of 12 in 1975 to a rank of 3 using 1970 data levels. It is interesting to note also

that when comparing the simple correlations between the two ADT variables and total development Y_{12}, the coefficients in 1970 for the two variables are almost the reverse of those in 1975.

These results suggest that the ADT on the interstate is more significant in determining the level of development around an interchange in its earlier stages, but that as an interchange grows and matures, the ADT on the cross route is a more significant factor in determining the degree of economic development.

As can also be seen in Table 6 using the 1970 data levels for the 128 complete interchanges, the age of the interchange is significantly correlated with all endogenous variables (except the one measuring public development).

Using the 1975 data levels at these same interchanges resulted in a drop in all correlations, with total development and highway oriented development showing very little correlation. These results are also reflected in the rankings shown in Table 7.

This suggests that for interchanges which have not been opened for an extended period of time, the age of the interchange might be an important factor in explaining the degree of development. For older interchanges, age becomes less important, expecially for explaining highway oriented service development.

As a next step in getting a "feel for the data" and to aid in the construction of a forecasting model, a multiple linear regression analysis was conducted by regressing each endogenous variable against all 12 exogenous variables. This was done for three different time periods or data levels, 1970, 1973, and 1975, in order to see what the resulting effect would be in the proportion of explained variations, number of statistically significant variables, and regression coefficients.

Table 7 - Comparisons of the rankings of the simple correlation coefficients of the three exogenous variables using 1970 and 1975 data levels

Endogenous Variable		X_1 ADT-Cross Route		X_2 ADT-Interstate		X_4 Age of Interchange	
		1975 Rank	1970 Rank	1975 Rank	1970 Rank	1975 Rank	1970 Rank
Y_7	Highway Oriented	1	2	12	3	6	1
Y_8	Public	2	5	8	4	10	2
Y_9	Industrial	8	7	1	1	5	2
Y_{10}	Other Commercial	4	6	3	3	5	4
Y_{11}	Total Non-Highway	4	6	3	1	6	2
Y_{12}	Total Development	1	4	4	2	8	1

Endogenous Variable		Proportion of Explained Variance R^2			Number Statistically Significant Variables**		
		1970	1973	1975	1970	1973	1975
SERVICE STATION DEVELOPMENTS							
Y_1	Number of Stations	.220	.202	.212	5	5	8
Y_2	Number of Gas Pumps	.200	.199	.204	9	4	9
RESTAURANT DEVELOPMENTS							
Y_3	Number of Restaurants	.284	.158	.153	8	6	5
Y_4	Number of Seats	.351	.231	.191	8	9	7
MOTEL DEVELOPMENTS							
Y_5	Number of Motels	.221	.231	.225	6	5	5
Y_6	Number of Rooms	.386	.269	.245	7	4	5
TOTAL HIGHWAY ORIENTED SERVICES							
Y_7	Highway Oriented Developments	.297	.214	.203	10	7	5
NON-HIGHWAY ORIENTED DEVELOPMENT							
Y_8	Public Developments	.097	.082	.093	3	2	2
Y_9	Industrial Developments	.233	.230	.288	5	3	4
Y_{10}	Other Commercial Establishments	.215	.309	.260	4	9	10
TOTAL NON-HIGHWAY ORIENTED DEVELOPMENT							
Y_{11}	Non-Highway Oriented Developments (sum of Y_8, Y_9, Y_{10})	.301	.348	.354	4	10	9
TOTAL DEVELOPMENT							
Y_{12}	Non-Highway and Highway Oriented (sum of Y_7 and Y_{11})	.356	.287	.262	7	6	6

* Obtained from multiple linear regression of the respective endogenous variable on all 12 exogenous variables.
** 10% level of significance.

Some of the results are summarized in Table 8 which gives each endogenous variable, the proportion of explained variation R^2, and the number of statistically significant variables when all 12 exogenous variables were used in each linear equation. The results were not especially encouraging since, in most cases, only 20 to 30 percent of the variations in the endogenous variables could be explained by all the exogenous variables. The lowest proportion of explained variation occurred with public development. This had been somewhat anticipated on the basis of the simple correlation analysis.

For the 1973 and 1975 data levels, the number of statistically exogenous variables in the multiple regressions ranged from a low of two for public development to a high of ten of the possible 12 for the non-highway oriented (other) commercial establishments in 1975, and total non-highway oriented development in 1973. For the 1970 data, the range was a low of 3 for public development to a high of 10 for highway oriented development. As can also be seen from Table 8, the proportion of explained variation for total highway oriented developments for the years 1970, 1973, and 1975 were .297, .214, and .203, respectively; the corresponding figures for total non-highway oriented developments were .301, .348, and .354.

Regression coefficients associated with the exogenous variables are not presented here for the sake of brevity, but for the most part, also varied in direct proportion to the variation in degree of explained variation. That is, as more variability occurred in the degree of explained variation from 1970 to 1975, greater differences occurred among the corresponding regression coefficients.

These results suggested that if the current variables were to be used in constructing a static growth model and in estimating its structural parameters, great care would have to be given to defining the population of interchanges for which the model might be applicable, especially with regard to age. Even so, it appears that such a model would not yield very great predictive ability on the basis of the explained variations in the preliminary ordinary multiple regression analysis.

Hence, other attempts at obtaining a higher degree of explained variation are being made before attempting to specify an entire structural model. One of these attempts involves the transformation of existing variables. For example, actual distance to the nearest urban center may have better been measured as the logarithm of distance or as the square root of distance. These as well as other logarithmic transformations of the variables are being conducted, along with the addition of some new variables.

Realizing the many pitfalls in arbitrary transformations of data and in using stepwise regression analysis to find significant variables, a prime consideration in the addition of a new variable or modification of existing variables is that a logical theoretical basis be established for such changes. In this regard, a new variable, which at this preliminary stage has shown promise in significantly increasing the proportion of explained variation, is population of the nearest urban center divided by the distance to the nearest urban center.

Another consideration, in the addition of new variables, is that either secondary data sources are readily available for their measurement or primary data collection is relatively easy, as for example, in measuring distances to nearby urban centers.

Further refinements and analyses are still in progress; hence, final results of the preliminary analysis cannot be presented at this time. However, the work thus far is encouraging and it is felt that a model can be developed that will be usable by planners and highway designers.

SUMMARY AND CONCLUSIONS

This paper presents the results of an attempt to develop a method for forecasting the type and intensity of economic development at non-urban interstate highway interchanges. Such information could be used by planners and highway designers to avoid premature obsolescence of highway facilities.

Some of the difficulties encountered in developing such a model involve proper definition of the interchange area or "interchange community" and the "economic growth" of the interchange community. Another problem involves the identification and quantification of certain factors that cause differences in the economic growth of interchange communities.

Still another very practical and important consideration is that the model be designed such that it can be implemented easily using secondary data. Although a model that requires an extensive primary data collection effort may have greater predictability for a specific location, it would have very limited general value.

The "interchange community" was considered as that area located within one-half mile of the interchange. The "economic growth" of an interchange community was considered to be determined by two types of factors

1) endogenous variables, i.e., those variables that describe the state or levels of economic development for the given community, and

2) exogenous variables, i.e., those variables that affect the level of economic development of the interchange community but which are not, in general, affected by the growth that takes place.

A general theoretical simultaneous equation model is discussed together with its assumptions and limitations.

In order to aid in the development of a particular structure of the general model, a preliminary analysis was conducted utilizing a sample of 144 non-urban interchanges on Pennsylvania's interstate highways. The preliminary analysis involved classification of developments into various types and performing simple and multiple linear correlation analyses. Twelve endogenous and twelve exogenous variables were analyzed.

In particular the analysis revealed that the exogenous variables differ in their influence over time as well as across various types of economic developments. Data levels for the years 1970, 1973, and 1975 were utilized in a multiple linear regression to see how much fluctuation would occur in the proportion of explained variations and the regression coefficients over time. In some instances, the results revealed strong differences between the earlier and later time periods.

Because of the low levels of explained variation, further preliminary analyses involving transformation of existing variables and creation of some new variables is currently being conducted. Some preliminary analysis of these further refinements have shown considerable improvement.

Once the refined static model has been tested empirically, it is hoped that for short run purposes, it may be able to provide a "rough" approximation for forecasting potential development. In the long run, however, a dynamic model, even a somewhat crude one, is probably most appropriate. The complexity involved in designing and determining the proper structure for such a dynamic model will be greatly aided by the analysis conducted in this on-going investigation.

REFERENCES

[1] United States Congress. 1956. **Federal-Aid Highway Act of 1956.** Public Law 627, Title I Section 108, 84th Congress, 2nd Session. Washington: U.S. Government Printer.

[2] Levin, D.R. 1961. "The Highway Interchange Land-Use Problem." **Land Use and Development at Highway Interchanges.** HRB Bull. 288, p. 1. Washington, D.C.: NRC, National Academy of Sciences.

[3] Ferber, R. and P. J. Verfoon. 1962. **Research Methods in Economics and Business.** p. 407. New York: Macmillan Company.

[4] Hood, W. C. and T.C. Koopmans. 1961. **Studies in Econometric Methods.** p. 112. New York: Wiley.

[5] Johnston, J. 1972. **Econometric Methods.** p. 376. New York: McGraw Hill.

[6] Pendleton, W.C. and R.D. Vlasin. 1961. "The Impact of Interstate Highways in Rural Areas, **"Engineering Bulletin of Purdue University** (Proceedings of the 47th Annual Road School, March 27-30, 1961). p. 106. Lafayette, Indiana: Purdue University.

[7] Lehr, R.L. **et al.** 1965. **The Relationship of the Highway Interchange and the Use of Land in the State of Oklahoma.** Pt. I, p. I-6. Oklahoma City: University of Oklahoma Research Institute.

[8] United States Department of Transportation. 1976. **Social and Economic Effects of Highways.** Washington, D.C.: Federal Highway Administration, USDOT.

[9] Malinvaud, E. 1966. **Statistical Methods of Econometrics.** P. 70. Chicago: Rand McNally.

[10] Goldberger, A. 1964. **Econometric Theory.** p. 329. New York: Wiley.

The effect of alternative urban forms on two-mode transportation system requirements

by
R.G. RICE
Department of Civil Engineering
University of Toronto

INTRODUCTION

The interrelationship between urban land use and urban transportation has long been recognized as a phenomenon worthy of attention at the policy level. It is common to regard the provision of transportation services as an important policy variable amongst what is generally considered to be a limited set of policy options available to government control. The ability to influence accessibility levels through the control of the design, construction, and operation of the transportation network is a controllable variable which must be utilized in a responsible and positive manner. In a similar way, it is essential that we understand the effect which urban development patterns have on travel demands and hence on the transportation networks required to accommodate these demands. The direction in which the interrelationship between transportation and land use is approached matters little, since it is much too complex to be able to attribute causality to either determinant. The importance of the interrelationship to the transportation engineer or urban planner lies in the understanding and utilization of the relationship in a positive manner, rather than the need to know which is the dependent and independent variable.

The question which is addressed by the research described in this paper has to do with the potential for reducing transportation system requirements and improving transportation efficiency through modification in urban density and spatial patterns. In other words, it attempts to assess the nature and degree of transport sensitivity to variations in urban land use. The measures of effectiveness which are developed relate to both the performance and efficiency of the transportation system. Implications for energy consumption may be determined from operating conditions and implications for capital investment requirements from derived network capacities and configurations.

The typical approach to the type of investigation proposed is to conduct a static comparison of a series of alternative end-state or horizon-year plans, and to make a choice of 'best' alternative on the basis of future travel demand accommodation at an acceptable level-of-service. This is a rather limited perspective, however, since the interrelationship between transportation service and land use is very much a dynamic one. In effect, it is the *time stream* of the interaction and its associated benefits and costs which should be the object of evaluation, and not the terminal state at the end of the planning period. [Rice and Nowlan (1975)]. The implication of this realization is that the true nature of the transportation/land-use relationship is not likely to be revealed by a comparison of transportation systems for a range of urban forms, but this does not imply that such an exercise is without value. In fact, it is likely that, from an efficiency point of view, the evaluation of planning actions through time will still require the definition of an end-state or boundary condition.

It is the objective of the research described in this paper, then, to determine the most effective combinations of road and transit systems to serve a defined number of cities with differing density and spatial patterns, and thereby to assess the effects of varying urban form on transportation investment and service requirements. While the results of such an analysis are of direct relevance to the planning of new towns, the implications may also be extended to expanding urban areas. This is of concern in Canada, for example, where it is estimated that cities with populations of 400,000 and over will double in size by 1990. The urban development consequences are even greater since the rate of household formation is expected to be larger than the rate of population growth.

REVIEW OF THE LITERATURE

Given the fact that research interest in coordinated urban transportation and land-use planning has only developed in the last ten to fifteen years, the literature available represents quite a range of techniques and conclusions. For the sake of simplicity the studies which have been done have been divided into two categories:

a) those dealing with *sensitivity analyses,* either of transportation service variations on land development, or of land use alternatives on transportation system requirements, and

b) those which attempt to describe the *interactive nature* of transportation/land-use relationships, allowing for appropriate feedback effects.

The first group of studies deal almost exclusively with the sensitivity of transportation requirements to variations in urban density and spatial patterns, and make use of the established four-stage transportation modelling procedure. Representative of this group are the studies by Voorhees, Barnes and Coleman (1962), Jamieson, et al (1967), Voorhees and Assoc. (1968), Milton Keynes Development Corporation (1970), Bellomo, Dial and Voorhees (1970), Sjovold (1973), and Zupan (1973). All of these provide interesting insights into the variability of travel demands with changing development patterns, but conclusions often conflict due to differences in assumptions and in the choice of output variables. The same type of results derive from a smaller sub-group of studies which assesses the same sensitivity question, but through the application of optimizing procedures. Most

447

notable among these are the research of Hemmens (1967), Black (1967), and Creighton et al (1964).

Very little research has been conducted on the sensitivity of the transportation/land-use relationship as perceived from the opposite direction: that is, the sensitivity of land-use growth patterns to changes in the transportation system. The research of simplest elegance in this area is that of Schneider (1968) and Hamburg, Brown and Schneider (1970), in which a model is postulated relating zonal growth to zone attractiveness and relative accessibility. The EMPIRIC growth allocation model has also been applied to this question [Hill, Brand and Hansen (1965)], where it is concluded that the provision of transportation facilities can result in a difference in land-use growth of as much as 20 percent.

The second major category of the literature which is relevant here relates to the two-way interaction of transportation and land use, so that not only is the effect of one on the other considered, but also the consequential feedback in the reverse direction. Most of the studies in this area make use of conventional transportation models and growth allocation models, and representative of these are Morison and Hansen (1968), Campbell (1968), Metropolitan Toronto Transportation Plan Review (1974), Putman (1974) and Maunsell and Partners Ltd. (1975). Once again, as was the case in the first area of the literature on sensitivity analyses, there have been a selective number of studies in this second area which approach the problem through the use of optimizing procedures. Most notable among these are the studies by Cockfield (1970) and Stewart and Grecco (1970).

In terms of the conclusions to be drawn from the two major areas of the literature, it is perhaps easiest to divide these into general results and those results which relate directly to particular urban forms. Generally, the primary result is simply that land-use distribution is a major determinant of urban travel requirements – the most important factor in this regard is the distribution and balance of employment opportunities and resident labour force, so that the adjustment of these land-use densities and their proximities may result in as much as a 10-30% decrease in travel. By way of modal comparisons, it appears that the roadway system is more flexible than the transit system, in that the forcer can support a wider range of land-use plans without changes in configuration or capacity. It is also true, however, that a mixed-mode plan is more desirable than a single-mode system, since improved travel conditions and greater modal operating efficiencies result. While it appears that the consideration of a range of land-use development alternatives produces an equally wide range of transit and road utilization, relatively little research has been conducted on the effect of development patterns on the use and requirements for the two travel modes.

An assessment of those conclusions in the literature which relate to the transportation requirements of particular urban forms indicates a high degree of conflict; however, this is almost always due to the difference of indicator measures utilized in each study. For example, the use of average trip length indicates that the central core city results in the lowest requirement and the low-density sprawl pattern the highest. The determination of capital costs of the transportation system indicate the converse, however.

While several studies are concerned with the transportation "mode mix", they avoid the complexity of land-use variation. Those research efforts which do address the full land-use/transportation problem typically conclude quite generally with regard to mode usage: for example, the need for corridors of a particular trip density for the efficient use of rapid transit, or the suitability of particular modes for the line-haul and feeder compo-

nents of urban travel. In essence, the assessment of the variation in mode utilization with changes in urban form remains basically unfulfilled.

RESEARCH METHODOLOGY

As has been indicated, it is the intent of the research described here to assess the effects of varying urban form on road and transit investment and service requirements. Given the perspective offered in the existing literature it is apparent that any effort in this area should allow, firstly, for full modal interdependence, permitting travel mode shifts with changes in land-use and socio-economic characteristics as well as level-of-service; and secondly, for a broader number and type of output indicators. In essence, the estimation of modal travel demands for each urban form must be sensitive both to the level-of-service supplied and to the spatial and density pattern of land-use activities. In order to permit the investigation of the transportation system characteristics for a range of urban patterns, there is a strong need for an analytical base which allows for the comparison of transportation measures between land-use plans. That is, the procedure for developing the transportation network and mode combination for each urban form must be consistent and not unduly bias any particular city pattern(s). Herein lies the central issue of the research procedure.

The description of the research method has been divided into three separate stages: the first deals with derivation of the range of hypothetical urban forms, the second with the estimation of peak-hour travel demands for each city type, and the third with the generation of optimal two-mode transportation networks to accommodate the estimated travel demands in each city. Each of these phases is described in turn in the next three sub-sections.

Development of the Urban Forms

Due to the complexities associated with transportation/land-use interrelationships hypothetical rather than actual urban forms were generated for testing in the research project. It was necessary that the range of hypothetical city types be defined such that they resulted in a significantly broad range of transportation conditions. To accomplish this, three elements or components of urban form were defined as follows:

a) *spatial organization* – the configuration of the urban area in two-dimensional space on the horizontal plane,

b) *activity distribution* – the distribution pattern of land-use activities within the spatial organization, in terms of both the type and density of land use, and

c) *transport connectivity* – the transportation network which provides linkages between the land-use activities and thereby services the spatial organization, in terms of both travel mode type and capacity and the extent to which it provides linkages between all zone pairs.

These three components are represented diagrammatically in Figure 1. Using these definitions, the objective of the research may now be re-stated as the analysis of the effect of urban spatial organization and activity distribution on the requirements and nature of the transport structure.

By analyzing a range of conditions associated with each of the three component elements and through a review of similar studies, six distinctive city types were defined. These were the central core, uniform density, multi-centred, radial corridor, linear, and satellite cities, as shown schematically in Figures 2 and 3. It was then possible to define population and employment distribution characteristics for a total population size of two million for each of the urban forms. This was accomplished through a series of realistic and empirically-derived constraints on density variation, socio-economic characteristics, and relative population and employment location. Since all of the city forms had at least some degree of central concentration, distance from the core was the primary structural variable, with random variations in population and employment characteristics permitted on a zone-to-zone basis. The details of this allocation procedure have been described elsewhere [Rice (1975)], although further summary characteristics for each of the six urban forms are provided in Table 1 and in Appendix 1.

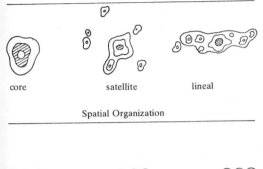

Spatial Organization

core   satellite   lineal

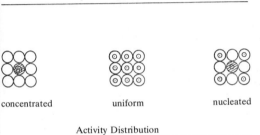

concentrated   uniform   nucleated

Activity Distribution

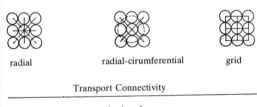

radial   radial-cirumferential   grid

Transport Connectivity

Figure 1 – components of urban form

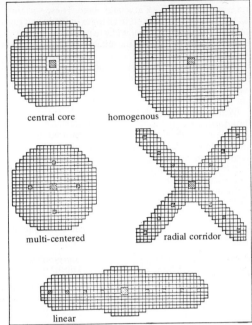

central core   homogenous

multi-centered   radial corridor

linear

Figure 2 – selected urban forms

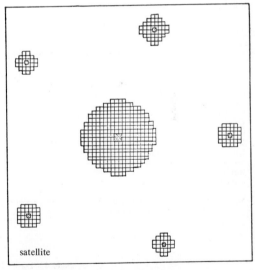

satellite

Figure 3 – selected urban form

Travel Demand Estimation

With the definition of the urban forms characteristics it becomes possible to estimate peak-hour travel demands. For this analysis attention was directed to the work trip, on the basis that it was this trip purpose which set the condition for the design of the transportation networks. The demand estimation procedure involved the use of the conventional four-stage process, applying zonal trip generation and attraction equations and the gravity model to produce a work-trip origin-destination matrix for each of the six urban forms. Trip distribution was assumed to be fixed, in spite of variations in the

Table 1 – General urban form characteristics

Urban Form	Population	Employment	Developed Area	Gross Pop. Density	Average Net Resid. Density	Number of Dwelling Units	Average Pers. Per Dwell. Unit
Central	2,000,000	800,000	484 mi²	4130 pers/mi²	28,600 pers/mi²	565,300	3.54
Homogeneous	2,000,000	803,000	856	2340	13,300	534,300	3.74
Multi-centred	2,000,000	804,700	484	4130	30,800	567,000	3.52
Radial Corridor	2,000,000	802,200	408	4900	33,800	567,000	3.52
Linear	2,000,000	803,000	496	4030	29,500	566,100	3.54
Satellite	2,000,000	800,300	444	4500	32,300	567,300	3.53

transportation network at a later stage. These variations were only allowed to result in changes in mode and route choice. This assumption of inelasticity of demand for the work trip was thought to be suitable in the light of the research objectives.

A comparison of the trip production estimates for the range of urban forms is provided in Table 2 and the person-trip hours for all trip purposes as estimated by the trip distribution model are indicated in Table 3.

Within the trip distribution phase of the travel estimation procedure, it was critical that differences in travel behaviour for the six city types be permitted. Since trip distribution deals with interchange patterns, the relative location and distribution of employment and population will be the primary determinants of average trip lengths and transportation system requirements. It is apparent then that each hypothetical urban form must have a unique travel impedance function associated with it. The determination of this function was achieved by relating average trip length to the work opportunity distribution as defined by Voorhees and Associates (1968). Since this distribution is uniquely defined for each city type, it was possible to determine an average work trip length and, from this, an impedance function for each of the six cities. Finally, the work trip origin-destination matrices were assigned to spider networks, resulting in the desire-line assignment results presented in Table 4[1]. The advantage of the desire-line assignment is that the volume flow condition that has been estimated is not constrained by the form or characteristics (capacity and mode) of the spider network. It therefore provides a relatively objective and consistent base for deriving more comprehensive two-mode transportation networks.

Table 2 – Trip production estimates by urban form

Urban* Form	Total Person-Trips/Day	Home-origin Trips/Day	Person-Trips by Purpose			Truck Vehicle-Trips
			Home-based work	Home-based non-work	Non-home-based	
UF-1A	4,250,000	1,830,000	1,524,000	2,130,000	596,000	425,000
UF-1B	4,420,000	1,900,000	1,526,000	2,274,000	620,000	440,000
UF-2	4,180,000	1,800,000	1,530,000	2,064,000	586,000	420,000
UF-3	4,100,000	1,750,000	1,526,000	2,000,000	574,000	410,000
UF-4	4,280,000	1,840,000	1,526,000	2,154,000	600,000	430,000
UF-5	4,180,000	1,795,000	1,520,000	2,074,000	586,000	420,000

* UF-1A	– central core	UF-3	– radial corridor
UF-1B	– homogeneous	UF-4	– linear
UF-2	– multi-centred	UF-5	– satellite

Table 3 – Person-trip hours by purpose and for all-day by urban form

Urban form	Trip purpose				Total for 24-Hours
	Home-work	Home-non-work	Non-home-based	Truck	
UF-1A	*64,766*	94,308	*43,580*	*31,274*	392,782
UF-1B	76,485	121,856	54,759	44,753	495,872
UF-2	65,187	*90,892*	45,007	33,700	*390,930*
UF-3	83,713	103,931	44,236	35,401	454,312
UF-4	81,598	118,645	48,591	36,968	485,268
UF-5	106,075	130,623	44,009	32,490	539,201
Ratio of high value to low	1.6	1.4	1.25	1.4	1.4

NOTE: The cursive values in the table indicate the lowest number of person-trip hours within each column (i.e., trip purpose).

Table 4 – Desire-line assignment summary

Urban form	Total network length (mi.)	Average link length (mi.)	no. of two-way links	ASSIGNMENT RESULTS							
				Total trips				Work Trips			
				Avg. Vol. per Link	Max. Link Volume	Total Pers.-Mi.	Total Pers.-Hrs.	Avg. Vol. per Link	Max. Link Volume	Total Pers.-Mi.	Total Pers.-Hrs.
UF-1A	376.4	3.6	104	32,710	104,500	20,550,000	342,470	5,465	34,600	3,400,000	56,700
UF-1B	462.4	4.2	108	31,360	103,000	27,030,000	450,230	4,900	24,000	4,150,000	69,200
UF-2	381.4	3.2	120	29,390	80,100	20,300,000	338,000	4,270	21,000	2,920,000	48,600
UF-3	289.9	3.5	82	50,800	170,500	23,700,000	395,000	8,530	47,100	3,730,000	62,200
UF-4	377.6	3.3	114	37,970	169,000	26,030,000	433,760	6,470	57,300	4,410,000	73,500
UF-5	597.0	4.9	122	30,520	107,300	30,340,000	505,640	5,130	28,800	5,740,000	95,700

Flow Diagram	Computer Programs

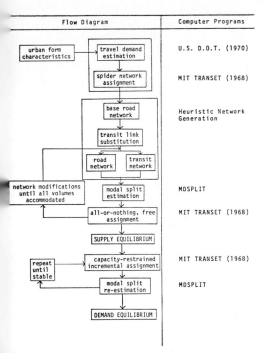

Figure 4 – Two-mode network generation procedure

were depleted in trip volume, thereby modifying the service available on these links in the next round of transit service substitution. Within an iterative sequence then, a network rationalization process takes place, involving both traveller route and mode choice, so that natural corridors of travel demand build up in accordance with network geometry and demand orientation.[4]

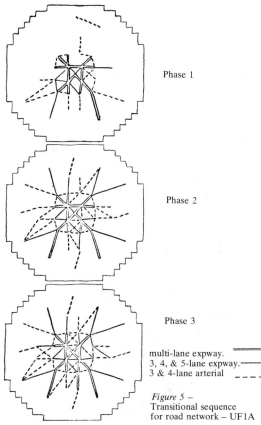

Phase 1

Phase 2

Phase 3

multi-lane expway. ════
3, 4, & 5-lane expway. ──────
3 & 4-lane arterial ─ ─ ─ ─

Figure 5 –
Transitional sequence
for road network – UF1A

Two-Mode Network Generation

The final phase of the research requires that a procedure be developed for generating a unique two-mode, capacity-restrained transportation network for each city type, thereby permitting a realistic and unbiased comparison of mode performance for the six urban forms. In very basic terms this procedure is dependent upon a definition of mode "balance" which might be stated as the condition in which both mode sub-systems are used effectively in and of themselves and in such a manner as to produce collectively optimal *total* system performance. [2]

The network generation procedure which was applied was a two-stage heuristic process, dependent on an initial division of mode service for each network link (the supply equilibrium cycle) and the refinement of model volumes in accordance with mode and route choices (the demand equilibrium cycle). This procedure is described in flow chart form in Figure 4, with an indication of the computer programs utilized in each step.

The supply equilibrium phase starts with the desire-line volumes from the spider assignment for each city type and defines an initial two-mode transportation network which is able to accommodate the expected demand. This was achieved by first designing a base road network which could just carry the estimated desire-line volumes. Modifications were then made to this initial "feasible" solution by substituting transit service on a link-by-link basis, such that a trade-off function between transportation facility space consumption and user travel time is always satisfied. [3] It is obvious that the introduction of transit mode service will have a substantial effect on both mode and route choice. It was necessary, therefore, to re-estimate modal split and trip assignment after the initial round of transit substitution. When this was done, however, it was found that the new routes selected take advantage of the higher level-of-service links, so that there is a natural aggregation of trip movements into specific modal corridors. In a similar manner, other links

The network rationalization process is most easily demonstrated by the diagrams in Figures 5 and 6. These diagrams represent the results for the road and transit networks of the central core city (UF-1A) for three phases of the iterative supply cycle. While these figures only represent the high-capacity links in the modal networks it is quite apparent that the road network expands and the transit network contracts. This is obviously a function of the modal split function, but this phenomenon did occur for all of the six urban forms, as demonstrated in Tables 5 and 6.

The supply equilibrium cycle is repeated until no further changes are required in each of the modal network links to accommodate the travel volumes estimated in the previous iteration of the cycle. It should be noted (Figure 4) that the trip assignment component of the supply cycle is a free or desire-line assignment, since the objective of network synthesis is to develop a natural expression of the required transportation system. In other words, network rationalization must be unconstrained by physical limitations; modal capacity is simply provided in accordance with traveller demand. This results, therefore, in the need for the demand equilibrium cycle, which re-estimates modal split and route assignment in an iterative sequence, under assumptions of capacity-restrained flow on all links. This cycle is also

451

Table 5 – Lane-mile summary by urban rorm

Urban Form	Link Type	Number of Lane-Miles		
		Phase 1	Phase 2	Phase 3
UF1A	road 1	172.0	256.6	258.1
	2	89.0	21.0	19.5
	3	801.6	905.2	856.8
	4	676.5	958.6	1123.7
	Total	1739.1	2141.4	2258.1
UF1B	road 1	162.0	229.8	233.8
	2	93.8	17.8	10.8
	3	1387.6	1479.4	1452.2
	4	375.7	814.4	972.4
	Total	2019.1	2541.4	2669.2
UF2	road 1	198.8	262.3	262.3
	2	77.6	18.2	18.2
	3	877.8	1029.0	884.4
	4	388.6	780.2	999.4
	Total	1542.8	2089.7	2164.3
UF3	road 1	197.8	228.0	228.0
	2	36.6	0.0	0.0
	3	392.0	416.6	394.0
	4	1063.0	1276.6	1287.4
	Total	1689.4	1921.2	1909.4
UF4	road 1	107.8	145.2	153.2
	2	56.2	20.0	12.0
	3	906.8	766.4	782.4
	4	1216.0	1677.4	1765.4
	Total	2286.8	2609.0	2713.0
UF5	road 1	480.2	476.0	484.0
	2	34.8	22.2	10.0
	3	945.6	727.2	709.8
	4	2015.0	2624.8	2694.0
	Total	3475.6	3850.2	3897.8

NOTE: 1. Road link type 1 – local
Road link type 2 – minor arterial
Road link type 3 – major arterial
Road link type 4 – expressway

2. Only link types 3 and 4 appear in Figures 60, 62, 64, 66, 68 & 70.

3. Since all links derive from the spider network with interzonal connections, many intra-zonal local and minor arterial links and lane-miles will not be represented in this table.

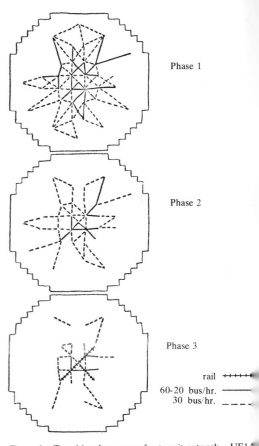

Figure 6 -- Transitional sequence for transit network – UF1A

indicated in the flow diagram of Figure 4. The system output from the four required steps of this cycle for th radial corridor city (UF-3) is shown in Figure 7, as a example of the operation of the demand equilibrium process.

Table 6 – Train/bus-mile summary by urban form

Urban Form	Link Type	Number of train/bus-miles		
		Phase 1	Phase 2	Phase 3
UF1A	rail	0.0	0.0	756
	bus	23,772	14,029	8,446
UF1B	rail	0.0	0.0	0.0
	bus	22,223	12,788	8,666
UF2	rail	0.0	0.0	0.0
	bus	19,730	10,676	6,815
UF3	rail	0.0	0.0	1,974
	bus	15,656	14,576	7,997
UF4	rail	0.0	0.0	1,356
	bus	23,378	16,729	9,508
UF5	rail	0.0	0.0	1,536
	bus	32,404	27,266	21,027

NOTE: Only a portion of the bus-miles are represented in Figures 61, 63, 65, 67, 69 and 71.

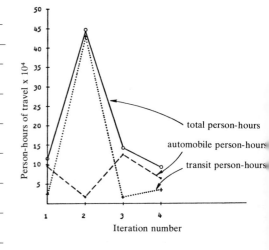

Figure 7 – System person-hour oscillation for UF3

Table 7 – Summary of final travel demand characteristics by urban form

Output Measure	URBAN FORM					
	UF1A	UF1B	UF2	UF3	UF4	UF5
Total System						
(a) total work trips	346,500	341,380	326,900	334,700	375,100	387,950
(b) person-hours	7.00×10^4	7.71×10^4	5.00×10^4	9.65×10^4	9.51×10^4	17.14×10^4
(c) mean trip length	11.68 min.	13.1 min.	9.07 min.	17.01 min.	14.49 min.	26.0 min.
(d) % transit	18.2%	8.0%	10.3%	33.8%	19.9%	8.0%
Road Network						
(a) work trips	293,100	313,900	293,500	221,200	300,350	357,950
(b) % on expwy.	63%	55%	59%	85%	75%	90%
(c) trip length						
– mean	11.78 min.	12.16 min.	8.30 min.	17.2 min.	13.58 min.	26.66 min.
– std. dev.	10.88 min.	7.64 min.	4.99 min.	18.8 min.	12.54 min.	40.8 min.
Transit Network						
(a) work trips	53,400	27,480	33,400	113,500	74,750	30,550
(b) % on rail	30%	0%	0%	51%	37%	26%
(c) trip length						
– mean	11.22 min.	24.06 min.	15.82 min.	16.62 min.	18.82 min.	18.39 min.
– std. dev.	8.27 min.	11.02 min.	8.98 min.	13.16 min.	13.94 min.	18.34 min.

COMPARATIVE ANALYSIS OF MODAL PERFORMANCE

The results of the network generation procedure are most easily demonstrated by the total system output measures in Table 7. The differences in travel conditions for the six cities are obviously quite significant. For both total person-hours and mean trip length, the first three urban forms (UF1A, UF1B and UF2) have lower conditions than the other three forms. This is not a function of mode usage, since modal split varies from 8% to 34%, and this variation occurs in both groups of cities.

The comparison of mode usage for the range of cities is indicated diagramatically in Figures 8 and 9. The percentage of trips using transit corresponds closely to the number of train-miles supplied, with the exception of the satellite city where the existence of rail transit has little effect on the use of public transit. With regard to the percentage of person-hours on the high-speed service links (expressway and rail), the two corridor cities (UF3 and UF4) and the satellite city (UF5) have the highest dependency on high service level facilities, as would be expected. While tranportation investment cost has not been estimated directly, it is possible to form some general conclusions on capital costs from the amount of high-service facilities required in each of the six city types. The two corridor plans and the satellite plan (UF3, UF4 and UF5) are dependent on high-service facilities for both modes, and hence will require high capital investment. The satellite plan easily claims the position of most expensive form, even though its rail service requirements are not the largest. The radial corridor plan is likely to be the cheapest of the corridor

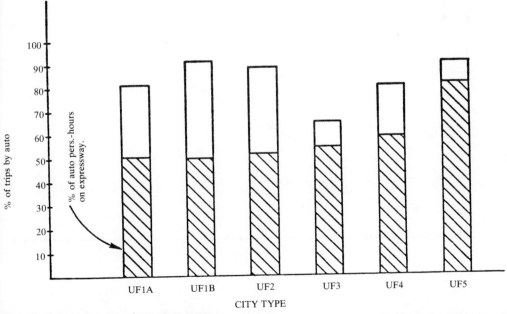

Figure 8 – Auto mode usage and expressway usage

453

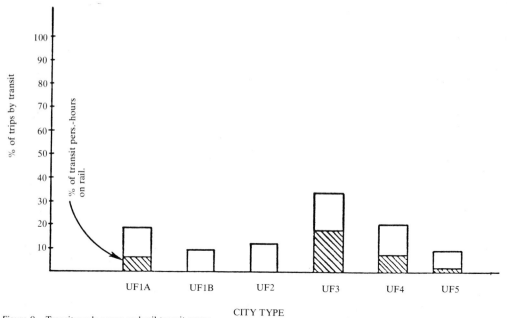

Figure 9 – Transit mode usage and rail transit usage

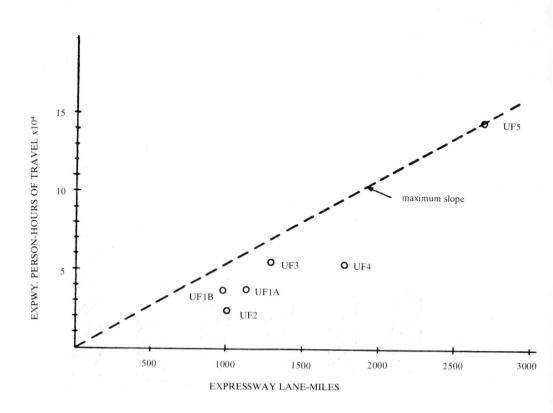

Figure 10 – Efficiency of expressway usage

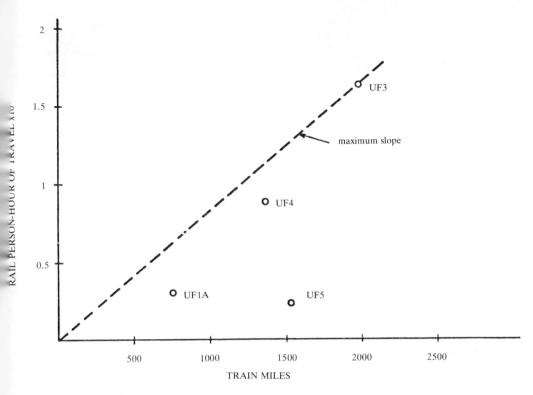

Figure 11 – Efficiency of rail transit usage

plans. The remaining three cities (central core, homogeneous, and multi-centred) require the lowest transportation investment, with the multi-centred city requiring the absolute minimum.

Finally, in order to measure the relative efficiencies of the high-service links in the modal networks Figures 10 and 11 have been constructed for expressway lane-miles and person-hours, and for rail transit train-miles and person-hours, respectively. It is apparent that for expressway efficiency, the satellite city (UF5) ranks at the top while the multi-centred (UF2) and the linear city (UF4) perform rather poorly. For rail transit, however, the networks of the radial corridor (UF3) and linear city (UF4) perform well and UF5 does exceedingly poorly. With regard to the efficiency of the total networks, including all link types, it may be concluded generally that it is more difficult to obtain an efficient transit network than it is to achieve the same for a road network. The satellite form is the primary example of this disparity, but it is demonstrated in the other urban forms as well. In terms of overall modal efficiency, the radial corridor city rates best in general, with little question. While this might be as expected, the homogeneous city takes second position. Even though this latter city has minimal transit service, what is available is effectively utilized.

CONCLUSIONS AND POLICY IMPLICATIONS

It is the task of this final section to indicate general observations and conclusions which derive from the analysis, to specify their relevance to policy considerations, and to describe the directions in which further research might be most profitably oriented.

The primary hypothesis assumed by the research reported upon in this paper is that, for a consistent set of assumptions, the transportation requirements of any particular urban form are uniquely defined. This hypothesis is strongly supported by the analysis in the previous section; in particular, average work trip lengths for the six cities differ by a factor of almost three. Also, the investment cost implications clearly indicate the relative inexpensiveness of the centrally-oriented city types (central core, homogeneous and multi-centred) relative to the two corridor plans and the satellite plan, and this conclusion is verified by the requirement for a large percentage of high-service links in the latter group of cities.

The verification of this hypothesis, therefore, generally supports similar research by Balkus (1967) and runs counter to the conclusions of Zupan (1973) and Hemmens (1967). With regard to specific urban forms, the research results are confirmed by Voorhees, Barnes and Coleman (1962), who conclude that the existence of sub-centres reduces average trip length, but conflict with Jamieson, et al (1967), who contend that the linear form is most efficient, rather than the radial corridor plan. In reference to the final conclusions of the Metropolitan Toronto Transportation Plan Review (1974), the research supports the contention that a nucleated pattern is preferable to a single core plan in terms of all transportation measures, but conflicts directly with the statement that a single transportation network is capable of supporting three different city forms.[5]

The first hypothesis of the research may be extended to relate to the effect which alternative urban forms have on transportation mode requirements. The analyses of the previous section indicate substantial variability in mode usage (8-34% transit use) between the six city types. In addition, the submode balance (rail/bus and expressway/arterial) is also dramatically different, with two urban forms (homogeneous and multi-centred) having no rail service at all.

The implications of these modal differences on user

455

travel costs and agency transportation investment costs should also prove to be significant for policy input. While neither type of costs have been estimated directly in this research, it is possible to compare average trip length and personhours of travel with network supply requirements. Since the ranking of the urban forms by trip length or person-hours gives identical results (multicentres, central core, homogeneous, linear, radial corridor, and satellite), the choice does not matter. Comparing this ranking with that for implied investment requirement, the same ordering from low to high cost is obtained for the first three urban forms, and a change in order for the linear and radial corridor form in the last three forms. However, it is even more instructive to use an efficiency measure (relating output per unit of input, such as person-hours/lane-mile or bus-mile). Such a comparison indicates that the radial corridor plan, followed by the homogeneous and multi-centred city, make the best use of transportation investment funds.

As is the case with much policy-oriented research, the directions which are identified for further analysis are often as significant as the product produced. It is quite apparent in this case that there are several internal modifications to the modelling procedure which could be proposed. These include the use of simultaneous destination, mode, and route choice models, the incorporation of transportation investment and user cost functions, the empirical verification of results, the inclusion of new transportation systems, and the application of the model procedure to cities of different population size. The most important implication of the research, however, has to do with the planning process needed to effectively evaluate long-range plans.

The perspective taken by this research of the interrelationship between urban land use and transportation has been one essentially oriented to the transportation implications of a number of static urban forms. It therefore represents a method suited to the assessment of an end-state condition, but not to the means required to produce such an end-state through time. In many ways it is the latter question which is of prime importance in urban planning; in fact, it is contended that the evaluation of any plan may *only* be accomplished by assessing the path by which that plan is achieved (or, to determine if it is even possible to get there from here).

This assertion requires that increased attention be given to the staging of transportation plans in such a way that selected urban states may be promoted. This type of dynamic policy orientation will require the use of land-use forecasting techniques in conjunction with the transportation methods used in this research. With this combination it would be possible to assess the balanced and inbalanced state of a transportation plan in relation to the urban activity pattern, and to make changes in accordance with perceived objectives.

ACKNOWLEDGEMENT
While the author accepts all responsibility for the research described here, personal acknowledgements are extended to Professors Richard M. Soberman and John Dakin for their encouragement and guidance, and to members of the Urban Transportation Policy Impact study group within the University of Toronto/York University Joint Program in Transportation for their collective contributions. The financial assistance offered by the Central Mortgage and Housing Corporation, the Ontario Department of Treasury, Economics and Intergovernmental Affairs, and the Transportation Development Agency is gratefully acknowledged.

REFERENCES
Balkus, Kozmas (1967), "Transportation Implications of Alternative Sketch Plans", **Highway Research Record Number**
180. Washington: Highway Research Board, pp. 52-70.

Bellomo, S.J., Dial, R.B., and Voorhees, A.M. (1970). "Factors, Trends, and Guidelines Related to Trip Length", **National Cooperative Highway Research Program Report No. 89.** Washington: Highway Research Board.

Black, Alan (1967). "Optimizing Density of Development with Respect to Transportation Cost", **Highway Research Record Number 207.** Washington: Highway Research Board. pp. 22-31.

Campbell, E. Wilson (1968). "An Evaluation of Alternative Land Use and Transportation Systems in the Chicago Area". Chicago Area Transportation Study. (October).

Cockfield, R.W. (1970). "A Design Method for the Preparation of a Preliminary Urban Land-Use/Transport Plan". Waterloo, Ontario: University of Waterloo (May).

Creighton, Roger L., Gooding, David, Hemmens, George, and Fidler, Jere (1964). "Optimum Investment in Two-Mode Transportation Systems", **Highway Research Record Number 47.** Washington: Highway Research Board. pp. 23-45.

Hamburg, John R., Brown, Geoffrey, J.H. and Schneider, Morton (1970). "Impact of Transportation Facilities on Land Development", **Highway Research Record Number 305.** Washington: Highway Research Board. pp. 172-178.

Hemmens, George C. (1967). "Experiments in Urban Form and Structure", **Highway Research Record Number 207.** Washington: Highway Research Board. pp. 32-41.

Hill, D.M., Brand, D. and Hansen, W.B. (1966). "Prototype Development of a Statistical Land-Use Prediction Model for Greater Boston Region", **Highway Research Record Number 114.** Washington: Highway Research Board. pp. 51-70.

Jamieson, G.B., et al (1967). "Transportation and Land-Use Structures", **Urban Studies,** Vol. 4, No. 3, (November) pp. 201-217.

Maunsell and Partners Ltd. (1975). "New Structures for Australian Cities", prepared for the Cities Commission, Canberra, Australia. (February).

Metropolitan Toronto Transportation Plan Review (1974). "Development of Land Use and Transportation Alternatives", Working Paper, Report no. 62. Toronto. (May).

Milton Keynes Development Corporation (1970). "The Plan for Milton Keynes", Volume Two, Report of the evidence presented by the consultants. United Kingdom. (March).

Morison, Ian W. and Hansen, Walter G. (1968), "Canberra: Toward a Scheme for Continuous Growth", **Highway Research Record Number 229.** Washington: Highway Research Board. pp. 7-20.

Putman, Stephen H. (1974). "Preliminary Results from an Integrated Transportation and Land-Use Models Package", **Transportation,** Vol. 3, No. 3. (October).

Rea, John C. (1972). "Designing Urban Transit Systems: An Approach to the Route-Technology Selection Problem", **Highway Research Record Number 417.** Washington: Highway Research Board. pp. 48-59.

Rice, R.G. (1975). "Performance Characteristics of Two-Mode Transportation Systems for Varying Urban Form", unpublished Ph. D. thesis manuscript. Toronto: University of Toronto, Department of Civil Engineering.

Rice, R.G. and Nowlan, D.M. (1975). "Toward a Dynamic Framework for Urban Transportation and Land-Use Planning", **Proceedings – Sixteenth Annual Meeting, Canadian Transportation Research Forum and Transportation Research Forum,** Vol. XVI, No. 1. pp. 91-106.

Schneider, M. (1968). "Access and Land Development", in **Urban Development Models,** Special Report No. 97. Washington: Highway Research Board. pp. 164-177.

Sjovold, A.R. (1973). "Investigation of the Sensitivity of Transportation Systems Performance to Changes in Land Use", **High-Speed Ground Transportation Journal,** Vol. IV, No. 2.

Stewart, W. Don, and Grecco, William L. (1970). "Plan Design Model for Urban Area Use Allocations", **Highway Research Record Number 305.** Washington: Highway Research Board. pp. 156-171.

Voorhees, A.M., and Assoc. (1968). "Factors and Trends in Trip Lengths", National Cooperative Highway Research Program Report No. 48. Washington: Highway Research Board.

Voorhees, A.M., Barnes, Charles F., and Coleman, Francis W. (1962). "Traffic Patterns and Land-Use Alternatives", **Highway Research Board Bulletin Number 347.** Washington: Highway Research Board, pp. 1-9.

Zupan, Jeffrey M. (1973). "Social Implications of Land Use and Mode Choice", **Transportation Engineering Journal, ASCE Paper 9750, T.E. 2.** (May) pp. 383-391.

FOOTNOTES

1. The spider networks developed for each of the six urban forms are described in Appendix 2.

2. A more detailed discussion of alternative definitions of mode balance and the possible use of this concept in planning is presented in Rice (1975).

3. This is somewhat akin to the space-time product used by Cockfield (1970), although he permits variations in both network connections and land-use activety location in an effort to minimize "wasted space-time content".

4. Rea (1972) also noted a similar network rationalization process in his research on the specification of transit technology and level of service.

5. Although in a dynamic sense this statement might be considered to be true; ie – alternative stagings of any transportation plan will produce different land-use configurations.

APPENDIX 1

– Comparative Urban Form Characteristics

The general population and employment characteristics of the six urban forms are very important for the subsequent travel demand analyses, so it is of some vulue to present further comparative information. Summary information on land-use distribution, employment distribution, and population and housing distributions is provided in Figures A-1 to A-6. In addition, Table A-1 indicates the degree of population and employment concentration in the central area of each of the six cities, and Figure A-7 presents the net residential density functions by distance from the core for each of the city types.

FIG. A-1

GENERAL CHARACTERISTICS GRAPHS — UF-1A

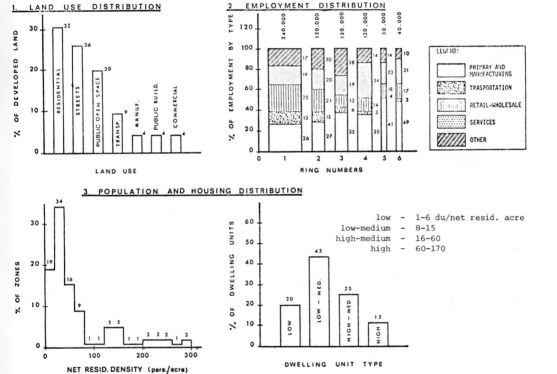

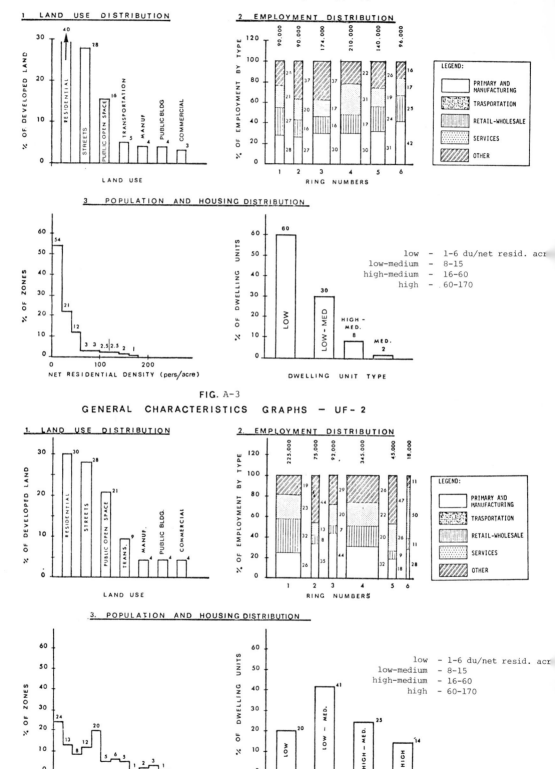

FIG. A-2

GENERAL CHARACTERISTICS GRAPHS — UF-1B

FIG. A-3

GENERAL CHARACTERISTICS GRAPHS — UF-2

458

GENERAL CHARACTERISTICS GRAPHS — UF-3

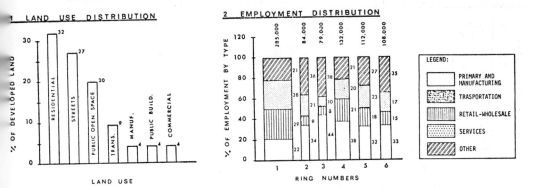

1 LAND USE DISTRIBUTION

2 EMPLOYMENT DISTRIBUTION

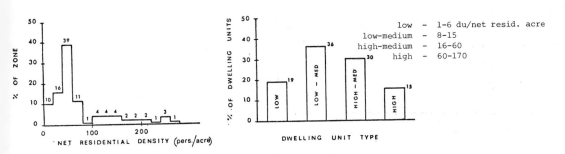

3 POPULATION AND HOUSING DISTRIBUTION

low — 1-6 du/net resid. acre
low-medium — 8-15
high-medium — 16-60
high — 60-170

GENERAL CHARACTERISTICS GRAPHS — UF-4

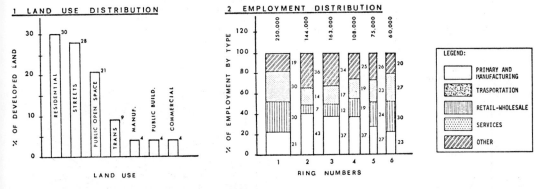

1 LAND USE DISTRIBUTION

2 EMPLOYMENT DISTRIBUTION

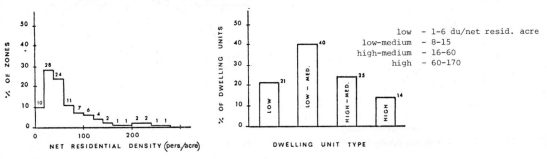

3 POPULATION AND HOUSING DISTRIBUTION

low — 1-6 du/net resid. acre
low-medium — 8-15
high-medium — 16-60
high — 60-170

FIG A-6
GENERAL CHARACTERISTICS GRAPHS — UF-5

1. LAND USE DISTRIBUTION

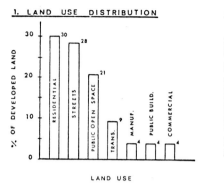

2. EMPLOYMENT DISTRIBUTION

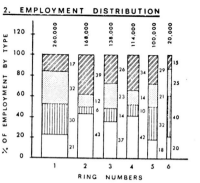

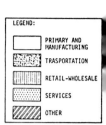

LEGEND:
- PRIMARY AND MANUFACTURING
- TRASPORTATION
- RETAIL-WHOLESALE
- SERVICES
- OTHER

3. POPULATION AND HOUSING DISTRIBUTION

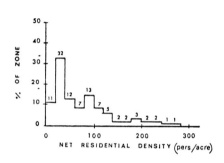

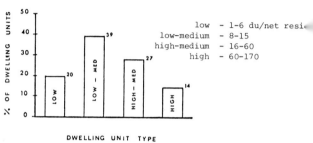

low — 1-6 du/net resi
low-medium — 8-15
high-medium — 16-60
high — 60-170

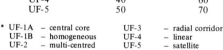

Table A-1 – Comparative distribution of population and employment

Urban Form*	% of Population in Central City	% of Employment in Central City
UF-1A	56%	70%
UF-1B	14	30
UF-2	24	45
UF-3	36	56
UF-4	40	60
UF-5	50	70

* UF-1A	– central core	UF-3	– radial corridor
UF-1B	– homogeneous	UF-4	– linear
UF-2	– multi-centred	UF-5	– satellite

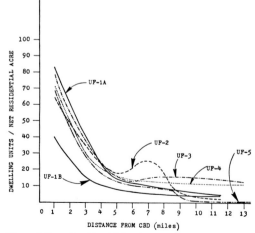

Figure A-7 – net residential density

APPENDIX 2
Spider Networks for the Six Urban Forms

It is the spider networks which form the initial basis for the network generation procedure so that their construction is of considerable importance to the research results. These are constructed in such a way that direct movement is possible between any trip origin and destination. The networks for the six city types are shown in Figures B-1 to B-6. These diagrams also indicate the zone system that was used throughout the transportation analysis.

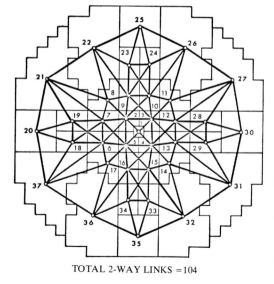

TOTAL 2-WAY LINKS =104

Fig. B-1 – Spider network UF-1A

460

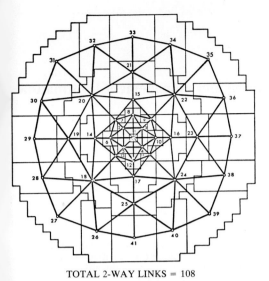

TOTAL 2-WAY LINKS = 108

Fig. B-2 – Spider network UF-1B

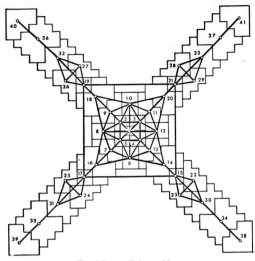

Total 2-way links = 82

Fig. B-4 – Spider network UF-3

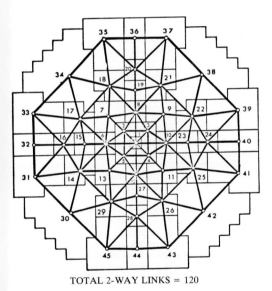

TOTAL 2-WAY LINKS = 120

Fig. B-3 – Spider network UF-2

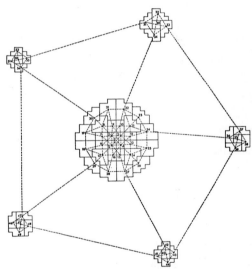

Total 2-way links = 122

Fig. B-6 – Spider network UF-5

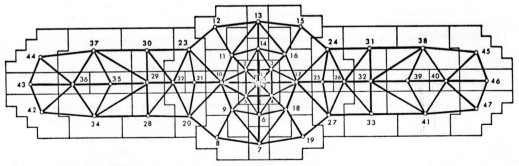

Fig. B-5 – Spider network UF-4   Total 2-way links = 114

An integrated system for airline planning and management information

by

Morton Ehrlich

Eastern Airlines, Inc., U.S.A.

INTRODUCTION

Eastern Air Lines is the third largest commercial airline in the world, superseded in passenger volumes only by Aeroflot and United Air Lines. During the year of 1976, Eastern carried twenty-nine million passengers on more than half a million flights. That is equivalent to eighty thousand passengers a day on one thousand five hundred flights operating between one hundred cities throughout North America and the Caribbean.

And not only is Eastern's operation large, it is also very complex. For instance, today at the Atlanta, Georgia airport Eastern's 250 operations will arrive with sixteen thousand passengers. Eight thousand of these will connect between the more than one thousand, three hundred origination and destination markets Eastern serves using the Atlanta airport as a connecting hub. These and eight thousand other Atlanta originating and connecting passengers from other airlines will then depart Atlanta on two hundred fifty scheduled departures. Eastern's Atlanta operation is the largest single carrier airport operation in the free world and as such I think you can appreciate the complexity of scheduling five hundred flight movements to provide daily service between the thirteen hundred markets served through this single facility.

I mention these statistics to illustrate not only the size of Eastern's operation but equally important – as evidenced by the Atlanta operation – is the complexity and interdependence of an air transportation system.

And, within this environment an air transport system needs to serve the requirements of the public by providing only those services demanded at the proper times and with appropriately sized aircraft and the services needed to operate with a high degree of punctuality.

We believe that Eastern has been somewaht succesful in providing customer demanded services. Our load factors and growth rates have recently been among the highest of all United States trunk carriers.

And, the punctuality demanded by our customers is evidenced by the completion of more than 99% of scheduled plane miles and the fact that more than 80% of our flights arrive within fifteen minutes of schedule.

These parameters do not permit more than a minimal occurence of marketing or operational slack – and certainly preclude any appreciable design or planning error.

So, the criteria by which we need to evaluate our Planning effectiveness is – to say the least – strict. There is little room for error.

I don't wish to make it sound as if Eastern is somehow unique – that is not the case. Most airlines in the world operate in a similar environment.

Where Eastern may be somewhat unique, has been in our committment to develop advanced systems that permit our management to function with the most accurate, timely and relevant information in making decisions that impact the future of the airline.

In today's discussion, I'll:

First: Outline the perspective that we at Eastern have utilized in developing management information systems that guide our decisions in planning the path the airline will travel.

Second: I'll describe some of these systems that today perform an integral function in the planning process. I think you'll find these to be among the more comprehensive and useful systems in operation in any transportation network. and

Finally: I'll review some of the current research and systems development projects now being pursued at Eastern.

SYSTEMS PERSPECTIVE

An airline can be viewed as a vast information system in that it depends on multiple levels and directions of information flows. This view is conceptually important in establishing an ideal set of information systems that foster an environment where decisions are made in context of the current state of the entire transportation network.

Functions of Systems in the Management Process

The systems involved in this structure are initially concerned with data collection and communication; both that which is endogenous to the airline and also that which defines the environment in which we operate.

After the raw data is gathered and summarized, it needs to be systematically reported and compared to objectives as part of a control mechanism.

As we proceed beyond that step to an analysis of the underlying causes of the observed results, we find more complex reporting systems that bring together data from various sources to fully clarify problems and opportunities. This is the intitial systematic process within the Planning function.

Proceeding yet further we have simple models that evaluate proposals for correcting problems and exploiting opportunities.

And finally, there exist complex models using operations research techniques that actually develop optimal solutions.

This progression outlines several distinct classes of systems. Initially providing for the capture and communication of information are data systems. Beyond that the process, whereby data is converted into varying degrees of useful management information, constitutes the higher level applications I classify as Management Information Systems.

Credit for assistance in the preparation of this report is given to Mr. D.C. Birdsall, Manager-Planning Systems, and Mr. O.F. Auten, Sr. Systems Analyst-planning, at Eastern Airlines.

Four Levels of Management Information Systems

These higher level applications can be categorized as follows:

LEVEL ONE: Basic reporting and communications systems usually focusing on a single source of data.

LEVEL TWO: Complex reporting systems bringing together various sources of data and focusing it on decision variables.

LEVEL THREE: Simple models that evaluate proposed plans, and

LEVEL FOUR: Complex models that actually develop solutions.

A "System of Sytems"

This conglomeration of successively complex management tools provide what we see as "A System of Systems" each dependent and largely integrated with those at the lower and higher levels. We began working towards the development of this "System of Systems" in the late 1960s.

Principles and Prerequisites

It was apparent at that time, as it is now, that if we were to implement systems proficient in advanced modeling and operations research techniques, there were a number of prerequisite systems and capabilities that would have to be developed.

Guidelines for our work were thus set:

− A good data system had to proceed any level of proficiency in Management Information Systems − be they as simple as LEVEL ONE or as complex as LEVEL FOUR Planning Systems. And to the extent that we could visualize eventual development of the LEVEL FOUR systems, it was necessary to devote more attention to the definition of complete data base systems. We knew then that the more advanced systems required more detailed information to function.

− We also knew that as we progressed through the evolution of each level of systems we had to maintain a purity of design. Each level could be developed only after complete definition of the prior level, as each depended to a large extent on the output of the lower level systems. This will be obvious to you in our discussion of Eastern's Planning Systems.

− And most importantly systems need to be decision oriented. And even oriented towards specific decisions. The information to be included and presented or analyzed has to have its origin in the mind of the decision maker. Only from an in-depth study of his needs within a decision process, can a system to fulfill those needs be defined. In this study one must identify, evaluate and modify traditional information flows to convert these flows into Management Information Systems that precipitate intelligent decisions.

− And the "System of Systems" must be permitted to evolve within the environment of their users. Very few of today's decision makers, for valid reasons, are prepared to casually accept systems that profoundly impact the traditional means by which they make and implement decisions. Therefore, most often, even if the systems planner could envision the ultimate manager/systems synthesis that would promote optimal decisions, he needs to implement this solution on a phased basis. Invariably, during the phased implementation, many improvements and refinements to the original system design will become apparent. A complex series of systems, like other live organisms need to germinate, build a solid root system and can then yield a product that is productive and symbiotic within its environment. Certainly systems that assist management in arriving at decisions need to have benefit of the symbiotic relationship.

These then, are some of what I think can perhaps be called a priori principles that need to serve as a guide in the development of any complex series of Management Information Systems.

DATA SYSTEMS

Data systems are a necessary prerequisite to a Management Information System. These are concerned with the capture and communication of raw data and the subsequent creation of a series of data bases.

The data capture and communication processes have undergone significant technological change in the decade of the seventies. Prior to this period this process was predominantly structured around the completion of paper forms and the physical transportation of these forms to a central site at which the information could be encoded via the keypunch process into machine readable form. This slow, cumbersome process was rather error prone due to the separation of the encoder from the physical operation of the airline and the necessary reliance on hand-written material for input to the data system.

Technological innovations in cable, microwave and satellite data transmission capabilities, complimented by the development of solid state electronics and high density storage media have fostered the migration of the data encoding process from the central site to operational locations, regardless of their geographical dispersion.

Now data can be entered directly into CRTs, equipped not only with a keyboard and display screen, but also with editing and feedback features that improve the accuracy of the data at its source. This technology was critical to many of the data capture systems surveyed. It also figured prominently in their economic productivity.

The operational, financial and marketing oriented data systems discussed here are but a sample of Eastern's total data systems but are those most critical to the Planning function.

Operational − SYSTEM INFORM

Technology made possible the design and implementation of an integrated series of on-line airline operations oriented data collection and communications subsystems. They provide for airport operating personnel to input and audit 178 elements of data defining the operation of each flight concurrent with the progress of the day's operation. This data is instantaneously transmitted from each airport to Eastern's Charlotte, North Carolina computer facility making this information available for query to all operating locations and also to central dispatch for real-time operational decisions.

It is then transmitted to Eastern's Miami, Florida commercial computer facility at 2:00 a.m. each day for the prior day's operation. As the data for approximately one thousand five hundred flights is received in Miami it is organized and structured into the data base we know as SYSTEM INFORM. It is this daily accumulation of raw operating information that provides the bulk of data available for higher level reporting and Management Information Systems.

Examples of the elements of data maintained for each flight are:

− Flight routings, equipment and departure and arrival times.

− Fuel loadings and consumption.

− Delay information.

− Passenger enplanements, deplanements and onboard counts and cargo movements as above.

SYSTEM INFORM has served as a critical data base system since 1971.

Financial-Expense & Revenue Accounting

Eastern's accounting systems have likewise been designed to collect and maintain expense and revenues at a low level of detail.

Expenditures are classified by location, department, general and specific expense account and aircraft type where applicable. The Accounting Ledger System (ALS) uses remote keyboard-CRT terminals for the input, coding, verification and payment of expense items.

Coupled with the expense system is the Earned Revenue System. It, like INFORM and ALS, uses terminals and minicomputers for data entry and auditing. The small computer aggregates the data for communication with the IBM 370 systems, which in addition to providing billing and receivables accounting, generates a fares data base containing sector price information.

Marketing – Traffic Information

One other system that I shall mention, only in passing at this point, provides a data base containing all connecting passenger flows between Eastern's on-line flights.

These data bases consitute the bulk of Eastern's historical data available as input to the airline planning process.

Scheduling – On-line Schedule Development System

Serving the planning process, in an iterative schedule development environment is an on-line minicomputer data entry system. This system audits proposed schedules, provides instant statistical summaries of operations and also communicates with Eastern's IBM/370 systems thereby supporting all schedule reporting, analysis and communication functions.

The system simultaneously supports two or more schedule development efforts in the future and current planning cycles in addition to schedules presently operating. It is so thoroughly integrated with the entire planning "Systems of Systems" that a single individual inputs schedule decisions and then provides machine instructions that automatically generate all necessary downline processing – including:

– the printing of reports
– printing of public timetabels
– creating schedule tapes as input to travel guides
– updating the reservations system, and
– updating operational systems

and so on through the entire communication process. Our ability to concentrate the responsibility for all schedule information needs under the control of a single person has been instrumental in substantially reducing Eastern's response time cycle in implementing schedule related planning decisions. The online system resides in the Schedules Department. There are three work stations each consisting of a keyboard and one or several CRT units. A printer, card reader, and magnetic tape and disk drive accessories are configured with the central processor and comprise the on-line hardware. As changes are made to the schedule, the operator keys them into the system. Airports, operating times, stations and other elements of data are audited to assure accuracy. The system rejects invalid data. Valid data is added into statistical summaries and the schedule flight operations are stored in the flight data base. This system has advanced technical features that make it easy to use and promote a high level of operator productivity. The reports generated by the system are discussed later as they fall under the category of LEVEL ONE Management Information Systems.

Competitive Information

In addition to internal data, Eastern Airlines operates in an environment that provides an extensive amount of competitive data. The bulk of this data is gathered by the Civil Aeronautics Board and made available to the certificated carriers in machine readable form.

Information obtained from this source includes:
– A quarterly 10% sample of domestic passenger movements providing their itineraries and carrier.
– Monthly flight segment data similar to that Eastern gathers in our SYSTEM INFORM, and
– Quarterly financial data providing revenue and expense details for each carrier, operating entity and aircraft type.

Eastern also purchases a data base detailing all competitive schedules in North America from the publishers of the North American Official Airline Guide.

The above coupled with Eastern's internal information provides a comprehensive network of data bases.

But data does not constitute a management information system.

MANAGEMENT INFORMATION SYSTEMS

Data has to be transformed into management information through initial processes of filtration, selection, organization and reporting. More complex processes involving comparisons, analysis, modeling techniques and the use of advanced mathematical forecasting tools are then used to generate very specific inputs to Planning's decision processes.

The four levels of Management Information Systems used at Eastern Airlines were defined earlier. In the balance of this discussion I will describe a number of those systems beginning with LEVEL ONE and progressing through to LEVEL FOUR systems. Most of these have been in use at Eastern for a number of years. Those currently under development reflect the natural evolutionary extension of the systems now serving the planning function.

A. LEVEL ONE – Management Information Systems

LEVEL ONE management information systems primarily fulfill basic reporting requirements. Within the Airline Planning function these are part of a control process that identifies areas where some Planning action may be required.

Eastern has a number of such systems. For the most part they reflect a single data source and show operating results that are often compared to either a plan or prior period, but do not attempt to analyze or explain the results.

Traffic Results

A series of these systems keep management well informed on traffic results both on a company-wide basis and for each market and flight within the airline. Timeliness is a necessary ingredient because changes to flight schedules involve lead times of two to six months from decision to implemention.

Eastern's traffic performance is measured using several systems, each with different degrees of timeliness and amounts of detail.

Daily System Performance – PIR Report

Aggregate totals of passengers, passenger miles and load factor, as well as aircraft departes, miles and seat miles are summed from the INFORM data base for the prior day's operations. These summaries are compared to expected results and reports are available to management at the start of each day.

These reports keep management apprised of strengths or weakness in aggregate system traffic and capacity levels and highlight deviations from expected results that need to be investigated in more detail.

Weekly Traffic and Load Factor Reports

Percentage traffic growth in each of more than 200 of Eastern's largest markets is measured weekly by a system that compares passenger volumes (using the IN-FORM database) versus the same data for the equivalent week in the prior years. Results in these markets are further summarized to six general market categories and compared to the prior year. These weekly comparisons alert management to trends in individual markets as well as in groups of business and vacation markets.

Load factors are similarly reported for nonstop markets and summarized for the six groups. Load factors on new services are highlighted. This system also produces a report detailing passenger volumes and load factors for each flight which is instrumental in researching problem markets.

Weekly statistics are summarized to show the month's performance and are reported in the context of the prior month's information.

Monthly System and Station Performance

Traffic data contained in the INFORM data base is summarized each month and transferred to a time-share environment. In the context of reporting, the current data is compared to forecasted amounts and reports specifying variances by marketing region and station are used for responsibility measurement. Division and station managers are held accountable to achieving forecasts for their stations.

A second report created within the timeshare environment compares Eastern's traffic growth and load factors to that of the other U.S. domestic trunk airlines. This report puts Eastern's traffic results in context of performance within the total industry.

Market Schedule Development – MSD System

A third series of monthly reports involve a more complex process where a number of elements of data from several sources are systematically combined to form a higher level data base unique to the needs of the Planning function. This compendium of data includes both Eastern and competitive information.

The prime value of this system is that is has broad flexibility in creating reports. When specific problems are identified this system provides analytic time series summaries of various traffic and capacity related statistics that are germane to the problem. The system also provides monthly traffic reports for directional and origin-destination markets and generates summaries for a rather diverse number of economic and geographic marketing economics.

This entire series of traffic oriented reporting systems is designed to assure that senior management at the corporate level and managers at all levels within the Airline Planning function are continually apprised of the airline's marketing position. Insofar as these systems are performance oriented, they predominantly report historical data.

Schedule Development System – SDS

Planning has another LEVEL ONE series of systems that is forward looking. This is the Schedules Development System which is an integrated processing network. It consists of an on-line minicomputer that provides data entry and some reporting functions and is linked with an IBM 370 which provides the bulk of applications and communications functions. This integrated network of systems is key to the iterative process that is necessary for optimizing schedules.

The aspects of the on-line system that facilitate the creation of the data base were discussed earlier. The on-line system also performs LEVEL ONE reporting functions.

It reports summaries of scheduled aircraft operating statistics, such as flight hours, available seat miles and aircraft utilization. This information is by aircraft type and for various periods within the schedule under development. The on-line system also stores statistical profiles of the corporate approved schedule operating plan and compares the current status of a schedule with those objectives.

There are several other reporting capabilities each of which provides aircraft schedulers with details of the planned operation that need to be monitored.

The on-line system provides magnetic tape input to Eastern's IBM 370. It is within that environment that the more extensive LEVEL ONE reporting and communication systems reside.

The 370 report generating programs provide the following:
– A flight listing showing the operating details of all schedule flights
– A nonstop segment report giving a chronological listing of all services in each market,
– A station activity report, and
– An aircraft flow listing

Each of these reports has been designed to fulfill the information requirements of managers within all marketing and operational departments of the airline.

The IBM 370 resident applications also construct passenger time-tables and create magnetic tapes which provide schedule input to airline guides, Eastern's reservations systems and other industry vendors and governmental agencies.

In terms of the breadth of its applications, the SDS series of sub-systems figures most prominently in the schedule development process. And most importantly, the integrated structure of the system assures that schedule decisions can be transformed into any of those outputs, even as involved as a complete timetable, by 9:00 a.m. of the following morning.

B. LEVEL TWO – Management Information Systems

The LEVEL TWO systems involve more complex reports involving the analytical treatment of the observed information. These systems need to provide decision makers with a knowledge, not only of what happened, but with an understanding of why these results occurred. Or with regard to future operations, there is a need to provide enough information so as to suggest a likely range of results.

Schedules Information System – SIS

The first of two systems surveyed here is the Schedules Information System. It produces flight, segment and station reports similar in structure to the LEVEL ONE SDS reports, but with complete historical passenger and cargo traffic information.

These reports show not only the volumes of passengers carried on each flight, but also the origination and final on-line destination point for each passenger. In addition, day of week traffic, the passengers total mileage on all Eastern segments, and connecting complex passenger counts detailing the exchanges between all flights are shown in these reports.

The SIS reports are the basic tool used by planners in designing future Eastern schedules. This system has recently been supplemented by another that provides similar reports, but with competitive schedules and traffic volumes.

Competitive Schedule Analysis

The Competitive Schedule Analysis system uses several data bases. Prior and future Eastern schedules, competitors' schedules, and passenger and cargo traffic are included in these reports.

The purpose of the report is to have Eastern management view the future placement of our flight schedules in context of competitors' schedules and traffic volumes. Schedules in a market for three successive periods are shown by departure time for all carriers. A competitor's prior period schedules are extrapolated into the future and can be modified to reflect assumed changes. Traffic volumes and projected load factors for each flight and market are included in the report. This process provides estimates of capacity changes and resultant load factors and market shares.

This system exists in a time-sharing environment, resident in Eastern's own IBM 370 computer. As such, it too communicates with other systems and will reflect Eastern's most up-to-date scheduling decisions.

It is also structured to provide a timely analysis of competitive schedules as rapidly as they are published in the airline guides. This capability is instrumental in focusing Eastern's sales and advertising efforts toward those markets where the competitive environment will be most challenging.

The two systems are very basic analytical ingredients in Eastern's schedule development efforts. In essence they represent the storehouse of knowledge from which most of our flights are planned.

C. LEVEL THREE – Management Information Systems

LEVEL THREE management information systems go one step beyond the reporting systems in that they provide not so much a report of past or future activity – but more significantly – a model of it.

The concept of the model is important as it implies that the system understands and emulates the process being observed.

Profit and Loss by Flight

One of Eastern's most useful tools is a financial model of the schedule. This system uses all the internal data sources referenced, and many not referenced. From these it constructs the revenues, expenses and profit associated with each flight in the airline. It is imperative that P & L by Flight be an accurate representation of the financial consequences associated with each service as decisions to add or delete flights are influenced, if not dictated, by their profitability. To assure a high degree of accuracy, costs are brought into the system at a low level of detail at which they can be associated with flight activity. This logic applies also to revenues which are calculated using actual passengers on each flight and their itineraries and observed prices in the various markets.

Costs are summarized to identify; first, direct costs for each flight, second, those costs that are highly correlated with a service, and lastly, system overhead costs that vary with the aggregate size of the airline but not directly with specific flights.

The availability of these levels of expense identification are important to estimating the marginal financial impact of adding or deleting services.

The P & L by Flight system produces flight level, market and aircraft type oriented reports. In terms of market and schedule planning, P & L by Flight provides a financial model that assures that the profits or losses from each scheduled flight are known to management. Correction or reaffirmation of scheduling decisions thereby becomes an ongoing process.

Operations Forecasting – FMS

The Frequency Management System is Eastern's long-range macro operations forecasting tool. It exists in the time-sharing environment as the basic reports, comparisons and analyses it generates are part of a highly iterative process. The forecasts cover a period up to

three years in the future. They provide operating management with projections upon which te make plans for their divisions.

The forecast is primarily an extrapolation of prior period operations. Aircraft acquisition and retirement programs and the resultant change in growth rates and changes in scheduling priorities are input to the system and future operations are parametrically altered to reflect these changes.

FMS produces high level statistical summaries upon which divisional operating and financial forecasts are made. The forecast cycle is repeated three times each year with the current portion of the final forecast being the next year's Operating Plan.

Traffic Forecasting Systems

The statistical output from FMS provides a capacity level for which traffic is forecasted. The traffic forecast system is linked to FMS in the time share environment. It, like FMS, is primarily a mathematical extrapolation of historical data that can be tempered for expected exogenous factors by control parameters. This system provides the airline with a traffic forecast from which future revenues are projected.

The macro level forecast is complimented by a station boardings forecast for the next twelve months. Station boardings are generated by a system that contains historical data that is projected forward and dynamically adjusted for variations in service levels by marginal load factor assumptions.

Together the latter two systems are the basic tools of management in projecting corporate revenues and providing a basis for performance measurement.

D. LEVEL FOUR – Management Information Systems

LEVEL FOUR management information systems have a high degree of complexity due to both the vast quantity of detail with which they operate and the use of advanced mathematical and operations research concepts. Much of the necessary computer technology and academic theory required for these systems is relatively new, and therefore, not many LEVEL FOUR applications are currently in use.

Flight Crew Scheduling – TPACS

An exception is the flight crew scheduling models that are widely used throughout the industry. These are deterministic models that utilize linear programming techniques to assing flight crews to trips so as to minimize the costs of flying the schedule. These models contain numerous parameters that constrain the scheduling of flight crews, but by evaluating a large number of potential solutions, the one that is most optimal is identified. Crew scheduling systems are one of the most prolific applications of LEVEL FOUR systems in the airline industry.

Flight Forecasting System

Just over a year ago we initiated at Eastern the development of a system that would provide passenger forecasts for each of about 180,000 discrete flight operations within a schedule period. Specific forecasts for each operation were necessary to estimate the number of seats on each flight to be made available for advance purchase discount fare programs.

The system was completed in April, 1976 and has been in use since then. Through it, full fare passenger demand is forecasted for each flight departure. Then using a statistical profile of that flight's history we are able to estimate the various probabilities of all demand levels. Knowing the fare discount, the system determines the optimal number of seats to be saved for expected full fare passengers in order to maximize total revenue. The remaining seats are made available to be sold at a discount.

The output from this system is fed into Eastern's reservations system and seat availability for the discount programs is automatically controlled by the reservations computer.

The statistical and mathematical processes involved in forecasting traffic and probabilities of demand are rather complex but this system is now generating flight forecasts, that when summed, are within two percent of Eastern's official aggregate traffic forecast.

The use of this capability has improved the revenue yield by more than two million dollars in 1976. The primary inputs to Flight forecasting are LEVEL ONE and LEVEL TWO SDS and SIS outputs.

This represents the most sophisticated forecasting system currently being used in Eastern as it operates at the lowest possible level of detail and maximizes revenue tradeoffs using higher level mathematics.

Airline Schedule Planning Evaluation Model – ASPEM

The Airline Schedule Planning and Evaluation Model (ASPEM) developed by MacDonnell Douglas Aircraft Corporation, evaluates airline schedules in attempting to estimate the traffic that each flight would carry. ASPEM receives as input all airline schedules in the markets to be evaluated and from these constructs a catalogue of all nonstop, direct and connecting services that would be available to each Origination-Destination market. The model then uses various parameters to assess the quality and time of day value of these services. The quality index is used to allocate the available traffic to the flights in the market.

The model has not yet been used extensively by airlines to arrive at schedule decisions, but Eastern is currently engaged in implementing a version of ASPEM that will be tested to determine its value to us as a schedule planning tool.

Aircraft Sizing Model

Eastern is also now evaluating a linear programming model that attempts to re-route aircraft so as to maximize the profitability of the deployment of a fleet. The model requires as input estimates of passengers gained or lost due to the availability of more or fewer seats for each flight. This application then, in a manner similar to TPACS, searches for the most optimal routing solution. Unlike TPACS the results are not deterministic and in fact often not even feasible. Much research remains before a model of this type can become an integral part of the schedule development process.

I mention schedule evaluation and aircraft routing models, primarily because in spite of their current unsettled status, there is a consensus with which I agree, that these types of models will be useful at some time in the future.

As I mentioned earlier, systems need to evolve in an orderly process. The value of both of these systems is largely dependent on the quality of available traffic forecasts. As traffic forecasting systems improve and gain the confidence of planners, the logical extensions of those systems will earn their place in the Planning process.

Concluding Remarks

I hope this discussion has served to illustrate not so much the specific systems that are used in Eastern's planning process, but more importantly the logical structure and sequential levels of proficiency through which the current state of affairs was achieved.

I believe that the use of advanced Management Information Systems is becoming increasingly important to the airline planning process.

With quantum improvements in aircraft technology now largely behind us, a substantial portion of the efficiency gains of the future will be derived through the development and use of advanced systems that provide management with the tools required to increase resource productivity.

For these reasons, continuing research and development, primarily with LEVEL FOUR systems is necessary for airlines to effectively perform their public and private roles.

COMPUTER SERVICES - COMMERCIAL COMPUTER SYSTEMS

EQUIPMENT SCHEMATIC

UNIT ADDRESSES IN ITALICS

TO EIGHT TSO TERMINALS WITH PRINTER ON 4TH FLOOR FOR PROGRAMMER USE

PTS-1020 RAYTHEON CPU 32K

PTS-1020 RAYTHEON CPU 32K

PTS-1020 RAYTHEON CPU 32K

360-65 CPU 768K
PROCESSOR STORAGE

370-158 CPU 3 MEG

370-168 CPU 4 MEG

370-168

360-30

ONLINE TEST SYSTEMS

PRODUCTION MAR-TRIM DATALINE

Simplified Communications

468

4 PHASE & RAYTHEON SYSTEMS

ON LINE DATA ENTRY SYSTEMS

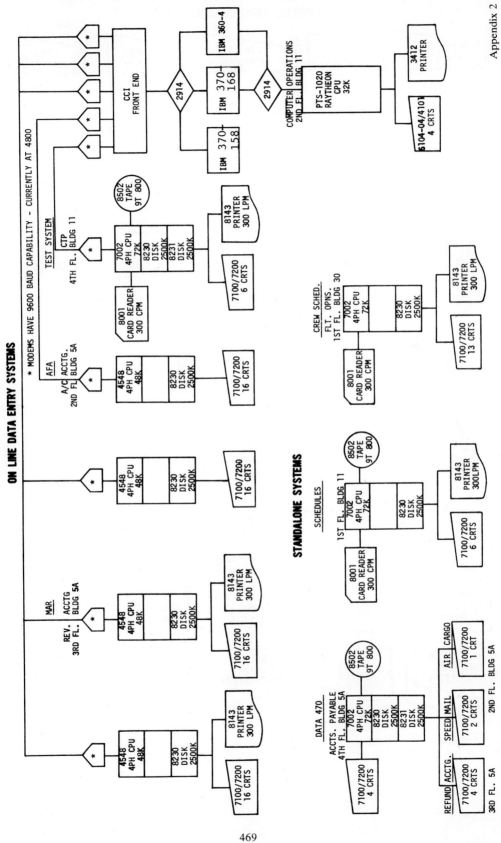

* MODEMS HAVE 9600 BAUD CAPABILITY - CURRENTLY AT 4800

STANDALONE SYSTEMS

Appendix 2

SYSTEM INFORM DATA BASE

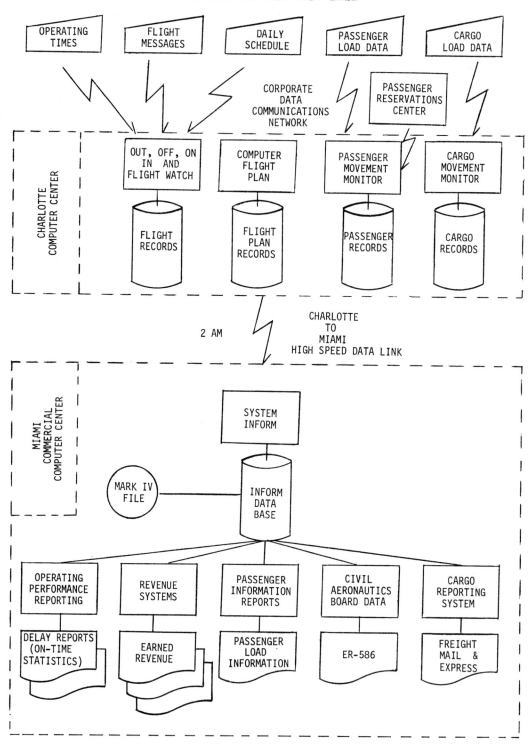

Appendix 3

ON LINE SCHEDULE DEVELOPMENT SYSTEM

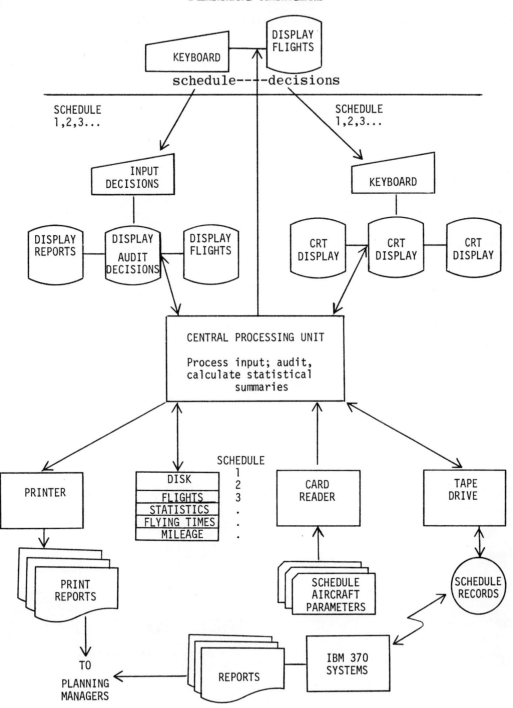

PLANNING MANAGERS

KEYBOARD

DISPLAY FLIGHTS

schedule----decisions

SCHEDULE 1,2,3...

SCHEDULE 1,2,3...

INPUT DECISIONS

KEYBOARD

DISPLAY REPORTS

DISPLAY AUDIT DECISIONS

DISPLAY FLIGHTS

CRT DISPLAY

CRT DISPLAY

CRT DISPLAY

CENTRAL PROCESSING UNIT

Process input; audit, calculate statistical summaries

PRINTER

DISK

SCHEDULE 1 2 3 . . .

FLIGHTS
STATISTICS
FLYING TIMES
MILEAGE

CARD READER

TAPE DRIVE

PRINT REPORTS

SCHEDULE AIRCRAFT PARAMETERS

SCHEDULE RECORDS

TO PLANNING MANAGERS

REPORTS

IBM 370 SYSTEMS

Appendix 4

Management information systems in local public transport

by

N.H. van der Woude

Economic Bureau for Road and Water Transport, The Netherlands

INTRODUCTION

Until the early sixties public transport was seen as an economic activity (for a considerable part carried out by private companies) and mostly run at a normal profit.

The fast growing popularity of the private car resulted in a sharp decline of the demand for public transport and huge deficits in operations.

At the same time it was acknowledged that the massive use of private cars had many negative aspects and that public transport could be an alternative to the use of the private car.

This has led to a policy of stimulating public transport and subsidizing its deficits, and as a consequence the central government in Holland now pays the integral deficits of public transport, in which local public transport plays an important part.

At the time when these fundamental decisions were made hardly anybody could foresee that those deficits would grow as tremendously as they did and at such a pace.

In the past decade the deficits in local transport had a growth rate of 20% per annum.

The direct causes of these fast growing deficits are mainly the following facts:

1. at a constant demand level the production of public transport has substantially been stepped up.

2. the fares the public has to pay hardly follow the increase of the cost of living.

3. the costs per output unit increased more rapidly than the cost of living index.

The deeper cause, however, was that the cost vs. revenue conception was abandoned. In fact, no other operational criteria were available for determining the:

– volume and quantity of services to be offered
– fares to be charged
– the cost level to be maintained

There were ample incidental studies on demand functions, however, with lessening attention to the actual demand. And there are a number of studies on cost models based on overall figures and cross-section analyses, but with little or no crities on the actual cost level.

Actually, a set of operational goals and an institutional framework to set up and control goals and performance was lacking.

PUBLIC TRANSP. PLANNING MODEL

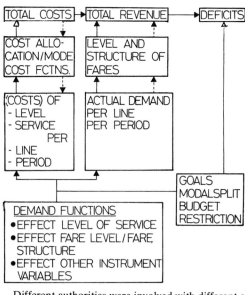

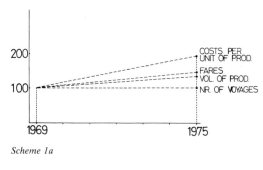

Scheme 1a

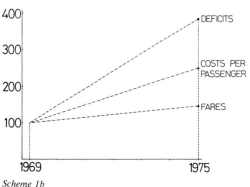

Scheme 1b

Different authorities were involved with different aspects of public transport. But even when this instrumental framework would be available, the instruments needed were not. This situation is not typical for local public transport, nor for Holland.

MODEL PHILOSOPHY

It may seem rather simple to define the ends and the tasks of public transport starting from a set of basic goals in the sphere of the modal split wanted and the budget to be put forward. This budget should be included in the basic decisions because it is competing with other social demands. Starting with these basic goals and a demand function, a level of service, fare rate and fare structure and the actual demand can be determined.

Cost functions, fare rates and fare structure give the total costs and the total revenues, from which the total deficits can be derived.

These total deficits can be confronted with the budget, and through a number of iterations an operational set of ends and tasks can be defined.

In practice, however, things are not that simple. The actual situation is that total costs and total revenues as well as deficits are (ex post) given data.

Furthermore, there is a level of service based on historical facts, incidental decisions etc.

The link between total costs and this level of service in the form of causal relations, however, is missing.

On the demand side mostly incidental information is available, but the total demand on the network, the relation between the demand on the different lines, as well as the use of the different types of tickets are not available.

Therefore it is necessary, before going into the model's philosophy, to chart the actual state of affairs and to get a grip on that state of affairs. This is a tremendous job, which includes the overall organization, organization on the different levels involved, and the setting up of an overall information system as well as a management information system at company level.

This paper will confine itself to some aspects of the management information system at company level. This system has been developed by the EBW (Economic Bureau for Road and Water Transport) in co-operation with nine local transport companies and initiated by the Netherlands Ministry of Transport.

TASKS OF THE MANAGEMENT INFORMATION SYSTEM

The basic philosophy of this system is that the overall policy and control are in the hands of the central government, which fixes:
- the total services to be rendered per city/town
- the fare level per city/town
- the budget per city/town

The details of level of service and fares should – in accordance with the general outlines agreed upon – be decided by the local government, and the execution by the transport company.

This means that starting with a detailed information system on company level, the information on local level is considerably less detailed, whereas the information for the central government can be an overall information, but should be consistent with the management information and open to verification by an external controler.

This management information system has the following tasks:

1) It should provide a cost accounting system that gives the causal link between initial costs and final activities on the line network.

2) It should provide a task-setting budget for the company in costs, physical input and physical output.

3) It should provide a registration system in the financial sphere as well as in the physical sphere to control reality against budget.

4) The registration system should be integrated as much as possible with the process management. This not only to save costs but primarily to ensure the registration of the right data.

In many companies – also private companies – there exist for the same subject (in this instance on km-production) more than one registration system on different places, for different purposes and with different answers.

These should be replaced by one registration, made on the spot where decisions are made and accesible to all who need the information.

5) The cost accounting system should be reversable in the sense that it gives the link between the level of service and the costs in the opposite direction (cost model).

The stress on the notion of costs, cost allocation, and cost in relation to output may seem overdone. Nevertheless, it is essential because analyses of costs differences among the companies involved and between these companies and regional bus companies show differences in cost level of units of tens of percents.

Moreover, the companies involved were run in the past as civil agencies (with monopoly) rather than as companies, and the traditional accounting systems in these companies were primarily set up to respond to income and expenditures and not to control efficiency.

BASIC FORM OF THE COST TYPE/AND COST CENTRE SYSTEM

The centre of the system is a conventional cost type/ cost centre system of which the principal construction is shown in scheme 2.

In this scheme three basic types of centres are distinguished.

General and additional cost centres

This type of cost centre renders services that either cannot be measured in performance units (for instance general management) or of which the performances are fixed during a period (for instance housing and garaging). These costs are charged to other centres on the basis of keys, defined in advance.

Production centres

The performance of these centres is measurable, and variable in total volume as well as in the distribution over other centres.

The costs of these centres can be calculated in an amount per unit of performance and charged to other centres according to the volume of services delivered.

Last production centres

These are the production centres of which the performances are directly charged to the final activities on performance basis. Prominent last production centres are:
- rolling stock
- driving personel
- infrastructure

The costs of these last production centres are charged to the final activities as shown in scheme 3.

Accountability per department

Based on the organisation of the company and the production process, the individual cost centres are defined in such a way that they form alone or in conjunction a center accountability.

This grouping into centres of accountability is necessary in order to put forward task-setting budgets.

The task-setting budget for the company as a whole can be subdivided in tasks per department, per subdepartment and on a lower level by task per individual

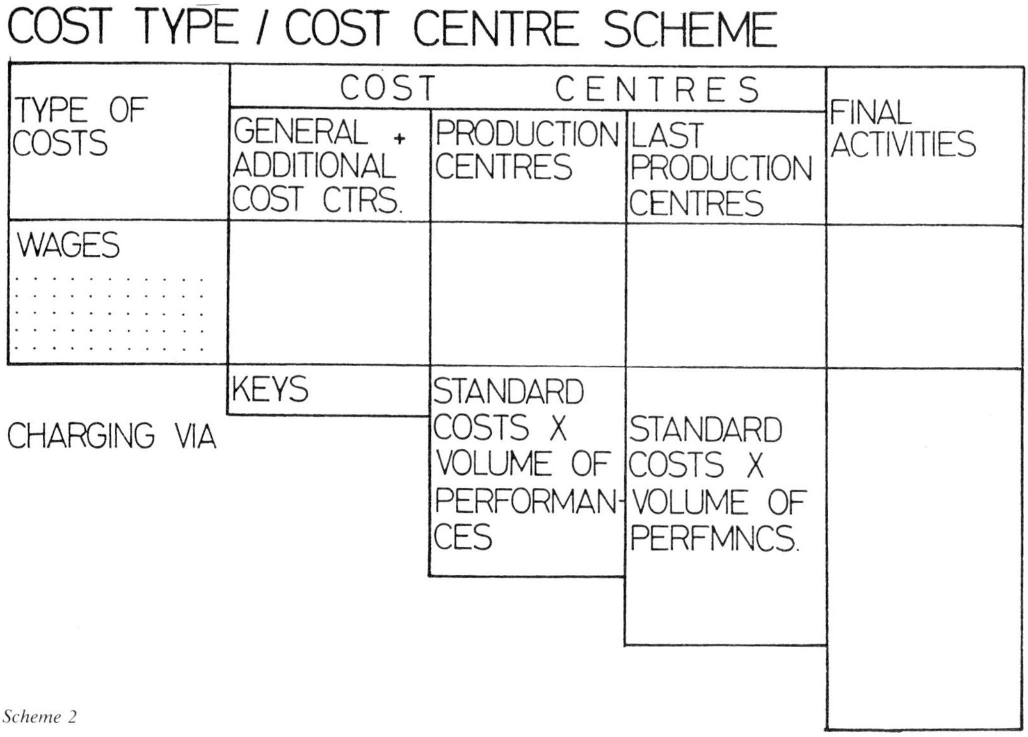

COST TYPE / COST CENTRE SCHEME
TYPE OF COSTS
COST CENTRES
GENERAL + ADDITIONAL COST CTRS.
PRODUCTION CENTRES
LAST PRODUCTION CENTRES
FINAL ACTIVITIES
WAGES
CHARGING VIA
KEYS
STANDARD COSTS X VOLUME OF PERFORMANCES
STANDARD COSTS X VOLUME OF PERFMNCS.

Scheme 2

NUMBER OF		COSTS PER		
VEHICLES	X	VEHICLES/YEAR	=	*f* ....
VEHICLE-DAYS	X	VEHICLE/DAY	=	*f* ....
VEHICLE-KMS	X	VEHICLE/KM	=	*f* ....
DRIVING-HOURS	X	DRIVING-HOUR	=	*f* ....
KM INFRASTRUCTURE	X	KM INFRASTRUCTURE	=	*f* ....
DIRECT COSTS OF INFRASTRUCTURE			=	*f* ....

Scheme 3

1. TECHNICAL DEPARTMENT
2.
GENERAL
BUS
TRAM
INFRA-STRUCTURE
3.
GENERAL BUS
REPAIR-SHOP A
REPAIR-SHOP B
4.
GENERAL REPAIR-SHOP A
SUB DEPMNT. 1
SUB DEPMNT. 2
SUB DEPMNT. 3

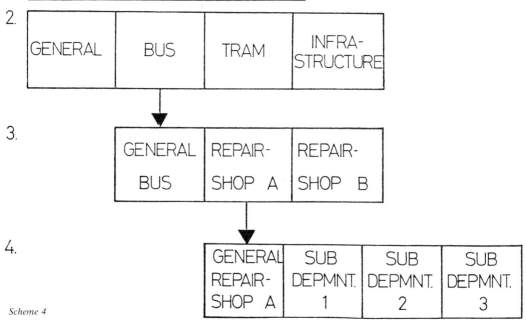

Scheme 4

centre of accountability, as shown in scheme 4.

By use of the computer this grouping and subgrouping is easy to achieve.

Charging of costs between cost centres

A problem in a cost centre model is that not only centre A charges to centre B, but that also the reverse situation exists.

With the help of a system of equations this problem is solved by computer routine that gives, in one calculation process, the equilibrium equation.

The results give in matrix form and per cost centre, the centres to which it charges its costs and the amounts

charged, as well as the centre that charges costs to this cost centre.

Prices and quantities

The initial cost amount per cost centre consists of a price, a physical quantity and an amount. Per cost centre these three elements are stated.

In the same way the charges from other cost centres are split up in quantity price and amount. From general cost centres the quantity consists of a percentage, whereas from productive centres the quantity consists of the amount of performance delivered.

COSTS CENTRES REPAIR BUSES

COST TYPE / COST CENTRE	UNIT	QUANTITY	PRICE	AMOUNT x f 1000	%
COSTS CHARGED TO THE CENTRE					
A. *INITIAL COSTS*					
wages	nr. of mechanics	65	30.000	1.800	35
social charges	Wage-sum in *fl.*	1.800.000	0,50	900	18
other initial costs	—	—	—	200	4
sub-total initial costs				*2.900*	*57*
B. *CHARGES FROM OTHER CENTRES*					
housing	m³	10.000	50	500	10
overhead of the department*)	% of total overhead dept.	100	1.500.000	1.500	29
charges from centres	—	—	—	200	4
sub-total charges other centres				*2.200*	*43*
TOTAL COSTS	NR. OF EFF. HRS.	100.000	51	5.100	100

COSTS CHARGED TO THE CENTRE					
C. *CHARGES TO OTHER CENTRES*					
bus-park	nr. of effective hrs.	70.000	51	3.570	70
investment account	nr. of effective hrs.	15.000	51	765	15
housing	nr. of effective hrs.	5.000	51	255	5
other cost centres	nr. of effective hrs.	10.000	51	510	10
TOTAL CHARGES	NR. OF EFF. HRS.	100.000	51	5.100	100

*) General overhead not included.

Scheme 5

This makes it possible, to calculate per computer the effects, in case of price changes or changes in quantity, and to present the new budget.

An example of the budget for a cost centre/centre of accountabillity is shown in scheme 5. In this way a cost allocation system integrated with a tasksetting budgeting system is set up per company.

Evaluation

The system described gives the causal relation between costs and performances, without, however, giving nominal costs.

Critical evaluation and intercompany comparison based on uniform accounting systems give the possibility for critical review and can show ways for improvement.

Very important in this sphere is the composition of the tariff per performance for the production centres.

wages costs incl. social changes direct
  personel per nominal hour   ————
cost of non production time   ————
cost of indirect production time   ————
cost per direct productive hour of
  direct personel   ————
costs of indirect personel per direct
  hour   ————
additional costs per direct hour
(housing, inventory, etc.)   ————
total costs per direct
  production hour   ————

Cost models

Reversing this cost allocation model from output to input leads to cost functions, that for instance give the

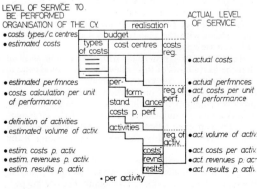

Scheme 6

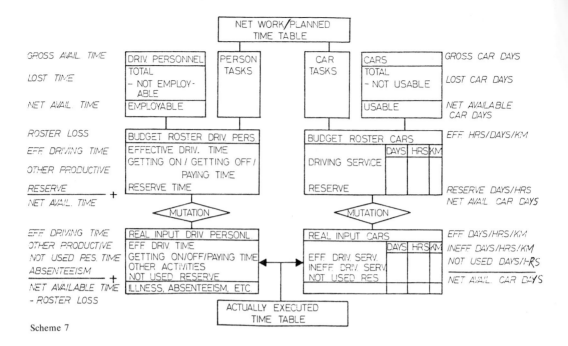

Scheme 7

relation between changes in output and change in input, and the cost effects of changes in organisation of the production process.

Registration systems

A budgeting system as described earlier only has meaning when the actual course of affairs is registered according to scheme 6).

Within this registration system three main groups can be distinguished:
1) The financial registration including the registration of quantities at the initial costs.
2) Registration of the times of direct personel
– drivers
– mechanics
3) Registration of the use of the rolling-stock.

Financial registration

The financial registration should – whenever detailed – conform with the cost type/cost centre system.

Per item is stated:
a) the cost type
b) the cost centre to be charged
c) the activity to be charged.

The activity is introduced mainly for purposes of controls in the technical department. The technicians want to know not only the costs of repairs and maintenance per 100 km, but also the costs per type of maintenance. This is solved by a seperate grouping of costs per type of activity.

The registration of time of direct personel and of rolling stock

Driving personel and rolling-stock

In public transport the most complicated registration is that of the performances of drivers and rolling-stock.

As in this sector most of the performances are planned and realisation is highly in accordance with the planning, the registration of what really is performed need not to be done in detail.

On the contrary, the planning is translated in planned performances and only the deviations from the planning are registered. The principle of this registration system can be found in scheme 7.

The level of service is translated in person tasks and car tasks. These tasks are confronted with the available driving personel and the available rolling-stock. From these data the planned performance is registered. The deviations are put into this planned performance and this automatically gives the actual performance.

The composition of the tasks as to effective driving time, indirect time, reserve time, etc. is not gathered in one stage.

Information on the lines (for instance km per line) is automatically linked to the standard car tasks, whereas the car tasks are linked to a high degree to the person tasks. Information on the drivers is linked via a code number to the tasks to be performed.

As these parts of the planning are fixed to a high degree, the planned performance and its details can be calculated with a few variable data.

With the help of a computer program in which the detailed planning is stored and deviation from planning are brought in, the real use of time of driving personel and of rolling-stock is calculated.

The results of these calculations are printed out in comparison with the planning in a series of tables for different viewpoints.

Experience in Amsterdam with this system showed that the extra costs of this procedure were moderate in comparison with the cost of previous non integrated detail registrations. Combination of this system with process management (for instance planning, scheduling of tasks, salary administration) which is for a large part realized, can even bring forward cost savings and can prevent errors caused by the manyfold rewriting of the same data.

Of course the real value of the system lies in the close control of the realisation that makes sharper planning possible. Marginal savings in the number of driving personel outweigh the cost of the system. In combination with the rest of the total M.I.S. in which the demand pattern is included, the possibilities of this system can be fully used.

Registration of mechanic time use

As to the time use of mechanics no detailed planning forward planning exists and this registration is set up as an integral observation of time used. As far as effective direct time is concerned, a notification is made of the type of activity and the car or car series for which the activity is carried out.

In practically all companies, this type of registration (more or less in detail) is available. The problems in this field are, who writes the time used and to what degree of exactness can this be done.

The new element is that the time used is combined with standard costs per hour and directly translated into costs.

Planification opérationnelle des transports urbains en commun: approches et applications

par
Matthias H. Rapp
W. & J. Rapp SA, Ingénieurs-Conseils, Bâle, Suisse
et
Philippe Mattenberger
Institut de technique des transports (ITEP)
Ecole polytechnique fédérale de Lausanne (Suisse)

ROLE DE LA PLANIFICATIOn OPERATIONELLE DANS UN PROCESSUS GENERAL DE PLANIFICATION

Il y a lieu de tenter tout d'abord d'identifier les problèmes essentiels auxquels seront confrontés les décideurs en matière de transports urbains en commun dans le proche avenir.

Les contraintes fixées par l'aménagement existant de l'espace urbain et par les possibilités financières des collectivités publiques justifient l'hypothèse que, dans les pays industrialisés surtout, l'essentiel de l'infrastructure des systèmes de transport en commun urbains est déjà en place et que les décisions porteront à l'avenir moins sur la réalisation de nouveaux systèmes que sur l'adaptation des réseaux à l'évolution de la demande et aux exigences des collectivités. Ces actions, visant à améliorer les performances du système de transport en commun, porteront en tout premier lieu sur l'organisation de l'exploitation, c'est-à-dire sur l'ajustement de la structure de réseaux de surface, en site banal, sur les horaires, l'acquisition de matériel roulant, la régulation des circulations, la tarification, la politique de stationnement et de réservation de couloirs aux transports en commun (Fig. 1).

Toutefois, dans certains cas, une part importante des budgets d'investissement destinés à l'amélioration des réseaux de transport est et restera encore réservée à la réalisation de projets coûteux qui s'étendent sur plusieurs années. Il s'agira, par exemple, de l'extension d'un réseau lourd, de la réalisation de nouvelles connexions. Chaque nouvelle étape doit certes s'incrire dans une conception globale cohérente, mais elle doit aussi apporter des améliorations immédiatement ressenties par les usagers. Elle sera ainsi remise en cause, réanalysée, voire optimisée, sur la base de l'état connu du système et des hypothèses de son évolution, au moment de la phase de réalisation (Fig. 2).

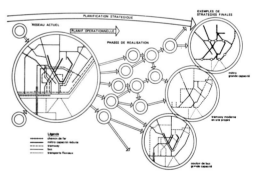

Fig. 2 - Evolution possible d'un système de transport, points de décision et phases de réalisation: illustration du cas de Libonne

Par ailleurs, la planification générale, stratégique, des systèmes de transport qui s'inscrit dans celle d'un plan directeur d'une agglomération repose généralement sur des hypothèses à long terme. Mais, l'incertitude, d'une part, concernant des hypothèses relatives à l'aménagement de l'espace, à l'évolution socio-économique et, d'autre part, les coûts internes et externes élevés des systèmes de transports justifient le recours à des instruments permettant de développer, d'évaluer, de faire émerger des propositions efficaces, réalistes et cohérentes n'hypothéquant pas de façon inacceptable l'avenir [1].

Ceci explique l'intérêt croissant d'études de *planifica-*

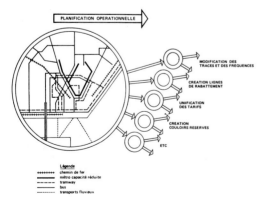

Fig. 1 - Possibilités d'actions sur l'organisation de l'exploitation d'un réseau de transport: illustration du cas de Lisbonne.

tion opérationnelle, portant sur le fonctionnement d'ensemble des réseaux multimodaux, avec pour objectif essentiel de faire le meilleur usage possible des infrastructures et équipements existants (fig. 3).

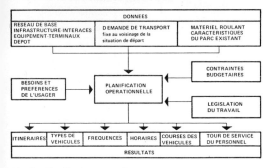

Fig. 3 - Planification opérationnelle: problème type.

METHODES D'APPROCHE

La démarche de la planification opérationnelle est donc apparentée à celle d'une optimisation. Cependant, la formulation des problèmes en termes de variables de décision, de contraintes et d'objectifs présente des particularités qui conditionnent fortement le choix d'une méthode d'approche.

Les variables de décision englobent tous les paramètres sur lesquels le planificateur peut agir pour modifier les performances de l'exploitation d'un système de transport en commun. Leur nombre est considérable et les possibilités de combinaisons difficilement dénombrables. Il y a lieu de citer, parmi celles qui sont les plus utilisées, l'itinéraire des lignes, l'organisation des circulations sur un tronçon donné, l'aménagement des interfaces, la structure des horaires, l'utilisation des véhicules.

Les contraintes expriment pour l'essentiel les limites que constituent les ressources disponibles. Il s'agit, dans le cas particulier, de celles qui ont trait à l'infrastructure du réseau, aux budgets d'investissement et d'exploitation des compagnies de transport, à certains éléments de la législation du travail . . . Il peut s'agir, par exemple, de conditions locales d'exploitation liées à la géométrie de l'infrastructure, à la régulation du trafic, à l'aménagement existant ou possible des interfaces, parfois même à certaines habitudes des usagers. La plupart d'entre elles n'ont donc pas un caractère définitif et sont difficilement quantifiables. Il importe donc de faire preuve d'une souplesse suffisante dans la prise en considération de telles contraintes.

Les objectifs de tout processus d'optimisation s'expriment sous forme de fonctions objectives, lorsqu'ils peuvent facilement être ramenés à un dénominateur commun, ces cas sont pratiquement inexistants au niveau des objectifs généraux. Il est en revanche possible de rencontrer de telles circonstances pour l'une ou l'autre étape conduisant à l'ensemble des mesures envisagées.

Les prises de décision en matière de transport résultent le plus souvent d'approches et d'évaluations multi-objectifs et multi-critères. L'aggrégation des variables d'évaluation ou de mesures d'impacts n'est pas souhaitable dans ces conditions, car elle constituerait ipso facto soit une véritable substitution des planificateurs aux décideurs, soit l'expression à priori de fonctions de préférence par ces mêmes décideurs (p.e. analyse coût-avantage), alors que de nombreux arbitrages ne se révèlent le plus souvent qu'en cours d'étude.

Le processus d'optimisation du fonctionnement d'un système de transport consiste donc à dégager des solutions pour une mise en oeuvre des ressources de façon à atteindre les meilleures performances, selon certains critères tels que réduction du nombre de transbordements, des temps moyens de parcours, des coûts d'exploitation, accroissement de l'accessibilité en provenance ou à destination de zones de la région d'étude (Fig. 4).

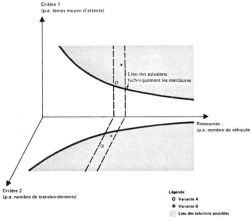

Fig. 4 - Evaluation de variantes selon plusieurs critères sur un domaine restreint de variation des ressources.

Le fonctionnement du système est représenté par des relations entre les variables de décision, les variables endogènes et exogènes et les variables d'évaluation qui constituent les bases de la modélisation. Il y a lieu, dans le cas de la planification opérationnelle, de rendre compte des modifications de l'équilibre offre-demande sous l'effet des actions sur l'offre, ainsi que des coûts qu'elles engendrent. Il s'agit donc des relations qui apparaissent, d'une part, dans les modèles de transport, et, d'autre part, dans les modèles de coût.

Les expressions qui interviennent sont complexes, elles ne peuvent pas être réduites, par exemple, à un système d'équations linéaires; elles font de plus intervenir des paramètres qu'il n'est possible d'appréhender que sur la base de l'analyse d'états de fait et en prenant pour hypothèse une certaine stabilité de comportement du système.

Compte tenu des remarques qui précèdent, les modifications qui peuvent être envisagées ne sauraient provoquer un bouleversement, mais il devrait s'agir de corrections successives qui conservent à la situation de départ un poids prédominant. Dans ces conditions, le fonctionnement du système peut être appréhendé par une méthode d'analyse du type „point pivot" ([2], chap. 1-3/17).

Les méthodes d'approches des problèmes d'optimisation peuvent être classées en deux groupes:
– l'approche directe basée sur une formalisation très poussée du problème, compatible avec l'existence d'un algorithme d'optimisation qui détermine les valeurs de la solution optimale;
– l'approche exploratoire qui repose sur un modèle de prédiction des impacts appliqué à chaque variante conçue à partir de solutions initiales, permettant ainsi, par corrections successives, d'approcher les solutions les meilleures (Fig. 5) [3].

(a) L' APPROCHE EXPLORATOIRE

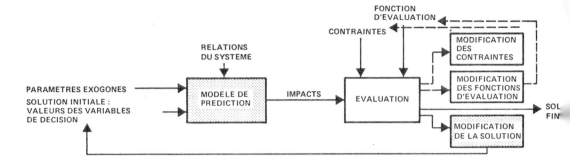

(b) L' APPROCHE DIRECTE

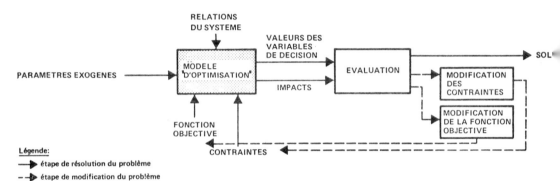

Légende:
⟶ étape de résolution du problème
--▶ étape de modification du problème

Fig. 5 - Les méthodes d'approche des problèmes de conception d'un système

Il apparaît clairement que les caractéristiques des problèmes de planification opérationnelle des transports en commun dont il a été question justifient une approche exploratoire. L'optimisation directe par des méthodes mathématiques, si elle était légitime et possible, exigerait des dépenses importantes et parallèlement des simplifications souvent incompatibles avec les exigences pratiques.

La recherche des solutions les plus prometteuses à l'aménagement et l'exploitation de réseaux de transport passe donc par le développement, l'évaluation puis l'amélioration de variantes dans un même processus. Il s'est avéré, dans les expériences réalisées depuis quelques années, que le recours à des modèles interactifs livrant des informations numériques et graphiques est particulièrement efficace pour ce genre d'activités [4].

Ils offrent à leur utilisateur la possibilité d'être informé très rapidement et de façon précise sur les conséquences des dispositions envisageables et de porter un jugement sur leur efficacité. Les opérateurs conservent tout au long de l'étude une vision globale des problèmes, ils peuvent ainsi exercer leurs capacités d'innovation et faire la synthèse de leurs démarches, alors qu'ils confient à l'ordinateur les tâches de calcul et de présentation des résultats (Fig. 6).

De telles méthodes offrent la souplesse désirée pour faire intervenir des contraintes et les arbitrages. Elles ont un effet de stimulation inventive qui favorise l'émergence des solutions dominantes.

Un certain nombre de méthodes d'étude et d'instruments ont été développés jusqu'ici pour la planification opérationnelle des systèmes de transport, ils sont utilisés, dans la pratique courante, pour les études sectorielles auxquelles ils semblent le mieux convenir: l'établissement des horaires, la rotation du matériel roulant et l'élaboration des tableaux de services.[1]

Mais les limites de telles pratiques résident dans la difficulté de tenir compte de l'interdépendance des problèmes allant du choix de la structure d'un réseau multimodal à l'élaboration des horaires, des plans de courses et des tours de services.

Fig. 6 - Illustration de l'utilisation d'un modèle interactif et graphique.

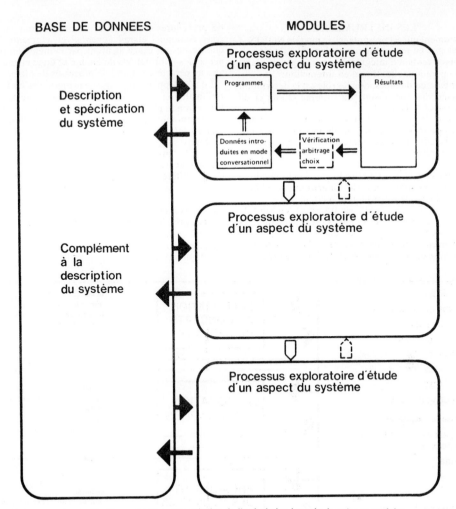

Fig. 7 - Instrument de planification opérationnelle: principe de l'articulation base de données et modules.

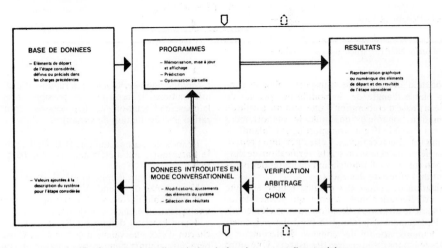

Fig. 8 - Instrument de planification opérationnelle: principe de fonctionnement d'un module.

LES INSTRUMENTS

L'instrument qui est présenté ici, le modèle NOPTS, a été développé en recourant non seulement à l'interactivité, mais en tentant d'intégrer diverses étapes de planification opérationnelle. Il met en interaction:

– une base de données, dont le rôle est la description permanente des composants du système étudié et de leurs interactions (Fig. 7);

– un certain nombre de modules ou programmes interactifs permettant de définir, de modifier, de compléter et d'analyser l'état du système étudié sous la forme où il est représenté (Fig. 8).

Une telle conception favorise la création et la mise à jour permanente d'une base de données unique et facilite le développement continu du modèle.

Dans la plupart des études de transport, en effet, le coût de la préparation des données est considérable et cet investissement est en grande partie perdu après les études souvent ponctuelles pour lesquelles il a été consenti. La mise en place d'une base de données et surtout de procédures d'examen et de mise à jour en mode conversationnel élargit l'éventail et augmente la fréquence de son usage assurant par là même en permanence des informations de qualité et donc mieux adaptées au caractère continu du processus de planification.

Le développement de nouveaux modules en fonction de l'évolution des connaissance et de la nature des objectifs est rendu plus aisé, puisqu'ils viennent se greffer sur un système informatique dont un grand nombre d'éléments sont utiles à l'étude de nouveaux aspects, favorisant ainsi tout à la fois l'extension et l'affinement progressif de l'instrument.

L'état actuel du développement du modèle NOPTS et de ses différents modules est représenté schématiquement dans la figure 9.

Conception et évaluation des réseaux

Leur premier module a pour objet l'étude du tracé ou de l'itinéraire des lignes, du type des convois et des fréquences d'exploitation suivant la démarche présentée à la figure 10.

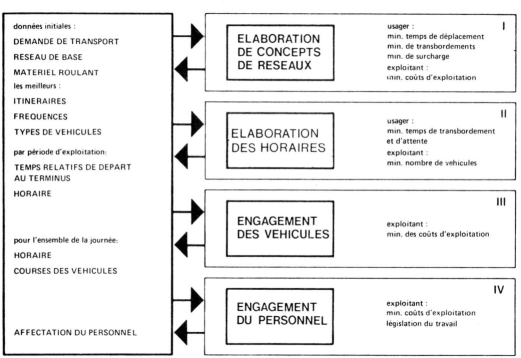

Fig. 9 – Modelle NOPTS: articulation des modules

Le modèle d'affectation des transports collectifs constitue la pierre d'angle de ce module qui permet de passer de la phase d'élaboration d'une variante à celle de son évaluation. Son rôle est de simuler le comportement des usagers face à l'offre de transport dont le planificateur définit les caractéristiques. Cette opération prépare donc les éléments nécessaires à la vérification de certaines contraintes et à l'appréciation de l'effet des paramètres et de l'efficacité des choix.

L'évaluation des choix des usagers repose sur une technique d'affectation multi-chemin qui permet de tenir compte de la diversité telle qu'opérations élémentaires de déplacement – parcours à bord des véhicules, transbordements, attente des convois, déplacements à pied – des réactions différenciées des usagers. Une autre caractéristique importante, qui a guidé le choix de la technique adoptée, touche à la rapidité d'exécution des informations, de façon à rendre possible l'intégration de la phase d'affectation dans le processus itératif d'élaboration et d'évaluation de variantes.

Le modèle multiplicatif que R.B. Dial a proposé pour le trafic individuel a été retenu comme base de travail [5].

Considérons un graphe G (V, E, d) avec:

V ensemble de noeuds V_i

E ensemble fini d'arcs directionnels et représentant une opération élémentaire de déplacement

d une fonction définie sur les arcs et qui associe à chacun d'eux une valeur non négative. Cette fonction peut être définie comme une mesure de l'utilité (ou conductivité) de l'arc

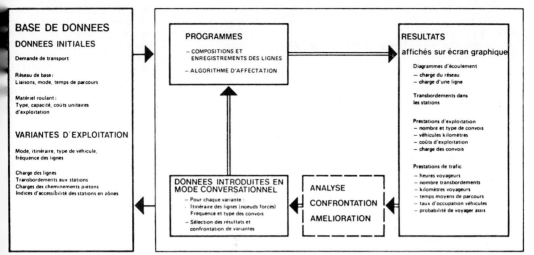

Fig. 10 - NOPTS phase 1: élaboration de concepts de réseaux.

L(e) caractéristique additive d'un arc; longueur ou coût généralisé

$P_{i,j}$ un chemin sur G de V_i à V_j

$P_{i,j}$ l'ensemble des chemins de V_i à V_j

Pr(p) mesure du poids (ou de la probabilité d'être emprunté d'un chemin)

Pr(e) mesure du poids d'un arc

Un modèle multiplicatif a la forme suivante:

$$Pr(p) = K\Pi_{e\epsilon E}d(e)^{\delta ep}$$

K: facteur de proportionnalité

$$\delta ep: \begin{cases} 1 \text{ si } e\epsilon p \\ 0 \text{ si } e\epsilon p \end{cases}$$

R.B. Dial a proposé d'adopter comme fonction de mesure de l'utilité des arcs une expression qui peut être ramenée à la forme suivante [6]:

si $e\epsilon p \vee p\epsilon P$

$d(e) = 0$

si $e\epsilon p \vee p\epsilon P$

$d(e) = \exp(-\varphi L(e))$

L'application de principes similaires au cas de réseaux de transport individuel comporte deux phases:

— la construction du graphe G à partir de la description des lignes, des cheminements piétons et des interfaces, cette opération est réalisée automatiquement, sur la base des informations disponibles dans la base de données pour chaque variante; il s'agit principalement du tracé des lignes, du type et de la fréquence des convois (Fig. 11a);

— l'attribution à chaque opération élémentaire de déplacements d'une fonction L(e) permettant d'exprimer et de mesurer la conductivité ou l'utilité des arcs, c'est à ce niveau que doivent être mises en évidence les valeurs relatives que l'usager place dans les diverses opérations élémentaires de déplacement et qui déterminent le choix de son itinéraire.

Des coefficients expriment ces relations entre les opérations de parcours à bord des véhicules, les transbordements, les délais d'attente des véhicules, les déplacements à pied.

La forme générale est: $L(e) = \alpha_i t_e$ où t_e est la durée de l'opération et α_i le coefficient de la catégorie à laquelle

appartient e, qui doit être déterminé statistiquement sur la base d'états de fait. Ces valeurs peuvent être attribuées pendant la phase de création du graphe. Font exceptions les opérations d'attente des convois qui dépendent des fréquences combinées des lignes disponibles et par là même de l'origine et de la destination des usagers.

Dès lors, le calcul des volumes de déplacement pour chaque arc d'un réseau multimodal comporte les mêmes étapes que celles d'un réseau homogène, unimodal.

Ce calcul est effectué successivement pour chaque origine de déplacement

— dans un *pas en avant,* les poids relatifs des arcs sont calculés à un facteur près, les noeuds étant traités dans un ordre topologique fixé par leur temps ou coût d'accès minimum depuis l'origine considérée. Cet ordre résulte dans notre cas de l'application de l'argorithme de Moore [7];

— dans un *pas en arrière,* les poids des arcs sont déterminés et simultanément les volumes de déplacement sur chacun d'eux; l'ordre topologique étant l'inverse du précédent.

Les charges des lignes, les mouvements de transbordement, les temps moyens de déplacements et d'attente, l'ensemble des variables caractérisant les déplacements des usagers peuvent être évalués (Fig. 11b) à partir des valeurs obtenues pour chaque opération élémentaire représentée dans le graphe.

Optimisation des horaires

Pour tirer profit au maximum d'un réseau des équipements du matériel roulant et d'un programme d'exploitation donné, les entreprises de transports publics sont placées, lors de l'établissement de l'horaire, face aux problèmes de l'ajustement des correspondances des lignes, de la succession des véhicules aux arrêts et sur les tronçons communs à plusieurs lignes.

L'objectif principal du deuxième module est de permettre à l'exploitant d'améliorer la qualité de service en réduisant les temps de transbordement résultant de l'attente des correspondances, tout en utilisant de façon efficace le matériel roulant (Fig. 12).

L'ajustement des horaires est réalisé pour diverses périodes d'exploitation de la journée, pendant lesquelles les lignes sont exploitées à des fréquences constantes.

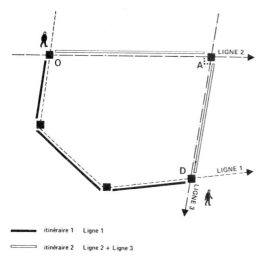

itinéraire 1   Ligne 1

itinéraire 2   Ligne 2 + Ligne 3

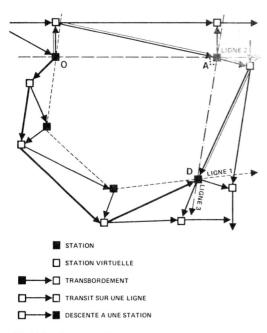

■ STATION

□ STATION VIRTUELLE

■→□ TRANSBORDEMENT

□→□ TRANSIT SUR UNE LIGNE

□→■ DESCENTE A UNE STATION

Fig. 11A - Représentation partielle d'un graphe créé à partir de la description des lignes.

Ces périodes correspondent à celles qui ont été choisies pour l'évaluation des concepts. Les résultats de l'affectation, notamment les mouvements de transbordement de ligne et au niveau de chaque noeud qui ont été enregistrés, sont alors utilisés pour l'étude des horaires.

L'ajustement des correspondances aux noeuds du réseau consiste à favoriser les mouvements préférentiels de ligne à ligne. Cependant, toute modification qui apporte des améliorations locales peut avoir globalement une incidence néfaste sur le temps total de transbordement.

Le problème est donc complexe et il s'est avéré utile de confier à l'ordinateur non seulement une tâche d'évaluation, mais également celle de dégager, par une heuris-

tique, du type "branch and bound", une solution optimale ou quasi optimale. L'opérateur peut agir par corrections successives, à partir d'une variante établie dans l'optique d'abaisser au maximum le temps total de transbordement, tout en maintenant le nombre de véhicules au niveau fixé pour les fréquences d'exploitation et les temps de pause minimums en fin de parcours. Les documents d'exploitation tels que les horaires graphiques peuvent être affichés à volonté sur l'écran et reproduits sur un support permanent. Ils donnent des indications utiles sur l'occupation des tronçons et la succession des convois.

Elaboration des courses et rotation du matériel

Les deux premiers modules sont utilisés pour une ou successivement plusieurs périodes d'exploitation journalières pendant lesquelles le fonctionnement du système est considéré comme invariable.

Le troisième module permet de composer le programme d'exploitation journalier du réseau de transport en commun étudié, à partir des tranches horaires définies préalablement (Fig. 13).

La transition d'une période d'exploitation, qui correspond par exemple à un faible niveau de demande, à la suivante, celle qui est exigée par un trafic d'une heure de pointe, est ajustée en mode conversationnel par l'utilisateur du modèle, vraisemblablement, à ce stade, par le service des horaires de l'exploitant. Cette opération achevée, il peut procéder à l'élaboration du tableau des courses de chaque véhicule. Les lignes, qui ont un terminus commun et dont le service peut être assuré successivement par les mêmes véhicules, doivent être regroupées. Il y a lieu de tenir compte enfin des temps de parcours entre terminus et dépôt.

Le tableau de formation des courses peut dès lors être élaboré grâce au modèle, à partir de l'horaire complet.

Chaque transfert possible des véhicules, d'un terminus ou d'un dépôt à un autre terminus ou dépôt, pour assurer le service, est représenté sur un graphe par un arc muni d'une capacité de borne inférieure à un ou zéro et de borne supérieure à un, ainsi que d'un coût unitaire de transfert. Le programme détermine alors le flot de coût minimal, compatible avec les bornes de capacités.

L'algorithme utilise la méthode out-of-kilter de Fulkerson [8].

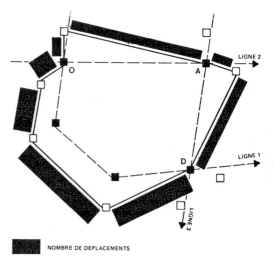

■ NOMBRE DE DEPLACEMENTS

Fig. 11B – Illustration partielle des résultats de l'affectation obtenus sur le graphe des opérations élémentaires de deplacement.

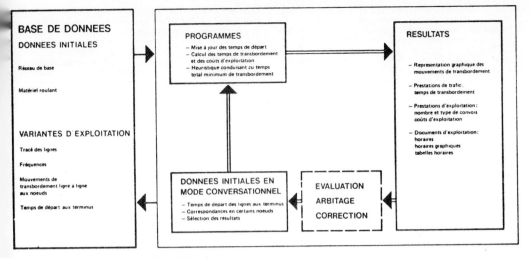

Fig. 12 – NOPTS phase II: élaboration des horaires

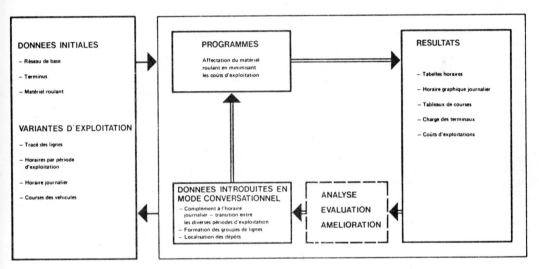

Fig. 13 - Nopts phase III: élaboration des courses des véhicules

L'utilisateur peut établir diverses stratégies de service en intervenant au niveau du groupement des lignes et du graphe composé des transferts possibles.

La phase traitant de la formation des tours de service et de l'engagement du personnel n'a pas encore été abordée sur le plan de la programmation.

APPLICATIONS ET ENSEIGNEMENTS

Le modèle NOPTS est opérationnel depuis près de trois ans. Il a été appliqué et l'est actuellement dans le cadre d'études des réseaux de transport de Lausanne, Bâle, Zurich, Turin, Lisbonne et Porto. Il a de plus été acquis par l'administration américaine des transports urbains (UMTA)[2] qui assurera sa distribution aux Etats-Unis[3].

Une brève description des objectifs, du contexte dans lequel elles se sont déroulées et des résultats de ces applications est donnée en appendice, à l'exception de celle de Turin[4], dont nous n'avons pas encore eu connaissance jusqu'ici de l'ensemble des résultats.

Un certain nombre d'enseignements peuvent être déjà tirés de ces expériences: *le fonctionnement et la qualité de service d'un réseau de transport en commun peut être souvent substantiellement amélioré tout en respectant la contrainte fixée par le niveau des coûts d'exploitation existants ou en consentant des investissements limités.*

L'étude de restructuration du réseau de Bâle a montré, par exemple, que même un réseau très bien géré peut voir son service amélioré en adaptant les itinéraires, par le jeu de lignes radiales et diamétrales, ainsi que les fréquences à l'évolution de la demande. Quelques éléments de comparaison entre la situation de départ (1975) et la variante retenue comme étant la mieux adaptée par le service des transports en commun, à l'issue de l'étude, sont rassemblés dans le tableau 1.

Tableau 1 – Comparaison réseau actuel, variante retenue (source: Basler Verkehrs-Betriebe „Netzoptimisierungssystem für die Netzstruktur der öffentlichen Nahverkehrsmittel in der Region Basel", Basel, Juni 1975).

Criteres	Réseau (1975) existant	Variante retenue	Amélioration relatives (%)
– Temps moyen de déplacement (min.)	17.0	16.9	0.6
– Mombre de transbordements (par heure de pointe)	17'550	15'830	8.2
– Degré de surcharge (% de passagers-km en véhicules surchargés)	4.8%	3.8%	20.8
– Probabilité d'obtenir une place assise	70.6%	68.4%	–3.1
– Mombre de véhicules engagés pour l'heure de pointe	202	204	–1.0
– Coûtes d'exploitation par heure (S.Fr.) (y compris l'amortissement du matériel)	19'287	20'139	–4.4

Sur le plan de l'adaptation des horaires, il a été possible de mettre en évidence, toujours pour le cas de Bâle, la possibilité de réduire considérablement les temps d'attente des correspondances en ajustant, pour les fréquences données, les temps de départ aux terminus. Cette opération n'entraîne aucun accroissement des coûts d'exploitation et respecte les temps minimums d'arrêts en bout de ligne, fixés par des conventions collectives.

Les gains obtenus sur les temps d'attente sont évidemment plus importants pour les périodes de la journée durant lesquelles la demande est faible, par exemple le soir et les fins de semaine où, à Bâle, la plupart des lignes sont exploitées avec cadence de 12 minutes. Le tableau 2 est établi pour un tel cas.

Tableau 2 – Comparaison horaire actuel et horaire optimisé en fonction d'une réduction de la durée d'attente des correspondances.

Critères	Horaire actuel	Horaire optimise	Amélioration relatives (%)
Temps moyen d'attente des correspondances (min.)	7.0	5.7	19
Nombre de véhicules engagés	82	82	—

La technique interactive, associant au modèle l'expérience du planificateur et de l'exploitant, favorise une approche exploratoire qui conduit à des solutions mieux adaptées à la situation existante et à son évolution, que les approches traditionnelles.
Des études parallèles ont été effectuées à Bâle, l'une, celle de la restructuration de l'optimisation de certains éléments du réseau existant de Bâle, à l'aide du modèle NOPTS et l'autre en s'appuyant sur des modèles de planification stratégique, cette dernière a été d'ailleurs proposée dans le cadre de l'établissement d'un plan directeur des transports.[5] Le réseau de transport en commun proposé dans ce plan pour une hypothèse donnée de l'évolution de l'occupation du sol a été comparé, sur la base de la demande actuelle à la variante développée à l'aide du NOPTS. Les résultats obtenus se présentent comme il suit:

Tableau 3 – Comparaison des variantes de réseaux de transport en commun résultant d'une approche exploratoire et d'une approche classique dans le cadre d'une planification stratégique.

Criteres	Réseau résultant de l'étude de restructuration NOPTS	Réseau propose dans le cadre du plan directeur (1)	Différences relatives (%)
– Temps moyen de déplacement (min.)	16.9	17.3	– 2.4
– Nombre de transbordements (heure de pointe)	15'830	23'830	– 50.5
– Degré de surcharge	4.8%	1.9%	+60.4
– Nombre de véhicules engagés	204	233	+ 14.2
– Coûts d'exploitation par heure de pointe	19'287	25'382	+31.6

Même si les données à partir desquelles sont bâties ces deux variantes sont différentes, il est intéressant de constater que la variante élaborée dans le cadre d'un plan directeur sur la base d'une évolution de la demande, qui reste hypothétique, représente, pour la situation existante, une solution mal adaptée.
Un modèle de planification opérationnelle utilisant une technique interactive graphique offre une possibilité intéressante de concilier les points de vue entre les différents services chargés de la gestion des réseaux et les différents groupes d'utilisateurs, en favorisant leur participation dans le processus d'élaboration et d'évaluation de variantes.
L'application de Bâle permet également d'illustrer ce point. Elle a été mandatée par trois services concernés par les transports en commun de la région: le service d'urbanisme de la ville, le service de planification régionale et la compagnie d'exploitation (Basler Verkehrs-Betriebe).
Un ou plusieurs professionnels de la planification, appartenant à chaque organisme, ont suivi une rapide mise au courant de l'utilisation du modèle avant de procéder, d'abord indépendamment, puis conjointement, à l'élaboration de diverses variantes. Cette approche qui rappelle celle des jeux d'entreprise a été réalisée à partir d'une base de données commune, mais parfois avec des objectifs différents.
La solution retenue à la fin de ces travaux a été le résultat d'une confrontation d'idées et d'objectifs, de négociations et d'arbitrages.
Par la suite, la solution retenue par les professionnels a été comparée, toujours en mode conversationnel, avec la structure des lignes proposée par une association d'usagers des transports publics.
La souplesse offerte par la technique interactive graphique, associée à la désagrégation de l'évaluation et de la représentation des impacts favorise l'examen détaillé du fonctionnement des réseaux sous de multiples aspects, en particulier celui de chaque action envisagée et prise isolément.
Même des actions mineures, relatives à l'exploitation, telles qu'une augmentation ou une diminution des fréquences, ainsi que des adaptations d'horaire provoquent des effets favorables pour certains groupes d'usagers et défavorables pour d'autres.
Il est dès lors très précieux d'être en mesure de comparer des variantes sur la base non seulement de valeurs globales, mais également au niveau des effets locaux. Par exemple, la représentation graphique d'indices de modi-

ñcation „d'accessibilité" permet de mettre en évidence les zones favorisées ou défavorisées par les mesures envisagées et de les tester sous l'angle de l'équité (Fig. 14).

CONCLUSIONS ET PERSPECTIVES

Il est souvent délicat d'évaluer, à partir d'une situation connue et de quelques scénarios d'occupation future du sol, ce que pourra être la demande dans un avenir plus ou moins lointain et d'en tirer des propositions précises sur le développement à donner à l'offre de transport.

De telles études permettent toutefois d'évaluer certains impacts d'options, à moyen terme, portant par exemple sur l'extension de l'ossature principale d'un réseau de transport en commun.

De telles options peuvent servir à orienter les corrections et transformations successives qui sont apportées aux réseaux de transport et à leur exploitation afin de les adapter à l'évolution progressive de l'aménagement de l'espace (voir fig. 2).

APPLICATION EXAMPLE BASEL, SWITZERLAND NETWORK OPTIMIZATION

COPY OF DESIGN 1000

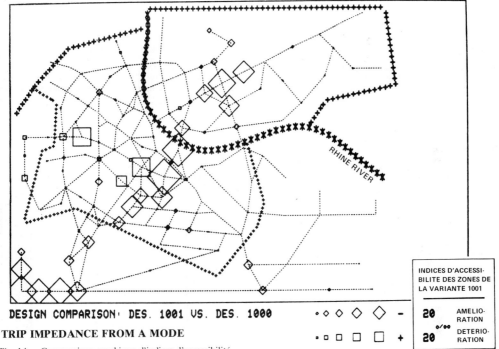

Fig. 14 - Comparaison graphique d'indices d'accessibilité

Bien que les études de planification de nombreux réseaux de transport se soient étendues sur plusieurs années, elles ont été basées sur des données représentant un état instantané. Une part non négligeable des moyens a été consacrée à la récolte et à la codification des données caractérisant un état de fait. Les efforts de mise à jour des données n'ont souvent pas été suffisants pour fournir au planificateur une source permanente d'informations durant le processus cyclique de planification, de décision et de réalisation qui conduit, étape après étape, aux véritables transformations d'un réseau.

Il importe donc de donner à l'établissement *d'une base de données et de procédures d'examen et de mise à jour* une importance de premier ordre.

Leur conception doit être guidée par le souci de livrer aux organismes chargés de la gestion des réseaux, les données et un instrument leur permettant de développer et d'évaluer eux-mêmes leurs solutions.

Le niveau de détail d'une telle base de données devrait être adapté, tout au moins à l'origine, aux problèmes qu'il est indiqué de résoudre en priorité et aux moyens à disposition. Un usage fréquent de ces moyens conduira progressivement à un affinement des informations et à un élargissement de l'éventail des questions auxquelles il serait possible d'apporter des réponses.

En effet, comment tirer d'un ensemble de données statiques des éléments d'appréciations, statistiquement valables, liés aux caractéristiques de la demande et plus particulièrement au choix modal? Seul le suivi des modifications réelles de l'équilibre offre – demande résultant des actions réalisées, peut créer une situation de connaissances de laquelle les impacts pressentis, tenant compte de l'évolution de la demande, pourront être appréhendés sur la base de méthodes du type point pivot.

C'est dans cette voie que le développement du NOPTS se poursuivra par l'introduction au niveau du modèle des relations entre les fonctions d'offre et de demande selon une approche par élasticité. Parallèlement, les applications devraient, par une accumulation, il est vrai assez lente, d'un matériel statistique indispensable permettre d'isoler dans chaque cas les paramètres dont l'influence est prépondérante, dans l'étude du compte offre – demande.

REMERCIEMENTS

Le modèle décrit dans cet article a été développé conjointement par l'Institut de technique des transports (ITEP) de l'Ecole polytechnique fédérale de Lausanne, sous la direction du Professeur D. Genton et par le bureau d'ingénieurs-conseils W. & J. Rapp SA à Bâle (WJR). Le développement principal de la première étape a été réalisé par les auteurs et H. Spiess (WJR), la seconde partie par H. Spiess (WJR) et la troisième par M. Crvcanin (ITEP).

Nous remercions les nombreux collaborateurs des deux partenaires et les représentants des organismes mandataires de leur précieuses contributions relatives aux applications du NOPTS. L'édition technique a été préparée à l'ITEP sous les bons offices de R. Echenard.

REFERENCES

sur la planification des transports et les méthodes interactives graphiques

[1] Genton David L., **„Planung von Verkehrssystemen unter Ungewissheit",** Vorträge und Studien aus dem Institut für Verkehrswissenschaft an der Universität Münster, Heft 16.

[2] Manheim Marvin L., **„Fundamentals of Transportation System Analysis",** Vol. I, Preliminary Edition, fourth revision; Department of Civil Engineering, MIT, August 1976.

[3] Rapp M.H., **„ Planning Demand-Adaptive Urban Public Transportation Systems: The Man-Computer Interactive Graphic Approach",** Dissertation University of Washington, Seattle, USA, NTIS PB 212 540, June 1972.

[4] Rapp M.H., **„Transit System Planning: A Man-Computer Interactive Graphic Approach",** Highway Research Record, No. 415, pp. 49-61, Washington, D.C., 1972.

[5] Dial Robert B., **„Probabilistic Assignment: A Multipath Traffic Assignment Model which Obviates Path Enumeration",** Highway Research Record no. 369, Transportation Research Board, Washington, D.C., 1971.

[6] Trahan Michel, **„Probabilistic Assignment: An Algorithm",** Transportation Research, Vol. 8, no. 4 (Nov. 1974).

[7] Moore E.F., **„The Shortest Path Through a Maze",** International Symposium on the Theory of Switching, Proceedings, Harvard University, Cambridge, Mass., 1957.

[8] Bray T.A., Witzgall C., **„Algorithm 336: NETFLOW (H), Boeing Scientific Research Laboratories, Seattle, Communications of the ACM, Vol. 11, Sept. 1968.**

sur le développement du modèle NOPTS

Rapp M.H., Mattenberger Ph., Piguet S., Robert-Grandpierre A., **„Rapport RHITUC Modèle Interactif Graphique pour la Recherche Heuristique d'Itinéraires de Transports Urbains Collectifs",** Institut de technique des transports ITEP/ EPF-L, Lausanne, Switzerland, July 1974.

Rapp M.H., Mattenberger Ph., Piguet S. and Robert-Grandpierre A., **„Interactive Graphic System for Transit Route Optimization",** Transportation-Research Record, no. 559, pp. 73-80, Washington. D.C., 1976.

Rapp M.H. and Gehner C., **„Transfer Optimization to Minimize Delays: Stage II of an Interactive Graphic System for**

VARIANTE DE BASE

BVB BU/Gr 18.3.75

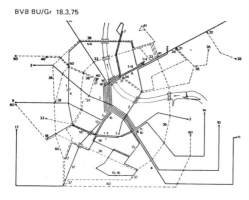

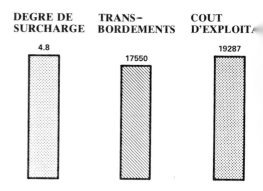

DEGRE DE SURCHARGE	TRANS-BORDEMENTS	COUT D'EXPLOIT/
4.8	17550	19287

NOUVELLE VARIANTE

BVB BU/Sü 1.4.75

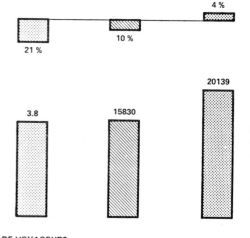

		4 %
21 %	10 %	
3.8	15830	20139

APPLICATION DU NOPTS AU RESEAU DE BALE:
COMPARAISON ETAT DE FAIT, NOUVELLE VARIANTE.

% DE VOYAGEURS
EN VEH. SURCHARGES   NOMBRE   Frs./h

Operational Transit Planning", Transportation Research Record, Washington, D.C., forthcoming.

CRVCANIN Milan, „OPTFLO, Détermination sur un réseau du flot compatible à coût minimal", bibliothèque des programmes de calcul du Département de génie civil de l'EPF-Lausanne.

ITEP and W. & J. Rapp AG:

– „NOPTS – Programmsystem für die Betriebsplanung im öffentlichen Verkehr", Allgemeine Beschreibung und Benützerhandbuch, Juni 1975.

– „NOPTS – Computer Program for Operational Planning in Public Transit", General Description and User Manual, June 1975.

– „NOPTS – Modèles de planification opérationnelle de systèmes de transports en commun", Aperçu général, février 1976.

– „NOPTS – Computer Program for Operational Planning in Public Transit", General Overview and Examples of Applications. Dec. 1976.

– „NOPTS – Modelos de Planificaçao Operacional de Sistemas de Transportes Colectivos", Generalidades e Manual do Utilizador, GEPP, Porto, 1976.

NOTES EN BAS DE PAGES

1. Voir le résumé des moyens d'études existant ou en développement donné dans la revue UITP no 1, 1975.
2. Par l'intermédiaire de Peat, Marwick, Mitchell & Co.
3. Sous le nom d'ITAM (Interactive Transit Assignment Model)
4. Etude entreprise par SITECO (Società Italiana Tecnica Consulenze SPA, Torino)
5. Prof. W. Grabe „Überprüfung der Struktur und Gesamtverkehrsplanung Basel", Institut für Verkehrswirtschaft, Strassenwesen und Städtebau, Technische Universität Hannover, Hannover, 1976.

ANNEXES: APPLICATIONS DU MODELE NOPTS

Étude du système des transports en commun de Bâle
Clients
Basler Verkehrsbetriebe (BVB, Société de transport en commun bâloise)
Stadtplanbüro Basel (Bureau de planification de la ville de Bâle)
Regionalplanungsstelle beider Basel (Bureau de planification régionale bâloise)

Date
1974/75

Objectifs
La société de transport en commun de Bâle exploite 12 lignes urbaines de transport par rail comprenant des lignes de tramways légers en site banal au centre-ville et dans les faubourgs et des lignes de tramways en site propre en banlieue, ainsi qu'un nombre identique de parcours de bus. Une autre compagnie assure le service de deux lignes de tramways de banlieue dont les itinéraires ne pénètrent pas jusqu'au centre-ville, ce qui oblige un grand nombre d'usagers à transborder sur le système de transport urbain.

Le but de cette application du NOPTS était d'examiner d'une part les possibilités de prolongement des lignes de banlieue jusqu'au centre urbain et d'établir d'autre part des lignes radiales (rocades) au niveau de la banlieue de façon à augmenter le nombre de parcours directs, cette amélioration devant amener à une réduction des mouvements de transbordement sans augmentation sensible du matériel roulant et du personnel.

Dimension du problème
– Population urbaine: 202'000
– Population de l'agglomération: 380'000
– Réseau de base: 150 noeuds, 520 liaisons (directionnelles), 26 lignes de transit (14/TRL, 12/bus urbains)
– Usagers: 150 mio. de passagers par an, 50'000 passagers par heure de pointe.

Sources des données
Les données de la demande ont été récoltées d'après plusieurs enquêtes O-D sur les passagers transportés (1962, 1968 et 1972). Pour le NOPTS, la matrice originale de 229x229 a été compactée en matrice de 150x150 et mise à jour en utilisant les comptages par écrans de 1974. Les caractéristiques de l'offre (liaisons, vitesses, coûts unitaires d'exploitation par véhicule,

etc.) ont été obtenues des statistiques courantes d'exploitation des BVB.

Cadre institutionnel
Etant donné que le réseau de la compagnie des transports bâlois couvre des entités politiques différentes, les décisions à prendre concernant les changements de parcours devaient être coordonnées entre trois autorités: le service des transports, les bureaux de planification de la ville et de la région. Une équipe de spécialistes réunissant des représentants des trois autorités fut créée. Le bureau conseil expert à mis le NOPTS à disposition, a préparé les données de base, a calibré le modèle et a donné l'assistance nécessaire pour former les membres de l'équipe à l'utilisation du modèle.

Résultats
80 Variantes ont été élaborées et évaluées, nécessitant environ 30 heures de dialogue avec l'ordinateur. Le procédé interactif graphique s'est avéré très efficace pour mettre en évidence les divers éléments d'arbitrage provenant d'objectifs de départ divergents et permettre ainsi d'isoler une dizaine de solutions recevant l'approbation de l'ensemble des membres. Parmi ces solutions, l'alternative offrant le rapport jugé le meilleur entre les coûts d'exploitation et la diminution du nombre de transbordements fut retenue.

Experts
W. & J. Rapp AG, Bâle, et Rudolf Keller, Muttenz, Suisse

Matériel utilisé
Ordinateur HP – 2100 avec CRT Tektronix 4014.

Étude d'adaptation des horaires

Client
Basler Verkehrsbetriebe (Société de transport en commun bâloise)

Date
1976

Objectif
Etude pilote dont le but est d'examiner l'utilisation potentielle du NOPTS II en tant qu'instrument permettant de réduire les temps d'attente des correspondances des passagers, en dehors des heures de pointe, en coordonnant au mieux les temps de départ des véhicules au terminus pour un tracé des lignes et une périodicité donnés (12 min. pour la plupart des lignes).

Dimension du problème
Voir ex. 1

Sources des données
Pour les données de la demande, voir ex. 1. Réseau de base avec vitesses en-dehors des heures de pointe fournies par les BVB. Périodes et heures de départ résultant des horaires existants.

Résultats
Comparé à l'horaire établi manuellement, l'horaire proposé à la suite de l'optimisation par le NOPTS réduit le temps d'attente total des correspondances de 20'500 pass.-min./hr. à environ 16'700 pass. – min./hr. pendant la période creuse de la soirée. Le matériel roulant (82 véhicules) reste stable. Ceci signifie qu'un gain d'environ 20% peut être obtenu sans augmenter les coûts de fonctionnement.

Expert
W. & J. Rapp AG, Bâle

Contribution de l'expert
Etude complète.

Matériel utilisé
Ordinateur HP – 2100 avec écran Tektronix 4014 CRT.

Évaluation de la ligne de metro Lausanne-Ouchy (L-O)
Client
Municipalité de Lausanne, Suisse

Date
1975-76

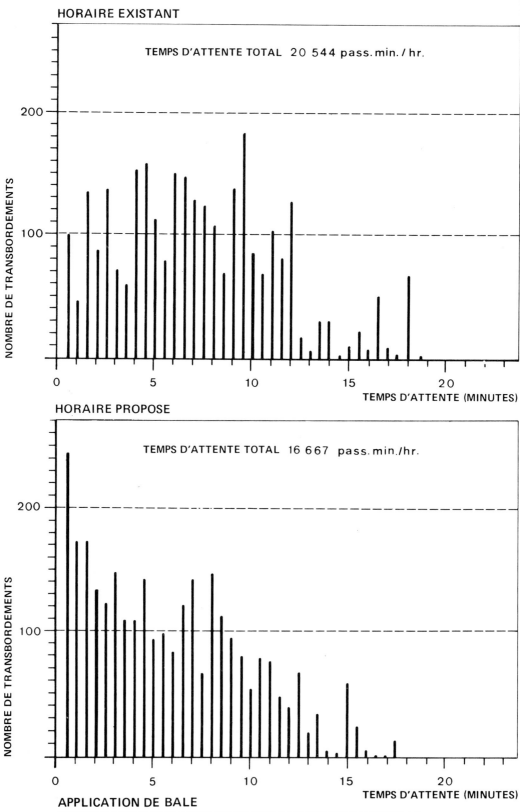

HORAIRE EXISTANT

TEMPS D'ATTENTE TOTAL 20 544 pass. min. / hr.

NOMBRE DE TRANSBORDEMENTS

TEMPS D'ATTENTE (MINUTES)

HORAIRE PROPOSE

TEMPS D'ATTENTE TOTAL 16 667 pass. min. / hr.

NOMBRE DE TRANSBORDEMENTS

TEMPS D'ATTENTE (MINUTES)

APPLICATION DE BALE
COMPARAISON DES DISTRIBUTIONS DES TEMPS D'ATTENTE
DES CORRESPONDANCES

Objectif

La compagnie du „métro" Lausanne-Ouchy exploite deux lignes urbaines parallèles dans la ville de Lausanne. Devant faire face depuis peu à des déficits croissants, le L-O hésite à supprimer ce service. Il incombait à la municipalité de Lausanne de décider si elle désirait reprendre ou abandonner l'exploitation du L-O. Deux alternatives furent évaluées: (1) maintenir l'exploitation de ces lignes en les intégrant au réseau municipal de bus ou (2) abandonner ce service et le remplacer par de nouvelles lignes de bus et des améliorations de fréquences.

Dimension du problème

- population de la région lausannoise: 235'000
- réseau de base: 132 noeuds, 344 liaisons (directionnelles) 30 lignes
- usagers: 55 mio. de pass. par an, 185'000 pass. par jour.

Source des données

Les données de la demande sont tirées de l'étude effectuée pour le plan de transport de la région lausannoise. Les caractéris-tiques de l'offre ont été obtenues du L-O et des Transports lausannois (service régional de bus).

Résultats

Pour des niveaux de service similaires, l'alternative 1 (maintien du système ferré urbain) est moins déficitaire que l'alternative 2 (remplacement par des lignes de bus), cette dernière ne permettant pas, en outre, d'assurer une même accessibilité dans le couloir métro où sont concentrés un grand nombre de postes de travail.

Expert

Robert-Grandpierre et Rapp SA, Ingénieurs-Conseils, Lausanne et ITEP, Lausanne.

Contribution des experts

Etude complète.

Matériel utilisé

CDC Cyber 7326 et Tektronix 4014

ETUDE DE LAUSANNE:
VARIANTES RELATIVES A L'EVALUATION DU METRO L-O

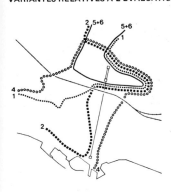
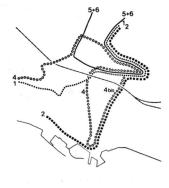

RESEAU ACTUEL   "METRO" INTEGRE, LIGNES DE BUS ADAPTEES   "METRO" SUPPRIME LIGNE DE BUS SUPPLEMENTAIRE

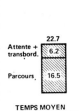
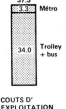
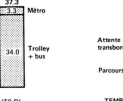
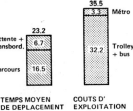
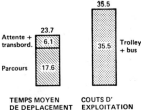

Étude d'evaluation du réseau des systémes de transport de Zürich

Client

Verkehrsbetriebe der Stadt Zürich (VBZ, compagnie des transports publics de Zürich)

Date

1976/77

Objectifs

1) Examen des conséquences de l'introduction d'une nouvelle ligne de tramways légers et de différents prolongements de quelques lignes existantes de bus et de tramways
2) Evaluation des possibilités offertes par le NOPTS en tant qu'instrument permanent de planification opérationnelle.

Dimension du problème

- population urbaine: 434'000
- population de la zone métropolitaine: 639'000
- réseau de base: 220 noeuds, 820 liaisons (directionnelles) 46 lignes (14 tram, 32 bus)
- usagers: 210 mio. de passagers par an. 76'600 pass. par heure de pointe.

Sources des données

Matrice des déplacements station à station (220x220) obtenue à partir du recensement détaillé des ménages effectué en 1969 dans toute la zone métropolitaine et mise à jour en 1976 par des comptages par écrans.

Résultats

Excellente concordance entre les valeurs déterminées par le modèle et les résultats d'enquêtes à bord des véhicules. Des résultats sur l'évaluation des variantes sont prévus pour le premier semestre 1977.

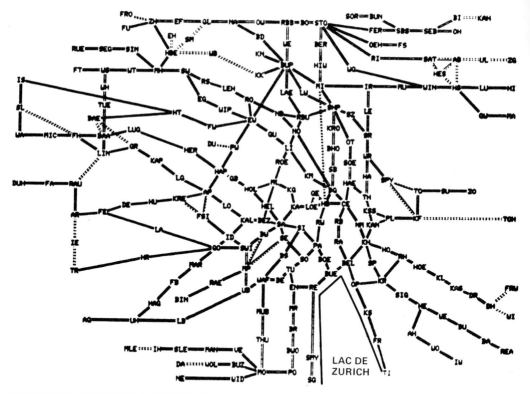

APPLICATION DE ZURICH : LIGNES EXISTANTES

VORSTUDIE VBZ ZUERICH   15 DEZEMBER 1976
UBZ ZUERICH VORSTUDIE ********** NETZ 65 **********

LINIEN:
2
4

APPLICATION DE ZURICH : CHARGE DES LIGNES

LAC DE
ZURICH

VARIANTE 6900   LINIENBELASTUNG   1000 FAHRTEN

Expert
W. & J. Rapp AG, Bâle et Rudolf Keller, Muttenz, Suisse.

Contribution des consultants
Préparation des données, calibrage du modèle, assistance technique durant les phases d'utilisation du NOPTS. Utilisation interactive du NOPTS par le personnel technique de la compagnie VBZ.

Matériel utilisé
Ordinateur HP-2100 avec écran Tektronix 4014 CRT

Étude des transports publics de la region de Lisbonne

Client
Direcçao-Geral de Transportes Terrestres (Public Transport Administration of Portuguese Transport Ministry)

Date
1976/77

Objectif
Étude du système des transports publics dans le cadre de la planification des transports de la région de Lisbonne. Evaluation des principales alternatives de développement à court et à moyen terme du système des transports publics, comprenant l'extension du réseau métro, le perfectionnement des chemins de fer subur-bains et des tramways, des conversions de mode tramway-bus, la restructuration du réseau urbain et suburbain de bus, l'adaptation de la capacité des lignes de transports fluviaux.

Dimension du problème
– population urbaine: 900'000
– population de l'agglomération: 2'250'000
– réseau de base traité par le NOPTS: 230 noeuds, 1100 liaisons, 160 lignes (4/trains, 2-5/métro, 7/bacs, 17/tramways, 60/bus urbains, 70/bus surburbains.
– usagers: 300'000 passagers à l'heure de pointe du matin.

Sources de données
Enquête à domicile origine-destination de 1973 mise à jour en 1975/76 par une série de comptages par écrans, sur les lignes et aux stations. La demande a été mise sous la forme d'une matrice 230x230 de station à station. Les données de l'offre ont été obtenues des principales compagnies de transport.

Cadre institutionnel
Sous la direction sur place d'un état-major du consultant, les divers services de planification ont rassemblé les informations et préparé les concepts à évaluer. L'élaboration et l'évaluation des alternatives sont réalisées au siège du consultant, mais l'installation Ju NOPTS sur place pourrait entrer en considération.

RÉSEAU TC DE LA REGION DE LIS-BONNE
CALIBRAGE DU 8 9 76 MATRICE NO 3

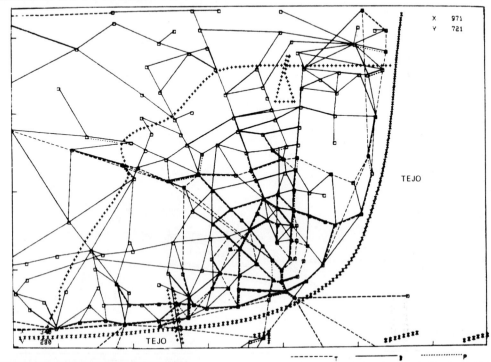

VARIANTE 1 RESEAU DE BASE

RESEAU TC DE LA REGION DE LIS-
BONNE
CALIBRAGE DU 8 9 76 MATRICE NO 3

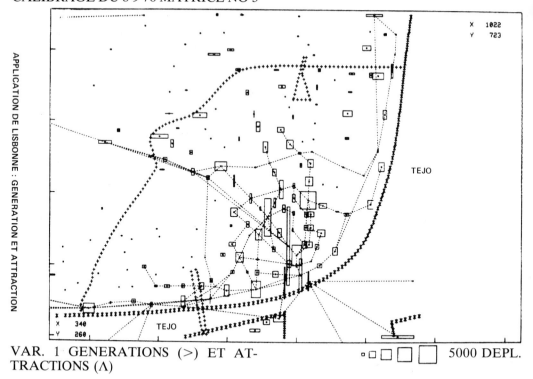

VAR. 1 GENERATIONS (>) ET AT-
TRACTIONS (Λ)   5000 DEPL.

RÉSEAU TC DE LA REGION DE LISBONNE CALIBRAGE DU 8 9 76 MATRICE N

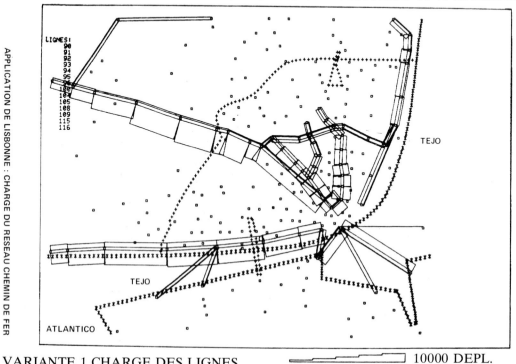

VARIANTE 1 CHARGE DES LIGNES   10000 DEPL.

Evaluation des résultats
Approximativement 25 variantes tirées de 9 concepts différents sont en phase de réalisation et d'évaluation.

Expert
ITEP, Lausanne, Suisse.

Matériel utilisé
Ordinateur CDC Cyber 7326 avec écran Tektronix 4014.

Étude des transports de Porto

Client
Direcçao-Geral de Transportes Terrestres (Département des transports publics du Ministère des transports portugais)

Date
1975/77

Objectifs
A partir d'une analyse détaillée des itinéraires, du matériel roulant, des fréquences ainsi que des interfaces sur l'ensemble du réseau des transports en commun de la région de Porto, faire des propositions pouvant porter sur des conversions de mode tramways, bus, trolleybus, tendant à améliorer les services à court et à moyen terme.

Dimension du problème
– population urbaine: 310'000
– population de l'aggl(o)mératoin: 860'000
– réseau de base traité par le NOPTS: 188 noeuds et 814 liaisons, 58 lignes (14/tramways, 10/trolleybus, 34/bus)
– usagers: 580'000 passagers par jour.

Sources des données
– enquêtes 1972/73 à bord des véhicules
– mesures des temps parcourus
– données de base de l'offre fournies par STCP (compagne des transports de Porto)

Evaluation et résultats
Prévu pour le deuxième trimestre 1977.

Cadre institutionnel
Une équipe à vocation interdisciplinaire a été mise sur pied. Elle comprend une quinzaine de spécialistes représentant les autorités publiques concernées (compagnie de transport, chemin de fer portugais, municipalités, ministère des transports) et elle se trouve sous la direction technique des représentants sur place du consultant.

Expert
W. & J. Rapp AG, Bâle, Suisse

Matériel utilisé
Ordinateur HP-2100 avec écran Tektronix 4014

PORTO ESTUDO DA REDE
STCP
REDE 1971   GEPP / RAPP

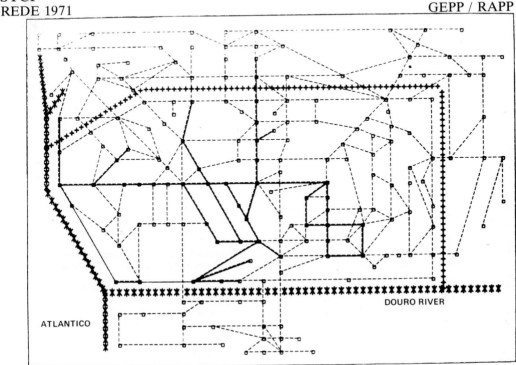

APPLICATION DE PORTO : RESEAU DE BASE

DESIGN 1 BASE NETWORK

——— R, ------- B,   P
Tramways   Bus   Piétons

Transport International et Pays en Voie de Développement

par

P. BAUCHET
Université de Paris no. 1, France

La croissance des Pays en Voie de Développement (P.V.D.) dépend très largement de leur commerce extérieur et plus particulièrement de l'exportation vers les pays développés de matières premières et de produits de base qui leur procurent l'essentiel de leurs recettes en devises. Ce commerce intéresse beaucoup plus les pays occidentaux que les nations socialistes de l'Est. Les relations Nord Sud jouent un rôle prépondérant dans le développement. Ce commerce utilise très largement le navire comme vecteur. Sans doute ne faut-il pas négliger le rôle croissant du transport aérien et des véhicules terrestres qui complètent une chaîne de transport. Mais le transport maritime est le lieu d'un conflit significatif entre P.D.V. et pays développés. Les premiers critiquent vigoureusement la politique menée par les nations occidentales qui possèdent encore plus de 80% de la flotte mondiale si l'on y inclut tous les pavillons de complaisance et qui useraient de cette arme sans considération des problèmes propres au développement. Les P.D.V. cherchent à mieux maîtriser le transport de leur traffic qui représente 40% du trafic total par des mesures d'intervention. Les nations occidentales n'ont pas manqué de réagir. Elles dénoncent les mesures de protection qui mettent en cause le principe du "Free Flow of Shipping" et qui sont, disent-elles, responsables au moins partiellement de la crise actuelle du transport. Le dialogue Nord Sud est donc aussi difficile dans le transport maritime que dans les autres domaines: il est nécessaire de prendre la mesure de l'importance de ce transport dans l'évolution des pays en voie de développement.

Nul ne peut contester que le transport international a eu un effet déterminant dans le développement des P.D.V. et que la politique menée ne leur a pas toujours été favorable. Mais les bouleversements actuels de l'économie mondiale sont en train de transformer les structures de l'échange et du transport international. Dans ce contexte s'élaborent de nouvelles règles du jeu dont l'observateur doit se demander si elles seront plus favorables au développement.

LE RÔLE DU TRANSPORT INTERNATIONAL DANS LE DÉVELOPPEMENT

Le commerce international est un facteur essentiel du développement du Tiers Monde, tant au plan des importations que des exportations. L'ouverture à l'échange international par les réseaux de communication maritime a constitué une condition fondamentale de leur croissance. Toutefois cette ouverture s'est située dans un contexte qui n'a pas favorisé le développement autant qu'on aurait pu l'espérer.

Dans un marché dominé par les pays développés acheteurs de matières premières, le transport maritime a exercé une influence considérable sur la production des P.V.D. Sans doute ne faudrait-il pas identifier au-

jourd'hui ces pays avec l'exportation de produits primaires; la valeur totale de ces produits exportés par les pays développés est plus importante. Toutefois les P.D.V. ont été et restent encore aujourd'hui malgré la croissance rapide de leurs exportations industrielles, spécialisés dans les exportations primaires, et souvent même dans la production d'un seul produit [1]. Or le prix de leur transport est relativement plus élevé -il peut être supérieur à 10% du prix total - que celui des produits manufacturés. Dans un contexte où la demande par les pays industriels est à la fois diversifiée et élastique face à une offre unitaire et peu élastique, les changements de prix du transport auront tendance à se répercuter sur l'offre et à exercer une influence déterminante sur le prix, donc le volume et la structure des exportations.

Le passé récent montre de nombreux exemples des variations des coûts de transport. Les frets de ligne régulières ont connu une hausse continue avec un doublement de 1970 à 1976, ceux du tramping des fluctuations importantes puisqu'après avoir doublé en 1973 ils sont revenus à leur point de départ en 1976. La répercussion des hausses de fret pour les matières premières à offre inélastique et à demande élastique se produit nécessairement sur le prix de vente F.O.B. de ces produits. L'histoire coloniale est remplie d'exemples, allant du cacao au bois, qui illustrent cette thèse. Ce sont les pays en voie de développement exportateurs de produits primaires qui vont subir les effets des hausses et souffrent des variations de fret. Comme importateurs de produits manufacturés dont ils ont le plus grand besoin, ils subiront aussi les hausses de prix sur le transport des "divers". L'absolue nécessité dans laquelle ils sont d'exporter pour couvrir des importations indispensables conduit donc les pays les plus pauvres à supporter les variations de fret [2]. A travers les prix les conditions du transport maritime modifient le volume et la structure des productions. On sait le rôle qu'ont joué dans le développement des mines de fer lointaines et l'extraction pétrolière, l'augmentation de la taille des navires. Et de la productivité faisant baisser les frets. A l'inverse des événements comme la fermeture du canal de Suez ont entraîné des difficultés dans certaines cultures exotiques d'Asie.

Le transport maritime pèse enfin sur les pays en voie de développement par le poids considérable que représente sur leur balance des paiements le coût en devises du transport maritime. L'illustration la plus récente en a été donnée par le Ministre Ivoirien de la marine [3] qui indique que, en cinq ans, le déficit de la balance des frets a été multiplié par trois. Si l'on tient compte de l'endettement écrasant des pays les plus pauvres cette charge supplémentaire parait insupportable.

Ce ne sont pas seulement la nature des marchés en présence et la part relativement faible des moyens de transport sous pavillons de P.V.D. qui expliquent la dépendance de ces pays par rapport au transport mariti-

496

me. Les pays les plus défavorisés mettent en cause devant les instances internationales et notamment devant la Conférence des Nations Unies pour le Commerce et le Développement (C.N.U.C.E.D.) les pratiques monopolistiques des armements occidentaux qui se cachent derrière le principe de la liberté des mers. L'existence des conférences pour le transport de ligne limitent la concurrence, favorise les discriminations de service et de prix. Les pratique anciennes de secret des tarifs et les ristournes occultes accréditent les thèses les plus avancées sur les pressions qu'exerceraient ainsi les pays développés contre la croissance de certaines activités dans les P.D.V. On cite fréquemment les exemples des industries du bois, du textile qui n'auraient pu se développer en raison de pratiques tarifaires qui auraient joué le rôle de véritables taxes à l'importation. Là où elles ne visaient pas des activités déterminées, les discriminations tendraient simplement à écarter les vrais prix des coûts et à faire peser sur les pays pauvres des frets exessifs.

Il est malheureusement difficile de mesurer avec précision la portée exacte de ces faits puisque nous manque jusqu'alors, pour la pluspart des produits transportés, un élément d'information fondamental, la connaissance des frets pratiqués notamment sur les transports de ligne. On pourrait mesurer l'influence des politiques de transport sur les prix si l'on connaissait au moins les prix F.O.B. des produits à la sortie du P.V.D. et les prix C.A.F. de ces produits à l'importation en Occident. La différence des deux éléments nous fournirait des indications utiles sur le rôle des coûts de transport et d'assurance pratiqués en fait sur un même produit suivant son origine. Mais si les prix des importations C.A.F. dans les pays développés sont bien connus, les prix F.O.B. à l'exportation des P.V.D. le sont mal sauf pour le pétrole et les quelques produits qui ont fait l'objet d'enquêtes de la C.N.U.C.E.D.. On ne saurait trop insister sur l'importance de la connaissance des prix F.O.B. à l'exportation des P.V.D. pour éclairer à l'avenir les politiques des Etats en matière de transport. Même en l'absence de données générales, on ne peut nier certains aspects négatifs qu'a pu avoir l'organisation actuelle du transport maritime sur le développement dans le contexte de marchés d'acheteurs et pratiques discriminatoires.

Toutefois des signes montrent qu'un renversement du contexte peut se produire. Nous n'en citerons qu'un aspect que les consommateurs occidentaux de café ne peuvent ignorer avec l'augmentation de son prix. Il n'est plus vrai que sur tous les produits primaires la demande soit inélastique et l'offre élastique. Après le pétrole où le renversement de la situation est spectaculaire, d'autres produits suscitent en Occident une consommation inélastique alors que leur offre s'assouplit. Que ce changement soit provoqué par des pénuries ou par un renforcement du pouvoir des producteurs, peu importe. En conséquence les fluctuations des prix de transport jouent aujourd'hui contre les importateurs de certains produits primaires et non plus contre les exportateurs. De façon plus générale, les changements intervenus dans la croissance mondiale sont en train de bouleverser les conditions et la structure du transport international. Il faut donc les examiner avant de voir quelles règles du jeu sont les plus favorables au développement.

L'EFFET DES TRANSFORMATIONS DE L'ÉCONOMIE MONDIALE SUR LE TRANSPORT INTERNATIONAL

Trois traits ne résument pas les transformations de l'économie mondiale mais mettent en valeur ce qui perturbe profondément le transport international: la fin du monopole industriel des pays développés, l'extension des entreprises multinationales et les changements dans les rythmes de croissance pour ce qu'ils comportent comme conséquences sur le transport.

Trois transformations de l'économie internationale
La fin du monopole industriel des pays développés
En 1974, la productions industrielle des P.V.D. représente seulement 7 à 8% de la production mondiale. Or la déclaration de Lima en 1974 envisageait suivant le trend de croissance de leur production, que ces pays pourraient occuper 25% de la production industrielle mondiale en l'an 2000. La fin du monopole industriel de l'Occident ne correspond certes pas nécessairement à la fin de l'hégémonie des grandes puissances. Mais elle signifie que sur tous ces continents, des pays neufs ont désormais les moyens en matières premières, en capital et en homme de développer des complexes industriels. Dans un contexte d'épuisement des ressources en matières premières des pays d'Europe et partiellement des U.S.A., le Tiers Monde cherche et est parfois parvenu à s'assurer la maîtrise de ses propres gisements. Il tend alors à élever le prix de ces richesses et singulièrement du pétrole. L'accumulation de devises qui en résulte permet un financement du développement indépendant de l'aide parcimonieuse de l'Occident. La récente conférence du Caire marque en ce sens une étape importante dans l'émergence d'un nouveau système de soutien de l'industrialisation du Tiers Monde plus indépendant du système financier occidental. Enfin les universités donnent à ces pays un personnel qualifié en nombre croissant. Tous les facteurs sont donc réunis pour que des pays neufs concurrencent et parfois freinent le développement de certaines industries occidentales comme le textile; l'habillement, le cuir, la chaussure, le meuble, la construction navale. Plus encore les P.V.D. cherchent à transformer directement sur place leurs matières premières pour en valoriser l'exportation; les activités de raffinage, l'industrie chimique de base, la sidérurgie, connaissent en Europe des difficultés qui ne sont pas étrangères au développement du Tiers Monde.

Sans doute tous les pays ne bénéficient pas de ce développement, mais on peut citer parmi les ''nouveaux Japons'' l'Arabie Saoudite, la Chine, la Corée, l'Inde, l'Irak, l'Iran la Malaisie, les pays d'Afrique du Nord, la Côte d'Ivoire, le Nigéria, l'Argentine, le Brésil, le Vénézuéla, le Mexique. Les exportations industrielles des pays du Tiers Monde ont en conséquence progressé de plus de 25% par an au cours de la dernière décade malgré les obstacles douaniers élevés par l'occident. Elles représentent aujourd'hui plus de 25% de leurs exportations totales contre 10% en 1950. Les entreprises multinationales contribuent beaucoup à ce développement industriel du tiers monde.

L'extension des entreprises multinationales
Phénomène récent il trouve sa source dans les investissements directs effectués par les Etats Unis et le Royaume Uni, la France, l'Allemagne de l'Ouest, le Japon et même des pays neufs comme l'OPEP. La force des multinationales provient non seulement de leur taille mais aussi de la combinaison internationale des facteurs et des produits qu'elles réalisent. Elles déplacent les capitaux et les connaissances des pays où ils sont le moins coûteux vers ceux où la main d'oeuvre est bon marché. A l'inverse elles amènent en Occident les produits intermédiaires déjà élaborés et les produits finis fabriqués dans le Tiers Monde. Ce double déplacement des facteurs et des produits facilité par le développement des voies de communication donne aux produits finis vendus par ces entreprises des avantages comparés considérables par rapport à ceux produits dans une nation.

Si ces capitaux s'orientaient jadis essentiellement vers les mines et le pétrole il n'en va plus de même aujourd'hui où ils intéressent principalement le secteur secondaire, voire les activités tertiaires comme l'hôtellerie. Ces capitaux s'orientent d'ailleurs vers des régions nouvelles et notamment l'Asie et l'Amérique du Sud. Les critiques souvent fondées ne manquent pas à l'égard de ces entreprises et le développement qu'elles provoquent n'est souvent pas celui souhaité par les P.V.D. Mais il faut constater qu'elles contribuent à renforcer la puissance économique de ces dernières et à créer une nouvelle division internationale du travail que comme l'apprenti sorcier, les pays développés n'ont pas toujours voulu au départ.

Surtout, la structure des échanges internationaux et donc celle des transports en n'est profondément transformée. Une partie du commerce mondial - certains disent 45% - n'est plus inter-nations mais intra-firmes qui ont ainsi possibilité de s'assurer une certaine maitrise du transport. Les vieilles lois de l'échange ne s'appliquent plus. Les coûts comparés entre nations ont aujourd'hui moins de sens que les coûts comparés entre deux firmes multinationales. Tout ceci contribue à un changement dans les rythmes et les modes de croissance des divers pays.

La rupture des rythmes et des modes de croissance

La croissance exceptionnelle que le monde connait depuis trente ans est essentiellement due à celle des pays développés de l'Europe dont le poids relatif et le pouvoir d'entraînement sur l'économie mondiale ont été déterminants. La poursuite de cette croissance pourrait être différente.

Nombreux sont les facteurs qui pourraient contribuer à un ralentissement de la croissance des pays industrialisés: épuisement des réserves de main d'oeuvre dans les secteurs à basse productivité comme l'agriculture, augmentation du prix des ressources énergétiques et des matières premières avec des conditions d'exploitation plus difficiles, productivité plus faible de nouveaux investissements, difficulté d'adaptation de l'offre à une demande saturée, hausse des coûts de la main d'oeuvre et chômage. Il faut ajouter les contraintes nouvelles des politiques de l'environnement et la concurence des pays neufs obligeant à un redéploiement coûteux des activités.

Les pays en voie de développement étroitement dépendants risquent de connaitre aussi des difficultés. Mais d'autres mieux armés reçoivent des transferts d'activité des plurinationales cherchant à fuir les rigidités des vieux pays et peuvent en profiter.

Au Mexique, Brésil, Vénézuela, la production de filiales plurinationales est beaucoup plus rapide que celle déjà élevée des autres activités industrielles [4]. De nombreux pays neufs poursuivent encore des croissances de 8% et plus alors que l'Europe est passée de son rythme trentenaire de 5% à 3%. Même si l'on admet que l'Europe est entrée dans la phase décroissante de son cycle Kondratieff, il faut se garder de généraliser une telle conclusion à l'ensemble de la planète. D'autres pays pourraient, au contraire, voir leur croissance s'accélérer.

Un tel mouvement en ciseau contribuerait lui aussi à transformer profondément la structure du transport international.

Ses effets sur le transport international

Les changements profonds dans le transport international toucheront le trafic lui-même, la structure des transports, les conditions de fixation et de répercussion des frets.

Les changements dans le trafic

Il faudrait pour préciser ces changements avoir une connaissance plus précise des relations qui unissent le taux de croissance de chaque catégorie de P.V.D. et son commerce international; de même il serait précieux de disposer d'études concernant les relations entre l'industrialisation des P.V.D. et les distances sur lesquelles sont transportées quelques grandes matières premières. La pauvreté de la littérature en la matière interdit des considérations autres que partielles tant en ce qui concerne les marchandises transportées que les centres de trafic.

Pour les marchandises transportées la simple extrapolation du passé conduirait à des erreurs grossières. Dans le cas des produits énergétiques le rattrapage encore modeste des quantités d'énergie consommées par tête dans les P.V.D. (0,4 tec) par rapport à la situation en Amérique du Nord (12,6 tec) ou en Europe (5 tec) contribue à accroître la part de la demande des pays du tiers monde. Pour le charbon les prévisions pour l'an 2000 envisagent un accroissement de la demande dans les pays producteurs eux-mêmes, Etats-Unis, URSS, pays de l'Est et Chine. Le doublement de la production sera largement consommé sur place. Mais des accroissements d'importations en Europe et au Japon [5]. Les transports de méthane pourraient, eux, sensiblement augmenter. Par contre, la croissance des transports de pétrole pourrait être assez fortement freinée. En effet, ce sont surtout les pays du tiers monde qui consommeraient davantage de ce produit particulièrement bien adapté à leurs besoins et dont ils souhaiteront réaliser la transformation sur place. L'autonomie croissante des pays neufs devrait donc conduire à une auto-suffisance continentale généralisée: Amerique du Nord avec le centre du continent, Amérique du Sud, les pays de l'Est, l'Europe et le moyen Orient. Cette perspective ne conduit pas à l'optimisme en ce qui concerne le transport pétrolier qui représente plus de la moitié du volume du transport maritime.

La volonté des pays neufs d'exploiter sur place leurs matières premières pourrait d'ailleurs provoquer une évolution identique pour le transport de vrac. La tendance des pays développés à redéployer leur industrie vers de la transformation fine et peut-être le ralentissement de leur rythme de croissance pourrait également peser sur le transport de vrac. Mais il est probable que l'augmentation des besoins alimentaires dans des pays arides ou surpeuplés devrait faire croître le trafic des céréales et celui des engrais.

Le transport des diverses devrait aussi profiter des transformations en cours. Le développement des industries des P.V.D. appelle une information de biens d'équipement et de demi-produits, particulièrement sensible dans les pays en voie d'industrialisation rapide. Par ailleurs, la hausse de leur niveau de vie est source d'importations de produits de consommation. D'autre part, nous avons déjà noté la croissance très rapide des exportations de produits manufacturés en provenance du tiers monde. Ajoutons que l'extension des multinationales qui vivent de la combinaison de produits et de facteurs venant de toutes les parties du monde multiplie les occasions d'échange sur les produits divers. Elle est un élément du succès du conteneur et du transport pluri modal. L'avion avec le navire devrait profiter de l'accroissement du trafic sur ces produits divers.

Il est probable que de nouveaux pôles d'échange se structureront dans un avenir proche. A la prééminence nord-américaine sont venues s'ajouter la zone d'attraction du marché commun, celle du Japon. Il n'est pas impensable que l'Amérique du Sud et le Sud-Est Asiatique constituent bientôt ces nouveaux pôles.

Ces trafics qui intéressent donc des pays neufs modifieront les structures actuelles du transport international.

Par structure, nous entendons ici l'appropriation et la

maîtrise du transport. La place des pavillons des P.V.D., moins de 8% du tonnage mondial si l'on exclut les pavillons de complaisance, indique assez leur dépendance. Pourtant, cette place a tendance à augmenter et les P.V.D. ont manifesté à plusieurs reprises leur volonté de posséder leur propre flotte maritime comme d'ailleurs leur flotte aérienne. Parmi les raisons avancées on retiendra outre le prestige, la volonté de peser sur les décisions des conférences pour obtenir de meilleures conditions de fret et de desserte, et indirectement la volonté de promouvoir leurs exportations dans les directions les plus profitables. S'y ajoute enfin le souci d'alléger leur balance.

Ces politiques se sont heurtées à des obstacles qui ont amené la CNUCED à des recommandations plus nuancées et ont freiné le développement des flottes. Pour les pays avancés comme le Brésil ou la Corée qui fabriquent eux-mêmes les navires, le gain en devises est plus certain que pour ceux, les plus nombreux, qui sont obligés de dépenser des devises pour acquérir les navires. Encore la construction navale est-elle une activité très conjoncturelle et donc dangereuse pour des économies fragiles. Outre le problème d'investissement se pose celui de la formation d'équipages et de l'embauche d'un encadrement étranger lui aussi coûteux en devises. Pour diminuer ces côuts, les P.V.D. ont eu recours à des formules autres que la création de flottes purement nationales. Si la constitution de flottes pluri-nationales est encore exceptionelle, on assiste au développement de Joint Venture - comme l'Eurandino - conclues entres pays développés et pays en voie de développement et les Consortiums.

La création de ces flottes sous pavillon national ou conjointes n'a pas rapporté autant que ces pays l'espéraient. Une baisse des frets n'a pas toujours pu être obtenue et lorsqu'elle l'a été elle a augmenté des déficits d'exploitation qui retombent lourdement, nous le savons pas expérience, sur les caisses publiques du pas propriétaire de la flotte [6]. L'incitation à exporter n'a pas toujours joué comme dans le cas exceptionnellement favorable de la Colombie avec ses ventes de café [7].

Mais il n'en reste pas moins que les flottes sous pavillon des P.V.D. ont tendance à se développer et qu'elles continueront probablement à le faire [8]. Ceci est très notable pour les pays pétroliers qui souhaitent maîtriser ainsi leurs exportations [9]. Ailleurs, outre les mobiles de prestige et d'entrainement des exportations, des considérations purement économiques sur lesquelles malheureusement nous manquons d'information pourraient jouer aussi, notamment le moindre coût de navigants dans les P.V.D. Compte-tenu des charges salariales importantes directes et indirectes ainsi que des nouvelles contraintes concernant la pollution et la protection de l'environnement, qui pèsent sur les flottes occidentales, il n'est pas invraisemblable que sous des formes diverses et notamment des joint venture, les capitaux occidentaux n'encouragent les développement de flottes de P.D.V. qui ne seraient pas de complaisance. Un meilleur contrôle par les P.V.D. des flottes sous pavillon de complaisance irait d'ailleurs dans le même sens et ferait d'eux des pays transporteurs. Ici encore le développement de financement international direct, et l'augmentation de la puissance industrielle de certains pays ne pourront que favoriser le changement de structure du transport aérien et maritime.

Les conditions de fixation et de répercussion des variations de fret changent aussi

La position des conférences n'est plus aussi forte qu'elle le fut. La création ou la menace de création de flottes nationales n'en est pas la seule cause. Les pays chargeurs usent de la concurrence du tramping sous forme d'affretement surtout dans les périodes où comme aujourd'hui le marché est en crise. Les conférences sont obligées d'entrer en négociation avec les Etats, les forces économiques des nations dont elles sont les transporteurs ou encore des organisations communes comme la C.O.W.A.C. (conférence de la Cote Ouest d'Afrique). Surtout elles doivent tenir compte des Cosneils de Chargeurs que les P.V.D. cherchent à organiser systématiquement pour peser sur les frets.

Ces conseils de chargeurs reçoivent des délégation pour négocier avec les transporteurs. Ils organisent le groupage de cargaisons qui permet l'affretement de navires dans des conditions qui abaissent sensiblement le coût du transport. Ils vont parfois jusqu'à créer des bureaux de fret qui informent leurs mandats et leur évitent de négocier isolément. Certains gouvernements ont même transformé ces bureaux en offices nationaux qui traitent de tous les problèmes de transport maritime [10].

En même temps, le gouvernements des P.V.D. prennent conscience de ce que le transport maritime aérien proprement dit n'occupe qu'une modeste part du coût de transport du fournisseur au client, environ 20%, et du handicap que constitue la faiblesse de leurs installations portuaires et aéroportuaires. A l'exemple des invoiriens qui développent à St Pedro un port en eau profonde avec une zone industrielle, ils cherchent à créer des complexes avec des installations de stockage et de transformation ainsi que des moyens de raccordement vers l'intérieur qui évitent les délais d'attente qui ont pesé si lourdement au cours des derniers moins sur le fret. Des aides étrangères de l'Ouest ou de l'Est - l'example le plus récent en est le chemin de fer chinois qui dégage le port de Dar Es Salam en Tanzanie - assurent le financement de ces opérations.

Tout ceci ne permet pas seulement aux P.V.D. de peser sur les frets. Ceux qui disposent d'une puissance industrielle ou d'un certain monople de matière première peuvent aujourd'hui répercuter sur le consommateur les variations de fret.

Un dernier élément modifie les conditions de fixation et de répercussion des frets: les règles internationales. Le Code de Conduite de la C.N.U.C.E.D. tente de faire prévaloir de nouvelles règles en matière de transport maritime. Il ne fait en réalité qu'accompagner toute une remise en cause de l'ordre établi en la matière. Le problème posé aujourd'hui est de savoir dans le contexte des changements profonds qui sont intervenus dans l'économiie internationale quelles sont les règles du jeu qui sont les plus favorables au développement.

III QUELLES SONT LES NORMES LES PLUS FAVORABLES AU DÉVELOPPEMENT?

Opposer un ordre ancien, celui de libéralisme, à un ordre nouveau, celui de la réglementation est une caricature. Toutefois il est cependant possible de tracer à grands traits ce qui sépare la situation passée de l'avenir qui se dessine.

Fondé sur le principe du free flow of shipping, la situation ancienne se caractérisait par le coexistence de deux domainees. Celui des lignes régulières oligopole de fait contrôlé par une ou plusieurs conférences ou consortiums. Là la concurrence était restreinte, sinon éliminée, les taux de fret fixés en commun à un niveau qui permet de rémunérer les partenaires. Si comme nous l'avons souligné de nouvelles conditions internationales limitent aujourd'hui ces situations oligopolistiques, elles n'en subsistent pas moins au profit des principaux signataires de l'entente et au détriment des absents. A côté, le marché des tramp présentait une situation largement concurrentielle limitée seulement par les spécialisations techniques des navires et l'existence de circuits captifs de transport que contrôlaient les grandes firmes, notamment pétrolières. Ce marché n'est donc pas purement libéral bien qu'il reste encore très souple et les P.V.D. s'opposent au maintien de cette fiction libérale que défendent l'O.C.D.E. et le G.A.T.T. pour promouvoir un cadre plus rigide et protectionniste.

Ce nouveau cadre en cours de gestation comprend en réalité trois aspects distincts. En premier lieu de nouvelles règles juridiques concernant le droit de la mer, le transport des marchandises par mer (qui renforce la responsabilité du transporteur), la réglementation du transport pluri-modal et les navires sub standard limitent la liberté d'entreprise mais ne modifient pas profondément les règles dus jeu. Il en va autrement du Code de Conduite des conférences maritimes qui introduit des règles de fixation des taux de fret et ouvrent un droit d'accès aux armateurs de chancun des pays desservis auxquels le code réserve 40% du traffic. L'insuccès des efforts de ratification de ce code et aussi la croissance des échanges avec les pays à commerce d'Etat a conduit a une troisième série d'innovations que constituent les accords bilatéraux: bien qu'ils ne soient pas généralisés, leur liste s'allonge et de nombreux pays en développement y ont dès maintenant recours, Algérie, Brésil, Egypte, Côte d'Ivoire. Ils incluent parfois une partage du trafic 50/50 encore plus rigoureux que celui du Code de Conduite et plus général puisqu'il concerne également le Tramping. Le dernier aspect du changement de cadre, plus net *encore mais* exceptionnel est la prise de décision unilatérale de pays qui se réservent purement et simplement certaines cargaisons.

Que le Code de Conduite soit ou non ratifié, et surtout s'il ne l'est pas, il est probable que nous allons vers une extension des accords bilatéraux et plus largement du protectionnisme des pays en voie de développement tant pour le trafic de ligne que pour le tramping qui reste jusqu'alors très peu réglementé. Mais les pays en voie de développement ont aujourd'hui une position ambigue à l'égard de l'ordre nouveau contenu dans ce code. Certains dénoncent les rigidités introduites par les accords de pool qu'encourage le code [11] sans leur apporter des avantages dont l'expérience prouve que dans le nouveau contexte économique international ils peuvent les obtenir par d'autres mesures. Ainsi, compte-tenu des changements en cours dans l'ordre international, un débat s'instaure sur les mérites de l'ancien et du nouveau système.

La comparaison de l'efficacité de l'ancien et du nouveau système peut se faire par comparaison des désordres que l'un et l'autres sons suceptibles d'entraîner.

Le système libéral entraîne des monopoles de conférences, dex fixations de prix abusifs, des dominations des pays les plus pauvres par l'absence de prise en compte des intérêts de leur développement. Dans sa partie concurrentielle le tramping, l'adaptation de l'offre à la demande s'est faite à tavers des cycles périodiques dont le dernier est très important. Les fluctuations erratiques de fret qui s'en sont suivies entraînent des irrégularités dans les circuits des échanges particulièrement graves pour les économies fragiles. Le désarmement ou la destruction d'une partie non négligeable du tonnage mondial [12] entraîne des pertes qui sont payées partiellement au moins, tôt ou tard, par les chargeurs: les gains de bonne conjuncture épongent les pertes des mauvaises années. Cette situation qui n'est finalement bonne ni pour les transporteurs, ni pour les chargeurs, ni pour les Etats appelle incontestablement une organisation plus rationnelle.

Le système d'intervention qui se met en place ne peut certes pas être tenu pour responsable de la crise actuelle du transport international qui, il est vrai, a éclaté au moment de cette mise en place: il concerne une part beaucoup trop faible du trafic mondial. Toutefois, son application généralisée conduirait à une rigidité peu compatible avec la nécessaire souplesse de l'échange international. La signature d'accords bilatéraux protectionnistes en ordre dispersé entraînerait une véritable désorganisation des relations internationales. Dès maintenant on note, dans le cadre des accords 50/50, des frets qui n'ont plus de rapport avec les coûts faute de concurrence. Par ailleurs, pour éviter des accords dont le fret est trop élevé se produisent des détournements de trafics par des pays tiers qui sont économiquement coûteux.

Mais le problème n'est pas seulement de savoir lequel des systèmes est le plus efficace; il est aussi de connaître ceux qui paient les désordres.

Qui paie les désordres?

Il est clair que le changement en cours des normes du transport international a eu pour objet moins de diminuer les désordres que d'empêcher qu'ils ne soient supportés par les P.D.V. comme par le passé. Or les mesures suggérées pourraient se retourner contre eux. Ainsi en est-il des mesures visant à transférer les coûts du chargeur sur le transporteur en matière d'assurance et de responsabilité. Ce transfert risque de coûter cher aux P.V.D. dans la mesure où ils deviennent transporteurs. En outre, ne retrouveront-ils pas dans les frets les frais supplémentaires encourus par le transporteur? De même, les difficultés de déchargement des navires dans les ports des P.V.D. sont retombées sur eux sous forme de charges d'immobilisation des navires (surestaries). Enfin, les baisses du fret conjuncturelles comme celle que nous connaissons ne profitent aux chargeurs que temporairement. Elles seront un jour récupérées par des frets plus élevés que les coûts. En réalité aucune règlementation juridique ne peut empêcher durablement la répercussion des charges du plus fort sur le plus faible. Les seules recettes valables pour empêcher cette répercussion sont soit de diminuer les désordres par une règlementation internationale qui tempèrerait les cycles et les phénomènes de domination, soit de rendre les "faibles" plus "forts".

A court terme un moyen pour les P.V.D de devenir forts est de se protéger par des mesures unilatérales discriminatoires dont les nations occidentales ne se sont pas privées dans le passé à des fins militaires ou commercials [13]. Mais à long aller les désordres du protectionisme risquent de peser sur les P.V.D. eux-mêmes. Les lois de partage des frets entre l'offreur et le demandeur d'une marchandise sont quasi-inéluctables: une offre élastique et (ou) dominée face à une demande inélastique et (ou) dominante paiera la plus grande partie du fret et vice versa. C'est la fragilité du commerce hollandais qui a permis à Cromwell de l'emporter et non pas l'"Acte de Navigation" en soi. Aussi ne sert-il de rien de modifier les normes du commerce international si elles ne réduisent pas les désordres et ne changent pas les rapports de force. A long terme changer les rapports de force signifie que les nations faibles renforcent avec leur potentiel économique, leur potentiel maritime, qu'elles disposent directement ou indirectement de flottes compétitives. Or les signes d'un tel changement sont aujourd'hui manifestes.

Les transformations dans l'économie mondiale permettent d'espérer l'apparition de pôles de développement dans des zones jusqu'alors considérées comme sous-développées en Asie, au Moyen Orient, en Amérique du Sud et dans certaines parties de l'Afrique. Cette émergence est la condition d'un rééquilibre du transport international. Elle permet d'éviter un protectionnisme qui n'a plus toujours l'excuse de la faiblesse et qui aurait érigé un nouvel ordre coûteux pour tous. Mais encore faut-il que tous les "forts" anciens et nouveaux acceptent une règlementation qui réduirait les désordres cycliques et les effets de domination qui ne manqueront pas de s'exercer à l'égard de ceux qui resent "faibles".

NOTES EN BAS DE PAGES

1. Denis Clair Lambert - Les Economies dur Tiers Monde - Armand Collin collection U 1976, p. 129-131. La Bolivie n'est past parvenue à réduire sa dépendance à l'égard de l'étain et le Chili a accru la sienne à l'égard du cuivre.

2. La hausse des frets aurait ainsi contribué à la dégration des term of trade sur laquelle d'ailleurs l'unanimité n'est pas faite (cf C. Godet).
Le choix de la période a une importance fondamentale sur les conclusions que l'on peut tirer de l'analyse des variations de prix. Pour la décade qui s'étend de 1963 à 1973 il ne fait pas de doute que les hausses de coût du fret ont contribué à dégrader les term of trade et, dans la mesure où les rapports de prix étaient établis sur des prix CAF-incluant la hausse du fret de produits primaires, à cacher cette dégradation.

3. Cf. Interview de Mr Lamine Fadika publié dans le Journal de la Marine Marchande 21/10/76, p. 2574.

4. cf. Denis Clair Lambert. Les Economies du Tiers Monde op. cit. p. 182

5. Entraîneraient de nouveaux trafics sauf gazéification sur place des combustibles minéraux solides et autres innovations techniques.

6. On estime que dans les pays développés, en France par exemple, un armement coûte à l'Etat du Pavillon 10% environ de son chiffre d'Affaires. Ceci est encore plus vrai des flottes aériennes. Encore doit-on noter que dans les P.D.V. la formation d'équpages nationaux a allégé les dépenses en devises des compagnies.

7. La création de la "Flotta Mercante Grancolombiana" avait permis à la Colombie d'améliorer ses exportations de café par une baisse sensible des frets.

8. Parmi les recommandations de la dernière conférence des pays non alignés figurent la création de conférences exclusives et d'entreprises communes aux P.V.D. pour la création de ports et de chantiers navals.

9. Toutefois l'exploitation déficitaire de l'Arab Maritime Petroleum Transport Company (AMPTC) fondée par 9 pays a incité les investisseurs privés arabes a se tourner vers des placements plu rémunérateurs.

10. Sans doute le dernier rapport de la CNUCED mentionne que les organisations de chargeurs ont eu plus d'efficacité en ce qui concerne les conditions de transport qu'en matière de niveau de fret; cf. Journal de la Marine Marchande Jeudi 7 avril p. 794.

11. cf. la critique de l'All India Shippers Council à l'égard des accords de pool passés par les Indian, Pakistan, Bangladesh Conférences citée par la revue Navigation Maritime p. 353, 1977

12. En juin 1976, 15% de la flotte pétrolière était désarmée. En outre, on estime que d'ici 1980, les commandes de navires neufs ne correspondraient qu'à 60% de la capacité actuelle de production des chantiers.

13. "L'Acte de Navigation" d'Olivier Cromwell (1651) interdisait l'accès des ports anglais aux navires étrangers important des marchandises en Grande Bretagne pour lutter contre la concurence de la Hollande. En 1811 l'Angleterre et la France décidaient chacune de leur côté le blocus des ports.

Infrastructural growth and developmental planning: A comparative study of road infrastructure in the national development of ASEAN countries

by

SEAH CHEE MEOW

University of Singapore

The road itself seems to speak to him: ". . . I shall change everything and everybody . . . . I am abolishing the old ways, the old ideas, the old law; I am bringing wealth and opportunity for good as well as vice, new powers to men and therefore new conflicts. I am the revolution. I am giving you plenty of trouble already, you governors, and I am going to give you plenty more. I destroy and I make new. What are you going to do about it? I am your idea. You made me, so I suppose you know" - Joyce Cary, Mister Johnson *(New York: Harper & Brothers, 1954), pp. 186-87.*

The importance of transportion in national development is generally accepted although the extent to which transportation (and its different modes) can play a catalytic role is questioned. Transportation is one form of social infrastructure; it is also a form capital formation for any society wishing to further economic growth. Galbraith, referring to economic development, has argued that "a highly efficient transportation and an economic and reliable source of power are indispensable. With these available, something is bound to happen; without them, we can be less sure". [1] A report by the U.N. Economic Commission for Africa, reiterated a common observation when it commented that the material development in that continent could be summed up in one word, namely, transport. It argued that "improved transport is certainly a prerequisite for any type of development". [2] The importance of improved transport infrastructure may be evinced from the large allocation to this sector: countries are known to invest between 25 to 30 percent of national capital formation in the transportation sector.

This emphasis is not too surprising. Transportation is the link between geographically dispersed markets and settlements whose growth is dependent on an infrastructure which can be provided in efficient amounts and at efficient rates. Leferber sums up neatly when he said that "efficient pricing of regionally separated activities requires that the difference between the prices of homogeneous goods at different locations should not exceed the marginal cost of transporting these goods". [3] Transportation facilities thus contribute in determining the patterns and rates of economic growth and whether the factors of production may be more optimatly matched.

On non-economic considerations, transport infrastructure is equally valued as a factor in social communication and national consolidation. The ability and speed in linking variously scattered communities affects accep-

tance of political authority. This is even more relevant for the bulk of the developing countries which have only a brief history of infant nationhood and which have still to tackle the problems of national consolidation. External threats by "less friendly" powers and domestic threats from groups with views radically different from those of the ruling elites continue to plague many of these nations. Infrastructural development, especially road transport, is viewed a priority item because it could be used to minimise these threats or conversely, strengthen the capabilities of the ruling regimes to confront them. For example, national governments are known to have re-routed communication links to "more friendly" countries even though the economic rationale for doing so may not exist while similarly, an expanded network of infrastructure in the country is also welcomed by security forces in facilitating logistics support against scattered insurgent groups. These non-economic reasons sometime outweigh the economic considerations in the planning of additional network capabilities.

While the importance of transport infrastructure is generally recognised, considerable differences exist on a range of concomitant issues. What, for example, should be the appropriate strategic-mix in terms of infrastructural facilities? How should the modes be financed and priced? What priority to be assigned to the build-up urbanised areas and the less developed regions and how will this determine strategy in economic development? Should infrastructural development preceed demand or should it be a response to needs? The list of questions can be extended.

There are no clear-cut solutions. Infrastructural development is not the exclusive concern of the planners (spatial and economic) even though they may help influence decisionmaking. Neither can the political leadership rely exclusively on economic considerations. Besides, not all the parameters, such as improved well-being among those affected by proposed infrastructural development, can be comprehensively accounted and adequately quantified. [4]

The governments are increasingly called to shoulder the cost of infrastructural development. Apart from the scale of the costs involved, it is generally argued that such developments affect the community and the government, rather than the private sector, should assume the cost as part of its responsibility to the society. Also, the returns to investments made in plant facilities (such as roads, railways, or airports) are difficult to ascertain partly because of different categories of user-demands, a feature more so in regard to road transportation.

Road transport is probably one mode which affects

the people most intensely. It is characterised by a general purpose capability and it is also the most flexible in that access is theoretically possible on all points of the roadways. Collector or feeder roads could always be connected to the main or primary distributory roads. Secondary development can grow along the lengths of these roads. Accessibility from point to point is also complemented by a wide range of available transport modes (such as cars, freight trucks and various other forms of public transport). Entrepreneurship is thus fostered while the diffusion of rudimentary technical skills for maintenance of transport vehicles can have considerable economic and educational potential. [5]

The responsibility for road development unfortunately does not end with the provision of these infrastructure; in most instances, it is only one aspect of a syndromic development ranging from infrastructural maintenance and expansion to regulation and coordination of these linkages. A wide range of human activities depends on this infrastructure which has become an indispensible aspect for the community's continued well-being. A large number of governmental agencies is thus involved in the various aspects of road development. Intra-agency and inter-agency cooperation and coordination is thus a premium, but because road transportation serves varied needs and various user intersts are involved (including governmental agencies) cooperation and coordination among these agencies may not always be attained. Indeed, a major bottleneck in road development is not just the physical constraints resulting from overloading of system capacities but the bottlenecks which resulted from failure to ensure effective cooperation and coordination of these agencies.

Finally, a major aspect of road development is that while it links the cities to the region, it also has the effect of aggravating the problems in the cities by channelling people from the rural areas to the cities. The phenomenal growth of cities both in the West and in developing countries is largely due to the ease with which the rural people are able to come to the cities. While the flow has to some extent slowed down in the West, for the developing countries this trend continues to persist. Short of drastic measures such as those implemented by the new regime in Kampuchea to "empty" the cities, the cities unfortunately have become repositories for excess people from the regions. Lured by the presumed attractions of city life and spurred by pervasive underemployment in the rural sectors, these "urban villagers" are often unequipped for the demands and skills required in the cities while their physical presence strain the available facilities and resource-base of the cities. They thus contribute much to the anomie and restlessness in the cities. Other factors such as the growing environmental costs due to pollution and the physical hazards of urban transportation add to the growing problems of cities. Road development thus may have mixed blessings.

This paper examines the relationship between infrastructural growth and development planning in the ASEAN countries. The scope is restricted to road transportation and the role it plays in national development. The first section discusses the state of infrastructural development in these countries and the extent to which road transport can assist in national development. The second section examines the administrative agencies involved in road development and the attendant problems of coordination and cooperation. The third section analyses some of the more common themes resulting from existing pattern(s) of road development such as the effect on urbanisation. It should be stressed that in a paer of this nature and because of the non-availability and sometimes, non-comparability of country data (because of different classification methods adopted), statistical analysis can very often be handicapped or accepted with certain caution. These qualifications, however, will not detract from the main context of the paper.

THE ASEAN COUNTRIES AND ROAD DEVELOPMENT

The five countries of Indonesia, Malaysia, Philippines, Singapore and Thailand grouped together to form the Association of Southeast Asian Nations (ASEAN) in 1967 as a concerted collaborative effort at regional cooperation. These five countries are under the control of regimes which are staunchly anti-communist; indeed, apart from neutralist Burma and the new state of Papua-New Guinea, the ASEAN countries constitute the only group of non-communist countries in Southeast Asia.

The ASEAN countries have enormous resources. They are responsible for the bulk of the world's primary commodities such as rubber and palm oil. Minerals, availability of arable land, and the more recent extensive exploitation of fuel and gas - all these indicate the range of resources in the region. This is not to underestimate the other resource - manpower - which, partly as a result of these congenial factors, has multiplied to approximately 210 million in 1970 (or a projected figure of 361 million by 1990) for the five countries.

It is necessary to point out the considerable differences which exist among the five countires as general statements tend to gloss over, and thus distort, the analysis. Differences exist among the five countries on ethnic composition, territorial size, pattern and rate of economic development. On the one extreme, there is the city-state of Singapore, limited to an area of 581 square kilometers and whose 2.2 million population has to depend on industrialisation and services to sustain what is generally accepted as the second highest level of income in Asia. On the other extreme, there is Indonesia which has 3,000 islands covering an area as large as the United States. It is the sixth most populated country in the world and is largely dependent on agriculture and extractive industries for economic growth The other countries - Malaysia, Thailand and Philippines

Table 1 - Some Basic Data on ASEAN Countries

Country	Populations (1970) (million)	Total Area (m.sq.km.)	Population Density (per square kilometer)	GNP (1970) in million US dollars	Per Capita income (US dollars)	Agriculture as percent of GDP	1970	
							Total imports (million US dollars)	Total exports
Indonesia	121.2	1.492	81	7881.9	67.9	44.8	809	883
Malaysia	10.8	0.33	32	3340.3	380.2	31.2	1757	1468
Philippines	38.5	0.300	128	8055.7	216.8	37.5	1967	1210
Singapore	2.0	0.001	3528	1555.7	770.2	2.9	1554	2461
Thailand	35.8	0.514	70	6230.4	179.3	28.6	697	1252

Source: U.N., *Statistical Yearbook for Asia and the Far East, 1970, Far Eastern Economic Review* and Statistical Yearbooks of ASEAN countries.

- fall somewhere along this continuum although they, like Indonesia, tend to depend more heavily on agriculture and extractive industries as absorbers of manpower. The details are summarised in Table 1.

The brief sketch does not indicate the complexity of the problems faced within these countries. Population and economic activities (except for Singapore) are not spread out evenly with implications for economic growth and political stability. In Indonesia, for example, more than 60 percent of the population are found in Java and Madura - two of the smaller islands of the country. Unless effective measures (such as transmigration of people to other islands or family planning) are initiated, these two highly populated islands are unable to absorb additions to their already high population concentrations notwithstanding the extremely fertile agricultural land or the over-expanded tertiary sector located in the capital city of Jakarta. In Malaysia, development in concentrated along the western belt of "Peninsula Malaysia"; in Thailand, activities and population centres are largely located in the Central Region; while in Philippines, the position is assumed by the main island of Luzon. For the ruling elites in this region, a primary task is to find possible solutions so that existing economic and population patterns can be modified without extreme dislocations or adverse effects on the economy. This is a most difficult challenge in view of the high population growth rates (around 2 to 3 percent a year) and the magnitude of other problems (political and economic) confronting them.

Developmental planning is often seen as the solution by the political elites. Through developmental planning, it is hoped that priorities can be clarified while problem areas identified and targetted for solutions. Malaysia, for example, has formal planning since 1955 when the First Malaya Plan was launched. It has completed two Five-Year Malaya Plans and is now on the Third Malaysia Plan. Indonesia is on the later stage of its second development plan or Repelita II. Thailand and Philippines have formal planning. Although Singapore discarded formal planning, it did experiment with formal planning when the first State Development Plan was initiated in 1960.

The use of formalised development strategies is thus aimed at ensuring optimum utilisation of resources and simultaneously improve the overall well-being of the people. The objectives of Repelita II, for instance, "provides guidelines for the creation of expanding employment opportunities . . . a rising level of income, a more equitable distribution of income, a more even distribution of the gains of development among the various regions of the country, greater economic and social integration of the regions into one effective national entity,

and an enhanced quality of life, including environmental, cultural and nutritional aspects of life . . ." [6]

With the exception of Singapore which does not have any significant rural base, the other ASEAN countries place priority to the rural sector. There is the underlying belief that the rural sectors (including the regions) have to be uplifted. This stress is made for various reasons ranging from desire to rectify imbalances in favour of the urbanised areas, to restructuring of society to favour a more balanced equitable distribution of job opportunities and income among the diverse ethnic groups.

To attain the outlined development objectives, the ruling elites place emphasis on road development. The two Malayan plans (1955-64) focus on provision of penetration or feeder roads to link outlying areas with existing transport network. This was regarded necessary for the attainment of other objectives. The first six year plan of Thailand (1961-66) allocated some 30 percent of total developmental expenditure to transportation and communications while Repelita I sought to upgrade and rehabilitate about 50 percent of existing roads as only 5 percent of the network was classified to be in "good" condition (that is, no potholoes or corrugations). It is hoped by the second plan period, the proportion of damaged roads would have dropped from the once-staggering figure of 41 percent to only 9 percent. Even in Philippines, road construction and improvements were assigned top priority. [7]

The attention on road infrastructure is welcome, if not belated. To begin with, the network as found in the ASEAN countries were constructed rather late and were not designed for the capacity found in present days. In Thailand, the first long range programme for highway development was prepared in 1936 on the basis of an economic survey then undertaken. Although it envisaged a total system of 14,900 kilometers, this figure was attained only lately and the system then was only expected to meet minimal traffic requirements of that period. Late construction in some instances were compounded by sheer neglect. In Indonesia, for instance, the network was largely prewar and it was left to deteriorate until the rehabilitation programme was initiated under Repelita I. Road shoulders and drainage were in disrepair. The magnitude of the rehabilitation programme of Repelita I can be seen from the rehabilitation or improvement to 17,225 of the 32,531 kilometers of roads and to 80,000 meters of bridges. [8]

Secondly, the physical environment takes a toll on existing infrastructure. The high rate of precipitation, the rugged terrain and climate (such as the typhoons) make it necessary to regularly maintain these roads before they are damaged or washed away. This is particularly so as not all roads are paved. As shown in Table 2,

Table 2 - Roads by Types of Surface Levels (percentages in parenthesis)

	Asphalt bituminous or equivalent		Gravel		Earth Surface		Total (kms)
Indonesia: (1972/73)	23633	(26.4)	45212	(50.6)	20533	(23.0)	89378
Malaysia: (i) Peninsula Malaysia (1971)	15098	(84.8)	2039	(11.5)	665	(3.7)	17802
(ii) East Malaysia (1970)	1004	(16.4)	3338	(54.6)	1771	(29.0)	6113
Philippines (1973)	17442	(18.8)	46149	(49.8)	29106	(31.4)	92697
Singapore (1974)	1665	(77.3)	—		490*	(22.7)	2155
Thailand (1971)	11462	(43.0)	6543	(24.6)	8630	(32.4)	26635

Sources: *Statistik Indonesia, 1972/73* (Jakarta: Biro Pusat Statistik, 1974); *UN Statistical Yearbook for Asia and the Far East, 1972; National Transportation System* (Manila: DPWTC, 1975); *Singapore Yearbook of Statistics, 1974/75.*

Note: * This refers to local unimproved roads. Some of these could have gravel surface level.

a large proportion of the roads in the ASEAN countries are largely gravel or earth roads, most of which are seasonal in use and with limited capacities. Even in paved roads, the toll resulting from overladen vehicles could be exacting as instances in Thailand and elsewhere have shown. [9] The deterioration is also speeded up if the soil surface is prone to periodic water-logging. [10]

The attention to road development is also prompted by the inadequacy of existing network. In Thailand, for instance, the major highways to the regions were constructed rather recently. The Bangkok-Korat-Nongkhai highway was completed in 1964 thereby effectively linking the capital with the Northeast region. Yet, on the whole, the ASEAN countries are far from attaining road sufficiency as shown in Table 3. Indeed, road development in most instances drop behind corresponding

Table 3 - Road Transport in ASEAN Countries: Basic Data for 1971

Countries	Total number of vehicles (excl. motor-cycles)	Length of road in km.	Total area	Density		Length of railways in km.
				Metres of road per sq.km.	Metres of road per vehicle	
Indonesia	392,100	84270	1492,000	56	214	6630
Malaysia *	385,300	23484	333,000	70	61	2313
Philippines	468,200	73532	300,000	245	157	1052
Singapore	204,000	1973	581	3396	10	negligible
Thailand	284,700**	26635	514,000	52	94	3765

Source: See Table 1.

* Peninsula Malaysia is very much more developed than East Malaysia. Thus while the overall density is 70 meters per sq.km. for the whole of Malaysia, the density in Peninsula Malaysia is 135.
** Figure for 1969 only.

increases in motor vehicles. In Philippines, for example, private motorcars doubled between 1968 and 1974. Hefty increases in vehicle population are noted in the other countries, except in Singapore where tough fiscal and regulatory measures led to a tapering off in car population.

The emphasis on infrastructural improvements will continue right into the foreseeable future. This is prompted by two other considerations. To begin with, the present network in the ASEAN countries have already attained or are rapidly attaining over-capacity as seen from the report of the Road Transport Survey of 1972. [11] Roads will continue to be the most popular mode of transport within these countries. The Road Transport Survey indicates that even in 1970, the five ASEAN countries would have 65.2 billion passenger-kilometers as compared to 8.2 and 2.0 for railway and air transport or 86.5 percent of all domestic passenger travel. Projections for intercity base into the 1990s indicate an annual growth rate in the ASEAN countries of 8.5 to 13.0 percent. Unless the network can be expanded considerably, a slowdown in pace of economic growth resulting from over-capacity in existing transport linkages is inevitable.

Secondly, the existing networks are unevenly distributed. The main islands or regions receive a fair share of the available road infrastructure; the outlying regions or islands are largely neglected. Thus in the Philippines, it is not surprising that the areas in or around Metro-Manila tend to have the densest network. In Indonesia, the islands of Java and Madura have 33 percent of total network although they constitute 7 percent of total land area. With the growing vehicle stock and with growing demands for greater mobility, the governments will be pressured to give even greater attention to expand such infrastructure. Already, in the four-year highway programme (1970/71 - 1973/74), the Philippine government envisaged an investment of 1.8 billion pesos which would be expended in strengthening 3,500 kilometers of primary roads, 2,200 kilometers of secondary roads and construction of 4,400 kilometers of new roads. It is hoped that these improvements would result in a structurally safe and adequate system of major roads supported by integral networks of secondary and feeder roads. [12]

As shown in Table 4 below, the total planned investments in highway development in the ASEAN countries between 1970 and 1990 is in the region of US$2.7 billion. This excludes investments on feeder roads which these governments would invariably undertake. By comparing to planned investment in railway in these countries over the same period (between US$261.2m and US$301.2m), it is beyond any doubt that the national governments' belief in the importance of road transportation remains unshaken.

Table 4 - Total Planned Investments in Highway Development of ASEAN Countries, 1970-90 US$ (in millions)

Indonesia	575.6
Malaysia	333.5
Philippines	445.2
Singapore	28.7
Thailand	1276.2
Total	2659.2

Source: Extracted from page 318, *Road Transport Survey* (Asian Development Bank, 1972), Volume Two, Part One.

Improvements to road infrastructure will thus take place in the form of addition to the existing network or improvements to existing roads. While these two aspects will be carried out simultaneously, differences in emphasis can be detected. In West Malaysia, the major additions are largely in the form of new links between the East and West (such as the East-West highway) as the arterial highways linking the capitals with the regions are completed. Attention is also focused on upgrading existing network either through improved surface treatment or expanding capacities by broadening the existing roads. In Singapore, the pattern of primary distributory roads or expressways is being constructed which would enable all parts of the island-state within direct accessibility without having to go through the densely built city areas. The primary distributory roads also link the public housing estates and the industrials areas, thus contributing to greater economic growth through reduction of journey and congestion time. At the same time, congested stretches of existing roads have also been widened. In Indonesia and Thailand the emphasis will largely be on improvements to existing network.

When then is the contribution of road infrastructure

to economic growth? In terms of capital formation, road infrastructure and transport equipment/stock form a sizable component. In Thailand, for instance, expenditure on transportation as a percentage of GDP has increased throughout the last decade, the bulk of which largely going to road transport. The extensive highway construction programme, rising costs of transport operation and vehicle ownership have contributed to a situation in which almost a quarter of the gross fixed capital formation was in transportation. Transport equipment tends to form a much higher percentage than the costs of transport construction projects. In Thailand in the period of 1966-69, the ratio was almost 2:1. As most of the equipment has to be imported and as the propensity for acquiring these will continue to increase, the effect on balance of payments is likely to be serious. This problem can be put in perspective for the ASEAN region when it is estimated that the purchase of vehicles, spare parts and oil between 1970-90 is likely to be ten times the investments allocated to highway development for the same period.

On the other hand, improved infrastructure does contribute to increased economic activities. As most of these ASEAN countries are dependent on export of primary produce and mineral extraction, an efficient infrastructural network is vital in reducing costs and also to make these exports possible. The Bangkok-Korat-Nongkhai highway in Thailand, for example, reduces travelling time between Bangkok and Nongkhai by 8 hours while the alignment of the highway results in a saving of 140 kilometers. Micro-surveys conducted elsewhere in Thailand and Malaysia also indicate an increase in economic activities and mobility resulting from construction of specific highways or roads. [13]

It should however be stressed that the mere provision of such infrastructure does not necessarily result in positive economic growth. Attitudinal changes among those people affected by such development and the presence of complementary social services necessary to support a self-sustaining process of investment, marketing and production is essential before tangible growth can be seen. A study on transportation and modernisation in Malaya noted that while road and rail act as an integrating link in the modernisation of that country, it was the rise of extractive industries like tin and later, rubber which provided the bases for spatial integration and development. As a result of these activities, the "administrative-transport web" was thus extended over the country while the impact of modernisation was diffused slowly to include peripheral areas serviced by feeder and interconnection linkages. [14]

Road infrastructure can accelerate modernisation and thus further national development. This belief underlines the strategies of the political elites when they seek to physically integrate their countries through this infrastructure. But improved well-being is not necessarily positively correlated with economic growth as available surveys show that the modern facilities (such as community centres, outpatient clinics and school) which came along with the road infrastructure are used by the people without any substantial changes in their income. [15] This is particularly so in areas in which subsistence agriculture plays a dominant aspect in the economic life of these people. More important to the national elites - than just economic growth - is the growing confidence and positive commitment to the national governments by these people who no longer feel neglected or who now perceive that they have access to larger socio-economic benefits. Indeed, this explains why infrastructural construction forms an integral aspect in counter-insurgency programme. The Accelerated Rural Development Programme which affected 42 provinces in Thailand seeks to provide economic and social betterment through the provision of roads (and thus, accessibility) and other development projects.

THE ADMINISTRATIVE AGENCIES IN ROAD TRANSPORTATION

As indicated in the introduction, a major problem is to ensure that agencies which are responsible for infrastructural development could establish a working relationship of reasonable harmony. The task of securing this relationship, is not easy notwithstanding the goodwill of all the agencies involved. Part of the difficulty in attaining this relationship stems from the numerous operations (and hence, the number of agencies) which are required in infrastructural development. Infrastructural development affects and is affected by land use and other forms of planning. Similarly, it leaves indelible impact on locations of economic activities, consumption and investment patterns and even other forms of lifestyles. There are thus many categories of users and user-needs. At the same, the government in meeting infrastructural linkages also have certain expectations and requirements. In providing these facilities, a number of agencies were created to handle these various issues. Problems are bound to arise with respect to provision, operation and utilisation of such facilities. Conflicting, as well as complementary, interests among the agencies are thus common. Smooth inter-agency and intra-agency cooperation could hardly be more emphasized. For example, the expansion in road network would invariably lead to the acquisition/importation of more transport equipment (such as vehicles) and it is necessary to weigh these induced imports against balance of payments and effect on patterns of consumption, savings or investment. Political elites are also under pressure to offset the costs of infrastructural investment by hiving these costs on to the motorists in the form of higher road and other taxes. While the major issues will have to be resolved by the political leadership, according to its set of priorities, nonetheless agency interests cannot be dismissed since the latter do influence decisionmaking with regard to such issues.

In the ASEAN countries, the more common agencies which are found to have a vested interest with regard to infrastructural development are those involved in budget-allocation, revenue-generating, public works, communications, and planning. Other agencies such as public housing, public utilities, and even security and defence do have an interest in plans pertaining to transport infrastructure as it could affect their own development plans and priorities. Generally, the communications agency would have a major - though not overriding - influence with regard to formulating and implementing communications policy. These could also include regulation and licensing of vehicles, approving different forms of public carriers (and the rates to be charged). The public works department, as the name implies would be responsible for construction of such projects according to acceptable design standards. The budget bureau would decide on priorities on disbursement of funds while the revenue-generating agency would seek various ways (including from users of transport facilities) to raise the necessary funds required. The planning department would seek to offer advice on land use and related needs and will try to integrate transport needs with other sectoral demands to ensure a more optimum use of resources. Then there are the regulatory bureaus such as the police which are usually responsible for other enforcement and related activities.

While the definition of responsibilities seems clearcut, the modus operandi is often compounded by other problems. The existence of different "layers" of government the presence of over-lapping authority, the continuation of ill-defined channels of communication, coordination and command, and inter-agency competition for power and influence are some of the common features which could slow down bureaucratic responsiveness with regard to provision and operation of these infrastructural development. A brief description of the agencies involved in these ASEAN countries in thus necessary to show how such problems could arise and what possible solutions have been proposed to overcome them.

In Indonesia, the responsibility for road development is shared between the central, provincial and municipal governments. The nationa government is responsible for the highways or major arterial routes in the country. The major agencies involved at the national level include Bappenas or the National Development Planning Agency, the Department of Finance, and Department of Public Works/Directorate-General of Highway Construction. The national communications agency, the Department of Transport, Communication and Tourism (DOC), is not responsible for highway planning, a function which is assumed by Public Works Department. This is quite surprising insofar as this ministry is responsible for planning and associated activities in the transport, communications and tourism sectors. Plan proposals for implementation had to be in line with the National Development Plans (Repelitas). The prior approval of Bappenas (which is involved in coordinating and integrating inter-sectoral planning) and the Department of Finance (for budget allocation) and the Ministry of Communications is necessary before any project can be implemented. Upon approval, Bappenas and Ministry of Communications would be responsible for monitoring these projects.

Coordination between the national and provincial levels are carried out through ad hoc steering committees of the agencies involved in the project (such as those at the local, provincial or municipal levels). Their proposals could be submitted directly to the Department of Communications or the Public Works Department directly or through their representative office at the region/provincial levels.

In Malaysia, the Economic Planning Unit (EPU) is responsible for overall macro-planning and like Bappenas in Indonesia, is responsible for ensuring that sectoral planning is integrated into the overall national planning. The plans of any sector have thus to be in line with the priorities as established in the national development plans. In Malaysia, the Ministry of Communications is responsible for formulation, evaluation and implementation of transport policies, development programmes and capital projects. The provision and maintenance of physical facilities come under the control of the Ministry of Works and Utilities and its two bureaus, namely, Highway Planning and Publc Transport Unit (HP & PTU) and the Roads Section of the Public Works Department (PWD). The demarcation of responsibilities is quite clear-cut with the HP & PTU responsible for the planning and coordinating of federal road network development while the PWD is involved in the implementing of highway projects. The need for extensive collaboration between these two agencies need not be overstressed and this is even more apparent when we examine the relationship of these agencies and those at the state level. At the state (i.e., provincial) level, the planning and development of state roads fall under the jurisdiction of the state PWDs which is under the control of the federal PWD. Similarly, in the construction of federal highways, the state PWDs are sometimes delegated the responsibility of constructing those stretches that are within the respective state boundaries. It seems necessary that even though the HP & PTU is not directly in control of the state PWDs, the latter had to consult the former to ensure that proposed linkages at the state level would fit into overall federal transport system. Inter-agency coordination is further institutionalised through the Implementation, Coordination and Development Administration Unit (ICDAU) of the Prime Minister's Department which acts as a secretariat for the National Action Council (NAC). The NAC receives reports from agencies while the ICDAU assists in carrying out spot checks to ensure that project implementation is sufficiently coordinated. Steering committees are also set up on a need basis to ensure that agency interests are consulted in provision of specific linkages, be it the federal or state level.

In Phillipines, the major agencies are National Economic and Development Authority (NEDA), the Department of Public Works, Transport and Communications (DPWTC) and the Department of Public Highway (DPH). NEDA is responsible for overall development plans and coordination of inter-sectoral planning. The DPWTC is responsible for establishing a network of transportation facilities and integration of such facilities with other public works and communications systems. It discharges these roles such as planning, production, operation, regulation and maintenance of infrastructural facilities and services through specialised bureaus such as the Bureaus of Public Works and Land Transport. The DPH was a bureau in DPWTC until it was made a separate agency on par with the latter in 1968. This agency is assigned the specific tasks of planning, maintaining and regulating highways in the country and the studies on traffic flows.

In Singapore, the major agencies involved are Ministry of Finance (in charge of overall development plans and budget allocation), the Ministry of National Development and its bureaus, the Planning Department and Public Works Department, and the Ministry of Communication (overall regulation and implementation of communications policies).

In Thailand, the Ministry of Communications, through its bureau, the Department of Land Transportation, is responsible for formulating and implementing transport policies. The Ministry of Interior is also involved in provision of road infrastructure - a role which is strengthened by its control over the PWD (responsible for engineering services and roads to provinces and municipalities), the Department of Local Administration (responsible for funds to provincial administration and funds for road construction at provincial level) and the Office of Accelerated Rural Development (or ARD) which, previously under the charge of the Prime Minister, is involved in developmental activities as part of the overall counter-insurgency programme. In addition, the Ministry of Interior is responsible for town and country planning (through its Town and Country Planning Agency) and transportation systems of Bangkok (through its Expressway and Rapid Transit Authority). The Ministry of Finance affects road development with regard to revenue-generation and the Ministry of Defence, as a priority transport user, has a dominant influence on matters pertaining to infrastructural development. The latter too constructs minor roads, though ostensibly for military use or to improve local logistics. The Prime Minister's Office is involved largely through its National economic and Social Development Board (NESDB) which prepares developmental policies and the Budget Bureau. Overall coordination is ensured by the NESDB which coordinates plans and programmes both within and outside the control of the Ministry of Communication, although a Transport and Communications Committee

(TCC) was set up in 1973 and which involves all agencies which are users or providers of infrastructural facilities and services. This is also the only committee in charge of inter-modal coordination and elaborating the national transport policy in an inter-sectoral context.

The brief description of agencies in the ASEAN region points to several interesting generalisations. First, with the exception of Singapore, there are many tiers of government involved and a major administrative problem is to ensure that these layers of government and the agencies involved could function harmoniously. This is not always attained partly because of differences in extent of control, and powers to generate revenue, and partly because of differences in perceptions of needs at these various levels. In Thailand, for example, a major problem is to ensure an effective working relationship between the Ministry of Communications (in charge of the national network) and the Ministry of Interior (in charge of provincial administration and funds).

The description also shows the importance of a central planning agency. While the ambit of power and influence varies, it would seem that these planning agencies like Bappenas, EPU, NEDA, the Ministry of Finance in Singapore, and NESDB, have considerable influence on how transport development should be staged. Because of their control over inter-sectoral development, it would seem therefore that transport development should harmonise with other sectoral developments since it has, like other activities, to compete for support and thus for the necessary funds.

Thirdly, there seems to be a separation between agencies involved in project implementation and those in policy regulation. In Philippines, this became clearer when the Department of Public Highways was created. This separation, has been justified in many of the Asean countries on the premise that construction of all development projects (of which infrastructural development forms a part) should be undertaken by a specialised agency. On the other hand, this may compound problems in coordination and sharpen inter-agency conflicts. In Philippines, the creation of DPH on par with DPWTC, while ostensibly achieving greater specialisation in the road transport activities, "may have structurally added to coordination and integration problems in transport sector planning and implementation". [16] In Thailand, the Ministry of Interior has been traditionally a much stronger agency - more so by its control over public works, local administration, accelerated rural development programme, planning, and transportation in the Bangkok region. It is thus unlikely that such an agency would merely wit for the cue from the Ministry of Communications and is just as likely to stage its own programme and pace on matters pertaining to road and infrastructural development.

Finally, there is the tendency to resort to coordinating committees. [17] While this is a solution to matters involving multiple agencies, and could have positive uses by ensuring that plan formulation and implementation would take into account other agency interests - either as providers or users - such committees tend to blur lines of responsibility while powerful agencies would try to elbow other organisations into accepting their views. Also, it is a common observation that such committees invariably lengthen the time lag in policy formulation and implementation.

Administrative measures have been proposed in streamlining and improving the administrative processes in each of these countries in studies undertaken elsewhere on the subject. [18] Suffice it to say, administrative feasibility and political convenience and between administrative feasibility and deep seated personal and agency interests do not also coincide. Fundamental administrative changes have been proposed in some of these countries, but they were not accepted. In Singapore, the proposal for an Inland Transport Authority to encompasss all agencies involved in the regulation, enforcement, construction and planning of traffic management schemes - which would have the effect of setting up a single agency to replace the existing practice of having numerous agencies dealing on these matters on a fragmented basis - was not accepted by many of the existing agencies. A major factor in rejecting this proposal was the fear that such a super-agency may reduce or even deprive the existing agencies of their roles although the practical problems of demarcating the roles to be assumed by such an agency were also mentioned. [19] In Philippines, the Integrated Reorganisation Plan of 1972 recommended the creation of a Bureau of Transportation which would, just as in the Singapore proposal assume responsibilities pertaining to transport infrastructural activities as well as the regulation, development and control of land, sea and air transportation. [20] The sub-systems of the transport system such as infrastructure (roads, bridges, rail, ports), modes of transport (rail, road, sea, or airplanes), and regulation (licensing, tariffs, etc.), would come under one department. The proposal seeks to cut across the labyrinth of agencies and committees thus simplying and expediting decision-making with regard to overall infrastructure and national development plans. As expected, this proposal encountered vigorous resistance from many of the existing bureaus. Agency interests could prevail over arguments for administrative rationalisation.

Short of changes, administrative reforms had to focus largely on reducing possible areas of conflicts and on personnel strengthening. Personnel strengthening has been suggested as one of the remedies as many of the ASEAN countries are confronted with a shortage of trained and specialised manpower to carry out the various facets of road development programmes. Indeed, a tendency for projects to be "contracted" out to private construction companies in many of these countries indicate not so much a fervent commitment to the spirit of the pro-capitalist enterprise but because of the shortage of skilled manpower in the agencies in carrying out these projects. Consequently the private contractors are often more experienced and effective than the governmental agencies that from an cost-effective perspective, these contractors had to be extensively relied on for the construction of developmental projects. Project-implementing agencies have *de facto* been reduced to a monitoring role.

Other proposals call for unambiguous lines of authority and communication, the shortening of time-lag between formulation and implementation and effective monitoring of implementation progress are some areas that could be looked into, although, ironically, many of such proposals would simply have the effect of adding more agencies/committees to the already complex administrative scene. [21]

FUNDING AND URBAN TRANSPORATION

A major problem, apparent in the discussion on inter-agency relationship, involves the issue of funding. The national governments have to satisfy a wide range of social and other needs and they are increasingly called to fulfil these needs. Indeed, an underlying factor in the ambitious development plans of the region is the desire to maximise satisfaction of such needs through careful allocation of resources.

Road development is a costly exercise. Even though local materials and manpower could be tapped for road development, expensive equipments, and land (right-of-way acquisition) had to be bought. Foreign funding, through technical assistance programme or borrowings, has been resorted to in specific road development projects or to top up funds resulting from policy commitments. Instances of such assistance would be the Friendship highway linking Saraburi to Korat in Thailand which was financed by the United States after an application to the World Bank bank was rejected in the early 1950s. This cost of this highway, stretching a distance of 310 kilometers, was US$15.6 million including right-of-way acquisition and construction or an average cost of $94,000 per kilometer. The loan from the Japanese government to the Philippines is another example of such assistance. This assisted project made possible a major transport infrastructure serving Luzon, Visayas and Mindanao, that is, a total length of 2,066 kilometers traversing 21 provinces and 11 major cities. From this highway, other secondary distributory linkages are constructed or made possible.

While foreign assistance would be useful and welcome, especially when it made possible purchases of equipment and materials, nonetheless there are various constraints in securing such funds. To begin with, the perceptions of needs (even when supplemented by feasibility and other cost studies) of the national government and those of the potential lenders may not coincide. The setting up of institutions like the Asian Development Bank could go a long way to securing cheap development funds, but the problem still persists. State-to-state lending, on the other hand, is influenced by other policy considerations especially the extent to which the proposed infrastructural developments would also secure the national interests of the lending countries. The willingness of the United States to participate in many highway construction projects in Southeast Asia in the 1960s was as much influenced by the extent to which such projects would help to promote better inter-state relationships between the United States and these countries and also the extent to which these assistance would improve logistics capabilities against communist insurgency. The major factors in deciding whether loans would be forthcoming would thus depend on the congruence of interests between the lending and borrowing countries and the leverage to which these countries would be able to exert on each other.

Ultimately, the national governments have to look to the domestic sources for funding. While revenue could come from other economic sectors (such as taxes from extractive activities), it is generally felt that users of facilities would have to pay for improvements to transport infrastructure. From points of political stability and social equity, the government could shift the incidence of the burden to selected user-groups while others such as the cyclists, the farmers using farm equipments, or the pedestrians would be exempted. The vehicle-users appear to be a major group of consumers made to pay. Toll practice is not widespread, being found only in isolated linkages where fees collected are generally used for infrastructural maintenance rather than for recoping of developmental costs. The acceptable approach has been to impose taxes on motorised vehicles and petroleum. This could take many forms from import taxes on vehicles to the annual "road" tax. The rates on these taxes would be varied accordingly to realize the funds required by the government after taking into account the incidence and impact of these taxes on economic activities.

The amounts realized can be substantial. In Singapore, it has been shown that the revenue collected through these sources exceeded annual expenditure on road development by wide margins. [22] Undoubtedly, the rates of taxes levied are also done with other implications, namely, as a deterrence to over-expansion of car-ownership. The Singapore case is interesting insofar as it illustrates the use of tax measures not merely for revenue-generation (welcome though this would be), but largely as a deterrent against ownership of cars. The over-riding factor is to prevent the city-state from suffering the slow strangulation resulting from a saturation of vehicles and inadequate room for mobility. V.P.D. (on many of the arterial roads in 1968) were reported to be 40,000. Apart from improving the public transport system, the taxes on cars and petroleum were periodically revised upwards to make car-operation in this city-state one of the costliest in the world. [23] Even then, the number of car-ownership tapers off rather than declining sharply. At the same time, an attempt at road pricing in the core areas of the city (the CBD) was attempted when fees were levied for vehicles seeking access to the CBD during morning peak hours. This arrangement (the Area Licensing Scheme or ALS) has the purpose of reducing car flow into the CBD. [24]

It would seem that enormous revenue could be realised from this form of domestic funding. These fiscal measures could also have the effect of ensuring a more orderly growth in car-ownership. To a great extent, the initiative will have to come from the political leadership which has to decide on which source of funds ought to be tapped and on whether it is willing to antagonise vested interest groups such as the road users. An attempt to impose road tax on cars on a sliding scale in Thailand, for example, resulted in vociferous denunication of the proposal.

On the other hand, it is clear that a major factor in car-ownership is its disproportionate concentration in urbanised areas, especially in the primate capital cities. It is true that the larger share of national wealth and tertiary activities are found in these cities - and hence the ability to pay for the vehicle-purchasing and maintenance - but the figures have been disquieting. An examination of the vehicle distribution in the ASEAN countries shows that more than half of the total vehicle population are concentrated in the capital cities. Thus, in Philippines, 58 per cent of the vehicles registration in 1973 was in Manila Bay region, as compared to the 13 percent in other parts of Luzon and Palawan, 14 percent in Visayas, 12 percent in Mindanao and 2 percent in the Bicol region. [25] In Malaysia, it is projected that by 1990, about 50 percent of the families in the metropolitan area of Kuala Lumpur will be car-owners. Translated into other terms, there were already 200 vehicles for every of the 192 kilometers of road in Kuala Lumpur in 1970 as compared to 39 vehicles per kilometer for the whole of peninsula Malaysia. If this car-kilometer ratio between Kuala Lumpur and the rest of the country were to be maintained, the city would require an additional 960 kilometers of roads to be constructed by 1990.

The problems of the primate cities are the large concentration of population and economic activities. In most instances, they have also attracted the bulk of the country's industrial activities. Mobility and accessibility in these cities are a premium, but these requirements have been hampered by many factors such as the inability of earlier city-planning designs to cope with the dimensions of the current problems, the rural-urban drift of people and the lack of other supporting facilities. In Jakarta, for example, basic utilities like electricity, water and sanitation have yet to cover all parts of the metropolis - the task of providing these services having been hampered by growing population and proliferating commercial/industrial activities. Daily trips in these cities exceeded the million mark and puts a considerable strain on existing transport modes and facilities.

Obviously, a solution to the transport problem (and

also, road development problem) in the capital cities is most urgent if economic activities are not to grind to a halt by the slowing down in mobility. Planning of transport development has to take into account a possible replanning of the cities, not just the often delapidated CBD but also the other industrial and commercial zones to ensure better use of land. Solution to congestion and traffic manoeuvrability cannot be adopted on a piecemeal basis (such as the construction of new roads) because of environmental constraints. It is thus not surprising that the replanning of the city areas has been initiated such as is occuring in Singapore or is currently been thought out in Manila. Hopefully, these new plans could provide for a more rational and effective use of land and other resources in the metropolitan areas.

At the same time it is increasingly clear to most policy-makers that a reduction of motor vehicle population is essential. This is done through construction of ring roads so that through-city traffic need not go through the city areas and thus reducing demand on city routes. In Singapore, as stated earlier, the Area Licensing Scheme is another regulative method to reduce traffic into the city areas through imposition of a fee. Governments are also made aware of the need to improve public transport such as rationalising the routes and tariffs or ensuring that public transport operators do have sufficient fleets. The unsatisfactory state of public transportation and the inevitable interest in public transport by the government (or the municipal authorities) invariably lead the authorities to a more extensive involvement on the operational issues of public transport.

The problem of urban transportation is thus a source of continuing concern. This can be seen from the number of reports or studies commissioned. [26] Most of these reports mentioned a series of proposals such as improved traffic management, reduction of through city traffic, curbs on car-ownership, and improvement of public transport. Each of these proposals, taking into account the complex urban administrative processes and the configuration of political support, would itself be a challenge. Yet, unless policy-initiative in these directions are made, the urban transportation problem is likely to be excerbated.

The other proposal which most of these expert-reports have generally recommended is the introduction of mass rapid transport system. [27] Unlike the other categories of proposals, the mass rapid transit system (MRT) requires a different approach to the urban transportation problem insofar as it called for the provision of right-of-way or grade segregation for selected transport mode, further investment in technology and equipment and a revival of the problem as to the extent of governmental involvement. Funding and recoping of investments on such a massive scale are likely to be major problems for the governmental authorities having to decide on whether such a system is essential. These decisions have to be made amidst other considerations such as the requirements of the rural and other less urbanised sectors, the availability of financing, and also, the need to prevent the urban sprawl in the primate cities from becoming unmanageable. Notwithstanding feasibility and other studies, any decision on whether to implement such a project or otherwise would ultimately have to be decid- • ed by the political leadership.

CONCLUSION

In this paper we try to examine the role of road infrastructure in the national development of ASEAN countries. This is largely an exploratory paper since studies on a comparative basis of this region in this aspect have been neglected and much of the data necessary for a full-scale study are not available. Nonetheless, it has been shown that the national leadership in these countries are committed to formal development as a optimal approach to accelerating economic growth and improving the welfare of the people. There is a general acceptance of the importance of infrastructural development, notably with regard to road infrastructure. The belief in a correlation between provision of road infrastructure and economic growth and improvement in overall national welfare has been justified by the feedbacks to the government which indicate that visible social and economic changes do result from investments in road infrastructure.

There are many constraints or bottlenecks in the provision of road infrastructure. There are even more bottlenecks on the other issues of maintenance and regulation. The major constraints have been noted to include the complexity and cumbersomeness of the existing administrative processes, the question of fundings, and the problems peculiar to primate capital cities. For the national government, all these problems are not exclusive to the road infrastructure. As indicated in the paper, these issues relate to the wider questions of resource allocation, opportunity costs, development strategies, inherited administrative processes and skills - all of these in an environment of limited resources at the disposal of the national elites. Yet, unless positive response to these issues are forthcoming, the question of maximising the use of limited resources will remain only partially answered. For the national governments, this could mean a slower response to satisfying the demands of national development and could limit the potentialities of road infrastructure to satisfy national and community needs.

REFERENCES

[1] K. E. Galbraith, **Economic Development** (Cambridge, Mass.: Harvard University Press, 1965), p. 73.

[2] UN Economic Commission for Africa, **Transport Problems in Relation to Economic Development in West Africa,** E/CN 14/63, p. 2.

[3] Louis Leferber, "Economic Development and Regional Growth", in Gary Fromm, ed., **Transport Investment and Economic Development** (Washington: Brookings Institution, 1965), p. 120.

[4] Some transport planners and economists feel that quantification is not an insurmountable obstacle. See, for example, Sei-Young Park, "Transportation and its role in socio-economic development", in ITC-UNESCO, **Seminar on Transportation Problems and Integrated Surveys** (Delft: ITC-UNESCO, 1968), especially pages 38-46.

[5] Local participation in both construction and maintenance of road facilities is possible. Such participation imparts experience in administration and greater inter-personal contacts. See G. W. Wilson, "Theory a Theory of Transport and Development", in G. W. Wilson, **et. al., The Impact of Highway Investment on Development** (Washington: Brookings Institution, 1966), pp. 190-218.

[6] **Indonesia Develops: Repelita II** (Jakarta: Department of Information, Indonesia, n.d.), p. 7.

[7] The total length of paved roads, for example, has increased from 10,208 kms. in 1966 to 15,540 in 1970 or 34.3 percent in 5 years. Also see Chapter 9 of **Four Year Development Plan, 1972-75** (Manila: National Economic Council, 1971) for details.

[8] Extracted from Table E-8, in **Southeast Asian Regional Transport Survey,** Vol. Three, Part Two (Manila: Asian Development Bank, 1972), p. 17.

[9] In Thailand, the policy in the 1960's was to construct all primary highways with base and sub-base layers to support a minimum load of 9,000 lbs. per single wheel. This figure has been raised to 12,000 lbs. in new design construction because frequent overloading contributed to rapid deterioration of roads built to lower standards. See D. K. Clark and A. C. Giarratana, **Transportation System of Thailand** (McLeen, Virginia: R. N. Corporation, 1966), p. 8.

[10] Erosion caused by floods and water logging is very common. See **ibid.,** pp. 13-14. Also see comments of **Evaluation**

510

of the First Six-Year Plan, 1961-66 (Bangkok: NEDB, 1967), Chapter 9.

[11] This survey carried out under the sponsorship of the Asian Development Bank, looks into highway development in Southeast Asia. The study was carried out by Arthur D. Little Inc., and Associated Consultants using materials and data supplied by countries included in the survey.

[12] See for example the National Transportation System Study made by the Department of Public Works, Transportation and Communications in collaboration with other related agencies.

[13] See for Example, Willian Hughes, "Social Benefits Through Improved Transport in Malaya", in E. T. Haefele, ed., **Transport and National Goals** (Washington: Brookings Institution, 1969), pp. 105-121; G. W. Wilson, *et. al.,* **op. cit.,** pp. 127-161; J. H. Jones, **Economic Benefits from Development Roads in Thailand** (Seato Graduate School of Engineering, Technical Note 15); Patrocinio S. Villanueva, **The Value of Rural Roads** (Manila: Community Development Research Council, 1968). Also see, G. Fromm, ed., **Transport Investment and Economic Development** (Washington: Brookings Institution, 1965).

[14] See T. Leinbach, **Transportation and Modernisation in Malaya** (Ph. D. dissertation, Pennsylvania State University, 1971) for details.

[15] See Hughes, **op. cit.**

[16] See, page 4 of G. U. Iglesias, *et. al.,* "Study of the Administration of Transport and Communications Projects, Plans, and Annual Budgets in the Philippines", in **Transport Planning Procedures** (Kuala Lumpur: ACDA, 1976).

[17] See the country-papers in **Transport Planning Procedures, ibid.,** for a description of the agencies and committees in the five Asean countries. In most instances, the list is staggering.

[18] See the country-papers in the **Transport Planning Proce-**dures. The respective writers for the country reports are M. Siregar (Indonesia); Abdul Halim bin Datuk Haji Abdul Rauf (Malaysia); G. U. Iglesias, J. B. Evidente, Jose R. Valdacanas and E. T. Gumayan (Philippines); Seah Chee-Meow (Singapore); and Pharani Kirtiputra (Thailand).

[19] See Chia Lin Sien, *et. al.,* **Organisation and Financing of Domestic Transportation in Singapore** (Kuala Lumpur: ACDA: 1976), p. 38.

[20] Iglesias, **op. cit.,** p. 70.

[21] Reforms that have a high degree of acceptance generally do not affect the core interests of certain competing agencies. These are likely to be in the form of more coordinating committees which would over-stretch the time and energy of the bureaucrats.

[22] Revenue from import duties, petroleum tax and fees collected by Registry of Vehicle has increased from $59 m. in 1969 to $134 m. in 1973. Expenditure has not matched revenue. Development expenditure in 1973 amounted to $29 m.

[23] For a detailed discussion of these rates see, Chia Lin Sien, *et. al.,* **op. cit.**

[24] See Tan Kee Tiang, **The Area Licensing Scheme in Singapore** (Academic Exercise, University of Singapore, 1975).

[25] **Philippine National Transportation Survey, op. cit.,** p. 4.

[26] For example, the studies on Singapore Mass Transit Study by Wilbur-Smith and Associates, Bangkok Transportation Study by the German Team of Experts, and the Urban Transport Policy and Planning Study for Metropolitan Kuala Lumpur by Wilbur Smith and Associates. Many of these studies are carried out with the financial assistance of international agencies such as the World Bank.

[27] Specific agencies, as in the case of the Singapore Mass Transit Planning Unit, could be set up to examine the issues specific to the implementation of rapid transit systems.

EMME:
A planning method for multi-modal urban transportation systems

M. Florian, R. Chapleau, S. Nguyen, C. Achim, L. James and J. Lefebvre
University of Montreal, Canada

INTRODUCTION

The purpose of this paper is to present a new multi-modal urban transportation planning method, EMME (Equilibre Multi-Modal/Multi-Modal Equilibrium), that is based on and is consistent with a general theory of equilibrium in transportation systems. The requirement that is often asked of transportation systems analysis methods is that they be policy responsive, in the sense that a considerable number of the variables considered are explicit policy variables: changes in these variables bring about changes in the distribution of transportation demands and flows between origins and destinations, over specified links, between modes or by time of day. EMME has been designed to respond, as much as is possible within the current state of the art of transportation systems modelling, to changes in these variables and is oriented to short term and medium term planning applications. The implementation of EMME exploits the considerable progress that has been achieved recently in the development of efficient algorithms for the computation of equilibrium flows in transportation networks and on advanced concepts for computer based systems and data bank design. Full advantage has been taken of the possibilities offered by the current computing technology, to facilitate the interaction of the user with the possibilities offered by EMME; the input data is provided in a form related to the originating activity and not to the internal file design and the specification of planning scenarios is achieved in a way that requires minimal user effort.

The paper is organized in the following way: first we describe the general notions of equilibrium in transportation systems, provide a spatially disaggregated interpretation of these notions and then indicate the specific modelling choices made in EMME that are consistent with this general framework; we discuss next, the innovations that are offered by EMME in modelling the road and transit networks, in the integration and use of travel demand functions and in the algorithms that are used to compute the equilibrium demands and flows; then we describe the computer systems design principles on which EMME is based and give an overall description of the design; last but not least we show how EMME may serve in the analysis of land use allocation and changes in the supply of transportation services provided.

EQUILIBRIUM IN TRANSPORTATION SYSTEMS

We begin our presentation with the formulation of the notion of equilibrium in transportation systems, such as exposed by Manheim [6] and Beckmann [3]. (Our presentation is inspired by Manheim's work although many of the details are different). The transportation system consists of the following main components:

T, the transportation infrastructure and its control or regulatory measures,

A, the socio-economic activities in the area spanned by T,

D, the transportation demands on T generated by A, and

L, the levels of service offered on T to demands D.

The fundamental relations that link the components of the system are:

D = G (A, L): the demands generated by the activities A depend on the level of service (or performance) L of the transportation infrastructure; as the service level decreases, the demand decreases.

L = C (T,D): the level of service depends on the transportation infrastructure T and on the realized demand D; as the demand increases, the level of service decreases and its perceived cost increases.

The simplest and most general definition of equilibrium is that *equilibrium is a steady state that is reached when the demand for transportation gives rise to a service level that maintains that demand.* The common pictorial representation of the equilibrium state is achieved supposing that the above relations are *continuous functions* for given A and T, and their intersection defines the equilibrium demand D_E and service level L_E. Sie Figure 1 below.

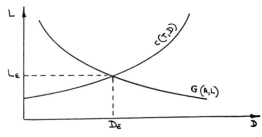

Figure 1

For a fixed A, we denote the restriction of the demand function $\tilde{G}(L)$ and similarly, for a fixed T, the restriction of the service (performance) function is $\check{C}(D)$. Then, the equilibrium state is (D_E, L_E) that satisfy

$$L_E = \tilde{C}(D_E) = \tilde{G}^{-1}(D_E) \qquad (1)$$

If the transportation infrastructure and its control measures is modified such that $T \rightarrow T^1$ or the activities change from $A \rightarrow A^1$, the demand and service level functions are displaced. The *basis of all impact analysis* is the prediction of changes in the demands $D_E \rightarrow D_E^1$ and service levels $L_E \rightarrow L_E^1$, which is the new equilibrium state. See Figure 2 below.

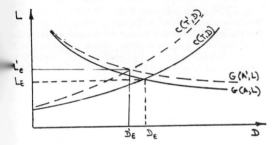

Figure 2

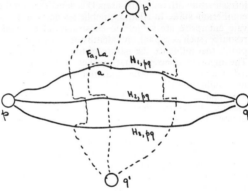

Figure 3

Before presenting a spatialized version of this notion of equilibrium we remark that both D and L are vectors, that is the demand functions may be specified by population subgroups, by time of day, by mode, etc. and the service levels may characterize each mode and may be travel time, distance, cost, comfort, etc. In this exposition our notation does not explicitly recognize this; rather than use vector notation and refer to demand vectors and service level vectors, we use simply demand and service level. We shall however make this distinction in describing the details of EMME.

The simple paradigm of equilibrium in a transportation system of Figure 1 is a reasonable representation for the aggregate of an urban area or for the analysis of a well defined corridor between 2 centers, where the distribution of activities in space and the details of the network of T are not relevant. The explicit consideration of the spatial distribution of the socio-economic activities A and of the network aspects of T makes the definition of equilibrium more tedious although the basis notion of equilibrium *remains intact.* We consider, as usual, that the urban area is subdivided into zones, a zone representing a (hopefully) homogenous subgroup of activities that generate and attract demands for transportation. The socio-economic activities A are subdivided by zone: A_p is the set of activities that generate travel demands at origin zone p and A_q is the set of activities that attract travel at destination q. Thus $A = \begin{pmatrix} \cup A_p \\ p \end{pmatrix} \cup \begin{pmatrix} \cup A_q \\ q \end{pmatrix}$

The service levels that are relevant are L_{pq}, that is between origins p and destinations q. The demand for travel between p and q is given by a demand function $D_{pq} = G_{pq} (A_p, A_q, L_{pq})$. Similarly T is the collection of T_a, the characteristics of all the links of the transportation network(s) and their control or regulatory measures. The service function L is specified for each link as a function of the *flows* on each link, F_a, induced by (or derived from) the travel demands $D_{pq} : L_a = c_a (T_a, F_a)$. The definition of the equilibrium travel demands and service levels is more tedious, as mentioned earlier, since the relation between L_{pq} and L_a must be determined in an unambiguous way. In order to achieve this it is also necessary to relate the origin destination demands D_{pq} to the link flows F_a.

The following discussion applies simultaneously to all origin destination pairs, however for simplicity of exposition we focus on a single origin destination pair (p, q). See Figure 3.

The travel demands D_{pq} use several paths, not entirely distinct, between p and q and induce path flows $H_{k,pq}$ and path service levels $L_{k,pq}$. The values of the path flows are a function of the demands and the path service levels

$$H_{k,pq} = \Phi (D_{pq}; L_{k,pq}, \text{all } k), \text{all } (p, q) \qquad (2)$$

and the flows *are conserved,* that is

$$D_{pq} = \sum_k H_{k,pq} \qquad (3)$$

Also, the origin to destination service level is a function of the path flows and service levels

$$L_{pq} = \Psi (H_{k,pq}, \text{all } k; L_{k,pq}, \text{all } k) \qquad (4)$$

Each of the paths is composed of several links a of T. For a given path, the arcs are identified by an indicator function $\delta_{ak,pq}$ which equals 1 if link a is used by the path k,pq and 0 otherwise. The service level $L_{k,pq}$ is then a function of the service (performance) levels associated with each link of the path, that is

$$L_{k,pq} = \Omega (L_a; \delta_{ak,pq}), \qquad (5)$$

and the service level of a link a depends on its induced flow F_a

$$L_a = c_a (T_a; F_a), \text{all } a \qquad (6)$$

The last relation which is necessary for the definition of the equilibrium demands and service levels, and consequently the equilibrium flows, is the way in which the link flows depend on the demand D_{pq}, that is

$$F_a = \sum_p \sum_q \sum_k \delta_{ak,pq} \cdot H_{k,pq} , \quad \text{all } a \qquad (7)$$

By considering the chain of relations and equations (2)-(7) it is easy to see that the service level L_{pq} depends on all the demands D_{pq}, that is

$$L_{pq} = C (T_a, \text{all } a; D_{pq}, \text{all } (p, q)), \text{all } (p,q) \qquad (8)$$

where C may be interpreted as the transformations, analytic or algorithmic, that are necessary to achieve (2)-(7). Thus, the equilibrium state is *the steady state that is reached when the demands for transportation give rise to link and path flows and corresponding service levels that maintain those demands.*

This is the definition given by Beckman [3]. More precisely, for fixed A_p, A_q, T_a, the equilibrium demands and service levels are

$$L_{pq}^E = \tilde{c} (D_{pq}^E , \text{all } (p,q)) = \tilde{G}_{pq}^{-1} (D_{pq}^E) , \text{all } (p,q) \qquad (9)$$

the equilibrium flows F_a^E , $H_{k,pq}^E$
are the flows that are induced by D_{pq}^E

as described by (2), (3), (7) and the link service levels L_a given by (6) correspond to $L_{k,pq}$ given by (5) and origin-destination service levels L_{pq} given by (4).

Particular choices of the functions Φ, Ψ and Ω result in different specific models of the equilibrium in the transportation system and the possibility of numerically computing the equilibrium state depends on the mathematical structure of the resulting models.

Before proceeding to describe the specific modelling choices imbedded in EMME, we touch briefly on the extension of this equilibrium notion to consider systematic changes in T. We postulate a supply relation $T = S(D_E, L_E)$, that is, the changes in the transportation infrastructure offered to the users D is dependent on the equilibrium state. In addition, public agencies and private enterprise are subject to constraints of available resources such as capital, and identify objectives, such as profit, that influence the nature of the above relation. The important concept is that *supplier's actions are related to the equilibrium state,* and, in a spatial context, to the equilibrium flows and service levels.

Similarly, $A = R (D_E, L_E)$ is the relation that we postulate to describe the changes in the level and distribution of activities.

EMME: THE EQUILIBRIUM MODEL AND THE SOLUTION ALGORITHM

The transportation infrastructure modelled in EMME consists of a road network, T^{au}, and a transit network, T^{tr}. The road network consists as usual of nodes and links a, which carry the flow of private cars and transit vehicles. The transit network consists of nodes, access and transfer links and transit line segments s. Certain links and segments of the two networks can be considered to coincide in the sense that all transit lines that use the road network share the use of the road links with the private cars. The interaction between the two networks, a major feature of EMME, is denoted by setting the indicator function $\Delta_{a,s} = 1$ whenever a line segment s uses link a and 0 otherwise. The road link service function depends on the link volumes F_a^{au} and the number of transit vehicles that use link a, F_a^{tr}. Thus

$$L_a = c_a (T_a^{au} ; F_a^{au} ; F_a^{tr} \text{ if } \Delta_{a,s} = 1) \quad (10)$$

The link service function may include both time and distance. If distance is not relevant then the link service functions are simply link volume delay functions. The transit segment service functions do not depend on the transit passenger volumes, F_s^{tr}, but depend on the corresponding service level on the road link if $\Delta_{a,s} = 1$

$$L_s = c_s (T_s^{tr} ; L_a , \text{ if } \Delta_{a,s} = 1) \quad (11)$$

See Figures 4 and 5.

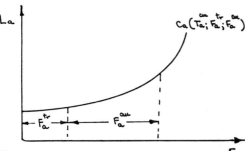

Figure 4

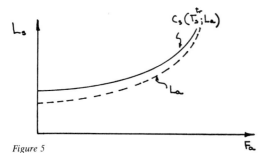

Figure 5

In EMME, the relations Φ and Ψ are subsumed by Wardrop's *user-optimized* principle [10], which states that the travel demands between origins and destinations is distributed among the utilized paths in such a way that no traveller can reduce his journey time by choosing a different path on the road network. As is well known, the implication is that all the utilized paths have equal service levels, that is

$$L_{k,pq}^{au} = L_{pq}^{au} \text{ if } H_{k,pq} > 0 , \text{ all } (p,q) \quad (12)$$

and all paths that do not carry flow have higher service levels

$$L_{k,pq}^{au} \geq L_{pq}^{au} \text{ if } H_{k,pq} = 0 , \text{ all } (p,q) . \quad (13)$$

The relation Ω is additive, that is

$$L_{pq}^{au} = \sum_a \delta_{ak,pq} \cdot L_a , \text{ all } (p,q) \quad (14)$$

On the transit nework, a similar *user optimized* flow distribution is used, that is

$$L_{k,pq}^{tr} = L_{pq}^{tr} = \sum_s \delta_{sk,pq} \cdot L_s, \text{ if } H_{k,pq}^{tr} > 0 , \text{ all } (p,q) \quad (15)$$
$$L_{k,pq}^{tr} \geq L_{pq}^{tr} \text{ if } H_{k,pq}^{tr} = 0$$

where $\delta_{sk,pq}$ is the indicator function which equals 1 if transit link or segment s is used in the transit path k from p to q.

The service times on the transit network identify separately, access and egress time, transfer time and in-vehicle travel time. Thus a path length is described by the above identified components and not by the total travel time.

The demand functions that EMME can accept are *zonal aggregate* functions of the general form

$$D_{pq}^{au} = G^{au} (A_p ; A_q ; L_{pq}^{au} ; L_{pq}^{tr})$$

and

$$D_{pq}^{tr} = G^{tr} (A_p ; A_q ; L_{pq}^{au} ; L_{pq}^{tr}) \quad (16)$$

The socio-economic variables A_p, A_q are fixed for the purposes of computing the equilibrium demands, flows and service levels. Therefore, we are only interested in the restrictions

$$D_{pq}^{au} = \tilde{G}^{au} (L_{pq}^{au} , L_{pq}^{tr})$$

and

$$D_{pq}^{tr} = \tilde{G}^{tr} (L_{pq}^{au} , L_{pq}^{tr}) \quad (17)$$

which are prepared by an internal manipulation imbedded in EMME.

It is important to remark that consistent with (17) are the so-called *direct demand* functions which include a trip generation effect, such as indicated in Figure 6 or simply *modal split* functions, where the demand for travel by all modes is fixed, say $\overline{D}_{pq} = D_{pq}^{tr} + D_{pq}^{au}$,

and the demand changes are only between modes, such as indicated in Figure 7.

Another important consideration is that these demand functions must be calibrated using service levels L_{pq}^{au}, L_{pq}^{tr} that are consistent with the modelling of the transportation network. If for instance, the travel time components are given different weights and these weights are calibrated using measures obtained from the network models, it is essential that these be consistent in the sense that the same L_{pq}^{tr} are found on the network using the results of the calibration. It is also worthwhile to note that it is not possible to exploit directly for EMME the recent advances in *disaggregate* demand modelling and calibra-

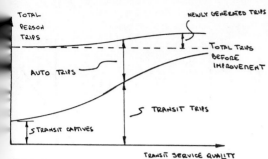

Figure 6

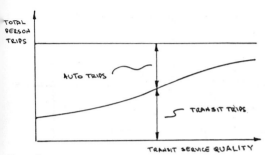

Figure 7

tion since the demand functions used are, as indicated earlier, zonal aggregate.

The resulting mathematical model is analysed in detail and the solution algorithm which is imbedded in EMME is described in [4]. The resulting model may be solved by a quasi-decomposition of the problem for each mode and results in a sequence of shortest path computations on the transit network and equilibrium demands, flows and service level computation on the road network. The oveall steps of the computational procedure, which yields a unique solution, is as follows:

Step 0: Select initial estimate of transit service levels $\bar{\tau}_s^{tr}$ (travel times) for all segments s such that $\Delta_{as} = 1$

Step 1: Compute shortest paths in the transit network and obtain transit service levels $\bar{\tau}_{pq}^{tr}$ for all (p, q)

Step 2: Solve an equilibrium problem on the road network using the demand functions $\tilde{G}_{pq}^{au}$ $(L_{pq}^{au}, \bar{\tau}_{pq}^{tr})$ for all (p, q) and obtain the equilibrium demands, flows and service levels, $\bar{L}_a$.

Step 3: If the current transit service levels $\bar{L}_s^{tr}$ are significantly different than those given by relations (11)

$$\bar{\bar{\tau}}_s^{tr} = c_s \ (\bar{L}_a \ , \text{ if } \Delta_{a,s}=1),$$

then replace $\bar{\tau}_s^{tr} \leftarrow \bar{\bar{\tau}}_s^{tr}$ and return to Step 1. Otherwise continue to Step 4.

Step 4: Determine the transit demands

$$D_{pq}^{tr} = \tilde{G}_{pq}^{tr} \ (\bar{L}_{pq}^{au} \ , \ \bar{L}_{pq}^{tr}) \ , \text{ all } (p,q)$$

and allocate these trips along the current shortest paths in the transit network.

Although we have shied away from using the term *assigment* due to the connotation that it has the fourth step in the classical sequence of generation, distribution, modal split and assignment, we shall refer, for simplicity, to the above procedure as a *bimodal assignment.*

EMME: THE NETWORK ALGORITHMS

Although EMME is evidently not as extensive a planning method as UTPS, that permits the execution of all the steps in the classical urban transportation planning format, it offers the following possibilities:

Given a fixed road demand $\bar{D}_{pq}^{au}$ compute the link and path flows and service levels according to Wardrop's user optimized principle. The computation is known (loosely) as the *equilibrium traffic assignment with fixed demand.* The algorithm imbedded in EMME is a further refinement [5] of the adaptation of the Frank and Wolfe algorithm for this problem realized in TRAFFIC [8], that was used extensively by us and other users.

Given a fixed transit demand $\bar{D}_{pq}^{tr}$ compute the link and path flows and service levels. This computation is a variation on the "all-or-nothing" transit assignment that considers diversion on common line segments, as realized in TRANSCOM [1], that was also used extensively before.

Given demand functions $\tilde{G}_{pq}^{au}$ compute the equilibrium demands, link and path flows and service levels according to Wardrop's user optimized principle. This computation is carried out by the adaptation of the Frank and Wolfe algorithm for this problem as described by Nguyen [7] and represents *the first time* that such an algorithm has been imbedded in an operational computer-based package.

Given demand functions $\tilde{G}_{pq}^{tr}$ compute shifts in the transit demands, link and path flows and service levels. This computation is necessary if a change in the transit services offered change the service levels significantly and induce a change in the transit demands.

Carry out the full bi-modal assignment outlined in the previous section.

It is important to remark that the algorithms imbedded in EMME, although rather sophisticated, may be used for planning purposes due to the development of the recent generation of computers that permits to complete seemingly cumbersome computations in reasonable total computing times. We estimate that the execution of the full bi-modal assignment for urban transportation networks of the order of 5000 links should take about 15-20 minutes of elapsed time on a CDC CYBER 74, or a cost of the order of $300.

EMME: CODING THE ROAD AND TRANSIT NETWORKS

One of the major features and innovations imbedded in EMME is an efficient interface between the road and transit networks. Particular attention was given to the way in which the data required by EMME is prepared by the user in order to ease the dialogue between the planner and the computer-based procedures.

The innovation of the coding procedure is that the road and transit networks may be coded independently if the user does not wish to use the interface feature and then, the minimal information necessary to achieve the interface is provided, if the interface feature is desired. The details of the coding procedure are described in [1]. We summarize in this paper the main concept used. We suppose that a road network is coded in a conventional way and is available. See Figure 8. Three types of transit networks are distinguished in the coding:

Type 1 network (low level of detail): represents the minimum data required to compute the transit flows and service levels given a fixed O/D matrix of transit demands. This type of network is used to represent only passenger movements. The only nodes used in this type network are line terminus, transfer nodes and access nodes. This type network is coded on the basic road network using road nodes, when they exist where required. If no road node exists but one is required, a new "transit" node is used. See Figure 9.

Type 2 network (intermediate level of detail): is required to perform the computation of transit flows and service levels with the EMME bi-modal equilibrium al-

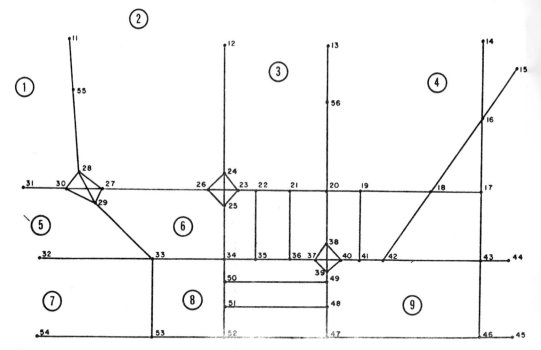

Figure 8

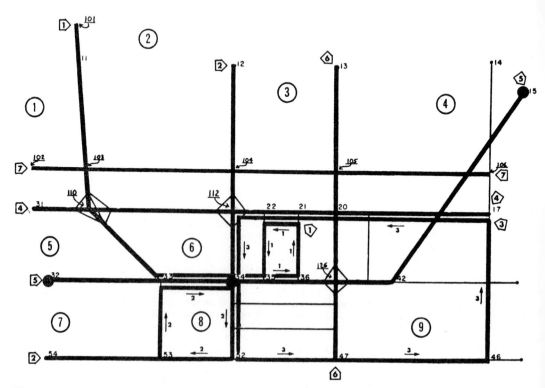

Figure 9

516

gorithm. It is obtained by inserting intermediate road nodes on the type 1 network, while ignoring the detail of "turning" road nodes at an intersection. A transit node, that corresponds to the expanded intersection, is coded to represent the intersection.

To permit interface with the coded road network, the user must define a correspondence table between transit nodes and road nodes for expanded intersection. Finally the user provides the access and egress links for the transit network. See Figure 10.

Then, the interface module in EMME generates internally a Type 3 network (high level of detail) which describes completely the transit vehicle movements by using coded road links. The module uses as input the type 2 network and the associated node correspondence table and each transit line is transformed into a sequence of road links. A byproduct of the interface is the possibility of determining transit vehicle travel time from the

travel time of the road link as indicated earlier.

Thus the coding of the transit network may be viewed as a useful exercise which gives the planner a global image of the complete transit network and its interrelationship with the road network, as well as the nitty-gritty details of modelling access and egress links which are specific to the transit network.

EMME: THE COMPUTER SYSTEMS DESIGN

The computer based implementation of EMME is designed to construct a data base containing the description of the urban road and transit networks, the socioeconomic activities and the coefficients of the demand functions. Data from the data base is then transformed into internal files that are used by EMME's assignment algorithms to predict the equilibrium demands for each mode, the link and path flows and service levels on each network.

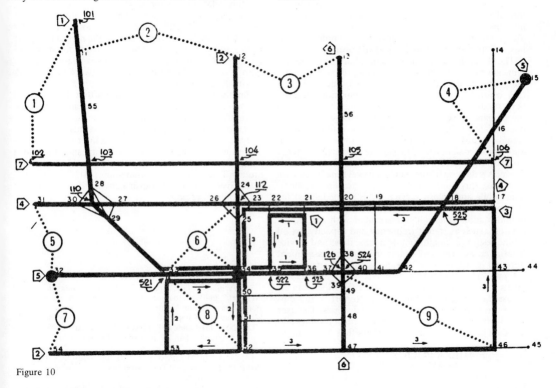

Figure 10

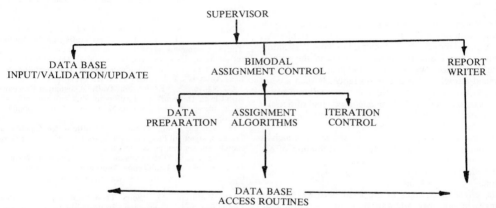

Figure 11 - EMME: System Hierarchy

517

EMME accepts a simple command language which permits the user to specify data base manipulations and request the execution of any one of the network algorithms outlined earlier. The commands are decoded by a supervisor which calls the relevant sections of the system.

The structure of the system is hierarchical, as shown in Figure 11. Within the hierarchy, the design is modular so that each section consists of a simple control procedure which calls different modules to perform the necessary functions. *Well defined files provide the interface between the modules.*

The design objective for the data base include efficient use of its random file structure and the ability to store and apply temporary modifications so that the user can easily investigate, for example, several different network configurations.

The Data Base Section include modules to read and validate the data provided by the user. It also includes modules to transform the node numbering system defined by the user to a form which enables the network algorithms to operate efficiently. This renumbering is however not apparent to the EMME user.

The Bi-modal Assignment Control Section of the system calls three types of modules: data preparation modules, network algorithm (assignment) modules and iteration control modules. The data preparation modules perform demand function manipulations and transform the demand depending for instance on the auto occupancy factors. The assignment modules with their associated subroutines perform the road traffic assignment and transit assignment. During the iterative bi-modal process, communication between the two assignment modules is defined by files such as travel time by auto on each link, travel time by transit on each line segment, automobile and transit service levels (impedances) for each origin-destination pair, etc... The iteration control modules adjust the values associated with the transit network, such as transit frequency and capacity, based on the resulting equilibrium demands, flows and service levels, and determines if another bi-modal assignment iteration is necessary. When an assignment terminates, the predicted equilibrium demands, flows and service levels for each mode are saved on files which can be accessed by the Report Writer. The Report Writer modules produce reports on the predicted values. The user may also use the files containing the predicted values and the data base to produce any reports that he requires.

EMME: A POLICY RESPONSIVE PLANNING METHOD

As remarked earlier, one of the principal aims of EMME is to aid in the efficient evaluation of alternative policy options. Most of the variables that are important for policy evaluation are likely to be independent explanatory variables in the demand functions (variables A_p, A_q, L_{pq}) and the others are contemplated network modifications that indirectly induce changes in the service levels L_{pq}. Thus, a well specified and properly calibrated demand model is of prime importance. If such a *good* demand function is available and the road and transit networks are modelled at the *adequate* level of detail a variety of changes in the *supply* of transportation may be evaluated. Some of these are:
− the effect of changes in public transit services such as line routing, line frequency, fares, introduction of express lines, exclusive bus lanes, etc...
− the effect of road pricing and changes in parking space availability and parking costs
− the effect of changes in the road network such as changes in one way orientation of streets, closing or opening of streets, etc.

Conceptually, this amounts to a large extent to recomputation of the equilibrium state (D_E, L_E) when actions dictated by relation(s) of the type $T = S (D_E, L_E)$ are contemplated. Thus, viewed in this way, EMME offers the possibility of interfacing supply decisions and, if available, explicit supply functions for transportation. So far, the supply decisions or functions have not been studied with the same intensity as demand functions. Future findings in this area will permit the generalization of EMME to include this component.

In a completely analogous way, EMME may be used to interface with decisions or systematic procedures that modify the socio-economic activities A according to relation(s) R (D_E, L_E), as outlined earlier. The challenge for the development of these expanded planning methods is one of sheer size: it remains to determine at what level of detail it is possible to apply and use such methods efficiently.

With relatively minor modification, the elastic demand network equilibrium computation of EMME may be used to estimate origin-destination matrices for *"windows"* in the network based on the method recently proposed by Nguyen [9]. This will enable the more detailed study of *subareas* without excessive data needs, requiring only observed times on the network and the link service level functions.

Finally, we would like to mention that the road and transit components of EMME have already been used successfully to evaluate changes in the supply of transportation services. The road component has been used to test the feasibility of introducing an intermediate capacity transit system in a Canadian city and the transit component has been used by the Montreal Urban Community Transportation Commission (MUCTC) to evaluate five scenarios of transit network development in the Montreal region.

REFERENCES
[1] Achim, C. and Chapleau, R., **"EMME-Coding the Transit Network"**, publication no. 49, Centre de recherche sur les transports, Université de Montréal (1976).
[2] Achim, C., Chapleau, R., Chriqui, C. and Robillard, P., **"TRANSCOM-Guide de l'utilisateur"**, publication no. 23, Centre de recherche sur les transports, Université de Montréal (1975).
[3] Beckman, M.J., McGuire, C.B. and Winsten, C.B., **"Studies in the Economics of Transportation"**, Yale University Press, New Haven, Conn. (1956).
[4] Florian, M., **"A Traffic Equilibrium Model of Travel by Car and Public Transport Modes"**, publication no. 32, Centre de recherche sur les transports, Université de Montréal (1975) To appear in Transportation Science, Vol. 11, No. 2 (1977).
[5] Florian, M., **"A Note on Accelerating an Equilibrium Traffic Assignment Algorithm"**, publication no. 56, Centre de recherche sur les transports, Université de Montréal (1977).
[6] Manheim, M.L. **"Fundamentals of Transportation Systems Analysis"**, Vol. 1, MIT Press (In Press) (1977).
[7] Nguyen, S., **"Equilibrium Traffic Assignment Procedure with Elastic Demand"**, publication no. 39, Centre de recherche sur les transports, Université de Montréal (1975). To appear in Transportation Science.
[8] Nguyen, S. and James, L., **"Traffic − An Equilibrium Traffic Assignment Program"**, publication no. 17, Centre de recherche sur les transports, Université de Montréal (1975).
[9] Nguyen, S., **"Estimating an OD Matrix from the Network Data: A Network Equilibrium Approach"**, publication no. 60, Centre de recherche sur les transports, Université de Montréal (1977).
[10] Wardrop, J.G., **"Some Theoretical Aspects of Road Traffic Research"**, Proceedings, Institute of Civil Engineering, Part II, pp. 325-378 (1952).

Scope for the substitution of labor and equipment in civil construction

A Progress Report

C. G. HARRAL, I. K. SUD and B. P. COUKIS

World Bank

INTRODUCTION

Widespread unemployment and underemployment in many developing countries has been a cause of increasing concern in recent years. It is generally acknowledged that productive employment opportunities must be created for large segments of population to foster economic development with distributional equity. In this regard, the present dominance of highly capital-intensive technologies in capital-scarce, labor-abundant economies has brought into question the appropriateness of the technology being transferred from the developed to the developing countries. It is argued that the pool of unemployed and underemployed labor is an important resource which could contribute to real capital formation and income if only "appropriate technologies" could be found which employ this resource productively.

Since 1971 the World Bank, in conjunction with several governments and other agencies, has undertaken to investigate the prospects for appropriate technologies in civil construction. [1] Although the question of appropriate technologies has been raised for a number of different sectors, the Bank study has been focused on civil construction for two main reasons. First, the need for appropriate technology is perhaps most apparent in civil construction, where a pronounced dichotomy exists between the modern capital-intensive technology and the traditional labor-intensive technology of civil construction. The output of a modern machine, typically costing in excess of US$100,000, is equivalent to the output of several hundred laborers. Second, civil works in the form of roads, irrigation channels, dams, reservoirs, etc., account for a major part of real domestic capital formation, and thus account for a significant part of lending by the World Bank and bilateral aid agencies. The employment potential of these investments is indeed substantial.

The initial phase of the study confirmed the technical feasibility of the substitution of labor for equipment for a wide range of construction activities. However, economic feasibility, which depends on relative factor prices and productivities, could not be assessed bacause of a lack of adequate information on the productivity of labor under different conditions. The second phase of the study, therefore, focused on collecting field observations of ongoing construction activities on 30 road, irrigation and dam construction sites in India and Indonesia to obtain the production relationships between varying inputs of equipment and labor and the output of different tasks of civil construction.

Based on the evidence on hand at the end of the second phase of the study, it was concluded that the traditional labor-intensive methods of construction that were being observed were not economically competitive with modern equipment even at extremely low wage rates. The reasons for this were believed to be:

a. the inefficiency of the technology employed;

b. a lack of proper organization and management; and

c. the fact that labor-intensive methods were observed under conditions where the primary emphasis was on employment creation rather than the productive use of labor.

Phase III of the study was initiated in late 1973 to examine ways in which the efficiency of labor-intensive methods could be enhanced by the introduction of improved hardware, project organization, management and incentives. The research is now sufficiently far-advanced so that the main conclusions have been established, which are significant enough to warrant a review at this stage. In future work the focus will be more on implementation and demonstration of the results rather than on research *per se*. This report is intended as a summary of the findings. For greater detail the reader is referred to the numerous technical memoranda and other reports listed in Appendix 1.

MAIN CONCLUSIONS

The following are the main conclusions of the work completed so far:

a. Labor-intensive methods are technically feasible for a wide range of construction activities and can generally produce the same quality of product as equipment-intensive methods.

b. Traditional labor-intensive civil works as observed in the course of this study are inefficient and economically inferior to [2] capital-intensive works except at extremely low wage levels. However, labor productivity can be improved very significantly by the introduction of certain organizational, management and mechanical improvements.

c. With superior tools, high incentives, and good management labor productivity can be improved to the point that labor-intensive methods can be fully competitive with equipment-intensive methods for wages under US$1.00 per day at present (1976) prices for equipment and fuel. For base wages above US$2.00 per day, labor-intensive methods are unlikely to be economically justifiable; for wages between US$1.00 and US$2.00 per day the economic viability will depend on various factors. Of course, these "break-even wages" would change with changes in the price of equipment and fuel.

d. Although there is considerable scope for increasing labor productivity by the use of available off-the-shelf hardware and improvements in the quality of tools, the prospect for developing new "intermediate technologies" for civil construction may be limited.

e. Prevalence of low wage rates (under US$1.00 per day) merely indicates the *potential* for the use of labor-intensive methods. Adequate organization and management particularly designed for labor-intensive projects is a critical consideration in adopting labor-intensive methods on a large scale.

f. The availability of adequate labor supply during the construction season is a much more significant factor than has generally been considered even in labor-abundant economies. Labor requirement for civil works is specific in time and space dimensions and it is therefore not sufficient to have an aggregate stock of surplus labor in a region. The required flow of labor at the construction site is the relevant consideration.

g. The health and nutrition status of construction workers has a significant effect on worker productivity. Several health/nutritional improvements at relatively low costs can result in major improvements in productivity and earnings of the workers. However, mechanisms available for large scale interventions in this area need to be further investigated.

h. Alteration of project design, can in some circumstances improve the feasibility of using labor-intensive technologies, but any resulting change or deferral in project benefits must be explicitly accounted for.

As is evident from the conclusions given above, the scope for using labor-intensive methods for civil construction is determined by a number of conditions, of which low wage rates is only one. Selection of tools of appropriate type and design can effect labor productivity, and therefore the economic viability of labor-intensive technologies. Organization and management considerations of labor recruitment, supervision and motivation are of critical importance.

The remainder of the paper is devoted to an elaboration of these and other considerations. In many developing countries with low wage rates, where labor-intensive methods could potentially be economical, many of the conditions given above are not met. The last section of the paper discusses the approach which will be followed in the future work program of the study which has as aim the development of the capacity for undertaking efficient labor-intensive projects. Areas which require further research are also discussed.

TECHNICAL AND ECONOMIC FEASIBILITY OF LABOR-INTENSIVE TECHNOLOGIES

Technical Feasibility

Civil construction basically consists of the integration of a small number of repetitive tasks, which in turn are comprised of a number of activities. Although the range of feasible technologies is large for some tasks and restricted for others, most of these tasks can be accomplished using a wide range of technology, from the most labor-intensive to the most capital-intensive. In theory any combination of technologies may be specified for the various tasks, but in practice the use of certain technology (say equipment) for any one task may indicate the use of a similar technology for some or all of the other tasks in the project.

Earthworks, including haulage of aggregates and other materials, is overall the single most important task of civil construction and typically accounts for up to 50 percent of expenditures on civil construction. Earthworks can be broken down into the activities of ripping (if required), excavation, loading of excavated material into a haulage vehicle, hauling, unloading, spreading and compaction, although more than one of these activities may be combined into a single operation in different technologies. Manual excavation and loading can be combined with a variety of haulage modes - headbaskets, wheelbarrows of different types, various types of animals, agricultural tractor/trailer combinations and flat-bed trucks - and manual unloading and spreading as necessary. Equipment-intensive methods of earthworks include bulldozers, excavators with haulage vehicles, and towed and motorized scrapers of various sizes and specifications. Compaction may be carried out by self-propelled and tractor or animal-towed rollers of various designs; although the compaction standards normally achieved by the latter are not comparable to those by fully mechanized rollers. Thus, it is often necessary to specify mechanical means of compaction on labor-intensive projects, even though the output of the compaction equipment is considerably higher than the labor gangs generally engaged on any one site, resulting in a low utilization of equipment.

Besides earthworks, production of aggregates and pavement construction are other major tasks of civil construction. Aggregate production can be carried out entirely by manual methods or by mechanical crushers of varying sizes, but hand crushing cannot economically achieve gradation standards comparable to those achieved by mechanical crushers. Although the larger crushing plants can be highly automated, a significant number of laborers can be employed with small-scale crushers for such activities as loading and hauling of stock piles. Pavement construction involves two main tasks which require a significant labor input. These are the laying of the base, e.g. water-bound macadam (WBM), and the laying of the surface, either premix carpet or bituminous surface dressing. The laying of WBM is peculiar to labor-intensive road construction and therefore no strictly comparable equipment-intensive methods are available. Most premix carpet can be laid either by conventional mechanical pavers, which have relatively high output rates, or by manual methods which may be suitable for working with smaller size hot-mix plants. However, the quality of machine-laid surface is normally superior as measured by its surface roughness.

Thus, from a technical point of view, most major tasks of civil construction can be carried out by various labor-intensive methods working generally to the same tolerances as machines. But for a few selected activities changes in design standard may be necessary to off-set the advantage of machinery with some loss of benefit (see the section 'Project Design' for further elaboration of this point).

Economic Feasibility

Whether or not labor-intensive methods are economically feasible depends on the productivity of different technologies and the relative prices of labor and equipment. For the different tasks of civil construction, productivity of different labor-intensive methods with alternative assumptions of wage rages can be compared with the cost of the same task by equipment-intensive methods to determine the economic 'break-even' wages for labor. The lower the productivity of labor, the lower would be the break-even wage, and vice versa. Early conclusions of the study (Phase II) indicated extremely low productivity of traditional labor-intensive technologies, which, at the prices for equipment and fuel then prevailing (1973), could not be economically competitive with equipment except at extremely low wages. Clearly the economic feasibility of labor-intensive techniques rests on increasing the productivity of labor.

Field work carried out in the study indicates that substantial improvements in labor productivity in certain tasks are achievable by improvements in basic tools, worker incentives and site management. Labor productivity in excavating hard soils, for example, can very from $2m^3$ per man-day to $5m^3$ per man-day with high incentives and better quality shovels. Further increases of 50-100 percent can be achieved by pre-ripping of soil by animal-drawn ploughs (see Technical Memorandum No. 19). Labor productivity in haulage by wheelbarrows can be up to twice the productivity of haulage by head-baskets depending on the length of haul, and productivity with a better designed wheelbarrow with ball-bearings can be 50 percent more than that with many conventionally available wheelbarrows (see Technical Memoranda No. 1 and 13). Use of rail wagons and aerial ropeways can increase labor productivity significantly in specific site conditions where large quantities of material are to be moved or where a substantial lift is involved (see Technical Memoranda No. 6, 22 and 23). Production of aggregates by manual methods can be improved by the use of specially designed hammers. With the types of productivity increases indicated above, the economic break-even wages for labor-intensive methods are much higher at current (1976) prices of equipment and fuel than were indicated in the earlier phase of the study. [3]

For generalized comparisons, break-even wages have been calculated by using international prices for equipment and fuel, while local labor costs have been expressed in US dollars. Obviously, the break-even wages will increase or decrease with any future variations in the price of equipment and fuel. Broadly speaking, base wage rates of US$1.00 to US$1.80 per day combined with and effective incentive system represent the upper limit (in 1976 prices) at which labor-intensive methods can be economically attractive. For base labor wages of over US$2.00 or US$2.50 per day, there is little prospect for labor-intensive methods being economically competitive with equipment. These wage rates represent the boundary conditions. Between the two, factors such as the nature of work, special site conditions, magnitude of the work, and set-up costs, will determine the economic feasibility of labor-intensive technologies.

Typical unit cost of earthworks for a few selected technologies at varying wage rates and alternative haul lengths is depicted in Figure 1. For each method, a lower and upper bound is given, reflecting the range of productivities under favorable conditions (high incentive wages and good supervision) and poor conditions (daily wages and poor supervision). Comparing extremes, it can be seen from the figures for all haul distances that the unimproved labor-intensive method is not economically competitive with efficient equipment-intensive methods except at wage rates of the order of US$0.40 to US$0.50 per day or less. However, by introducing small scale equipment, improved supervision and high wage incentives, productivity can be increased several fold and labor-intensive methods become economical at base wage rates up to about US$1.20 per day when compared to the more efficient equipment-intensive operation, or as high as US$1.60 to US$1.80 per day when compared to less efficient equipment operations. This comparison includes allowances for the cost of the equipment, for wage incentive supplements equal to the base daily wage (to compensate for additional effort and skills), and an additional overhead allowance of thirty percent for the cost of superior supervision, as consistent with field observations. [4]

Technical considerations would dictate the use of mechanical compaction even on labor-intensive projects. On a larger project this would pose no special difficulties as the cost of compaction would generally be only a small part of the total project cost. However, on many smaller and scattered labor-intensive jobs (e.g. feeder road construction), such compaction equipment would have a very low utilization because of the small quantities of work involved and it may be more economical to use animal-or tractor-towed rollers with an acceptable reduction of compaction standards (see Technical Memorandum No. 17). These are explicit tradeoffs which must be considered in the design and organization of the project, as discussed below.

Break-even wages have also been computed for other important tasks. For aggregate production, larger size aggregates (greater than 25 mm) can be produced more economically by labor with proper incentives at wages under US$1.00 per day, whereas small aggregates for shippings, etc. are produced more economically by mechanical crushers. However, limited evidence from the study suggests that at low wage rates, smaller size aggregates may be produced more economically by first pre-breaking of larger stones by hand to about 50 mm size and then crushing by machine. It should be noted that manual stone breaking itself is a semi-skilled task. Using hammers of improved design can increase productivities as much as 50 percent, but there appears little prospect for increasing productivity by further altering the technology short of switching to a mechanical crusher.

Laying of hot premix carpet can be accomplished much more economically by labor for typical project conditions in developing countries where the quantity of work and the output rate required may be relatively small. This is because the available paving machines are of high capacity (70-80 tons per hour) and consequently entail considerable idle time. In one instance in India, the cost of laying premix carpet by hand was estimated to be US$0.06 per ton and by mechanical paver to be US$0.85 per ton when both methods were used in conjunction with a 25-30 ton/hour capacity hot mix plant (see Technical Memorandum No. 5). However, the quality of machine-laid surface was markedly superior. In this case, the increased user costs resulting from lowered surface standard had to be weighed against the reduction in the cost of surfacing. User cost considerations may be significant for highly trafficked roads but are less important for feeder roads or roads with heavy volumes of slow moving traffic.

The conclusions about the relative costs of different technologies should, of course, be recognized as being boundary conditions. Each individual situation has to be analyzed to determine any deviations from these conditions Factors such as available skills both in the use of machines and labor, set-up costs and site conditions, would determine these deviations. Moreover, project management considerations will influence the overall economic feasibility of labor-intensive methods, as will be discussed in the section below.

Prospects for 'Intermediate' Technologies

The extreme dichotomy between the available labor-intensive technologies and the modern equipment-intensive technologies has prompted the study to focus attention on the development of 'intermediate' technologies. It was believed that technologies could be developed between the two extremes which require considerably less capital per unit of output, a smaller investment per machine (less lumpiness), and which would enhance labor productivity such that these technologies would be economically efficient at higher labor wage rates than the traditional labor-intensive technologies. Development of intermediate technologies can be envisaged in two ways. Starting with the equipment-intensive end of the spectrum the size and production capacity of equipment can be reduced in steps thereby decreasing the capital content and increasing the labor content of any given task. Various earthmoving machines, for example, can be replaced by smaller size equipment. Alternatively, starting from the labor-intensive end, capital can be substituted for labor in small increments for some of the activities of a task in such a way that the overall labor productivity is enhanced, which can more than offset the incremental increase in the capital cost. For example, labor productivity in earthworks can be increased by the use of superior excavating and loading tools, substituting wheelbarrows for headbaskets, introduction of improved design wheelbarrows, use of rail carts, animal-drawn carts, etc. The latter approach was pursued in the Bank study which has

explored the development of intermediate technologies principally from the labor-intensive end of the spectrum. Field trials were carried out not only with the available off-the-shelf hardware and tools with improved designs, but also innovations in hand and animal carts, winches, animal and tractor-drawn scrapers, lever cranes, monorails, etc. However, while substantial improvements in labor productivity were obtained by the proper selection and adaptation of conventional hardware, the more innovative devices did not prove to be very successful. It appears that for most tasks of civil construction and under the general site conditions encountered on civil works projects, the available hardware may represent the practical limit of intermediate technologies and the prospects for any new intermediate technologies is not clear.

Two factors support this conclusion. First, output of

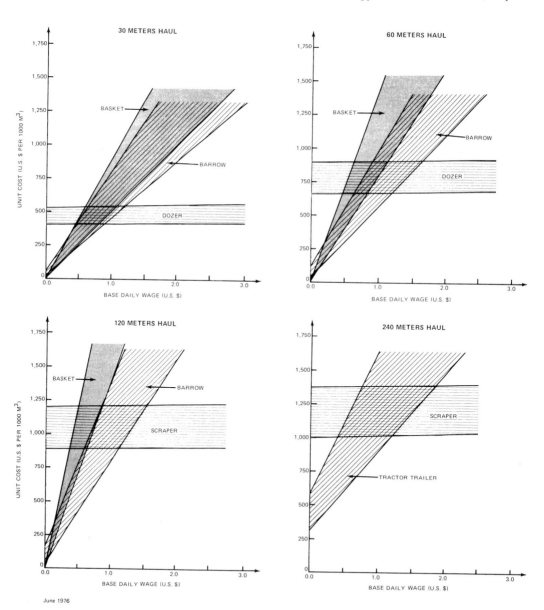

June 1976

Figure 1 - Comparative unit costs of earthworks by different methods as a function of haul distance and wage rate

labor based technologies is limited by the physical constraints of energy of a worker (see Technical Memorandum No. 11). Various types of mechanical advantages (wheels, levers, inclined planes, etc.) can be provided to an individual to ensure that only a minimum of energy is wasted. The conventional hardware generally serves this purpose. Further increases in productivity are only possible by switching to a machine generated source of power, which in turn entails a major jump in labor productivity and a major increase in capital intensity of the task. Once a switch is made to machine-based technologies, there is a minimum size of machines below which the machine operation is not economical. Thus, although a farm tractor could be used in excavation, its cost per unit of output is considerably higher than that of a conventional dozer, because it does not have the horsepower and weight necessary for ripping or shearing the soil efficiently.

The second reason for the lack of success with new intermediate technologies seems to be the complexity they introduce in the execution of the task. Introduction of these technologies for one or more activities of a task requires a close coordination with the remaining activities to be able to realize the expected gains in productivity. For example, haulage by wheelbarrows and carts, which already represents a major improvement on haulage by headbaskets, could be further improved in some circumstances by resorting to a fixed rail system. But this requires a proper set-up of the rails and the balancing of loaders and unloaders at the two ends of the system to match the haulage cycle of the rail, without which the rail haulage becomes much less efficient. Such close coordination is often not achievable under typical site conditions in civil construction projects. Similary, switching to machine based technologies for any one part of a task generally dictates the use of machines for all other activities of the task because of the large imbalances between men and machine productivities.

Thus the prospect for developing intermediate technologies between the limits of an efficient labor-intensive technology based on human muscle and modern equipment technologies based on other sources of energy are not very encouraging. Such a technology would hinge on the development of small scale equipment which could efficiently substitute other sources of energy for human muscle. However, the evidence to date suggests that there are limits on the degree to which equipment can be fragmented without experiencing losses due to the inherent economies of scale to be found in fossil produced sources of energy. The employment effects of using such a technology will also be small compared to human muscle based technologies and will primarily involve the use of skilled labor. Undoubtedly there are some improvements that can be made in adapting modern machine based technologies to conditions found in developing countries and it will certainly be worthwhile to do so; but their employment effects are likely to be marginal.

ORGANIZATION AND MANAGEMENT REQUIREMENTS

Much of the discussion on the economic efficiency of labor-intensive methods has in the past been primarily based on the type of micro-level cost comparisons of alternative technologies described above. However, such comparisons merely indicate the range of wage rates (and other factor costs) for which labor-intensive methods can be economical. Whether labor-intensive methods can be economically implemented at the project and program level is determined by the organization and management capabilities of the public works authority or contractor concerned to recruit, mobilize, organize and supervise large numbers of labor. Without effective project organization and management, inefficiencies in the form of multiple handling of materials, long project gestation periods and low labor productivity are commonly observed. Thus prevalence of labor wage rates at or below the economic break-even wage is a necessary but not sufficient condition for the adoption of labor-intensive technologies.

Of course, the need for effective project organization and management exists irrespective of the technology employed. However, what is often not appreciated is the fact that the organization and management requirements of labor-intensive projects are quite different from those of equipment-intensive projects. There are unique problems associated with recruitment, supervision and motivation of labor which call for different supervision skills and a different framework for project organization. These factors are often overlooked by many public works authorities thereby resulting in a mismatch of supervisory skills and an inappropriate project organization. This may well be the major cause of the inefficiencies which are often observed in labor-intensive works. [5] These issues are discussed in more detail in the following.

Labor Mobilization

Availability of an adequate supply of labor at the project site is obiously a critical consideration in the planning and execution of labor-intensive projects. The labor supply conditions determine not only the relative economics of labor-intensive methods but also the length of time required for project completion. Even in the most labor abundant economies, the supply of labor to civil construction projects is often inadequate, contributing to long project delays. This is particularly true during the seasons when earnings opportunities in agriculture rise sharply. The tradeoffs between higher wages necessary to attract an adequate labor force and the economic loss from deferred project benefits caused by insufficient labor must be explicitly accounted for.

Most of the arguments in favor of using labor-intensive methods in construction (as in other sectors) are based on the assumption of the existence of surplus labor in agriculture. It has been hypothesized that a stock of surplus labor exists, particularly in the slack agricultural season, which could be diverted to other productive activities without a significant loss in agricultural production. However, the existence of a stock of surplus labor during certain seasons does not ensure labor will be available for employment in civil construction at the specific times when it is required. The willingness of labor to work in civil construction depends on earning differentials (both short-term and long-term) relative to alternative employment, on the "wealth" of the individual (e.g. extent of landholdings, if any), any additional work-related costs of food, housing and transport, and on the disutility of work in terms of leisure foregone. In addition, substantial underemployment may be interspersed with essential part-time employment such that it is difficult to utilize productively the time that is available.

Limited empirical evidence has been collected in the Bank studies on the determinants of labor supply for civil construction, [6] but the importance of seasonal variations in agriculture is clearly established. In India agricultural wages typically increase from 30 to 80 percent or more during peak seasons, which are encountered about four months out of the year in rainfed cultivation but may extend to eight months in irrigated areas. Because of the shortage of labor during this period, and because of climatic factors, civil construction is normally halted from sometime in June until October, and periodic interruptions of work occur during the rest of the year. An important fact to be determined is the extent to which labor may be more freely available on a part-time basis more suitable for periodic activities (such as maintenance) near to their homes than for construction activities which demand full time and require substantial travel.

Labor demand for construction also fluctuates as the work progresses over the construction season. This consideration normally dictates employing labor on a casual basis, i.e. labor is employed as and when necessary. The ability of the project authorities to recruit labor in this context is governed by their sensitivity and responsiveness to the changing labor market conditions. Unless wage rates can be revised in response to changing site conditions or seasonal considerations, wide fluctuations in labor availability can occur. On many sites, it becomes necessary to import labor from other labor surplus regions, which may sometimes be located several hundred miles from the site. In order to attract labor from such distant places, it is generally necessary to provide labor with mobilization advances, travel fares and sometimes even food supplies and shelter for their assignment. Government construction authorities are not well suited to perform such functions as they often require long and personal contacts with these communities. Intermediaries or special contractors are commonly used to perform such functions, as discussed below.

In India large migratory labor populations have emerged which provide the bulk of the labor force for large scale civil works projects. Migration of hundreds of thousands of workers and their families for construction work, usually in response to specific recruitment drives by contractors, is an annual phenomenon. The existence of this large mobile population, combined with relatively low costs of migration in India [7] tends to limit wage differentials between regions. The propensity to seasonal migration is higher in those areas and among those classes which have been relatively impoverished over a long term; notable reluctance to migrate has been observed among those affected even severely by temporary or recent events such as drought or floods. Field investigations in northern and central India in fact show that almost all migrant laborers on construction work are either landless or possess very small holdings. The investigations also confirm that contractors have a strong preference for migrant laborers whom they consider more productive, reliable and disciplined. Migrant workers tend to specialize in particular activities, developing skills and often much higher productivities and earnings than casual laborers recruited locally.

The important point to be stressed is that even in seemingly labor-abundant areas, the availability of an adequate supply of labor for civil works cannot be assumed without a careful investigation of the local labor market conditions. Examples of labor-intensive projects which have remained uncompleted for years are unfortunately all too common. The cost of having large sums of capital tied-up in unfinished projects does not seem to be fully recognized. An explicit recognition of labor supply constraints may well dictate a redesign of the project or the selection of a more capital-intensive technology.

Labor Management
Supervisory Skill Requirements

For the same rate of output, supervision requirements of labor-intensive projects are much greater than those for equipment-intensive projects. The output of a single piece of equipment is generally equivalent to the output of several hundred laborers working in several small gangs. For example, the output of a bulldozer employed in earthworks can be as high as 1,000 cubic meters per day, which may be equivalent to the output of 200-300 laborers working in groups of 20-30 each. The work of the bulldozer may be carried out by one or two skilled workers, but it would require more than a dozen supervisors to supervise the work of the equivalent number of labor. In addition, labor is often deployed over a wider geographical area requiring a dispersal of supervision, which further increases supervision requirements.

The skills needed for the supervision of labor rather than machines are also quite different; the former requiring the leadership qualities to motivate large groups of human beings over long periods. Labor is more heterogenous in its characteristics than equipment and therefore the "style" of supervision is likely to vary widely for labor-intensive projects. Moreover, a task which can be performed in one machine operation may require several gangs of labor working in the different component activities. This imposes an important responsibility on the supervisor to coordinate and sequence the different activities efficiently. For instance, on a road construction project in India it was found that with a proper balance of excavators and haulers and with a more appropriate sequence of performing the excavation, labor productivity could be more than doubled. (See Technical Memorandum No. 2). In another instance of canal construction in Indonesia, when wheelbarrows were introduced for haulage instead of headbaskets, the expected increase in productivity could not be realized because of the site supervisor's apparent inability to understand the need for a proper balance between the excavators, loaders and haulers -- the haulers speeded up, but only to be delayed in queues because the rate of excavation and loading was inadequate. Other aspects of site supervision of labor-intensive projects which have a major bearing on productivity are the proper selection and maintenance of work tools, which require a good understanding by the supervisors of the principles of manual work.

Unfortunately, such supervision skills require a certain inclination and training for the site supervisors which often do not exist. Even in countries like India and Indonesia, where labor-intensive methods of construction have been traditionally used, many of the site supervisors are graduates of polytechnics or engineering schools where the education tends to be oriented towards design engineering and the use of equipment. Frequently these supervisors possess no prior experience in working with labor, and they rarely (if ever) come up from the labor ranks. Indeed, labor-intensive civil works are often seen by governments as a way to absorb the unemployed technical graduates. Under these conditions, the role of these site supervisors in project execution is more like the measurement and checking of work done by 'quantity surveyors' rather than the labor management and supervision work done by a 'foreman'.

Thus, for labor-intensive projects to be implemented on a wide scale, it is essential that sufficient numbers of site supervisors be available who are specifically trained in labor supervision and management. In most countries availability of such skilled staff will be a critical constraint in the adoption of labor-intensive methods. A substantial effort is required to develop and implement training programs specifically oriented to labor-intensive works. The nature of the work suggests that on the job training would be the most suitable approach.

Wage and Incentive Systems

As indicated earlier in the paper, management systems which provide incentives for efficiency are of paramount concern in labor-intensive works programs. The evidence indicated that incentive payment methods may result in labor productivities up to three times greater than daily wage systems. (See Technical Memoranda No. 12, 19). However, the development and administration of incentive systems is a large and difficult task; at a minimum, job analyses must be carried out and a schedule of productivity norms established. The payment basis must be fully understood and felt to be fair by the labor force, and wage payments must be made regularly and promptly. There must be flexibility so that rates can be revised to reflect particular site conditions. In the case of the Chinese sponsored road projects in Nepal, elaborate piece rate systems were developed which provided different rates for each task under varying conditions. Development and administration of such incentive schemes can only be done by the site level supervisors, who must therefore possess the necessary skills and authority for this purpose.

Health/Nutrition Considerations

Sufficient evidence has been collected in the study to indicate a significant effect of health and nutrition status of workers on productivity. Several of these deficiencies can be corrected at relatively modest cost and yield high benefits. Studies of adult male plantation workers in Indonesia indicated a significant correlation between iron deficiency anemia and the output of rubber plantation workers. [8] A simple iron supplementation program at a cost of US$0.50 per worker resulted in increased productivity by up to 25 percent. The benefit/cost ratio of such a program is obviously large. A similar study in India of road construction workers (Technical Memorandum No. 4) and an independent study in Jamaica [9] of sugar plantation workers indicated correlation between output and body weight and dimensions. This would suggest a possible relationship between work output and caloric consumption which can be augmented by locally available food supplements. Present work underway in Kenya is attempting to study the benefits and costs of caloric supplementation. Various public health measures can also be used to reduce the incidence of certain health deficiencies which may limit worker productivity and/or availability. However, there is inadequate knowledge of the delivery mechanisms which may be used for nutritional/health interventions on a scale larger than the experimental level, and further work needs to be done in this area.

Organizational Framework

The unique requirements of labor recruitment, payment, supervision and motivation, combined with the geographical dispersion of sites and the major influence of site variables on labor productivity, suggests three main organizational requirements for labor-intensive public works programs:

a. as much of the decisionmaking as feasible must be delegated to the site level supervisor in order to enable him to respond quickly to changes in site conditions;

b. sufficient flexibility must be given to site supervisors to revise wage rates and an incentive built in for the site manager to ensure that labor is employed productively; and

c. the organization must be responsive to the relative prices of labor and equipment, to ensure that labor-intensive methods are adopted in low wage situations where such methods may be more economical than equipment.

The first two considerations would tend to favor the use of private contractors, while the last consideration may necessitate the use of force account construction particularly in countries where labor-intensive methods have not been traditionally used in spite of the prevalence of low wage rates. However, both of these systems have certain weaknesses which limit their application to labor-intensive projects.

Private contractors have the necessary flexibility and incentives for carrying out construction projects efficiently. However, established contractors show little inclination in using labor-intensive methods, even in countries like Indonesia where such methods may be more profitable on certain projects. The larger contractors have generally developed specialized expertise in the use of equipment and perceive the use of labor-intensive methods as being management-intensive, time consuming and generally inefficient; the element of risk is large in dealing with unfamiliar methods. In countries where these contractors can find sufficiently large and specialized jobs (e.g., major bridge contracts in India and large civil works contracts in Indonesia), the smaller jobs are regarded by them to be marginal and therefore they prefer to leave them to the smaller contractors. Moreover, many construction authorities consider access to equipment as a major criterion to judge the contractors' ability to execute works. These and similar regulations inhibit the contractors from adopting labor-intensive methods. In the circumstances it seems unlikely that large contractors will opt for labor-intensive methods even if they are free to choose their technology.

The system of "petty" contracting which is widely used in India is oriented specifically to the use of labor-intensive methods. Under this system works are sliced into a large number of small contracts varying in value form $10,000 to $100,000 per year. The contractors by virtue of their small size and fragmented works, have virtually no access to capital and therefore own little or no equipment. Their principal characteristic is the ability to perform labor-intensive works, as the only capital outlays these works require are the funds for the payment of small labor advances and for their current payroll expenditures.

While the petty contractor method is effective in ensuring that the contractors will choose labor-intensive methods without the construction authority having to specify this administratively, this system suffers from some drawbacks which limits the efficient use of labor. Because of their small size, the petty contractors generally possess little or no formal skills in contracting or construction management. Their financial status is so limited that they cannot afford to experiment with unfamiliar technologies. Essential items of equipment, e.g., rollers, must normally be provided by the construction authority. The individual slices of works which are given to the petty contractors tend to be not only small but also limited in scope, as they commonly specialize in particular tasks, e.g., earthworks, stone production, or transport of materials. But fragmentation of this type imposes a major responsibility on the construction authority to schedule and sequence the various contractors' works. In practice this often proves to be a difficult undertaking and numerous instances are observed in the field where the inability of just a single contractor to complete his part of the job prevents other contractors from completing their works.

By using force account construction, it is possible to specify the appropriate technology to be used. However, force account construction normally implies a centralized, hierarchical management structure and experience indicates that it is difficult to provide the flexibility required for site staff to respond to varying conditions and to the needs for labor recruitment and payment. Force account construction also generally suffers from a lack of financial discipline and control. With dispersion of sites and fragmentation of resources, financial control of labor intensive projects becomes even more difficult. However, despite the potential difficulties, force account may provide the only feasible avenue for introduction of labor-intensive methods in those countries where modern equipment has become the established technology. In these circumstances force account programs may be used to test the efficiency of alternative labor-intensive methods, evaluate different management schemes and develop a reservoir of skilled manpower familiar with the use of labor-intensive methods. By demonstrating through such programs that labor-intensive methods can be cost effective, the element of risk will be reduced and the adoption of similar methods by the contracting industry encouraged. The Kenya Rural Access Roads program, which is discussed in the section 'Future Work' below, is one example of this approach.

PROJECT DESIGN

The issue of the choice of technology is closely linked with the question of appropriate design of the project. Treating the project design as "fixed" may in many instances preclude the use of labor-intensive methods. Under certain circumstances, it may be possible to alter the design to facilitate adoption of manual methods and build a facility with essentially the same performance characteristics or with only a limited loss of benefits. This is indeed a common practice in countries where labor-intensive construction methods are commonly used.

There are three ways in which the design of a civil works project can be altered to make the project amenable to construction by labor-intensive methods. These are:

a. Selection of a basic design concept or type or project which has a high labor component, e.g., in the irrigation sector a choice may sometimes be possible between surface water schemes, which can largely be carried out by labor-intensive methods, and ground water schemes which are generally capital-intensive.

b. Variation in project scale and timing to conform to the availability of labor, e.g., a large irrigation channel can sometimes be subdivided into two smaller channels, a road can be constructed to low standards initially and upgraded in subsequent stages as labor is available.

c. Variation in engineering design and specifications, e.g., earthworks in irrigation channels may be reduced by lining the channels, and the use of masonry rather than concrete lining materials creates further employment; similarly relaxation of aggregate gradation standards and specification of larger size stone in pavement construction will enhance the feasibility of labor-intensive methods.

Where a labor-intensive design solution which yields the same or similar performance standards cannot be found, labor-intensive methods may be more competitive for lower design standards or slower implementation schedules. In these cases the reduced or deferred benefits must be explicitly recognized and a comparison of benefit and cost streams made for alternative designs. Further research is being undertaken to determine the performance of alternative designs and specifications in roadworks and to explore various avenues in the adaption of engineering design to facilitate labor-intensive methods of construction.

FUTURE WORK
Measures to Promote Labor-Intensive Technologies

The results of the Bank study to date have highlighted the conditions necessary for the successful (economical) implementation of labor-intensive technologies. Availability of labor for civil construction at low wage (or opportunity cost) is, of course, a prerequisite, and the extent to which labor-intensive methods can be adopted would depend upon the elasticity of labor supply. But whether labor-intensive methods could be implemented on a large scale is determined by the organization and management capabilities of the construction authorities. Development of such capabilities must be undertaken simultaneously with the adoption of labor-intensive technologies, particularly in countries where such methods have not been traditionally employed. This is likely to be a slow and difficult process and the effort required for it should not be underestimated. It would be necessary initially to provide major inputs of technical assistance for training of staff from the foreman to the supervisory engineers and project planners on pilot construction programs. These programs, while providing training for staff, could also serve as "demonstration programs" for labor-intensive technologies and expanded in their coverage as the organizational capability is developed. Ultimately, the programs should aim at the development of a local contracting industry which would be geared towards the use of labor-intensive methods. As the research findings of the Bank have been generally established, future work is now primarily focussed on such demonstration/training programs. Kenya and Honduras have been selected as two countries for the implementation of the study recommendations.

Demonstration/training programs being undertaken in both Kenya and Honduras have been designed with the following considerations:

a. The works involved (feeder road construction) are relatively small which do not require large numbers of labor at one site. This permits an evaluation of the labor market potential for such works below the maximum break-even wages.

b. The program horizon is medium to long-term (5-10 years) which permits a gradual expansion of the program. In Kenya the program employed 1,000 laborers in the first year, and this is to be expanded to 20,000 laborers in about 10 years.

c. A training program for site supervisory staff has been initiated to produce the requisite supervisory staff as the program expands.

d. A detailed monptoring and evaluation program is concurrently undertaken to evaluate and improve the technologies used.

The initial phase of the program in Kenya, which has been underway since early 1975, has required a considerable amount of management input. A team of three engineers and an organization and management specialist provided from the study funds is assisting the Ministry of Works in implementing the program. A labor economist will investigate the local labor market conditions in the areas of the construction sites. Since many of the tools normally required for labor-intensive methods are not locally produced in Kenya or are of poor quality and design, a small scale industry specialist will explore possible ways of developing local manufacturing capability in this area. In addition, the senior management positions are presently occupied by expatriate staff. Thus, in the initial stages, while the direct costs of the program have been very competitive indeed because of the prevalent wage rates (about $0.75 per day), management costs have been quite substantial. At present, the program is carried out entirely by force account, but consideration is now being given to the development of local contractors. Ultimately, the success would depend on whether the program can sustain itself without the need for an inordinate amount of management input.

The work in Honduras is currently in the planning stages and actual constructions is expected to get underway by late 1976. More recently, assistance has also been provided to initiate similar programs in Lesotho and Chad as a part of Bank financed projects. The results of all these efforts would be monitored closely in the study to evaluate their effectiveness. It is likely to be a long and tedious process, and if the experience from the study so far is a guide, it is unlikely that any quick solutions can be developed.

Research

WHile the main thrust of future work will be on implementation of efficient labor-intensive technologies, certain gaps in knowledge remain which require further research, as listed below. As most of these issues are pertinent to the Kenya and Honduras programs, many facets of the research will be encompassed within those programs; in addition, separate efforts will be undertaken through research institutions in other countries which by virtue of their established capacity have an advantage in executing more complex, long term research.

(i) *Labor supply.* The seemingly paradoxical problems of labor shortages in labor abundant economies has been discussed above. Regional and seasonal conflicts in demand with agriculture and other sectors constitute one of the most important constraints in the use of labor-intensive methods. A good understanding of the exact nature of the available labor supply is essential in planning any labor-intensive works programs. Through continuing investigation of labor supply conditions in India and Kenya, an attempt will be made to develop simple predictive models which can be applied at the project or micro district level to forecast available labor, both local and migrant, on a seasonal basis.

(ii) *Adaption of Engineering Designs.* Research should be pursued of the performance characteristics of alternative road designs which may extend the feasible range for labor-intensive technologies. Possible areas for investigation include: compaction standards, aggregate gradation standards, use of larger aggregates in pavements, and surface tolerance specifications for premix surfaces.

(iii) *Equipment Research and Development.* While the introduction of suitable tools and equipment selected from existing technologies has resulted in significant productivity improvements compared to traditional manual methods, the limited research that has been undertaken to develop and test more innovative concepts has not been encouraging, as discussed in the third section.

At this stage it is not clear to what extent further research can lead to useful investigations, particularly with respect to scaling down of equipment. Attention is being given to identifying specific areas where the scope for development of new or modified equipment would appear most promising. Subsequent research would then be subcontracted to institutions with established capacities in design engineering.

FOOTNOTES

1. The World Bank study is being supported by the Governments of Canada, Denmark, Finland, Germany, Japan, Norway, Sweden, United Kingdom and United States, and by the World Bank. The Governments of India and Indonesia have collaborated with the Bank in the study. The International Labour Organization has also been examining similar issues within the broad framework of the World Employment Programme.

2. The term 'wage rate' as used in this paper may be interpreted either as the market wage (including any allowances for housing, transport, etc.) if these reflect the real economic cost of employing labor, or as the opportunity cost of labor if distortions exist in the labor market. However, in cases where the market wage is above the break-even wages for labor-intensive methods but the opportunity cost of labor is lower there are special problems associated with implementation of labor-intensive methods which are not treated in the present paper.

3. Prices of equipment have increased substantially (about 75 percent) since 1973, thus improving the competitiveness of labor methods.

4. Cost comparisons for earthworks are treated in greater detail in Technical Memoranda No. 3.7.12.13.17.18.19 and 20.

5. See World Bank Staff Working Paper No. 224, "Public Works Programs in Developing Countries" (February 1976) for a comparative review of 24 labor-intensive works programs in 14 countries.

6. See World Bank Staff Working Paper No. 223, "Some Aspects of Unskilled Labor Markets for Civil Construction in India: Observations Based on Field Investigation" (November 1975). Follow-up work is continuing.

7. The migratory labor are provided with either extremely modest or no accomodation at all on site. Low-cost huts are built by the labor for accommodation.

8. See "Iron Deficiency Anemia and the Productivity of Adult Males in Indonesia", **IBRD Staff Working Paper No. 175** (April 1974)

9. Heywood, Peter F., "Malnutrition and Productivity in Jamaican Sugar Cane Cutters", Ph. D. Dissertation (unpublished), Cornell University, Ithaca, Cornell, 1974

WORLD BANK STUDY OF THE SUBSTITUTION OF LABOR & EQUIPMENT IN CIVIL CONSTRUCTION
Reports and Technical Memoranda

A. Study Reports

Study of the Substitution of Labor and Equipment in Road Construction, Phase I: Final Report (IBRD, October 1971)

Study of the Substitution of Labor and Equipment in Civil Construction, Phase II: Final Report (IRBD, Staff Working Paper No. 172, January 1974).

Iron Deficiency Anemia and the Productivity of Adult Males in Indonesia (IBRD, Staff Working Paper No. 175, April 1974)

Some Aspects of Unskilled Labor Markets for Civil Construction in India: Observations Based on Field Investigations (IBRD, Staff Working Paper No. 223, November 1975).

B. Technical Memoranda Available as at June 30, 1976
Technical Memorandum No. 1
Comparison of Alternative Design Wheelbarrows for Haulage in Civil Construction Tasks, January 1975

A comparison is made of productivity in haulage of different design of wheelbarrows. Two-wheel and one-wheel barrows,

solid tired v.s. pneumatic rubber tired barrows, and ball-bearing vs. bushed bearing wheels for barrows are investigated. On the basis of 6 weeks of trials, it is concluded that a lightweight, single-wheel barrow with a scooter-tire and ball-bearing wheels, is the most economicial type of wheelbarrow of earth haulage. (See also Technical Memorandum No. 13 (October 1975)).

Technical Memorandum No. 2
Increasing Output of Manual Excavation By Work Reorganization: An Example of Passing Place Construction on a Mountain Road
January 1975

The Paper demonstrates the need for proper organization of labor-intensive tasks of civil construction. It is shown that for excavation and hauling activities, labor productivity can be increased two to three fold with

  (i) proper work organization,
  (ii) incentive payment methods, and

(iii) proper selection and maintenance of hand tools.

Work was carried out on a passing place construction on a mountain road in northern India. Using the improved organization and work procedures, output per man-hour for excavation and haulage of earth was increased from 0.11 cubic meters to 0.28 cubic meters.

Technical Memorandum No. 3
Comparison of Different Modes of Haulage in Earthworks
June 1975

A comparison is made of the economics of earthmoving using different combinations of labor and capital. The range of alternatives varies from entirely labor-intensive methods to fully equipment-intensive methods. Intermediate technologies are introduced based on the usage of better modes of manual haulage and with the use of animals. The intermediate technologies are found to be generally economical for unskilled labor wage rates of $0.75 per day or less. Equipment-intensive methods are found to be optimal for wage rates of over $1.00 per day. The traditional labor-intensive methods are not found to be efficient under any assumptions of wage rates.

Technical Memorandum No. 4
Effect of Health and Nutrition Status of Road Construction Workers in Northern India on Productivity
January 1975

A pilot study was conducted to assess the health and nutrition status of a population of road construction workers in the mountainous region of Northern India. Clinical, dietary and biochemical analyses were carried out for a sample of 198 workers belonging to two distinct groups. In addition, the output of workers in haulage was measured over a period of six weeks. A number of health and nutritional deficiencies were observed. Among these were vitamins A and B complex, calories, fats, serum folic acid and red cell folate. Significant variations in work output were observed. Output of one population labor was positively correlated with homatocritic levels, but no such correlation existed for the other population. For both groups, output was strongly correlated with height, weight and arm circumference. However, because of several limitations of data, it was not possible to relate work output to any of the other health and nutrition variables. It is believed that these effects would be discernible in an intervention study in which intervention is undertaken to correct one or more deficiencies. Future work is planned in this direction.

Technical Memorandum No. 5
Comparison of Hand-Laid and Machine-Laid Road Surfaces
February 1975

A comparison is made of the quality of hand-laid with machine-laid road surfaces on a surfacing project in India. The machine-laid surface was found to be markedly superior with a rideability ratio of 2.5. Densities of asphaltic concrete for the two methods were similar. However, the cost of hand-laid surface was considerably lower than that of the paver-laid surface under Indian conditions. It should be noted that the surfacing by hand was carried out using labor who had no training in the operation and who did not employ even elementary tools. It is felt that the quality of hand-laid surface could be significantly improved by making a few simple changes. Future work is planned in this area.

Technical Memorandum No. 6
Haulage with Lift of Materials: Lifting Sand by Ropeway
February 1975

In labor-intensive haulage activities, labor productivity is reduced substantially if the materials have to be lifted over more than a certain height. This paper describes an experiment in which sand was to be hauled over a distance of 100 meters and a lift of 18 meters. Manual productivity was increased three-fold by the introduction of a ropeway arrangement which was manually operated. Applications of such an arrangement are possible in construction of embankments and in haulage of excavated materials from canal beds.

Technical Memorandum No. 7
Productivity Rates of Earthmoving Machines
May 1975

This paper attempts to arrive at some agreement as to what could be considered as "average" productivity of machines used for earth haulage. It studies the productivities of four basic machines -- bull-dozers, motorized scrapers, towed scrapers, and

front-end loaders -- from various sources and under varying conditions. By comparing the various sources of productivity and the way machine productivity is affected by both the mechanical and the job condition characteristics, the paper recommends some adjustment factors that could be used to calculate machine productivities of Caterpillar equipment.

A "Supplement to Technical Memorandum No. 7" was published in August 1975.

Technical Memorandum No. 8
A Field Manual for the Collection of Productivity Data from Civil Construction Projects
July 1975

The collection of productivity data is the first (and last) step in any systematic procedure for choosing the "appropriate" technology to carry out a particular civil construction project. This manual describes a system for productivity data collection that is simple and concise enough for field use. It is specifically designed for application to labor-intensive construction projects.

Technical Memorandum No. 9
Report of First Road Demonstration Project
August 1975

A summary is given of observations and measurements taken during one construction season (1974) for a mountain road project in northwest India. In addition to recording overall productivities for the season's work, experiments and/or studies were made of the main operations, including earthworks (formation cutting), aggregate production, the transportation of materials, the laying of sub-base and base layers, and surfacing work. It was concluded that measurable improvements in productivity of labor-intensive tasks was achieved by the re-organization of work procedures and/or the use of modified or new equipment.

Technical Memorandum No. 10
A System of Deriving Rental Charges for Construction Equipment
August 1975

This paper investigates the requirements and aims of costing procedures for plant and equipment on civil engineering projects with particular reference to developing countries. Various existing systems of equipment rental charges are examined and a particular system is recommended for use by public works authorities in developing countries. Methods for derivation of the various elements of the charging system are described in detail.

Technical Memorandum No. 11
A Literature Review of the Ergonomics of Labor-Intensive Civil Construction
August 1975

This is a summary report of a literature study of the ergonomics of labor-intensive civil construction tasks. Some examples of potential uses of the subject are included in the appendices. The conclusion is reached that further work is necessary to make full use of this science.

Technical Memorandum No. 12
Haulage by Headbaskets, Shoulder Yokes and Other Manual Load-Carrying Methods
October 1975

This memorandum describes the use of headbaskets, shoulder yokes and other manual load-carrying methods traditionally used in civil construction. In addition, relationships for estimating productivity using headbaskets are presented, based on a simple theoretical work cycle "calibrated" by using the results of production studies currently available. An illustrative example is also given showing how the cost of headbasket haulage can be calculated by using the productivity data presented.

Technical Memorandum No. 13
The Use of Wheel barrows in Civil Construction
October 1975

This memorandum describes the characteristics of wheelbarrows, the mechanics of their use, various aspects of their design and features of wheelbarrow working, all with particular reference to the task of haulage in civil construction. In addition, relationships for estimating productivity using wheelbarrows are presented, based on a simple work cycle that has been calibrated by using the results of productivity studies currently available.

An earlier memorandum (No. 1) dealt with some limited experiments with wheelbarrows. This memorandum describes new work which is complementary to those experiments.

Technical Memorandum No. 14
Hardware Research Summary
October 1975
This memorandum outlines the investigations into the field of hardware made in the Study to date. A summary is given of the scope of future work planned, or needed, in construction hardware research for labor-intensive and intermediate technologies, primarily in connection with tasks related to earthworks.

Technical Memorandum No. 15
The Planning and Control of Production, Productivity and Costs in Civil Construction Project
October 1975
The planning and efficient control of production, productivity and costs in a civil construction project is the major task of site management. This memorandum briefly discusses planning and describes a control system which should assist site managers to make sound decisions based on measurements and should assist planners to have more reliable data for future projects. The system described is complementary to and compatible with the Manual for Productivity Data Collection, already issued as Technical Memorandum No. 8 of this series. It is specifically designed for use in labor-intensive construction projects.

Technical Memorandum No. 16
Lever Cranes
October 1975
This memorandum describes the testing of two types of manually-powered lever cranes on a canal excavation site in Indonesia. Traditionally soil is moved by headbaskets on such sites and this involves the haulers lifting their own bodyweight as well as their payload when working over a rising grade. It was felt that by lifting the load alone some improvement in productivity could be obtained. The report shows that if lever cranes are used for this haulage activity several factors combine to reduce the productivity markedly below that for headbasket haulage and concludes that manually-powered lever cranes appear to have little application in civil construction, except for a very few special circumstances.

Technical Memorandum No. 17
Compaction
December 1975
This paper reviews the techniques applicable to compaction on labor-intensive projects. It does not purport to be a treatise on compaction, but discusses the on-going processes as noted by observers in various countries and examines the results of an intervention study carried out on a canal construction project in Indonesia where the productivity of various types of simple equipment, powered by animals or humans, was measured.

Technical Memorandum No. 18
Spreading Activities in Civil Construction
December 1975
Spreading is a common but frequently minor activity in civil construction. During the study observations have been made of on-going methods in earthworks and pavement construction, including surfacing. This memorandum summarises the results of these observations and concludes that for non-bituminous materials there is a relationship between the productivity (expressed as output per man-hour, etc.) and the layer thickness. It also appears that spreading bituminous materials requires less effort than that needed for non-bituminous materials of similar thickness.

Technical Memorandum No. 19
Excavation
February 1976
The activity of excavation is basic to all civil engineering projects to a greater or lesser extent. This paper presents excavation data from sites in India and Indonesia largely from observations of on-going work, but in some instances intervention techniques, such as pre-ripping by plough, were applied. It is found that in many cases the excavation activity is inextricably connected with the loading activity and that in general labor-intensive methods are very similar in cost to, and often somewhat cheaper than, equipment-intensive methods. The use of tracked or wheeled machines for excavation alone is substantially more expensive than manual excavation.

Technical Memorandum No. 20
Loading and Unloading Activities
February 1976
The loading and unloading of materials into or from vehicles and other equipment are activities which occur on all civil construction projects. During the study observations have been made of manual loading and unloading of a variety of equipment using hard tools. This memorandum summarizes the results of these observations. A full statistical analysis of the data shows that productivity is significantly affected by the payment method being used and the level of supervision.

Technical Memorandum No. 21
A Literature Review of the Work Output of Animals with Particular Reference to their Use in Civil Construction
February 1976
This is a summary report of a literature study of the work output of animals and the factors which affect animal productivity. It is intended as a complementary memorandum to Technical Memorandum No. 11 on human ergonomics, and should be read in conjunction with it. The conclusion is reached that further work is necessary and that special attention should be paid to the work of animals when used on civil construction tasks and to particular problems this work may cause.

Technical Memorandum No. 22
Haulage Using Aerial Ropeways
June 1976
This paper discusses the results of experimental field studies with ropeways, and outlines the scope for using aerial ropeways in labor-intensive construction work. It is shown that in appropriate circumstances a simple ropeway installation can give significant reduction in unit cost of haulage compared with manual load carrying.
(Note: Part of the technical material in this paper formed the subject of a previous memorandum in this series (No. 6) entitled 'Haulage with Lift of Materials, Lifting Sand by Ropeway'.)

Technical Memorandum No. 23
The Use of Rail Systems in Civil Construction
June 1976
This memorandum describes the methods of assessing the suitability of rail systems for haulage work in civil construction and describes various types of systems used experimentally for such work in India.

Technical Memorandum No. 24
The Use of Agricultural Tractor/Trailer Combinations
June 1976
This memorandum describes the use of agricultural tractors to haul construction materials in trailers, it explains the problems in their use and ways of overcoming these problems. Various options are discussed, such as the choice between two- and four-wheeled trailers, tipping trailers and ballasting of the tractor. A large portion of the memorandum is devoted to the question of load transfer from trailer to tractor and to the manner in which this affects the traction available to the tractor. The paper gives a numerical guide to the selection of appropriate combinations of tractor and trailer size for a given haul route surface and gradient, followed by an explanation of how to calculate the numbers of laborers and trailers required. Detailed instructions for calculating productivity and unit costs are given, and the relative merits, in cost terms, of truck and tractor/trailer haulage are discussed. The memorandum ends with a review of other implements available for use in conjunction with tractors, such as rippers, graders and rollers.

Technical Memorandum No. 25
Aggregate Production
June 1976
Aggregates are extensively used in civil construction and the cost of their production is often a significant part of the total project cost. If suitable aggregates can be gathered (with or without screening) from sources close to the site, then this will probably be the cheapest method of production. However, it is usually necessary to crush or break quarried rock and/or collected boulders to produce aggregate of an acceptable size, shape and strength. These tasks are carried out by equipment-intensive crushers or by labor-intensive methods using hammers. Although a crushing plant can be highly automated, a significant number of laborers can be employed with small-scale equipment for such activities as loading and hauling to stockpiles.

This memorandum discusses aggregate production with particular reference to labor-intensive and semi-labor-intensive methods, and given the results of field observations of productivity. As a result of these observations it is concluded that for hand-breaking of stone the size, shape and construction of the hammer is important, and more attention needs to be given to the steel used for the hammer head. In addition, there appears to be a relationship between manpower required for manual breaking and the size of product, reduction factor, and hardness of the rock being processed.

Cost comparisons at a daily wage rate of U.S. $0.5 suggest that there is a break-even aggregate size between 15 and 25 mm above which manual breaking is generally cheaper than using crushers. At that wage rate and for 1975 costs, the cost of producing aggregates are, typically, about U.S. $0.1 per tonne for 150 mm output size, U.S. $0.8 per tonne for 50 mm size and U.S. $2.0 per tonne for 15 mm size.

Rural road planning in developing countries

by

E. D. TINGLE

Overseas Unit, Transport and Road Research Laboratory, England

INTRODUCTION

In an age of uncertainty one thing is certain: the poor of the world are getting poorer while the rich are getting richer. It is now seen that in the last 25 years of national and international effort the pattern of development has often resulted in growing disparities between the living standards of countries and also in many developing countries between classes in the same country. In an age that has seen massive economic growth for the world as a whole there are still about 40 developing countries where the annual income per head is less than $200. Thirty per cent of the world's population, 1200 million people, live in these countries. Even in those countries of the Third World which are above this poverty line it is often the case that the benefit of over half the national income goes to less than one quarter of the population. The poor countries are those that rely almost entirely on agricultural production and where 80-90 per cent of the population live in rural areas by subsistence or near subsistence farming. It is these facts that have led to new thinking nationally and internationally about directions for development and new policies of aid to developing countries. Indeed "a widespread current view among analysts of the development process is that, unless specific action is taken to assist the poorest groups directly, relative poverty will increase and any reduction in the numbers of people living in a state of absolute poverty will be painfully slow". This view implies that more should be done to ensure that a higher proportion of aid should directly benefit not only the poorest countries but the poorest people in these countries. As most of these people live in rural areas, any new aid strategy should not only put new emphasis on programmes oriented towards the relief of poverty within countries but should give specific emphasis to rural development.

This emphasis, present in much international thinking about development, highlights the need for improved transport in rural areas and requires a re-appraisal of conventional methods of rural transport planning. Following a recommendation adopted by the OECD Steering Committee for Road Research a Joint Working Group was formed with the OECD Development Centre to consider the problems of planning roads and other transport facilities in rural areas of developing countries. It is the object of this paper to discuss the wider issues involved in the light of the conclusions of this Joint Working Group.

TRANSPORT PLANNING METHODS

In the ideal situation a transport planner sets out to devise transport facilities to help a society to achieve the wider economic and social goals it has set itself. He cannot properly begin his task before these goals are described in sufficient detail for him to translate them into the needs for moving goods and people. Far too often, however, the planner's task has been seen only in terms of improving an existing facility for the benefit of those who will use it.

Transport planning techniques have been substantially developed only in industrialised countries and where there was in existence an extensive and largely unplanned transport system. Inadequate track standards and traffic congestion was already leading to costly delays to users and to pollution of the environment. The problems first appeared in extreme form in cities. The main techniques which were devised were oriented to the alleviation of these urban problems and were developed for application within the constraints of the urban scene.

The beneficiaries of improvements could be closely identified as present and future users of the system. There was considerable experience of the past growth and characteristics of traffic which could be used with some confidence to predict future growth. Since high levels and already been reached growth was relatively small and prediction that much more certain.

In developing countries the role of transport has often been seen in the past as "catalytic" to development in the sense that provision of a transport facility has been assumed to be sufficient in itself to open up a region and so stimulate economic growth and improve social conditions within its area of influence. Roads were needed in rural areas where no vehicle yet moved. It is paradoxical therefore that the techniques adopted for planning transport intended to stimulate growth in rural areas were derived very largely from the existing complex methods devised to alleviate the urban congestion in industrialised countries. This is paradoxical but not surprising. Some success had been claimed for the application of existing transport planning techniques, mainly in cities in North America. No tested alternative existed for a developing country to use. Foreign experts commissioned to help with transport planning tended to use the techniques with which they were familiar in their own country.

In most recent years the deficiences of the 'transferred technology' approach to transport planning in developing countries were clearly seen and several attempts to broaden the basis for planning were made. In particular research workers have attempted to clarify the relationship between transport investment and increased agricultural production. These broadened approaches have been reviewed by the OECD Working Party in their report. The conclusion was that there was no tried and tested method of allocating finance for transport that could achieve optimum development impact.

RURAL ROAD TRANSPORT APPRAISAL

It is probably true to say that the broader issues of transport planning have received less attention than the appraisal of discrete transport projects. Developing countries, international lending agencies and aid donor countries have concentrated their efforts in finding answers to two main questions:

Is the project to construct a transport facility justifiable in economic terms?

How can competing projects be ranked in priority order?

The urgency with which these questions have been posed, often occasioned by the conviction that transport was a seminal requirement for development, have tended to deflect thinking into the confines of sectoral planning and away from comprehensive development planning and the need to reconcile physical, economic and social aspects.

Again, methods of transport project appraisals in developing countries have in the past relied heavily on these familiar methods established in industrialized countries for projects to relieve traffic congestion. Some form of conventional cost-benefit analysis was used. At its simplest this implied first assessing the cost of constructing or improving the facility, in most cases a road. The benefits were then identified as cost savings accruing to the vehicle operators using the road. Existing traffic was measured in volume and weight. It is crucial both to the calculation of cost and of benefit that an accurate estimate is made of future volumes, weights and speeds of traffic which will use the facility. The structural standards to which the road is designed begin with consideration of the load it will bear in terms of repetitions of application of axle-weights; the geometric standard to considerations of volume dimensions and speed of traffic. The standards adopted determine the cost of construction or improvements.

The aim of the project was normally envisaged as relief of congestion and thus benefits could be uniquely identified as road user cost saving in time, vehicle operating costs, accident cost savings and the like. Again the estimate of cost savings is directly related to future traffic volumes.

Future increases in traffic are usually predicted in three categories, normal, diverted and generated. Normal traffic is defined as the traffic that will materialize whether the road investment is made or not. Forecasts are made from a knowledge of past trends in traffic growth, sometimes by linear extrapolation but more usually by sophisticated methods using relationships between income and vehicle ownership and usage or between land-uses and trip making. Diverted traffic is that which switched from use of another road or another mode because of a perceived cost saving if the new facility is used. Generated traffic is defined as that traffic other than diverted traffic which is induced to use the projected road by the reduction in transport costs.

Those traffic estimates used in conventional cost-benefit analyses of road transport projects encounter difficulties and inadequacies when applied to roads in rural areas in developing countries. In these areas of low traffic and low economic activity it is obviously inadequate to use past traffic trends as a basis for future forecasting. When the aim is to increase economic activity rapidly and perhaps to modify drastically the mode of agricultural production, it is unlikely that a study of the present situation will give any useful guide to the planned future. It is indeed very unlikely that improved transport will be the sole input needed to stimulate the changes although it may be essential. Thus in the conventional analysis benefits are measured too specifically and attributed too narrowly.

In these circumstances it is surprising how much reliance was placed on appraisal methods for road projects in developing countries that were only a slight modification of those conventionally used in developed countries. These necessarily favoured projects for inter-urban roads, highways in which traffic was already appreciable and often growing rapidly. It is arguable that such infrastructure was, in any case, a prerequisite framework into which future development of feeder roads could be fitted. On the other hand application of conventional appraisal technique was inappropriate for the myriad of low-volume, low-cost roads needed for a strategy of regional development of agriculture and small scale industry. Investment in these roads was difficult to appriase and they were neglected.

A BROADENED APPROACH TO RURAL ROAD APPRAISAL

Case-studies of road planning in rural areas in developing countries were critically reviewd by the OECD Working Group. Many of these measured an increase in agricultural production that occured when roads were built. They pointed to one fairly obvious method of improving road project appraisal. The benefits derived from this increased producer surplus could be added to those derived from road user savings. This is a sensible approach but in application has shown many deficiencies. For increased agricultural production investments in fertilisers, irrigation, agricultural extension services may be equally necessary and may be large. Thus those analyses that attribute the total increase in production to road investment alone are clearly inadequate. Even those that go further and deduct the cost of other investments from the cost side of the equation perpetuate the fallacy by assuming that these other investments have no net benefit.

The World Bank, aware of the deficiencies in project appraisal for the sharpened emphasis it was giving to policies to benefit the small farmer in rural areas, have developed a broadened approach to the economic appraisal of rural roads. [1] The method devised does not represent a sharp break with current practice but by focussing on the analysis of changes in farm income, explicitly orients the evaluation towards the main target beneficiaries of rural road projects. A 'producer surplus' analysis is made which quantifies the developmental impact of transport cost savings and complementary investments within the area of influence of a road. This area is estimated as extending as far as the transport cost savings of the road project have an effect on agricultural production.

The forecast of developmental impact is based on a careful evaluation of the rural economy that is influenced. Three essential issues are examined: [2]

Producer Response

How will producers respond to higher farmgate prices, lower input costs and improved quality of service? Will the likely increase in farmgate prices be of sufficient magnitude to stimulate increased production?

Distribution of benefits

To whom do the transport cost savings accrue? How are they distributed among producers, truckers, traders, consumers and others affected by the road? What is the relation between the distribution of benefits and the structure of the economy reflected, for instance by land tenure patterns and the structure of the trucking industry?

Non-transport constraints

What constraints exist which might prevent the producer from responding to the incentive provided by the road project? Does the producer have the required resources, attitudes and risk preferences? And if he does not, what else needs to be done, by whom and when, to get the maximum impact from the road investment?

The net income (producer surplus) of farmers and transporters prior to the proposed investment is determined from an analysis of baseline data on crop areas and yields, production costs, ex-farm prices, marketed output and local consumption together with transport costs and prices. Changes in these data are then forecast if the proposed investment is made and subtracted from those changes that would have occured without the investment. By these means a benefit can be summed year by year and compared with costs of the project. A calculation is then made of a rate of return of the package of investments in transport combined with other complementary investments.

It is not suggested by the IBRD that this complex analysis is needed for all road projects in rural areas. It is accepted that there are cases in which the level of economic activity is high and the traffic demand sufficient to allow the traditional methods of road project appraisal to be used with confidence. As a guide the World Bank method suggests that roads with traffic levels of greater than 20-50 vehicles per day fall into this category. However, it is strongly recommended that estimated transport cost savings measured on the basis of predicted traffic levels should be supplemented by consideration of the distribution of their benefits. It may also be necessary to consider whether complementary investments are needed before the road project will produce the calculated benefit.

A second case applies to areas where the need for development is greatest, where economic activity is low and where the market economy is very weak. There may be no motorable roads or those that there are carry less than 20-50 vehicles per day. In most areas the considerably extended investigation of agricultural production, distribution and marketing systems required in the 'producer surplus' analysis outlined above is vital. Without it the justification of a transport investment is pure guess work.

After examination of the concepts and methods described by the World Bank in this broadened appraisal procedure the OECD Working Group concluded that it represented the best approach currently available - and strongly recommended its adoption. The Group and the World Bank recognise that no 'universal' method of project appraisal is conceivable and recognise also that the recommended approach has deficiencies. In basic concept it still relies very heavily on the assumption that an analysis in economic terms is sufficient. Consideration of stimulus to development from non-transport investments and from social, non-economic influences are treated as secondary. In practice the recommended method would require a massive data collection that may make the analysis of a project unacceptably high compared with its cost. Further research, some of it already under way, and experience from application of the method is still required. Never-the-less it is advocated in the interim to OECD member countries as a basis for a harmonised approach to investment studies of rural road transports.

TRANSPORT IN PLANNED RURAL DEVELOPMENT

For a truly fresh look at the problems of transport planning and transport project appraisal it is best to return to considering planning for rural development in a wide sense. Given that in the great majority of developing countries the basic infrastructure of main roads exists, even in rural areas, it is necessary to drop completely the concept that transport has any unique role: it is no more an initiator of growth than many other forms of investment. Successful rural development must be based on increased agricultural production of all kinds but it is probable that in the vast majority of cases this increase will not be stimulated by a separate sectoral investment. It seems probable that emphasis on planning for economic returns will not achieve alleviation of the poverty of the rural masses, nor stimulate the changes in rural society that will be necessary. Social factors that hinder progress should be analysed: for example provision of schools and hospitals may be equally necessary. Although literacy and health of the rural population may be goals in themselves they may also be indispensable steps for increased agricultural production. This argues that planning must integrate elements of economic and social advance with planned improvement of the physical infrastructure in a comprehensive policy for development. It should be made appropriate for the particular region at the particular time. In short there should be, in a fashionable phrase, integrated rural development.

Transport projects should now be seen as one element in a planned package of investments identified as needed for development. There can be little doubt that improved transport will be an urgent need in rural areas where there is emphasis on increasing agricultural production above subsistence levels. Crops must be grown for sale in the market. They must be carried to the market. The means of carriage is almost everywhere in these regions so inefficient and expensive that over very short distances the returns to farmer are negated. [3] Improved transport is vitally necessary although not of itself sufficient to effect the change to the market economy.

It is this ambiguity about the role of transport in development that has hidden what should come first. If development is to improve the level of living of the rural poor then development plans start with benefits to this group through increases in production and income, better health and literacy. Better transport is not a primary goal, it is a service to the achievement of the more basic goals. The benefits of better transport should not be relied on to 'trickle-down' to the poorer groups. Improved means of moving people and goods, improved transport infrastructure should be provided in a development programme only to the extent necessary to match the specific need for movement if the other basic goals are to be met. Where resources are scarce over-emphasis on transport can be counter-productive.

There are two important consequences for the appraisal and justification of road projects in an integrated approach to rural development if the view of the 'service' role of transport as expressed above is accepted. Provision of improved transport will in most cases be vital to the success of the development programme but no attempts will be made to attribute benefits to transport alone. In the economic analysis made to justify the investment package, benefits will be quantified in terms of achievement of economic and social goals. For example, in terms of the value of increased agricultural production or of improved health and education of the target group. The costs of transport provision, which include expenditure on road construction and maintenance will be added to the costs of the other inputs.

The second consequence affects the role of the transport planner in the multi-disciplined team necessary for pre-investment studies. In feasibility studies for ad-hoc transport projects the transport planner has normally been required to estimate the numbers of vehicles of various types which will use the proposed new or improved facility in the years after installation, in other words to assess accurately transport demand. But transport has an influence on nearly every aspect of integrated planning. An iterative approach showing how different levels of transport provision affect levels, spacing and timing of other inputs is an essential part of the process. The transport planner should, therefore, be a member of the planning team from the outset so that his particular expertise can be fed into the overall conceived in more fundamental terms than in terms of vehicle flows. The assessment of the nature, quantity and timing of goods movements and the requirements for personal mobility should properly be the role of those concerned with development of the natural resources of the region and of the planners of social advance, of improvements in health and education. It is the agricultural planner who should estimate how much tonnage of product should be moved and the marketing planner where it should be moved. The education planner should determine the need for children to move to the schools he plans; the medical planner how many people require access to the health centre.

The main role of the transport planner in the team will be to devise cost-effective ways of meeting this fundamental transport demand, not of assessing it. He should then adopt a 'system' approach in which there is an evaluation of the interaction between costs of track construction and maintenance on one hand and the cost of vehicle operation on the other. He should look into the important but neglected field of provision of vehicles that are more appropriate to the transport needs of specific developments and to the primitive tracks on which they may have to travel. He will also be freer than at present to consider using other transport modes and their co-ordination with road transport.

There is one particular area of transport improvement that may be of main importance in increasing the productivity of the farmer. It has been largely neglected by transport planners. This is in the movement of goods off the road or track. At present loads of produce are carried to the road by human porterage. Materials needed on the cultivated land such as fertilisers or anti-pest sprays are similarly loaded on heads or backs. Since the possible distances are low the area of cultivation and the penetration of improved agricultural practices are similarly limited. A careful examination is required of the needs for this kind of transport. An economic analysis, which takes into account social constraints and physical conditions of the terrain, should be made of ways of improving the efficiency of human muscle power by using bicycles, carts or barrows. Consideration of vehicles pulled by animals or moved by engines should follow. Where disposable income is very low even individual ownership of an imported bicycle may be impossible - so that questions of organisation of use and local manufacture of appropriate vehicles may be crucial.

FUTURE RESEARCH
Evaluation of transport projects

In the critical analysis made by the OECD Working Group of current methods of planning and appraising road projects in developing countries one of the notable features was the shortage of well-documented follow-up studies to ascertain the efficiency of evaluation procedures. Although the Group put forward the view that the broadened approach recommended by the World Bank is sufficiently developed to enable it to be used now as the basis for a common approach to transport investment appraisal in developing countries, it was concluded that there was need for more research.

The main emphasis should be to validate and improve the methods of transport planning and project evaluation for use in integrated rural development. The best approach will be to monitor socio-economic changes induced by a planned transport project. Beginning with the active cooperation of developing countries a number of rural development projects should be implemented on the basis of the integrated investment approach. It was recommended that there should be international cooperation to coordinate the research so that maximum impact could be rapidly obtained.

The studies envisaged are similar to and could complement those being carried out by the World Bank in Brazil, Ethiopia, Kenya, Madagascar and the Yemen. These studies use extensive and comprehensive collection of socio-economic data to describe the post-evaluation situation and the post-implementation situation as it develops. This data collection is likely to be an expensive exercise but it should be designed to provide information that will be of value for monitoring the total investment package and not solely the transport element.

A rapid international build-up of information will require a number of such post-evaluation studies carefully chosen to reinforce and complement one another. Land classification, a mapping technique involving the identification of natural patterns of landscape (land systems) from aerial photography, satellite imagery and field survey is being increasingly used to assess potential for agricultural development. It can thus be used for selection of research areas for the investment studies that are of similar potential and also for transfer of conclusions from one area to another. It could be used to aid research using cross-sectional as well as time-series analysis on a number of projects in a given region. The use of the imagery involved is well established for monitoring changes in agricultural land-use.

In this research, the need to simplify and cheapen planning and evaluation procedures for the low-cost rural transport required should be kept in the forefront. If good plans for this urgent development need are to be made they should be pragmatic and accomodated to the level of achievement of the developing country in question so that the plans can be implemented.

Research on cost-effective transport systems for rural areas

It is central to the ideas advocated by the Working Group that the provision of rural road transport should be as cost-effective as possible. There are already gaps in the knowledge of rural road construction which research should fill before integrated transport demand can be satisfied as effectively and as cheaply as possible. The Working Group made recommendations for a number of engineering research activities which should provide this essential information. These are concerned with the development of standards of construction and maintenance of extremely low cost roads; the cost effectiveness of simpler, cheaper and more flexible vehicles than those at present imported for use on the rural roads of less developed countries; the better use of indigenous materials for truly low cost roads, and further work on labour-intensive road construction methods which take account of the recent experience of countries which have adopted such methods with considerable success.

A Road Transport Investment Model [4] has been developed through international cooperation and the mathematical relationships from which it is constructed have been calibrated by field work in developing countries. Further development of the model and extension of the relationships are needed before it can be used to help decisions such as choice of road standards for the lowest level of rural road provision. Research is needed on the relationship for instance, of vehicle operating cost to roughness and geometry of earth roads.

The present choice of motorized vehicles for use on

rural roads in developing countries is at present often confined to those imported from industrialized countries. Research is needed on the trade-offs between road design and vehicle design to enable decisions on appropriate transport systems to be made. There is considerable evidence that a potential transport bottle-neck in rural areas in developing countries is lack of suitable vehicles for off-road, field or farm to road movements. Research is required on simple vehicles, motorized or muscle-powered for this purpose.

Roads in rural areas must use the earth materials of the terrain traversed; importation of material from any distance can increase the costs of construction many fold. The information on the occurrence and the basic properties of tropical soils and rock that does exist is inadequate and selection standards for road use borrowed from the practice in industrialized countries are inappropriate both to the materials and to the methods of construction best suited to developing countries. Research is needed to establish cost-effective procedures for using indigenous materials. The first step is to identify the resources of road building materials and to map their occurrence. This should be followed by measurement of basic properties in suitable laboratory tests and by performance testing in scientifically designed full-scale road experiments.

Rural areas in most developing countries have large scale unemployment or under employment. The decision needs to be made as to how far efforts should be made to use labour-intensive methods of building and maintaining roads, so providing jobs for a large workforce and using and developing local skills. The decision needs to take account of more than the strictly economic analysis of comparative costs of transport provision by capital-intensive versus labour-intensive means. In addition the possibility of continuing social effects of the alleviation of under-employment and the local acquisition of managerial and organisational skills of projects are accomplished by successful labour-intensive methods. Much work has recently been carried out by ILO [5] and the World Bank [6] into the comparison between labour and capital intensive methods of road construction. The studies have provided guidelines for the economic use of labour-intensive work but have concluded that in particular further research is needed into methods of work organisation. In this regard the special efforts and experience of countries such as Mexico and India should receive special study to determine how their successful methods can be translated into other environments.

Besides the question as to how far labour can be substituted for machines in transport technology, there is also the question for the Third World of developing and using in a new alternative technology appropriate to the physical environment, social condition and state of development and capable of evolving as development proceeds. Such a technolxgy should embrace both the building and maintenance of roads and eventually the vehicles which use them. It should be characterised by low capitalization costs and almost certainly by high employment of labour but should also embody the latest scientific understanding of the bases of the processes employed. Development of this appropriate technology would seem to be an ideal area for cooperation between transport research institutes in industrialised and less-developed countries.

ACKNOWLEDGEMENT

The work described in this paper forms part of the programme of the Transport and Road Research Laboratory and the paper is published by permission of the Director.

Grateful thanks are due to the members of the OECD Joint Working Group from France, Germany, Norway, Spain, the United States of America and the World Bank. It was their contributions and constructive criticism that enabled members of the Overseas Unit of the TRRL to fulfil the task of preparing the report which is summarised above.

REFERENCES

[1] Carnemark C., J. Biderman and D. Bovet. The economic analysis of rural road projects. **World Bank Staff Working Paper** No 241. Washington, August 1976. (International Bank for Reconstruction and Development)

[2] Carnemark, C., The World Bank and rural roads. **Paper presented to the International Road Federation III African Highway Conference, Abidjan, 24-30 October 1976.** (International Bank for Reconstruction and Development)

[3] Clark, C and M. R. Haswell. **Economics of subsistence agriculture.** London 1964. (MacMillan)

[4] Bulman J. N. and R. Robinson. A road transport investment model for developing countries. **Paper to be presented to the World Conference on Transport Research,** Rotterdam, 26-28 April 1977

[5] Sud I. K., C. G. Harral and B. P. Coukis. Scope for the substitution of labour and equipment in civil construction. **Paper for Panel Discussion, Indian Roads Congress 37th Annual Session, Bhopal, December 1976.** (Indian Roads Congress)

[6] Allal M. and G. A. Edmonds (in collaboration with A. S. Bhalla). **Manual on the planning of labour-intensive road construction.** Geneva 1977. (International Labour Office)

Mobility problems and solutions for elderly, handicapped, and poor persons in the United States

by

ARTHUR SALTZMAN

University of California, Irvine, California

ALICE E. KIDDER

Transportation Institute

North Carolina Agricultural and Technical State University,
Greensboro, N.C.

with the assistance of

RICHARD WATT

INTRODUCTION

At some time in his life, virtually everyone has been transportation disadvantaged. The most common occurrence that restricts mobility is when a person temporarily does not have an automobile available to make a trip. A good example is when the one-family auto needs repairs and it is out of commission or temporarily being used by another member of the family. The simple solution to this mobility problem is to wait for the auto to return home or get it repaired.

A more serious problem occurs when a person is unable to drive an automobile or is not sufficiently wealthy to purchase and maintain one. It is this group that is generally defined as "transportation disadvantaged".

Practically all of the research, demonstration and legislation concerning persons who could be considered transportation disadvantaged have focused on three sub-sets of this group; namely elderly persons, persons who are physically or mentally handicapped, and poor persons. These groups are by no means small. Various estimates indicate that in the United States between 70 million [3] and 100 million [4] are either elderly, handicapped or poor. This wide numerical range is indicative of the definitional problem inherent in trying to count the number of persons who are transportation disadvantaged. For example, the definition of who is elderly is somewhat arbitrary. Usually persons above 65 years are considered elderly by Federal and State agencies, but some local social service programs are extended to all those over 55. A more serious issue is that not all persons over 65 have severe mobility problems. Equating age with immobility is a gross oversimplification.

Defining all persons who are physically or mentally handicapped as transportation disadvantaged, also poses some problems. First, there is no professional consensus on who is handicapped. Second, not all handicapped persons have severe transportation problems.

The problem of classifying poor persons is one that has vexed every agency that has tried to deal with low-income individuals. What should be the measure of poverty? It is generally accepted that household income is a reasonable measure of wealth and the ability to purchase adequate transportation is directly dependent on income level, as will be seen in another portion of this paper. Since some low-income persons do not own a car, but use

other auto-oriented solutions to journey to work, the term "transportation disadvantaged" may apply for some trip purposes but not others.

Adequate public transportation would seem to be the solution for the transportation disadvantaged. But there are many indications that current transit systems are far from being adequate. Both rail rapid transit lines and fixed-route bus operations offer a solution to some transportation demands, but the services they offer are not sufficient to serve all the needs of those with mobility problems. Barriers to the use of conventional mass transit include some which are physical, and others which are operational. For example, the difficulty a handicapped person would have in negotiating a high step on a bus is a physical barrier, whereas insufficient route coverage resulting in long walks to bus stops would be an operational barrier for many of the elderly. In addition to these physical and operational factors are psychological barriers, such as fear of assault which can affect any potential rider. Finally, there is the standard transit fare which can be an economic barrier to the poor.

Perhaps the overriding barrier in conventional public transportation is that it does not take people to where they want to go. On the level of ubiquity, transit is still radially oriented and does not usually allow for good service unless the destination or origin of travel is the central business district. With respect to convenience, conventional transit cannot provide door-to-door service.

Moreover the transit industry has until recently paid very little attention to the mobility needs of the transportation disadvantaged. It is extremely costly to provide the specialized transportation needed by this group. In an era of declining patronage, most operators have been concerned with cutting costs rather than with expanding services for any special sub-groups. Thus, providing special services for elderly, handicapped and poor persons has been a low priority item for transit operations. [1]

There have been a few isolated cases of innovation by the transit operator but this has usually occurred when general services were being substantially improved as a result of a newly implemented dial-a-ride system, as for example in Rochester, New York. At other times innovation has occurred when a public planning agency has made and implemented a specific policy on serving elderly and handicapped persons. For example, the Regional Transit District in Denver decided to provide a special service for elderly and handicapped persons and implemented an effective but rather costly system. Few have followed Denver's commitment to a substantial effort to serve the transportation disadvantaged. However, as a result of recent legislation which would deny them federal funds unless they include the transportation disadvantaged in their planning, virtually every transit system in the country now has transportation disadvantaged as one of its priorities.

A plethora of social service and health agencies have responded to the lack of adequate transit for their clients by initiating their own transit systems. These systems range in size from single vehicles that provide monthly trips to large (e.g. 300 vehicles), statewide coordinated systems such as the Delaware Authority for Special Transportation. It is not surprising that these health and social service agencies have opted for non-conventional, para-transit, transportation operations. These para-transit options are usually more demand-responsive than the conventional fixed-route, fixed-schedule transit. Vehicles are dispatched only when some demand has been established. Operations are personalized, and frequently provide door-to-door service in small vehicles.

These systems were not initiated by transportation planners. Agency directors who perceived mobility needs among many of their clients decided to start a system to handle their needs. This is a significant fact and should not be overlooked in the future planning of transit for the transportation disadvantaged. The persons who developed these systems usually had no technical expertise in transit per se. They simply recognized the problem and went at it the best way they knew how.

Fortunately, few of them were aware of the "urban transportation planning process" and did not use sophisticated models to develop their systems. Using a "seat of the pants" approach, they identified the location of their clients and tried to provide door-to-door service to meet their most critical transportation needs.

Various government surplus vehicles were acquired and elderly or unemployed drivers were often hired. Sometimes repairs were being done by local garages or county maintenance departments, and when social service agency vehicles did not have priority, a reliable pattern of vehicle availability was not assured. In most cases a preventive maintenance schedule did not exist.

It is very easy to be critical of the poor planning and management exhibited by most of these systems, but these operations have provided door-to-door services that have had significant positive impact on their passengers.

TRAVEL NEEDS

The introductory statement defined the transportation disadvantaged as those who have no access to an automobile. While this is a useful statement for general descriptive purposes, a more precise and analytical definition is necessary in considering this group's travel needs, as well as proposed solutions. [2] More precision can be achieved by using a measure that can be compared among each of the disadvantaged groups. Thus for describing the degree of disadvantage, data on trip frequency per person will be the prime determinant. A transportation disadvantaged person is defined as one who takes fewer trips per person per day than one who is not disadvantaged. This procedure is modified from one used by researchers on a detailed study on the urban transportation disadvantaged. [6] Some caution is necessary in using this measure. Although the relative degree of transportation disadvantaged can be indicated by comparing trip rates among groups, it should not be assumed that the transportation disadvantaged will utilize as many daily trips as the general population, when a transit, as opposed to a personal auto, mode is available. Thus, planners should be warned against using this gap analysis technique as a way of predicting, for example, the additional trips a group of elderly persons will take if an innovative transit system is provided. Even when provided with vastly improved transit, few among the disadvantaged will take the number of trips per day of the non-disadvantaged population.

Trip rates do however, provide one measure of transportation disadvantage. In the following sections the trip rates, major travel problems, and characteristics of each of the prime groups identified as being transportation disadvantaged, will be discussed.

The poor

The poor are one of the most readily identifiable groups of the transportation disadvantaged. They are, because of lack of sufficient income, unable to meet conveniently their travel needs and desires. Low incomes result in low trip making rates as indicated in Table I. The household trip rate for those with annual in-

Table I – Annual passenger car trip rates, vehicle-miles of travel per household, and average trip length by household income

Annual Household Income	Trip Rate per Household	Vehicle-miles per Household	Average Trip Length
Dollars	Number	Number	Miles
Under 4,000	580	4,708	8.1
4,000-9,999	1,433	12,262	8.6
10,000-14,999	1,949	17,497	9.0
15,000 and over	2,526	24,410	9.7

Source: Report No. 7 of the National Personal Transportation survey. "Household Travel in the United States," Federal Highway Administration, Washington, D. C., December 1972.

comes over $4,000 is much higher than for those with lower incomes. Many trips desired by the poor are not being made. Of course, the intervening variable between incomes and trip rates is auto ownership. Data from 1971 show that while only 20% of all U. S. households were without an auto, 46% of households with under $3,000 annual earnings did not own an auto. [6] Furthermore, since many of the autos owned by the poor are old and not in good operating condition, the mere availability of an auto does not necessarily guarantee mobility.

If income is held constant, members of carless households seem to take about one trip less per person per day than did people from one-car households. The difference in the total number of trips is much greater, however, between zero and one-car households than between one and two-car households. [6]

The location of carless individuals also has a considerable effect on available transportation alternatives and, therefore, on trip making rates.

In the larger cities where public transportation is more readily available, the trip frequency gap between individuals with and without an auto is reduced. In these cities, transit is used for a much larger percentage of trips taken by carless individuals. The situation is different in sparsely populated areas. In smaller cities, ride sharing and car borrowing by carless households exist to a much greater degree.[8] These informal methods, however, do not allow poor residents of smaller cities the mobility afforded them by the better transit systems of the larger cities.

Inner city poor and non-whites

There are special transportation problems associated with the poor and non-whites, including Blacks, Puerto Ricans, Chicanos, Orientals and American Indians, who live in inner cities of major metropolitan areas. The lack of adequate areawide coverage by many inner city public transit systems has been, in part, responsible for the lack of access to jobs, and very critical services. More specifically, the decentralization of jobs and services as a result of suburban growth, has not been followed by the development of a convenient transit system that inner city residents can use to reach desired work and non-work destinations. [9]

The relationship between race and transportation is also an important issue because even when income is held constant, minority group members across the nation take from .4 to .9 fewer non-work trips per person per day than do whites. [5] Non-whites are most disadvantaged, when compared with whites, in their trip rates to social/recreational activities and in the frequency with which they shop.

Mode choice data are also revealing. When comparing the percent of public transportation used by both inner city whites and non-whites, one finds that non-whites are more dependent on public transportation than whites. This relationship is true within each income group of inner city residents.

Finally, many of the trips made by the non-whites and the poor are walking trips, partly because of the densely populated neighborhoods in which many of them live. This larger number of walking trips, however, does not negate the fact that the poor and non-whites make considerably less trips than higher income persons.[6].

The elderly

One group of the transportation disadvantaged which has been the focus of considerable attention from researchers in recent years has been the elderly of our society. The elderly are a significant portion of our population and will continue to increase as a proportion of our total population. In 1970, there were 20 million Americans over age 65, of which about 65 percent lived in urban or suburban areas. It is estimated that there will be 28 million by the year 2000.[10]

There are two major factors associated with the elderly's transportation problems. The first is that many have limited income and are not able to pay for automobile or taxi expenses. The second factor relates to the physical health of the elderly as a handicap in operating an automobile, as well as in riding conventional transit systems. Auditory and visual problems of many senior citizens considerably reduce their ability to operate an automobile in safety.

The elderly are inhibited by a number of problems in using conventional public transportation. The design related problems such as high entrance steps, overhead grips, and fast-acting doors act to their disadvantage. In addition, other problems occur when too many transfers are required, and long waits are necessary at stops. An elderly person subjected to these discomforts and inconveniences, is discouraged from using public transportation.

Some of the effects of not being able to afford an auto

and the barriers to using public transit are evident in Table II. The average number of trips per person per day, by income, age, and trip purposes, are given for SMSA residents. Because of the aforementioned factors, the trip-making rate for the elderly is considerably lower than that of the non-elderly within each income group. The effect of income on trip-making rates for the elderly is also shown in Table II. As income increases, the elderly take more trips for both work and non-work purposes.

Mode choice data indicate that although the elderly are described as 'captive riders', they do not use transit for a large number of their trips. In fact, they tend to use transit for a smaller proportion of their total trips than the nonelderly, according to nationwide data on the elderly within SMSA's.[6]

No description of the transportation characteristics of the elderly would be complete without some mention of the importance of transportation used, solely as an activity for many of the elderly. "Transportation for the elderly needs to be provided not purely for getting from "here to there" but also as an "antidote" for the entire process of aging".[10]

Handicapped persons

The major transportation problem of the handicapped, like the elderly, lies in their inability to find a convenient mode of transportation which does not cause them serious discomforts. Of all the handicapped persons in the United States, the Department of Transportation has calculated the total number who cannot use transit or who use transit with difficulty. A list of the dysfunctions of the transportation handicapped is shown in Table III. It should be noted that 53 per cent of the handicapped are elderly persons. As discussed in the previous section, the problems of the elderly in driving and riding conventional modes of transportation are, to a large extent, associated with their physical impairment.

Their difficulties in getting to the bus stop, boarding high entrance steps, safely riding buses, and getting to their destinations mean that the handicapped only ride public transit when absolutely necessary.[10] Their attempts to use inadequate public transit result in both physical endangerment and psychological frustrations.

The travel patterns of the handicapped, as a result of some of the above mentioned impediments, result in a large gap between the trip frequencies of the handicapped and the non-handicapped. Data from a study in Boston showed that the handicapped took 1.13 trips per day compared to an average of 2.23 trips per day by the general population.[12]

Finally, a look at modal split of the handicapped shows that a significant number of trips by the handicapped are taken by taxi. The handicapped, for example, take 15 per cent of their trips by taxi compared with two per cent of the nonhandicapped. Although the handicapped are generally less able to afford the taxi fare, they need the door-to-door taxi service.[12]

FEDERAL ROLE

This section will trace the various programmatic efforts that have been made to solve the transportation problems of the poor, elderly, and handicapped persons. The focus will be on the advent of federal responses to the problem. The impact at state and local levels, will be emphasized.

The poor

The first use of federal funds for the transportation disadvantaged occurred in the mid-1960's when the Department of Housing and Urban Development (HUD) initiated a series of demonstration projects that were

Table II – Average number of trips per person per day by income, age and trips purposes for SMSA residents

Household Income and Age

Trip Purposes	Poverty $0-4,000 Elderly	Non-Elderly	Low $4-6,000 Elderly	Non-Elderly	Middle $6-10,000 Elderly	Non-Elderly	High $10,000+ Elderly	Non-Elderly
Work	.11	.88	.19	.48	.39	.56	.37	.59
Shopping	.29	.24	.27	.28	.24	.42	.27	.44
Social/Recreational	.38	.46	.41	.42	.49	.72	.29	.44
Personal Business	.10	.22	.24	.31	.24	.41	.20	.41
Other	.62	.77	.52	.76	1.07	.63	.69	.67
Total Non-Work	1.39	1.69	1.44	1.77	2.04	2.18	1.45	2.26
Total	1.50	2.07	1.63	2.25	2.43	2.74	1.82	2.85

Sample Size: 5,187 persons SMSA, Standard Metropolitan Statistical areas
Source: Nationwide Personal Transportation Survey, 1969-70 as reported in Abt Associates, *Transportation Needs of the Handicapped.*

Table III – The national numbers of handicapped with transportation dysfunctions*

Handicap Class	Elderly Handicapped	Non-Elderly Handicapped	Total Handicapped
Non-Institutional Chronic Conditions			
Visually impaired	1,460,000	510,000	1,970,000
Deaf	140,000	190,000	330,000
Uses Wheelchair	230,000	200,000	430,000
Uses Walker	350,000	60,000	410,000
Uses Other Special Aids	2,290,000	3,180,000	5,470,000
Other Mobility Limitations	1,540,000	1,770,000	3,310,000
Acute Conditions	90,000	400,000	490,000
Institutionalized	930,000	30,000	960,000
TOTALS	7,030,000	6,340,000	13,370,000

Sources: HEW National Center for Health Statistics 1960 and 1970 Census of Population in *The Handicapped and Elderly Market for Urban Mass Transit* prepared by the Transportation Systems Center for the Urban Mass Transportation Administration, October, 1973.

*1970 Estimate, persons, who cannot use transit or who use transit with difficulty.

Table IV – Transportation projects serving older Americans by type of service as of july 1974

Type of Service	Number	Percent
Demand-Responsive	112	35.77
Combined Demand-Responsive & Fixed Route/Schedule	88	28.0
Fixed Route/Schedule	55	17.5
Volunteer Systems	48	15.2
Taxi: Reduced Fares	11	3.6
Total of Identified Projects	314	100.0%
Not identified by Service	606	—
Total	920	—

Source: Administration on Aging, *Transportation for the Elderly: The State of the Art,* prepared by Joe Revis, Institute of Public Administration, Washington, D. C., January 1975

aimed at solving some of the transportation problems of the poor. [8] These projects were in response to the national prominence that had come to the issue of the immobility of the poor with the 1965 racial riots of Watts. Inadequate transportation to employment centers had been identified by the McCone Commission as a factor leading to high unemployment rates in Watts.[18]

In response to these conditions, federally-supported demonstration projects were launched in riot-prone major metropolitan areas. Buses would provide daily door-to-door service from workers' homes to outlying suburban jobs. These services had a number of demand-responsive characteristics. Routes were usually changed daily or weekly to accommodate new clients. Pickups were made at the clients' door or very close to it and provided direct access to their place of employment. Some of these projects improved employment access

enormously, more than justifying the large initial investment in the operation by consequent increase in lifetime earnings of new job holders. Others suffered from waning ridership and were not continued beyond the demonstration phase.

In addition to these employment facilitation efforts, the poor have been the focus of a number of other federally-funded demand-responsive transportation services primarily planned for non-work-related trips. Model Cities' agencies in Columbus, Ohio; Detroit and Grand Rapids, Michigan; and Buffalo, New York, each have experimented with dial-a-ride services that are allowing residents better access to health and social service agencies. [8] In Grand Rapids, for example, a special supplement to the fixed route system is providing increased mobility to the poor and elderly. A demonstration grant to the Grand Rapids Transit Authority from the Urban Mass Transportation Administration (UMTA) has provided for a demand-responsive transportation system within the Model Cities' neighborhood. Five small buses provide services to or from anywhere in the city, as long as one end of the trip is in the Model Cities' neighborhood. [3]

The Office of Economic Opportunity (OEO) was a prime mover behind efforts to provide demand-responsive transportation to the transportation disadvantaged in rural areas. Prototype public transportation systems have been started in rural areas with demonstration grants from OEO. In their effort to help people out of the poverty cycle, local OEO funded Community Action Agencies (CAA's) had consistently identified transportation as a major problem area. In response to these needs by 1972, there had been over 50 rural transportation projects funded by OEO.[19] The dispersed nature of the trips and lack of high population densities have dictated that few of these systems have conventional fixed routes or schedules. These are primarily social service delivery systems that provide door-to-door service for agency clients. The conversion of OEO programs to a new funding basis under the Community Services Act has seen the retention of some financial commitment to transportation services. Typically, the funding is largely federal in source, and spent for a target population of low income. Many programs did not survive federal spending cutbacks.

Elderly and handicapped

UMTA and the Administration on Aging (AOA) are the two federal agencies that have been active in developing demand-responsive transportation to serve the elderly and handicapped.

UMTA

The Urban Mass Transportation Administration (UMTA) of the U. S. Department of Transportation has the Congressional mandate to ensure that elderly and handicapped persons are provided access to mass transit. A series of legislative enactments have indicated the intent of Congress. Starting with the Urban Mass Transportation Act of 1964 as amended in 1970, and more recently the National Mass Transportation Assistance Act of 1974, these enactments have emphasized the need to provide for the mobility of elderly and handicapped persons.

UMTA has funded a number of demonstrations that have included demand-responsive transportation for the elderly and handicapped. Under its Service and Methods Demonstration Program, UMTA is experimenting with innovative transportation services for those with mobility constraints. A project in the Lower Naugatuck Valley, Connecticut, has a demand-responsive component which is providing transportation services to clients of health and social service agencies.[20] Telephone requests for the door-to-door demand service are made in advance and served by six vehicles, five of which were modified to meet the special needs of the elderly and handicapped. The Valley Transit District also offers other specialized transportation services including charters available to the local agencies. The project also features a new concept in automated fare collection which uses credit cards instead of cash and allows agencies to pay all or part of a client's trip through a feature called FAIR-SHARE. Demand for the service has grown to the point that the system is saturated and the operators have moved to expand the system by more than doubling the size of the fleet. As the system matured, some demand-responsive service was converted to fixed-route, and the State of Connecticut enters as a larger source of financial support than when the project was first initiated.

Financial support of the project has also been received from AOA. These additional funds have been used to help the agencies pay for client transportation. UMTA and AOA officials are hopeful that the consolidation of social and health service agency transportation needs and the flexible service developed in this demonstration will be a model for serving the transportation needs of many small to medium sized communities.[3]

Another UMTA project started in 1973 in St. Petersburg, Florida, is dubbed "TOTE" which stands for Transportation Of The Elderly. Handicapped and aged persons receive door-to-door service within a ten square mile area which contains the central business district and where a large majority of the citizens are senior citizens. Riders call 24 hours in advance of the intended trip for 35¢ per trip or request a higher priced same day demand-responsive service which is available on a limited basis.

Ridership on the TOTE system has increased steadily. The public acceptance and utilization of the service was slower than anticipated by the sponsors but those who did use the service were pleased with it and many of them became steady riders.[20]

In addition to these and other projects of the Service Development Program, there are other UMTA funded projects that provide demand-responsive transportation services. However, the only major demonstration of the dial-a-ride concept, conducted in Haddonfield, New Jersey, was halted in early 1975 for lack of funds. This system was not specifically designed for the elderly and handicapped, but it did have significant impact on their mobility. Elderly and handicapped persons, as well as housewives and young people, found that the new service decreased their dependence on friends or on the family car. One specially equipped bus accommodated wheelchair passengers and others with handicaps which prevent them from using conventional transit vehicles.

AOA

The Administration on Aging (AOA) of the Department of Health, Education and Welfare (HEW) was authorized to conduct transportation research and demonstration programs under Title III and Title VII of the Older Americans Act.

One of the first pilot projects funded by AOA was the YMCA Senior Citizens Mobile Service which was funded from September 1966 through November 1969. Two seven-passenger vans provided door-to-door service to participating elders on request. Service to health centers, welfare agencies, supermarkets, senior citizens, and libraries was provided to senior citizens who called in their requests for transportation one day in advance. The project has shown that isolated persons living in a large city would use a free demand-responsive service to get where they needed and wanted to go.[21]

The foregoing is just one of some 920 projects involving the provision of transportation for the elderly enumerated by a research project conducted for the AOA.[11] All of this activity is being implemented through local and state governments, and a majority of the projects are receiving funds under Titles III and VII of the Older Americans Act and Titles XIX and XX of the Social Security Act.

An enumeration of these services makes a strong case for the superiority of demand-responsive over fixed-route systems. Of the 314 projects that reported on the type of service, some form of demand-responsive service accounted for 36%; fixed-route 18%; combination of fixed-routes and demand-responsive systems 28%; volunteer systems 15%; and taxi reduced fares 4%, as seen in Table IV. There were, thus, 255 projects involved in routing of vehicles. Of these, only 55 or 22% did not have a demand-responsive component. Clearly, local agencies are recognizing the benefits of demand-responsive transportation for the elderly.

Consolidation of resources

The way to have the most profound impact on transportation for clients of social service agencies is to find ways to utilize more efficiently the equipment and manpower that are currently used to provide para-transit transportation services. This means that if in one county there are ten different agencies providing services for the elderly, they should be able to put their vehicles and drivers into one consolidated system that could provide better service at a lower cost per passenger trip. Recent data suggest that considerable economies occur by spreading management and maintenance costs over larger scales of operations. [24]

But why does not public policy move toward capturing these advantages of large scale operation and what should be done to facilitate this consolidated effort? At the federal level there are a very large number of funding sources for transportation, but the regulations that determine their use are frequently interpreted by local implementing agencies as quite restrictive. Therefore, we must change the regulations that do not allow flexibility in the use of currently available transportation funds. Unfortunately, the institutional impediments to changing these regulations are found at every level of government, starting with laws enacted by Congress which must ultimately be implemented by local agencies. For example, there is legislative intent to restrict use of 16(b)2 vehicles to the service of elderly and handicapped.

Laws that affect rural public transportation are developed by many different Congressional committees. These various pieces of legislation have not in the past been coordinated to see that they do not create overlapping programs, or to ensure that they allow for sufficient flexibility so that some consolidation is possible. Of course this is not unique to the area of transportation. The interfacing of many federal social service programs is made difficult by the uncoordinated nature of the Congressional committee structure.

On a more positive note are some recent efforts towards coordination of transportation legislation by a number of Senate committees, including the Special Committee on Aging and the Subcommittee on Transportation. One task being considered to facilitate this coordination would be a study of the total amount being spent on special transportation services by all federal agencies. The General Accounting Office has been asked to enumerate these programs.

An interagency task force of the Southern Federal Regional Council has been studying rural public transportation. Ms. Suanne Brooks of this task force has documented the administrative jungle created by the many separate sources of federal funds for providing transportation service. She indicated that:

"The Departments of Health, Education, and Welfare; Labor, Transportation and the U. S. Office of Economic Opportunity fund no less than fifty (50) human service categorical and formula grant programs that authorize the provision of a payment for transportation services . . ." Many needful people who are categorically ineligible go unserved as a result (23).

The same problem exists among the various state sponsored special transportation services. There are too many uncoordinated, restricted funding sources for transportation programs. Suggested improvements for state governments, however, need not stop with better coordination. In addition to enacting better legislation and implementing coordinated programs, the states can establish umbrella agencies that are empowered to consolidate disparate sources of funds. Probably the best example of a state-created agency which was established to coordinate specialized transportation service is found in Delaware. The Delaware Authority for Specialized Transportation (DAST) embodies a successful approach for funding and operating specialized transportation services on a statewide basis. In essence, the legislature created an authority that could provide transportation services to a wide range of client agencies under purchase-of-service contracts.

Local county governments, the United Fund of Delaware and numerous private agencies now contract with DAST to provide transportation services for their clients. In almost every case, the cost to the agency is less than was previously the case. This may not be a feasible solution in every area, but it is certainly indicative of the strong role a state agency can play in coordinating specialized transportation services.

Local efforts at coordination are also helpful in reducing costs and providing better services. Some rural transit systems have been successful in providing transportation services to more than just one agency. Typically, these systems were started as a result of a grant from OEO and were initially used to provide service to clients of local Community Action Agencies (CAA's). A number of enterprising CAA directors recognized that they were not fully utilizing their vehicles, while other agencies in same county were experiencing transportation problems associated with delivery of services to their clients. Thus, in a number of counties arrangements were made by CAA's to provide transportation to clients from other agencies. Of course, this was feasible only where the regulations mentioned earlier were flexible enough to allow for purchase-of-service arrangements.

THE FEDERAL OUTLOOK

Although legislation designed to enhance the mobility of elderly and handicapped persons was enacted in the early 1970's, many representatives of disadvantaged groups felt that there had been little or no changes because of this law. Thus during 1974-75, a number of court cases were initiated to force the Federal Department of Transportation to implement the legislation that was passed by Congress. In Baltimore for example, the city was enjoined from purchasing a large number of vehicles for its public transit system because they were not designed to accept a person in a wheelchair. UMTA finally agreed to provide a set of rules governing the provision of transit for elderly and handicapped persons. An initial set of rules was published for comment and a number of hearings were held to receive transit industry and public input, before final publication of the UMTA rules.

Major issues addressed in the rules are:

1. *Accessibility versus Mobility:*

Should every vehicle in transit service be accessible to all handicapped persons including those in wheelchairs or is it sufficient that some mobility is provided to elderly and handicapped persons by a specialized service?

2. *Service Levels:*

What are appropriate service levels for providing transit for elderly and handicapped persons?

3. *Vehicle Design:*

Some vehicle design criteria are being developed. These engineering specifications will be mandatory for any vehicles purchased with federal funds.

4. *Planning Needs:*

What specific planning tasks that relate to the transportation disadvantaged will be required before a city is deemed eligible for federal funds?

The majority of subsidy monies going to social service

agencies to furnish transportation services have resulted in proliferation of independent, uncoordinated services. Some funds to reimburse clients for use of existing public transit or taxi facilities; but, in the main, the expenditures result in a proliferation of inefficient transportation units. In general, the services provided by social service agencies are fragmented, very costly, and not widely advertised to the general public. Poor or high-cost maintenance of vehicles results from nonconsolidation. Social service agency staffs divert time from important professional duties to engage in chauffering functions.

The staffs of the agencies recognize these problems; but in the absence of an adequate public transit system, especially in small areas, these staffs prefer to retain the agency-based system. The vehicles used for clients are also a visible sign of an organization. They play a role in advertising the current operations of a nonprofit organization.

In general, bus and taxi operators in small and mid-sized cities are not aware of the many forms of indirect subsidies to transportation available to social service agencies. Transit operators are aware of the existence of some of the more prominent organizations, but do not typically interact with the agency directors to plan route or schedule changes. The more vocal social service agency professionals are often highly critical of public transit, citing inconvenience, slow speed, and poor schedules. The social service agency staffs, in general, are unfamiliar with routes and schedules, taxi fare structures, or the transportation planning process.

The transportation planners in many small and mid-sized cities could derive useful information from social service agencies about travel needs of clients; but, in general, the agencies are not invited or funded to conduct such studies. Transportation planners, operating under the time constraint of deadlines for proposal submission, frequently express the view that there are too many disparate agencies and that it is too much work to try to get them together. Planners also fear that agencies will not be in agreement among themselves on transit priorities, and thus will compound the political difficulties in getting a plan inplemented. Planners at the state level, in general, appear willing to offer financial incentives to encourage moves toward consolidation, but are timid about applying sanctions against localities which tolerate costly, inefficient proliferation of independent transportation programs. Despite the potential for gubernatorial encouragement to consolidation, few states currently promote this approach.

The underlying assumption of federal revenue sharing is that local governments close to the people will best be able to spend tax dollars in an efficient manner. Knowledge of local conditions is claimed to foster rationality, and consolidation of budgetary power in the hands of local elected officials is expected to permit agencies un-

der those officials to coordinate efforts at the local level. In fact, the actual behavior of system participants suggests that these assumptions are unwarranted in many instances. Even where several social service agencies expend public monies at the city or county level, they may be under no pressure to rationalize the supply of transit services. Transportation planners working for mayors or county commissioners do not, in many instances, interact with local welfare officials for the purposes of improving transportation services to social agencies.

The reasons for these problems seem to be that even in "small" cities there are too many bureaucracies, too many intermediaries, and too many rules which inhibit the development of consolidated transportation systems. No one agency is charged as the "lead" agency; no one agency is taxed by the diseconomies of the current approach to transportation services. No one agency is to blame as the individual agencies cope unsuccessfully with the issue of mobility for the disadvantaged.

Since it may be posited that lack of transportation services decreases access to jobs, medical services, food stamps, and many other programs which raise the standard of living for the poor, the state of nonconsolidation has important long-run consequences for the well-being of the citizenry.

Cost studies show great diversity in system costs despite some similarity in purpose, clientele, and market prices of the inputs used in the system. There is a need for good prior planning to achieve economies of scale.

Currently public policy in the area of transportation for social service agency clients does not appear to promote the formation of large coordinated systems, since agencies can obtain vehicles under the 16(b)2 program without belonging to a coordinated program such as the Rhode Island or Delaware systems. More research should be done to explore how to achieve a higher level of coordination, thus effecting greater economies.

Public transit companies which fear that demand-responsive service for the elderly and handicapped is very expensive may be interested in the findings that some well-managed systems are able to operate on a cost per passenger mile of less than twenty cents (See Table V). Success in keeping unit costs low appears to involve:

a. agglomerations of elderly which facilitate the bunching of demand

b. spreading management costs thinly over a large scale of operation

c. avoiding a large artificial distortion of costs resulting from a short-term massive federal demonstration grant

d. controlling wage costs by using drivers part-time as needed

CONCLUSION

In the United States between 70 million and 100 mil-

Table V – Costs and selected characteristics by system type

	Number of Passenger Miles Per Annum		Cost Per Passenger Mile		Name of Lowest Cost System
Fixed Route Systems with	Range:	212,000 to 677,000	Range:	$ .25 to $1.35	Broward County, Florida
Special Service to	Mean:	417,000	Mean:	$ .72	
Elderly & Handicapped	Median:	361,000	Median:	$ .56	
Demand-Responsive Other	Range:	9,900 to 1,520,000			Logansport, Indiana
Than Taxi	Mean:	485,000	Mean:	$1.19	
	Median:	280,000	Median:	.70	
Taxi	Range:	161,112 to 4,800,000	Range:	$ 42 to $ .69	Hicksville, New York
	Mean:	—	Mean:	—	
	Median:	—	Median:	—	
Mixed Demand/Responsive	Range:	1,951,000	Range:	—	Merritt Island, Florida
and Fixed Route	Mean:	—	Mean:	—	
	Median:	—	Median:	$ .13	

lion persons are either elderly, handicapped or poor. From these population classes come the preponderance of the transportation disadvantaged, the autoless in an auto-oriented society. Funding to solve the transportation problems of these groups has flowed from many channels, federal, state, and local as well as non-profit agencies.

The problem has been tackled by addressing particular needs of a selected client target group, usually only a fraction of the transportation disadvantaged. Recently, researchers and planners are starting to address the issue of a public transportation problem to be solved through the consolidation of separate programs into a local para-transit operation. Alternatively sharing of experiences and problems at the local level begins to reveal the extent of duplicative services or unmet needs. The diversity of local conditions makes difficult any blanket federal policy but public funds might well be invested in the startup costs of providing the organizational impetus for coordination and/or consolidation of these vital transportation programs.

ACKNOWLEDGEMENTS
This report was produced in part from data obtained under a grant from the program of Research and Training in Urban Transportation, sponsored by the Urban Mass Transportation Administration of the U.S. Department of Transportation. The results and views expressed are the independent product of university research and not necessarily concurred in by the Urban Mass Transportation Administration.
The assistance of George Amedee, Lalita Sen, Doug McKelvey, Jan Williams, Denese Lavender, and J. Wilder is gratefully acknowledged.

REFERENCES
[1] Kidder, Alice E., and Amedee, George, **Assuming Responsibility for Mobility of Elderly and Handicapped: the Roles of Transit Properties, Transit Planners and Social Service Agencies in Small Cities** (NTIS, and Transportation Institute, North Carolina A & T State University, Greensboro, 1976).

[2] Saltzman, Arthur, and Amedee, George, "Servicing the Transportation Disadvantaged With Demand-Responsive Transportation," forthcoming in the Transportation Research Record, Washington, D. C.

[3] Sahaj, Lynn, "Mobility for the Disadvantaged" in **Transportation Topics for Consumers,** Vol. 1, No. 4, Office of Consumers Affairs, Department of Transportation, Washington, D. C., November 1973.

[4] Crain, John, "Transportation Problems of Transit Dependent Persons", in **Conference on Transportation and Human Needs in the 70's,** held at the American University, Washington, D.C., June 1972, under the sponsorship of the Urban Mass Transportation Administration.

[5] Saltzman, Arthur, "Para-Transit: Taking the Mass Out of Transit," **Technology Review,** Volume 75, Number 8, Cambrigde. Massachusetts, July/August 1973, pp. 46-53.

[6] Abt Associates, Inc., **Transportation Needs of the Urban Disadvantaged,** U.S. Department of Transportation, Federal Highway Administration, March 1974.

[7] Paaswell, Robert E., "Problems of the Carless in the United Kingdom and the United States," prepared for the Organization for Economic Cooperation and Development, Department of Civil Engineering, State University of New York at Buffalo, New York, August 1972.

[8] Kidder, Alice E. and Saltzman, Arthur, "Mode Choice Among Autoless Workers in Auto-Oriented Cities." (A&T-TI-06-RR-73) Proceedings, International Conference on Transportation Research, Bruges, Belgium, June 1973.

[9] Notess, Charles B., "Shopping and Work Trips in Black Ghetto" in **Proceedings of The American Society of Civil Engineers,** Journal of the Urban Planning and Development Division, Vol. 98, No. 65 UPI, July 1972.

[10] U. S. Department of Transportation, 1972 National Transportation Report: Office of the Assistant Secretary for Policy and International Affairs, Superintendent of Documents, Stock Number 5000-00058, Washington, D.C., July 1972.

[11] Administration on Aging, **Transportation for the Elderly: The State of the Art,** prepared by Joe Revis, Institute of Public Administration, Washington, D.C., January 1975.

[12] Abt Associates, Inc., **Travel Barriers: Transportation Needs of the Handicapped,** Department of Transportation, Office of Economic and Systems Analysis, 1969. (RB 187 327)

[13] Golob, Thomas F., **et. al.,** "Analysis of Consumer Preferences For A Public Transportation System", **Transportation Research, March** 1972, pp. 81-102.

[14] Butts, Michael Vern and Loobey, Phyllis Price, **Transportation Alternatives for the Physically Limited and Elderly,** prepared for the Lane Transit District, Eugene, Oregon, March 1974.

[15] Gurin, Douglas and Wofford, John, **Implications of Dial-A-Ride For the Poor,** USL-70-18, Urban Systems Lab., Massachusetts Institute of Technology, March 1971. (PB 199-406)

[16] Transportation Systems Center, **The Handicapped and Elderly Market for Urban Mass Transit,** prepared for Urban Mass Transportation Administration, Washington, D.C. October 1973. (PB 224-821)

[17] Technology Sharing, Transportation Systems Center, **Demand-Responsive Transportation: State of the Art Overview,** U.S. Department of Transportation, Cambridge, Massachusetts, August 1974.

[18] McCone, John M., **Violence in the City: An End or a Beginning: A Report by the Governors Commission on the Los Angeles Riots,** prepared for submission to California Governor Edmund T. Brown, 1975.

[19] Kaye, Ira, "Transportation Problems of the Older American in Rural Areas" in **Rural Development.** A report printed for use of the U.S. Senate on Agriculture and Forestry, (U.S. Government Printing Office, Washington, D.C., 1972).

[20] RRC International, Inc., **Valley Transit District: Elderly/Handicapped Transportation,** prepared for Lower Naugatuck Valley Community Council, Ansonia, Connecticut, July 1974.

[21] St. Petersburg, Florida, **Transportation of the Elderly (TOTE):** Interim Report on a Pilot Project to Develop Mobility for the Elderly and Handicapped, April, 1974.

[22] Bell, John H., "Senior Citizens Mobile Service' in **Transportation and Aging:** Proceedings of the Interdisciplinary Workshop on Transportation and Aging, edited by E. J. Cantilli and J. L. Shmelzer, Washington, D.C., May 24-26, 1970, (Stock No. 1762-0042) Superintendent of Documents, Washington, D.C.

[23] Brooks, Suanne, "Funding Specialized Transportation Systems: Policies and Problems" in Proceedings of Fourth Annual Transportation Conference on the Transportation Disadvantaged, edited by William G. Bell and William T. Olsen, Florida State University, Tallahassee, Florida, December, 1974.

[24] Kidder, Alice E. et al., **Costs of Alternative Systems to Serve Elderly and Handicapped in Small Urban Areas,** Greensboro: Transportation Institute, North Carolina A & T State University, 1977.

Social assessment of technology and its application to urban transportation

by

FRANÇOIS HETMAN

Organization for Economic Co-operation and Development

Technical change derives from the inherent endeavour to modify the outside world so as to smooth out the risks of existence. By challenging nature with his crafts, Man has progressively created a functional link between science, technology and economy. This has led to societal systems where technology is geared to maximising economic growth and the average expectancy of material well-being.

MAN-MADE SYSTEMS

As a matter of fact, technology has been the major factor in liberating man – at least in technologically advanced countries – from his main ancestral fears, hunger, illness and insecurity. This seems to explain why technology has won support from all sides. It has come to be considered as a kind of bounty, transcending individuals and societies as an autonomous force.

However, such a fatalistic fostering of technology and of its unconditional diffusion has led to new threats to human existence, such as nuclear destruction, ecological disaster, depletion of natural resources, malnutrition owing to the failure to curb the population explosion. At the same time, technical change makes obsolete whole categories of knowledge, production processes, professional skills and occupational patterns. This gives rise to economic and social disruptions, and a feeling of frustration both on the social and individual levels.

Thus, as a consequence of the very "success" of scientific research and technological change, mankind is now faced with new risks and dangers. These are man-made. There are no natural or supra-natural correcting mechanisms which can be applied. From now on, men will have to come to new terms with technology-induced human systems and devise new ways of bringing technological innovation and proliferation of techniques under some kind of social control.

This runs counter to a largely accepted and almost unquestioned conviction that technology is a basic factor of social change which acts upon society in an irresistible and self-enhancing way. Such a conviction is commonly held by the followers of most prevailing political doctrines and is based on several currently admitted views.

TECHNOLOGICAL DETERMINISM

An oft-repeated contention is that technological innovation is by definition a self-contained process. By its inner logic – i.e. the pursuit of an improvement in a specific performance or an increase in productivity – each separate technology creates opportunities for constant innovation. In a sense, innovators are merely the "revealers" of new and gradual steps forward in a basic trend along a given functional trajectory. Further, technological innovators are stimulated by scientific discoveries which become available through research and development, while scientific research in turn is stimulated by the firmly held belief in scientific freedom.

Dialectically, this technological determinism is frequently opposed to the apparent capriciousness and instability of social phenomena. Such an opposition is interpreted as the progressive inability of man and society to adapt to the pace set by technological development. According to this interpretation, while technology is advancing at an accelerating pace, human adaptability and social structures in general are stagnating if not actually regressing. This discrepancy ends by provoking a feeling of frustration which contributes to accentuating the lack of confidence in existing social institutions and to the prevalence of a gloomy view of increasing alienation.

Whatever the grounds on which this way of thinking is based, it reinforces the thesis of technological determinism in that it accepts as evidence that human, social and ethical phenomena lag behind technological developments. It implies that social problems tend to derive from technological change. Impacts are generated by technology and move in a linear fashion from technology to society. Society merely reacts, through feedback loops, in a rather haphazard and incongruous manner.

Arguments like these reveal a basic misinterpretation of the essence and societal role of technology. A comparison between the rates of technological advance and the evolution of society is quite irrelevant. Technology is only one method for coping with various social problems – one of the possible methods. A given technological development can provide an improved means, but cannot determine the rationale and content of a social achievement.

NEW ATTITUDE TOWARDS TECHNOLOGICAL CHANGE

The new threats and problems created by technology make it more and more obvious that "technological" change does not automatically and necessarily mean "technological" progress, real economic growth and still less an actual increase in social welfare and human satisfaction. Conventional criteria of economic growth appear to be of limited significance and the so-called indicators of "progress" are increasingly contested.

Consequently, new tools for decisionmaking in the field of technology are needed. Since it has been recognised that technology can be the source of both benefits and undesirable effects, a drastic change in thinking and general attitude towards technological change is now taking place.

This calls for a new course of policy for which neither governments nor individuals have been prepared. Governments continue to favour technological innovation as a means to attain and maintain full employment of available resources and sustained economic growth. At

544

he same time, they are solicited to take strong action to reduce the negative effects of technology, and above all, to define new policies likely to make it possible to direct technology towards socially desirable ends.

How can such broad and diffuse, fundamental but also partly contradictory goals be pursued? As an answer to this question a new aid to decisionmaking has been suggested: technology assessment or rather social assessment of technology (SAT).

The term was coined some ten years ago by the Science, Research and Development Sub-Committee of the U.S. Congress. It was then defined as a form of policy research, a method of analysis that systematically appraises the nature, significance, status and merit of technological progress with a view to identifying policy issues, assessing the impact of alternative courses of action and presenting findings.

As the notion spread, various activities and conceptual constructs have been subsumed under the same label. However, a review of the experience gained suggests that there are two main tendencies diverging in approach and basic philosophy.

CHALLENGE TO ANALYSTS

The first tendency can be called the technologist's approach. It considers that technology assessment examines the impacts of all alternative policies which can be followed, but does not come out with a specific recommendation involving value systems. Assessment ends at the frontiers of the broadened technological analysis, leaving the rest to traditional, existing, social and political processes.

The second tendency, on the contrary, regards management of technology as a part of overall planning or "social engineering". In its extreme formulation, it starts by spelling out values, social policies and objectives and works down to technology assessment in order to clarify the most appropriate technical options.

These two points of view may be considered as extreme lines of definitional mapping between which social assessment of technology can take a great variety of forms. They are not mutually exclusive but rather complementary as they address themselves to the same cluster of problems, but from a different angle and at a different level of the decisionmaking process. At the present stage, both challenge scientists and engineers to develop a better understanding of inter-relationships between technology and society. They also challenge decisionmakers, from individual organisations to central government, to evolve new procedures and institutional forms which can help them to build up a firmer basis for their technology policies.

Such procedures and mechanisms should serve to indicate new directions for technology and for scientific research. They will also have to make clear the possible detrimental effects at an early enough stage for remedial measures to be considered by policy-makers. However, the difficulty is to ensure that policies and instruments are not so rigid as to hamper technological change and inhibit genuine social progress.

Theoretically, six main areas can be identified as starting points for technology assessment studies: technology, economy, society, the individual, the environment and value systems. However, for some of these and particularly for society, environment, the individual and value systems, there is as yet little knowledge available on relationships with technology. Most frequently, therefore, technology assessment studies are merely divided into two broad categories:
    (a) technology-initiated, and
    (b) problem-initiated.
In a broad sense, from the technologist's point of view,

the great majority of assessments are technology-initiated whereas from the social engineer's standpoint most assessments should be considered as problem-oriented.

Available examples of technology assessment studies are mostly of the technology-initiated type. This can easily be explained by the fact that the first generation of assessment took place in direct response to questions concerning the particular environmental impacts of selected technologies.

CHALLENGE TO DECISIONMAKERS

The concept of social assessment of technology leads to a reappraisal of the role of science and technology in contemporary society, both with deeper understanding of the nature of technology, and of the innovation process, as well as consideration of the consequences of alternative technological decisions and a new approach to a better informed decisionmaking.

Social assessment of technology can be defined as a process of analysis, forecasting and assessment of technological futures and their impacts on society resulting in action options for the decisionmakers. On the analyst's side, it encompasses the study of technological parameters, the elaboration of technological forecasts, the analysis of social, environmental, cultural and political factors, the general assessment of all relevant effects and possible consequences of a technology and an evaluation of alternatives.

On the decisionmaker's side, it implies appropriate institutional mechanisms which make it possible to: identify demands for technological change; gear scientific and technological knowledge to societal needs; make the choice of socially desirable and politically feasible technological variants; determine suitable means of action; plan the appropriate phases of implementation.

There is a close and permanent interplay between assessment study and decisionmaking. It takes the form of convergent iterations which are necessary to evaluate the consequences of technological change on society and to determine the channels through which the societal objectives can exercise their influence on the future course of technological development.

This can be represented as a threefold systemic approach which integrates the processes of analysis, of decisionmaking and of information into one dynamic continuum – as illustrated in the chart attached. The analysis process itself is a multi-iterative feedback process which combines forecasting and evaluation methods to explore relevant societal aspects, of a given technological development and to evaluate their impacts and consequences.

INSTITUTIONAL STATUS OF SAT

Ideally, social assessment of technology should examine closely all virtualities of a technology. This implies that analysts are able to consider and evaluate all possibilities both as to their beneficial and negative effects. However, any new technological development entails an infinite number of unpremeditated consequences. There is no scientist or technologist who can take into account all of these consequences which go far beyond the capability of any group of people to understand and to draw the "social path" of a given technological event.

These are important and sobering limitations. It is obvious that social assessment of technology is not a technical device but rather a change in attitude towards technology and a new approach to a better informed decisionmaking in this field. It is not concerned with technical expertise per se but mainly with socio-political answers to the impacts of technology. If the analysts are to provide useful information their involvement, assumptions, sources of data and methods of reporting to decisionmakers must be made clear so as to set workable boundaries to their effort.

What can be the institutional status of social assessment of technology? Is it an outgrowth of science and technology policy? Or is it a new branch of general policy stemming from the reaction to the "disenchantment" with science and technology and the subsequent questioning of the ends of scientific activity and passive acceptance of technological developments?

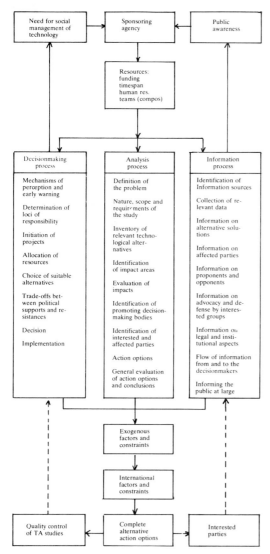

One would expect that it should be closely linked to technology policy. However, there has not been such a thing so far. From the institutional point of view, technology has no place of its own. Both in national governmental agencies and relevant committees of the international organisations, the word technology was only recently added to that of science. Although this marks an increased concern for questions of technology the couple, science and technology, remains illmatched. While government agencies for science policy are now established with pretty well defined attributions, this is not the case for technology. Deep investigations are still necessary to

understand the mechanisms of technological advance and of the interplay between technology and society before technology policy can be outlined in relevant operational terms.

EXPERIENCE OF PRINCIPAL INDUSTRIALISED COUNTRIES

As a new concept and a new approach to technological change and social policy in general, social assessment of technology has still to find its place within the institutional set-up and decisionmaking mechanisms. It may therefore be of some interest to review shortly the experience of principal industrialised countries.

The most straightforward solution is to create a specific institution. This is the case of the *United States*. After five years of discussion, an Office of Technology Assessment was set up in 1972, under Congress with the aim of providing early indications of the probable beneficial and adverse impacts of the applications of technology, and to develop other coordinate information which may assist the legislative branch of Government. The Office started its activity in 1973. It has a limited inhouse capability which is to be progressively extended, but contracts most of the studies to outside organisations.

As far as the executive is concerned, several governmental agencies undertake, or finance, technology assessment studies. Since the last reorganisation of the institutional framework for scientific and technological policy, the National Science Foundation is the most active in this field, in particular under its programme, 'Research Applied to National Needs' (RANN). The NSF contracts are widely dispersed among the various types of institutions; however, university groups have been preferred so far.

In the *Federal Republic of Germany*, a proposal to create a similar parliamentary institution as in the United States was made by the Opposition. This initiative was not supported by the Government and the final decision was postponed sine die. In the executive, it is mainly the Federal Ministry for Research and Technology that have for years done work related to technology assessment and is now financing important assessments in the field of transportation and communications. The Commission for Economic and Social Change – a study group with limited life-time which was disbanded last year – has financed a number of studies with a technology assessment character. A number of systems studies were carried out by the Nuclear Research centres in Karlsruhe and Jülich, the Studiengruppe für Systemforschung in Heidelberg and the Battelle Institute in Frankfurt.

Apart from the United States, the most active country in the field of technology assessment has been *Japan*. After the striking environmental deterioration which followed the forced pace of industrialisation, management of technology is considered now as an essential element in the future orientation of economic and social development. Technology assessment studies are undertaken in the executive by the Science and Technology Agency on one side, and the Ministry of Trade and Industry on the other. Since 1971, a number of studies were completed on subjects ranging from energy to transportation, building, telecommunications, pesticides, etc. Both agencies use both in-house capacity and outside contractors, in particular, universities.

In the *United Kingdom*, the Programme Analysis Unit has been working on specific evaluation studies since 1967. This Institution is financed jointly by the Department of Trade and Industry and the Atomic Energy Authority. Until recently, its main role was a technicoeconomic appraisal of R&D projects with a view to guiding the allocation of government funds. During the last few years, it completed studies on topics of current interest, for example air pollution, inter-city transportation, security of vehicles, etc. These studies are generally confidential.

A special type of technology assessment study is constituted by some Public Inquiries which are held on the initiative of the responsible ministries. A well-known example is the large scale study on the siting of the third London Airport (known as the Roskill Commission).

In *France,* evaluating economic consequences of technical developments has been an intrinsic part of the planification process of the Planning Agency. Apart from this specific approach, some recent studies in the field of environmental protection and land-use can be regarded as technology assessment studies. The concept of technology assessment was introduced in 1972 into the activities of the working group, "Development of techniques and new technologies relating to the environment" of the Inter-Ministerial Group for Environment Problems. An important inventory of literature and technology assessment activities was realized under this Group.

In *Sweden,* a number of studies of technology assessment character were realized by the Office for Technological Development and the Swedish Academy of Engineering Sciences. Since 1973, social assessment of technology has been a central part of the activities initiated by the Secretariat for Future Studies, special staff service created under the Prime Minister.

In the *Netherlands,* in addition to specialised "planning" agencies, the Government created the Scientific Council for Government Policy, an autonomous body which is entrusted with study of future trends and societal developments. Establishment of research councils for future studies is contemplated in both *Norway* and *Denmark.*

Several large international organisations have significant activities in the area of technology assessment.

For a number of years, the *United Nations* have been exploring the various aspects of technological change, in particular from the angle of transfer of technologies and evaluation of technical projects.

NATO has been active in this field since 1972, when they organised, together with the International Institute for Management of Technology, an International Seminar on this subject.

The most recent initiateve is the project *Europe plus Thirty.* On request by the Commission of European Economic Community, a comprehensive report on the need for studies of future developments has just been completed by a group of external experts. This document examines the essential aspects of the "forecasting and assessment function" and its use in policymaking. It is intended to serve as a basis for discussions within the EEC with a view to establishing a special European Office for Future studies and social assessment of technology on a European level.

OECD PROGRAMME ON SAT

OECD work in the area of social assessment of technology was initiated in compliance with the new orientations for science policy, outlined by the Ministers of Science in their 1971 meeting. Exploratory research began with the organisation, in January 1972, of the first international seminar on technology assessment in which participated some 40 distinguished scholars, technologists and politicians. This seminar was devoted to discussions of possible approaches and usable methods, as well as of the first experiences in the field.

This exchange of information was a starting point for an in-depth exploration of the state-of-the-art which led to the publication of "Society and the Assessment of Technology", a comprehensive OECD report, examining the general philosophy of social assessment of technology, conceptual starting points and methodological frameworks, reviewing the available experience, establishing a general typology of assessment studies, exposing the methods of cost/benefit analysis, outlining the possible areas for use of assessment studies, examining the institutional problems and relationships between analysts and decisionmakers.

Another initiative was the establishment of an Advisory Group on Control and Management of Technology. This group was composed of high officials from a number of OECD Member countries. Its main role was to inform the OECD Secretariat on national policy developments related to technology and its impacts on society. The discussions of this group were of great help in clarifying the needs, and in formulating the OECD programme in the area of social assessment of technology.

Both the theoretical work accomplished and identification of national views pointed towards the desirability of stimulating national studies and enhancing international cooperation. The need was perceived to elucidate methodological issues and to set up guidelines which might be used by the Member countries and the international community at large.

This work was undertaken with the help of a panel of experts and it led to the publication of "Methodological Guidelines for Social Assessment of Technology". A general framework for social assessment studies is outlined in this document. It is an attempt to reconcile the exigency of a comprehensive set of guidelines with the legitimate concern for practical usefulness. Obviously, such a framework implies a number of caveats and raises questions as to its adaptability to any specific subject. These points and other comments by the experts are included in the same volume.

Simultaneously was started an activity which was intended to test the social assessment approach in applying it to real problems of the interested Member countries. From a great number of topics suggested by national authorities, three subjects were selected for studies to be launched within the OECD programme. These were:
– New Urban Transportation Systems – efficient modes of collective rapid transportation;
– Humanised Working Conditions – new modes of organising work and working conditions;
– Telecommunication technologies as an instrument of regional planning and balanced regional economic and social development.

From the beginning, two possible approaches were suggested by the OECD Secretariat: studies in cooperation by pooling available national resources in a common effort and studies in co-ordination leaving each country free to organise the work at national level. This second approach was preferred by the interested Member countries. Consequently, the studies were to be carried out in parallel by national research teams, the OECD Secretariat assuring mainly exchange of information and co-ordination.

The final objective was to make a comparative study of the national contributions with a view to identifying the main aspects where further improvements appear desirable in future technology assessment activities.

PROJECT: NEW URBAN TRANSPORTATION SYSTEMS

Finally, a sufficient commitment could be secured only for the first subject: New Urban Transportation Systems. By now, this project is nearly completed. National reports from six participating countries were assembled and the comparative synthesis is under preparation. A closing session of the project leaders will be held in the near future to discuss both the national contributions and the results of the comparative study. Their comments will be taken into account in the final document which will be submitted to the OECD Committee for Scientific and Technological Policy.

The project was carried out within the timespan of about two years, following the first exploratory stage, devoted mainly to defining the practicability and operational steps of the methodological approach and to identification of national studies which could be retained in the framework of the project.

To facilitate this identification the OECD Secretariat prepared an outline of the general procedure along the lines of the "Methodological Guidelines for Social Assessment of Technology". At the same time two discussion papers were distributed, which had been prepared by external experts. One was technology-oriented and reviewed the main features and technical characteristics of new urban transportation system families[1]. The second was methodology-oriented and dealt with conceptual considerations likely to emerge in the process of application of social assessment of technology to problems of urban transportation systems[2].

The succeeding meetings of the national project leaders made it clear that none of the national organisations involved were ready, or had the possibility to devote a sufficient part of its resources to a specifically designed social assessment study. Instead, proposals were made to derive some kind of contribution from the current work. In order to obtain at least some degree of similarity with respect to the format, a list of 12 "common points" was drawn up as a guidance, with the hope that all participating research teams would be able to contribute to these items and, if not, to bring out explicitly the difficulties of assessment (See list attached).

As a result, even if compared with an extremely limited common frame of reference, the national contributions received could hardly be considered as social assessment studies of technology. Most often they were parts of broader projects undertaken within the current programme and responsibility of the respective research organisation. Frequently, they were merely derived from an already completed work which had been carried out with a quite different objective in mind. Each of them was thus devoted to a particular aspect or point of interest so that it was particularly difficult to identify common areas on which a meaningful comparison could bear.

In general, however, a certain effort was made to introduce the idea of social assessment of technology either as an additional category of conceptualisation or, more wholeheartedly as a promising methodological tool, allowing for exploration of aspects often neglected in traditional technical feasibility studies.

The attention of the participating research teams, was progressively focused on two elements of the social assessment of technology, considered as a particularly useful broadening of the analysis, i.e. the establishment of societal scenarios and the involvement of concerned groups. This explains that among the six national contributions, two were devoted mainly to designing and evaluating scenarios of future states of society with respect to a given type of transportation technology. Two other contributions reported almost exclusively on experiences gained with simulated implementation of the public involvement in the case of an introduction of a specific mode of transportation.

This is not a negligible result if one considers that the main thrust of the OECD programme must have been to draw attention to the ideas and methodology of the social assessment of technology with a view to making both the researchers and decisionmakers aware of it potential value to policy-making.

One can argue that it would be unfair to insist on the lack of homogeneity of these various national contributions and particularly on the absence of most of the basic categories of information which constituted a full-fledged social assessment of technology, since these contributions were not undertaken as assessment studies per se.

Common points of the national studies

1. New balance between public transportation and the motor car

Technological assessment of transport systems should be carried out, based on the assumption of a possible modification of the present balance between private cars and public transport which would favour the latter. The future role of private cars in cities should also be considered and broadly defined.

2. The assessment will be based on social needs

The assessment would focus on social needs of the various population groups concerned; special attention being paid to the distributive aspects of the impacts of a given technology (distribution effects of the impacts, among the groups of any given group).

3. Long-range indirect impacts

Long-range indirect impacts of the technologies will be analysed; i.e. impacts on living modes, on the evolution of some activities, on urban development, on societal organisation and disparities.

4. Consideration of technical performance of systems

As far as possible, the evaluation of the expected system's performance would be based on field results, rather than desk-research. The problems of data veracity and uncertainty require special attention; it is important that sources of uncertainty as well as the level of uncertainty be clearly identified.

5. Local projects evaluation

The technological assessment should be based on the study of local projects, integrated into a specific environment, so that the specific constraints become evident, and that interdependencies with urban development be taken into account. Attention should also be paid to the interdependence of the movement of goods in urban areas.

6. Local policy context

The technological assessment should be conducted within the framework of the general policy at the local level; due account being taken of the political power structure and of the various institutions involved.

7. Consideration of impacts on the transport-manufacturing industry

The analysis should be performed with regard to at least two aspects: i) the influence on industrial structures; and ii) the problems of manpower, employment, etc.

8. Societal scenarios

The hypothesis concerning societal developments, on which the development of technology (environment, economic context, social relations, public safety, urban development ...) will depend, should be specified through simplified scenarios. However, a strictly qualitative approach which would lead to the assembly of heterogeneous elements in society which dilutes any serious analysis of transport systems, should be avoided.

9. Involvement of concerned groups in the social assessment of technology

Although its application is difficult, the involvement of concerned groups in a social assessment of technology, is most desirable, as it offers a means by which the real meaning of the impacts at the groups' level may be understood.

10. Comparison with marginal improvements of existing systems

The assessment of the technologies under consideration implies that these technologies be compared with less innovative alternatives; in particular, marginal improvements (that do not consist of a modification of the technology) to existing systems should be considered as alternatives to the technological innovations under review.

11. Transition problems

Assessing a technology under the assumption of its eventual implementation is insufficient. It is equally important to make an appraisal of the problems raised by its progressive introduction into the urban system, in order to identify possible blockages, the chances of success, as well as the effects of this transition phase, which may extend over a long period of time.

12. Operating conditions and statutory provisions

The statutory provisions and operating conditions (especially concerning safety) are adjusted slowly, depending on technological progress. It appears essential to specify possible modifications and restraints to modifications in this area, that could influence the technological assessment.

WORK OF THE U.S. OFFICE OF TECHNOLOGY ASSESSMENT

In comparison with this experience, one would expect that the studies carried out by the U.S. Congressional

Office of Technology Assessment come much closer to the concept of a full-fledged social assessment of technology. From the start of its activities in January 1974, it has benefited from an already considerable amount of work carried out in this field by the National Science Foundation. Given its unique position and status, OTA can avail itself of important autonomous resources which make it possible to continuously improve its procedures and to call upon a broad range of knowledgeable people from different disciplines and horizons.

In the field of transportation policy, OTA conducted, in particular, several coordinated studies to evaluate the potential of new mass transit technologies to meet urban transportation problems[3]. Its methods of work and importance of effort can be illustrated by the example of the assessment of Automated Guideway Transit.

The objectives of this assessment were:

i) to provide the Senate Appropriations Committee with information on the current status and the social and economic aspects of these technological developments;

ii) to evaluate the key problems associated with these technologies as perceived by potential users, the communities and the transit industry;

iii) to identify major policy issues and automated guideway programme alternatives and to explore their implications.

The assessment was conducted by a team of more than 30 experts in the field, drawn from universities, consulting organisations, transit planning and operating agencies, manufacturers public agencies and concerned citizens. They were organised into five panels – current developments in the United States, economics, social acceptability, operations and technology, international developments – whose findings were included as supporting material to the final report written by the OTA staff. The panels consulted with other interested individuals including representatives of urban planning organisations, transit operators, industry and other groups who could make a significant contribution.

In all OTA studies major emphasis is put on identifying policy alternatives and their implications for allocation of government research and development funds. The best explored aspects are, quite naturally, the technological systems under consideration with a profusion of technical details and, where possible, empirical operational data. Important attention is paid also to cost/benefit analysis and economics of operations. An effort is made to identify social problems raised by the use of automated systems.

However, no attempt is made to integrate the various categories of findings so as to present to the decisionmaker an array of global alternative pictures. The need for more social and economic information is emphasized. The less known factors are those related to planning and decisionmaking at the local level, and in particular to questions of acceptance, impacts on population, safety, quality of service and land use.

DIFFICULTIES AND PROSPECTS OF SAT

As a new concept and a new approach to technological change and social policy in general, SAT has still to find its place within the institutional set-up and decisionmaking mechanisms.

With the exception of the United States and their Office of Technology Assessment, there are no special institutions for SAT. As is illustrated hereabove by the experience of OECD, the major obstacle to SAT, both within the country and at the international level, is the absence of technology policy and a government body responsible for it.

In the present situation, it is extremely difficult to find for any candidate for SAT, the appropriate institution which is willing, able and authorized to undertake such assessment studies. There is a wide dispersion of competences among the various ministries and agencies. Furthermore, institutions which show an interest for SAT – and there are often several of them, each responsible for only one aspect of a given technology – are hampered by their narrowly defined responsibilities; they have the greatest difficulty in modifying their programmes in order to devote some resources to SAT.

In addition to these well-known phenomena of structural rigidity and institutional inertia, there is the fact that the concept of SAT is still badly understood and hardly propagated. For all these reasons, its usefulness is minimised and its implementation resisted.

As a rule, technology is developed as a trial and error process with opportunities for feedback from social, economic and legal institutions. Such a feedback should allow technologists to modify and reshape a technology and to adapt it better to social objectives. In reality, there is little adaptation because the social consequences are difficult to clarify and impossible to attest objectively, and because practical and political involvements make it generally difficult to modify the course of action. This makes decisionmakers hesitant and ready to justify on-going technological trends, rather than to challenge them.

It should be recalled that the fundamental rationale of social assessment of technology is that from now on various social groups other than the actual initiators and proponents of a technology are claiming the right to have their say in decisions concerning the future application and diffusion of a technology. There are several basic characteristics which distinguish the social assessment of technology approach, making it potentially far-reaching in shaping the decisionmaking process:

i) Social assessment of technology requires to be conducted in a "systemic way", i.e. the problem under consideration is studied as a system, as a dynamic whole whose components are defined both per se and through the mutual relationships.

ii) Its central part is a systematic inventory of the possible impacts on society, both direct and indirect, short- and long-term.

iii) The crucial phase is the attempt to evaluate all these impacts including, besides the usual technical and economic ones, the impacts on individuals, social groups, social structures, the environment and value systems.

iv) Not only promoters and interested parties have to be taken into account. In particular, the options and socio-political weight of those social groups who have previously been considered as external to the decisionmaking process must enter into the analysis of impacts and especially into the formulation of policy.

v) The expected outcome of genuine social assessment of technology is to present an array of coherent action options to the decisionmaker.

The assessment implies therefore, a multi-disciplinary approach allowing for a simultaneous tracing of the pathways between technological developments and societal impacts. It can be performed only as a multi-iterative feedback process where the analysis of a technological development interacts with generation of new knowledge about its impacts and with needs for action options likely to optimise the societal benefits of the course decided upon.

With such a wide range of phenomena, variables and relationships to be considered, social assessment of technology is of necessity a particularly complex matter and an extremely extensive and demanding activity which is hardly possible without incessant evaluation of those states of society which relate social and economic developments to technological change.

REFERENCES

[1] G. Hupkes: **New Urban Transportation System Families.**

[2] Alain Bieber and Xavier Godard: **Notes on the Social Assessment of Technology in the Case of Urban Transport.**

[3] **An Assessment of Community Planning for Mass Transit. Automated Guideway Transit:** an Assessment of PRT and Other New Systems. Automatic Train Control in Rail Rapid Transit.

The state of mobility research

Heinz Hautzinger and Peter Kessel

Prognos, European Center for Applied Economic Research

Basel, Switzerland

INTRODUCTION

Mobility research is concerned with the description, explanation and forecast of the extent to which individuals carry out movements in space. For a large part, it thus stands for transport research as such. In an attempt to present a brief outline of this field, it will therefore hardly be possible to give a complete survey, and the selection of topics will always be somewhat arbitrary.

As a personal characteristic, mobility is usually measured by the number of trips a person completes during a specified time period. The necessity and urgency of making trips results from the compulsions and/or desires of an individual to carry out social and economic activities. Whether subjective mobility desires become an actual mobility demand is largely determined by the mobility opportunities of an individual, which are characterized by the availability of transport modes, the ability and inclination to buy transport services and the physical driving or riding capability.

Initially, mobility research was almost exclusively descriptive in nature and in transport planning the future level of mobility was treated as an exogenous quantity like motorization. Although the necessity of a behavioural and causal explanation of mobility has been recognized at a fairly early stage, suitable models have been developed only in recent years. In order to evaluate what has been reached in mobility research up to now.

- the characteristics of mobility,
- the determinants of mobility and, finally,
- the state of the art in mobility modelling

are discussed in the remainder of this paper.

CHARACTERISTICS OF MOBILITY

As indicated above, the mobility of an individual is usually measured by its trip frequency. The total number of trips e.g. per day, however, is only a very crude measure since mobility is an extremely heterogeneous phenomenon. The various components of an individual mobility pattern may for instance be as different from each other as a charter flight to Majorca or a little walk to the cigarette automat on the corner. Trips as the natural elements of any mobility pattern can show quite divergent qualities and features and their completion may depend on quite different compulsions and choices regarding the purpose, spatial destination, transport mode and route.

Mobility research has therefore first of all to deal with these different features of trips. This refers mainly to the following detail aspects:

- The functional distribution of trips according to the various travel purposes
- The spatial distribution of trips (origin-destination relationships)
- The modal distribution of trips
- The distribution of trips according to length and duration
- The distribution of trips according to time of completion.

Since the empirical findings on the temporal, spatial, modal, and functional distribution of trips are generally well documented, it is not necessary to repeat them here. However, a few remarks should be made on the functional aspect i.e. the travel purposes. These are of particular importance as they predetermine to a large extent the mobility behaviour of individuals with regard to the choice of transport modes, and the other aspects of trip making. According to the purpose (motive) of a trip the following types of trips are usually distinguished: work, education, business, shopping, recreation, and passenger services. If a further division according to weekday and weekend travel is undertaken, the mobility components which have thus been defined are much more homogeneous in themselves than the heterogeneous overall mobility of an individual. The current situation in the Federal Republic of Germany (FRG) is characterized as follows [1]: work 29%, shopping 27%, recreation 21%, education 12%, business 7%, and service 4%.

According to the importance of travel purposes wide attention has been paid to this aspect within the scope of mobility research. The analysis of the "purpose structure" of travel behaviour is increasingly shifting from an isolated consideration of single trips to the investigation of complete daily travel patterns. For the transition from a certain transport purpose (activity) to the next – not necessarily different - purpose, specific transition probabilities can be identified. We shall refer to this again later on in more detail. An important starting base for further investigation of trip patterns is the empirical result that the daily trip sequences of individuals are strongly concentrated on only a few basic types. An analysis of the travel behaviour of approximately 16,000 persons yielded nearly 1,200 different trip patterns. Half of all mobile persons did however have one of the following six trip patterns:

home-work-home (20.6%)
home-shopping-home (10.1%)
home-education-home (9.8%)
home-education-home-recreation-home (3.4%)
home-recreation-home (3.2%), and
home-work-home-recreation-home (2.9%).

In the widest sense, all types of spatial movements including walks on foot should be considered as part of the individual mobility pattern. Such a comprehensive approach is becoming increasingly important in view of the potential substitutability and actual substitution of walks on foot by vehicular trips and vice versa. In spite of this fact, walks have up to now received relatively little attention in mobility research and few analyses have been made. Past data are almost exclusively available for vehicular trips.

These data indicate a strong growth of vehicular mobility in all industrialized countries. In the FRG, for instance, in 1950 only 0.5 daily trips per capita were carried out. In 1975, this figure was already 1.3 trips per person and day, i.e. the growth amounted to approximately 180%. The length of trips has also increased distinctly. In 1950, the average of length of a trip was about 10 km, in 1975 approximately 20 km [2]. A more detailed analysis shows that the development up to now has been marked by partially extreme changes in the relative and absolute importance of the various travel purposes. While the average number of work trips per person and weekday has been stagnating for quite some time, the business and recreational mobility in the FRG has alone during the last decade about doubled in volume. Shopping trips per person trebled and mainly due to specific developments in the German education system the number of school trips has grown fivefold [1,3].

DETERMINANTS OF MOBILITY BEHAVIOUR

A large number of different influential factors can be identified as the causes of the described development of mobility, depending on its multi-layered, multidimensional structure. From a macro viewpoint, the primary causes of the characteristics, scope, and development of the demand for mobility can be classified as follows:

– **Economic factors:** these are mainly the income of private households and growing labour division in the organization of economic processes.

– **Demographic structures:** the most important are the age structure of the population, activity and education rates, and size of households.

– **Settlement and spatial structure:** the impacts of these causal components are probably most easily discernible. Mobility demand results from the spatial separation of basic activities, i.e. place of residence, work, shopping and recreation. The way these activities are spatially mixed or disentangled determines the necessity and scope for each individual of connecting by trips his

various activities during the course of a day.

– **Social behavior patterns:** in this context, the previous development has been marked by an increasing number of social positions and rôles of the individuum, not last on account of more leisure time. The growing number of positions inside the family, at the workplace, in societies, associations of political parties can be observed in all industrialized societies as typical accompaniment of the economic development. It increases quite inevitably the necessity of communication and integration and thus the demand for mobility [4].

– **Transport network and transport mode supply conditions:** the previous development in practically all industrialized countries was largely characterized by mass motorization, forced extensions of road networks and, at the same time, decreasing intensity of services in public passenger transport. These supply conditions have a direct and immediate impact on mobility, for instance by way of inducing trips through the initial purchase of a car, regardless of whether the resulting additional demand is actually "new" or whether it has already been latently existent. Indirectly, transport supply affects mobility by influencing also the other causal components mentioned above. Since without transport supply mobility cannot materialize, the demand for mobility is a "coupled" demand for trips, and for the means of transport they necessitate.

The possibilities to quantify the relations between the macro-type determinants as described above and the demand for mobility are very limited. Gross national product, income and motorization can be used only as crude indicators for the level of mobility. For example, the close connection between the mean number of daily trips per person and the motorization level of a certain town or region has already been identified during the early descriptive phase of mobility research [3, 5]. Any real explanation of mobility, however, presupposes a consideration of the socio-economic conditions of the individual. Despite this, personal and household characteristics have only recently been included in studies of mobility behaviour which utilize individual instead of zonal aggregated data.

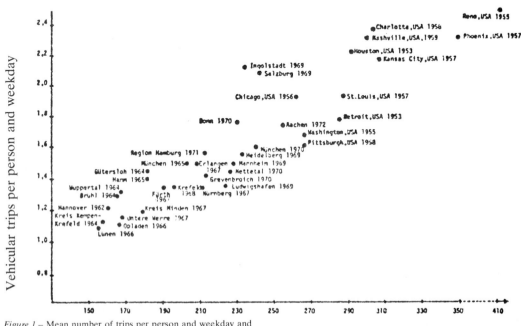

Figure 1 – Mean number of trips per person and weekday and motorization level in 38 towns and regions.

Cars per 1000 inhabitants

The analysis of major causal determinants of mobility which was initially undertaken rather qualitatively and globally from a macro viewpoint can be carried out much more concretely within a micro analytic framework with the individual as the study object. In several previous studies, the following central socio-economic factors have been identified [1, 6, 7, 8].
– Regularly recurring **demand compulsions,** as mainly characterized by the occupational status;
– The individual **mobility potential,** i.e. the ability to undertake trips, as for instance characterized by the possession of a driving license, of an automobile or by age;
– The **social status,** as for instance expressed by household income or the education level of an individual.
Of the socio-economic factors described in the foregoing, those which are closest related to the total number of daily trips, are – as expected – the most important factors of influence also in mode-specific analyses.

If the frequency of daily trips which an individual undertakes by car, public transit modes, bicycle or on foot, is analysed, in context with its socio-economic features, the following dependencies become apparent:
– The number of trips, which an individual undertakes is for each single transport mode largely determined by the same characteristics, above all by the possession of a driving license, possession of a car, and by occupational status.
– If a person is occupied and possesses both driving licence and a car, the individual number of automobile trips will, of course, be usually large. At the same time, total mobility tends also to be high.
– The number of trips a person undertakes on foot, by bicycle or public transport modes is chiefly determined by the automobile availability of that individual. The quality of supply with public transport facilities for instance has a much less significant influence on the usage of this mode. This confirms available experience from specific transport mode choice studies.

Table 1 – Relative importance of various determinants of trip frequency for different types of transport modes [1].

No.	Total trips	Walks	Bicycle trips	Car trips (Driver)	Bus trips
1	Licence poss.	Sex	Licence poss.	Car ownership	Licence poss.
2	Car ownership	Car ownership	Car ownership	Licence poss.	Car ownership
3	Occup. status	Housing conditions	Age	Occup. status	Age
4	Education	Occup. status	Occup. status	Pos. in household	Pos. in household
5	Age	Licence poss.	Pos. in household	Sex	Age (head of household)

Except age all variables appearing in this list are binary. No income data available.

In Table 1 various variables are ranked according to their importance in determining mobility. In interpreting these results it should be noted, however, that the occupational status was treated here as a binary variable (employed, not employed). If instead the full "range" of this characteristic (i.e. the categories employed, housewife, scholar, retired) was considered, the occupational status of a person proves to be the clearly dominating factor in most cases.

These empirical results have been obtained using a variety of statistical techniques. It seems, however, that the potential of methods of statistical inference has not yet been fully utilized. This is especially true for multivariate methods.

MODELS OF MOBILITY
General requirements for mobility models
By the "condensation" of available empirical knowledge about the study subject mobility into a number of *a priori* hypotheses, a mobility model is created. The development of such models must naturally be oriented by the concrete information needs of transport policy and planning. Statements on expected future developments of mobility and on the probable effect of measures which influence mobility will take a prominent position. From these two major functions, the standards can be derived which have to be required of models of mobility demand. They can be summarized as follows:
– **Explanatory value:** The model should be multivariate, i.e. it should contain statements on structural interrelations and thus provide the basis for an analysis of the effects of changing conditions.
– **Forecasting capacity:** The model should take into account the intrinsic dynamics of mobility behaviour and its interrelations with the relevant socio-economic and technical systems.
– **Policy sensitivity:** The model should, in an opera-

tional form, contain as variables all determining factors which can be influenced politically or by planning. Thus it should be suited to detect ways and means of achieving certain targets.

As shown by the following critical assessment of approaches which have been developed up to now, no comprehensive mobility model exists yet which meets all these requirements.

Currently existing models
Model typology
For a systematic study of currently existing models, a distinction should first of all be made between macro and micro models of transport mobility. While for *macro models,* spatial or socio-economic aggregates of individuals are the object of model design, *micro models* always attempt to reflect the behaviour of single individuals. With a micro model statements on behavioural characteristics of certain populations are therefore only possible after applying suitable aggregation methods. Macro models are estimated on the basis of aggregated data, while the statistical estimation of micro models requires disaggregated individual data.

A classification according to the time element leads to *static* and *dynamic* mobility models. While models of the first category contain no time-dependent variables, dynamic models are characterized by explicit time dependence of the variables. Temporal aspects can, within the scope of static models, at best be taken into account by comparative static analyses.

A third differentiation is finally undertaken according to the question to what extent the models are based on explicit behavioural hypotheses. Models which answer this qualification are usually called *behaviour-oriented.*

This classification results in altogether eight different categories of mobility models, to which the models developed so far can be assigned. As will be shown later, only six of these eight model categories have so far become apparent. Therefore, in the subsequent discussion a distinction will be made only between macro and micro models, the latter being additionally divided into static and dynamic approaches.

Macro-analytical mobility models

Seen from a historical point of view, macro-analytical *zonal trip generation models* represent the first mobility models altogether. The issue of model design in this case is first of all the estimation of the relationship between the number T of trips starting out from a traffic zone and certain characteristics x_j $(j=1, \ldots, q)$ of this zone (e.g. number of inhabitants or number of cars per zone). Typically, a linear stochastic relationship of the form

$$T = \alpha_0 + \alpha_1 x_1 + \ldots + \alpha_q x_q + \varepsilon \qquad (1)$$

is assumed, with $\alpha_0, \alpha_1, \ldots, \alpha_q$ being parameters, and ε a random disturbance variable, representing all non-systematic influences on the number of zonal trips. On the further assumptions of the classical linear regression model, estimates $\hat{\alpha}_j$ for the unknown parameters can be determined from zonally aggregated random sampling data. Given forecast values x_j^* of the exogenous variable, the expected number τ^* of trips starting out from an individual zone at a certain time interval in the future is estimated by means of the relation

$$\hat{\tau}^* = \hat{\alpha}_0 + \hat{\alpha}_1 x_1^* + \ldots + \hat{\alpha}_q x_q^* \qquad (2)$$

Zonal trip generation models have quite a number of weaknesses which have already been examined very thoroughly in the literature [9, 10]. The main points of this criticism have been the following:

– The assumptions of the classical linear regression model which form the basis of parameter estimation and testing of hypotheses, are in reality often violated to such an extent that the derived results are practically worthless.

– Zonal trip generation models explain only the variation of travel behaviour between different zones and thus not the real causes of the observed behaviour discrepancies. High values of the multiple correlation coefficient ($R=0.95$ is not rare) pretend a non-existing explanatory quality.

– The results – in particular the parameter estimates – depend heavily on the division into traffic zones and are therefore not spatially transferable.

– Macro-analytical trip frequency models of the type (1) do on account of their zonal aggregated character as a rule do not contain policy sensitive variables in a form which would make an analysis of the effects of alternative measures possible.

A recent *two-stage mobility forecasting model* [11] can also be classified as macro approach. In this model the mean daily trip frequency T of the inhabitants of a town or region is assumed to depend on the prevailing car density x (number of cars per 1000 inhabitants):

$$T = \alpha_0 + \alpha_1 x + \varepsilon \qquad (3)$$

The car density is largely regarded as an indicator variable for the individual transport mode supply conditions and the general economic status of the area under survey. The parameters α_0, α_1 of the regression model (3) have been estimated on the basis of the values indicated in Figure 1 ($\hat{\alpha}_0 = .118$, $\hat{\alpha}_1 = .006$). By means of the Gompertz-function

$$x_t = \xi \exp(-\beta_0 \beta_1^t) \qquad (4)$$

a forecast of the car density has been carried out for the Federal Republic of Germany, with t denoting the time (the base year (t=1) was 1952). With an exogenously given saturation level of $\hat{\xi} = 400$ cars per 1000 inhabitants the parameter estimates $\hat{\beta}_0 = 3.682$ and $\hat{\beta}_1 = .906$ resulted. A combination of the results of the regression analysis and the car density forecast yielded

$$\hat{\tau}_t^* = \hat{\alpha}_0^t + \hat{\alpha}_1 x_t^* = .188 + 2.400 \exp\{(-3.682) (.906)^t\} \qquad (5)$$

i.e. the forecasted value of the average daily vehicular trip frequency for the FRG in year t. Naturally, $\hat{\tau}_t^*$ has the character of a conditional point forecast of the mean trip frequency for a given car density forecast x_t^*. Starting out from a current mobility level of 1.9 vehicular trips per person and day (weekdays) this number rises according to (5) to 2.2 by 1980 and to 2.4 trips per person and day by 1985. For the year 1990 the value 2.5 follows, with the saturation level of average daily trip frequency being at just 2.7 trips per day. In addition to this point forecast, the limits of the respective (conditional) forecast intervals for arbitrary future dates have been determined. See Figure 2.

This approach has the advantage of being fully dynamic, since the temporal development of mobility is described by means of the saturation model (5). Its effectiveness is of course limited mainly due to the high aggregation level of this model. In principle however further refinements seem to be possible, for instance by means of stronger disaggregation and introduction of additional (causal) explanatory variables.

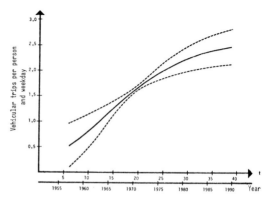

Figure 2 – Point and interval forecast of mean number of vehicular trips per person and weekday for the Federal Republic of Germany.

With some reservations, also *category analysis* [12] can be regarded as a mobility model. In order to characterize the mobility behaviour of households, these are first of all broken down into individual categories by means of household characteristics which have a significant influence on mobility (e.g. household income, car ownership, family structure). To these household categories specific mean trip rates will then be attributed. Accordingly, in category analysis for forecasting purposes the shares of individual household categories, on the one hand, and the related mean trip frequencies, on the other hand, must be estimated.

The category analysis approach is only to be classified with reservations as a mobility model in as much as it does not yield an explicit relation between mobility and its determinants. There is in particular, no possibility within the scope of this approach to assess the relative significance of the various influential factors. The major forecasting steps (forecast of category shares and specific categorial mobility levels) are taking place outside the actual "model".

Static micro-analytical mobility models

Contrary to the macro approach, in micro-analytical mobility models the individual or the household represent the study unit whose mobility behaviour is to be explained. *Linear regression models of individual trip frequency* are based on a stochastic relation of the type (1) with the exception that in this case T denotes the daily trip frequency of a person or a household, and the variables $x_1, \ldots, x_q$ represent characteristics of individuals or households (occupational status, car ownership, age, etc.), characteristics of the supply with public transport facilities (e.g. distance to stops) as well as characteristics of the opportunity potential (e.g. number of accessable leisure time institutions). For an estimation of the constant α_0 as well the variable weights $\alpha_1, \ldots, \alpha_q$ disaggregated random sampling data on persons or households are necessary.

As to whether the individual or the household are the better suited study unit, opinions differ. In an empirical study by the authors [1], the characteristics of the individual (in particular the occupational status) were distinctly confirmed as major determinants of the individual mobility level and accordingly the individual as the best suited study unit. From other sides, however, it has been requested to make the household the subject of analysis [13], since household characteristics, as for instance income and car ownership, are also of considerable importance for the mobility behaviour of individuals. The fact that mobility models on the household level leave a considerable part of total variability of trip frequency (i.e. behaviour variability within households) unexplained, is borne out by the fact that the coefficient of determination which reaches up to $R^2 \approx 0.4$ with household regression models [14] is generally distinctly below 0.3 with individual models.

It is evident that the problems of multiple regression analysis (non-normality, heteroskedasticity, multicollinearity) which are sufficiently known from statistical literature, also occur in the development of regression models of travel mobility. A discussion of relevant questions can be found in [13, 14, 15], where in addition specification problems and further aspects, as for instance the use of dummy variables and stepwise multiple regression, are dealt with.

On the whole, it can be observed that a micro approach of the type mentioned has considerable advantages over macro analytical regression models of mobility. The most important advantage is to be seen in its causal character and in the fact that it is much more easily transferable, spatially as well as temporally, due to its independence of special zonal divisions. On account of these stability properties it is particularly suited for forecasting purposes.

The linear regression model of individual mobility behaviour explains the observed behaviour divergencies by inter-personal differences of the values of certain variables – or more precisely – it assumes a linear dependence of the expected individual trip frequency on its determining factors. It does, on the other hand, not contain any explicit hypotheses on the origin of these behaviour patterns. This theoretical weakness is at least partially overcome by the so-called *behaviour-oriented trip frequency models*, which are based on the theory of qualitative choice behaviour [16].

It is not necessary to deal in detail with this approach which in the meantime is very much in use within the field of transport research. Models of this type explain the probability

$$p_j = P\{T=j\} \quad (j=0,1,\ldots,n) \tag{6}$$

that an arbitrary person undertakes exactly j trips for a certain purpose during a specific time interval as follows: The individual attributes to each "alternative" j a certain utility U_j, depending on the characteristics of this alternative which are combined in a vector x_j, and on the vector s of the socio-economic characteristics of the individual, i.e. $U_j = U(x_j, s)$. It is assumed that the individual chooses that alternative which offers the greatest utility.

Of course, for a randomly selected individual, U_j is a random variable. According to the decision rule mentioned above, we have

$$\{T=j\} \text{ if and only if } \{U_j = \max_{0 \le k \le n} U_k\} \tag{7}$$

Without loss of generality, U_j may be represented in the form $U_j = u(x_j, s) + \varepsilon(x_j, s)$ where u is non-stochastic and ε is a random variable. If the value of the h_{th} explanatory variable for alternative j is denoted by y_{hj} where y_{hj} depends on x_j and s, and if it is assumed that for $u_j = u$ (x_j, s) we have

$$u_j = \sum_{h=1}^{q} \alpha_h y_{hj} \quad (j=0,1,\ldots,n) \tag{8}$$

it can be shown that under the additional assumption of independent Weibull-distributed variables $\varepsilon_0, \varepsilon_1, \ldots, \varepsilon_n$ the multinomial logit model

$$P_j = \exp(u_j) / \sum_{k=0}^{n} \exp(u_k) \quad (j=0,1,\ldots n) \tag{9}$$

results. The unknown parameters $\alpha_1, \ldots, \alpha_q$ of this model can be estimated according to well-known statistical methods [16].

The expected value of the individual trip frequency is given by

$$\tau = E(T) = \sum_{j=0}^{n} j p_j \tag{10}$$

According to (8) and (9) it depends on the alternative-specific values y_{hj} of the explanatory variables as well as on the parameters α_h, which express the relative importance of the individual variables.

As compared with other aspects of travel behaviour (in particular transport mode choice) logit models have up to now only rarely been used for the estimation of trip frequency. Referring to initial applications as, for instance, described in [17] it seems promising to further develop trip frequency models of the type and to analyze the influence especially of socio-economic variables on an improved sampling data basis. The potential range of application of choice models is to be seen mainly in non-compulsory travel (i.e. shopping and recreational trips) since the completion of work and school trips is almost completely determined by the occupational status of a person.

Dynamic micro-analytical mobility models

Owing to the exceptional importance of travel purposes in the analysis of mobility it is advisable to formulate separate trip frequency models for each travel purpose. With such a breakdown of the overall mobility of a person, of course, the sequential aspect of trip making cannot be captured. Since quite a number of mobility phenomena can, however, only be explained by the optimizing behaviour of the individual in the planning of his daily activity program it seems only logical to develop appropriate dynamic models. Currently three different approaches can be roughly distinguished in this field:

– Markov chain models of the linking of activities,
– models which are based on hypotheses on the length of trip chains, and
– models which assume a trip generating process of need accumulation

If the activities carried out by a person are interpreted as states of a stochastic process, and his trips as transitions between subsequent states, a highly developed mathematical instrumentarium can be resorted to for the description of the mobility behaviour. Particularly specific statements are achieved if it is assumed that the described stochastic process is a finite homogenous Markov Chain. By means of such *Markovian trip chain models*, the distribution of population consisting of n persons over the set of various activities after completion of their i^{th} trip can be determined by using the recursion formula

$$s_i = s_{i-1}P \qquad (i=1,2,\ldots) \qquad (11)$$

The jth component s_{ij} of the row vector s_i is the number of persons who carry out an activity of type j ($j=1,\ldots,m$) before undertaking the $(i+1)^{th}$ trip, and the elements p_{jk} ($p_{jk}=0$) of the $(m \times m)$ matrix P denote the probability of a person's passing on to an activity of type k ($k=1,\ldots,m$) as next state, if it is just occupied with an activity of the type j. Apparently

$$\sum_{j=1}^{m} s_{ij} = n \qquad \text{and} \qquad \sum_{k=1}^{m} P_{jk} = 1$$

for all $i=0,1,2,\ldots$ and $j=1,\ldots,m$, respectively. The vector s_0 is called initial state and P is referred to as transition matrix of the process.

If the state (activity) "home" is split into two states, "from home" and "to home" (the latter being absorbing), this model yields the expected frequency of trip chains of any type, the expected frequency of the incidence of a certain trip purpose within a trip chain, and the expected "length" of a trip chain (number of trips until the return to the home). For the calculation of these expected values, merely the initial state s_0 and the transition matrix P must be known, since these two quantities completely determine the Markov chain.

The weak points of this simple Markovian model are obvious and are, for one thing, due to the Markov property of the model, i.e. to the assumption that the probability of a trip to a certain activity only depends on the last previous activity, and for another, to the homogeneity assumption that this transition probability is independent of the fact where the particular trip in question is ranking within the trip chain. Another weakness is the fact that temporal aspects (travel time, duration of an activity) are not taken into account. The first papers which were published as early as the 1960s [18, 19, 20] have in the meantime been generalized into various directions [21, 22].

The basic inadequateness of this type of model however is its descriptive nature: Transition probabilities must always be determined empirically, the model does not offer the possibility of estimating them on the basis of land-use, transport supply, and socio-economic data. A critical evaluation of these models should however not underestimate the fact that Markovian trip chain models represent the first approaches into a direction of research which is today regarded as the right one.

Besides Markovian trip chain models which build up on hypotheses regarding the linking of activities by trips, a second type of dynamic micro mobility models is based on assumptions on the probability of returning home from a non-home activity [24, 25]. Starting out from the empirically proven fact that short trip chains occur more frequently than long ones, in [24] the following assumption is made on the probability $p(t)$ of carrying out an additional trip to a non-home activity (in this instance: shopping) given that t trips have already been carried out since the last stay at home:

$$p(t) = \exp(-t/\lambda) \qquad (t=1,2,\ldots) \qquad (12)$$

In (12) the parameter λ is identified with the mean length of a trip chain and has to be determined empirically.

The model developed in [25] is mainly concentrated on the connexion between the process of linking trips and the number of daily activities outside the home. If this number is denoted by n and it is assumed that an individual is just staying at its kth non-home activity ($k \leq n$), the destination of the next trip may be one of the $n-k$ places which have not yet been visited or the home,

i.e. altogether $n-k+1$ destinations. If $p(k|n)$ denotes the probability of the event "trip back home from the kth non-home activity provided that altogether n activities outside the home are carried out", the fundamental hypothesis of the model can be depicted as follows:

$$p(k|n) = 1/(n-k+1) \qquad (13)$$

i.e. the probability of a return to the home is the smaller the more unattended activities are still on the daily program of the person in question. Since from (13) it follows for the expected value of the number C_n of daily trip chains of a person visiting n non-home activities

$$E\{C_n\} = \sum_{i=1}^{n} \frac{1}{i}$$

the model is called *harmonic seris trip chain model*. Under the hypothesis (13) the distribution of the length of trip chains and the expected value of the individual daily trip frequency can be obtained in dependence on n.

The advantages of the harmonic series model are to be seen in the fact that it seeks to describe the entire daily mobility pattern of persons in a distinct manner and not only single trip chains from such a pattern. Moreover, it creates an immediate connexion between travel behaviour and number of daily activities. On the other hand, it is a disadvantage that the model is based on an assumption (Eq. (13)) which seems very specific, that no activities of differing types are taken into account, and that the ultimate results depend only on the distribution of the number n of non-home activities. If the model is calibrated, only the distribution of n, but not the observed mobility behaviour would be taken into consideration. The model also has a descriptive character, since it does not contain any explanatory variables. This criticism indicates at the same time possible approaches toward an improvement of the model.

A third, very interesting approach starts out from a classification into so-called "fixed" and "substitutable" activities [26, 27]. While activities of the first kind are carried out regularly at certain times and certain places (e.g. work), the latter are marked by free choice of time and place – at least within certain limits. Their occurence depends on whether the respective need has exceeded a certain threshold value. This threshold value depends on the expected utility which is connected with the activity in question, and on the distance from the place where the activity is carried out. While the expected utility of each substitutable activity can be regarded as fixed, the distance of the individual from the places of substitutable activities changes in the course of its movements in space which are induced by the fixed activities. In this context it is assumed that given the expected utility of a substitutable activity the threshold of the need increases with the distance from the activity place. Consequently, for each distance there is a minimum strength of the need required to incite a trip to the respective substitutable activity, One of the focal points of the model is the assumption that, starting out from a zero position, the intensity of need grows as long as it takes to reach the threshold value. After that, the respective activity will be carried out and the need drops to the starting value to begin accumulating again.

This principle of accumulation of need results in the fact that in the demand for substitutable activities, two alternative types of demand can be distinguished. In those cases where a person is staying at a "base place" (e.g. its home), and the need has been accumulated long enough to exceed the respective threshold value, we may speak of an autonomous demand. A controlled demand is the case when the accumulation of need is not far enough advanced to incite an autonomous demand, but that during the course of a trip from the base to a fixed activity, the distance of the person from the place of the

556

substitutable activity is reduced to such an extent as to make the accumulated need exceed the lower threshold of need attributed to this distance.

In [26] several travel pattern models of this type have been developed with varying degrees of complexity. The case of exponentially distributed time intervals between two subsequent fixed activities and an accumulation of need following a Poisson process has for instance been discussed. After complete specification, such a model yields, besides a number of interesting expected values (e.g. length of a trip chain, time interval between two trip chains, and frequency of trips of a certain type during a time interval) also estimates for the probability of a trip chain to contain certain types of activities. These quantities could however only be determined in simpler cases by analytical methods. For the more complicated models this was not possible, and simulation techniques had to be resorted to.

Without doubt, the *need accumulation model* represents an important contribution to the development of mobility models since it explains the generation of travel demand by the needs of persons for certain activities and by the individual utility resulting therefrom. In its present state of development it is however still as far removed from practical applicability as the other trip chain and travel pattern models. The problem of integration of personal and activity characteristics as explanatory variables is also still unsolved to a large extent.

Summary of Model Evaluation

The review of currently existing models in the field of transport mobility has demonstrated the great variety of all hitherto developed approaches. As shown in Table 2

with the exception of behavioural macro models all categories in the sense of the typology used here can be found.

If it is now attempted to assess in the form of a summary to what extent these models fulfill the three requirements of explanatory quality, forecasting capacity and policy sensitivity, the following can be said:

– Explanatory quality: This characteristics, as far as the integration of causal explanatory variables is concerned, is most markedly present in multinomial logit and individual regression (multivariate linear) trip frequency models. The explanatory potential of trip chain models is currently still very limited due to lacking consideration of socio-economic variables. Only a light explanatory quality can be accorded to all macro models.

– Forecasting capacity: This characteristic can probably at best be attributed to the regression model of the micro type and the dynamic macro mobility forecasting model. In the case of the logit model, the questions connected with the aggregation problem have not yet been solved to complete satisfaction. The zonal regression model is not very suitable on account of its parameter instability. Trip chain models can at the moment not be considered at all for longer-term forecasts, mainly due to their descriptive character.

– Policy sensitivity: The integration of policy sensitive variables in an operational form seems at best possible with micro models of the multinomial logit and multivariate linear type. With macro models, this is more difficult due to their high degree of aggregation, and with trip chain models, not even first approaches exist at the present time.

Table 2 - Classification of existing mobility models.

Type of model	Static		Dynamic	
	Behavioural	*Non behavioural*	*Behavioural*	*Non behavioural*
Macro	—	Zonal regression model (Category analysis)	—	Two-stage mobility forecasting model
Micro	Multinomial logit model	Individual regression model	Need accumulation model Harmonic series model	Markovian trip chain model

DIRECTIONS OF FUTURE MOBILITY RESEARCH

This survey of the present state of mobility research has made two major issues quite clear. For one thing, it could be demonstrated that empirical knowledge of the characteristics and determining factors of mobility have already reached a comparatively high standard. For another, it has become apparent that mobility research is suffering from a deficit in theories which should not be underestimated: no really satisfactory model of travel mobility exists yet.

Behavioural micro-analytical trip frequency models, for instance, have the advantage of being based on explicit behavioural hypotheses and containing the significant socio-economic explanatory variables. Their weakness, on the other hand, is the oversimplified description of individual mobility behaviour merely by daily trip frequency. The dynamic trip chain models, for their part, characterize mobility much more precisely, but are at the present time still lacking in the integration of causal determining factors.

From this disproportion between the empirical and theoretical state of knowledge the emphases of future theoretical mobility research are directly derived. The aim should in this case plainly be the development of models which explain the mobility behaviour of persons by the pattern of daily activities with the help of plausible assumptions on the individual decision behaviour. Approaches of this kind could for instance be the further development of the harmonic trip chain model or the need accumulation model. It would in this context also appear a promising undertaking to follow up the travel time budget approach [28] as well as the journey structures approach [29].

All currently existing micro models are of a short-term nature. No method exists so far which shows how to use these short-term behavioural models for long-term forecasts. A stronger concentration of research activities on the long-term forecasting problem should bring the necessary complementation of the aspect of model calibration which has been strongly emphasized up to now.

Applied mobility research should in the future be

more concentrated on actual mobility problems of our society. Of particular urgency in this context seems to be the identification of individual social groups, which are at a particular disadvantage on account of insufficient mobility opportunities, and the investigation of their mobility problems. The analysis of the possibilities of influencing mobility in order to reach an overall social optimum distribution of mobility should also be seen in this context.

REFERENCES

[1] Hautzinger, H., and P. Kessel: **Mobilität im Personenverkehr,** Untersuchung im Auftrag des Bundesverkehrsministeriums, Bonn, Prognos AG, Basel, 1976.

[2] Der Bundesminister für Verkehr: Verkehr in Zahlen 1976, Bonn, 1976.

[3] Kessel, P.: Verhaltensweisen im werktäglichen Personenverkehr, **Strassenbau und Strassenverkehrstechnik,** Heft 132, Bonn, 1972.

[4] Spiegel, E.: Stadtstruktur und Gesellschaft, in: **Zur Ordnung der Siedlungsstruktur,** Veröffentlichungen der Akademie für Raumforschung und Landesplanung, Hannover, 1974.

[5] Curran, and Stegmaier: Travel patterns in 50 Cities, **Highway Research Record,** No. 230, 1958.

[6] Mossman, F., and A.J. Faria: Mobility Index Based on the Socioeconomic Characteristics of Households, Traffic Quarterly, Vol. 29, 347-367, 1975.

[7] Tardiff, T.J.: Comparison of Effectiveness of Various Measures of Socioeconomic Status in Models of Transportation Behavior, **Transportation Research Record,** No. 534, 1975, 1-9.

[8] Kannel, E.J., and K.W. Heathington: Structural Model for Evaluating Urban Travel Relationships, **Transportation Research Record,** No. 526, 73-82, 1974.

[9] McCarthy, G. M.: Multiple-Regression Analysis of Household Trip Generation - A Critique, **Highway Research Record,** No. 298, 31-43, 1969.

[10] Lewis, R.J., and A.A. Douglas: Trip Generation Techniques, **Traffic Engineering and Control,** Vol. 12, 428-431, 1970.

[11] Kessel, P., and H. Hautzinger: Verkehrsmobilität: Meinungen – Analysen – Prognosen, **Zeitschrift für Verkehrswissenschaft,** 47. Jahrgang, Heft 1, 1976, 31-44.

[12] Wootton, H.J., and G.W. Pick: A Model for Trips Generated by Households, **Journal of Transport Economics and Policy,** Vol. 1, No. 2, 1967, 137-153.

[13] Douglas, A.A., and R.J. Lewis: Trip Generation Techniques, **Traffic Engineering and Control,** Vol. 12, 477-479, 1971.

[14] White, M.T.: An Examination of Residual Distributions in Ordinary Least Squares (OLS) Household-Based Trip Generation Models, **Transportation Research,** Vol. 10, 249-254, 1976.

[15] Hautzinger, H.: Statistical Analysis of Travel Behaviour, (forthcoming).

[16] McFadden, D.: Conditional Logit Analysis of Qualitative Choice Behaviour, in: Zarembka, P. (ed.): **Frontiers in Econometrics,** Academic Press, New York, 1974.

[17] Charles River Associates: **A Disaggregate Behavioral Model of Urban Travel Demand,** Federal Highway Administration, U.S. Department of Transportation, Washington, D.C., 1972.

[18] Hemmens, G.C.: **The Structure of Urban Activity Linkages,** Center for Urban and Regional Studies, Chapel Hill, 1966.

[19] Horton, F.E., and W.E. Wagner: A Markovian Analysis of Urban Travel Behavior: Pattern Response by Socioeconomic-Occupational Groups: **Highway Research Record,** No. 283, 1969, 19-29.

[20] Marble, D.F.: A Simple Markovian Model of Trip Structures in a Metropolitan Region, **Papers of the Regional Science Association,** Western Section, 1964.

[21] Kondo, K.: Estimation of Person Trip Patterns and Modal Split, in: Buckley, D.J. (ed.): **Transportation and Traffic Theory,** Elsevier, New York, 1974.

[22] Gilbert, G., G.L. Peterson and J.L. Schefer: Markov Renewal Model of Linked Trip Travel Behaviour, **Transportation Engineering Journal,** Proceedings of the American Society of Civil Engineers, TE 3, 1972, 691-704.

[23] Jones, P.M.: **The Analysis and Modelling of Multi-Trip and Multi-Purpose Journeys,** Transport Studies Unit/University of Oxford, Working Paper No. 6 (Revised), May, 1976.

[24] Nystuen, J.D.: A Theory and Simulation of Intraurban Travel, in: Garrison, W.L., and D.F. Marble (ed.): **Quantitative Geography,** Northwestern University, Studies in Geography, No. 13, 1967, 54-83.

[25] Vidakovic, V.S.: A Harmonic Series Model of the Trip Chains, in: See Ref. 21.

[26] Westelius, O.: **The Individual's Pattern of Travel in an Urban Area,** National Swedish Building Research, Document D 2, 1972.

[27] Westelius, O.: **The Individual's Way of Choosing Between Alternative Outlets,** National Swedish Building Research, Document D 17, 1973.

[28] Zahavi, Y.: **Travel Time Budgets and Mobility in Urban Areas,** Final Report No. PL 8183, prepared for the U.S. Federal Highway Administration, Washington, D.C., 1974.

[29] Hensher, D.A.: **The Structure of Journeys and Nature of Travel Patterns: Some Conceptual Issues,** Transport Studies Unit/University of Oxford, Working Paper No. 15, January, 1976.

Accessibility and its application to a dynamic model of spatial land-use distribution

by

BEAT GREUTER

University of Dortmund Federal Republic of Germany

Transportation planning is based on the assumption that the distribution of land-uses determines the relations between them. With the help of appropriate models, it is possible to estimate the volumes which must be handled by the interconnecting transport links. The volumes, then determine the required quality of transportation infra-structure. On the other hand, experts have pointed out, that the development of transportation infra-structure does have an impact on the distribution of land-uses and also, for certain trip purposes, on the number of trips. This kind of feedback – inconvenient as it may be – can indeed render previous decisions obsolete. It may very well happen, that actual volumes of new urban roads serving the city centre will be much larger than originally calculated, since the improved level of service generates an intensified location of certain land-uses in the city centre. The response of the transportation planners and the politicians alike was mostly such, that they demanded further improvements in service quality for the links concerned without being aware of the fact that, owing to this action, the negative feedbacks would only be intensified. Instead of achieving a reduction in transportation, new and heavier volumes would be the result. This effect was observed in most of the cities of mid-west U.S.A. The consequence was a drain of the city centres, first of residential land-use, and later on also of workplaces, since the growing difficulties in transportation increasingly aggravated the exchange of people and commodities between the city centre and the periphery.

From the above, the question arises, whether one could not succeed in formulating a model which would make the growth and the distribution of land-uses in an urban region dependent on the quality of exchange-relations in the whole urban area and in individual sub-areas. Such a model could demonstrate and forecast this counterflow relationship which is not considered in gravitation models.

Although this basic hypothesis of my simulation model cannot yet be verified statistically, it is very probable as soon as the inner relations of an urban region, owing to the increasing sectoral and spatial differentiation of urban land-uses, become more significant than its external relations. In this case, the so-called 'urban multiplier', i. e. the development of the external relations, will no longer solely determine the growth of a city – although is still being presumed by some new models which aim at the same objective. The hypothesis is also substantiated by the observation, that a growing number of urban development planners deliberately or intuitively imply, that it is the spatial structure of a city which determines growth. Thus, for instance, the Hamburg economist Jürgensen once warned not to underestimate the significance of the internal urban land-use and spatial structure for the growth of a city. The interesting aspect is, that while urban development planning is based on future economic growth, this is now seen to depend largely on structural assets and not only on general national economic development which, according to previous practices of economists, has never been transformed into a spatial structure.

A model, which makes the development of urban land-uses dependent on interior urban exchange relations, must have two characteristics:

1. It must of necessity be dynamic, i. e. include a time dimension, since we are confronted with land-use changes.

2. The dynamic process must be inherent, i. e. the structure of the system itself determines its development and not some external factors.

The first, and in my opinion, the only scientists to explicitly introduce these two concepts of dynamic into their models are two Americans, J.W. Forrester (Industrial Dynamic and Urban Dynamic) and his assistant Meadow, who became noted for his so-called World Model ("Limitations of Growth").

I myself have adopted Forrester's dynamic simulation method for my model, but only with respect to format and not to its substance, since Forrester does not subdivide the urban system into sub-areas and essentially considers an other problem, i. e. the question of vertical mobility versus horizontal mobility which is my field of interest.

The general schematic of the feedback process shows that the internal structure of the land-use transportation system controls the changes of its elements. One distinguishes between level variables which together indicate the present state of the system, and flow values – the so-called rate variables – which show the absolute change of level variables per unit of time. Since it is of course not only the level variable illustrated here which determines its own change, but several other or all level variables are involved, the feedback-arrow was drawn as a dotted line.

To construct the model we must first define and then combine all level and rate variables. In doing so, we distinguish between workplaces and residential land-use which, however, as far as the model structure is concerned, differ only in detail from each other.

The level variables always indicate the quantity of a certain land-use, both in the urban region as a whole, and in a given sub-area i

For residential land-use, the rate variables are as follows:

1. New residential population moves into the urban

559

region (NWG).

2. New residential population moves into sub-area i (NWT$_i$).

This rate variable is composed of

a) persons coming from areas outside the urban region,

b) persons having migrated or having been displaced from other sub-areas.

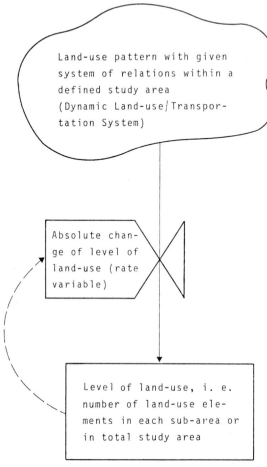

Fig. 1 – Schematic of feed-back process

3. Residential population migrates from sub-area i ('voluntary' migration AWT$_i$) 'Voluntary', however, does not imply that there are no social pressures.

4. Residential population is displaced from sub-area i ('forced' migration VWT$_i$). 'Forced' migration means, that one land-use is displaced from a sub-area by another land-use which is socially more powerful and curtails its former share of land.

5. Natural growth of residential population in sub-area i (NET$_i$).

6. Residential population leaves the urban region (AWG).

The rate variables for workplaces are of the same tenor, with the only exception that now there is no 'natural growth'. This is not quite correct, since the location of workplaces depends on whether an enterprise is already in the sub-area concerned or not, i. e. whether it is a newcomer or wishes to expand. Neither the theoretical

nor the empirical data, however, allow to differentiate between these two categories.

Next, the feedbacks, i. e. the values of the rate variables must be determined hypothetically. This is done by means of so-called determining factors which must be composed of the level or other rate variables respectively. To illustrate the two most important determining factors, let us look at the rate variable 'new residential land-use moves into sub-area i'.

We consider two land-uses (residential and work) and the relationships between them (commuters). Moreover, it is assumed that the land-uses are distributed over three sub-areas, and that the workingplaces are socially stronger and thus able to displace residential land-use. The feedbacks are then as follows:

1. All level variables have a two-fold influence on the determining factor 'accessibility' (E$_i$):

(i) in a direct manner, via the relation between the two land-uses,

(ii) indirectly via the loads on the transport infrastructure which, in turn, influence spatial interaction (deterrence function, $w_{ij}{}^{-1}$). Thus, accessibility is a measure of the present quality of the spatial ralations of a particular sub-area with respect to the exchange-process between land-uses. It may adopt values ranging from 0 to 1, 1 indicating optimal conditions of exchange. Since we have only one relation, value E_1 (B) for the relation is equivalent to value E_1 (F) for the land-use.

2. The quantity of residential population in sub-area 1 (W)$_1$, minus the number of residents prepared to migrate from sub-area 1 (AWT$_1$), yields the present total area demand for housing in subarea 1 (GN$_1$). Total demand, GN$_1$, in turn, represents the area factor (RF(F)) which signifies the additional growth potential due to available residential land reserves. This factor, too, may range between 0 and 1, 1 indicating optimum growth potential.

The area factor (RF(F)) is furthermore influenced by the proportion of land assigned to residential use in sub-area 1 (RA$_i$(F)) which is constantly threatened by possible displacement through workplaces. Furthermore it also depends on the value assigned to available residential land in the eye of demand, i. e. on what is known as 'potential' which indicates the quantity of attractions (in this case represented by workplaces). No matter how large the area, if there are no attractions, the area factor will still be 0.

3. The determining factors accessibility, area factor, and the absolute quantity of residential land-use in sub-area 1, now control the value of the rate variable 'new residential population moves into sub-area 1', using the absolute number of residential population as weight or agglomeration factor. Presenting only this one rate variable demonstrated the variety and complexity of feedback processes. In the following our task will be to determine, for each individual rate variable, the dependence on its determining factors. Thus, we shall arrive at the basic hypotheses of the simulation model.

1. DETERMINING FACTORS AND BASIC HYPOTHESIS FOR THE RATE VARIABLE 'NEW WORKPLACES MOVE INTO THE URBAN AREA' (NAG)

The rate variable 'new workplaces move into the urban area' is controlled by the weighted total accessibility. This is the sum of the accessibilities of all individual sub-areas and describes the quality of interrelationships within the urban system. Weighting will include both the relative quantity of land-uses in each sub-area and its area factor, i.e. the indicator for land which is still at disposal. It may

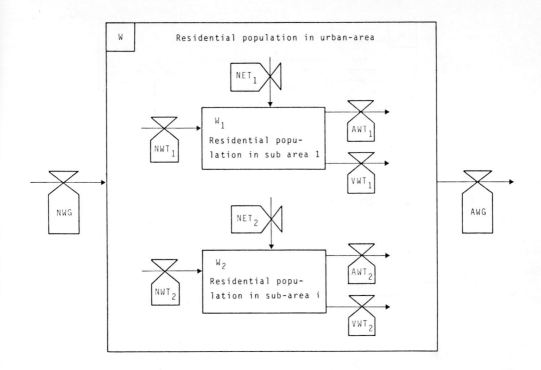

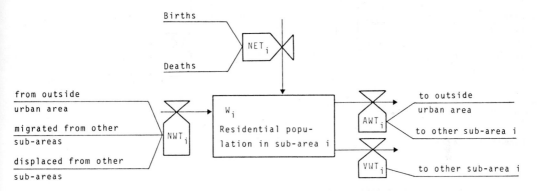

Legend of rate variables:

NWG   =   new residential population moves into urban-area

NWT_i =   new residential population moves into urban-area i

AWT_i =   residential population migrates from sub-are i (voluntary migration)

VWT_i =   residential population is desplaced from sub-area i (forced migration)

NET_i =   natural growth of residential population in sub-area i (difference between births and deaths which, unlike all values of other change variables, may also be negative)

AWG   =   residential population leaves urban-area

Fig. 2 – Model structure (for residential population) and combination of rate variables for a given sub-area.

561

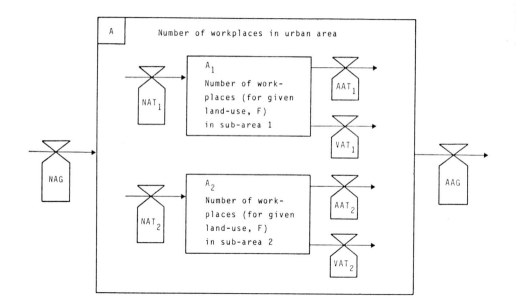

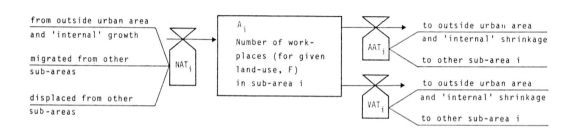

Legend of rate variables:

NAG   =   new workplaces move into urban area

NAT_i =   new workplaces move into sub-area i

AAT_i =   workplaces migrate from sub-area i (voluntary migration)

VAT_i =   workplaces are displaced from sub-area i (forced migration)

AAG   =   workplaces leave urban area

Fig. 3 – Model structure (for workplaces) and combination of rate varables for a given sub-area

562

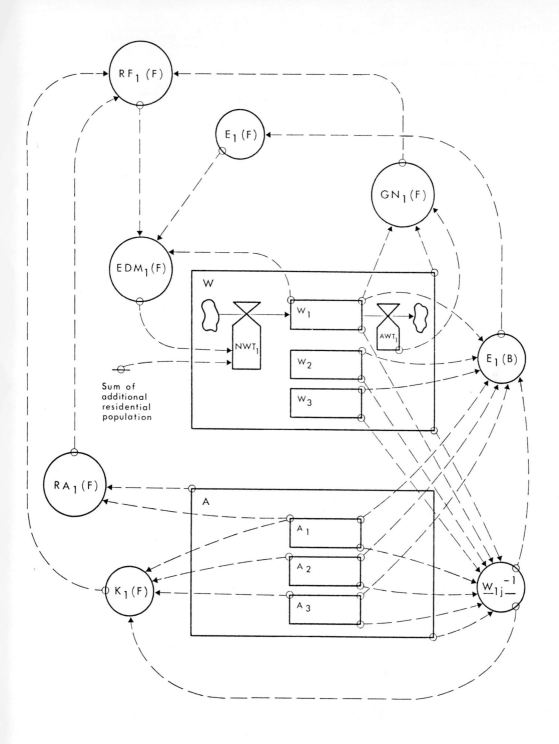

Fig. 4 – The complex influence of all level variables of the system on the rate variable NWT $_1$ (new residential population moves into sub-area 1)

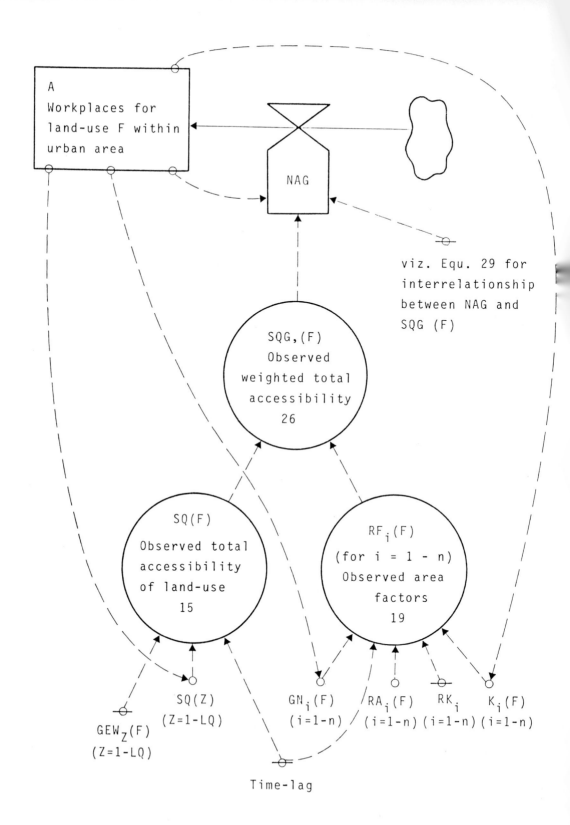

Fig. 5 – Relationship between rate variable NAG and its determining factors

happen, for example, that a land-use which is primarily concentrated in the city centre and has a comparatively high accessibility, is assigned a lower weighted total accessibility, if land reserves in the city centre are small. We shall see, that this is a very important fact to be considered in the model.

The first basic hypothesis now reads as follows:

The higher the total accessibility of workplaces in an area (it may also adopt values ranging between 0 and 1), weighted by area factors, the higher will be the percentage of gross growth within that area.

In combination with the present absolute quantities of land-uses in the urban area (level variable) the rate variable 'new workplaces move into the urban area', can be determined for each period of time.

This hypothesis does not apply to the corresponding rate variable for residential land-use. Since in a closed system the number of employees must always be equivalent to the number of workplaces, the quantity of new residential land-use will only be calculated at the end of overall balancing.

Since the following hypotheses apply to both residential land-uses and workplaces, there will no longer be any differentiation between them.

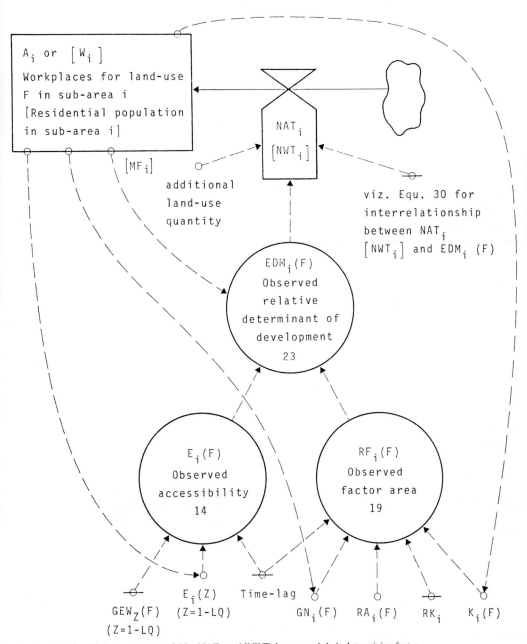

Fig. 6 - Relationship between rate variables NAT_i and $[NWT_i]$, resp. and their determining factors

2. DETERMINING FACTORS AND BASIC HYPOTHESIS FOR THE RATE VARIABLE 'NEW LAND-USES MOVE INTO A PARTICULAR SUB-AREA i' (NAT$_i$ AND NWT$_i$, RESPECTIVELY)

We have already discussed the determining factors. Accessibility, area factor, and present absolute quantity of land-uses are combined, by multiplication, to so-called development determinants. Then the hypothesis reads:

The higher the relative development determinant of a sub-area, the higher will be the proportion of the quantity of land-uses to be established in the urban system.

3. DETERMINING FACTORS AND BASIC HYPOTHESIS FOR THE RATE VARIABLE 'LAND-USES MIGRATE FROM SUB-AREA i' (VOLUNTARY MIGRATION, AAT$_i$ AND AWT$_i$, RESPECTIVELY)

'Voluntary' migration depends solely on the accessibility of a sub-area. The hypothesis reads:

The higher the accessibility of sub-area i for a given land-use, the lower the proportion of 'voluntary' migration from the sub-area considered.

The rate variable can be calculated for each period of time together with the present absolute quantity of land-use in each sub-area.

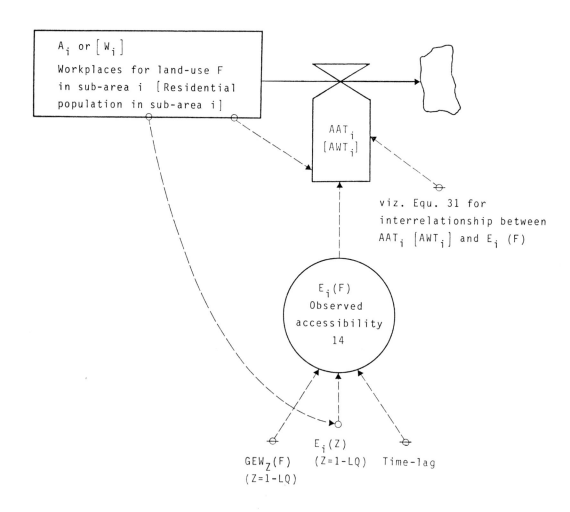

Fig. 7 – Relationship between rate variables AAT$_i$ and [AWT$_i$], resp., and their determining factors

4. DETERMINING FACTORS AND BASIC HYPOTHESIS FOR THE RATE VARIABLE 'DISPLACEMENT OF SOCIALLY WEAKER LAND-USES' ('FORCED' MIGRATION, VAT$_i$, VWT$_i$).

The quantity of a displaced land-use depends on its own degree of land-occupancy and on the degree of land-occupancy of other uses which are socially stronger. The degree of land-occupancy for each land-use and sub-area is defined as the ratio between total land demand and the corresponding land supply. The hypothesis reads:

The higher the degree of land-occupancy of a socially stronger land-use, the higher will be the quantity of displaced land-uses, of a socially weaker nature, provided that these have exhausted their share of land and total land within the sub-area cannot be extended.

The arguments for this hypothesis lie in the fact, that a high degree of occupancy limits further growth. Powerful land-uses will therefore attempt, at the expense of other land-uses, to increase their share of land in attractive sub-areas. In our economic and social system this is done via the price of land.

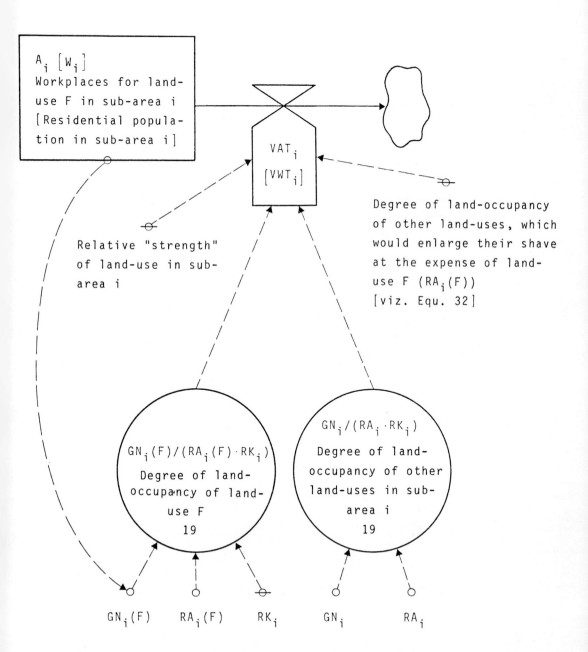

Fig. 8 – Relationship between rate variables VAT$_i$ and [VWT$_i$], resp., and their determining factors

567

5. DETERMINING FACTORS AND BASIC HYPOTHESIS FOR THE RATE VARIABLE 'LAND-USES LEAVE THE URBAN AREA' (AAG, AWG, RESPECTIVELY).

The rate variable 'land-uses leave the urban area' is determined by the total accessibility of the system. However, there is no weighting by use of area factors as was the case when dealing with new land-uses. Thus, it is assumed that, as for 'voluntary' migration from sub-area i, the area still at disposal has no influence on the rate variable 'land-uses leave the urban area'. The hypothesis reads:

The higher the total accessibility of a land-use within the urban system, the lower the proportion of migrants sumultaneously leaving the urban area out of each sub-area.

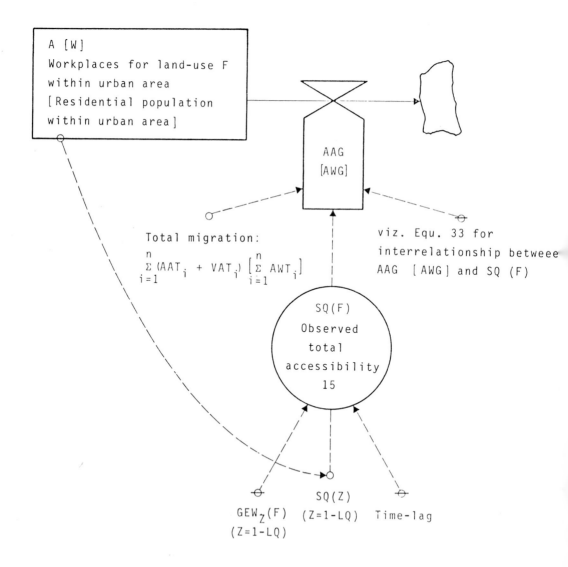

A [W]

Workplaces for land-use F within urban area

[Residential population within urban area]

AAG

[AWG]

Total migration:

$$\sum_{i=1}^{n} (AAT_i + VAT_i) \left[\sum_{i=1}^{n} AWT_i \right]$$

viz. Equ. 33 for interrelationship betweee AAG [AWG] and SQ (F)

SQ(F)

Observed total accessibility

15

GEW$_Z$(F) SQ(Z) Time-lag
(Z=1-LQ) (Z=1-LQ)

Fig. 9 – Relationship between rate variables AAG and [AWG], resp., and their determining factors

Two other important variables have also not yet been considered in the feedback-process:

Area demand of transportation infrastructure and commuter mobility. There are, however, no difficulties to integrate them at a later stage.

For the simulation model the hypotheses are now transformed into mathematical functions. These functions must be calibrated, and for this, additional investigations are necessary. I should emphasize, however, that it is more important to combine the hypothetical interrelationships into a model of the complex social urban system than to endulge into extensive empirical analysis. This is the only way to analyse feedback phenomena, even if they do not exaxtly correspond to reality as far as their quantities are concerned.

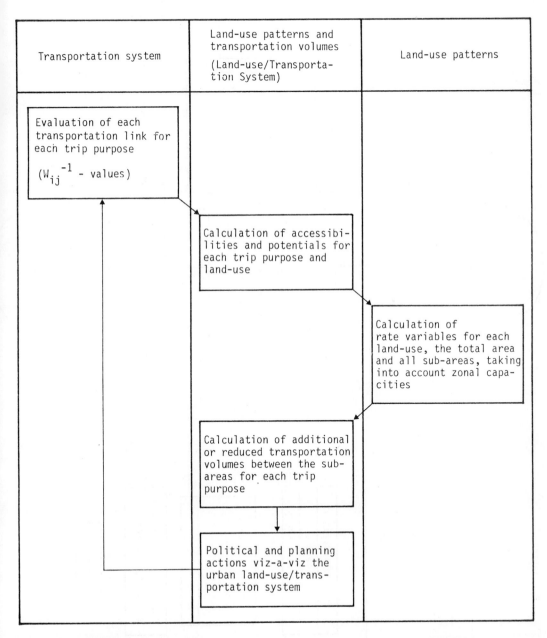

Transportation system	Land-use patterns and transportation volumes (Land-use/Transportation System)	Land-use patterns
Evaluation of each transportation link for each trip purpose (W_{ij}^{-1} - values)		
	Calculation of accessibilities and potentials for each trip purpose and land-use	
		Calculation of rate variables for each land-use, the total area and all sub-areas, taking into account zonal capacities
	Calculation of additional or reduced transportation volumes between the sub-areas for each trip purpose	
	Political and planning actions viz-a-viz the urban land-use/transportation system	

Fig. 10 – General schematic of model sequence

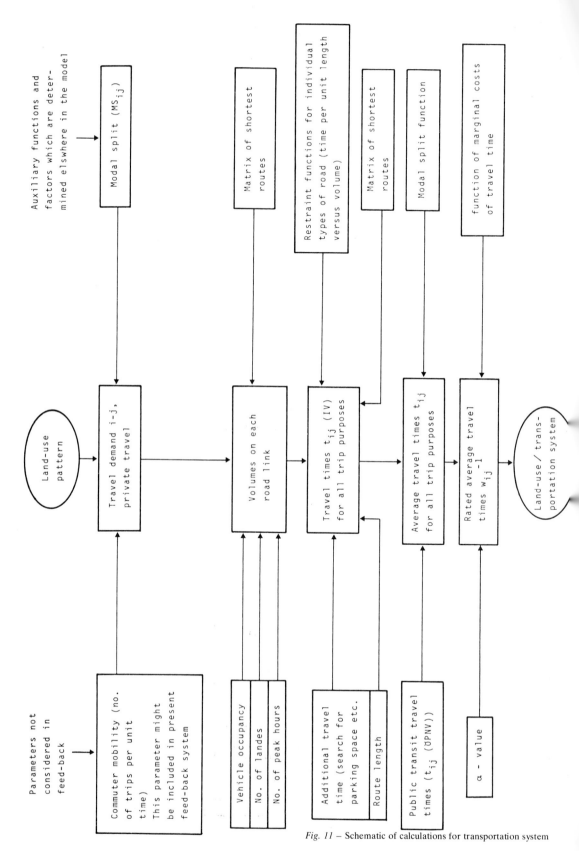

Fig. 11 – Schematic of calculations for transportation system

Next, let us have a look at the general model sequence.

1. In a first step, the individual transportation links between the sub-areas are evaluated for each trip purpose. The value factors w_{ij}^{-1} are a particular function of distance.

2. By means of the value factors, we now calculate accessibility and potentials (i. e. the determing factors) for each trip purpose and land-use. A more detailed and closer mathematical description would be too extensive here.

3. In a third step, the rate variables for each land-use, the total urban area and each sub-area may be determined while considering area capacities. The required hypothetical interconnections, have been explained above.

4. From the new quantities of land-use, which were determined by overall balancing, the additional or reduced quantities of transportation demand between the sub-areas can be estimated for each trip purpose. This is done by LEONTIEF's multi-regional input-output model, which is based on a concept of gravitation.

5. In a fifth step, there is the possibility to introduce political and planning interference into the land-use/transportation system. This can be done on the basis of the results obtained in steps 1-4. After this, a simulation period (e. g. one year) is terminated, and one may start again with step 1 (evaluation of transportation links) for the next period.

A closer observation of step 1 (evaluation of transportation links) shows the necessary parameters and supplemental functions which are not or only partially integrated into the feedback procedure. For the greater part, these are subject to changes in the course of political and planning interference into the system. Among these are: the commuter mobility, public-transport travel times, additional travel times, e. g. for finding a parking space etc., number of lanes of a given type of urban roads, number of passengers per automobile, number of peak-hours per given trip purpose (in this context, staggering of work hours comes into play) and last not least the parameter, α, of the deterrence function. Another function relates to modal split; this is, however, partially integrated into the feedback-process, since it depends on automobile travel times.

The actions mentioned in connection with step 5, however, not only relate to transportation but also to direct measures aimed at influencing urban growth and distribution of land-uses. Thus direct influences can be exerted on the parameters of the rate variables, e.g. on mobility in relation to land-uses or on potential displacements. In addition, land-use policies may be introduced to correct the distribution of land-uses generated by the determining factors, or to control total growth.

Our next task is now, to find out how urban development proceeds on the basis of the simulation model. Doing this, we are able to examine the effect of certain measures, i. e. parameter changes. Criteria for this are individual accessibilities as well as the non-weighted total and total accessibilities weighted by the area factors. Unweighted total accessibility indicates the qualitative development of the exchange situation within the urban area; weighted total accessibility indicates growth potential of individual urban land-uses. To facilitate the analysis, a so-called entropy-factor is introduced which indicates the degree of concentration or deconcentration of the land-uses. The entropy-factor, may also adopt values between 0 and 1, value 1 signalling the highest concentration of a certain land-use which is weighted by its accessibility.

For the simulation there are the following requirements:

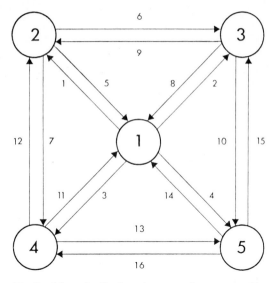

Fig. 12 – Schematic of land-use / transportation system used in test examples

We assume a fictitious land-use/transportation system including 5 sub-areas, a city centre and four decentralized sub-areas (sub-centres). Thus, we have a monocentric urban region, i.e. there is only one dominating city centre.

Not counting internal relations, the 5 sub-areas imply 20 possible relations for which 16 links of the transportation network are available. Among these, there are eight tangential links, which directly interconnect the sub-centres and 8 radial links, which lead to or away from the city centre.

Two land-uses are distributed over the sub-areas – residential and workplaces – which are connected by one relation, e.g. home-to-work commuting and v. v. With reference to the exchange process, workplaces are supply land-use (if offers places of work) residential land-use represents demand (for workplaces).

The initial situation for the simulation is as follows: As in all simulations, the level variables must have initial values. We assume, that both land-uses show a relatively high concentration, but that the concentration of workplaces is considerably higher.

The area capacities are such that there will soon be a shortage of land in the city centre, whereas there are sufficient land reserves in the sub-centres. Zoning in the city centre corresponds to the initial occupation.

Now the parameters for the calculation of the rate variables must be defined. Considering displacement, we assume, that the workplaces are the socially stronger land-use type. When land-occupancy in the city centre reaches .87, displacement in the city centre begins.

For the spatial relations among the sub-areas, the modal split ratio (it is not yet integrated into the feedback-process) and the value factor, α, for the travel time must be determined. In the first example, α, has been assigned a relatively large value, i.e. there is little resistance against covering large distances. This means, that spatial restrictions against the division of labour are small, the dynamic of the system and with this, growth, are, however, very high. Next there are statements concerning the above parameters of transportation demand, transportation supply and land-use programs. We assume that there are no land-use programs, i.e. no additional interferences into the system on the part of the government.

Finally, statements are required concerning the simulation period and the reaction time following changes in the system structure, the so-called time-lag. The simulation period is 20 years, the time-lag is 7 years.

Results of the simulation and interferences into the system

With the initial conditions as described above, the first simulation run yields the following result:

Considering total accessibilities, weighted with the area factors, there are four phases of development. (X = workplaces, ☆ = residential land-use, 0 = average of workplaces and residential land-use, which for the purpose of simplifying the test examples also represents total growth):

1. The phase prior to displacement, i. e. prior to the intensified deconcentration of residential land-use. During this phase, the extension of workplaces is restricted as their share of land in the city centre has been utilized. Unweighted total accessibility remains relatively high, since there are sufficiently large transport capacities.

2. The phase of intense deconcentration of residential land-use due to start of displacement. As more decentralized areas become involved in the exchange process, there is an increase in the chance of growth, i.e. the weighted total accessibility of residential land-use.

Through displacement, workplaces can compensate for their loss of growth potential.

Although volumes on the radial transportation links increase, there is, on the whole, no major reduction in total accessibility as yet.

Phase 2 is characterized by the fact, that additional area potential temporarily safeguards the further growth of residential land-use (at the periphery) and of workplaces (through displacement).

3. During the third phase of development, the advantages of a larger land supply at the periphery are to a certain extent diminished because of growing volumes on the radial links. Weighted total accessibility is reduced more. In addition to growing volume-capacity ratios on the transportation links, increasing area restrictions against workplaces in the city centre may come into play as soon as further displacement of residential land-use is no longer possible. As regards workplaces, we notice a higher loss in growth potential. The reason for this is the extremly long time-lag. A delayed response to structural changes results in excessive growth in favour on the city centre, thus prolonging the phase of structural redesign.

Therefore phase 3 is characterized by the fact, that a future structural redesign is being prepared, i.e. the deconcentration of workplaces, in order to escape from restrictions in both land-use and transportation capacities. The entropy curve shows how abruptly the spatial restructing is being initiated.

4. The preparations for restructuring during phase 3 now enable a regeneration of accessibilities as well as of chances of growth, i. e. of the total accessibilities weighted with area factors. We denote this development period as regeneration phase during which the exchange process increasingly moves to the tangents of the urban system, where there are still sufficient area and transportation capacities.

If one assumes a higher deterrence of distance, i. e. larger spatial restrictions against interchange, the four phases of development cannot be so easily distinguished. There is not such an intense restructuring, in particular, phase 3 blends fairly direct into the regeneration phase (4). Displacement of residential land-use is also considerably smaller. This is, however, done at the expense of reduced growth, i. e. a lesser system dynamic.

Going back to the example based on low sensitiveness

to distance, we shall now examine some measures which might be employed to prevent losses of accessibility and growth.

Firstly, transportation supply on the radials is improved, at the beginning of phase 3 (year 10) by increasing the modal split ratio from .333 to .5.

The consequence is, that losses of accessibility (cf. unweighted total accessibility) can be reduced over an extended period of time. This, however, prevents an early preparation of restructuring in favour of workplaces in the sub-centres, i. e. displacement in phase 2 will be strongly intensified, so that in year 13, when further displacement is no longer possible, area restrictions for workplaces come into full effect: Major losses of growth are unavoidable. Preventing one early negative feedback (congestion on the transportation links) has initiated another negative feedback (area restriction) at an earlier stage and with much greater intensity.

Now one might think of additionally increasing the area within the city centre (from 100.000 to 150.000) in the year 13. The consequences are disastrous. The measure relatively quickly leads to another strong reduction of accessibilities and growth potentials since a further concentration of workplaces in the city centre rapidly absorbs the additional radial transportation capacities.

Instead of enlarging the central area, one could initiate a land-use program (along with increasing the modal split ratio) which would influence, beginning with the year 10, the distribution of workplaces in favour of the sub-centres.

The result shows that, although losses in growth potential are being reduced, from year 15 onwards another major drop in the Unweighted total accessibilities cannot be avoided, since total growth will be higher: A new negative feedback of the system in terms of volumes versus the existing transportation capacities. The negative feedback will have an even stranger effect on area restrictions against workplaces in the city centre, with the result that, in year 14, the weighted total accessibility will again decrease, once displacement of residential land-use is no longer possible.

To avoid this negative feedback, let us now try to exercise an additional influence on migration of city-centre workplaces, and on the timelag. Increasing migration of city-centre workplaces aims at launching an early deconcentration of workplaces (in phase 2 already), while shortening the time-lag (from 7 to 2 years) intens an early adjustment to changing realities and thus a reduction of overall growth. Both measures relieve the city centre. Since despite or even because of these measures overall growth might again be too large, involving new negative feedback effects, there will also be a restrictive policy concerning overall growth from year 10 onwards. The result shows, that now the most important negative feedbacks of the system have been eliminated: phase 3 merges continuously into regeneration phase 4. The entropy curve shows the continuous deconcentration of workplaces (weighted by accessibility). We have outwitted the system.

The example proved that, with the help of appropriate interferences into the urban system, major losses of accessibility and growth may be avoided. Individual measures alone, however, are insufficient; it is imperative to employ whole packets of measures, where the individual components offset the negative feedback of others, i. e. where all measures are carefully coordinated. This is a basic concept, which was already distinctly emphasized by Forrester.

The examples, however, also show that measures are required which, in our economic and social system are difficult to implement i.e. for which there is no political means. In this context, I venture to say that we are

572

confronted with a barbarian form of society which, is capable of constructing and using sub-ways and other modern means of transport, but unable to exert a purposeful influence on mobility and growth and other social and economic phenomena of our time.

It has now been attempted to calibrate the model for forecasting purposes on the basis of development data for the city of Zurich between 1955 and 1965. The result of this forecast for the individual sub-areas – measured by the deviation of calculated from actual development

after a period of 10 years – (viz. Fig. 20-23) is not yet fully satisfactory. Several reasons are responsible for this: insufficient data basis, inappropriate zoning, missing variables of influence, a partly too high degree of aggregation for the variables used, a too small number of interrelations considered (job and retail commuters only), defective model construction. Should it be possible to work out the required modifications and to improve the data basis, more reliable forecasting can be achieved in the future.

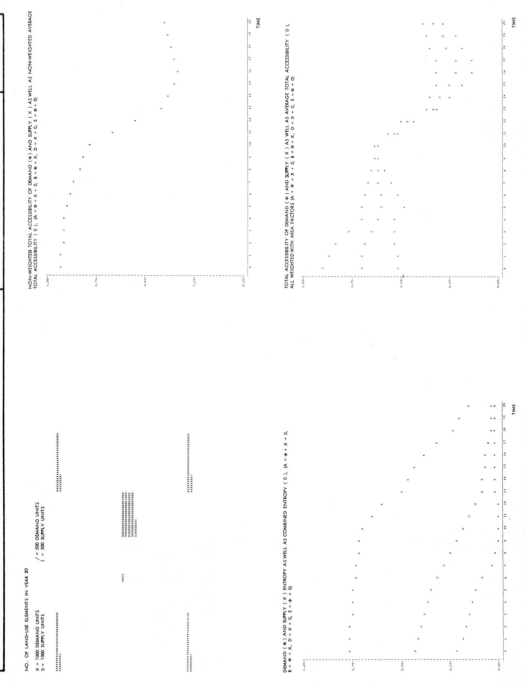

Fig. 13

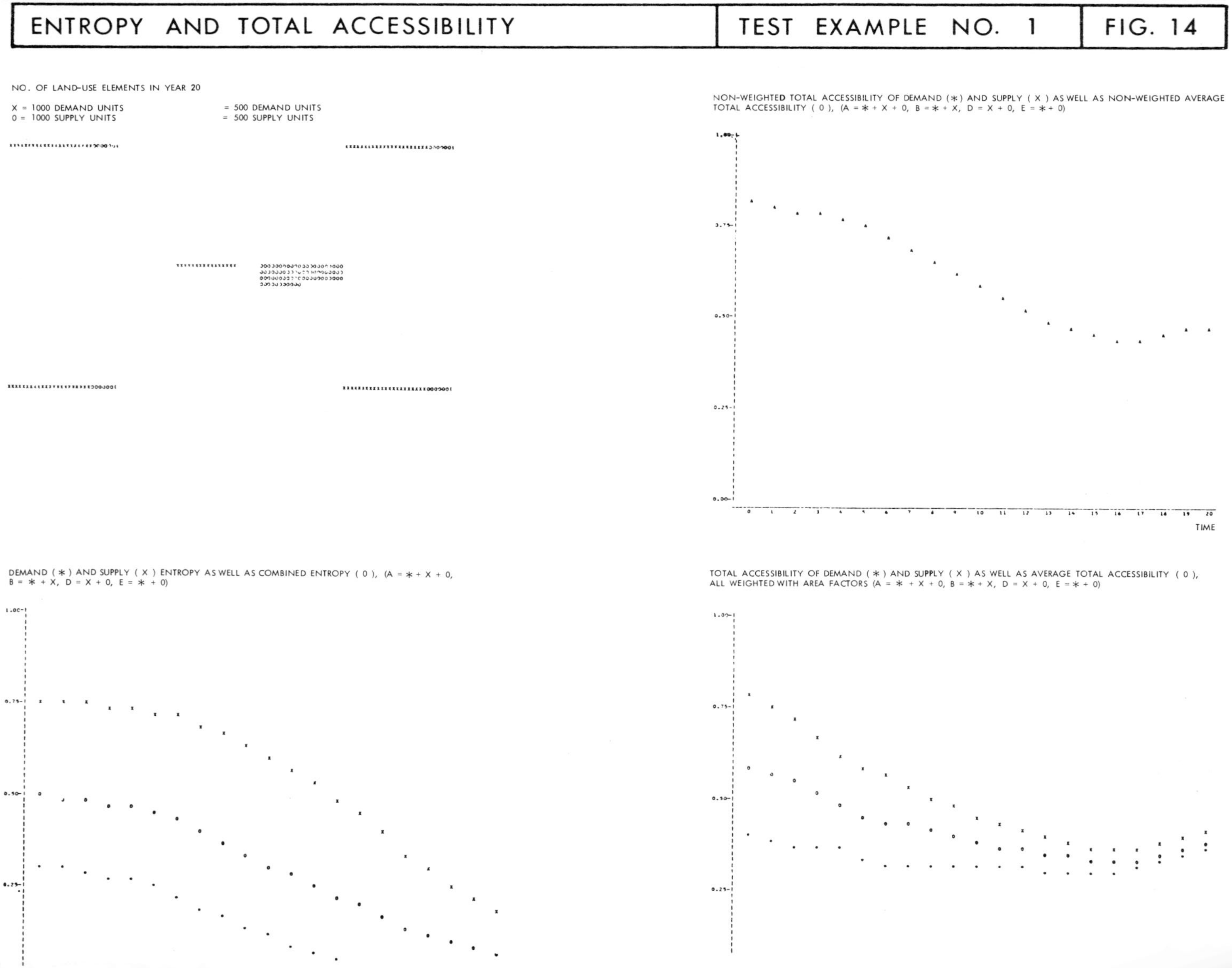

ENTROPY AND TOTAL ACCESSIBILITY | TEST EXAMPLE NO. 1 | FIG. 14

NO. OF LAND-USE ELEMENTS IN YEAR 20

X = 1000 DEMAND UNITS   = 500 DEMAND UNITS
0 = 1000 SUPPLY UNITS   = 500 SUPPLY UNITS

NON-WEIGHTED TOTAL ACCESSIBILITY OF DEMAND (*) AND SUPPLY (X) AS WELL AS NON-WEIGHTED AVERAGE
TOTAL ACCESSIBILITY (0), (A = * + X + 0, B = * + X, D = X + 0, E = * + 0)

DEMAND (*) AND SUPPLY (X) ENTROPY AS WELL AS COMBINED ENTROPY (0), (A = * + X + 0,
B = * + X, D = X + 0, E = * + 0)

TOTAL ACCESSIBILITY OF DEMAND (*) AND SUPPLY (X) AS WELL AS AVERAGE TOTAL ACCESSIBILITY (0),
ALL WEIGHTED WITH AREA FACTORS (A = * + X + 0, B = * + X, D = X + 0, E = * + 0)

Fig. 14

574

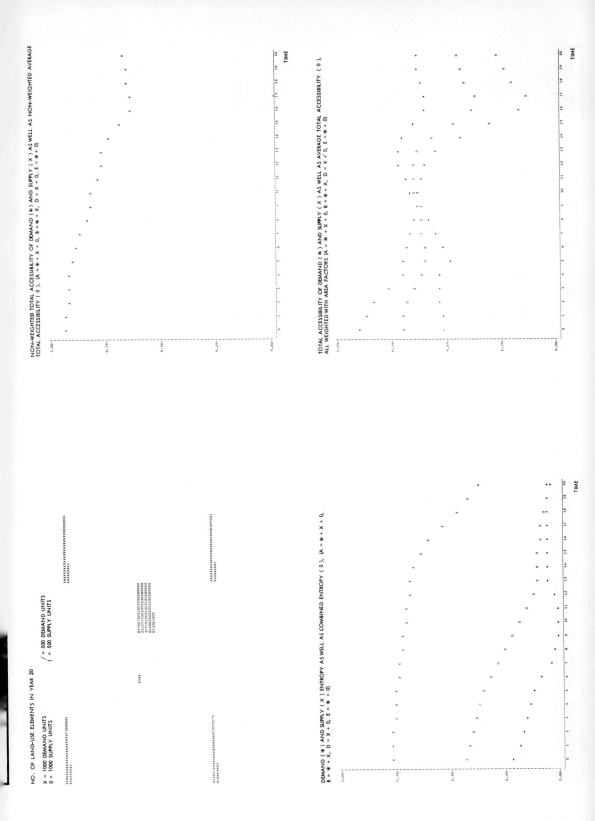

Fig. 15

575

ENTROPY AND TOTAL ACCESSIBILITY	TEST EXAMPLE NO. 9	FIG. 16

NO. OF LAND-USE ELEMENTS IN YEAR 20

X = 1000 DEMAND UNITS / = 500 DEMAND UNITS
0 = 1000 SUPPLY UNITS (= 500 SUPPLY UNITS

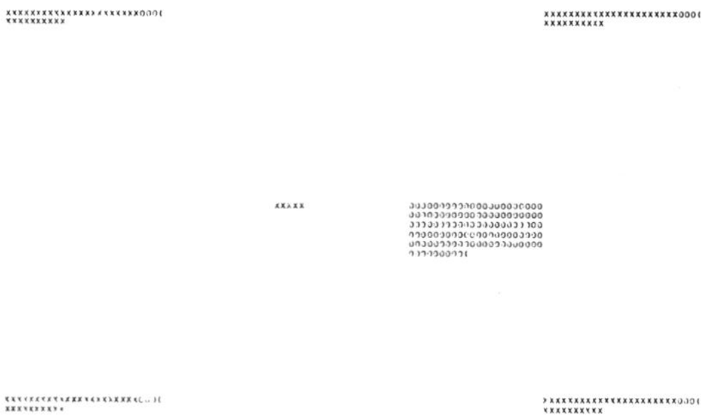

NON-WEIGHTED TOTAL ACCESSIBILITY OF DEMAND (*) AND SUPPLY (X) AS WELL AS NON-WEIGHTED AVERAGE TOTAL ACCESSIBILITY (0), (A = * + X + 0, B = * + X, D = X + 0, E = * + 0)

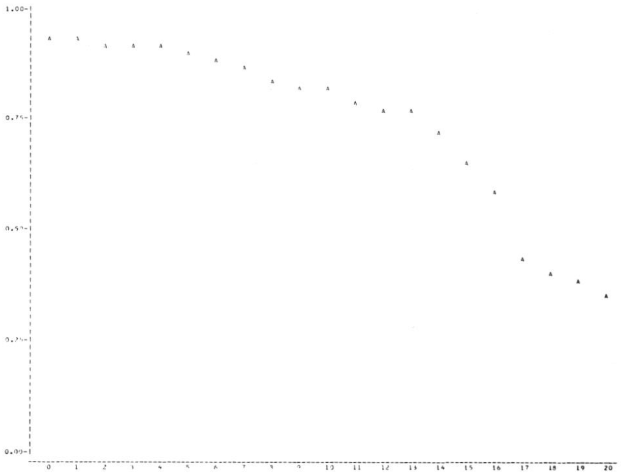

DEMAND (*) AND SUPPLY (X) ENTROPY AS WELL AS COMBINED ENTROPY (0), (A = * + X + 0, B = * + X, D = X + 0, E = * + 0)

TOTAL ACCESSIBILITY OF DEMAND (*) AND SUPPLY (X) AS WELL AS AVERAGE TOTAL ACCESSIBILITY (0), ALL WEIGHTED WITH AREA FACTORS (A = * + X + 0, B = * + X, D = X + 0, E = * + 0)

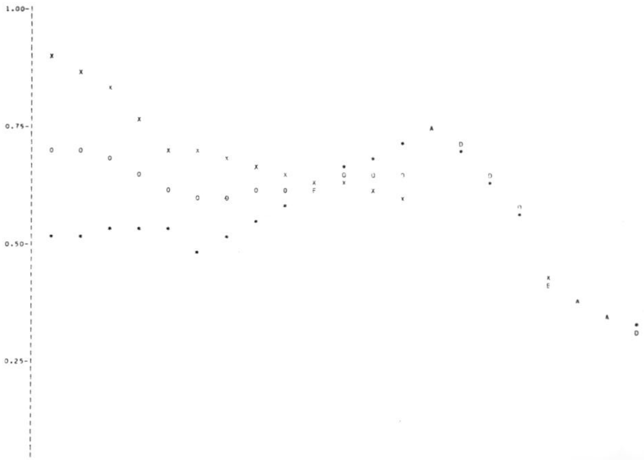

Fig. 16

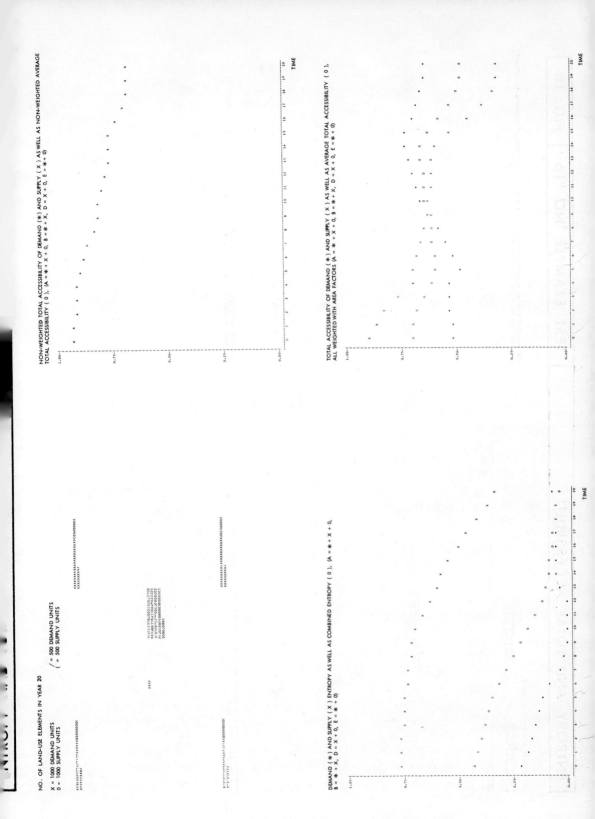

Fig. 17

NO. OF LAND-USE ELEMENTS IN YEAR 20

X = 1000 DEMAND UNITS   / = 500 DEMAND UNITS
0 = 1000 SUPPLY UNITS   (= 500 SUPPLY UNITS

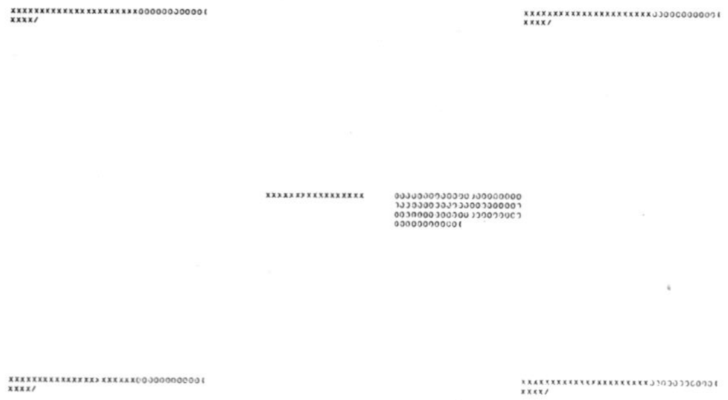

NON-WEIGHTED TOTAL ACCESSIBILITY OF DEMAND (*) AND SUPPLY (X) AS WELL AS NON-WEIGHTED AVERAGE
TOTAL ACCESSIBILITY (0), (A = * + X + 0, B = * + X, D = X + 0, E = * + 0)

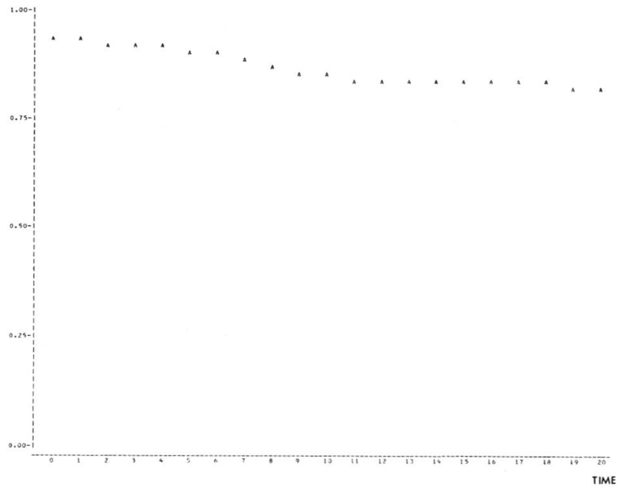

DEMAND (*) AND SUPPLY (X) ENTROPY AS WELL AS COMBINED ENTROPY (0), (A = * + X + 0,
B = * + X, D = X + 0, E = * + 0)

TOTAL ACCESSIBILITY OF DEMAND (*) AND SUPPLY (X) AS WELL AS AVERAGE TOTAL ACCESSIBILITY (0),
ALL WEIGHTED WITH AREA FACTORS (A = * + X + 0, B = * + X, D = X + 0, E = * + 0)

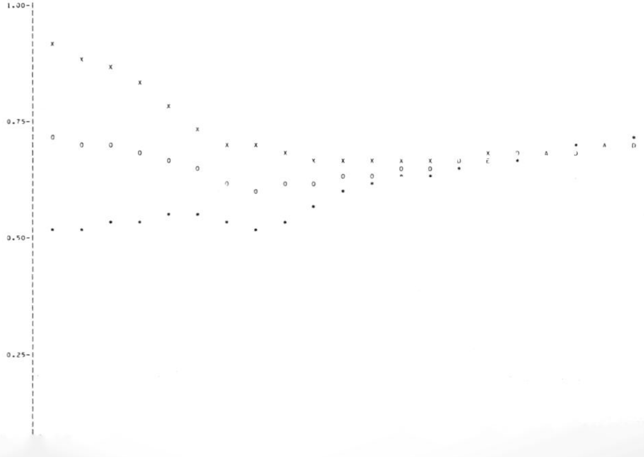

Fig. 18

Residential land-use, year 10

Zone	Available in year 0	Available	Ind [3]	Growth/ Decrease	Positive migration	Negative migration	Displace- ment	Natural develop- ment	Accessibility	Potential	Area factor	Land- occupancy [%]
1	52513	43868	10	-395	7569	7531	399	8	0.851	0.707	0.953	28.81
2	31966	31026	4	-338	5206	5226	334	20	0.900	0.674	0.934	45.24
3	21480	23491	0	0	2047	2971	0	16	0.789	0.574	0.755	77.75
4	3308	11300	0	0	1491	1509	0	76	0.749	0.621	0.845	92.05
5	46264	44415	10	-285	6622	6620	285	76	0.867	0.663	0.013	61.85
6	67792	67545	8	-450	10953	10934	450	-18	0.907	0.663	0.022	74.55
7	26109	35155	5	-318	4439	4450	319	11	0.359	0.655	0.935	62.60
8	37111	35798	7	-275	6422	6335	275	-20	0.946	0.651	0.940	64.57
9	2698	7103	0	674	1489	804	1	62	0.716	0.564	0.877	89.58
10	25333	34801	0	0	4585	5199	0	613	0.671	0.522	0.720	89.72
11	35523	43278	2	-72	6535	6800	72	356	0.919	0.531	0.837	60.21
12	23140	41823	0	1355	6272	5324	0	695	0.698	0.523	0.703	85.90
13	33453	48830	0	0	7342	7829	0	445	0.812	0.590	0.943	65.79
14	22053	32366	0	1104	5267	4470	0	227	0.693	0.370	0.827	78.23
15	3729	17247	0	379	3041	2330	0	316	0.673	0.374	0.272	84.00
16	10200	15168	0	393	2237	1941	0	143	0.741	0.273	0.702	65.00
17	14376	22840	0	1301	3613	2930	0	313	0.743	0.130	0.803	69.00
18	6678	13210	0	583	2467	1700	0	204	0.685	0.120	0.256	75.00
19	6689	12100	0	681	2075	1551	0	167	0.721	0.233	0.823	74.00
20	1454	2734	0	192	526	367	0	34	0.687	0.296	0.904	81.00
21	2402	5116	0	413	1011	650	0	52	0.720	0.412	0.903	86.00
22	7323	9693	0	370	1632	1391	0	133	0.469	0.205	0.877	78.00
23	1816	2664	0	120	474	407	0	53	0.626	0.341	0.902	78.00
24	7503	10316	0	324	1813	1704	0	115	0.761	0.420	0.928	61.00
25	2207	16720	0	203	2807	2364	0	370	0.469	0.315	0.900	74.00
26	3275	6302	0	443	1168	805	0	170	0.661	0.243	0.944	80.00
27	701	1841	0	171	367	210	0	22	0.757	0.233	0.973	77.00
28	33033	42438	0	1122	6926	6501	0	526	0.636	0.172	0.878	66.00
29	4590	5980	0	244	1037	922	0	127	0.626	0.364	0.909	87.00
30	2073	4595	0	372	865	573	0	21	0.727	0.255	0.963	63.00
31	1661	4576	0	373	900	566	0	99	0.733	0.233	0.903	77.00
32	2769	4112	0	238	741	552	0	55	0.686	0.311	0.903	74.00
33	1966	3754	0	267	694	516	0	63	0.674	0.413	0.937	67.00
34	5918	13766	0	345	2414	1325	0	256	0.705	0.210	0.971	74.30
35	3608	21144	0	1452	2740	2760	0	404	0.702	0.262	0.872	63.30
36	7743	14080	0	352	2596	1921	0	186	0.716	0.401	0.972	65.00
37	2652	5031	0	345	918	663	0	93	0.705	0.326	0.500	81.00
38	3572	20668	0	1792	3003	2561	0	424	0.733	0.416	0.902	72.00
39	5034	10061	0	714	1800	1344	0	130	0.683	0.265	0.971	75.00
40	2745	4536	0	329	800	696	0	105	0.667	0.356	1.000	75.00
41	13421	23205	0	1014	3943	3033	0	337	0.714	0.352	0.863	72.00
42	847	2056	0	199	425	261	0	26	0.703	0.353	1.003	84.00
43	8166	20518	0	1302	4153	2426	0	175	0.762	0.502	0.563	85.00
44	14431	29620	0	1553	5150	3725	0	120	0.723	0.370	0.935	72.00
45	2497	5000	0	384	1001	632	0	72	0.677	0.225	0.965	82.00
46	12777	17172	0	223	2572	2300	0	137	0.704	0.233	0.722	72.00
47	7716	12151	0	611	2144	1653	0	150	0.682	0.155	0.934	71.00
48	9968	13575	0	326	2030	1921	0	200	0.703	0.112	0.676	70.00
G	673222	794895	0	32414	17175 [1]	10933 [1]	-	8550	0.767	-	0.680 [2]	-

1) employees
2) total accessibility, weighted with area factors
3) no. of years of negative development

Retail land-use, year 10

Zone	Available in year 0	Available	Ind [3]	Growth/ Decrease	Positive migration	Negative migration	Displace- ment	Natural develop- ment	Accessibility	Potential	Area factor	Land- occupancy [%]
1	22370	37264	0	417	1708	1291	0	-	0.708	1.570	0.551	25.92
2	6193	10015	0	276	583	307	0	-	0.786	1.620	0.633	15.50
3	1465	2150	0	7	71	64	0	-	0.834	0.553	0.312	7.19
4	228	456	0	32	43	12	0	-	0.883	0.590	0.952	4.74
5	4193	6557	0	222	490	187	0	-	0.941	0.632	0.684	9.68
6	5656	8209	0	283	521	237	0	-	0.789	0.652	0.709	9.60
7	4431	6901	0	193	404	211	0	-	0.765	0.615	0.647	13.16
8	5277	6923	0	193	403	210	0	-	0.731	0.615	0.612	13.13
9	124	252	0	19	25	6	0	-	0.800	0.556	0.934	3.90
10	785	1536	0	107	146	33	0	-	0.609	0.576	0.932	5.11
11	3027	5433	0	287	430	152	0	-	0.541	0.694	0.736	9.13
12	1143	2199	0	144	200	57	0	-	0.834	0.574	0.911	7.72
13	2654	4815	0	270	400	134	0	-	0.865	0.444	0.306	4.00
14	1636	2029	0	7	66	60	0	-	0.807	0.442	0.061	4.00
15	595	1146	0	79	100	30	0	-	0.848	0.350	0.767	6.00
16	782	1325	0	63	101	37	0	-	1.030	0.350	0.693	7.00
17	1470	2380	0	115	184	69	0	-	0.856	0.171	0.934	6.70
18	611	1051	0	62	93	31	0	-	0.369	0.236	0.679	7.30
19	642	1146	0	67	99	31	0	-	0.990	0.373	0.994	5.00
20	116	225	0	16	22	6	0	-	0.801	0.405	0.707	3.00
21	178	335	0	18	27	9	0	-	0.835	0.402	1.000	5.00
22	625	954	0	34	62	28	0	-	0.835	0.407	0.672	5.00
23	94	172	0	11	16	5	0	-	0.834	0.406	0.886	6.00
24	581	1036	0	59	88	23	0	-	0.858	0.397	0.933	7.30
25	641	1178	0	77	100	22	0	-	0.882	0.316	0.937	4.30
26	204	291	0	27	37	10	0	-	0.897	0.211	0.926	4.30
27	64	124	0	9	12	2	0	-	0.897	0.230	0.906	4.00
28	3669	4924	0	161	336	175	0	-	0.683	0.330	0.831	7.00
29	226	415	0	25	37	12	0	-	0.838	0.467	0.943	2.00
30	191	374	0	27	36	10	0	-	0.806	1.451	1.000	5.00
31	172	335	0	24	32	9	0	-	1.058	0.325	0.901	6.00
32	185	352	0	24	32	9	0	-	0.870	0.400	0.903	4.00
33	96	180	0	12	17	5	0	-	0.470	0.513	1.000	5.00
34	617	1095	0	65	94	29	0	-	0.873	0.330	0.867	5.00
35	1867	2943	0 [3]	151	244	93	0	-	0.752	0.492	1.000	14.00
36	706	1281	0	93	118	25	0	-	0.455	0.507	0.995	6.30
37	223	436	0	31	42	11	0	-	0.901	0.427	0.886	5.00
38	805	1539	0	110	149	40	0	-	0.502	0.516	0.999	6.00
39	405	740	0	49	67	20	0	-	0.874	0.330	0.985	4.20
40	153	291	0	20	28	7	0	-	0.854	0.405	1.000	4.00
41	1233	2063	0	111	171	61	0	-	0.815	0.363	0.003	6.00
42	73	147	0	11	15	4	0	-	0.917	0.449	1.000	4.00
43	876	1520	0	57	95	42	0	-	0.879	0.551	0.493	5.00
44	1527	2662	0	134	208	74	0	-	0.866	0.449	0.750	7.30
45	289	471	0	26	40	14	0	-	0.785	0.313	0.994	7.30
46	1282	1716	0	40	92	52	0	-	0.837	0.270	0.555	6.00
47	665	1116	0	60	92	32	0	-	0.830	0.274	0.801	7.00
48	1338	1755	0	52	109	57	0	-	0.744	0.161	0.730	3.00
G	92439	132557	0	4361	5009	648	-	-	0.783	-	0.560 [2]	-

2) total accessibility, weighted with area factors
3) no. of years of negative development

Fig. 19 – Level and changes for 4 selected land-uses in 1965 at low distance sensibility

Industrial land-use, year 10

Zone	Available in year 0	Available	Ind [3]	Growth/ Decrease	Positive migration	Negative migration	Displace-ment	Natural develop-ment	Accessibility	Potential	Area factor	Land-occupancy [%]
1	29950	26842	10	-82	1426	1507	0	–	0.709	0.577	1.384	20.00
2	12946	14103	0	8	733	725	0	–	0.770	0.578	0.341	22.36
3	2370	3448	0	1	171	169	0	–	0.809	0.598	0.311	12.50
4	160	233	0	2	12	11	0	–	0.860	0.552	0.292	2.06
5	13348	15705	0	33	792	758	0	–	0.821	0.599	0.308	23.70
6	7098	6969	8	-1	340	341	0	–	0.811	0.621	0.306	8.27
7	1842	2172	0	5	109	105	0	–	0.820	0.595	0.309	5.88
8	5949	7008	0	19	362	343	0	–	0.810	0.588	0.319	13.50
9	89	252	0	23	33	10	0	–	0.913	0.629	0.768	3.87
10	1279	1759	0	16	96	80	0	–	0.868	0.548	0.308	4.83
11	14282	17673	0	109	967	858	0	–	0.816	0.574	0.333	26.26
12	1777	2993	0	71	205	135	0	–	0.871	0.545	0.375	6.97
13	10469	15347	0	206	952	745	0	–	0.808	0.542	0.349	23.33
14	4606	6033	0	89	382	294	0	–	0.811	0.586	0.349	14.00
15	1277	2134	0	59	155	95	0	–	0.872	0.395	0.435	7.00
16	3547	5203	0	152	414	262	0	–	0.786	0.295	0.501	25.00
17	4214	7253	0	337	685	348	0	–	0.796	0.202	0.411	21.00
18	1559	3038	0	205	351	146	0	–	0.776	0.144	0.810	17.00
19	1379	2706	0	151	274	123	0	–	0.829	0.253	0.633	16.00
20	158	408	0	38	55	18	0	–	0.824	0.729	0.919	12.00
21	327	701	0	40	72	31	0	–	0.844	0.431	0.610	8.00
22	1352	2225	0	90	203	113	0	–	0.755	0.241	0.624	15.00
23	237	513	0	33	65	26	0	–	0.730	0.353	0.956	15.00
24	4328	5263	0	84	367	233	0	–	0.731	0.439	0.477	30.00
25	2042	3784	0	195	378	183	0	–	0.783	0.353	0.660	15.00
26	502	1278	0	119	175	56	0	–	0.818	0.773	0.943	15.00
27	220	528	0	45	68	23	0	–	0.847	0.240	0.828	15.00
28	13401	15374	0	292	1285	992	0	–	0.609	0.180	0.715	23.00
29	496	1086	0	79	131	52	0	–	0.768	0.419	0.847	3.00
30	402	1031	0	110	156	47	0	–	0.832	0.402	0.994	30.00
31	459	1048	0	81	127	46	0	–	0.842	0.285	0.773	13.00
32	463	1178	0	106	159	53	0	–	0.798	0.368	0.946	17.00
33	353	901	0	76	119	43	0	–	0.771	0.471	0.955	23.00
34	1623	3357	0	228	381	153	0	–	0.816	0.267	0.741	19.00
35	1764	3702	0	292	473	181	0	–	0.774	0.452	0.879	12.00
36	2294	4970	0	374	610	236	0	–	0.777	1.469	0.855	27.00
37	444	1051	0	82	128	46	0	–	0.833	0.397	0.782	12.00
38	1807	4507	0	375	567	191	0	–	0.863	0.482	0.775	14.00
39	1521	2818	0	156	293	137	0	–	0.776	0.361	0.701	15.00
40	453	1168	0	113	165	52	0	–	0.806	0.460	0.992	13.00
41	4093	7267	0	333	676	344	0	–	0.807	0.330	0.589	23.00
42	83	241	0	25	35	10	0	–	0.879	0.414	0.938	7.00
43	767	1751	0	98	171	73	0	–	0.910	0.519	0.920	7.00
44	2219	3696	0	110	273	167	0	–	0.859	1.412	0.429	10.00
45	384	848	0	61	99	38	0	–	0.828	0.383	0.745	9.00
46	3420	4552	0	103	331	227	0	–	0.783	0.242	0.471	19.00
47	1731	2649	0	96	227	131	0	–	0.783	0.232	0.565	12.00
48	2431	3309	0	98	269	171	0	–	0.750	0.142	0.561	16.00
G	168654	222347	0	5341	7155	1814	–	–	0.767	–	0.357 [2]	–

2) total accessibility, weighted with area factors
3) no. of years of negative development

Administrative land-use, year 10

Zone	Available in year 0	Available	Ind [3]	Growth/ Decrease	Positive migration	Negative migration	Displace-ment	Natural develop-ment	Accessibility	Potential	Area factor	Land-occupancy [%]
1	31349	35288	0	467	1602	1135	0	–	0.789	0.623	0.335	25.17
2	7360	10559	0	188	537	313	0	–	0.810	0.413	0.332	16.30
3	531	667	0	0	21	20	0	–	0.818	0.543	0.223	2.27
4	75	138	0	1	5	4	0	–	0.842	0.544	0.233	1.15
5	2529	3234	0	69	163	94	0	–	0.838	0.617	0.243	4.76
6	5217	6542	0	169	361	192	0	–	0.827	0.644	0.353	7.58
7	3617	5097	0	112	260	147	0	–	0.832	0.627	0.333	13.36
8	3686	4440	0	75	207	131	0	–	0.820	0.623	0.350	9.50
9	83	235	0	20	26	6	0	–	0.675	0.652	0.706	2.75
10	413	558	0	2	18	18	0	–	0.833	0.562	0.221	1.53
11	2020	3135	0	63	157	94	0	–	0.815	0.593	0.374	4.54
12	634	923	0	3	30	27	0	–	0.644	0.550	0.220	1.34
13	1552	2453	0	14	89	75	0	–	0.807	0.568	0.342	3.50
14	555	1236	0	92	128	36	0	–	0.784	0.336	0.812	4.00
15	221	514	0	37	51	14	0	–	0.830	0.495	0.717	2.00
16	212	637	0	42	62	20	0	–	0.752	0.301	0.783	4.00
17	700	1200	0	52	88	38	0	–	0.758	0.205	0.572	3.00
18	243	471	0	30	44	15	0	–	0.756	0.142	0.765	2.00
19	277	560	0	32	49	16	0	–	0.704	0.250	0.443	5.00
20	62	146	0	11	15	4	0	–	0.512	0.337	0.775	2.00
21	133	277	0	18	27	9	0	–	0.622	0.438	0.603	3.00
22	199	343	0	15	26	11	0	–	0.744	0.349	0.503	2.00
23	49	103	0	8	11	3	0	–	0.717	0.360	0.662	2.00
24	152	325	0	25	35	10	0	–	0.737	0.451	0.726	3.00
25	194	420	0	35	48	13	0	–	0.754	0.353	0.742	3.00
26	61	141	0	12	16	4	0	–	0.770	0.377	0.733	1.50
27	13	40	0	3	4	1	0	–	0.706	0.267	0.567	1.00
28	1676	2660	0	98	204	106	0	–	0.606	0.183	0.766	4.00
29	66	150	0	13	17	5	0	–	0.744	0.416	0.837	3.00
30	93	240	0	23	29	7	0	–	0.813	0.433	0.877	2.00
31	109	265	0	22	30	8	0	–	0.400	0.278	0.677	4.00
32	50	118	0	10	13	3	0	–	0.778	0.363	0.823	1.00
33	128	278	0	22	30	8	0	–	0.743	0.467	0.735	4.00
34	285	521	0	25	40	16	0	–	0.764	0.259	0.576	2.00
35	1203	2630	0	224	307	83	0	–	0.747	0.350	0.642	11.00
36	207	469	0	37	50	14	0	–	0.772	0.465	0.744	2.00
37	85	205	0	16	22	6	0	–	0.813	0.385	0.838	2.00
38	252	661	0	66	84	18	0	–	0.836	0.470	0.902	4.00
39	159	236	0	24	35	10	0	–	0.754	0.352	0.846	2.00
40	49	110	0	11	14	3	0	–	0.777	0.457	0.909	2.00
41	457	817	0	36	62	26	0	–	0.757	0.323	0.575	2.00
42	20	78	0	6	8	2	0	–	0.858	0.414	0.743	1.00
43	331	817	0	53	75	22	0	–	0.890	0.533	0.845	4.00
44	714	1511	0	76	119	43	0	–	0.838	0.471	0.510	4.00
45	73	177	0	14	19	5	0	–	0.783	0.391	0.945	2.00
46	419	796	0	46	70	25	0	–	0.756	0.240	0.706	4.00
47	231	487	0	36	51	15	0	–	0.763	0.198	0.863	4.00
48	667	1201	0	32	73	40	0	–	0.823	0.135	0.493	5.00
G	69942	95055	0	2484	2954	470	–	–	0.775	–	0.388 [2]	–

2) total accessibility, weighted with area factors
3) no. of years of negative development

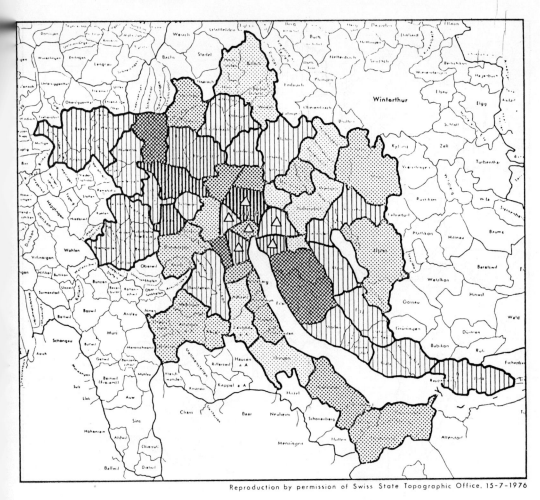

Overestimated sub-areas B F$_i$ (F) >1

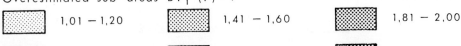

| | 1,01 – 1,20 | | 1,41 – 1,60 | | 1,81 – 2,00 |
| | 1,21 – 1,40 | | 1,61 – 1,80 | | > 2,00 |

| △ | Sub-areas showing negative development |

Underestimated sub-areas B F$_i$ (F) <1

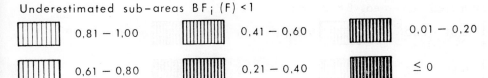

| | 0,81 – 1,00 | | 0,41 – 0,60 | | 0,01 – 0,20 |
| | 0,61 – 0,80 | | 0,21 – 0,40 | | ≤ 0 |

Fig. 20 – Comparison of actual and forecast development of residential land-use at low distance sensibility (Simulation 1a)

581

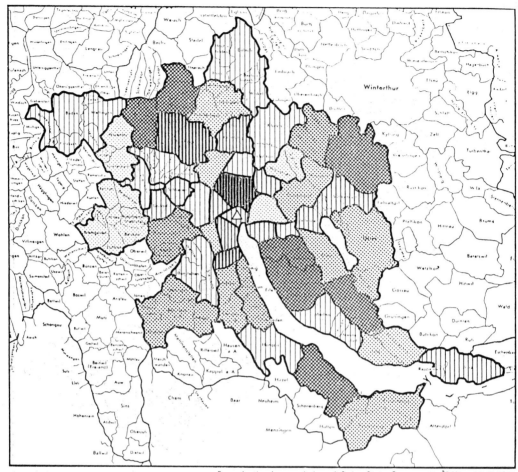

Reproduction by permission of Swiss State Topographic Office, 15-7-1976

Overestimated sub-areas $BF_i (F) > 1$

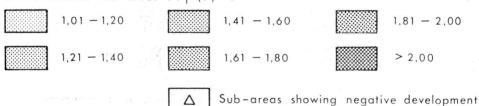

| | 1,01 − 1,20 | | 1,41 − 1,60 | | 1,81 − 2,00 |
| | 1,21 − 1,40 | | 1,61 − 1,80 | | > 2,00 |

$\triangle$ Sub-areas showing negative development

Underestimated sub-areas $BF_i (F) < 1$

| | 0,81 − 1,00 | | 0,41 − 0,60 | | 0,01 − 0,20 |
| | 0,61 − 0,80 | | 0,21 − 0,40 | | ≤ 0 |

Fig. 21 – Comparison of actual and forecast development of industrial land-use at low distance sensibility (Simulation 1a)

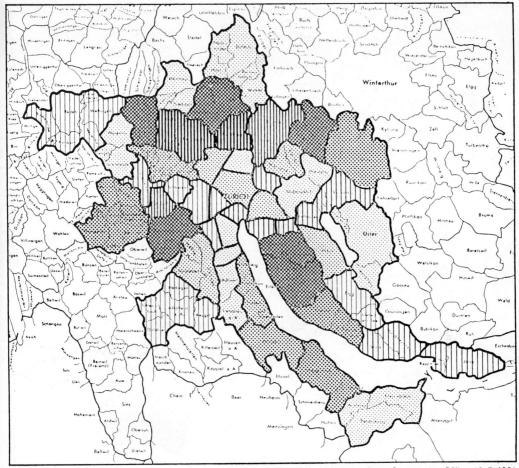

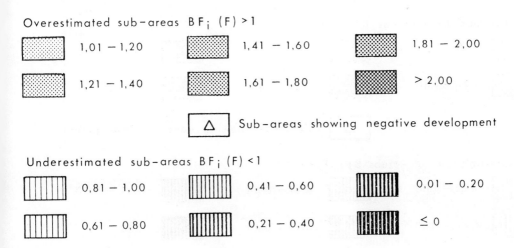

Overestimated sub-areas $BF_i (F) > 1$

▓	1,01 — 1,20
▓	1,21 — 1,40
▓	1,41 — 1,60
▓	1,61 — 1,80
▓	1,81 — 2,00
▓	> 2,00

△ Sub-areas showing negative development

Underestimated sub-areas $BF_i (F) < 1$

▓	0,81 — 1,00
▓	0,61 — 0,80
▓	0,41 — 0,60
▓	0,21 — 0,40
▓	0,01 — 0,20
▓	≤ 0

Fig. 22 – Comparison of actual and forecast development of retail land-use at low distance sensibility (Simulation 1a)

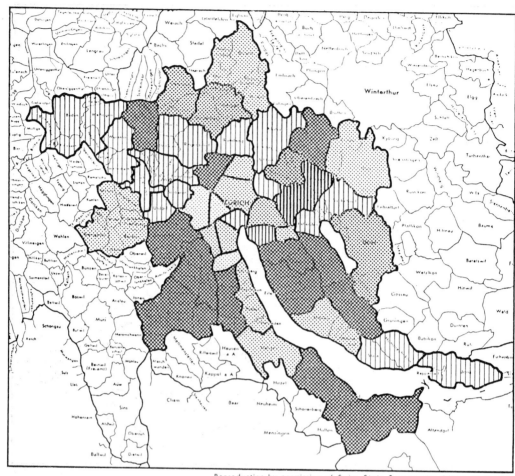

Reproduction by permission of Swiss State Topographic Office, 15-7-1976

Overestimated sub-areas BF$_i$ (F) >1

▒	1,01 − 1,20	▒	1,41 − 1,60	▒	1,81 − 2,00
▒	1,21 − 1,40	▒	1,61 − 1,80	▒	> 2,00

△ Sub-areas showing negative development

Underestimated sub-areas BF$_i$ (F) <1

▕▏	0,81 − 1,00	▕▏	0,41 − 0,60	▕▏	0,01 − 0,20
▕▏	0,61 − 0,80	▕▏	0,21 − 0,40	▕▏	≤ 0

Fig. 23 – Comparison of actual and forecast development of administrative land-use at low distance sensibility (Simulation 1a)

REFERENCES

[1] Abler, R., Adams, J. S., Gould, P., **'Spatial Organization, The Geographer's View of the world,'** Prentice-Hall Inc., New Jersey 1971

[2] Alonso, W., **'Location Theory,'** Regional Development and Planning, A Reader, edited by J. Friedmann and W. Alonso, The MIT-Press, Cambridge 1964, pp. 88 and following.

[3] Anderson, T.R., Egeland, J.A., **'Spatial Aspects of Social Area Analysis,'** American Sociological Review, Vol 26, Number 1, 1961.

[4] Batty, M., **'Dynamic Simulation of an Urban System,'** Geographical Papers No 12, The University of Reading Department of Geography, Whiteknights Park 1971.

[5] Cordey-Hayes, M., **'Dynamic frameworks for spatial models,'** centre for Environmental Studies, CES WP 76, London 1971.

[6] Crecine, J.P., **'A Dynamic Model of Urban Structure,'** Rand Memo P3803, 1968.

[7] Forrester, J. W., **'Urban Dynamics,'** The MIT-Press, Cambridge, Massachusetts, 1969.

[8] Hansen, W. G., **'How Accessibility Shapes Land Use,'** Journal of Am. Inst. of Planners, Vol 25 (1959) No 2.

[9] Ingram, D.R., **'The Concept of Accessibility: A search for an Operational Form,'** Regional Studies, Vol 5, 1971, pp. 101 and following.

[10] Isard, W., **'Methods of Regional Analysis: an Introduction to Regional Science,'** MIT-Press, Cambridge, Massachusetts, 1960.

[11] Kristensson, F., **'People, Firms and Regions, A Structural Economic Analysis,'** The Economic Research Institute at the Stockholm School of Economics, 1967 (unpublished manuscript).

[12] Lachene, R., **'Networks and the Location of Economic Activities,'** Regional Science Association, Papers XIV, 1965, pp. 183 and following.

[13] Leontief, W., **'Die multiregionale Input-Output-Analyse,'** Arbeitsgemeinschaft für Forschung des Landes NRW, Heft 123, Düsseldorf 1962.

[14] Lowry, I. S., **'Model of Metropolis,'** RM-4035-RC, Rand Corporation, Santa Monica 1964.

[15] Richardson, H.W., **'Regional growth theory,** Macmillan Press LTD, London 1973.

[16] Wilson, A. G., **'Notes on some concepts in social physics,'** Centre for Environmental Studies, Working Paper 4, to be published, Papers and Proceedings of Regional Science Association, London 1968.

[17] Wilson, A. G., **'Entropy in urban and regional modelling,'** Centre for Environmental Studies, Working Paper CES WP 26, London 1969.

[18] Wilson, A. A., **'Entropy in urban und regional modelling,'** Pion, London 1970.

Freight transport models as a tool for management

J. VAN ES
Netherlands Institute of Transport

INTRODUCTION
1.1 General features of policy information systems

The transport industry as well as the government are continuously confronted with situations where they have to make decisions in order to reach certain future objectives. Those decisions can influence each other strongly and are to a more or less extent based on concrete policy targets and on the choice of specific policy instruments.

Policy information systems now do have the object to prepare the decisionmaking of the transport industry and the government in the best possible way. Decisionmaking however suggests that the objectives are formulated and the most efficient instruments are chosen in order to reach the mentioned objectives. This does not mean that the development of policy information systems has to wait on the ultimate formation of the policy targets and the determination of the instruments. In real live policy targets and the choice of policy instruments are subject to a process of evolution and can not be determined once and for all.

It must be clear that policymaking not only includes short term market policies, which can only react to given actual situations, but that it includes also medium and long term policies, which have the object to influence structural situations.

It will be clear too that policymaking is not only done by the government but that the developments in transport life are the combined results of the policies of transport firms, government and organized transport industry as well.

If a policy information system want to be a real help for policymaking, it must include two essential characteristics:

1. It must give actual information on transport and the underlying factors.

2. It must be based on the existing interrelations between the transport sector and the rest of the economy and on the interrelations within the transport sector itself.

The complementary position of freight transport in the overall economic life makes those interrelations very complex and multi-dimensional. This can be easily understood, considering that freight transport has to deal with:

1. a great diversity of economic activities

(production and consumption activities) each of which has its own very specific transport needs.

Supply and demand pattern per economic activity can differ strongly with respect to:
- transport volume per time unit
- commodity groups
- appearance of the cargo
- size of shipment
- geographical distance
- origin resp. destination
- technical organisation of the physical distribution process
- seasonal, conjunctural and structural dependencies etc., etc.

2. An environmental dispersion of the economic activities

Which influence considerably the geographical transportation pattern. That is to say the realized need for transport per commodity group. Changes in the environmental dispersion can influence the transport pattern on the medium and the longterm the transport pattern in a great deal.

3. The possibility of using different modes of transport for the carriage of goods (road transport, rail transport, inland navigation, maritime transport and so on).

To some extent these transport modes compete with one another and to some extent they complement each other; this situation can vary a great deal from one section of the transport market to another.

4. A great number of professional transport firms which are most of the time acting in competitive markets

In addition the number of competitive firms can be quite different per mode of transport.

5. Technological developments

Which can have great influence on certain parts of the transport market (e.g. the development of container transport).

6. Changes in social and economic thinking (environmental aspects, avoiding air and noise pollution).

An example of this is the desire to keep heavy lorries out of town centres, a possible solution being a switch to freight depots.

From this summing up it must be clear that only via systematic and methodologically reliable research it will be possible to uncover this complex structure and make it manageable for the purpose of policymaking.

1.2. Types of policymakers

It is very important to understand that there are different types of policymakers, each of them have their own needs for information. A distinction can be made between the individual transport firms, the government and the organized transport industry. The first group has by their policy actions (investment policy, pricing policy, choice of submarkets etc.) a great influence on the real course of things in the transport market.

Beside the transport firms the government has its own responsibility in creating a general transport policy based on its overall objectives which leads to a general framework in which the transport firms are functioning. It must be clear however that consultation between the government and the transport industry is necessary, because in the end the objectives of the government have to be realized by the companies.

The needs of a third policymaking body comes logically from the above mentioned consulting process. The organized industry has as its main task the protection of the joint interests of the transport industry.

1.3. Levels of management information and time-scale distinction in policymaking

To get a clear understanding of all types of management information needed, first of all a distinction has to be made between different levels of aggregation. Normally the following classification is suitable:

– macro level (concerning the transport sector as a whole c.q. per mode of transport placed in an interregional framework)

– meso level (concerning subsectors, various markets per mode of transport)

– micro level (concerning individual transport firms)

Although the macro and meso level primarily concern the field of responsibility of the government and the organized industry, it is often very important for the firm's policy and strategy too. On the other hand micro information on the firm's level is the source of the more aggregated macro and meso information on which the government's policy has to be based.

A second important aspect concerns the difference in time-scaling periods.

Normally policymaking can be distinghuished in:

a. long term policy (general outline of the objectives and instruments to be used)

b. medium term policy (gives a more concrete form of the mentioned general outline)

c. short term policy (application of policy instruments to actual situations)

Medium term policy can hardly be used to create on conjunctural deviations or incidental problems of every day. Here short term policy is needed which must be consistent with long term and medium term policy. On the short term many structures can be considered as fixed by which reason the extent of influence as well as the choice of instruments remain restricted. On the long term however it is possible to influence the underlying structures in a real way.

1.4. The interrelations between policy information flows

For a real understanding of the policy information system it is not enough to identify the different policymakers and their need for information for short term, medium term and long term decisionmaking.

Although the need for information for the three groups of policymakers differ in degree of detail, the basic data have to come for a large part from the same sources, the transport firms. Otherwise the creation of a consistent policy is not possible. The accessibility to these sources however is most of the time different for the mentioned groups of policymakers.

Consequently, after defining the policy information needed, by each of the groups it should be determined:

i) who has access to the sources of information and who is equipped for which type of information collection

ii) at what level of aggregation or in what detail the data from the various sources should be available to the government, organized industry and the firms.

Only then it is possible to have sophisticated policy information systems with reliable recent information at minimum costs, for each interested party.

The interrelationships between information patterns are given in fig. 1. In this train of thought the organized industry is, as it were, the interface between the govern-

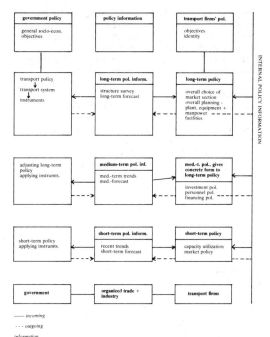

Fig. 1

ment and the firms; it should be involved in the policymaking of each of the two groups and in particular be responsible for reconciling the interests of individual firms with the interests of the branch of industry as a whole.

Based on this philosophy the Netherlands Institute of Transport (NVI) and the Economic Bureau for Road and Water transport have developed and are still developing policy information systems for the freight transport sector (government and transport industry). In this research work there is a continuous tendency to integrate macro and micro aspects of the transport sector, whereby more and more macro-systems are joining, based on the micro-structure derived from individual firms. Given the time available only attention can be given to the policy information systems developed at the macro and meso level.

THE POLICY INFORMATION SYSTEM DEVELOPED AT MACRO AND MESO LEVEL

2.1 The basic model structure

Since the completion of an Integral Traffic and transportstudy in the Netherlands 1972, during which study the proto-type of a freight forecasting model was developed, an important amount of research has been done to improve the mentioned forecasting system.

With regard to the further improvement and development of the model already in an early stage two basic requirements were formulated. In the first place the model should be set up as a policy information system. Which means that with the aid of the system all kinds of consequences of alternative economic developments and alternative transportpolicy strategies could be quantified. Only in this way the system could function in the preparation of policymaking for the government as well for the transport industry. The second requirement which was formulated concerned the utilization of the computerprograms on the basis of the freight models developed.

The programs should be flexible enough to handle a lot of policy problems and the costs of using these programs should remain relatively low, in order to fulfil a real function in the policymaking process.

Now - 1977 - it can be said that the policy information system for freight transport, available in an operational form, is complying to a great extent with these requirements.

However before describing the basic structure of the model in a more detailed way it should be mentioned that the set-up of the model system was especially meant for freight forecasting (domestic and international transport) on medium- and long term, whereby the application for the long term is partly restricted to the condition that the environmental planning is not changed to a great extent. However the possibilities of using the model system would be underestimated if the model would only be seen in the light of forecasting the volume and composition of freight transport. As a policy information system the model forms also the base for determining the consequences of alternative transport policy strategies. The basic structure of the model developed can best be shown as a whole in figure 2. It is obvious from this diagram that the transportmodel is part of a larger system: the policy information system.

The transportmodel is fed by three categories of data, i.e.
 – the general objectives
 – the economic and technological variables exogenous for the transport sector
 – the instrumental variables (kind and level)

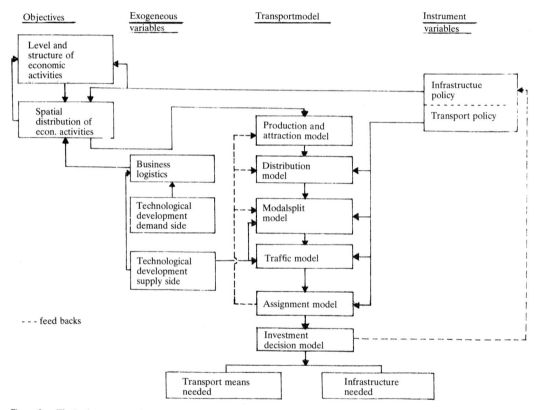

Figure 2 - The basic structure of the freight policy information system

Furthermore the feed-backs from the transportmodel to the three categories of data are explicitly shown in the diagram. It would appear that in many cases these categories of data are also in themselves the results of model systems which form an interdependent system with the transportmodel. The structure of the transportmodel (a set of submodels) in the narrow sense can best be shown in figure 3, whereby the commodity transport from, to and within the Netherlands is taken as a starting point. In the total cycle of submodels a distinction is made between two main categories: domestic transport and international transport.

Domestic transport includes the commodity transport with origin and destination within the Netherlands, as well as import overseas and export overseas; international transport includes import en export via land frontiers as well as transit without transhipment. Initially the demand for freight transport is split into domestic and international transport. The most important reasons for this are:
 a) the structure with the base of explanation of the two categories
 b) the way in which the statistical data for commodity transport are coming available

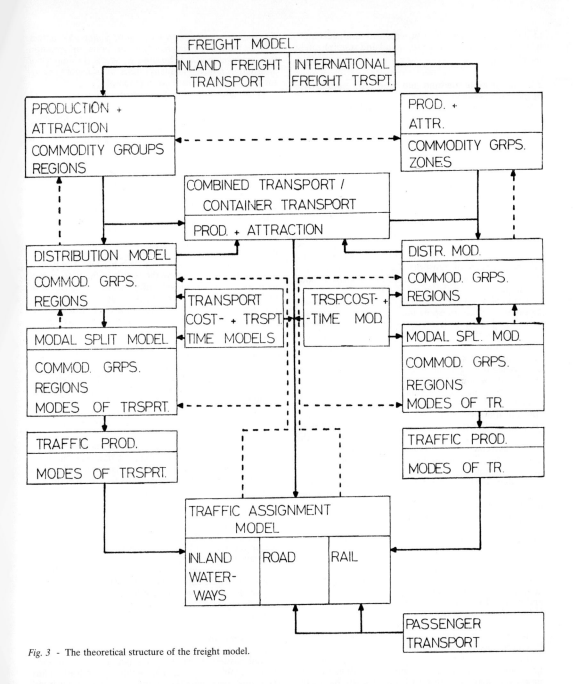

Fig. 3 - The theoretical structure of the freight model.

In view of the complexity of freight transport demand, both domestic and international transport are split into different phases. A sub-model was developed for each phase. Thus the production and attraction model determines the supply and demand per commodity group per region (number of tons); the distribution model determines the transport volume per transport relation per commodity group; the modalsplit model distributes the transport volume per commodity group per transport relation between the modes available, after which the traffic model converts the tonnages carried into both loaded and empty trips. After generation and attraction per zone have been determined the appropriate transport package for container transport is substracted or since this type of transport clearly has different transport characteristics than the remaining freight transport. The finally determined traffic production for domestic transport is assigned, together with the traffic production for international transport (both excluding container transport) and where appropriate together with the traffic production for passenger transport, to the relevant infrastructure networks.

Since after the above mentioned traffic assignment travel times and transport costs per relation may not be the same as the values initially introduced into the preceding models, there has to be a feedback from the beginning into the afore going models (from the traffic assignment model to the other submodels). By means of an iterative calculation process the ultimate equilibrium for the entire model (demand and supply) can be determined.

2.2 The possible medium and long term applications of the basic system

Before going into the possible applications of the policy information systems it may be useful to give a general indication of the ways the model results can be influenced substantially. Clearly the volume and composition of the freight transport demand is very dependent on
- the level and composition of economic activities
- the geographical spread of these activities

Changes in the economic development, both in general and in individual sectors, can exert a considerable influence on goods transport demand per transport relation. Such changes in transport demand cause changes in the transport and traffic infrastructure requirements, and in the scale and composition of the transport service offered per mode of transport, thereby causing changes in the amount and composition of the capacity needed per mode.

In addition, however, developments influencing the supply side of the transport market may cause changes in the size and composition of the goods transport package (total traffic). Technological changes in the despatch of goods, changes in the scale and the quality of the transport infrastructure available, changes in the legal regulations for the various modes of transport, changes in operating systems (e.g. the railways), changes in the amount and composition of the transport capacity available, and changes in consignment sizes etc. all affect absolute transport costs and journey times, and influence the relative transport costs and haulage times of the various modes of transport, and thereby influence the volume and composition of the freight transport pattern, as well as the distribution thereof between the transport modes available.

In other words, the model results may be influenced both by spatially differentiated economic development and the elements which independently from transport demand determine the supply of transport services.

Some examples of the potential applications of the basic freight transport model are given below:

(a) Medium- and long term goods transport forecasting

By making assumptions about economic growth (in general and for individual sectors) in the Netherlands and abroad forecasts can be made of:
(i) the volume of domestic commodity transport by commodity groups and market section
(ii) the volume of international commodity transport by commodity (15) groups and market section
(iii) the geographical split of commodity transport per commodity group over transport relations for domestic international transport (in the present model the Netherlands is split into 76 zones, but any other subdivision is possible)
(iv) the share of the transport modes (railways, roads and inland water ways) per transport relation commodity group
(v) the number of vehicle movements, both loaded and empty, per transport mode (lorry journeys, movements of shipping and wagons) per carrying capacity class and per transport relation
(vi) the traffic intensity for the different types of transport infrastructue (rail, road, water) depending on the kind and size of traffic networks brought into the model, with the possibility of a subsequent comparison of traffic intensity and capacity.

(b) Impact assessment for transport policy alternatives

In addition to making forecasts, the policy information system developed can be used to assess the impact of alternative policies in many areas of transport policy, for the statistics described in (a) above.

These alternatives may concern:
(i) measures designed to alter the conditions of competition between the transport modes (e.g. by influencing transport costs and rates)
(ii) measures designed to alter despatch arrangements (e.g. the railways)
(iii) measures designed to improve transport infrastructure and infrastructure policy (e.g. by means of transport infrastructure goods stations)

2.3 Other potential applications of the available policy information system

Other applications than those interdict as support for the preparation of policy by the government and the transport industry as described in the preceding paragraph, are possible, using extra sub-models. The principal methods is to combine the results of the basic model with specific (micro-level) information on the level of individual transport firms. In this way, policy information can be obtained as a support for the following areas of government policy and/or the policy of transport-firms.

a. Transport capacity
(i) Estimate of the future size and composition of the inland shipping fleet and the lorry fleet required to handle the freight package (total transport demand) quantitatively and qualitatively

The capacity required depends on the volume and composition of the forecast transport demand (all aspects)
(ii) a comparison of the above mentioned size and composition of the inland shipping fleet and the lorry fleet with the capacity currently available provides information about necessary extensions to, or reductions in the various components of supply.

b. Support for ratemaking

The results of the traffic assignment model can be used for the purpose or ratemaking in the inland waterway sector and the road sector; using the empty trip model allowance can be made in the tariff basis for the geographical likelihood of return freight. It is also possible to investigate the extent to which constraints on the capacity of the inland waterway infrastructure (waterways, locks, bridges, etc.) increase costs for the various types of vessel.

c. Infrastructure

The model results can form the main basis for sophisticated costbenefit analyses for decisions on transport infrastructure projects. This applies to infrastructure decisions concerning the inland waterways, road transport and rail transport as well.

d. Ports

The model results can also be used to assess the quality of the hinterland connections for the major Dutch ports.

e. Support for structure surveys

After appropriate extensions have been made, the model system can be used as the principal tool in carrying-out transport structure surveys. The above mentioned capacity estimates for the inland shipping fleet and the lorry fleet can be linked to this system. The requisite investments can be established, and the profitability trends forecased, and so on.

f. Combined transport systems

The model results can be used to investigate in greater detail the potential marketing outlets for container transport and combined transport systems (e.g. rail/road).

g. Policy with regard to spatial integration (land-use planning)

The incorporation of long-term freight demand functions in the system available makes it possible to analyse more closely the consequences of structural changes in spatial integration policy and regional economic policy, on the one hand and in transport policy (particularly as regards infrastructure policy), on the other.

This impact assessment concerns in particular the interrelationships between the various areas of policy.

The extent to which the spatial integration of economic activities can be altered in the light of the existing financial and physical "elbow-room" in infrastructure policy, or the extent to which the spatial integration of economic activities can be altered in the desired direction with the help of infrastructure policy, are questions which can be answered using the policy information model.

h. Support for short-term policy

The distinction between time scales in policymaking has not been explicitly discussed with regard to the potential applications described so far. Clearly, this distinction adds an extra dimension to the potential applications of the policy information system.

After bringing short-, medium- and long-term demand functions into the policy information system, information relating to policy for the period concerned can be obtained in a suitable form for the abovementioned applications. In theory, the same basic model structure is used as a starting point.

As regards the use of the various sub-models, it is possible, depending on the time periods concerned, to regard certain structures described by these sub-models as constants. For the short term, this applies for example to the modal split and physical distribution systems. For the long term, the changes in all the sub-models are part of the total calculating process.

The short term system offers vast possibilities for monitoring freight trends, particularly as regards the short term aspect of transport. Short term trends in economic activity can be converted into probable freight transport market trends, the latter being reflected in the most important market indicators. For example, information concerning:

(i) the price trend of each market section
(ii) the capacity utilization of each market section
(iii) the profitability trend of each market section
(iv) equipment utilization planning and reserving of equipment (the railways)

2.4 Geographical application of the freight model system

Although the in section 2.3 mentioned models were specific developed for the Dutch situation, the basic structure of the model is, in adapted form, applicable for almost every geographical area.

At this moment a complete model system will be developed on behalf of the European Commission for the European Community (9 countries). This model will mainly be used by the Commission for the preparation of their infrastructure policy for rail, road and inland waterway shipping.

Such a policy will depend upon the long term development of variables such as population, economic growth, technical advancement etc. It will be clear that the future development of these variables (and others) will be very uncertain. In order to reduce the degree of uncertainty as much as possible the model will be set up as a sensitivity model; thus it will be possible to determine the consequences of alternative assumptions on the future development of the variables mentioned. A coherent set of assumptions on these variables is called a "scenario". The model will make forecasts of the expected traffic flows and the corresponding loadings of the infrastructure. By comparing the results of various scenarios one can ascertain the relative importance of the above variables. An additional factor to be considered is the influence of alternatives within the transport policy itself, not only as far as the market forces (taxes, etc.) are concerned, but also concerning the infrastructure. A coherent set of assumptions made here is called a "strategy".

After having decided on a certain scenario the model results for that scenario will enable to judge the merits of alternative strategies.

It should be mentioned here that a model of this type needs a great deal of data. Moreover for many variables (e.g. the traffic flows) these data need to be spatially differentiated. A preliminary survey carried out by the NVI has shown that there are in general sufficient data available in the different countries. The first stage of the actual project - that started at the end of 1975 - consists of collecting, screening and ordering the data available. It will be noted that the reliability and the degree of detail of the model that will eventually be constructed will depend upon the quality of the data provided by the various countries.

In the ultimate set up of the freight model system a distinction will be made between domestic models (as far as possible one model for every country) and an international model with which the commodity and traffic flows between the regions of the different countries are forecasted. Although the first idea was to develop only an international model, statistical data showed that only 5% of the total commodity transport volume should be covered by this model. To get a right insight in the traffic intensities, caused by commodity transport, of the different infrastructure networks made it necessary to incorporate the domestic transport too (83% of the total transport volumes). To give an idea about the dimensions of the freight model systems in development the following can be mentioned:

The model system will deal with:
- three detailed European infrastructure networks
  - road
  - rail
  - inland waterway
- fourteen commodity groups
- a large number of regions
  - for international transport the 70 so called E.C. transport regions will be used
  - for domestic transport the number of regions vary with the geographical size of the countries concerned

To give a few examples:

Germany - 79 regions
United Kingdom - 134 regions
France - 95 regions
Netherlands - 13 regions

At this moment the project is in the data collection phase. Statistical data on commodity transport per geographical relation are collected to fill the different origin and destination tables. At the same time socio-economic data are collected for the different countries and their regions to form the basis for development of the different production and attraction models. Infrastructure network data (level of service variables), transport cost data etc. are collected for the development of transportation cost models which are necessary to develop the distribution and modalsplit models.

The model development itself will start in the second half of this year and will probably be finished in one year. The model development will not only take place for the E.C.-area, some ECMT-countries like Spain will be integrated in the same model system too.

A second example of geographical application of the models can be mentioned for the case of Switzerland. On behalf of the National Committee responsible for the general transportation plan of Switzerland a large part of the described freight system has been developed as a part of an integral transport and traffic model. A very interesting point here is the integration of commodity transport models and passenger transport models. In a simultaneous assignment procedure the traffic flows caused by commodity transport and passenger transport are assigned to different infrastructure networks. This gives the possibility to get a clear picture of the total traffic intensity and their interdependencies on the networks. Via feedback calculations the ultimate equilibrium can be established.

A last example concerns some Federal Republics of Yugoslavia. Also for these areas it is intended to develop the same kinds of freight transport models, of course after the necessary adaption to the local situation.

The conclusion which can be drawn from all these applications is that the theoretical model structure can be maintained for different social, economic and political situations. In most cases the number of necessary local data can be reduced to the minimum, because a lot of extra data can be produced by analog methods (for example cost functions).

Minimizing uncertainties in master planning the transport sector of a developing country

by
ANTOINE G. HOBEIKA
Virginia Polytechnic Institute and State University,
Blacksburg, Virginia, U.S.A.

INTRODUCTION

Transportation provides the basic infrastructure for economic and social development. Clearly, the services of transportation are not ends in themselves. They are means to other objectives. These objectives are economic as well as non-economic. Non-economic objectives include promoting political cohesiveness, strengthening national defenses or bringing about socially desirable demographic patterns. These classes of objectives, whether economic, social or defense related, are often in conflict within and between themselves. The development of an overall transportation plan is an outcome of the resolution and conciliation of these conflicts within the existing and expected budgetary and administrative constraints.

This paper is based on the work done to evaluate and prioritize the transportation projects proposed by the Iraq Ministry of Transportation and the Iraq Ministry of Communications, Baghdad, Iraq and the development of five year transport plan for Iraq ending year 1980 *. The proposed projects, which comprised about 75 individual undertakings, covered all modes including rail, air, land, river, coastal and sea and were mostly related to facility improvements and equipment acquisition.

A necessary ingredient to a sound evaluation and analysis is a well formulated and developed overall national framework within which individual transportation projects are assessed and their priorities ordered.

In the light of the foregoing need, the objectives of the study were to:

1. Develop a framework of national transportation requirements.
2. Evaluate and rank the proposed projects.
3. Identify modal and intermodal gaps, inconsistencies and new projects, and reorder priorities in light of the requirements of national transportation plans.

This paper will focus only on the planning methodology used in this study, and will highlight at the end some of the topics that need to be researched to enhance the transport planning in developing countries.

METHODOLOGY

The systems approach followed in the study as shown in Figure 1 consists of three major tasks. Task I concerns with the development of a feasible physical network based on the existing and proposed projects. Task II, performed in parallel with the foregoing task, concerns with the development of the hypothetical network based on the projected national requirements for transportation. Task III, a concluding task for the study, accomplished the evaluation, ranking and ordering of the total

set of feasible projects after the combatibility of the physical network and the hypothetical network had been checked.

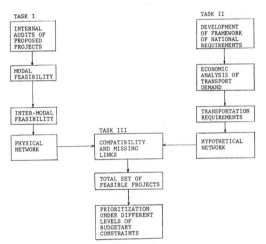

Figure 1 - Schematic of overall study approach

This approach followed in the study to achieve the above objectives, did not only define and evaluate the projects within the context of national development goals and ends, but it also avoided internal contradictions, blind spots, and consequent serious error of omission. Moreover, the systems approach used, avoids the tendency to suboptimize at the national expense.

Task I is based on three rings of analysis. The first and smaller ring consists of engineering and cost review of the specific projects proposed. This task is confined to internal engineering and technical auditing of proposed projects with respect to accuracy, adequacy and reliability of assumptions and of the data utilized in each project. At this level, each project is examined independently with respect to the respective economic and engineering parameters and to the soundness of the conclusions affecting its successful initiation and completion. The following tasks were performed on each individual transportation project:

1. Adequacy of engineering specifications.
2. Listing and analysis of possible alternatives.
3. Sufficiency of project supports.
4. Reasonableness of cost estimates.
5. Expected earnings and effectiveness.

The second level of analysis or the middle ring which encompasses the first one, evaluates the projects within their respective modes. It provides a compatibility analysis of each project within its existing and proposed modal network. In the case of a new airport development, compatibility is examined in the light of the total aviation system network, and its modal feasibility is consequently determined. At this stage, any missing links, or gaps in the modal network are identified and new lists of projects within the mode are formed and examined. Part of the test of modal feasibility is the time phasing of the project. If the project is part of an existing or planned network, it is important to determine whether its schedule of completion will coincide with the operations of the existing or planned system. This test of time phasing of projects is also carried out in the third level of analysis, where intermodal dependence of projects is determined essential to the completion of a project.

The third level of analysis or the larger ring determines the intermodal compatibility of the proposed projects within the existing and proposed transport system network. Inconsistencies and gaps in the total network are identified which resulted in the rejection and re-evaluation of certain projects and the formulation and analysis of new ones. The result of this analysis is a feasible and compatible network based on the existing and planned system.

This network which is developed from the physical systems approach, namely "network feasibility", is then checked against the hypothetical network developed from the framework of projected national requirements for transportation. The hypothetical network involves a broader systems approach to include economic analysis of the demand for transportation and the feasibility of various alternatives to satisfy the demand such as to yield optimal solutions.

The economic analysis of the demand for transportation comprised the following major tasks in this study:

1. Determination of national objectives for development in terms of short range (five years) and long range (twenty-five years). It is more respect to the long range plans that national development goals impact the planning of transportation projects. These projects have a long life, as a rule, and their impact and value must be justified in the long term as well as in the immediate or near term.

2. Development of a forecast of basic sector activities and growth. The basic sectors included services, agriculture, industry, mining and petroleum, import, tourism and transit goods.

3. Determination of a demand profile utilizing present flows of passenger and goods.

4. Development of costs of transportation for passenger and freight by relevant modes.

5. Development of additional economic aspects of demand for transportation such as price elasticity and related economic considerations which contributed to the final analysis of prioritizing the projects

The national objectives for development included other than primary economic objectives, such as social and defense goals. These objectives were then detailed and specified as they affect the development of the transportation infrastructure of the five-year plan.

The economic analysis determined the growth of the basic sector activities and the growth of demand for transportation over a twenty-five year period. The development of forecasts for basic sector activities and growth consisted of two elements:

The first involved identification of economic development plans and evaluation of probable exogenous impact of these development plans upon the transporta-

tion sector during the twenty-five-year period and more specifically during the five-year period under study.

The second element consisted of generating basic economic sector activity projections from historic trends utilizing statistical multiple correlation techniques relating the basic economic activities to appropriate dependent variables. Micro-econometric models and input/output models were not used due to unavailability of data and limitation of time.

The forecasts of demand for transportation utilized existing patterns of flows modified by exogenously planned activities super-imposed upon historic patterns. Passenger projections were made based on projections of population demographic patterns. In the projection of demand three levels were included; high, low and intermediate.

Given the growth of the basic sector activities, and the growth of demand for transportation, the operational flow of passengers and goods were determined by spatial distribution of surpluses and deficits using linear programming. Transportation flows were assigned from surplus regions in Iraq to deficit ones utilizing linear programming techniques whose objective function is to minimize the transportation distance between sources and links. The final results of projected flows were reallocated by mode based on cost effectiveness of each mode.

Shipper costs by mode were developed by leading commodity classes. Cost data were generated from available records and supported by data available from other sources than Iraq. For freight movements, five commodity groups were used to distinguish between value of goods transported, type of handling and equipment needed, and desirable transit times. For passenger movement, three classes of movements were considered to reflect differences between demand for passenger transportation for motor, air and rail transport.

The developed physical systems network is then checked against the hypothetical network, which is based on projected demand for transportation. Gaps in the present and proposed supply of transportation are identified. Present or proposed links that dit not have sufficient capacity or desirable features, or the absence of feasible links became transportation gaps to be evaluated in the context of the projects proposed.

The final step in the systems analysis approach is the prioritization of the total feasible set of projects. Prioritization of projects is not a sole function of one criterion but the combination of several criteria. Projects that are less economically justifiable than others may nevertheless have a higher priority because they constitute an integral part of other feasible projects in existence or planned.

The prioritization of projects is based on assigning ordinal values to each project for the following criteria:

1. Cost/Benefit and Internal Rate of Return Analysis:

The stream of benefits for each project included both direct and indirect benefits. Indirect benefits include the project social and military values, and its impact upon primary sectors. The impact areas and sectors of each project are determined and the "opportunity cost" of not having that project undertaken and completed is assessed. A rate of return analysis is also made for each project. It is based on a time profile of the discounted flow of costs and patterns under the lifetime of each project.

2. Physical Network Value:

The importance of each project within its mode and within the system to provide a compatible and feasible network is determined.

594

3. Relationship to Expressed National Goals and Objectives.

4. Likelihood of Completion and Successful Operation:

The success of completion and operation of each project is determined in terms of the ease of acquiring the construction equipment and materials and availability of contractors, in terms of the ease of operating and maintaining the project as specified, and in terms of the cadre and technical support required.

A second level of prioritization of projects is considered assuming only a certain percentage of the budget requirements is made available. Two levels of funding were assumed, 80% and 60% of the total sum of requested funds. Under each level of funding, a subset of the total projects is selected and consequently prioritized.

This two-way systems approach to master planning the transport sector of a developing country, which starts at one-end from the physical systems network and at the other-end from the projected hypothetical network to develop an integrated and feasible set of transport projects, minimizes the uncertainties facing the transport planner and provides the decisionmaker with alternative transportation plans under different budgetary and administrative constraints.

The basic advantages of this methodology could be summarized as follows:

1. It considers and utilizes the projects proposed by the local governments and the Ministry of Planning.

2. It familiarizes the transport planner with the importance as well as the difficulties of each project.

3. It provides two independent approaches of analysis. One approach assumes that the proposed projects are justified, and determines the improvements needed to produce a feasible and sound network. The second approach determines another network based on the economic analysis of national requirements for transportation. This dual analysis provides a safeguard against the failures in any of the approaches.

4. It avoids the serious errors of omission, internal contradictions and blind spots.

5. It considers in the analysis the time phasing of projects and the likelihood of their successful completion.

6. It evaluates and prioritizes different sets of feasible projects under different levels of budgetary constraints.

7. It requires less time for execution in comparison with similar studies.

RESEARCH TOPICS

In conducting this study, many areas in the transport sector of a developing nation are found to need extensive study and research to improve the total master planning efforts. Among these areas are the following important topics:

1. Basic Data Requirements for Transport Planning

The lack of basic transport data (such as inventories of demand, characteristics of the transport system, transport socio-economic indicator, etc.), on the urban and on the national scale hinders and limits the scope of analysis of transport planning and subjects the transport planner to personal evaluations and rough estimations. Although the data may vary with the planning methodology used, yet there is basic data requirements which is common to most planning methods, and which should be stored in the data bank and available for updating the five-year transport plans of the developing countries. This research activity should investigate and identify the types of data needed, the mechanism and the methodologies of collection and storage required.

2. Impact Studies of Commuter Railroads and Urban Freeways

Little has been done to assess the socio-economic and environmental impacts of different modes of transport in developing countries. The socio-economic impacts of feeder roads are under study by the World Bank, but other impacts are as necessary and urgent as well, such as commuter railroads, and urban Freeways. They are very useful in the evaluation of the mode itself and in the comparison between two alternative modes. The purpose of this research should be to determine the socio-economic and environmental impacts of these two modes.

3. Minimize Risk of Transport Investments Under Uncertainties of Planning Conditions

Abrupt and unforeseeable changes in the transport conditions could easily occur in a developing nation (such as the discovery of a new ore, the opening of a new border due to the relief of hostilities between two neighboring nations, etc.). These new conditions of demand may upset the transport master planning of the nation and may require some costly changes in already invested projects. The planner in planning for total transport investments, which may amount to 25% of the gross national product of the nation, may want to minimize the risk involved in these investments under the uncertainties of demand. This research should investigate and develop ways of determining these uncertainties and incorporating them in the master planning efforts.

4. Low Cost Solutions to Traffic Problems in Urban Areas

High capital investment solutions to urban traffic problems are practically unfeasible in most developing nations. Most city officials are looking to low-cost solutions to their traffic problems. Solutions that require low-key investments and that maximize the use of the existing transport facilities and equipments. Techniques to help solve traffic problems in developing urban centres at low costs are needed. Techniques in traffic management and operations, such as, banning the private car from certain congested sectors of the town, higher pricing of parking facilities in downtown areas, preferential treatment of buses (special bus lanes), the use of high-capacity buses (articulated-bus), the use of trolley cars, these and other techniques should be researched and developed.

5. The Role of Low-Cost Airports in Interurban Transportation Systems

Air transport would provide a faster and cheaper mode of travel in low density corridors of most large-area developing nations, such as Sudan and Saudi-Arabia. A research to help investigate the feasibility of these low-cost airports for different travel and environmental conditions, and to determine the necessary physical and operating requirements is also needed.

6. The Role of River Transport in Intra-Urban Passenger Transportation Systems

Most cities of developing nations are built around rivers, where they still constitute a high density corridor of travel, yet the river itself is no more being used for passenger transport, such as the Nile River in Cairo, Egypt. The purpose of this study is to investigate the potential use of river transport in intra-urban passenger transport and to determine the feasibility of its implementation.

7. Transportation Information Centres

Most neighboring developing nations, that geographically formulate a transportation region, depend on one another's transportation facilities for the movement of passengers and goods. Bottlenecks occurring at the sea-port or at the over-land transport of one nation may halt the development of its sister nation that depends on these facilities. To better utilize the existing transport facilities and to better schedule the transport traffic among these nations, the exchange of transport informa-tion is becoming a necessity. A transportation Informa-tion Centre in the region would collect, classify and distribute this information.

The proposed research should be directed basically to determine the feasibility of such a concept and to esta-blish the different elements needed to develop such a transportation centre.

ACKNOWLEDGEMENTS

For the preparation of the Transport Plan Study, special thanks are to Director and Staff, Transport Division, Ministry of Planning, Baghdad, Iraq, and to Arab Projects and Develop-ment Staff, Consultants, Beirut, Lebanon. The materials presen-ted in this article reflect the view of the author, and is responsible for errors and omissions.

FOOTNOTE

* "Evaluation and Prioritization of Transportation Projects and Development of Five Year Transport Plan Ending 1980". Three Volumes, Iraq Ministry of Planning, Baghdad, Iraq, 1975.

Traffic research relating to both short-term and long-term traffic planning

by

LARS NORDSTRÖM

University of Gothenburg, Sweden

Traffic planning is a term covering a wide range of varying activities and comprising all different means of traffic. An attempt to illustrate future traffic planning in more general terms can therefore be extremely difficult. However, we can no doubt benefit from certain experiences when considering the problems facing us.

Generally speaking, traffic planning has so far been a relatively isolated activity performed by experts and researchers, technicians and economists. The planning process can very briefly be described as follows: the politicians have determined certain aims – the fulfilment of specified traffic requirements – after which the traffic planners have supplied the technical and economic solutions, for instance the building of roads or railways, the improvement of collective traffic systems, etc. The planners have often presented a separate solution to each problem.

For a number of years Sweden, like most other countries, has successively built up the necessary know-how for the development and implementation of traffic planning. This planning has covered different levels – local, regional and nationwide traffic – and applies both to individual and collective traffic, passenger and freight traffic. It would be far from true to claim that this planning is now perfect and equals all reasonable demands. On the contrary, we are still only at the beginning of a long process towards ever-improving traffic resources and knowledge of how to achieve them.

What are the chief aims of present-day traffic planning? One might say that, both in the case of individual and collective traffic as well as passenger and freight traffic, efforts have been concentrated partly on increasing *accessibility* and partly on making travelling and transport *economically possible* for the individual or the firm. I shall in the following be limiting myself to passenger traffic only. However, the same conception applies also to freight traffic.

Passenger traffic planning has been included in the overall societal planning as a means to create swift and cheap traffic solutions on the basis of the existing structure of *private dwellings – places of work* and *service facilities*. This has created an ambition to make work and service more accessible and to stimulate and increase (in the short-term view) the traffic input. Several different methods have been used in this connection. In the case of individual traffic it has chiefly been a case of improving the road network, creating shorter routes which permit faster traffic, etc. In order to increase the passability of the collective traffic the most important factors are to increase the regularity, concentrate the bus or train line networks, and increase the speed. In latter years the additional most important method has been to lower the fares for collective travelling by introducing subsidies.

All the measures now mentioned have aimed to increase the capacity of the traffic machine, increase traffic output and reduce the dependence on distance as such. The main obstacle facing these efforts has been the possibilities of society to meet the traffic requirements by means of tax revenue.

The role played by traffic researchers in this planning process has been comparatively simple. It has been their job to suggest measures and point to methods which would make it easier for the planners to achieve their main goal – good accessibility. The researchers have thus studied how, given certain prices, the traffic is divided amongst different means of traffic, the effects of reduced travelling times, the influence of the convenience factor, etc. Behind all these studies we find the assumption that the consumer, that's to say the traveller, should be comparatively free to choose the means of travel which he/she prefers. This attitude has resulted in the tremendous expansion of private motorism all over the world. Existing differences between the number of cars per 1 000 inhabitants in various countries are almost entirely related to variations in economic development. On the other hand, the views with regard to the motorcar as a means of traffic are fairly similar, or rather have been fairly similar.

The traffic planning which has taken place in our major cities has thus aimed at building up traffic systems which can transport large numbers of people swiftly and cheaply. The governing principles for the construction of these systems have often been of a fairly short-term nature, whereas the solutions chosen often have had exceedingly long-term effects, for instance motor highways and underground railway lines, which are built to solve current traffic problems but which have consequences affecting societal development for perhaps up to 100 years after their creation.

It is here we find one of the most serious failings within present-day traffic research and there is every reason to consider this matter. I shall revert later on with some examples of the conflicts with regard to aims which can arise when adopting short term, alternatively long-term approaches to traffic problems. First, however, I think there is cause to dwell somewhat on the working technique often adopted by researchers when making long-term assessments instead of the more usual short-term forecasts.

As I mentioned just now, it is quite an ordinary technique within traffic research and traffic planning to have a comparatively short planning horizon – at best up to about 15 years. Based on forecasts for such a period of time, the planners suggest to the politicians that a highway or underground railway line, etc., should be built. Then one leaves it to the traveller to choose the means of traffic he/she finds most suitable. Now, should a politician begin to worry about what the future will look like after the 15 years have elapsed, the planner approaches the researcher with a request for a scenario for the future or a long-term prognosis. This is where the responsibility of the researcher enters the picture. A scrutiny of such long-term forecasts almost invariably shows that they are to a very small degree related to all the investments we have already made or are making and which will be in good working order for maybe 100 years ahead.

What is the reason for this? Well, traffic researchers have to a great extent simply not been interested in tying together the future with the present. One may perhaps sympathize with such omissions within other sectors of society, but it is a dangerous matter when it comes to traffic, since all investments we make in that field have such a long life, compared for instance with investments made within the engineering industry.

The following two figures illustrate what I mean in diagrammatic form.

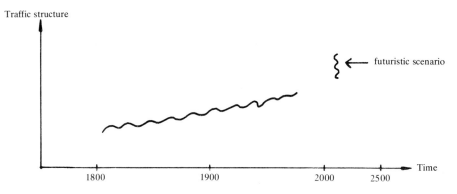

Fig. No. 1.

Fig. No. 1 illustrates a certain factual development of the traffic machine. It could for instance show how the road network has developed. For the years immediately following 1975 there are certain tangible plans which can be indicated with a certain degree of accuracy. Later on, when a more long-term prognosis is to be made, same often hangs in the air, completely separated from all previous investments. It is at this stage that different more or less fantastic projects see the light of day. They may be possible from a technical point of view, but lack all economic relevancy.

Instead, we traffic researchers should strive to develop our methods so that they also include determining the long-term effects and ties of the investments which have already been made or may be executed. The figure would then have the following appearance.

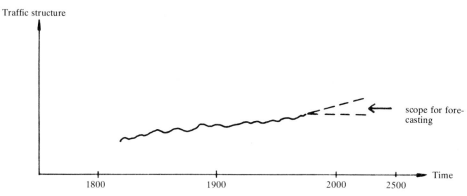

Fig. No. 2

The ties resulting from the often short-term decisions are as a rule so great also in the long-term view that the scope for a prognosis, not least within the traffic sector, is very limited indeed.

This type of approach is by no means a new phenomenon. It has been discussed in many connections among futurologists. However, tangible studies and more thoroughly prepared proposals about such studies are more rare within the traffic sector. This is all the more regrettable in view of the fact that traffic planning is facing a number of really formidable trials which will place great demands both on researchers, planners and politicians.

There are many circumstances which would seem to indicate that this very roughly outlined earlier planning procedure can now be regarded as more or less unsuitable and due for development along other lines. Based on experiences mainly in Sweden, it seems reasonable to me to claim that politicians – and in this case I refer to politicians active at the central decision level – have a desire to participate in and also actually do engage themselves in the entire planning process, thereby exerting an influence on the technical solutions successively evolved. This is mainly a consequence of the fact that traffic planning already has been or will soon be given an entirely different dimension.

I initially mentioned that traffic planning has hitherto primarily aimed at increasing accessibility, that's to say transporting people between two points in a *swift and cheap manner.* Consequently, all forecasts and futuristic scenarios have been governed by this rather simple principle, and the same applies to the methods chosen.

The new feature of special interest for the future is that traffic planning in all probability will be governed not by *one* aim alone but by perhaps four or five different goals. To the principle of *high accessibility* can be added *a reduction in the negative effects on the environment,* efforts to *minimize energy consumption, a high degree of traffic safety* and, last but not least, an integration of traffic planning into the general welfare policy with *traffic being regarded as an economic equality factor.*

There is no exaggeration in venturing to say that a number of serious conflicts will arise as to which aim should take precedence over the other and, seeing that different aims call for different methods, future traffic planning will become extremely complicated and delicate.

I should like to briefly comment on some of these aims and their probable effects, with particular emphasis on the aspects of energy consumption, illustrating how that principle clashes with other aims, above all the desire to achieve a high degree of accessibility.

The demands for *a traffic machine which is less ruthless to the environment* have increased in step with our growing knowledge of the connection between serious illnesses and pollution, the long-term effects on vegetation caused by the discharge of sulphur, etc.

As a result, traffic solutions previously regarded as being both rational and natural are now considered completely unthinkable by both policians and public opinion. We can in fact expect more and more frequent restrictions where traffic – above all private motoring, road transport and air-borne traffic – is concerned.

This makes it obvious that the aim of achieving high accessibility in many cases will directly clash with the demands concerning the environment. One can be fairly sure of the fact that, in the long-term view, the environmental demands will be more and more accentuated.

Traffic safety is yet another question which in recent years has become increasingly important and, politically speaking, an evermore burning issue. In an age when tremendous efforts are being made to cure illnesses, prevent epidemics, etc., more and more people are beginning to question the justification for the death of hundreds of thousands annually in traffic accidents.

The aims relating to traffic safety will no doubt also affect traffic planning far stronger in the future, despite the fact that great achievements have already been made in this field.

A third aspect I should like to dwell on briefly is a line of development which is becoming increasingly noticeable in more and more countries, namely the view that good traffic resources should be regarded as a *social right.* At least as far as private traffic is concerned, this means that we are beginning to regard traffic in the same light as schools, medical care, etc. This results i.a. in collective traffic to an ever increasing degree being financed by public funds and in public agencies becoming responsible for both planning and running. This of course automatically leads to the question of traffic resources becoming a political issue. It also results in harder priorities between different means of traffic or, in other terms, a political directing of the traffic to certain means of traffic and traffic solutions. A debate is presently in progress in Sweden regarding these questions and corresponding discussions are also being increasingly held in other countries as well. Not least the future demands for a society which economizes with existing resources will require increased Government intervention, which in turn presupposes the need of an increased societal economic input. The free choice of traffic servi-

ces, to which we have become accustomed, can in future be severely restricted.

This brings me to the question of resources and the effect which efforts to reduce the consumption of energy can have on traffic planning.

First of all, it should be emphasized that a general aim to reduce energy consumption within the traffic sector can constitute an excellent example of the risks of *sub-optimations.* Efforts to reduce energy consumption within the traffic sector could for instance result in increased consumption within another sector, which might lead to an increase of the total energy consumption. Without exhaustive ananlyses of the intersectorial connections relating to energy consumption the risks of such effects should definitely not be ignored. However, in the following I shall simplify matters by assuming that such risks do not in fact exist. I therefore base myself on the simplified assumption that efforts to reduce the consumption of energy within the transport sector constitutes a meaningful policy. In order to further simplify the discussion only passenger traffic will be dealt with.

Efforts to reduce energy consumption in connection with passenger traffic can be regarded in a short-term and a long-term perspective.

Attempts to reduce energy consumption can be divided into four different sub-goals or rather methods of achieving the aims. The first aim can be termed a *reduction of the total traffic sector* or the *prevention of a continued growth of the total traffic sector,* see Fig. No. 3.

Aim	Method	
	Short-term	Long-term
Reduction of the total traffic sector	Restrictions	Alterations of the settlement structure
	Increased fares	
	Increased petrol prices	
	Reduced collective traffic	

Fig. No. 3

In the *short-term* view the aim can be achieved by introducing different types of restrictions on travelling, for instance petrol rationing, imposing a ban on driving, increased energy tax on petrol, increased collective fares, a reduction in collective traffic, etc. These methods are in stark contrast to what has earlier been indicated as the usual aim of traffic planning, that's to say accessibility, and implies a reorientation of the entire traffic policy. Corresponding measures in the *long-term* view could be to change the settlement structure so that private housing, service facilities and work places are located close to one another. It is difficult to prophesy as to how this would affect freedom of choice as regards work, recreational possibilities, etc. In all probability scattered building in sparsely populated areas would be made impossible and this aim might also mean the death of all small places. Even our present major cities might prove to be unsuitable. However, a long-term effort to reduce the total traffic sector might still prove to be necessary and therefore increased knowledge of regional variations within the traffic sector is highly desirable.

Another aim of energy resource policy could be to *transfer traffic from an individual to a collective basis.* Behind this goal we have the conception that collective traffic per person is less energy-consuming than individual traffic (see Fig. No. 4).

Aim	Method	
	Short-term	Long-term
Transfer from individual to collective traffic	Restrictions on individual traffic	Fully developed collective infrastructure
	Increased petrol prices	Reduced road-building
	Reduced collective fares	
	Fully developed collective traffic	

Fig. No. 4

The *short-term* measures which can be adopted are restrictions on individual traffic, increased petrol prices, reduced fares for collective traffic and a fully developed collective traffic. It is quite apparent that some of these measures are entirely contrary to the aims which were intended to reduce the total traffic sector. As far as the *long-term* measures are concerned one can mention a development of the collective infrastructure and abstaining from further roadbuilding for individual traffic. This aim becomes particularly interesting when being compared with the two following goals which aim to reduce energy consumption within the individual sector respectively the collective sector.

The aim of reducing *energy consumption within the individual traffic sector* could, in the short-term view, be accomplished by increased petrol prices and energy tax, restrictions, the stimulation of co-driving and the use of smaller and energy-saving cars (see Fig. No. 5). In this case the means agree with what I have said previously concerning the other aims.

Aim	Method	
	Short-term	Long-term
Reduced energy consumption within the individual traffic sector	Increased petrol prices	Increased passability on the road network by building away queues and straigthening out roads
	Restrictions	
	Stimulation of co-driving	
	Reduced energy consumption per car	

Fig. No. 5

In the *long-term* view these methods can no doubt be augmented by measures aiming to improve passability by building away queues, straightening out the road network so that the driving distances become shorter, etc. In this latter respect the measures chosen comply with present-day road policy. Efforts to reduce energy consumption within the individual traffic sector are probably easiest to fit into present traffic planning. However, there can be no doubt that a far-reaching one-sided aim to reduce individual traffic would have considerable effects on other parts of social-welfare policy, such as for instance the efforts to achieve equality within employment policy and as regards regional policy.

The fourth aim, finally, is to attempt to *reduce energy consumption within collective traffic* (see Fig. No. 6.)

Aim	Method	
	Short-term	Long-term
Reduction of energy consumption within collective traffic	Reduced frequency	Increased passability by infrastructural measures
	Increased fares	
	Increased combined running	
	Smaller vehicles	

Fig. No. 6.

These measures may seem drastic. However, they were to a certain extent applied during the latest energy crisis. The *short-term* methods are reduced frequency – above all during off-peak hours – , increased fares, a reduced number of lines, which means more changes and reduced travelling speed. All these measures are directly contrary to the traffic planning which has been common during latter years. The establishment of such an aim thus means a radical rethinking within the planning, In the *long-term* view the measures previously mentioned could be augmented by the infrastructural development of new collective traffic routes, roads, etc., that's to say methods which form part of presentday road policy.

In the light of what I have just said there is reason to try to connect the earlier discussion on planning and futurology with existing signs of new aims making themselves felt within the traffic sector. It is in this context that the role of the traffic researcher becomes particularly interesting.

Now let's revert to the figure shown earlier. The hypothetical development shown by the curves illustrates a traffic structure which has been based on the principle of a high degree of accessibility. (See Fig. No. 7).

Traffic structure

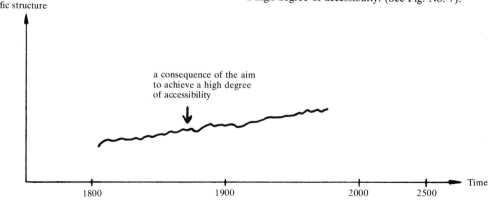

a consequence of the aim to achieve a high degree of accessibility

1800   1900   2000   2500   Time

Fig. No. 7

When discussing the future the question now arises how much of the earlier investments must be considered incorrect and therefore abandoned due to the introduction of new aims.

It is here that the researcher has a vital part to play. When the politician – whether he himself wants it or not – has defined his aims for a traffic policy, it is the task of the researcher to show the resultant effects and develop methods indicating for instance which previous investments are thereby made valueless. The fact of introducing new aims which are in conflict with old goals and which are also at variance with one another can hypothetically lead to the curve having the following appearance: (see Fig. No. 8)

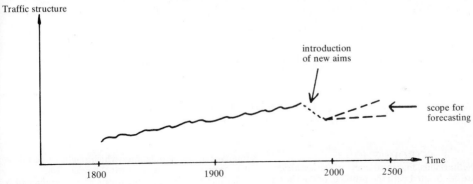

Fig. No. 8.

The scope for prognosticating which then arises differs from that resulting from traffic planning with unaltered aims.

The traffic researcher thus has a very important role to play when it comes to long-term planning and the establishment of long-term goals for the planning. The responsibility of the researcher will also increase considerably, seeing that the results which he presents will guide the politicians when making decisions with extremely long-lasting effects. At the same time the parts played by politicians and planners will change in a manner so as to make them more and more dependent on the researchers.

Another conclusion to be drawn from what I have said here to-day is that traffic planning can no longer be considered solely a matter of traffic technique and traffic economy but instead is becoming increasingly a question of societal economy and societal politics. This change calls for entirely different means of planning compared to those previously adopted. These altered circumstances will place great demands on planners, researchers and others engaged in evolving these new means of influence and new priorities. The new situation I have described has so far primarily been noticeable in questions relating to collective traffic. In due course, however, planners etc. engaged in private motor traffic, airborne traffic, shipping, port activities and railways will gradually become aware of similar tendencies. I do not consider it an exaggeration to claim that we are facing a revolution within the field of traffic planning.

The planning of an airport system, a comprehensive approach

Schiphol Airport Authority, The Netherlands

and

R. P. van der Kind
Netherlands Institute of Transport

1. INTRODUCTION

In the Netherlands, like in so many other countries, we are confronted with the problem of the shortfall of capacity of existing airports. Although the problem, in consequence of the recent stagnation of economic development would appear to be less urgent, it should, however, be borne in mind, that world air traffic, despite the recession, still shows a reasonable growth of approx. 6% a year, while future expectations in general range around 8% per year. The problem accordingly continues to exist, though it is likely to manifest itself in a somewhat milder form.

In the present structure of society it is no longer possible to consider the airport capacity problem from the narrow viewpoint of transport economics. Many other aspects also feature in such a problem: town and country planning, the overall traffic problem, in the air as well as on the surface, and the balanced repartition of same, traffic congestion and the inherent problem of mobility in general, international relations, employment, etc.

Neither is it conceivable in the present social configuration that a decision for a substantial expansion of the airport capacity should exclusively be taken at one decision level without other official bodies and persons directly involved being enabled to participate in that decision. Such a decision in fact so fundamentally affects the national budget, the proportionate distribution of costs (and benefits – which in connection with airports sometimes tends to be overlooked) and other national policy objectives that it could not be taken without due consultation with interested parties.

In the Netherlands attempts have of late been made towards achieving an adequate solution to the airport problem, in which both aspects, i.e. the linking-up of the airport problem with other aspects of overall national policy, and a decision-initiation approach under which all parties concerned are enabled to take part in the decision process, are being taken into account.

The following review, which is rather a case study of an experience of a wide-scope decision than an in-depth theoretical paper, therefore only claims to be comprehensive in the following two ways, viz.

a. by including in the considerations, apart from the airport capacity proper, also the consequences in other sectors of society besides the air traffic sector proper, and

b. by also paying attention, besides to the technical planning problems, to decision-taking procedures and consultation structures (including government bodies, trade and industry, research institutions as well as representatives of the population), which ought to be taken into account in arriving at a suchlike decision.

The fact that the present paper is the product of a co-operation between two authors, one being engaged in industry and the other in a government agency and the research side, may go to show that it is possible to reach such a co-operation in the latter field, in spite of the fact that the aims of the two interest groups do not always run parallel.

2. BRIEF DESCRIPTION OF THE PRESENT COMPLEX OF PROBLEMS

2.1. Description of the present system

The airport system in the Netherlands comprises, besides a number of minor airfields for general aviation and gliders, one major central airport (Schiphol), where 92% of the total air traffic to and from this country is concentrated, and five airports of less importance. The largest of these five airports is the airport of Rotterdam, which accounts for approx. 7% of total air traffic; the other four airfields, two of which are military ones being partly open to civil aviation, between them account for a few per cent of total air traffic. (See fig. 1).

It may therefore be argued that the future growth of air traffic in the situation given will be determined by the coping abilities of Schiphol airport, the more so since the only other airport of national importance, i.e. Rotterdam, is destined to be closed down, while the remaining four airports in their present form will certainly not be able to accommodate any substantial sections of the air traffic.

2.2. Capacity of Schiphol airport (see fig. 2)

The capacity of Schiphol is largely determined by the runway system, in the use of which account is to be taken of the noise-sensibility of the airport's surroundings. This sensibility to noise and the consequent pressure from the neighbourhood towards limiting the resultant disturbance have led to a system of preferential runway use being introduced at Schiphol, as a result of which a maximized utilization of available runway capacity is no longer possible.

On the basis of this restricted utilization the capacity of Schiphol's current runway system may be estimated at approx. 235,000 air traffic movements, a volume which according to the latest estimates is anticipated to be reached by 1990.

Apart from the runway system and the neighbourhood's noise sensibility, some additional factors which may possibly have al limiting effect on capacity can be

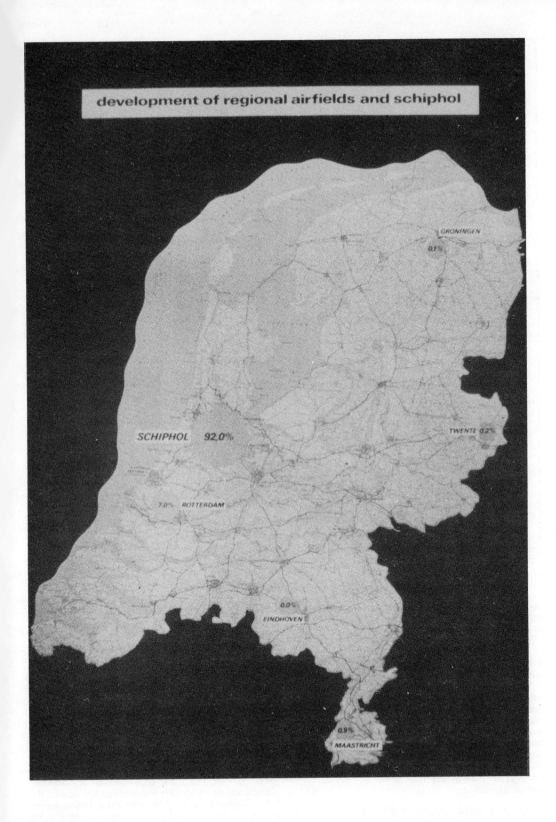

development of regional airfields and schiphol

Fig. 1.

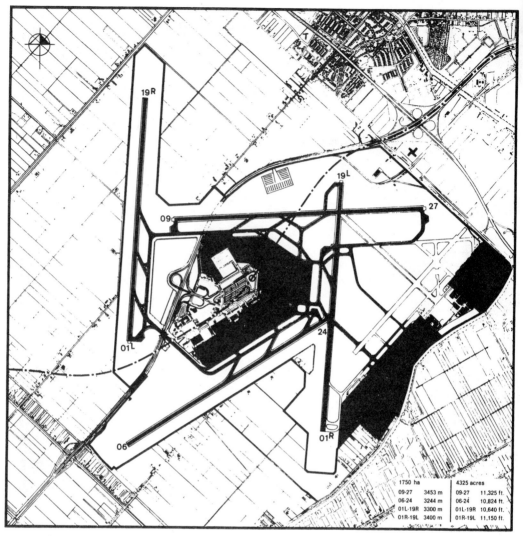

Figure 2 - Schiphol the present

1750 ha		4325 acres	
09-27	3453 m	09-27	11,325 ft.
06-24	3244 m	06-24	10,824 ft.
01L-19R	3300 m	01L-19R	10,640 ft.
01R-19L	3400 m	01R-19L	11,150 ft.

designated, i.e. the surface traffic infra-structure around the airport, the terminal facilities etc. at the airport, and the urbanization problems which ensue from the development of employment at Schiphol.

2.3. Possibilities of utilization of the regional airfields

With the regard to the possibilities of utilization of the other airfields it may likewise be noted that substantial pressure from the neighbourhood of these airfields towards restriction is being exerted. In the case of the Rotterdam airport this has even assumed such proportions that a principle decision has already been passed by the municipal council to close the airport altogether. Intervention on the part of the central government has however resulted in this resolve not yet having been carried into effect.

3. POSSIBILITIES OF ACHIEVING A SOLUTION

When reviewing the foregoing it appears that a number of alternatives are open in order to bring the future

supply and demand of airport capacity into harmony with each other. In discussions between government bodies, aviation authorities and other professional people on the one hand and research people on the other hand, a programme of studies has gradually come into existence in which all these alternatives have been given more elaborate consideration. In view of the urgency that was being assumed to exist at the time (Schiphol was supposed to reach saturation in 1983) the study which was aimed at the creation of a Second National Airport (SNA) was given priority, also in view of the expected complexity of the problems concerned. This study was initiated by the Civil Aviation Authority. Right from the start it was being taken for granted that also other aspects besides air traffic aspects should be included in the considerations. This led to the setting-up of a Steering Committee, on which were also represented, besides the CAA, representatives of the Physical Planning Agency, the Ministry of Traffic and Transport, the Central Planning Agency etc., all these bodies being directly involved in a possible creation of a SNA. It was ultimately this Steering Committee which to a large extent determined the course and content of the actual work as far as the SNA study was concerned.

Apart form the government bodies directly concerned, however, also the participation of less directly interested parties was to be safeguarded. To this end a consultative body between the Steering Committee and these interested parties was set up, comprising local government authorities, other ministries and similar bodies.

The terms of reference of this group, besides contributing to the forming of opinions, was to ensure also the communication between researchers and interested parties, such as neighbours, action groups, trade and industry, etc. It was particularly the forming of judgments within this group which has effected the gradual widening of scope from the mere SNA problem to consideration of overall problems relating to airport capacity.

During these consultations it was already becoming apparent that each of these alternatives had its advantages and disadvantages. These advantages and disadvantages will be briefly dealt with below.

3.1. Extension of Schiphol

Enabling it to cater for the total traffic demand. From the aviation optic this solution is obviously to be preferred: split operations are not necessary, interlining can take place without difficulty, full utilization of investments takes place, while the additional investments will be relatively low, and the problems of aviation politics will not be more difficult than they have been so far. The drawbacks of this solution are situated outside the direct aviation sphere: the disturbance to the neighbourhood, despite the fact that aircraft engine noise will decrease in the future, is likely to remain a significant factor, the open area will gradually be affected and the infrastructure is bound to become very heavy.

3.2. The solution through the creation of a Second National Airport (SNA)

This is a very expensive solution, which may however adequately solve the problem, particularly if the location is carefully chosen and future potentialities of expansion are taken into account. The advantages of this solution are obvious: the disturbance around Schiphol can be kept to a limited level, the open area can to a large extent remain open, air traffic growth will not be hampered, etc. The drawbacks, however, are likewise obvious: the solution is expensive, both from the viewpoint of investments and from the viewpoint of duplicate operation, it will be a long time before the SNA is operational, problems of aviation politics will arise due to the fact that operations will have to be distributed among the two airports, and ATC problems with two major airports in the relatively small air space available to the Netherlands, will by no means become easier.

3.3. The third solution

that may be envisaged might be found in improving the existing regional airfields in such a way that these may take over part of Schiphol's air traffic. This solution is less than optimal in so far as only a relatively minor increase of airport capacity can be achieved, and this at relatively high cost (although the cost will be lower than in the case of a second National Airport). A significant advantage, however, might be the fact that by way of employing these airfields in this manner, a gain of time is achieved.

A far-reaching decision like the construction of a SNA may then be taken under less pressure. From a physical point of view the solution referred to will bring about a spreading of activities to the country's periphery which, in view of the centralization trends towards the western

conurbation, would be a welcome development. The drawbacks are rather significant, though; distribution of operations among several airfields; in view of the location of the regional airfields (close to built-up centres) a substantial increase of the number of noise-affected people is to be anticipated; a very complicated set of ATC problems. Also the problems related to aviation politics, associated with the division of the traffic among the airfields, will by no means be simple.

3.4. The most drastic solution

is that which by means of a purposeful policy aims at keeping the demand for air traffic limited to such an extent that an extension of capacity can be dispensed with. From the aviation point of view this is clearly not the most desirable solution. In view of the important position that the transport sector occupies in the Dutch economy (cf. diagram), it is not the best solution from the economic optic either. A number of advantages in the way of conservation of the environment and physical planning can however be indicated: reduction of disturbance, reduced encroachment upon the scarce open areas and a less extensive infrastructure.

4. STRUCTURE AND RESULTS OF THE STUDIES

The foregoing is a rough outline of current airport problems along with an indication of possible solutions. It is clearly unfeasible, within the framework of the present paper, for the various possible intermediate forms of the four solutions considered to be thoroughly dealt with.

In the following an equally broad description will be given of the way in which the problems referred to have been tackled on the research side.

Also some results of the studies carried out will be presented and a number of tentative conclusions drawn. In the last chapter the way in which the results of the studies are being brought into the political decision process as well as the interplay arising between decision preparation and decision implementation will be briefly dealt with.

4.1. Extension of Schiphol airport (see fig. 3)

In the study relating to the possibilities of extension of Schiphol [1] the following are reviewed:

a. what possibilities are still left for Schiphol to be expanded without the disturbance to the neighbourhood increasing;

b. what possibilities still exist to restrict the nuisance to the neighbourhood, without the capacity having to be enlarged.

Accordingly only the supplement to the present capacity is being evaluated; the functioning of Schiphol in its present form is not gone into. Taking these starting points into account, two variants ultimately remained, one under which the present runway system would be extended by the addition of a parallel N/S 5th runway, and one under which the existing fourth runway would be turned in such a way that an alleviation of the noise disturbance could be expected. The latter alternative naturally did not produce any capacity gain. The solution with the parallel 5th runway did produce a capacity gain; this was calculated at 50,000 to 60,000 movements, i.e. an increase compared to present capacity of 20 to 25%. That this gain is only 20 to 25% is mainly due to the fact that by the addition of a fifth runway an unbalanced runway system is created (3 runways N/S, 2 runways E/W). As a result the gain in capacity was limited to the maximum acceptable supplementary load in the direction with the least capacity. In order to obtain a larger capacity gain, another (6th) runway would have to be provided in this

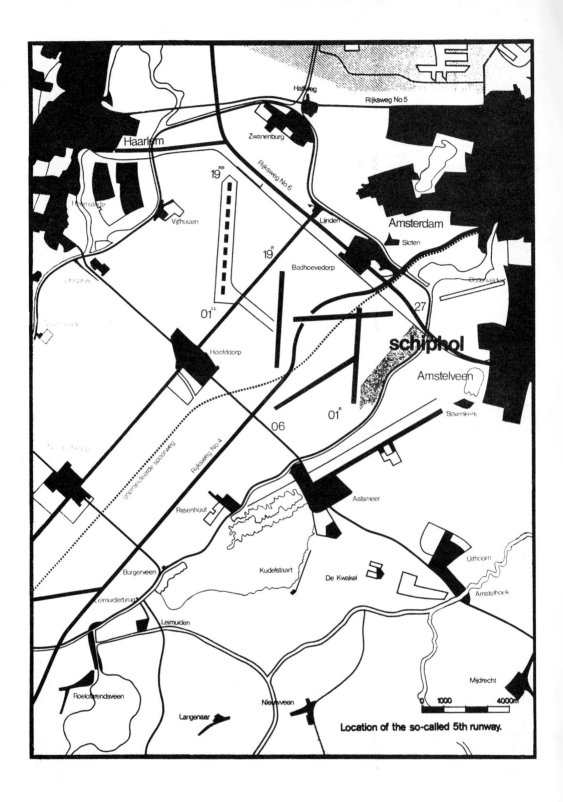

Location of the so-called 5th runway.

Fig. 3

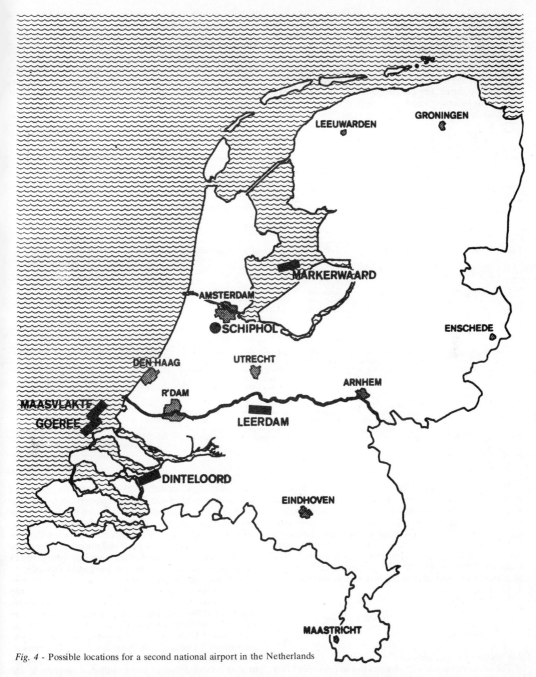

Fig. 4 - Possible locations for a second national airport in the Netherlands

latter direction as well. In view of the fact that an area in the extension of this possible 6th runway has meanwhile been assigned to residential housing, the extension of Schiphol is only possible by means of a 5th runway and its inherent other facilities. On the basis of the latest forecasts such an extension would result in Schiphol not being saturated by 1990 but around 1995.

4.2. Schiphol plus SNA

In view of the far-reaching consequences which the creation of a new airport may entail, it is not surprising that this alternative for the solution to the capacity problem has been thoroughly studied. Not only has the question of the possible location been gone into, but it has also been investigated whether from a socio-economic point of view the creation or non-creation of a SNA would in itself be a paying proposition. For both analyses (the location as well as the socio-economic acceptability of a SNA) cost/benefit analysis techniques have been employed; the ins and outs of these will however not be discussed in the present paper. For those interested it may be noted that English translations of both studies have been published [2]. In order nevertheless to give an impression of the multitude of aspects that have been considered in the study, the broad outline of the model structure employed is shown in Annex 1.

In this paper only a general idea of the structure and results of this study will be given. The study was started in 1972 when in an inter-departmental commission, which had been set up to review the physical planning situation around Schiphol, the conclusion had been reached that the airport on the basis of the growth forecasts drawn up at the time, would reach saturation in the first part of the eighties. The commission then decided first to start a site selection analysis in regard to five possible locations and only after that to answer the question as to whether another airport would in fact be expedient from a socio-economic point of view.

The site selection analysis

The five locations to be considered are shown in fig. 4. From this plan it is clear that there are marked differences between the locations. In table 1 the main differences, split up according to a number of the most important aspects, are shown.

Table 1 - Advantages and disadvantages of the locations

location	cost (soc.-econ.)	employment	planning	accessibility	ATC	defense	noise
1. MARKERWAARD	relatively low	relatively favourable	empty area integration easily feasible, favourable for decentralisation from western conurbation	passable	passable	no major problems	favourable
2. LEERDAM	relatively high reason: land improvement defense	neutral	fine scenery; preferably to be kept open; unfavourable	excellent	passable	poor: transfer of a number of mil. bases	poor
3. DINTELOORD	relatively low	relatively favourable, reverse of commuter flow	relatively favourable no special scenery favourable for decentralisation	passable	poor in view of nearness of Belgium	no major problems	relatively poor
4. GOEREE	high, reason: construction of island + cross runways + infrastructure	relatively unfavourable	unfavourable owing to intersection of scenic areas and urbanisation	poor, one-sided (no distribution of traffic)	passable	no problems	favourable
5. MAASVLAKTE	very high, reason: construction of island + cross runways + infrastructure	unfavourable: labour market already tight	relatively unfavourable in view of construction of infrastructure	poor (one-sided, no distribution of traffic)	passable	no problems	favourable

The qualitative assessment of the various aspects shown in table I has been valuated in the cost/benefit analysis as much as possible in terms of money. Where this was not possible, because either the conversion into money implied a political judgement (e.g. employment) or because the appraisal methods failed, the aspects have been quantified as much as possible in terms of their own units. The ultimate order which emerged from the survey of material and immaterial aspects was as follows:

1. Markerwaard
2. Dinteloord
3. Leerdam
4. Goeree
5. Maasvlakte

The socio-economic analysis

The socio-economic c/b analysis has in principle been carried out on the same data as the location analysis. In this analysis the problem of the viability of a new major airport in the Netherlands is approached from two angles. First, it has been examined, through a conventional analysis based on differences in journey time with and without the second airport, wat "costs" the non-construction of an SNA would entail on air transport users. This amounted to a computation of the difference in consumers surplus between the two situations. Apart from these advantages on the consumer side, however, an investigation has been made into the effect which an investment in airport capacity may have on the productive sectors of the Dutch economy. To this end use has been made of the models employed for the forecasting of the development of the Dutch economy up to the year 2000 (Central Planning Agency). From this highly complex link-up of models a division has been made for this purpose in such a way that one sector describes the "air traffic and transport activities" and the other sector "the rest of the economy". Both sectors are interconnected by means of so-called forward and backward linkages.

With the aid of these model structures it was now possible to ascertain what shiftings and effects will crop up in the Dutch economy following a missive investment in the "air traffic and transport" term, as compared with a situation without a SNA. These shiftings and effects, expressed in terms of money, together with the consumers surplus, constitute the benefits of the SNA project, which benefits are set off against the costs, as these had to a substantial extent been collected already in the location analysis. Obviously in this analysis, as this had in fact also been done in the location analysis, several variants have been worked out. We will confine ourselves here to indicating only a few major variants.

socio-economic return of an SNA

	B/C ratio
High Forecast	3.76
Medium Forecast	2.16
Low Forecast	1.23

The conclusion was that the creation of a SNA would be an attractive proposition from the socio-economic viewpoint. Nevertheless there were also considerable uncertainties, as is also apparent fromt the effect of e.g. the forecasts in the above table. It likewise appeared, for instance, that the B/C ratio differed rather substantially according to location. A supplementary analysis to the results showed that 49% of these uncertainties were attributable to uncertainties in relation to future policy (consequently to be influenced, like the choice of the location, the division of traffic between the airports, etc.) and that 51% of the uncertainties concerned genuine uncertainty, that is to say caused by the inability to appraise future developments with any accuracy (e.g. forecast, development of income, etc.).

4.3. Capacity increase through regional airports [3]

Simultaneously with the SNA study, an investigation into the possibilities of development of the regional airports was carried out. This study however was not so much directed towards drawing up an overall cost/benefit assessment as on determining the maximum traffic volume which *in favourable conditions* might be accommodated at these airfields. These favourable conditions were interpreted in such a way that the package of services of the regional airfields was very substantial. The effect of great differences in frequency between for instance Schiphol and regional airfields was thus eliminated.

The choice of the airport is then determined by the following factors, viz.

    a. the airport's accessibility
    b. distribution of the population in the Netherlands
    c. the propensity to fly per region
    d. the choice of destination

The above does mean that the results found, as far as the regional airports are concerned, will be too optimistic. The intention was to ascertain to what extent these airfields would be able to relieve Schiphol's capacity problem. To this end an analysis of the airport selection behaviour of air travellers was made on the basis of extensive surveys, held virtually simultaneously at Schiphol and the regional airfields.

This study was likewise designed in such a way that policy-relevant alternatives could be rapidly elaborated. In total over 25 variants were worked out. In tables 2 and 3 the most important ones are given. From table 2 it appears that although the shares of the regional airfields do increase to some extent, the overall effect is not of such a nature as to bring about a very substantial lessening of the pressure on Schiphol.

The most significant influence lies with Rotterdam and Welschap (Eindhoven). These two airports, however, are precisely the ones (notably Rotterdam) whose closing or restriction is being contemplated. In order to ascertain what the effect of this closing or restriction will be, a variant can be worked out in which these two airports are assumed to be closed. This variant is shown in table 3.

Table 3 - Development of regional airfields, in favourable conditions and closing of Rotterdam and Eindhoven (% of total)

	Schip-hol	Rotter-dam	Maas-tricht	Twente	Gronin-gen	Eind-hoven
1973 (actual)	92	7	0.9	0.2	0.1	– (100)
1980 (forecast)	86.2	–	4.2	6.2	3.4	– (100)
1985 (forecast)	86.5	–	4.5	5.5	3.5	– (100)

From the latter table it appears that the closing of Rotterdam and Eindhoven would lead to a substantial proportion of Schiphol's capacity gain in variant I being lost again. Particularly if it is realized that the assumption of equal service packages imparts a flattered picture of the proportions of the regional airfields, it may be argued that involving these airfields will not produce an adequate solution to Schiphol's capacity problem. It may be a possible interim solution, though, which may offer some relief for a couple of years.

4.4. Restriction of the demand [4]

The solution through a purposeful policy directed on restraining the demand is associated with the evasive and comprehensive problem of the restraining of mobility. It is therefore understandable that the studies on this possible solution have been less concrete than the solutions described in the foregoing. On the other hand it may be expedient to point out that putting a restraint on the demand for air transport will contribute only to a limited extent to the overall restraining of mobility. Of the total number of medium and long distance transport movements only a small percentage relate to movements by air. The effects of restraining the demand have nevertheless been looked into yet. In doing so, there have been two approaches one directed from actual practice and one from a more theoretic point of view.

4.4.1. The theoretic approach

is mainly directed on holiday air traffic, since this is the sector in which the largest growth of air is anticipated. On the basis of the data of observed holiday habits of the Dutch it has been tried to assess with the aid of disaggregated model techniques how the choice of holidays is likely to develop in the future. Although the analysis concerned also comprises the choice between going and non-going on holiday as well as the choice between domestic and foreign holiday destinations, the outcome most relevant to the problem in hand is a description of the modal split conduct of the holiday-goers in the future.

The results of the forecast under unchanged policy conditions are shown in table 4 Variant III. More interesting for the present considerations is, however, the variant in which it is assumed that owing to some as yet undefined policy measure flying for holiday purposes is rendered impossible. The results of this variant are also reflected in table 4 Var. IV. On comparing the two situations it will be seer that the frustrated air travellers split up among the other modes of transport, the majority opting for the motor car – which is not likely to be the most desirable effect envisaged by such measure. (See also table 5).

4.4.2. The practical approach

does not so much base itself on the effect which a policy measure might have on general mobility as on the possibilities and instruments which are available to implement such a measure, the following factors having been

Table 2 - Development of regional airfields and Schiphol in favourable conditions (% of total)

	Schip-hol	Rotter-dam	Maas-tricht	Twente	Gronin-gen	Eind-hoven
1973 (actual)	92	7	0.9	0.2	0.1	– (100)
1980 (forecast)	75	13	1.9	3.4	2.2	5.8 (100)
1985 (forecast)	76	11	2.4	3.5	2.7	5.5 (100)

Table 4 - Modal Split Foreign Holidays

	Variant III air included			Variant IV air excluded			change
	1980	1985	1990	1980	1985	1990	1980, 1985, 1990
Camping							
– car	27,9	26,4	24,8	33,0	31,4	29,6	+ 2,2
– other	2,2	2,2	2,1	2,9	2,9	2,8	+ 9,1
Other types of holidays							
– plane	17,2	17,4	17,8	–	–	–	–
– car	35,1	36,1	37,2	42,3	43,5	45,0	+ 26,8
– train	8,8	9,4	10,1	11,3	12,1	13,0	+ 40,9
– bus	5,8	5,6	5,3	7,5	7,2	6,9	+ 53,4
– other	3,0	2,9	2,7	3,0	2,9	2,7	+ 6,6

Table 5 - Changes in mode, due to suppression of airtransport mode type of holiday

Camping	
– car	+ 30
– other	+ 4
Other types	
– plane	– 100
– car	+ 41
– train	+ 15
– bus	+ 10
– other	+ 0

considered, viz. quota restriction, price measures, measures of aviation politics and licencing systems. Here, too, the possibilities of retraining non-business traffic have been reviewed. A major difficulty in this connection, however, is the fact that an increasingly growing proportion of this traffic takes place on normal scheduled services also catering for business traffic, and it will certainly not be intended to frustrate the latter category, in view of the significance of international commercial traffic to the Dutch economy (a large percentage of the Dutch GNP is achieved through international trade). By way of tackling the non-business traffic sector accordingly not only holiday charter transport but also the service level of scheduled traffic will be affected. Moreover, aviation political consequences will no doubt crop up owing to foreign airlines getting fewer chances than before with, in consequence, further impairment of scheduled traffic. In general the conclusion therefore was that there were only few instruments qualifying for achieving the desired result, i.e. restraining part of the air traffic: the instruments either operate unduly rigorously thus defeating the object to be attained (quota restriction, licencing, aviation politics) or they were insufficiently effective.

An instance of a low-effect instrument was price setting. In fact the government and the airport authorities can only exert influence on a minor part of overall flying costs, i.e. by way of landing charges. An analysis of the possible consequences of a drastic increase of landing charges (by 50%) led to the conclusion that this would produce only marginal effects, both on scheduled and charter traffic, i.e. of the order of 0,5% on long hand and appr. 2,5% on short distance. [5] This is partly due to the relatively small proportion of airport charges in overall flying costs, since landing charges represent only some 6% of flying costs, so that a 50% increase will lead to an increase of only 3% of flying costs, the effect of the price elasticity consequently being limited, partly this is also due to the competition among airlines which may tend to part of the increase not being passed on, thus reducing

the returns to the airlines, which may possibly induce airlines to transfer their services to other airports nearby offering more favourable terms. However this effect on further analysis also appeared to be extremely weak. The conclusion of this approach therefore was that even if it should be contemplated to try to restrain air traffic, the possibilities for this are limited and that the consequences of such a measure through the modal split effect might well counteract other policy measures such as restraining road vehicle traffic.

4.5. Correlation between the studies

It is clear that the studies described above correlate with each other. This is partly due to the fact that there is a causal connection (for instance between the Second National Airport study and the study of the Regional Airfields), partly also because when a study was submitted to policymaking authorities, new queries were called forth, which again led to further studies (for instance Second National Airport and restraining of air traffic demand). As a matter of fact the comprehensive approach had not been planned in advance, but rather grew as a gradual process following the consistent consultations between researchers and users, as described earlier.

The ultimate result of this gradually grown situation is a set of consistently linked up models, with which several intermediate variants of the aforementioned solution potentials may be solved. Thus situations may be imagined in which no major second airport will be constructed, but a new, relatively favourably located regional airport in addition to Schiphol and the existing regional airfields. It may then be assessed with the aid of a combination of the SNA-model and the model for the regional airfields what will be the effect of such an airport on airport capacity in the Netherlands. By the same token situations with a SNA, closing down of one or more of the regional airfields and, for example, closing of Schiphol, can be worked out. It will be clear that this system of models may in theory constitute a significant aid in the further decisionmaking processes in respect of airport capacity in this country. Fortunately this turns out to be the case also in practice. The results of the studies have been submitted to the policy-making bodies, following which elaborate discussions ensued. The queries and problems arising from these discussions were fed back to the researchers who with the aid of the instruments developed appeared to be able to answer at short notice the majority of the problems posed.

The questions asked ranged from e.g. the influence of lower or higher forecasts, the calculation of the business economic returns in the case of one airport or in a system of two airports, the passenger load factor of railways under various alternatives, the expected volume of em-

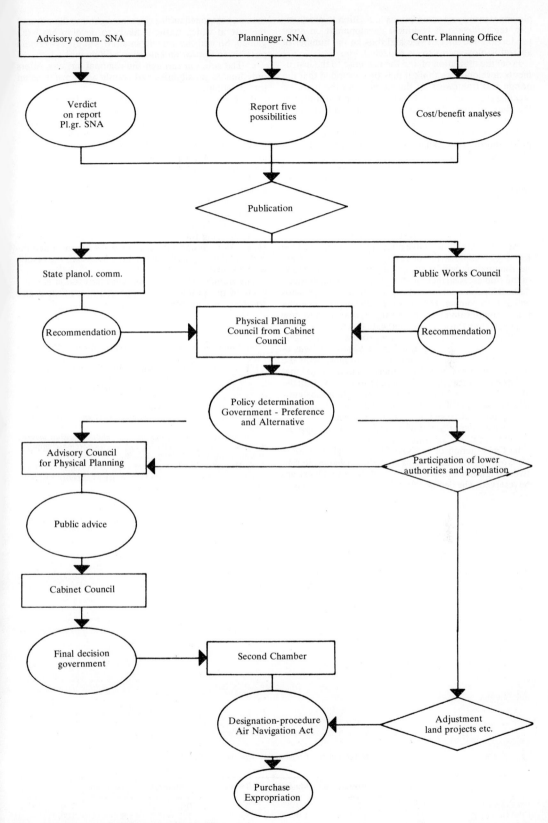

Fig. 5 - Procedure of participation of choice SNA

ployment in varying assumptions in relation to productivity, the influence of technical development on noise production and aircraft size and thus on the number of air traffic movements to be expected, etc.

From the utilization of and the response to the instruments developed we think it may be concluded that the design and framework of the studies and the mode of tackling the problems, in which already in the course of the phase of study the participation and involvement of future users is ensured, has been a success.

The model system developed has turned out to be a policy information system not only in theory, but it has also appeared to be used as such in practice, which for the user leads to alertness in his evaluations and for the researcher to a considerable amount of satisfaction in his work.

5. THE FURTHER PROGRESS: POLITICAL DECISIONMAKING AND THE EFFECT OF THE STUDIES THEREON

Although the studies have undoubtedly influenced the forming of opinions, this does not mean that the ultimate decisionmaking will be completely based on the results of the studies. Also there is still a long way to go before a definite decision on airport capacity in the Netherlands will be forthcoming. The relevant decision process is of a rather complicated nature (see fig. 5) which up to now has been gone through only halfway. It is to be anticipated that as further progress in this process is being made an increasingly growing number of arguments will emerge, which cannot be answered any more with the instruments developed. Nevertheless it may be said that on the basis of the studies the initial problem, with all the alternatives still open, has been reduced to a substantially simpler problem, current alternatives essentially having been narrowed down to the following:

a. Extension of Schiphol by a fifth runway – approx. 50,000 additional air traffic movements.

b. Construction of a SNA: Of the original 5 locations only 2 have remained as more or less viable alternatives. It is contemplated that one of these two locations be reserved. The decision to effectuate construction may then be postponed until a clearer insight into the way and the rate at which traffic is likely to develop has been gained. Should this remain small, it will always remain possible to opt for an extension of Schiphol.

c. The solution through the regional airfields offers only limited possibilities and is only appropriate as an interim solution.

d. Restraining of the demand is considered as a serious alternative by only very few people.

When reviewing the overall picture we think it may be said that in spite of the fact that the aims of the various bodies co-operating in the study did not always run parallel, in the elaboration of the various alternatives such harmony of consultation has prevailed that the remaining aspects of the problem have become comparatively simple. Naturally this does not mean that in the further decision process conflicting objectives could not emerge again. By way of the continuous co-operation structures it is nevertheless likely that a greater mutual understanding for each other's viewpoints also in this stage will be found than if the parties involved had directly and one-sidedly been confronted with the results of the study.

The framework is there for consultations on new aspects of the problem to be pursued in a positive and constructive consultative atmosphere.

REFERENCES

[1] **Vijfde baan rapport** Rijksluchtvaartdienst Den Haag 1975.

[2] a. **Second National Airport Site selection,** Government publishing office (Staatsuitgeverij) Den Haag 1974.
b. **Cost Benefit Analysis, Second National Airport** (Staatsuitgeverij) 1974.

[3] **Ontwikkelingsmogelijkheden van de regionale luchtvaartterreinen tot 1985,** Nederlands Vervoerswetenschappelijk Instituut, Rijswijk, Holland.

[4] **Summary of the Study on the holiday decision making process of Dutch people,** Nederlands Vervoerswetenschappelijk Instituut, Rijswijk, Holland, december 1976.

[5] **Het effect van luchthavenbelastingen** (The effect of airportcharges), Nederlands Vervoerswetenschappelijk Instituut, Rijswijk, Holland, september 1976.

Development of regional airfields and Schiphol

	Schiphol	Rotterdam	Maastricht	Twente	Groningen	Eindhoven	
1973 (actual)	92	7	0,9	0,2	0,1	–	100
1980 (forecast)	75	13	1,9	3,4	2,2	5,8	100
1985 (forecast)	76	11	2,4	3,5	2,7	5,5	100

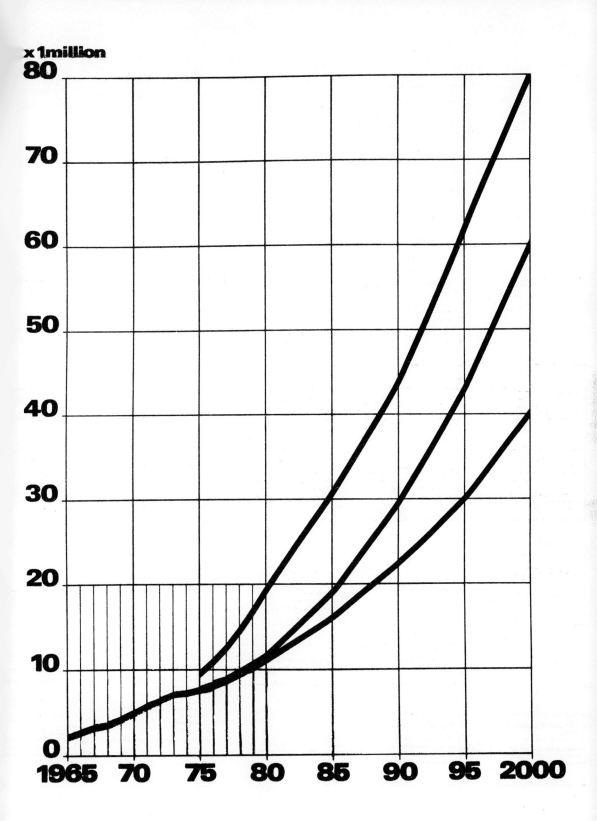

x 1million

FORECAST OF PASSENGER MOVEMENTS
(excluding direct transit)

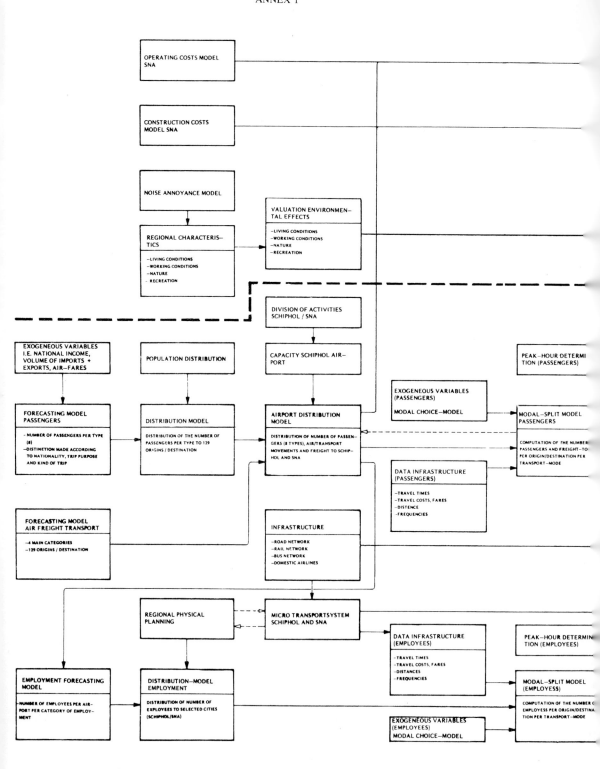

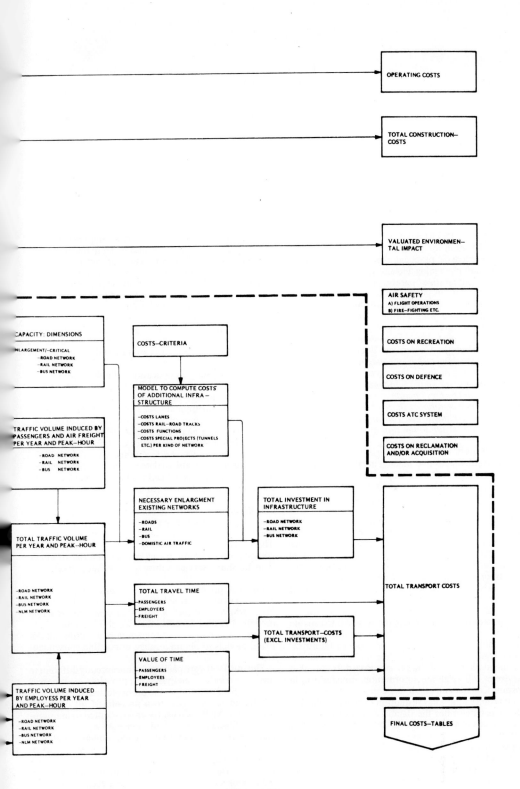

OPERATING COSTS

TOTAL CONSTRUCTION—COSTS

VALUATED ENVIRONMEN—TAL IMPACT

AIR SAFETY
A) FLIGHT OPERATIONS
B) FIRE—FIGHTING ETC.

COSTS ON RECREATION

COSTS ON DEFENCE

COSTS ATC SYSTEM

COSTS ON RECLAMATION AND/OR ACQUISITION

CAPACITY: DIMENSIONS

ENLARGEMENT/—CRITICAL
—ROAD NETWORK
—RAIL NETWORK
—BUS NETWORK

COSTS—CRITERIA

MODEL TO COMPUTE COSTS OF ADDITIONAL INFRA—STRUCTURE

—COSTS LANES
—COSTS RAIL—ROAD TRACKS
—COSTS FUNCTIONS
—COSTS SPECIAL PROJECTS (TUNNELS ETC.) PER KIND OF NETWORK

TRAFFIC VOLUME INDUCED BY PASSENGERS AND AIR FREIGHT PER YEAR AND PEAK—HOUR
—ROAD NETWORK
—RAIL NETWORK
—BUS NETWORK

NECESSARY ENLARGMENT EXISTING NETWORKS
—ROADS
—RAIL
—BUS
—DOMISTIC AIR TRAFFIC

TOTAL INVESTMENT IN INFRASTRUCTURE
—ROAD NETWORK
—RAIL NETWORK
—BUS NETWORK

TOTAL TRAFFIC VOLUME PER YEAR AND PEAK—HOUR
—ROAD NETWORK
—RAIL NETWORK
—BUS NETWORK
—NLM NETWORK

TOTAL TRAVEL TIME
—PASSENGERS
—EMPLOYEES
—FREIGHT

TOTAL TRANSPORT—COSTS (EXCL. INVESTMENTS)

TOTAL TRANSPORT COSTS

VALUE OF TIME
—PASSENGERS
—EMPLOYEES
—FREIGHT

TRAFFIC VOLUME INDUCED BY EMPLOYESS PER YEAR AND PEAK—HOUR
—ROAD NETWORK
—RAIL NETWORK
—BUS NETWORK
—NLM NETWORK

FINAL COSTS—TABLES

— — — — — — traffic model.

615

CANPASS:
A Strategic Planning Capability for Intercity Passenger Transportation

by

JOHN C. REA, M. J. WILLS and J. B. PLATTS
Strategic Planning Group, Transport Canada

INTRODUCTION

The specification for the CANPASS System derives from extensive practical experience in multimodal transportation planning and analysis. The system was designed as an integrative operational tool to support the activities of the various policy and administrative groups within Transport Canada. In any large highly structured organization dealing with a wide range of problems, coordination can present a problem. The need for a capability such as the CANPASS System was foreseen in a report issued by the Conference Board in 1972: [1]
,, The policy-making task is of a magnitude and variety that precludes the possibility that decisionmaking can be centralized in any one spot... Independent actions may result in chaos unless they operate within some intellectual framework, some commonly shared body of knowledge, prediction and argument that can impart a measure of coherence and direction to the sum of independent decisions." [2]

Since transportation is increasingly being evalutated in holistic terms, effective management requires both information and the means of applying that information to specific types of problems in a rapid effective manner. To quote again from the Conference Board Report: [3]
"...there are relatively few integrated basic research projects involving systems formulation, software, hardware and mathematical models. But, these total applications of information technology are necessary for effective management of today's large scale economic and social problems such as health care, environmental control, public transportation, land use and resource allocation."

The CANPASS System is an integrated system of database, software and mathematical models oriented to multimodal intercity passenger transportation (hence the designation). The purpose of the system is to provide a common source of data and analysis capabilities for use by the policy/evaluation groups and model administrations in Transport Canada. It is hoped, in line with the recommendations in the Conference Board Report, that the system will facilitate information transfer within Transport Canada and result in a common definition of problems and in the joint resolution of these problems.

The paper describes the database, software and demand model elements of the CANPASS System. The description of each component is necessarily brief, but it is hoped to convey an outline of the capability of the system and its relevance to multimodal planning by a central government agency. The next section provides an overview of the CANPASS System.

AN OVERVIEW

To give an initial overview of the system, the various major elements and their interrelationships are shown in Figure 1. The database describes in detail the infrastructure and supply of intercity passenger transport services between 700 communities across Canada. Modal fares and modal origin-destination demand are also included. The software consists of three linked packages each designed to address a particular type of problem.

The CANPASS-3 software is designed to provide reports from the detailed database, to provide extensive analyses of itineraries through the modal systems and give detailed reports on accessibility and interaction potential.

For comparing the implications of policy options, one does not need the detail available at the CANPASS-3 level. It would be very onerous, time consuming and expensive to manipulate real-time schedules and detailed fare data when examining a wide range of options. To simplify such analyses, the CANPASS-2 software is designed to analyse modal systems described in terms of frequency of service and fare functions.

To utilize the wealth of data available in the database, a module entitled NETAGG has been designed to transform and aggregate data from the CANPASS-3 to the CANPASS-2 level. In a few hours, one can establish the "background" activity system and modal supply definitions upon which one can easily impose specific policy options, be they demographic, system or fare changes. The CANPASS-2 software is then used to explore the consequences of these policy options in terms of modal demand shifts, service patronage, revenues, accessibility, etc.

For such policy analyses, one needs demand models. This capability is provided by a module entitled DEMEX which is, in fact, a library of calibrated demand models. The user specifies the model most appropriate for his purpose or he can sequentially use different demand models to obtain a range of possible consequences.

The third software package is conceptually different to the previous analysis approaches. Whereas CANPASS-2 determines the probable demand response to offered services (i.e. to a predefined set of modal services), CANPASS-1 software is oriented to multimodal equilibrium analyses of transport supply and demand. Here, the calibrated demand models are used to represent the demand functions and explit schedules of transport supply for equivalent levels of demand are specified. The software defines the modal network configurations and levels of service when each modes' supply and demand are in equilibrium as a result of intermodal competition.

The CANPASS System thus provides both data and

COMMUNITIES AND SOCIO-ECONOMIC DATA

	AIR	BUS	RAIL	HIGHWAY
facilities	,,	,,	,,	Highway
access links	,,	,,	,,	Link
carriers	,,	,,	,,	Attributes
services	,,	,,		
schedules	,,	,,	,,	,,
O-D flows	,,	,,	,,	
fares	,,	,,	,,	

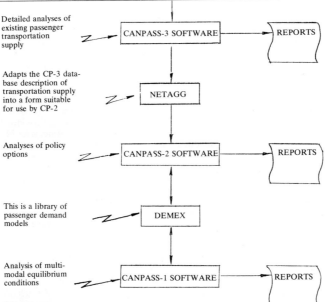

Detailed analyses of existing passenger transportation supply → CANPASS-3 SOFTWARE → REPORTS

Adapts the CP-3 database description of transportation supply into a form suitable for use by CP-2 → NETAGG

Analyses of policy options → CANPASS-2 SOFTWARE → REPORTS

This is a library of passenger demand models → DEMEX

Analysis of multimodal equilibrium conditions → CANPASS-1 SOFTWARE → REPORTS

Figure 1 - The CANPASS system

the means to apply the data to a wide range of problems. As such, the system has the potential to serve a basic integrative role in policy planning and administration, and constitutes the basis of an effective decision support system.

THE CANPASS DATABASE

The database is designed to serve four functions:

1. to support national and regional multimodal passenger transportation studies of existing modal systems and the consequences of policy options;

2. to serve a data retrieval function;

3. to serve as an historical record, i.e. an archival function. This presupposes that the database is maintained on an annual basis;

4. to provide a framework for integrating data collected in other areas of Transport Canada.

In establishing a transportation database, the first problem is to define the extent of the activity system. Since the basic objective of passenger transportation is to provide for interaction between people, it was decided to orient the database to intercommunity service. This implies that a basic set of communities must be defined as a framework for the database. To do this, a National Urban Classification [4] was undertaken in conjunction with the Department of Regional Economic Expansion. This study selected 701 communities across Canada and ranked them in a seven tier hierarchy or class system corresponding to their importance within their regional context. The communities encompass 77.6% of the Canadian population.

The CANPASS database addresses the intercity air, bus, rail, ferry and highway modes and consists of ten principal files. A very straightforward approach was adopted to facilitate the incorporation of additional data and to make the database as flexible as possible. An outline of each of these files is given below:

1. Community File:
defines the name, class, geocode and a unique structured number for each of the 701 communities. Socio-economic data required by the demand models is also provided (e.g. population, linguistic characteristics, etc.) both for historic censal years and future "scenarios". Additional communities may be included as required.

2. Enumeration Area File:
each community is defined in terms of its constituent enumeration areas with their geocodes. This allows access to the Census of Canada data files to obtain more detailed socio-economic community data as required.

3. Facility File:
defines the name, quality, geocode and a unique structured number for all air, bus, rail and ferry access/egress points (i.e. airports, railway stations etc.) serving the above communities. Attributes of the facilities are also provided, such as minimum inter-portal transfer times, entry time, etc.

4. Access Link File:
provides the distance, time and cost from the commu-

nity population centroid to each modal facility plus inter-facility data where a community has more than one facility.

5. Carrier File:
gives the name and designation of all modal operators offering passenger service between any of the communities. Additional carrier data (e.g. employment, revenues, etc.) may be added.

6. Scheduled Service File:
defines the route structure of all modal services and the arrival and departure times at all facilities on the route: a unique identifying number is assigned to each service.

7. Service File:
provides for each of the above scheduled services such data as days of operation, equipment used, amenities provided. Additional service data such as energy usage, revenue and operating cost data may be added.

8. Fare File:
details the "basic" fare between each pair of facilities for each mode of transport.

9. Highway Link File:
defines characteristics (e.g. number of lanes, speed limit, traffic volumes) of each link of the highway network connecting the 701 communities. Additional data pertaining to physical characteristics and traffic flows may be added.

10. Origin-Destination Demand:
provides modal origin to destination demand for each community pair.

A more complete description of the database files is given in Appendix A.

CANPASS SOFTWARE
The software which consists of some 52 major programming elements has been designed from a user point of view and makes extensive use of the Wylbur preprocessor system to simplify use of the system. The user is guided by a sequence of questions as to his requirements and can call for "help" at any stage of the process. When the user requirements are specified, the Wylbur system assembles the necessary software and data elements and submits the "job" for batch processing. The system can thus be considered interactive to a certain degree, but the use of "foreground" interactive capability such as TSO was not considered necessary for this type of application. Use is made of variety of languages (e.g. Cobol, Fortran, PLI) as judged appropriate for the task at hand.

Although the system is designed primarily to produce formal reports, the need to provide for other analyses has been recognised. The flow of processed data within the system can be tapped and reformatted for use with the Statistical Package for the Social Sciences (SPSS). Additional software capabilities have been developed to supplement the CANPASS system. These include DEMON, a statistical capability for calibrating demand models and a model for estimating O-D from link flow data. [5] These elements are however not described here.

CANPASS-3 SOFTWARE
The CANPASS-3 package is designed to act on and analyse the air, bus, rail and ferry data at the detailed level given in the CANPASS database. A parallel software package carries out similar functions for the highway mode.

The package provides capabilities in four areas as follows:

1. Manipulation of the database
a. Subfile: this module allows the user to establish a subset of the master national database oriented to a particular study area, i.e. a problem area database.

b. Update: this capability allows the user to change an element in his problem area database, e.g. change services, route structure, schedules, insert or delete facilities, etc. The user can thus fine tune existing systems to improve coordination, integration, level of service, accessibility, etc.

2. Reports from the database
a. The user can request reports from any of the files in the database, impose "screens" to eliminate unwanted data, and asked for data associations (e.g. detail modal services at all facilities accessible by residents of a town).

3. Intercity Itineraries
a. Detailed Itineraries: provides times, distance, fare and speed data for all itineraries between specified city pairs on a specified day. The user can impose constraints such as "within X% or Y hours of fastest time".

b. Summary Itineraries: details only the maximum, minimum and average itinerary attributes from the above.

c. Return Trip Analysis: details the possibility of a day (or "n" day) return trip starting out and arriving back in user-specified periods of the day for specified city pairs.

4. Accessibility Analyses
a. Accessibility detail report: shows "best" times, distance, speed, time and fare from a specified community to all other communities arranged in order of class.

b. Summary Accessibility report: provides distributions of time, cost, etc. in user-specifiable intervals from subject community to classes of community, and population.

The above capability directly addresses problems of modal performance, efficiency, coordination, integration, level of service, accessibility, equity, adequacy and, of course, the control, direction, subsidy and evaluation functions of a central government agency. It provides the information and analyses to facilitate communication, problem definition and problem resolution within the central agency and between the central government and the provincial, regional or local governments.

CANPASS-2 SOFTWARE
The CANPASS-2 software is oriented towards policy exploration – the "what if" type of analysis. As discussed earlier, a more "abstract" level of system representation is appropriate for comparative analysis of policy options. The conceptual organisation of a CANPASS-2 application is shown in Figure 2.

The existing modal supply situation is first defined using data already available in the database. A module entitled NETAGG is used to establish this "background" definition. The module enables the user to define a suitable "activity system" from the 701 communities by selecting and aggregating communities as required. The existing modal systems serving the new "activity system" are extracted and redefined in terms of frequency of service by NETAGG. In a few hours the analyst can thus "set up" to do any type of policy analysis.

Phase A of CANPASS-2 analyses each modal system sequentially to establish modal supply attribute files (i.e.

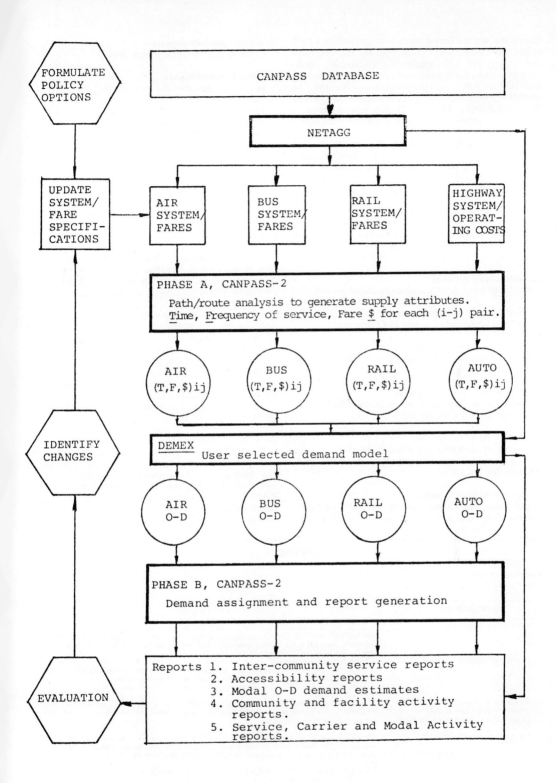

Figure 2 - Flow Chart for CANPASS-2 application

619

travel time, service frequency, travel cost between each origin and destination). These provide the necessary inputs (together with appropriate community socio-economic data) for a calibrated demand model to estimate both total and modal passenger travel demand. The modal O-D estimates are now available for use by Phase B of CANPASS-2. Modal O-D demand is assigned to routes and services and an array of reports are generated.

The analyst can now evaluate the reports, identify possible changes to the modal systems or fare structures and impose these on the previous system/fare descriptions using the update capability.

The reports generated by CANPASS-2 include:

1. Inter-community service reports:
the time, distance, fare, speed etc. by six types of route (e.g. one segment, multi segment/non stop, "n" stop, etc.). The user can specify which level of detail he requires and can obtain any one of five reports.

2. Accessibility reports:
similar to the CANPASS-3 accessibility reports.

3. Modal Origin-Destination reports:
matrices of estimated modal O-D demand.

4. Excessive Transfer reports:
identifies instances where direct service would be possible.

5. Community Activity reports:
originating and destined modal demand by community in terms of the facility utilised.

6. Facility Activity reports:
originating, destined and through demand, services, capacity provided and transferring passengers and average transfer times.

7. Service Activity reports:
utilisation, load factors, capacity, revenues, costs profit/loss, energy consumption etc. for each modal service.

8. Carrier Activity reports:
as above aggregated for each carrier.

9. Modal System report:
as above aggregated for each mode.

This extensive range of reports provides most of the data required to evaluate alternative policy options in comparative terms. Detailed submodels to deal with such items as noise incidence at airports etc. could, of course, be added but it is essential to preserve a balance between level of detail and the confidence one can assign to such detail in this type of modelling. Certainly the CANPASS-2 software provides the type of analysis capability required by central agencies to comparatively evaluate various policy options. Once one or two are selected, these can be examined in detail – perhaps at the CANPASS-3 level.

PASSENGER DEMAND MODELS

A library of fully specified and calibrated aggregate demand models is provided by the DEMEX module of the CANPASS System. More than one model is included for two reasons:

a. different models with different functional forms produce different elasticities and consequently a range of simulation results;

b. one general model specification cannot adequately address all problems. For example, an international model which focuses on air travel would naturally exhibit different definitions and parameters than a regional model intended to analyse all modes symmetrically.

Further details on the nature of the demand models is given in Appendix B.

CANPASS-1 SOFTWARE

The CANPASS-2 and 3 software are traditional in concept. The modal systems, either existing or proposed, are predefined and the question is to determine the modal demand response to the offered services. The CANPASS-1 software which is based on the Service Specification Model [6] is quite different in concept in that it is oriented to equilibrium analyses. Inputs to

APPENDIX A

Community file

Table A1

ELEMENT	COMMENT
1. SEQUENCE NUMBER	Each of the 700 communities in the database has its own unique four digit identifying number. The first digit identifies provincial location. In general, the number sequence runs from east to west. Gaps have been left in the number sequence to facilitate the addition of other communities at a later date.
2. CLASS OF COMMUNITY	All communities are classified within a seven tier hierarchical National Community Classification Scheme. This is a functional classification scheme based on the population and facilities available in the community; ranking ranges from "1" for the largest metropolitan centres to "7" for communities of about 1000 population. Class ranking is a surrogate for "inter-action" potential and need for passenger services.
3. NAME OF COMMUNITY (20X)	The name by which the community is listed in the Official List for the 1971 Census of Canada.
4. COMMUNITY TIME BAND DIFFERENCE FROM GREENWICH MEAN TIME	Passenger service arrival and departure times are "local" times. This data element allows the elapsed travel times to be computed.
5. LATITUDE OF COMMUNITY	These data refer to the population "centroid" of the community, i.e. the "centre of gravity" of the population. The data permit the calculation of intercommunity "airline" distances, and "airline"
6. LONGITUDE OF COMMUNITY	distance from the population centroid to modal facilities (e.g. airport), as well as allowing computer graphic mapping.
7. POPULATION	The total population of the community is the sum of the populations of the enumeration areas which define the community (see Enumeration Area File). The data were obtained from the 1971 Census of Canada. Preliminary counts from the 1976 Census were also included.
8. PERCENTAGE ENGLISH SPEAKING	The percentage of the population whose mother tongue is English: obtained from 1971 census data.

Note:
This file may be expanded to include (a) data from the 1961 and 1966 Census of Canada, and (b) additional socio-economic data contained on census tapes – tertiary employment, disposable income, and so on.

CANPASS-1 include explicit modal supply functions and modal demand functions. The calibrated demand models serve as the latter. The supply functions take the form of a schedule of service quality (i.e. technology, frequency and performance) which the modal operator would be willing to offer for corresponding ranges in demand.

The potential spatial extent of each modal network is also predefined using a link node format. The function of CANPASS-1 is to determine the service quality of each link in the modal networks (technology, frequency and performance) when modal supply and demand are in equilibrium. The procedure is an iterative one in which the modes compete for a share of the market during each iteration. The final modal network configurations indicate the equilibrium status of each mode given their respective supply functions.

The CANPASS-1 software is operational for multimodal equilibrium analyses using the 1972 pseudo abstract mode model as the "arbitrator" in the intermodal competition. However, the software is still considered experimental at present and considerable scope for refinements and coding efficiencies remain. This type of equilibrium analysis has obvious importance for exploring such concepts as "user pay", commercial viability, subsidy policy, equity and adequacy.

CONCLUSIONS

The synthesis of database, analytical software and passenger demand models makes the CANPASS System an extremely powerful tool. Certainly it is able to support the functions of strategic planning. However, it also constitutes a tool for "imparting a measure of coherence and direction" within the disparate functional groups in a central government agency such as Transport Canada. The database offers the opportunity for rapid accurate information transfer, for a "pooling" of information and for a common definition of problems. The analytical software offers a capability which supercedes empirical "back of an envelope" approaches to policy development and evaluation. Although the system has been operational only for a short time, it has already been well received by professional staff in other areas of Transport Canada and indeed has been used for a variety of purposes. It will be interesting to see if the integrative possibilities of the CANPASS System can be realised and if its role as a management decision system can be put into effect.

Enumeration area file

Table A2

ELEMENT	COMMENT
	Note:
	1. This file defines a community in terms of its constituent enumeration areas.
	2. The file is not an active file in the CANPASS-3 database, but it is used to compute the value of data elements in the community file.
1. COMMUNITY SEQUENCE NUMBER	The community's unique identification number.
2. ENUMERATION AREA CODE	Each enumeration area has a unique identification number given in the 1971 Census Official List.
3. LATITUDE OF ENUMERATION AREA	The latitude and longitude of the population centroid as given in the 1971 Census Official List. These data allow one to determine the location of the community population centroid.
4. LONGITUDE OF ENUMERATION AREA	
	The data in items 2, 3 and 4 is given for each enumeration area comprising the community.
5. POPULATION OF ENUMERATION AREA	Obtained from 1971 census tapes.
6. PERCENTAGE ENGLISH SPEAKING	Obtained from 1971 census tapes.
7. POTENTIAL FOR EXPANSION	Similar data items to those described in the Community File, provided that the data exist on census tapes.

Facility file

Table A3

ELEMENT	COMMENT
	Note:
	1. A facility means an airport, a bus or ferry terminal, or a railway station.
	2. Only important ferries are included.
1. MODE	Air, bus, rail or ferry.
2. FACILITY SEQUENCE NUMBER	Each facility has its own unique identification number.
3. QUALITY	This is an index number from 1 thru 8 based on ranking within a subjective scale based on the size of the facility. Size was used as a surrogate for quality and number of amenities available at a facility. The element is included as a first attempt to include "quality" in transport system appraisal. Obviously, further research is needed to define a more sophisticated index.
4. NAME	The name by which the facility is usually known.
5. FACILITY TIME BAND DIFFERENT FROM GREENWICH MEAN TIME	Passenger service arrival and departure times are "local" times. This data allows the elapsed travel times to be computed.
6. LATITUDE OF FACILITY	These data allow "airline" distance to the community, and inter-facility "airline" distances to be computed as well as permitting computer graphic mapping.
7. LONGITUDE OF FACILITY	
8. ENTRY TIME INTO THE FACILITY	Entry time refers to the period from arrival at the facility (e.g. the car park) to actually boarding the service (i.e. boarding an aircraft).
9. EXIT TIME FROM FACILITY	Exit time refers to the period from deboarding a service to actually departing from the facility.
10. CONNECT TIME AT THE FACILITY	Connect time refers to the minimum time required to transfer from an inbound service to an outbound service at the facility.

Access link file

Table A4

ELEMENT	COMMENT
	Note:
	1. An access link may be from a community (centroid) to a modal facility or from one facility to another facility.
	2. It is assumed that the access link attributes are the same in each direction.
	3. The user has the opportunity to insert specific distance, time and fare values, if so required.
1. ORIGIN	The identification number of:
	a. the community in the case of a "community to facility" access link; In general, each community is linked to at least one facility for each mode (provided that there is road access)
	b. the facility in the case of a "facility to facility" access link.
	In general, facilities are connected only if they are located within the same community.
2. DESTINATION	The identification number of the facility.
3. LINK LENGTH	The "air line" length of the access link which is *computed endogenously* by CANPASS-3 software using the latitude and longitude of the origin and destination.
4. LINK TRAVEL TIME	The automobile travel time to traverse the above link length is computed endogenously by CANPASS-3 software using a travel time formula.
5. LINK TRAVEL FARE	In the same manner as above, automobile travel fare is computed endogenously on the basis of link distance using a cost formula.

Carrier file

Table A5

ELEMENT	COMMENT
	Note:
	This file lists the carriers providing scheduled service between any of the 700 communities.
1. MODE	Air, bus, rail of ferry.
2. CARRIER IDENTIFICATION CODE	A unique two letter identification code for each carrier.
3. CARRIER NAME	The name of the carrier, abbreviated to 20 letters.
4. POTENTIAL FOR EXPANSION	This file could be extended to include such company information as type of ownership, revenue class, and so on.

Scheduled service file

Table A6

ELEMENT	COMMENT
	Notes:
	1. This file describes the actual schedule and route structure of every service offered between any of the 700 communities. It consists of a sequence of facilities with associated mileages, arrival and departure times.
	2. A service will normally consist of a single mainline. In exceptional cases, a service may have a branch, i.e. a 4-RDC train may split into two 2-RDC trains. In such cases, the branching service is assigned a unique branch number. Branch characteristics are described following the description of the mainline service to which they are attached.
1. MODE	Air, bus, rail or ferry.
2. CARRIER	The identification code of the carrier offering the service.
3. SERVICE NUMBER	The identification number of the service or branch to which the subsequent data pertain. Each scheduled service has its own unique number.
5. FACILITY	The identification number of the facility at which service is provided. These are listed in order of distance from the origin point.
6. MILEAGE	The cumulative mileage from the service origin point to the above facility.
7. ARRIVAL TIME	The "local" arrival time at the facility.
8. DEPARTURE TIME	The "local" departure time at the facility.
	The five data elements above are repeated for each facility on the service or branch.

622

Carrier service file

ELEMENT	COMMENT
	Note: *This file provides descriptive data about each of the services provided by the carriers other than the actual operating schedule.*
1. MODE	Air, bus, rail or ferry.
2. SERVICE NUMBER BRANCH NUMBER	A number which uniquely identifies every scheduled service in the database.
3. CHANGE POINT	This identifies the location in a mainline service or branch service at which some change in the characteristic of the service occurs (e.g. change in equipment).
4. DAYS OF OPERATION	The days on which the service operates are identified by a sequence of seven binary digits representing Monday thru' Sunday. A "1" indicates that service operates on that day while a "0" indicates the absence of service on that day.
5. EQUIPMENT TYPE	This is a two digit code which is keyed to a table of equipment characteristics (e.g. "08" represents a DC-9 aircraft).
6. SEATING CAPACITY	The number of seats provided on each log of an itinerary.
7. POTENTIAL FOR EXPANSION	This file may be extended to record historic service-related data, e.g. operating cost, subsidy, revenue, passengers carried, energy consumed.
	The file could also conveniently record historical data, if required.

Highway link file

ELEMENT	COMMENT
	Note: *This file describes the highway system connecting the 700 communities in the database in terms of nodes and links. A link is identified by the nodes at the beginning and end of the link. The characteristics and attributes of each link are then recorded.*
1. "A" NODE	The number of the node at one end of the link (A-B).
2. "B" NODE	The number of the node at the other end of the link (A-B).
3. LINK LENGTH	The distance from node A to node B along the highway link.
4. NUMBER OF LANES	The *total* number of vehicle lanes provided.
5. AVERAGE OPERATING SPEED	The average operating speed limit on each link of highway network. Travel times can be calculated from this information.
6. AADT	The Average Annual Daily Traffic along each link.
7. SADT	Summer Average Daily Traffic.
8. WADT	Winter Average Daily Traffic.
9. POTENTIAL FOR EXPANSION OR TRAFFIC FLOWS	This file may be extended to include other physical inventory data elements, if required, such as shoulder widths, speed limits and weight restrictions.

APPENDIX B

Mathematically, the models are quasi-direct in form. They are essentially direct in that the demand for travel by mode is related to attributes of the transport system and the socio-economic environment by a single equation. However, the models exhibit a separability between the demand for travel, independent of mode, and the choice of mode. This separability is imposed and exploited in the estimation of parameters which is partitioned into two stages, the second of which is linked to the first by substitution of a calibrated modal impedance term.

The majority of the models are of the following structure:

$$T_{mht} = T_{ht} (A_{ht}, C_{mht}) \cdot S_{mht} (C_{mht})$$

where T_{mht} = the demand for travel by mode m on city pair h at time t

$$T_{ht} = \sum_m T_{mht} \tag{1}$$

S_{mht} = the share of travel using mode m
A_{ht} = a vector of socio-economic activity variables
C_{mht} = a vector of modal attributes

The separability of (1) gives rise to the following additive property of the modal attribute elasticities:

$$\frac{\partial T_m}{\partial C_{mk}} \left(\frac{C_{mk}}{T_m} \right) = \frac{\partial T}{\partial C_{mk}} \left(\frac{C_{mk}}{T} \right) + \frac{\partial S_m}{\partial C_{mk}} \left(\frac{C_{mk}}{S_m} \right) \tag{2}$$

Thus, for example, the fare own elasticity of demand by mode is composed of the sum of two effects: the elasticity of total intercity demand, and the elasticity of market share, of mode m with respect to its own fare.

Whereas the models may be estimated using either cross-sectional or time-series data or both, the work to date has employed only cross-sectional data from some 230 city pairs in Canada for 1972 and 1976. In terms of the modal share component, one form of the model [7] is specified by:

$$S_{mh} = U_{mh} \left[\sum_m U_{mh} \right]^{-1}$$

$$\text{where} \quad U_{mh} = \exp \left(\alpha_{om} + \alpha_1 C_{mh}^{(\lambda_1)} + \alpha_2 H_{mh}^{(\lambda_1)} + \alpha_3 D_{mh}^{(\lambda_3)} \right) \tag{3}$$

$$C_{mh}^{(\lambda_1)} = \frac{C_{mh}^{\lambda_1} - 1}{\lambda_1} \quad \text{is a Box and Cox transformation}$$

C_{mh} = travel cost or fare by mode m on city pair h
H_{mh} = travel time in hours
D_{mh} = departure frequency per week

The quasi-abstract model with generalised functional form possesses own-attribute modal share elasticities of

$$\frac{\partial s_m}{\partial c_{mk}} \left(\frac{c_{mk}}{s_m}\right) = \alpha_k \, c_{mk}^{\lambda_k} \, (1 - s_m) \tag{4}$$

which may be computed either on a city-pair specific, or city-pair class specific, basis or at the sample mean of the observations on the original variables.

Aggregate demand for travel is similarly specified as

$$T_h^{(\lambda_0)} = \beta_0 + \beta_1 \, P_h^{(\lambda_1)} + \beta_2 \, L_h^{(\lambda_2)} + \beta_3 \, Y_h^{(\lambda_3)} + \gamma u_h^{(\lambda_4)} \tag{5}$$

where P_h = population product for city pair h
$L_h = 1 - |L_i - L_j|$ a linguistic pairing index for the bilingual case
L_i = proportion speaking English in city i
Y_h = average per capita disposable income

$u_h = \sum_m u_{mh}$ an impedance index

The elasticity of (5) with respect to a modal attribute is therefore

$$\frac{\partial T}{\partial c_{mk}} \left(\frac{c_{mk}}{T}\right) = \alpha_k \, c_{mk}^{\lambda_k} \, T^{-\lambda_0} \, \gamma \, u^{\lambda_4} \, s_m \tag{6}$$

Both (4) and (6) reduce to conventional cases for $\lambda = 0$ and the generalised unimodal gravity model if, in addition, $S_m = 1$. Detailed empirical analyses of the effect of the specification of functional form on elasticities are available elsewhere. [8]

REFERENCES

[1] **"Information Technology: Initiatives for Today – Decisions that Cannot Wait".** Part 2 of a study on "Information Technology, Some Critical Implications for Decision Makers 1971-1990" by the Senior Executives Council of the Conference Board. Report 577, 1972.

[2] Quote by Max Way in Fortune Magazine taken from the Conference Board Report 577, p. 6.

[3] Conference Board Report 577, p. 20.

[4] **A Classification of Canadian Communities According to Their Importance as Generators of Intercity Passenger Travel.**

DREE/ADMSP, October 1976.

[5] Wills, M.J. – **Linear and NON-Linear Estimates of the O-D Matrix.** Ph.D. dissertation, University of British Columbia, forthcoming.

[6] J.C. Rea, **Designing Urban Transit Systems: An Approach to the Route-Technology Selection Problem.** Highway Research Record No. 417, 1972.

[7] M.J. Wills, Op.cit.

[8] Gaudry, M. and M.J. Wills. **Estimating the functional form in the demand for travel,** publication 63, Centre de Recherche sur les Transports, Université de Montréal, forthcoming.

Transport policy models and transport policy development a major challenge or a search for a "Philosopher's stone"?

K.W. STUDNICKI-GIZBERT
Canadian Transport Commission, Canada

As I was going up the stair
I met a man who wasn't there
He wasn't there again today
I wish, I wish, he'd stay away

HUGHES MEARNS

INTRODUCTION

The last two decades have witnessed numerous attempts to develop formal comprehensive models in the field of transport policy.[1] "Comprehensive Models" are defined here as models aimed at the analysis of large (national, regional, metropolitan areas) transport systems which treat explicitly interactions between transport and socio-economic environment; they can be contrasted with "specific models", i.e. models dealing with the analysis and evaluation of individual projects or programs or the revision of a specific set of policy measures. Comprehensive policy models are essentially normative; their aim is to generate policy alternatives. Another common characteristic of this work is that the interrelationships taken into account are formalized as a relatively closed system of equations; the number of exogeneous inputs is kept to the minimum through the extension of the model to internalize most of the key variables; the assumed relationships are considered to be quantifiable and the models conceived as an exercise in quantitative economic policy modelling. The normative characteristics of the models and the stress on quantification force the model builders into an explicit formulation of the objective function, or at least into the development of quantitative policy assessment rules, which, in turn, assures that the objective function is known either by the model builders or that it can be explicitly displayed by the "decisionmakers".

The impressive effort by the model-builders has raised many expectations. It is not coincidental that the policy models' development had taken place at the time when "government efficiency through systems approach", benefit-costs analysis, PPBS and similar attempts to produce quantitative aids to the decisionmaking flourished. Yet, the promises of a major improvement in policy making which were explicit in all this effort have hot materialized. Admittedly, through the process of model building much has been learned about transport systems and transport/non-transport activities' interaction, and many important issues were classified in the process. Yet, doubts about the quantitative policy models have been growing, and are being, at least implicitly acknowledged even by most devoted model builders.[2] The question then arises whether we should continue to elaborate the models, include explicitly more inter-connections, search for more data, i.e. whether constructing better models is a major challenge which is to be met by more efforts, or whether we should admit that the task set by model builders is inherently impossible, and abandon it as the early scientists abandoned the search for a philosopher's stone.

It appears proper to close this introductory section by making explicit its intended limitations. Although a rather lengthy list of references is enclosed, this essay is not meant as a "survey article" or an assessment of the state of the art.[3] It should also be noted that references to studies by consultants and staff papers released by governmental organizations have been omitted although a large part of the pioneer work first appeared in this form; this material is too voluminous to cover and, eventually the findings and descriptions of methodology employed in these efforts are reflected in academic or professional publications.

2. THE NATURE OF TRANSPORT POLICY MODELS

In the analysis of policy models it is useful to make a clear distinction between the "positive" or "descriptive" models or parts of models and the "normative" or "prescriptive". This distinction, incidentally, does not necessarily reflect the policy use of a model. A transport demand model, for example, may be developed in response to expressed needs of the "policy maker" and the outputs of such a model may be used as important inputs into decision making. However, the model as such is strictly policy neutral, even if model builders put a special stress on modelling parts of the system which they know are likely to relate to major policy decisions.

Normative models must necessarily relate to an "objective function" of the decision maker.[4] From this objective function, choice or evaluation criteria are derived. Depending on the nature of the system analysed and specific needs of the decision maker[5] a policy model may have to identify policy instruments. Many transport policy models are in fact "transport investment policy models". In this case, a particular policy instrument has been chosen (transport investment); however, the existence of other instruments and controls which affect either transport system or activities which generate transport demand should be considered explicitly.

Waters [67] makes an interesting distinction between "impact" and "evaluation" studies: "the purpose of impact studies is to estimate (and preferably quantify) effects of a certain measure on other parts of the economic and/or social system or environment; given considerable interdependence and complex linkages of the modern socio-economic system and in particular numerous inter-relationships between transport and other sectors, impact studies (conducted at a different level of sophistication) are important inputs into a decision making process.[6] Evaluation studies are intended to assess the relative merit of one project as opposed to another . . . From the information contained in an impact study, items must be selected to be considered for evaluation purposes . . . Next it is necessary to assign weights or values to the various impacts to arrive at some measure of the net economic merit of this project . . . To do this it is necessary that planning or policy objectives be quite explicit (along with the relative weights if multiple objectives are being pursued)." Project or program or policy "evaluation" – as contrasted with "impact analysis" – may still constrain the scope of the study and require very limited information of the decision maker's objective function; for example, if the decision maker selected a specific set of projects for evaluation and stated evaluation criteria.

Obviously, once the scope of the analytical effort is extended to the review and analysis of the transport system, or its major sub-system, and this analysis is to be directly interpreted with the generation of a set of transport policies, the problem of identification of the over-all objective function becomes the key part of the effort. This logically should lead to explicit structuring of goals and objectives as well as formalization and ranking of "community-values."[7]

Depending on the scope of the model, and preferences of model builders, one of the following policy objectives are assumed[8]:

a. minimization of costs of a transport system (to be understood broadly as the minimization of transport and related social and private costs);

b. achievement of non-transport objectives, which can be understood in two ways, *viz.*

(i) shifts in transport patterns believed to be socially beneficial (eg. shift towards public transport) or

(ii) through the working of a transport system affecting the distribution of population and/or economic activities in a more desirable manner;

c. a mix of transport and non-transport objectives derived from formalized social and/or distributional goals.

Logically, a transport policy model will

a. model transport flows and inter-action between transport and other sectors of the economy and derive from it projections of the future states of the system;

b. rigorously compare probable states of the system in the absence of positive intervention with the desirable states of the system (which implies knowledge of the objective function);

c. identify *feasible* policy instruments and quantify to the largest extent possible the effectiveness of their use;

d. define targets.

Thus, the effectiveness of the policy model depends on:

a. adequacy of the analysis of the working of the system;

b. availability of an operationally meaningful set of objectives;

c. identification of feasible policy instruments and quantification of their efficiency.

Major failures of policy models tend to be associated with problems related to (b) and (c). However, it is the difficulty in formulating an adequate model of the actual working of the transport system and its interactions which tends to be most stressed. Furthermore, the blame for the failure to model the working of the system is usually attributed to the "data problem".

Clearly, perfection is not achievable and the existence of failures need not preclude future successes. However, from the point of view of research strategy, it is important to consider the prospects for improvement of different areas of endeavour. It is my contention that, with the accumulated experience, the quality of positive or analytical descriptive models will continue to improve

both because of better techniques and because of cumulatively increasing understanding of how the system works. Furthermore, the improvement of the knowledge of the system is bound to improve our ability to utilize available and to generate more efficiently the potentially available information. Paradoxically as it may sound, a good or more realistic model design is less likely to fail because of the estimating difficulties[9] and less likely to be frustrated by non-availability of data.[10] This general optimism should be tempered by the realization of the inherent difficulties in this field, some of which have been accentuated by over-ambitious design and often by the neglect of a simple rule that it is easier and more fruitful to start with simpler models and to accept "open ends", asymmetries and inelegant linkages of sub-models and then progress towards greater realism, complexity and analytical elegance, than to start with over-complex structure which has to be simplified to meet arising estimating and data problems.[11]

If one can be moderately optimistic about future positive models, this guarded optimism appears not to be justified about the future of normative models; to quote the famous saying of a police recruit: "you can't get from here to there; to get there you have to start from somewhere else".

3. THE INTELLECTUAL ANTECEDENTS OF POLICY MODELS

It is an impossible task to attempt to determine the precise intellectual sources of a vast array of professional effort generated by specialists from different disciplines, together with a vast amount of cross-fertilization. It is possible, however, to identify major intellectual sources; these, I submit, are:

a. modern welfare economics;

b. the theory of quantitative economic policy, largely based on Tinbergen's work;

c. systems analysis and policy applications of operations research.

The two main themes of modern welfare economics have been:

(i) vigorous analysis of the limits of "value free," positive analysis and the legitimacy of policy recommendations which economists, as scientists, can give,[12] and

(ii) analysis of the nature and derivation of a social welfare function and its application to economic policy choices. These two themes are strongly inter-related; it is not difficult to name economists who having rigorously identified problems of derivation and application of social welfare function have also done extensive work in applied welfare economics and benefit-cost analysis. Essentially, the social welfare function is derived from individual preference functions, modified – in the case of public goods – through the working of the political system. In the growing area of public goods provision, the theory of public choice (which can legitimately be considered as an extension of welfare economics) relates individual to collective preferences. In spite of the recognition of analytical difficulties inherent in the formulation of a social welfare function, an objective function of the decision making is asserted to exist, and this objective function should correspond to the subjective valuation of the members of the society.[13]

From the very beginning of welfare economics – Pigou's *Economics of Welfare* – the problem of external or indirect effects and the divergence between private and social costs has been one of the central issues discussed; indeed the existence of externalities was according to Baumol [7] a major justification for state intervention. The identification and evaluation of externalities is, of course, the essence of benefit-cost analysis which has played an important part in planning of public investments. The step from analysis of externalities in project evaluation to a comprehensive investigation of interactions between the transport sector and the economy has been logical, and the identification of divergencies between private and social costs could be accepted as indications of government actions within the framework of criteria of economic efficiency.

Tinbergen's work on theory of economic policy can well be regarded as an operational extension of welfare analysis.[14] The introduction of the concept of policy instruments, target variables and the strong stress on quantification (at least potential quantification) provided the framework within which policy analysis, policy administration and empirical investigation could be logically integrated.[15] The greatest impact of this work was on macro-economic policy analysis, but this approach provided challenge and inspiration to sectoral planning model builders. However, in the latter applications new problems arise, some of which relate to a much greater specificity, an increased number of policy instruments, lengthening of time-lags, and the irreversibility of major decisions.

Systems analysis influence on transport policy modelling is direct. Transport policy analysis by its very nature implies investigation of a great number of interdependencies. Successful application of systems analysis, operations research and computers to the resolution of complex management problems created great expectations and ambitions to adapt management tools to transport policy problems. The background of the first practitioners of systems analysis and operations research was close enough to that of planning engineers to facilitate what appeared to be a technological transfer. Two important group characteristics of system analysts have to be stressed here:

(i) insistence on direct relevance for problem solving or decision making – thus models are conceived not as general aid to the decision maker by providing him with a set of relevant information and improved understanding of the reality which he may use for a variety of purposes but as an input for specific recommendations; the goal: "design a system which meets a given objective" is translated as "design a policy which meets a given objective";

(ii) "the logical precision of the model enforces corresponding precision of the objectives that the operation is intended to attain" (Dorfman [17]).

4. THE SEARCH FOR OBJECTIVES

The key importance of a rigorous definition of the objective function has been admitted by the policy model builders. Considerable effort has been expanded in this area and the difficulties have been recognized.

One of the major approaches to an operational identification and definition of the objective function is directly related to the theoretical work of welfare consultants. This intellectual tradition has profoundly affected benefit/ cost analysis.[16] The social welfare function considered is derived from individual preferences corrected for externalities. In its operational application, economic evaluation analysis relies heavily on market generated prices and costs, supplemented, and if necessary, substituted by a consistent set of macro-economically determined shadow prices.

An approach, which stems from a different intellectual tradition, but is not necessarily in conflict with that of the economists, is an engineering systems analysis, which is primarily geared to the identification and evaluation of system bottlenecks. Its aim is to optimize system efficiency; the evaluation criteria tend to be user benefits and costs of improvements – in this way one can view this approach as an operational and restricted version of benefit-cost analysis.

The difficulties associated with the determining of an operation version of a social welfare function from welfare analysis, led to a search for an identifiable policy-maker's objective function. Basic to this approach was viewing an analyst as a technical advisor to the decision maker whose role is "to select the optimum course of action from a number of complex action alternatives available to a certain decision maker by weighing the degrees of realization of the decisionmaker's multiple objectives that can be achieved with alternative strategies ..." [56] p. 157. Identification of the policy maker's objective function is by no means a trivial problem. Where policy instruments are reasonably well identified and their efficacy reasonably well appreciated, the problem can, to some extent, be reduced to the one of the "subsidiary decisionmaking", i.e. target choice. Assuming a consistency in the policy-making process, through the selection of specific targets, the objective function can be revealed. Or, to put it in common sense expression – through the participation in a continuous decision-making process, the analyst acquires an implicit, but adequate, appreciation of the policy maker's objectives, and both the analyst and the decision maker acquire increasing knowledge of the efficacy of policy instruments and the type of information inputs required. It may be useful to make such a process explicit, and formalize it into quantitative policy model.

The problem becomes inherently more difficult if either "the policy maker" is difficult to identify – i.e. the policy process involves a number of actors, with some common values and goals, but also with conflicting goals; or if the decision making process is discontinuous. This is particularly difficult in the case of urban transport planning where the preparation of "comprehensive plans" is infrequent, where planning work is performed by outsiders, and where direct expression of views by affected groups is less institutionalized than in the case of more senior governments. The analyst is therefore often forced into a consideration of "community values" or community objective functions.

Attempts to determine community objective functions and to produce an operational assessment tool led to the evolvement of the "planning balance-sheet"[17] and "Goal Achievement Matrix"[18] approaches. There has also been extensive discussion of analytically different but conceptually related approaches, based on weighing the desirability of possible outcomes, but also introducing probability evaluations.[19] Somewhere in the middle, between a pragmatic or "revealed preference of the decisionmaker's" approach and attempts to construct a rigorous and quantified (or at least ordinal) explicit objective function, one may classify Manheim's "search and choice" work [43] [44] [45]. Some initial knowledge of the objective function is assumed, and used in the generation of a preliminary plan; the results of such a plan are subsequently displayed and discussed. This may lead to a re-definition of objectives and introduction of new objectives of constraints, i.e. to a reformulation of the objective function, (or "fuller revealing of the community or decisionmaker's preferences"). [20]

5. ANALYTICAL WORK AND THE DECISION-MAKING PROCESS

Since the developers of comprehensive transport policy models consider their work as a contribution to improved decisionmaking, it is appropriate that this effort be judged according to the criteria of usefulness in a "real life" context. The obvious limitations of specific, narrowly defined project appraisal efforts were early recognized. Firstly, transport itself can properly be considered as a system of inter-connecting and interdependent elements. Secondly, obvious and important inter-relationships exist between transport and other sectors, especially between transport and spatial policies (whether viewed as transport and land use or transport and regional planning). In the context of development policies, these realizations led to serious large scale modelling efforts, conceived either as network models with transport developmental impacts explicitly recognized (eg. [16]) or as large scale macro-economic/transport models.[21] On the other side of the spectrum, urban road models started initially as network models with user benefits as the evaluation criteria and later developed – at least in theory – into more comprehensive urban transport/land use models.[22] Comprehensive transport planning also became generally accepted in regional and nation-wide system planning in developed countries.[23]

Extensive effort, profusely financed, must have borne some relation to the need. It is interesting to observe that this need, in many cases, has not been precisely stated. True enough, in the case of developing countries, a system of general and sectoral planning mechanisms establishing overall priorities and relating to available resources was necessary to meet the requirements not only of the countries concerned but of international and national lending and aid agencies. To some extent, a parallel can be drawn between the role of lending and aid agencies and senior governments' financial contributions to urban administrations. Major review of problems, priorities and programs has given rise to other large scale modelling exercises.

In general, policy development and administration is a continuous and adoptive process, something much more than the implementation of a comprehensive long range plan or a grand policy design (especially, since the rate of obsolence of long range plans is quite high). The success of policy implementation depends on the institutional ability to "learn by doing" and to absorb new information inputs.[24] (New information inputs also affect objectives and assessment of constraints). The continuity and adaptability of the policy process has a number of implications for analytical work:

1. The stability of the objective function is likely to be low, not only because social or economic goals, objectives, aspiration levels and concerns change over time, but also because the increase of knowledge changes social preferences. Ability to construct a "synthetic" objective function by analogy with the theory of individual decision under conditions of perfect knowledge is crucially dependent on the assumption that all relevant objectives are known and can be ordered, and that additional knowledge will not introduce new objectives or constraints, which in turn will not affect ordering of objectives previously taken into account.[25]

2. The key role which knowledge of an objective function plays in normative models, and the difficulty in identifying an objective function becomes somewhat spurious – the key role is now occupied by the continuous interchange of information and policy instructions.

3. Policy process is largely a steering and control process; even decisions, such as large investment decisions, which appear as discontinuities from the point of view of sectorial management are affected by the continuous steering process of the economy as a whole.

4. The role of large scale sectorial or system models is to provide information relevant to the decision process – this implies continuous adaptability of the model to provide *inter alia* information on specific, direct and indirect effects of policy changes, to monitor the working of the system and to give advanced warning of arising concerns.

Viewed in this context, a "comprehensive policy model" should not be considered as a once-for-all exercise,

but as a framework for provision of information on the workings of the system, the directions of change and the interactions of relevant elements. This implies not only periodic re-estimation of the model, i.e. re-estimation of relationships specified by the model's structure, but also the restructuring of the model itself. Thus, the adaptability of a large scale policy model becomes a matter of concern. Complexity in the structure (as indicated by the number of feedbacks and assumed inter-relationships) tends to adversely affect adaptability. In addition, a model whose structure dictates rigid and highly specific data inputs is likely to be prone to "data failures". A "modular structure", which permits easy partitioning of the model and changing one part without forcing an overall model reformulation, may produce a less satisfactory initial version, but be more adjustable with time.

6. CONCLUSIONS

In 1965 Garrison speculated about the nature of urban transportation planning models which would exist in 1975 [23]; his conclusions were:

a. "not much will be available in 1975 which is not already on view to-day";

b. "while we can speak quite articulately about goals and the measurement of goals and about formal decisionmaking schemes, it is difficult to believe that the next decade will see great strides in these areas";

c. "with respect to information, however, it would appear that a considerable amount of development and new flexibility is in view"

d. the need, neglected so far, is for greater exploration of self-adapting models for current adjustment and control.

In the light of developments in the last ten years, it is difficult to fault Garrison's 1965 assessment. Regarding the future, the following conjectures may be made:

a. We have indeed made great strides in our ability to digest and use information, even if we have made little progress in understanding available and potentially available information. It is probable that we shall see in the next decade significant progress in this respect which will affect the methodology of model building.

b. Intensive exploration of goals-objectives formal decision making structures has produced a large literature but few relevant worthwhile results.[26] If one were optimistic, one might expect that systematic investigation of actual decisionmaking processes could have a fruitful effect on the uses of models and hence on their structures.

c. One may expect significant results in evaluating the efficacy of policy instruments and the reaction-lags associated with their use. In transport, this problem is particularly bothersome – in a nutshell, we have a situation where reaction time to determine and implement transport policy changes can be larger than the terms of office of elected politicians, and even longer than the period of stability of social goals and aspirations.

d. One would hope that the problem of self-adapting mechanisms and short-term instruments for "steering" the sytem will receive increasing attention.

e. Lastly, one can expect some good results from the current disillusionment and questioning of existing main-stream methodologies.

The question posed in the title of this paper was: are large scale transport policy models a useful development or a "search for a philosopher's stone"? Undoubtedly, much of the activity in this field was similar to that of alchemists of the past – goals set were often unrealistic, conceptual difficulties in constructing complex large scale models were underestimated, and the relationship of model-building to the actual policy-making process was often at best tangential. However, at the same time much has been learned about the proper framework within which transport problems should be discussed and about the actual working of the transport system.

The alchemists did not find the philosopher's stone but, in searching for it they made worthwhile discoveries. Similarly, while I doubt whether an adequate comprehensive transport policy model serving metropolitan, regional or national transport policy needs will ever be developed, we have made significant progress in developing models analyzing traffic movements and transport demand as we have improved our understanding of the structure of the transport industries on the "supply side" and the linkages between transport and other sectors. One may also be optimistic about future work on transport policy instruments and the efficacy of using transport as an instrument for the achievement of non-transport objectives. Progress in all these areas has been vastly increased through large scale policy model building – *ex tenebris lux!*

REFERENCES

List of Abbreviations

AER: *American Economic Review*
ARS: *The Annals of Regional Science*
EC: *Economica*
EJ: *Economic Journal*
HRR: *Highway Research Board: Highway Research Record*
HSGT: *High Speed Ground Transportation Journal*
IJTE: *International Journal of Transport Economics*
JTEP: *Journal of Transport Economics and Policy*
JAIP: *Journal of American Institute of Planners*
JTPI: *Journal of the Town Planning Institute*
JWHCE: *Journal of the Waterways, Harbours and Coastal Engineering Division, ASCE*
OEP: *Oxford Economic Papers*
OR: *Operations Research*
PDR: *Population and Development Review*
QJF: *Quarterly Journal of Economics*
RE: *Regional Studies*
SEPS: *Socio-Economic Planning Sciences*
TEJ: *Transportation Engineering Journal* TEJ/PASCE: *Transportation Engineering Journal* Proceedings of ASCE
TJ: *Transportation Journal*
TPT: *Transportation Planning and Technology*
TQ: *Traffic Quarterly*
TR: *Transportation*
TRF: Transportation Research Forum, *Papers,* after 1970: *Proceedings*
TRR: *Transportation Research*

[1] H.E. Adler, **Economic Appraisal of Transport Projects,** Bloomington: Indiana Univ. Press, 1971.
[2] Wm. Alonso, **"Predicting Best with Imperfect Data",** JAIP, 1968.
[3] G.C. Archibald, **"Welfare Economics, Ethics and Essentialism",** EC 1959.
[4] W.B. Arthur and G. McNicoll, **"Large Scale Simulation Models in Population Development: What Use to Planners"?** PDR 1975.
[5] D.W. Barrel and P.J. Hills, **"The Application of Cost-Benefit Analysis to Transport Investment in Britain"** TR 1972.
[6] K.W. Bauer, **"The Comprehensive Plan in Transportation Planning",** TEJ/PASCE 1970.
[7] W.J. Baumol, **Welfare Economics and the Theory of the State** (2nd ed.) Cambridge, Mass: Harvard Univ. Press, 1965.
[8] A. Bieber, "Transportation Planning and Systems Analysis: A Preliminary Bibliography" in organization for Economic Co-Operation and Development, **The Urban Planning Transportation Planning Process,** Paris OECD.
[9] G. Blanwens, **"The Optimum Output of Transportation in an Imperfect Economic Environment",** JTEP, 1972.
[10] H.W. Bruck, M.L. Manheim and P.W. Shuldiner, **"Transportation System Planning as a Process: the Northeast Corridor Example",** TRF 1907.
[11] H.W. Bruck, S.H. Putman and W.E. Steger, **"Evaluation of Alternative Transportation Proposals: the Northeast Corridor"** JAIP 1966.
[12] A.J. Catanese, **"Urban System Planning: Restrospect**

and Prospect, HSGT 1969.
[13] A.J. Catanese and A.W. Steiss, **"Systematic Planning"** JTPI, 1968.
[14] R. de Neufville, **"Towards a Comprehensive Systems Analysis for Transportation Planning: An Urban Example"** TRF 1967.
[15] R. de Neufville and R.L. Keeney, "Use of Decision Analysis in Airport Development for Mexico City" in R. de Neufville and D. Marks (eats) **Systems Planning and Design,** Englewood Cliffs, 1974.
[16] Wm. H. Dodge, **"Network Analysis of Central American Regional Highway System",** TRF 1969.
[17] R. Dorfman, "Operations Research" in Economic Association American and Royal Economic Society **Surveys of Economic Theory,** vol. III, London: MacMillan 1956.
[18] J.W. Drake, **The Administration of Transportation Modelling Projects,** Lexington: Heath & Co. 1973.
[19] J.W. Drake, **"The Background and Value Systems of Transportation Modelling Participants and their Effects on Project Success",** TRF 1973.
[20] M.S. Feldstein, **"Net Social Benefit Calculation and the Public Investment Decision",** OEP, 1964.
[21] K.A. Fox, J.K. Sengupta and E. Thorbecke, **The Theory of Quantitative Economic Policy** (2nd ed.) Amsterdam North Holland 1973.
[22] A. Mynick Freeman, "Project Design and Evaluation with Multiple Objectives" in R.H. Haveman and J. Margolis (edts) **Public Expenditure and Policy Analysis,** Chicago: Markham, 1970.
[23] W.L. Garrison, **"Urban Planning Models in 1975"** JAIP, 1965.
[24] K.W. Gwilliam, **"Economic Evaluation of Urban Transport Projects: the State of the Art",** TPT, 1972.
[25] P. Halm, Introduction [to] A. Karkvist **et al, Dynamic Allocation of Urban Space,** Farnborough: Saxon House, 1975.
[26] F. Hayek, "Economics and Knowledge", EC 1937, reprinted in J.M. Buchanan and G.F. Thirlby, **LSE Essays on Cost,** London: Weidenfeld and Nicolson, 1973.
[27] M. Hill, **"A Method for the Evaluation of Transportation Plans"** HRR 1967 (No. 180).
[28] M. Hill, **"A Goods Achievement Matrix for Evaluating Alternative Goals",** JAIP 1968.
[29] C. Hitch, **"Operations Research and National Planning – A Dissent",** OR 1957.
[30] J. Hoffman and M.E. Goldsmith, **"A Comprehensive Evaluation of Transportation Alternatives for a Large Urban Area",** TRF 1974.
[31] B.J. Hutchison, **"An Approach to the Economic Evaluation of Urban Transportation Investments"** HRR 1970 (No. 314).
[32] A.M. Khan, **"Transport Policy Decision Analysis: An Expected Utility Approach",** HSGT 1971.
[33] A.M. Khan, **"Transport Policy Decision Analysis: A Decision Theoretic Framework,"** SEPS 1971.
[34] A.M. Khan, **"Transport Policy Decision Analysis: Recent Developments in the Techniques of Investment Planning"** HSGT 1972.
[35] A.M. Khan, **"Land Use and Transport Interaction: Policy and Planning Implications",** HSGT 1974.
[36] Du W.A. Kock, **"Implications of Systems Analysis to Inland Navigation,"** JWHCE 1971.
[37] H.J. Koelman, **"Transportation Planning Integrated in the Overall Planning Process,"** TO 1974.
[3I] N. Litchfield, **"Cost Benefit in City Planning"** JAIP 1960.
[39] N. Litchfield, **"Evaluation Methodology of Urban and Regional Plans – A Review",** RS 1970.
[40] I.M.D. Little, **A Critique of Welfare Economics,** Oxford: Oxford University Press (2nd ed) 1957.
[41] A. Maas, **"Cost-Benefit Analysis: Its Relevance to Public Investment Decisions",** QJE, 1966.
[42] J.H. Makin, **"Constraints on Formulation of Models for Measuring Revealed Preferences of Policy Makers,"** KYKLOS, 1976.
[43] M.L. Manheim, **"Principles of Transport System Analysis",** TRF 1966.
[44] M.L. Manheim, **"Search and Choice in Transport System Analysis",** HRR 1969 (No. 293).
[45] M.L. Manheim, E.R. Ruiter and K.U. Bhatt, **Search and Choice in Transport Systems Planning,** Cambridge, Mass: MIT Transportation Systems Division (Research Report R 68-40) 1968.

[45a] B. Martin and C. Warden, **"Transportation Planning in Developing Countries"**, TQ 1965.

[46] F.J. Mishan, **Cost Benefit Analysis,** London: Allen and Unwin, 1971.

[47] E.J. Mishan, **"Flexibility and Consistency in Project Evaluation"**, EC 1974.

[48] C.A. Nash, D. Pearce and J. Stanley, **"Criteria for Evaluating Project Evaluation Techniques"**, JAIP, 1975.

[49] A.R. Prest and R. Turvey, "Theories of Cost Benefit Analysis – A Survey", EJ 1965 (reprinted in **Surveys of Economic Theory**, vol. III, London: MacMillan 1966).

[50] S.H. Putman, **"Urban Law Use and Transportation Models: A State of the Art Summary"**, TR 1975.

[51] P.O. Roberts, **"Multi-Viewpoint Evaluation of Transportation Projects and Systems"**, TRF 1966.

[52] P.O. Roberts and D.N. Dewees, **"Problems in the Application of Systems Simulation to Transport Planning"**, TRF 1968.

[53] P.O. Roberts and D.T. Kresge, **"Simulation of Transport Policy Alternatives for Columbia"**, AER

[54] G.B. Rodgers, R. Wery and M.J.D. Hopkins, **"The Myth of the Cavern Revisited: Are Large-Scale Behavioural Models Useful?"**, PDR 1976.

[55] A. Saltzman, A.E. Kidder, F.V. Sowell and S.H. Evans, **"Transportation Research for Community Objectives"** TEJ/PASCE, 1972.

[56] T. Sarrazin, F. Spreer and M. Tietzel, **"Logical Decision-making Techniques to Evaluate Public Investment Projects: Cost-Benefit Analysis, Cost-Effectiveness Analysis, Utility Analysis – A Criteria Comparative Approach"**, IJTE.

[57] A.L. Silvers, **"Analysing the Impact of Transportation in a Public Investment Program for Economic Development"**, TRF 1969.

[58] J.K. Stanley, **"A Cardinal Utility Approach for Project Evaluation"**, SEPS, 1974.

[59] D.N.M. Starkie, **Transportation Planning and Public Policy,** Oxford: Pergamon Press 1973.

[60] D.N.M. Starkie, **"Transport Planning and the Policy-Modelling Interface"**, TR 1974.

[61] K.W. Studnicki-Gizbert, "Transport Policy: Objectives and Policy Instruments" in K.W. Studnicki-Gizbert (ed), **Issues in Canadian Transport Policy,** Toronto: MacMillan of Canada 1974.

[62] E.N. Thomas and J.L. Schafer, **Strategies for the Evaluation of Alternative Transportation Plans,** Washington: Highway Research Board 1970 (National Co-Operative Highway Research Program, Report 96).

[63] T.A. Tillman, **"Model for Planning a Transportation System"**, TEJ, 1970.

[64] J. Tinbergen, **On the Theory of Economic Policy,** Amsterdam: North Holland 1952.

[65] Transport Canada, **Transportation Policy – A Framework for Transport in Canada,** Ottawa: Information Canada 1975.

[66] U.S.A. Department of Commerce, **Highways and Economic and Social Changes,** Washington: US Gov't Printing Office 1964.

[67] U.S.A. Department of Transportation, **Preparation and Appraisal of Transport Projects,** Washington: US Gov't. Printing Office 1968.

[68] W.G. Waters II, **"Impact Studies and the Evaluations of Public Projects"**, ARS, 1976.

[69] K.W. Webb, "Models in Transportation" in S.I. Gass and R.L.S. Sisson (edts), **A Guide to Models in Governmental Planning and Operations,** Potomac, MD: Sauger Books 1975.

[70] M. Wohl, **Transportation Investment Planning,** Lexington: Heath & Co., 1972.

FOOTNOTES

1. Drake [18] [19] quotes estimates of costs of transport modelling by US government of the order of $800 mil. in the Decade of the 1960's. Adding the expenditures of other national governments, states, provinces, municipalities, international institutions etc. transport modelling expenditures may well exceed $150 mil. p.a., with large scale policy models accounting for at least a quarter of this sum.

2. For example, in an introduction to a recent symposium, Per Holm writes: "we can mention why the extensive planning contributions have not given the expected results. The first is that theoretical foundations for policy decisions are rather weak . . . and secondly, there is a scarcity of planning models which are applicable [to] practical planning problems and which can be

used in the decision process. [25] pxvi. Interestingly enough, similar criticism has been raised in other fields; for a critique of population policy models see Arthur and McNicoll [4] and for a reasoned reply Rogers *et al* [54].

3. Aspects of transport modelling work, mostly in the urban context have been reviewed, *inter alia*, by Alain Bieber [8], K.W. Gwilliam [24] and S.H. Putman [5]. "The concepts of systems analysis as they may be applied to the transport planning process" is reviewed by E.N. Thomas and J.L. Schofer [62], which contain extensive bibliographies. International Bank for Reconstruction and Development released a number of staff summaries/staff assessment reports dealing with more important models prepared by the Bank's consultants dealing with transport-economic development aspects.

4. However, in practice such an "objective function" may have to be deduced from either observations of past choices ("revealed preferences of decisionmakers") or from the choice and establishment of policy targets, "The fixation of Ω (objective function) is a difficult matter; generally it will not be considered consciously but intuitively by those responsible for policy . . . In practice the stage of fixing Ω and trying to maximize it will often be paved over and the targets chosen directly" Tinbergen [64].

5. The term "decision maker" is used here wisely – which is a normal practice of the policy model builders. Later on the term will be discarded, and we shall refer to the "decision making process"; at this stage "decisionmakers or makers" are defined as those directly and substantively involved in the decision process.

6. Impact studies of highway projects have been particularly numerous; for a review of U.S. practice see [66].

7. For a comprehensive presentation of this approach and extensive review of the literature of this genre see Thomas and Schlofer [62].

8. An interesting and somewhat different approach was adopted in Transport Canada policy document [65]: over-all goals of transport policy were stated, but the objectives and intensity of government intervention varies depending on the state of a particular part of a transport system which is described by the use of two scales: "maturity" and "competitiveness".

9. Alonso's [2] thoughtful remarks are relevant here.

10. Contrary to common complaint, the transport sector generates vast amounts of information; with a systematic improvement of the management information systems, volume and quality of information is likely to improve further. Secondly, the understanding of the logic why some data are generated while others are not throws considerable light on the decision process within the sector. Complaints that data are not available, while large volumes of information are not utilized is likely to be a symptom of poor model design!

11. The related problem is that in order to salvage an over-complex model low quality data derived from doubtful estimates may impair the overall reliability of empirical material. A mixture of low and high quality data in the same set of estimates introduces unknown biases. A less ambitious model may give us fewer answers but in many circumstances will produce less trash.

12. The classic contribution is by Little [40]. Also see Archibald [3].

13. The following quotations from Mishan, a leading welfare economist are relevant here: "If there is to be any consensus on the weights to be used in a cost-benefit analysis, it should be reached in advance, and therefore independently of, the critical sets of weights yielded by any particular project" ([47] p. 94), i.e. objective function ranking all relevant factors for public choice exists prior to and independent of the evaluation process. Regarding the nature of the welfare function: "[economists] should not overlook the fact that once they accept from the political process prices or weights that have no necessary correspondence with the relevant subjective valuation of the members of the society, they not only cease to offer the public an independent economic appraisal of any plan or project . . . they may be unable to provide a coherent interpretation of their resulting calculations . . ." *ibid* p. 95. Derivation of the "necessary correspondence" since it is necessary must be feasible – or at least that is what Mishan believes.

14. "As the broadest object of the theory of economic policy we consider the determination of the optimum policy, given the individual preference indicators of the citizens of the community. The object is very broad and implies, among other things (i) the fixation of a collective preference indicator" Tinbergen [64] p. 3.

15. For a comprehensive discussion of theory of quantitative economic policy see Fox *et al* [21]. The difficulties inherent in Tinbergian formulation which permitted no trade-offs between

targets and required equality between number of targets and instruments for the existence of an optimum policy was removed through reaction function analysis, which assumes the existence of a suitable form of policy maker's welfare function; see Makin [42] and sources quoted by him.

16. The literature of the subject is quite extensive and cannot be reviewed here. The comprehensive review is by Poest and Turvey [49]; recent definitive work is by Mishan [46]; for a review of applications to urban transport see Barrel and Hills [5] and Gwilliam [24]; for "manual approach" related to developing countries see Alder [1] and US Department of Transportation [67]; also see Hutchinson [31] and Wohl [70] for an engineer's view of the problem. An important critical contribution is by Feldstein [20]; for application of economic controls to transport see Blanwens [9].

17. See Litchfield [38] [39].

18. Hill [27] [28].

19. See Khan [32] [33] [34] [35] for useful sympathetic review of this work; on specific application to an airport problem see de Neufville and Keeney [15].

20. Numerous contributions stress the iterative nature of goals or objectives determination through planned/community interaction, inter-sectoral or inter-disciplinary interaction.

21. The most influential was the "Harvard Model" [53] [45a] which led to the development of a wide range of planning models, usually simplifying the "Harvard Model" structure and substituting "judgmental" or "sector assessment" inputs for large, systematic and "closed" macro-economic part. Although formally quasi-Harvard models differ from, and are less elegant, than the original, the intellectual influence of the Harvard Model is discernible.

22. See Starkie [59] [60], Catanese [12], survey by Putman [50].

23. See Bauer [6], Bruck, Manheim and Shuldiner [10], Bruck, Putman and Steger [11], as examples.

24. For the elaboration of the relationship between institutional structure, absorption of information and selection of solutions see Studnicki-Gizbert [61].

25. Hayek's essay on "Economics and Knowledge" [26] is highly relevant here. Imperfect knowledge is quite distinct from uncertain outcomes and cannot be handled through a scheme of probability assignments.

26. "Real life" applications of formal decision/choice analysis have often produced interesting theoretical contributions; solutions obtained, however, have tended to be trivial, or obvious from problem statement.

Application of demographic and econometric models to regional transportation planning*

by

C. CHARLES KIMM

Battelle Memorial Institute, Columbus, Ohio, U.S.A.

INTRODUCTION

One of the most pressing problems facing the transportation planner today is the ability to identify, design, and implement a reliable methodology to relate uncertain future socioeconomic conditions to the transportation system requirements needed to support the demand. To complicate the matter further, factors such as resource limitations, environmental degradation, and problems related to interregional integration of widely dispersed people and productive units, which are more recent issues facing the planning, must also be recognized as important factors affecting overall transportation needs.

The United States Transportation System is expected to face new challengers in coming years due to the scarcity of energy resources, increasing costs to construct new facilities and to maintain existing networks, and increasing Federal interest in using the Highway Trust Fund as a source to finance a wider variety of transportation improvement programs. At a time when all these developments are taking place, energy conservation measures are expected to cause a reduction in motor-fuel tax revenues of many states, since the major highway funding source is a gallonage tax on fuel sold to highway users.

In recognition of these problems and uncertain future transportation requirements, Battelle researchers have developed two modeling frameworks as an alternative attempt to project transportation demands, for both passengers and freight, by modes and origin-destination links. The first forecasting model is built around Battelle Demographic and Economic Modeling System (DEMOS) to project passenger travel and vehicle-miles of travel (VMT). The second forecasting model is based on Battelle's regional input/output (I/O) model to project freight transportation. The use of these models in a regional setting will be described in this paper.

DEMOS MODEL

DEMOS is a dynamic simulation model which is composed of various submodels. The model is a simulation as opposed to an optimizing model; it begins with a set of initial conditions, but does not provide optimal values as a result of any simultaneous solutions. It is dynamic as opposed to static: it generates values for many subsequent time periods rather than for a given point in time.

Through the use of DEMOS, subregional level forecasts for population, employment, vehicle ownership and trip generation were obtained. From the subregional level, projections were aggregated by geographic zones. The aggregation was done on the basis of similarity of socioeconomic characteristics such as large urban area influence zones, small urban area influence zones, and rural area influence zones.

The model is composed of three submodels – the demographic submodel, the economic submodel, and the feedback mechanism. Each segment incorporates real world relationships which are structured into a system operating within a simulated time frame. The ability of the variables to change and interact over time gives the model its dynamic nature.

For purpose of inclusion in the model, real world relationships have been identified, expressed in mathematical form, and estimated by means of regression analysis. Although not all relationships which exist in the real world are incorporated in the model, those felt to be most important in terms of their potential effects on the projected variables are included. Figure 1 summarizes the structure of the DEMOS model and indicates the interrelationships among its components.

Demographic Submodel

The demographic submodel is based upon the cohort-survival method of projecting population. In this method the three components of population change – births, deaths, and migration – are summed over time and added to the previous year's population to give a new age specific population for the subregional units.

Since the population changes vary by age group, the three components of population are age specific. The population is separated into 1-year age cohorts and to these cohorts are applied their respective rates. The net natural change in population plus the net migration are then summed to give the new population. This process is reiterated for every year simulated.

Subregion specific births are determined by birth rate equations which are adjusted for current fertility trends. Deaths are calculated by applying age specific mortality rates to the various population cohorts. Age and subregion specific migration is calculated through use of a migration equation in which migration is a function the difference between the local and national unemployment rates.

Changes in birth and migration rates over time are brought into play by means of the feedback mechanism which will be discussed later. These changes over time are changes that occur within the model, a result of its dynamic nature, and not changes related to the alternate assumptions concerning fertility and migration rates which are discussed at a latter point.

* *This paper is based on research work conducted by Battelle Columbus Laboratories for the Commonwealth of Kentucky in 1975.*

Economic Submodel

Employment projections by industry are the result of the economic submodel. The actual employment structure used is confined to those sectors shown in Table 1. As in the demographic submodel, real world relationships are simulated over time to generate employment projections within the various industries in the subregional economy. Basically, this submodel consists of various relationships among the subregional export industries, household serving industries, and business serving industries. Employment in each of these industrial sectors responds and changes for different reasons.

Export Employment

Export employment is defined as that employment serving a demand external to the specific subregion. Generally, export employment is limited to the agriculture, mining, and manufacturing sectors. Since export sectors produce goods and services which are exported to markets outside the subregion, the employment required within a given export industry and the changes in that employment over time depend upon factors beyond the control of the subregion's economy. As a result, the manner in which export industries grow is assumed to be exogenous. Generally, that growth is based on national economic forecasts.

Business Serving Employment

Business serving employment in a subregion is a function of the total employment within the subregion. Since demand for business serving industries depends, by definition, upon other businesses, it follows that as total employment increases, business serving employment increases and vice versa. Given a change in subregion-based export industry employment, there will be a corresponding change in total employment and thus busi-

Table 1 – List of economic sectors considered for each subregional unit in the regional DEMOS model

Agricultural, Forestry, and Fishing
Mining
Construction
Furniture, Lumber, and Wood
Metals Industry
Machinery, Excluding Electrical
Electrical Machinery
Transportation Equipment
Other Durable Goods
Food and Kindred Products
Textile and Textile Products
Printing and Publishing
Chemicals
Other Nondurable Goods
Railroad
Trucking
Other Transportation
Communications
Utilities and Sanitary Service
Wholesale Trade
Food and Dairy Stores
Eating and Drinking Places
General Merchandising
Motor Vehicle Retailing
Other Retail Trade
Finance
Insurance and Real Estate
Business and Repair Services
Private Households
Other Personal Services
Entertainment
Hospitals
Other Health Services
Government Education
Private Education
Other Educational Services
Religions and Nonprofit Organizations
Professional Organizations
Public Administration

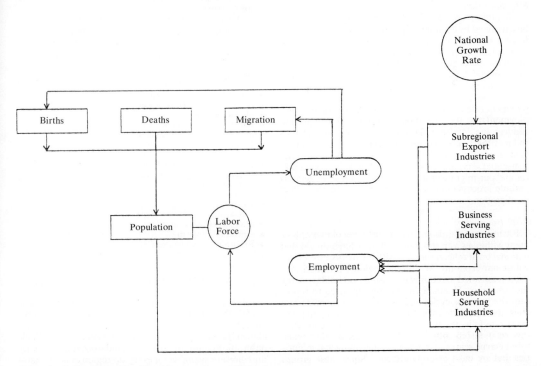

Figure 1 – Regional demographic and economic modeling system

ness serving employment within the subregion. The availability of labor in the subregion also affects the magnitude of the employment change in the business serving sector. For example, as employment in the export sector increases, the unemployment rate decreases making less labor available for any given job. Business within the subregion must now compete for the available labor supply and a specific business may not be able to hire all the labor it would like. This factor is represented within the model, and it dampens the relationship between business serving employment and total employment within the subregion.

Household Serving Employment

Household serving employment is a function of total population within the subregion. Household serving employment provides goods and services to the subregion population; as the population and their demand increase, so does employment in the household serving sector. Examples of household serving industries are hospitals, entertainment, eating and drinking places, and retail trade.

As before, the amount of labor desired by any particular household serving industry is adjusted to take account of the current labor availability in the subregion. Thus, desired change in employment may not be equal to actual change.

Feedback Sector

The feedback sector of the subregional DEMOS model relates the economic and demographic submodels of the system. The basic concept of the feedback sector is the relationship between unemployment and other variables within the model. The unemployment rate within a subregion serves as an indication of the subregion's economic vitality. Migration rates, labor force participation rates, and birth rates are all affected by the degree of unemployment within a given subregion.

Migration Rates

Migration, especially for the working ages, can largely be explained by economic opportunity. People gravitate toward areas having relatively low unemployment rates. This relationship between migration rates and unemployment has been incorporated into the feedback sector of the model. Basically, as the subregion unemployment rate becomes less than the national unemployment rate, there is net in-migration; and as the subregion unemployment rate becomes greater than the national unemployment rate, there is net out-migration. Out-migration reduces the total population in a subregion and thus reduces the household serving sector of the economy. Changes in total employment caused by changes in the household serving sector affect the business serving sector and out-migration may be further increased. A comparable process operates in a reverse manner to affect in-migration.

Birth Rates

Blirht Rates are also related to the level of unemployment within a given subregion. Studies have shown that national birth rates respond positively to business cycles within our economy. Within the regional DEMOS model it is assumed that this relationship also holds true for the subregion. Unemployment rates are used to represent the business cycle; and as the unemployment rate rises, the birth rate falls. Conversely, as the unemployment rate falls, the birth rate increases. One can sense this relationship intuitively by considering that when jobs become scarce, it is generally the young and minorities that are most severely affected. Since these groups are the most fertile groups in our society, and since

family planning (including marriage) and personal income (including income derived from employment) are closely related, the relationship between unemployment rates and birth rates becomes apparent.

Labor Force Participation Rates

The labor force participation rate is an important link between the economic and demographic submodels. It is defined as the percentage of the population, age 16 and over, that is working or actively seeking employment. The labor force participation rate is computed for specific age groups within the model since actual rates vary by age group, geographic area, and over time. Past investigations have indicated that labor force participation rates are inversely related to the unemployment rates. As the unemployment rate increases and the number of jobs available becomes smaller, some workers become discouraged and withdraw from the labor force. Conversely, as the economic situation improves and the number of jobs increase, the number of persons seeking employment increases. As labor force participation rates change, they affect unemployment rates and other variables within the model, and once again the model's dynamitics come into play.

Registrations and Trips

In addition to the demographic and economic variables, other variables pertaining to vehicle registrations and trip generations were also projected. The actual variables forecast are:
- Automobile registration by subregion
- Passenger cars, trucks, farm trucks, trailers, and other
- Trips generated by subregion.

The equations used to forecast vehicle registrations are generally linear while the equation used to generate trips is multiplicative. The actual relationships used are as follows:

    a. Passenger cars and truck registrations = f (total employment)

    b. Farm truck registrations = f (time)

    c. Trailer registrations = f (total population)

    d. Other registrations = f (total employment)

    e. Trips = f (total registration, total population).

Table 2 – Data inputs used in the regional DEMOS model

- Male population by 5-year age group
- Female population by 5-year age group
- Military workers
- Inmates of institutions
- Male labor force participation rate
- Female labor force participation rate
- Export serving employment
- Household serving employment
- Business serving employment
- Birth rate
- Annual migration rate by 5-year age group
- Labor force – civilian
- Esimated nonresident college students
- Motor vehicle registrations
- Census fertility series
- Export industry employment growth rate

DATA INPUTS TO THE REGIONAL DEMOS MODEL

Table 2 indicates the initial data inputs for the basic model. The DEMOS model is constructed so that it uses published secondary data inputs. These data are obtainable in Bureau of the Census of other generally available publications, and the data are standardized in the sense that they are available for every subregion or administrative unit in the region.

The use of various assumptions, such as different fertility trends or migration rates, allow us to simulate subregion specific conditions. It also, when future conditions are uncertain, allows us to simulate a range of possible conditions so that a range of possible outcomes can be generated.

The socioeconomic forecast generated by the Regional DEMOS are subregional unit specific. For each region's subregional unit DEMOS provides a dynamic simulation of future economic activity and generates forecasts of population, population distribution, migration patterns, employment by 39 economic sectors, labor force participation rates, and other variables for the projected years.

As shown in Figure 2, the outputs from DEMOS were used in a Gravity and Fratar Model to forecast passenger trips and vehicle-miles of travel. Since automobile travel has been and is expected to be the predominant mode of passenger transportation, greater emphasis is given for this mode of transportation. A Gravity model is used to forecast intraregional trips as well as extraregional trips using the region's highway in transit. The Gravity model develops an index of attraction between two points as a function of the population at each point and the distance between them. To operationalize the Gravity model, a vector of trips by zone is first generated. Since the trip behavior of people differ as a function of the area in which they live and work, a separate trip equation for

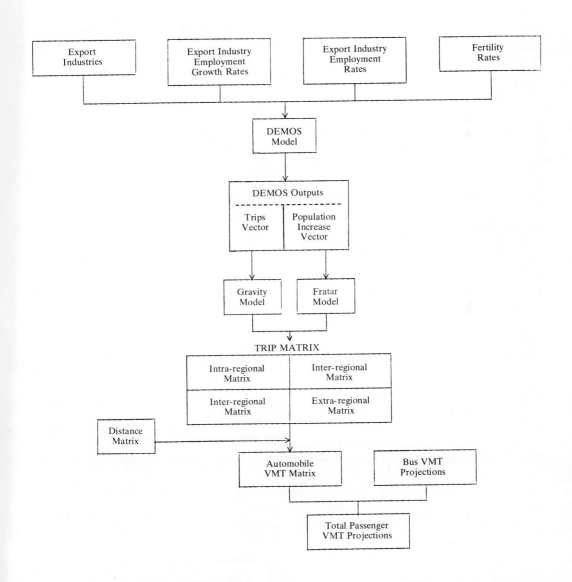

Figure 2 – Methodology to forecast automobile passenger demand

635

large urban, small urban, and rural influence zones is estimated. Based on the Household Travel Survey, a stepwise linear analysis was performed for a linear and logarithmic equation. In all three areas the linear equation was selected on the basis of the coefficients and determination (R^2) and F statistics. After the trips per zone are generated by using the appropriate equation, the Gravity model was used to assign trips to destinations.

The form of the equation is as follows:

$$T_{ij} = \left(\frac{\frac{P_i P_j}{D_{ij}}}{\sum\limits_{i=1}^{n} \frac{P_i P_j}{D_{ij}}} \right) T_i \quad (i \neq j)$$

$$T_{ij} = \left(\frac{2 \frac{P_i P_j}{D_{ij}}}{\sum\limits_{i=1}^{n} \frac{P_i P_j}{D_{ij}}} \right) T_i \quad (i = j)$$

where

T_{ij} = number of trips per day from i to j
P_i = population of origin zone i
P_j = population of destination zone j
D_{ij} = distance between i and j
T_i = trips originating in zone i.

When i = j (intra-zonal trips) a weighting factor of 2 is used to account for greater interaction within the zone.

The Fratar model is a proportional method of estimating link flows between nodes by distributing trips in proportion to the attractiveness of each zone. "Attractiveness" in this study being represented by the population of each zone. It is an interative method whereby observed zonal interchange was estimated for traffic between each pair of zones. For example, trips between zone i and zone j are estimated by distributing the total flow as originating either from i or from j, in proportion to the respective populations of the zones. The arithmetic average of the two estimates is taken as the estimate from the first iteration, and the computed number of trip-ends for each zone is obtained by summing the estimated zonal transfers to each zone. So then, the ratio of the originally forecasted trip-ends to the computed number of trip-ends represents the growth factor for the second iteration. This process is repeated with new growth factor until the ratio of forecasted to computed trip-ends for all zones are sufficiently close to one. The algebraic formulation of the Fratar model is as follows.

The number of trips between zones i and j computed at zone i is:

$$t_{ij}(i)' = \left(\sum_{j \neq i} t_{ij} \right) F_i \left[\frac{t_{ij} F_j}{\sum\limits_{j \neq i} t_{ij} F_j} \right].$$

The number of trips between zones i and j is the same basic equation with j substitute for i at appropriate places:

$$t_{ij}(j)' = \left(\sum_{i \neq j} t_{ij} \right) F_j \left[\frac{t_{ij} F_i}{\sum\limits_{i \neq j} t_{ij} F_i} \right].$$

The first approximation to t_{ij}' is the arithmetic mean of $t_{ij}(i)$' and $t_{ij}(j)$ as follows:

$$t_{ij}' = \frac{t_{ij}(i)' + t_{ij}(j)'}{2}$$

The second approximation proceeds in a similar fashion, with:

$$t_{ij}(i)' = \left(\sum_{i \neq j} t_{ij}' \right) F_i' \left[\frac{t_{ij}' F_j'}{\sum\limits_{i \neq j} t_{ij}' F_j'} \right].$$

And it continues in this manner while the desired accuracy is obtained between two iterations.

Using Gravity and Fratar models, a matrix of 0-D trips was created for the Regional DEMOS model. When this matrix is multiplied by a matrix of highway distances, the VMT matrix, by automobile, was generated.

Bus travel was found not to be linked to demographic or economic factors. A separate forecast of bus VMT was therefore compiled, based on historical growth trends.

INPUT/OUTPUT MODEL

A regional input/output model was developed to serve as a basis for freight transportation forecasting. The input/output model is a representation of region's economy in terms of inter-industry consumption and output. The Battelle model, currently operational at a 127-industry sector detail:

• Can be regionalized into any subregional administrative unit

• Reflects present or future technologies, i.e., is *not* confined, as are most other I/O models, to the technological situation that existed 8 or more years ago

• Produce an I/O table that allows distinctions to be made between those inputs into the region's industries which are produced within the region and those that must be imported; thus, it permits identifying purely regional impacts.

The overall purpose for deriving this particular set of tables was to provide accurate estimates of freight transportation needs by mode required to produce and deliver regions industrial output by sector for each of the projected years.

Preparation of the regional tables involves three basic steps:

1. Deriving the base year "unbalanced" table from the base year Battelle national table

2. "Balancing" the base table, i.e., distinguishing between the share of regional output retained in study region to satisfy total regional requirements (intermediate plus final demand) and the share which must be imported

3. Simulating the effects of estimated growth rates for each of a region's 127 producing sectors over the projected years.

There are several assumptions that lie behind the derivation of the regional input/output table from the national table, the most important of which are:

1. That region's share of national output for any given industry is proportional to its share of national employment in that industry.

2. That the technology employed by each industry in the region is that of the national average for that industry.

3. That regional productivity is the same as the national productivity.

4. That a sector's output is homogeneous in the sense that industry i's output can be used by any forwardly linked industry i.

Because of these four assumptions, the resulting I/O tables must be treated as being normative rather than precisely definitive. Nevertheless, it is felt that this type of table provides a good assessment of the amounts and levels of economic activity taking place within the region.

In actually deriving the tables, the region's share of total national output was obtained for each of the account sectors. These outputs were derived directly from the base year estimates of national total output, assuming that the region's total output has the same relationship to national total output as the relationship of the region's employment to national employment. That is, for each sector classification, the ratio of the employment in region to the total national employment was calculated. This ratio was then multiplied by total output for the national sector to provide the estimate of total regional output in that sector.

After estimating total output, similar estimates were made for final demands originating in the region. The personal consumption component of final demand was assumed to have the same distribution as personal consumption in the national table. The estimates of personal consumption expenditures in the region were obtained by multiplying each entry in the U.S. PCE (Personal Consumption Expenditures) table column by the ratio of personal income in the region to personal income in the nation.

Estimates of regional demand for gross private fixed capital formation were similarly obtained using the regional/national ratio for income arising in contract construction. The assumption implicit here is that all other plant and equipment expenditures are proportional to construction.

Similarly, the ratio of incomes paid by the Federal Government in the region to incomes paid by the Federal Government at the national level was used to estimate the component of final demand attributable to Federal activities in the region. This procedure is repeated to obtain final demand resulting from activities at the regional and subregional levels.

Estimates of gross imports (gross imports are defined here as foreign imports) were calculated in two ways. For about two-thirds of the sectors, gross imports were estimated by using the regional/national ratio used to estimate total output. For the remaining sectors, the ratio between regional total intermediate output and national total intermediate output was applied. The second procedure eliminates the possibility for significant amounts of foreign imports of more primary oriented products to enter a regional economy which has no apparent use for them, e.g., importing iron ore into a region which has no primary iron and steel processing.

The two remaining components of final demand, gross exports and inventory change, were estimated by assuming the regional/national ratio for each sector to be the same one used to estimate the regional total output. In this connection, attention is called to the fact that only the region's share of the nation's exports to other countries is under consideration here.

Intermediate (intra-industry) requirements were calculated by multiplying the national direct technical coefficients by the vector of estimated regional total output for the applicable industry. The result of this process is an *unbalanced* regional table which indicates regional final demand, total output, and intermediate requirements. Total requirements may equal, exceed, or fall short of actual regional output. The residual between regional requirements and output is then entered as interregional imports or interregional exports, depending upon whether the residual is negative or positive.

The next step was to determine the percentage of regional output retained in the region in order to satisfy total regional requirements (intermediate plus final demand). This determination was made in one of two ways, depending upon available data for each industry. The first involved personal knowledge or the use of actual survey information. In this case, people knowledgeable of the region's economy or representatives of the actual manufacturing concerns were questioned to determine the percentage of local output retained within the region.

The second procedure involved the use of a form of location quotient which compared the ratio of regional demand and supply to the ratio of national demand and supply for the same industry.

Once a determination of the region's output retained to satisfy regional demand was known, that amount was separated into the portion going to final demand and the portion going to intermediate demand. As personal knowledge did not dictate otherwise, this separation was consistent with the share between intermediate and final demand requirements of total requirements in the unbalanced tabel.

The second step involved reducing the unbalanced regional table to a balanced regional table. This step was accomplished by assuming that the national direct coefficients were reduced in region in proportion to the ratio of regional output retained to satisfy region's intermediate requirements to total regional intermediate requirements or:

$$r_{ij} = (a_{ij}) \left[\frac{t_{ri}}{T_{ri}} \right]$$

where

r_{ij} = regional direct technical coefficients from industry i to industry j

a_{ij} = national direct technical coefficients from industry i to industry j

t_{ri} = total region's output of industry i retained to satisfy regional intermediate demand

T_{ti} = total regional intermediate demand for industry i's output.

Given the set of regional direct technical coefficients, the regional table was balanced and inverted, and the total direct and indirect impacts resulting from the projected industrial growth rates were calculated.

For example, to simulate the effects of increasing the output of a sector, the regional exports final demand subvector was increased by the amount of the projected increase in output. Additionally, another final demand subvector, personal consumption expenditures, was changed as the increased output of the sector generated additional income which generated additional final demand. The inverted coefficients were then multiplied by the new final demand, and new values of total output, employment, income, etc., were generated. The impact was then calculated as the difference between the two sets of results.

In matrix notation the process is as follows:

$$X = (I - A)^{-1} Y$$

where

X = total output for the baseline conditions
$(I - A)^{-1}$ = inverted table of region's direct technical coefficients
Y = region's final demand for the baseline conditions.

$$X^* = (I - A)^{-1} Y^*$$

where

X* = the vector of total region's output after the output of a particular sector has been increased
Y* = new vector of final demand.

$$I = X^* - X$$

where

I = total direct and indirect impact generated by the direct change in output.

To a large degree, projected national growth rates for each of the 127 account sectors were applied to regional industries. However, where possible, more precise regional sector growth rates have been substituted for the expected national growth rates.

637

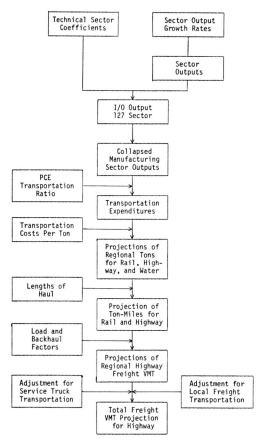

Figure 3 – Methodology to forecast freight transportation demand

As shown in Figure 3, the freight demand analysis for all sectors was based on conversion of the input/output table's sector output (in dollars) to a unit of transportation demand. In order to do this, it was necessary to first get a measure of the regional freight accounted for by each dollar of industrial output. This was done through use of the U.S. Department of Commerce, Bureau of Economic Analysis Personal Consumption Expenditure (PCE) "Poridge tables". These tables indicate transpor-

tation and other add-ons to producer prices. To convert transportation costs by sector to traffic volume expressed in tons, rate estimates derived from Interstate Commerce Commission and a series of interviews with the region's shippers representing the major industries were used. This application resulted in volume estimates by rail, truck, and water in the Input/Output model. Because ton-miles are not a meaningful indication of volume of inland waterway transportation, especially if the region's navigable waterways lie on regional boundaries, further freight forecasts in ton-miles were confined to rail and truck transportation. Rail and highway ton-miles were computed by multiplying the projected volumes by estimated average distance traveled within the region. Distance data were derived from the Censuses of Transportation and Manufacturing and the above-mentioned shipper interviews. In the case of truck transportation, it was necessary to go a step beyond ton and ton-miles forecasts. VMT projections in truck transportation were needed to add on to the VMT forecasts of passenger travel. To calculate vehicle-miles, the ton-miles were divided by the average load factor with allowance made for empty backhauls.

The input/output model's 127 industrial sector detail can be collapsed, based on the similarity of physical property of commodities and transportation characteristics, or any sector can be studied at greater depth exogenous to input/output model framework.

CONCLUSIONS

The DEMOS and Input/Output models provide an invaluable opportunity to transportation agencies, at all levels to evaluate the national, regional, and subregional based impacts of alternative growth levels in a wide variety of industries. The capabilities of these models have further been enriched to project freight vehicle-miles of travel and freight transportation demand as a function of complex socioeconomic interaction. In addition, the Gravity and Fratar models provide an added capability to project passenger origin-destination trips and vehicle-miles of travel. The transportation demand projections can be used to assess future system requirements and region's revenues as a source for funding transportation projects.

This comprehensive framework is expected to offer a unique opportunity to nations as an efficient tool in regional transportation planning. It will provide an input to facilitate the planning coordination of all modes in both public and private sectors.

New trends in rural feeder roads planning

by
HAROLD KURZMAN
Louis Berger International, Inc., U.S.A.

A. THE NEW TRENDS

International lending agencies are rapidly moving, as a matter of policy, towards focusing their road infrastructure investments on rural feeder roads.

For AID this is in response to a "Congressional Mandate" that infrastructure projects should directly benefit the small farmer. Therefore the distribution of benefits is at least as important as the total value of the producer surplus created or the balance of payments effect, and the measurement of benefits involves social welfare as well as incremental income valuation. Consequently, priority is given to farm to market roads as compared to feeder roads which provide point to point links with marketing centers. The former are not viewed as forming part of the future national road network.

IBRD's approach is in the same direction but less single-minded. It will continue to finance a broad spectrum of road works but is trying to correct past neglect of farm access and secondary roads. This implies an acceptance of lower engineering standards, a departure from economic justifications based on vehicle operating savings alone, and a commitment to more local cost financing. Moreover, IBRD is sponsoring a substantial amount of research to improve the economic and engineering techniques for design, justification and evaluation of rural road projects.

This attention to rural roads is part of the growing emphasis that international financing agencies are placing on the rural sector, especially on efforts to raise productivity and income levels of the rural poor through generally a multi-disiplinary approach involving in a number of cases integrated rural development projects. It reflects a recognition that subsistence sector cannot be modernized simply by migration of labor out of agriculture into the modern sector. Employment opportunities in the non-rural sector cannot be generated sufficiently fast to absorb the under-employment or low productivity of labor in the rural areas, as well as relatively rapid natural growth in population characteristic of most of the less developed subsistence economies.

There is little agreement on how high a priority should be placed on roads relative to other resource inputs in integrated rural developing planning. Access to marketing and service centers are generally agreed to be an essential component of any rural development planning. There are numerous examples which demonstrate that investment in rural roads alone does not necessarily yield a greater producer surplus or improvement in rural standards of living. The particular national, regional, local environment within which rural development is planned conditions to a large extent the success of investments. An important characteristic of the environment is the density of the existing rural road system as related to population density and the extent to which this system permits all-weather access. However, much of the effort in rural development projects is directed towards increasing outputs and incomes of low-income producers by the introduction and expansion of technological change at the farm level.

"The assumption underlying this effort is that three basic conditions must be met if changes are to be brought about: producers must know how to increase their output; they must have access to the means of increasing their output; and they must have incentive to make the effort and accept the risks associated with increasing their output. Agriculture is atomistic in the sense that there are many producers each with little influence over the prices he receives (though improved marketing techniques can often raise prices at the farm gate). Consequently, most projects tend to be focused on cost effective ways and means of delivering to farmers the goods and services that they need. These include all inputs and those that investment and infrastructure, such as irrigation and transport, will provide." [1]

The principal attempt of this paper is to draw the reader's attention to the fact that the planning and evaluation of rural feeder roads is a much more complicated, interdisciplinary and uncertain task, than the traditional engineering and cost/benefit analysis used for developing justification for and the implementation planning of capital investment in transport. Roads are the mode of attention since they represent the most flexible and lest cost means of providing transportation services to rural populations, with the exception of a few areas where rivers may provide an alternative. Although the percapita investment may be relatively small, the absolute needs on a regional or nationwide basis are often very large and consequently require very substantial investments. They are spatially widely dispersed, and involve the development of new implementing organizations, training, and management skills. Furthermore, the risks or uncertainties of success, i.e. of accomplishing project objectives no matter how defined or quantified, are often substantially greater than for traditional investment projects. Moreover, relatively little careful research has been devoted to determining what makes for a successful project and whether the successful components can be replicated from one area to another within a single country and still more conjecturally whether the experience in one country can provide good guidelines for planning in others.

B. DEFINITION OF RURAL FEEDER ROADS

There is still some fuzziness in defining the term rural feeder road. For the purposes of this paper the following characteristics are implied, which are broad enough to encompass both the AID and IBRD views.

1. The purpose of the road is primarily to provide improved farmer access to producer markets and to markets supplying goods and services to farmers.

2. The road will generally be intra-provincial, either linking farms to a small marketing center, or these centers to the provincial centers.

3. The investment cost per kilometer will not exceed $30,000, except in difficult terrain.

4. The roads may be either dry-weather or all-weather but will not have asphalt or concrete paving or a formation greater than 6 meters.

5. Existing traffic will not exceed 100 VPD, most frequently will be less than 50 VPD, and therefore road user savings are not a reliable or sufficient measure of benefits.

C. MAJOR ISSUES

The planning and justification of such roads raises the following major issues:

1. How rapidly can a country embark on a rural roads program given the constraints of budget, managerial and technical skills, and availability of workforce?

2. What are the appropriate criteria for determing priorities? Among the broad alternatives are:

a. Highest priority to areas of highest population density and development potential. This implies a high value assigned to economic efficiency.

b. Highest priority to areas whose development has been neglected relative to other parts of the country. This alternative implies a social equity criteria, i.e., the use of roads program to narrow income or social welfare disparities between regions.

c. Highest priority to roads which compliment or are a part of comprehensive regional development schemes. This implies that a specific set of complimentary inputs are necessary for the roads to generate a significant economic response.

3. Closely associated with the issue of appropriate criteria is the question of who should set the criteria. Some would argue that for a nationwide program, utilizing in part or in total national funds, this can only be determined at the highest political level and be translated into operating guidelines by technicians of a ministry planning bureau. Others contend that rural road programs will never succeed unless priorities are determined at the local level by the people who are to directly benefit from the investment and who may be asked to contribute some money or labor to the project.

4. How is one to forecast economic activity and associated transport demand, particularly where roads are not a part of an integrated rural development package? How much time and expense are warranted in making such forecasts? Are the tools for evaluation which may be developed and the interrelationships they may postulate applicable, beyond the spatial confines of the area studied, either to other regions within a country or to other countries?

5. What design standards and construction techniques are appropriate? What are the trade-offs between construction and maintenance costs and labor and capital intensive techniques? Is cost efficiency to be the primary guide for evaluating these choices? What impact should the policies of aid donors have on these choices?

6. How should a rural roads program be organized and financed? If one believes that he who holds the purse strings also determines the way the program will be designed and executed, the organization and its financing are closely related. Among the possible alternatives are:

a. The provincial and local authorities are primarily responsible and are provided with the financial capacity to undertake the program. They may contract for services and equipment not locally available.

b. An entirely new works organization may be established.

c. Rural roads programs may be organized and undertaken by public agencies responsible for agriculture, livestock, community development and the like, as an additional but complimentary activity to those for which the agency is already responsible.

d. Private commercial enterprises, with a special interest in road access and conditions in a particular area, (cooperatives, agro-industries, mining or forestry enterprises) may take upon themselves road building and maintenance, with or without some financial or technical assistance from public authorities.

7. *Trained Manpower* Since it is the intent to build rural roads to minimum standards and costs consistent with the traffic to be served, it is unlikely that one can afford detailed engineering proceeding construction. Therefore the critical individual, both for detailed planning and works execution, will be the on-site construction supervisor. These minor road works are likely to be unattractive to large private contractors and also difficult to execute by contract without detailed specifications. Therefore construction will be done by public works agencies (force account) or by small private contractors who have relatively unsophisticated management skills or financial resources. Therefore the responsible public agency will have to greatly increase its pool of works supervisors. Can this be accomplished rapidly and what types of skills and training are appropriate?

The supervisor will have to have some engineering planning, and administrative skills. He will have to be innovative and self-reliant to a much greater extent than if he were working on a larger job, to detailed plans, under close supervision by an engineer. If works are to be accomplished largely by labor intensive techniques, will he know how to obtain the best productivity under these conditions? Will he have the personality required to effectively manage a large labor force or to negotiate for labor with the leaders of local communities? Must one train manual labor in the use of tools and other small implements?

8. *Maintenance.* The issues here are who will have maintenance responsibility for the roads once built, what level of maintenance is necessary, does it require seasonal peak efforts and if so how can the effort be assured at times and places required, who will finance it, and should it be a labor or capital intensive activity or some mix of both?

Economics dictate that one can only afford to spend a few hundred dollars a year on routine maintenance of rural feeder roads. This eliminates machine intensive maintenance as an alternative except in areas of very sparse population. The best alternative appears to be to use persons living in proximity to the roads to perform routine maintenance, with each person or gang responsible for a specific road section that is within walking distance of their homes. This solution has many advantages:

a. Maintenance labor can be held specifically responsible for physical sections of road both by local communities (their peers) and by the agency supervising their work.

b. The laborers are always on-site to identify road deterioration and make necessary repairs.

c. The cost of labor is relatively low as compared to laborers permanently employed by a works agency whose cost, when minimum wages, fringe benefits, works camp expenses, and transport are incurred, may be four times higher.

Supervision of maintenance requires more planning and perhaps staff but this cost can be minimized by careful organization. One can have the lowest level supervisor using a bicycle, then his supervisor covering more area with a motorcycle, and finally a senior supervisor in a motorized vehicle. Where hauling of materials is necessary, this can be scheduled as an intensive motorized task a few times a year with materials stockpiled at locations convenient for placement by hand labor.

Periodic maintenance, required at intervals of one to three years, may remain a more centralized responsibility undertaken with more mechanization.

D. PROJECT EVALUATION

Traditionally, the analysis of transportation investment projects has relied on the concept of economic efficiency (benefit/cost). In the traditional transportation benefit/cost analysis, it is assumed that the economy is in equilibrium and the constituency consists only of users of the transportation system. Under this assumption, economic benefits accruing to current and prospective users are evaluated against the economic costs of constructing and maintaining the facilities or equipment. While the impact on users is a vitally important component of a benefit/cost analysis, experience had demonstrated that transportation investments may have a far greater socio-economic impact upon the people who live near the facility and upon the communities and towns served by the facility.

While the transportation planner was, in one instance, faced with the requirements for highly sophisticated and advanced planning techniques, on the other hand, he was increasingly criticized for his failure to deal with social equity, income distribution, rural development, and in recent years environmental considerations. Transportation planning was faulted for evaluating project benefits in the form of savings or benefits which were received by the monetrized or modern sectors of a developing economy. These recipients were the relatively prosperous urban and modern farming sectors.

In undertaking such rural road evaluation studies, the analyst must first ascertain the extent to which the present lack of adequate access has significantly distorted the development potential of a region. Then, the analyst must identify on a micro-level the present structural and socioeconomic characteristics of the economy of the area, including non-transport institutional constraints, the available human natural resources, the development potential, and the region's comparative economic advantage and income distribution to analyse why the region has trailed the national economy or other equally endowed regions in economic development. Such studies involve multidisciplinary analysis and raise significant problems of input compatibility (e.g. how does one compare agricultural production with improved health and welfare).

E. NEW TECHNOLOGY AND RESEARCH

These issues are very challenging. They call for new or adapted technology, engineering design, construction work methods, management, and finance. In this paper it is only possible to briefly summarize the steps that many organizations are taking to improve the state of the arts.

The IBRD, through its Transportation Research Department, is sponsoring substantial research. It is attempting to identify the developmental impact of rural roads, namely the classification, magnitude, and distribution of benefits and farmer response to perceived benefits. This is being accomplished through the following:

1. In-house position papers outlining the need and methods of a new analytical approach.

2. Operations research systems to support application of these methods.

3. Research programs in Brazil, Ethiopia, Malagasy, Yemen and probably Kenya to monitor the socioeconomic impact of new rural roads through long-term before and after construction studies.

IBRD and ILO are also concentrating on studies of labor/equipment substitution in civil construction. IBRD has sponsored a series of technical memoranda based largely on field work in Northwest India and Indonesia undertaken by Scott Wilson Kirkpatrick in collaboration with government counterparts. ILO has sponsored several closely controlled pilot construction projects in various countries utilizing largely labor and special equipment adopted for use with draft animals.

The UK Transportation and Road Research Laboratory (TRRL) is undertaking research on the feasibility of using a variety of in-situ materials for gravel surfacing in E. Africa and is studying the effects of various methods and degrees of compaction in an attempt to lower rural road surfacing costs.

The TRRL and MIT have both developed new models for analyzing vehicle operating costs and road wear for gravel roads with traffic in the 100 VPD and higher range.

Our firm is also rapidly gaining experience in this field and is increadingly being called upon to take the lead in assisting to find answers to the critical issues. In the last twelve months we have completed work in Haiti, Tanzania, Kenya and Ethiopia which have had as a principal focus the planning of rural feeder roads.

United States Agency for International Development has prepared new guidelines for the planning (project design) of rural development projects. These guidelines are used by USAID missions around the world and by consultants that they may employ to prepare project justifications responsive to the "Congressional Mandate" mentioned earlier and require specific consideration of most of the points raised in this paper. Included in these guidelines is a complete new section requiring social soundness analysis in the planning of all new rural projects and specific consideration of simple technology, high-labor use techniques for project execution. Consultants who have better access to the multi-discipline expertise required for these types of analysis, are increasingly being called in by USAID to prepare these projects. Furthermore, the guidelines normally require that a specific evaluation program be planned for study of the project during its construction and for several years thereafter. This includes the establishment within the implementing host government agency of an evaluation function capability. This is a recognition of the fact that there may be important lessons to be learned from careful monitoring of the project implementation and ex post facto experience, in a field where careful empirical lessons are far and few between.

In Southeast Asia AID is assisting SEATAC in financing a research study specifically directed to evaluate the impact of transportation projects in four of its member countries. Namely, the Phillipines, Malaysia, Thailand and Indonesia. Louis Berger International. Inc. has been employed as consultants to SEATAC for this study which will be launched in May. Each of these countries has organized a multi-disciplinary study team to evaluate projects in their own countries and consultants will help them develop methodology, provide training seminars and an operations manual for their guidance. The terms of reference of this study are appended to this paper.

In Upper Volta the IDA is financing a study for the purpose of evaluating the construction, maintenance and economic impact of the various road projects included in several agricultural projects financed by the IDA. In fact a great deal of the financing for rural road construction projects is subsumed under various agriculture or rural development projects. The study will serve to define the methodology to be utilized in future projects of rural road improvement in Upper Volta in order to permit an analysis of the relative advantages of several possibilities and to choose the best method of obtaining these. The study will extend over a three year period. Traffic rarely exceeds 10-15 light vehicles per day. Most of the main secondary roads are unpaved and there is a vast kilometrage of non-classified roads or tracks. The study will begin with a critique of the economic analysis that was made in the original feasibility studies, such as cost of transport, projection of traffic, and distribution of benefits, comparing these with the ex post facto situation. It will consider the mechanism by which farmers received benefits, the estimated traffic induced by the road improvement and the mechanism by which this traffic was generated. It will also evaluate certain technical engineering aspects such as the geometric characteristics that were used and their rationale, and the methods of construction used, particularly labor intensive efforts. Finally, the study will produce an adapted methodology which can be used for analysis of projects in the future. The methodology will take account of all the quantifiable aspects as well as the social variables.

REFERENCE

[1] **"Integrated Rural Development Projects: The Bank's Experience"**. Montague Yudelman, *Finance and Development,* March 1977.

ANNEX 1

Seatac study
Terms of Reference

I. The Louis Berger International, Inc. team in cooperation with SEATAC and the local study teams would undertake the intire scope of work presented in the Request for Proposal:

A. Collect copies of reports and documentation on the impact of transport investment on socioeconomic development and take account of these reports in the selection of analytical methods relevant to the ex-post analysis or the types of projects included in the study.

B. Review the extent and specific contents of the data the local study teams have collected or are collecting and recommended changes, if any.

C. Upon receipt of data collected by the local study teams, to apply the appropriate method of analysis to each of four selected transport projects to determine the impact of each investment in relieving poverty, improvement of the life of the poor and improving the socioeconomic possibilities of the area. Variations of different analytical methods may be necessary to arrive at an optimum general methodology or methodologies for the different types of transport projects. This process of selecting methodologies and their utilization will be discussed with leaders of the local study teams as training to facilitate the application of the operations manual in the respective COORDCOM member countries.

D. Present appropriate methodologies and findings from the analysis of data as well as their implications at a workshop meeting among study participants including members of local study teams.

E. Prepare a report describing the major findings of the work undertaken during Phase I of this study and to provide specific guidelines for preparation of new projects during Phase II.

F. Draft an operations manual reflecting the findings and conclusions of Phase I of the study for the use of government and other agencies responsible for transport planning and social and economic development programs in remote areas. The manual will be primarily for project preparation and will include guidelines for calculating not only the direct economic benefits of projects but also, more importantly, the impact of the project investment in relieving poverty, enhancing the quality of life of the poor, and improving the economic possibilities of the area. (This manual, may be revised in accordance with the results obtained in Phase II).

II. The work would be completed within an eight month period, utilizing approximately 20 man-months of effort.

Panel discussion

Panel discussion

Panel Members

H. J. NOORTMAN (chairman)
Director of the Netherlands Institute of Transport
The Netherlands

D. J. FRENZEL
Director of the Federal Ministry of Research and Technology
Federal Republic of Germany

M. FRYBOURG
Director of the Institute for Transport Research
France

Prof. M. L. MANHEIM
Massachusetts Institute of Technology
U.S.A.

A. SILVERLEAF
Director of the Transport and Road Research Laboratory
U.K.

A. de WAELE
Senior Administrator of the E.C.M.T.
France

C. G. HARRAL
Chief of the Transportation Research Division of the World Bank
U.S.A.

W. SUCHORZEVSKI
Deputy Director General of the Research Institute on Environmental Protection
Poland

R. P. BAFFOUR
Chairman Ghana Highway Authority
Ghana

What overall economic and social issues will be relevant in the coming decade and what is their impact on transport

Mr. Silverleaf

There are of course many major changes taking place in economic and social conditions in both developed and developing countries, which are bound to have a considerable impact on transport research in the next decade. All I will try to do is to open the discussion, and mention one or two points which seem to me to be among the more important.

The first we should recognize is that we are in a period of uncertainty. We are always in a period of uncertainty in the sense that we are quite unaware of what next year is likely to bring and it is almost invariably true that next year is different from what we expect.

But I think that we also agree that we are in a greater period of uncertainty at present than we have been for some considerable time. Certainly in the developed world. I think we are probably in a period of transition in both national attitudes and economies. There is a general feeling that the economic growth pattern of the last decade is unlikely to be repeated in the next decade. But undoubtedly we also feel that there will be differences between different countries even in the developed world within the next decade. Also there will be considerable changes in social attitudes which will reflect themselves on transport and on the research that we should carry out to help that transition most effectively.

I think that I would add only two things. The first is that there is a growing awareness that in general terms, economic and social terms, and more particularly so far as we are concerned in transport, we must pay greater attention to the very considerable disparities between the general group of developed countries and that very substantial group of developing countries. Mr. Willoughby gave us some dramatic figures which illustrate that vast gap and many of us who are familiar with that and have worked in that context feel that we can look forward in the next decade to a growing recognition of the need to pay greater attention to these disparities and to try to reduce them and hope that this will be reflected in our transport attitudes, as dr. Baffour said, making transport a world-wide responsibility.

Finally in the developed world we can look forward to a period in which there will be a greater emphasis on making the most of what we have, rather than taking it for granted that we will have resources to increase what we have already in a substantial way. We shall see it in many ways in the slowing down of car ownership rates, in the slowing down of new construction for major roads, in a much greater thoughtfulness about major investments for guided-track railways and other systems. That coupled with a growing awareness of social needs, trying to provide the transport that people want will provide a new and significantly different framework for the next decade.

Mr. Manheim

In addition to what Mr. Silverleaf has stated I would like to emphasize the particular issue of equity and the related issue of participation. The equity at a broad international scale, among regions of the world and countries at various stages of development, equity within regions of countries which was an issue clearly brought out in papers on intercity transport and in other sessions and equity within a particular region, an urban area or rural in terms of the distribution of benefits of transport among the users of different modes, among travellers for different purposes and among the operators and among those who are concerned about environmental issues.

This is an issue that becomes particularly pertinent even more in the age of uncertainty because we have seen in a number of the sessions a clear recognition of the fact that uncertainty is a certainty. But I am seriously concerned about the ability of the public to adapt to the age of uncertainty that so many of the papers of this conference have accepted as a natural event. As people are concerned about equity, who gets what benefits and at what costs and as people look at a more and more uncertain future and as they also demand more participation in the decisionmaking and more participation in the technical analysis, how much will the fear of the future change the nature of our planning and decisionmaking and the kinds of research that we should be doing.

Mr. Frybourg

Nous sommes tous conscients de l'importance des effets négatifs dan les transports de ce qu'on appelle en anglais les "adverse effects", qui portent en particulier sur les nuisances et l'environnement. Mais sans doute nous nous rendons compte mieux maintenant qu'à côté de ces effets négatifs, il y a les effets en retour, à plus long terme, non prévus, de la politique menée pour répondre à des sollicitations qui étaient claires à court terme.

C'est un phénomène que certains appelleraient de récupération, qui se fait bien souvent au profit des plus forts et au détriment des plus faibles. La recherche peut contribuer à limiter de tels effets notamment en se penchant sur la gestion des entreprises de transport, particulièrement difficile dans cette période économiquement instable, car le poids des investissements d'infrastructure rend les entreprises financièrement très vulnérables et lorsqu'on regarde les conditions de leur gestion, on constate que bien souvent, jouant avec une réglementation inadaptée et incontrôlable, ces entreprises sont en prise avec une cliéntele qui n'hésite pas à utiliser la faiblesse économique et financière du secteur pour transférer les charges sur le contribuable ou sur les plus défavorisés. Si effets en retour il y a, cela ne doit pas pour autant donner mauvaise conscience au chercheur, même si certains prétendent que bien souvent la recherche n'est pas idéologiquement neutre.

En fait les transports n'ont pas à supporter la responsabilité des changements d'orientation de la société. Ce qu'il importe pour nous c'est de déceler 'a temps ces changements d'objectifs et d'être capables d'éclairer sur l'ensemble les effets 'a long terme d'une politique dont l'oerientation à court terme est évidemment plus facile à déceler.

Mr. De Waele

Je pense que restrictions n'est pas synonyme d'incertitude. Au contraire plusieurs des restrictions, plusieurs des certitudes - c'est des certitudes négatives bien entendu - rendent les choix plus sûrs; par exemple le fait de savoir qu'il y aura moins de pétrole ne laisse plus autant de choix disponibles.

Il y a une certitude plus au moins grande sur beaucoup de faits, que ce soit sur un urbanisme, au moins pour les pays développés que nous connaissons, sur des réseaux qui existent et que nous n'allons pas fondamentalement modifier dans les années à venir, sur nos revenues sur lesquelles nous sommes à peu près fixés, sur nombre d'autres facteurs. L'incertitude à mon sens réside essentiellement dans le comportement des individus et des groupes vis-à-vis de faits qui eux sont plus ou moins prédéterminés.

Du point de vue politique une très grande importance revient à l'étude des motivations et des comportements, à savoir pourquoi la réaction est telle ou telle, et aussi à la possibilité pour les responsables d'informer le public d'une façon appropriée sur les intentions.

Mr. Frenzel

According to the general theme - transport decisions in an age of uncertainty - I am glad that there is uncertainty, because that is the demand as well as the justification for transport research.

If we were sure of what will come, we did not have to do anything. But because we are not sure, and in general we cannot be sure of tomorrow we must do something. We must act we should not react. We should not be paralyzed by the problems of today as they were in the world yesterday and will be tomorrow. But we have to do something. We should get things done and leave it to the market and to society to decide what is a good solution or what has to be abandoned. We should divide between the aspects of transportation and what is the demand and what is needed. What will people's need be tomorrow, in this changing world, what energy consumption and environmental protection, economy, and development will there be.

We should try, and try hard, to have a set of solutions or thoughts put forward to others in a political scene who have to decide what will happen. Most of the things we do today are fixed for centuries, because a new street, a new track of a railroad is a decision for 100 years at least and therefore we have to anticipate a lot in that period of uncertainty.

Mr. Baffour

There is a great deal of similarity in terms of methodologies in evaluating transport problems. The developed countries have a very highly sophisticated system of different types and about all tending towards the same system and basis, the analysis of problems, identification of the problems and the research effort, although they may vary from country to country, they all came from the very same direction and I believe the same can be said for developing countries. There are many stages of development in transport research in the developing countries. Some countries have no scientific basis at all, no personnel. Others are very much in their infancy. Others have by a system of linking with developed countries' research organizations, built up a sizable beginning which with patience and with mutual assistance and help in the right direction could rise to useful standards. In the developing countries, there is this emphasis on the need to establish research organizations to enable them to evaluate the need to establish their own systems of adapting their own material, the socio-economic basis of analysis, identification of problems of transport and for most of all the need to enhance the research efforts of these developing countries' units in order to first of all establish a state of confidence between themselves and the respective governments.

It is through the action and policies of governments that transport efforts at all can be made. Development in the direction of real transport can be achieved in these developing countries. Therefore there has been the general feeling that developed country research units should endeavour to establish links with developing countries and establish between themselves a comradery and understanding, a trust which should be mutual, which should give developed countries' research organizations the opportunities to try out their results, at the same time correcting some mistakes that have been made in the past and also encourage and enhance the image of these research organizations in developing countries such that they may achieve the confidence of their respective governments and so enable them to influence the decisions of these governments. I also can see that there is a stress to establish information centres where research findings and results may be stored, enabling developing countries to utilize these research findings of the developed countries.

Mr. Suchorzevski

I would like to express a feeling of great satisfaction because of the comprehensive approach of transport research. And I am really very proud to be a member of the group. Not always I had this feeling in the past. To illustrate the evolution I will use an example what happened about ten years ago at one of the large international meetings of transport people, both policymakers, practicians and researchers from the whole world. During the highly professional debate one of the speakers proposed that social and environmental factors should be taken into account by transport people who usually are orientated towards narrow objectives of their sector. What happened was that in the final report of this conference you could find that planners and politicians, would have to pay much more attention to social and environmental factors. The proportion of time we are devoting here to the more general objectives of transport systems gives reasons for some optimism even in this age of uncertainty.

Mr. Harral

Mr. Silverleaf and also Mr. Manheim have named 2 of the 5 principal socio and economic issues that we will be confronting in the next decade. Certainly we anticipate that the gap between rich and poor nations will grow wider. Certainly there is already set in train a greater concern for the issues of social equity, not only within nations but between nations. I would like to add to these two points three additional factors which will concern us all in the coming years. In the developing countries the problems of unemployment will be growing more severe in many cases, compelling the need for further attention to the problems of technology adaptation in the development of these countries. The efforts to stimulate income growth in the rural sector of the developing nations will certainly be intensified. Finally we must recognize that the rural urban migration process which has largely been completed in the rich nations, is only really beginning in much of the world. We can look forward perhaps with some apprehension to the development of massive cities in the poor countries which will generate enormous demands for investment funds, for development of urban infrastructure pressing still harder on the scarcity of funds in those countries.

What could be the impact of uncertainties, especially for transport and what is the way in which transport could be used as one of the instruments to cope with some of the uncertainties

Mr. Suchorzevski

We should be very cautious with solutions which are appropriate in other social and economic situations. We are in the period when we are too optimistic when looking at the methodology, techniques and tools which have been developed by research people. I might say that the main problem I am facing is how to make a proper use of these advanced sophisticated methods, techniques and tools.

It is particularly important when trying to face the problems in developing countries. I do not like the words "developing countries". It seems to me that this division of the world between developed and developing was invented by those who think that they are developed. When looking at the cultural development we would have quite different borders between different parts of the world. It reminds me of one experience I had with one of the so-called developing countries. I was visiting a group of experts and one of them was a transportation planner in this city, and I asked him what is your major problem. He said, "my problem is how to improve the vehicular traffic at this two directional road in which this vehicular traffic is to a very high extent slowed down by intensive bicycle movement". So I asked, "what are the traffic volumes," and he said, "the situation is that there are between 5 and 7 thousand bikes per hour in two directions carrying 10 to 12 thousand people". The average per bike was 1.5, much larger, than the one of the automobile. And as far as vehicular traffic is concerned there were 50 to 100 passengercars, carrying about 200 people. So the objective which was formulated by this European transport planner was how to enable these 200 people to move faster at the cost of 10.000. Are we really right in advising others to follow our common mistakes instead of thinking how to help in cultivating some elements of travel behaviour and some elements of this time of life which are sometimes more sound than advocated by so-called developed countries.

Mr. Manheim

One of the issues which clearly was raised, for example in the discussion on systems analysis in workshop 3 and cost analysis in session 3:4, was that of uncertainty. They also pointed in some directions in which transport research could attempt to deal with uncertainty such as through first of all explicitly recognizing that uncertainty exists and admitting it in our research and planning studies.

Secondly trying to quantify uncertainties, to put ranges on it and third to try to find designs that can be capable of dealing with uncertainty. The chairman of this particular workshop used the phrase designs that can be modified as construction proceeds or after it is completed to adapt to conditions departing from original assumptions. I would like to extend that thought but I think the way it was phrased, designs that can be modified, implies that we are dealing primarily with infrastructural improvements. But in fact a key element of developing transport strategies that are flexible in the face of uncertainty, is through institutional innovations, designing organizations which can deliver a variety of different transport services to a variety of different means. The infrastructure can also be progressively upgraded over time and so this clearly is a very important area of research. How to design organizations in developed countries as well as developing countries which can grow and change adaptively in the face of uncertainty as the needs of the users and as the concerns of the public change over time. We have, in the transport sector, very unflexible organizations and in another workshop on systems analysis and planning there was a very clear concern that the planning process itself has to recognize this and as a consequence becomes much more focussed on short range operational planning, to the total neglect of long-term consequences.

Mr. Frybourg

Je crois qu'il faut distinguer, dans les incertitudes que nous rencontrons, deux niveaux et pour chacun de ces niveaux les contremesures que nous pouvons adopter sont différentes. Le premier niveau concerne les paramètres extérieurs au transport, qu'ils soient économiques, démographiques ou sociaux. La connaissance de cette incertitude nous conduit évidemment à donner moins d'importance peut-être à une planification fine à long terme, pour se concentrer davantage sur les étapes intermédiaires et les aménagements progressifs.

Je crois également qu'il faut que nous développions les méthodes interactives ou itératives, et il faut, pour bien suivre ces cheminements, ne pas éviter la recherche sur les rapports de force dans le processus des décisions et spécialement la signification des conflicts dont l'aménagement de l'espace et les transports sont l'enjeu. C'est à travers cette recherche de type institutionnel que l'on pourra développer la nécessaire relation entre la politique et la technique. Le deuxième niveau d'incertitude concerne les méthodes scientifiques dont nous disposons. La diversité des méthodes qui ont été exposées ici, montre à quel point actuellement les experts s'interrogent sur la nécessaire refonte de la méthodologie dont nous disposons.

Nous avons notamment vu triompher les modèles dits désagrégés, mais si nous poussons la désagrégation jusqu'à sa limite, c'est la notion même de modèle qui est mise en cause. Il faudrait, pour nous permettre de progresser dan nos méthodes d'investigations, que nous améliorions la collecte et la mise en ordre des données de base. Celles existantes reflètent trop les préoccupations internes, commerciales et financières des exploitants de transport; elles sont souvent difficiles à utiliser pour la recherche, particulièrement intermodale. On a pu même constater dans certains cas que les données nécessaires pour la recherche ne sont pas disponibles, car elles ne correspondent pas à des préoccupations de gestion sectorialisée.

Mr. Silverleaf

You asked me how we saw the impact of transport on the economic and social changes which we were discussing. From the papers given to the conference, from the discussions, from the summaries that we have had from chairmen of sessions, I draw certain general conclusions which may not be supported of course by everyone. The first is that I see a declining perhaps even a terminating trend and that is the belief in high technology as providing a major contribution to the solution of transport problems. We can see this throughout the world in urban transport in developed countries and equally perhaps in road construction methods for developing countries. It is perhaps however more true for ground transport than it is for air and sea transport, where I think there is still probably a higher belief in advanced technology as a natural continuing trend. Secondly in contrast I see a growing trend in making the best possible use of what we have and that means as Mr. Manheim was saying a move from interest and investment in infrastructure towards operational procedures.

I think that there has been throughout our conference a recognition that in transport and in transport research, we are paying much more attention now in the last few years towards moving people and goods rather than counting vehicles and finally we can see a clear recognition that transport decisions and investment must be related more closely than in the past to broader policies, both urban policies and rural development policies and that I am sure that we shall find a growing recognition of the need not to consider transport as an end in itself or as a stimulance in itself but as part of a much more comprehensive group of development investments.

Mr. De Waele

La politique des transports des dernières années n'a pas résolu grand chose. Comme vous le saves très bien, le problème des chemins de fer s'est aggravé, le problème de nos villes s'est aggravé, le problème des subsides s'est aggravé, tous les problèmes se sont aggravés. Donc, il ne fallait même pas une crise ou ce que vous appelez l'incertitude pour avoir des préoccupations politiques et par conséquent de appuis dans la recherche. Mais cependent il y a quelques élements neufs qui m'autorisent a peut-être proposer des thèmes de réflexions qui de toutes les manières complètent ou soulignent simplement ce qu'ont dit mes collègues déjà. En effet ces dernières années au niveau de nos budgets d'Etat, nous constatons un transfert assez sensible de moyens en faveur d'une priorité que nous avons dû donner à l'objectif social parce qu'il s'agissait de maintenir le pouvoir d'achat d'une partie de la population qui risquait de s'appauvrir ou même de n'avoir plus d'emplois du tout.

Ce qui a eu comme contrepartie par exemple que dans becaucoup de nos pays à un certain moment le trafic de marchandises a sérieusement diminué tandis que le trafic de voyageurs a continué d'augmenter.

Ce qui a comme conséquence également que très souvent au niveau de l'individu, le citoyen n'est pas conscient de la crise que connaissent seulement les entreprises et les Etats. C'est une réalité très importante qui a comme conséquence que les investissements devront être sélectionnés par des critères plus affinés. il s'y ajoute le renchérissement du transport qui intervient à un moment particulièrement fâcheux pour des raisons de coûts de la main d'oeuvre et là il y a peut-être un thème à développer beaucoup à l'avenir. C'est l'économie des trois-quart du coût des transports. Nous avons écrit des bibliothèques sur l'infrastructure, sur des choses tout à fait subsidiaires, mais la part essentielle du transport, c'est l'homme, c'est une énergie qui aux chemins de fer coûte douze fois plus que l'énergie dont nous ne cessons de parler et qui en termes constants n'a pas varié pendant les dernières années en effet la main d'oeuvre en 1970 comme en 1975 coûte aux chemins de fer 10 à 12 fois plus que l'énergie proprement dite. C'est donc là un thème de recherche.

Mr. Harral

On the basic question what is the impact of transportation on the social and economic problems of the next decade the main point I would like to indicate is the emphasis and the role that transportation development will play in developing rural sectors in the poor countries. Certainly we foresee a major increase in infrastructural investment in that particular area but we have to look beyond just transportation to the other sectors and the complementary investments and services which must be provided.

Mr. Baffour

There is a steady decline in the foreign currency earnings in most of the developing countries for reasons other than transportation.

There is a steady drift from the rural areas to urban centres, imposing considerable strain on existing transport, particularly with respect to road transport, and its effect on agricultural and other infrastructural work development in the developing countries. I foresee a greater need for investment to increase the social and economic standing of rural areas to reverse the drift, to improve transportation, the distribution of commodities, particularly for the feeding of the people, which is essential to any meaning of development at all in a developing country. This would claim priority of attention to subsidizing transport and so the need for a long term planning in developing countries, the planning of roads becomes of great importance because it might be necessary and I think it is essential for a country to spend more for constructing better roads of lasting value, than short term planning involving extensive amounts of money annually in repairing and maintaining poor quality roads.

Mr. Frenzel

We do not have many possibilities for new main lines we can follow up, especially in the much developed countries. We have so much infrastructure, we have so many operating organizations, most people are used to use traffic and transport systems. Traffic and transport is no matter for specialists, everyone uses it every day so we must make clear what we think, what politicians should think and what people wish to have, and these wishes should be identified.

Mr. P. Patin, France

Je suis venu à cette conférence mondiale sur la recherche dans les transports un peu sur la foi du titre et sur la foi du menu. En ce qui concerne le titre je pense que quelqu'un qui nous verrait de l'extérieur se demanderait si la recherche dans les transports est vraiment limitée à la politique et à la socio-économie. La technique, on n'en a pas parlé, je pense qu'on ne devrait pas en parler beaucoup, mais peut-être aurait-on pu y faire quelques allusions.

Je suis venu aussi, je le dis, en fonction du menu et justement je reste un peu sur ma faim, pour conserver une comparaison gastronomique.

Précisément je m'attendais à ce qu'on nous donne des directives. Tout à l'heure je crois que c'est monsieur Silverleaf qui a parlé d'une baisse dans la confiance dans la technique. Pendant quelques années, dans la dernière décennie, on a laissé faire les techniciens.

Les techniciens commencent par inventer et ensuite construisent un moyen de transport autour de leur invention. Ce n'est pas une bonne méthode.

J'ai un peu l'impression que les problèmes n'ont pas été posés. Le rôle des politiciens c'est de se tourner vers nous, techniciens, en disant ce qu'il faut faire.

Faut-il que nous donnions par exemple en matière de transport urbain de la vitesse, du confort, de la capacité, de la fréquence? Nous ne le savons pas. En matière de transport interurbain, faut-il donner de la vitesse, faut-il faire de l'économie d'énergie, faut-il faire de l'économie de personnel comme Monsieur de Waele l'a dit tout à l'heure, nous ne le savons pas. Tout à l'heure Monsieur de Waele a parlé du coût du personnel. Biens sûr c'est 12 fois celui de l'énergie mais si nous prenons les pays dits en voie de développements, ils ont de l'énergie, ils ont du personnel et en général le personnel ne risque pas de manquer, au contraire, il y a du chômage.

Par contre, l'énergie commence à manquer partout. Alors que faut-il faire? Est-ce le personnel ou l'énergie qu'il faut économiser? Voilà toutes sortes de questions que nous nous posons et sur ces questions il me semble que nous restons un peu sans réponse.

Mr. M. Esteve Rios, Spain

J'approuve Monsieur Patin à propos du fait qu'ici il manque l'étude de quelques problèmes que je trouve fondamentaux. Tous ces modèles sont très bien structurés, très bien étudiés, mais je crois que la plupart oublient une chose fondamentale. Au moment d'appliquer ces modèles il y a une institution, il y a un gourverment qui exprime ses choix limités d'investissement. A mon avis la plupart des modèles, des idées qui sont exposées ici, ont oblié d'une façon assez nette tous les aspects économiques-financiers qui amènent à la réalité un projet concret.

Mr. K. Vonk, The Netherlands

We are sure that the world is moving and is moving rather quickly. There will be a certain shortage of materials, of energy; there is a shortage of money - inflation is a shortage of money - and that action is needed in a rather short time.

Politicians are not free in their choice, they are free to choose for confusion or for a certain equilibrium but that is the choice they have to make.

Research has to make clear to politicians that they are very limited in the possibility of choice if they want to avoid confusion. Research should not only deal with economic matters and technology but also with organization, organization of public matters, to bring together the development of law and the development of law at a point of social organization, the development of economic decision and the decisions about technology. These are three main points and if they are not followed, we are up to confusion within a decade what depends on the situation in the different countries and the different regions.

Mr. G. C. Meeuse, The Netherlands

Transportation is moving with a break-neck speed from bottleneck to bottleneck. I have learned much of the break-neck speed these days. The bottle-necks have been touched on briefly in this conference.

I should like to emphasize that in the coming decade more emphasis should be put on another aspect of transportation.

Transportation includes the movement, the conveyance, the transhipment and the storage. So trade transport models should include the storage aspects, because these could affect in a considerable way the reduction of waste of materials and of values, being the inventories, the stocks which are all around the world and which can be minimized considerably if transportation is developed in an optimization model.

Mr. L. Sjoestedt, Sweden

Is the adaptivity of the research society itself large enough to cope with a period of rapidly changing priorities. I should like to illustrate that with one example. During the last ten years there has been a great interest in developing completely new systems for transport, requiring also completely new infrastructure. But as Mr. Silverleaf stated, the interest in such new systems has diminished rather rapidly, which means that we are now interested in improving the existing systems.

This means that we are no longer dealing with complete systems, we are dealing with components of systems. And this changes very much the demand for professional skill from the research society. At least in Sweden we have noted that we now have a much greater demand for mechanical engineers than for civil engineers. And without going too much into this I think this might have someting to do with these changed priorities.

Mr. A. Hussain, Irac

I want to make a comment on the attitude of transport planners and transport industry. I think there is one aspect which the transport industry has to look at in more detail and that is the depletion of resources. In the field of transportation, the traffic engineer, the transportation planner, the manufacturers and the decisionmakers are responsible for creating new standards. If we take as an example the energy use in urban areas and look at the way the energy resources are used by the vehicles, little has been done. Research has not concentrated on this matter. There are some institutes e.g. the TRRL that are doing research on commercial vehicles, the hauling system, that is using energy to its optimum.

Is it using this energy in the right way? So many resources are depleted. I can not see that there is an acceptance or an intensification of research in this field and I do feel that there is a need to broaden the field of the traffic engineer and the transport planner in this respect.

Mr. Suchorzevski

From the point of view of somebody who takes part in the research establishment in the field of urban transportation in my country and being to some extent responsible for the assignment of resources to different projects I am of such an opinion:

A lot of money has been spent during the last dozen or so years for about 500 products, aiming at the development of completely new or almost new innovative transport systems or elements of these systems.

And now we are in the situation of a great disappointment of the results which we achieved from new innovative systems as far as energy consumption is concerned. We can spend 10 or 100 times more energy if we accept some of these solutions or inventions.

Therefore an emphasis has been put to software solutions rather than to hardware solutions.

Mr. Frybourg

Je voudrais également intervenir sur ce thème de la recherche technique. Monsieur Patin, à juste titre, a constaté une absence quasi-complète d'interventions sur ce sujet, qui est bien un sujet de recherche dans les transports et cela tient notamment à une participation certainement insuffisante des industries du matériel de transport. Nous aurions souhaité que des chercheurs appartenant à cette industrie puissent davantage participer et c'est un point que nous devons garder en mémoire pour les prochaines manifestations. Cependant en restant au niveau de ce que certains appellent les caractéristiques fonctionelles des systèmes de transports qui permettent d'orienter la recherche technique, certaines interventions ont confirmé plutôt qu'apporté des idées nouvelles sur ce qui peut être fait pour orienter cette recherce. Nous savions que dans le domaine des transports collectifs il est impossible pour fixer les performances de ne considérer que le seul véhicule. Il faut tenir compte également des conditions d'exploitation de ce véhicule, notamment des flottes et de la politique tarifaire, et il faut également tenir compte bien sûr des possibilités d'insertion de l'infrastructure. En dehors des difficultés financières qui certainement vont limiter les possibilités de réalisations de systèmes entièrement nouveaux, par rapport à la situation que nous avions connue dans les dix dernières années, il est clair que les systèmes de transports nouveaux, qui reposaient sur des infrastructures entièrement nouvelles et une automatisation très poussée, rencontrent des difficultés pour leur déploiement en site réel à cause des réticences des populations de voir insérer en surface une infrastructure entièrement nouvelle, et bien entendu de la baisse de motivations pour les objectifs d'automatisation, à un moment où les perspectives de l'emploi son préoccupantes. Cependant, et ce point a été clairement établi, les gouvernements s'efforcent de ne pas fermer prématurément les voies prometteuses et par conséquent continuent à financer certaines recherches d'amont sur des composants ou des sous-ensembles des systèmes de transport qui sont apparus comme particulièrement importants, à l'occasion des développements passés sur les systèmes automatiques à cabine. Et cette recherche sur les composants qui n'engagent pas des moyens financiers considérables, si nous réussissons à la maintenir active, aura ce mérite d'avoir éventuellement des possibilités d'application sur les systèmes classiques existants, car les recherches sur les composants ne sont pas liées à un système particulier, et de permettre si les conditions évoluent, de redémarrer des travaux sur des systèmes entièrement nouveaux. Il est donc important de maintenir vivant le potentiel scientifique qui a été éveillé au cours de ces dix dernières années sur le thème des transports terrestres collectifs, thème qui avait été pour le moins délaissé dans

651

le passé, mais pour le maintenir vivant il faudra certainement davantage le concentrer sur les composants et les sous-ensembles que sur les systèmes entièrement nouveaux.

Mr. Manheim

I think the question raised by mr. Sjoestedt is one that ought to be one of the main focal points of the discussion. Does the research community and the institutions in which we participate have the capability to adjust to a new era of dynamic change. Can we start searching for The single technology or The magic number of desired speed, can we stop searching for The best plan for the year 2000, can we stop training ourselves to only build facilities or build equipment instead. Can we design organizations. Can we, who are teachers or administrators educate students and personnel to be comfortable with a world in which there are no definite answers, in which next year's problems, next years services, next year's budget and next year's organization may be very different from this year?

Mr. Frenzel

I will try to give some remarks to the question of energy.

There are a lot of studies as well as real improvements where we can improve existing sytems or implement systems of less energy consumption. On the other hand there are some alternatives, for instance for fuels, on an other basis then crude oil, hydrogin for instance.

Furthermore not by improving technology the best reduction of energy consumption can be found but in changing the organization of traffic and transportation of today as well as the behaviour of the users.

At least there are thoughts to solve the problems, to totally abandon traffic and transportation. For instance by new means as broad-band communication; no physical communication as in traffic and transportation.

I do not know whether it is possible to have meetings, not by sitting together physically but by telecommunication.

These are possibilities which have been studied and will be studied but there is no solution immediately as well as there is no solution immediately of these new technologies which were debated some years ago.

Mr. Silverleaf

I would like to return to the question Mr. Sjoestedt asked, a key question, which effects many of us here as individuals and to which prof. Manheim added a few essential comments.

Can the transportation research community cope with the rapidly changing situation in which it has found itself and will find itself. Perhaps because I am an optimist by nature I want to give an unqualified yes to that question as an answer. I believe that the answer depends perhaps more than anything else on two factors.

The quality of the research workers in transport and not their initial disciplines and secondly the quality of the research managers, preferably in the research institutes. Many of you will know that the laboratory or research institute of which I am director has a staff of over 1000 and during the past ten years we have made, what we believe to be, radical changes in the nature and extent of our programme of work.

A whole new transport group e.g. has been essentially formed within that decade. But also we have changed the nature of the work in the traditional areas very considerably. All of it is now very much more policy-oriented, than project-oriented or technology-oriented. And we have done this partly by recruiting new people and expanding the range of disciplines within the staff so that we have now sociologists as well as medical staff, as well as engineers, mathematicians and physicists. But we have done it more I think by changing the activities of those who came in with a totally or very considerably different purpose from that which they are now pursuing.

What we need to know is the direction in which we should go. We must have new directions, new policy objectives clearly set for us and sometimes also new criteria of success. I think if you had been working in technological research there is a natural assumption that if the child you create is not adopted by someone else and brought up and expanded, that you have failed. I do not believe that. Even in technological research if your research has shown clearly what would be involved in implementing the results of that research, so that the decision can then be made not to implement it and that decision is broadly and soundly based, you have succeeded as a research worker. Now that is an attitude that we have had to introduce and to convince many of our staff a few years ago when one or two projects on which many had worked hard were shelved, they felt they had failed. I do not believe that they feel the same way now. Provided what they do is properly recognized, they can feel a proper sense of success and are ready to move into new fields, new attitudes, new approaches.

Mr. Noortman

We were talking about the economic and social issues that will be of relevance in the coming decade and we discussed too the impact of these issues on our transport system and vice versa, the impact of transport on the economic and environmental development.

Now I would like to raise another point, namely given what was discussed before, do we have a reason to change the priorities in research compared to what has been done up to now. And in the second place is there enough communication between the research people and the decisionmakers to be sure that an optimum use is made of the know-how that is available and if not what measures should be taken to improve the situation.

Mr. Manheim

It is important to note that the discussion before the break did not imply a negative feeling but a positive feeling of a real challenge in terms of research priorities. There is a very important challenge in terms of adapting our research directions to these new circumstances or perhaps not so new as mr. Silverleaf insisted. Mr. Meeuse for example talked about the storage of goods and there were papers in some of the sessions e.g. on rail systems research talking about the more effective utilization of existing resources, rail vehicles etc.

The same kind of research can be done in bus fleet management, in truck fleet management and looking at integrated multi-modal systems with a primary emphasis on the impact of service on users and of costs to the operator and with an emphasis on finding innovative ways to improve the operation of a system effectively. That is a very interesting research challenge in both the public and the private sectors, which requires new kinds of approaches, new methodologies, substantial new data; that is a very exciting opportunity. This reaches into the design of specific methods within operating organizations for utilizing this research and methods for getting this research established, accepted by the staff of operating organizations.

That to me is also an interesting research challenge which I find exciting and not negative.

Mr. Silverleaf

I like to agree very strongly with prof. Manheim. In

fact I was surprised when Mr. Eldin suggested that there was a malaise among research workers. I certainly do not detect that in my own group and in any people I meet and I very much doubt that many of you here feel that transport research is in a bad way in that sense. I believe that there will be quite significant continuing changes in the directions of research and in research priorities. This morning at one of the sessions Mr. Hetman from OECD used a phrase about societal approach to technological problems. I think that perhaps this is a little too broad and equally perhaps a little too narrow, but I think that it does generally express the broad direction in which transport research will continue to go in the next decade. It will really be a societal approach to a wide range of technical and operational problems which will differ in emphasis according to the nature of the society for which the solutions are required.

We will not forget some of the key differences between developed and developing countries. That distinction of course being made only in economic terms and no other way. But I believe that broadly speaking this is the sort of way in which we would go. I will be a little more specific and quote two or three examples. One is the greater emphasis on finding improved operational methods for conventional means of transport, both in urban and in rural situations. There will be a need for research to give us a better understanding of individual transport requirements and equally how to aggregate these in a way which will lead to socially acceptable policies. The third point I would mention is perhaps a negative one. I think that in setting our research priorities within a broad transport in the next few years, we need to avoid to put an excessive emphasis on what appears to be very major problems at the moment. It may turn out to be no more than transient difficulties. As we have been reminded not only does transport itself has a long time history but so does transport research. And I believe that we could make the mistake of concentrating too much attention on problems which are not perhaps as important as they seem. There I suggest that energy requirements for transport come into that category. I have myself never believed even when I did fail to get any petrol for my own car for a couple of days, that there was a crisis of the kind that was being described. I believe it illustrates one of our dangers but we do not think sufficiently about identifying the broad long term purposes of our research and which could easily be diverted into short term irrelevances.

If we do that we will fail to put enough effort into what may really be the basic enduring problems.

Mr. Baffour

There is a serious challenge to research work in developing countries. Particularly more at this time than later because we are faced with the problem of laying down higher standards and producing better results, utilizing research findings more closely than before.

It was comparatively recently that heavy equipment has come into use for roadbuilding, therefore placing emphasis on specialization, mechanical engineering, handling of equipment and managerial organization.

The unfortunate situation is, that the governments of developing countries as I said before, are finding it extremely difficult to finance these new roads, because it does really mean that what they would spend on these roads will have to be taken out of other priorities in the socio-economic situation of the countries. And therefore it does mean that research has got to go in the direction of finding substitutes for materials that have to be imported.

These are the challenges that face research organizations in developing countries and what I know of them is that they are equal to the task but a great deal more depends on what assistance they can get in the way of exchanging experience with research organizations in developed countries.

Mr. Frybourg

Mon intervention portera sur deux points, le transport international et les modèles. A l'occasion d'une conférence mondiale, il me paraît normal de mettre l'accent sur le problème du transport international.

Il fait appel à de nombreux acteurs, les états, les transporteurs, les chargeurs, les pays développés et les pays en voie de développement. Le transport international est le support d'objectifs nombreux, le commerce extérieur, moyen du développement économique, l'indépendance, la possibilité pour les Etats de contribuer, en conservant leur spécificité, au progrès mondial. Les transformations dans l'économie mondiale permettent d'espérer l'apparition de pôles de développement dans des zones jusqu'alors considerées comme sous-développées, en Asie, au Moyen-Orient, en Amérique du Sud et dans certaines parties de l'Afrique.

Cette émergence est la condition d'un rééquilibre du transport international. Elle permet d'éviter un protectionnisme qui n'a plus toujours l'excuse de la faiblesse et qui aurait érigé un nouvel ordre coûteux pour tous. Mais encore faut-il que tous les forts anciens et nouveaux acceptent une reglémentation qui réduirait les désordres cycliques et les effets de domination qui ne manqueront pas de s'excercer à l'égard de ceux qui restent faibles. Il y a là un domaine privilégié pour la recherche qu'il me paraît utile de mettre en évidence.

La deuxième intervention concerne les modèles qui ont toujours fait la joie des chercheurs. En bien ces modèles devront pour l'avenir davantage intégrer les informations provenant du fonctionnement actuel des transports et de leur évolution récente. Il faut donc rapprocher plus que nous l'avons fait dans le passé ce que l'on a appelé la planification opérationnelle et les grandes fresques de l'organisation de l'espace à un horizon éloigné. Pour cela nous savons que nous manquons encore cruellement de données adaptées à l'approche plurimodale, qui s'impose si l'on veut continuer à donner à l'analyse des systèmes de transport et de leur interaction avec l'organisation de l'espace, l'ambition et le sens qui nous paraîssent indispensables à une meilleure insertion des transports dans les objectifs généraux de la collectivité.

Mr. De Waele

A la première question, j'ai répondu tout à l'heure. Je repète donc brièvement que les priorités de recherche à mon sens sont surtout dans la direction des études de motivations et dans la recherche d'une amélioration de l'information.

Mais pour moi le grand problème est celui de la communication entre la recherche et la décision: identifier d'abord le décideur ou celui qu'on appelle décideur, parce que en effet on appelle parfois décideurs une personne qui ne prend pas jamais de décisions. Cela peut être également la définition de l'homme politique, celui qui ne prend pas de décisions. C'est la remarque que Monsieur Patin nous a faite tout à l'heure: mais au lieu de supposer tout ce que les décideurs auraient pu demander, est-ce que il n'aurait pas été possible de le demander aux décideurs eux-mêmes.

Dans un gouvernement il y a à peine un ministre qui ne soit pas concerné par les problèmes de transport. Même ceux de l'agriculture et de l'éducation, ont de très bonnes raisons de s'occuper du transport. Ceci est un premier problème tout à fait typique des transports. Il faut savoir ensuite si ce sont les ministres qui prennent ces décisions, ou si ce sont les groupes de pression derrière les ministres, à quel niveau le parlement travaille encore. Il faut également se demander quelle est la relation ministre-fonctionnaire. Bref il faudrait pratiquement démonter tout le rouage d'une société bloquée pour voir comment se prennent les décisions, si on en prend encore et si en fait nous ne sommes pas plutôt propulsés par une série d'automatismes que nous avons créés. Pour ma part je pense que ce que nous appelons déjà depuis quelque temps incertitude, est essentiellement de la confusion politique, voire même de l'irresponsabilité institutionelle. Je voudrais quand même essayer de réprondre à la question, à supposer qu'il ait une identification des décideurs: que doit être le contact alors entre le décideurs et le chercheur? Puisque nous sommes dans des mutations rapides et que de toute façon le décideur est régulièrement confronté à des échéances électorales, je pense qu'il sera essentiellement concerné par des problèmes à moyen terme. Et il ne faut pas que le chercheur se trouve particulièrement vulgaire si on lui demande ce que peut faire un ministre, lorsqu'il n'a pas beaucoup d'argent, lorsque le problème est urgent et lorsque il voudrait quand même faire quelque chose. Je crois que ce sont des problèmes très intéressants et que par là le chercheur peut se rendre utile, indispensable ou tout simplement crédible, beaucoup plus qu'avec des démonstrations très savantes de grandes formules qui n'intéressent plus les ministres.

Mr. Harral

I will be a bit more specific and run over a list of several items that are of great importance for research on the problems of transportation in developing countries. These really constitute four broad headings of engineering research on low cost technologies, management research and management economic research, broader studies on the socio-economic impact of investments and finally urban problems.

Addressing first the issue of technological research for low cost and appropriate technologies I might like to take exception to certain of the remarks of my distinguished panel member Mr. Baffour on the issue of how to design strategies. There has been in recent years a great deal of research set in motion which will be continuing at least for another 5 years on the whole issue of highway design and making strategies looking at the costs of construction, maintenance and vehicle operating costs and attempting to identify economically appropriate or optimal design and maintenance strategies. I would like to submit that we do not yet know definitively the answer to the question that Mr. Baffour raised.

Is it in fact better to build roads to very high standards initially and in effect capitalize future maintenance cost streams or rather to build on very low standards and have to worry with the future maintenance. I might suggest that in the course of coping with uncertainties in transport and road investments one of the major tools we have is in fact time staging of investments. And certainly this is an important element in road construction policies.

There is the issue of the transferability of the research that has been set on the way in Kenya, Brasil and India and in other countries in the developing world and I might add that the research probably has almost as much meaningfulness for the rich countries of the world than for the poor countries, when we look at the poor state of knowledge, of management decisionmaking tools in establishing the levels of highway maintenance which is just as poor in the rich countries as it is in the low income countries.

The second area is the issue of appropriate factor mix in the various facets. We have looked at the issue of construction of infrastructure, where we have in fact found that more labour intensive methods would appear to be economically feasible potentially in at least some 40 or 60 countries of the world. The next decade really should see the completion of several demonstration projects in various countries which will be the ultimate test of the feasibility of these methods in the developing world today.

Finally in the area of low cost technology I must draw attention to the problem of rural transport. Take countries such as India for example with one of the world's largest railway systems. Still the major mode of transportation there is the bullock cart. In other countries in Africa and Latin America, animals and indeed human porterage are still significant means of transport in rural areas. There is need for investigation of the technological alternative, not advanced technology but the very simplest technology that helps to solve the problems of rural transportation.

Shifting now to the second broad area of management and economics research, I would merely call attention to the need for further integrated studies of the transportation process from the original manufacturer to the recipient of goods, a neglected dimension in the first half of the panel session. We do anticipate increasing specialization, a growing role of the developing countries in the manufacturing of many products.

The development of systems suitable for rapid transportation of manufactured products is something that must receive some attention. Also in this general area of research, the whole problem of subsidization of transportation. What is the role of railways, what is the role of public transport, what are the circumstances under which we feel it economically appropriate to consider the allocation of extremely scarce resources to the area of subsidizing modes of transport which would not otherwise be viable.

The third general area to which I would like to call attention is the problem of measuring the socio-economic impact of rural roads and rural investment generally. As I indicated earlier this is a major field of increasing emphasis in the developing world and further attention is needed there. I think it emerged from this conference that theoretical models of analysis have generally gone beyond the state of the data base and further understanding of these problems can really come about only through development of institutions for collection of primary data on the underlined phenomena.

Finally the issue of urban problems as we have indicated. The cities will be growing enormously, unlike the cities of Europe which are in a static situation. Therefore there are both opportunities and need for the research on land use planning and control as a measure for reducing transport demand. There is a need for further research on the role of public transport particularly as it effects the poor people and finally the role of the bicycle.

The poorest people in these countries will not have access to unsubsidized motorized transport. And measures to enhance the feasibility of the use of the bicycle in urban transport is perhaps one of the more important areas of urban transport research.

Mr. J. H. Doyen, World Bank

There is one assumption that seems to be prevalent among the panel members as well as the conference. Transport infrastructure is there and is taken for granted. The problem is to limit its expansion or to guide it and to use it to the best benefit of the people.

Now this may be very well so in the situation of the so-called developed world but it is far from being so in the situation of the developing countries. They are still struggling very hard with the establishment of their basic infrastructure. Not only the establishment but also the maintenance of their basic infrastructure. And my conviction from working in these countries is that it will be increasingly difficult for these countries to expand the highway infrastructure which accounts for 80% in most of the countries for the freight and passenger transport. Not to expand this infrastructure but to conserve it. In many countries the highway infrastructure that is the primary network is regressing. I can name Peru, I can certainly name Zaire, a country which has gone through the various ranges of the developing process. And why is this happening?

Because the costs of maintaining the infrastructure which has been built cheaply as Dr. Baffour mentioned, are increasing. The traffic is increasing rapidly and so are the constant costs for the infrastructure just to be maintained in many countries. This would imply an increase in budget appropriation for strict maintenance and conservation of existing infrastructure to 10 to 15% per year.

There is tremendous pressure on the budget in these countries and the country cannot afford this. As a result in many countries, especially over the last 5 years, we have seen that there is a process of regression; what used to be paved roads are now gravel roads, roads which used to be graveled are now regressing to a state of deteriorated earth roads. And now this is giving particular relevance to the subject of research which Mr. Harral mentioned. The problem of managing a highway network, how to conserve this network from the point of view of government. There is so much money available, what should we do with it.

Should we put all in maintenance, should we do a mixture of rehabilitation and maintenance, should we wait until all the roads are down the drain and then rebuild them. This is a very real problem and it is not an isolated one and it is a problem which I can only propose as a subject which needs acute research. The problem what is the best use of a limited amount of money.

The other question which I feel should be the subject of particular attention in developing countries is the problem of the trucking industry, which accounts for sometimes more than 80% of the freight transport. Trucking industry has developed in an unregulated environment, an environment of regulation not being enforced. Now the problem of renewing the stock, expanding it to meet the demand implies the use of scarce foreign exchange resources.

How to manage the trucking industry? How much should be regulated and what is the experience in other countries?

Another problem is the partitioning of the trucking industry. There is a very modern part which is intermodal, the container and the trailer trucks, which are very expensive and foreign owned and foreign operated and on the other side you have very small truckers which have a very low loading factor. How to integrate this best. Tremendous saving can be achieved there.

Speaker's name unknown

J'interviens comme ressortissant d'un pays pour lequel les problèmes de transport ont une importance majeure. Il s'agit de l'Empire centrafricain, pays enclavé situé à 1.200 kms de l'Océan Atlantique et auquel tout ce qui est importation et exportation se solde par des coûts très élévés. Je suis venu à cette conférence comme profane car personellement je ne suis pas versé dans ce domaine très technique que j'ai suivi depuis hier avec beaucoup d'intérêt. J'ai été donc désigné par mon gouvernement pour suivre ces débats et ensuite faire rapport sur les conclusions qui en seront tirées.

L'impression d'abord que j'ai, à la lecture du titre, est une sorte de découragement car on parle des décisions sur les transports dans un période d'incertitude. Et il a été développé beaucoup de points d'incertitude. Mais j'ai en même temps tiré beaucoup de réconfort à la lecture de la deuxième part du titre -conférence *mondiale* sur la recherche dans les transports.

Je me permets de dire à mon niveau que la recherche en matière de transport, contrairement à ce qui a pu être dit, a beaucoup d'avenir, de perspectives, et M. Frybourg disait tout à l'heure en parlant de transports internationaux, que justement vous aviez beaucoup à faire. Aujourd'hui on parle de restructurer le monde, on parle d'un nouvel ordre économique international et un monde dans lequel on espère que chaque Etat apportera sa contribution de par ses ressources naturelles etc. Aujourd'hui on se plaint de manque d'énergie. Mais le manque d'énergie n'est pas certain car il y a encore des pays dont les ressources énergétiques ne sont pas encore exploitées. Ces pays ne demandent qu'à être développés dans leurs moyens de transport pour que à leur tour ils puissent apporter leur contribution. On a parlé des difficultés bien sûr dans le transport urbain des pays Européens. Mais dans d'autres pays, la plupart des pays d'Afrique, d'Asie et d'Amérique, ce n'est pas seulement le transport urbain, c'est le transport rural, c'est le transport pour développer l'économie nationale, et cela est vrai plus particulièrement pour les pays enclavés dans l'Afrique et il y en a un certain nombre, comme le Niger, le Mali, la Haute-Volta, le Burundi, le Rwanda, l'Ouganda, le Centrafrique etc. et en Amérique également; ces pays-là, quoique actuellement dits sous-développés, ont en réalité des potentialités que demain peuvent contribuer à l'enrichissement du monde. On peut ajouter aussi une note d'utopie. Je pense que les chercheurs devraient être considérés un peu comme des utopistes et dans cette perspective je ne pense pas qu'on puisse voir la chose avec pessimisme.

Et je dis donc, comme l'a dit tout à l'heure Monsieur de Waele, que peut-être il y a des difficultés qu'il faut résoudre du côté des gouvernements. Il y a des problèmes politiques et des problèmes financiers, mais il y a peut-être aussi lieu de penser également au statut des chercheurs; il serait peut-être intéressant de trouver un statut international pour les chercheurs qui seraient indépendants des gouvernements et qui pourraient alors faire des recherches sur les routes dans les pays riches, dans les villes etc. et qui constitueraient une banque de données dans laquelle les Etats iraient puiser suivant le cas.

On pourrait donc concevoir dans cette perspective d'un nouvel ordre économique international que les chercheurs indépendants -vous êtes certes indépendants, mais il faut tenir compte des enveloppes financières qu'on vous propose- internationaux et non représentants de tel institut national, mettent à la disposition des gouvernements des données exploitables, suivant les moyens financiers et les données politiques de chacun, pour contribuer à leur développement. On doit concevoir le développement du transport comme lié au développement des Etats, comme lié à l'établissement d'un nouvel ordre économique mondial et dans cette optique, les chercheurs dans le domaine du transport international ont beaucoup à faire et on peut leur souhaiter bonne route.

Mr. D. L'Huillier France

J'ai l'impression que si on pouvait arriver à cette conférence avec l'idée que le transport était en accusation, on a tendance à terminer avec l'idée que la recherche dans les transports est, elle, en accusation. Je ne pense pas qu'il faille quand même faire preuve d'un peu trop de masochisme, tout n'est pas perdu. Je pense surtout que nous avons réalisé peut-être un peu tard que le transport en lui-même dans l'activité économique et sociale est un prélèvement sur la production sociale, sur la plus-value ajoutée chaque année à une société donnée. Mais c'est un fait qui a existé de tout temps, il a été masqué parce que peut-être la croissance de la mobilité, de l'échange et de la division internationale du travail a fait qu'on essayait de produire toujours plus de transport pour produire toujours plus d'utilités de biens économiques et de services. Alors peut-être effectivement, comme le disaient Monsieur Harral et Monsieur Frenzel, il est temps de se demander si on peut pas vivre mieux avec moins de transport en changeant les structures et je propose que l'on fasse des modèles sur les voyages évitables, "the avoidable trips". Cela pourrait être un concept intéressant justement pour voir dans quelle mesure, il est possible en analyse de système de réagir un peu contre une croissance anarchique du transport. Et je pense que dans cette optique globale il serait intéressant de faire porter notre étude sur tous les phènomènes de captivité qui existent à l'intérieur du système de transport.

Et pour terminer sur une note optimiste dans le domaine de la recherche, je pense que s'amorce aussie cette nécessité d'interaction, non pas seulement entre les politiques et les chercheurs, mais à l'intérieur du milieu de la recherche lui-même. Je pense que nous devons être prêts à adopter une attitude véritablement transdisciplinaire qui fasse travailler ensemble des gens d'horizons différents et sur des problèmes semblables, comme le disait Monsieur Silverleaf, mais également que nous devons accepter le fait que différentes approches méthodologiques, voire parfois idéologiques, peuvent contribuer au meilleur éclaircissement de l'infini diversité de notre champ.

Mr. A. Kanafani, U.S.A.

At the risk of striking a pessimistic note I think it would be productive for us to recognize that research is limited in its contribution towards solving transportation problems. I would like to propose that some of the most difficult problems and questions in transportation planning, particularly long range transportation planning, can only be answered by the imagination and foresight of decisionmakers. I think that these are things that cannot be researched and I would appreciate hearing various comments from the distinguished panel as to how they see the limitations of research.

Mr. P. K. Wheeler, U.S.A.

I would like to take two remarks of the panel out of the context and just say a couple of things briefly. One was that the research should be more in policy, should be more responsive to the wishes of the users and second that policy objectives need to be more clearly set for the researchers.

I think the first, the wishes of the users are clearly being expressed in a system where research costs are not being charged to the users. There have been a lot of national interests, a lot of sectional and industrial interests and the response to the present system, that is the way users are expressing their demands, may be very misleading. We should always pay very close attention to this distortion within the transport sector and often between various modes.

The second point I would like to mention is that the decisionmakers have some uncertainties also and it is very difficult to put forward an operable, a sustainable policy objective. It is very hard to formulate one and it is very hard to attach one to a real world situation. I think this may be asking too much of a decisionmaker. I have spent the past two years trying to find some clear-cut policy objectives expressed in the will and doings of our legislative bodies and I have yet to discover anything of this nature. However research, while not making the final decision it needs to become much richer, it must contain more alternatives and more broad views of what the ramifications of persuing various policies will be.

If research can do this, then the decisionmakers will have a much richer background, when a policy decision comes along. I think research must also attempt a bit more to the institutional factors in the transportation sector. It seems to me that researchers should quit taking the institutional setting as given. They must be able to really look through some of the regular things like licencing, labour practice and modal separation problems and suggest more solutions in those areas.

Mr. A. L. Webster, U.S.A.

We have become increasingly aware of both financial and social aspects of transportation, but on the benefit side we are still operating somewhat in the dark ages. I suggest that mobility is one form of freedom. It allows us to increasingly live where we are most comfortable, to work where we are most productive and to play where we have the most fun.

We need to have ways of assessing the value of such attributes. In an economic sense transportation makes possible the acquisition of resources from a broader field, makes possible reasonable specialization, economies of scale of production, increased competition in markets, thus it can mean greater choice at less costs for all of us.

We need to be able to estimate such benefits. In an uncertain environment we may do very well to concentrate on processes rather than on a series of improducts. For instance I would pose the following questions. How can we improve the market and governmental procedures by which resources will be allocated to the evolution of transportation in the future.

Can we cut off the ways in which markets fail and design ways to ameliorate the conditions and to make the part-markets operate more perfectly in allocating resources to transportation and society.

Can we design methods of governmental regulation, research allocation which complement more perfect markets and encourage evolutionary transportation developments which are increasingly in the broad public interest. I think Mr. Harral touched on this when he commented on subsidy for instance. In summary an orientation where we try to maximize the social profits of transportation rather than think in terms of least-cost systems may be warranted.

Mr. Noortman

The topic of our discussions was decisionmaking in an age of uncertainty. We started to discuss what are those uncertainties, and a whole range of them were presented this afternoon. There was one certainty and that is that there are uncertainties and we can even locate them, at least the most important of them. Only we do not know at what time they will be of serious importance and in what direction exactly they will go. There were some pessimistic elements in it, that is the widening gap in economic development level between the now so-called economic developed areas and the less developed areas. There was a rather pessimistic uncertainty, that is to say to what level unemployment will increase. Probably it is an uncertainty that it increases. Perhaps pessimistic as well was the statement that we will be confronted with a migration from the rural areas towards the more urban areas. From several points of view you can consider that as a negative development.

On the other hand, more positive, the trend to social equity, trends to better understanding, that we have a world responsibility to cope with the problems we are confronted with in the future. To cope with them from our responsibility as a human being as a member of mankind.

On the on hand the responsibility of decisionmakers. They have to come to decisions. It was mentioned that we know a lot of decisionmakers, but where are the decisions. Not taking a decision is a decision as well. So how uncertain the future may be, the decisionmaker has to go on, or he has to step aside. The researcher has to try to give him support as much as possible from his professional know-how. Therefore the increasing importance of policy oriented research, not ivory tower research, but policy oriented, down to earth, willing to abandon old fashioned approaches, willing to start new ways. A lot has been explained these days about what was wrong in the ways we went in the past and what are the possibilities in the future.

A whole list of whishes was formulated during the discussions. Not all these wishes can be answered. Certainly not at the same time. But anyhow there was a general trend to optimism. Optimism that we are able to cope with the problems we are confronted with. That we are not denying to chose new roads to the future.

There are enormous gaps in our equipment. There are enormous gaps in our know-how but at least there is the willingness to go new roads and to go those roads together. Not isolated but on a world-wide scale.

I think that this is a very positive point.

What trends can we see in new research developments. I think it was a common opinion during the discussions that we need multi-modal approaches, that we need multi-sectoral approaches and multi-disciplinary approaches. It has the danger that we are trying to broaden our models in such a way that we can embrace all the problems at the same time. That is an impossibility. We will have to make some abstractions, but anyhow we understand the necessity to see transport as a part of a much wider field of decisionmaking. A much wider field of economic and social activities. It was mentioned that transport is not the point of how to move vehicles. The point is to transport human beings and goods from origin to destination.

We want to look behind the actual transport activity. We want to look into the systems that form the basis of our total activity.

In order to do that it is necessary to improve the communication not only between the research people but certainly between the research people and the decisionmakers. That means and it was mentioned several times, that research should use words that are to be understood by people, normal human beings; they should not talk in a mistic way, they should not talk only in a jargon that cannot get beyond their own studies. At the same time it is expected from the decisionmaker that he is willing to formulate precisely his problem. Only then it is possible to communicate. And this trend to humanize research underlines the necessity not to think so much in the development of master plans or short term plans but in the necessity to train human beings to form organizations of research people that are able to build continuous flows of research results to the world's decisionmakers. Especially in the period of uncertainty it is impossible to do a job once and then go to rest. To be flexible it is necessary to create a continuous flow of information. Otherwise the decisionmaker cannot make use of the research results. He needs his answer today. The answer for the next years has only historical value.

We cannot isolate research from training. What sense does it make to ask people to develop very highbrow systems and methods if not at the same time in the area where the model has to be used the people are available to operate with the model. It should be integrated as well in the area where the models should be used. And a continuous effort to combine research and training should be recommended. And I think just to bridge the gap between the researcher and the decisionmaker it is vital to come to more simplified procedures than using research as a tool to support the decisionmakers, whether it is a political decisionmaker or a manager. Simplify procedures that make it possible to get an answer today on the problem of today. This does not mean that we should return to naive models. The simpler the procedure, the more serious research efforts are necessary to develop these simplified models.

The more simple the model, the broader the basis must be in research to create this operational simple model. It is not the researcher that has the responsibility for decisions. It is the political man and it is the business man that has to take his decision. If policy-oriented research sets a task for the research people it has to make this research more human and I understand that it is not in the first place necessary to concentrate on new technological research. To make the optimum use of available resources means optimal management. Let us understand that this does mean new roads in research. If you are obliged to develop better management information systems that means at the same time that you have to create new resources as input for your more policy-oriented research models. The more sophisticated these models are, the broader is the stream of empirical information which is needed as input for those models. The marriage of management information systems and policy-oriented systems is a happy marriage. I have the feeling that we made a step forward. A step on a very long road, but as long as we are willing to go together on that road I am convinced that we will make progress. It will be possible to transpose the research results to other areas, not only from developed areas to developing areas but the other way round as well. It will be necessary to create new forms of communication between research people. It is necessary to come to international research institutes that are independent from governments. Some institutes are already existing.

It is more important to open the ways to reach these research institutes and to bring their efforts together.

I would not like to end this conference without thanking the people that have given their effort to bring the results we have in front of us. I would like to mention in the first place the authors that presented such excellent papers. I would like to mention the chairmen of the sessions. I would like to thank the members of the panel that did such a very good job, the steering committee that made such an effort to make the best of this conference. Last but not least I would like to thank the secretary of the steering committee Mr. Visser and his staff that after all had to do the job and also I would like to thank the interpreters.

This is the end of the formal part of this conference.

Mr. Suchorzevsky

I would like in my own name and I am convinced that all participants would also join me to express the warmest thanks and feeling of gratitude to the host country, to its government and the institute involved. To all the Rotterdam people, to the organizers of this conference, to the steering committee, technical staff and interpreters for everything they have done to make this conference not only an interesting and successful but also an exciting and unforgettable event. I feel that special thanks should be expressed to two people, one is the secretary of the conference Mr. Visser, the other is Mr. Noortman for his excellent leadership.